STATUTORY INSTRUMENTS 1969

PART II
(in two Sections)
SECTION 1

Published by Authority

LONDON
HER MAJESTY'S STATIONERY OFFICE
1969

SBN 11 840039 8

Preface

Scope and arrangement of the Volume

1. This volume gives the full text of the statutory instruments registered in the year 1969 which were classified as general, and gives particulars of those which were classified as local(**a**). Other instruments are contained in the Appendix (as to which see para. 3 below).

2. The general instruments are arranged according to their S.I. numbers(**b**), that is to say, in the order of their registration as statutory instruments. The volume is published in three Parts, containing the instruments registered between 1st January and 30th April, 1st May and 31st August, and 1st September and 31st December respectively.

Contents of the Volume

3. **Parts I and II.** At the beginning of each of these Parts is a list of the instruments whose text is contained in that Part, showing their S.I. numbers and titles. The list is followed by the text of the statutory instruments registered in the relevant period and an **Appendix of Instruments not registered as Statutory Instruments** issued in that period. This Appendix includes Orders in Council issued under the royal prerogative or otherwise outside the definition of a statutory instrument, Royal Proclamations which are of a legislative nature, and Letters Patent and Royal Instructions which relate to the constitutions, etc. of overseas territories.

At the end of each Part is a Table showing the modifications to legislation and an Index. Each Table is confined to the instruments in its own Part and gives particulars of those Acts and instruments which have been amended, extended, excluded, repealed or revoked by instruments in the Part. The Index to Part II will be cumulative to both Parts.

4. **Part III.** At the beginning is a list of the instruments in Part III similar to the lists in Parts I and II. It is followed by the text of the instruments comprising Part III, as in Parts I and II.

At the end of Part III are the features which are required by reg. 10 of the Statutory Instruments Regulations 1947 to be included in the Annual Volume of Statutory Instruments. They cover the instruments in all three Parts. In the order in which they occur in the Volume, they are as follows:—

The **Classified List of Local Instruments** gives particulars, including the dates of making, and the S.I. numbers of, all local statutory instruments registered in the S.I. series of the year to which the Annual Volume relates. They are grouped in classes according to their subject-matter.

(**a**) *See* Statutory Instruments Regulations 1947 (S.I. 1948/1 (Rev. XXI, p. 498: 1948 I, p. 4002)), reg. 4 of which provides that S.I. which are in the nature of public general Acts of Parliament shall be classified as general and those which are in the nature of local and personal or private Acts shall be classified as local.

(**b**) Reg. 3 of the Statutory Instruments Regulations 1947 provides for instruments to be numbered in a separate series for each calendar year. Certain instruments bear a subsidiary number—

C. Commencement Orders (bringing an Act or part of an Act into operation).
L. Instruments relating to fees or procedure in courts in England or Wales.
S. Instruments made by a Scottish rule-making authority and applying to Scotland only.

The **Tables.** "Table A" gives particulars of the Acts of Parliament, and "Table B" particulars of statutory and other instruments, the operation of which was affected by the instruments appearing in the Volume. They include the information as to amendments, repeals, revocations, etc., already given in tables of "Modifications to Legislation" in Parts I and II and corresponding information with respect to the instruments in Part III, and also give particulars of Acts or instruments modified or restricted by general instruments throughout the Volume. In addition, Table B gives particulars of general instruments whose operation was affected expressly by Public General Acts of the year in question, or which ceased to operate through becoming spent during that year as a result of legislation of the year.

The **Numerical and Issue List** gives particulars of all statutory instruments which were printed and put on sale by the Queen's Printer of Acts of Parliament under the provisions of the Statutory Instruments Act 1946(a), during the year, with, in each case, the date of making and the date of first issue by Her Majesty's Stationery Office.

The **Index** will be cumulative to Parts I and II.

Definition of a statutory instrument

5. To determine whether or not any instrument is required to be a statutory instrument, reference must be made to s. 1 of the Statutory Instruments Act 1946, reg. 2 of the Statutory Instruments Regulations 1947, and arts. 1 and 2 of the Statutory Instruments (Confirmatory Powers) Order 1947(b).

The definition of what constitutes a statutory instrument, as respects instruments made under Acts passed before the commencement (1 Jan. 1948) of the 1946 Act, is governed by definitions contained in the Rules Publication Act 1893(c) (which was repealed and replaced by the 1946 Act); for those made under Acts passed after the commencement of the 1946 Act, the document is a statutory instrument if it is an Order in Council or if it is made by a Minister of the Crown and the Act provides that the power is to be exercisable by statutory instrument.

Citation

6. For the purposes of citation, most statutory instruments are given a title. In addition, all statutory instruments may be identified by the year and number. The first instrument in Part I of this Volume would, by this method, be cited as "S.I. 1969/1". When a statutory instrument is referred to in another statutory instrument, a lettered footnote is provided in the latter, giving the identification of the first instrument as above, and also its Part and page reference in the Annual Volume. The footnote reference for the same instrument would therefore be "S.I. 1969/1 (1969 I, p. 1)".

If the text of the instrument is set out in the current edition of *S.R. & O. and S.I. Revised* (Third Edition, as at 31st Dec., 1948) the footnote references give the volume reference in that edition as well as the page reference in the Annual Volume (see, for example, footnote (b) below). If a footnote contains the references of a number of instruments, they may in certain circumstances be run together, so as to give all the instrument numbers together and all the volume references together, e.g. "S.R. & O. 1946/157; S.I. 1948/1073, 1961/1942 (1946 II, p. 26; 1948 II, p. 13; 1961 III, p. 2650)".

(a) 1946 c. 36.   (b) S.I. 1948/2 (Rev. XXI, p. 504: 1948 I, p. 4008).
(c) 1893 c. 66.

Production in Court

7. Under section 2 of the Documentary Evidence Act 1868(**a**), read with section 2 of the Documentary Evidence Act 1882(**b**), *prima facie* evidence of any proclamation, order or regulation made by certain rule-making authorities may be given in courts of justice by production of a copy purporting to be printed by the Government Printer or under the superintendence or authority of Her Majesty's Stationery Office. The Act of 1868 has since been extended by numerous Acts(**c**) to rules, etc., made thereunder by other rule-making authorities. The copies of proclamations, orders, regulations, etc., made by the authorities referred to above as printed in these volumes may therefore be produced as *prima facie* evidence.

Up to date information on statutory instruments

8. The *Index to Government Orders* contains, under subject headings, summaries of all powers to make subordinate legislation conferred by statute on H.M. in Council, the Privy Council, government departments and certain other public bodies. Below each summary appear particulars of any general instruments made in exercise of it which were in force at the date of publication of the *Index*. Details are also given of certain instruments made under prerogative powers. The work contains also a Table of Statutes showing the subject headings under which references to particular sections of enabling Acts appear. (The *Index* is published every two years by H.M.S.O.)

9. Information as to whether any instrument is still in operation, or whether anything has happened to it since it was made, can be obtained from the *Table of Government Orders*. This Table lists general statutory rules and orders and statutory instruments in numerical order, and gives the history of those which have been affected (i.e. revoked, amended, etc.) by subsequent legislation, whether statute or subordinate legislation, identifying the Act or instrument in question. Where any instrument has been amended, the Table gives particulars of the article, section, rule, etc., affected. A user who is interested in one particular provision only of the earlier instrument can thus ascertain whether or not he need consult the text of the amending enactment at all. The *Table of Government Orders* is published annually by H.M.S.O. and is cumulative. A Noter-Up is issued twice yearly.

Authority for Publication

10. The Annual Volumes of Statutory Instruments are published in pursuance of reg. 10 of the Statutory Instruments Regulations 1947 and are prepared under the direction of the Statute Law Committee. Any suggestion or communication relating to their contents should be addressed to the Editor, Statutory Publications Office, Queen Anne's Chambers, 41, Tothill Street, S.W.1.

(**a**) 1868 c. 37. (**b**) 1882 c. 9.
(**c**) *See* the entries relating to extensions of the 1868 Act in the *Chronological Table of the Statutes*.

Abbreviations

Addnl. Instructions	...	Additional Instructions.
A.S.	...	Act of Sederunt.
am., amdg., amdt.	...	amended, amending, amendment.
appx.	...	appendix.
art(s).	...	article(s).
bd(s).	...	board(s).
c.	...	chapter(s).
cl(s).	...	clause(s).
Cmd., Cmnd.	...	Command Paper.
Cont.	...	continued.
ct(s).	...	court(s).
E.	...	England.
exc.	...	except, excepted.
excl.	...	excluded.
expl.	...	explained.
ext.	...	extended.
G.B.	...	Great Britain.
gen.	...	generally.
govt.	...	government.
H.C.	...	House of Commons Paper.
H.M.	...	Her Majesty, Her Majesty's.
incl.	...	included, including.
instrt.	...	instrument.
L.P.	...	Letters Patent.
Min(s).	...	Minister(s).
mod., mod(s).	...	modified, modification(s).
N.	...	North.
N.I.	...	Northern Ireland.
No.	...	number.
O.	...	Order(s).
O. in C., O. of C.	...	Order(s) in Council, Order(s) of Council.
p., pp.	...	page(s).
para(s).	...	paragraph(s).
prerog.	...	prerogative.
prosp.	...	prospectively.
prov.	...	provisional, proviso.
pt.	...	part.
r.	...	revoked.
R.C.	...	Rules of the Court of Session.
R. Instructions	...	Royal Instructions.
R. Warrant	...	Royal Warrant.
reg(s).	...	regulation(s).
rep.	...	repealed.
restr.	...	restricted.
retrosp.	...	retrospectively.
Rev.	...	Statutory Rules and Orders and Statutory Instruments Revised (Third Edition, 1948).
Rev. 1903	...	Statutory Rules and Orders Revised (Second Edition, 1903).
revn.	...	revocation.
S.	...	Scotland.
s., ss.	...	section(s).
S.I.	...	Statutory Instrument(s).
S.R. & O.	...	Statutory Rule(s) and Order(s).

ABBREVIATIONS

sch(s).	...	...	...	schedule(s).
Secy.	...	...	...	Secretary.
susp.	...	...	...	suspended.
temp.	...	...	...	temporarily.
transfd.	...	...,	...	transferred.
Treas.	...	...	...	Treasury.
U.K.	...	...	...	United Kingdom of Great Britain and Northern Ireland.
vol.	...	...	...	volume.
W. ...	...	...	...	Wales.

Statutory Instruments in Part II

1969/	Title	Page
632	Wages Regulation (Cotton Waste Reclamation) O.	1749
635	Capital Allowances (Comparable N.I. Grants) O.	1754
636	Abortion (Amdt.) Regs.	1756
637	Isles of Scilly (Housing) (Amdt.) O.	1758
638	Isles of Scilly (Housing) O.	1759
639	Building (Fourth Amdt.) Regs.	1762
640	Wages Regulation (Hair, Bass and Fibre) O.	1775
641	Wages Regulation (Hair, Bass and Fibre) (Holidays) O. ...	1781
654	Wages Regulation (Rope, Twine and Net) O.	1789
655	Wages Regulation (Licensed Non-residential Establishment) (Managers and Club Stewards) O.	1804
659	Teachers Superannuation (S.) (Amdt.) Regs.	1820
660	Increase of Pensions (Teachers Family Benefits) (S.) Regs. ...	1822
664	Price Stability of Imported Products (Rates of Levy No. 10) O.	1824
665	Superannuation (Commission on Industrial Relations) O. ...	1827
667	Motor Vehicles (International Circulation) (Amdt.) Regs. ...	1829
668	Motor Vehicles (International Motor Insurance Card) Regs....	1831
670	Rates Support Grant (S.) (Amdt.) Regs.	1843
672	Cereals (Guarantee Payments) (Amdt.) O.	1844
676	Price Stability of Imported Products (Rates of Levy No. 11) O.	1847
677	Importation of Plants and Plant Produce (Health) (G.B.) (Amdt.) O.	1849
679	Rules of Procedure (Air Force) (Amdt.) Rules...	1851
680	Rules of Procedure (Army) (Amdt.) Rules	1853
686	Smoke Control Areas (Exempted Fireplaces) (S.) O. ...	1855
687	Trustee Savings Banks (Rate of Interest) O.	1857
688	Income Tax (Employments) (No. 4) Regs.	1859
689	Industrial Training (Ceramics, Glass and Mineral Products Bd.) O.	1860
690	Asbestos Regs.	1871
691	Wages Regulation (Industrial and Staff Canteen) O.... ...	1879
692	Merchant Shipping (Fees) (Amdt.) Regs.	1901
693	Beef Cow (E. and W.) (Amdt.) Scheme	1905
694	Beef Cow Subsidy Payment (E. and W.) (Amdt.) O. ...	1907
695	Hill Cattle (Breeding Herds) (E. and W.) (Amdt.) Scheme ...	1909
696	Hill Cattle Subsidy (Breeding Herds) (E. and W.) Payment (Amdt.) O.	1911
697	Hill Sheep (E. and W.) (Amdt.) Scheme	1913
698	Beef Cow (N.I.) (Amdt.) Scheme	1915
699	Beef Cow Subsidy Payment (N.I.) (Amdt.) O....	1916
700	Hill Cattle (Breeding Herds) (N.I.) (Amdt.) Scheme	1918
701	Hill Cattle Subsidy (Breeding Herds) (N.I.) Payment (Amdt.) O.	1920
702	Hill Sheep (N.I.) (Amdt.) Scheme	1922
703	Industrial Training Levy (Ceramics, Glass and Mineral Products) O.	1924
707	Hill Cattle Subsidy Payment (S.) (Amdt.) O.	1930
708	Beef Cow Subsidy Payment (S.) (Amdt.) O.	1931

1969/	Title	Page
709	Education (No. 2) Act 1968 (Commencement No. 1) O.　...	1933
710	Superannuation (Local Govt. and Other Employments) Interchange Rules	1934
713	Motor Cars (Driving Instruction) (Amdt.) Regs.　　...　　...	1944
716	National Insurance (Industrial Injuries) (Colliery Workers Supplementary Scheme) Amdt. O.	1947
722	Pneumoconiosis, Byssinosis and Miscellaneous Diseases Benefit (Amdt.) Scheme	1949
723	Police Pensions (Amdt.) Regs. ...　　...　　...　　...　　...	1952
724	Special Constables (Pensions) (Amdt.) Regs. ...　　...　　...	1958
731	Cutlery Wages Council (G.B.) (Abolition) O.　　...　　...	1960
732	Increase of Pensions (India, Pakistan and Burma) Regs.　...	1962
733	International Coffee Organisation (Immunities and Privileges) O.	1966
734	International Sugar Organisation (Immunities and Privileges) O.	1972
735	Foreign Compensation (Union of Soviet Socialist Republics) O.	1978
736	Turks and Caicos Islands (Constitution) O.　...　　...　　...	1992
737	Aliens O. ...　　...　　...　　...　　...　　...　　...　　...	2018
738	Dangerous Drugs Act 1965 (Modification) O.　　...　　...	2020
739	Genocide Act (Guernsey) O.　...　　...　　...　　...　　...	2021
740	Merchant Shipping Act 1965 (Isle of Man) O.　　...　　...	2022
741	Merchant Shipping Act 1965 (Jersey) O.　　...　　...　　...	2024
742	Central Banks (Income Tax Schedule C Exemption) O.　...	2026
743	Copyright (Bermuda: Protection of Foreign Broadcasts) O....	2027
747	Industrial Training Levy (Water Supply) O.　...　　...　　...	2029
752	Home-Grown Cereals Authority (Rates of Levy) O. ...　...	2033
753	Wages Regulation (Licensed Residential Establishment and Licensed Restaurant) O.	2036
756	Urban District Council Election Rules　　...　　...　　...	2080
757	Rural District Council Election Rules ...　　...　　...　　...	2107
758	Price Stability of Imported Products (Levy Arrangements) (Amdt.) O.	2137
759	National Health Service (Designation of Teaching Hospitals) O.	2139
760	British Nationality Regs.　　...　　...　　...　　...　　...	2142
761	Wages Regulation (General Waste Materials Reclamation) O.	2163
762	Wages Regulation (General Waste Materials Reclamation) (Holidays) O.	2170
763	Matrimonial Causes (Amdt.) Rules　　...　　...　　...　　...	2176
767	Assistance for House Purchase and Improvement (Qualifying Lenders) O.	2178
769	Ploughing Grants Scheme　　...　　...　　...　　...　　...	2180
770	Anti-Dumping (Provisional Charge to Duty) O.　　...　　...	2184
776	Fertilizers (U.K.) Scheme　　...　　...　　...　　...　　...	2186
778	Ploughing Grants (S.) Scheme ...　　...　　...　　...　　...	2191
779	Price Stability of Imported Products (Rates of Levy No. 12) O.	2195
783	British Commonwealth and Foreign Post Amdt. (No. 4) Regs.	2198
784	British Commonwealth and Foreign Parcel Post Amdt. (No. 4) Regs.	2200

1969/	Title	Page
785	Teachers Superannuation Account (Rates of Interest) (S.) Regs.	2203
790	Superannuation (Scottish Teaching and English Local Govt.) Interchange Rules	2207
791	Increase of Pensions (Extention) Regs.	2225
793	National Insurance (Modification of Local Govt. Superannuation Schemes) Regs.	2227
794	Sale of Venison (Forms etc.) (S.) Regs.	2272
804	Mines and Quarries (Tips) Act 1969 (Commencement No. 1) O.	2276
805	Mines and Quarries (Tips) Act 1969 (Commencement No. 2) O.	2277
806	Mines and Quarries (Tips) (Rate of Interest) O.	2278
807	Disused Mine and Quarry Tips (Prescribed Forms) Regs. ...	2280
808	Ionising Radiations (Sealed Sources) Regs.	2296
813	Fees of Appointed Factory Doctors (Amdt.) O.	2316
820	Industrial Training Levy (Furniture and Timber) O. ...	2317
822	Price Stability Imported Products (Rates of Levy No. 13) O....	2322
826	Road Safety Act 1967 (Commencement No. 3) O.	2324
833	Civil Aviation (Investigation of Accidents) Regs.	2325
834	Air Corporations (General Staff, Pilots and Officers Pensions) (Amdt.) Regs.	2338
839	Import Duties (Temporary Exemptions) (No. 4) O.	2341
840	Aliens (Approved Ports) O.	2347
841	Education Authority Bursaries (S.) O.	2349
842	Foreign Compensation Commission (Union of Soviet Socialist Republics) Rules Approval Instrt.	2359
843	Agriculture (Poisonous Substances) (Amdt.) Regs.	2375
844	Public Health (Infectious Diseases) (Amdt.) Regs.	2378
848	Training of Teachers (Amdt.) Regs.	2380
849	Nurses (Regional Nurse-Training Committees) (S.) Amdt. O.	2381
850	Cycle Racing on Highways (Special Authorisation) (S.) Regs.	2384
851	Irish Land (Finance) (Amdt.) Regs.	2386
854	Antarctic Treaty (Specially Protected Area) O.	2388
855	Bahrain (Amdt.) O.	2390
856	Qatar (Amdt.) O.	2392
857	St. Helena Supreme Ct. O.	2394
858	Admiralty Jurisdiction (St. Helena and its Dependencies) O....	2399
859	Trucial States (Amdt.) O.	2402
860	Southern Rhodesia (United Nations Sanctions) (Channel Islands) O.	2405
861	Southern Rhodesia (United Nations Sanctions) (Isle of Man) O.	2424
862	County Ct. Judges (Maximum Number) O.	2444
863	Registration of Title O.	2445
864	Double Taxation Relief (Taxes on Income) (South Africa) O.	2446
865	Patents Etc. (Laos) (Convention) O.	2461
866	Vehicle and Driving Licences Act 1969 (Commencement No. 1) O.	2462
867	Selective Employment Payments Variation O.	2463
868	Wages Regulation (Linen and Cotton Handkerchief etc.) O....	2465

1969/	Title	Page
869	Wages Regulation (Linen and Cotton Handkerchief etc.) (Holidays) O.	2470
870	Mines and Quarries (Tips) Act 1969 (Commencement No. 3) O.	2477
871	Meat (Sterilisation) Regs.	2478
873	Welfare Foods (N.I.) O.	2487
875	Television Act 1964 (Additional Payments) O.	2488
876	Agriculture (Spring Traps) (S.) O.	2490
878	Price Stability of Imported Products (Rates of Levy No. 14) O.	2492
879	Industrial Training (Road Transport Bd.) O....	2495
880	Industrial Training Levy (Road Transport) O.	2503
881	Military Pensions (Ministry of Overseas Development) Regs.	2509
882	Hosiery and Knitwear Industry (Scientific Research Levy) O.	2511
884	Industrial Training (Iron and Steel Bd.) O.	2517
886	Friendly Societies (Halfpenny) Regs.	2523
887	Industrial Assurance (Halfpenny) Regs.	2525
888	'Pelican' Pedestrian Crossing Regs. and General Directions...	2527
889	Sugar (Rates of Surcharge and Surcharge Repayments) (No. 5) O.	2549
890	Composite Sugar Products (Surcharge and Surcharge Repayments—Average Rates) (No. 5) O.	2552
894	Wages Regulation (Button Manufacturing) O.	2556
895	Anti-Dumping Duty (No. 1) O.	2563
896	Acquisition of Land (Rate of Interest after Entry) (No. 2) Regs.	2565
897	Acquisition of Land (Rate of Interest after Entry) (S.) (No. 2) Regs.	2566
901	Wages Regulation (Baking) (E. and W.) O.	2567
902	Heavy Goods Vehicles (Drivers' Licences) (Commencement) O.	2580
903	Heavy Goods Vehicles (Drivers' Licences) Regs.	2582
904	Representation of the People Regs.	2602
905	Representation of the People (N.I.) Regs.	2666
906	National Health Service (Charges for Appliances) Regs. ...	2715
909	Wages Regulation (Brush and Broom) (Amdt.) (No. 2) O. ...	2718
911	Police (Amdt.) (No. 2) Regs.	2724
912	Representation of the People (S.) Regs.	2726
913	Vehicle and Driving Licences Act 1969 (Commencement No. 2) O.	2790
915	Equine Arrivals (Importation) O.	2791
918	National Health Service (Charges for Appliances) (S.) Regs.	2797
921	Legal Aid (Extension of Proceedings) Regs.	2800
922	Legal Aid (Assessment of Resources) (Amdt.) Regs.	2802
923	Legal Aid (General) (Amdt.) Regs.	2804
927	Police (S.) Amdt. (No. 3) Regs.	2805
929	Wages Regulation (Hollow-ware) (Holidays) O.	2807
930	Wages Regulation (Hollow-ware) O.	2815
931	Pensions Appeal Tribunals (E. and W.) (Amdt.) Rules... ...	2823
936	Grading of Produce (Apples) (Amdt.) Regs.	2825
937	Grading of Produce (Pears) (Amdt.) Regs.	2827
939	Savings Banks (Ordinary Deposits) (Limits) O.	2829

1969/	Title	Page
940	Post Office Savings Bank (Investment Deposits) (Limits) O.	2832
941	Trustee Savings Banks (Special Investments) (Limits) (Amdt.) O.	2834
942	Trustee Savings Banks (Current Account Deposits) (Limits) (Amdt.) O.	2836
944	Agricultural Lime Scheme (Extension of Period) O.... ...	2838
953	Awards and Settlements (Temporary Continuation of Stand-still) (No. 2) O.	2840
954	Goods Vehicles (Production of Test Certificates) Regs. ...	2842
955	Legal Aid (Extension of Proceedings) (S.) Regs.	2846
962	Motor Vehicles (Designation of Approval Marks) (No. 2) Regs.	2847
963	Mines (Notification of Dangerous Occurrences) (Amdt.) O....	2851
964	Quarries (Notification of Dangerous Occurrences) (Amdt.) O.	2853
972	Milk (Great Britain) (Amdt.) O.	2855
973	Milk (Northern Ireland) (Amdt.) O.	2859
974	Rules of the Air and Air Traffic Control (Amdt.) Regs. ...	2861
975	Superannuation (Local Govt. and Overseas Employment) Interchange Rules	2866
976	Water Resources (Succession to Licences) Regs.	2881
978	Small Farm (Business Management) Scheme	2892
987	A.S. (Extension of Sessions of Ct.)	2901
988	Export of Goods (Control) (Amdt.) O....	2902
989	Special Constables (Pensions) (S.) Amdt. Regs.	2903
995	Clean Air Act 1968 (Commencement No. 2) O.	2905
997	Superannuation (Local Govt. and Approved Employment) Interchange Rules	2906
998	Local Loans (Increase of Limit) O.	2941
999	Bacon Curing Industry Stabilisation (Variation) Scheme ...	2943
1001	Firemen's Pension Scheme (Amdt.) O.	2945
1003	Housing Subsidies (Representative Rates of Interest) O. ...	2949
1006	Clean Air Act 1968 (Commencement No. 2) (S.) O. ...	2951
1007	Bankruptcy (Amdt.) Rules	2952
1008	Judicial Offices (Salaries) O.	2953
1014	A.S. (Extension of Sessions of Ct. No. 2)	2955
1015	White Fish (Inshore Vessels) and Herring Subsidy (U.K.) Scheme	2956
1018	National Insurance Act 1969 (Commencement) O.	2966
1019	Licensing (S.) O.	2970
1020	Price Stability of Imported Products (Rates of Levy No. 15) O.	2973
1021	Plant Breeders' Rights Regs.	2976
1022	Plant Breeders' Rights (Fees) (Amdt.) Regs.	3003
1023	Plant Breeders' Rights (Herbaceous Perennials) Scheme ...	3005
1024	Plant Breeders' Rights (Trees, Shrubs and Woody Climbers) Scheme	3011
1025	Plant Breeder's Rights (Conifers and Taxads) Scheme ...	3024
1026	Plant Breeders' Rights (Narcissi, Freesias and Gladioli) Scheme	3027
1027	Plant Varieties (Index) Regs.	3030
1028	Plant Varieties (Performance Trials) Regs.	3041
1034	Import Duty Drawbacks (No. 1) O.	3054
1035	Personal Injuries (Civilians) (Amdt.) Scheme	3055

1969/	Title	Page
1036	Supplementary Benefit (Determination of Requirements) Regs.	3065
1037	Industrial and Provident Societies (Group Accounts) Regs....	3067
1038	Food (Control of Irradiation) (S.) Amdt. Regs.	3073
1039	Food (Control of Irradiation) (Amdt.) Regs. ...	3075
1042	Motor Vehicles (Construction and Use) (Amdt.) (No. 2) Regs.	3077
1046	Superannuation (Teaching and Public Bds.) Interchange (S.) Rules	3080
1052	Iron and Steel (Pensions) (Dependants) Regs....	3093
1053	Injuries in War (Shore Employments) Compensation (Amdt.) Scheme	3101
1058	Milk (Extension of Period of Control of Maximum Prices) O.	3103
1059	Evidence (Republic of Ireland) O.	3104
1060	Hong Kong Divorce Jurisdiction (Amdt.) O.	3106
1061	Merchant Shipping (British Solomon Islands Protectorate) Maritime O.	3107
1062	Merchant Shipping (New Hebrides) Maritime O.	3109
1063	Reciprocal Enforcement of Foreign Judgements (the Netherlands) O.	3111
1064	Saint Vincent Electoral Provisions O.	3120
1065	Virgin Islands Constitution (Amdt.) O.	3122
1066	Post Office Act 1969 (Appointed Day) O.	3123
1067	Transfer of Functions (Safety of Reservations) O.	3124
1068	Double Taxation Relief (Taxes on Income) (Denmark) O. ...	3126
1069	Double Taxation Relief (Taxes on Income) (Jamaica) O. ...	3134
1070	Crown Office (Commissions of the Peace) Rules	3138
1071	Crown Office (Writs of Summons) Rules	3141
1072	Civil Defence (Designation of the Minister of Posts and Telecommunications) O.	3143
1073	Medical Practitioners (Antigua) O.	3144
1074	Medical Practitioners (Barbados) O.	3145
1075	Medical Practitioners (Dominica) O.	3146
1076	Medical Practitioners (Grenada) O.	3147
1077	Medical Practitioners (Guyana) O.	3148
1078	Medical Practitioners (Jamaica) O.	3149
1079	Medical Practitioners (Saint Christopher, Nevis and Anguilla) O.	3150
1080	Medical Practitioners (Saint Lucia) O.	3151
1081	Medical Practitioners (Trinidad and Tobago) O.	3152
1082	Air Navigation (Fourth Amdt.) O.	3153
1083	Carriage by Air Acts (Application of Provisions) (Amdt.) O	3156
1084	Merchant Shipping (Load Lines Convention) (Various Countries) (No. 2) O.	3157
1085	Oil in Navigable Waters (Convention Countries) (Southern Yemen) O.	3159
1086	Motor Vehicles (International Circulation) (Amdt.) O. ...	3160
1089	Housing Subsidies (Representative Rates of Interest) (S.)O. ...	3162
1090	Remuneration of Teachers (S.) Amdt. O.	3164
1091	Industrial Training Levy (Food, Drink and Tobacco) O. ...	3166
1092	Town and Country Planning (Inquiries Procedure) Rules ...	3171
1093	Provision of Milk and Meals (Amdt.) Regs.	3182
1095	Northern Pennines Rural Development Bd. O.	3184

1969/	Title	Page
1096	Slaughter of Poultry Act 1967 (Commencement) O.	3198
1099	Betting Premises (Licence Duty) Regs.	3199
1100	Bingo Duty Regs.	3207
1101	Gaming Machine (Licence Duty) Regs.	3214
1103	Industrial Training Levy (Cotton and Allied Textiles) O. ...	3222
1104	Civil Evidence Act 1968 (Commencement No. 2) O.	3227
1105	Rules of the Supreme Ct. (Amdt.)	3228
1106	Education (No. 2) Act 1968 (Commencement No. 2) O. ...	3239
1107	Rate Support Grants (Pooling Arrangements) (Amdt.) Regs.	3240
1108	Gaming Act 1968 (Commencement No. 4) O.	3242
1109	Gaming Act (Registration under Pt. III) Regs.	3244
1110	Gaming Clubs (Licensing) Regs.	3251
1115	Gaming Clubs (Licensing) (S.) Regs.	3260
1116	Gaming Act (Registration under Pt. III) (S.) Regs. ...	3269
1117	Social Work (Compensation) (S.) Regs.	3275
1118	Social Work (Transfer of Staff) (S.) Regs.	3311
1120	Sugar (Rates of Surcharge and Surcharge Repayments) (No. 6) O.	3320
1121	Composite Sugar Products (Surcharge and Surcharge Repayments—Average Rates) (No. 6) O.	3324
1125	Industrial Training Levy (Construction Bd.) O.	3328
1126	Price Stability of Imported Products (Rates of Levy No. 16) O.	3333
1127	Disused Mine and Quarry Tips (Prescribed Forms) (S.) Regs. ...	3335
1130	Transport (London) Act 1969 (Commencement No. 1) O. ...	3351
1132	National Insurance and Industrial Injuries (Stamps) Regs....	3353
1133	National Insurance (Assessment of Graduated Contributions) Amdt. Regs.	3363
1134	Restriction of Merger O.	3369
1135	Family Allowances, National Insurance and Industrial Injuries (Post Office Act 1969 Consequential) Regs.	3371
1136	Anti-Dumping (Provisional Charge to Duty) (Revn.) O. ...	3377
1137	Horse Breeding (Amdt.) Rules	3378
1138	Licensing of Boars (E. and W.) (Amdt.) Regs.	3380
1139	Licensing of Bulls (E. and W.) Regs.	3385
1140	Family Law Reform Act 1969 (Commencement No. 1) O. ...	3400
1141	Mines and Quarries (Notification of Tipping Operations) Regs.	3401
1149	Indian Civil Service Family Pension Fund (Amdt.) Rules ...	3402
1152	Local Land Charges (Amdt.) Rules	3406
1153	Small Farm (Business Management) (S.) Scheme	3409
1154	Improvement of Livestock (Licensing of Bulls) (S.) Amdt. Regs.	3418
1155	Improvement of Livestock (Licensing of Boars) (S.) Amdt. Regs.	3421
1161	National Health Service (Nottingham University Hospital Designation) O.	3426
1162	Bankruptcy (Amdt. No. 2) Rules	3428
1167	Price Stability of Imported Products (Rates of Levy No. 17) O.	3430
1168	National Insurance (Industrial Injuries) (Increase of Benefit and Miscellaneous Provisions) Regs.	3432

1969/	Title	Page
1169	Supplementary Benefit (Claims and Payments) Amdt. (No. 2) Regs.	3438
1170	County Courts (Bankruptcy and Companies Winding-up Jurisdiction) (Amdt.) O.	3440
1171	Motor Vehicles (Tests) (Amdt.) Regs.	3443
1172	Wages Regulation (Paper Box) O.	3447
1173	Wages Regulation (Paper Box) (Holidays) O.	3456
1174	Schools (Amdt. No. 2) Regs.	3464
1177	Companies (Winding-up) (Amdt.) Rules	3465
1178	County Ct. Districts (Miscellaneous) (No. 2) O.	3467
1179	Land Registration (Official Searches) Rules	3474
1184	Rent Regulation (Forms etc.) (E. and W.) Regs.	3483
1187	Wages Regulation (Paper Bag) O.	3505
1188	Wages Regulation (Paper Bag) (Holidays) O.	3513
1189	Sugar (Rates of Surcharge and Surcharge Repayments)(No. 7)O.	3522
1190	Composite Sugar Products (Surcharge and Surcharge Repayments—Average Rates) (No. 7) O.	3525
1195	Workmen's Compensation (Supplementation) Amdt. Scheme	3529
1196	Pneumoconiosis, Byssinosis and Miscellaneous Diseases Benefit (Amdt.) (No. 2) Scheme	3531
1203	A. S. (Alteration of Sheriff Ct. Fees) O.	3533
1204	Sugar (Rates of Surcharge and Surcharge Repayments)(No. 8)O.	3535
1205	Composite Sugar Products (Surcharge and Surcharge Repayments—Average Rates) (No. 8) O.	3538
1206	Increase of Pensions (Past Prime Ministers) Regs.	3542
1209	Docks and Harbours Act 1966 (Amdt. No. 5) O.	3544
1210	Industrial Training (Man-made Fibres Producing Industry Bd.)O.	3545
1211	Governors' Pensions (Maximum Amounts) O.	3550
1214	Import Duties (General) (No. 1) O.	3552
1215	Import Duties (Temporary Exemptions) (No. 5) O.	3554
1216	Anti-Dumping Duty (Temporary Suspension) O.	3560
1219	Firearms Rules	3561
1229	Sugar (Rates of Surcharge and Surcharge Repayments)(No. 9)O.	3580
1230	Composite Sugar Products (Surcharge and Surcharge Repayments—Average Rates) (No. 9) O.	3583
1231	Post Office (Guernsey) O.	3587
1232	District Registries O. in C.	3588
1234	Industrial Training Levy (Gas) O.	3591
1235	Industrial Training Levy (Rubber and Plastics Processing) O.	3595

OTHER INSTRUMENTS IN PART II

Title or description	Page
Gibraltar Constitution O.	3602
Proclamation calling in Halfpennies	3651
Disablement and Death Pensions etc. (Military), 1914 World War Service, and Service subsequent to 2nd Sept. 1939 (Amdt.) R. Warrant	3652
Disablement and Death Pensions etc. (Air Forces), 1914 World War Service, and Service subsequent to 2nd Sept. 1939 (Amdt.) O.	3682
Disablement and Death Pensions etc. (Naval Forces), 1914 World War Service, and Service subsequent to 2nd. Sept. 1939 O. in C.	3712

STATUTORY INSTRUMENTS

1969 No. 632

WAGES COUNCILS

The Wages Regulation (Cotton Waste Reclamation) Order 1969

Made - - -		*30th April* 1969
Coming into Operation		*2nd June* 1969

Whereas the Secretary of State has received from the Cotton Waste Reclamation Wages Council (Great Britain) the wages regulation proposals set out in the Schedule hereto ;

Now, therefore, the Secretary of State in exercise of her powers under section 11 of the Wages Councils Act 1959(**a**), and of all other powers enabling her in that behalf, hereby makes the following Order :—

1. This Order may be cited as the Wages Regulation (Cotton Waste Reclamation) Order 1969.

2.—(1) In this Order the expression "the specified date" means the 2nd June 1969, provided that where, as respects any worker who is paid wages at intervals not exceeding seven days, that date does not correspond with the beginning of the period for which the wages are paid, the expression "the specified date" means, as respects that worker, the beginning of the next such period following that date.

(2) The Interpretation Act 1889(**b**) shall apply to the interpretation of this Order as it applies to the interpretation of an Act of Parliament and as if this Order and the Order hereby revoked were Acts of Parliament.

3. The wages regulation proposals set out in the Schedule hereto shall have effect as from the specified date and as from that date the Wages Regulation (Cotton Waste Reclamation) Order 1968(**c**) shall cease to have effect.

Signed by order of the Secretary of State.

A. A. Jarratt,
Deputy Under Secretary of State,
30th April 1969.   Department of Employment and Productivity.

(**a**) 1959 c. 69.   (**b**) 1889 c.63.
(**c**) S.I. 1968/1355 (1968 II, p.3759).

Article 3 SCHEDULE

The following minimum remuneration shall be substituted for the statutory minimum remuneration fixed by the Wages Regulation (Cotton Waste Reclamation Order) 1968 (Order C.W. (78)).

STATUTORY MINIMUM REMUNERATION

PART I

GENERAL

1. The minimum remuneration payable to a worker to whom this Schedule applies for all work except work to which a minimum overtime rate applies under Part III of this Schedule is:—

(1) in the case of a time worker, the general minimum time rate payable to the worker under Part II of this Schedule;

(2) in the case of a worker employed on piece work, piece rates each of which would yield, in the circumstances of the case, to an ordinary worker at least the same amount of money as the general minimum time rate which would be payable to the worker under Part II of this Schedule if he were a time worker.

PART II

GENERAL MINIMUM TIME RATES

MALE WORKERS

2. The general minimum time rates payable to male workers are as follows:—

	Per hour
	s. d.
Aged 21 years or over	4 7½
„ 20 and under 21 years	4 4½
„ 19 „ „ 20 „	4 2½
„ 18 „ „ 19 „	3 11¼
„ 17 „ „ 18 „	3 7½
„ 16 „ „ 17 „	3 2¾
„ under 16 years	3 0¼

FEMALE WORKERS

3. The general minimum time rates payable to female workers are as follows:—

	Per hour
	s. d.
Aged 18 years or over	3 11¼
„ 17 and under 18 years	3 6¾
„ 16 „ „ 17 „	3 2¾
„ under 16 years	3 0¼

PART III

OVERTIME AND WAITING TIME—ALL WORKERS

MINIMUM OVERTIME RATES

4.—(1) Subject to the provisions of this paragraph, minimum overtime rates are payable to any worker as follows:—

(a) on any day other than a Saturday, Sunday or customary holiday—

(i) for the first 2 hours worked in excess of 9 hours ... time-and-a-quarter

(ii) thereafter ... ... time-and-a-half

(b) on a Saturday—

(i) for the first 2 hours worked ... ... time-and-a-quarter

(ii) thereafter ... ... time-and-a-half

(c) on a Sunday or a customary holiday,

for all time worked ... ... double time

(d) in any week (exclusive of any time in respect of which any minimum overtime rate is payable under the foregoing provisions of this sub-paragraph)—

(i) for the first 2 hours worked in excess of *40 hours* ... time-and-a-quarter

(ii) thereafter ... ... time-and-a-half

(2) Notwithstanding the provisions of (a)(i), (b)(i) and (d)(i) of sub-paragraph (1) of this paragraph, overtime at the rate of time-and-a-quarter shall not be paid for more than an aggregate of 2 hours worked in any week and any overtime so worked in excess of 2 hours in the aggregate shall be paid for at the overtime rate of time-and-a-half.

(3) In this paragraph the expression "customary holiday" means:—

(a) (i) In England and Wales—

Christmas Day (or, if Christmas Day falls on a Sunday, such week day as may be appointed by national proclamation, or, if none is so appointed, the next following Tuesday), Boxing Day, Good Friday, Easter Monday, Whit Monday and August Bank Holiday.

(ii) In Scotland—

New Year's Day (or, if New Year's Day falls on a Sunday, the following Monday);

the local Spring Holiday;

the local Autumn holiday; and

three other days (being days on which the worker normally works for the employer) in the course of a calendar year to be fixed by the employer and notified to the worker not less than three weeks before the holiday;

or (b) In the case of each of the said days (other than a day fixed by the employer in Scotland and notified to the worker as aforesaid) a day substituted by the employer therefor, being a day recognised by local custom as a day of holiday in substitution for the said day, or a day substituted by agreement between the employer and the worker or his representative.

(4) In this paragraph the expressions "time-and-a-quarter", "time-and-a-half" and "double time" mean respectively one and a quarter times, one and a half times, and twice the minimum remuneration payable to the worker for work to which a minimum overtime rate does not apply.

WAITING TIME

5.—(1) A worker is entitled to payment of the minimum remuneration specified in this Schedule for all time during which he is present on the premises of his employer, unless he is present thereon in any of the following circumstances:—

(a) without the employer's consent, express or implied;

(b) for some purpose unconnected with his work and other than that of waiting for work to be given to him to perform;

(c) by reason only of the fact that he is resident thereon;

(d) during normal meal times, in a room or place in which no work is being done, and he is not waiting for work to be given to him to perform.

(2) The minimum remuneration payable under sub-paragraph (1) of this paragraph to a piece worker when not engaged on piece work is that which would be payable if he were a time worker.

PART IV

APPLICABILITY OF STATUTORY MINIMUM REMUNERATION

6. This Schedule applies to workers in relation to whom the Cotton Waste Reclamation Wages Council (Great Britain) operates, that is to say, workers employed in Great Britain in the Cotton Waste Branch of the Waste Materials Reclamation trade as specified in the Schedule to the Trade Boards (Waste Materials Reclamation Trade, Great Britain) (Cotton Waste Branch) (Constitution and Proceedings) Regulations 1929(a), which Schedule is as follows:—

"1. For the purposes of this Schedule the expression 'reclamation' means all operations (including the operations of willowing and garnetting) performed on any waste material or waste article.

The expression 'cotton waste establishment' means an establishment in which the operations specified in paragraphs 2(a) and 2(b) hereof and operations connected therewith constitute the principal business carried on.

The expression 'establishment' means any establishment or any branch or department of an establishment.

2. Subject to the provisions of this Schedule the Cotton Waste branch of the Waste Materials Reclamation trade consists of the following operations:—

(a) reclamation wherever performed of cotton waste;

(b) making engine cleaning waste;

(c) reclamation of any other waste material or article where performed in or in connection with a cotton waste establishment;

(d) making (whether from new or waste material) or repairing sacks or bags in a cotton waste establishment except where the bags are made or repaired:—

(i) otherwise than for use in the establishment; and

(ii) in an establishment wholly or mainly engaged in the making or repairing of sacks or bags;

and operations connected therewith.

3. Notwithstanding anything in this Schedule the following operations are not operations in the Cotton Waste branch of the Waste Materials Reclamation trade:—

(a) reclamation of any waste material or waste article in an establishment (other than a cotton waste establishment) in which that material or article is produced or is used as material for manufacture or as a container or wrapper for other articles manufactured in the establishment, and operations connected therewith;

(a) S.R. & O. 1929/3 (1929, p. 1378).

(b) production of shoddy or mungo or woollen flock or any operations performed in an establishment in which the production of shoddy or mungo or woollen flock is the principal business carried on;

(c) repairing or overhauling machinery or plant;

(d) collecting, transporting, packing, warehousing, or despatching when performed by workers in the direct employment of an employer who is not otherwise engaged in the Waste Materials Reclamation trade;

(e) cleaning or washing when performed in an establishment where the cleaning or washing is mainly of articles other than those specified in paragraph 2 hereof;

(f) cleaning of premises by charwomen;

(g) caretaking;

(h) clerical work;

(i) reclamation of cotton waste and making engine cleaning waste when performed in, or in connection with, a general waste material establishment (as defined in the Schedule to the Trade Boards (Waste Materials Reclamation Trade, Great Britain) (General Waste Branch) (Constitution and Proceedings) Regulations 1933(a)), except where performed in or in connection with:—

    (i) a branch or department of a general waste materials establishment which constitutes a cotton waste establishment, or

    (ii) a branch or department of a cotton waste establishment which constitutes a general waste materials establishment."

EXPLANATORY NOTE

(This Note is not part of the Order.)

This Order, which has effect from 2nd June 1969, sets out the statutory minimum remuneration payable in substitution for that fixed by the Wages Regulation (Cotton Waste Reclamation) Order 1968 (Order C.W. (78)) which Order is revoked.

New provisions are printed in italics.

(a) S.R. & O. 1933/833 (Rev. XXIII, p. 497: 1933, p. 2056).

STATUTORY INSTRUMENTS

1969 No. 635

INCOME TAX

The Capital Allowances (Comparable Northern Ireland Grants) Order, 1969

Made - - - - 25th *April* 1969

The Treasury in pursuance of powers conferred on them by Section 36(3), Finance Act 1966(**a**), do hereby make the following Order :—

1. Each of the following grants, provided that it is paid (or, but for any reduction by reference to a grant made under the Capital Grants to Industry Acts (Northern Ireland) 1954 to 1967 would be paid) at a rate not less than the forty per cent rate, is hereby declared to be comparable to a grant falling within paragraph (*a*) of the said section 36(3)—

(*a*) a grant made under the Industrial Investment (General Assistance) Act (Northern Ireland) 1966(**b**) otherwise than under section 5 of that Act ; and

(*b*) a grant made under the Industries Development Act (Northern Ireland) 1966(**c**) so far as it is made towards expenditure in respect of which a grant such as is mentioned in paragraph (*a*) above may be made.

2. In this Order the expression " the forty per cent rate " means the rate of forty per cent specified in sections 1(6), 2(2), 4(3) and 7(3) of the Industrial Investment (General Assistance) Act (Northern Ireland) 1966, or the rate for the time being substituted for it by an Order under section 8 of that Act.

3. This Order may be cited as the Capital Allowances (Comparable Northern Ireland Grants) Order 1969.

25th April 1969.

Walter Harrison,

B. K. O'Malley.

Two of the Lords Commissioners of Her Majesty's Treasury.

(**a**) 1966 c. 18.　　　(**b**) 1966 c. 41 (N.I.).　　　(**c**) 1966 c 36 (N.I.).

EXPLANATORY NOTE

(This Note is not part of the Order.)

Section 36, Finance Act 1966 entitles the Treasury to prescribe grants payable under Northern Ireland enactments to be " comparable " to investment grants payable in Great Britain at the higher rate for development areas with the consequence that expenditure in respect of which the grant is paid will not be eligible for " free depreciation " (the computation of annual and writing down allowances for tax purposes at a rate specified by the taxpayer). This instrument so prescribes certain grants made under the Industrial Investment (General Assistance) Act (Northern Ireland) 1966 and the Industries Development Act (Northern Ireland) 1966.

STATUTORY INSTRUMENTS

1969 No. 636

MEDICAL PROFESSION

The Abortion (Amendment) Regulations 1969

Made - - -	*30th April* 1969
Laid before Parliament	*8th May* 1969
Coming into Operation	*1st June* 1969

The Secretary of State for Social Services, in exercise of his powers under section 2 of the Abortion Act 1967(**a**), as amended by the Transfer of Functions (Wales) Order 1969(**b**) and of all other powers enabling him in that behalf, hereby makes the following regulations :—

1.—(1) These regulations may be cited as the Abortion (Amendment) Regulations 1969 and shall come into operation on 1st June 1969.

(2) The Interpretation Act 1889(**c**) shall apply to the interpretation of these regulations as it applies to the interpretation of an Act of Parliament.

2. The Abortion Regulations 1968(**d**) shall be amended as follows :—

(1) For regulation 4 (Notice of termination of pregnancy and information relating thereto) there shall be substituted the following regulation :—

"4.—(1) Any practitioner who terminates a pregnancy in England, excluding Monmouthshire, shall within 7 days of the termination give to the Chief Medical Officer of the Department of Health and Social Security notice thereof and the other information relating to the termination in the form set out in Schedule 2 to these regulations, and any such notice and information shall be sent in a sealed envelope to the Chief Medical Officer, Department of Health and Social Security, Alexander Fleming House, Elephant and Castle, London, S.E.1.

(2) Any practitioner who terminates a pregnancy in Wales or Monmouthshire shall within 7 days of the termination give to the Chief Medical Officer of the Welsh Office notice thereof and the other information relating to the termination in the form set out in Schedule 2 to these regulations, and any such notice and information shall be sent in a sealed envelope to the Chief Medical Officer, Welsh Office, Cathays Park, Cardiff".

(2) In regulation 5 for the words from the beginning to the end of paragraph (*a*)(i) there shall be substituted the following :—

"5. A notice given or any information furnished to a Chief Medical Officer in pursuance of these regulations shall not be disclosed except that disclosure may be made—

(*a*) for the purposes of carrying out their duties,

(**a**) 1967 c. 87.   (**b**) S.I. 1969/388 (1969 I, p. 1070).
(**c**) 1889 c. 63.   (**d**) S.I. 1968/390 (1968 I, p. 1060).

(i) to an officer of the Department of Health and Social Security authorised by the Chief Medical Officer of that Department, or to an officer of the Welsh Office authorised by the Chief Medical Officer of that Office, as the case may be, or".

(3) In Schedule 2 for the note at the end there shall be substituted the following note :—

"This form is to be completed by the operating practitioner and sent in a sealed envelope within seven days of the termination of the pregnancy—

(a) if the termination of the pregnancy took place in England, excluding Monmouthshire, to the Chief Medical Officer, Department of Health and Social Security, Alexander Fleming House, Elephant and Castle, London, S.E.1. or

(b) if the termination of the pregnancy took place in Wales or Monmouthshire, to the Chief Medical Officer, Welsh Office, Cathays Park, Cardiff".

3. These regulations shall apply in respect of any termination of a pregnancy which takes place on or after 1st June 1969.

R. H. S. Crossman,
Secretary of State for Social Services.

30th April 1969.

EXPLANATORY NOTE
(This Note is not part of the Regulations.)

These Regulations amend the Abortion Regulations 1968 by providing that in respect of any termination of a pregnancy in Wales and Monmouthshire notification and the other information required by the Regulations are to be given to the Chief Medical Officer of the Welsh Office instead of to the Chief Medical Officer of the Department of Health and Social Security. They also make some consequential drafting amendments in regulation 5 of the Abortion Regulations 1968.

STATUTORY INSTRUMENTS

1969 No. 637

HOUSING, ENGLAND AND WALES
The Isles of Scilly (Housing) (Amendment) Order 1969

Made - - - -	1*st May* 1969
Laid before Parliament	9*th May* 1969
Coming into Operation	19*th May* 1969

The Minister of Housing and Local Government, upon the application of the Council of the Isles of Scilly and in exercise of his powers under section 134 of the Housing Act 1957(a), and of all other powers enabling him in that behalf, hereby makes the following order:—

1.—(1) This order may be cited as the Isles of Scilly (Housing) (Amendment) Order 1969 and shall come into operation on 19th May 1969.

(2) The Interpretation Act 1889(b) shall apply for the interpretation of this order as it applies for the interpretation of an Act of Parliament.

2. The Isles of Scilly (Housing) Order 1946(c) as amended by the Isles of Scilly (Housing) (Amendment) Order 1963(d) shall be further amended by the inclusion in article 3(2) of the said order of 1946, at the end, of the following proviso:—

"Provided that no such contribution shall be payable in respect of any dwelling falling within paragraph (*a*) or (*b*) of section 1(3) of the Housing Subsidies Act 1967(e).".

Given under the official seal of the Minister of Housing and Local Government on 1st May 1969.

(L.S.)

Anthony Greenwood,
Minister of Housing and Local Government.

EXPLANATORY NOTE
(*This Note is not part of the Order.*)

This order further amends the Isles of Scilly (Housing) Order 1946 as amended by the Isles of Scilly (Housing) (Amendment) Order 1963 by providing that no annual contribution of £40 for sixty years shall be payable to the Council of the Isles of Scilly in respect of any dwelling falling within paragraph (*a*) or (*b*) of section 1(3) of the Housing Subsidies Act 1967. Part I of the Act of 1967 has been applied to the Isles of Scilly by the Isles of Scilly (Housing) Order 1969 (S.I. 1969/638) and accordingly housing subsidies will be payable in respect of any such dwelling under the provisions of the said Part I.

(a) 1957 c. 56.   (b) 1889 c. 63.   (c) S.R. & O. 1946/2105 (Rev.XII, p. 572: 1946 I, p. 980).
(d) S.I. 1963/1722 (1963 III, p. 3342).   (e) 1967 c. 29.

STATUTORY INSTRUMENTS

1969 No. 638

HOUSING, ENGLAND AND WALES

The Isles of Scilly (Housing) Order 1969

Made - - -	*1st May* 1969
Coming into Operation	*19th May* 1969

The Minister of Housing and Local Government, in exercise of his powers under section 57 of the Housing (Financial Provisions) Act 1958(**a**), as applied by section 22 of and paragraph 7 of Schedule 3 to the Housing Subsidies Act 1967(**b**) (hereinafter called "the Act of 1967"), and of all other powers enabling him in that behalf, hereby makes the following order :—

1.—(1) This order may be cited as the Isles of Scilly (Housing) Order 1969 and shall come into operation on 19th May 1969.

(2) The Interpretation Act 1889(**c**) shall apply for the interpretation of this order as it applies for the interpretation of an Act of Parliament.

2.—(1) The provisions of Part I of the Act of 1967 which are specified in column (1) of the Schedule to this order shall extend to the Isles of Scilly.

(2) The said provisions as so extended shall have effect subject to the adaptations and modifications specified in respect thereof in column (2) of the said Schedule.

SCHEDULE

(1) Provision	(2) Adaptations and modifications
Section 1, with the exception of subsection (3)(*c*) and (*d*).	In section 1(1), the words from "and exchequer subsidies" onwards shall be omitted; in section 1(3), paragraphs (*c*) and (*d*) shall be omitted; in section 1(5), for the words "sections 2, 4 to 8 and 10 of this Act" there shall be substituted the words "sections 2, 5(1), 7 and 10 of this Act".

(**a**) 1958 c. 42.   (**b**) 1967 c. 29.   (**c**) 1889 c. 63.

SCHEDULE

(1) Provision	(2) Adaptations and modifications
Section 2.	In section 2(3), after the words "The rate so specified" there shall be added the words "shall in relation to approved dwellings provided by the Council of the Isles of Scilly in respect of the financial years commencing on 1st April 1966, 1st April 1967 and 1st April 1968 be that respectively specified in article 2(*a*)(ii) and (iii) of the Housing Subsidies (Representative Rates of Interest) Order 1967 and article 2(*a*) of the Housing Subsidies (Representative Rates of Interest) Order 1968 and in respect of any subsequent financial year" and after the words "the Greater London Council" there shall be added the words "the Council of the Isles of Scilly".
Section 3.	
Section 5, with the exception of subsection (2).	In section 5(3), for the words "under either" to "the same dwelling" there shall be substituted the words "under subsection (1) of this section shall not".
Section 7.	
Sections 10 to 12.	
Section 13.	In section 13(1), the words "or such contributions under section 9 thereof" shall be omitted.
Section 14.	In section 14(1), for the words "before the commencement of this Act" there shall be substituted the words "before the date on which the Isles of Scilly (Housing) Order 1969 comes into operation".
Section 15.	
Sections 19 and 20.	
Section 21.	In section 21(1) in the definition of "local authority", at the end, there shall be added the words "and the Council of the Isles of Scilly".
Sections 22 and 23.	
Schedules 1, 2, 3 and 4.	

Given under the official seal of the Minister of Housing and Local Government on 1st May 1969.

(L.S.)

F. J. Ward,
Under Secretary,
Ministry of Housing and Local Government.

EXPLANATORY NOTE

(This Note is not part of the Order.)

This order extends, subject to adaptations and modifications, certain provisions of Part I of the Housing Subsidies Act 1967 to the Isles of Scilly and thereby enables the Minister to give financial assistance to the Council of the Isles of Scilly towards the provision of new dwellings and to housing associations. The order also extends to the Isles certain consequential and supplemental provisions relating to housing subsidies.

STATUTORY INSTRUMENTS

1969 No. 639

BUILDING AND BUILDINGS

The Building (Fourth Amendment) Regulations 1969

Made - - - -	*1st May* 1969
Laid before Parliament	*13th May* 1969
Coming into Operation	*1st July* 1969

The Minister of Housing and Local Government, in exercise of the powers conferred on him under sections 61 and 62 of the Public Health Act 1936(a), as amended by section 11 of and Schedule 1 Part III to the Public Health Act 1961(b) and sections 4 and 6 of the Public Health Act 1961, and as read with the Transfer of Functions (Building Control) Order 1964(c) and the Transfer of Functions (Building Control and Historic Buildings) Order 1966(d), and of all other powers enabling him in that behalf, after consultation with the Building Regulations Advisory Committee and such other bodies as appear to him to be representative of the interests concerned, hereby makes the following regulations:—

PART I

GENERAL

1. These regulations may be cited as The Building (Fourth Amendment) Regulations 1969 and shall come into operation on 1st July 1969.

2.—(1) In these regulations, unless the context otherwise requires—

   (*a*) "the principal regulations" means The Building Regulations 1965(e) as amended by The Building (Second Amendment) Regulations 1966(f) and by The Building (Third Amendment) Regulations 1967(g), and other words and expressions have the same meaning as in the principal regulations; and

   (*b*) any reference to a regulation or Schedule shall be construed as a reference to a regulation of, or Schedule to, the principal regulations.

(2) The Interpretation Act 1889(h) shall apply for the interpretation of these regulations as it applies for the interpretation of an Act of Parliament.

3. These regulations shall not apply to any work which was—

   (*a*) completed before the date of the coming into operation of these regulations; or

---

(a) 1936 c.49.

(b) 1961 c. 64.

(c) S.I. 1964/263 (1964 I, p.457).

(d) S.I. 1966/692 (1966 II, p.1558).

(e) S.I. 1965/1373 (1965 II, p.3890).

(f) S.I. 1966/1144 (1966 III, p.2750).

(g) S.I. 1967/1645 (1967 III, p.4494).

(h) 1889 c.63.

(b) completed after that date in accordance with plans deposited with the local authority before that date, with or without any departure or deviation from those plans;

and for the purpose of this regulation "work" means the erection of a building, the alteration or extension of a building, the execution of any works or the installation of any fittings.

PART II

AMENDMENTS OF THE PRINCIPAL REGULATIONS

4. In regulation A2—

(a) in paragraph (1) there shall be inserted after the definition of "combustible" the following definition:

" "conservatory" includes only a conservatory of which the roof (and the ceiling, if any) is transparent or translucent;"; and

(b) there shall be substituted for sub-paragraph (b) of paragraph (5) the following sub-paragraph:

"(b) Any reference in these regulations to a publication shall be construed as follows—

(i) in regulation B2 and in any other case where no date is included in the reference, the reference is to the edition thereof current at 31st May 1968, together with any amendments, supplements or addenda thereto published at that date;

(ii) in Schedule 1 reference to the Standard Industrial Classification is a reference to the edition thereof published in September 1968;

(iii) in any other case where a date is included in the reference, the reference is to the edition of that date, together with any amendments, supplements and addenda thereto published at 31st May 1968; and

(iv) reference to any publication is a reference to so much only thereof as is relevant in the context in which such publication is quoted.".

5. In regulation A9—

(a) at the beginning of paragraph (1) there shall be substituted for the words "Any person who intends to—" the words "Subject to the provisions of paragraphs (2) and (3) of this regulation, any person who intends to—";

(b) there shall be deleted from paragraph (1)(c) the words "(subject to paragraphs (2) and (3) of this regulation)"; and

(c) there shall be substituted for paragraphs (2) and (3) the following paragraphs:

"(2) The provisions of paragraph (1) relating to the making of a structural alteration shall not apply to the carrying out of structural work associated with an operation to which either sub-paragraph (3)(a) or (3)(b) of this regulation relates if the extent of the work does not exceed that described therein.

(3) The provisions of paragraph (1) relating to the installation of fittings shall not apply to—

(a) the installation of an appliance to which Part M relates (other than a high-rating appliance or an appliance described in sub-paragraph (b) of this paragraph) by way of replacement of an existing appliance if compliance with the relevant regulations in that Part does not require the carrying out of any structural work other than such work as may be necessary in order to comply with regulation M4(10); or

(b) the installation, whether or not by way of replacement, of a Class II gas appliance or of a Class I or Class II incinerator which employs gas as a means of igniting refuse if—

    (i) the appliance is installed by, or under the supervision of, an Area Board established under the Gas Act 1948(a); and

    (ii) compliance with the relevant regulations in Part M does not require the carrying out of any structural work other than the construction of a flue pipe which is wholly within the room or internal space in which the appliance is installed and conveys the products of combustion from the appliance to an existing flue in a chimney or flue pipe or to the external air through an existing opening in an external wall; or

(c) the installation of a fitting to which Part N, P or Q relates by way of replacement of an existing fitting if compliance with the relevant regulations in that Part does not require the carrying out of any structural work.

(4) In paragraph (3) of this regulation, words and expressions have the same meaning as in Part M.".

6.—(1) In the sub-heading to the Table to regulation B3 there shall be substituted for the words "(Materials unsuitable for permanent buildings)" the words "(Materials unsuitable for use in permanent buildings as the weather-resisting parts of external walls or roofs)".

(2) In item 12 (Sheet steel) of the Table to regulation B3 there shall be substituted for the reference "BS 2989: 1958" in both places in which it occurs the reference "BS 2989: 1967".

(3) In the Table to regulation B3 for each of the entries in columns (2) and (3) in respect of item 13 (Asbestos-cement sheeting) there shall be substituted both in column (2) and in column (3) the following entry—

"Unsuitable except (subject to the footnote to this Table) asbestos-cement sheets conforming with BS 690: 1963 or BS 4036: 1966".

(4) At the end of the Table to regulation B3 there shall be inserted the following footnote:

"*Note* (*Item* 13): Asbestos-cement sheets which fail to conform with BS 690: 1963 only because their profile is not listed in figures 4 to 8 thereof shall not be deemed to be unsuitable if—

(a) in the case of symmetrically corrugated sheets, the average extreme fibre stress as determined by test in accordance with Appendix B of

---

(a) 1948 c.67.

BS 690: 1963 is not less than 2,275 pounds per square inch, the width of the test specimens being the width of the sheet as manufactured and the span at which each sheet is tested being not less than the width of the test specimen; or

(b) in the case of asymmetrically corrugated sheets, the average extreme fibre stress as determined by test in accordance with Appendix A of BS 690: 1963 is not less than 2,800 pounds per square inch, the test being carried out on flat pieces cut from the sheet length and the test bearers being placed at right angles to the direction of the fibres.".

7. For regulation B5 there shall be substituted the following regulation:

"*Deemed-to-satisfy provisions for the special treatment of softwood timber in certain areas*

B5. *The requirements of regulation B4(2) shall be deemed to be satisfied if—*
(a) *the timber is treated in accordance with the provisions of BS 4072: 1966; or*

(b) *the timber, when freshly felled and milled and having an average moisture content of not less than 50% of its oven-dry weight, is treated by diffusion with sodium borate to produce a net dry salt retention of not less than 0·33 pound of boric acid equivalent per cubic foot; or*

(c) *the timber is completely immersed for not less than 10 minutes in an organic-solvent type wood preservative containing at least 1 part of gamma BHC, dieldrin or other persistent organochlorine contact insecticide in every 200 parts of the preservative solution (the parts being measured by weight) and any surfaces subsequently exposed by cutting the timber for fitting into the building are thoroughly treated by dipping, spraying or brushing those surfaces with the same type of preservative.".*

8. In regulation D14 there shall be added after the reference "*CP 112: 1952*" in both places in which it occurs the word and reference "*or CP 112: 1967*".

9. In regulation E1 there shall be added after paragraph (3) the following paragraph:

"(4) If any part of a building other than a single storey building—

(i) consists of a ground storey only;

(ii) has a roof to which there is only such access as may be necessary for the purposes of maintenance or repair; and

(iii) is completely separated from all other parts of the building by a compartment wall or compartment walls in the same continuous vertical plane,

that part may be treated, for the purposes of this Part, as a part of a single storey building.".

10. In regulation E9—

(a) in paragraph (1)(a) there shall be substituted for the words "an opening fitted with a door which complies with the requirements of regulation E11 and has fire resistance which is not less than—" the words "an opening fitted with a door which has fire resistance for the following minimum period and complies with the provisions of regulation E11 or E11A—"; and

(b) in paragraph (1)(e) there shall be substituted for the words "Part L" the words "paragraphs (5) and (6) of this regulation and of Part L".

11. In regulation E10—

(a) there shall be substituted for item (ii) of paragraph (5)(b) the following item:

"(ii) an opening fitted with a door which has fire resistance complying with the provisions of paragraph (7) of this regulation and complies with the provisions of regulation E11 or E11A;"; and

(b) in paragraph (7) there shall be substituted for the words "Any fire-resisting door" to "minimum periods—" the words "Any door fitted in an opening in protecting structure shall have fire resistance for the following minimum period—".

12. In regulation E11—

(a) there shall be substituted for paragraph (1) the following paragraph:

"(1) Subject to the provisions of regulation E11A, this regulation shall apply to any door which is required to have fire resistance by the provisions of this Part.";

(b) there shall be substituted for sub-paragraph (a) of paragraph (3) the following sub-paragraph:

"(a) Any door fitted in an opening in protecting structure as defined in regulation E10(3) may consist of any single or double leaf door (the leaf or each leaf of which swings in one or both directions), other than a double leaf door both leaves of which swing in one and the same direction and have rebated meeting stiles, if—

(i) the door is not required by the provisions of regulation E10(7) to have fire resistance of more than half an hour; and

(ii) the door opens into a hall, lobby or corridor enclosed by walls or partitions having fire resistance of not less than half an hour."; and

(c) there shall be deleted from paragraph (3)(c) the words "falling within sub-paragraph (a)(iii) or (iv)".

13. After regulation E11 there shall be inserted the following regulation:

"Exceptions permitting use of certain doors in lift shafts

E11A.—(1) Notwithstanding the requirements of regulation E11, there may be provided, in an opening in the structure which encloses a protected shaft containing exclusively a lift or lifts, a door which is not fitted with a self-closing device if either—

(a) the door has fire resistance for a period not less than half an hour and there is also provided in the opening another door which is fitted with an automatic self-closing device actuated by a fusible link and has fire resistance for a period not less than that prescribed by the relevant provisions of this Part for the structure surrounding the opening; or

(b) (unless the opening is in a compartment wall and is one of two openings provided at the same level to allow access to a lift from different sides) the door has fire resistance for a period not less than that prescribed by the relevant provisions of this Part for the structure surrounding the opening.

(2) Any door specified in this regulation shall, if exposed to test by fire in accordance with Section 3 of BS 476: Part 1: 1953, satisfy the requirements of that test, when fitted in its frame, as to freedom from collapse and resistance to passage of flame for the period prescribed by sub-paragraph (*a*) or (*b*) of paragraph (1) of this regulation as the case may be (but with no minimum period in respect of insulation).

(3) For the purposes of this regulation, the expression "automatic self-closing device" does not include rising butt hinges.".

14. In regulation E14(2) there shall be inserted after the words "paragraph (3)" the words "of this regulation and to the provisions of regulation E14A".

15. After regulation E14 there shall be inserted the following regulation:

"Exceptions permitting use of ceiling panels of plastics materials

E14A.—(1) Notwithstanding the provisions of regulation E14, the surface of the ceiling of a room or circulation space may consist in whole or in part of a panel or panels of plastics material as permitted by paragraph (2) of this regulation, provided that the upper and lower surfaces of any part of the ceiling which does not consist of a panel of plastics material and the surface of any other structure enclosing the space over the ceiling are of a class not lower than that required by regulation E14 for the ceiling of such a room or circulation space.

(2) The said panel or panels may consist of one or more sheets or membranes of either—

   (*a*) polyvinyl chloride which has a degree of flammability of not more than 3 inches when tested in accordance with method 508C of BS 2782: Part 5: 1965 or which has very low flammability when tested and classified in accordance with method 508D of BS 2782: Part 5: 1965, if—

      (i) the nominal thickness of the sheet or membrane (or, if a panel consists of two or more sheets or membranes, their nominal aggregate thickness) does not exceed 0·04 inch; and

      (ii) no panel has an area exceeding 40 square feet; or

   (*b*) any plastics material which has a softening point of not more than 120°C when tested by method 102C of BS 2782: Part 5: 1965 and a burning rate of not more than 2 inches per minute when tested in a thickness of 0·125 inch in accordance with method 508A of BS 2782: Part 5: 1965, if—

      (i) the nominal thickness of the sheet or membrane (or, if a panel consists of two or more sheets or membranes, their nominal aggregate thickness) does not exceed 0·125 inch;

      (ii) the aggregate area of the plastics material, if situated in a building or compartment of purpose group II, III or VII, does not exceed 30% of the floor area of the room or 15% of the floor area of the circulation space, as the case may be, or, if situated in a building or compartment of any other purpose group, does not exceed 50% of the floor area of the room or 15% of the floor area of the circulation space, as the case may be;

    (iii) no panel has any side exceeding 16 feet in length or an area exceeding 40 square feet if situated in a room or 20 square feet if situated in a circulation space ; but if two or more panels are grouped so that each is less than 23 inches from another, the said maximum dimensions shall be applied to the smallest rectangle which would wholly enclose all such panels ; and

    (iv) every panel is loosely mounted in such a way that it will fall out of its mountings when softened by heat.

    (3) For the purpose of this regulation, words and expressions shall have the meaning assigned to them by regulation E14(4).".

16. In regulation H1(1) there shall be substituted for the definitions of "common stairway" and "private stairway" the following definitions respectively :

    " "common stairway" means an internal or external stairway of steps with straight nosings on plan which forms part of a building and is intended for common use in connection with two or more dwellings ;"

    " "private stairway'" means an internal or external stairway of steps with straight nosings on plan which forms part of a building and is either within a dwelling or intended for use solely in connection with one dwelling ;".

17. In regulation L1(1) in the definition of "appliance"—

    (*a*) there shall be substituted for sub-paragraph (*b*) the following sub-paragraph :

    "(*b*) an incinerator employing any means of igniting refuse, including electricity ;"; and

    (*b*) there shall be deleted all the words following the said sub-paragraph (*b*).

18. In regulation L2 after paragraph (4) there shall be added the following paragraph :

    "(5) If provision is made for a solid fuel fire to burn directly on a hearth, secure means of anchorage for an effective fireguard shall be provided in the adjoining structure.".

19. In regulation L6 there shall be added at the end of paragraph (1) the following proviso :

    "Provided that, notwithstanding the requirements of this paragraph, a chimney may be lined with a flexible flue liner if—

    (i) the chimney is already lined or constructed in accordance with this paragraph ; or

    (ii) the chimney is not so lined or constructed but was erected under former control.".

20. In regulation L8(*b*) there shall be substituted for the reference "BS 835 : 1959" the reference "BS 835 : 1967".

21. In regulation L14—

    (*a*) at the beginning of paragraph (1) there shall be substituted for the words "Any chimney serving a Class II appliance" the words "Subject to the provisions of paragraph (5) of this regulation, any chimney serving a Class II appliance" ;

(b) in paragraph (1)(a)(ii) there shall be substituted for the words "either specification (a) or specification (b)" the words "specification (a)" ; and

(c) there shall be added after paragraph (4) the following paragraph:

"(5) Notwithstanding the requirements of paragraph (1) of this regulation, a chimney serving a Class II appliance (not being an appliance ventilation duct) may be lined with a flexible flue liner if—

(a) the chimney is already lined or constructed in accordance with that paragraph ; or

(b) the chimney is not so lined or constructed but was erected under former control.".

22. In regulation L16(f)(i) there shall be substituted for the reference "*BS 835 : 1959*" the reference "*BS 835 : 1967*" and for the reference "*BS 567 : 1963*" the reference "*BS 567 : 1968*".

23. In regulation L17 there shall be substituted for paragraph (2) the following paragraph:

"(2) *A flue pipe serving a Class II appliance (being a pipe which is situated neither in the room or internal space in which the appliance is installed nor in an enclosed space to which no person has access) shall be deemed to satisfy such requirements of regulation L2(3)(a) as relate to the placing and shielding of a pipe within a building if—*

(a) *it is enclosed, either separately or together with one or more other flue pipes serving Class II appliances, in a casing constructed of suitable, but not necessarily imperforate, non-combustible material ; and*

(b) *there is a distance of at least 1 inch between the inside of the casing and the outside of any flue pipe ; and*

(c) *no combustible material is built into, or enclosed within, the casing.".*

24. In regulation L18(1) there shall be inserted after the words "Class II appliance" the words "(except where any part of that flue is in a ridge terminal)".

25. In regulation M1 there shall be added the following proviso :

"Provided that neither "appliance" nor "incinerator" shall in this Part include an incinerator employing electricity as a means of igniting refuse.".

26. In regulation M4 after paragraph (9) there shall be added the following paragraph :

"(10) An appliance which is an open fire and is not capable of being used as a closed stove shall not be installed unless secure means of anchorage for an effective fireguard are, if not provided in the appliance itself, provided in the adjoining structure.".

27.—(1) In Schedule 1, PART A—BUILDINGS in the entry relating to Class 6 in column (1) there shall be substituted for the words "(other than a building included in Class 7)" the words "(other than a building included in Class 7 or Class 8)".

(2) In Schedule 1, at the end of PART A—BUILDINGS—there shall be added the entry relating to a new Class 8 which is set out in the Schedule to these regulations.

(3) In Schedule 1, PART B—WORKS AND FITTINGS in the second entry in column (1) there shall be substituted for the words "Classes 3, 5 and 6" the words "Classes 3, 5, 6 and 8".

28.—(1) In Schedule 2, Rule A, Item 2 there shall be substituted—

(a) for the words "not less than 1 inch to every 8 feet" the words "not less than 1/100"; and

(b) for the words "not less than 1 inch to every 16 feet" the words "not less than 1/200".

(2) In Schedule 2, Rule C there shall be substituted for the words "(b) a building in Classes 4, 5 or 6 in that Schedule:" the words "(b) a building in Classes 4, 5, 6, 7 or 8 in that Schedule:".

(3) In Schedule 2, Rule F there shall be deleted all the words from "other than" to "and no structural work is involved:".

29. In Schedule 4 there shall be inserted in the list of local authorities—

(a) at the beginning of the list the words "Bagshot Rural District Council";

(b) after "Easthampstead Rural District Council" the words "Egham Urban District Council"; and

(c) after "Walton and Weybridge Urban District Council" the words "Windsor Rural District Council".

30. In Schedule 6—

(a) there shall be substituted for Rule 2(a)(i) the following:

"(i) *the member either consists of timber of a species classified as Softwood, Group II in CP 112 : 1952 or consists of timber which is of a species named in the list at the end of this rule and is of a grade not inferior to that noted against its name, the grade being determined in accordance with CP 112 : 1967 ; and*" ; and

(b) there shall be inserted at the end of Rule 2 the following:

LIST OF SPECIES OF TIMBER

(1) Imported timber	(2) Grade	(3) Home-grown timber	(4) Grade
Douglas fir	40	Douglas fir	50
Pitch pine	40	Larch	50
Canadian spruce	50	Scots pine	50
Parana pine	50		
Redwood	50		
Western hemlock (commercial)	50		
Western hemlock (unmixed)	50		
Whitewood	50		

SCHEDULE

Regulation 27 (2)

New entry to be inserted in Schedule 1, PART A—BUILDINGS, to the principal regulations

Class	(1)	(2)	(3)	(4)
8	A building which is wholly detached and is used exclusively for the accommodation of plant or machinery designed for any of the processes specified against Minimum List Headings 262, 271, 272, 276, 277, 278, 279.2 and 279.4 of the Standard Industrial Classification (3rd Edition, 1968) issued by the Central Statistical Office (whether or not such plant or machinery forms any part of the structure) if:— (i) it forms part of and is within the curtilage of a works; and (ii) the only persons habitually employed in it are employed solely in the general care, supervision, regulation or maintenance of such plant or machinery.	Regulations A9 and A10	Part B	Part D (in relation to any part of the building which comprises more than one storey) Regulation E5 (unless the building is so situated that each side may in accordance with regulation E7 consist entirely of an unprotected area) Regulation E7 Regulation E15 Regulation K3 Part L

Given under the official seal of the Minister of Housing and Local Government on 1st May 1969.

(L.S.)

Anthony Greenwood,
Minister of Housing and Local Government.

EXPLANATORY NOTE
(This Note is not part of the Regulations.)

These regulations make further amendments to The Building Regulations 1965, as already amended by The Building (Second Amendment) Regulations 1966 and The Building (Third Amendment) Regulations 1967 (the 1965 regulations, as amended in 1966 and 1967, being referred to as "the principal regulations"). These further amendments are, by virtue of Part I, brought into operation on 1st July 1969 but do not apply to work which has been completed, or for which plans have been deposited with local authorities, before that date.

Part II contains the amendments. By regulation 4(*a*) it is made clear that for the purposes of the building regulations, a 'conservatory' means a conservatory with a transparent or translucent roof.

Regulation 4(*b*) amends regulation A2(5)(*b*) so that account may be taken, for the purposes of regulation B2, of British Standards and British Standard Codes of Practice which were current on 31st May 1968, and also, in connection with any publication mentioned in the principal regulations, of any amendments, supplements or addenda published on or before that date.

Regulation 6(2), 20 and 22 substitute references to revised versions of certain British Standards specifically mentioned in the principal regulations.

Regulation 6(3) and (4) removes certain types of asbestos-cement sheeting from the list of materials prescribed as unsuitable for use in permanent buildings as the weather-resisting parts of external walls or roofs.

Regulation 7 replaces the existing regulation B5 by a new regulation containing revised methods for satisfying the requirements of regulation B4 as to treatment of softwood timber to prevent infestation by the house longhorn beetle, and regulation 29 extends the application of regulation B4 to three more local authority areas.

Regulations 8 and 30 amend the deemed-to-satisfy provisions relating to structural work of timber to take account of the current code, CP 112: 1967, but the continued use of CP 112: 1952 is allowed as an alternative.

Regulation 9 provides that under certain conditions, a single storey part of a multi-storey building may be treated for the purposes of Part E (Structural Fire Precautions) as if it were part of a single storey building.

Regulations 10, 11, 12(*a*) and 13 provide that under certain conditions, a door without a self-closing device may be fitted as a fire-resisting door in a lift shaft.

Regulation 12(*b*) modifies the requirements for certain types of fire-resisting door.

Regulations 14 and 15 permit the use, subject to certain conditions, of plastics materials in ceiling panels.

Regulation 16, by re-defining 'common stairway' and 'private stairway' extends the application of Part H of the principal regulations to the construction of external, as well as internal, stairways serving dwellings.

Regulations 17 and 25 extend the control exercised by Part L of the principal regulations to the construction of a chimney or flue pipe intended to serve an electrical incinerator and to the construction of parts of a building in close proximity to such an appliance.

Regulations 18 and 26 amend regulations L2 and M4 of the principal regulations so as to require the provision of means of securing a fireguard in front of an open fire.

Regulations 19 and 21 permit the insertion of a flexible flue liner in chimneys in certain circumstances.

Regulation 27, together with the schedule, widens the exemption from the building regulations for industrial buildings housing plant or machinery associated with certain chemical or similar processes. The publication entitled Standard Industrial Classification (3rd Edition, 1968), referred to in the new entry, is obtainable from Her Majesty's Stationery Office.

Regulation 28(1) alters the minimum scales for drawings submitted for building regulation purposes in order to facilitate the use of metric dimensions.

In addition, regulations 5, 6(1), 23, 24 and 28(2) and (3) make minor adjustments of detail in various particular provisions.

STATUTORY INSTRUMENTS

1969 No. 640

WAGES COUNCILS

The Wages Regulation (Hair, Bass and Fibre) Order 1969

Made - - -		1*st May* 1969
Coming into Operation		23*rd May* 1969

Whereas the Secretary of State has received from the Hair, Bass and Fibre Wages Council (Great Britain) the wages regulation proposals set out in the Schedule hereto ;

Now, therefore, the Secretary of State in exercise of her powers under section 11 of the Wages Councils Act 1959(**a**), and of all other powers enabling her in that behalf, hereby makes the following Order :—

1. This Order may be cited as the Wages Regulation (Hair, Bass and Fibre) Order 1969.

2.—(1) In this Order the expression "the specified date" means the 23rd May 1969, provided that where, as respects any worker who is paid wages at intervals not exceeding seven days, that date does not correspond with the beginning of the period for which the wages are paid, the expression "the specified date" means, as respects that worker, the beginning of the next such period following that date.

(2) The Interpretation Act 1889(**b**) shall apply to the interpretation of this Order as it applies to the interpretation of an Act of Parliament and as if this Order and the Order hereby revoked were Acts of Parliament.

3. The wages regulation proposals set out in the Schedule hereto shall have effect as from the specified date and as from that date the Wages Regulation (Hair, Bass and Fibre) Order 1968(**c**) shall cease to have effect.

Signed by order of the Secretary of State.

1st May 1969.

A. A. Jarratt,
Deputy Under Secretary of State,
Department of Employment and Productivity.

SCHEDULE

Article 3

The following minimum remuneration shall be substituted for the statutory minimum remuneration fixed by the Wages Regulation (Hair, Bass and Fibre) Order 1968 (Order H.B. (69)).

(**a**) 1959 c. 69.
(**c**) S.I. 1968/133 (1968 I, p. 357).

(**b**) 1889 c. 63.

STATUTORY MINIMUM REMUNERATION

Part I

GENERAL

1. The minimum remuneration payable to a worker to whom this Schedule applies for all work except work to which a minimum overtime rate applies under Part IV is:—

(1) in the case of a time worker, the general minimum time rate payable to the worker under Part II or Part III of this Schedule;

(2) in the case of a worker employed on piece work, piece rates each of which would yield, in the circumstances of the case, to an ordinary worker at least the same amount of money as the piece work basis time rate applicable to the worker under Part II or Part III of this Schedule, or, where none is applicable, at least the same amount of money as the general minimum time rate which would be payable to the worker if he were a time worker.

Part II

MALE WORKERS

GENERAL MINIMUM TIME RATES

2.—(1) The general minimum time rates payable to male workers are as follows:—

(a) where the worker is employed in any of the occupations specified in sub-paragraph 2 of this paragraph and his experience in any one or more of them totals not less than 3 years:—

and the worker is aged—	Per hour
	s. d.
21 years or over	6 1½
20 and under 21 years	5 5
19 „ „ 20 „	4 11
18 „ „ 19 „	4 3½

(b) where the worker, not being a worker to whom sub-paragraph (1)(a) of this paragraph applies, is aged—

	Per hour
	s. d.
21 years or over	5 8½
20 and under 21 years	5 0
19 „ „ 20 „	4 4½
18 „ „ 19 „	3 10½
17½ „ „ 18 „	3 3
17 „ „ 17½ „	3 0
16½ „ „ 17 „	2 9½
16 „ „ 16½ „	2 7½
15½ „ „ 16 „	2 5½
Under 15½ years	2 3½

Provided that the general minimum time rate payable during his first 12 months' employment in the trade to a worker specified in this sub-paragraph who enters or has entered the trade for the first time at or over the age of 17 years shall be that applicable to a worker in the age group immediately junior to his age group.

(2) The occupations referred to in (a) of sub-paragraph (1) of this paragraph and in sub-paragraph (1) of paragraph 4 are as follows:—

HAIR DRESSING—Dresser, Opener, Washer, Dyer, Bleacher, Sorter, Hackler or Comber, Drawer or Drafter, Firster, Seconder, Knocker-up, Buncher, Finisher;

HAIR WEAVING (Power loom weaving, damask seating hand loom weaving or carpet weaving)—Weaver, Dyer, Starcher, Hair Carpet Picker;

BASS DRESSING—Sorter, Dyer, Cutter, Rougher, Hackler or Comber, Shaker-up, Roller-up, Mixer or Blender, Jumper, Drawer or Drafter, Bundler, Buncher or Tyer-up, Tightener;

FIBRE DRESSING—Dyer, Bleacher, Hackler or Comber, Shaker-up, Mixer or Blender, Drawer or Drafter, Polisher, Bundler, Buncher or Tyer-up, Hand Trimmer.

PIECE WORK BASIS TIME RATE

Per hour
s. d.

3. The piece work basis time rate applicable to a male worker specified in (a) of sub-paragraph (1) of paragraph 2 is 6 8

PART III

FEMALE WORKERS

GENERAL MINIMUM TIME RATES

4. The general minimum time rate payable to female workers are as follows:—

Per hour
s. d.

(1) where the worker is employed in any of the occupations specified in sub-paragraph (2) of paragraph 2 and her experience in any one or more of them totals not less than 3 years 3 11½

(2) where the worker, not being a worker to whom (1) of this paragraph applies, is aged—

							s.	d.
18 years or over	...	...	...	...	...	...	3	8
17½ and under 18 years		...	...	...	...	...	3	3
17 „ „ 17½ „	...	...	...	...	...	...	3	0
16½ „ „ 17 „	...	...	...	...	...	...	2	10
16 „ „ 16½ „	...	...	...	...	...	...	2	7½
15½ „ „ 16 „	...	...	...	...	...	...	2	5½
Under 15½ years	...	...	...	...	...	...	2	3½

Provided that the general minimum time rate payable during her first 12 months' employment in the trade to a worker who enters or has entered the trade for the first time at or over the age of 16 years shall be that applicable to a worker in the age group immediately junior to her age group.

PIECE WORK BASIS TIME RATE

Per hour
s.   d.

5. The piece work basis time rate applicable to a female worker specified in sub-paragraph (1) of paragraph 4 is **4   1½**

PART IV

OVERTIME AND WAITING TIME—ALL WORKERS

MINIMUM OVERTIME RATES

6. Subject to the provisions of this paragraph, minimum overtime rates are payable to any worker as follows:—

(1) In any week, exclusive of any time for which double time is payable under the provisions of (2) or (3) of this paragraph, for time worked in excess of 40 hours—

    (*a*) for the first 3 hours so worked   ...   .   time-and-a-quarter

    (*b*) thereafter   ...   .   time-and-a-half

    Provided that where in any week a worker is allowed a holiday on any day of customary holiday the said period of 40 hours shall be reduced by 8 hours in respect of each such holiday which is allowed on a day normally worked by the worker.

(2) On a Sunday or a customary holiday—
for all time worked   ...   .   double time

(3) On a Saturday—
for all time worked after noon   ...   .   double time

7. In this Part of this Schedule—

(1) The expressions "time-and-a-quarter", "time-and-a-half" and "double time" mean respectively:—

    (*a*) in the case of a time worker, one and a quarter times, one and a half times and twice the general minimum time rate otherwise payable to the worker;

    (*b*) in the case of a piece worker to whom a piece work basis time rate otherwise applies under paragraph 3 or 5,

        (i) a time rate equal respectively to one quarter, one half and the whole of the said piece work basis time rate and, in addition thereto,

        (ii) piece rates each of which would yield, in the circumstances of the case, to an ordinary worker, at least the same amount of money as the said piece work basis time rate;

    (*c*) in the case of any other worker employed on piece work,

        (i) a time rate equal respectively to one quarter, one half and the whole of the general minimum time rate which would be payable under Part II or Part III of this Schedule if the worker were a time worker and a minimum overtime rate did not apply and, in addition thereto,

        (ii) piece rates each of which would yield, in the circumstances of the case, to an ordinary worker, at least the same amount of money as the said general minimum time rate.

(2) The expression "customary holiday" means—

  (*a*) (i) In England and Wales—

Christmas Day (or, if Christmas Day falls on a Sunday, such week-day as may be appointed by national proclamation, or, if none is so appointed, the next following Tuesday), Boxing Day, Good Friday, Easter Monday, Whit Monday and August Bank Holiday.

    (ii) In Scotland—

New Year's Day (or if New Year's Day falls on a Sunday, the following Monday);

the local Spring holiday;

the local Autumn holiday; and

three other days (being days on which the worker normally works) in the course of a calendar year, to be fixed by the employer and notified to the worker not less than three weeks before the holiday;

or (*b*) in the case of each of the said days (other than a day fixed by the employer in Scotland and notified to the worker as aforesaid) a day substituted therefor by the employer, being a day recognised by local custom as a day of holiday in substitution for the said day.

WAITING TIME

8.—(1) A worker is entitled to payment of the minimum remuneration specified in this Schedule for all time during which he is present on the premises of his employer unless he is present thereon in any of the following circumstances:—

  (*a*) without the employer's consent, express or implied,

  (*b*) for some purpose unconnected with his work and other than that of waiting for work to be given to him to perform,

  (*c*) by reason only of the fact that he is resident thereon,

  (*d*) during normal meal times in a room or place in which no work is being done, and he is not waiting for work to be given to him to perform.

(2) The minimum remuneration payable under sub-paragraph (1) of this paragraph to a piece worker when not engaged on piece work is that which would be payable if he were a time worker.

PART V

APPLICABILITY OF STATUTORY MINIMUM REMUNERATION

9. This Schedule does not apply to workers employed in the weaving of hair machine belting or in any preparatory, finishing, warehousing or packing operation incidental to or appertaining to such weaving, but save as aforesaid applies to workers in relation to whom the Hair, Bass and Fibre Wages Council (Great Britain) operates, that is to say, workers to whom the Schedule to the Hair, Bass and Fibre Wages Council (Great Britain) (Variation) Order 1964(a) applies namely:—

Workers employed in Great Britain in any of the following occupations:—

The drafting, dressing or mixing of bass, whisk or similar fibres or horse hair or other hairs and the weaving of hair or fibre or of mixed hair and fibre, and all

---

(a) S.I. 1964/585 (1964 I, p. 1085).

preparatory, finishing, warehousing or packing operations incidental to or appertaining to all or any of the above processes, but excluding:—

(*a*) any of the above operations or processes where they are carried on in association with or in conjunction with the manufacture of brushes or brooms;

(*b*) the drafting, dressing or mixing of hair or fibre preparatory to the curling of hair or fibre or of mixed hair and fibre and all preparatory, finishing, warehousing or packing operations incidental to or appertaining to all or any of the last above-mentioned processes, and

(*c*) the dressing of animal skins.

EXPLANATORY NOTE

(*This Note is not part of the Order.*)

This Order, which has effect from 23rd May 1969, sets out the statutory minimum remuneration payable in substitution for that fixed by the Wages Regulation (Hair, Bass and Fibre) Order 1968 (Order H.B. (69)), which Order is revoked.

New provisions are printed in italics.

STATUTORY INSTRUMENTS

1969 No. 641

WAGES COUNCILS

The Wages Regulation (Hair, Bass and Fibre) (Holidays) Order 1969

Made - - -		*1st May* 1969
Coming into Operation		*23rd May* 1969

Whereas the Secretary of State has received from the Hair, Bass and Fibre Wages Council (Great Britain) the wages regulation proposals set out in the Schedule hereto ;

Now, therefore, the Secretary of State in exercise of her powers under section 11 of the Wages Councils Act 1959(**a**), and of all other powers enabling her in that behalf, hereby makes the following Order :—

1. This Order may be cited as the Wages Regulation (Hair, Bass and Fibre) (Holidays) Order 1969.

2.—(1) In this Order the expression "the specified date" means the 23rd May 1969, provided that where, as respects any worker who is paid wages at intervals not exceeding seven days, that date does not correspond with the beginning of the period for which the wages are paid, the expression "the specified date" means, as respects that worker, the beginning of the next such period following that date.

(2) The Interpretation Act 1889(**b**) shall apply to the interpretation of this Order as it applies to the interpretation of an Act of Parliament and as if this Order and the Order hereby revoked were Acts of Parliament.

3. The wages regulation proposals set out in the Schedule hereto shall have effect as from the specified date and as from that date the Wages Regulation (Hair, Bass and Fibre) (Holidays) Order 1962(**c**), shall cease to have effect.

Signed by order of the Secretary of State.

A. A. Jarratt,
Deputy Under Secretary of State,
Department of Employment and Productivity.

1st May 1969.

(**a**) 1959 c. 69.   (**b**) 1889 c. 63.
(**c**) S.I. 1962/790 (1962 I, p. 844).

Article 3 SCHEDULE

The following provisions as to holidays and holiday remuneration shall be substituted for the provisions as to holidays and holiday remuneration set out in the Wages Regulation (Hair, Bass and Fibre) (Holidays) Order 1962 (hereinafter referred to as "Order H.B. (58)").

Part I

APPLICATION

1. This Schedule applies to every worker (other than an outworker) for whom statutory minimum remuneration has been fixed.

Part II

CUSTOMARY HOLIDAYS

2.—(1) An employer shall allow to every worker in his employment to whom this Schedule applies a holiday (hereinafter referred to as a "customary holiday") in each year on the days specified in the following sub-paragraph, provided that the worker has been in his employment for a period of not less than eight weeks immediately preceding the customary holiday and has worked for the employer during the whole or part of that period and (unless excused by the employer or absent by reason of the proved illness of the worker) has worked for the employer throughout the last working day on which work was available to him immediately preceding the customary holiday.

(2) The said customary holidays are:—

    (a) (i) In England and Wales—

Christmas Day (or, if Christmas Day falls on a Sunday, such week-day as may be appointed by national proclamation, or, if none is so appointed, the next following Tuesday), Boxing Day, Good Friday, Easter Monday, Whit Monday and August Bank holiday.

    (ii) In Scotland—

New Year's Day (or, if New Year's Day falls on a Sunday, the following Monday);

the local Spring holiday;

the local Autumn holiday; and

three other days (being days on which the worker normally works) in the course of a calendar year to be fixed by the employer and notified to the worker not less than three weeks before the holiday;

or (b) In the case of each of the said days (other than a day fixed by the employer in Scotland and notified to the worker as aforesaid) a day substituted therefor by the employer, being a day recognised by local custom as a day of holiday in substitution for the said day.

(3) Notwithstanding the preceding provisions of this paragraph, an employer may (except where in the case of a woman or young person such requirement would be unlawful) require a worker who is otherwise entitled to any customary holiday under the foregoing provisions of this Schedule to work thereon and, in lieu of any holiday on which he so works, the employer shall allow to the worker a day's holiday (hereinafter referred to as a "holiday in lieu of a customary holiday") on a week-day within the period of two months next ensuing.

(4) A worker who is so required to work on a customary holiday shall be paid:—

    (a) for all time worked thereon, the statutory minimum remuneration then appropriate to the worker for work on a customary holiday; and

    (b) in respect of the holiday in lieu of the customary holiday, holiday remuneration in accordance with paragraph 8.

PART III

ANNUAL HOLIDAY

3. Subject to the provisions of paragraph 4, in addition to the holidays specified in Part II of this Schedule, an employer shall, between the date on which the provisions of this Schedule become effective and 30th September 1969 and in each succeeding year between 6th April and 30th September allow a holiday (hereinafter referred to as an "annual holiday") to every worker in his employment to whom this Schedule applies who has been employed by him during the twelve months immediately preceding the commencement of the holiday season for any of the periods of employment (calculated in accordance with the provisions of paragraph 13) set out in the Table below, and the duration of the annual holiday shall, in the case of each such worker, be related to his period of employment during that twelve months as follows:—

Period of employment					Duration of annual holiday where the worker's normal working week is:—		
					5 days	4 days	3 days
At least 48 weeks	..	..	..	..	10 days	8 days	6 days
„ „ 44 „	..	..	..	..	9 „	7 „	5 „
„ „ 40 „	..	..	..	..	8 „	6 „	5 „
„ „ 36 „	..	..	..	..	7 „	6 „	4 „
„ „ 32 „	..	..	..	..	6 „	5 „	4 „
„ „ 28 „	..	..	..	..	5 „	4 „	3 „
„ „ 24 „	..	..	..	..	4 „	4 „	3 „
„ „ 20 „	..	..	..	..	3 „	3 „	2 „
„ „ 16 „	..	..	..	..	2 „	2 „	2 „
„ „ 12 „	..	..	..	..	2 „	2 „	1 day
„ „ 8 „	..	..	..	..	1 day	1 day	1 „

4.—(1) An annual holiday under this Schedule shall be allowed on consecutive working days, being days on which the worker is normally called upon to work for the employer, and days of holiday shall be treated as consecutive notwithstanding that a Sunday, a customary holiday on which the worker is not required to work or a holiday in lieu of a customary holiday intervenes:

Provided that—

(a) where the duration of an annual holiday which the employer is required to allow to a worker exceeds the period constituting the worker's normal working week the said holiday may by agreement in writing made between the employer and the worker be allowed in two separate periods of such consecutive working days, if one of such periods is not less than the period constituting the worker's normal working week;

(b) one day of an annual holiday may be allowed on a non-consecutive working day falling within the holiday season or with the consent of the worker on any working day prior to the commencement of the next holiday season where the said annual holiday or such separate period, as the case may be, is allowed immediately after a customary holiday on which the worker is not required to work or so that such a customary holiday intervenes;

(c) the duration of the worker's annual holiday in the holiday season ending on 30th September 1969 shall be reduced by any days of annual holiday duly allowed to him by the employer under the provisions of Order H.B. (58) between 6th April 1969 and the date on which the provisions of this Schedule become effective.

(2) Subject to the provisions of sub-paragraph (1) of this paragraph, any day of annual holiday *or additional annual holiday* under this Schedule may be allowed on a day on which the worker is entitled to a day of holiday or to a half-holiday under any enactment other than the Wages Councils Act 1959.

(3) In this Schedule the expression "holiday season" means, in relation to an annual holiday during the year 1969, the period commencing on 6th April 1969 and ending on 30th September 1969 and, in relation to each subsequent year, the period commencing on 6th April and ending on 30th September in that year *and in relation to an additional annual holiday means a period of one year commencing on 6th April.*

ADDITIONAL ANNUAL HOLIDAY

5. *Subject to the provisions of this paragraph, in addition to the holidays specified in paragraphs 2 and 3 an employer shall in each year commencing on 6th April allow a holiday (hereinafter referred to as an "additional annual holiday") to every worker in his employment to whom this Schedule applies who has been employed by him at the preceding 5th April for a continuous period of two years or more (calculated in accordance with paragraph 13) and the duration of the additional annual holiday shall be related to his continuous period of employment as follows:—*

(a) *2 years but less than 4 years' continuous employment—1 day;*

(b) *4 years or more continuous employment—2 days.*

6. *Where a worker becomes entitled to any days of additional annual holiday in accordance with the provisions of paragraph 5 those days of additional annual holiday shall be allowed by the employer, by agreement with the worker, on a day or days on which the worker is normally called upon to work for the employer, at any time (or times) during the period of 12 months immediately following 5th April upon which the worker becomes entitled as aforesaid.*

GENERAL

7. *An employer shall give to a worker notice of the commencing date or dates and duration of the period or periods of his annual holiday and the date or dates of his additional holiday. Such notice shall be given at least 28 days before*

(a) the first day of the annual holiday or, where under the provisions of paragraph 4 an annual holiday is allowed in more than one period, before each separate period; *and*

(b) *the said date or dates of the additional annual holiday.*

Notice may be given individually to the worker or by the posting of a notice in the place where the worker is employed.

PART IV
HOLIDAY REMUNERATION
A—CUSTOMARY HOLIDAYS AND HOLIDAYS IN LIEU OF CUSTOMARY HOLIDAYS

8.—(1) Subject to the provisions of this paragraph, for each day of holiday which a worker is allowed under Part II of this Schedule he shall be paid by the employer as holiday remuneration whichever of the following sums is the greater, that is to say either:—

(a) (i) in the case of a worker whose normal working week is five days, one-fifth

(ii) in the case of a worker whose normal working week is four days, one-quarter

(iii) in the case of a worker whose normal working week is three days, one-third

of the average weekly earnings (exclusive of overtime but including holiday remuneration) of the worker during the twelve months ended on 5th April immediately preceding the holiday such average weekly earnings to be determined by dividing, by the number of weeks of employment with the employer during the said period, the total remuneration (as defined in paragraph 14) paid to him by the employer during that period:

Provided that when Good Friday or Easter Monday in England and Wales or the local Spring holiday in Scotland (or days substituted therefor under the provisions of sub-paragraph (2)(*b*) of paragraph 2 or holidays in lieu of such customary holidays) fall after 5th April in any year, the holiday remuneration for any such holiday under this sub-paragraph shall be one-fifth, one-quarter or one-third, as the case may require, of the average weekly earnings (exclusive of overtime but including holiday remuneration) of the worker (calculated as aforesaid) during the twelve months ended on 5th April in the preceding year; or

(*b*) a sum equal to the appropriate statutory minimum remuneration to which he would have been entitled if the day had not been a day of holiday and he had been employed on work entitling him to statutory minimum remuneration for the time normally worked by him on that day of the week:

Provided that payment of the said holiday remuneration is subject to the condition that the worker (unless excused by the employer or absent by reason of the proved illness of the worker) presents himself for employment at the usual starting hour on the first working day following the holiday.

(2) The holiday remuneration in respect of any customary holiday shall be paid by the employer to the worker on the pay day on which the wages for the pay week including the customary holiday are paid.

(3) The holiday remuneration in respect of any holiday in lieu of a customary holiday shall be paid on the pay day on which the wages for the week including that holiday in lieu of a customary holiday are paid: Provided that the said payment shall be made immediately upon the termination of the worker's employment if he ceases to be employed before being allowed such holiday in lieu of a customary holiday and in that case the condition specified in sub-paragraph (1) of this paragraph shall not apply.

B—ANNUAL HOLIDAY

9.—(1) Subject to the provisions of paragraph 11, a worker qualified to be allowed an annual holiday under this Schedule shall be paid as holiday remuneration by his employer in respect thereof not later than the last pay day preceding such annual holiday—

(*a*) in the case of a worker who has been in the employment of the employer during the whole of the twelve months up to and including the 5th April immediately preceding the commencement of the holiday season whichever of the following sums is the greater, that is to say either:—

(i) a sum equal to two fifty-seconds of the total remuneration (as defined in paragraph 14) paid to him by the employer during the said twelve months; or

(ii) one day's holiday pay in respect of each day of annual holiday;

(*b*) in the case of any other worker:—
one day's holiday pay in respect of each day of annual holiday.

(2) Where under the provisions of paragraph 4 an annual holiday is allowed in more than one period the holiday remuneration shall be apportioned accordingly.

C—ADDITIONAL ANNUAL HOLIDAY

10. *A worker entitled to be allowed an additional annual holiday under this Schedule shall be paid by his employer in respect thereof on the last pay day preceding such additional annual holiday as follows:—*

(*1*) *Where (a) of paragraph 5 applies:—*

Where the worker's normal working week is 5 days ...	...	*one-tenth*
" " " " " " " 4 days ...	...	*one-eighth*
" " " " " " " 3 days ...	...	*one-sixth*

of the amount he would be entitled to receive at the date of the holiday for an annual holiday of two normal working weeks determined in accordance with paragraph 9.

(2) Where (b) of paragraph 5 applies:—

Where the worker's normal working week is 5 days ...   ...   one-fifth
     "   "   "   "   "   "   " *4 days ...   ...   one-quarter*
     "   "   "   "   "   "   " *3 days ...   ...   one-third*

of the amount he would be entitled to receive at the date of the holiday for an annual holiday of two normal working weeks determined in accordance with paragraph 9.

(3) Where an employer allows the days of additional annual holiday otherwise than on consecutive days the remuneration shall be apportioned accordingly.

11. Where any accrued holiday remuneration has been paid by the employer to the worker (in accordance with paragraph 12 of this Schedule or Order H.B. (58)) in respect of employment during any of the periods referred to in paragraph 12 of this Schedule, the amount of holiday remuneration payable by the employer in respect of any annual holiday for which the worker has qualified by reason of employment during the said period shall be reduced by the amount of the said accrued holiday remuneration unless that remuneration has been deducted from a previous payment of holiday remuneration made under the provisions of this Schedule or of Order H.B. (58).

ACCRUED HOLIDAY REMUNERATION PAYABLE ON TERMINATION OF EMPLOYMENT

12. Where a worker ceases to be employed by an employer after the provisions of this Schedule become effective, the employer shall, immediately on the termination of the employment pay to the worker as accrued holiday remuneration:—

(1) (*a*) in respect of employment in the twelve months up to and including the immediately preceding 5th April a sum equal to the holiday remuneration for any days of annual holiday for which he has qualified except days of annual holiday which he has been allowed or has become entitled to be allowed before leaving his employment; and

(*b*) *in respect of employment up to and including the immediately preceding 5th April a sum equal to the holiday remuneration for any days of additional annual holiday for which he has qualified except any day or days of additional annual holiday which he has been allowed or has become entitled to be allowed before leaving his employment;*

(2) in respect of any employment since the said 5th April a sum equal to the holiday remuneration which would have been payable to him if he could have been allowed an annual holiday in respect of that employment at the time of leaving it, and if paid at the rate of one day's holiday pay in respect of each day thereof.

PART V

GENERAL

13. For the purposes of calculating any period of employment qualifying a worker for an annual holiday *or additional annual holiday* or for any accrued holiday remuneration under this Schedule, the worker shall be treated—

(*a*) as if he were employed for a week in respect of any week in which—

(i) he has worked for the employer on not less than three days and has performed some work for which statutory minimum remuneration is payable; or

(ii) he has been absent throughout the week by reason of the proved illness of or accident to, the worker, but not exceeding four weeks in the aggregate in the period of twelve months immediately preceding the commencement of the holiday season; and

(b) as if he were employed on any day of holiday allowed under the provisions of this Schedule, and for the purposes of the provisions of sub-paragraph (a) of this paragraph, a worker who is absent on such a holiday shall be treated as having worked thereon for the employer on work to which statutory minimum remuneration applies.

14. In this Schedule, unless the context otherwise requires, the following expressions have the meanings hereby respectively assigned to them, that is to say:—

"APPROPRIATE RATE OF STATUTORY MINIMUM REMUNERATION" means—

(a) in the case of a worker who is usually wholly employed as a time worker, the general minimum time rate ordinarily applicable to the worker;

(b) in the case of a worker who is usually employed on piece work,

   (i) where the worker is aged over 18 years and a piece work basis time rate is applicable, a time rate equal to the piece work basis time rate ordinarily applicable to the worker;

   (ii) in any other case the general minimum time rate which would be ordinarily applicable to the worker if he were employed as a time worker:
Provided that for the purposes of this definition—

   (i) a rate ordinarily applicable to a worker shall be ascertained by reference to the work on which he has been mainly employed in the twelve months immediately prior to the holiday in the case of a customary holiday, the commencement of the holiday season in the case of an annual holiday *or additional annual holiday* or the termination date where accrued holiday remuneration is payable;

   (ii) where a worker is usually employed partly on time work and partly on piece work, he shall be treated as having been usually employed wholly on piece work.

"NORMAL WORKING WEEK" means the number of days on which it has been usual for the worker to work in a week in the employment of the employer during the twelve months immediately preceding the commencement of the holiday season, or, where under paragraphs 11 and 12, accrued holiday remuneration is payable on the termination of the employment, in the twelve months immediately preceding the termination date:

Provided that:—

   (i) part of a day shall count as a day; and

   (ii) no account shall be taken of any week in which the worker did not perform any work for which statutory minimum remuneration has been fixed.

"ONE DAY'S HOLIDAY PAY" means the appropriate proportion of the remuneration which the worker would be entitled to receive from his employer at the date of the annual holiday (or, where the holiday is taken in more than one period, at the date of the first period), *or date or dates of additional annual holiday* or at the termination date, as the case may be, for one week's work if working his normal working week and the number of daily hours normally worked by him (exclusive of overtime), and if paid at the appropriate rate of statutory minimum remuneration for work to which statutory minimum remuneration applies and at the same rate for any work for the same employer to which such remuneration does not apply, and in this definition "appropriate proportion" means—

where the worker's normal working week is five days — one-fifth
   "   "   "   "   "   "   " four " — one-quarter
   "   "   "   "   "   "   " three .. — one-third

"STATUTORY MINIMUM REMUNERATION" means statutory minimum remuneration (other than holiday remuneration) which has been fixed by a wages regulation order.

"TOTAL REMUNERATION" means any payments paid or payable to the worker under his contract of employment, for time (other than hours of overtime) worked or piece work done by him, holiday remuneration, any productivity or long service bonus payable to the worker on a weekly, fortnightly or monthly basis and merit payments so payable but does not include any other payments.

"WAGES REGULATION ORDER" means a wages regulation order made by the Secretary of State to give effect to proposals submitted to her by the Hair, Bass and Fibre Wages Council (Great Britain).

"WEEK" means pay week.

15. The provisions of this Schedule are without prejudice to any agreement for the allowance of any further holidays with pay or for the payment of additional holiday remuneration.

EXPLANATORY NOTE

(*This Note is not part of the Order.*)

This Order, which has effect from 23rd May 1969, sets out the holidays which an employer is required to allow to workers and the remuneration payable for those holidays in substitution for the holidays and holiday remuneration set out in the Wages Regulation (Hair, Bass and Fibre) (Holidays) Order 1962 (Order H.B. (58)), which Order is revoked.

New provisions are printed in italics.

STATUTORY INSTRUMENTS

1969 No. 654

WAGES COUNCILS

The Wages Regulation (Rope, Twine and Net) Order 1969

Made - - - -	*5th May* 1969
Coming into Operation	*21st May* 1969

Whereas the Secretary of State has received from the Rope, Twine and Net Wages Council (Great Britain) the wages regulation proposals set out in Schedules 1 and 2 hereof;

Now, therefore, the Secretary of State in exercise of her powers under section 11 of the Wages Councils Act 1959(a), and of all other powers enabling her in that behalf, hereby makes the following Order:—

1. This Order may be cited as the Wages Regulation (Rope, Twine and Net) Order 1969.

2.—(1) In this Order the expression "the specified date" means the 21st May 1969, provided that where, as respects any worker who is paid wages at intervals not exceeding seven days, that date does not correspond with the beginning of the period for which the wages are paid, the expression "the specified date" means, as respects that worker, the beginning of the next such period following that date.

(2) The Interpretation Act 1889(b) shall apply to the interpretation of this Order as it applies to the interpretation of an Act of Parliament and as if this Order and the Order hereby revoked were Acts of Parliament.

3. The wages regulation proposals set out in Schedules 1 and 2 hereof shall have effect as from the specified date and as from that date the Wages Regulation (Rope, Twine and Net) Order 1967(c) shall cease to have effect.

Signed by order of the Secretary of State.

A. A. Jarratt,
Deputy Under Secretary of State,
Department of Employment and Productivity.

5th May 1969.

SCHEDULE 1   Article 3

The following minimum remuneration shall be substituted for the statutory minimum remuneration fixed by the Wages Regulation (Rope, Twine and Net) Order 1967 (Order R. (149)).

(a) 1959 c. 69.   (b) 1889 c. 63.
(c) 1967/757 (1967 II, p. 2233).

STATUTORY MINIMUM REMUNERATION

PART I

GENERAL

1. The minimum remuneration payable to a worker to whom this Schedule applies for all work except work to which a minimum overtime rate applies under Part III of this Schedule is:—

(1) in the case of a time worker, the general minimum time rate, *or, where appropriate, the minimum weekly remuneration* payable to the worker under Part II of this Schedule;

(2) in the case of a worker employed on piece work—

(*a*) where a general minimum piece rate applies under Part II of this Schedule, that piece rate increased by *33⅓ per cent.*, or

(*b*) where no general minimum piece rate applies, piece rates each of which would yield, in the circumstances of the case, to an ordinary worker at least the same amount of money as the piece work basis time rate applicable to the worker under Paragraph 3 (5) of this Schedule.

DEFINITIONS

2. In this Schedule, unless the context otherwise requires,

(1) SHIFT WORKER means a worker employed on a shift system in accordance with which—

(*a*) a 24-hour period is divided into two or more shifts, one of which is a night shift; or

(*b*) there is no night shift and the remainder of the day is divided into two or more shifts;

and for the purposes of this definition NIGHT SHIFT means a turn of duty which includes some period of employment between 10 p.m. on one day and 6 a.m. on the next following day.

(2) HARD FIBRES mean manilla, sisal, maguey fibre, New Zealand hemp or coir or a mixture thereof;

SHRINK NETTING means that the netting is made by shrinking or gaining, that is to say, the process of putting two meshes into one mesh or vice versa in order to obtain the required taper, shrink or gain;

PLAIN NETTING is ordinary braiding, single selvedge, the net mesh when straight hanging diamond;

A RAN SHORT REEL is the amount of twine wound on a reel 69 inches in circumference in 400 revolutions or 766⅔ yards;

SIZE OF MESH means in the case of all nets, other than the stack nets referred to in paragraph 9, the total length of two adjacent sides of the mesh, measured from the inside of one knot to the outside of the other.

PART II

ALL SECTIONS OF THE TRADE
GENERAL MINIMUM TIME RATES, MINIMUM WEEKLY REMUNERATION AND PIECE WORK BASIS TIME RATES

3.—(*1*) *Subject to the provisions of sub-paragraphs* (*2*) *to* (*4*) *of this paragraph, the general minimum time rates payable to male and female workers specified in Column 1 of the next following Table are the rates set out in Column 2 of that Table.*

(2) *Where, in any week, the remuneration payable to a worker for the hours worked (excluding overtime) in that week, calculated at the appropriate general minimum time rate, together with any bonus payments or holiday remuneration payable to the worker in that week amounts to less than the minimum weekly remuneration specified for that worker in Column 3 of the next following Table, the minimum remuneration (exclusive of any amount payable in respect of overtime) payable to that worker in that week shall be the minimum weekly remuneration so specified.*

(3) *For the purposes of the preceding sub-paragraph the minimum weekly remuneration shall be reduced proportionately according as the number of hours worked (excluding overtime) is less than 40 where—*

(a) *the worker is a part-time worker who normally works for the employer for less than 40 hours a week by reason only of the fact that he does not hold himself out as normally available for work for more than the number of hours he normally works in the week;*

or (b) *the worker works for less than 40 hours in any week by reason of absence at any time during that week with the consent of the employer or because of proved incapacity due to illness or injury.*

(4) *Except as provided by sub-paragraph (3)(b) of this paragraph, the minimum weekly remuneration specified in column 3 of the next following Table shall not be payable to a worker in any week in which that worker at any time in that week is absent from work without the consent of the employer.*

Table of General Minimum Time Rates and Minimum Weekly Remuneration

TIME WORKERS	General Minimum Time Rate	Minimum Weekly Remuneration
Column 1	Column 2	Column 3
MALE WORKERS OTHER THAN SHIFT WORKERS (including home-workers) being aged—	per hour s. d.	s. d.
18 years or over	5 4½	240 0
17 and under 18 years	3 5½	138 4
16 ,, ,, 17 ,, ...	2 10½	115 0
under 16 years	2 4½	95 0
FEMALE WORKERS OTHER THAN SHIFT WORKERS (including home-workers) being aged—		
18 years or over	4 1½	180 0
17½ and under 18 years	3 6½	141 8
17 ,, ,, 17½ ,, ...	3 1	123 4
16½ ,, ,, 17 ,, ...	2 10	113 4
16 ,, ,, 16½ ,, ...	2 6	100 0
under 16 years	2 4½	95 0
MALE SHIFT WORKERS, WHEN EMPLOYED ON DAY SHIFTS, being aged—		
18 years or over	6 0	270 0
17 and under 18 years	3 9¼	150 10
16 ,, ,, 17 ,, ...	3 1¾	125 10
FEMALE SHIFT WORKERS, WHEN EMPLOYED ON DAY SHIFTS, being aged—		
18 years or over	4 7	202 6
17½ and under 18 years	3 10¾	155 10
17 ,, ,, 17½ ,, ...	3 4¾	135 10
16½ ,, ,, 17 ,, ...	3 1½	125 0
16 ,, ,, 16½ ,, ...	2 9	110 0

TIME WORKERS	General Minimum Time Rate	Minimum Weekly Remuneration
Column 1	Column 2	Column 3
MALE SHIFT WORKERS, WHEN EMPLOYED ON NIGHT SHIFTS, being aged—		
18 years or over	6 5	288 0
PROVIDED THAT the following rates shall apply to new entrants who enter or have entered the trade for the first time at or over the age of 18 years:—		
MALE WORKERS—for the first eight weeks of employment...	5 4½	215 0
FEMALE WORKERS—for the first eight weeks of employment...	4 1½	165 0

(5) *The piece work basis time rates applicable to the male or female workers specified in Column 1 of the next following Table, when employed on piece work with the materials specified in Column 2 or 3 as the case may be, are the rates set out in Column 2 or 3 respectively.*

Table of Piece Work Basis Time Rates

WORKERS EMPLOYED ON PIECE WORK	Fibres other than man-made fibres of continuous filament	Man-made fibres of continuous filament
Column 1	Column 2	Column 3
	s. d.	s. d.
Male workers other than shift workers	5 6	—
Female „ „ „	4 3	4 8
Male shift workers on day shift „	6 1½	—
Female „ „ „ „ „	4 7½	5 1
Male workers on night shift	6 6½	—

(6) *In this paragraph*—

"*bonus payments*" *means any production, merit, incentive or similar bonus payments payable at intervals of not more than one month;*

"*the Trade*" *means the Rope, Twine and Net Trade as specified in paragraph 14.*

GENERAL MINIMUM PIECE RATES

MAKING COTTON NORSELLS

4. The general minimum piece rates payable per pound to female home-workers for making cotton norsells are as follows:—

11 inches and upwards:—

	s. d.			s. d.
32s/18 ply norsells ...	11 2	32s/36 ply norsells ...		4 9
32s/21 „ „ ...	9 3	32s/42 „ „ ...		3 9⅜
32s/24 „ „ ...	7 4⅞	32s/48 „ „ ...		3 5½
32s/27 „ „ ...	6 6½	32s/54 „ „ ...		3 1½
32s/30 „ „ ...	5 7	32s/60 „ „ ...		2 8¼

MAKING HEMP NORSELLS

5. The general minimum piece rates payable per 1,000 to female home-workers for making hemp norsells are as follows:—

		Natural Colour	Tanned			Natural Colour	Tanned
		s. d.	s. d.			s. d.	s. d.
18 inch	...	5 7	6 7½	36 inch	...	9 6	11 2
20 „	...	5 8	6 9¾	42 „	...	10 9¼	12 4¾
22 „	...	5 11	7 1	48 „	...	12 4¾	13 10⅛
24 „	...	6 8⅝	7 6¼				

HANDBRAIDING, HANDKNOTTING OR HANDBAITING NETS FROM FIBRES NOT BEING HARD FIBRES OR MAN-MADE FIBRES OF CONTINUOUS FILAMENT

NETS MADE FROM SINGLE TWINE

6.—(1) The general minimum piece rates set out in the next following Table are per dozen rans short reel or per 9,200 yards and are payable, subject to the provisions of this paragraph, to female home-workers employed on handbraiding, handknotting or handbaiting nets made from single twine (of sizes up to and including 36 lbs. per dozen rans short reel or per 9,200 yards) from fibres not being hard fibres or man-made fibres of continuous filament.

(2) The length of the nets referred to in Columns 3 to 8 inclusive of the said Table is the length measured by stretched mesh or through the hand.

(3) Where the twine is of a size larger than 36 lbs. per dozen rans short reel or per 9,200 yards the general minimum piece rates payable to the said workers are the rates set out in the said Table increased as follows:—

Size of Twine   Additions

									s.	d.
Over	36 lbs. and up to and including	48 lbs.	...	...	...	...			10	1
„	48 „ „ „ „ „ „	60 „	...	...	...	...			20	4
„	60 „ „ „ „ „ „	84 „	...	...	...	...			31	4
„	84 „ „ „ „ „ „	96 „	...	...	...	...			32	0
„	96 „ „ „ „ „ „	108 „	...	...	...	...			36	0
„	108 „ „ „ „ „ „	120 „	...	...	...	...			42	0
„	120 „ „ „ „ „ „	132 „	...	...	...	...			48	0
„	132 „ „ „ „ „ „	144 „	...	...	...	...			54	0
„	144 „ „ „ „ „ „	156 „	...	...	...	...			60	0
„	156 „	...	...	...	...	...	...	...	66	0

(4) Where the work is double knotted work, the general minimum piece rates payable to the said workers shall be one and two-thirds times the rates payable for single knotted work.

TABLE OF PIECE RATES

Twines of sizes up to and including 36 lbs. per dozen rans short reel or per 9,200 yards

Size of mesh	Plain netting	Shrink or square mesh work irrespective of numbers of meshes begun or ended (single or double selvedge) and plain netting with double selvedge	Netting braided in the form of a hose or bag including shrimp and landing nets, billiard table pockets and other fancy nets					
			Length 30 inches and over	Length 20 inches and over but under 30 inches	Length 15 inches and over but under 20 inches	Length 10 inches and over but under 15 inches	Length 5 inches and over but under 10 inches	Length under 5 inches
	Column 1	Column 2	Column 3	Column 4	Column 5	Column 6	Column 7	Column 8
	s. d.	s. d.	s. d.	s. d.	s. d.	s. d.	s. d.	s. d.
Over 7 inch	88 5½	93 0½	97 7	111 10½	123 5	132 8	139 3½	146 3
5 inch and over up to and including 7 inch	92 7½	97 6	101 11½	117 3	128 11	138 7	145 6½	152 10
4 inch and over up to but not including 5 inch ...	99 8½	105 0½	109 10	126 3½	138 11	149 4	156 9½	164 7
Rows per yard:—								
Over 18 and up to and including 21	106 3	111 2½	116 10	134 5	147 10	158 11	166 10½	175 2½
" 21 " " 24	111 9½	117 4½	123 3	141 9	155 11	167 7½	175 11½	184 9
" 24 " " 27	117 4½	123 3	129 2½	148 7	163 5½	175 8½	184 5½	193 8
" 27 " " 30	123 3	129 6	135 7½	155 11½	171 6½	184 5½	193 7½	203 4
" 30 " " 33	128 7½	135 3½	141 9½	163 0½	179 4½	192 9½	202 5½	212 7
" 33 " " 36	134 6	141 6	147 11½	171 1½	187 2½	201 2½	211 3	221 10
" 36 " " 39	140 1½	146 10½	154 1	177 2½	194 11	209 6	220 0	231 0
" 39 " " 42	145 11½	152 11	160 6	184 7	203 0½	218 3	229 1½	240 8
" 42 " " 45	151 3½	158 10	166 5	191 5	210 6½	226 4	237 8	249 6
" 45 " " 48	157 2½	164 11½	172 11	198 10	218 9	235 1½	246 10½	259 2½
" 48 " " 54	168 4	176 11½	185 6	213 4	234 8	252 3	264 10½	278 1½
" 54 " " 60	179 10	188 10½	197 9½	227 5½	250 2½	268 11½	282 5	296 5½
" 60 " " 66	191 1	200 11	210 5	241 11	266 2½	286 1½	300 5	315 5
" 66 " " 72	202 6	212 3½	222 8½	256 0½	281 8½	302 10	317 11½	333 10½
" 72 " " 78	213 9	224 4	235 1	270 4	297 4½	319 8	335 8	352 5½
" 78 " " 84	225 3	236 4½	247 7½	284 9	313 3	336 9	353 7	371 3
" 84 " " 90	236 4½	248 3	260 3	299 3	329 2	353 10½	371 7	390 2
" 90 " " 96	247 7	260 2½	272 7½	313 6	344 10	370 8½	389 3	408 8½
" 96 " " 108	270 5	283 10	297 5	342 0½	376 1½	404 5	424 8	445 11
" 108 " " 120	292 11½	307 10	322 1½	370 5	407 6	438 1	459 11½	482 11½
" 120 " " 132	315 9	331 5½	347 5½	399 7	439 6½	472 6	496 1½	520 11
" 132 " " 144	338 6	355 2	372 5	428 3	471 1	506 5	531 9	558 4
" 144 " " 162	372 5	390 9	409 10	471 4	518 5½	557 4	585 2½	614 4½

NETS MADE FROM DOUBLE OR TREBLE TWINE

7. The general minimum piece rates payable to female home-workers employed on handbraiding, handknotting or handbaiting nets made from double or treble twine from fibres not being hard fibres or man-made fibres of continuous filament are respectively three-quarters and two-thirds of the general minimum piece rates which would be payable under paragraph 6 if the nets were made from single twine.

HANDBRAIDING OF TRAWL, SEINE OR OTHER NETS FROM HARD FIBRES

8.—(1) The general minimum piece rates set out in the next following Table are per lb. of twine and are payable, subject to the provisions of this paragraph, to female workers (including home-workers) employed in the handbraiding of trawl, seine or other nets (other than stack nets to which paragraph 9 applies) from hard fibres.

(2) The general minimum piece rates set out in the said Table are payable where the needles are filled at the expense of the worker. Where the needles are filled at the expense of the employer, the said rates shall be reduced by ten per cent.

(3) Where a net section contains meshes of more than one size, the general minimum piece rate payable for the whole section is that for a mesh size ascertained by a weighted average arrived at as follows: Multiply the number of rows of each separate mesh size by the size of the mesh, add the product, and divide the result by the total number of rows in the net section.

For example: The belly of a new trawl net consisting of 75 rows of 3-inch mesh, 50 rows of 4-inch mesh, 25 rows of 5-inch mesh: Calculation of weighted average mesh—

$$75 \times 3 = 225$$
$$50 \times 4 = 200$$
$$25 \times 5 = 125$$

Weighted average mesh size $= \dfrac{550}{150} = 3\frac{2}{3}$ inches.

$$\overline{150} \quad \overline{550}$$

The whole net section must be paid for as though the mesh was $3\frac{2}{3}$ inches throughout, viz., under Col. 8 of the said Table.

TABLE OF PIECE RATES

	Col. 1		Col. 2		Col. 3		Col. 4		Col. 5		Col. 6	
Size of mesh: less than ...	2 in.		2¼ in.		2½ in.		2¾ in.		3 in.		3¼ in.	
and not less than ...	—		2 in.		2¼ in.		2½ in.		2¾ in.		3 in.	
Twine used as: S.=Single, D.=Double ...	S.	D.	S.	D.	S.	D.	S.	D.	S.	D.	S.	D.
Twine sizes:—	s. d.	s. d.	s. d.	s. d.	s. d.	s. d.	s. d.	s. d.	s. d.	s. d.	s. d.	s. d.
Up to and including 60 yds. per lb. ...	4 11⅝	3 4⅜	3 2¾	2 3	2 9⅝	1 11¼	2 5½	1 8⅜	2 1¼	1 6	1 9¼	1 3⅛
Over 60 up to and including 75 yds. per lb. ...	5 3½	3 6⅝	3 5⅛	2 4⅜	2 11½	2 0½	2 6¾	1 9¼	2 2½	1 6⅝	1 10⅞	1 3⅞
„ 75 „ „ 90 „ „ ...	5 8⅛	3 9⅜	3 8	2 5⅞	3 2⅛	2 2⅛	2 8⅝	1 10⅞	2 4½	1 8⅛	2 0¼	1 5¼
„ 90 „ „ 105 „ „ ...	6 1¾	4 1	3 11½	2 7¾	3 4¾	2 3⅛	2 11¼	2 0⅛	2 6⅝	1 8⅞	2 2½	1 6¼
„ 105 „ „ 120 „ „ ...	6 7½	4 5	4 3⅝	2 10	3 7¾	2 4⅞	3 2⅛	2 1¾	2 8⅝	1 10½	2 4⅝	1 7¼
„ 120 „ „ 135 „ „ ...	7 2⅝	4 9½	4 8¼	3 1¼	3 11¾	2 6½	3 5¼	2 3⅝	2 11⅝	1 11⅞	2 7⅛	1 9
„ 135 „ „ 150 „ „ ...	7 11⅛	5 2⅜	5 1⅞	3 4¾	4 4⅞	2 10⅞	3 8¾	2 5⅞	3 2¾	2 1⅞	2 9¾	1 11
„ 150 „ „ 165 „ „ ...	8 9¼	5 8	5 8⅜	3 9	4 10¾	3 3	4 1⅛	2 8⅞	3 6⅝	2 4⅜	3 1⅜	2 1
„ 165 „ „ 180 „ „ ...	9 8⅜	6 3⅛	6 3⅝	4 1⅜	5 5⅝	3 6⅞	4 6½	3 0⅛	3 11½	2 7½	3 5⅜	2 3¾
„ 180 „ „ 195 „ „ ...	10 11	6 11½	7 0¾	4 6½	6 1⅝	3 11¼	5 1⅜	3 4¼	4 5⅞	2 10⅞	3 10⅞	2 6⅝
„ 195 „ „ 210 „ „ ...	12 3½	7 8⅜	7 10¾	5 0⅛	6 10⅜	4 4⅜	5 9⅜	3 9⅛	5 1⅜	3 3¼	4 5⅜	2 10¼
„ 210 „ „ 255 „ „ ...	15 3⅞	9 6⅞	9 9¾	6 2⅞	8 5½	5 4⅝	7 2⅞	4 8⅛	6 3¼	4 0	5 7	3 7

	Col. 7		Col. 8		Col. 9		Col. 10		Col. 11		Col. 12	
Size of mesh: less than ...	3½ in.		3¾ in.		4 in.		4¼ in.		4½ in.		4¾ in.	
and not less than ...	3¼ in.		3½ in.		3¾ in.		4 in.		4¼ in.		4½ in.	
Twine used as {S.=Single, D.=Double} ...	S.	D.	S.	D.	S.	D.	S.	D.	S.	D.	S.	D.
Twine sizes:—	s. d.	s. d.	s. d.	s. d.	s. d.	s. d.	s. d.	s. d.	s. d.	s. d.	s. d.	s. d.
Up to and including 60 yds. per lb. ...	1 6¼	1 0¾	1 4⅝	11½	1 3¼	10¾	1 2¼	10	1 1⅜	9½	1 0¾	8⅞
Over 60 up to and including 75 yds. per lb. ...	1 7⅜	1 1½	1 6	1 0½	1 4⅜	11½	1 3⅜	10¾	1 2¾	10¼	1 2⅛	9⅝
" 75 " " 90 " " ...	1 9	1 2⅞	1 7	1 1¼	1 5⅝	1 0½	1 4⅝	11⅝	1 4⅛	11⅛	1 3¼	10¾
" 90 " " 105 " " ...	1 11	1 3⅝	1 9	1 2¼	1 7¼	1 1¼	1 6¼	1 0⅝	1 5⅜	1 0⅜	1 4⅞	11⅝
" 105 " " 120 " " ...	2 0¾	1 5¼	1 11	1 3⅝	1 9⅛	1 2¾	1 8¼	1 1¾	1 7¼	1 1¼	1 6⅝	1 0¾
" 120 " " 135 " " ...	2 2⅞	1 6⅝	2 1⅛	1 5⅜	1 11⅜	1 4¼	1 10½	1 3⅜	1 9¼	1 2¾	1 8¾	1 2¼
" 135 " " 150 " " ...	2 5¾	1 8½	2 3⅞	1 7⅛	2 2¼	1 6⅛	2 1	1 5¼	2 0⅛	1 4⅜	1 11¼	1 3⅝
" 150 " " 165 " " ...	2 9½	1 10½	2 6⅞	1 9	2 4¾	1 7⅞	2 3⅛	1 7⅛	2 2⅝	1 6½	2 1¾	1 6
" 165 " " 180 " " ...	3 0⅜	2 0¾	2 10	1 11	2 7⅞	1 10	2 6½	1 9	2 5⅝	1 8⅜	2 4⅜	1 8⅛
" 180 " " 195 " " ...	3 5⅛	2 3¾	3 2½	2 1⅞	3 0⅛	2 0½	2 10⅜	1 11⅜	2 9½	1 10¾	2 7⅞	1 9⅞
" 195 " " 210 " " ...	3 10½	2 6½	3 7½	2 4½	3 4¾	2 3⅛	3 3¼	2 2¼	3 1⅜	2 1¼	3 0⅛	2 0½
" 210 " " 255 " " ...	4 11⅜	3 2½	4 6	2 11¾	4 2⅞	2 10¼	4 1	2 8⅝	3 10¾	2 7⅝	3 9	2 6¾

	Col. 13		Col. 14		Col. 15		Col. 16		Col. 17		Col. 18	
Size of mesh { less than	5 in.		5¼ in.		5½ in.		5¾ in.		6 in.		—	
and												
not less than	4¾ in.		5 in.		5¼ in.		5½ in.		5¾ in.		6 in.	
Twine used as { S.=Single D.=Double }	S.	D.	S.	D.	S.	D.	S.	D.	S.	D.	S.	D.
Twine sizes:—	s. d.	s. d.	s. d.	s. d.	s. d.	s. d.	s. d.	s. d.	s. d.	s. d.	s. d.	s. d.
Up to and including 60 yds. per lb.	1 0½	8¾	11⅞	8⅝	11⅝	8½	11½	8	11⅛	7⅞	10¾	7¾
Over 60 up to and including 75 yds. per lb.	1 1⅜	9½	1 1⅛	9⅜	1 0⅝	8⅞	1 0½	8¾	11⅞	8⅝	11⅝	8½
„ 75 „ „ 90 „ „	1 2¾	10¼	1 2¼	10	1 1¾	9⅝	1 1⅜	9½	1 1⅛	9⅜	1 0¾	8⅞
„ 90 „ „ 105 „ „	1 4⅜	11⅛	1 3⅝	10⅞	1 3⅜	10¾	1 3⅛	10½	1 2¾	10¼	1 2½	10
„ 105 „ „ 120 „ „	1 6¼	1 0½	1 5⅜	1 0⅜	1 5⅛	11⅝	1 4½	11½	1 4¼	11⅛	1 3⅞	10⅞
„ 120 „ „ 135 „ „	1 8⅜	1 1¾	1 7⅜	1 1¼	1 7	1 0¾	1 6½	1 0⅝	1 6¼	1 0½	1 6	1 0½
„ 135 .... 150 „ „	1 10⅞	1 3⅜	1 10⅜	1 2⅞	1 9¼	1 2½	1 8⅞	1 2¼	1 8⅜	1 2⅛	1 8¼	1 1⅝
„ 150 „ „ 165 „ „	2 1	1 5¼	2 0¼	1 4½	1 11⅜	1 4¼	1 11⅛	1 3⅞	1 10¾	1 3⅝	1 10½	1 3½
„ 165 „ „ 180 „ „	2 3⅞	1 7⅛	2 2⅞	1 6⅝	2 2½	1 6¼	2 2	1 6	2 1⅛	1 5⅝	2 1	1 5⅜
„ 180 „ „ 195 „ „	2 7⅛	1 9	2 6	1 8¾	2 4⅞	1 8⅛	2 4½	1 7⅞	2 4⅛	1 7¼	2 3⅞	1 7⅛
„ 195 „ „ 210 „ „	2 10⅜	1 11⅜	2 9½	1 11	2 8	1 10½	2 7⅝	1 9⅞	2 7⅛	1 9¾	2 6¾	1 9¼
„ 210 „ „ 255 „ „	3 6⅞	2 5¾	3 5⅝	2 4½	3 3½	2 3⅛	3 2⅜	2 2⅝	3 1¼	2 1⅞	2 11¾	2 1

HANDBRAIDING OF STACK NETS

9.—(1) The general minimum piece rates set out in the next following Table are payable to female workers (including home-workers) employed in the handbraiding of stack nets and shall apply to the making by hand of all such nets irrespective of the method of manufacture and the type of material used.

(2) The general minimum piece rates set out in the said Table are payable where the needles are filled at the expense of the worker. Where the needles are filled at the expense of the employer, the said rates shall be reduced by ten per cent.

TABLE OF PIECE RATES

Diamond mesh throughout		Square mesh throughout	
Size of mesh	Per dozen meshes	Size of mesh	Per square yard
	d.		d.
		Less than 6 ins.	$1\frac{3}{8}$
		Not less than 6 ins. but less than 7ins.	$1\frac{5}{16}$
Less than 16 ins.	1	Not less than 7 ins. but less than 8 ins.	$1\frac{1}{4}$
Not less than 16 ins. but less than 18 ins.	$1\frac{3}{16}$	Not less than 8 ins. but less than 9 ins.	$1\frac{3}{16}$
Not less than 18 ins. but less than 20 ins.	$1\frac{5}{16}$	Not less than 9 ins. but less than 10 ins.	$1\frac{1}{8}$
Not less than 20 ins. but less than 22 ins.	$1\frac{9}{16}$	Not less than 10 ins. but less than 11 ins.	$1\frac{1}{16}$
Not less than 22 ins. but less than 24 ins.	$1\frac{3}{4}$	Not less than 11 ins. but less than 12 ins.	$\frac{15}{16}$
Not less than 24 ins. but less than 26 ins.	2	Not less than 12 ins. but less than 13 ins.	$\frac{7}{8}$
Not less than 26 ins. but less than 28 ins.	$2\frac{1}{8}$	Not less than 13 ins. but less than 14 ins.	$\frac{13}{16}$
28 ins. and over	$2\frac{5}{16}$	14 ins. and over	$\frac{3}{4}$

(3) For the purposes of this paragraph—

(a) Square yardage shall be calculated by multiplying in feet the length by the breadth of the net and dividing the result by nine.

(b) SIZE OF MESH is—

(i) in the case of diamond mesh, the total length of two adjacent sides of the mesh measured from the inside of one knot to the outside of the other;

(ii) in the case of square mesh, the length of one side of the mesh measured from the inside of one knot to the outside of the other.

Part III

OVERTIME AND WAITING TIME

10. This Part of this Schedule applies to a worker in any section of the Trade, not being—

(1) a home-worker employed in the net section on piece work or

(2) a female home-worker employed in a section other than the net section.

MINIMUM OVERTIME RATES

11.—(1) Subject to the provisions of sub-paragraph (2) of this paragraph, minimum overtime rates are payable to any worker to whom this Part of this Schedule applies as follows:—

(a) on any day other than a Saturday, Sunday or a customary holiday—

    (i) for the first two hours worked in excess of 8 hours   time-and-a-quarter

    (ii) thereafter ... ... time-and-a-half

(b) on a Saturday, not being a customary holiday—

    (i) for the first two hours worked ... ... time-and-a-quarter

    (ii) thereafter ... ... time-and-a-half

(c) on a Sunday or a customary holiday—
for all time worked ... ... double time

(2) Where the employer and the worker by agreement in writing fix in respect of each weekday the number of hours after which a minimum overtime rate shall be payable and the total number of such hours amounts to 40 weekly, the following minimum overtime rates shall be payable in substitution for those set out in sub-paragraph (1) of this paragraph:—

(a) on any day other than a Saturday, Sunday or a customary holiday—

    (i) for the first two hours worked in excess of the agreed number of hours ... ... time-and-a-quarter

    (ii) thereafter ... ... time-and-a-half

(b) on a Saturday, not being a customary holiday—
for all time worked in excess of the agreed number of hours ... ... time-and-a-half

Provided that where the said agreement provides that Saturday shall not normally be a working day, the following minimum overtime rates shall apply—

    (i) for the first two hours worked ... ... time-and-a-quarter

    (ii) thereafter ... ... time-and-a-half

(c) on a Sunday or a customary holiday—
for all time worked ... ... double time

12. In this Part of this Schedule,

(1) The expression "customary holiday" means:—

(a) (i) In England and Wales:—

    Good Friday, Easter Monday, Whit Monday (or where another day is substituted therefor by national proclamation, that day), August Bank Holiday (or, in the case of August Bank Holiday, such day, other than a weekly short day, as may be substituted therefor by the employer, being a day which is by local custom recognised as a day of holiday and which falls within three months of the day for which it is substituted), Christmas Day (or, if Christmas Day falls on a Sunday, such weekday as may be appointed by national proclamation, or, if none is so appointed, the next following Tuesday) and Boxing Day;

    (ii) In Scotland:—

    The New Year's holidays (2 days),

    The local Spring holiday (1 day),

    The local Autumn holiday (1 day) and

    two other weekdays (being days upon which the worker normally attends for work) in the course of a calendar year, to be fixed by the employer and notified to the workers not less than three weeks before the holiday;

or (*b*) in the case of each of the said days, such weekday falling between 1st April and 30th September as may be substituted therefor by agreement between the employer and the workers.

(2) The expressions "time-and-a-quarter", "time-and-a-half" and "double time" mean respectively:—

(*a*) in the case of a time worker, one and a quarter times, one and a half times and twice the general minimum time rate otherwise payable to the worker;

(*b*) in the case where a piece work basis time rate is otherwise applicable to a piece worker,

 (i) a time rate equal respectively to one quarter, one half and the whole of the said piece work basis time rate, and, in addition thereto,

 (ii) the piece rates otherwise applicable under paragraph 1(2);

(*c*) in the case where a general minimum piece rate is otherwise payable to a piece worker employed in the net section of the trade on hand net braiding, knotting or baiting,

 (i) a time rate equal respectively to one quarter, one half and the whole of the piece work basis time rate which would be applicable to a female worker under the provisions of paragraph 3 if a minimum overtime rate did not apply and, in addition thereto,

 (ii) the said general minimum piece rate.

WAITING TIME

13.—(1) A worker is entitled to payment of the minimum remuneration specified in this Schedule for all time during which he is present on the premises of the employer, unless he is present thereon in any of the following circumstances:—

(*a*) without the employer's consent, express or implied;

(*b*) for some purpose unconnected with his work and other than that of waiting for work to be given to him to perform;

(*c*) by reason only of the fact that he is resident thereon;

(*d*) during normal meal times in a room or place in which no work is being done and he is not waiting for work to be given to him to perform.

(2) The minimum remuneration payable under sub-paragraph (1) of this paragraph to a piece worker when not engaged on piece work is that which would be payable if he were a time worker.

PART IV

APPLICABILITY OF STATUTORY MINIMUM REMUNERATION

14. This Schedule applies to workers in relation to whom the Rope, Twine and Net Wages Council (Great Britain) operates, that is to say, workers employed in Great Britain in the branches of work specified in the Schedule to the Trade Boards (Rope, Twine and Net Trade, Great Britain) (Constitution and Proceedings) Regulations 1933(**a**), but excluding therefrom the splicing or braiding of rope, cord or twine performed by hand or machine when incidental to, or carried on in association with or in conjunction with, the operations specified in paragraphs 1 and 2 of the Appendix to the Trade Boards (Made-up Textiles) Order 1920(**b**), or any other processes or operations which are specifically mentioned in the said Appendix.

The Schedule to the said Regulations reads as follows:—

"The Rope, Twine and Net Trade, that is to say—

(1) The making or re-making of (*a*) rope (including driving rope and banding), (*b*) cord (including blind and window cord, but excluding silk, worsted and other fancy cords), (*c*) core for wire-ropes, (*d*) lines, (*e*) twine (including binder and trawl twine), (*f*) lanyards, (*g*) net and similar articles.

(**a**) S.R. & O. 1933/1023 (1933, p. 2049). (**b**) S.R. & O. 1920/1901 (1920 II, p. 782).

(2) The bleaching, teazing, hackling, carding, preparing and spinning of the materials required for the making or re-making of any of the articles (*a*) to (*g*) above when carried on in the same factory or workshop as such making or re-making.

(3) The manufacture of packings, gaskins, and spun yarns, when carried on in the same factory or workshop as the making or re-making of any of the articles (*a*) to (*g*) above.

(4) The braiding or splicing of articles made from rope, cord, twine or net.

(5) The mending of nets and the winding, twisting, doubling, laying, polishing, dressing, tarring, tanning, dyeing, balling, reeling, finishing, packing, despatching, warehousing and storing of any of the above articles, where these operations or any of them are carried on in a factory or workshop in which any of the articles (*a*) to (*g*) above are made or re-made;

but excluding the making of wire rope (unless made in the same factory or workshop as hemp or similar rope or core for wire rope), and also excluding the making of net in connection with the lace-curtain trade and the weaving of cloth."

Article 3

SCHEDULE 2

HOLIDAYS AND HOLIDAY REMUNERATION

The Wages Regulation (Rope, Twine and Net) (Holidays) Order 1968(a) (Order R.(151)) shall have effect as if in the Schedule thereto—

1. for sub-paragraph (1) (*b*) (i) of paragraph 6 there were substituted the following:—

"(*b*) (i) Payment of the said holiday remuneration is subject to the condition that the worker presents himself for employment at the usual starting hour on and works throughout the first working day following the holiday or, if he fails to do so, such failure is by reason of the proved *incapacity* of the worker *due to illness or injury* or with the consent of the employer;"

2. for the expression "one day's holiday pay" in paragraph 11 there were substituted the following expression:—

" 'one day's holiday pay' means—

the appropriate proportion of the amount which the worker would be entitled to receive from his employer, at the beginning of the holiday or the first period of the holiday, as the case may be, for a week's work, if working his normal working week and the number of daily hours usually worked by him (exclusive of overtime), and if paid—

(*a*) in the case of a time worker, at the appropriate rate of statutory minimum remuneration for time work, for work to which that rate applies and at the same rate for work (if any) to which that rate does not apply;

(*b*) in the case of a piece worker, the appropriate *statutory minimum remuneration* that would have been applicable to him if he had been employed as a time worker.

In this definition 'appropriate proportion' means—

where the worker's normal working week is six days						...	one-sixth
„	„	„	„	„	„ „ five days	...	one-fifth
„	„	„	„	„	„ „ four days	...	one-quarter
„	„	„	„	„	„ „ three days or less		one-third"

(a) S.I. 1968/1051 (1968 II, p. 2761).

EXPLANATORY NOTE

(This Note is not part of the Order.)

This Order has effect from 21st May 1969. Schedule 1 sets out the statutory minimum remuneration payable in substitution for that fixed by the Wages Regulation (Rope, Twine and Net) Order 1967 (Order R. (149)), which Order is revoked, and Schedule 2 sets out the amendments to the holiday remuneration provisions of the Wages Regulation (Rope, Twine and Net) (Holidays) Order 1968 (Order R. (151)) consequential upon the changes introduced by the said Schedule 1.

New provisions are printed in italics.

STATUTORY INSTRUMENTS

1969 No. 655

WAGES COUNCILS

The Wages Regulation (Licensed Non-residential Establishment) (Managers and Club Stewards) Order 1969

Made - - -	*5th May* 1969
Coming into Operation	*15th June* 1969

Whereas the Secretary of State has received from the Licensed Non-residential Establishment Wages Council the wages regulation proposals set out in the Schedule hereto ;

Now, therefore, the Secretary of State in exercise of her powers under section 11 of the Wages Councils Act 1959(**a**), and of all other powers enabling her in that behalf, hereby makes the following Order :—

1. This Order may be cited as the Wages Regulation (Licensed Non-residential Establishment) (Managers and Club Stewards) Order 1969.

2.—(1) In this Order the expression "the specified date" means the 15th June 1969, provided that where, as respects any worker who is paid wages at intervals not exceeding seven days, that date does not correspond with the beginning of the period for which the wages are paid, the expression "the specified date" means, as respects that worker, the beginning of the next such period following that date.

(2) The Interpretation Act 1889(**b**) shall apply to the interpretation of this Order as it applies to the interpretation of an Act of Parliament and as if this Order and the Orders hereby revoked were Acts of Parliament.

3. The wages regulation proposals set out in the Schedule hereto shall have effect as from the specified date and as from that date the Wages Regulation (Licensed Non-residential Establishment) (Managers and Club Stewards) Order 1967(**c**) and the Wages Regulation (Licensed Non-residential Establishment) (Managers and Club Stewards) (Amendment) Order 1968(**d**) shall cease to have effect.

Signed by order of the Secretary of State.

5th May 1969.

A. A. Jarratt,
Deputy Under Secretary of State,
Department of Employment and Productivity.

(**a**) 1959 c. 69.   (**b**) 1889 c. 63.
(**c**) S.I. 1967/645 (1967 I, p. 2000).   (**d**) S.I. 1968/1598 (1968 III, p. 4399).

ARRANGEMENT OF SCHEDULE

PART I

REMUNERATION FOR EMPLOYMENT

MANAGERS, TRAINEE MANAGERS, MANAGERESSES, RELIEF MANAGERS, RELIEF MANAGERESSES AND THE WIVES OF MANAGERS, TRAINEE MANAGERS AND RELIEF MANAGERS

	Paragraph
Remuneration for a Manager, a Trainee Manager or a Manageress	1
Table of weekly minimum remuneration	2
Staff hours basis for determining categories	3
Remuneration for the wife of a Manager, Trainee Manager or a Relief Manager	4
Remuneration for a Relief Manager	5
Remuneration for a Relief Manageress	6
Benefits or advantages where full board is supplied	7
Work on the weekly day of rest	8
Work on a public holiday	9

CLUB STEWARDS, CLUB STEWARDESSES AND THE WIVES OF CLUB STEWARDS

	Paragraph
Remuneration for a Club Steward or a Club Stewardess	10
Table of weekly minimum remuneration	11
Staff hours basis for determining categories	12
Minimum overtime rates	13
Remuneration where less than 34 hours a week are ordinarily worked by a Club Steward or Club Stewardess	14
Remuneration for a Club Steward's wife	15
Benefits or advantages where full board is supplied	16
Work on the weekly day of rest	17
Work on a public holiday	18

PART II

ANNUAL HOLIDAY AND HOLIDAY REMUNERATION

	Paragraph
Annual holiday	19–21
Remuneration for annual holiday	22
Accrued holiday remuneration payable on termination of employment	23–25
Calculation of employment	26

PART III

GENERAL

	Paragraph
Definitions	27
Workers to whom the Schedule applies	28–29
Illegal deductions, etc.	30

Article 3   SCHEDULE

The following minimum remuneration and provisions as to holidays and holiday remuneration shall be substituted for the statutory minimum remuneration and the provisions as to holidays and holiday remuneration set out in the Wages Regulation (Licensed Non-residential Establishment) (Managers and Club Stewards) Order 1967 (Order L.N.R. (71)) and the Wages Regulation (Licensed Non-residential Establishment) (Managers and Club Stewards) (Amendment) Order 1968 (Order L.N.R. (74)).

PART I

REMUNERATION FOR EMPLOYMENT

MANAGERS, TRAINEE MANAGERS, MANAGERESSES, RELIEF MANAGERS, RELIEF MANAGERESSES AND THE WIVES OF MANAGERS, TRAINEE MANAGERS AND RELIEF MANAGERS

1. The minimum remuneration payable to a Manager, a Trainee Manager or a Manageress, other than a Relief Manager or a Relief Manageress, for any week in which he is employed and during any part of which he is capable of and available for work, whether he performs any work for his employer in that week or not and irrespective of the number of hours worked, shall be in accordance with the table in paragraph 2:

Provided that the minimum remuneration payable under this paragraph shall be reduced in any week by the amount of any holiday remuneration paid to the worker in respect of any day or days of annual holiday allowed in that week to the worker under Part II of this Schedule.

2. The table of weekly minimum remuneration is as follows:—

Column 1 Manager or Manageress	Column 2 Where the employer provides accommodation		Column 3 Where the employer does not provide accommodation	
	Manager	Manageress	Manager	Manageress
	£ s. d.	£ s. d.	£ s. d.	£ s. d.
Trainee	11 11 6	—	14 4 0	—
Category A	12 10 0	10 9 6	15 2 6	13 2 0
,, B	13 0 6	10 18 0	15 13 0	13 10 6
,, C	13 11 0	11 6 6	16 3 6	13 19 0
,, D	14 1 6	11 14 6	16 14 0	14 7 0
,, E	14 11 0	12 1 0	17 2 0	14 13 6
,, F	14 17 6	12 7 6	17 10 0	15 0 0
,, G	15 7 6	12 15 6	18 0 0	15 8 0
,, H	16 8 0	13 12 0	19 0 6	16 4 6
,, I	17 8 6	14 8 6	20 1 0	17 1 0
,, J	18 9 6	15 5 0	21 2 0	17 17 6

3.—(1) For the purposes of paragraph 2 the category of a Manager or a Manageress in a licensed non-residential establishment (other than a club) in which no staff hours are worked in a week or the number of staff hours worked in a week does not exceed 35 shall be A.

(2) The category of a Manager or a Manageress in a licensed non-residential establishment (other than a club) in which the number of staff hours worked in a week exceeds that specified in Column 2 of the table to this sub-paragraph but does not exceed that in Column 3 shall be that specified in Column 1 of that table.

Column 1					Column 2	Column 3
Category B	...	...	...	...	35 hours	70 hours
,, C	...	...	...	...	70 ,,	105 ,,
,, D	...	...	...	...	105 ,,	175 ,,
,, E	...	...	...	...	175 ,,	280 ,,
,, F	...	...	...	...	280 ,,	420 ,,
,, G	...	...	...	...	420 ,,	560 ,,
,, H	...	...	...	...	560 ,,	735 ,,
,, I	...	...	...	...	735 ,,	980 ,,
,, J	...	...	...	...	980 ,,	1,330 ,,

(3) For the purpose of sub-paragraphs (1) and (2) of this paragraph—

(a) the staff hours shall be calculated as follows:—in any week there shall be counted all hours including overtime actually worked by workers for whom statutory minimum remuneration has been fixed and who are employed in the licensed non-residential establishment (other than a club) by the employer, but excluding any time worked by the Manager, Trainee Manager or Manageress, a Relief Manager or Relief Manageress or the wife of the Manager, Trainee Manager or Relief Manager and excluding also any time worked by any worker in an ancillary business the profits from which are taken by the Manager, the Trainee Manager, the Manageress or the wife of the Manager or Trainee Manager;

(b) the number of staff hours worked in a week shall be the total of weekly staff hours calculated as in (a) of this sub-paragraph averaged over the period of 52 weeks preceding the last Saturday in February in each year and the resulting figure shall determine the category of the Manager or the Manageress for the 26 weeks beginning with the fifth week following the last Saturday in February. For the following period of 26 weeks the number of staff hours worked in a week shall be the total of weekly staff hours calculated as in (a) of this sub-paragraph averaged over the period of 52 weeks preceding the last Saturday in August in each year and the resulting figure shall determine the category of the Manager or Manageress for the purposes of remuneration for that period of 26 weeks:

Provided that where the licensed non-residential establishment (other than a club) is newly opened or has been under management for less than 52 weeks immediately preceding the last Saturday in February or the last Saturday in August in any year, the category of the Manager or the Manageress in any week shall be determined by the staff hours worked in the previous week calculated as in (a) above until the establishment shall have been under management for not less than 52 weeks preceding the last Saturday in February or the last Saturday in August as the case may be.

4. Where the wife of a Manager, a Trainee Manager or of a Relief Manager is required by the employer to assist in the work of the licensed non-residential establishment (other than a club) she shall be paid not less than 60s. for any week in which she is employed and during any part of which she is capable of and available for work whether she performs any work for her employer in that week or not and irrespective of the number of hours she works:

Provided that the minimum remuneration payable under this paragraph shall be reduced in any week by the amount of any holiday remuneration paid to the worker in respect of any day or days of annual holiday allowed in that week to the worker under Part II of this Schedule.

5.—(1) The remuneration for a Relief Manager whether accommodation is provided by the employer or not shall be not less than £14 2s. 0d. for any week in which he is employed on the duties of a Relief Manager on more than one day and during any part of which week he is capable of and available for work, whether he performs any work for his employer in that week or not and irrespective of the number of hours he works:

Provided that the minimum remuneration payable under this paragraph shall be reduced in any week by the amount of any holiday remuneration paid to the worker in respect of any day or days of annual holiday allowed in that week to the worker under Part II of this Schedule.

(2) The remuneration for a Relief Manager who is employed on not more than one day in any week shall be not less than £2 7s. 0d. for such day of employment.

6.—(1) The remuneration for a Relief Manageress whether accommodation is provided by the employer or not shall be not less than £11 19s. 6d. for any week in which she is employed on the duties of a Relief Manageress on more than one day and during any part of which she is capable of and available for work, whether she performs any work for her employer in that week or not and irrespective of the number of hours she works:

Provided that the minimum remuneration payable under this paragraph shall be reduced in any week by the amount of any holiday remuneration paid to the worker in respect of any day or days of annual holiday allowed in that week to the worker under Part II of this Schedule.

(2) The remuneration for a Relief Manageress who is employed on not more than one day in any week shall be not less than £1 19s. 11d. for such day of employment.

BENEFITS OR ADVANTAGES

MANAGERS, TRAINEE MANAGERS OR MANAGERESSES SUPPLIED WITH FULL BOARD

7. For the purpose of calculating the weekly minimum remuneration of a Manager, a Trainee Manager or a Manageress, the Wages Council authorises the following benefits or advantages, being benefits or advantages provided in connection with the employment by the employer or by some other person under arrangements with the employer and not being benefits or advantages illegally provided, to be reckoned as payment of wages by the employer in lieu of payment in cash:—

    (1) full board supplied to a Manager and his wife or a Trainee Manager and his wife;

    (2) where (1) above is not provided, full board supplied to a Manager, a Trainee Manager or a Manageress;

and the Wages Council defines the value at which such benefits or advantages are to be reckoned at 57s. a week and 33s. 0d. a week respectively.

WEEKLY DAY OF REST

8. Where a worker to whom the foregoing paragraphs apply is required to work on the weekly day of rest he shall be paid in respect of the week in which no weekly day of rest has been allowed, in addition to the weekly minimum remuneration to which he is entitled under the provisions of those paragraphs, an amount equal to one-sixth of that weekly minimum remuneration.

PUBLIC HOLIDAYS

9. Where a worker to whom the foregoing paragraphs apply is required to work on a public holiday, or where such public holiday falls on a day of annual holiday, and his employer has neither (a) during the four weeks immediately preceding the public holiday allowed him on a week-day other than the weekly day of rest or a day of annual holiday, a day of holiday in lieu of the public holiday, nor (b) agreed to allow him such a day of holiday within four weeks of the public holiday, the worker shall be paid in respect of the public holiday in addition to the minimum remuneration to which he is entitled under the provisions of paragraphs 1 to 7 an amount equal to one-sixth of that weekly minimum remuneration.

CLUB STEWARDS, CLUB STEWARDESSES AND THE WIVES OF CLUB STEWARDS

10. Subject to the provisions of paragraph 13 relating to overtime, the minimum remuneration payable to a Club Steward or a Club Stewardess who ordinarily works for the employer for not less than 34 hours a week on work to which this Schedule applies for any week in which he is employed and during any part of which he is capable of and available for work, whether he performs any work for his employer in that week or not, shall be in accordance with the table in paragraph 11:

Provided that the minimum remuneration payable under this paragraph shall be reduced in any week by the amount of any holiday remuneration paid to the worker in respect of any day or days of annual holiday allowed in that week to the worker under Part II of this Schedule.

11. The table of weekly minimum remuneration is as follows:—

Column 1 Club Steward or Club Stewardess	Column 2 Where the employer provides accommodation		Column 3 Where the employer does not provide accommodation	
	Club Steward	Club Stewardess	Club Steward	Club Stewardess
	£ s. d.	£ s. d.	£ s. d.	£ s. d.
Category A	9 15 0	7 17 0	12 0 0	10 1 6
„ B	10 5 0	—	12 10 0	—
„ C	10 5 0	8 5 0	12 10 0	10 9 6
„ D	10 15 0	8 13 0	13 0 0	10 17 6
„ E	11 5 0	9 1 0	13 10 0	11 5 6
„ F	11 15 0	9 9 0	14 0 0	11 13 6
„ G	12 5 0	9 17 0	14 10 0	12 1 6
„ H	12 15 0	10 5 0	15 0 0	12 9 6
„ I	13 5 0	10 13 0	15 10 0	12 17 6
„ J	14 5 0	11 9 0	16 10 0	13 13 6
„ K	15 5 0	12 5 0	17 10 0	14 9 6
„ L	16 5 0	13 1 0	18 10 0	15 5 6

12.—(1) For the purposes of paragraph 11 the category of a Club Steward or a Club Stewardess shall be determined in the following manner:—

(a) Where no staff hours are worked in a week in a club and, in the case of a Club Steward, his wife is not required by the employer to assist in the work of the club, the category shall be A.

(b) Where no staff hours are worked in a week in a club, but the wife of the Club Steward is required by the employer to assist in the work of the club, the category shall be B.

(c) Where the number of staff hours worked in a week in a club does not exceed 35, the category shall be C.

(d) Where the number of staff hours worked in a week in a club exceeds that specified in Column 2 of the table to this sub-paragraph but does not exceed that in Column 3 the category shall be that specified in Column 1 of that table.

Column 1					Column 2	Column 3
Category D	...	...	...	...	35 hours	70 hours
„ E	...	...	...	...	70 „	105 „
„ F	...	...	...	...	105 „	175 „
„ G	...	...	...	...	175 „	280 „
„ H	...	...	...	...	280 „	420 „
„ I	...	...	...	...	420 „	560 „
„ J	...	...	...	...	560 „	735 „
„ K	...	...	...	...	735 „	980 „
„ L	...	...	...	...	980 „	1,330 „

(2) For the purpose of sub-paragraph (1) of this paragraph—

(a) the staff hours shall be calculated as follows:—in any week there shall be counted all hours, including overtime, actually worked by the following grades or descriptions of workers employed in the club:—

(i) Cellarmen (England or Wales);

(ii) Barmen (England or Wales) or Barmen (Scotland only);

(iii) Barmaids (Great Britain);

(iv) Club Waiters (Great Britain) who are under the control of the Club Steward or Club Stewardess;

(v) Club Waitresses (Great Britain) who are under the control of the Club Steward or Club Stewardess;

(vi) Workers employed in cleaning the bar and such other parts of the club, for the cleanliness of which the Club Steward or Club Stewardess is required by the employer to be responsible:

Provided that hours worked by a worker relieving a Club Steward or a Club Stewardess in his absence shall not be included for the purpose of calculating the number of staff hours;

(b) the number of staff hours worked in a week shall be the total of weekly staff hours calculated as in (a) of this sub-paragraph averaged over the period of 52 weeks preceding the last Saturday in February in each year and the resulting figure shall determine the category of the Club Steward or the Club Stewardess for the 26 weeks beginning with the fifth week following the last Saturday in February. For the following period of 26 weeks the number of staff hours worked in a week shall be the total of weekly staff hours calculated as in (a) of this sub-paragraph averaged over the period of 52 weeks preceding the last Saturday in August in each year and the resulting figure shall determine the category of the Club Steward or the Club Stewardess for the purposes of remuneration for that period of 26 weeks:

Provided that where a club has been in existence for less than 52 weeks immediately preceding the last Saturday in February or the last Saturday in August in any year, the category of the Club Steward or the Club Stewardess in any week shall be determined by the staff hours worked in the previous week calculated as in (a) above until the club shall have been in existence for not less than 52 weeks preceding the last Saturday in February or the last Saturday in August as the case may be.

13. Minimum overtime rates are payable to Club Stewards and Club Stewardesses who ordinarily work for the employer for not less than 34 hours a week on work to which this Schedule applies as follows:—

(1) for the first four hours worked in excess of 50½ hours exclusive of time worked on a rest day ... time-and-a-quarter

(2) thereafter ... ... time-and-a-half

14. The minimum remuneration for a Club Steward or a Club Stewardess who ordinarily works for his employer for less than 34 hours a week on work to which this Schedule applies shall be—

(1) where the employer does not provide the worker with accommodation— at the rate of 4s. 3d. an hour for each hour worked;

(2) where the employer provides the worker with accommodation—

(a) at the rate of 2s. 2d. an hour for each of the first 22 hours worked in any week;

(b) at the rate of 4s. 2d. for each hour worked thereafter in that week.

15. Except as is otherwise provided in this paragraph the minimum remuneration for the wife of a Club Steward who is required by the employer to assist in the work of the club, shall be at the rate of 3s. 7d. per hour for all time worked:

Provided that where the wife of a Club Steward performs all or the greater part of the duties of her husband during his absence on any day of annual holiday allowed him under Part II of this Schedule (hereafter in this paragraph referred to as a day of special duties), the minimum remuneration for each day of special duties shall be one-sixth of the remuneration payable under the provisions of paragraph 11 to a Club Stewardess of the same category as the husband or, where the husband is a Club Steward of category B, one-sixth of the remuneration payable to a Club Stewardess of category C.

BENEFITS OR ADVANTAGES

CLUB STEWARDS OR CLUB STEWARDESSES SUPPLIED WITH FULL BOARD

16. For the purpose of calculating the weekly minimum remuneration of a Club Steward or Club Stewardess, the Wages Council authorises the following benefits or advantages, being benefits or advantages provided in connection with the employment by the employer or by some other person under arrangements with the employer and not being benefits or advantages illegally provided, to be reckoned as payment of wages by the employer in lieu of payment in cash:—

    (1) full board supplied to a Club Steward and his wife;

    (2) where (1) above is not provided, full board supplied to a Club Steward or a Club Stewardess;

and the Wages Council defines the value at which such benefits or advantages are to be reckoned at 41s. 6d. a week and 24s. 6d. a week respectively.

WEEKLY DAY OF REST

17. Where a worker to whom paragraph 10, 11, 14, 15 or 16 applies, but excluding such worker who ordinarily works for the employer for less than 18 hours a week, is required by the employer to work on the weekly day of rest, he shall be paid in respect of the pay week in which no weekly day of rest has been allowed, in addition to the minimum remuneration to which he is entitled under the provisions of this Schedule, apart from this paragraph, an amount equal to one-sixth of the weekly remuneration specified in the table in paragraph 11 in the case of a worker to whom that paragraph applies, and in the case of a worker to whom paragraph 14 or 15 applies, one-sixth of the minimum remuneration to which the worker is entitled for a week's work under the provisions of this Schedule if working the number of hours ordinarily worked by him in a week, exclusive of hours worked on the weekly day of rest.

PUBLIC HOLIDAYS

18. Where a worker to whom paragraph 10, 11, 14, 15 or 16 applies, not being a worker who ordinarily works for the employer for less than 18 hours a week, is required by the employer to work on a public holiday, or when such public holiday falls on a day of annual holiday, and his employer has neither (a) during the four weeks immediately preceding the public holiday allowed him on a week-day other than the weekly day of rest or a day of annual holiday, a day of holiday in lieu of the public holiday, nor (b) agreed to allow him such a day of holiday within four weeks of the public holiday, the worker shall be paid in respect of the public holiday in addition to the minimum remuneration to which he is entitled under the provisions of this Schedule, apart from this paragraph, an amount equal to one-sixth of the weekly minimum remuneration specified in the table in paragraph 11 in the case of a worker to whom that paragraph applies, and in the case of a worker to whom paragraph 14 or 15 applies, one-sixth of the minimum remuneration to which the worker is entitled for a week's work under the provisions of this Schedule if working the number of hours ordinarily worked by him in a week, exclusive of hours worked on the weekly day of rest.

PART II

ANNUAL HOLIDAY AND HOLIDAY REMUNERATION
ANNUAL HOLIDAY

19. An employer shall, between the date on which the provisions of this Schedule become effective and 31st December 1969, and in each succeeding year between 1st January and 31st December (hereinafter referred to as the "holiday season"), allow an annual holiday to every worker to whom this Schedule applies (other than a worker who is a Club Steward, a Club Stewardess or the wife of a Club Steward, and who ordinarily works for the employer for less than 18 hours a week). The dates between which the annual holiday is to be allowed shall be agreed between the employer and the worker, or if no agreement is reached, it shall be allowed so as to terminate not later than 31st December.

20. The duration of the annual holiday shall be determined by reference to the worker's period of employment during the 12 months immediately preceding the commencement of the holiday season, in the following manner:—

Period of employment							Duration of holiday	
At least	1 month	...	...	...	...	...	1	day
„	„ 2 months	...	...	...	...	...	2	days
„	„ 3 „	...	...	...	...	...	3	„
„	„ 4 „	...	...	...	...	...	4	„
„	„ 5 „	...	...	...	...	...	5	„
„	„ 6 „	...	...	...	...	...	6	„
„	„ 7 „	...	...	...	...	...	7	„
„	„ 8 „	...	...	...	...	...	8	„
„	„ 9 „	...	...	...	...	...	9	„
„	„ 10 „	...	...	...	...	...	10	„
„	„ 11 „	...	...	...	...	...	11	„
„	„ 12 „	...	...	...	...	...	12	„

Provided that—

(1) the number of days of annual holiday to which a worker is entitled in any year shall not exceed twice the number constituting the worker's normal working week;

(2) the number of days of annual holiday which an employer is required to allow to a worker during the year 1969 under the provisions of this Schedule shall be reduced by the number of any days of paid annual holiday allowed to the worker under the provisions of Order L.N.R. (71) during 1969 prior to the date on which this Schedule becomes effective.

21. An annual holiday shall be allowed on consecutive working days, being days upon which the worker is normally called upon to work, and days of holiday shall be treated as consecutive notwithstanding the intervention of a public holiday or a day of holiday in lieu of a public holiday:

Provided that where a worker is entitled to more days of annual holiday than the number of days constituting his normal working week, his annual holiday may be allowed in two or more separate periods of which one shall consist of at least the number of days constituting his normal working week.

REMUNERATION FOR ANNUAL HOLIDAY

22. Holiday remuneration for the annual holiday shall be paid on the last pay day preceding the holiday as follows:—

(1) Where a worker is not provided by the employer, for the duration of the holiday, with full board—for each day of holiday allowed in accordance with the provisions of paragraph 20—

(a) in the case of Managers, Trainee Managers, Manageresses, Relief Managers, Relief Manageresses and the wives of Managers, Trainee

Managers or Relief Managers where such wives are required by the employer to assist in the work of the licensed non-residential establishment (other than a club), not less than one-sixth of the statutory minimum remuneration to which the worker would be entitled at the date of the holiday for a week's work if he were not provided by the employer with full board;

(b) in the case of Club Stewards, Club Stewardesses and the wives of Club Stewards where such wives are required by the employer to assist in the work of the club, not less than one-sixth of the statutory minimum remuneration to which the worker would be entitled at the date of the holiday for a week's work if he worked his normal weekly hours of work and if he were not provided by the employer with full board.

(2) Where a worker is provided by the employer, for the duration of the holiday, with full board—for each day of holiday allowed in accordance with paragraph 20—

(a) in the case of Managers, Trainee Managers, Manageresses, Relief Managers, Relief Manageresses and the wives of Managers, Trainee Managers or Relief Managers where such wives are required by the employer to assist in the work of the licensed non-residential establishment (other than a club), not less than one-sixth of the statutory minimum remuneration to which the worker would be entitled in cash at the date of the holiday for a week's work if he were provided by the employer with full board;

(b) in the case of Club Stewards, Club Stewardesses and the wives of Club Stewards where such wives are required by the employer to assist in the work of the club, not less than one-sixth of the statutory minimum remuneration to which the worker would be entitled in cash at the date of the holiday for a week's work if he worked his normal weekly hours of work and if he were provided by the employer with full board:

Provided that where under the provisions of paragraph 21 an annual holiday is taken in more than one period the holiday remuneration shall be apportioned accordingly.

ACCRUED HOLIDAY REMUNERATION PAYABLE ON TERMINATION OF EMPLOYMENT

23. If a worker (other than a worker who is a Club Steward, a Club Stewardess or the wife of a Club Steward, and who ordinarily works for the employer for less than 18 hours a week) ceases to be employed by an employer after the provisions of this Schedule become effective, the employer shall immediately on the termination of the employment (hereinafter referred to as "the termination date") pay to the worker accrued holiday remuneration in accordance with the provisions of paragraph 24.

24. Subject to the provisions of this paragraph, accrued holiday remuneration shall be payable to a worker in respect of such period of his employment with the employer in the 12 months immediately preceding the termination date as has not already been counted as employment for the purpose of any day or days of annual holiday, as follows:—

For each month's employment—

(1) in the case of Managers, Trainee Managers, Manageresses, Relief Managers, Relief Manageresses and the wives of Managers, Trainee Managers or Relief Managers, where such wives are required by the employer to assist in the work of the licensed non-residential establishment (other than a club), not less than one-sixth of the statutory minimum remuneration to which the worker would be entitled at the termination date for a week's work if he were not provided by the employer with full board;

ld

(2) in the case of Club Stewards, Club Stewardesses and the wives of Club Stewards where such wives are required by the employer to assist in the work of the club, not less than one-sixth of the statutory minimum remuneration to which the worker would be entitled at the termination date for a week's work if he worked his normal weekly hours of work and if he were not provided by the employer with full board:

Provided that—

(a) no worker shall be entitled to the payment by his employer of accrued holiday remuneration if—

(1) he is dismissed on either of the following grounds, that is to say—

(i) dishonesty, or

(ii) misconduct involving contravention of the licensing laws, and is so informed by the employer at the time of dismissal; or

(2) he leaves his employment without having notified his employer, not less than one week before terminating his employment, of his intention to do so;

(b) the amount of any accrued holiday remuneration payable at the termination date shall be reduced by the amount of any sum paid by the employer to the worker—

(i) as accrued holiday remuneration under the provisions of this Schedule or of Order L.N.R. (71) in so far as such sum is attributable to the period for which the accrued holiday remuneration is payable;

(ii) in respect of any day or days of holiday for which the worker had not qualified under the provisions of this Schedule or of Order L.N.R. (71) and allowed during the period in respect of which the accrued holiday remuneration is payable;

(c) accrued holiday remuneration is not payable in respect of any period of employment for which the worker has become entitled to be allowed an annual holiday under the provisions of this Schedule or of Order L.N.R. (71).

25. Where under the provisions of this Schedule or of Order L.N.R. (71) any accrued holiday remuneration has been paid by the employer to a worker prior to the allowance of an annual holiday in accordance with the provisions of this Schedule, the amount of holiday remuneration payable by the employer in respect of the said annual holiday under the provisions of paragraph 22 shall be reduced by the amount of any previous payment of accrued holiday remuneration in so far as it is attributable to any part of the period of employment in respect of which the said holiday has been allowed.

CALCULATION OF EMPLOYMENT

26. For the purposes of calculating any period of employment qualifying a worker for an annual holiday or for any accrued holiday remuneration under this Schedule a worker shall be treated as having been employed:—

(1) for a month in respect of any month in which he has worked for the employer for not less than two weeks and has qualified for payment of statutory minimum remuneration;

(2) when absent from work in any of the following circumstances:—

(a) during annual holiday, public holidays or days in lieu of public holidays;

(b) during proved sickness or accident up to and not exceeding eight weeks in the aggregate during any such period as aforesaid;

(c) by leave of the employer.

PART III

GENERAL

DEFINITIONS

27. In this Schedule unless the context otherwise requires the following expressions have the meanings hereby respectively assigned to them:—

"ACCOMMODATION" means living premises, including the supply of light and heat.

"CATERING UNDERTAKING" means any undertaking or any part of an undertaking which consists wholly or mainly in the carrying on (whether for profit or not) of one or more of the following activities, that is to say, the supply of food or drink for immediate consumption, the provision of living accomodation for guests or lodgers or for persons employed in the undertaking and any other activity so far as it is incidental or ancillary to any such activity as aforesaid of the undertaking.

"FULL BOARD" means not less than three meals per day of good and sufficient quality and quantity one of which shall be dinner.

"LICENSED NON-RESIDENTIAL ESTABLISHMENT" means—

    (1) a public house, inn, hotel or other premises, being an establishment—

    (*a*) at which it is lawful for intoxicating liquor to be sold for consumption on the premises or to be supplied for consumption on the premises by reason of the fact that part of the premises is habitually used for the purposes of a registered club; and

    (*b*) which is not a residential establishment within the meaning of this Schedule;

    (2) a club—

    (*a*) at which it is lawful for intoxicating liquor to be supplied for consumption on the premises; and

    (*b*) which is not a residential establishment within the meaning of this Schedule,

but does not include—

    (i) any such establishment or club as aforesaid if the main activity there carried on consists of the supply of food or drink for immediate consumption at one or more of the following places, that is to say, a restaurant, dining room, cafe or similar place;

    (ii) any hostel or similar establishment provided by or by arrangement with an employer wholly or mainly for the purposes of accommodating persons employed by him.

"MONTH" means the period commencing on a date of any number in one month of the calendar and ending on the day before the date of the same number in the next month, or if the commencing date is the 29th, 30th or 31st and there is no date of the same number in the next month, then on the last day of that month.

"NORMAL WEEKLY HOURS OF WORK" means the number of hours which have been most frequently worked by the worker in a week in the employment of the employer in the 12 months immediately preceding the commencement of the annual holiday, or where accrued holiday remuneration is payable on the termination of the employment, in the 12 months immediately preceding the termination date.

"NORMAL WORKING WEEK" means the number of days on which the worker has most frequently worked in a week in the employment of the employer in the 12 months immediately preceding the commencement of the annual holiday, or where accrued holiday remuneration is payable on the termination of the employment, in the 12 months immediately preceding the termination date.

"PUBLIC HOLIDAY" means—

(1) In England and Wales—

Christmas Day (or, if Christmas Day falls on a Sunday, such week-day as may be prescribed by national proclamation, or, if no such day is prescribed, the next following Tuesday), Boxing Day, Good Friday, Easter Monday, Whit Monday, August Bank Holiday and any day proclaimed as an additional Bank Holiday or a general holiday;

(2) In Scotland—

(a) New Year's Day (or the following day if New Year's Day falls on a Sunday), the local Spring holiday, the local Autumn holiday and any day proclaimed as an additional Bank Holiday or a general holiday; and

(b) any other week-days in the course of a calendar year locally recognised as days of public holiday, not exceeding three in any one year.

"RAILWAY REFRESHMENT ESTABLISHMENT" means any place of refreshment at a railway station being a place of refreshment:—

(1) at which it is lawful for intoxicating liquor to be sold for consumption on the premises; or

(2) the activities of which are carried on by a railway company or any Board established by the Transport Act 1962 or any subsidiary thereof;

and for the purpose of this definition "place of refreshment" means a place used either regularly or occasionally as, or for the purposes of, a restaurant, dining room, cafe, tea shop, canteen or similar place or coffee stall, buffet or bar.

"RESIDENTIAL ESTABLISHMENT" means an establishment which either contains four or more rooms ordinarily available as sleeping accommodation for guests or lodgers or if it contains less than four such rooms which contains sleeping accommodation ordinarily available for not less than eight guests or lodgers.

"STATUTORY MINIMUM REMUNERATION" means minimum remuneration (other than holiday remuneration) fixed by a wages regulation order made by the Secretary of State to give effect to proposals submitted to her by the Wages Council.

"TIME-AND-A-QUARTER" and "TIME-AND-A-HALF" mean, respectively, one and a quarter times and one and a half times the hourly rate obtained by dividing by $50\frac{1}{2}$ the minimum weekly remuneration to which the worker would be entitled if he were employed in the circumstances specified in Column 3 of paragraph 11.

"TRAINEE MANAGER'S CONTRACT" means a written contract of employment which contains the following provisions or provisions substantially to the same effect and no provisions contrary thereto:—

(1) the worker of his own free will (and if he is under the age of 21 years with the consent of his guardian) binds himself to serve the employer as a trainee in the business of a licensed non-residential establishment and the duties of a Manager thereof;

(2) the employer undertakes to instruct the worker or cause him to be instructed in the business of a licensed non-residential establishment and the duties of a Manager thereof.

"WAGES COUNCIL" means the Licensed Non-residential Establishment Wages Council.

"WEEK" means pay week.

"WEEKLY DAY OF REST" means—

(1) in a licensed non-residential establishment open on seven days in the week—

    (*a*) a day fixed by agreement between the employer and the worker, being a day which may be changed by agreement between the employer and the worker; or

    (*b*) if no such day has been fixed or agreed—Wednesday;

(2) in a licensed non-residential establishment closed on Sunday—Sunday;

(3) in any other case—

    (*a*) a day fixed by agreement between the employer and the worker, being a day which may be changed by agreement between the employer and the worker; or

    (*b*) if no such day has been fixed or agreed—the first day in the week on which the licensed non-residential establishment is closed.

"BARMAID (Great Britain)" means a female worker wholly or mainly employed in dispensing or in dispensing and serving refreshment.

"BARMAN or BARMAN-WAITER (England or Wales)" means a male worker aged 21 years or over who is employed in England or Wales and who is wholly or mainly employed in dispensing or in dispensing and serving refreshment.

"BARMAN (Scotland only)" means a male worker aged 21 years or over who is employed in Scotland and who is wholly or mainly engaged in preparing, supplying and serving refreshment.

"CELLARMAN (England or Wales)" means a male worker aged 21 years or over who is employed in England or Wales and who is wholly or mainly employed in receiving, bottling or binning beers, wines, spirits or minerals, and who is responsible for the custody, issue and keeping records thereof, and for the satisfactory condition of beer and beer pipes and for seeing that beer is ready for sale.

"CLUB STEWARD" or "CLUB STEWARDESS" means a worker aged 21 years or over who is responsible for the stock and management of the bar or bars in a club.

"CLUB WAITER (Great Britain)" or "CLUB WAITRESS (Great Britain)" means a worker aged 21 years or over who is wholly or mainly employed in serving refreshment in a club and who is under the control of a Club Steward or a Club Stewardess.

"MANAGER" or "MANAGERESS" means the person responsible to the employer for the cleanliness, care and supervision of the premises and equipment of a licensed non-residential establishment (other than a club), for the keeping of records and for the correct handling of the cash and stocks, for the control of the staff where any are employed and for the conduct of the establishment as required by the law.

"RELIEF MANAGER" or "RELIEF MANAGERESS" means a worker who is appointed by the employer to take charge of a licensed non-residential establishment (other than a club), in the absence of the Manager or Manageress and who is not in receipt of statutory minimum remuneration other than the remuneration provided for a Relief Manager or a Relief Manageress.

"TRAINEE MANAGER" means a worker during the first year of his employment under a Trainee Manager's contract or a continuous series of such contracts with any one employer.

WORKERS TO WHOM THE SCHEDULE APPLIES

28. Subject to the provisions of paragraph 29, the provisions of this Schedule apply to the following workers employed in Great Britain in a catering undertaking who are employed by the person or body of persons carrying on that undertaking, that is to say:—

> (1) a Manager, Trainee Manager, Manageress, Relief Manager, Relief Manageress, Club Steward, Club Stewardess; and

> (2) the wife of a Manager, a Trainee Manager, a Relief Manager or of a Club Steward if she is required by the employer to assist in the work of an establishment

and who are so employed either

> (a) for the purposes of such of the activities of the undertaking as are carried on at a licensed non-residential establishment; or

> (b) in connection with the provision of food or drink or living accommodation provided wholly or mainly for workers employed for the purposes of any of the activities of the undertaking specified in (a) of this sub-paragraph;

and who are engaged on any of the following work, that is to say:—

> (i) the preparation of food or drink;
> (ii) the service of food or drink;
> (iii) work incidental to such preparation or service;
> (iv) work connected with the provision of living accommodation;
> (v) work in connection with any retail sale of goods at a licensed non-residential establishment;
> (vi) transport work;
> (vii) work performed at any office or at any store or warehouse or similar place or at any garage or stable or similar place;
> (viii) any work other than that specified in sub-paragraphs (i) to (vii) hereof performed in or about a licensed non-residential establishment, including work in connection with any service or amenity provided in or about such establishment.

29. This Schedule does not apply to any of the following workers in respect of their employment in any of the following circumstances, that is to say:—

> (1) workers who are employed by the same employer partly in a catering undertaking and partly in some other undertaking, if their employment in the catering undertaking is confined to work specified either in sub-paragraph (vi) or sub-paragraph (vii) of paragraph 28 or partly to work specified in the said sub-paragraph (vi) and partly to work specified in the said sub-paragraph (vii) and they are mainly employed on work in or in connection with that other undertaking;

> (2) workers who are employed for the purposes of any of the activities carried on at a theatre, music hall or other place of entertainment ordinarily used for the public performance of stage plays or variety entertainments;

> (3) workers who are employed for the purposes of any of the activities carried on in a railway train;

> (4) workers employed for the purposes of the activities carried on at a railway refreshment establishment;

> (5) workers who are employed by the Crown;

> (6) workers in relation to whom the Industrial and Staff Canteen Undertakings Wages Council operates, in respect of any employment which is for the time being within the field of operation of that Wages Council.

30. Nothing in the provisions of this Schedule shall be construed as authorising the making of any deduction or the giving of any remuneration in any manne that is illegal by virtue of the Truck Acts 1831 to 1940(a), or of any other enactment.

(a) 1831 c. 37; 1887 c. 46; 1896 c. 44; 1940 c. 38.

EXPLANATORY NOTE

(This Note is not part of the Order.)

This Order, which has effect from 15th June 1969, sets out the statutory minimum remuneration payable and the holidays to be allowed to workers in substitution for the statutory minimum remuneration fixed, and the holidays provided for, by the Wages Regulation (Licensed Non-residential Establishment) (Managers and Club Stewards) Order 1967 (Order L.N.R. (71)) and the Wages Regulation (Licensed Non-residential Establishment) (Managers and Club Stewards) (Amendment) Order 1968 (Order L.N.R. (74)), which Orders are revoked.

New provisions are printed in italics.

STATUTORY INSTRUMENTS

1969 No. 659 (S.53)

EDUCATION, SCOTLAND

The Teachers Superannuation (Scotland) (Amendment) Regulations 1969

Made - - -	*5th May* 1969
Laid before Parliament	*13th May* 1969
Coming into Operation	*14th May* 1969

In exercise of the powers conferred upon me by sections 18 and 21(3)(*b*) of the Teachers Superannuation (Scotland) Act 1968(**a**) as amended by the Minister for the Civil Service Order 1968(**b**) and of all other powers enabling me in that behalf and after consultation with representatives of education authorities, teachers and other bodies appearing to me to be likely to be affected as required by section 18(5) of the said Act, and with the consent of the Minister for the Civil Service, I hereby make the following regulations—

Citation and commencement

1. These regulations may be cited as the Teachers Superannuation (Scotland) (Amendment) Regulations 1969 and shall come into operation on 14th May 1969 but, subject to the provisions of section 18(7) of the Teachers Superannuation (Scotland) Act 1968, shall be deemed to have had effect from and including 1st February 1969.

Interpretation

2. The Interpretation Act 1889(**c**) shall apply for the interpretation of these regulations as it applies for the interpretation of an Act of Parliament.

Amendment of the Teachers Superannuation (Scotland) Regulations 1969

3. In regulation 78 of the Teachers Superannuation (Scotland) Regulations 1969(**d**) (which relates to amendment of enactments) the following paragraph shall be inserted after paragraph (2)—

"(3) The Pensions (Increase) Acts of 1944, 1947, 1952, 1956, 1959, 1962 and 1965 shall apply to an annual allowance payable under section 1 of the Act of 1968 as if it were a pension specified in Part I of the relevant Schedule to each of the aforesaid Acts of 1944, 1952, 1956, 1959 and 1965. For the purposes of this paragraph 'the relevant Schedule' in relation to the Pensions (Increase) Act of any year means the Schedule to that Act which lists the pensions qualifying for increase under section 1 of the Act."

William Ross,
One of Her Majesty's
Principal Secretaries of State.

St. Andrew's House,
Edinburgh, 1.
5th May 1969.

(**a**) 1968 c. 12.
(**c**) 1889 c. 63.

(**b**) S.I. 1968/1656 (1968 III, p. 4485).
(**d**) S.I. 1969/77 (1969 I, p. 133).

Consent of the Minister for the Civil Service given under his Official Seal on 5th May 1969.

J. E. Herbecq,
Authorised by the Minister for
the Civil Service.

EXPLANATORY NOTE

(This Note is not part of the Regulations.)

These Regulations provide for the Pensions (Increase) Acts of 1944 to 1965 to apply to annual allowances payable under the Teachers Superannuation (Scotland) Regulations 1969.   For pensions increase purposes a teacher's annual allowance is deemed to begin on the day after cessation of service, which in some cases can occur many years before the allowance comes into payment.   In so far as such allowances come into payment after 31st January 1969 and are therefore paid under the Teachers Superannuation (Scotland) Regulations 1969, it is necessary to amend those Regulations to provide that these allowances may attract increases as appropriate under the Pensions (Increase) Acts before that of 1969.   The Pensions (Increase) Act 1969 itself provides for increases of these allowances under that Act.

The Regulations have retrospective effect from 1st February 1969 (the date of coming into operation of the Teachers Superannuation (Scotland) Regulations 1969) by virtue of section 18(7) of the Teachers Superannuation (Scotland) Act 1968.

STATUTORY INSTRUMENTS

1969 No. 660 (S.54)

PENSIONS

The Increase of Pensions (Teachers Family Benefits) (Scotland) Regulations 1969

Made - - -	*5th May* 1969
Laid before Parliament	13th *May* 1969
Coming into Operation	14th *May* 1969

In exercise of the powers conferred upon me by paragraphs 12 and 14 of Schedule 2 to the Pensions (Increase) Act 1969(**a**) and with the consent of the Minister for the Civil Service, I hereby make the following regulations—

Citation and commencement

1. These regulations may be cited as the Increase of Pensions (Teachers Family Benefits) (Scotland) Regulations 1969 and shall come into operation on 14th May 1969 but shall be deemed to have had effect from and including 1st April 1969.

Interpretation

2.—(1) The Interpretation Act 1889(**b**) shall apply for the interpretation of these regulations as it applies for the interpretation of an Act of Parliament.

(2) References in these regulations to a regulation shall, unless the context otherwise requires, be construed as references to a regulation of the Regulations.

Definitions

3.—(1) In these regulations, unless the context otherwise requires—

"the Act" means the Pensions (Increase) Act 1969 ;

"the Regulations" means the Teachers Superannuation (Family Benefits) (Scotland) Regulations 1969(**c**).

(2) Other expressions used in these regulations to which meanings are assigned by the Regulations shall, unless the context otherwise requires, have the same respective meanings in these regulations.

Exceptions from the Act

4. In relation to pensions payable under the Regulations, section 1(1) of the Act shall apply subject to the exception therefrom of—

(*a*) a short service widow's pension payable under regulation 46 ; and
(*b*) a children's pension payable under regulation 49.

Widow's Minimum Pension

5.—(1) In relation to a widow's pension payable under regulation 43 of which the annual rate is either—

(*a*) the minimum sum of £115 by reason of regulation 44(1)(*b*) ; or

---

(**a**) 1969 c. 7.   (**b**) 1889 c. 63.   (**c**) S.I. 1969/78 (1969 I, p. 192).

(b) a proportion of the minimum sum of £115 by reason of regulation 44(1)(b) as affected by regulation 52,

section 1(1) of the Act shall apply subject to the modifications specified in paragraphs (2) and (3) of this regulation.

(2) In a case to which sub-paragraph (a) of paragraph (1) of this regulation applies the amount of the increase shall be the amount, if any, of the excess over £115 of the aggregate of—

(a) the annual rate of the pension if it were determined under paragraph (2) or (3) of regulation 44 ; and

(b) the amount of the increase of the annual rate so determined if section 1(1) and (2) of the Act were applicable thereto.

(3) In a case to which sub-paragraph (b) of paragraph (1) of this regulation applies the amount of the increase shall be the amount, if any, of the excess over the annual rate of the pension of the aggregate of—

(a) the annual rate of the pension if it were determined under paragraph (2) or (3) of regulation 44 and were subject to regulation 52 ; and

(b) the amount of the increase of the annual rate so determined if section 1(1) and (2) of the Act were applicable thereto.

William Ross,
One of Her Majesty's
Principal Secretaries of State.

St. Andrew's House,
Edinburgh, 1.
5th May 1969.

Consent of the Minister for the Civil Service given under his Official Seal on 5th May 1969.

J. E. Herbecq,
Authorised by the Minister for
the Civil Service.

EXPLANATORY NOTE

(This Note is not part of the Regulations.)

These Regulations except from increase under the Pensions (Increase) Act 1969 pensions payable under the Teachers Superannuation (Family Benefits) (Scotland) Regulations 1969 to the widow of a teacher with less than ten years' service and to the children of a teacher.

They also provide that where a widow's pension is payable at the minimum rate of £115 a year (or, in the case of a teacher with service elsewhere in the British Isles, as a proportion of that minimum) the increase shall be limited to the amount (if any) by which the total of the pension and increase, if both were determined by the normal methods, would exceed £115 (or, if such is the case, the proportion of that sum being paid).

The Regulations have retrospective effect from 1st April 1969 by virtue of paragraph 14 of Schedule 2 to the Pensions (Increase) Act 1969.

STATUTORY INSTRUMENTS

1969 No. 664

AGRICULTURE

The Price Stability of Imported Products (Rates of Levy No. 10) Order 1969

Made - - - -	*6th May* 1969
Coming into Operation	*7th May* 1969

The Minister of Agriculture, Fisheries and Food, in exercise of the powers conferred upon him by section 1(2), (4), (5), (6) and (7) of the Agriculture and Horticulture Act 1964(a) and of all other powers enabling him in that behalf, hereby makes the following order :—

1. This order may be cited as the Price Stability of Imported Products (Rates of Levy No. 10) Order 1969 ; and shall come into operation on 7th May 1969.

2.—(1) In this order—

" the Principal Order " means the Price Stability of Imported Products (Levy Arrangements) Order 1966(b), as amended by any subsequent order and if any such order is replaced by any subsequent order the expression shall be construed as a reference to such subsequent order ;

AND other expressions have the same meaning as in the Principal Order.

(2) The Interpretation Act 1889(c) shall apply to the interpretation of this order as it applies to the interpretation of an Act of Parliament and as if this order and the order hereby revoked were Acts of Parliament.

3. In accordance with and subject to the provisions of Part II of the Principal Order (which provides for the charging of levies on imports of certain specified commodities)—

(*a*) the rate of general levy for such imports into the United Kingdom of any specified commodity as are described in column 2 of Part I of the Schedule to this order in relation to a tariff heading indicated in column 1 of that Part shall be the rate set forth in relation thereto in column 3 of that Part;

(*b*) the rate of country levy for such imports into the United Kingdom of any specified commodity as are described in column 2 of Part II of the Schedule to this order in relation to a tariff heading indicated in column 1 of that Part shall be the rate set forth in relation thereto in column 3 of that Part.

4. The Price Stability of Imported Products (Rates of Levy No. 9) Order 1969(d) is hereby revoked.

In Witness whereof the Official Seal of the Minister of Agriculture, Fisheries and Food is hereunto affixed on 6th May 1969.

(L.S.)

R. J. E. Taylor,
Assistant Secretary.

(a) 1964 c. 28.   (b) S.I. 1966/936 (1966 II, p. 2271).   (c) 1889 c. 63.
(d) S.I. 1969/571 (1969 I, p. 1532).

SCHEDULE

PART I

1. Tariff Heading	2. Description of Imports	3. Rate of General Levy
		per ton £ s. d.
	Imports of:—	
10.01	Denatured wheat	5 0
10.01	Any wheat (other than seed wheat the value of which is not less than £34 per ton, denatured wheat and durum wheat) for which a minimum import price level is prescribed	5 0
10.03	Barley	1 10 0

11.02	Cereal meals—
	   of barley .. ..
	   of maize .. ..
		5 10 0
		6 15 0

11.02	Rolled, flaked, crushed or bruised cereals— barley	5 15 0

PART II

1. Tariff Heading	2. Description of Imports	3. Rate of Country Levy
		per ton £ s. d.
	Imports of:—	
10.01	Denatured wheat which has been grown in and consigned to the United Kingdom from Belgium, the French Republic, the Kingdom of the Netherlands or the Kingdom of Sweden	5 0
10.01	Any wheat (other than seed wheat the value of which is not less than £34 per ton, denatured wheat and durum wheat) for which a minimum import price level is prescribed and which is grown in and consigned to the United Kingdom from the French Republic or the Kingdom of the Netherlands ..	5 0
10.03	Barley which has been grown in and consigned to the United Kingdom from Canada	1 10 0

EXPLANATORY NOTE
(This Note is not part of the Order.)

This order, which comes into operation on 7th May 1969, re-enacts with amendments the Price Stability of Imported Products (Rates of Levy No. 9) Order 1969. It:—

(a) reduces to 5s. per ton the general levy on imports of denatured wheat;

(b) reduces to 5s. per ton the country levy on imports of denatured wheat which has been grown in and consigned to the United Kingdom from Belgium, France, the Netherlands or Sweden;

(c) reduces to 5s. per ton the general levy on wheat (other than seed wheat the value of which is not less than £34 per ton, denatured wheat and durum wheat);

(d) reduces to 5s. per ton the country levy on such wheat which is grown in and consigned to the United Kingdom from France or the Netherlands;

(e) increases to 30s. per ton the general levy on barley;

(f) increases to 30s. per ton the country levy on barley which has been grown in and consigned to the United Kingdom from Canada;

(g) removes the country levy on barley which has been grown in and consigned to the United Kingdom from Australia, Belgium, Denmark, Finland, France, the Netherlands or Sweden;

(h) increases to 135s. per ton the general levy on maize meal; and

(i) reimposes unchanged the general levies on barley meal and rolled, flaked, crushed or bruised barley.

STATUTORY INSTRUMENTS

1969 No. 665

PENSIONS

The Superannuation (Commission on Industrial Relations) Order 1969

Made - - -	*6th May* 1969
Laid before Parliament	*13th May* 1969
Coming into Operation	*14th May* 1969

The Minister for the Civil Service, in exercise of the powers conferred on him by section 98(5) and (9) of the Superannuation Act 1965(**a**) and article 2(1)(*c*) of the Minister for the Civil Service Order 1968(**b**), hereby makes the following Order :—

1. This Order may be cited as the Superannuation (Commission on Industrial Relations) Order 1969, and shall come into operation on 14th May 1969.

2. The Interpretation Act 1889(**c**) shall apply for the interpretation of this Order as it applies for the interpretation of an Act of Parliament.

3.—(1) Employment by the Commission on Industrial Relations shall be added to the employments listed in Schedule 8 to the Superannuation Act 1965.

(2) This article shall have effect as from 1st March 1969.

Given under the official seal of the Minister for the Civil Service on 6th May 1969.

(L.S.)

J. E. Herbecq,
Authorised by the Minister
for the Civil Service.

(**a**) 1965 c. 74.
(**c**) 1889 c. 63.

(**b**) S.I. 1968/1656 (1968 III, p. 4485).

EXPLANATORY NOTE

(This Note is not part of the Order.)

Section 98(4) of the Superannuation Act 1965 provides that service in employment of the kinds listed in Schedule 8 to that Act shall be treated as service in the civil service of the State for the purposes of pensions and other superannuation benefits. This Order adds employment by the Commission on Industrial Relations to the list in that Schedule. Under the powers of section 98(9) of the Act the Order has retrospective effect as from 1st March 1969.

STATUTORY INSTRUMENTS

1969 No. 667

ROAD TRAFFIC

The Motor Vehicles (International Circulation) (Amendment) Regulations 1969

Made - - -	6*th May* 1969
Laid before Parliament	15*th May* 1969
Coming into Operation	1*st June* 1969

The Minister of Transport in exercise of his powers under sections 8, 16 (as amended by section 46 of the Road Traffic Act 1962(**a**)), and 23 of the Vehicles (Excise) Act 1962(**b**), and Articles 5 and 6 of the Motor Vehicles (International Circulation) Order 1957(**c**), as varied by the Motor Vehicles (International Circulation) (Amendment) Order 1962(**d**) and the Motor Vehicles (International Circulation) (Amendment) Order 1968(**e**), and of all other powers him enabling in that behalf, hereby makes the following Regulations :—

1. These Regulations shall come into operation on the 1st June 1969, and may be cited as the Motor Vehicles (International Circulation) (Amendment) Regulations 1969.

2. The Motor Vehicles (International Circulation) Regulations 1965(**f**) shall have effect as though :—

(1) Regulation 1 (which relates to furnishing of particulars etc. by persons bringing vehicles temporarily into Great Britain) were omitted ;

(2) Regulation 5 (which relates to the keeping of certain records by registration authorities) were omitted ;

(3) in Regulation 6—

(*a*) paragraph (1) (which relates to the preservation by the Greater London Council of certain particulars) were omitted ;

(*b*) in paragraph (3), the words from "any documents" to "Northern Ireland and" were omitted ;

(4) in Regulation 7(1), the definitions of "certificate of insurance", "certificate of security", "insurance card" and "duplicate page" were omitted ;

(5) the Schedule (which relates to particulars to be furnished to registration authorities) were omitted.

Given under the Official Seal of the Minister of Transport the 6th May 1969.

(L.S.)

Richard Marsh,
Minister of Transport.

(**a**) 10 & 11 Eliz. 2 c. 59.   (**b**) 10 & 11 Eliz. 2 c. 13.
(**c**) S.I. 1957/1074 (1957 II, p. 2154).   (**d**) S.I. 1962/1344 (1962 II, p. 1483)
(**e**) S.I. 1968/1111 (1968 II, p. 3068).   (**f**) S.I. 1965/329 (1965 I, p. 1067).

EXPLANATORY NOTE

(This Note is not part of the Regulations.)

These Regulations amend the Motor Vehicles (International Circulation) Regulations 1965 by:—

1. providing that persons resident outside the United Kingdom who bring vehicles temporarily into Great Britain need no longer furnish registration authorities with the particulars specified in the Schedule to the 1965 Regulations with respect to those vehicles or produce to those authorities insurance documents relating to those vehicles ;

2. terminating the need for certain records to be made by registration authorities in respect of vehicles temporarily in Great Britain and for copies of those records to be preserved by the Greater London Council.

STATUTORY INSTRUMENTS

1969 No. 668

ROAD TRAFFIC

The Motor Vehicles (International Motor Insurance Card) Regulations 1969

Made - - - -	*6th May* 1969
Laid before Parliament	*15th May* 1969
Coming into Operation	*1st June* 1969

ARRANGEMENT OF REGULATIONS

Regulation

Commencement and Citation 1

Revocation 2

Interpretation 3

Validity of insurance card 4

Third-party risks arising out of the use of motor vehicles by visitors 5, 6 and 7

Production of insurance card on application for excise licence ... 8

Requirements in connection with duplicate pages 9

Special provision for motor vehicles from Northern Ireland ... 10

Form of insurance card ... ... (Part I) Schedule

Form of duplicate page ... ... (Part II)

The Minister of Transport in exercise of his powers under sections 211 and 215 of the Road Traffic Act 1960(a), and section 23 of the Vehicles (Excise) Act 1962(b), and of all other enabling powers and after consultation with representative organisations in accordance with the provisions of section 260(2) of the Road Traffic Act 1960, hereby makes the following Regulations:—

Commencement and Citation

1. These Regulations shall come into operation on the 1st June 1969 and may be cited as the Motor Vehicles (International Motor Insurance Card) Regulations 1969.

Revocation

2. The Motor Vehicles (International Motor Insurance Card) Regulations 1963(c) are hereby revoked.

(a) 8 & 9 Eliz. 2. c.16.   (b) 10 & 11 Eliz.2.c.13.

(c) S.I. 1963/436 (1963 I, p.492).

Interpretation

3.—(1) In these Regulations—

"the Act" means the Road Traffic Act 1960;

"authorised insurer" has the same meaning as in Part VI of the Act;

"British Bureau" means the Motor Insurers' Bureau incorporated under the Companies Act 1929**(a)**, and having its registered office at Aldermary House, Queen Street, London, E.C.4.;

"chief officer of police", and "police area", in relation to England and Wales, have respectively the same meanings as in the Police Act 1964**(b)**, and, in relation to Scotland, have respectively the same meanings as in the Police Pensions Act 1921**(c)**;

"Foreign Bureau" means a central organisation set up by motor insurers in any country outside the United Kingdom, the Isle of Man and the Channel Islands for the purpose of giving effect to international arrangements for the insurance of motorists against third-party risks when entering countries where insurance against such risks is compulsory, and with which organisation the British Bureau has entered into such an arrangement;

"hired motor vehicle" means a motor vehicle which is:—

    (*a*) designed for private use and with seats for not more than eight persons excluding the driver, and

    (*b*) specified in an insurance card, and

    (*c*) last brought into Great Britain by a person making only a temporary stay therein, and

    (*d*) owned and let for hire by a person whose business includes the letting of vehicles for hire and whose principal place of business is outside the United Kingdom;

"hiring visitor" means a person to whom a hired motor vehicle is let on hire, who is making only a temporary stay in Great Britain and is named as the insured or user of that vehicle in the insurance card in which that vehicle is specified;

"insurance card" means an international motor insurance card issued under the authority of a Foreign Bureau or of the British Bureau which is green in colour and, either in English or a foreign language, in the form specified in Part I of the Schedule to these Regulations and which in the case of each entry into the United Kingdom of the motor vehicle specified in the card during the period of validity so specified has attached thereto one or more pages green in colour and, either in English or a foreign language, in the form specified in Part II of the said Schedule, each of which said pages is hereinafter referred to as a "duplicate page";

"the Minister" means the Minister of Transport;

"trade licence" has the same meaning as in the Vehicles (Excise) Act 1962;

"visitor" means a person bringing a motor vehicle into Great Britain, making only a temporary stay therein and named in an insurance card as the insured or user of the vehicle, and includes a hiring visitor who brings a hired motor vehicle into Great Britain, but no other hiring visitor.

(a) 19 & 20 Geo. 5.c.23.   **(b)** 1964 c.48.
(c) 11 & 12 Geo. 5.c.31.

(2) Any reference in these Regulations to any provision in an Act of Parliament or in subordinate legislation shall be construed as a reference to that provision as amended by any other such provision.

(3) The Interpretation Act 1889(a) shall apply for the interpretation of these Regulations as it applies for the interpretation of an Act of Parliament and as if for the purposes of section 38 of that Act these Regulations were an Act of Parliament and the Regulations revoked by Regulation 2 of these Regulations were an Act of Parliament thereby repealed.

Validity of insurance card

4.—(1) An insurance card shall be valid for the purposes of these Regulations only if—

(a) the card bears on page 1 thereof the name of the Foreign Bureau or the British Bureau, as the case may be, under whose authority the card was issued;

(b) the motor vehicle specified in the card is brought into the United Kingdom during the period of validity so specified;

(c) the application of the card in Great Britain is indicated thereon;

(d) all relevant information provided for in the card has been inscribed therein;

(e) the card has been duly signed by the visitor, by the insurer named in the card and, in the case of a hired motor vehicle, by every hiring visitor who is named in the card as the insured or user thereof.

(2) The information required to be inscribed in paragraphs (2), (3) and (8) on page 3 of the card is:—

(a) in the said paragraph (2), the name of the Foreign Bureau or the British Bureau, as the case may be, under whose authority the card was issued; and

(b) in the said paragraph (3), the name and address of the insured visitor and of every person who is, as respects a hired motor vehicle, a hiring visitor; and

(c) in the said paragraph (8), the name and address of the insurer authorised to issue the card by the Foreign Bureau or the British Bureau, as the case may be, and by whom the card was issued.

Third-party risks arising out of the use of motor vehicles by visitors

5.—(1) As respects the use on a road of a motor vehicle specified in a valid insurance card, being use by the visitor to whom the card was issued, or by any hiring visitor named therein, or by any other person on the order or with the permission of the said visitor or of any such hiring visitor, section 201 of the Act shall have effect as though the said card were a policy of insurance complying with the requirements of and having effect for the purposes of Part VI of the Act in relation to such use;

Provided that where the said motor vehicle remains in the United Kingdom after the expiry of the period of validity specified in the card, then as respects any period whilst it so remains during which the vehicle is in Great Britain the

(a) 52 & 53 Vict. c.63.

said card shall not be regarded as having ceased to be in force for the purposes of the said section 201 by reason only of effluxion of the period of validity specified in the card.

For the purposes of this paragraph a motor vehicle shall be deemed not to have left the United Kingdom whilst it is only in transit between different parts of the United Kingdom.

(2) Any reference in this Regulation and in the next two following Regulations to the use on a road of a motor vehicle shall not include any use of the vehicle for the purpose of delivering it to or for the visitor at some place other than the place of entry of the vehicle into Great Britain, which is authorised under a trade licence.

6.—(1) For the purposes of sections 226, 230 and 231 of the Act, a valid insurance card shall have effect as though it were a certificate of insurance issued by an authorised insurer and in relation to any claim in respect of any such liability as is required to be covered by a policy of insurance under section 203 of the Act and arising out of the use on a road of a motor vehicle specified in such a card by the visitor to whom it was issued, by any hiring visitor named therein, or by any other person on the order or with the permission of the said visitor or of any such hiring visitor, the person against whom the claim is made shall in lieu of making the statement and giving the particulars referred to in section 209(1) of the Act, give to the person making the claim, on his demand, the serial letter or letters and number shown in the card, the name of the Bureau under whose authority it was issued and the name and address of the person specified therein as the insured.

(2) Any person making or intending to make any such claim as is mentioned in the preceding paragraph of this Regulation shall give notice of the claim in writing to the British Bureau as soon as practicable after the happening of the event out of which the claim arose specifying the nature of the claim and against whom it is made or intended to be made.

(3) Where owing to the presence on a road of a motor vehicle specified in an insurance card, an accident occurs involving personal injury to a person other than the driver of the vehicle, and by reason of section 226 or 230 of the Act, as modified by paragraph (1) of this Regulation, the insurance card, together with a duplicate page, is produced to a police constable or at a police station, that police constable or a police constable at that station may detach the duplicate page from the card and arrange for its retention for the purposes of recording or producing insurance particulars relating to the accident.

7. In any civil proceedings in respect of any such liability as is required to be covered by a policy of insurance under section 203 of the Act and arising out of the use on a road of a motor vehicle specified in a valid insurance card, the production of the duplicate page detached by a police constable in pursuance of paragraph (3) of the last preceding Regulation shall be evidence that the person specified in the card as the insured has duly signed the form of authority specified in paragraph (4) on page 4 of the card unless the contrary is proved.

Production of insurance card on application for excise licence

8. Any visitor or hiring visitor applying for a licence under the Vehicles (Excise) Act 1962 for a motor vehicle specified in a valid insurance card in which he is named as the insured may, during the period of validity specified in the

card, in lieu of producing to the licensing authority such evidence as is required by Regulation 9 of the Motor Vehicles (Third Party Risks) Regulations 1961(a), produce such a card to the licensing authority.

Requirements in connection with duplicate pages

9. The chief officer of police of each police area shall without charge:—

(a) furnish to the Minister, or the British Bureau on request or to an authorised insurer on request by the British Bureau any information relating to the contents of a duplicate page which may have been detached by a police constable under Regulation 6(3) of these Regulations in connection with an accident in that area; and

(b) forward to the British Bureau or to an authorised insurer on request by the British Bureau any such duplicate page and the British Bureau or the authorised insurer, as the case may be, shall as soon as practicable, return the duplicate page to the chief officer of police by whom it was forwarded.

Special provision for motor vehicles from Northern Ireland

10. In the case of a motor vehicle brought from Northern Ireland into Great Britain by a person making only a temporary stay in Great Britain, a policy of insurance or a security which complies with the Motor Vehicles and Road Traffic Act (Northern Ireland) 1930 and which covers the driving of the motor vehicle in Great Britain and any certificate of insurance or certificate of security issued in pursuance of that Act and the Regulations made thereunder in respect of such policy or security shall have effect as a policy of insurance or a security or a certificate of insurance or certificate of security respectively for the purposes of Part VI of the Act, and of the Motor Vehicles (Third Party Risks) Regulations 1961.

Given under the Official Seal of the Minister of Transport the 6th May 1969.

(L.S.)

Richard Marsh,
Minister of Transport.

(a) S.I. 1961 /1465(1961 II, p.2967).

THE SCHEDULE

(See Regulation 3)

(In this Schedule, references to the Convention of 1949 are references to the Convention on Road Traffic concluded at Geneva in the year 1949(a).)

PART I

FORM OF INSURANCE CARD

PAGE 1

INTERNATIONAL MOTOR INSURANCE CARD
CARTE INTERNATIONALE D'ASSURANCE AUTOMOBILE

Issued under the Authority of

By

(a) Cmnd. 7997.

PAGE 2

(This page may contain Notes by the Insurer for the information of the Insured)

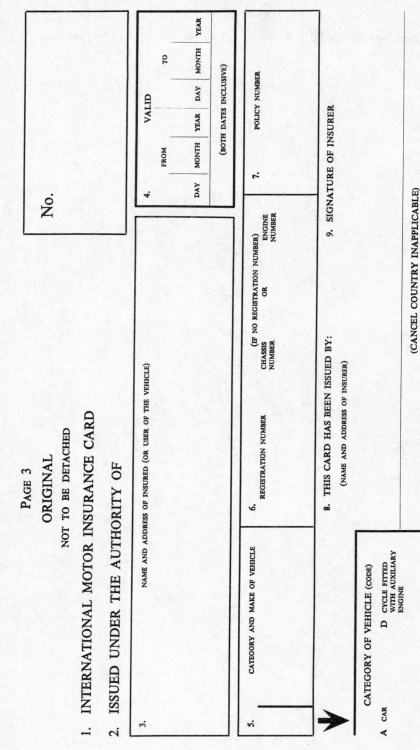

PAGE 3

ORIGINAL

NOT TO BE DETACHED

1. INTERNATIONAL MOTOR INSURANCE CARD

2. ISSUED UNDER THE AUTHORITY OF

No.

3. NAME AND ADDRESS OF INSURED (OR USER OF THE VEHICLE)

4. VALID

FROM | TO
DAY | MONTH | YEAR | DAY | MONTH | YEAR

(BOTH DATES INCLUSIVE)

5. CATEGORY AND MAKE OF VEHICLE

6. REGISTRATION NUMBER

CHASSIS NUMBER   (IF NO REGISTRATION NUMBER)   OR   ENGINE NUMBER

7. POLICY NUMBER

8. THIS CARD HAS BEEN ISSUED BY:

(NAME AND ADDRESS OF INSURER)

9. SIGNATURE OF INSURER

CATEGORY OF VEHICLE (CODE)

A CAR

B MOTOR CYCLE

C LORRY OR TRACTOR

D CYCLE FITTED WITH AUXILIARY ENGINE

E BUS

F TRAILER

(CANCEL COUNTRY INAPPLICABLE)

(Print here the Distinguishing Signs, according to the Convention of 1949, of the countries participating in the International Motor Insurance Card System on the first day mentioned in paragraph 4 above).

PAGE 4

(1) In each country visited, the Bureau of that country assumes, in respect of the use of the vehicle referred to herein, the liability of an Insurer in accordance with the laws relating to compulsory insurance in that country.

(2) After the date of expiry of this Card, liability is assumed by the Bureau of the country visited, if so required by the law of such country or by any agreement with its Government.

(3) In such case, the within-mentioned Insured undertakes to pay the premium due for the duration of the stay after the date for which the Insurance Card is valid has passed.

(4) I, the within-mentioned Insured, hereby authorise the Motor Insurers' Bureau and the Bureaux of any mentioned countries, to which it may delegate such powers, to accept service of legal proceedings, to handle and eventually settle, on my behalf, any claim for damages in respect of liability to third parties required to be covered under the compulsory insurance laws of the country or countries specified herein, which may arise from the use of the vehicle in that country (those countries).

(5) Signature of the Insured

(6) For visitors to Great Britain and Northern Ireland only.
Signature of any other persons who may use the vehicle

....

(This Insurance Card is only valid when signed by the Insured.)

Cards applicable to the following countries must contain detachable copies of the form on the preceding page:—

Great Britain & Northern Ireland
Switzerland

LAST PAGE

Note to the Insured

In regard to (*a*) damage to the insured vehicle, however caused ; (*b*) personal injuries sustained by the Insured ; the Bureau of the country visited should not be approached but notification should be given (unless otherwise instructed by the Insurer) direct to the Insurer.

NAMES AND ADDRESSES OF BUREAUX

(Print here the Distinguishing Sign of each country where the International Motor Insurance Card System is in force at the time of issue of this card, and opposite the signs the names and postal addresses of the Bureaux)

PART II

FORM OF DUPLICATE PAGE
(DUPLICATE)

1. INTERNATIONAL MOTOR INSURANCE CARD

2. ISSUED UNDER THE AUTHORITY OF

No.

4.	VALID							
	FROM				TO			
	DAY	MONTH	YEAR		DAY	MONTH	YEAR	
	(BOTH DATES INCLUSIVE)							

3. NAME AND ADDRESS OF INSURED (OR USER OF THE VEHICLE)

5. CATEGORY AND MAKE OF VEHICLE

6. REGISTRATION NUMBER   CHASSIS NUMBER   (IF NO REGISTRATION NUMBER) OR ENGINE NUMBER

7. POLICY NUMBER

8. THIS CARD HAS BEEN ISSUED BY:
(NAME AND ADDRESS OF INSURER)

9. SIGNATURE OF INSURER

(CANCEL COUNTRY INAPPLICABLE)

(Print here the Distinguishing Signs, according to the Convention of 1949, of the countries participating in the International Motor Insurance Card System on the first day mentioned in paragraph 4 above).

CATEGORY OF VEHICLE (CODE)

A CAR

B MOTOR CYCLE

C LORRY OR TRACTOR

D CYCLE FITTED WITH AUXILIARY ENGINE

E BUS

F TRAILER

EXPLANATORY NOTE

(This Note is not part of the Regulations.)

These Regulations re-enact with amendment the Motor Vehicles (International Motor Insurance Card) Regulations 1963. The principal changes are:—

1. The requirement in Regulation 9 of the 1963 Regulations that visitors bringing a motor vehicle into Great Britain which is specified in an international motor insurance card shall surrender to a registration authority a duplicate page (showing certain insurance particulars) of the card at the place of entry of the vehicle into Great Britain is not re-enacted;

2. Provision is made for a police constable to retain a duplicate page of an international motor insurance card for insurance record purposes in the event of certain accidents involving a motor vehicle specified in such a card (Regulation 6(3));

3. The requirements in Regulations 9, 10 and 11 of the 1963 Regulations relating to the making by registration authorities of certain records in connection with international motor insurance cards and the preservation by the Greater London Council of these records are discontinued;

4. New provision is introduced requiring a chief officer of police to make available on request by specified authorities information about duplicate pages (Regulation 9).

1969 No. 670 (S.56)

LOCAL GOVERNMENT, SCOTLAND

The Rate Support Grant (Scotland) (Amendment) Regulations 1969

Made - - -	*5th May* 1969
Laid before Parliament	*15th May* 1969
Coming into Operation	*16th May* 1969

In exercise of the powers conferred on me by paragraph 5 of Part 1 of Schedule 1 to the Local Government (Scotland) Act 1966(**a**) and of all other powers enabling me in that behalf, and after consultation with such associations of local authorities as appear to me to be concerned, I hereby make the following regulations :—

1. These regulations may be cited as the Rate Support Grant (Scotland) (Amendment) Regulations 1969 and shall come into operation on 16th May 1969.

2. The Interpretation Act 1889(**b**) shall apply for the interpretation of these regulations as it applies for the interpretation of an Act of Parliament.

3. The Rate Support Grant (Scotland) Regulations 1967(**c**) as amended by the Rate Support Grant (Scotland) (Amendment) Regulations 1968(**d**) shall be further amended as follows :—

In paragraph (7) of regulation 4 there shall be added after the words "health visitors" the words ", district nurses,".

William Ross,

One of Her Majesty's Principal Secretaries of State.

St. Andrew's House,
Edinburgh.
5th May 1969.

EXPLANATORY NOTE

(This Note is not part of the Regulations.)

These Regulations further amend the existing Regulations dealing with the pooling (by means of adjustments to rate support grants) of expenditure incurred by certain local authorities among all local authorities, by adding expenditure on the training of district nurses to the items of expenditure to be pooled.

(**a**) 1966 c. 51.   (**b**) 1889 c. 63.
(**c**) S.I. 1967/715 (1967 II, p. 2162).   (**d**) S.I. 1968/1889 (1968 III, p. 5033).

STATUTORY INSTRUMENTS

1969 No. 672

AGRICULTURE

GUARANTEED PRICES AND ASSURED MARKETS

The Cereals (Guarantee Payments) (Amendment) Order 1969

Made - - -	*7th May* 1969
Laid before Parliament	15*th May* 1969
Coming into Operation	1*st July* 1969

The Minister of Agriculture, Fisheries and Food, the Secretaries of State respectively concerned with agriculture in Scotland and Northern Ireland and the Secretary of State for Wales, acting jointly, in exercise of the powers conferred upon them by sections 1 and 35(3) of the Agriculture Act 1957(a), as read with the Transfer of Functions (Wales) Order 1969(b), and of all other powers enabling them in that behalf, with the consent of the Treasury and after consultation with such bodies of persons as appear to the said Ministers to represent the interests of producers of cereals, hereby make the following order :—

Citation, commencement and interpretation

1.—(1) This order may be cited as the Cereals (Guarantee Payments) (Amendment) Order 1969 ; and shall come into operation on 1st July 1969.

(2) The Interpretation Act 1889(c) shall apply to the interpretation of this order as it applies to the interpretation of an Act of Parliament.

Amendment of the principal order

2. The Cereals (Guarantee Payments) Order 1964(d), as amended (e), shall be further amended as follows :—

    (*a*) by substituting in article 2(1) thereof for the definitions of "guaranteed price", "target indicator price", "standard quantity", "annual production" and "average realised price" the following definitions :—

        " 'guaranteed price', 'target indicator price' and 'average realised price' mean respectively the prices determined or ascertained pursuant to article 3 of this order ;";

(a) 1957 c. 57.   (b) S.I. 1969/388 (1969 I, p. 1070).

(c) 1889 c. 63.   (d) S.I. 1964/840 (1964 II, p. 1796).

(e) S.I. 1966/484, 1968/767 (1966 I, p. 995; 1968 II, p. 2148).

(b) by deleting therefrom paragraph (2) of article 3 thereof ;

(c) by substituting for paragraph (3) of article 3 thereof, the following paragraph : —

> "(2) In respect of each year the Minister shall ascertain in such manner and at such time as appears to him proper the average realised price per hundredweight obtained by producers for wheat and barley respectively." ;

(d) by substituting for article 4 thereof the following article : —

> "4. The guarantee payment for wheat and for barley respectively shall be the amount, if any, by which the guaranteed price thereof exceeds the average realised price thereof, or the target indicater price thereof, whichever is the higher.".

In Witness whereof the Official Seal of the Minister of Agriculture, Fisheries and Food is hereunto affixed on 28th April 1969.

(L.S.)   *Cledwyn Hughes,*
                          Minister of Agriculture, Fisheries and Food.

Given under the Seal of the Secretary of State for Scotland on 30th April 1969.

(L.S.)   *William Ross,*
                               Secretary of State for Scotland.

Given under the hand of the Secretary of State for the Home Department on 5th May 1969.

                                            James Callaghan,
                          Secretary of State for the Home Department.

Given under my hand on 6th May 1969.

George Thomas,
Secretary of State for Wales.

We consent
7th May 1969.

Joseph Harper,
E. Alan Fitch,
Two of the Lords Commissioners of
Her Majesty's Treasury.

EXPLANATORY NOTE

(This Note is not part of the Order.)

This order further amends the Cereals (Guarantee Payments) Order 1964, as amended, and provides for changes in the arrangements for guarantee payments to producers of cereals following the determinations of the Ministers after a review held under section 2 of the Agriculture Act 1947.

The changes effected by the order relate only to barley. Provision is made for the abolition of the standard quantity and for the ending of the arrangement under which, when annual production is below the standard quantity and the average realised price is below the target indicator price, the deficiency payment is abated within a range of production determined by the Ministers.

The provisions relating to wheat, rye, oats and mixed cereals remain unchanged.

STATUTORY INSTRUMENTS

1969 No. 676

AGRICULTURE

The Price Stability of Imported Products (Rates of Levy No. 11) Order 1969

Made - - - -	*8th May* 1969
Coming into Operation	*9th May* 1969

The Minister of Agriculture, Fisheries and Food, in exercise of the powers conferred upon him by section 1(2), (4), (5), (6) and (7) of the Agriculture and Horticulture Act 1964(a) and of all other powers enabling him in that behalf, hereby makes the following order :—

1. This order may be cited as the Price Stability of Imported Products (Rates of Levy No. 11) Order 1969 ; and shall come into operation on 9th May 1969.

2.—(1) In this order—

" the Principal Order " means the Price Stability of Imported Products (Levy Arrangements) Order 1966(b), as amended by any subsequent order and if any such order is replaced by any subsequent order the expression shall be construed as a reference to such subsequent order ;

AND other expressions have the same meaning as in the Principal Order.

(2) The Interpretation Act 1889(c) shall apply to the interpretation of this order as it applies to the interpretation of an Act of Parliament.

3. In accordance with and subject to the provisions of Part II of the Principal Order (which provides for the charging of levies on imports of certain specified commodities), and notwithstanding the provisions of Article 3(*a*) of the Price Stability of Imported Products (Rates of Levy No. 10) Order 1969(d), the rate of general levy for such imports into the United Kingdom of any specified commodity as are described in column 2 of the Schedule to this order in relation to a tariff heading indicated in column 1 of that Schedule shall on and after 9th May 1969 be the rate set forth in relation thereto in column 3 of that Schedule.

In Witness whereof the Official Seal of the Minister of Agriculture, Fisheries and Food is hereunto affixed on 8th May 1969.

(L.S.)

R. J. E. Taylor,
Assistant Secretary.

(a) 1964 c. 28. (b) S.I. 1966/936 (1966 II, p. 2271). (c) 1889 c. 63.
(d) S.I. 1969/664 (1969 II, p. 1822).

SCHEDULE

1. Tariff Heading	2. Description of Imports	3. Rate of General Levy
		per ton £ s. d.
11.02	Imports of :— Cereal meal— of barley	7 5 0

EXPLANATORY NOTE

(This Note is not part of the Order.)

This order, which comes into operation on 9th May 1969, increases on and after that date the general levy on imports of barley meal to 145s. per ton.

1969 No. 677

PLANT HEALTH

The Importation of Plants and Plant Produce (Health) (Great Britain) (Amendment) Order 1969

Made - - - -	*8th May* 1969
Laid before Parliament	*16th May* 1969
Coming into Operation	*20th May* 1969

The Minister of Agriculture, Fisheries and Food and the Secretary of State, by virtue and in exercise of the powers vested in them respectively by section 2 of the Plant Health Act 1967(**a**) and of every other power enabling them in that behalf, order as follows:—

Citation, extent and commencement

1.—(1) This Order may be cited as the Importation of Plants and Plant Produce (Health) (Great Britain) (Amendment) Order 1969, and the Importation of Plants and Plant Produce (Health) (Great Britain) Order 1965(**b**) (hereinafter referred to as "the principal Order"), the Importation of Plants and Plant Produce (Health) (Great Britain) (Amendment) Order 1966(**c**) and this Order may be cited together as the Importation of Plants and Plant Produce (Health) (Great Britain) Orders 1965 to 1969.

(2) This Order shall apply to England and Wales and Scotland and shall come into operation on 20th May 1969.

Interpretation

2. The Interpretation Act 1889(**d**) shall apply to the interpretation of this Order as it applies to the interpretation of an Act of Parliament.

Amendment of principal Order

3. Schedule 1 to the principal Order is hereby amended as follows:—

(*a*) In place of the words in the second column describing item (1) in Part IA there shall be substituted the words "Annual and biennial plants grown in any place outside Europe and beet, mangold, fodder beet and sugar beet (*Beta* spp.) and spinach (*Spinacia* spp.) grown in Europe.".

(*b*) In place of the words in the second column describing item (3) in Part IA there shall be substituted the words "Sloe, bullace, cherry plum, plum, apricot, peach (*Prunus spinosa* L., *P. insititia* L., *P. cerasifera* Ehrh., *P. domestica* L., *P. salicina* Lindl., *P. armeniaca* L., *P. persica* (L.) Batsch, *P. tribola* Lindl., *P. tomentosa* Thunb.) grown in Bulgaria, Czechoslovakia, Hungary, Poland, Rumania or Yugoslavia.".

(*c*) For the figure " (3) " appearing in the entry relating to *Prunus* L. in the second column in the description of item (6) in Part IC there shall be substituted the figure " (12) ".

(**a**) 1967 c. 8.
(**b**) S.I. 1965/1426 (1965 II, p. 4228).
(**c**) S.I. 1966/1308 (1966 III, p. 3635).
(**d**) 1889 c. 63.

(*d*) In place of the words in the second column describing item (11) in Part IC there shall be substituted the words " Sloe, bullace, cherry plum, plum, apricot, peach (*Prunus spinosa* L., *P. insititia* L., *P. cerasifera* Ehrh., *P. domestica* L., *P. salicina* Lindl., *P. armeniaca* L., *P. persica* (L.) Batsch, *P. tribola* Lindl., *P. tomentosa* Thunb.) grown in any country in Europe other than those named in item (3) of this Schedule or grown in any country outside Europe in which the virus disease Sharka (Plum Pox) is known to occur.".

(*e*) In place of the words in the second column describing item (12) in Part IC there shall be substituted the words "*Prunus* L. (including *Amygdalus* L., *Armeniaca* Mill., *Cerasus* Adan., *Laurocerasus* Roem., *Padus* Mill. and *Prunophora* Neck.) spp. plants grown in any country in which the disease Bacterial Spot (*Xanthomonas pruni* (E. F. Smith) Dowson) is known to occur.".

(*f*) Item (13) in Part IC described in the second column together with the words in the third column opposite thereto shall be omitted.

(*g*) In place of the words in the second column describing item (22) in Part IIIA there shall be substituted the words " Raw cherries grown in Italy, Portugal or Spain.".

(*h*) In place of the words in the second column describing item (23) in Part IIIA there shall be substituted the words " Raw cherries grown in Austria, Bulgaria, that part of France which is south of latitude 46° North, Hungary or Yugoslavia.".

In Witness whereof the official seal of the Minister of Agriculture, Fisheries and Food is hereunto affixed on 7th May 1969.

(L.S.)   *Cledwyn Hughes,*
Minister of Agriculture, Fisheries and Food.

Given under the seal of the Secretary of State for Scotland on 8th May 1969.

(L.S.)   *William Ross,*
Secretary of State for Scotland.

EXPLANATORY NOTE

(*This Note is not part of the Order.*)

This Order further amends Schedule 1 to the Importation of Plants and Plant Produce (Health) (Great Britain) Order 1965.

Article 5 of that Order imposes prohibitions and restrictions on the landing in Great Britain of plants, seeds and raw fruit described in the first Schedule. The present Order removes one item from that Schedule and amends the descriptions of a number of others.

1969 No. 679

DEFENCE

The Rules of Procedure (Air Force) (Amendment) Rules 1969

Made - - - -	*8th May* 1969
Laid before Parliament	*16th May* 1969
Coming into Operation	*1st June* 1969

The Secretary of State in exercise of the powers conferred upon him by sections 103, 104, 105 and 106 of the Air Force Act 1955(a) and of all other powers enabling him in that behalf hereby makes the following Rules:—

Citation and Commencement

1. These Rules may be cited as the Rules of Procedure (Air Force) (Amendment) Rules 1969 and shall come into operation on the 1st June 1969.

Interpretation

2. The Interpretation Act 1889(b) shall apply to the interpretation of these Rules as it applies to an Act of Parliament.

Amendment to the Rules of Procedure (*Air Force*) 1956

3.—(1) The Rules of Procedure (Air Force) 1956(c), as amended (d), shall be further amended in accordance with the following provisions of this Rule.

(2) In Rule 62 there shall be added and shall stand as paragraph (4):—
"(4) Where the accused is not represented by a defending officer or counsel, then, whether or not he himself has given evidence, the prosecutor shall not make a closing address unless the accused has called witnesses as to the facts of the case".

(3) In the Third Schedule (RECORD OF PROCEEDINGS BEFORE AN APPROPRIATE SUPERIOR AUTHORITY) for the words "forfeiture of a sum from pay" in paragraph 5 there shall be substituted the words "a fine".

(4) In Form (5) of the Fourth Schedule (RECORD OF PROCEEDINGS OF A COURT-MARTIAL) the part D5, being the PROCEEDINGS ON PLEA(S) OF NOT GUILTY (*continued*), shall be amended as follows:—

(a) 1955 c. 19. (b) 1889 c. 63.
(c) S.I. 1956/163 (1956 II, p. 2020).
(d) The relevant amending instruments are S.I. 1961/2152, 1964/1282, 1968/1173 (1961 III, p. 3884; 1964 II, p. 2955; 1968 II, p. 3187).

In the first paragraph the blank space after the word "The" shall be replaced by the word "prosecutor" and in the second paragraph the blank space after the word "The" shall be replaced by the word "accused".

At the end of the first paragraph and at the end of the second paragraph there shall be inserted the notation "2".

Dated 8th May 1969.

Denis Healey,
One of Her Majesty's Principal
Secretaries of State.

EXPLANATORY NOTE

(*This Note is not part of the Rules.*)

These Rules amend the Rules of Procedure (Air Force) 1956 so as to take account of:

(*a*) the practice in the civil criminal courts where the accused is not represented and calls no witnesses as to fact. In such a case the prosecutor is not permitted to make a closing address. The amendments bring the procedure at courts-martial into line with this practice (Rule 3(2));

(*b*) the replacement of the punishment of forfeiture of a sum from pay by a fine (Rule 3(3));

(*c*) the amendment by S.I. 1964/1282 of Rule 62(2) which, as amended, provides for an accused in all cases to make his closing address after the closing address by the prosecutor (Rule 3(4)).

STATUTORY INSTRUMENTS

1969 No. 680

DEFENCE

The Rules of Procedure (Army) (Amendment) Rules 1969

Made - - -	*9th May* 1969
Laid before Parliament	*16th May* 1969
Coming into Operation	*1st June* 1969

The Secretary of State in exercise of the powers conferred upon him by sections 103, 104, 105 and 106 of the Army Act 1955(a) and of all other powers enabling him in that behalf hereby makes the following Rules :—

Citation and Commencement

1. These Rules may be cited as the Rules of Procedure (Army) (Amendment) Rules 1969 and shall come into operation on 1st June 1969.

Interpretation

2. The Interpretation Act 1889(b) shall apply to the interpretation of these Rules as it applies to an Act of Parliament.

Amendment to the Rules of Procedure (Army) 1956(c)

3.—(1) The Rules of Procedure (Army) 1956, as amended (d), shall be further amended in accordance with the following provisions of this Rule.

(2) In Rule 5 the words "and a copy thereof shall be sent direct to the Director of Army Legal Services or his representatives" shall be omitted.

(3) In Rule 62 there shall be added and shall stand as paragraph (4) :—

"(4) Where the accused is not represented by a defending officer or counsel, then, whether or not he himself has given evidence, the prosecutor shall not make a closing address unless the accused has called witnesses as to the facts of the case".

(4) In Form (1) of the First Schedule the words "To : Director of Army Legal Services" and footnote 1 shall be omitted. Footnotes 2 and 3 shall be re-numbered 1 and 2 respectively.

(5) In paragraph 5 of the Third Schedule (Record of Proceedings before an Appropriate Superior Authority) there shall be substituted for the words "forfeiture of a sum from pay" the words "a fine".

(a) 1955 c.18.   (b) 1889 c.63.
(c) S.I. 1956/162 (1956 I, p.213).
(d) The relevant amending instruments are S.I. 1961/2223, S.I. 1964/1006 (1961 III, p.3903; 1964 II, p.2256).

(6) In Form 5 of the Fourth Schedule (Record of Proceedings of a Court-Martial) the Part D 5, being the Proceedings on Plea(s) of Not Guilty (continued), shall be amended as follows :—

In the first paragraph the blank space after the word "The" shall be replaced by the word "prosecutor" and in the second paragraph the blank space after the word "The" shall be replaced by the word "accused".

At the end of the first paragraph and at the end of the second paragraph there shall be added the notation "2".

Denis Healey,
One of Her Majesty's Principal
Secretaries of State.

Dated 9th May 1969.

EXPLANATORY NOTE

(This Note is not part of the Rules.)

These Rules amend the Rules of Procedure (Army) 1956 so as to take account of :—

(a) a change in administrative procedure concerning the reports required by sub-section (2) of section 75 of the Army Act 1955. (Rule 3(2) and (4)).

(b) the practice in the civil criminal courts where the accused is not represented and calls no witnesses as to fact. In such a case the prosecutor is not permitted to make a closing address. The amendments bring the procedure at courts-martial into line with this practice (Rule 3(3)).

(c) the punishment of forfeiture of a sum from pay having been replaced by the punishment of a fine (Rule 3(5)).

(d) the amendment by S.I. 1964/1006 of Rule 62(2) which, as amended, provides for an accused in all cases to make his closing address after the closing address by the prosecutor (Rule 3(6)).

1969 No. 686 (S.58)

CLEAN AIR

The Smoke Control Areas (Exempted Fireplaces) (Scotland) Order 1969

Made - - -	*7th May* 1969
Laid before Parliament	*21st May* 1969
Coming into Operation	*2nd June* 1969

In exercise of the powers conferred on me by section 11(4), as read with section 34(1) of the Clean Air Act 1956(a), and of all other powers enabling me in that behalf, and being satisfied that fireplaces of the classes described can be used for burning fuel other than authorised fuel without producing a substantial quantity of smoke, I hereby make the following order :—

Title and commencement

1. This order may be cited as the Smoke Control Areas (Exempted Fireplaces) (Scotland) Order 1969 and shall come into operation on 2nd June 1969.

Interpretation

2. The Interpretation Act 1889(b) shall apply for the interpretation of this order as it applies for the interpretation of an Act of Parliament.

Classes of fireplace exempted from section 11 of the Clean Air Act 1956

3. In Scotland the classes of fireplace described in column (1) of the Schedule hereto shall, subject to the conditions specified in column (2) opposite the description of the fireplace, be exempted from the provisions of section 11 of the Clean Air Act 1956 (which empowers a local authority to declare the whole or any part of their district to be a smoke control area).

William Ross,

One of Her Majesty's Principal
Secretaries of State.

St. Andrew's House,
  Edinburgh.

7th May 1969.

(a) 1956 c. 52.   (b) 1889 c. 63.

SCHEDULE

(1) Classes of fireplace	(2) Conditions
The fireplace known as the House-warmer and manufactured for the National Coal Board by Ideal Standard Limited.	The fireplace shall be installed, maintained and operated so as to minimise the emission of smoke and in accordance with the instructions for operation as supplied with the fireplace by or on behalf of the National Coal Board. No fuel shall be used other than washed coal singles.
The fireplace known as the Wood Chip Fired Air Heater manufactured by Air Plants Limited.	The fireplace shall be installed, maintained and operated so as to minimise the emission of smoke, and in accordance with the manufacturer's instructions for operation as supplied with the fireplace. No fuel shall be used other than clean wood waste of a size within the limits referred to in those instructions.

EXPLANATORY NOTE

(This Note is not part of the Order.)

Section 11 of the Clean Air Act 1956 empowers local authorities to declare the whole or any part of their district to be a smoke control area in which the emission of smoke is, generally, prohibited. This Order exempts the "House-warmer" and the Wood Chip Fired Air Heater fireplaces from the provision of that section, upon certain conditions as to proper operation.

STATUTORY INSTRUMENTS

1969 No. 687

SAVINGS BANKS

The Trustee Savings Banks (Rate of Interest) Order 1969

Made - - -	13*th May* 1969
Laid before Parliament	20*th May* 1969
Coming into Operation	21*st May* 1969

The Treasury, in exercise of the powers conferred upon them by section 27(2) of the Trustee Savings Banks Act 1954(**a**), as amended by section 7(3) of the Trustee Savings Banks Act 1964(**b**) and section 1 of the Trustee Savings Banks Act 1968(**c**), and of all other powers enabling them in that behalf, hereby make the following Order :—

1. This Order may be cited as the Trustee Savings Banks (Rate of Interest) Order 1969, and shall come into operation on 21st May 1969.

2. The Interpretation Act 1889(**d**) shall apply for the interpretation of this Order as it applies for the interpretation of an Act of Parliament.

3. The rate at which interest is to be paid or credited on sums standing to the credit of trustee savings banks in the Fund for the Banks for Savings representing savings account deposits or current account deposits shall be £3 13s. 0d. per cent. per annum.

4. The Trustee Savings Banks (Rate of Interest) Order 1968(**e**) is hereby revoked.

Walter Harrison,
Joseph Harper,

Two of the Lords Commissioners
of Her Majesty's Treasury.

13th May 1969.

(**a**) 1954 c. 63. (**b**) 1964 c. 4.
(**c**) 1968 c. 6. (**d**) 1889 c. 63.
(**e**) S.I. 1968/765 (1968 II, p. 2141).

EXPLANATORY NOTE

(*This Note is not part of the Order.*)

This Order provides that the rate of interest allowed to trustees of trustee savings banks on sum standing to the credit of trustee savings banks in the Fund for the Banks for Savings shall be increased from £3 10s. 0d. per cent. to £3 13s. 0d. per cent. per annum.

STATUTORY INSTRUMENTS

1969 No. 688

INCOME TAX

The Income Tax (Employments) (No. 4) Regulations 1969

Made - - -	14*th May* 1969
Laid before the	
House of Commons	20*th May* 1969
Coming into Operation	22*nd June* 1969

The Commissioners of Inland Revenue, in exercise of the powers conferred upon them by Section 157 of the Income Tax Act 1952**(a)**, hereby make the following Regulations:—

1.—(1) These Regulations may be cited as the Income Tax (Employments) (No. 4) Regulations 1969, and shall come into operation on the 22nd day of June 1969.

(2) The Interpretation Act 1889**(b)** shall apply for the interpretation of these Regulations as it applies for the interpretation of an Act of Parliament.

(3) In these Regulations the expression "the Principal Regulations" means the Income Tax (Employments) Regulations 1965**(c)** as amended by the Income Tax (Employments) (No. 2) Regulations 1966**(d)** and the Income Tax (Employments) (No. 3) Regulations 1969**(e)**.

2. Regulations 19 and 29 of the Principal Regulations shall have effect, as regards payments of emoluments made on or after the 22nd day of June, 1969, as if for any reference to a rate of £5 5s. 0d. or more a week there were substituted a reference to a rate of £6 5s. 0d. or more a week, and as if for any reference to a rate of £22 15s. 0d. or more a month there were substituted a reference to a rate of £27 or more a month.

By Order of the Commissioners of Inland Revenue.

J. Webb,
Secretary.

14th May 1969.

EXPLANATORY NOTE

(*This Note is not part of the Regulations.*)

These Regulations provide for raising the limit of weekly or monthly pay above which an employer has to operate the Pay As You Earn scheme for every employee, to take into account the increased Income Tax allowances proposed in the Finance Bill 1969.

(a) 15 & 16 Geo. 6 & 1 Eliz. 2. c. 10.   **(b)** 52 & 53 Vict. c. 63.
(c) S.I. 1965/516 (1965 I, p. 1321).   **(d)** S.I. 1966/1373 (1966 III, p. 3691).
(e) S.I. 1969/170 (1969 I, p. 440).

STATUTORY INSTRUMENTS

1969 No. 689

INDUSTRIAL TRAINING

The Industrial Training (Ceramics, Glass and Mineral Products Board) Order 1969

Made - - -	13*th May* 1969
Laid before Parliament	27*th May* 1969
Coming into Operation	30*th May* 1969

The Secretary of State after consultation with the Ceramics, Glass and Mineral Products Industry Training Board and with organisations and associations of organisations appearing to be representative respectively of substantial numbers of employers engaging in the activities hereinafter mentioned and of substantial numbers of persons employed in those activities and with a body established for the purpose of carrying on under national ownership an industry in which the said activities are carried on to a substantial extent and in exercise of her powers under section 9 of the Industrial Training Act 1964(**a**) and of all other powers enabling her in that behalf hereby makes the following Order :—

Citation, commencement and interpretation

1.—(1) This Order may be cited as the Industrial Training (Ceramics, Glass and Mineral Products Board) Order 1969 and shall come into operation on 30th May 1969.

(2) In this Order—

(*a*) "the Act" means the Industrial Training Act 1964 ;

(*b*) "the Board" means the Ceramics, Glass and Mineral Products Industry Training Board ;

(*c*) "levy Order" means the Industrial Training Levy (Ceramics, Glass and Mineral Products) Order 1967(**b**), or the Industrial Training Levy (Ceramics, Glass and Mineral Products) Order 1968(**c**) ;

(*d*) "the principal Order" means the Industrial Training (Ceramics, Glass and Mineral Products Board) Order 1965(**d**).

(3) The Interpretation Act 1889(**e**) shall apply to the interpretation of this Order as it applies to the interpretation of an Act of Parliament and as if this Order and the principal Order were Acts of Parliament.

Activities of the Board

2. The activities in relation to which the Board exercises the functions conferred by the Act upon industrial training boards shall, in lieu of the activities specified in Schedule I to the principal Order, be the activities specified in the Schedule to this Order, and accordingly in the principal Order the latter Schedule shall be substituted for the former Schedule.

(**a**) 1964 c.16.
(**c**) S.I. 1968/342 (1968 I, p.976).
(**e**) 1889 c. 63.

(**b**) S.I. 1967/841 (1967 II, p.2507).
(**d**) S.I. 1965/1391 (1965 II, p.4062).

Transitional provisions

3.—(1) The chairman and other members of the Board on the day upon which this Order comes into operation shall continue to be members of the Board and to hold and vacate their offices in accordance with the terms of the instruments appointing them to be members.

(2) The provisions of this Order shall not—

(a) extend the operation of either levy Order ;

(b) affect the operation of either levy Order in relation to the assessment of an employer within the meaning of that Order in respect of an establishment engaged in the first levy period or the second levy period, as the case may be, wholly or mainly in activities included in the Schedule to this Order ;

(c) affect the operation of any assessment notice served by the Board under the provisions of either levy Order before the date upon which this Order comes into operation or any appeal or other proceedings arising out of any such notice.

13th May 1969.

> *Barbara Castle,*
> **First Secretary of State and**
> Secretary of State for Employment and Productivity.

Article 2

SCHEDULE

The Ceramics, Glass and Mineral Products Industry

1. Subject to the provisions of this Schedule, the activities of the ceramics, glass and mineral products industry are the following activities in so far as they are carried out in Great Britain :—

(a) the lifting or extracting of mineral deposits or products of minerals from the earth or of mineral deposits from the bed of a lake or river or of the sea ;

(b) the crushing, grinding, washing, drying, grading or screening of sand, gravel or fluorspar ;

(c) the crushing, grinding, washing, drying, foaming, grading, screening, cutting, splitting, dressing, polishing or mixing of mineral deposits (not being sand, gravel or fluorspar) or products of minerals or any similar operation, being activities carried out—

    (i) by an employer (or an associated company of the employer, being a company) engaged in any activities specified in sub-paragraph (a) of this paragraph ; and

    (ii) on land in or adjacent to a mine or quarry and in conjunction with the operation thereof ;

(d) the burning of limestone or the hydration of lime ;

(e) the production of cement, plaster, or whiting ;

(*f*) the production of ready-mixed concrete or ready-mixed mortar or the batching or mixing of ingredients in connection with such production ;

(*g*) the exfoliation of vermiculite or any similar material ;

(*h*) the production of coated material for the purpose of the construction or repair of roads or footways ;

(*i*) the processing of slag, clinker or breeze ;

(*j*) the manufacture of—

    (i) articles consisting mainly of bonded abrasive material or coated with abrasive material ;

    (ii) glass ;

    (iii) calcium silicate bricks ;

(*k*) the manufacture of articles or other products wholly or mainly from—

    (i) asbestos cement ;

    (ii) clay or any mixture of clay and calcined or burnt animal bones ;

    (iii) concrete, cast stone, or cement, or from any mixture of aggregate together with a cementing or bonding agent ;

    (iv) glass ;

    (v) plaster ; or

    (vi) one or more refractory materials ;

(*l*) the manufacture, wholly or mainly from concrete and tiles or from stone set in concrete, of fire-places ;

(*m*) the milling, grinding or mixing of any material for the purpose of the manufacture of pottery ;

(*n*) the calibrating, graduating or toughening of glass or glass articles ;

(*o*) any activities, being—

    (i) related activities incidental or ancillary to principal activities of the ceramics, glass and mineral products industry ; or

    (ii) activities undertaken in the administration, control or direction of one or more establishments, being establishments engaged wholly or mainly in principal activities of that industry, in related activities incidental or ancillary thereto, or in the administration, control or direction of one or more other establishments engaged in such principal or related activities ;

and carried out, in either case, by the employer engaged in those principal activities or, where that employer is a company, by the company or by an associated company of the company ;

(*p*) any activities of industry or commerce (other than ceramics, glass and mineral products activities) carried out at or from an establishment mainly engaged—

    (i) in ceramics, glass and mineral products activities ; or

    (ii) in ceramics, glass and mineral products activities and in activities described in the Appendix to this Schedule, but to a greater extent in ceramics, glass and mineral products activities than in activities described in that Appendix in relation to any one industry.

2. Notwithstanding anything contained in this Schedule, there shall not be included in the activities of the ceramics, glass and mineral products industry : —

    (*a*) the activities of any establishment engaged—

        (i) mainly in activities not being ceramics, glass and mineral products activities or activities described in the Appendix to this Schedule ; or

        (ii) to a less extent in ceramics, glass and mineral products activities than in activities described in that Appendix in relation to any one industry ;

(b) the activities of any establishment engaged wholly or mainly in related activities, being activities—

    (i) incidental or ancillary to the activities of one or more establishments (in this sub-paragraph hereafter referred to as "the principal establishment") engaged wholly or mainly in any activities not being principal activities of the ceramics, glass and mineral products industry ; and

    (ii) carried out by the employer carrying on the principal establishment or, where that employer is a company, by the company or by an associated company of the company ;

(c) the activities of any establishment engaged wholly or mainly in one or more activities of a kind specified in an entry in the second column of the next following Table (being activities undertaken in relation to all or any of the products comprised in the group specified in the corresponding entry in the third column of that Table) or in two or more of such entries :

TABLE

No.	Activities	Group of Products
1.	Quarrying, mining or (for the purpose of smelting) treatment or preparation.	Iron ore.
2.	Quarrying, in association with any of the following activities, that is to say, quarrying or mining iron ore, treating or preparing iron ore for smelting, smelting iron ore in a blast furnace with or without other metalliferous materials, producing iron by any other process or producing steel by any process.	Limestone.
3.	Getting, winning, screening or washing.	Coal.
4.	Preparation for building or monumental purposes.	Stone.
5.	Manufacture.	Industrialised building components or sections and prefabricated buildings or sections of buildings, being components, sections or buildings framed in wood.
6.	Construction on the premises on which they are to be installed or prefabrication elsewhere by the employer engaged in the installation.	Shop, office or similar fittings.
7.	Cutting, bevelling, silvering or decorating.	Flat glass.
8.	Manufacture, where the manufacturer is engaged in the installation thereof.	Leaded lights and leaded windows.

No. *Activities*	*Group of Products*
9. Manufacture.	(a) Ophthalmic lenses and articles embodying a lens or prism.
	(b) Primary cells, batteries and electric accumulators.
	(c) Electric cables, electric filament lamps, electric discharge lamps and photographic flashbulbs.
	(d) Thermionic, cold cathode or photo-cathode valves or tubes, cathode-ray tubes and electric capacitors or resistors.
	(e) Micro-electronic circuits, devices using ferrite or quartz crystals for electrical purposes and semi-conductor or piezo-electric devices.
10. Machining.	Carbon articles.
11. Manufacture.	Painters' rollers.
12. Manufacture.	Woven fabrics.
13. Searching, boring for or getting.	Petroleum.
14. Processing.	Plastics material.
15. Manufacture.	Printers' rollers.
16. Manufacture.	Buttons.
17. Manufacture.	(a) Natural or synthetic pigments and their intermediates.
	(b) Carbon black, activated carbon and diamonds.
	(c) Paints of any kind, enamels (not being vitreous enamels), lacquers, stains and varnishes.
	(d) Medical or pharmaceutical products.
	(e) Cosmetic or toilet compounds, mixtures and preparations.
18. Manufacture (not being an activity mentioned in paragraph 1(c) or 1(d) of this Schedule).	Fertilisers and conditioners of the soil.
19. Pumping or raising from a shaft, well, spring or mine or from the sea or processing.	Brine.
20. Mining.	Rock salt.
21. Processing or manufacture of any derivative therefrom.	Fuller's earth.
22. Manufacture.	(a) Toys.
	(b) Jewellery.
	(c) Artificial teeth or crowns for teeth.

(d) the activities of any establishment engaged wholly or mainly in the activities following, that is to say—

  (i) any operations in building or civil engineering work ;

  (ii) any operations in agriculture or horticulture ;

  (iii) display writing ; or

  (iv) dredging for the primary purpose of maintaining or improving the navigation of a harbour, estuary or water-way or for the benefit of vessels coming to, leaving or using any dock or other premises ;

(e) the activities of a harbour authority when acting in that capacity ;

(f) the activities of a local authority ;

(g) the activities of any company, association or body that is required by its constitution to apply its profits, if any, or other income in promoting its objects and is prohibited thereby from paying any dividend to its members, and that has for its sole or principal object or among its principal objects the provision of facilities for any of the purposes mentioned in section 15(1) of the Disabled Persons (Employment) Act 1944(a) (which relates to the provision for registered persons who are seriously disabled of work or training) ;

(h) any work, occupation or training that is provided in accordance with arrangements made by a local authority under the Disabled Persons (Employment) Act 1958(b) or any other enactment that authorises or requires the provision of arrangements for persons suffering from illness, severe physical defect or disability or from mental disorder, or for persons who have been suffering from illness or whose care is undertaken with a view to preventing them from becoming ill, or for old people ;

(i) dock work performed by a registered dock worker ; or

(j) the supply of food or drink for immediate consumption.

3. In this Schedule unless the context otherwise requires—

"aggregate" includes clinker, fly-ash, shale, slag, vermiculite and similar materials and wood wool ;

"articles" includes parts and components of articles ;

"asbestos" means any fibrous silicate mineral or any admixture containing any such mineral whether crude, crushed or opened ;

"building or civil engineering work" means—

  (a) the construction, alteration, repair or demolition of a building or part of a building or of an erection in the nature of a building ;

  (b) the construction or demolition of a railway-line, siding or monorail ;

  (c) the construction, structural alteration, repair or demolition of any aerodrome, airport, bridge, road, viaduct, dock, harbour, pier, quay, wharf, coast protection, river or drainage work, aqueduct, canal, inland navigation, reservoir, waterworks, bore-hole, well (other than an oil well), filter bed, sewage works, sewer, cooling tower or pond, tunnel, heading, adit, chimney, furnace, carbonising or gas-making plant, nuclear or thermal power station, hydro-electric station, electric line or any structure designed for its support, cable trench or duct, oil refinery, pipe-line or defence installation ;

  (d) the sinking of a shaft or bore-hole in a mine of coal, stratified ironstone, shale or fireclay, or the construction of a road below ground in such a mine ;

  (e) the construction or repair of a swimming pool or other bathing place, or of a playing field or ground for sporting or recreational purposes, or the laying out of a cemetery ;

(a) 1944 c. 10.   (b) 1958 c.33.

(f) the preparation of the site or the laying down of a foundation or sub-structure in connection with any operations above mentioned in this definition or with the erection of structural metalwork ;

(g) the manufacture, wholly or mainly from concrete or cast stone, on the site, and for the purposes, of any operations above-mentioned in this definition, of any of the following products, that is to say, industrialised building components or sections, prefabricated buildings or sections of buildings, beams, columns, piles, caissons, tunnel segments or other civil engineering sections or structures or parts of structures ;

(h) the working of coal by opencast operations or the screening, washing or other preparation of coal on the site of opencast workings ; or

(i) the restoration of land affected by the working of coal by opencast operations, or of land which has been excavated in the course of winning or working ironstone by opencast operations ;

"cement" includes Portland cements, high alumina cements and cements of a similar character ;

"ceramics, glass and mineral products activities" means any one or more of the principal activities of the ceramics, glass and mineral products industry and the activities included in that industry by virtue of paragraph 1(o) of this Schedule ;

"clay" includes shale, brick earth, China stone and any similar materials ;

"coal" means bituminous coal, cannel coal or anthracite ;

"coated material" means any mixture consisting of bitumen, tar or asphalt together with slag or one or more minerals ;

"company" includes any body corporate, and "subsidiary" has the same meaning as by virtue of section 154 of the Companies Act 1948(a) it has for the purposes of that Act ;

"concrete" includes pre-cast, pre-stressed, reinforced or autoclaved aerated concrete ;

"dock work" and "registered dock worker" have the same meanings as in the Docks and Harbours Act 1966(b) ;

"fire-places" includes any mantelpiece, curb or other part of the surround ;

"glass" includes glass fibres and laminated glass ;

"harbour authority" means a harbour authority within the meaning of the Harbours Act 1964(c) ;

"jewellery" includes any articles of personal adornment, whether or not containing stones ;

"local authority" means—

(a) in relation to England and Wales, a local authority within the meaning of the Local Government Act 1933(d) or the Common Council of the City of London, and includes a joint board or joint committee of such authorities ;

(b) in relation to Scotland, a county council, town council or district council, and includes any joint board or joint committee of such authorities appointed under any enactment, order or scheme ;

"manufacture" includes assembly and any process or operation incidental or appertaining to manufacture or assembly ;

"mine" and "quarry" have the same meanings as in the Mines and Quarries Act 1954(a) ;

"mineral deposits" includes any natural deposits (except peat) capable of being lifted or extracted from the earth or from the bed of a lake or river or of the sea ;

"office premises" has the same meaning as in section 1(2) of the Offices, Shops and Railway Premises Act 1963(b) ;

"petroleum" includes any mineral oil or relative hydrocarbon and natural gas existing in its natural condition in strata, but does not include coal or bituminous shales or other stratified deposits from which oil can be extracted by destructive distillation ;

"plaster" means calcium sulphate, lime plaster or plaster of a similar character;

"plastics material" means any material made wholly or mainly by addition, polyaddition, condensation, polycondensation, polymerisation, copolymerisation, esterification or other similar chemical process, or regenerated or modified cellulose, or hardened proteins, or natural resin modified by fusion or esterification, and includes any such material reinforced by, or bonding, glass fibres ;

"principal activities of the ceramics, glass and mineral products industry" means activities which, subject to the provisions of paragraph 2 of this Schedule, are specified in paragraph 1, other than sub-paragraphs (o) and (p) thereof, as activities of the ceramics, glass and mineral products industry ;

"processing" in relation to plastics material means any of the following operations, that is to say, masticating, compounding, mixing, calendering, extruding, moulding, pressing, thermoforming, blowing, casting, dipping, coating, encapsulating, heat sealing, laminating, filament winding, machining, cutting, vulcanising or foaming ;

"refractory materials" includes andalusite, bauxite, chromite, dolomite, fireclay, ganister, kyanite, magnesite, mica, silica and sillimanite ;

"related activities" means any of the following activities, that is to say—

(a) research, development, design or drawing ;

(b) buying, selling, letting out on hire, testing, advertising, packing, distribution, transport or any similar operations ;

(c) operations of a kind performed at office premises or laboratories, or at stores, warehouses or similar places ;

(d) cleaning, washing or garaging vehicles, or carrying out running repairs or minor adjustments thereto ;

(e) training of employees or apprentices ;

"site" in relation to any operations mentioned in heads (a) to (f) of the definition of "building or civil engineering work" contained in this paragraph, includes any place other than the site of such operations if that place is occupied temporarily by the person carrying out such operations for the manufacture, wholly or mainly from concrete or cast stone and solely for the purposes of the said operations, of any products specified in head (g) of the said definition.

4.—(1) References in this Schedule to the provisions of any enactment shall be construed as references to those provisions as amended by or under any subsequent enactment.

(2) For the purposes of this Schedule two companies shall be taken to be associated companies if one is a subsidiary of the other, or both are subsidiaries of a third company, and "associated company" shall be construed accordingly.

(a) 1954 c. 70.   (b) 1963 c. 41.

The activities that would be included in an industry specified in Column 1 hereof by virtue of the industrial training order specified in the corresponding entry in Column 2, if the provisions specified in Column 3 were omitted from that order.

Column 1	Column 2	Column 3
The wool, jute and flax industry	The Industrial Training (Wool Industry Board) Order 1964 as amended by the Industrial Training (Wool, Jute and Flax Board) Order 1968(a)	Schedule 1 Paragraph 1(s)
The iron and steel industry	The Industrial Training (Iron and Steel Board) Order 1964(b)	Schedule 1 Paragraph 1(j)
The construction industry	The Industrial Training (Construction Board) Order 1964 as amended by the Industrial Training (Construction Board) Order 1967(c)	Schedule 1 Paragraph 1(l)
The engineering industry	The Industrial Training (Engineering Board) Order 1964 as amended by the Industrial Training (Engineering Board) Order 1968(d)	Schedule 1 Paragraph 1(m)
The shipbuilding industry	The Industrial Training (Shipbuilding Board) Order 1964 as amended by the Industrial Training (Shipbuilding Board) Order 1968(e)	Schedule 1 Paragraph 1(g)
The furniture and timber industry	The Industrial Training (Furniture and Timber Industry Board) Order 1965(f)	Schedule 1 Paragraph 1(r)
The man-made fibres producing industry	The Industrial Training (Man-made Fibres Producing Industry Board) Order 1966(g)	Schedule 1 Paragraph 1(d)
The carpet industry	The Industrial Training (Carpet Board) Order 1966 as amended by The Industrial Training (Carpet Board) Order 1968(h)	Schedule 1 Paragraph 1(f)
The knitting, lace and net industry	The Industrial Training (Knitting, Lace and Net Industry Board) Order 1966(i)	Schedule 1 Paragraph 1(j)
The cotton and allied textiles industry	The Industrial Training (Cotton and Allied Textiles Board) Order 1966(j)	Schedule 1 Paragraph 1(p)
The agricultural, horticultural and forestry industry	The Industrial Training (Agricultural, Horticultural and Forestry Board) Order 1966(k)	Schedule 1 Paragraph 1(m)
The road transport industry	The Industrial Training (Road Transport Board) Order 1966(l)	Schedule 1 Paragraph 1(o)

(a) S.I. 1964/907, 1968/898 (1964 II, p. 1928; 1968 II, p. 2376).
(b) S.I. 1964/949 (1964 II, p. 2127).
(c) S.I. 1964/1079, 1967/924 (1964 II, p. 2384; 1967 II, p. 2757)
(d) S.I. 1964/1086, 1968/1333 (1964 II, p. 2402; 1968 II, p. 3694).
(e) S.I. 1964/1782, 1968/1614 (1964 III, p. 3928; 1968 III, p. 4432).
(f) S.I. 1965/2028 (1965 III, p. 5998).
(g) S.I. 1966/143 (1966 I, p. 257).
(h) S.I. 1966/245, 1968/1882 (1966 I, p. 499; 1968 III, p. 5017).
(i) S.I. 1966/246 (1966 I, p. 506).   (j) S.I. 1966/823 (1966 II, p. 1907).
(k) S.I. 1966/969 (1966 II, p. 2333).   (l) S.I. 1966/1112 (1966 III, p. 2712).

APPENDIX (contd.)

Column 1	Column 2	Column 3
The hotel and catering industry	The Industrial Training (Hotel and Catering Board) Order 1966(a)	Schedule 1 Paragraph 1(e)
The civil air transport industry	The Industrial Training (Civil Air Transport Board)Order 1967(b)	Schedule 1 Paragraph 1(h)
The petroleum industry	The Industrial Training (Petroleum Board) Order 1967(c)	Schedule 1 Paragraph 1(h)
The rubber and plastics processing industry	The Industrial Training (Rubber and Plastics Processing Board) Order 1967(d)	Schedule 1 Paragraph 1(k)
The chemical and allied products industry	The Industrial Training (Chemical and Allied Products Board) Order 1967(e)	Schedule 1 Paragraph 1(s)
The paper and paper products industry	The Industrial Training (Paper and Paper Products Board) Order 1968(f)	Schedule 1 Paragraph 1(j)
The printing and publishing industry	The Industrial Training (Printing and Publishing Board) Order 1968(g)	Schedule 1 Paragraph 1(n)
The distributive industry	The Industrial Training (Distributive Board) Order 1968(h)	Schedule 1 Paragraph 1(h)
The food, drink and tobacco industry	The Industrial Training (Food, Drink and Tobacco Board) Order 1968(i)	Schedule 1 Paragraph 1(q)
The footwear, leather and fur skin industry	The Industrial Training (Footwear, Leather and Fur Skin Board) Order 1968(j).	Schedule 1 Paragraph 1(v)

(a) S.I. 1966/1347 (1966 III, p. 3669).   (b) S.I. 1967/263 (1967 I, p. 968).
(c) S.I. 1967/648 (1967 I, p. 2032).   (d) S.I. 1967/1062 (1967 II, p. 3151).
(e) S.I. 1967/1386 (1967 III, p. 4049).   (f) S.I. 1968/787 (1968 II, p. 2194).
(g) S.I. 1968/786 (1968 II, p. 2185).   (h) S.I. 1968/1032 (1968 II, p. 2709).
(i) S.I. 1968/1033 (1968 II, p. 2721).   (j) S.I. 1968/1763 (1968 III, p. 4785).

EXPLANATORY NOTE

(This Note is not part of the Order.)

The Ceramics, Glass and Mineral Products Industry Training Board was established on 23rd July 1965 by the Industrial Training (Ceramics, Glass and Mineral Products Board) Order 1965, which defined the ceramics, glass and mineral products industry in relation to which the Board exercises its functions. This Order re-defines that industry. The principal changes in the definition are set out below.

Among the activities henceforth to be included in the industry are :

(*a*) the crushing, grinding, washing, drying, grading or screening of sand, gravel or fluorspar whether or not carried out on land adjacent to a mine or quarry ;

(*b*) the processing of clinker or breeze ;

(*c*) the manufacture of articles from any mixture of clay and calcined or burnt animal bones.

The manufacture of prefabricated buildings or sections of buildings will henceforth be excluded from the industry only where they are framed in wood or are constructed on a building or civil engineering site wholly or mainly from concrete or cast stone.

STATUTORY INSTRUMENTS

1969 No. 690

FACTORIES

The Asbestos Regulations 1969

Made - - - -	13th May 1969
Laid before Parliament	22nd May 1969
Coming into Operation	14th May 1970

ARRANGEMENT OF REGULATIONS

Reg.

PART I	Application, Interpretation and General	1 — 6
PART II	Exhaust Ventilation and Protective Equipment ...	7 and 8
PART III	Cleanliness of Premises and Plant	9 — 14
PART IV	Storage and Distribution	15 — 17
PART V	Accommodation for and Cleaning of Protective Equipment	18 and 19
PART VI	Young Persons	20
SCHEDULE	Processes specified for the purposes of Regulation 13	

REGULATIONS

The Secretary of State—

(a) by virtue of her powers under sections 62, 76 and 180(6) and (7) of the Factories Act 1961(a) and of all other powers enabling her in that behalf; and

(b) after publishing, pursuant to Schedule 4 to the said Act of 1961, notice of the proposal to make the Regulations and not having received any objection to the draft in regard to which she is required by the said Schedule to direct an inquiry to be held,

hereby makes the following special Regulations:—

PART I

APPLICATION, INTERPRETATION AND GENERAL

Citation, commencement and revocation

1.—(1) These Regulations may be cited as the Asbestos Regulations 1969 and shall come into operation on 14th May 1970.

(2) The Asbestos Industry Regulations 1931(b) are hereby revoked.

(3) The Shipbuilding and Ship-repairing Regulations 1960(c) shall have effect as if the following provisions were omitted—

(a) in Regulation 3(2), the definition of the word "asbestos";

(b) in Regulation 76(1), sub-paragraphs (a) to (d); and

(c) in Regulation 77, paragraphs (a) to (d).

Interpretation

2.—(1) The Interpretation Act 1889(d) shall apply to the interpretation of these Regulations as it applies to the interpretation of an Act of Parliament, and as if these Regulations and the Regulations hereby revoked were Acts of Parliament.

(a) 1961 c. 34.   (b) S.R. & O. 1931/1140 (Rev. VII, p. 181: 1931 p. 410).
(c) S.I. 1960/1932 (1960 II, p. 1427).   (d) 1889 c. 63.

(2) In these Regulations, unless the context otherwise requires, the following expressions have the meanings hereby assigned to them respectively, that is to say—

"approved" means approved for the time being by certificate of the Chief Inspector;

"asbestos" means any of the following minerals, that is to say, crocidolite, amosite, chrysotile, fibrous anthophyllite and any mixture containing any of the said minerals;

"factory" includes any premises and place to which these Regulations apply;

"protective clothing" means overalls and headgear, which (in either case) will when worn exclude asbestos dust;

"the principal Act" means the Factories Act 1961 as amended by or under any other Act.

(3) References in these Regulations to asbestos dust shall be taken to be references to dust consisting of or containing asbestos to such an extent as is liable to cause danger to the health of employed persons.

Application of Regulations

3.—(1) These Regulations shall apply to the following premises and places in which any process to which these Regulations apply is carried on, that is to say, factories and all premises and places to which the provisions of Part IV of the principal Act with respect to special regulations for safety and health are applied by the following provisions of that Act, namely, section 123 (which relates to electrical stations), section 124 (which relates to institutions), so much of section 125 as relates to warehouses other than warehouses within any dock or forming part of any wharf or quay, section 126 (which relates to ships) and section 127 (which relates to building operations and works of engineering construction).

(2) These Regulations apply to every process involving asbestos or any article composed wholly or partly of asbestos, except a process in connection with which asbestos dust cannot be given off.

(3) The provisions of these Regulations are in substitution for the provisions of so much of section 1(2) of the principal Act as relates to the cleaning of parts of factories, being parts in which any process to which these Regulations apply is carried on or into which any asbestos dust from any such process carried on in the factory is liable to escape, and of so much of section 63(1) of that Act as relates to the measures to be taken against asbestos dust, but save as aforesaid are in addition to and not in substitution for or in diminution of other requirements imposed by or under the principal Act.

Certificates of exemption

4. The Chief Inspector may (subject to such conditions, if any, as may be specified therein) by certificate in writing (which he may in his discretion revoke at any time) exempt from all or any of the requirements of these Regulations—

(a) any factory or part of any factory; or

(b) any class or description of factories or of parts thereof; or

(c) any machine, plant, apparatus or process or any class or description of machines, plant, apparatus or processes; or (*d*) the employment of any person or class or description of persons.

if he is satisfied that the requirements in respect of which the exemption is granted are not necessary for the protection of persons employed or are impracticable.

Obligations under Regulations

5.—(1) Except in the case of any place where building operations or works of engineering construction are carried on it shall be the duty—

(*a*) of every employer (whether or not an occupier) who is undertaking in a factory any process to which these Regulations apply to comply with the requirements of these Regulations in relation to any person employed by him, any plant or material under his control, and any part of the factory in which he is carrying on the process or into which asbestos dust in connection with that process is liable to escape;

(*b*) of every occupier of any factory (whether or not such an employer as aforesaid) where any such process is being carried on to comply with the requirements of Regulations 8, 18 and 19 in relation to any person employed in the factory (other than any person employed by an employer who is undertaking in the factory any process to which these Regulations apply) and with the requirements of Part III of these Regulations; and

(*c*) of every person who is undertaking in a factory any process to which these Regulations apply and who employs no other person in the carrying on of that process to comply, for the protection of employed persons working there, with the requirements of these Regulations (other than Regulations 8, 14 and 18 to 20) with which he would have to comply if he were the employer of a person doing there the work which he does himself.

(2) In the case of places where building operations or works of engineering construction are carried on it shall be the duty of every contractor and of every employer who is undertaking any process to which these Regulations apply to comply with the requirements of these Regulations in relation to any person employed by him and any person employed there who is liable to be exposed to asbestos dust in connection with any process carried on by the contractor or employer (as the case may be), and in relation to any plant or material under his control and any part of the site where he is carrying on the process or where asbestos dust in connection with that process is liable to escape.

(3) It shall be the duty of every person employed to comply with the requirements of such of these Regulations as relate to the performance of or refraining from an act by him.

Notifications

6.—(1) Where at the date of the coming into operation of these Regulations a person is undertaking in a factory any process involving crocidolite (including the removal from any surface of lagging consisting of or containing crocidolite), he shall within 28 days of that date give written notice to the inspector for the district that he is undertaking such a process and of the address of the factory at which he is doing so.

(2) Before a person first begins after the coming into operation of these Regulations to undertake in a factory any such process as aforesaid, he shall give not less than 28 days written notice to the inspector for the district, or such shorter notice as the inspector may agree to accept, of the date on which and of the address of the factory at which he will begin to do so.

PART II

EXHAUST VENTILATION AND PROTECTIVE EQUIPMENT

Exhaust ventilation

7.—(1) Subject to the provisions of the next following Regulation, no process to which these Regulations apply shall be carried on in any factory unless equipment is provided, maintained and used which produces an exhaust draught which prevents the entry into the air of any workplace of asbestos dust:

Provided that the foregoing requirements of this Regulation shall not apply where any such process is carried on in such a manner as to be as safe as it would be if the said requirements were complied with.

(2) Exhaust ventilation equipment provided in accordance with this Regulation shall while any work of maintenance or repair to the machinery, apparatus or other plant or equipment in connection with which it is provided is being carried on, be kept in use so as to produce an exhaust draught which prevents the entry into the air of any workplace of asbestos dust.

(3) Exhaust ventilation equipment provided in accordance with this Regulation shall be inspected at least once in every seven days and shall be thoroughly examined and tested by a competent person at least once in every period of fourteen months, and a report of the results of every such examination and test containing approved particulars and signed by the person making or responsible for the carrying out of the examination and test shall be made within fourteen days after the examination and test.

(4) Every such report as aforesaid shall be attached to the general register and be preserved and kept available for inspection by any inspector for a period of two years after it is made.

Protective equipment

8.—(1) Where in any factory the requirements of paragraph (1) or (2) of the last foregoing Regulation apply, but it is impracticable to comply with those requirements, there shall be provided for the use of each person employed in any part of the factory, being a part into which asbestos dust from a process to which these Regulations apply is liable to escape—

(a) approved respiratory protective equipment; and

(b) protective clothing.

(2) All respiratory protective equipment and protective clothing provided in pursuance of the foregoing paragraph of this Regulation shall be maintained.

(3) All respiratory protective equipment and protective clothing so provided shall be used by the persons for whom they are provided while employed in any such part of the factory as aforesaid.

(4) No respiratory protective equipment so provided which has been worn by a person shall be provided for the use of another person unless it has been thoroughly cleaned and disinfected since last being worn.

(5) No person shall be employed to perform any work for which respiratory protective equipment is provided in pursuance of this Regulation unless he has been fully instructed in the proper use of that equipment.

PART III

CLEANLINESS OF PREMISES AND PLANT

Duty to keep clean

9. All machinery, apparatus, work benches and other plant and equipment used in any factory for the purposes of any process to which these Regulations apply, all external surfaces of exhaust ventilation equipment provided in pursuance of these Regulations and all floors, inside walls, ceilings, ledges and other internal surfaces of any part of a building or of any ship, being a part in which any process to which these Regulations apply is carried on or into which asbestos dust from any such process carried on in the factory is liable to escape, shall, so far as is practicable, be kept in a clean state and free from asbestos waste and dust in accordance with the provisions of this Part of these Regulations.

Cleaning by dustless method

10. The cleaning required by the last foregoing Regulation shall, so far as is practicable, be carried out—

(*a*) by means of vacuum cleaning equipment so designed and constructed and so used; or

(*b*) by some other suitable method such,

that asbestos dust neither escapes nor is discharged into the air of any workplace.

Cleaning where cleaning by dustless method is impracticable

11.—(1) In so far as it is impracticable to carry out the cleaning required by Regulation 9 in accordance with the provisions of the last foregoing Regulation, such cleaning shall be carried out in accordance with the provisions of this Regulation.

(2) Protective clothing and approved respiratory protective equipment shall be provided for and used by every person present in any part of a factory while such cleaning is being carried out in that part otherwise than in accordance with Regulation 10.

(3) No respiratory protective equipment so provided which has been worn by a person shall be provided for the use of another person unless it has been thoroughly cleaned and disinfected since last being worn.

(4) No person shall be employed to perform any work for which respiratory protective equipment is provided in pursuance of this Regulation unless he has been fully instructed in the proper use of that equipment.

(5) Any surface on which asbestos waste or dust is deposited as a result of the carrying out of cleaning in pursuance of this Regulation, not being a surface of the cleaning equipment used, shall be cleaned forthwith.

Vacuum cleaning equipment

12. Vacuum cleaning equipment used for cleaning in accordance with the provisions of this Part of these Regulations shall be maintained and have all external surfaces kept in a clean state and free from asbestos waste and dust.

Requirements as to construction of buildings before first use for certain processes

13. After the date of the coming into operation of these Regulations no process specified in the Schedule to these Regulations shall be carried on in a building by the occupier of the building unless any part of such building where any such process is carried on and has not previously been carried on—

(*a*) is so constructed that all its interior surfaces are smooth and impervious and is so designed and constructed as to have in it as few surfaces as is practicable on which asbestos dust can settle; and

(*b*) has a vacuum cleaning system which has filters and a source of suction located at a fixed central point with pipes throughout the building fitted with suitably placed inlets to which portable cleaning implements can be attached and is a system which is so designed and constructed that asbestos dust cannot escape or be discharged from it into the air of any workplace:

Provided that the requirements of this Regulation shall not apply where a process or processes so specified are carried on in a factory for a total number of hours not exceeding eight in any week.

Cleanliness of accommodation for clothing

14. Where there is provided for the use of employed persons under section 59 (accommodation for clothing) of the principal Act or under any regulations made under that Act accommodation for clothing not worn during working hours, the accommodation so provided shall be such or shall be so situated that asbestos dust is not deposited on any such clothing in the said accommodation.

PART IV

STORAGE AND DISTRIBUTION

Storage

15. All loose asbestos in a factory shall when not in use be kept in suitable closed receptacles which prevent the escape of asbestos dust therefrom, and all asbestos waste in a factory shall, when stored, be kept in such receptacles.

Distribution, etc.

16. No loose asbestos or asbestos waste shall be despatched from or as far as is practicable received into a factory except in suitable closed receptacles which prevent the escape of asbestos dust therefrom or shall be distributed within a factory except in such receptacles or in a totally enclosed system of conveyance.

Marking of receptacles

17. All such receptacles as aforesaid shall, where they contain crocidolite, be clearly and boldly marked with the words "Blue asbestos—do not inhale dust".

PART V

ACCOMMODATION FOR AND CLEANING OF PROTECTIVE EQUIPMENT

Accomodation, etc. for protective clothing and respiratory protective equipment

18.—(1) Suitable accomodation in a conveniently accessible position shall be provided for the use of persons employed when putting on or taking off respiratory protective equipment and protective clothing provided in pursuance of these Regulations and for the storage of such clothing and equipment when it is not in use.

(2) All protective clothing and respiratory protective equipment which has been provided in pursuance of these Regulations for the use of persons employed shall when not required for use be kept in the accommodation for storage provided in pursuance of paragraph (1) of this Regulation, except when it is necessary for it to be removed for cleaning or replacement.

(3) So far as practicable, the same protective clothing shall (until it becomes necessary to replace it) be available for use by a person employed on each occasion on which he requires to wear it in pursuance of these Regulations.

Cleaning of protective clothing

19.—(1) All protective clothing provided in pursuance of these Regulations shall at suitable intervals be cleaned.

(2) The said cleaning shall be carried out within the factory where the clothing is provided:

Provided that this requirement shall not apply in the case of protective clothing which before despatch from the factory for cleaning is properly packed in suitable containers which prevent the escape of asbestos dust therefrom and the containers in which it is packed are clearly and boldly marked with the words "Asbestos contaminated clothing".

PART VI

YOUNG PERSONS

Employment of young persons

20. No young person shall be employed—

(*a*) in any process to which these Regulations apply or in any part of a factory into which asbestos dust from any such process carried on in the factory would otherwise be liable to escape unless the requirements of Regulation 7 are complied with in respect of that process; or

(*b*) in carrying out any cleaning in accordance with Part III of these Regulations otherwise than by means of vacuum cleaning equipment or other suitable method in accordance with the provisions of Regulation 10.

13th May 1969.

Barbara Castle,
First Secretary of State and Secretary
of State for Employment and Productivity.

SCHEDULE

Regulation 13

Processes specified for the purposes of Regulation 13

1. Breaking, crushing, disintegrating, opening and grinding of asbestos, and the mixing of asbestos (including the mixing of asbestos with any other material) or the sieving of asbestos, and all processes involving manipulation of asbestos incidental thereto.

2. All processes in the manufacture of yarn or cloth composed of asbestos or asbestos mixed with any other material, including preparatory and finishing processes.

1e

3. The making of insulation slabs or sections, composed wholly or partly of asbestos, and processes incidental thereto.

4. The making and repairing of insulating mattresses, composed wholly or partly of asbestos, and processes incidental thereto.

5. Any other process in the manufacture of articles composed wholly or partly of asbestos in connection with which asbestos dust is given off.

EXPLANATORY NOTE

(This Note is not part of the Regulations.)

These Regulations impose requirements for the safety and welfare of persons employed in factories and in other premises and places to which the Factories Act 1961 applies, where processes are carried on which involve asbestos or any article composed wholly or partly of asbestos and are capable of giving rise to asbestos dust.   The Regulations require that the processes be carried on under an exhaust draught or in some other equally safe way, or that protective clothing and respiratory protective equipment be provided for the use of persons employed. The Regulations also impose requirements as to the cleaning of premises and plant, the construction of buildings newly used for the processes, the storage and distribution of asbestos, the accommodation to be provided for protective equipment and the cleaning of protective clothing.   The employment of young persons in connection with processes to which the Regulations apply and in cleaning work is prohibited except in specified circumstances. The Regulations also require that notification of processes involving crocidolite be sent to the inspector for the district.

The Asbestos Industry Regulations 1931 and certain provisions concerning asbestos of the Shipbuilding and Ship-repairing Regulations 1960 are revoked.

STATUTORY INSTRUMENTS

1969 No. 691

WAGES COUNCILS

The Wages Regulation (Industrial and Staff Canteen) Order 1969

Made - - -	13*th May* 1969
Coming into Operation	30*th June* 1969

Whereas the Secretary of State has received from the Industrial and Staff Canteen Undertakings Wages Council the wages regulation proposals set out in the Schedule hereto ;

Now, therefore, the Secretary of State in exercise of her powers under section 11 of the Wages Councils Act 1959(**a**) and of all other powers enabling her in that behalf, hereby makes the following Order :—

1. This Order may be cited as the Wages Regulation (Industrial and Staff Canteen) Order 1969.

2.—(1) In this Order the expression "the specified date" means the 30th June 1969, provided that where, as respects any worker who is paid wages at intervals not exceeding seven days, that date does not correspond with the beginning of the period for which the wages are paid, the expression "the specified date" means, as respects that worker, the beginning of the next such period following that date.

(2) The Interpretation Act 1889(**b**) shall apply to the interpretation of this Order as it applies to the interpretation of an Act of Parliament and as if this Order and the Order hereby revoked were Acts of Parliament.

3. The wages regulation proposals set out in the Schedule hereto shall have effect as from the specified date and as from that date the Wages Regulation (Industrial and Staff Canteen) Order 1967(**c**) shall cease to have effect.

Signed by order of the Secretary of State.

A. A. Jarratt,

13th May 1969.

Deputy Under Secretary of State,
Department of Employment and Productivity.

(**a**) 1959 c. 69.   (**b**) 1889 c. 63.
(**c**) S.I. 1967/939 (1967 II, p. 2866).

ARRANGEMENT OF SCHEDULE

PART I

REMUNERATION FOR EMPLOYMENT

	Paragraph
Workers other than night workers, shift workers and split duty workers	1
Night workers	2
Shift workers	3
Split duty workers	4
Workers temporarily transferred to higher grade work	5
Workers provided with meals or full board and lodging, overalls and headwear	6
Workers not provided with meals, full board, lodging, overalls or headwear	7
Hours on which remuneration is based	8 and 8A
Guaranteed weekly remuneration for full-time workers	9 and 9A
Overtime rates—workers other than shift and split duty workers ...	10 and 10A
„ „ —shift workers	11 and 11A
„ „ —split duty workers	12 and 12A
„ „ —Jewish undertakings	13
Work on customary holidays	14
Special provisions relating to workers provided with full board and lodging	15

PART II

HOLIDAYS AND HOLIDAY REMUNERATION

Customary holidays	16-17
Remuneration for customary holidays	18
Annual holiday	19-24
Remuneration for annual holiday	25-26
Accrued holiday remuneration payabie on termination of employment	27

PART III

DEFINITIONS

Time-and-a-quarter, time-and-a-half and double time	28 and 28A
Grades or descriptions of workers	29
Other definitions	30

PART IV

GENERAL

Workers to whom the Schedule applies	31
Illegal deductions, etc.	32

SCHEDULE

Article 3

The following minimum remuneration and provisions as to holidays and holiday remuneration shall be substituted for the statutory minimum remuneration and the provisions as to holidays and holiday remuneration set out in the Wages Regulation (Industrial and Staff Canteen) Order 1967 (hereinafter referred to as "Order I.S.C. (41)").

Part 1

REMUNERATION FOR EMPLOYMENT

WORKERS OTHER THAN NIGHT WORKERS, SHIFT WORKERS AND SPLIT DUTY WORKERS

1. The minimum weekly remuneration for workers (other than night workers, shift workers and split duty workers) who are employed in the circumstances specified in paragraph 6 shall be in accordance with the following Table.

Where an increase in remuneration becomes payable under the provisions of paragraphs 8A, 9A, 10A, 11A or 12A on a day other than the first day of a pay week it shall become effective on the first day of the first full pay week following the date upon which the increase would otherwise become payable under those provisions.

	Column 1 Workers employed in the circumstances specified in Paragraph 6(1)		Column 2 Paragraph 6(2)
	London area	Other areas	All areas
	s. d.	s. d.	s. d.
A. FEMALE WORKERS—			
CANTEEN ATTENDANT	132 6	130 0	105 2
Provided that where a Canteen Attendant in the course of her duties on any day or night is engaged in the cooking of prepared food she shall receive for that day or night in addition an allowance of 8d.			
Provided also that where a Canteen Attendant is deputed to supervise staff for a minimum consecutive period of one hour, she shall receive in addition for all time during which she is so employed an allowance of 1d. per hour.			
ALL WORKERS UNDER 18 YEARS OF AGE—			
17 and under 18 years of age	107 0	104 6	86 4
16 „ „ 17 „ „ „	84 6	82 0	70 5
Under 16 years of age	73 0	70 0	60 1
CASHIER	136 6	134 0	109 2
ASSISTANT COOK	142 6	140 0	115 2
COOK	156 6	154 0	129 2
HEAD COOK	171 6	169 0	144 2
CANTEEN SUPERVISOR, MANAGERESS OR STEWARDESS—			
Grade X	161 0	158 6	133 8
Grade A	169 0	166 6	141 8
Grade B	179 0	176 6	151 8
Grade C	189 0	186 6	161 8
Grade D	199 0	196 6	171 8
B. MALE WORKERS—			
PORTER OF 21 YEARS OF AGE OR OVER ...	178 6	176 0	151 2
Provided that where a Porter is deputed to supervise staff for a minimum consecutive period of one hour, he shall receive in addition for all time during which he is so employed an allowance of 1d. per hour.			
ASSISTANT COOK	197 6	195 0	170 2
COOK	217 6	215 0	190 2
HEAD COOK	230 6	228 0	203 2
CANTEEN SUPERVISOR, MANAGER OR STEWARD—			
Grade A	225 6	223 0	198 2
Grade B	235 6	233 0	208 2
Grade C	245 6	243 0	218 2
Grade D	255 6	253 0	228 2

	Column 1 Workers employed in the circumstances specified in Paragraph 6(1)		Column 2 Paragraph 6(2)
	London area	Other areas	All areas
	s. d.	s. d.	s. d.
APPRENTICE COOKS—			
First year of apprenticeship	92 6	90 0	79 6
Second year of apprenticeship	115 0	112 6	99 0
Third year of apprenticeship	138 0	135 6	119 0
Fourth year of apprenticeship	160 0	157 6	138 0
Fifth year of apprenticeship	182 0	179 6	157 0

Provided that for the purpose of determining the "year of apprenticeship" any period by which the 5 years' apprenticeship is reduced under the proviso to the definition of "APPRENTICE COOK" in paragraph 29 shall be treated as a period of apprenticeship.

	London area	Other areas	All areas
ALL OTHER MALE WORKERS aged			
21 years or over	178 6	176 0	151 2
20 and under 21 years	152 6	150 0	125 2
19 „ „ 20 „	137 0	134 6	112 6
18 „ „ 19 „	117 0	114 6	96 10
17 „ „ 18 „	100 6	97 6	83 1
16 „ „ 17 „	81 0	78 6	66 11
Under 16 years	69 6	67 0	57 1

NIGHT WORKERS

2. The minimum remuneration for a night worker who is employed in the circumstances specified in sub-paragraph (1) or (2) of paragraph 6 and who is not a shift worker or a split duty worker is that for the corresponding description of worker in the same area specified in paragraph 1 INCREASED IN EACH CASE BY ONE-FIFTH.

SHIFT WORKERS

3. The minimum remuneration for a shift worker who is employed in the circumstances specified in sub-paragraph (1) or (2) of paragraph 6 is that for the corresponding description of worker in the same area specified in paragraph 1 with the ADDITION OF 1d. per hour.

SPLIT DUTY WORKERS

4. The minimum remuneration for a split duty worker who is employed in the circumstances specified in paragraph 6(2) is that for the corresponding description of worker specified in Column 2 of paragraph 1 with the ADDITION OF 2d. per hour.

WORKERS TEMPORARILY TRANSFERRED TO HIGHER GRADE WORK

5. Where a worker is required temporarily to perform the duties of a worker entitled to a higher minimum remuneration than himself and is engaged on such higher graded duties for four or more hours on any day he shall be paid for the whole of his time on that day not less than the minimum remuneration appropriate to the worker of the higher grade.

WORKERS PROVIDED WITH MEALS OR FULL BOARD AND LODGING, OVERALLS AND HEADWEAR

6.—(1) The minimum remuneration in Column 1 of paragraph 1 is payable to a worker not being a worker to whom sub-paragraph (2) hereof applies who is employed in the circumstances that he is provided by the employer, subject in the case of (b) to the requisite supplies being available, with—

(a) such meals as are available during the time the worker is on duty and as are provided for the persons using the canteen; and

(b) a reasonable supply in good repair of clean overalls and (except in the case of a supervisor, manager, manageress, steward, stewardess or porter) of clean headwear for the use of the worker while at work.

(2) The minimum remuneration in Column 2 of paragraph 1 is payable to a worker employed in the circumstances that he is provided by the employer, subject in the case of (b) to the requisite supplies being available, with—

(a) full board and lodging for 7 days a week; and

(b) a reasonable supply in good repair of clean overalls and (except in the case of a supervisor, manager, manageress, steward, stewardess or porter) of clean headwear for the use of the worker while at work.

WORKERS NOT PROVIDED WITH MEALS, FULL BOARD, LODGING, OVERALLS OR HEADWEAR

7. The minimum remuneration for a worker who is not employed in the circumstances specified in paragraph 6(1) or 6(2) is:—

(1) In the case of a worker who is not provided by his employer with meals as specified in paragraph 6(1)(a) or full board and lodging, the remuneration specified in paragraph 1 (Column 1), 2, 3 or 5 for the corresponding description of worker in the same area INCREASED BY 17s. PER WEEK.

(2) In the case of a worker who is provided by his employer with full board or lodging (but not full board and lodging) the remuneration specified in paragraph 1 (Column 2), 2, 3 or 5 for the corresponding description of worker in the same area increased by the following amounts:—

(a) Where lodging is provided but not full board:—

   (i) Workers 17 years of age or over ... ...   AN INCREASE of 27s. 5d. per week of seven days or 3s. 11d. per day.

   (ii) Workers under 17 years of age   ...   AN INCREASE of 19s. 3d. per week of seven days or 2s. 9d. per day.

(b) Where full board is provided but not lodging:—

   (i) Workers 17 years of age or over   ...   AN INCREASE of 15s. 2d. per week of seven days or 2s. 2d. per day.

   (ii) Workers under 17 years of age   ...   AN INCREASE of 8s. 9d. per week of seven days or 1s. 3d. per day.

(3) In the case of any worker who is not provided by his employer with a reasonable supply in good repair of clean overalls and headwear as specified in paragraph 6(1)(b) or (2)(b) the remuneration specified in paragraph 1, 2, 3, 4 or 5 for the corresponding description of worker in the same area INCREASED BY 2s. 6d. PER WEEK.

GUARANTEED WEEKLY REMUNERATION AND OVERTIME RATES

FOR THE PERIOD UP TO AND INCLUDING 29TH JUNE 1970

HOURS ON WHICH REMUNERATION IS BASED

8.—(1) *Up to and including 29th June 1970* the weekly remuneration specified in this Schedule except as provided in paragraph 7(2) relates to a week of *41 hours* and, except as provided in paragraph 9, is subject to a proportionate reduction according as the number of hours worked is less than *41*.

(2) In calculating the remuneration for the purposes of this Schedule recognised breaks for meal times shall be excluded.

GUARANTEED WEEKLY REMUNERATION FOR FULL-TIME WORKERS

9.—(1) *Up to and including 29th June 1970*, where in any week a full-time worker works for the employer for less than *41 hours* he shall, subject to and in accordance with the provisions of this paragraph, be paid in respect of that week not less than the guaranteed weekly remuneration.

(2) The guaranteed weekly remuneration payable in respect of any week to a full-time worker

(*a*) who normally works for the employer for less than 40 hours in the week, is the remuneration to which he would be entitled under this Schedule (calculated as in paragraph 8) for 40 hours' work;

(*b*) who normally works for the employer for 40 hours or more in the week, is the remuneration to which he would be entitled under this Schedule for *41 hours*' work;

(*c*) who normally works for the employer for less than *41 hours* in the week by reason only of the fact that he does not hold himself out as available for work for more than the number of hours he normally works in the week and who has so informed the employer in writing, is the remuneration (calculated as in paragraph 8) for the number of hours normally worked by the worker for the employer.

(3) Guaranteed weekly remuneration is not payable in respect of any week unless the worker is capable of and available for work (except as respects any time allowed to him as a holiday)

(*a*) in the case of a worker to whom sub-paragraph (2)(*a*) applies, for 40 hours in that week, including the hours normally worked by him;

(*b*) in the case of a worker to whom sub-paragraph (2)(*b*) applies, for *41 hours* in that week, including the hours normally worked by him; and

(*c*) in the case of a worker to whom sub-paragraph (2)(*c*) applies, for the number of hours normally worked by him;

and is willing to perform such duties outside his normal occupation as may reasonably be required by the employer when work is not available for him in his normal occupation in the undertaking.

(4) If the employer is prevented from providing employment by reason of strikes or other circumstances outside his control and has given the worker not less than four days, notice of his inability to provide such employment and the notice has expired, the provisions in regard to the guaranteed payment shall not apply and the worker shall be entitled in that week to payment in respect of hours actually worked.

(5) In order to ascertain for the purposes of sub-paragraph (1) of this paragraph whether a full-time worker has worked in any week for less than *41 hours*, any day or days allowed and taken as holidays by the worker under Part II of this Schedule shall be treated as a day or days on which the worker worked for the number of hours usually worked by him on that day of the week or those days of the week as the case may be.

(6) Where in any week any day or days have been allowed and taken as holidays by a worker under Part II of this Schedule the guaranteed weekly remuneration which that worker would be entitled to under the preceding sub-paragraphs of this paragraph shall be reduced by the amount of remuneration received or receivable by him in respect of the day or days of holiday aforesaid.

OVERTIME RATES

WORKERS OTHER THAN SHIFT AND SPLIT DUTY WORKERS

10.—(1) *Up to and including 29th June 1970* and subject to the provisions of paragraphs 13 and 15, overtime rates shall be paid as follows:—

(*a*) to workers other than night workers, shift workers and split duty workers:—

For the first 2 hours worked in excess of 8 hours on any of five week-days in the week other than the weekly short day or in excess of 4 hours on the weekly short day	Time-and-a-quarter.
For all time worked thereafter on any of those days ...	Time-and-a-half.
For all time worked on Sunday	Double time.
For all time worked in excess of *41 hours* in any week exclusive of any time in respect of which overtime rates are payable under the foregoing provisions of this sub-paragraph	Time-and-a-quarter.

The weekly short day shall be Saturday or any other week-day substituted therefor by agreement between an employer and a worker or his representative:

Provided that in the case of a worker who is customarily required to attend only on five days a week the following overtime rates shall apply:—

For the first 2 hours worked in excess of 9 hours on any week-day on which he is customarily required to attend	Time-and-a-quarter.
For all time worked thereafter on any of such days ...	Time-and-a-half.
For the first 2 hours worked on a sixth day (not including any time worked on Sunday) on which attendance is not customarily required	Time-and-a-quarter.
For all time worked thereafter on that day (not including any time worked on Sunday)	Time-and-a-half.
For all time worked on Sunday	Double time.
For all time worked in excess of *41 hours* in any week exclusive of any time in respect of which overtime rates are payable under the foregoing provisions of this proviso	Time-and-a-quarter.

(*b*) to night workers other than shift workers and split duty workers:—

For the first 2 hours worked in excess of 9 hours on any day from Monday to Friday inclusive	Time-and-a-quarter.
For all time worked thereafter on any of such days ...	Time-and-a-half.
For the first 2 hours worked on Saturday	Time-and-a-quarter.
For all time worked thereafter on Saturday	Time-and-a-half.
For all time worked on Sunday	Double time.

For all time worked in excess of *41 hours* in any week
exclusive of any time in respect of which overtime
rates are payable under the foregoing provisions of (*b*)
of this sub-paragraph ...   .   Time-and-a-quarter.

(2) The whole of a worker's turn of duty shall be counted for the purpose of ascertaining the overtime rate payable and, where the turn extends beyond midnight, shall be regarded as having been worked on the day upon which it commences.

(3) Notwithstanding the provisions of sub-paragraphs (1) and (2) of this paragraph all time worked between midnight on Saturday and midnight on Sunday shall be paid at double time and all time worked on Monday which is part of a turn of duty which normally commences on Sunday shall be regarded as overtime and paid as follows:—

For such time as is required to complete 2 hours from
the commencement of the turn of duty   ...   ...   Time-and-a-quarter.

For the remainder of the time   ...   .   Time-and-a-half.

The time worked on Monday aforesaid shall not be included in calculating overtime on any turn of duty which commences on Monday.

Shift Workers

11.—(1) *Up to and including 29th June 1970* and subject to the provisions of paragraph 15, overtime rates shall be paid to shift workers as follows:—

(*a*) to workers whose shift comprises six full turns of duty:—

For the first 2 hours worked in excess of $7\frac{1}{2}$ hours on any
of the six turns of duty ...   .   Time-and-a-quarter.

For all time worked thereafter on such turns of duty   ...   Time-and-a-half.

For all time worked on a seventh turn of duty or on the
normal rest day   ...   .   Double time.

For all time worked in excess of *41 hours* in any week
exclusive of any time in respect of which overtime rates
are payable under the foregoing provisions of this
sub-paragraph ...   .   Time-and-a-quarter.

(*b*) to workers whose shift comprises five full turns and one short turn of duty:—

For the first 2 hours worked in excess of 8 hours on any
of the five full turns of duty or in excess of 4 hours on
the one short turn of duty   ...   .   Time-and-a-quarter.

For all time worked thereafter on any such turns
of duty ...   .   Time-and-a-half.

For all time worked on a seventh turn of duty or on the
normal rest day   ...   .   Double time.

For all time worked in excess of *41 hours* in any week
exclusive of any time in respect of which overtime rates
are payable under the foregoing provisions of (*b*) of
this sub-paragraph   ...   .   Time-and-a-quarter.

(*c*) to workers whose shift comprises five turns of duty:—

For the first 2 hours worked in excess of 9 hours on any
turn of duty   ...   .   Time-and-a-quarter.

For all time worked thereafter on any turn of duty   ...   Time-and-a-half.

For all time worked on the first day of the week on which
attendance is not normally required   ...   .   Time-and-a-quarter.

For all time worked on the second day of the week on
which attendance is not normally required   ...   ...   Double time.

For all time worked in excess of *41 hours* in any week
exclusive of any time in respect of which overtime rates
are payable under the foregoing provisions of (*c*) of
this sub-paragraph   ...   .   Time-and-a-quarter.

(2) A shift worker shall in addition to the above be paid an amount calculated at the rate of 1d. per hour for all overtime worked in respect of which an overtime rate is payable as above.

(3) For the purpose of calculating the time worked in any week a shift worker who is allowed and has taken a holiday in any week under Part II of this Schedule shall be treated as having worked on any such day of holiday the number of hours usually worked by him on the turn of duty which he would otherwise have worked if the holiday had not been allowed.

SPLIT DUTY WORKERS

12.—(1) *Up to and including 29th June 1970* and subject to the provisions of paragraph 15, overtime rates shall be paid to split duty workers as follows:—

For the first 4 hours worked in excess of *41 hours* in any
week on days other than the normal rest day   ...   Time-and-a-quarter.

For all time worked thereafter on days other than the
normal rest day   ...   .   Time-and-a-half.

For all time worked on a normal rest day   ...   ...   Double time.

(2) A split duty worker shall in addition to the above be paid an amount calculated at the rate of 2d. per hour for all overtime worked in respect of which an overtime rate is payable as above.

(3) For the purpose of calculating the time worked in any week a split duty worker who is allowed and has taken a holiday in any week under Part II of this Schedule shall be treated as having worked on any such day of holiday the number of hours usually worked by him on the turn of duty which he would otherwise have worked if the holiday had not been allowed.

GUARANTEED WEEKLY REMUNERATION AND OVERTIME RATES FOR THE PERIOD ON AND AFTER 30TH JUNE 1970

HOURS ON WHICH REMUNERATION IS BASED

8A.—(1) *On and after 30th June 1970* the weekly remuneration specified in this Schedule except as provided in paragraph 7(2) relates to a week of *40 hours* and, except as provided in paragraph 9A, is subject to a proportionate reduction according as the number of hours worked is less than *40*.

(2) In calculating the remuneration for the purposes of this Schedule recognised breaks for meal times shall be excluded.

GUARANTEED WEEKLY REMUNERATION FOR FULL-TIME WORKERS

9A.—(1) *On and after 30th June 1970*, where in any week a full-time worker works for the employer for less than *40 hours* he shall, subject to and in accordance with the provisions of this paragraph, be paid in respect of that week not less than the guaranteed weekly remuneration.

(2) The guaranteed weekly remuneration payable in respect of any week to a full-time worker

(*a*) who normally works for the employer for less than 40 hours in the week, is the remuneration to which he would be entitled under this Schedule (calculated as in paragraph 8A) for 40 hours' work;

(*b*) who normally works for the employer for less than *40 hours* in the week by reason only of the fact that he does not hold himself out as available for work for more than the number of hours he normally works in the week and who has so informed the employer in writing, is the remuneration (calculated as in paragraph 8A) for the number of hours normally worked by the worker for the employer.

(3) Guaranteed weekly remuneration is not payable in respect of any week unless the worker is capable of and available for work (except as respects any time allowed to him as a holiday)

 (a) in the case of a worker to whom sub-paragraph (2)(a) applies, for 40 hours in that week, including the hours normally worked by him; and

 (b) in the case of a worker to whom sub-paragraph (2)(b) applies, for the number of hours normally worked by him;

and is willing to perform such duties outside his normal occupation as may reasonably be required by the employer when work is not available for him in his normal occupation in the undertaking.

(4) If the employer is prevented from providing employment by reason of strikes or other circumstances outside his control and has given the worker not less than four days' notice of his inability to provide such employment and the notice has expired, the provisions in regard to the guaranteed payment shall not apply and the worker shall be entitled in that week to payment in respect of hours actually worked.

(5) In order to ascertain for the purposes of sub-paragraph (1) of this paragraph whether a full-time worker has worked in any week for less than *40 hours*, any day or days allowed and taken as holidays by the worker under Part II of this Schedule shall be treated as a day or days on which the worker worked for the number of hours usually worked by him on that day of the week or those days of the week as the case may be.

(6) Where in any week any day or days have been allowed and taken as holidays by a worker under Part II of this Schedule the guaranteed weekly remuneration which that worker would be entitled to under the preceding sub-paragraphs of this paragraph shall be reduced by the amount of remuneration received or receivable by him in respect of the day or days of holiday aforesaid.

OVERTIME RATES

Workers other than Shift and Split Duty Workers

10A.—(1) *On and after 30th June 1970* and subject to the provisions of paragraphs 13 and 15, overtime rates shall be paid as follows:—

 (a) to workers other than night workers, shift workers and split duty workers:—

For the first 2 hours worked in excess of *7½ hours* on any of five week-days in the week other than the weekly short day or in excess of 4 hours on the weekly short day ... ... Time-and-a-quarter.

For all time worked thereafter on any of those days ... Time-and-a-half.

For all time worked on Sunday ... ... Double time.

For all time worked in excess of *40 hours* in any week exclusive of any time in respect of which overtime rates are payable under the foregoing provisions of this sub-paragraph ... ... Time-and-a-quarter.

The weekly short day shall be Saturday or any other week-day substituted therefor by agreement between an employer and a worker or his representative:

Provided that in the case of a worker who is customarily required to attend only on five days a week the following overtime rates shall apply:—

For the first 2 hours worked in excess of *8 hours* on any week-day on which he is customarily required to attend ... ... Time-and-a-quarter.

For all time worked thereafter on any of such days ... Time-and-a-half.

For the first 2 hours worked on a sixth day (not including any time worked on Sunday) on which attendance is not customarily required ... ... Time-and-a-quarter.

For all time worked thereafter on that day (not including any time worked on Sunday) ...   .   Time-and-a-half.

For all time worked on Sunday ...   .   Double time.

For all time worked in excess of *40 hours* in any week exclusive of any time in respect of which overtime rates are payable under the foregoing provisions of this proviso   ...   .   Time-and-a-quarter.

    (b) to night workers other than shift workers and split duty workers:—

For the first 2 hours worked in excess of *8 hours* on any day from Monday to Friday inclusive...   ...   ...   Time-and-a-quarter.

For all time worked thereafter on any of such days   ...   Time-and-a-half.

For the first 2 hours worked on Saturday   ...   ...   Time-and-a-quarter.

For all time worked thereafter on Saturday   ...   ...   Time-and-a-half.

For all time worked on Sunday ...   .   Double time.

For all time worked in excess of *40 hours* in any week exclusive of any time in respect of which overtime rates are payable under the foregoing provisions of (b) of this sub-paragraph   ...   .   Time-and-a-quarter.

(2) The whole of a worker's turn of duty shall be counted for the purpose of ascertaining the overtime rate payable and, where the turn extends beyond midnight, shall be regarded as having been worked on the day upon which it commences.

(3) Notwithstanding the provisions of sub-paragraphs (1) and (2) of this paragraph all time worked between midnight on Saturday and midnight on Sunday shall be paid at double time and all time worked on Monday which is part of a turn of duty which normally commences on Sunday shall be regarded as overtime and paid as follows:—

For such time as is required to complete 2 hours from the commencement of the turn of duty   ...   ...   Time-and-a-quarter.

For the remainder of the time   ...   .   Time-and-a-half.

The time worked on Monday aforesaid shall not be included in calculating overtime on any turn of duty which commences on Monday.

Shift Workers

11A.—(1) *On and after 30th June 1970* and subject to the provisions of paragraph 15, overtime rates shall be paid to shift workers as follows:—

    (a) to workers whose shift comprises six full turns of duty:—

For the first 2 hours worked in excess of *7 hours* on any of the six turns of duty   ...   .   Time-and-a-quarter.

For all time worked thereafter on such turns of duty   Time-and-a-half.

For all time worked on a seventh turn of duty or on the normal rest day ...   .   Double time.

For all time worked in excess of *40 hours* in any week exclusive of any time in respect of which overtime rates are payable under the foregoing provisions of this sub-paragraph   ...   .   Time-and-a-quarter.

    (b) to workers whose shift comprises five full turns and one short turn of duty:—

For the first 2 hours worked in excess of $7\frac{1}{2}$ *hours* on any of the five full turns of duty or in excess of 4 hours on the one short turn of duty   ...   .   Time-and-a-quarter.

For all time worked thereafter on any such turns of duty   Time-and-a-half.

For all time worked on a seventh turn of duty or on the normal rest day   . .   ..   Double time.

For all time worked in excess of *40 hours* in any week exclusive of any time in respect of which overtime rates are payable under the foregoing provisions of (*b*) of this sub-paragraph	Time-and-a-quarter.

(*c*) to workers whose shift comprises five turns of duty:—

For the first 2 hours worked in excess of *8 hours* on any turn of duty	Time-and-a-quarter.
For all time worked thereafter on any turn of duty ...	Time-and-a-half.
For all time worked on the first day of the week on which attendance is not normally required	Time-and-a-quarter.
For all time worked on the second day of the week on which attendance is not normally required	Double time.
For all time worked in excess of *40 hours* in any week exclusive of any time in respect of which overtime rates are payable under the foregoing provisions of (*c*) of this sub-paragraph	Time-and-a-quarter.

(2) A shift worker shall in addition to the above be paid an amount calculated at the rate of 1d. per hour for all overtime worked in respect of which an overtime rate is payable as above.

(3) For the purpose of calculating the time worked in any week a shift worker who is allowed and has taken a holiday in any week under Part II of this Schedule shall be treated as having worked on any such day of holiday the number of hours usually worked by him on the turn of duty which he would otherwise have worked if the holiday had not been allowed.

SPLIT DUTY WORKERS

12A.—(1) *On and after 30th June 1970* and subject to the provisions of paragraph 15, overtime rates shall be paid to split duty workers as follows:—

For the first 4 hours worked in excess of *40 hours* in any week on days other than the normal rest day ...	Time-and-a-quarter.
For all time worked thereafter on days other than the normal rest day	Time-and-a-half.
For all time worked on a normal rest day	Double time.

(2) A split duty worker shall in addition to the above be paid an amount calculated at the rate of 2d. per hour for all overtime worked in respect of which an overtime rate is payable as above.

(3) For the purpose of calculating the time worked in any week a split duty worker who is allowed and has taken a holiday in any week under Part II of this Schedule shall be treated as having worked on any such day of holiday the number of hours usually worked by him on the turn of duty which he would otherwise have worked if the holiday had not been allowed.

JEWISH UNDERTAKINGS

13. Where it is, or becomes, the established practice in a Jewish undertaking for the employer to require attendance on Sunday instead of Saturday, the provisions of paragraph 10 or 10A, as the case may be, shall apply in like manner as if in such provisions Sunday were treated as a week-day and as if:—

(1) in sub-paragraph (1) thereof the word "Sunday" were substituted for "Saturday" and the word "Saturday" for "Sunday"; and

(2) in sub-paragraph (3) thereof the word "Friday" were substituted for "Saturday", the word "Saturday" for "Sunday" and the word "Sunday" for "Monday".

WORK ON CUSTOMARY HOLIDAYS

14. Notwithstanding the foregoing provisions of this Schedule where a worker is required to work—

(1) on any day of customary holiday for which he has qualified under Part II of this Schedule; or

(2) a turn of duty which commences on the day preceding any day of customary holiday and extends beyond midnight or a turn of duty which commences on the day of customary holiday and extends into the following day,

he shall, in addition to the minimum remuneration appropriate to him under the foregoing provisions, be paid for all time so worked between midnight and midnight on the day of customary holiday, one-half of the minimum remuneration which would be appropriate to the corresponding description of worker in the same area employed in the circumstances specified in sub-paragraph (1) of paragraph 6.

SPECIAL PROVISIONS RELATING TO WORKERS PROVIDED WITH FULL BOARD AND LODGING

15.—(1) The provisions of this paragraph apply in the case of a worker who is provided by his employer with full board and lodging.

(2) Where a worker to whom this paragraph applies works on a seventh turn of duty or on a normal rest day pursuant to an agreement in writing with his employer that the employer will allow the worker an equivalent time off within a period of one month in lieu of time so worked, the worker shall for the purposes of the provisions of this Part of this Schedule be treated as though during such turn of duty or on that day as the case may be he had performed no work to which the Schedule applies.

(3) Where a worker to whom this paragraph applies is allowed time off pursuant to an agreement as is specified in sub-paragraph (2) of this paragraph he shall be treated for the purposes of the provisions of this Part of this Schedule as though in respect of that time he had been employed by the employer in his usual occupation.

PART II

HOLIDAYS AND HOLIDAY REMUNERATION
CUSTOMARY HOLIDAYS

16. An employer shall (except as provided in paragraph 17) allow to every worker to whom this Schedule applies, who at the date of the holiday has been in his employment for not less than six days and (unless excused by the employer or absent by reason of proved sickness) has worked for the employer the number of hours ordinarily worked by him on the last working day on which work was available to him preceding a holiday, a holiday on each of the following days:—

(1) In England and Wales—Christmas Day (or, if Christmas Day falls on a Sunday, such week-day as may be prescribed by national proclamation or the next following Tuesday), Boxing Day, Good Friday, Easter Monday, Whit Monday (or where another day is substituted therefor by national proclamation, that day), August Bank Holiday and all nationally proclaimed holidays;

(2) In Scotland—

    (a) New Year's Day (or the following day if New Year's Day falls on a Sunday), the local Spring holiday, the local Autumn holiday, and all nationally proclaimed holidays;

    (b) three other week-days in the course of a calendar year, to be fixed by the employer and notified to the worker not less than three weeks before the holiday, or any other day or days falling within the same calendar year which may be substituted for such day or days by agreement between the employer and the worker or his representative:

Provided that where, in any establishment it is not the custom or practice to observe such days as are specified in sub-paragraph (1) or (2)(*a*) of this paragraph as holidays, other days not fewer in number may, by agreement between the employer and the worker or his representative, be substituted for the above-mentioned days.

17. A worker may be required to work on any day specified in paragraph 16 above, or on any day substituted therefor under the proviso to that paragraph, and if so required he shall be allowed a day of holiday in lieu thereof within the period of eight weeks from the day on which he is so required to work unless it is agreed in writing between the employer and the worker or his representative that the day in lieu be granted at another date not later than the last day of February next following:

Provided that, in the case of a worker who is ordinarily employed on turns of duty extending beyond midnight, another day of holiday shall not be allowed in lieu of a day of customary holiday if the worker having worked on one turn of duty which finishes or commences on the customary holiday has not been required to work on another turn of duty which he would otherwise be required to work and which would commence or finish on the customary holiday.

REMUNERATION FOR CUSTOMARY HOLIDAYS

18.—(1) Subject to the provisions of sub-paragraph (2) of this paragraph, for each day allowed as a holiday under paragraphs 16 and 17, the worker shall be paid the appropriate statutory minimum remuneration to which he would have been entitled had the day not been a day of holiday and he had worked the number of hours usually worked by him on that day of the week, and

(*a*) in the case of a worker other than a worker to whom the provisions of (*b*) of this sub-paragraph apply, AN ADDITION OF 2s. 10d. for each day of holiday, or

(*b*) in the case of a worker who is employed in the circumstances that he is provided by his employer with full board and lodging or either full board or lodging, AN ADDITION OF—

(i) 6s. 1d. if the worker is 17 years of age or over, or

(ii) 4s. 0d. if the worker is under 17 years of age

for each day of holiday except where board and lodging is available to the worker on that day.

(2) Notwithstanding the provisions of the foregoing sub-paragraph, payment of remuneration in respect of the said holiday is subject to the condition that the worker (unless excused by the employer or absent by reason of proved sickness) worked for the employer the number of hours ordinarily worked by him on the first working day on which work was available to him following the holiday.

ANNUAL HOLIDAY

19.—(1) Subject to the provisions of paragraphs 22 and 23, in addition to the customary holidays provided in paragraphs 16 and 17, an employer shall, between the date on which this Schedule becomes effective and 31st October 1969, and in each succeeding year between 1st March and 31st October, allow a holiday (hereinafter referred to as an "annual holiday") to every worker to whom this Schedule applies who was employed or engaged to be employed by him during the 12 months immediately preceding the commencement of the holiday season (hereinafter referred to as the "qualifying period") for any of the periods of employment set out in the appropriate column of the table below, and the duration of the annual holiday shall, in the case of each such worker, be related to that period as follows:—

Where the worker's normal working week is:—

Period of Employment	Six days			Five days			Four days or less		
	Duration of annual holiday in 12 months commencing 1st March			Duration of annual holiday in 12 months commencing 1st March			Duration of annual holiday in 12 months commencing 1st March		
	1969	1970	1971 and thereafter	1969	1970	1971 and thereafter	1969	1970	1971 and thereafter
	Days	Days	Days	Days	Days	Days	Days	Days	Days
At least 4 weeks	1	1	1	1	1	1	—	—	—
" 8 "	2	2	2	2	2	2	1	1	1
" 12 "	3	3	3	3	3	3	2	2	2
" 14 "	3	4	4	3	3	3	2	2	2
" 16 "	4	5	5	4	4	4	2	3	3
" 18 "	4	6	6	4	4	5	3	3	3
" 20 "	5	6	7	5	5	5	3	4	4
" 22 "	5	8	8	5	5	6	4	4	4
" 24 "	6	8	8	6	6	7	4	5	5
" 26 "	7	9	9	6	6	8	5	6	6
" 28 "	7	10	10	7	7	9	5	7	7
" 30 "	8	11	11	7	8	9	6	7	7
" 32 "	8	12	12	8	8	10	6	8	8
" 34 "	9	12	13	8	9	11	7	8	8
" 36 "	10	13	14	9	9	11	7	9	9
" 38 "	11	14	15	9	10	12	8	9	9
" 40 "	12	14	16	10	10	13	8	10	10
" 42 "	12	15	17	10	11	13	9	10	10
" 44 "	13	16	18	11	12	14	9	11	11
" 46 "	14			11	13	14	10	11	11
" 48 "				12	14	15	10	12	12

(2) Notwithstanding the provisions of the last foregoing sub-paragraph—

(a) (i) the number of days of annual holiday which an employer is required to allow to a worker in respect of a period of employment during the 12 months immediately preceding 1st March 1969 shall not exceed in the aggregate twice the number of days constituting the worker's normal working week, *plus two days;*

(ii) the number of days of annual holiday which an employer is required to allow to a worker in respect of a period of employment during the 12 months immediately preceding 1st March 1970 shall not exceed in the aggregate—

in the case of a worker with a normal working week of four days or more, *twice the number of days constituting the worker's normal working week, plus four days;* and

in the case of a worker with a normal working week of less than four days, *three times the number of days constituting the worker's normal working week;* and

(iii) the number of days of annual holiday which an employer is required to allow to a worker in respect of a period of employment during the 12 months immediately preceding 1st March 1971 and during the 12 months immediately preceding 1st March in any succeeding year shall not exceed in the aggregate *three times the number of days constituting the worker's normal working week;*

(b) the worker's annual holiday during the holiday season ending on 31st October 1969, shall be reduced by any days of annual holiday duly allowed to him by the employer under the provisions of Order I.S.C. (41) between 1st March 1969, and the date on which the provisions of this Schedule become effective.

(3) In this Schedule the expression "holiday season" means in relation to the year 1969 the period commencing on 1st March 1969, and ending on 31st October 1969, and in each succeeding year, the period commencing on 1st March and ending on 31st October of the same year.

20. For the purpose of calculating any period of employment referred to in paragraph 19, 23 or 27 qualifying the worker for an annual holiday or for any accrued holiday remuneration, a worker shall be treated as having been employed:—

(1) For a week in respect of any week in which he has performed some work for the employer which would entitle him to statutory minimum remuneration.

(2) When absent from work in any of the following circumstances:—

(a) on customary holidays and annual holidays as provided in this Part of this Schedule or in the Schedule to Order I.S.C. (41);

(b) during proved sickness or accident up to and not exceeding a maximum of eight weeks in the aggregate during any such period as aforesaid;

(c) by leave of the employer.

21. An annual holiday shall be allowed on consecutive days and days of holiday shall be treated as consecutive notwithstanding that a Sunday (or in the case of a shift worker or split duty worker the normal day of rest), or a holiday allowed under the provisions of paragraph 16 or 17 intervenes:

Provided that—

(a) Where the number of days of annual holiday for which a worker has qualified exceeds the number of days constituting his normal working week, *but does not exceed twice that number*, the holiday may be allowed in two periods of consecutive working days; so, however, that when a holiday is so allowed, one of the periods shall consist of a number of such days not less than the number of days constituting the worker's normal working week.

(b) *Where the number of days of annual holiday for which a worker has qualified exceeds twice the number of days constituting his normal working week the holiday may be allowed as follows:—*

   (i) *as to the period comprising twice the number of days constituting the worker's normal working week, in accordance with sub-paragraph (a) of this paragraph; and*

   (ii) *as to the additional days, on working days to be fixed by agreement between the employer and the worker or his representative, either during the holiday season or before the beginning of the next following holiday season.*

22.—(1) Notwithstanding the provisions of paragraph 19, days of annual holiday may be allowed after the end of the holiday season and before the commencement of the next following holiday season if it is agreed before the end of the holiday season in writing between the employer and the worker or his representative.

(2) Where by agreement in writing between the employer and the worker or his representative at any time during the qualifying period immediately preceding the commencement of the holiday season in any year, the employer allows the worker, in respect of employment within that qualifying period, any day or days of holiday (not being days of customary holiday) and pays him holiday remuneration in respect thereof calculated in accordance with the provisions of paragraph 25, then—

   (a) the annual holiday to be allowed in accordance with paragraph 19 in the holiday season in that year shall be reduced by the day or days of holiday so allowed prior to the commencement of that holiday season; and

   (b) for the purpose of calculating accrued holiday remuneration under paragraph 27 any day or days of holiday deducted in accordance with (a) hereof shall be treated as if they had been allowed as a day or days of annual holiday.

23. Notwithstanding the provisions of paragraph 19, an employer may make application to the Wages Council to vary the holiday season to meet special circumstances, either by providing for its commencement earlier than 1st March or extending its duration beyond 31st October in any year, provided that any such application is made, in the case of the commencement of the holiday season on an earlier date, not less than six weeks before the date on which it is desired that the holiday season shall commence, and in the case of the extension of the holiday season, before 1st August.

Where the holiday season has been varied under this provision so as to commence earlier than 1st March, the qualifying period in respect of the worker or workers concerned shall be the 12 months immediately preceding the commencement of the holiday season as varied.

24. An employer shall give to a worker reasonable notice of the commencing date or dates and duration of his annual holiday and such notice may be given individually to a worker or by the posting of a notice in the place where the worker is employed.

REMUNERATION FOR ANNUAL HOLIDAY

25.—(1) Subject to the provisions of paragraph 26, a worker qualified to be allowed an annual holiday under this Schedule shall be paid by his employer in respect thereof, on the last pay day preceding such annual holiday, one day's holiday pay in respect of each day thereof.

(2) Where under the provisions of this Schedule an annual holiday is taken in more than one period the holiday remuneration shall be apportioned accordingly.

26. Where in accordance with the provisions of paragraph 27 of this Schedule, or of Order I.S.C. (41), accrued holiday remuneration has been paid by the employer to the worker in respect of any period of employment in the 12 months immediately preceding the holiday season within which an annual holiday is allowed by the employer to the worker in accordance with the provisions of this Schedule, the amount of holiday remuneration payable by the employer in respect of the said annual holiday under the provisions of paragraph 25 shall be reduced by the amount of the said accrued holiday remuneration.

ACCRUED HOLIDAY REMUNERATION PAYABLE ON TERMINATION OF EMPLOYMENT

27. Subject to the provisions of this paragraph, where a worker ceases to be employed by an employer after the provisions of this Schedule become effective, the employer shall, immediately on the termination of the employment, pay to the worker as accrued holiday remuneration:—

(1) in respect of employment in the 12 months up to the commencing date of the current holiday season, a sum equal to the holiday remuneration for any days of annual holiday for which he has qualified, except days of annual holiday which he has been allowed or has become entitled to be allowed before leaving the employment; and

(2) in respect of any employment since the commencing date of the current holiday season, or if no holiday season is then current, the commencing date of the last holiday season, a sum equal to the holiday remuneration which would have been payable to him if he could have been allowed an annual holiday in respect of that employment at the time of leaving it:

Provided that—

(a) the amount of the accrued holiday remuneration payable to a worker who leaves his employment without the consent of his employer before giving one week's notice of termination of employment or before one week has elapsed from the time of giving such notice, shall be the amount payable under the foregoing provisions of this Schedule less an amount equal to the holiday remuneration which would have been payable to him if at the termination of his employment he had been allowed an annual holiday of the number of days constituting his normal working week;

(b) accrued holiday remuneration shall not be payable to a worker if he is dismissed on the grounds of dishonesty and is so informed by his employer at the time of dismissal;

(c) where, during the period or periods in respect of which the said accrued holiday remuneration is payable, the worker has been allowed any day or days of holiday for which he had not qualified under the provisions of this Schedule or of Order I.S.C. (41), not being days of holiday referred to in paragraph 22(2) of this Schedule, any accrued holiday remuneration payable as aforesaid shall be reduced by the amount of any sum paid by the employer to the worker in respect of such day or days of holiday.

PART III

DEFINITIONS

28. *For the purposes of paragraphs 8 to 12 of this Schedule* the expressions "time-and-a-quarter", "time-and-a-half" and "double time" mean in the case of any worker whether employed as a day worker, a night worker, a shift worker or a split duty worker, respectively, one and a quarter times, one and a half times and twice the hourly rate obtained by dividing by *41* the minimum weekly remuneration specified in paragraph 1 for the corresponding description of worker employed in the same area and in the circumstances specified in sub-paragraph (1) of paragraph 6.

28A. *For the purposes of paragraphs 8A to 12A of this Schedule* the expressions "time-and-a-quarter", "time-and-a-half" and "double time" mean in the case of any worker whether employed as a day worker, a night worker, a shift worker or a split duty worker, respectively, one and a quarter times, one and a half times and twice the hourly rate obtained by dividing by *40* the minimum weekly remuneration specified in paragraph 1 for the corresponding description of worker employed in the same area and in the circumstances specified in sub-paragraph (1) of paragraph 6.

29. In this Schedule the following expressions have the meanings hereby respectively assigned to them, that is to say:—

"APPRENTICE COOK" is a male worker under the age of 21 years who is employed during the whole of his time under a written contract of apprenticeship which has been duly executed and which contains the provisions set out in (1) and (2) below or provisions substantially to the same effect and no provisions contrary thereto:—

(1) the worker of his own free will and with the consent of his guardian binds himself to serve the employer as his apprentice for a term of not less than five years;

(2) the employer will employ the worker as his apprentice during the said term and to the best of his power, skill and knowledge, instruct the worker or cause him to be instructed by a Head Cook in the underlying principles of cookery including the preparation, cooking and service of fish, meat, poultry, game, vegetables, eggs, pastry, cakes and sauces:

Provided that the minimum period of five years' apprenticeship under sub-paragraph (1) above shall be reduced—

(a) where the worker has after attaining the age of 15 years received a course of instruction in cookery in a technical class at any university, college, school or similar establishment, by a period equal to the duration of such course of instruction subject to a maximum reduction of two years;

(b) where the worker has after attaining the age of 16 years continued to receive at a school full time general education which does not include a course of instruction in cookery in a technical class, by a period equal to the duration of such full time general education received after he attained the age of 16 years subject to a maximum reduction of one year;

but so that the total reduction in the minimum period of any worker's apprenticeship shall not be more than two years.

"ASSISTANT COOK" is a male worker of 21 years of age or over, or a female worker of 18 years of age or over, wholly or mainly engaged in assisting in the preparing and cooking of food under the instructions of a cook or of a canteen supervisor, manager, manageress, steward or stewardess who is required to perform the duties of a cook.

"CANTEEN ATTENDANT" is a female worker of 18 years of age or over employed as a waitress, counter assistant, service worker, washer-up, cleaner, tea girl, or kitchen assistant whose duties may include vegetable preparation.

"CANTEEN SUPERVISOR", "MANAGER OR MANAGERESS", "STEWARD OR STEWARDESS" is a person of one of the undermentioned grades who is in direct control of the staff of a canteen and immediately responsible for its operation including such a person required to perform the whole or part of the duties of a cook:—

Grade	Staff (exclusive of the supervisor, manager or manageress, steward or stewardess) normally employed in the canteen under his or her direct control
X (Female only)	Not less than 2 and not more than 4 persons
A	„ „ „ 5 „ „ „ „ 10 „
B	„ „ „ 11 „ „ „ „ 20 „
C	„ „ „ 21 „ „ „ „ 30 „
D	„ „ „ 31 „ „ „ „ 40 „

In computing the number of persons normally employed on the staff of the canteen both full-time workers and workers other than full-time workers shall be included except that in the case of workers other than full-time workers the number to be counted shall be the number disregarding fractions obtained by dividing by 36 the aggregate of the hours usually worked in the week by all such workers.

"CASHIER" is a female worker of 18 years of age or over wholly or mainly engaged in taking cash or giving change.

"COOK" is a male or female worker of 21 years of age or over wholly or mainly engaged in the preparing and cooking of food requiring the mixing of two or more ingredients and/or the preparing and the cooking of meat, poultry or game.

"HEAD COOK" is a cook experienced in all departments of the kitchen who is capable of training inexperienced staff and has not less than 3 cooks or assistant cooks under his or her control and whose duties mainly consist in cooking, planning menus, ordering supplies and who may be required to control kitchen staff.

30. In this Schedule the following expressions have the meanings hereby respectively assigned to them, that is to say:—

"AREAS"—

"LONDON AREA" means the Metropolitan Police District, as defined in the London Government Act 1963(a), the City of London, the Inner Temple and the Middle Temple.

"OTHER AREAS" means all areas other than the London area.

"FULL-TIME WORKER" means a worker whose usual hours of employment amount to 36 hours or more per week.

"FULL BOARD" means four meals per day which shall be of good and sufficient quality and quantity and shall consist of dinner and three other meals.

"LODGING" means clean and adequate accommodation and facilities for eating, sleeping, washing and leisure.

"NIGHT WORKER" is a worker whose usual turn of duty includes not less than four hours' work between 8.30 p.m. on one day and 6.30 a.m. on the next day and who is not a shift worker or a split duty worker.

"NORMAL WORKING WEEK" means the number of days on which it has been usual for the worker to work in a week in the employment of the employer during the 12 months immediately preceding the commencement of the holiday season or, where accrued holiday remuneration is payable under paragraph 27 on the termination of the employment, during the 12 months immediately preceding the date of the termination of the employment.

"ONE DAY'S HOLIDAY PAY" means the appropriate proportion of the remuneration which the worker would be entitled to receive from his employer at the date of the annual holiday (or, where the holiday is allowed in more than one period, at the date of the first period) or at the date of termination of the employment as the case may be for one week's work if working his normal working week and the number of daily hours usually worked by him (exclusive of overtime) and if paid at the appropriate rate of statutory minimum remuneration for work for which statutory minimum remuneration is payable and at the same rate for any work for the same employer for which such remuneration is not payable with the ADDITION of the following amounts—

(1) in the case of a worker, other than a worker to whom the provisions of (2) apply, an addition of 2s. 10d.;

(a) 1963 c. 33.

(2) in the case of a worker who is employed in the circumstances that he is provided by his employer with full board and lodging or either full board or lodging—

　(*a*) 6s. 1d. if the worker is 17 years of age or over; or

　(*b*) 4s. 0d. if the worker is under 17 years of age.

In this definition "appropriate proportion" means—

where the worker's normal working week is six days ... ... one-sixth
where the worker's normal working week is five days ... ... one-fifth
where the worker's normal working week is four days or less ... one-quarter.

"SHIFT WORKER" means a worker employed on a shift system in accordance with which—

(1) a 24-hour period is divided into three turns of duty; or

(2) there is no night turn of duty and the remainder of the day is divided into two or more turns of duty;
and the worker is employed for not less than five out of the seven days in any week on the same turn and changes turns periodically in accordance with a pre-arranged plan.

"SPLIT DUTY WORKER" means a worker who is employed in the circumstances that he is provided by the employer with full board and lodging for seven days in any week and whose normal hours of daily duty are spread over a period exceeding 10 hours inclusive of meal times but not exceeding 14 hours inclusive of meal times.

"STATUTORY MINIMUM REMUNERATION" means minimum remuneration (other than holiday remuneration) which has been fixed by a wages regulation order made by the Secretary of State to give effect to proposals submitted to her by the Wages Council; and

"APPROPRIATE STATUTORY MINIMUM REMUNERATION" means the statutory minimum remuneration payable to the worker at the date of the holiday or the date when the employment ceases, as the case may be, but excluding any part of such remuneration payable thereunder solely by reason of the fact that meals, board, lodging, or overalls and headwear are not provided by the employer.

"WEEK" means "pay week".

PART IV

GENERAL

WORKERS TO WHOM THE SCHEDULE APPLIES

31. The provisions of this Schedule apply to the following workers, that is to say:—

Workers employed in Great Britain by the person or body of persons carrying on an industrial or staff canteen undertaking who are so employed in the said undertaking, and who are engaged on any of the following work, that is to say:—

　(*a*) the preparation of food or drink;

　(*b*) the service of food or drink;

　(*c*) work incidental to such preparation or service;

　(*d*) any work performed on or about premises where food or drink is prepared or served, including work in connection with any service or amenity provided at such premises;

　(*e*) transport work;

　(*f*) work performed at any office, depot, store or similar place;

but excluding transport workers and workers at any office, depot, store or similar place who are employed by the person or body of persons carrying on the undertaking mainly on work not in connection with the undertaking.

DEFINITION OF INDUSTRIAL OR STAFF CANTEEN UNDERTAKING

An industrial or staff canteen undertaking consists of any undertaking or any part of an undertaking which is wholly or mainly engaged in supplying food or drink for immediate consumption and activities incidental or ancillary thereto, and which is carried on for the use of employed persons in connection with their employment:—

(a) by their employer or employers; or

(b) by the employed persons themselves; or

(c) by the employed persons and their employer or employers jointly; or

(d) by any other person or body of persons in pursuance of an arrangement or arrangements with the employer or employers of the employed persons, or with the employed persons themselves, or with the employed persons and their employer or employers jointly; or

(e) by a dock authority or by any person or body of persons under an arrangement with a dock authority;

but excluding any such undertaking carried on:—

(1) directly by the Crown; or

(2) by an employer or by workers and their employer jointly, wholly or mainly for the use of workers employed by the employer:—

(i) in the business of supplying food or drink for immediate consumption by the general public; or

(ii) at or in connection with a shop, if the shop includes a restaurant, café or similar place where meals are served to the general public; or

(iii) at or in connection with an hotel, boarding house, hostel or other similar establishment; or

(iv) at or in connection with any hospital, nursing home or other similar establishment; or

(v) at or in connection with any university, college, school or other similar establishment.

For the purpose of this definition "dock authority" means any person or body of persons whether incorporated or not who are authorised to construct or are owners or lessees of any dock authorised by or under any Act, and "dock" includes a wharf or quay.

32. Nothing in this Schedule shall be construed as authorising the making of any deduction or the giving of any remuneration in any manner which is illegal by virtue of the Truck Acts 1831 to 1940(a) or of any other enactment.

EXPLANATORY NOTE

(This Note is not part of the Order.)

This Order, which has effect from 30th June 1969, sets out the statutory minimum remuneration payable and the holidays to be allowed to workers in substitution for the statutory minimum remuneration and holidays set out in the Wages Regulation (Industrial and Staff Canteen) Order 1967 (Order I.S.C. (41)), which is revoked.

New provisions are printed in italics.

(a) 1831 c. 37; 1887 c. 46; 1896 c. 44; 1940 c. 38.

STATUTORY INSTRUMENTS

1969 No. 692

MERCHANT SHIPPING

The Merchant Shipping (Fees) (Amendment) Regulations 1969

Made - - -	*14th May* 1969
Laid before Parliament	*22nd May* 1969
Coming into Operation	*29th May* 1969

The Board of Trade, with the approval of the Treasury and in exercise of their powers under section 33 of the Merchant Shipping (Safety Convention) Act 1949(**a**) as having effect by virtue of the Transfer of Functions (Shipping and Construction of Ships) Order 1965(**b**), and of all other powers enabling them in that behalf, hereby make the following Regulations :—

1.—(1) These Regulations may be cited as the Merchant Shipping (Fees) (Amendment) Regulations 1969 and shall come into operation on 29th May 1969.

(2) The Interpretation Act 1889(**c**) shall apply to the interpretation of these Regulations as it applies to the interpretation of an Act of Parliament.

2. The Merchant Shipping (Fees) Regulations 1967(**d**) shall be amended by substituting for Parts 12 and 13 of the Schedule thereto the following :—

"PART 12. FEES FOR ENGAGEMENT AND DISCHARGE OF SEAMEN (OTHER THAN MEMBERS OF THE CREWS OF FISHING BOATS)

1. In this Part, "seamen" does not include members of the crews of fishing boats within the meaning of Section 390 of the Merchant Shipping Act 1894.

2. *Enactment*	*Service*	*Fee* £ s. d.
Section 2(2) of the Fees (Increase) Act 1923	(1) For the engagement or discharge of seamen otherwise than on board ship before a superintendent or his duly appointed deputy:—	
	(*a*) (i) For each of the first 100 men engaged	12 6
	(ii) For each man engaged in excess of 100 but not in excess of 500 ...	8 0
	(iii) For each man engaged in excess of 500	4 0

(**a**) 1949 c. 43.
(**c**) 1889 c. 63.

(**b**) S.I. 1965/145 (1965 I, p. 438).
(**d**) S.I. 1967/1611 (1967 III, p. 4432).

Enactment	Service	Fee
		£ s. d.
	(b) (i) For each of the first 100 men discharged	12 6
	(ii) For each man discharged in excess of 100 but not in excess of 500 ...	8 0
	(iii) For each man discharged in excess of 500	4 0
	(2) Subject to (3) and (4), for the engagement or discharge of seamen on board ship	The appropriate fee shown in (1) plus an additional fee in respect of each visit by the superintendent or his duly appointed deputy to the ship as follows:—
	(a) (i) If not more than 36 men are engaged during the visit, for each man	6 0
	(ii) If more than 36 men are so engaged	10 15 0 plus £2. 18s. 0d. for every 50, or fraction of 50, men so engaged in excess of 100.
	(b) (i) If not more than 36 men are discharged during the visit, for each man	6 0
	(ii) If more than 36 men are so discharged	10 15 0 plus £2. 18s. 0d. for every 50, or fraction of 50, men so discharged in excess of 100.
	(3) Subject to (4), if any seamen are re-engaged on board a ship immediately after their discharge on board that ship the additional fee payable in respect of such seamen by reason of their re-engagement on board ship shall be half the fee payable in respect of them under (2)(a).	

Enactment	Service	Fee £ s. d.
	(4) The minimum additional fee for any visit of a superintendent or his duly appointed deputy to a ship for the purpose of the engagement, discharge or re-engagement of seamen shall (whether or not one or more of those services is carried out during the visit) be	4 16 0

PART 13. FEES FOR SERVICES IN CONNECTION WITH AGREEMENTS OPENED IN INDIA OR PAKISTAN

Enactment	Service	Fee £ s. d.
Section 125(3) of the Merchant Shipping Act 1894.	For certifying that a further agreement is a proper agreement in all respects under section 125 of the Merchant Shipping Act 1894 ...	4 0 0"

William Rodgers,

Minister of State,
Board of Trade.

14th May 1969.

We approve the making of these Regulations.

Joseph Harper,

Walter Harrison,

Two of the Lords Commissioners of
Her Majesty's Treasury.

14th May 1969.

EXPLANATORY NOTE

(This Note is not part of the Regulations.)

These Regulations increase by approximately 75% the fees prescribed by the Merchant Shipping (Fees) Regulations 1967 for the engagement and discharge of seamen before a superintendent or his deputy and for services in connection with agreements opened in India or Pakistan.

STATUTORY INSTRUMENTS

1969 No. 693

AGRICULTURE

LIVESTOCK INDUSTRIES

The Beef Cow (England and Wales) (Amendment) Scheme 1969

Made - - - -	14*th May* 1969
Laid before Parliament	22*nd May* 1969
Coming into Operation	23*rd May* 1969

The Minister of Agriculture, Fisheries and Food and the Secretary of State, acting jointly, in pursuance of section 12 of the Agriculture Act 1967(**a**), as read with the Transfer of Functions (Wales) Order 1969(**b**), and all their other enabling powers, with the approval of the Treasury, hereby make the following scheme:—

Citation, commencement and interpretation

1. This scheme, which may be cited as the Beef Cow (England and Wales) (Amendment) Scheme 1969, shall come into operation on 23rd May 1969 and shall be construed as one with the Beef Cow (England and Wales) Scheme 1967(**c**).

Amendment of 1967 scheme

2.—(1) In paragraph 4(1)(*b*) of the Beef Cow (England and Wales) Scheme 1967 (which restricts the number of cows in any herd in respect of which subsidy payments may be made to one cow for each $2\frac{1}{2}$ acres of grass and forage crops available for the maintenance of the herd), for the words " $2\frac{1}{2}$ acres " there shall be substituted the words " two acres ".

(2) Nothing in this scheme shall affect subsidy payments relating to the prescribed dates in the years 1967 or 1968.

In Witness whereof the Official Seal of the Minister of Agriculture, Fisheries and Food is hereunto affixed on 7th May 1969.

(L.S.) *Cledwyn Hughes,*
Minister of Agriculture, Fisheries and Food.

Given under my hand on 8th May 1969.

George Thomas,
Secretary of State for Wales.

We approve,
14th May 1969.

Joseph Harper,
Walter Harrison,
Two of the Lords Commissioners of
Her Majesty's Treasury.

(**a**) 1967 c. 22.   (**b**) S.I. 1969/388 (1969 I, p. 1070).   (**c**) 1967/1555 (1967 III, p. 4317).

EXPLANATORY NOTE
(This Note is not part of the Scheme.)

This scheme amends the Beef Cow (England and Wales) Scheme 1967 by altering the maximum stocking ratio from one cow for each $2\frac{1}{2}$ acres to one cow for each two acres. This improvement applies to payment of subsidy for each of the years 1969 to 1971 inclusive.

1969 No. 694

AGRICULTURE

LIVESTOCK INDUSTRIES

The Beef Cow Subsidy Payment (England and Wales) (Amendment) Order 1969

Made - - -	14*th May* 1969
Laid before Parliament	22*nd May* 1969
Coming into Operation	23*rd May* 1969

The Minister of Agriculture, Fisheries and Food and the Secretary of State, acting jointly, in pursuance of sub-sections (4) and (7) of section 12 of the Agriculture Act 1967(**a**), as read with the Transfer of Functions (Wales) Order 1969(**b**), and all their other enabling powers, with the approval of the Treasury, hereby make the following order :—

Citation and commencement

1. This order, which may be cited as the Beef Cow Subsidy Payment (England and Wales) (Amendment) Order 1969, shall come into operation on 23rd May 1969.

Interpretation

2.—(1) Unless the context otherwise requires, expressions used in this order have the same meaning as in the Beef Cow (England and Wales) Scheme 1967(**c**).

(2) The Interpretation Act 1889(**d**) shall apply to the interpretation of this order as it applies to the interpretation of an Act of Parliament.

Increase in subsidy payments

3. Article 3 of the Beef Cow Subsidy Payment (England and Wales) Order 1967(**e**), as amended (**f**), (which specifies the amount of a subsidy payment under the Beef Cow (England and Wales) Scheme 1967) shall have effect in relation to prescribed dates in 1969 and subsequent years with the substitution of £10 for £9.

(**a**) 1967 c. 22.
(**c**) S.I. 1967/1555 (1967 III, p. 4317).
(**e**) S.I. 1967/1559 (1967 III, p. 4326).

(**b**) S.I. 1969/388 (1969 I, p. 1070).
(**d**) 1889 c. 63.
(**f**) S.I. 1968/967 (1968 II p. 2576).

In Witness whereof the Official Seal of the Minister of Agriculture, Fisheries and Food is hereunto affixed on 7th May 1969.

(L.S.)

Cledwyn Hughes,
Minister of Agriculture, Fisheries and Food.

Given under my hand on 8th May 1969.

George Thomas,
Secretary of State for Wales.

We approve,
14th May 1969.

Joseph Harper,
Walter Harrison,
Two of the Lords Commissioners of
Her Majesty's Treasury.

EXPLANATORY NOTE

(*This Note is not part of the Order.*)

This order increases the amount of the Beef Cow subsidy for each of the years 1969 to 1971 inclusive from £9 to £10 per cow.

STATUTORY INSTRUMENTS

1969 No. 695

AGRICULTURE

HILL LANDS

The Hill Cattle (Breeding Herds) (England and Wales) (Amendment) Scheme 1969

Made - - -	14*th May* 1969
Laid before Parliament	22*nd May* 1969
Coming into Operation	23*rd May* 1969

The Minister of Agriculture, Fisheries and Food and the Secretary of State, acting jointly, in pursuance of sections 13, 14, 15 and 17 of the Hill Farming Act 1946(**a**), as extended by section 43 of the Agriculture Act 1967(**b**) and as read with the Transfer of Functions (Wales) Order 1969(**c**), and all their other enabling powers, with the approval of the Treasury, hereby make the following scheme :—

Citation, commencement and interpretation

1. This scheme, which may be cited as the Hill Cattle (Breeding Herds) (England and Wales) (Amendment) Scheme 1969, shall come into operation on 23rd May 1969 and shall be construed as one with the Hill Cattle (Breeding Herds) (England and Wales) Scheme 1968(**d**).

Amendment of 1968 scheme

2.—(1) In paragraph 10(1)(*b*) of the Hill Cattle (Breeding Herds) (England and Wales) Scheme 1968 (which restricts the number of cattle in any herd in respect of which subsidy payments may be made to one cow for each five acres of hill land available for the maintenance of the herd) for the words "five acres" there shall be substituted the words "four acres".

(2) Nothing in this scheme shall affect subsidy payments in respect of the year 1968.

(**a**) 1946 c. 73. For change of title of the Minister, see S.I. 1955/554 (1955 I, p. 1200).
(**b**) 1967 c. 22. (**c**) S.I. 1969/388 (1969 I, p. 1070).
(**d**) S.I. 1968/875 (1968 II, p. 2310).

In Witness whereof the Official Seal of the Minister of Agriculture, Fisheries and Food is hereunto affixed on 7th May 1969.

(L.S.)　　　　　　　　　　　　　　　*Cledwyn Hughes,*
　　　　　　　　Minister of Agriculture, Fisheries and Food.

Given under my hand on 8th May 1969.

　　　　　　　　　　　　　　　　George Thomas,
　　　　　　　　　Secretary of State for Wales.

We approve,

14th May 1969.

　　　　　　　　　　　　　　　　Joseph Harper,
　　　　　　　　　　　　　　　　Walter Harrison,
　　　　　　　Two of the Lords Commissioners of
　　　　　　　　　Her Majesty's Treasury.

EXPLANATORY NOTE

(This Note is not part of the Scheme.)

This scheme amends the Hill Cattle (Breeding Herds) (England and Wales) Scheme 1968 by altering the maximum stocking ratio from one cow for each five acres to one cow for each four acres. This improvement applies to payment of subsidy for each of the years 1969 to 1972 inclusive.

STATUTORY   INSTRUMENTS

1969 No. 696

AGRICULTURE

HILL LANDS

The Hill Cattle Subsidy (Breeding Herds) (England and Wales) Payment (Amendment) Order 1969

Made - - - -	*14th May* 1969
Laid before Parliament	*22nd May* 1969
Coming into Operation	*23rd May* 1969

The Minister of Agriculture, Fisheries and Food and the Secretary of State, acting jointly, in pursuance of sections 14(3) and 17 of the Hill Farming Act 1946(**a**), as amended by section 8 of the Livestock Rearing Act 1951(**b**) and as read with the Transfer of Functions (Wales) Order 1969(**c**), and all their other enabling powers, with the approval of the Treasury, hereby make the following order:—

Citation and commencement

1. This order, which may be cited as the Hill Cattle Subsidy (Breeding Herds) (England and Wales) Payment (Amendment) Order 1969, shall come into operation on 23rd May 1969.

Interpretation

2.—(1) Unless the context otherwise requires, expressions used in this order shall have the same meaning as in the Hill Cattle (Breeding Herds) (England and Wales) Scheme 1968(**d**).

(2) The Interpretation Act 1889(**e**) shall apply to the interpretation of this order as it applies to the interpretation of an Act of Parliament.

Increase in subsidy payments

3. Article 3 of the Hill Cattle Subsidy (Breeding Herds) (England and Wales) Payment Order 1968(**f**) (which specifies the amount of a subsidy payment under the Hill Cattle (Breeding Herds) (England and Wales) Scheme 1968) shall have effect in relation to subsidy payments in respect of 1969 and subsequent years with the substitution of £22 5s. for £21 5s.

In Witness whereof the Official Seal of the Minister of Agriculture, Fisheries and Food is hereunto affixed on 7th May 1969.

(L.S.)   *Cledwyn Hughes,*
                    Minister of Agriculture, Fisheries and Food.

Given under my hand on 8th May 1969.

                                        George Thomas,
                              Secretary of State for Wales.

(**a**) 1946 c. 73. For change of title cf the Minister, see S.I. 1955/554 (1955 I, p. 1200).
(**b**) 1951 c. 18.   (**c**) S.I. 1969/388 (1969 I, p. 1070).   (**d**) S.I. 1968/875 (1968 II, p. 2310).   (**e**) 1889 c. 63.   (**f**) S.I. 1968/876 (1968 II, p. 2317).

We approve,
14th May 1969.

Joseph Harper,
Walter Harrison,
Two of the Lords Commissioners of
Her Majesty's Treasury.

EXPLANATORY NOTE

(This Note is not part of the Order.)

This order increases the amount of the Hill Cattle subsidy for each of the years 1969 to 1972 inclusive from £21 5s. to £22 5s. per cow.

STATUTORY INSTRUMENTS

1969 No. 697

AGRICULTURE

HILL LANDS

The Hill Sheep (England and Wales) (Amendment) Scheme 1969

Made - - -	14*th May* 1969
Laid before Parliament	22*nd May* 1969
Coming into Operation	23*rd May* 1969

The Minister of Agriculture, Fisheries and Food and the Secretary of State, acting jointly, in pursuance of sections 13, 14, 15 and 17 of the Hill Farming Act 1946(**a**), as extended by section 43 of the Agriculture Act 1967(**b**) and as read with the Transfer of Functions (Wales) Order 1969(**c**), and all their other enabling powers, with the approval of the Treasury, hereby make the following scheme :—

Citation, commencement and interpretation

1. This scheme, which may be cited as the Hill Sheep (England and Wales) (Amendment) Scheme 1969, shall come into operation on 23rd May 1969 and shall be construed as one with the Hill Sheep (England and Wales) Scheme 1967(**d**).

Amendment of 1967 scheme

2.—(1) In paragraph 9(1)(*c*) of the Hill Sheep (England and Wales) Scheme 1967 (which restricts the number of ewes in any flock in respect of which subsidy payments may be made to two ewes for each acre of hill land on which the flock is grazed), for the word "two" there shall be substituted the figure "$2\frac{1}{2}$".

(2) Nothing in this scheme shall affect subsidy payments relating to the relevant days in the years 1967 or 1968.

(**a**) 1946 c. 73. For change of title of the Minister, see S.I. 1955/554 (1955 I, p. 1200).
(**b**) 1967 c. 22. (**c**) S.I. 1969/388 (1969 I, p. 1070).
(**d**) S.I. 1967/1869 (1967 III, p. 5072).

In Witness whereof the Official Seal of the Minister of Agriculture, Fisheries and Food is hereunto affixed on 7th May 1969.

(L.S.)   *Cledwyn Hughes,*
                    Minister of Agriculture, Fisheries and Food.

Given under my hand on 8th May 1969.

                              George Thomas,
                    Secretary of State for Wales.

We approve,

14th May 1969.

                              Joseph Harper,
                              Walter Harrison,
                    Two of the Lords Commissioners of
                    Her Majesty's Treasury.

EXPLANATORY NOTE

(This Note is not part of the Scheme.)

This scheme amends the Hill Sheep (England and Wales) Scheme 1967 by altering the maximum stocking ratio from two ewes per acre to 2½ ewes per acre. This improvement applies to payment of subsidy for 1969 and subsequent years of the scheme.

1969 No. 698

AGRICULTURE

The Beef Cow (Northern Ireland) (Amendment) Scheme 1969

Made - - - -	14*th May*, 1969
Laid before Parliament	22*nd May*, 1969
Coming into Operation	23*rd May*, 1969

The Minister of Agriculture, Fisheries and Food, in pursuance of section 12 of the Agriculture Act 1967(**a**) and all his other enabling powers, with the approval of the Treasury, hereby makes the following scheme : —

Citation, commencement and interpretation

1. This scheme, which may be cited as the Beef Cow (Northern Ireland) (Amendment) Scheme 1969, shall come into operation on 23rd May, 1969 and shall be construed as one with the Beef Cow (Northern Ireland) Scheme 1967(**b**).

Amendment of 1967 scheme

2.—(1) In paragraph 4(1)(*b*) of the Beef Cow (Northern Ireland) Scheme 1967 (which restricts the number of cows in any herd in respect of which subsidy payments may be made to one cow for each $2\frac{1}{2}$ acres of grass and forage crops available for the maintenance of the herd), for the words "$2\frac{1}{2}$ acres" there shall be substituted the words "two acres".

(2) Nothing in this scheme shall affect subsidy payments relating to the prescribed dates in the years 1967 or 1968.

In Witness whereof the Official Seal of the Minister of Agriculture, Fisheries and Food is hereunto affixed on 7th May, 1969.

(L.S.)

Cledwyn Hughes,
Minister of Agriculture, Fisheries and Food.

We approve,
14th May 1969.

Joseph Harper,
Walter Harrison,
Two of the Lords Commissioners of
Her Majesty's Treasury.

EXPLANATORY NOTE

(*This Note is not part of the Scheme.*)

This scheme amends the Beef Cow (Northern Ireland) Scheme 1967 by altering the maximum stocking ratio from one cow for each $2\frac{1}{2}$ acres to one cow for each two acres. This improvement applies to payment of subsidy for each of the years 1969 to 1971 inclusive.

(**a**) 1967 c. 22.   (**b**) S.I. 1967/1976 (1967 III, p. 5405).

STATUTORY INSTRUMENTS

1969 No. 699

AGRICULTURE

LIVESTOCK INDUSTRIES

The Beef Cow Subsidy Payment (Northern Ireland) (Amendment) Order 1969

Made - - - -	14th May 1969
Laid before Parliament	22nd May 1969
Coming into Operation	23rd May, 1969

The Minister of Agriculture, Fisheries and Food, in pursuance of sub-sections (4) and (7) of section 12 of the Agriculture Act 1967(a) and all his other enabling powers, with the approval of the Treasury, hereby makes the following order :—

Citation and commencement

1. This order, which may be cited as the Beef Cow Subsidy Payment (Northern Ireland) (Amendment) Order 1969, shall come into operation on 23rd May 1969.

Interpretation

2.—(1) Unless the context otherwise requires, expressions used in this order have the same meaning as in the Beef Cow (Northern Ireland) Scheme 1967(b).

(2) The Interpretation Act 1889(c) shall apply to the interpretation of this order as it applies to the interpretation of an Act of Parliament.

Increase in subsidy payments

3. Article 3 of the Beef Cow Subsidy Payment (Northern Ireland) Order 1967(d), as amended(e), (which specifies the amount of a subsidy payment under the Beef Cow (Northern Ireland) Scheme 1967) shall have effect in relation to prescribed dates in 1969 and subsequent years with the substitution of £10 for £9.

In witness whereof the Official Seal of the Minister of Agriculture, Fisheries and Food is hereunto affixed on 7th May 1969.

Cledwyn Hughes,
Minister of Agriculture, Fisheries and Food.

We approve,

14th May 1969.

Joseph Harper,
Walter Harrison,
Two of the Lords Commissioners of
Her Majesty's Treasury.

(a) 1967 c. 22.　　(b) S.I. 1967/1976 (1967 III, p. 5405).　　(c) 1889 c. 63.
(d) S.I. 1967/1977 (1967 III, p. 5409).　　(e) S.I. 1968/968 (1968 II, p. 2578).

EXPLANATORY NOTE

(This Note is not part of the Order.)

This order increases the amount of the Northern Ireland Beef Cow subsidy for each of the years 1969 to 1971 inclusive from £9 to £10 per cow.

STATUTORY INSTRUMENTS

1969 No. 700

AGRICULTURE

HILL LANDS

The Hill Cattle (Breeding Herds) (Northern Ireland) (Amendment) Scheme 1969

Made - - -	14*th May* 1969
Laid before Parliament	22*nd May* 1969
Coming into Operation	23*rd May* 1969

The Minister of Agriculture, Fisheries and Food, in pursuance of Sections 13, 14, 15 and 17 of the Hill Farming Act 1946(**a**), as extended by section 43 of the Agriculture Act 1967(**b**), and all his other enabling powers, with the approval of the Treasury, hereby makes the following scheme :—

Citation, commencement and interpretation

1. This scheme, which may be cited as the Hill Cattle (Breeding Herds) (Northern Ireland) (Amendment) Scheme 1969, shall come into operation on 23rd May 1969 and shall be construed as one with the Hill Castle (Breeding Herds) (Northern Ireland) Scheme 1968(**c**).

Amendment of 1968 scheme

2.—(1) In paragraph 9(1)(*b*) of the Hill Cattle (Breeding Herds) (Northern Ireland) Scheme 1968 (which restricts the number of cattle in any herd in respect of which subsidy payments may be made to one cow for each five acres of hill land available for the maintenance of the herd), for the words "five acres" there shall be substituted the words "four acres".

(2) Nothing in this scheme shall affect subsidy payments in respect of the year 1968.

(**a**) 1946 c. 73.   For change of title of the Minister, see S.I. 1955/554 (1955 I, p. 1200).
(**b**) 1967 c. 22.   (**c**) S.I. 1968/965 (1968 II, p. 2569).

In Witness whereof the Official Seal of the Minister of Agriculture. Fisheries and Food is hereunto affixed on 7th May 1969.

(L.S.)

Cledwyn Hughes,
Minister of Agriculture, Fisheries and Food.

We approve,
14th May 1969.

Joseph Harper,
Walter Harrison,
Two of the Lords Commissioners of
Her Majesty's Treasury.

EXPLANATORY NOTE

(This Note is not part of the scheme.)

This scheme amends the Hill Cattle (Breeding Herds) (Northern Ireland) Scheme 1968 by altering the maximum stocking ratio from one cow for each five acres to one cow for each four acres. This improvement applies to payment of subsidy for each of the years 1969 to 1972 inclusive.

STATUTORY INSTRUMENTS

1969 No. 701

AGRICULTURE

HILL LANDS

The Hill Cattle Subsidy (Breeding Herds) (Northern Ireland) Payment (Amendment) Order 1969

Made - - -	*14th May* 1969
Laid before Parliament	*22nd May* 1969
Coming into Operation	*23rd May* 1969

The Minister of Agriculture, Fisheries and Food, in pursuance of Sections 14(3) and 17 of the Hill Farming Act 1946(**a**), as amended by section 8 of the Livestock Rearing Act 1951(**b**), and all his other enabling powers, with the approval of the Treasury, hereby makes the following order :—

Citation and commencement

1. This order, which may be cited as the Hill Cattle Subsidy (Breeding Herds) (Northern Ireland) Payment (Amendment) Order 1969, shall come into operation on 23rd May 1969.

Interpretation

2.—(1) Unless the context otherwise requires, expressions used in this order shall have the same meaning as in the Hill Cattle (Breeding Herds) (Northern Ireland) Scheme 1968(**c**).

(2) The Interpretation Act 1889(**d**) shall apply to the interpretation of this order as it applies to the interpretation of an Act of Parliament.

Increase in subsidy payments

3. Article 3 of the Hill Cattle Subsidy (Breeding Herds) (Northern Ireland) Payment Order 1968(**e**) (which specifies the amount of a subsidy payment under the Hill Cattle (Breeding Herds) (Northern Ireland) Scheme 1968) shall have effect in relation to subsidy payments in respect of 1969 and subsequent years with the substitution of £22 5s. for £21 5s.

(**a**) 1946 c. 73.   For change of title of the Minister, see S.I. 1955/554 (1955 I, p. 1200).
(**b**) 1951 c. 18.   (**c**) S.I. 1968/965 (1968 II, p. 2569).
(**d**) 1889 c. 63.   (**e**) S.I. 1968/966 (1968 II, p. 2574).

In Witness whereof the Official Seal of the Minister of Agriculture, Fisheries and Food is hereunto affixed on 7th May 1969.

(L.S.)

Cledwyn Hughes,
Minister of Agriculture. Fisheries and Food.

We approve,
14th May 1969.

Joseph Harper,
Walter Harrison,
Two of the Lords Commissioners of
Her Majesty's Treasury.

EXPLANATORY NOTE
(This Note is not part of the Order.)

This order increases the amount of the Northern Ireland Hill Cattle subsidy for each of the years 1969 to 1972 inclusive from £21 5s. to £22 5s. per cow.

1969 No. 702

AGRICULTURE

HILL LANDS

The Hill Sheep (Northern Ireland) (Amendment) Scheme 1969

Made - - - -	14*th May* 1969
Laid before Parliament	22*nd May* 1969
Coming into Operation	23*rd May* 1969

The Minister of Agriculture, Fisheries and Food, in pursuance of sections 13, 14, 15 and 17 of the Hill Farming Act 1946(**a**), as extended by section 43 of the Agriculture Act 1967(**b**) and all his other enabling powers, with the approval of the Treasury, hereby makes the following scheme:—

Citation, commencement and interpretation

1. This scheme, which may be cited as the Hill Sheep (Northern Ireland) (Amendment) Scheme 1969, shall come into operation on 23rd May 1969 and shall be construed as one with the Hill Sheep (Northern Ireland) Scheme 1968(**c**).

Amendment of 1968 scheme

2.—(1) In paragraph 9(1)(*c*) of the Hill Sheep (Northern Ireland) Scheme 1968 (which restricts the number of ewes in any flock in respect of which subsidy payments may be made to two ewes for each acre of hill land on which the flock is grazed), for the word " two " there shall be substituted the figure " $2\frac{1}{2}$ ".

(2) Nothing in this scheme shall affect subsidy payments relating to the relevant days in the years 1967 or 1968.

In Witness whereof the Official Seal of the Minister of Agriculture, Fisheries and Food is hereunto affixed on 7th May 1969.

(L.S.)   *Cledwyn Hughes,*
Minister of Agriculture, Fisheries and Food.

We approve,
14th May 1969.

Joseph Harper,
Walter Harrison,
Two of the Lords Commissioners of
Her Majesty's Treasury.

(**a**) 1946 c. 73.   For change of title of the Minister, see S.I. 1955/554 (1955 I, p. 1200).
(**b**) 1967 c. 22.   (**c**) S.I. 1968/830 (1968 II, p. 2241).

EXPLANATORY NOTE

(This Note is not part of the Scheme.)

This scheme amends the Hill Sheep (Northern Ireland) Scheme 1968 by altering the maximum stocking ratio from two ewes per acre to 2½ ewes per acre. This improvement applies to payment of subsidy for 1969 and subsequent years of the scheme.

STATUTORY INSTRUMENTS

1969 No. 703

INDUSTRIAL TRAINING

The Industrial Training Levy (Ceramics, Glass and Mineral Products) Order 1969

Made - - -	*14th May* 1969
Laid before Parliament	*27th May* 1969
Coming into Operation	*2nd June* 1969

The Secretary of State after approving proposals submitted by the Ceramics, Glass and Mineral Products Industry Training Board for the imposition of a further levy on employers in the ceramics, glass and mineral products industry and in exercise of her powers under section 4 of the Industrial Training Act 1964(a) and of all other powers enabling her in that behalf hereby makes the following Order:—

Title and commencement

1. This Order may be cited as the Industrial Training Levy (Ceramics, Glass and Mineral Products) Order 1969 and shall come into operation on 2nd June 1969.

Interpretation

2.—(1) In this Order unless the context otherwise requires:—

(*a*) "an appeal tribunal" means an industrial tribunal established under section 12 of the Industrial Training Act 1964;

(*b*) "assessment" means an assessment of an employer to the levy;

(*c*) "the Board" means the Ceramics, Glass and Mineral Products Industry Training Board;

(*d*) "business" means any activities of industry or commerce;

(*e*) "ceramics, glass and mineral products establishment" means an establishment in Great Britain engaged in the third base period wholly or mainly in the ceramics, glass and mineral products industry for a total of twenty-seven or more weeks or, being an establishment that commenced to carry on business in the third base period, for a total number of weeks exceeding one-half of the number of weeks in the part of the said period commencing with the day on which business was commenced and ending on the last day thereof;

(*f*) "the ceramics, glass and mineral products industry" means any one or more of the activities which, subject to the provisions of paragraph 2 of the Schedule to the industrial training order, are specified in paragraph 1 of that Schedule as the activities of the ceramics, glass and mineral products industry;

(a) 1964 c. 16.

(g) "emoluments" means all emoluments assessable to income tax under Schedule E (other than pensions), being emoluments from which tax under that Schedule is deductible, whether or not tax in fact falls to be deducted from any particular payment thereof;

(h) "employer" means a person who is an employer in the ceramics, glass and mineral products industry at any time in the third levy period, but does not include a person in whose case the sum of the emoluments paid or payable to all persons in his employment in the said industry in the third base period and (if the employer is a company) to all persons in the employment of an associated company of the company in the said industry in the said period is less than £5,000;

(i) "the industrial training order" means the Industrial Training (Ceramics, Glass and Mineral Products Board) Order 1969(a);

(j) "the levy" means the levy imposed by the Board in respect of the third levy period;

(k) "notice" means a notice in writing;

(l) "pottery" includes bone china, vitreous china, porcelain, earthenware, wall tiles, sanitary fire clay ware, sanitary earthenware and similar wares;

(m) "related or administrative activities" has the meaning assigned to that expression in paragraph 3 of the Schedule to this Order;

(n) "the third base period" means the period of twelve months that commenced on 6th April 1968;

(o) "the third levy period" means the period commencing with the day upon which this Order comes into operation and ending on 31st March 1970;

(p) other expressions have the same meaning as in the industrial training order.

(2) In the case where a ceramics, glass and mineral products establishment is taken over (whether directly or indirectly) by an employer in succession to, or jointly with, another person, a person employed at any time in the third base period at or from the establishment shall be deemed, for the purposes of this Order, to have been so employed by the employer carrying on the said establishment on the day upon which this Order comes into operation, and any reference in this Order to persons employed in the third base period shall be construed accordingly.

(3) Any reference in this Order to an establishment that commences to carry on business or that ceases to carry on business shall not be taken to apply where the location of the establishment is changed but its business is continued wholly or mainly at or from the new location, or where the suspension of activities is of a temporary or seasonal nature.

(4) For the purposes of this Order no regard shall be had to the emoluments of any person employed as follows:—

(a) by a harbour authority when acting in that capacity;

(b) wholly as a registered dock worker in dock work;

(c) wholly in the supply of food or drink for immediate consumption.

(5) The Interpretation Act 1889(b) shall apply to the interpretation of this Order as it applies to the interpretation of an Act of Parliament.

(a) S.I. 1969/689 (1969 II, p. 1858).   (b) 1889 c. 63.

Imposition of the Levy

3.—(1) The levy to be imposed by the Board on employers in respect of the third levy period shall be assessed in accordance with the provisions of this Article.

(2) The levy shall be assessed by the Board separately in respect of each ceramics, glass and mineral products establishment of an employer, but in agreement with the employer one assessment may be made in respect of any number of such establishments, in which case those establishments shall be deemed for the purposes of that assessment to constitute one establishment.

(3) Subject to the provisions of this Article, the levy assessed in respect of a ceramics, glass and mineral products establishment of an employer shall be an amount equal to 0.75 per cent. of the sum of the emoluments of all the persons employed by the employer at or from that establishment in the third base period.

(4) In respect of any ceramics, glass and mineral products establishment described in the Schedule to this Order the amount of the levy shall be twice the amount determined in accordance with the foregoing paragraph.

(5) The amount of the levy imposed in respect of a ceramics, glass and mineral products establishment that ceases to carry on business in the third levy period shall be in the same proportion to the amount that would otherwise be due under paragraph (3) or (4) of this Article as the number of days between the commencement of the said levy period and the date of cessation of business (both dates inclusive) bears to the number of days in the said levy period.

Assessment Notices

4.—(1) The Board shall serve an assessment notice on every employer assessed to the levy, but one notice may comprise two or more assessments.

(2) An assessment notice shall state the amount of the levy payable by the person assessed to the levy, and that amount shall be equal to the total amount (rounded down where necessary to the nearest £1) of the levy assessed by the Board under Article 3 of this Order in respect of each establishment included in the notice.

(3) An assessment notice shall state the Board's address for the service of a notice of appeal or of an application for an extension of time for appealing.

(4) An assessment notice may be served on the person assessed to the levy either by delivering it to him personally or by leaving it, or sending it to him by post, at his last known address or place of business in the United Kingdom or, if that person is a corporation, by leaving it, or sending it by post to the corporation, at such address or place of business or at its registered or principal office.

Payment of the Levy

5.—(1) Subject to the provisions of this Article and of Articles 6 and 7, the amount of the levy payable under an assessment notice served by the Board shall be due and payable to the Board one month after the date of the notice.

(2) The amount of an assessment shall not be recoverable by the Board until there has expired the time allowed for appealing against the assessment by Article 7(1) of this Order and any further period or periods of time that the Board or an appeal tribunal may have allowed for appealing under paragraph (2) or (3) of that Article, or, where an appeal is brought, until the appeal is decided or withdrawn.

Withdrawal of Assessment

6.—(1) The Board may, by a notice served on the person assessed to the levy in the same manner as an assessment notice, withdraw an assessment if that person has appealed against that assessment under the provisions of Article 7 of this Order and the appeal has not been entered in the Register of Appeals kept under the appropriate Regulations specified in paragraph (5) of that Article.

(2) The withdrawal of an assessment shall be without prejudice—

(*a*) to the power of the Board to serve a further assessment notice in respect of any establishment to which that assessment related; or

(*b*) to any other assessment included in the original assessment notice, and such notice shall thereupon have effect as if any assessment withdrawn by the Board had not been included therein.

Appeals

7.—(1) A person assessed to the levy may appeal to an appeal tribunal against the assessment within one month from the date of the service of the assessment notice or within any further period or periods of time that may be allowed by the Board or an appeal tribunal under the following provisions of this Article.

(2) The Board by notice may for good cause allow a person assessed to the levy to appeal to an appeal tribunal against the assessment at any time within the period of four months from the date of the service of the assessment notice or within such further period or periods as the Board may allow before such time as may then be limited for appealing has expired.

(3) If the Board shall not allow an application for extension of time for appealing, an appeal tribunal shall upon application made to the tribunal by the person assessed to the levy have the like powers as the Board under the foregoing paragraph.

(4) In the case of an establishment that ceases to carry on business in the third levy period on any day after the date of the service of the relevant assessment notice, the foregoing provisions of this Article shall have effect as if for the period of four months from the date of the service of the assessment notice mentioned in paragraph (2) of this Article there were substituted the period of six months from the date of the cessation of business.

(5) An appeal or an application to an appeal tribunal under this Article shall be made in accordance with the Industrial Tribunals (England and Wales) Regulations 1965(**a**) as amended by the Industrial Tribunals (England and Wales) (Amendment) Regulations 1967(**b**) except where the establishment to which the relevant assessment relates is wholly in Scotland in which case the appeal or application shall be made in accordance with the Industrial Tribunals (Scotland) Regulations 1965(**c**) as amended by the Industrial Tribunals (Scotland) (Amendment) Regulations 1967(**d**).

(6) The powers of an appeal tribunal under paragraph (3) of this Article may be exercised by the President of the Industrial Tribunals (England and Wales) or by the President of the Industrial Tribunals (Scotland) as the case may be.

Evidence

8.—(1) Upon the discharge by a person assessed to the levy of his liability

---

(**a**) S.I. 1965/1101 (1965 II, p. 2805).   (**b**) S.I. 1967/301 (1967 I, p. 1040).
(**c**) S.I. 1965/1157 (1965 II, p. 3266).   (**d**) S.I. 1967/302 (1967 I, p. 1050).

under an assessment the Board shall if so requested issue to him a certificate to that effect.

(2) The production in any proceedings of a document purporting to be certified by the Secretary of the Board to be a true copy of an assessment or other notice issued by the Board or purporting to be a certificate such as is mentioned in the foregoing paragraph of this Article shall, unless the contrary is proved, be sufficient evidence of the document and of the facts stated therein.

14th May 1969.

Barbara Castle,
First Secretary of State and
Secretary of State for Employment and Productivity.

Article 3(4)

SCHEDULE

ESTABLISHMENTS TO WHICH ARTICLE 3(4) OF THIS ORDER APPLIES

1. Any ceramics, glass and mineral products establishment that was engaged wholly or mainly in the activities specified in paragraph 2 of this Schedule.

2. The said activities are the activities following or any of them, that is to say—

(*a*) the manufacture of glass;

(*b*) the manufacture of articles or other products wholly or mainly from glass;

(*c*) the calibrating, graduating or toughening of glass or glass articles;

(*d*) the milling, grinding or mixing of any material for the purpose of the manufacture of pottery;

(*e*) the manufacture of pottery;

(*f*) related or administrative activities.

3. "Related or administrative activities" means activities of a kind to which paragraph 1(*o*) of the Schedule to the industrial training order applies, being activities undertaken in relation to any activities specified in the last foregoing paragraph.

EXPLANATORY NOTE

(*This Note is not part of the Order.*)

This Order gives effect to proposals submitted to the Secretary of State for Employment and Productivity by the Ceramics, Glass and Mineral Products Industry Training Board for the imposition of a further levy upon employers in the ceramics, glass and mineral products industry for the purpose of raising money towards the expenses of the Board.

The levy is to be imposed in respect of the third levy period commencing with the day on which this Order comes into operation and ending on 31st March 1970. The levy will be assessed by the Board and there will be a right of appeal against an assessment to an industrial tribunal.

STATUTORY INSTRUMENTS

1969 No. 707 (S.59)

AGRICULTURE

HILL LANDS

The Hill Cattle Subsidy Payment (Scotland) (Amendment) Order 1969

Made - - - -	16*th May* 1969
Laid before Parliament	23*rd May* 1969
Coming into Operation	24*th May* 1969

In exercise of the powers conferred on me by section 14(3) of the Hill Farming Act 1946(a) as amended by section 8 of the Livestock Rearing Act 1951(b), and of all other powers enabling me in that behalf, and with the approval of the Treasury, I hereby make the following order:—

Citation, commencement and interpretation

1.—(1) This order may be cited as the Hill Cattle Subsidy Payment (Scotland) (Amendment) Order 1969 and shall come into operation on 24th May 1969.

(2) The Interpretation Act 1889(c) shall apply for the interpretation of this order as it applies for the interpretation of an Act of Parliament.

Increase in amount of subsidy payment

2. Article 2 of the Hill Cattle Subsidy Payment (Scotland) Order 1968(d) (which specifies the amount of a subsidy payment under the Hill Cattle (Scotland) Scheme 1968(e)) shall have effect in respect of the year 1969 and each of the three next succeeding years with the substitution of £22 5s. 0d. for £21 5s. 0d.

William Ross,
One of Her Majesty's Principal
Secretaries of State.

St. Andrew's House,
Edinburgh.
13th May 1969.

We approve.

J. McCann,
Walter Harrison,
Two of the Lords Commissioners
of Her Majesty's Treasury.

16th May 1969.

EXPLANATORY NOTE

(*This Note is not part of the Order.*)

The Hill Cattle (Scotland) Scheme 1968 sets out the conditions subject to which subsidy payments may be made in the year 1968 and each of the next four succeeding years in respect of breeding cows grazed and maintained on hill land in Scotland. This Order increases the amount of such payments for 1969 and each of the three following years from £21 5s. to £22 5s. per cow.

(a) 1946 c. 73.   (b) 1951 c. 18.   (c) 1889 c. 63.
(d) S.I. 1968/982 (1968 II, p.2598).   (e) S.I. 1968/981 (1968 II, p.2590).

STATUTORY INSTRUMENTS

1969 No. 708 (S.60)

AGRICULTURE

LIVESTOCK INDUSTRIES

The Beef Cow Subsidy Payment (Scotland) (Amendment) Order 1969

Made - - - -	16*th May* 1969
Laid before Parliament	23*rd May* 1969
Coming into Operation	24*th May* 1969

In exercise of the powers conferred on me by section 12(4) and (7) of the Agriculture Act 1967(a) and of all other powers enabling me in that behalf, and with the approval of the Treasury, I hereby make the following order:—

Citation, commencement and interpretation

1.—(1) This order may be cited as the Beef Cow Subsidy Payment (Scotland) (Amendment) Order 1969 and shall come into operation on 24th May 1969.

(2) The Interpretation Act 1889(b) shall apply for the interpretation of this order as it applies for the interpretation of an Act of Parliament.

Increase in amount of subsidy payment

2. Article 3 of the Beef Cow Subsidy Payment (Scotland) Order 1967(c) as amended (d) (which specifies the amount of a subsidy payment under the Beef Cow (Scotland) Scheme 1967(e)) shall have effect in relation to the prescribed date in the year 1969 and in each of the two next succeeding years with the substitution of £10 for £9.

William Ross,
One of Her Majesty's Principal
Secretaries of State.

St. Andrew's House,
Edinburgh.
13th May 1969.

We approve.
16th May 1969.

J. McCann,
Walter Harrison,
Two of the Lords Commissioners
of Her Majesty's Treasury.

(a) 1967 c. 22.   (b) 1889 c. 63.   (c) S.I. 1967/1561 (1967 III, p. 4333).
(d) S.I. 1968/983 (1968 II, p. 2600).   (e) S.I. 1967/1560 (1967 III, p. 4328).

EXPLANATORY NOTE

(This Note is not part of the Order.)

The Beef Cow (Scotland) Scheme 1967 sets out the conditions subject to which subsidy payments may be made in respect of cows comprised in herds kept primarily for breeding calves for beef. This Order increases the amount of such payments for 1969 and each of the two following years from £9 to £10 per cow.

STATUTORY INSTRUMENTS

1969 No. 709 (C. 16)

EDUCATION, ENGLAND AND WALES

The Education (No. 2) Act 1968 (Commencement No. 1) Order 1969

Made - - - *15th May* 1969

The Secretary of State for Education and Science, in exercise of the powers conferred upon him by Section 4(1) of the Education (No. 2) Act 1968(a), hereby orders as follows:—

1. This Order may be cited as the Education (No. 2) Act 1968 (Commencement No. 1) Order 1969.

2. The appointed day for the coming into force of the Education (No. 2) Act 1968 for the purposes of colleges of education shall be 1st July 1969.

Given under the Official Seal of the Secretary of State for Education and Science on 15th May 1969.

(L.S.)

Edward Short,
Secretary of State for
Education and Science.

EXPLANATORY NOTE
(This Note is not part of the Order.)

This Order appoints 1st July 1969 as the day by which local education authorities must make instruments and articles of government for colleges of education maintained by them.

(a) 1968 c. 37.

STATUTORY INSTRUMENTS

1969 No. 710

PENSIONS

The Superannuation (Local Government and Other Employments) Interchange Rules 1969

Made - - -	*16th May* 1969
Laid before Parliament	*27th May* 1969
Coming into Operation	*1st July* 1969

The Minister of Housing and Local Government, in exercise of his powers under sections 2 and 15 of the Superannuation (Miscellaneous Provisions) Act 1948(a), as amended by section 11(6) of the Superannuation (Miscellaneous Provisions) Act 1967(b), and of all other powers enabling him in that behalf, hereby makes the following rules:—

Title and commencement

1. These rules may be cited as the Superannuation (Local Government and Other Employments) Interchange Rules 1969 and shall come into operation on 1st July 1969.

Interpretation

2. The Interpretation Act 1889(c) shall apply for the interpretation of these rules as it applies for the interpretation of an Act of Parliament.

Amendment of Interchange Rules

3. The rules specified in column (1) of the schedule to these rules shall be amended by adding thereto in each case the following three rules (which shall be numbered as specified in column (2) thereof), namely :—

"*Extension of time*

(1) Notwithstanding any other provision of these rules, the authorities may at any time, on the application of a person who desires these rules to apply to him, agree to extend any of the following periods, namely—

    (*a*) a period of 12 months after the person ceased to be employed in employment of a class to which these rules apply ;

    (*b*) a period of 6 months after any period of national service ; or

    (*c*) a period of 3 months within which the person must notify in writing that he desires these rules to apply to him.

(2) An authority to whom a person must furnish particulars of service or pay an amount equal to any sum paid to him by way of return of contributions may at any time, on the application of that person, extend the period within which he must take such action.

(a) 1948 c. 33.   (b) 1967 c. 28.
(c) 1889 c. 63.

(3) Where a period is extended pursuant to paragraph (1)(*a*) of this rule in respect of a person who—

    (*a*) ceased to be in local government employment before 1st July 1968 and

    (*b*) entered the employment of the other authority before 1st July 1969.
then, notwithstanding any other provision of these rules, the transfer value payable by the authority maintaining the fund to which he was a contributor shall be calculated by reference to his age on 1st July 1969.

(4) Where a period is extended pursuant to paragraph (1)(*a*) of this rule in respect of a person who—

    (*a*) has ceased to be in local government employment and

    (*b*) entered the employment of the other authority on or after 1st July 1969,
then, notwithstanding any other provision of these rules, the transfer value payable by the authority maintaining the fund to which he was a contributor shall be calculated by reference to his age on entering the employment of the other authority.

Interest on returned contributions

(1) Where a period is extended pursuant to paragraph (1)(*a*) of the last preceding rule in respect of a person who has ceased to be in local government employment, that person may be required by the authority maintaining the fund to which he was a contributor to make a payment by way of compound interest on any sum paid to him by way of return of contributions, other than voluntary contributions, on or after ceasing to be in that employment at a rate of 3% per annum with half-yearly rests for a period beginning either with the date 12 months after the date on which he left that employment or, where this is later, the date on which he received such sum, and ending with the date on which he notified in writing that he desired these rules to apply to him.

(2) The interest payable under this rule shall not exceed a sum equal to one-half of the difference between the transfer value payable by virtue of paragraph (3) or (4) of the last preceding rule, as may be applicable, and the transfer value which would be payable if calculated by reference to the person's age on ceasing to be in that employment.

(3) A person required to pay interest under this rule shall pay it to the authority whose employment he has entered, together with any amount he may be required to pay in respect of returned contributions ; and the authority maintaining the superannuation fund to which he was a contributor before leaving local government employment shall reduce the transfer value payable by them by a corresponding amount.

Termination of entitlement

Notwithstanding anything in the Act of 1937 or any local Act scheme, when these rules become applicable to a person who has ceased to be in employment in which he was a contributory employee or local Act contributor, he shall cease to be entitled to any payment out of the superannuation fund to which he contributed while in that employment in respect of any service of which account was taken in calculating the transfer value payable under these rules out of that fund, other than a payment by way of return of voluntary contributions.".

The Superannuation (English Local Government and Isle of Man) Interchange Rules 1951

4. The Superannuation (English Local Government and Isle of Man) Interchange Rules 1951**(a)** shall be further amended as follows :—

(*a*) after rule 1(2) (which relates to interpretation) there shall be inserted the following paragraph : —

"(2A) In rules 12 and 13 of these rules "the authorities" means an Isle of Man authority and the authority maintaining the superannuation fund to which a person is or first became a contributor or, as the case may be, was a contributor ; and "authority" means one of the authorities." ;

(*b*) in rule 2(1) (which relates to transfers from local government employment to the employment of an Isle of Man authority and provides that the rules may apply to a person who inter alia has not become entitled to any benefit), before the words "any benefit under the Act of 1937", there shall be inserted the words "and received payment of" ;

(*c*) at the end of proviso (*a*) to rule 4(1) (which relates to transfers from the employment of an Isle of Man authority to local government employment and provides that the rules may apply to a person who inter alia pays certain sums), there shall be added the words "together with any interest which he may be required to pay" ;

(*d*) rule 7 (which terminates the right to a return of contributions where rule 2 has become applicable) shall cease to have effect.

The Superannuation (English Local Government and Northern Ireland) Interchange Rules 1952 and 1958

5. The Superannuation (English Local Government and Northern Ireland) Interchange Rules 1952**(b)** as amended **(c)** shall be further amended as follows :—

(*a*) after rule 1(2) (which relates to interpretation) there shall be inserted the following paragraph : —

"(2A) In rules 12 and 13 of these rules "the authorities" means the Committee or the Corporation, as the case may be, and the authority maintaining the superannuation fund to which a person is or first became a contributor or, as the case may be, was a contributor ; and "authority" means one of the authorities." ;

(*b*) in rule 2(1) (which relates to transfers from local government employment to the employment of a Northern Ireland employing authority and provides that the rules may apply to a person who inter alia has not become entitled to any benefit), before the words "any benefit under the Act of 1937", there shall be inserted the words "and received payment of" ;

(*c*) at the end of proviso (*a*) to rule 4(1) (which relates to transfers from the employment of a Northern Ireland employing authority to local government employment and provides that the rules may apply to a person who inter alia pays certain sums), there shall be added the words "together with any interest which he may be required to pay" ;

(*d*) rule 7 (which terminates the right to a return of contributions where rule 2 has become applicable) shall cease to have effect ;

(a) S.I. 1951/309 (1951 II, p. 148).   **(b)** S.I. 1952/937 (1952 II, p.2354).
(c) S.I. 1958/2136 (1958 II, p.1822).

(*e*) at the end thereof there shall be added the following rule :—

"Calculation of transfer value following extension of time

15. Where an extension of time is granted pursuant to rule 12(1)(*a*) of these rules in respect of a person who enters local government employment, any provision of these rules requiring payment of a transfer value calculated in accordance with the transfer value regulations shall be read as requiring payment of a transfer value calculated as if the person were ceasing to be in local government employment and entering the employment of the other authority under these rules.".

*The Superannuation (Local Government and National Health Service)
Interchange Rules* 1955

6. The Superannuation (Local Government and National Health Service) Interchange Rules 1955(**a**) shall be further amended as follows :—

  (*a*) after rule 2(1) (which relates to interpretation) there shall be inserted the following paragraph :—

  "(1A) In rules 13 and 14 of these rules "the authorities" means the Secretary of State for Social Services and the authority maintaining the superannuation fund to which a person is or first became a contributor or, as the case may be, was a contributor ; and "authority" means one of the authorities." ;

  (*b*) rule 3(2), (3) and (4) (which contain provisions for the extension of periods of time) shall cease to have effect ;

  (*c*) in rule 4(1) (which relates to transfers from local government employment to employment in the National Health Service and provides that the rules may apply to a person who inter alia has not become entitled to any benefit)—

  (i) before the words "any benefit under the Acts of 1937 to 1953", there shall be inserted the words "and received payment of" ; and

  (ii) proviso (*d*) shall cease to have effect ;

  (*d*) rule 8 (which terminates the right to a return of contributions where rule 4 has become applicable) shall cease to have effect.

The Superannuation (English Local Government and Northern Ireland Civil Service) Interchange Rules 1957

7. The Superannuation (English Local Government and Northern Ireland Civil Service) Interchange Rules 1957(**b**) shall be further amended as follows :—

  (*a*) after rule 2(1) (which relates to interpretation) there shall be inserted the following paragraph :—

  "(1A) In rules 13 and 14 of these rules "the authorities" means the Ministry of Finance and the authority maintaining the superannuation fund to which a person is or first became a contributor or, as the case may be, was a contributor ; and "authority" means one of the authorities." ;

  (*b*) in rule 3(1) (which relates to transfers from local government employment to the Civil Service of Northern Ireland and provides that the rules may apply to a person who inter alia has not become entitled to any benefit)—

  (i) in sub-paragraph (*b*) the words from "but owing to causes" to the

---

(**a**) S.I. 1955/1494 (1955 II, p. 1758).   (**b**) S.I. 1957/1155 (1957 II, p. 1774).

words "twelve months", and in sub-paragraph (d) the words from "but owing to causes" to the end of the sub-paragraph, shall cease to have effect ;

(ii) in proviso (iii), for the words "who became entitled on leaving his former employment to any benefit", there shall be substituted the words "who on leaving his former employment became entitled to and received payment of any benefit" ;

(c) in rule 5 (which relates to transfers from the Civil Service of Northern Ireland to local government employment and provides that the rules may apply to a person who inter alia has not been granted a pension), for the words "having been granted", there shall be substituted the words "being granted and receiving payment of" ;

(d) rule 6 (which contains provisions with respect to breaks in service) and rule 9 (which terminates the right to a return of contributions where rule 3 has become applicable) shall cease to have effect ;

(e) at the end thereof there shall be added the following rule : —

"Calculation of transfer value following extension of time

16. Where an extension of time is granted pursuant to rule 13(1)(a) of these rules in respect of a person who enters local government employment, any provision of these rules requiring payment of a transfer value calculated in accordance with the transfer value regulations shall be read as requiring payment of a transfer value calculated as if the person were ceasing to be in local government employment and entering the employment of the other authority under these rules.".

The Superannuation (English Local Government and Northern Ireland Health Service) Interchange Rules 1957

8. The Superannuation (English Local Government and Northern Ireland Health Service) Interchange Rules 1957(**a**) shall be further amended as follows :—

(a) after rule 2(1) (which relates to interpretation) there shall be inserted the following paragraph : —

"(1A) In rules 12 and 13 of these rules "the authorities" means the Ministry and the authority maintaining the superannuation fund to which a person is or first became a contributor or, as the case may be, was a contributor ; and "authority" means one of the authorities.";

(b) rule 3(2), (3) and (4) (which contain provisions for the extension of periods of time) shall cease to have effect ;

(c) in rule 4(1) (which relates to transfers from local government employment to employment in the Northern Ireland Health Service and provides that the rules may apply to a person who inter alia has not become entitled to any benefit)—

(i) before the words "any benefit under the Acts of 1937 to 1953", there shall be inserted the words "and received payment of" ;

(ii) proviso (d) shall cease to have effect ;

(d) at the end of proviso (a) to rule 6(1) (which relates to transfers from employment in the Northern Ireland Health Service to local government employment and provides that the rules may apply to a person who inter alia pays certain sums), there shall be added the words "together with any interest which he may be required to pay" ;

(**a**) S.I. 1957/2197 (1957 II, p.1783).

(*e*) rule 8 (which terminates the right to a return of contributions where rule 4 has become applicable) shall cease to have effect.

The Superannuation (Local Government, Social Workers and Health Education Staff) Interchange Rules 1959

9. The Superannuation (Local Government, Social Workers and Health Education Staff) Interchange Rules 1959(**a**) shall be further amended as follows :—

(*a*) after rule 2(1) (which relates to interpretation) there shall be inserted the following paragraph : —

"(1A) In rules 13 and 14 of these rules "the authorities" means the appropriate Committee and the authority maintaining the superannuation fund to which a person is or first became a contributor or, as the case may be, was a contributor ; and "authority" means one of the authorities." ;

(*b*) rule 3(2) and (3) (which contain provisions for the extension of periods of time) shall cease to have effect ;

(*c*) in rule 4(1) (which relates to transfers from local government employment to social welfare or health education employment and provides that the rules may apply to a person who inter alia has not become entitled to any benefit), before the words "any benefit under the Acts of 1937 to 1953", there shall be inserted the words "and received payment of" ;

(*d*) in rule 4, the proviso to sub-paragraph (*c*) of paragraph (2) (which provides for extension of time) and paragraph (5) (which relates to transfer values) shall cease to have effect ;

(*e*) in rule 7(1) (which relates to transfers from social welfare or health education employment to local government employment and provides that the rules may apply to a person who inter alia has not been granted a pension), for the words "having been granted", there shall be substituted the words "being granted and receiving payment of" ;

(*f*) rule 8 (which terminates the right to a return of contributions where rule 4 has become applicable) shall cease to have effect.

The Superannuation (English Local Government and Jersey) Interchange Rules 1961

10. The Superannuation (English Local Government and Jersey) Interchange Rules 1961(**b**) shall be further amended as follows :—

(*a*) after rule 2(1) (which relates to interpretation) there shall be inserted the following paragraph : —

"(1A) In rules 11 and 12 of these rules "the authorities" means the employing authority and the authority maintaining the superannuation fund to which a person is or first became a contributor or, as the case may be, was a contributor ; and "authority" means one of the authorities." ;

(*b*) in rule 3(1) (which relates to transfers from local government employment to pensionable employment in the Island of Jersey, and provides that the rules may apply to a person who inter alia has not become entitled to any benefit)—

(i) in proviso (ii), the words "or within such longer period as the

(**a**) S.I. 1959/1573 (1959 II, p. 2015).   (**b**) S.I. 1961/316 (1961 I, p.501).

employing authority may in any particular case allow" shall cease to have effect;

    (ii) in proviso (iii), for the words "who became entitled on leaving his former employment to any benefit" there shall be substituted the words "who on leaving his former employment became entitled to and received payment of any benefit";

  (c) in rule 5 (which relates to transfers from pensionable employment in the Island of Jersey to local government employment and provides that the rules may apply to a person who inter alia has not become entitled to any benefit), for the words "having become entitled to or been granted" there shall be substituted the words "becoming entitled to and receiving payment of";

  (d) rule 7 (which terminates the right to a return of contributions where rule 3 has become applicable) shall cease to have effect;

  (e) at the end thereof there shall be added the following rule:—

"Calculation of transfer value following extension of time

14. Where an extension of time is granted pursuant to rule 11(1)(a) of these rules in respect of a person who enters local government employment, any provision of these rules requiring payment of a transfer value calculated in accordance with the transfer value regulations shall be read as requiring payment of a transfer value calculated as if the person were ceasing to be in local government employment and entering the employment of the other authority under these rules.".

The Superannuation (Local Government and Public Transport Services) Interchange Rules 1965

11. The Superannuation (Local Government and Public Transport Services) Interchange Rules 1965(**a**) shall be further amended as follows :—

  (a) after rule 2(1) (which relates to interpretation) there shall be inserted the following paragraph:—

    "(1A) In rules 12 and 13 of these rules "the authorities" means the transport authority and the authority maintaining the superannuation fund to which a person is or first became a contributor or, as the case may be, was a contributor; and "authority" means one of the authorities.";

  (b) rule 3(2) and (3) (which contain provisions for the extension of periods of time) shall cease to have effect;

  (c) in rule 4 (which relates to transfers from local government employment to transport employment and provides that the rules may apply to a person who inter alia has not become entitled to any benefit)—

    (i) in paragraph (1), before the words "any benefit under the Acts of 1937 to 1953", there shall be inserted the words "and received payment of";

    (ii) in paragraph (2), the words from "or within such longer period" to the word "allow", where it first occurs, and the proviso to subparagraph (c), shall cease to have effect; and

    (iii) paragraph (5) shall cease to have effect;

(a) S.I. 1965/1676 (1965 III, p.4771).

(d) in rule 6(1) (which relates to transfers from transport employment to local government employment and provides that the rules may apply to a person who inter alia has not been granted a pension)—

 (i) for the words "having been granted", there shall be substituted the words "being granted and receiving payment of"; and

 (ii) in proviso (i), the words from "or within such longer period" to the word "allow" shall cease to have effect;

(e) rule 8 (which terminates the right to a return of contributions where rule 4 has become applicable) shall cease to have effect.

Rule 3

SCHEDULE

NUMBERING OF NEW RULES

(1)	(2)		
	Number of new rule		
Title of rules	Extension of time	Interest on returned contributions	Termination of entitlement
The Superannuation (English Local Government and Isle of Man) Interchange Rules 1951	12	13	14
The Superannuation (English Local Government and Northern Ireland) Interchange Rules 1952	12	13	14
The Superannuation (Local Government and National Health Service) Interchange Rules 1955	13	14	15
The Superannuation (English Local Government and Northern Ireland Civil Service) Interchange Rules 1957	13	14	15
The Superannuation (English Local Government and Northern Ireland Health Service) Interchange Rules 1957	12	13	14
The Superannuation (Local Government, Social Workers and Health Education Staff) Interchange Rules 1959	13	14	15
The Superannuation (English Local Government and Jersey) Interchange Rules 1961	11	12	13
The Superannuation (Local Government and Public Transport Services) Interchange Rules 1965	12	13	14

Given under the official seal of the Minister of Housing and Local Government on 16th May 1969.

(L.S.)   *Anthony Greenwood,*
                    Minister of Housing and Local Government.

EXPLANATORY NOTE

(This Note is not part of the Rules.)

These Rules add three new, identical, provisions to each of eight sets of rules which relate to the superannuation rights of persons transferring in either direction between employment in English local government and other pensionable employment—namely, employment under certain public authorities in (1) the Isle of Man, (2) Northern Ireland and (3) Jersey, and employment in (4) the National Health Service, (5) the Northern Ireland Civil Service, (6) the Northern Ireland Health Service, (7) Social Welfare and Health Education and (8) Public Transport.

The new provisions—

(i) give the old and the new pension fund authorities discretion to extend the permissible length of any break between employments and the time limit for compliance with various conditions ;

(ii) provide, where such a break has been extended, for the payment of interest by a person who holds superannuation contributions returned on leaving local government employment ;

(iii) terminate any right to any payment out of a local government superannuation fund when the rules have been applied to a person (in substance replacing an existing provision the terms of which have given rise to doubts).

They are given retrospective effect to a limited extent under the express powers of, and subject to the safeguards required by, section 2(5) of the Superannuation (Miscellaneous Provisions) Act 1948.

The eight sets of rules are then further amended individually as follows :—

(a) a definition is added as a link with the new provisions ;

(b) existing (more limited) provisions relating to the subject matter of the new provisions are revoked, and some minor consequential amendments are made ;

(c) an unrelated amendment extends the scope of the rules to include persons who have become entitled to a pension in respect of their old employment but have not started to receive payment.

STATUTORY INSTRUMENTS

1969 No. 713

ROAD TRAFFIC

The Motor Cars (Driving Instruction) (Amendment) Regulations 1969

Made - - -	16*th May* 1969
Laid before Parliament	30*th May* 1969
Coming into Operation	31*st May* 1969

The Minister of Transport, in exercise of his powers under sections 10 and 18 of the Road Traffic (Driving Instruction) Act 1967(**a**) and of all other powers enabling him in that behalf, hereby makes the following Regulations:—

1. These Regulations shall come into operation on the 31st May 1969 and may be cited as the Motor Cars (Driving Instruction) (Amendment) Regulations 1969.

2. The Interpretation Act 1889(**b**) shall apply for the interpretation of these Regulations as it applies for the interpretation of an Act of Parliament.

3. The Motor Cars (Driving Instruction) Regulations 1969(**c**) shall have effect as though, for the Schedule, there were substituted the Schedule set out in the Schedule to these Regulations.

4. A certificate issued before the date of the coming into operation of these Regulations to a person whose name was in the Register of Approved Driving Instructors as evidence of his name being therein, in the form set out in the Schedule to the Motor Cars (Driving Instruction) Regulations 1969 as in force immediately before the coming into operation of these Regulations, shall, whilst it remains valid, be treated as being in a form prescribed by the said Regulations of 1969 as amended by these Regulations.

Given under the Official Seal of the Minister of Transport the 16th May 1969.

(L.S.)

Richard Marsh,
Minister of Transport.

(**a**) 1967 c. 79.
(**c**) S.I. 1969/85 (1969 I, p. 248).

(**b**) 52 & 53 Vict. c. 63.

SCHEDULE

SCHEDULE

Regulation 12(2)

Form of certificate of registration

MINISTRY OF TRANSPORT APPROVED DRIVING INSTRUCTOR

ROAD TRAFFIC (DRIVING INSTRUCTION) ACT 1967

On behalf of the Minister of Transport, I certify that

is included in the Register of Approved Driving Instructors as qualified to give instruction in the driving of motor cars.

This certificate

is valid until the last day of

No.

SIGNED

DATE

REGISTRAR

SIGNATURE OF HOLDER:—

EXPLANATORY NOTE
(This Note is not part of the Regulations.)

These Regulations amend the Motor Cars (Driving Instruction) Regulations 1969 by prescribing a new form of Certificate as evidence of an instructor's name being in the Register of Approved Driving Instructors (Regulation 3). Certificates already issued in the previous form will remain legal so long as they remain valid (Regulation 4).

STATUTORY   INSTRUMENTS

1969 No. 716

SOCIAL SECURITY

The National Insurance (Industrial Injuries) (Colliery Workers Supplementary Scheme) Amendment Order 1969

Laid before Parliament in draft

Made -	-	-	-		20th May 1969
Coming into Operation					3rd June 1969

Whereas the National Committee for the time being constituted in accordance with the Supplementary Scheme set out in Schedule 1 to the National Insurance (Industrial Injuries) (Colliery Workers Supplementary Scheme) Amendment and Consolidation Order 1963(a) as subsequently varied and amended(b) is the body charged with the administration of that Scheme and has requested the Secretary of State to vary and amend the provisions of the said Supplementary Scheme in manner set out in the following Order :—

Now, therefore, the Secretary of State, in exercise of his powers under section 47(1)(*a*)(ii) of the National Insurance Act 1965(c) as applied by section 82(2) of the National Insurance (Industrial Injuries) Act 1965(d) and of all other powers enabling him in that behalf, hereby makes the following Order, a draft of which has been laid before Parliament and has been approved by resolution of each House of Parliament :—

Citation, commencement and interpretation

1.—(1) This Order, which may be cited as the National Insurance (Industrial Injuries) (Colliery Workers Supplementary Scheme) Amendment Order 1969, shall come into operation on 3rd June 1969.

(2) In this Order " the Scheme " means the Supplementary Scheme set out in Schedule 1 to the National Insurance (Industrial Injuries) (Colliery Workers Supplementary Scheme) Amendment and Consolidation Order 1963 as varied and amended.

Amendment of Article 12 *of the Scheme*

2.—(1) At the end of paragraph (3) of Article 12 of the Scheme there shall be added the words " or any other Act or Regulations, increasing such rate or amount, which may be passed or made after 3rd June 1969 and come into force or operation before 3rd December 1969 " ; and that paragraph shall accordingly have effect as set out in the Schedule to this Order.

(a) S.I. 1963/934 (1963 II, p. 1559).   (b) The relevant amending instruments are
S.I. 1967/1550, 1968/83, 1896 (1967 III, p. 4313; 1968 I, p. 266; III, p. 5039).
(c) 1965 c. 51.   (d) 1965 c. 52.

(2) In paragraph (4)(*a*) of Article 12 of the Scheme for the date " 3rd June 1969 " there shall be substituted the date " 2nd December 1969 ".

Signed by authority of the Secretary of State for Social Services.

David Ennals,
Minister of State,
Department of Health and Social Security.

20th May 1969.

Article 2 SCHEDULE

ARTICLE 12(3) OF THE SCHEME AS AMENDED BY THIS ORDER*

(3) For the purpose of calculating the rate of any supplementary benefit in accordance with this Article any reference in the foregoing paragraphs to the rate of injury benefit or to the amount of any sums paid by way of a disablement pension or by way of a disablement or other gratuity shall be construed as referring to such rate or such amount as the beneficiary would have been entitled to or as would have been paid but for the coming into force or operation of the National Insurance Act 1967 and the National Insurance (Industrial Injuries) (Increase of Benefit and Miscellaneous Provisions) Regulations 1967(a) *or any other Act or Regulations, increasing such rate or amount, which may be passed or made after 3rd June* 1969 *and come into force or operation before 3rd December* 1969.

EXPLANATORY NOTE

(*This Note is not part of the Order.*)

This Order amends the provisions of the National Insurance (Industrial Injuries) Colliery Workers Supplementary Scheme by extending until 2nd December 1969 the period during which the rates of certain supplementary benefits that are related on a fractional basis of calculation to benefits payable under the National Insurance (Industrial Injuries) Act 1965 are not affected by any increase in such benefits payable under the said Act under or by virtue of the National Insurance Act 1967 and the National Insurance (Industrial Injuries) (Increase of Benefit and Miscellaneous Provisions) Regulations 1967 ; and by making comparable provision in respect of any such increases which may become payable under or by virtue of any further legislation taking effect during the relevant period.

* The words added by this order are shown in italics.
(a) S.I. 1967/1223 (1967 II, p. 3565).

1969 No. 722

SOCIAL SECURITY

WORKMEN'S COMPENSATION

The Pneumoconiosis, Byssinosis and Miscellaneous Diseases Benefit (Amendment) Scheme 1969

Laid before Parliament in draft

Made	-	-	*20th May* 1969
Coming into Operation			*27th May* 1969

Whereas a draft of the following Scheme was laid before Parliament and approved by a resolution of each House of Parliament :

Now, therefore, the Secretary of State for Social Services, with the consent of the Treasury, in exercise of his powers under section 5 of the Industrial Injuries and Diseases (Old Cases) Act 1967(a) as extended by section 3(2) of the National Insurance Act 1967(b) and of all other powers enabling him in that behalf, hereby makes the said Scheme :—

Citation, interpretation and commencement

1. This Scheme, which may be cited as the Pneumoconiosis, Byssinosis and Miscellaneous Diseases Benefit (Amendment) Scheme 1969, shall be read as one with the Pneumoconiosis, Byssinosis and Miscellaneous Diseases Benefit Scheme 1966(c) as amended (d) (hereinafter referred to as "the principal Scheme") and shall come into operation on 27th May 1969.

Amendment of Schedule 1 to the principal Scheme

2. Schedule 1 to the principal Scheme shall be amended by the addition, at the end of the first and second columns thereof respectively, of the disease specified in the first column of Schedule 1 hereto and of the occupations set against the said disease in the second column of that Schedule.

Amendment of Article 2 of the principal Scheme

3. In Article 2 of the principal Scheme (benefit payable) for sub-paragraph (*b*) of paragraph (1) there shall be substituted the following paragraph :—

"(*b*) who is a person who is totally or partially disabled (such disablement being likely to be permanent) as a result of any of the diseases set out in the first column of Schedule 1 hereto or who dies or has died as a result of any of those diseases at any time after, in each case, the date set out in Schedule 6 hereto against the number corresponding to the number given to that disease in the first column of the

---

(a) 1967 c. 34.   (b) 1967 c.73.
(c) S.I. 1966/164 (1966 I, p. 303).
(d) The relevant amending instrument is S.I. 1967/1233 (1967 II, p. 3594).

said Schedule 1, if he was a person who has been employed in Great Britain before 5th July 1948 in any of the occupations set against that disease in the second column of the said Schedule 1 : or".

Addition of further Schedule to the principal Scheme

4. After Schedule 5 to the principal Scheme there shall be added the Schedule, to be entitled Schedule 6, set out in Schedule 2 to this Scheme.

Signed by authority of the Secretary of State for Social Services.

> *David Ennals,*
> Minister of State,
> Department of Health and Social Security.

20th May 1969.

We Consent,

> *Joseph Harper,*
> *Walter Harrison,*
> Two of the Lords Commissioners
> of Her Majesty's Treasury.

20th May 1969.

SCHEDULE 1

Article 2

Description of Disease	Nature of occupation
6. Adeno-carcinoma of the nasal cavity or associated air sinuses.	Any occupation involving: attendance for work in or about a building where wooden furniture is manufactured.

SCHEDULE 2

Article 4

SCHEDULE ADDED AFTER SCHEDULE 5
TO THE PRINCIPAL SCHEME

SCHEDULE 6

Article 2

Dates after which death from diseases correspondingly numbered and set out in Schedule 1 must have occurred for provisions of this Scheme to apply.

Number of disease in Schedule 1	Date after which death must have occurred
1	31st December 1949
2	31st December 1949
3	27th July 1967
4	27th July 1967
5	27th July 1967
6	27th May 1969

EXPLANATORY NOTE

(This Note is not part of the Scheme.)

This Scheme amends the Pneumoconiosis, Byssinosis and Miscellaneous Diseases Benefit Scheme 1966 so as to add to the list of diseases, in respect of which benefit is payable out of the Industrial Injuries Fund under the principal Scheme, a further disease falling within the category of malignant or potentially malignant neoplasms.

STATUTORY INSTRUMENTS

1969 No. 723

POLICE

The Police Pensions (Amendment) Regulations 1969

Laid before Parliament in draft

Made - - -	*20th May* 1969
Coming into Operation	*1st June* 1969

In exercise of the powers conferred on me by sections 1 and 3 of the Police Pensions Act 1948**(a)** (read with Article 2(1) of the Minister for the Civil Service Order 1968**(b)**), as extended and amended by section 43 of the Reserve and Auxiliary Forces (Protection of Civil Interests) Act 1951**(c)**, section 5(3) of the Overseas Service Act 1958**(d)** and Schedule 2 thereto, section 1(1) of the Police Pensions Act 1961**(e)**, sections 40, 43(4), 45(4) and 63 of the Police Act 1964**(f)** and Schedules 6 and 9 thereto, sections 35 and 38(4) of the Police (Scotland) Act 1967**(g)** and section 1(4) of the Pensions (Increase) Act 1969**(h)** and paragraph 6 of Schedule 2 thereto, and after consultation with the Police Council for Great Britain, I hereby, with the consent of the Minister for the Civil Service, make the following Regulations, a draft of which has been laid before Parliament and has been approved by resolution of each House of Parliament:—

PART I
GENERAL

1. These Regulations may be cited as the Police Pensions (Amendment) Regulations 1969.

2. These Regulations shall come into operation on 1st June 1969 and shall take effect—

    (*a*) for the purposes of Part II thereof, as from 1st April 1969, and
    (*b*) for the purposes of Part III thereof, as from 1st June 1969.

3. In these Regulations any reference to the principal Regulations is a reference to the Police Pensions Regulations 1966**(i)**, as amended **(j)**.

PART II
PROVISIONS RELATING TO INCREASES IN WIDOWS' PENSIONS AND CHILDREN'S ALLOWANCES AND TAKING EFFECT AS FROM 1ST APRIL 1969

4. For Regulation 73(5) of the principal Regulations (which in certain circumstances authorises the payment to the widow of a policeman of a pension at the basic rate of 33s. 3d. a week in lieu of a gratuity) there shall be substituted the following provision:—

    "(5) The weekly amount of any pension payable under paragraph (4)(*a*) shall be 39s. 4d., increased in accordance with Regulation 93(2) and (4).".

(a) 1948 c. 24.   (b) S.I. 1968/1656 (1968 III, p. 4485).   (c) 1951 c. 65.
(d) 1958 c. 14.   (e) 1961 c. 35.   (f) 1964 c. 48.
(g) 1967 c. 77.   (h) 1969 c. 7.   (i) S.I. 1966/1582 (1966 III, p. 4894).
(j) The relevant amending instrument is S.I. 1968/530 (1968 I, p. 1269).

5. For Regulation 93(3) and (4) of the principal Regulations (which relates to the application of the Pensions (Increase) Act 1962(**a**)) there shall be substituted the following provisions:—

"(3) The appropriate amount mentioned in paragraph (2) shall be the weekly amount of—

(*a*) 42s. 4d., where the weekly amount which falls to be increased under that paragraph is 65s. 2d.;

(*b*) 33s. 10d., where the weekly amount which falls to be so increased is 52s. 3d.;

(*c*) 25s. 6d., where the weekly amount which falls to be so increased is 39s. 4d.

(4) Where such an amount as is mentioned in paragraph (2) is increased in accordance with that paragraph—

(*a*) the amount of the increase under paragraph (2) shall be increased in accordance with Regulation 94 and for the purposes thereof shall be treated as if it were a pension which began for the purposes of the Pensions (Increase) Act 1965(**b**) before 1st April 1957, and

(*b*) the amount of the increase under paragraph (2) (increased as aforesaid) shall be further increased in accordance with Regulation 94A and for the purposes thereof shall be treated as if it were a pension which began for the purposes of the Pensions (Increase) Act 1969 before 1st July 1955.".

6. After Regulation 94 of the principal Regulations (which relates to the application of the Pensions (Increase) Act 1965) there shall be inserted the following Regulation:—

"*Application of Pensions (Increase) Act 1969*

94A.—(1) Where it is provided in these Regulations that an amount shall be increased in accordance with this Regulation or this Part of these Regulations, it shall be increased by the amount, if any, by which a pension of the amount first mentioned would be increased under the Pensions (Increase) Act 1969 if—

(*a*) the person concerned were in receipt of such a pension; and

(*b*) that pension were specified in Part I or II of Schedule 1 to that Act.

(2) For the purposes of this Regulation the reference in section 1(1) of the Pensions (Increase) Act 1969 to an annual rate and the reference in paragraph 2 of Schedule 2 to that Act to an aggregate annual rate shall be construed, respectively, as a reference to the amount which falls to be increased expressed as an annual rate and as a reference to that amount, after any increase thereof in accordance with Regulations 89, 90, 91, 92, 93 and 94, expressed as an annual rate.

(3) Where it is provided in these Regulations that an amount shall be increased in accordance with this Part of these Regulations, any increase in accordance with this Regulation shall be additional to any increase in accordance with any other provision of this Part of these Regulations.".

7. In Regulation 95(*b*) of the principal Regulations (which relates to the duration of an increase in a child's allowance) for the words "the Pensions (Increase) Acts of 1959, of 1962 and of 1965" there shall be substituted the words "the Pensions (Increase) Acts of 1959, of 1962, of 1965 and of 1969".

(**a**)   11 & 12 Eliz. 2 c. 2.   (**b**)   1965 c. 78.

8. For paragraph 3(1) of Part I of Schedule 2 to the principal Regulations (which provides that a widow entitled to an ordinary pension at the standard rate may elect to receive a pension of an amount determined by reference to her husband's rank in lieu of one calculated by reference to his average pensionable pay) there shall be substituted the following provision:—

"3.—(1) Where in respect of any period a widow so elects, then, subject to paragraph 4, the weekly amount of her ordinary pension in respect of that period shall be, if her husband at the time when he ceased to be a regular policeman—

(a) held a rank higher than that of inspector, 65s. 2d.;

(b) held the rank of inspector, 52s. 3d.;

(c) held a rank lower than that of inspector, 39s. 4d.".

9. For paragraph 1 of Scheme I set out in Part II of Schedule 2 to the principal Regulations (which provides that a widow who is entitled to an ordinary pension at the preserved rate and in whose case Scheme II does not apply shall receive a pension of an amount determined by reference to her husband's rank) there shall be substituted the following provision:—

"1. Subject to paragraphs 2, 3 and 4 of this Scheme, the weekly amount of a widow's ordinary pension shall be, if her husband at the time when he ceased to be a regular policeman—

(a) held a rank higher than that of inspector, 65s. 2d.;

(b) held the rank of inspector, 52s. 3d.;

(c) held a rank lower than that of inspector, 39s. 4d.".

10. For paragraphs 1 and 2 of Part I of Schedule 3 to the principal Regulations (which provide that a child entitled to an ordinary allowance shall receive an allowance determined by reference to the parent's rank) there shall be substituted the following paragraphs:—

"1. Subject to this Part and to Parts III and IV of this Schedule, where one of a child's parents is alive, the child's ordinary allowance shall be the weekly amount in the second column of the following Table set opposite to the rank in the first column of the said Table which the parent in respect of whose death the allowance is payable held at the time when he ceased to be a regular policeman:—

TABLE

Parent's Rank	Weekly Amount
	s. d.
Higher than Inspector	19 9
Inspector	15 11
Lower than Inspector	13 4

2. Subject to this Part and to Parts III and IV of this Schedule, where the parent in respect of whose death the allowance is payable was the child's only surviving parent, or in respect of the period after the death of the child's other parent, the child's ordinary allowance shall be the weekly amount in the second column of the following Table set opposite to the rank in the first column of the said Table which the parent in respect of whose death the allowance is payable held at the time when he ceased to be a regular policeman:—

TABLE

Parent's Rank	Weekly Amount
	s. d.
Higher than Inspector	29 6
Inspector	23 9
Lower than Inspector	19 10 ,,

11. For paragraph 1(1) of Part III of Schedule 3 to the principal Regulations (which provides for the discretionary increase of a child's allowance) there shall be substituted the following provision:—

"(1) Where both parents of the child are dead—

    (*a*) subject to the provisions of the following sub-paragraphs and of Part IV of this Schedule, the weekly amount of a child's ordinary allowance may be increased to an amount not exceeding the amount in the second column of the following Table set opposite to the rank in the first column of the said Table which the parent in respect of whose death the allowance is payable held at the time when he ceased to be a regular policeman:—

TABLE

Parent's Rank	Increased Amount
	s. d.
Higher than Inspector	39 4
Inspector	31 6
Lower than Inspector	26 4

    (*b*) subject to sub-paragraph (4) and to Part IV of this Schedule, the weekly amount of a child's special allowance may be increased to an amount equal to the amount, increased in accordance with Part XI of these Regulations, of 2 fifteenths of the average pensionable pay for a week of the parent in respect of whose death the allowance is payable.".

PART III

MISCELLANEOUS PROVISIONS TAKING EFFECT AS FROM 1ST JUNE 1969

12. In Regulation 1(2)(*b*) of the principal Regulations (which relates to ordinary pensions) after the words "assistant chief constable, or a" there shall be inserted the words "deputy assistant commissioner,".

13. In Regulation 66(1)(*b*)(ii) of the principal Regulations (which relates to compulsory retirement on account of age) after the words "if he is a" there shall be inserted the words "deputy assistant commissioner,".

14. For paragraph 2(2) of Part III of Schedule 3 to the principal Regulations (which, as set out in Regulation 7(2) of the Police Pensions (Amendment) Regulations 1968, specifies the amounts up to which children's allowances, in certain cases, may be increased) there shall be substituted the following provision:—

"(2) The appropriate amount referred to in the preceding sub-paragraph shall be—

(a) irrespective of the date of the father's death, 45s. 6d. in the case of the only or eldest child included in a family within the meaning of the Family Allowances Act 1965(a) or of the Family Allowances Act 1945(b), either as originally enacted or as amended by any subsequent enactment;

(b) where the father dies on or after 1st June 1969—

  (i) 32s. 6d., in the case of the second child so included, and

  (ii) 30s. 6d., in the case of each subsequent child so included;

(c) where the father died on or after 9th April 1968 but before 1st June 1969—

  (i) 35s. 6d., in the case of the second child so included, and

  (ii) 33s. 6d., in the case of each subsequent child so included;

(d) where the father died before 9th April 1968—

  (i) 39s. 6d., in the case of the second child so included;

  (ii) 37s. 6d., in the case of the third child so included, and

  (iii) 35s. 0d., in the case of each subsequent child so included.".

James Callaghan,

One of Her Majesty's Principal
Secretaries of State.

20th May 1969.

Consent of the Minister for the Civil Service given under his Official Seal on 20th May 1969.

(L.S.)

K. H. McNeill,

Authorised by the Minister for
the Civil Service.

(a) 1965 c. 53.   (b) 1945 c. 41.

EXPLANATORY NOTE

(This Note is not part of the Regulations.)

These Regulations amend the Police Pensions Regulations 1966.

Part II of the present Regulations relates to increases in widows' pensions and children's allowances. Regulation 2 provides that, for the purposes of Part II, the Regulations shall have effect as from 1st April 1969, the date from which increases authorised by the Pensions (Increase) Act 1969 are payable; this provision is made in exercise of the power conferred by paragraph 6 of Schedule 2 to the 1969 Act.

The 1966 Regulations provide for the increase of widows' pensions and children's allowances (other than flat-rate awards), in accordance with Part XI thereof, by reference to the Pensions (Increase) Acts. They also provide for the increase of flat-rate widows' pensions, in accordance with Regulation 93(2), at age 70 by reference to section 2 of the Pensions (Increase) Act 1962.

Regulation 6 of the present Regulations adds Regulation 94A to Part XI of the 1966 Regulations. Regulation 94A provides for increases or additional increases by reference to the Pensions (Increase) Act 1969 in awards which fall to be increased in accordance with Part XI and also (by virtue of Regulation 5 of the present Regulations) in the amount of the increase at age 70, referred to above, in flat-rate widows' pensions.

The other amendments made by Part II of the present Regulations provide for increases in the flat-rates by reference to which the amounts of certain widows' pensions and children's allowances are determined.

Part III of the present Regulations contains miscellaneous amendments which, by virtue of Regulation 2, take effect as from 1st June 1969, the date on which the Regulations come into operation.

Regulations 12 and 13 of the present Regulations provide that a member of the metropolitan police force holding the newly adopted rank of deputy assistant commissioner shall be treated, as respects entitlement to an ordinary pension and compulsory retirement on account of age, in the same way as such a member holding the rank of commander.

Paragraph 2 of Part III of Schedule 3 to the 1966 Regulations provides, subject to conditions, for a discretionary increase in a child's allowance where the mother would have been entitled to national insurance widow's benefit or retirement pension had her husband satisfied the contribution conditions therefor. Regulation 14 of the present Regulations alters the amounts up to which an allowance payable to a second or subsequent child may be increased where the father dies on or after the coming into operation of the Regulations. (The rates of corresponding national insurance benefits were adjusted by the Family Allowances and National Insurance Act 1968 (c. 40).)

1969 No. 724

POLICE

The Special Constables (Pensions) (Amendment) Regulations 1969

Made - - -	*20th May* 1969
Laid before Parliament	*29th May* 1969
Coming into Operation	*1st June* 1969

In exercise of the powers conferred on me by section 34 of the Police Act 1964(**a**) (as read with section 1(2) of the Police Pensions Act 1961(**b**)) and section 1(4) of the Pensions (Increase) Act 1969(**c**) and paragraph 6 of Schedule 2 thereto, I hereby make the following Regulations :—

1.—(1) These Regulations may be cited as the Special Constables (Pensions) (Amendment) Regulations 1969.

(2) These Regulations shall come into operation on 1st June 1969 and shall have effect—

(*a*) for the purposes of Regulation 3(1)(*a*) thereof, as from 1st April 1969 ;

(*b*) for the purposes of Regulation 3(1)(*b*) thereof, as from 1st June 1969.

2. In these Regulations any reference to the Instrument of 1966 is a reference to the Special Constables (Pensions) Regulations 1966(**d**), as amended (**e**).

3.—(1) In the application of the Police Pensions Regulations 1966(**f**) to the calculation of the pension of the widow, or the allowance of a child, of a special constable under the Instrument of 1966, those Regulations shall apply as amended by—

(*a*) Part II of the Police Pensions (Amendment) Regulations 1969(**g**), and

(*b*) Part III of the said Regulations of 1969,

(which amendments relate, respectively, to increases in widows' and children's awards and alterations in discretionary increases in children's awards).

(2) In accordance with paragraph (1) of this Regulation, for Regulation 15(1) of the Instrument of 1966 (which, as set out in the Special Constables (Pensions) (Amendment) Regulations 1968(**h**), defines the expression "the principal Regulations") there shall be substituted the following paragraph :—

'(1) In these Regulations the expression "the principal Regulations" means the Police Pensions Regulations 1966, as amended by the Police

---

(**a**) 1964 c. 48.
(**b**) 1961 c. 35.
(**c**) 1969 c. 7.
(**d**) S.I. 1966/1590 (1966 III, p. 5008).
(**e**) The relevant amending instrument is S.I. 1968/1989 (1968 III, p. 5420).
(**f**) S.I. 1966/1582 (1966 III, p. 4894).
(**g**) S.I. 1969/723 (1969 II, p. 1950).
(**h**) S.I. 1968/1989 (1968 III, p. 5420).

Pensions (Amendment) (No. 2) Regulations 1967(**a**), the Police Pensions (Amendment) Regulations 1968(**b**) and the Police Pensions (Amendment) Regulations 1969.'

James Callaghan,
One of Her Majesty's Principal
Secretaries of State.

Home Office,
Whitehall.
20th May 1969.

EXPLANATORY NOTE

(This Note is not part of the Regulations.)

These Regulations amend the Special Constables (Pensions) Regulations 1966 which give to special constables and their dependants certain pension benefits for which members of police forces and their dependants are eligible.

The Police Pensions (Amendment) Regulations 1969 provide, with effect from 1st April 1969 (the date from which increases authorised by the Pensions (Increase) Act 1969 are payable), for the increase of certain benefits payable to the widows and children of members of police forces and, with effect from 1st June 1969, for alterations in certain discretionary increases in children's allowances.

These Regulations, with effect from the same dates, make similar provision as respects the benefits payable to widows and children of special constables. (Provision for the retrospective increase of benefits is made in exercise of the power conferred by paragraph 6 of Schedule 2 to the Pensions (Increase) Act 1969.)

(**a**) S.I. 1967/1500 (1967 III, p. 4204). (**b**) S.I. 1968/530 (1968 I, p. 1269).

STATUTORY INSTRUMENTS

1969 No. 731

WAGES COUNCILS

The Cutlery Wages Council (Great Britain) (Abolition) Order 1969

Made - - -		21*st May* 1969
Laid before Parliament		2*nd June* 1969
Coming into Operation		15*th July* 1969

Whereas the Minister of Labour in accordance with section 4 of and Schedule 1 to the Wages Councils Act 1959 **(a)** published notice of his intention to make an order abolishing the Cutlery Wages Council (Great Britain):

And whereas objections were made with respect to the draft order referred to in the said notice:

And whereas under paragraph 5(*b*) of the said Schedule 1 the Minister referred the said draft order to a commission of inquiry for inquiry and report, and in accordance with paragraph 6 of the said Schedule 1 notified to the commission the objections which he wished the commission to take into account:

And whereas the said commission of inquiry made a report recommending the abolition of the said Wages Council, which report the Secretary of State has considered:

Now, therefore, the Secretary of State in exercise of her powers under section 4 of the said Act, and of all other powers enabling her in that behalf, hereby makes the following Order:—

1. The Cutlery Wages Council (Great Britain) is hereby abolished.

2.—(1) This Order may be cited as the Cutlery Wages Council (Great Britain) (Abolition) Order 1969 and shall come into operation on 15th July 1969.

(2) The Interpretation Act 1889**(b)** applies to the interpretation of this Order as it applies to the interpretation of an Act of Parliament.

21st May 1969.

Barbara Castle,
First Secretary of State and Secretary of State
for Employment and Productivity.

EXPLANATORY NOTE

(*This Note is not part of the Order.*)

The Cutlery Trade Board (Great Britain) was established in 1933 under the Trade Boards Acts 1909 and 1918. It became a Wages Council upon the coming

---

(**a**) 1959 c. 69. (**b**) 1889 c. 63.

into force of the Wages Councils Act 1945, by virtue of section 20 of that Act, and was continued in existence by virtue of section 26 of, and Schedule 5 to, the Wages Councils Act 1959.

The Wages Council operated in relation to certain workers employed in the cutlery industry in Great Britain and their employers. This Order abolishes the Wages Council.

1969 No. 732

PENSIONS

The Increase of Pensions (India, Pakistan and Burma) Regulations 1969

Made - - -	22*nd May* 1969
Laid before Parliament	30*th May* 1969
Coming into Operation	31*st May* 1969

The Minister for the Civil Service, in exercise of the powers conferred upon him by section 1(4) of the Pensions (Increase) Act 1969(**a**) and paragraphs 13 and 14 of Schedule 2 to that Act, and of all other powers enabling him in that behalf, hereby makes the following Regulations :—

1. These Regulations may be cited as the Increase of Pensions (India, Pakistan and Burma) Regulations 1969, and shall come into operation on 31st May 1969.

2.—(1) In these Regulations the expression "the Act of" any specified year means the Pensions (Increase) Act of that year.

(2) In these Regulations the expressions "the Regulations of" or "the Rules of" any specified year mean the Increase of Pensions (India, Pakistan and Burma) Regulations or Rules (as the case may be) of that year.

(3) Any reference in these Regulations to the provisions of any enactment or regulations shall be construed, unless the context otherwise requires, as a reference to those provisions as re-enacted or amended by any subsequent enactment or regulations.

(4) The Interpretation Act 1889(**b**) shall apply for the interpretation of these Regulations as it applies for the interpretation of an Act of Parliament.

3. The Act of 1969 shall apply in relation to any pension specified in Part I of Schedule 1 hereto as if it were specified in Part I of Schedule 1 to the Act of 1969.

4. The Act of 1969 shall, subject to Regulations 5 and 6 hereof and to the modifications and adaptations specified in Schedule 2 hereto, apply to any pension specified in Part II of Schedule 1 hereto as if it were specified in Part I of Schedule 1 to the Act of 1969.

5. In relation to a pension deriving from any of the Transferred Funds specified in Part I of Schedule 3 hereto :—

(*a*) for the purpose of calculating the adjusted rate of such a pension in accordance with paragraph 2 of Schedule 2 to the Act of 1969, the annual rate of the pension before any relevant increase thereof shall be taken to be whichever is the less of the following amounts :—

(i) the amount of the pension from time to time payable in accordance with the Rules of that Fund ; or

---

(**a**) 1969 c. 7.   (**b**) 1889 c. 63.

(ii) the amount which would have been payable if the pension had been paid under the Rules of the corresponding Untransferred Fund specified in Part II of Schedule 3 hereto ;

(b) where an increase of such a pension payable to any person by virtue of the Regulations of 1963(a) and 1966(b) falls to be reduced by the amount specified in Regulation 5(b) of the Regulations of 1963, and that amount is greater than the increase so payable, the increase payable to that person by virtue of these Regulations shall be reduced by the excess.

6. Any pension which is described as a Supplementary pension in the Rules of the Indian Civil Service Family Pension Fund (Transferred), the Indian Military Widows' and Orphans' Fund (Transferred) and the Indian Military Service Family Pension Fund (Transferred) shall be disregarded for the purposes of the provisions of these Regulations, and any amount by which the annual amount of a pension, determined in accordance with the provisions of Regulation 5(a) hereof, exceeds the amount of a pension which would have resulted from subscription to the compulsory section of the Superior Services (India) Family Pension Fund (Transferred) and the Superior Services (India) Family Pension Fund (Untransferred) shall be similarly disregarded.

7. Whenever for the purpose of ascertaining any increase payable under these Regulations or the Regulations or Rules of 1957(c), 1959(d), 1963 or 1966 it is necessary to convert into sterling a basic pension initially payable in a currency other than sterling, the rate of exchange to be taken for the purpose of any such conversion shall be the rate of exchange between that currency and sterling in force on 6th May 1955 :

Provided that where a basic pension is converted by the paying authority into sterling at a privileged rate of exchange, then the rate of exchange to be taken shall be the said privileged rate.

8. Any increase authorised by these Regulations may take effect as from 1st April 1969.

(L.S.)

J. E. Herbecq,
Authorised by the Minister
for the Civil Service.

22nd May 1969.

(a) S.I. 1963/881 (1963 II, p. 1429).
(c) S.I. 1957/223 (1957 II, p. 1821).
(b) S.I. 1966/446 (1966 I, p. 957).
(d) S.I. 1959/1542 (1959 II, p. 2060).

SCHEDULE 1

PART I

PENSIONS TO WHICH THE ACT OF 1969 IS APPLIED

1. Any pension specified in paragraph 1 of Part I of the Second Schedule to the Pensions (India, Pakistan and Burma) Act 1955(a) which is a pension payable in respect of service as a member of either:—

    (a) the establishment of the Secretary of State in Council of India or

    (b) the staff of the High Commissioner for India or

    (c) the staff of the High Commissioner for Pakistan or

    (d) the staff of the Auditor of the Accounts of the Secretary of State for India in Council or

    (e) the staff of the Auditor of Indian Home Accounts.

2. Any pension specified in paragraphs 2 or 3 of Part I of the said Second Schedule.

PART II

PENSIONS TO WHICH THE ACT OF 1969 IS APPLIED SUBJECT TO MODIFICATIONS AND ADAPTATIONS

1. Any pension specified in paragraph 1 of Part I of the Second Schedule to the Pensions (India, Pakistan and Burma) Act 1955, as amended by section 4(1) of the Act of 1962(b), which is not such a pension as is specified in Part I of this Schedule.

2. Any pension specified in paragraph 4 of Part I or in Part II of the said Second Schedule.

SCHEDULE 2

MODIFICATIONS AND ADAPTATIONS OF THE ACT OF 1969

In its application to any pension specified in Part II of Schedule 1 hereto the Act of 1969 shall have effect as if:—

    (a) in section 1(1) the words "which began not later than 1st July 1967" were omitted and for the words from "an amount" to the end of the subsection there were substituted the words "eighteen per cent of the adjusted rate of that pension";

    (b) sub-section 1(2) were deleted;

    (c) the definition of "pension" in section 7(1) of the Act of 1959(c) as applied by section 4(1) of the Act of 1969 were modified by adding at the end of section 7(1) of the Act of 1959 the words "unless the commutation was made after 31st March 1969, in which case those provisions shall have effect as if the commutation had not been made";

    (d) in section 4(1) in the definition of "pension authority", for the reference to the authority by whom the pension is payable there were substituted a reference to the Minister of Overseas Development;

    (e) in section 4(1) in the definition of "relevant increase", there were added at the end of the definition the words "and any increase corresponding to any such increase".

    (a) 1955 c. 22.   (b) 1962 c. 2.   (c) 1959 c. 50.

SCHEDULE 3

PART I

TRANSFERRED FUNDS

Any pension which is such a pension as is specified in paragraph 1 of Part I of the Second Schedule to the Pensions (India, Pakistan and Burma) Act 1955 and is also a pension payable in accordance with the rules of the following Funds:—

The Indian Civil Service Family Pension Fund (Transferred)

The Superior Services (India) Family Pension Fund (Transferred)

The Indian Military Widows' and Orphans' Fund (Transferred)

The Indian Military Service Family Pension Fund (Transferred)

PART II

UNTRANSFERRED FUNDS

The Indian Civil Service Family Pension Fund (Untransferred)

The Superior Services (India) Family Pension Fund (Untransferred)

The Indian Military Widows' and Orphans' Fund (Untransferred)

The Indian Military Service Family Pension Fund (Untransferred)

EXPLANATORY NOTE

(This Note is not part of the Regulations.)

These Regulations authorise the Minister of Overseas Development to increase certain pensions, specified in the Regulations, arising from former India, Pakistan and Burma service. The increases are those authorised by the Pensions (Increase) Act 1969, in some cases with modifications, and in accordance with the provisions of paragraph 14 of Schedule 2 to that Act they take effect retrospectively from 1st April 1969.

STATUTORY   INSTRUMENTS

1969 No. 733

DIPLOMATIC AND INTERNATIONAL IMMUNITIES AND PRIVILEGES

The International Coffee Organisation (Immunities and Privileges) Order 1969

Laid before Parliament in draft
Made - - - - 23rd May 1969
*Coming into Operation   On a date to be notified in
the London Gazette*

At the Court at Holyroodhouse, the 23rd day of May 1969

Present,

The Queen's Most Excellent Majesty in Council

Whereas a draft of this Order has been laid before Parliament in accordance with section 10 of the International Organisations Act 1968(a) (hereinafter referred to as the Act) and has been approved by a resolution of each House of Parliament:

Now, therefore, Her Majesty, by virtue and in exercise of the powers conferred on Her by sections 1 and 12(6) of the Act or otherwise in Her Majesty vested, is pleased, by and with the advice of Her Privy Council, to order, and it is hereby ordered, as follows:—

PART I

GENERAL

Citation and Entry into Force

1. This Order may be cited as the International Coffee Organisation (Immunities and Privileges) Order 1969. It shall come into operation on the date on which the Headquarters Agreement between the Government of the United Kingdom of Great Britain and Northern Ireland and the International Coffee Organisation(b) enters into force. This date shall be notified in the London Gazette.

Interpretation

2.—(1) For the purposes of this Order, the official activities of the International Coffee Organisation shall include its administrative activities and those undertaken pursuant to the International Coffee Agreement 1968(c) or any subsequent agreement which replaces it.

(a) 1968 c. 48.   (b) Cmnd. 3915.   (c) Cmnd. 3648.

(2) In this Order "the 1961 Convention Articles" means the Articles (being certain Articles of the Vienna Convention on Diplomatic Relations signed in 1961) which are set out in Schedule 1 to the Diplomatic Privileges Act 1964(**a**).

(3) The Interpretation Act 1889(**b**) shall apply for the interpretation of this Order as it applies for the interpretation of an Act of Parliament, and as if this Order and the Order hereby revoked were Acts of Parliament.

Revocation

3. The International Coffee Organisation (Immunities and Privileges) Order 1962(**c**) is hereby revoked.

PART II

THE ORGANISATION

4. The International Coffee Organisation (hereinafter referred to as the Organisation) is an Organisation of which Her Majesty's Government in the United Kingdom and the governments of foreign sovereign Powers are members.

5. The Organisation shall have the legal capacities of a body corporate.

6.—(1) The Organisation shall have immunity from suit and legal process except:—

(*a*) to the extent that the Organisation shall have expressly waived such immunity in a particular case ;

(*b*) in respect of a civil action by a third party for damage arising from an accident caused by a motor vehicle belonging to, or operated on behalf of, the Organisation, or in respect of a motor traffic offence involving such a vehicle ; and

(*c*) in respect of the enforcement of an arbitration award made under Article 24, Article 25 or Article 28 of the Headquarters Agreement between the Government of the United Kingdom of Great Britain and Northern Ireland and the International Coffee Organisation.

(2) The provisions of the preceding paragraph shall not prevent the taking of such measures as may be permitted by law in relation to the property and assets of the Organisation in so far as they may be temporarily necessary in connection with the prevention of, and investigation into, accidents involving motor vehicles belonging to, or operated on behalf of, the Organisation.

7. The Organisation shall have the like inviolability of official archives and premises as, in accordance with the 1961 Convention Articles, is accorded in respect of the official archives and premises of a diplomatic mission.

8. Within the scope of its official activities, the Organisation shall have the like exemption or relief from taxes, other than customs duties and taxes on the importation of goods, as is accorded to a foreign sovereign Power.

9. The Organisation shall have the like relief from rates on its official premises as in accordance with Article 23 of the 1961 Convention Articles is accorded in respect of the premises of a diplomatic mission.

(**a**) 1964 c. 81.   (**b**) 1889 c. 63.   (**c**) S.I. 1962/2785 (1962 III, p. 3975).

10. The Organisation shall have exemption from customs duties and taxes on the importation of goods imported by the Organisation and necessary for the exercise of its official activities, or on the importation of any publications of the Organisation imported by it, such exemption to be subject to compliance with such conditions as the Commissioners of Customs and Excise may prescribe for the protection of the Revenue.

11. The Organisation shall have exemption from prohibitions and restrictions on importation or exportation in the case of goods imported or exported by the Organisation and necessary for the exercise of its official activities and in the case of any publications of the Organisation imported or exported by it.

12. The Organisation shall have relief, under arrangements made either by the Secretary of State or by the Commissioners of Customs and Excise, by way of refund of customs duty paid on any hydrocarbon oils (within the meaning of the Customs and Excise Act 1952(**a**)) which are bought in the United Kingdom and necessary for the exercise of the official activities of the Organisation, such relief to be subject to compliance with such conditions as may be imposed in accordance with the arrangements.

13. The Organisation shall have relief, under arrangements made by the Secretary of State, by way of refund of purchase tax paid on any goods which are necessary for the exercise of the official activities of the Organisation, such relief to be subject to compliance with such conditions as may be imposed in accordance with the arrangements.

Part III
Representatives

14.—(1) Except in so far as in any particular case any privilege or immunity is waived by the Government of the Member country whom they represent, representatives of Member countries of the Organisation on any of its organs shall enjoy:—

(*a*) in respect of words spoken or written and all acts done or omitted to be done by them in the exercise of their functions, the like immunity from suit and legal process as is accorded to the head of a diplomatic mission ;

(*b*) while exercising their functions and during their journeys to and from the place of meetings convened by the Organisation, the like immunity from personal arrest or detention and the like inviolability for all their official papers and documents as is accorded to the head of a diplomatic mission ;

(*c*) while exercising their functions and during their journeys to and from the place of meetings convened by the Organisation, the like exemptions and privileges in respect of their personal baggage as in accordance with Article 36 of the 1961 Convention Articles are accorded to a diplomatic agent.

(2) Part IV of Schedule 1 to the Act shall not operate so as to confer any privilege or immunity on the official staff of representatives of Member countries of the Organisation, other than alternate representatives.

(3) Neither the provisions of the preceding paragraphs of this Article nor those of Part IV of Schedule 1 to the Act shall operate so as to confer any privilege or immunity on any person as the representative or alternate

---

(a) 1952 c. 44.

representative of Her Majesty's Government in the United Kingdom or on any person who is a citizen of the United Kingdom and Colonies.

(4) Part IV of Schedule 1 to the Act shall not operate so as to confer any privilege or immunity on families of representatives or alternate representatives.

PART IV

OFFICERS

High Officers

15.—(1) Except in so far as in any particular case any privilege or immunity is waived by the Council of the Organisation, there shall be accorded to or in respect of the Executive Director of the Organisation, and, in his absence or incapacitation, the officer designated to act in his place:—

(*a*) the like immunity from suit and legal process, the like inviolability of residence and the like exemption or relief from taxes and rates, other than income tax in respect of his emoluments and customs duties and taxes on the importation of goods, as are accorded to or in respect of a diplomatic agent ;

(*b*) the like exemption from customs duties and taxes on the importation of articles imported for his personal use or the use of members of his family forming part of his household, including articles intended for his establishment, as in accordance with paragraph 1 of Article 36 of the 1961 Convention Articles is accorded to a diplomatic agent ;

(*c*) the like exemption and privileges in respect of his personal baggage as in accordance with paragraph 2 of Article 36 of those Articles are accorded to a diplomatic agent ;

(*d*) relief, under arrangements made either by the Secretary of State or by the Commissioners of Customs and Excise, by way of refund of customs duty paid on any hydrocarbon oils (within the meaning of the Customs and Excise Act 1952(**a**)) which are bought in the United Kingdom by him or on his behalf, such relief to be subject to compliance with such conditions as may be imposed in accordance with the arrangements ;

provided that the provisions of this Article shall not apply to any person who is a citizen of the United Kingdom and Colonies or a permanent resident of the United Kingdom.

(2) Part IV of Schedule 1 to the Act shall not operate so as to confer any immunity or privilege on the families of officers to whom this Article applies.

All Officers

16. Except in so far as in any particular case any privilege or immunity is waived by the Executive Director of the Organisation or (in the case of the Executive Director) by the Council of the Organisation, all officers of the Organisation with the exception of those who are recruited locally and assigned to hourly rates of pay shall enjoy :—

(*a*) immunity from suit and legal process in respect of words spoken or written and all acts done or omitted to be done by them in the course

(a) 1952 c. 44.

of the performance of their official duties, except in the case of a motor traffic offence committed by an officer or in the case of damage caused by a motor vehicle belonging to or driven by him ;

(b) as from the date on which the emoluments received by them as officers of the Organisation become subject to taxation by the Organisation for its benefit, exemption from income tax in respect of such emoluments ;

(c) unless they are citizens of the United Kingdom and Colonies, the like exemption from customs duties and taxes on the importation of articles which—

(i) at or about the time when the officer first enters the United Kingdom as an officer of the Organisation are imported for his personal use or that of members of his family forming part of his household, including articles intended for his establishment, and

(ii) are articles which were in his ownership or possession or that of such a member of his family, or which he or such a member of his family was under contract to purchase, immediately before he so entered the United Kingdom,

as in accordance with paragraph 1 of Article 36 of the 1961 Convention Articles is accorded to a diplomatic agent ;

(d) unless they are citizens of the United Kingdom and Colonies or permanently resident in the United Kingdom, exemptions whereby, for the purposes of the National Insurance Acts 1965 to 1969(a), the National Insurance (Industrial Injuries) Acts 1965 to 1968(b), any enactment for the time being in force amending any of those Acts, and any enactment of the Parliament of Northern Ireland corresponding to any of those Acts or to any enactment amending any of those Acts,—

(i) services rendered by them for the organisation shall be deemed to be excepted from any class of employment which is insurable employment, or in respect of which contributions are required to be paid, but

(ii) no person shall be rendered liable to pay any contribution which he would not be required to pay if those services were not deemed to be so excepted.

PART V
EXPERTS

17.—(1) Except in so far as in any particular case any privilege or immunity is waived by the Executive Director of the Organisation, experts (other than officers of the Organisation) serving on any committee of the Organisation or employed on missions on its behalf shall, so far as is necessary for the carrying out of their functions, including during journeys made in carrying out their functions and in the course of such missions, enjoy : —

(a) immunity from suit and legal process in respect of words spoken or written and all acts done or omitted to be done by them in the exercise of their functions, except in the case of a motor traffic offence committed by an expert or in the case of damage caused by a motor vehicle belonging to or driven by him ;

(a) 1965 c. 51; 1966 c. 6; 1967 c. 73; 1968 c. 40; 1969 c. 4.
(b) 1965 c. 52; 1967 c. 25; 1968 c. 40.

(*b*) while they are employed by the Organisation, the like inviolability for all their official papers and documents as is accorded to the head of a diplomatic mission :

(*c*) while carrying out their functions and during their journeys made in carrying out their functions and in the course of such missions, the like exemptions and privileges in respect of their personal baggage as in accordance with Article 36 of the 1961 Convention Articles are accorded to a diplomatic agent, provided that the provisions of this sub-paragraph shall not apply to any person who is a citizen of the United Kingdom and Colonies or a permanent resident of the United Kingdom.

(2) Part IV of Schedule 1 to the Act shall not operate so as to confer any privilege or immunity on the official staff or on families of experts to whom the provisions of paragraph (1) of this Article apply.

W. G. Agnew.

EXPLANATORY NOTE

(This Note is not part of the Order.)

This Order replaces the International Coffee Organisation (Immunities and Privileges) Order 1962, and confers privileges and immunities upon the International Coffee Organisation, its officers, representatives on its organs, and experts serving on committees or employed on missions on its behalf. These privileges and immunities are conferred in accordance with :—

(i) Article 22 of the International Coffee Agreement (Cmnd. 3648), opened for signature in New York on 18th March, 1968 ;

(ii) a Headquarters Agreement which has been negotiated between the Government of the United Kingdom and the International Coffee Organisation (Cmnd. 3915): this Order will enable Her Majesty's Government to give effect to the Agreement, which will enter into force on signature.

1969 No. 734

DIPLOMATIC AND INTERNATIONAL IMMUNITIES AND PRIVILEGES

The International Sugar Organisation (Immunities and Privileges) Order 1969

Laid before Parliament in draft

Made - - - - 23rd May 1969

Coming into Operation   On a date to be notified
in the London Gazette

At the Court at Holyroodhouse, the 23rd day of May 1969

Present,

The Queen's Most Excellent Majesty in Council

Whereas a draft of this Order has been laid before Parliament in accordance with section 10 of the International Organisations Act 1968(**a**) (hereinafter referred to as the Act) and has been approved by a resolution of each House of Parliament:

Now, therefore, Her Majesty, by virtue and in exercise of the powers conferred on Her by sections 1 and 12(6) of the Act or otherwise in Her Majesty vested, is pleased, by and with the advice of Her Privy Council, to order, and it is hereby ordered, as follows:—

PART I

GENERAL

Citation and Entry into Force

1. This Order may be cited as the International Sugar Organisation (Immunities and Privileges) Order 1969. It shall come into operation on the date on which the Headquarters Agreement between the Government of the United Kingdom of Great Britain and Northern Ireland and the International Sugar Organisation(**b**) enters into force. This date shall be notified in the London Gazette.

Interpretation

2.—(1) For the purposes of this Order, the official activities of the International Sugar Organisation shall include its administrative activities and those undertaken pursuant to the International Sugar Agreement 1968(**c**) or any subsequent agreement which replaces it.

(2) In this Order " the 1961 Convention Articles " means the Articles (being certain Articles of the Vienna Convention on Diplomatic Relations signed in 1961) which are set out in Schedule 1 to the Diplomatic Privileges Act 1964(**d**).

(**a**) 1968 c. 48.   (**b**) Cmnd. 3926.   (**c**) Cmnd. 3887.   (**d**) 1964 c. 81.

(3) The Interpretation Act 1889(a) shall apply for the interpretation of this Order as it applies for the interpretation of an Act of Parliament, and as if this Order and the Order hereby revoked were Acts of Parliament.

Revocation

3. The International Sugar Council (Immunities and Privileges) Order 1958(b) is hereby revoked.

PART II

THE ORGANISATION

4. The International Sugar Organisation (hereinafter referred to as the Organisation) is an Organisation of which Her Majesty's Government in the United Kingdom and the governments of foreign sovereign Powers are members.

5. The Organisation shall have the legal capacities of a body corporate.

6.—(1) The Organisation shall have immunity from suit and legal process except:—

(a) to the extent that the Organisation shall have expressly waived such immunity in a particular case ;

(b) in respect of a civil action by a third party for damage arising from an accident caused by a motor vehicle belonging to, or operated on behalf of, the Organisation, or in respect of a motor traffic offence involving such a vehicle ; and

(c) in respect of the enforcement of an arbitration award made under Article 24, Article 25 or Article 28 of the Headquarters Agreement between the Government of the United Kingdom of Great Britain and Northern Ireland and the International Sugar Organisation.

(2) The provisions of the preceding paragraph shall not prevent the taking of such measures as may be permitted by law in relation to the property and assets of the Organisation in so far as they may be temporarily necessary in connection with the prevention of, and investigation into, accidents involving motor vehicles belonging to, or operated on behalf of, the Organisation.

7. The Organisation shall have the like inviolability of official archives and premises as, in accordance with the 1961 Convention Articles, is accorded in respect of the official archives and premises of a diplomatic mission.

8. Within the scope of its official activities, the Organisation shall have the like exemption or relief from taxes, other than customs duties and taxes on the importation of goods, as is accorded to a foreign sovereign Power.

9. The Organisation shall have the like relief from rates on its official premises as in accordance with Article 23 of the 1961 Convention Articles is accorded in respect of the premises of a diplomatic mission.

10. The Organisation shall have exemption from customs duties and taxes on the importation of goods imported by the Organisation and necessary for the exercise of its official activities, or on the importation of any publications of the Organisation imported by it, such exemption to be subject to compliance with such conditions as the Commissioners of Customs and Excise may prescribe for the protection of the Revenue.

(a) 1889 c. 63.   (b) S.I. 1958/2191 (1958 I, p. 956).

11. The Organisation shall have exemption from prohibitions and restrictions on importation or exportation in the case of goods imported or exported by the Organisation and necessary for the exercise of its official activities and in the case of any publications of the Organisation imported or exported by it.

12. The Organisation shall have relief, under arrangements made either by the Secretary of State or by the Commissioners of Customs and Excise, by way of refund of customs duty paid on any hydrocarbon oils (within the meaning of the Customs and Excise Act 1952(a)) which are bought in the United Kingdom and necessary for the exercise of the official activities of the Organisation, such relief to be subject to compliance with such conditions as may be imposed in accordance with the arrangements.

13. The Organisation shall have relief, under arrangements made by the Secretary of State, by way of refund of purchase tax paid on any goods which are necessary for the exercise of the official activities of the Organisation, such relief to be subject to compliance with such conditions as may be imposed in accordance with the arrangements.

PART III

REPRESENTATIVES

14.—(1) Except in so far as in any particular case any privilege or immunity is waived by the Government of the Member country whom they represent, representatives of Member countries of the Organisation on any of its organs shall enjoy :—

(*a*) in respect of words spoken or written and all acts done or omitted to be done by them in the exercise of their functions, the like immunity from suit and legal process as is accorded to the head of a diplomatic mission ;

(*b*) while exercising their functions and during their journeys to and from the place of meetings convened by the Organisation, the like immunity from personal arrest or detention and the like inviolability for all their official papers and documents as is accorded to the head of a diplomatic mission ;

(*c*) while exercising their functions and during their journeys to and from the place of meetings convened by the Organisation, the like exemptions and privileges in respect of their personal baggage as in accordance with Article 36 of the 1961 Convention Articles are accorded to a diplomatic agent.

(2) Part IV of Schedule 1 to the Act shall not operate so as to confer any privilege or immunity on the official staff of representatives of Member countries of the Organisation, other than alternate representatives.

(3) Neither the provisions of the preceding paragraphs of this Article nor those of Part IV of Schedule 1 to the Act shall operate so as to confer any privilege or immunity on any person as the representative or alternate representative of Her Majesty's Government in the United Kingdom or on any person who is a citizen of the United Kingdom and Colonies.

(4) Part IV of Schedule 1 to the Act shall not operate so as to confer any privilege or immunity on families of representatives or alternate representatives.

(a) 1952 c. 44.

PART IV

OFFICERS

High Officers

15.—(1) Except in so far as in any particular case any privilege or immunity is waived by the Council of the Organisation, there shall be accorded to or in respect of the Executive Director of the Organisation, and, when the office is vacant, the officer specially designated to act in his place:—

(*a*) the like immunity from suit and legal process, the like inviolability of residence and the like exemption or relief from taxes and rates, other than income tax in respect of his emoluments and customs duties and taxes on the importation of goods, as are accorded to or in respect of a diplomatic agent ;

(*b*) the like exemption from customs duties and taxes on the importation of articles imported for his personal use or the use of members of his family forming part of his household, including articles intended for his establishment, as in accordance with paragraph 1 of Article 36 of the 1961 Convention Articles is accorded to a diplomatic agent ;

(*c*) the like exemption and privileges in respect of his personal baggage as in accordance with paragraph 2 of Article 36 of those Articles are accorded to a diplomatic agent ;

(*d*) relief, under arrangements made either by the Secretary of State or by the Commissioners of Customs and Excise, by way of refund of customs duty paid on any hydrocarbon oils (within the meaning of the Customs and Excise Act 1952(**a**)) which are bought in the United Kingdom by him or on his behalf, such relief to be subject to compliance with such conditions as may be imposed in accordance with the arrangements ;

provided that the provisions of this Article shall not apply to any person who is a citizen of the United Kingdom and Colonies or a permanent resident of the United Kingdom.

(2) Part IV of Schedule 1 to the Act shall not operate so as to confer any immunity or privilege on the families of officers to whom this Article applies.

All Officers

16. Except in so far as in any particular case any privilege or immunity is waived by the Executive Director of the Organisation or (in the case of the Executive Director) by the Council of the Organisation, all officers of the Organisation with the exception of those who are recruited locally and assigned to hourly rates of pay shall enjoy:—

(*a*) immunity from suit and legal process in respect of words spoken or written and all acts done or omitted to be done by them in the course of the performance of their official duties, except in the case of a motor traffic offence committed by an officer or in the case of damage caused by a motor vehicle belonging to or driven by him ;

(*b*) as from the date on which the emoluments received by them as officers of the Organisation become subject to taxation by the Organisation for its benefit, exemption from income tax in respect of such emoluments ;

(**a**) 1952 c. 44.

(c) unless they are citizens of the United Kingdom and Colonies, the like exemption from customs duties and taxes on the importation of articles which—

   (i) at or about the time when the officer first enters the United Kingdom as an officer of the Organisation are imported for his personal use or that of members of his family forming part of his household, including articles intended for his establishment, and

   (ii) are articles which were in his ownership or possession or that of such a member of his family, or which he or such a member of his family was under contract to purchase, immediately before he so entered the United Kingdom,

as in accordance with paragraph 1 of Article 36 of the 1961 Convention Articles is accorded to a diplomatic agent ;

(d) unless they are citizens of the United Kingdom and Colonies or permanently resident in the United Kingdom, exemptions whereby, for the purposes of the National Insurance Acts 1965 to 1969(**a**), the National Insurance (Industrial Injuries) Acts 1965 to 1968(**b**), any enactment for the time being in force amending any of those Acts, and any enactment of the Parliament of Northern Ireland corresponding to any of those Acts or to any enactment amending any of those Acts,—

   (i) services rendered by them for the Organisation shall be deemed to be excepted from any class of employment which is insurable employment, or in respect of which contributions are required to be paid, but

   (ii) no person shall be rendered liable to pay any contribution which he would not be required to pay if those services were not deemed to be so excepted.

PART V

EXPERTS

17.—(1) Except in so far as in any particular case any privilege or immunity is waived by the Executive Director of the Organisation, experts (other than officers of the Organisation) serving on any committee of the Organisation or employed on missions on its behalf shall, so far as is necessary for the carrying out of their functions, including during journeys made in carrying out their functions and in the course of such missions, enjoy : —

(a) immunity from suit and legal process in respect of words spoken or written and all acts done or omitted to be done by them in the exercise of their functions, except in the case of a motor traffic offence committed by an expert or in the case of damage caused by a motor vehicle belonging to or driven by him ;

(b) while they are employed by the Organisation, the like inviolability for all their official papers and documents as is accorded to the head of a diplomatic mission ;

(c) while carrying out their functions and during their journeys made in carrying out their functions and in the course of such missions, the like exemptions and privileges in respect of their personal baggage as in accordance with Article 36 of the 1961 Convention Articles are

(**a**) 1965 c. 51; 1966 c. 6; 1967 c. 73; 1968 c. 40; 1969 c. 4.
(**b**) 1965 c. 52; 1967 c. 25; 1968 c. 40.

accorded to a diplomatic agent, provided that the provisions of this sub-paragraph shall not apply to any person who is a citizen of the United Kingdom and Colonies or a permanent resident of the United Kingdom.

(2) Part IV of Schedule 1 to the Act shall not operate so as to confer any privilege or immunity on the official staff or on families of experts to whom the provisions of paragraph (1) of this Article apply.

W. G. Agnew.

EXPLANATORY NOTE

(This Note is not part of the Order.)

This Order replaces the International Sugar Council (Immunities and Privileges) Order 1958, and confers privileges and immunities upon the International Sugar Organisation, its officers, representatives on its organs, and experts serving on committees or employed on missions on its behalf. These privileges and immunities are conferred in accordance with:—

(i) Article 20 of the International Sugar Agreement (Cmnd. 3887), opened for signature in New York on 2nd December, 1968 ;

(ii) a Headquarters Agreement which has been negotiated between the Government of the United Kingdom and the International Sugar Organisation (Cmnd. 3926): this Order will enable Her Majesty's Government to give effect to the Agreement, which will enter into force on signature.

STATUTORY INSTRUMENTS

1969 No. 735

FOREIGN COMPENSATION

The Foreign Compensation (Union of Soviet Socialist Republics) Order 1969

Made - - -	*23rd May* 1969
Laid before Parliament	*30th May* 1969
Coming into Operation	*16th June* 1969

At the Court at Holyroodhouse, the 23rd day of May 1969

Present,

The Queen's Most Excellent Majesty in Council

Whereas Her Majesty is authorised to make provision by Order in Council under section 3 of the Foreign Compensation Act 1950(a) (hereinafter referred to as " the Act of 1950 ") as amended by section 2(1) of the Foreign Compensation Act 1969(b) (hereinafter referred to as " the Act of 1969 ") for the determination by the Foreign Compensation Commission (hereinafter referred to as " the Commission ") of claims to participate in compensation received under an agreement with the government of any other country, and for the distribution by the Commission of such compensation:

And Whereas Her Majesty is authorised by section 2(2) of the Act of 1969 to make the like provision by Order in Council under the said section 3 with respect to money paid to the Commission by virtue of section 1(3) or (4) of the Act of 1969:

And Whereas, consequent upon a settlement reached on 12th February 1967 and the formulation thereof contained in the Agreement entered into on 5th January 1968 between Her Majesty's Government in the United Kingdom and the Government of the Union of Soviet Socialist Republics, it is intended to pay money to the Commission as aforesaid:

Now, therefore, Her Majesty, by virtue and in exercise of the powers in that behalf by the Acts of 1950 and 1969 or otherwise in Her Majesty vested, is pleased, by and with the advice of Her Privy Council, to order, and it is hereby ordered, as follows:

(a) 1950 c. 12.   (b) 1969 c. 20.

PART I

COMMENCEMENT, CITATION AND INTERPRETATION

1. This Order shall come into operation on 16th June 1969, and may be cited as the Foreign Compensation (Union of Soviet Socialist Republics) Order 1969.

2.—(1) The Interpretation Act 1889(**a**) shall apply to the interpretation of this Order as it applies to the interpretation of an Act of Parliament, and as if this Order were an Act of Parliament.

(2) In this Order:—

" Baltic State " means Estonia, Latvia or Lithuania (including Memel and the city and territory of Vilna);

" British national " means—

(*a*) any individual who was at the material time, or who as regards any material time prior to 1st January 1949 would have been had the British Nationality Act 1948(**b**) and the British Protectorates, Protected States and Protected Persons Order in Council 1949(**c**) been in force at that time, a citizen of the United Kingdom and Colonies, a British subject by virtue of section 2, 13 or 16 of that Act or the British Nationality Act 1965(**d**), or a British protected person within the meaning of the said Act of 1948; provided that, as regards any material time prior to 16th May 1948, the expression " British protected person " shall be deemed to include a person who was at that time a Palestinian citizen under the Palestinian Citizenship Orders 1925 to 1942(**e**);

(*b*) any individual who as regards any material time after 31st December 1949 was a citizen of Southern Rhodesia or a citizen of Rhodesia and Nyasaland;

(*c*) any individual who as regards any material time after 31st October 1957 and prior to 17th September 1963 was a citizen of Singapore;

(*d*) any corporation, firm or association incorporated or constituted under the laws in force in the United Kingdom or in any territory for whose international relations Her Majesty's Government in the United Kingdom were, at the material time, responsible.

" Ceded territory " means territory ceded to the Union of Soviet Socialist Republics—

(*a*) by Czechoslovakia under an Agreement of 29th June 1945;

(*b*) by Finland under the Treaty of Peace between the ·Union of Soviet Socialist Republics and the Republic of Finland of 12th March 1940;

(*c*) by Finland under an Agreement of 19th September 1944, which cession was confirmed by the Treaty of Peace with Finland of 10th February 1947;

(*d*) by Finland under an Agreement of 3rd February 1947;

(*e*) by Poland under an Agreement of 16th August 1945;

(**a**) 1889 c. 63.   (**b**) 1948 c. 56.   (**c**) S.I. 1949/140 (1949 I, p. 522).   (**d**) 1965 c. 34.
(**e**) S.R. & O. 1925/777 ; 1931/671 ; 1939/863 ; 1941/1121 ; 1942/1177 ; (1925 p. 474 ;
1931 p. 467 ; 1939 II, p. 1658 ; 1941 I, p. 356 ; 1942 I, p. 216).

(*f*) by Poland under an Agreement of 15th February 1951; or

(*g*) by Rumania under an Agreement of 28th June 1940, which cession was confirmed by the Treaty of Peace with Rumania of 10th February 1947.

" Company " includes a body corporate.

" Debt " means a sum due or owing, or a claim for unliquidated damages, or a sum deposited in a bank in a Baltic State or ceded territory but not transferred, in respect of—

(*a*) a contract for the sale of goods or a bill of exchange given for the discharge of obligations under any such contract,

(*b*) the servicing, preservation, transport, insuring or advertising of goods in the course of trade, whether or not the goods are the subject of any such contract as aforesaid,

(*c*) an agency contract, other than one relating to a contract of insurance or to a treaty or contract of reinsurance,

(*d*) a contract for the payment of royalties or for the manufacture of goods under licence,

(*e*) professional charges or disbursements,

(*f*) a contract of insurance (including life and endowment assurance but not including a treaty or contract of reinsurance) concluded with an insurance company incorporated or constituted in a Baltic State or ceded territory,

(*g*) shipping or transport services, or

(*h*) an advance, loan, acceptance credit, or other facility originally granted in the course of business.

" External bond " means a bond forming part of a bond issue specified in column 1 of Schedule 1 to this Order.

" Internal bond " means a bond or other document of title in respect of a loan or obligation issued or guaranteed after 27th June 1919 and before the relevant date by the Government of a Baltic State or by a municipal authority in a Baltic State or ceded territory, other than an external bond.

" Material time " means any time or date at which it is material for the purposes of this Order to determine whether or not a person is a British national.

" Predecessor in title " means any person from whom, whether directly or indirectly, a person making application under this Order (including a trustee) has succeeded, whether by assignment or otherwise, to the property or claim to which the application relates. For the purpose of considering any question of succession, every claim shall be deemed (i) to have arisen at the relevant date but no claim shall be barred by any lapse of time thereafter, and (ii) to have been capable of transfer and transmission in the same manner as the property to which it relates.

" Property " includes all rights or interests of any kind in property.

" Relevant date " means in relation to each of the areas described in column 1 of Schedule 2 to this Order the date in column 2 of the said Schedule in respect of that area or, in the case of an application under Article 13 of the Order if the person making the application so elects, such other date after the said date in column 2 of the Schedule and before 13th February 1967 as he may establish to the satisfaction of the Commission to be the date on which he or his predecessor in title or, if he is a trustee, the person for whom he is a trustee or the predecessor in title of such person was deprived of the title to or enjoyment of the property to which the application relates.

" Rules of the Commission " means rules made by the Commission with the approval of the Lord Chancellor under section 4(2) of the Act of 1950 regulating the procedure of the Commission in determining applications made under this Order.

" Share " includes stock, a debenture, debenture stock and any funded obligation of a company.

" State Note " means any of the Union of the Soviet Socialist Republics State Notes issued either

(a) to the Tetiuhe Mining Corporation Limited, or

(b) to Lena Goldfields Limited.

" Trustee " includes a personal representative of a deceased person or a nominee; and " beneficiary " shall have a corresponding meaning.

PART II

THE FUND

3. The Commission shall pay into a fund to be called the Union of Soviet Socialist Republics Compensation Fund (hereinafter referred to as " the Fund ") all such sums as may be paid to them by virtue of section 1(3) or (4) of the Act of 1969.

4.—(1) Any sums standing to the credit of the Fund may be temporarily invested by the Commission in such manner as the Treasury may authorise.

(2) All interest, dividends and other sums received by the Commission as a result of any investment made by them of any sum standing to the credit of the Fund shall be paid into the Fund.

5. When it appears to the Secretary of State that all payments to be made into the Fund have been made and that all payments which it is practicable to make out of the Fund have been made, he may direct that the Fund shall be wound up and that any sum remaining therein shall be paid into the Consolidated Fund.

PART III

GENERAL PROVISIONS CONCERNING THE ESTABLISHMENT OF CLAIMS

6.—(1) An application shall not be entertained by the Commission for the purposes of this Order unless it has reached the Commission on or before 31st December 1969.

(2) An application shall not be entertained by the Commission for the purposes of this Order unless it is made in accordance with the Rules of the Commission.

7. Each application made under this Order shall be determined by not less than two members of the Commission, provided that—

(*a*) if the aggregate of all amounts claimed by an applicant under Parts IV and VI of the Order does not exceed £10,000, the provisional determination of the application may be made by one member of the Commission;

(*b*) notwithstanding paragraph (*a*) of this Article, no claim shall be dismissed except upon determination by not less than two members of the Commission.

8. Subject to the provisions of this Order, the Commission shall assess the amount of loss with respect to each claim established under the Order as may seem just and equitable to them having regard to all the circumstances, and shall dismiss each claim which is not so established.

9. Where any amount which is material to the determination of an application made under this Order is expressed in a unit of foreign currency, the value in sterling of that amount shall be determined in accordance with the rate of exchange for that currency set forth in columns 3 and 4 of Schedule 2 to this Order in respect of the area to which the claim relates, or, if there is no such rate, such rate as the Treasury may determine.

10. In assessing the amount of loss or interest with respect to any claim established under this Order the Commission shall have regard to any compensation, recoupment or payment in respect of that loss or interest that the person making the application or his predecessor in title or any trustee for such person or predecessor in title or, if the person making the application is a trustee, any beneficiary or any predecessor in title of any beneficiary has received or may, if he exercises diligence, be reasonably expected to receive from any source other than the Fund.

PART IV

Claims in respect of Debts, Bank Balances, Shares, Internal Bonds and other Property

11. No application may be made under this Part of the Order in respect of an external bond, a State Note, or any matter referred to in Part V of the Order.

12.—(1) The following persons shall be qualified to make application to the Commission for the purpose of establishing claims under this Part of the Order—

(*a*) Her Majesty's Government in the United Kingdom and the Government of any territory for the international relations of which Her Majesty's Government in the United Kingdom were, on the date of coming into operation of this Order, responsible;

(*b*) any person who was a British national on the date of coming into operation of this Order;

(*c*) any person who after the date of coming into operation of this Order has succeeded, whether by assignment or otherwise, to the claim of any person qualified under sub-paragraph (*b*) above; and

(*d*) a trustee for any person qualified under sub-paragraph (*b*) or (*c*) above.

(2) An application under this Part of the Order may be made by a trustee qualified under paragraph (1) of this Article or by a beneficiary so qualified.

An application by a trustee shall, however, be entertained by the Commission only in so far as the beneficial interest in the property or in the claim to which the application relates was, at the material times, owned by a British national.

(3) If application under this Part of the Order is made by a trustee and by a beneficiary in relation to the same claim, and both the trustee and the beneficiary are qualified under paragraph (1) of this Article, the Commission may entertain the application made by the trustee in preference to that made by the beneficiary, or entertain the application made by the beneficiary in preference to that made by the trustee. The Commission shall dismiss the application by the trustee or by the beneficiary, as the case may be, which it has decided not to entertain.

13.—(1) To establish a claim under this Part of the Order in respect of property (other than a debt, a balance in a bank, a share or an internal bond), any person making application to the Commission shall be required to establish to the satisfaction of the Commission—

(*a*) that he is a person qualified under Article 12 of this Order to make such application;

(*b*) that immediately before the relevant date the property to which the application relates was situated in a Baltic State or ceded territory and was British property (as provided in paragraph (2) of this Article), provided that in the case of property situated in the area described in paragraph 8 of Schedule 2 to this Order it shall be sufficient to satisfy the Commission that the property was, or would but for any act of the kind referred to in paragraph (*c*) of this paragraph have been, British property immediately before 16th August 1945; and

(*c*) that he or his predecessor in title or, if he is a trustee, the person for whom he is a trustee or the predecessor in title of such person has been deprived, on or after the relevant date and before 13th February 1967, of title to or enjoyment of such property by any act of confiscation, national-isation, expropriation or other similar official act of dispossession and has suffered loss thereby.

(2) Property shall be deemed to be British property to the extent that it was beneficially owned by a British national.

(3) For purposes of sub-paragraph (*c*) of paragraph (1) of this Article, the Commission may, if they think fit, assume, without proof of any specific act of deprivation, that a person referred to in that sub-paragraph has been de-prived of title to or enjoyment of the property by any act of the kind referred to in that sub-paragraph, if they are satisfied that he has lost the use or enjoy-ment of the property as a result of any action or course of conduct, on or after the relevant date, of the authorities of the area in which the property was situated.

14.—(1) To establish a claim under this Part of the Order in respect of a debt or a balance in a bank, any person making application to the Commission shall be required to establish to the satisfaction of the Commission—

(*a*) that he is a person qualified under Article 12 of this Order to make such application;

(*b*) that his application relates—

(i) to a debt which at any time after 31st August 1939 and before the relevant date was owing to a British national from a person (other than a British national) resident or carrying on business in a Baltic State or ceded territory and which is still unpaid; or

(ii) to a balance which was held by a British national immediately before the relevant date in a bank in a Baltic State or ceded territory and which is still outstanding; and

(c) that he is the person to whom the debt or the outstanding bank balance is owing.

(2) For the purposes of paragraph (1) of this Article and of Article 10 of this Order, the Commission may assume, if they think fit, that a debt or balance was irrecoverable on or after the relevant date.

15. To establish a claim under this Part of the Order in respect of a share, any person making application to the Commission shall be required to establish to the satisfaction of the Commission—

(a) that he is a person qualified under Article 12 of this Order to make such application;

(b) that the share was, or would but for any act of the kind referred to in sub-paragraph (d) of this paragraph have been, beneficially owned on 23rd November 1959 by a British national;

(c) that the company to which the share related was incorporated or constituted in a Baltic State or ceded territory and was carrying on business at any time within three months immediately before the relevant date; and

(d) that he or his predecessor in title or, if he is a trustee, the person for whom he is trustee or the predecessor in title of such person has suffered loss in respect of the share as a result of any act of confiscation, nationalisation, expropriation or other similar official act of dispossession applied in a Baltic State or ceded territory on or after the relevant date to the share or to the company or any of its assets.

16. To establish a claim under this Part of the Order in respect of an internal bond, any person making application to the Commission shall be required to establish to the satisfaction of the Commission—

(a) that he is a person qualified under Article 12 of the Order to make such application;

(b) that he is, or would but for any official act of confiscation, cancellation or dispossession effected since the relevant date have been, the owner or beneficial owner of the bond;

(c) that the bond was, or would but for any act of the kind referred to in sub-paragraph (b) of this paragraph have been, beneficially owned on 23rd November 1959 by a British national; and

(d) that the whole or part of the loan or obligation to which the bond relates has not been repaid or discharged.

17. If any transfer of property to which a claim relates was effected in a Baltic State or ceded territory after 31st August 1939 and before the relevant date, that transfer shall be deemed for the purposes of this Part of the Order to have been null and void if it was effected under fraud or duress or without the consent of the person to whom the property belonged at the date of such transfer.

18. Subject to Article 17 of this Order, for the purposes of this Part of the Order any transfer or transmission of property before the relevant date shall be deemed to have been governed by the law as on 31st August 1939 of the country in which the property was situate and the Commission may assume that the estate of a deceased person devolved as on an intestacy unless the contrary be shown.

19. Subject to Article 10 of this Order, the Commission shall, in assessing the amount of loss with respect to each claim established under this Part of the Order, add to the amount of the capital loss assessed by the Commission simple interest thereon at the rate of four per cent per annum for the period from the relevant date to 12th February 1967 (both dates inclusive).

PART V

CLAIMS IN RESPECT OF SHIPPING SERVICES AND SUPPLIES

20. Her Majesty's Government in the United Kingdom shall be qualified to make application to the Commission for the purpose of establishing a claim under this Part of the Order in respect of the provision, under the Ships' Expenses and Freights Agreement between Her Majesty's Government in the United Kingdom and the Government of the Union of Soviet Socialist Republics of 22nd June 1942, of services and supplies connected with shipping for the benefit of the Government of the Union of Soviet Socialist Republics.

21. To establish a claim under this Part of the Order, Her Majesty's Government in the United Kingdom shall be required to establish to the satisfaction of the Commission the amount outstanding in respect of charges made by Her Majesty's Government in the United Kingdom for such services and supplies after taking into account the value of services and supplies provided by the Government of the Union of Soviet Socialist Republics for the benefit of Her Majesty's Government under the said Agreement of 22nd June 1942.

22. The Commission shall, in assessing the amount of the loss with respect to a claim established under this Part of the Order, add to the amount of the capital loss assessed by the Commission simple interest thereon at the rate of four per cent per annum for the period from 27th December 1947 to 12th February 1967 (both dates inclusive).

PART VI

CLAIMS IN RESPECT OF EXTERNAL BONDS AND STATE NOTES

23. To establish a claim in respect of an external bond under this Part of the Order, any person making application to the Commission shall be required to establish to the satisfaction of the Commission—

(*a*) that he or, if he is a trustee, the person for whom he is a trustee was the beneficial owner of the bond on the date of making application to the Commission;

(*b*) that he or, if he is a trustee, the person for whom he is trustee was the beneficial owner of the bond on the date of coming into operation of this Order; or, if the beneficial owner on the date of coming into operation of the Order has died, that the person making application to the Commission has since the death become the owner or the beneficial owner of the bond by transfer or transmission;

(c) that the beneficial owner of the bond on the date of coming into operation of this Order was a British national; and

(d) that the beneficial owner of the bond on 23rd November 1959 was a British national.

24. To establish a claim in respect of a State Note under this Part of the Order, any person making application to the Commission—

(a) shall be required to establish to the satisfaction of the Commission (i) that he is the holder of the State Note, and (ii) that the State Note has not been redeemed and has not previously been stamped by the Commission under subparagraph (b) of this Article; and

(b) shall thereafter produce the State Note to the Commission for stamping.

25. The Commission shall assess the amount of loss with respect to each claim established under this Part of the Order and, for this purpose,

(a) the value of a bond shall, notwithstanding anything to the contrary stated therein, be taken to be the value specified in column 2 of Schedule 1 to this Order, together with simple interest thereon computed at the rate per annum specified in column 3 of the said Schedule for the period from the date specified in column 4 of the said Schedule to 12th February 1967 (both dates inclusive), and

(b) the value of a State Note shall be taken to be its nominal value, together with simple interest thereon computed at four per cent per annum for the period from 1st October 1940 to 12th February 1967 (both dates inclusive) in the case of the Tetiuhe Mining Corporation Limited and from 1st November 1940 to 12th February 1967 (both dates inclusive) in the case of the Lena Goldfields Limited.

PART VII

PAYMENTS OUT OF THE FUND

26.—(1) The Commission shall make payments out of the Fund to every person who has established a claim under this Order and who applies to the Commission for payment.

(2) If any person who has established a claim under this Order shall have died before the amounts payable to him under Articles 27 and 28 of the Order have been paid to him, such payments or the balance thereof shall be made to his personal representatives if they apply to the Commission for payment, provided that, if the Commission are satisfied that no grant of administration of his estate has been made in the United Kingdom and that the assets of his estate (including the amount payable under this Order) do not exceed £500 in value, the Commission may, at their discretion and subject to such conditions as the Commission think proper, make such payment either to any person who has taken out administration in any other part of the Commonwealth, or to the person who shall appear to the Commission to be the person who, being a widower, widow, child, father, mother, brother or sister of the deceased person, would, under the law of England, have the prior right to a grant of administration of the estate of the deceased person if such deceased person had died intestate domiciled in England.

(3) If any person whose claim has been established under this Order is an infant at the date when the amounts payable to him under Articles 27 and 28 of this Order are due to be paid, the Commission may make payment thereof into the Supreme Court, or, if the amount thereof does not exceed £500, into the County Court for the district in which the infant resides, under the provisions of the Trustee Act 1925(**a**), or, if the amount does not exceed £50, may place the same on deposit in the name of the Commission in any bank for such time as the person remains an infant.

27.—(1) The payment in respect of each claim established under this Order shall be a fraction of the distributable amount of the Fund equal to the proportion which the assessed amount of the claim bears to the total of the amounts assessed with respect to all claims established under the Order.

(2) The distributable amount shall be the total of all sums paid into the Fund, after the deduction of any payments made therefrom into the Consolidated Fund in accordance with any Order in Council made under section 7(2) of the Act of 1950 as originally enacted and as applied by section 3(3) of the Foreign Compensation Act 1962(**b**).

28.—(1) Whether or not all claims under this Order against the Fund have been finally determined, the Commission may, at such time or times as they may decide, make from the Fund interim payments to any of the persons who have established claims under the Order.

(2) Interim payments made under the provisions of this Article shall be made—

(*a*) on account of payments to be made in accordance with Article 27 of this Order, and

(*b*) at a uniform rate upon the assessed amount of the claim. The uniform rate of payment shall be determined by the Commission; for this purpose the Commission shall estimate the total liability likely to fall upon the Fund.

(3) For the purposes of the present Article—

(*a*) a claim shall be deemed to be established under this Order even though the determination thereof may be provisional and subject to review under the Rules of the Commission;

(*b*) the assessed amount of the claim shall be deemed to be the amount so provisionally determined subject to review unless before the date of payment the Commission shall have made a final determination on review.

29.—(1) Subject to the provisions of paragraph (2) of this Article, the Commission shall, as a condition of the making of any payment to any person under this Order, require him to surrender to the Commission all available documents of title, if any, relating exclusively to the claim to which the payment relates and shall require him to sign and deliver to the Commission a document in such form as the Commission may determine declaring that he renounces all those claims which he has established under the Order.

(2) If the person for whose benefit a payment is to be made is an infant, the Commission shall, as a condition of the making of any payment into Court or placing the same on deposit under paragraph (3) of Article 26 of this Order, require the person who, in accordance with the Rules of the Commission, has

(**a**) 1925 c. 19.   (**b**) 11 & 12 Eliz. 2 c. 4.

made an application for payment on the infant's behalf to surrender to the Commission the documents of title, if any, under his control relating exclusively to the claim and to sign and deliver to the Commission a document in such form as the Commission may determine declaring that the infant renounces all claims to which the payment relates; and the document so signed shall operate as a valid surrender by the infant of all such claims.

(3) All documents which are delivered to the Commission under paragraphs (1) and (2) of this Article shall remain in their custody until the Fund is wound up and the Commission shall then deliver them to Her Majesty's Principal Secretary of State for Foreign and Commonwealth Affairs.

W. G. Agnew.

SCHEDULE 1

EXTERNAL BONDS

Column 1 External Bond	Column 2 Value of each Bond	Column 3 Rate of Interest	Column 4 Date
1. Republic of Estonia (Banking and Currency Reform) 7% Sterling Loan 1927.	The value in sterling specified as the nominal value on the bond.	7%	2nd July 1940
2. Republic of Estonia (Banking and Currency Reform) 7% Dollar Loan 1927.	The value specified as the nominal value on the bond converted into sterling at the rate of U.S. $4·03=£1.	7%	2nd July 1940
3. City of Riga 4½% Sterling Loan 1913 (" un-assented " bonds).	The value in sterling specified as the nominal value on the bond reduced by £40 per cent.	4%	15th May 1940
4. City of Riga 4½% Sterling Loan 1913, as modi-fied pursuant to an offer made in 1934 (" assented " bonds).	The value in sterling specified as the nominal value on the bond as reduced by endorsement by £40 per cent.	4%	15th May 1940
5. City of Wilno (Vilna) 5% Loan 1912	The value in sterling specified as the nominal value on the bond.	5%	16th May 1939
6. City of Wilno (Vilna) 5% Sterling Conversion Loan 1931.	The value in sterling specified as the nominal value on the bond.	5%	16th May 1939

SCHEDULE 2

RELEVANT DATES AND EXCHANGE RATES

	Column 1 Area	Column 2 Date	Column 3 Currency	Column 4 Rate per £1
1.	Estonia	21st July 1940	Estonian kroner	14¾
2.	Latvia	21st July 1940	Latvian lats U.S. dollars	19¼ 4·03
3.	Lithuania (including Memel and the city and territory of Vilna).	21st July 1940	Lithuanian lits German Reichsmarks U.S. dollars	21⅝ 10·77 4·03
4.	Territory ceded by Czechoslovakia to the Union of Soviet Socialist Republics under an Agreement of 29th June 1945.	29th June 1945	Czech crowns	118·97
5.	Territory ceded by Finland to the Union of Soviet Socialist Republics under the Treaty of Peace between the Union of Soviet Socialist Republics and the Republic of Finland of 12th March 1940.	12th March 1940	Finmarks	193
6.	Territory ceded by Finland to the Union of Soviet Socialist Republics under an Agreement of 19th September 1944, which cession was confirmed by the Treaty of Peace with Finland of 10th February 1947.	19th September 1944	Finmarks	196
7.	Territory ceded by Finland to the Union of Soviet Socialist Republics under an Agreement of 3rd February 1947.	3rd February 1947	Finmarks	547
8.	Territory ceded by Poland to the Union of Soviet Socialist Republics under an Agreement of 16th August 1945.	29th September 1939	Polish zlotys	22·87
9.	Territory ceded by Poland to the Union of Soviet Socialist Republics by an Agreement of 15th February 1951.	15th February 1951	—	—
10.	Territory ceded by Rumania to the Soviet Socialist Republics by an Agreement of 28th June 1940, which cession was confirmed by the Treaty of Peace with Rumania of 10th February 1947.	28th June 1940	Rumanian lei	800

EXPLANATORY NOTE

(This Note is not part of the Order.)

This Order, which is made pursuant to the Foreign Compensation Act 1969, provides—

(i) for the determination by the Foreign Compensation Commission of claims to participate in the compensation fund established in consequence of the Agreement of 5th January 1968 between Her Majesty's Government in the United Kingdom and the Government of the Union of Soviet Socialist Republics concerning the Settlement of Mutual Financial and Property Claims (Cmnd. 3517); and

(ii) for the distribution of the aforesaid compensation fund by the Commission to applicants who have established claims under the Order.

1969 No. 736

CARIBBEAN AND NORTH ATLANTIC TERRITORIES

The Turks and Caicos Islands (Constitution) Order 1969

Made - - - -	*23rd May* 1969
Laid before Parliament	*30th May* 1969
Coming into Operation	*On a day to be appointed under section* 1 (2).

ARRANGEMENT OF ORDER

PART I

Introductory

Section
1. Citation, publication, commencement and revocation.
2. Interpretation.

PART II
The Governor
3. Functions of Governor.
4. Governor may perform Administrator's functions.

PART III
The Administrator
5. Office of Administrator and functions of Administrator.
6. Emoluments of Administrator.
7. Acting Administrator.
8. Administrator's deputy.

PART IV
The State Council
9. The State Council.
10. Qualifications for elected membership.
11. Disqualifications for nominated and elected membership.
12. Term of office of nominated and elected members.
13. Vacation of seats of members.
14. Vacation of seat on sentence.
15. Temporary members of State Council.
16. General elections.
17. Reconstitution of State Council.

Section
18. Determination of questions as to membership of State Council.
19. Penalty for sitting or voting when unqualified.
20. Qualifications of voters.
21. Right to vote at elections.

PART V

Executive Functions

22. Functions of State Council and Administrator.
23. Committees of State Council.
24. Administrator may authorise committee to exercise statutory functions.

PART VI

Legislation

25. Power to make laws.
26. Administrator's reserved power.
27. Assent to Bills.
28. Return of Bills by Administrator.
29. Disallowance of laws.

PART VII

Procedure of State Council

30. Oaths by members of Council.
31. Summoning of Council.
32. Holding of proceedings of Council in public or private.
33. Presiding in Council.
34. Quorum.
35. Submission of questions to State Council.
36. Restriction on proceedings upon certain measures.
37. Voting.
38. Participation of Administrator and other persons in certain proceedings.
39. Council may transact business notwithstanding vacancies.
40. Rules of procedure.

PART VIII

Miscellaneous

41. Court of Appeal.
42. Grants of land.
43. Powers of pardon, etc.
44. Offices and appointments.
45. Discipline.
46. Privileges of State Council and members.
47. Power reserved to Her Majesty.

PART IX

Transitional

Section

48. Existing laws.

49. Existing offices and officers.

50. First State Council.

51. Transitional provision relating to certain bills and laws passed or made under existing constitution.

SCHEDULE.

At the Court at Holyroodhouse, the 23rd day of May 1969

Present,

The Queen's Most Excellent Majesty in Council

Her Majesty, by virtue and in exercise of the powers conferred upon Her by section 5 of the West Indies Act 1962(a), and of all other powers enabling Her in that behalf, is pleased, by and with the advice of Her Privy Council, to order, and it is hereby ordered, as follows:—

PART I

INTRODUCTORY

Citation, publication, commencement and revocation. **1.**—(1) This Order may be cited as the Turks and Caicos Islands (Constitution) Order 1969.

(2) This Order shall come into operation on such day as the Administrator, acting in his discretion, may, by proclamation published in the Gazette, appoint, which day shall not be earlier than 31st May 1969.

(3) The Turks and Caicos Islands (Constitution) Order in Council 1965(b), the Turks and Caicos Islands (Constitution) (Amendment) Order 1967(c), the Turks and Caicos Islands (Constitution) (Amendment) (No. 2) Order 1967(d), the Turks and Caicos Islands (Constitution) (Amendment) Order 1968(e) and the Turks and Caicos Islands (Constitution) (Amendment) Order 1969(f) are revoked.

Interpretation. **2.**—(1) In this Order, unless the context otherwise requires,—

"Administrator" means the person for the time being holding the office of Administrator of the Islands, and includes any person for the time being acting in that office and, to the extent to which a deputy appointed under section 8 of this Order is authorised to act, that deputy;

"appointed day" means the day appointed under section 1(2) of this Order;

"the existing Constitution" means Schedule I to the Turks and Caicos Islands (Constitution) Order in Council 1965 as amended by section 2(3) of that Order and by the other Orders referred to in section 1(3) of this Order;

(a) 1962 c. 19.
(b) S.I. 1965/1861 (1965 III, p. 5609).
(c) S.I. 1967/977 (1967 II, p. 2960).
(d) S.I. 1967/1139 (1967 II, p. 3370).
(e) S.I. 1968/728 (1968 II, p. 2107).
(f) S.I. 1969/591 (1969 I, p. 1648).

" functions " includes powers and duties ;

" Gazette " means the Turks and Caicos Islands Government Gazette ;

" Governor " means the person for the time being holding the office of Governor and Commander-in-Chief of the Bahama Islands and includes any person for the time being acting in that office save when any such person is so acting by reason of the absence of the holder of the office for the purpose of visiting the Turks and Caicos Islands ;

" the Islands " means the Turks and Caicos Islands ;

" law " includes any subsidiary instrument ;

" public office " means, subject to the provisions of the next following subsection, an office of emolument in the public service ;

" public officer " means the holder of any public office, and includes a person appointed to act in any public office ;

" the public service " means the service of the Crown in a civil capacity in respect of the government of the Islands ;

" sitting " means, in relation to the State Council, a period during which the Council is sitting continuously without adjournment and includes any period during which the Council is in committee ;

" the specified public service matters " means the appointment (including the appointment on promotion or transfer, appointment on contract and appointment to act in an office) of any person to any public office, the suspension, dismissal, termination of employment or retirement of any public officer or taking of disciplinary action in respect of such an officer, the application to any public officer of the terms and conditions of employment of the public service (including salary scales, allowances, leave, passages or pensions) for which financial provision has been made, or the organisation of the public service to the extent that it does not involve new financial provision ;

" subsidiary instrument " means any proclamation, regulation, order, rule or other like instrument having the force of law.

(2) For the purposes of this Order, a person shall not be considered as holding or acting in a public office by reason only that he—

(a) is in receipt of any remuneration or allowance as a member of the State Council ;

(b) is in receipt of a pension or other like allowance in respect of service under the Crown ; or

(c) is on leave of absence pending relinquishment of a public office ;

and a provision in any law for the time being in force in the Islands that a person shall not be disqualified for appointment as a nominated member or election as an elected member of the State Council by reason of his holding or acting in any public office or class of public office specified therein shall have effect as if it were included in this Order.

(3) Any person who has vacated his seat in the State Council or has vacated any office constituted by this Order may, if qualified, again be appointed or elected as a member of that body or to that office, as the case may be, from time to time.

(4) Where the holder of any office constituted by or under this Order is on leave of absence pending the relinquishment of that office, the person or authority having power to make appointments to that office may appoint another person thereto ; and where two or more persons concurrently hold the same office by virtue of an appointment made in pursuance of this subsection, the person last appointed shall, in respect of any function conferred on the holder of that office, be deemed to be the sole holder thereof.

(5) Any power conferred by this Order to make any proclamation, rules or order or to give any directions shall be construed as including a power exercisable in like manner to amend or revoke any such proclamation, rules, order or directions.

(6) Where a person is required by this Order to make an oath he shall if he so desires be permitted to comply with that requirement by making an affirmation in the form provided for in the Schedule to this Order.

(7) For the purposes of this Order the resignation of a member of the State Council or the holder of any office constituted by this Order that is required to be addressed to any person shall, unless otherwise expressly provided, be deemed to have effect from the time at which it is received by that person.

(8) For the purposes of this Order a person shall not be regarded as absent from the Islands or as unable to perform the functions of his office by reason only that he is in passage from one part of the Islands to another.

(9) The Interpretation Act 1889(a) shall apply with the necessary adaptations for the purpose of interpreting this Order and otherwise in relation thereto as it applies for the purpose of interpreting and in relation to an Act of Parliament.

PART II

THE GOVERNOR

Functions of Governor.

3. The Governor shall have such functions in relation to the Islands as may be conferred upon him by or under this Order or any other law for the time being in force in the Islands and such other functions in relation to the Islands as Her Majesty may assign to him and, subject to the provisions of this Order and, in the case of functions conferred upon him by or under any other law, subject to the provisions of that law, shall perform all such functions according to such instructions, if any, as Her Majesty may give him :

Provided that the question whether or not the Governor has in any matter complied with any such instructions shall not be enquired into in any court of law.

Governor may perform Administrator's functions.

4. The Governor may, when he is present in the Islands, perform any of the functions conferred on the Administrator by or under this Order or any other law and references in this Order or in any such law to the Administrator in relation to any function conferred on the Administrator shall, to the extent to which the Governor performs that function, be construed as including references to the Governor.

(a) 1889 c. 63.

PART III

THE ADMINISTRATOR

5.—(1) The office of Administrator of the Islands is hereby constituted.

(2) The Administrator shall be appointed by the Governor in pursuance of instructions given by Her Majesty through a Secretary of State and shall hold office during Her Majesty's pleasure.

(3) A person appointed to the office of Administrator shall, before assuming the functions of that office, make the oaths of allegiance and for the due execution of that office in the forms set out in the Schedule to this Order.

(4) The Administrator shall have such functions as may be conferred upon him by or under this Order or any other law and such other functions as Her Majesty or the Governor may assign to him and, subject to the provisions of this Order and, in the case of functions conferred upon him by or under any other law, subject to the provisions of that law, shall perform all such functions (including functions which are expressed by this Order to be exercisable in his discretion or which he is directed by this Order to exercise in his own deliberate judgment) according to such instructions, if any, as may be given to him by Her Majesty or by the Governor :

Provided that the question whether or not the Administrator has in any matter complied with any such instructions shall not be enquired into in any court of law.

Office of Administrator and functions of Administrator.

6.—The holder of the office of Administrator shall receive such emoluments as may for the time being be fixed by a Secretary of State by directions in writing, and those emoluments are hereby charged on and shall be paid out of the revenues of the Islands.

Emoluments of Administrator.

7.—(1) Whenever the office of Administrator is vacant or the holder thereof is absent from the Islands or is for any other reason unable to perform the functions of his office, such person as may for the time being be designated in that behalf by instructions given by Her Majesty through a Secretary of State or, subject thereto, by the Governor by instrument in writing under his hand, shall, during Her Majesty's pleasure, act in the office of Administrator and perform the functions of that office accordingly.

Acting Administrator.

(2) A person shall not assume the functions of the office of Administrator under this section until he has made the oaths of allegiance and for the due execution of that office in the forms set out in the Schedule to this Order.

(3) A person shall not continue to perform the functions of the office of Administrator under this section after the person holding that office or some other person having a prior right to perform those functions has notified him that he is about to assume or resume those functions.

(4) For the purposes of this section (and without prejudice to the provisions of section 2(8) of this Order), the Administrator shall not be regarded as absent from the Islands or as unable to perform the functions of his office at any time when there is a subsisting appointment of a deputy under the next following section.

(5) The reference in subsection (3) of this section to a prior right to perform the functions of the office of Administrator shall not be construed as including a reference to the Governor's right to perform those functions under section 4 of this Order.

Administrator's deputy.

8.—(1) Whenever the Administrator—

(a) has occasion to be absent from the seat of government but not from the Islands ; or

(b) has occasion to be absent from the Islands for a period which he has reason to believe will be of short duration ; or

(c) is suffering from an illness which he has reason to believe will be of short duration,

he may, by instrument under the public seal, appoint any person in the Islands to be his deputy during such absence or illness and in that capacity to perform on his behalf such of the functions of the office of Administrator as may be specified in that instrument.

(2) The power and authority of the Administrator shall not be abridged, altered or in any way affected by the appointment of a deputy under this section and, subject to the provisions of this Order and of any law by or under which any function which the deputy is authorised to perform is conferred, the deputy shall conform to and observe all instructions that may from time to time be given to him by Her Majesty through a Secretary of State or by the Governor or the Administrator :

Provided that the question whether or not the deputy has in any matter complied with any such instructions shall not be enquired into in any court of law.

(3) A person appointed as deputy under this section shall hold that office for such period as may be specified in the instrument by which he is appointed but his appointment may be revoked at any time by Her Majesty through a Secretary of State or by the Governor or the Administrator.

(4) In this section " the Administrator " does not include a deputy appointed under this section.

(5) In the exercise of any power conferred upon him by this section, the Administrator shall act in his discretion.

(6) In subsection (1) of this section the reference to the functions of the office of Administrator does not include a reference to any functions conferred upon the Administrator by any Act of the Parliament of the United Kingdom or by any Order in Council or other instrument made under such an Act other than this Order.

PART IV

THE STATE COUNCIL

The State Council.

9.—(1) There shall be a State Council for the Islands.

(2) Subject to the provisions of this Order, the State Council shall consist of—

(a) the Treasurer ;

(b) one official member appointed by the Administrator, by instrument under the public seal, in pursuance of instructions given to him by Her Majesty through a Secretary of State from among persons holding public office who possess legal qualifications ;

(c) if it is for the time being so directed by instructions given as aforesaid, one additional official member appointed by the Administrator, by instrument under the public seal, in pursuance of such instructions from among persons holding public office ;

(d) not less than two nor more than three nominated members (as may for the time being be directed by instructions given as aforesaid) appointed by the Administrator, by instrument under the public seal, in pursuance of such instructions from among British subjects of the age of twenty-one years or upwards ; and

(e) nine elected members.

(3) For the purpose of the election of the elected members of the State Council the Islands shall be divided into such electoral districts as may be prescribed by any law for the time being in force in the Islands and, subject to the provisions of this Order, such number of members shall be elected to the State Council for each such district in such manner as may be so prescribed.

(4) In subsection (2) of this section " the Treasurer " includes any person for the time being acting in that office.

10.—(1) Subject to the provisions of the next following section, a person shall be qualified to be elected as a member of the State Council if, and shall not be qualified to be so elected unless, he— *Qualifications for elected membership.*

(a) is a person who belongs to the Islands ;

(b) is of the age of twenty-one years or upwards ; and

(c) either has resided in the Islands for a period of twelve months immediately preceding the date of his nomination for election, or is domiciled in the Islands and is resident therein at that date.

(2) For the purposes of paragraph (a) of the foregoing subsection. a person shall belong to the Islands who is a British subject and who

(a) was born in the Islands ;

(b) was born outside the Islands of a father and mother who were born in the Islands ;

(c) has been granted a certificate under the next following subsection ;

(d) has been granted a certificate of naturalisation by the Administrator under the British Nationality Act 1948 ; or

(e) is the wife of a person to whom any of the foregoing paragraphs apply who is not living apart from such person under a decree of a competent court or a deed of separation.

(3) The Administrator may, if application therefor is made to him by any British subject of the age of twenty-one years or upwards who satisfies him that he has been ordinarily resident in the Islands throughout the period of seven years immediately preceding the application and that he is of good character, grant to him a certificate that he belongs to the Islands for the purposes of this section.

11.—(1) No person shall be qualified to be appointed as a nominated member or to be elected as a member of the State Council who—- *Disqualifications for nominated and elected membership.*

(a) is, by virtue of his own act, under any acknowledgement of allegiance, obedience or adherence to a foreign power or state ;

(b) holds, or is acting in, any public office ;

(c) has been adjudged or otherwise declared bankrupt under any law in force in any part of the Commonwealth and has not been discharged ;

(d) is a person certified to be insane or otherwise adjudged to be of unsound mind under any law in force in the Islands ;

(e) is under sentence of death imposed on him by a court in any part of the Commonwealth, or is serving a sentence of imprisonment (by whatever name called) exceeding twelve months imposed on him by such a court or substituted by competent authority for some other sentence imposed on him by such a court, or is under such a sentence of imprisonment the execution of which has been suspended ;

(f) is a party to, or a partner in a firm or a director or manager of a company which is a party to, any contract with the Government of the Islands for or on account of the public service and, in the case of a nominated member, has not disclosed to the Administrator the nature of such contract and his interest, or the interest of any such firm or company, therein or, in the case of an elected member, has not, within the period of one month immediately preceding the day of election, published in the Gazette a notice setting out the nature of such contract and his interest, or the interest of any such firm or company, therein ;

(g) is disqualified for membership of the State Council by any law in force in the Islands relating to offences connected with elections ; or

(h) in the case of an elected member, is disqualified for election by any law in force in the Islands by reason of his holding, or acting in, any office the functions of which involve—

(i) any responsibility for, or in connection with, the conduct of any election ; or

(ii) any responsibility for the compilation or revision of any register of voters.

(2) For the purposes of paragraph (e) of the foregoing subsection—

(a) where a person is serving two or more sentences of imprisonment that are required to be served consecutively he shall, throughout the whole time during which he so serves, be regarded as serving a sentence exceeding twelve months if (but not unless) any one of those sentences exceeds that term ; and

(b) no account shall be taken of a sentence of imprisonment imposed as an alternative to or in default of the payment of a fine.

Term of office of nominated and elected members.

12. Subject to the next following section, the term of office of a nominated member or an elected member of the State Council shall commence upon the day upon which he assumes his seat in the Council in accordance with section 17 of this Order and shall end on the day, following the next general election to the Council after his appointment or election, upon which the Council is reconstituted.

Vacation of seats of members.

13.—(1) An official member and a nominated member of the State Council shall hold his seat in the State Council during Her Majesty's pleasure.

(2) The seat of an official member of the State Council shall become vacant—

(*a*) if he ceases to hold a public office ; or

(*b*) if he resigns his seat by writing under his hand addressed to the Administrator, and the Administrator, acting in his discretion, accepts his resignation.

(3) The seat of a nominated or an elected member of the State Council shall become vacant—

(*a*) if he is absent from the meetings of the Council in such circumstances and for such period as may be prescribed by the rules of procedure of the Council ;

(*b*) if he ceases to be a British subject ;

(*c*) in the case of an elected member, if he ceases to belong to the Islands for the purposes of paragraph (*a*) of section 10(1) of this Order ;

(*d*) if he resigns his seat by writing under his hand addressed to the Administrator ;

(*e*) if he becomes a party to any contract with the Government of the Islands for or on account of the public service, or if any firm in which he is a partner or any company of which he is a director or manager becomes a party to any such contract, or if he becomes a partner in a firm or a director or manager of a company which is a party to any such contract:

Provided that the Administrator, acting after consultation with the State Council, may exempt any nominated member from vacating his seat under the provisions of this paragraph and the State Council may exempt any elected member from so vacating his seat if the member, before becoming a party to the contract, or before or as soon as practicable after becoming otherwise interested in the contract (whether as a partner in a firm or as a director or manager of a company) discloses to the Administrator or, as the case may be, the Council the nature of the contract and his interest or the interest of the firm or company therein and if in the circumstances it appears to the Administrator or, as the case may be, the Council to be just to do so ;

(*f*) if any circumstances arise that, if he were not a member of the State Council, would cause him to be disqualified for appointment or election thereto by virtue of paragraph (*a*), (*b*), (*c*), (*d*) or (*g*) of section 11(1) of this Order or, in the case of an elected member, would cause him to be disqualified for election thereto by virtue of paragraph (*h*) of the said section 11(1) ; or

(*g*) in the circumstances specified in the next following section.

14.—(1) Subject to the provisions of this section, if a nominated or an elected member of the State Council is sentenced by a court in any part of the Commonwealth to death or to imprisonment (by whatever name called) for a term exceeding twelve months, he shall forthwith cease to perform his functions as a member of the State Council, and his seat in the State Council shall become vacant at the expiration of a period of thirty days thereafter: Vacation of seat on sentence.

Provided that the Administrator, acting in his discretion, may, at the request of the member, from time to time extend that period for thirty days to enable the member to pursue any appeal in respect of his conviction or sentence, so however that extensions of time exceeding in the aggregate three hundred and thirty days shall not be given without the approval of the State Council signified by resolution.

(2) If at any time before the member vacates his seat he is granted a free pardon or his conviction is set aside or his sentence is reduced to a term of imprisonment of twelve months or less or a punishment other than imprisonment is substituted, his seat in the State Council shall not become vacant under the provisions of the foregoing subsection, and he may again perform his functions as a member of the State Council.

(3) For the purposes of this section—

(*a*) where a person is sentenced to two or more terms of imprisonment that are required to be served consecutively, account shall be taken only of any of those terms that exceed twelve months ; and

(*b*) no account shall be taken of a sentence of imprisonment imposed as an alternative to or in default of the payment of a fine.

Temporary members of State Council.
15.—(1) Whenever an official or a nominated member of the State Council is by reason of his illness or absence from the Islands or for any other reason incapable of performing the functions of his office, the Administrator, acting in his discretion, may, by instrument under the public seal, appoint to be a temporary member of the State Council—

(*a*) in the case of the incapacity of an official member, a person who holds a public office ; or

(*b*) in the case of the incapacity of a nominated member, a person qualified for appointment as a nominated member.

(2) A person appointed under this section to be a temporary member of the State Council—

(*a*) shall hold his seat in the State Council during Her Majesty's pleasure ; and

(*b*) shall vacate his seat when he is informed by the Administrator, acting in his discretion, that the member on account of whose incapacity he was appointed is again able to perform his functions as a member of the State Council or when the seat of that member becomes vacant.

(3) The Administrator shall forthwith report to Her Majesty through a Secretary of State and to the Governor any appointment made under this section.

(4) Subject to the provisions of this section, the provisions of this Order shall apply to a person appointed to be a temporary member of the State Council as they apply to the member on account of whose incapacity he was appointed.

General elections.
16.—(1) A general election of elected members of the State Council shall be held on such day, being not less than four years and nine months and not more than five years after the Council was last constituted or reconstituted, as the Administrator may, by proclamation published in the Gazette, appoint:

Provided that the Administrator, acting in his discretion, but with the prior approval of the Governor, may, if he considers that it would be in the interests of the Islands to do so, appoint, in like manner, an earlier day for a general election of elected members of the Council.

(2) A person shall be eligible for election at a general election of new members of the Council notwithstanding that he is a member of the Council then in being.

17.—(1) When a general election of elected members of the State Council has been held under the last foregoing section the Administrator shall, by proclamation published in the Gazette, appoint a day upon which the Council shall be reconstituted, and upon that day the newly appointed nominated members and the newly elected members shall assume their seats therein.

Reconstitution of State Council.

(2) An elected member of the State Council elected otherwise than at a general election shall assume his seat at the next meeting of the Council after his election, and a nominated member of the Council appointed otherwise than upon the reconstitution of the Council or an official or temporary member of the Council shall assume his seat therein at the next meeting of the Council after his appointment.

18.—(1) Any question whether—

(a) a person has been validly appointed as an official or a nominated member of the State Council ;

(b) an official or a nominated member of the State Council has vacated his seat therein ; or

(c) a nominated member of the State Council is required, under the provisions of section 14 of this Order, to cease to perform his functions as such,

shall be determined by the Administrator.

Determination of questions as to membership of State Council.

(2) The Supreme Court of the Islands shall have jurisdiction to hear and determine any question whether—

(a) any person has been validly elected as an elected member of the State Council ; or

(b) any elected member of the State Council has vacated his seat or is required, under the provisions of section 14 of this Order, to cease to perform his functions as such.

(3) An application to the Supreme Court for the determination of—

(a) any question under paragraph (a) of the last foregoing subsection may be made by any person entitled to vote in the election to which the application relates or by any person who was a candidate at that election or by the Administrator ; or

(b) any question under paragraph (b) of the last foregoing subsection may be made by any person registered as an elector in the electoral district for which the member concerned was elected or by any elected member of the State Council or by the Administrator ;

and, if an application under this subsection is made by a person other than the Administrator, the Administrator may intervene and may then appear or be represented in the proceedings.

(4) Provision may be made by any law for the time being in force in the Islands with respect to—

(a) the circumstances and manner in which and the imposition of conditions upon which any application may be made to the Supreme Court for the determination of any question under this section ; and (*b*) the powers, practice and procedure of the Supreme Court in relation to any such application.

(5) No appeal shall lie from any determination by the Supreme Court in proceedings under this section.

(6) In the exercise of his functions under this section the Administrator shall act in his discretion.

Penalty for sitting or voting when unqualified. **19.**—(1) Any person who sits or votes in the State Council knowing or having reasonable grounds for knowing that he is not entitled to do so shall be liable to a penalty not exceeding twenty pounds for each day upon which he so sits or votes.

(2) Any such penalty shall be recoverable by civil action in the Supreme Court of the Islands at the suit of the Administrator, acting in his discretion.

Qualifications of voters. **20.**—(1) Subject to the provisions of the next following subsection, and to such provision with respect to the procedure for the registration of voters and for securing that a person is not registered as a voter in more than one electoral district at the same time as may be made by any law in force in the Islands, a person shall be entitled to be registered as a voter in an electoral district if, and shall not be so entitled unless, on the qualifying date he—

(*a*) is a British subject of the age of twenty-one years or upwards ;

(*b*) either has resided in the Islands for the immediately preceding period of twelve months, or is domiciled in the Islands and is resident therein ; and

(*c*) is ordinarily resident in that district.

(2) A person shall not be entitled to be registered as a voter in any electoral district who, on the qualifying date—

(*a*) is under sentence of death imposed on him by a court in any part of the Commonwealth, or is serving a sentence of imprisonment (by whatever name called) exceeding twelve months imposed on him by such a court or substituted by competent authority for some other sentence imposed on him by such a court, or is under such a sentence of imprisonment the execution of which has been suspended ;

(*b*) is a person certified to be insane or otherwise adjudged to be of unsound mind under any law in force in the Islands ; or

(*c*) is disqualified for registration as an elector by any law in force in the Islands relating to offences connected with elections.

(3) The provisions of section 11(2) of this Order shall apply for the purposes of paragraph (*a*) of the foregoing subsection as they apply for the purposes of paragraph (*e*) of section 11(1).

(4) In this section " the qualifying date " means such date as may be prescribed by or under any law in force in the islands as the date with reference to which a register of voters for the electoral district concerned shall be compiled or revised.

21.—(1) Any person who is registered as a voter in an electoral district shall be entitled to vote in such manner as may be prescribed by law at any election for that district unless he is prohibited from so voting by any law in force in the Islands—

(a) because he is a returning officer ;

(b) because he has been concerned in any offence connected with elections ; or

(c) because he has previously voted in some other electoral district on the same day :

Provided that no such person shall be entitled so to vote if on the date appointed for polling he is in lawful custody or, except in so far as may be otherwise provided by any law in force in the Islands, he is for any other reason unable to attend in person at the place and time appointed for polling.

(2) No person shall vote at any election for any electoral district who is not registered as a voter in that district.

PART V

EXECUTIVE FUNCTIONS

22.—(1) Subject to the following provisions of this section, it shall be a function of the State Council to advise the Administrator in the government of the Islands and accordingly, subject as aforesaid, the Administrator shall consult with the Council in the formulation of policy and the exercise of functions conferred upon him by this Order or any other law for the time being in force in the Islands.

(2) The Administrator shall not be obliged to consult with the State Council with respect to—

(a) any function conferred upon him by any provision of this Order which is expressed to be exercisable in his discretion or in pursuance of instructions given to him by Her Majesty through a Secretary of State or by the Governor ;

(b) any function conferred upon him by any other law in terms authorising him to exercise that function without consulting the Council ;

(c) any question of policy or any function that in his opinion relates to defence, external affairs, internal security, the police or the specified public service matters ;

(d) any case in which, in his judgment, the question for decision is too routine in nature to require the Council's advice or is one to which any previous determination of policy applies ; or

(e) any case in which, in his judgment, the urgency of the matter requires him to act before the Council can be consulted ;

but in any case falling within paragraph (e) of this subsection he shall, as soon as practicable, communicate to the Council the measures he has adopted and the reasons therefor.

(3) Subject to the next following subsection, the Administrator shall act in accordance with the advice of the State Council in any case in which he is required by the preceding provisions of this section to consult with the Council.

(4) The Administrator may act against the advice given to him by the Council in any such case if, in his judgment, it is expedient to do so in the interests of public faith or the welfare of the Islands :

Provided that he shall not so act against the advice of the Council without first obtaining the approval of a Secretary of State or the Governor.

(5) Nothing in the foregoing provisions of this section shall apply to the exercise of—

(*a*) any function conferred upon the Administrator by any provision of Part VI of this Order ;

(*b*) the functions of the Administrator relating to the regulation of the procedure of the State Council at any meeting of the Council at which he is presiding ; or

(*c*) the functions conferred upon the Administrator by the proviso to section 13(3)(*e*), section 33(1) and section 43 of this Order ;

and where the Administrator has consulted with the State Council in pursuance of any provision mentioned in paragraph (*c*) of this subsection he shall exercise the function concerned in his own deliberate judgment.

(6) The question whether the Administrator has, in pursuance of the provisions of this section or of any provision mentioned in subsection (5)(*c*) of this section, acted after consultation with, or in accordance with the advice of, the State Council shall not be enquired into in any court of law.

Committees of State Council. **23.**—(1) The Administrator may, by directions in writing, establish one or more committees of the State Council having such functions in relation to the conduct of the business of the Government of the Islands in relation to such matters as may be prescribed by such directions, and (without prejudice to the generality of the foregoing power) directions establishing a committee under this subsection may include provision—

(*a*) with respect to the tenure of office of members of the committee ;

(*b*) regulating the manner in which the committee shall perform its functions and the procedure of the committee.

(2) A committee of the State Council established under this section shall act in accordance with the policies of the Government of the Islands and with any directions given to the committee by the Administrator :

Provided that the question whether it has so acted shall not be enquired into in any court of law.

(3) The functions of a committee of the State Council established under this section shall not include functions in relation to the conduct of business in respect of defence, external affairs, internal security, the police or the specified public service matters.

(4) The provisions of this section shall be without prejudice to the establishment, by or under the rules of procedure of the State Council, of committees of the Council for the purpose of the exercise of its functions under Part VI of this Order or the establishment by the Administrator of committees of the Council for special purposes relating to any of the matters mentioned in the last foregoing subsection.

24.—(1) Where any committee of the State Council has been established under the last foregoing section the Administrator may, by order published in the Gazette, provide that, subject to such limitations and conditions as may be prescribed in the order, any of the powers or duties under any local enactment of the Administrator or of any public officer or public authority that are specified in the order may be exercised or shall be performed by that committee. *Administrator may authorise committee to exercise statutory functions.*

(2) Where an order under the foregoing subsection is in force with respect to any such power or duty—

(*a*) the Administrator or public officer or public authority, as the case may be, shall not exercise that power or perform that duty ;

(*b*) the committee by which the power is exercisable or the duty is to be performed may vary or rescind anything previously done in the exercise or performance thereof to the same extent as the Administrator or public officer or public authority, as the case may be, could have done.

(3) Where, by reason of the revocation or amendment of an order under subsection (1) of this section, a power or duty ceases to be exercisable or is no longer to be performed by a committee of the State Council anything done by the committee in the exercise or performance thereof and having effect immediately before the revocation or amendment shall continue to have effect, but without prejudice to the power of the Administrator or public officer or public authority or any other committee authorised under this section to exercise the power or perform the duty to vary or rescind the same.

(4) Nothing in this section shall apply to—

(*a*) any power or duty to make any subsidiary instrument ; or

(*b*) any power or duty of any judge, magistrate or court of law.

(5) In this section—

" local enactment " means any law made under this Order, any subsidiary instrument made under any such law and any existing law for the purposes of section 48 of this Order ;

" public authority " means a corporation, board or committee established for public purposes by or under a local enactment.

PART VI

LEGISLATION

25.—(1) Subject to the provisions of this Order, the Administrator, with the advice and consent of the State Council, may make laws for the peace, order and good government of the Islands. *Power to make laws.*

(2) The power to make laws conferred by this section shall be exercised by bills passed by the State Council and assented to in accordance with section 27 of this Order.

(3) In the making of laws under this section the Administrator and the State Council shall conform as nearly as may be to the directions contained in any Instructions under Her Majesty's Sign Manual and Signet which may from time to time be addressed to the Administrator in that behalf.

(4) Nothing in this section shall be construed as requiring subsidiary instruments to be made in the manner prescribed by this section.

Adminis-
trator's
reserved
power.

26.—(1) If the Administrator considers that it is expedient—

(*a*) in the interests of public order, public faith or good government (which expressions shall, without prejudice to their generality, include the responsibility of the Islands as a territory within the Commonwealth and all matters pertaining to the creation or abolition of any public office or to the salary or other conditions of service of any public officer) ; or

(*b*) in order to secure detailed control of the finances of the Islands during such time as the Islands are receiving financial assistance from Her Majesty's Exchequer in the United Kingdom, for the purpose of balancing the annual budget or otherwise, upon condition that such control should be exercisable by Her Majesty's Government,

that any bill introduced, or any motion to which this section applies proposed, in the State Council should have effect, then, if the Council fail to pass the bill or to carry the motion within such time and in such form as the Administrator thinks fit, and notwithstanding any provisions of this Order or of any other law in force in the Islands or of any rules of procedure of the Council, the Administrator may declare that the bill or motion shall have effect as if it had been passed or carried by the Council either in the form in which it was introduced or proposed or with such amendments as the Administrator thinks fit which have been moved or proposed in the Council or any committee thereof ; and the bill or the motion shall be deemed thereupon to have been so passed or carried, and the provisions of this Order, and in particular the provisions relating to assent to bills and disallowance of laws, shall have effect accordingly.

(2) The Administrator shall not make any declaration under this section without the prior approval of a Secretary of State or the Governor.

(3) If any member of the State Council objects to any declaration made under this section, he may, within fourteen days of the making thereof, submit to the Administrator a statement in writing of his reasons for so objecting, and a copy of the statement shall, if furnished by the member, be forwarded by the Administrator as soon as practicable to a Secretary of State and to the Governor.

(4) This section applies to—

(*a*) any motion relating to or for the purposes of a bill ;

(*b*) any motion proposing or amending a resolution which, if passed by the State Council, would have the force of law ; and

(*c*) any motion proposing or amending a resolution upon which the coming into force or continuance in force of a subsidiary instrument depends.

Assent to
Bills.

27.—(1) A bill shall not become a law until—

(*a*) the Administrator has assented to it in Her Majesty's name and on Her Majesty's behalf and has signed it in token of his assent ; or

(*b*) Her Majesty has given Her assent to it through a Secretary of State and the Administrator has signified Her assent by proclamation published in the Gazette.

(2) When a bill is presented to the Administrator for his assent, he shall, subject to the provisions of this Order and of any Instructions addressed to him under Her Majesty's Sign Manual and Signet or through a Secretary of State or by the Governor, declare that he assents, or refuses to assent, to it, or that he reserves the bill for the signification of Her Majesty's pleasure :

Provided that the Administrator shall reserve for the signification of Her Majesty's pleasure—

(a) any bill which is in any way repugnant to, or inconsistent with, the provisions of this Order ; and

(b) any bill which determines or regulates the privileges, immunities or powers of the State Council or of its members ;

unless he has been authorised by a Secretary of State to assent to it.

28. The Administrator may return to the State Council any bill presented to him for his assent, transmitting therewith any amendments which he may recommend, and the Council shall deal with such recommendation. _{Return of Bills by Administrator.}

29.—(1) Any law to which the Administrator has given his assent may be disallowed by Her Majesty through a Secretary of State. _{Disallowance of laws.}

(2) Whenever a law has been disallowed by Her Majesty the Administrator shall, as soon as practicable, cause notice of the disallowance to be published in the Gazette and the law shall be annulled with effect from the date of the publication of that notice.

(3) The provisions of section 38 (2) of the Interpretation Act 1889 shall apply to the annulment of any law under this section as they apply to the repeal of an Act of Parliament, save that any enactment repealed or amended by or in pursuance of that law shall have effect as from the date of the annulment as if that law had not been made.

PART VII

PROCEDURE OF STATE COUNCIL

30. Before assuming his functions a member of the State Council shall make before the Administrator, or some other person authorised in that behalf by the Administrator, an oath of allegiance and an oath for the due execution of his functions in the forms set out in the Schedule to this Order. _{Oaths by members of Council.}

31.—(1) The State Council shall not be summoned except by the authority of the Administrator, acting in his discretion. _{Summoning of Council.}

(2) Any meeting of the State Council for the purpose of proceedings to be held in public shall be summoned by the Administrator by notice published in the Gazette.

(3) Where the State Council meets in pursuance of a summons under the last foregoing subsection the meeting may be adjourned from time to time to a subsequent time ; but for the purpose of that subsection a meeting shall be regarded as having been terminated if the Council is adjourned sine die.

Holding of proceedings of Council in public or private.

32.—(1) The proceedings of the State Council for the purpose of consultation by the Administrator with the Council, whether in pursuance of section 22 of this Order or any provision mentioned in subsection 5(*c*) of that section or otherwise, shall be held in private.

(2) Other proceedings of the State Council (including in particular proceedings for the purpose of the exercise of its functions under Part VI of this Order and proceedings relating to any such motion as is mentioned in paragraph (*b*) or (*c*) of section 26(4) of this Order) shall be held in public.

(3) Where in his opinion it would not be contrary to the public interest so to do, the Administrator may, to such extent as he may specify, authorise any nominated or elected member of the State Council to disclose in proceedings of the Council held in public or otherwise to make public the position taken by that member with regard to any matter in proceedings of the Council held in private.

Presiding in Council.

33.—(1) There shall be a Speaker of the State Council, who shall be appointed by the Administrator, acting after consultation with the State Council, by instrument under the public seal, from among the nominated members of the Council.

(2) The Speaker shall vacate his office whenever the State Council is reconstituted or if he ceases to be a nominated member of the State Council or if he resigns his office by writing under his hand addressed to the Administrator.

(3) The Speaker shall preside at any sitting of the State Council held in public, and if the office of Speaker is vacant or the Speaker is absent from any such sitting there shall preside at that sitting such member of the Council as the Council may elect for the sitting.

(4) When the Governor is present in the Islands he may attend any sitting of the State Council held in private and when he does so he shall preside.

(5) The Administrator shall, so far as is practicable, attend the sittings of the State Council held in private and when he does so and the Governor is absent he shall preside ; and if both the Governor and the Administrator are absent from any such sitting there shall preside such member of the Council as the Administrator, acting in his discretion, may either generally or specially appoint.

Quorum.

34.—(1) No business except that of adjournment shall be transacted in the State Council if a quorum of the Council is not present.

(2) A quorum of the State Council shall consist of five members of whom not less than three are elected members.

Submission of questions to State Council.

35.—(1) Subject to the provisions of this Order and of the rules of procedure of the State Council, any member of the Council may submit any question for consideration by the Council.

(2) Nothing in the last foregoing subsection shall be construed as preventing the Administrator from submitting any question for consideration by the Council in proceedings held in private.

36.—(1) Except on the recommendation of the Administrator, the State Council shall not— Restriction on proceedings upon certain measures.

(a) proceed in any meeting held in public upon any bill (including any amendment to a bill) which, in the opinion of the member presiding in the Council, makes provision for imposing or increasing any tax, for imposing or increasing any charge on the revenues or other funds of the Islands or for altering any such charge otherwise than by reducing it or for compounding or remitting any debt due to the Islands ;

(b) proceed in any such meeting upon any motion (including any amendment to a motion) the effect of which, in the opinion of the member presiding in the Council, is that provision would be made for any of the purposes aforesaid.

37.—(1) Subject to the provisions of this Order, all questions proposed for decision at any proceedings of the State Council held in public shall be determined by a majority of the votes of the members present and voting. Voting.

(2) The member presiding shall not vote on any such question unless the votes are equally divided, in which case he shall have and exercise a casting vote.

(3) Where in any proceedings at any meeting of the State Council held in private the Administrator or other person presiding considers it desirable so to do for the purpose of determining what advice is given to the Administrator in any case referred to in section 22(3) of this Order, he may require a vote of the members of the Council to be taken upon the question, and thereupon any advice on that matter shall be regarded as the advice of the Council if a majority of the votes of the members present and voting are cast in favour thereof :

Provided that if the votes cast are equally divided the person presiding may give a casting vote.

38.—(1) When in his opinion the business before the State Council makes it desirable, the Administrator, acting in his discretion, may address the Council or otherwise take part in proceedings thereof held in public as if he were a member of the Council. Participation of Administrator and other persons in certain proceedings.

(2) The person presiding at any sitting of the State Council may, when in his opinion the business before the Council makes it desirable, summon any person to a sitting of the Council, and any person so summoned may, subject to the rules of procedure of the Council, take part in the proceedings of the Council relating to the matter in respect of which he was summoned as if he were a member of the Council.

(3) Nothing in this section shall be construed as entitling any person who is not a member of the State Council to vote upon any question before the Council.

39. Subject to section 34 of this Order, the State Council shall not be disqualified for the transaction of business by reason of any vacancy in the membership thereof (including any vacancy not filled when the Council is first constituted or is reconstituted at any time) and any proceedings therein shall be valid notwithstanding that some person who was not entitled to do so took part therein. Council may transact business notwithstanding vacancies.

Rules of procedure.
40.—(1) Subject to the provisions of this Order and of any Instructions under Her Majesty's Sign Manual and Signet, the State Council may make rules for the regulations and orderly conduct of its own proceedings and the despatch of business at meetings of the Council held in public and for the publication, passing, entitling and numbering of bills and their presentation to the Administrator for assent ; but no such rules shall have effect until approved by the Administrator in his discretion.

(2) Subject as aforesaid and to any rules of procedure, the procedure of the Council at any sitting shall be determined by the person presiding at the sitting.

PART VIII
MISCELLANEOUS

Court of Appeal.
41.—(1) The Court of Appeal for the Bahama Islands (hereinafter referred to as " the Court of Appeal ") shall have jurisdiction to hear and determine such appeals (including cases stated and questions of law reserved) from the courts of the Islands as may be prescribed by or under any law for the time being in force in the Islands, and for the purposes of hearing and determining such appeals the Court of Appeal may sit either in the Islands or in the Bahama Islands as the President of the Court may from time to time direct.

(2) Subject to any provision that may be made by any such law as aforesaid, the provisions of any law for the time being in force in the Bahama Islands shall apply, with the necessary adaptations, qualifications, modifications and exceptions, in relation to the powers, practice and procedure of the Court of Appeal when exercising its jurisdiction under this section (whether sitting in the Islands or in the Bahama Islands) and in relation to the powers conferred and the duties imposed upon other persons or authorities in connection with the exercise of that jurisdiction as those provisions apply in relation to the like matters in connection with the exercise of the jurisdiction of the Court of Appeal in respect of appeals from the courts of the Bahama Islands.

(3) Any power exercisable by a single judge of the Court of Appeal may, at any time when there is no such judge present in the Islands or in the Bahama Islands and able to perform the functions of his office, be performed by a judge of the Supreme Court of the Islands or a judge of the Supreme Court of the Bahama Islands as if that judge were a judge of the Court of Appeal.

Grants of land.
42. Subject to the provisions of any law for the time being in force in the Islands, the Administrator or any person duly authorised by him in writing under his hand may, in Her Majesty's name and on Her behalf, make and execute under the public seal grants and dispositions of any land or other immovable property within the Islands that may be lawfully granted or disposed of by Her Majesty.

Powers of pardon, etc.
43.—(1) The Administrator may, in Her Majesty's name and on Her behalf—

   (*a*) grant to any person convicted of any offence against any law in force in the Islands, a pardon, either free or subject to lawful conditions ;

(*b*) grant to any person a respite, either indefinite or for a specified period, from the execution of any punishment imposed on him for such an offence ;

(*c*) substitute a less severe form of punishment for that imposed by any sentence for such an offence ; or

(*d*) remit the whole or any part of any sentence passed for such an offence or of any penalty or forfeiture otherwise due to Her Majesty on account of such an offence.

(2) In the exercise of his powers under this section the Administrator shall consult with the State Council unless in any particular case not falling within the next following subsection he considers the matter to be too urgent to permit such consultation.

(3) Where any person has been sentenced to death (otherwise than by a court-martial) for an offence the Administrator shall cause a written report of the case from the trial judge, together with such other information derived from the record of the case or elsewhere as he may require, to be taken into consideration at a meeting of the State Council.

44.—(1) The Administrator, in Her Majesty's name and on Her behalf, may constitute such offices for the Islands as may lawfully be constituted by Her Majesty and, subject to the provisions of any law in force in the Islands, may make appointments to any such office ; and any person so appointed shall, unless it is otherwise provided by any such law, hold office during Her Majesty's pleasure. *Offices and appointments.*

(2) The reference in the last foregoing subsection to appointments shall be construed as including a reference to appointments on promotion or transfer, appointments on contract and appointments to act in an office during any period when it is vacant or the holder thereof is absent from the Islands or is for any other reason unable to perform the functions thereof.

45.—(1) Subject to the provisions of this section and of any law in force in the Islands, the Administrator may for cause shown to his satisfaction dismiss or suspend from the exercise of his office any person holding a public office, or take such disciplinary action with respect to such a person as may seem to him to be desirable. *Discipline.*

(2) When the Administrator proposes—

(*a*) to dismiss any officer whose annual salary exceeds such sum as may for the time being be prescribed for the purposes of this section by the Administrator in pursuance of instructions given to him by the Governor ;

(*b*) to award such an officer punishment by way of fine, reduction in rank or otherwise ;

(*c*) to require such an officer to retire from the public service in the exercise of any power in that behalf conferred by any law in force in the Islands ; or

(*d*) to refuse to exercise in relation to such an officer any power conferred by any such law to permit officers to retire from the public service,

the Administrator shall by notice inform the officer of the action he proposes to take and the officer may apply to the Administrator, in writing within seven days of the date of that notice, for the case to be referred to the Governor ; and thereupon the case shall be transferred to the Governor who shall take, or direct the Administrator to take, such action in respect of that officer as he sees fit.

(3) When a case falling within paragraph (*a*) or (*b*) of the last foregoing subsection is referred to the Governor, the Administrator may suspend the officer from the exercise of his office pending the determination of the reference to the Governor ; and any such suspension may at any time be revoked by the Governor.

(4) References in this section to the dismissal of any person holding a public office shall be construed as including references to the termination of a contract on which a person is employed in a public office.

(5) An officer who is suspended from the exercise of his office shall be paid such salary, not being less than half his rate of salary for the period of suspension, as the Administrator may determine.

Privileges of State Council and members.
46. A law enacted under this Order may determine and regulate the privileges, immunities and powers of the State Council and its members, but no such privileges, immunities or powers shall exceed those of the Commons' House of Parliament of the United Kingdom or of the members thereof.

Power reserved to Her Majesty.
47. Her Majesty hereby reserves to Herself power, with the advice of Her Privy Council, to make laws for the peace, order and good government of the Islands.

PART IX

TRANSITIONAL

Existing laws.
48.—(1) Subject to the provisions of this section, the existing laws shall be construed with such modifications, adaptations, qualifications and exceptions as may be necessary to bring them into conformity with the provisions of this Order.

(2) The Administrator may by regulations at any time within twelve months after the appointed day make such modifications or adaptations to any existing law as appears to him to be necessary or expedient for bringing that law into conformity with the provisions of this Order or otherwise for giving effect or enabling effect to be given to those provisions ; and any existing law shall have effect accordingly from such day (not being earlier than the appointed day) as may be specified in the regulations.

(3) Regulations made under this section may be amended or revoked in relation to any existing law effected thereby by any authority competent to amend or revoke that law.

(4) For the purposes of this section " existing law " means any law (including any law made, or having effect as if made, under or

by virtue of the existing Constitution) that has effect as part of the law of the Islands immediately before the appointed day (whether or not it has then come into operation), but does not include any Act of the Parliament of the United Kingdom or any Order in Council or other instrument made under such an Act.

49.—(1) Any office established by the Administrator under the existing Constitution or continued by that Constitution as if so established and subsisting immediately before the appointed day shall on and after that day be deemed to be an office constituted under section 44 of this Order. Existing offices and officers.

(2) Any person who, immediately before the appointed day, holds or is acting in the office of Administrator or any office mentioned in the last foregoing subsection shall, on and after that day, continue to hold or to act in that office as if he had been appointed to hold or to act in it in accordance with the provisions of this Order.

(3) Any person to whom the last foregoing subsection applies who, before the appointed day, has made any oath or affirmation required to be made by him before assuming the functions of his office shall be deemed to have made any like oath or affirmation so required by this Order or any other law.

50.—(1) The persons who immediately before the appointed day are nominated or elected members of the Legislative Assembly established by the existing Constitution (in this section referred to as " the Assembly ") shall as from that day be nominated or elected members of the State Council as if they had been appointed or elected as such and had assumed their seats in pursuance of this Order and shall hold their seats in the Council in accordance with the provisions of this Order. First State Council.

(2) Paragraph (a) of section 10(1) of this Order shall not have effect in relation to the election of any member of the State Council prior to the first general election of members of the Council and paragraph (c) of section 13(3) of this Order shall not have effect until the Council is reconstituted after that general election.

(3) For the purposes of section 16(1) of this Order the State Council shall be deemed to have been constituted on 2nd October 1967 (being the date on which the Assembly first met after the general election of elected members thereof last preceding the appointed day).

(4) Without prejudice to the provisions of section 48 of this Order, the Voters Registration and Election Regulations 1959 (as in force immediately before the appointed day) made under section 64 of the Turks and Caicos Islands (Constitution) Order in Council 1959(a) shall have effect on and after that day as if they were a law made under this Order and references therein to the Assembly were references to the State Council.

(a) S.I. 1959/864 (1959 I, p. 533).

(5) The Standing Orders of the Assembly as in force immediately before the appointed day shall, except as may be otherwise provided under section 40(1) of this Order, have effect on and after that day as if they had been made under that section as rules of procedure of the State Council, but shall be construed with such modifications, adaptations, qualifications and exceptions as may be necessary to bring them into conformity with this Order.

(6) Nothing in subsection (1) of this section shall be construed as exempting any person from complying with the requirements of section 30 of this Order.

Transitional provision relating to certain bills and laws passed or made under existing Constitution.
51. The provisions of sections 27 and 28 of this Order shall apply in relation to any bill passed by the Legislative Assembly established by the existing Constitution but not assented to before the appointed day as they apply in relation to any bill passed by the State Council; and the provisions of section 29 of this Order shall apply in relation to any law to which the Administrator has given his assent under the existing Constitution as they apply in relation to any law to which he has given his assent under this Order.

W. G. Agnew.

SCHEDULE

FORMS OF OATHS AND AFFIRMATIONS

1. *Oath of Allegiance*

I .... do swear that I will be faithful and bear true allegiance to Her Majesty Queen Elizabeth the Second, Her Heirs and Successors, according to law. So help me God.

2. *Oath for the due execution of office of Administrator.*

I .... do swear that I will well and truly serve Her Majesty Queen Elizabeth the Second, Her Heirs and Successors, in the office of Administrator. So help me God.

3. *Oath for the due execution of the functions of a member of the State Council.*

I, ... being a member of the State Council, do swear that I will to the best of my judgment, at meetings of the State Council, freely give my counsel and advice and, when required, cast my vote for the good management of the public affairs of the Turks and Caicos Islands, and I do further swear I will not on any account, at any time whatsoever, make public the counsel, advice, or vote of any other particular member given or cast at any meeting of the State Council held in private and that I will not, except to such extent as may be authorised by the Governor or the Administrator, make public my own counsel, advice or vote or the business or proceedings of the State Council at any meeting held in private or the nature or contents of any documents or any other matter communicated to me solely for the purpose of any such meeting, and that in all things I will be a true and faithful member of the State Council. So help me God.

4. *Affirmations.* In the forms above respectively set forth, for the word " swear " there shall be substituted the words " solemnly and sincerely affirm and declare ", and the words " So help me God " shall be omitted.

EXPLANATORY NOTE

(*This Note is not part of the Order.*)

This Order provides a new Constitution for the Turks and Caicos Islands in place of the Constitution established by the Turks and Caicos Islands (Constitution) Order 1965. It makes provision for constituting the office of Administrator and for the establishment of a State Council. It also provides for the functions of the Governor and Commander-in-Chief of the Bahama Islands in relation to the Turks and Caicos Islands.

STATUTORY INSTRUMENTS

1969 No. 737

ALIENS

The Aliens Order 1969

Made - - - -	23rd *May* 1969
Laid before Parliament	30th *May* 1969
Coming into Operation	2nd *June* 1969

At the Court at Holyroodhouse, the 23rd day of May 1969

Present,

The Queen's Most Excellent Majesty in Council

Her Majesty, in pursuance of section 1 of the Aliens Restriction Act 1914(a), as amended by the Aliens Restriction (Amendment) Act 1919(b), of section 21(5) of the Immigration Appeals Act 1969(c), and of all other powers enabling Her in that behalf, is pleased, by and with the advice of Her Privy Council, to order, and it is hereby ordered, as follows:—

Citation, date of operation and interpretation

1.—(1) This Order may be cited as the Aliens Order 1969.

(2) This Order shall come into operation on 2nd June 1969.

(3) In this Order—

" the principal Order " means the Aliens Order 1953(d) as amended by the Aliens Order 1957(e), the Aliens Order 1960(f), the Aliens Order 1964(g), the Aliens Order 1967(h) and the Aliens Order 1968(i);

" an Appeals Order " means any Order made by virtue of section 14 of the Immigration Appeals Act 1969;

and any other expression which is also used in the principal Order has the same meaning as in that Order.

Liability of owners or agents of ships and aircraft for expenses incurred in respect of aliens directed to be removed from the United Kingdom

2.—(1) Subject to the provisions of this Article, where directions are given under Article 8 of the principal Order for the removal of an alien from the United Kingdom the owners or agents of the ship or aircraft in which he arrived shall be liable to pay to the Secretary of State, on demand, any expenses incurred by the latter in respect of the custody, accommodation or maintenance of that alien at any time after his arrival while he was detained or liable to be detained under paragraph (4) of that Article.

(a) 1914 c. 12.
(b) 1919 c. 92.
(c) 1969 c. 21.
(d) S.I. 1953/1671 (1953 I, p. 94).
(e) S.I. 1957/597 (1957 I, p. 142).
(f) S.I. 1960/2214 (1960 I, p. 291).
(g) S.I. 1964/2034 (1964 III, p. 5116).
(h) S.I. 1967/1282 (1967 II, p. 3712).
(i) S.I. 1968/1649 (1968 III, p. 4471).

(2) The foregoing paragraph shall not apply to expenses in respect of an alien who, when he arrived in the United Kingdom, held—

(*a*) a valid visa for his journey to the United Kingdom; or

(*b*) a current permit of the kind mentioned in Article 4(1)(*b*) of the principal Order (employment permits);

and for the purposes of this paragraph a document purporting to be such a visa or permit shall be treated as genuine unless its falsity is reasonably apparent.

(3) If an alien is granted leave to land before the directions for his removal have been carried out, or he is granted such leave thereafter in consequence of the determination in his favour of an appeal under an Appeals Order (being an appeal against a refusal of leave to land by virtue of which the directions were given or against the directions themselves), no sum shall be demanded under paragraph (1) of this Article for expenses incurred in respect of that alien and any such sum already demanded and paid shall be refunded.

(4) In paragraph (1) of this Article " directions " does not include directions which by virtue of an Appeals Order have ceased to have effect or are for the time being of no effect; and the expenses to which that paragraph applies include expenses in conveying the alien in question to and from the place where he is detained or accommodated unless the journey is made for the purpose of attending an appeal by him under an Appeals Order.

W. G. Agnew.

EXPLANATORY NOTE

(This Note is not part of the Order)

This Order provides for the recovery of certain expenses incurred by the Secretary of State, in respect of an alien directed to be removed from the United Kingdom, from the owners or agents of the ship or aircraft in which he arrived. Its provisions correspond to those in section 21 of the Immigration Appeals Act 1969 in relation to Commonwealth citizens.

STATUTORY INSTRUMENTS

1969 No. 738

DANGEROUS DRUGS

The Dangerous Drugs Act 1965 (Modification) Order 1969

Made - - - *23rd May* 1969

Coming into Operation *16th June* 1969

At the Court at Holyroodhouse, the 23rd day of May 1969

Present,

The Queen's Most Excellent Majesty in Council

Whereas it appears to Her Majesty that a decision of the Commission on Narcotic Drugs of the Economic and Social Council of the United Nations to alter Schedule I to the Single Convention on Narcotic Drugs signed at New York on 30th March 1961 so as to add the substance bezitramide thereto requires the addition of that substance to Part I of the Schedule to the Dangerous Drugs Act 1965(a):

Now, therefore, Her Majesty, in pursuance of the powers conferred on Her by section 12 of the Dangerous Drugs Act 1965, is pleased, by and with the advice of Her Privy Council, to order, and it is hereby ordered, as follows:—

1. This Order may be cited as the Dangerous Drugs Act 1965 (Modification) Order 1969 and shall come into operation on 16th June 1969.

2. In paragraph 1 in Part I of the Schedule to the Dangerous Drugs Act 1965 (which specifies substances dealings in which are subject to control under Part III of the Act) after the word "Betaprodine" there shall be inserted the word "Bezitramide".

W. G. Agnew.

EXPLANATORY NOTE

(This Note is not part of the Order.)

This Order brings under control under Part III of the Dangerous Drugs Act 1965 the substance bezitramide and its salts, and any preparation, admixture, extract or other substance containing any proportion of those substances. The result of such control will be that it will not be lawful to import or export those substances except under licence, and that those substances will be subject to control under Part II of the Dangerous Drugs (No. 2) Regulations 1964— (S.I. 1964/1811).

(a) 1965 c. 15.

STATUTORY INSTRUMENTS

1969 No. 739

GENOCIDE

The Genocide Act (Guernsey) Order 1969

Made - - - -	*23rd May* 1969
Coming into Operation	*1st June* 1969

At the Court at Holyroodhouse, the 23rd day of May 1969

Present,

The Queen's Most Excellent Majesty in Council

Her Majesty, in pursuance of the power conferred upon Her by section 3(2) of the Genocide Act 1969(a), is pleased, by and with the advice of Her Privy Council, to order, and it is hereby ordered, as follows:—

1. This Order may be cited as the Genocide Act (Guernsey) Order 1969 and shall come into operation on 1st June 1969.

2. In this Order "Guernsey" means the Bailiwick of Guernsey and the territorial waters adjacent thereto.

3. Sections 1 and 4 of, and the Schedule to, the Genocide Act 1969 shall extend to Guernsey subject to the exceptions specified in the Schedule to this Order.

W. G. Agnew.

SCHEDULE

EXCEPTIONS TO THE EXTENSION OF THE GENOCIDE ACT 1969 TO GUERNSEY

1. In section 1(2) the words "on indictment" shall be omitted.
2. Section 1(3), (4) and (5) shall be omitted.

EXPLANATORY NOTE

(This Note is not part of the Order.)

This Order extends to the Bailiwick of Guernsey, with the appropriate exceptions, the provisions of the Genocide Act 1969 creating the offence of genocide.

(a) 1969 c. 12.

1969 No. 740

MERCHANT SHIPPING

The Merchant Shipping Act 1965 (Isle of Man) Order 1969

Made - - - -	23rd *May* 1969
Laid before Parliament	30th *May* 1969
Coming into Operation	1st *June* 1969

At the Court at Holyroodhouse, the 23rd day of May 1969

Present,

The Queen's Most Excellent Majesty in Council

Her Majesty, in pursuance of section 6 of the Merchant Shipping Act 1965**(a)**, is pleased, by and with the advice of Her Privy Council, to order, and it is hereby ordered, as follows:—

1.—(1) This Order may be cited as the Merchant Shipping Act 1965 (Isle of Man) Order 1969 and shall come into operation on 1st June 1969.

(2) The Interpretation Act 1889**(b)** shall apply for the purpose of the interpretation of this Order as it applies for the purpose of the interpretation of an Act of Parliament.

2. The Merchant Shipping Act 1965 shall extend to the Isle of Man subject to the exceptions, adaptations and modifications specified in the Schedule to this Order.

W. G. Agnew.

SCHEDULE

EXCEPTIONS, ADAPTIONS AND MODIFICATIONS IN THE MERCHANT SHIPPING ACT 1965 AS EXTENDED TO THE ISLE OF MAN

1. Any reference to the commencement of the Act shall be construed as a reference to the coming into operation of this Order.

2. In section 1(1) for the words "the Board of Trade by statutory instrument" there shall be substituted the words "the Isle of Man Harbour Board with the approval of Tynwald".

3. In section 1(4) for the words "the Board of Trade" there shall be substituted the words "the Isle of Man Harbour Board" and the words following that expression shall be omitted.

(a) 1965 c. 47.   (b) 1889 c. 63.

4. In section 1(6) for the words "United Kingdom" there shall be substituted the words "Isle of Man".

5. Section 1(7) shall be omitted.

6. In section 2 after the words "1932" there shall be inserted the words "as extended to the Isle of Man by the Merchant Shipping Load Line Convention (Isle of Man) Order 1935(a)".

7. Sections 4 and 5 shall be omitted.

8. Paragraphs (b) and (c) of section 6 shall be omitted.

9. Section 8(4) shall be omitted.

10. In Schedule 1 the entry relating to the Crown Proceedings Act 1947(b) shall be omitted.

EXPLANATORY NOTE

(*This Note is not part of the Order.*)

This Order extends the provisions of the Merchant Shipping Act 1965 to the Isle of Man with exceptions, adaptations and modifications.

(a) S. R. & O. 1935/714 (Rev. XIV, p. 378: 1935, p. 1173).
(b) 1947 c. 44.

STATUTORY INSTRUMENTS

1969 No. 741

MERCHANT SHIPPING

The Merchant Shipping Act 1965 (Jersey) Order 1969

Made - - -	*23rd May* 1969
Laid before Parliament	*30th May* 1969
Coming into Operation	*1st June* 1969

At the Court at Holyroodhouse, the 23rd day of May 1969

Present,

The Queen's Most Excellent Majesty in Council

Her Majesty, in pursuance of section 6 of the Merchant Shipping Act 1965(**a**), is pleased, by and with the advice of Her Privy Council, to order, and it is hereby ordered, as follows :—

1.—(1) This Order may be cited as the Merchant Shipping Act 1965 (Jersey) Order 1969 and shall come into operation on 1st June 1969.

(2) The Interpretation Act 1889(**b**) shall apply for the purpose of the interpretation of this Order as it applies for the purpose of the interpretation of an Act of Parliament.

2. The Merchant Shipping Act 1965 shall extend to the Bailiwick of Jersey subject to the exceptions, adaptations and modifications specified in the Schedule to this Order.

W. G. Agnew.

SCHEDULE

EXCEPTIONS, ADAPTATIONS AND MODIFICATIONS IN THE MERCHANT SHIPPING ACT 1965 AS EXTENDED TO THE BAILIWICK OF JERSEY

1. In section 1(1) for the words "the Board of Trade by statutory instrument" there shall be substituted the words "order of the Harbours and Airport Committee of the States of Jersey".

2. In section 1(4) for the words "the Board of Trade" there shall be substituted the words "the Harbours and Airport Committee of the States of Jersey" and the words following that expression shall be omitted.

3. In section 1(6) for the words "United Kingdom" there shall be substituted the words "Bailiwick of Jersey".

(**a**) 1965 c. 47. (**b**) 1889 c. 63.

4. For section 1(7) there shall be substituted the following subsection : —

"(7) The Subordinate Legislation (Jersey) Law 1960 shall apply to any order under this section and any such order may be revoked or amended by another such order.".

5. In section 2 after the words "1932" there shall be inserted the words "as extended to the Bailiwick of Jersey by the Merchant Shipping Load Line Convention (Jersey) Order 1933(a)".

6. Sections 4 and 5 shall be omitted.

7. Paragraphs (a) and (c) of section 6 shall be omitted.

8. For section 8(4) there shall be substituted the following subsection : —

"(4) This Act shall come into operation upon its registration in the Royal Court of Jersey but any reference to the commencement of this Act shall be construed as a reference to the coming into operation of the first order to be made under section 1 thereof.".

9. In Schedule 1 the entry relating to the Crown Proceedings Act 1947(b) shall be omitted.

EXPLANATORY NOTE

(*This Note is not part of the Order.*)

This Order extends the provisions of the Merchant Shipping Act 1965 to the Bailiwick of Jersey with exceptions, adaptations and modifications.

(a) S.R. & O. 1933/53 (Rev. XIV, p. 374: 1933, p. 1363).
(b) 1947 c. 44.

STATUTORY INSTRUMENTS

1969 No. 742

INCOME TAX

The Central Banks (Income Tax Schedule C Exemption) Order 1969

Laid before the House of Commons in draft
Made - - - *23rd May* 1969

At the Court at Holyroodhouse, the 23rd day of May 1969

Present,

The Queen's Most Excellent Majesty in Council

Whereas it appears to Her Majesty that the Bank Negara Malaysia (Central Bank of Malaysia) is not resident in the United Kingdom and is entrusted by the government of a territory outside the United Kingdom with the custody of the principal foreign exchange reserves of that territory :

And whereas a draft of this Order was laid before the Commons House of Parliament in accordance with the provisions of section 22(3) of the Finance Act 1957(a) and has been approved by resolution of that House :

Now, therefore, Her Majesty, in exercise of the powers conferred on Her by section 22(2) of the said Finance Act 1957 and of all other powers enabling Her in that behalf, is pleased, by and with the advice of Her Privy Council, to order, and it is hereby ordered, as follows :—

1. This Order may be cited as the Central Banks (Income Tax Schedule C Exemption) Order 1969.

2. Section 22 of the Finance Act 1957 shall apply to the Bank Negara Malaysia.

W. G. Agnew.

EXPLANATORY NOTE

(This Note is not part of the Order.)

Section 22 of the Finance Act 1957 exempts from income tax under Schedule C the interest on United Kingdom Government securities held by banks, or the issue departments of banks, to which that section applies, and empowers Her Majesty by Order in Council to direct that the section shall apply to any bank, or to the issue department of any bank, not resident in the United Kingdom, which is entrusted by the government of a territory outside the United Kingdom with the principal foreign exchange reserves of that territory.

This Order specifies the Bank Negara Malaysia (or, in English, the Central Bank of Malaysia) as a bank to which section 22 is to apply.

(a) 5 & 6 Eliz. 2. c. 49.

1969 No. 743

COPYRIGHT

The Copyright (Bermuda : Protection of Foreign Broadcasts) Order 1969

Made - - -	*23rd May* 1969
Laid before Parliament	*30th May* 1969
Coming into Operation	*23rd August* 1969

At the Court at Holyroodhouse, the 23rd day of May 1969

Present,

The Queen's Most Excellent Majesty in Council

Her Majesty, in pursuance of the powers conferred upon Her by section 31 of the Copyright Act 1956(**a**) and of all other powers enabling Her in that behalf, is pleased, by and with the advice of Her Privy Council, to direct, and it is hereby directed, as follows :—

1. This Order may be cited as the Copyright (Bermuda : Protection of Foreign Broadcasts) Order 1969 and shall come into operation on 23rd August 1969.

2. The Interpretation Act 1889(**b**) shall apply to the interpretation of this Order as it applies to the interpretation of an Act of Parliament.

3. Part II and (so far as relevant thereto) Part III of the Copyright (International Conventions) Order 1964(**c**) shall extend to Bermuda subject to the modifications specified in the Schedule hereto.

W. G. Agnew.

SCHEDULE

Modifications to Part II of the Copyright (International Conventions) Order 1964

1. In article 8, the words "other than section 40(3)" shall be omitted.

(**a**) 1956 c. 74.
(**c**) S.I. 1964/690 (1964 II, p. 1319).
(**b**) 1889 c. 63.

2. In article 9, the words "other than section 37(4), section 40(3) and Schedule 5" and paragraph (a) shall be omitted.

3. In Schedule 5, to the countries listed in column 1 there shall be added Czechoslovakia, Denmark, Brazil and the Federal Republic of Germany (and Land Berlin), and the date included in column 2 in relation to each country named in column 1 shall be 23rd August 1969.

4. In Schedule 6, France shall be deleted from and Czechoslovakia, Brazil and the Federal Republic of Germany (and Land Berlin) shall be added to the countries listed in column 1, and the date included in column 2 in relation to each country named in column 1 shall be 23rd August 1969.

EXPLANATORY NOTE

(This Note is not part of the Order.)

The United Kingdom proposes to declare Bermuda to be a territory to which the International Convention for the Protection of Performers, Producers of Phonograms and Broadcasting Organisations shall extend.

This Order implements the obligations thereby undertaken in respect of foreign sound and television broadcasts by extending to Bermuda those provisions of the Copyright (International Conventions) Order 1964 which protect foreign broadcasts.

The law of Bermuda already gives performers of literary and artistic works and producers of phonograms the protection required by the Convention.

STATUTORY INSTRUMENTS

1969 No. 747

INDUSTRIAL TRAINING

The Industrial Training Levy (Water Supply) Order 1969

Made - - - -	*23rd May* 1969
Laid before Parliament	*4th June* 1969
Coming into Operation	*9th June* 1969

The Secretary of State after approving proposals submitted by the Water Supply Industry Training Board for the imposition of a further levy on employers in the water supply industry and in exercise of her powers under section 4 of the Industrial Training Act 1964(a) and of all other powers enabling her in that behalf hereby makes the following Order:—

Title and commencement

1. This Order may be cited as the Industrial Training Levy (Water Supply) Order 1969 and shall come into operation on 9th June 1969.

Interpretation

2.—(1) In this Order unless the context otherwise requires :—

(*a*) " activities of the water supply industry " means any activities which, subject to the provisions of paragraph 2 of Schedule 1 to the industrial training order, are specified in paragraph 1 of that Schedule as activities of the water supply industry ;

(*b*) " an appeal tribunal " means an industrial tribunal established under section 12 of the Industrial Training Act 1964 ;

(*c*) " assessment " means an assessment of an employer to the levy ;

(*d*) " emoluments " means all emoluments assessable to income tax under Schedule E (other than pensions), being emoluments from which tax under that Schedule is deductible, whether or not tax in fact falls to be deducted from any particular payment thereof ;

(*e*) " employer " means an employer in the water supply industry, being on the day upon which this Order comes into operation statutory water undertakers or a regional water board ;

(*f*) " the fourth base period " means the period of twelve months that commenced on 6th April 1968 ;

(*g*) " the fourth levy period " means the period commencing with the day upon which this Order comes into operation and ending on 31st March 1970 ;

(*h*) " the Industrial Training Board " means the Water Supply Industry Training Board ;

(a) 1964 c. 16.

(*i*) " the industrial training order " means the Industrial Training (Water Supply Board) Order 1965(**a**) ;

(*j*) " the levy " means the levy imposed by the Board in respect of the fourth levy period ;

(*k*) " local water authority " means a local water authority within the meaning of the Water (Scotland) Act 1946(**b**) ;

(*l*) " notice " means a notice in writing ;

(*m*) " regional water board " means a regional water board within the meaning of the Water (Scotland) Act 1967(**c**) ;

(*n*) " statutory water undertakers " means any statutory water undertakers within the meaning of the Water Act 1945(**d**).

(2) The Interpretation Act 1889(**e**) shall apply to the interpretation of this Order as it applies to the interpretation of an Act of Parliament.

Imposition of the Levy

3.—(1) The levy to be imposed by the Industrial Training Board on employers in respect of the fourth levy period shall be assessed in accordance with the provisions of this Article.

(2) The levy shall be assessed by the Industrial Training Board in respect of each employer.

(3) The amount of the levy imposed on an employer shall be a sum equal to 1·6 per cent. of the emoluments of the persons following—

(*a*) in the case of statutory water undertakers, all persons employed by the employer in the fourth base period in activities of the water supply industry and any other persons employed at any time in that period in a water undertaking or part of a water undertaking that on the day upon which this Order comes into operation forms part of the water undertaking of the employer ;

(*b*) in the case of a regional water board, all persons employed in activities of the water supply industry in the fourth base period by the regional water board or by a local water authority whose functions have been transferred in whole or in part to that regional water board under the Water (Scotland) Act 1967, being, in the case of a local water authority, persons who were solely employed in connection with the functions so transferred.

Assessment Notice

4.—(1) The Industrial Training Board shall serve an assessment notice on every employer.

(2) An assessment notice shall state the address of the said Board for the service of a notice of appeal or of an application for an extension of time for appealing.

(3) An assessment notice may be served on an employer by sending it by post to the employer's registered or principal office.

Payment of the Levy

5.—(1) Subject to the provisions of this Article and of Articles 6 and 7, the amount of an assessment appearing in an assessment notice served by the Industrial Training Board shall be payable to the Board in two equal instalments, which shall be due respectively one month and six months after the date of the notice.

(**a**) S.I. 1965/1258 (1965 II, p. 3556).   (**b**) 1946 c. 42.   (**c**) 1967 c. 78.
(**d**) 1945 c. 42.   (**e**) 1889 c. 63.

(2) An instalment of an assessment shall not be recoverable by the Industrial Training Board until there has expired the time allowed for appealing against the assessment by Article 7(1) of this Order and any further period or periods of time that the said Board or an appeal tribunal may have allowed for appealing under paragraph (2) or (3) of that Article or, where an appeal is brought, until the appeal is decided or withdrawn.

Withdrawal of Assessment

6.—(1) The Industrial Training Board may, by a notice served on the person assessed to the levy in the same manner as an assessment notice, withdraw an assessment if that person has appealed against that assessment under the provisions of Article 7 of this Order and the appeal has not been entered in the Register of Appeals kept under the appropriate Regulations specified in paragraph (4) of that Article.

(2) The withdrawal of an assessment shall be without prejudice to the power of the Industrial Training Board to serve a further assessment notice on the person assessed to the levy.

Appeals

7.—(1) A person assessed to the levy may appeal to an appeal tribunal against the assessment within one month from the date of the service of the assessment notice or within any further period or periods of time that may be allowed by the Industrial Training Board or an appeal tribunal under the following provisions of this Article.

(2) The Industrial Training Board by notice may for good cause allow a person assessed to the levy to appeal to an appeal tribunal against the assessment at any time within the period of four months from the date of the service of the assessment notice or within such further period or periods as the Board may allow before such time as may then be limited for appealing has expired.

(3) If the Industrial Training Board shall not allow an application for extension of time for appealing, an appeal tribunal shall upon application made to the tribunal by the person assessed to the levy have the like powers as the Board under the foregoing paragraph.

(4) An appeal or an application to an appeal tribunal under this Article shall be made in accordance with the Industrial Tribunals (England and Wales) Regulations 1965(a) as amended by the Industrial Tribunals (England and Wales) (Amendment) Regulations 1967(b) except in the case of a regional water board when the appeal or application shall be made in accordance with the Industrial Tribunals (Scotland) Regulations 1965(c) as amended by the Industrial Tribunals (Scotland) (Amendment) Regulations 1967(d).

(5) The powers of an appeal tribunal under paragraph (3) of this Article may be exercised by the President of the Industrial Tribunals (England and Wales) or by the President of the Industrial Tribunals (Scotland) as the case may be.

Evidence

8.—(1) Upon the discharge by a person assessed to the levy of his liability under an assessment the Industrial Training Board shall if so requested issue to him a certificate to that effect.

(a) S.I. 1965/1101 (1965 II, p. 2805).
(c) S.I. 1965/1157 (1965 II, p. 3266).
(b) S.I. 1967/301 (1967 I, p. 1040).
(d) S.I. 1967/302 (1967 I, p. 1050).

(2) The production in any proceedings of a document purporting to be certified by the Secretary of the Industrial Training Board to be a true copy of an assessment or other notice issued by the Board or purporting to be a certificate such as is mentioned in the foregoing paragraph of this Article shall, unless the contrary is proved, be sufficient evidence of the document and of the facts stated therein.

Signed by order of the Secretary of State.

23rd May 1969.

Roy Hattersley,
Joint Parliamentary Under-Secretary of State,
Department of Employment and Productivity.

EXPLANATORY NOTE

(This Note is not part of the Order.)

This Order, which is made by the Secretary of State for Employment and Productivity, gives effect to proposals submitted by the Water Supply Industry Training Board for the imposition of a further levy on employers in the water supply industry for the purpose of raising money towards the expenses of the Board.

The levy is to be imposed in respect of the fourth levy period commencing with the date on which this Order comes into operation and ending on 31st March 1970. The levy will be assessed by the Industrial Training Board and there will be a right of appeal against an assessment to an industrial tribunal.

STATUTORY INSTRUMENTS

1969 No. 752

AGRICULTURE

CEREALS MARKETING

The Home-Grown Cereals Authority (Rates of Levy) Order 1969

Made - - - -		*23rd May* 1969
Laid before Parliament		*4th June* 1969
Coming into Operation		*1st July* 1969

Whereas the Home-Grown Cereals Authority (hereinafter referred to as "the Authority"), established by the Cereals Marketing Act 1965(a) (hereinafter referred to as "the Act"), have prepared and submitted to the Ministers hereinafter named, pursuant to section 13(1)(*a*) of the Act, an estimate of the amount required to be raised by levy for the period of twelve months beginning with 1st July 1969 (hereinafter referred to as "the relevant year") for the purposes of the Authority's functions under Part I of the Act:

And whereas pursuant to section 13(2) of the Act the Authority duly submitted to the Ministers with such estimate proposals as to the kinds of home-grown cereals in respect of which a levy should be imposed and as to the apportionment of the amount specified in the estimate as between those kinds of home-grown cereals:

And whereas the Ministers have determined that the amount to be raised by levy for the relevant year for such purposes shall be £1,440,000 and have determined that the kinds of home-grown cereals in respect of which the levy is to be imposed for that year shall be wheat and barley:

And whereas the Ministers have apportioned the amount so determined as between those kinds of home-grown cereals:

And whereas by virtue of section 14 of the Act the levy in respect of the relevant year will be imposed as mentioned in section 15(1) of the Act:

Now, therefore, the Minister of Agriculture, Fisheries and Food, the Secretaries of State respectively concerned with agriculture in Scotland and Northern Ireland and the Secretary of State for Wales, acting jointly in exercise of the powers conferred upon them by section 13 of the Act, as read with the Transfer of Functions (Wales) Order 1969(b), and of all other powers enabling them in that behalf, hereby make the following order:—

Citation and commencement

1. This order may be cited as the Home-Grown Cereals Authority (Rates of Levy) Order 1969; and shall come into operation on 1st July 1969.

Interpretation

2.—(1) In this order—

"cereals (guarantee payments) order" means an order under section 1 of the Agriculture Act 1957(c) which provides for payments to growers of home-grown cereals;

(a) 1965 c. 14.
(c) 1957 c. 57.   (b) S.I. 1969/388 (1969 I, p. 1070).

"cereals (protection of guarantees) order" means an order made under section 5 of the Agriculture Act 1957 for the purpose of supporting any arrangements in force by virtue of a cereals (guarantee payments) order;

"deficiency payment" means a payment made in pursuance of any cereals (guarantee payments) order;

"home-grown cereals" means cereals grown in the United Kingdom and being either wheat, barley, oats or rye, and "home-grown wheat" and "home-grown barley" shall be construed accordingly;

"registered buyer" means a person for the time being registered as a buyer of barley for the purposes of any cereals (protection of guarantees) order;

"registered grower" means a person for the time being registered as a grower for the purposes of any cereals (guarantee payments) order.

(2) The Interpretation Act 1889(a) shall apply to the interpretation of this order as it applies to the interpretation of an Act of Parliament.

Rates of levy

3. The rate of levy for the relevant year, which appears to the Ministers to be sufficient (but not more than sufficient) to meet the amount apportioned to—

(*a*) home-grown wheat, shall be 1·8d. per cwt;

(*b*) home-grown barley shall be 1·4d. per cwt. and 9d. per acre;

and the rate of levy shall apply respectively in respect of the quantity of home-grown wheat delivered and the quantity of home-grown barley delivered and the acreage of land used for the growing of such barley as determined in accordance with the following provisions of this order.

Home-grown wheat subject to levy

4. The quantity of home-grown wheat on which the relevant levy is to be imposed shall be that quantity (any quantity of less than 1 cwt. to be ignored)—

(*a*) which is delivered by or on behalf of registered growers during the relevant year to, or in accordance with the instructions of, purchasers thereof; and

(*b*) in respect of which deficiency payments would, apart from section 15 of the Act, be paid to or in respect of the registered growers thereof.

Home-grown barley subject to levy

5.—(1) The quantity of home-grown barley on which the relevant part of the levy in respect of that barley is to be imposed shall be that quantity (any quantity of less than 1 cwt. to be ignored)—

(*a*) which is delivered by or on behalf of registered growers during the relevant year to, or in accordance with the instructions of, registered buyers thereof; and

(*b*) in respect of which deductions or additions would be made in accordance with a cereals (guarantee payments) order from or to deficiency payments which would, apart from section 15 of the Act, be paid to or in respect of the registered growers thereof.

(2) The acreage of land on which the relevant part of the levy in respect of home-grown barley is to be imposed shall be the acreage of land (any area of less than one quarter of an acre to be ignored) used for the growing of home-grown

---

(a) 1889 c. 63.

barley for harvesting during the relevant year being land in relation to which deficiency payments would, apart from section 15 of the Act, be paid to or in respect of the registered growers of such barley.

In Witness whereof the Official Seal of the Minister of Agriculture, Fisheries and Food is hereunto affixed on 16th May 1969.

(L.S.)

Cledwyn Hughes,
Minister of Agriculture, Fisheries and Food.

Given under the Seal of the Secretary of State for Scotland on 19th May 1969.

(L.S.)

William Ross,
Secretary of State for Scotland.

Given under the hand of the Secretary of State for the Home Department on 23rd May 1969.

James Callaghan,
Secretary of State for the Home Department.

Given under my hand on 22nd May 1969.

George Thomas,
Secretary of State for Wales.

EXPLANATORY NOTE

(This Note is not part of the Order.)

This order specifies, in respect of home-grown wheat and home-grown barley, the rates of levy to be raised in respect of the year beginning with 1st July 1969 to meet the amounts apportioned by the Ministers to these kinds of home-grown cereals to finance the Home-Grown Cereals Authority in the performance of their non-trading functions under Part I of the Cereals Marketing Act 1965. These functions include the implementation of bonus payment schemes for growers of wheat and barley.

The order also includes provisions as to the quantity of wheat or barley, and acreage of land used for growing barley, in respect of which the levy is to be imposed.

The levy will be recovered as mentioned in section 15 of the Act, which provides for recovery by deduction from cereals deficiency payments.

STATUTORY INSTRUMENTS

1969 No. 753

WAGES COUNCILS

The Wages Regulation (Licensed Residential Establishment and Licensed Restaurant) Order 1969

Made - - - -	*27th May* 1969
Coming into Operation	*7th July* 1969

Whereas the Secretary of State has received from the Licensed Residential Establishment and Licensed Restaurant Wages Council the wages regulation proposals set out in the Schedule hereto;

Now, therefore, the Secretary of State in exercise of her powers under section 11 of the Wages Councils Act 1959(a), and of all other powers enabling her in that behalf, hereby makes the following Order:—

1. This Order may be cited as the Wages Regulation (Licensed Residential Establishment and Licensed Restaurant) Order 1969.

2.—(1) In this Order the expression "the specified date" means the 7th July 1969, provided that where, as respects any worker who is paid wages at intervals not exceeding seven days, that date does not correspond with the beginning of the period for which the wages are paid, the expression "the specified date" means, as respects that worker, the beginning of the next such period following that date.

(2) The Interpretation Act 1889(b) shall apply to the interpretation of this Order as it applies to the interpretation of an Act of Parliament and as if this Order and the Order hereby revoked were Acts of Parliament.

3. The wages regulation proposals set out in the Schedule hereto shall have effect as from the specified date and as from that date the Wages Regulation (Licensed Residential Establishment and Licensed Restaurant) Order 1968(c), shall cease to have effect.

Signed by order of the Secretary of State.

C. F. Heron,
Deputy Under Secretary of State,
Department of Employment and Productivity.

27th May 1969.

(a) 1959 c. 69.   (b) 1889 c. 63.
(c) S.I. 1968/54 (1968 I, p. 116).

Article 3

ARRANGEMENT OF SCHEDULE

PART I

REMUNERATION FOR EMPLOYMENT

Paragraphs

Remuneration for employment 1
Definition of grades or descriptions of workers 2
Other definitions relating to Tables of minimum remuneration 3
Tables of minimum remuneration:
    workers other than apprentice cooks, trainee cooks and extra waiting
    staff 4
Two-year and four-year trainee cooks 5
Workers supplied with full board and lodging 6
Workers supplied with meals but not with full board and lodging ... 7
Service workers employed under a written agreement relating to gratuities 8
Full-time workers not provided with laundry 9
Workers required to wear uniform or protective clothing of a distinctive
    character not provided by the employer 10
Extra waiting staff 11
Additional payment for night work 12
Payment for spreadover of hours of work 13
Payment for emergency duty 14
Special provisions relating to intervals for rest 15
Workers temporarily transferred to higher grade work 16
Hours on which remuneration is based 17
Guaranteed remuneration 18
Overtime 19
Special provisions relating to rest days 20
Special provisions relating to full-time workers who are not required to
    work on a customary holiday 21
Special provisions relating to full-time workers who work on a customary
    holiday 22
Night work in relation to customary holidays 23

PART II

ANNUAL HOLIDAY AND HOLIDAY REMUNERATION

Duration of annual holiday 24–25
Spells of annual holiday 26
Agreement to allow annual holiday outside the holiday season 27
Applications to vary the holiday season 28
General 29–30
Remuneration for annual holiday 31–32
Accrued holiday remuneration payable on termination of employment ... 33
Calculation of employment 34

PART III

GENERAL

Definitions 35
Workers to whom the Schedule applies 36–37
Illegal deductions, etc. 38

1k

SCHEDULE

PART I

REMUNERATION FOR EMPLOYMENT

1. Subject to the provisions of this Schedule—

the minimum remuneration for workers to whom this Schedule applies (other than trainee cooks, extra head waiters, extra waiters and extra waitresses) shall be in accordance with paragraph 4 hereof;

the minimum remuneration for trainee cooks shall be in accordance with paragraph 5 hereof; and

the minimum remuneration for extra head waiters, extra waiters and extra waitresses shall be in accordance with paragraph 11 hereof.

Provided that—

(a) an employer shall be treated as supplying full board and lodging or meals to a worker if he makes them available to the worker;

(b) in calculating the remuneration for the purposes of this Schedule recognised breaks for mealtimes shall be excluded;

(c) the minimum remuneration for a worker aged under 21 years who is employed as a waiter or waitress, and who has received a Certificate of Service under an apprenticeship scheme for waiters or waitresses administered by the National Joint Apprenticeship Council of the Hotel and Catering Industry or the Hotel and Catering Industry Training Board, shall be that for a waiter or waitress as the case may be, aged 21 years or over.

2. In this Schedule the following expressions have the meanings hereby respectively assigned to them; and shown against each grade (in column 2) is the number where applicable of the appropriate group in the Tables of remuneration in paragraph 4.

Grade or description of worker	No. of appropriate group in Tables of remuneration
Column 1	Column 2
APPRENTICE COOK has the meaning assigned to it in paragraph 5.	—
ASSISTANT MANAGER OR ASSISTANT MANAGERESS is a worker wholly or mainly engaged on catering work who assists the Manager or Manageress and who takes charge of the establishment during the absence of the Manager or Manageress.	—
BARMAID is a female worker aged 21 years or over who is wholly or mainly employed in dispensing, or in dispensing and serving, refreshment at a bar or dispense, or on duties ancillary to any of these duties and who is not a cocktail barmaid.	19
BARMAID, COCKTAIL is a female worker who is wholly or mainly employed in serving, or in dispensing and serving, refreshment at a cocktail bar.	*31*
BARMAID, HEAD is a barmaid who supervises not less than three barmen or barmaids, and who is responsible for the bar and the records.	22
BARMAN, COCKTAIL is a male worker who is wholly or mainly employed in serving, or in dispensing and serving refreshment at a cocktail bar.	11
BARMAN, DISPENSE, ETC., is a male worker aged 21 years or over who is wholly or mainly employed in dispensing, or in dispensing and serving, refreshment at a dispense, lounge, saloon or private bar, or on duties ancillary thereto and who is not a cocktail barman.	2
BARMAN, HEAD is a barman who supervises not less than three barmen or barmaids, and who is responsible for the bar and the records.	3
BARMAN, HEAD COCKTAIL is a barman who supervises not less than three barmen or barmaids who are wholly or mainly employed in dispensing at a cocktail bar, and who is responsible for the bar and the records.	13
BARMAN, PUBLIC is a male worker aged 21 years or over who is wholly or mainly employed in dispensing, or in dispensing and serving, refreshment at a public bar, or on duties ancillary to any of these duties.	1
BUTCHER is a male worker aged 21 years or over who is responsible for the storage of meat and who is wholly or mainly employed in the cutting up or dressing and preparation for cooking of meat.	6
BUTCHER, ASSISTANT is a male worker aged 21 years or over whose duties consist wholly or mainly in assisting a butcher.	4
CARVER is a male worker aged 21 years or over who is wholly or mainly employed in carving meat, poultry or game.	6
CASHIER, DINING-ROOM AND RESTAURANT is a female worker aged 21 years or over who is wholly or mainly employed on one or more of the following duties, that is to say, receiving payment from and giving change to customers in a dining-room or restaurant, keeping records of sums received and balancing cash taken with the records kept, or on duties ancillary to any of these duties.	19

Grade or description of worker	No. of appropriate group in Tables of remuneration
Column 1	Column 2
CELLARMAN is a male worker aged 21 years or over who is wholly or mainly employed on one or more of the following duties, that is to say, bottling, racking, receipt, custody, issue or keeping records of beers, wines, spirits and minerals.	2
CELLARMAN, HEAD is a cellarman who supervises not less than three cellar staff.	4
CHAMBERMAID OR ROOM MAID is a female worker who is wholly or mainly employed on one or more of the following duties, that is to say, making beds and cleaning and tidying bedrooms or bathrooms, taking orders for, or serving, meals and refreshment required in bedrooms or similarly attending to visitors, or on duties ancillary to any of these duties.	31
CHEF OR HEAD COOK (MALE) is a male worker aged 21 years or over experienced in all departments of the kitchen, who is wholly or mainly employed on the preparation and cooking of food requiring the mixing of two or more ingredients, or the preparation and cooking of meat, poultry, game or fish, and who supervises not less than three cooks or assistant cooks, whether male or female.	8
CHEF ENTREMETIER (HEAD VEGETABLE OR SOUP COOK) is a male worker aged 21 years or over who is wholly or mainly employed on one or more of the following duties, that is to say, the cooking, or supervising the cooking, of vegetables or the preparation and cooking, or supervising the preparation and cooking, of egg dishes or of soups, and who is assisted by one or more commis cooks whose duties he supervises.	9
CHEF GARDE-MANGER (HEAD LARDER COOK) is a male worker aged 21 years or over who is responsible for the larder or cold store, and who is wholly or mainly employed in preparing, or in supervising the preparation of, cold dishes containing meat, fish or poultry, and of garnishes, and who is assisted by one or more commis cooks whose duties he supervises.	9
CHEF PATISSIER (HEAD PASTRY COOK) is a male worker aged 21 years or over who is wholly or mainly employed in the making and preparation for the table, or in supervising the making and preparation for the table, of pastries, cakes, sweets, ices, puddings, pies and similar articles and who is assisted by one or more commis cooks whose duties he supervises.	9
CHEF DE PARTIE (SECTIONAL COOK) is a chef saucier, a chef patissier, a chef garde-manger, a chef rotisseur, a chef poissonnier, a chef entremetier, a head breakfast cook or a head grill cook.	—
CHEF POISSONNIER (HEAD FISH COOK) is a male worker aged 21 years or over who is wholly or mainly employed in cooking and preparing for the table, or in supervising the cooking and preparation for the table, of fish and fish dishes and who is assisted by one or more commis cooks whose duties he supervises.	9
CHEF ROTISSEUR (HEAD ROAST COOK) is a male worker aged 21 years or over who is wholly or mainly employed in cooking, or in supervising the cooking, of joints, poultry or game, and who is assisted by one or more commis cooks whose duties he supervises.	9

Grade or description of worker	No. of appropriate group in Tables of remuneration
Column 1	Column 2
CHEF SAUCIER (HEAD SAUCE COOK) is a male worker aged 21 years or over who is wholly or mainly employed in preparing, or in supervising the preparation of, sauces and the cooking and serving, or in supervising the cooking and serving, of entrees, and who is assisted by one or more commis cooks whose duties he supervises.	9
CLEANER is a female worker aged 21 years or over who is wholly or mainly employed in cleaning any part of the premises.	17
CLERK OR RECEPTIONIST is a worker aged 21 years or over who is wholly or mainly employed on clerical, office or reception work.	Male 4: Female 23
CLERK OR RECEPTIONIST, HEAD is a clerk or receptionist who supervises not less than three clerks or receptionists, whether male or female.	Male 6: Female 27
CLOAKROOM AND TOILET ATTENDANT is a worker who is wholly or mainly employed on one or more of the following duties, that is to say, the receipt, custody and issue of personal effects deposited in the cloakroom, or the charge of, and responsibility for cleaning, or for the cleanliness of, toilets.	Male 10: Female 29
COMMIS COOK is a male worker aged 21 years or over who has undergone not less than three years' training under a chef de cuisine or a chef de partie, or has completed training as a four-year trainee cook (as defined in paragraph 5), and who is employed under the immediate supervision of a chef de partie.	5
COOK (FEMALE) is a female worker aged 21 years or over (not being an assistant cook), or a female worker who has completed training as a four-year trainee cook (as defined in paragraph 5), who is wholly or mainly employed in the preparation and cooking of food requiring the mixing of two or more ingredients, or the preparation and cooking of meat, poultry, game or fish, and duties ancillary to any of these duties.	25
COOK (MALE) is a male worker aged 21 years or over (not being an assistant cook or a commis cook), or a male worker who has completed training as a four-year trainee cook (as defined in paragraph 5), who is wholly or mainly employed in the preparation and cooking of food requiring the mixing of two or more ingredients, or the preparation and cooking of meat, poultry, game or fish, and duties ancillary to any of these duties.	5
COOK, ASSISTANT is a worker aged 21 years or over, or a worker who has completed training as a two-year trainee cook (as defined in paragraph 5), who is wholly or mainly employed in assisting a chef or head cook, or cook, whether male or female, in the preparation and cooking of food (not being mainly the preparation of vegetables or salads).	Male 3: Female 20
COOK, HEAD (FEMALE) is a female worker aged 21 years or over experienced in all departments of the kitchen, who is wholly or mainly employed in the preparation and cooking of food requiring the mixing of two or more ingredients, or the preparation and cooking of meat, poultry, game or fish, and who supervises not less than three cooks or assistant cooks, whether male or female.	28
COOK, HEAD BREAKFAST is a male worker aged 21 years or over who is responsible for the preparation and cooking of breakfast dishes, and who is assisted by one or more commis cooks whose duties he supervises.	9
COOK, HEAD GRILL is a male worker aged 21 years or over who is wholly or mainly employed in the cooking, or in supervising the cooking, of grills, and who is assisted by one or more commis cooks whose duties he supervises.	9

Grade or description of worker	No. of appropriate group in Tables of remuneration
Column 1	Column 2
FIREMAN (PATROL) is a male worker aged 21 years or over who patrols the premises and who is responsible for the maintenance in good and efficient order of fire prevention appliances and for taking the necessary measures to deal with any outbreak of fire.	3
FISHMONGER-POULTERER is a male worker aged 21 years or over who is responsible for the storage of fish, poultry or game and who is wholly or mainly employed in the preparation for cooking of fish, poultry or game.	6
FISHMONGER-POULTERER, ASSISTANT is a male worker aged 21 years or over whose duties consist wholly or mainly in assisting a fish-monger-poulterer.	4
HOUSEKEEPER is a female worker aged 21 years or over who is employed on general household administration, selection and control of domestic staff, and who is responsible for domestic stores and the general cleanliness of the establishment.	—
HOUSEKEEPER GRADE I is a housekeeper who is employed in an establishment where she is the only housekeeper or where she is appointed to supervise not more than two other housekeepers.	26
HOUSEKEEPER GRADE II is a housekeeper who performs her duties under the supervision of another housekeeper or of a head housekeeper.	25
HOUSEKEEPER, HEAD is a housekeeper who supervises three or more housekeepers.	28
HOUSEMAID is a female worker aged 21 years or over who is wholly or mainly employed on one or more of the following duties, that is to say, cleaning in bedrooms, bathrooms, corridors, staircases, lounges, dining-rooms, restaurants, attending to fires, or on duties ancillary to any of these duties.	17
LIFT ATTENDANT is a worker aged 21 years or over who is wholly or mainly employed in operating a lift.	Male 1: Female 17
LINEN KEEPER, HEAD is a female worker aged 21 years or over who is responsible for the house linen, and who supervises not less than three linen or sewing maids.	21
MAID, HEAD STILLROOM is a stillroom maid who supervises not less than three stillroom maids.	21
MAID, KITCHEN, SCULLERY OR VEGETABLE is a female worker aged 21 years or over who is wholly or mainly employed on one or more of the following duties, that is to say, cleaning the kitchen or scullery, or kitchen or scullery apparatus, washing dishes or cooking utensils, cleaning fish, plucking poultry or game, cleaning and preparing raw vegetables or fruit, or on duties ancillary to any of these duties.	17
MAID, LINEN OR SEWING is a female worker aged 21 years or over who is wholly or mainly employed on one or more of the following duties, that is to say, the receipt, checking, folding, stacking, despatch or issue of house or visitors' linen or laundry, sewing repairs, or on duties ancillary to any of these duties.	19

Grade or description of worker	No. of appropriate group in Tables of remuneration
Column 1	Column 2
MAID OR FEMALE ATTENDANT, STAFF is a female worker aged 21 years or over who is wholly or mainly employed on the duties of a housemaid in connection with those parts of the premises used mainly by the staff.	17
MAID, STILLROOM is a female worker aged 21 years or over who is wholly or mainly employed on one or more of the following duties, that is to say, the preparation and dispensing of beverages or light refreshments, cleaning the stillroom, or on duties ancillary to any of these duties.	18
MANAGER OR MANAGERESS is the person responsible to the employer for the cleanliness, care and supervision of the premises and equipment of an establishment and for the handling of the cash and stocks, for the control of the staff where any is employed and for the conduct of the establishment as required by law.	—
OTHER WORKER is a worker whose *grade or description is not a grade or description* defined elsewhere in this Schedule.	Male 1: Female 17
PLATE OR PANTRY WOMAN OR CROCKERY ATTENDANT is a female worker aged 21 years or over who is wholly or mainly employed on one or more of the following duties, that is to say, collecting, cleaning, washing or sorting plate, cutlery, crockery or glass, or on duties ancillary to any of these duties.	17
PLATEMAN OR PANTRYMAN, HEAD OR FOREMAN is a plateman or pantryman who supervises not less than three platemen or pantrymen.	3
PORTER, HOUSE, BASEMENT, CELLAR OR STORE is a male worker aged 21 years or over (other than a night porter) who is wholly or mainly employed on any one or more of the following duties, that is to say, portering goods (other than luggage) or supplies, cleaning premises, furniture or fittings (including the cleaning of windows, glazed doors or partitions), attending to fires or boilers, or on duties ancillary to any of these duties.	1
PORTER (HALL OR FLOOR) OR BOOTS is a male worker (other than a night porter) who is wholly or mainly employed on any one or more of the following duties, that is to say, carrying luggage, supplying information to guests or customers, calling cars or taxis, or similarly attending to guests or customers, or cleaning boots or shoes.	10
PORTER, KITCHEN OR PLATEMAN, PANTRYMAN OR CROCKERY ATTENDANT is a male worker aged 21 years or over who is wholly or mainly employed on one or more of the following duties, that is to say, cleaning the kitchen, service or scullery, or kitchen, service or scullery apparatus; cleaning and preparing raw vegetables or fruit or fish or plucking poultry or game; collecting, cleaning, washing or sorting plate, cutlery, crockery or glass, or on duties ancillary to any of these duties.	1
PORTER, HEAD HALL is a hall porter who supervises all porters except these employed in or about the kitchen and who is employed in an establishment where not less than five hall porters (including himself) are employed.	15

Grade or description of worker	No. of appropriate group in Tables of remuneration
Column 1	Column 2
PORTER, NIGHT is a male worker who is normally employed on night work and whose duties consist of any one or more of the following duties, that is to say:— attending to the requirements of visitors, acting as night watchman, carrying out household duties (including cleaning premises, furniture or fittings, attending to fires or boilers, cleaning boots or shoes) or duties ancillary to any of these duties.	13
PORTER, SECOND HEAD HALL is a hall porter who is appointed to exercise supervisory authority under a head hall porter and to perform his duties when he is absent.	13
PORTER, SINGLE OR LEADING is a porter who is either the only porter employed in the establishment or is the leading porter in an establishment where not more than four male workers, including himself, are employed on portering (other than kitchen portering) or as cloakroom or toilet attendants.	11
SALAD HAND is a worker aged 21 years or over who is wholly or mainly employed on one or more of the following duties, that is to say, the washing of vegetables especially for salads or hors d'oeuvres, the preparation of salads or hors d'oeuvres, the making of sauces especially for salads or hors d'oeuvres, or on duties ancillary to any of these duties.	Male 3: Female 20
SERVICE DISPENSER is a worker who is not an attendant (railway refreshment establishment), is aged 21 years or over and is wholly or mainly employed in dispensing, or dispensing and serving, food or beverages (other than serving at table), cleaning the dispense counter, and on duties ancillary to these duties.	Male 2: Female 18
SERVICE WORKER is a worker whose grade or description is identified in this paragraph as appropriate to one of the groups numbered 10 to 16 in respect of male workers and 29 to 33 in respect of female workers, the rates for which are set out in paragraph 4 in Tables numbered A2, B2 and C2; *and A4, B4 and C4.*	Males 10 to 16: Females 29 to 33
STILLROOM MAN is a male worker aged 21 years or over who is wholly or mainly employed on one or more of the following duties, that is to say, the preparation and dispensing of beverages or light refreshments, cleaning the stillroom, or on duties ancillary to any of these duties.	2
STORESMAN is a male worker aged 21 years or over who is wholly or mainly employed in the storeroom and is responsible for the receipt, custody, issue and records of goods in his charge.	2
STORESMAN, HEAD is a storesman who supervises not less than three storeroom staff.	4
STOKER is a male worker aged 21 years or over who is wholly or mainly employed in the firing and regulating of boilers.	3
TELEPHONE OPERATOR (FEMALE) is a female worker aged 21 years or over who is wholly or mainly employed on one or more of the following duties, that is to say, operating a telephone switchboard or section thereof, obtaining calls for customers or guests in a telephone call box, making the appropriate charges to the customers or guests therefor.	21
TELEPHONE OPERATOR (MALE) is a male worker aged 21 years or over who is wholly or mainly employed in operating a telephone switchboard or section thereof.	2

Grade or description of worker	No. of appropriate group in Tables of remuneration
Column 1	Column 2
TELEPHONE OPERATOR, HEAD is a telephone operator (female) who supervises not less than six telephone operators, whether male or female.	23
TIMEKEEPER is a male worker aged 21 years or over who is wholly or mainly employed on one or more of the following duties, that is to say, recording the times of arrival or departure of staff, or ensuring that proper use is made by the staff of any time-recording system in operation, as a watchman responsible for preventing unauthorised ingoing or outgoing of goods or persons, or on duties ancillary to any of these duties.	3
TRAINEE COOK has the meaning assigned to it in paragraph 5.	—
VALET is a male worker who is wholly or mainly employed in caring for guests' clothing and including such a worker required to perform the duties of a floor porter, or on duties ancillary to any of these duties.	11
WAITER is a male worker who is wholly or mainly employed in the serving of food or drink at table, the preparation and laying and clearing of tables, or on duties ancillary to any of these duties.	12
WAITER, EXTRA is a waiter who is engaged on either an hourly or a day to day basis.	—
WAITER, EXTRA HEAD is a male worker aged 21 years or over who supervises not less than 12 waiting staff and who is engaged on either an hourly or a day to day basis.	—
WAITER, HEAD is a male worker who supervises not less than 12 waiting staff in an establishment where not less than 12 such workers are normally employed.	16
WAITER, HEAD WINE is a waiter who supervises not less than three waiters who are wholly or mainly employed in the serving of drink at table.	14
WAITER, LEADING OR CHARGE is a male worker who is a waiter who exercises general supervision over not less than four and less than 12 waiting staff.	14
WAITER, SECOND HEAD is a male worker who is appointed to exercise supervisory authority under a head waiter and to perform the head waiter's duties in his absence.	15
WAITRESS is a female worker who is wholly or mainly employed in the serving of food or drink at table, the preparation and laying and clearing of tables, or on duties ancillary to any of these duties.	*31*
WAITRESS, EXTRA is a waitress who is engaged on either an hourly or a day to day basis.	—
WAITRESS, HEAD is a waitress who supervises more than four waitresses.	33
WAITRESS, SECOND HEAD is a waitress who supervises not more than four waitresses.	32
WINDOW CLEANER is a male worker aged 21 years or over who is wholly or mainly employed on cleaning windows and whose work includes the external cleaning of windows above street level.	3

3. In this Schedule the following expressions have the meanings hereby assigned to them, that is to say:—

"AREA A" means the Metropolitan Police District, as defined in the London Government Act 1963(a), the City of London, the Inner Temple and the Middle Temple.

"AREA B" means—

(1) in England and Wales—the areas for the time being of the following County Boroughs:—Birmingham, Bradford, Bristol, Cardiff, Coventry, Kingston-upon-Hull, Leeds, Leicester, Liverpool, Manchester, Newcastle-upon-Tyne, Nottingham, Sheffield and Stoke-on-Trent;

(2) in Scotland—the areas for the time being of the following Counties of Cities:—Edinburgh and Glasgow.

"AREA C" means all areas other than those in Area A or Area B.

"DOUBLE TIME" means twice the rate appropriate to the worker set out under column 3 of the Tables;

"SINGLE TIME RATE" means the rate appropriate to the worker set out under column 3 of the Tables.

"TIME-AND-A-HALF" means the rate appropriate to the worker set out under column 5 of the Tables.

"TIME-AND-A-QUARTER" means the rate appropriate to the worker set out under column 4 of the Tables.

4. The minimum remuneration for workers employed in Areas A, B and C (as defined in paragraph 3) whose grades or descriptions are identified in paragraph 2 as appropriate to one of the groups in the Tables set out in this paragraph, shall be the amount specified in the Tables according to the Area and group number.

Provided that—

(1) *where a worker is supplied by the employer with full board and lodging for seven days a week, the minimum remuneration payable under this paragraph shall be subject to the reduction specified in paragraph 6;*

(2) *where a worker is not supplied by the employer with full board and lodging for seven days a week but is supplied by him with such meals as are normally available in the establishment during the time the worker is on duty, the minimum remuneration payable under this paragraph shall be subject to the reduction specified in paragraph 7.*

(a) 1963 c. 33.

TABLE A1 AREA A—MALE WORKERS OTHER THAN SERVICE WORKERS

Column 1 Groups into which workers are classified in accordance with paragraph 2	Per week of 44 hours Column 2	Per hour		
		Column 3 single time	Column 4 time-and-a-quarter	Column 5 time-and-a-half
	s. d.	s. d.	s. d.	s. d.
Group 1	217 0	4 $11\frac{1}{2}$	6 2	7 5
„ 2	222 0	5 1	6 4	7 7
„ 3	227 0	5 2	6 $5\frac{1}{2}$	7 9
„ 4	238 0	5 5	6 $9\frac{1}{2}$	8 $1\frac{1}{2}$
„ 5	248 0	5 8	7 1	8 $5\frac{1}{2}$
„ 6	258 0	5 $10\frac{1}{2}$	7 4	8 10
„ 8	278 0	6 4	7 11	9 6
„ 9	288 0	6 7	8 $2\frac{1}{2}$	9 10
Workers in Group 1 aged under 21 years— Aged 20 and under 21 years	205 0	4 8	5 10	7 0
„ 19 „ „ 20 „	193 0	4 5	5 6	6 7
„ 18 „ „ 19 „	182 0	4 2	5 $2\frac{1}{2}$	6 $2\frac{1}{2}$
„ 17 „ „ 18 „	151 6	3 $5\frac{1}{2}$	4 4	5 2
„ 16 „ „ 17 „	139 6	3 $2\frac{1}{2}$	4 0	4 $9\frac{1}{2}$
„ 15 „ „ 16 „	131 6	3 0	3 9	4 6

TABLE A2 AREA A—MALE SERVICE WORKERS

Column 1 Groups into which workers are classified in accordance with paragraph 2	Per week of 44 hours Column 2	Per hour Column 3 single time	Column 4 time-and-a-quarter	Column 5 time-and-a-half
	s. d.	s. d.	s. d.	s. d.
Group 10	171 0	3 11	4 10½	5 10
„ 11	176 0	4 0	5 0	6 0
„ 12	181 0	4 1½	5 2	6 2½
„ 13	186 0	4 3	5 3½	6 4½
„ 14	191 0	4 4½	5 5½	6 6½
„ 15	201 0	4 7	5 9	6 10½
„ 16	221 0	5 0½	6 3½	7 6½
Workers in the above-mentioned groups aged under 21 years—				
Aged 20 and under 21 years	168 0	3 10	4 9½	5 9
„ 19 „ „ 20 „	158 6	3 7½	4 6½	5 5
„ 18 „ „ 19 „	146 0	3 4	4 2	5 0
„ 17 „ „ 18 „	124 6	2 10	3 6½	4 3
„ 16 „ „ 17 „	115 0	2 7½	3 3½	3 11½
„ 15 „ „ 16 „	108 6	2 6	3 1	3 8½

TABLE A3 AREA A—FEMALE WORKERS OTHER THAN SERVICE WORKERS

Column 1 Groups into which workers are classified in accordance with paragraph 2	Per week of 44 hours Column 2	Per hour Column 3 single time	Column 4 time-and-a-quarter	Column 5 time-and-a-half
	s. d.	s. d.	s. d.	s. d.
Group 17	170 0	3 10½	4 10	5 10
,, 18	175 0	4 0	5 0	6 0
,, 19	179 6	4 1	5 1½	6 1½
,, 20	182 6	4 2	5 2½	6 3
,, 21	185 6	4 3	5 3½	6 4
,, 22	190 6	4 4	5 5	6 6
,, 23	196 0	4 5½	5 7	6 8½
,, 25	201 0	4 7	5 9	6 10½
,, 26	208 6	4 9	5 11½	7 1½
,, 27	213 6	4 10½	6 1	7 3½
,, 28	223 6	5 1	6 4½	7 7½
Workers in Group 17 aged under 21 years—				
Aged 20 and under 21 years	162 6	3 8½	4 7½	5 6½
,, 19 ,, ,, 20 ,,	154 6	3 6½	4 5	5 3½
,, 18 ,, ,, 19 ,,	145 6	3 4	4 2	5 0
,, 17 ,, ,, 18 ,,	120 0	2 9	3 5	4 1½
,, 16 ,, ,, 17 ,,	110 0	2 6	3 1½	3 9
,, 15 ,, ,, 16	104 6	2 4½	3 0	3 7

TABLE A4 AREA A—FEMALE SERVICE WORKERS

Column 1 Groups into which workers are classified in accordance with paragraph 2	Per week of 44 hours Column 2	Per hour		
		Column 3 single time	Column 4 time-and-a-quarter	Column 5 time-and-a-half
	s. d.	s. d.	s. d.	s. d.
Group 29	136 6	3 1½	3 11	4 8
„ 31	147 0	3 4½	4 2½	5 0½
„ 32	156 6	3 7	4 5½	5 4½
„ 33	161 6	3 8½	4 7½	5 6½
Workers in the above-mentioned groups aged under 21 years—				
Aged 20 and under 21 years	133 6	3 0½	3 10	4 7
„ 19 „ „ 20 „	129 6	2 11½	3 8½	4 5
„ 18 „ „ 19 „	121 6	2 9½	3 5½	4 2
„ 17 „ „ 18 „	103 6	2 4½	2 11½	3 6½
„ 16 „ „ 17 „	97 0	2 2½	2 9½	3 4
„ 15 „ „ 16 „	90 6	2 1	2 7	3 1½

TABLE B1 AREA B—MALE WORKERS OTHER THAN SERVICE WORKERS

Column 1	Per week of 44 hours	Per hour		
	Column 2	Column 3	Column 4	Column 5
Groups into which workers are classified in accordance with paragraph 2		single time	time-and-a-quarter	time-and-a-half
	s. d.	s. d.	s. d.	s. d.
Group 1	215 0	4 11	6 1½	7 4
" 2	220 0	5 0	6 3	7 6
" 3	225 0	5 1½	6 5	7 8½
" 4	236 0	5 4½	6 8½	8 1
" 5	246 0	5 7½	7 0	8 5
" 6	256 0	5 10	7 3½	8 9
" 8	276 0	6 3½	7 10½	9 5
" 9	286 0	6 6	8 1½	9 9
Workers in Group 1 aged under 21 years—				
Aged 20 and under 21 years	203 0	4 7½	5 9½	6 11½
" 19 " " 20 "	191 0	4 4½	5 5½	6 6½
" 18 " " 19 "	180 0	4 1½	5 1½	6 2
" 17 " " 18 "	149 6	3 5	4 3	5 1½
" 16 " " 17 "	137 6	3 1½	3 11	4 8½
" 15 " " 16 "	129 6	2 11½	3 8½	4 2

TABLE B2 AREA B—MALE SERVICE WORKERS

Column 1 Groups into which workers are classified in accordance with paragraph 2	Per week of 44 hours Column 2	Per hour Column 3 single time	Column 4 time-and-a-quarter	Column 5 time-and-a-half
	s. d.	s. d.	s. d.	s. d.
Group 10	169 0	3 10½	4 10	5 9½
,, 11	174 0	3 11½	4 11½	5 11½
,, 12	179 0	4 1	5 1½	6 1½
,, 13	184 0	4 2½	5 3	6 3½
,, 14	189 0	4 4	5 4½	6 5½
,, 15	199 0	4 6½	5 8	6 9½
,, 16	219 0	5 0	6 3	7 6
Workers in the above-mentioned groups aged under 21 years—				
Aged 20 and under 21 years	166 0	3 9½	4 9	5 8
,, 19 ,, ,, 20 ,, ...	156 6	3 7	4 5½	5 4½
,, 18 ,, ,, 19 ,, ...	144 0	3 3½	4 1½	4 11
,, 17 ,, ,, 18 ,, ...	122 6	2 9½	3 6	4 2½
,, 16 ,, ,, 17 ,, ...	113 0	2 7	3 3	3 10½
,, 15 ,, ,, 16 ,, ...	106 6	2 5½	3 0½	3 8

TABLE B3 AREA B—FEMALE WORKERS OTHER THAN SERVICE WORKERS

Column 1 Groups into which workers are classified in accordance with paragraph 2	Per week of 44 hours Column 2	Per hour		
		Column 3 single time	Column 4 time-and-a-quarter	Column 5 time-and-a-half
	s. d.	s. d.	s. d.	s. d.
Group 17	168 0	3 10	4 9½	5 9
„ 18	173 0	3 11½	4 11	5 11
„ 19	177 6	4 0½	5 1	6 1
„ 20	180 6	4 1½	5 2	6 2
„ 21	184 0	4 2½	5 3	6 3½
„ 22	188 6	4 3½	5 4½	6 5½
„ 23	194 0	4 5	5 6½	6 7½
„ 25	199 0	4 6½	5 8	6 9½
„ 26	206 6	4 8½	5 10½	7 0½
„ 27	211 6	4 10	6 0½	7 3
„ 28	221 6	5 0½	6 4	7 7
Workers in Group 17 aged under 21 years— Aged 20 and under 21 years	160 6	3 8	4 7	5 6
„ 19 „ „ 20 „	152 6	3 6	4 4	5 2½
„ 18 „ „ 19 „	143 6	3 3½	4 1	4 11
„ 17 „ „ 18 „	118 0	2 8½	3 4½	4 0½
„ 16 „ „ 17 „	108 0	2 5½	3 1	3 8½
„ 15 „ „ 16 „	102 6	2 4	2 11	3 6

TABLE B4 AREA B—FEMALE SERVICE WORKERS

Column 1 Groups into which workers are classified in accordance with paragraph 2	Per week of 44 hours Column 2	Per hour Column 3 single time	Column 4 time-and-a-quarter	Column 5 time-and-a-half
	s. d.	s. d.	s. d.	s. d.
Group 29	134 6	3 1	3 10	4 7
,, 31	145 0	3 4	4 1½	4 11½
,, 32	154 6	3 6½	4 5	5 3½
,, 33	159 6	3 7½	4 6½	5 5½
Workers in the above-mentioned groups aged under 21 years—				
Aged 20 and under 21 years	131 6	3 0	3 9	4 6
,, 19 ,, ,, 20 ,, ...	127 6	2 11	3 7½	4 4½
,, 18 ,, ,, 19 ,, ...	119 6	2 9	3 5	4 1
,, 17 ,, ,, 18 ,, ...	101 6	2 4	2 11	3 6
,, 16 ,, ,, 17 ,, ...	95 0	2 2	2 8½	3 3
,, 15 ,, ,, 16 ,, ...	88 6	2 0½	2 6½	3 0½

TABLE C1 AREA C—MALE WORKERS OTHER THAN SERVICE WORKERS

Column 1 Groups into which workers are classified in accordance with paragraph 2	Per week of 44 hours	Per hour		
	Column 2	Column 3 single time	Column 4 time-and-a-quarter	Column 5 time-and-a-half
	s. d.	s. d.	s. d.	s. d.
Group 1	212 0	4 10	6 0½	7 3
„ 2	217 0	4 11½	6 2	7 5
„ 3	222 0	5 1	6 4	7 7
„ 4	233 0	5 4	6 7½	7 11½
„ 5	243 0	5 6½	6 11	8 3½
„ 6	253 0	5 9	7 2½	8 7½
„ 8	273 0	6 2½	7 9½	9 4
„ 9	283 0	6 5½	8 0½	9 8
Workers in Group 1 aged under 21 years—				
Aged 20 and under 21 years	200 0	4 7	5 8½	6 10
„ 19 „ „ 20 „	188 0	4 3½	5 4½	6 5
„ 18 „ „ 19 „	177 0	4 0½	5 0½	6 0½
„ 17 „ „ 18 „	146 6	3 4	4 2	5 0
„ 16 „ „ 17 „	134 6	3 1	3 10	4 7½
„ 15 „ „ 16 „	126 6	2 10½	3 7½	4 4

TABLE C2 AREA C—MALE SERVICE WORKERS

Column 1 Groups into which workers are classified in accordance with paragraph 2	Per week of 44 hours Column 2	Per hour Column 3 single time	Column 4 time-and-a-quarter	Column 5 time-and-a-half
	s. d.	s. d.	s. d.	s. d.
Group 10	166 0	3 9½	4 9	5 8
,, 11	171 0	3 11	4 10½	5 10
,, 12	176 0	4 0	5 0	6 0
,, 13	181 0	4 1½	5 2	6 2½
,, 14	186 0	4 3	5 3½	6 4½
,, 15	196 0	4 5½	5 7	6 8½
,, 16	216 0	4 11	6 2	7 4½
Workers in the above-mentioned groups aged under 21 years—				
Aged 20 and under 21 years	163 0	3 8½	4 8	5 7
,, 19 ,, ,, 20 ,, ...	153 6	3 6	4 4½	5 3
,, 18 ,, ,, 19 ,, ...	141 0	3 3	4 0½	4 10
,, 17 ,, ,, 18 ,, ...	119 6	2 9	3 5	4 1
,, 16 ,, ,, 17 ,, ...	110 0	2 6	3 1½	3 9
,, 15 ,, ,, 16 ,, ...	103 6	2 4½	2 11½	3 6½

TABLE C3 AREA C—FEMALE WORKERS OTHER THAN SERVICE WORKERS

Column 1 Groups into which workers are classified in accordance with paragraph 2	Per week of 44 hours Column 2	Per hour		
		Column 3 single time	Column 4 time-and-a-quarter	Column 5 time-and-a-half
	s.　d.	s.　d.	s.　d.	s.　d.
Group 17	165　0	3　9	4　8½	5　7½
,,　　18	170　0	3　10½	4　10	5　10
,,　　19	174　6	4　0	4　11½	5　11½
,,　　20	177　6	4　0½	5　1	6　1
,,　　21	181　0	4　1½	5　2	6　2½
,,　　22	185　6	4　3	5　3½	6　4
,,　　23	191　0	4　4½	5　5½	6　6½
,,　　25	196　0	4　5½	5　7	6　8½
,,　　26	203　6	4　7½	5　9½	6　11½
,,　　27	208　6	4　9	5　11½	7　1½
,,　　28	218　6	5　0	6　2½	7　5½
Workers in Group 17 aged under 21 years—				
Aged 20 and under 21 years	157　6	3　7	4　6	5　4½
,,　19　,,　　,,　20　,,	149　6	3　5	4　3	5　1½
,,　18　,,　　,,　19　,,	140　6	3　2½	4　0	4　9½
,,　17　,,　　,,　18　,,	115　0	2　7½	3　3½	3　11½
,,　16　,,　　,,　17　,,	105　0	2　5	3　0	3　7
,,　15　,,　　,,　16　,,	99　6	2　3½	2　10	3　5

TABLE C4 AREA C—FEMALE SERVICE WORKERS

Column 1 Groups into which workers are classified in accordance with paragraph 2	Per week of 44 hours Column 2	Per hour		
		Column 3 single time	Column 4 time-and-a-quarter	Column 5 time-and-a-half
	s. d.	s. d.	s. d.	s. d.
Group 29	131 6	3 0	3 9	4 6
„ 31	142 0	3 3	4 0½	4 10½
„ 32	151 6	3 5½	4 4	5 2
„ 33	156 6	3 7	4 5½	5 4½
Workers in the above-mentioned groups aged under 21 years—				
Aged 20 and under 21 years	128 6	2 11½	3 8	4 5
„ 19 „ „ 20 „	124 6	2 10	3 6½	4 3
„ 18 „ „ 19 „	116 6	2 8	3 4	4 0
„ 17 „ „ 18 „	98 6	2 3	2 10	3 4½
„ 16 „ „ 17 „	92 0	2 1½	2 7½	3 2
„ 15 „ „ 16 „	85 6	1 11½	2 5½	2 11

TRAINEE COOKS

5.—(1) *A trainee cook is a worker who is employed during the whole of his time under a written agreement approved by the Hotel and Catering Industry Training Board (or, as a trainee cook or apprentice cook, under an existing written contract, or a contract of apprenticeship which has been duly executed, and which commenced before 1st September 1967) and which contains the provisions set out in (a) and (b) below or provisions substantially to the same effect and no provisions contrary thereto:—*

(a) *the worker of his own free will and with the consent of his guardian binds himself to serve the employer, or any subsequent employer to whom the agreement is transferred with the approval of the Hotel and Catering Industry Training Board, as his trainee for a period of not less than two years in the case of a two-year trainee cook and not less than four years in the case of a four-year trainee cook;*

(b) *the employer will employ the worker as his trainee during the said term and teach and instruct him to the best of his knowledge and ability or cause him to be taught the business and trade of a cook and all things relating thereto, according to the agreed standard decided upon by the Hotel and Catering Industry Training Board.*

(2) *The minimum remuneration for trainee cooks who are employed in Area A, B or C (as defined in paragraph 3) shall be respectively in accordance with the Tables in sub-paragraphs (3) (a) or (3) (b) of this paragraph.*

Provided that in the case of a four-year trainee—

(i) *the period under sub-paragraph (1) (a) above shall be reduced where the worker has after attaining the age of 15 years received a course of instruction in cookery approved by the Hotel and Catering Industry Training Board in a technical class at any university ,college, school or similar establishment by a period equal to the duration of such a course of instruction subject to a maximum reduction of two years; and*

(ii) *any such period shall be treated as a period of training for the purpose of determining the "year of training" in the Tables in sub-paragraph (3) (b) of this paragraph.*

(3)(a) TWO-YEAR TRAINEE COOKS

	Per week of 44 hours	Per hour		
	Column 2	Column 3	Column 4	Column 5
		single time	time-and-a-quarter	time-and-a-half
	s. d.	s. d.	s. d.	s. d.
AREA A				
MALE WORKERS—				
First year of training	115 6	2 7½	3 3½	3 11½
Second „ „ „	127 0	2 11	3 7½	4 4
FEMALE WORKERS—				
First year of training	101 0	2 3½	2 10½	3 5½
Second „ „ „	112 6	2 7	3 2½	3 10½
AREA B				
MALE WORKERS—				
First year of training	113 6	2 7	3 3	3 10½
Second „ „ „	125 0	2 10½	3 7	4 3½
FEMALE WORKERS—				
First year of training	99 0	2 3	2 10	3 4½
Second „ „ „	110 6	2 6½	3 2	3 9½
AREA C				
MALE WORKERS—				
First year of training	110 6	2 6½	3 2	3 9½
Second „ „ „	122 0	2 9½	3 6	4 2
FEMALE WORKERS—				
First year of training	96 0	2 2½	2 9	3 3½
Second „ „ „	107 6	2 5½	3 1	3 8

(3)(b) FOUR-YEAR TRAINEE COOKS

| | Per week of 44 hours | Per hour | | |
	Column 2	Column 3 single time	Column 4 time-and-a-quarter	Column 5 time-and-a-half
	s. d.	s. d.	s. d.	s. d.
AREA A				
MALE WORKERS—				
First year of training	115 6	2 $7\frac{1}{2}$	3 $3\frac{1}{2}$	3 $11\frac{1}{2}$
Second „ „ „	127 0	2 11	3 $7\frac{1}{2}$	4 4
Third „ „ „	153 0	3 6	4 $4\frac{1}{2}$	5 3
Fourth „ „ „	200 6	4 7	5 $8\frac{1}{2}$	6 $10\frac{1}{2}$
FEMALE WORKERS—				
First year of training	101 0	2 $3\frac{1}{2}$	2 $10\frac{1}{2}$	3 $5\frac{1}{2}$
Second „ „ „	112 6	2 7	3 $2\frac{1}{2}$	3 $10\frac{1}{2}$
Third „ „ „	133 0	3 $0\frac{1}{2}$	3 $9\frac{1}{2}$	4 $6\frac{1}{2}$
Fourth „ „ „	174 0	3 $11\frac{1}{2}$	4 $11\frac{1}{2}$	5 $11\frac{1}{2}$
AREA B				
MALE WORKERS—				
First year of training	113 6	2 7	3 3	3 $10\frac{1}{2}$
Second „ „ „	125 0	2 $10\frac{1}{2}$	3 7	4 $3\frac{1}{2}$
Third „ „ „	151 0	3 $5\frac{1}{2}$	4 $3\frac{1}{2}$	5 2
Fourth „ „ „	198 6	4 $6\frac{1}{2}$	5 8	6 $9\frac{1}{2}$
FEMALE WORKERS—				
First year of training	99 0	2 3	2 10	3 $4\frac{1}{2}$
Second „ „ „	110 6	2 $6\frac{1}{2}$	3 2	3 $9\frac{1}{2}$
Third „ „ „	131 0	3 0	3 9	4 6
Fourth „ „ „	172 0	3 11	4 11	5 $10\frac{1}{2}$
AREA C				
MALE WORKERS—				
First year of training	110 6	2 $6\frac{1}{2}$	3 2	3 $9\frac{1}{2}$
Second „ „ „	122 0	2 $9\frac{1}{2}$	3 6	4 2
Third „ „ „	148 0	3 $4\frac{1}{2}$	4 $2\frac{1}{2}$	5 1
Fourth „ „ „	195 6	4 $5\frac{1}{2}$	5 7	6 8
FEMALE WORKERS—				
First year of training	96 0	2 $2\frac{1}{2}$	2 9	3 $3\frac{1}{2}$
Second „ „ „	107 6	2 $5\frac{1}{2}$	3 1	3 8
Third „ „ „	128 0	2 11	3 8	4 $4\frac{1}{2}$
Fourth „ „ „	169 0	3 $10\frac{1}{2}$	4 10	5 $9\frac{1}{2}$

WORKERS SUPPLIED WITH FULL BOARD AND LODGING

6. *Where a worker is supplied by the employer with full board and lodging for seven days a week, the minimum remuneration shall be that payable under the other provisions of this Schedule to a worker of the same grade or description employed in the same area for the same hours REDUCED by the appropriate amount as follows:—*

	Area A		Area B		Area C	
	Male	Female	Male	Female	Male	Female
	per week		per week		per week	
	s. d.	s. d.	s. d.	s. d.	s. d.	s. d.
Workers other than Service Workers—						
Aged 21 years or over	60 0	57 6	59 0	56 6	58 0	55 6
„ 20 and under 21 years	57 6	55 0	56 6	54 0	55 6	53 0
„ 19 „ „ 20 „	53 6	51 0	52 6	50 0	51 6	49 0
„ 18 „ „ 19 „	49 0	46 6	48 0	45 6	47 0	44 6
„ 17 „ „ 18 „	37 6	37 0	36 6	36 0	35 6	35 0
„ 16 „ „ 17 „	33 6	32 6	32 6	31 6	31 6	30 6
„ 15 „ „ 16 „	30 6	29 6	29 6	28 6	28 6	27 6
Service Workers—						
Aged 21 years or over	50 6	49 6	49 6	48 6	48 6	47 6
„ 20 and under 21 years	48 6	46 6	47 6	45 6	46 6	44 6
„ 19 „ „ 20 „	45 0	43 0	44 0	42 0	43 0	41 0
„ 18 „ „ 19 „	41 0	39 0	40 0	38 0	39 0	37 0
„ 17 „ „ 18 „	33 0	32 0	32 0	31 0	31 0	30 0
„ 16 „ „ 17 „	29 6	28 6	28 6	27 6	27 6	26 6
„ 15 „ „ 16 „	26 6	25 6	25 6	24 6	24 6	23 6
Two-year Trainee Cooks—						
First year of training .. }	36 0	35 0	35 0	34 0	34 0	33 0
Second „ „ „ .. }						
Four-year Trainee Cooks—						
First year of training .. }	36 0	35 0	35 0	34 0	34 0	33 0
Second „ „ „ .. }						
Third „ „ „	38 0	37 0	37 0	36 0	36 0	35 0
Fourth „ „ „	46 6	43 0	45 6	42 0	44 6	41 0

WORKERS SUPPLIED WITH MEALS BUT NOT WITH FULL BOARD AND LODGING

7. *Where a worker (other than an extra waiter, extra waitress or head waiter) is not supplied by the employer with full board and lodging on seven days a week but is supplied by him with such meals as are normally available in the establishment during the time the worker is on duty, the minimum remuneration shall be that payable under the other provisions of this Schedule to a worker of the same grade or description employed in the same area for the same hours REDUCED, for the first 44 hours worked by him in any week, by the appropriate amount as follows:—*

	All Areas Per hour
Workers other than Service Workers—	
Aged 21 years or over	6d.
„ 20 and under 21 years	5½d.
„ 19 „ „ 20 „	5d.
„ 18 „ „ 19 „	5d.
„ 17 „ „ 18 „	3½d.
„ 16 „ „ 17 „	3½d.
„ 15 „ „ 16 „	3d.
Service Workers—	
Aged 21 years or over	5½d.
„ 20 and under 21 years	5d.
„ 19 „ „ 20 „	5d.
„ 18 „ „ 19 „	4½d.
„ 17 „ „ 18 „	3d.
„ 16 „ „ 17 „	3d.
„ 15 „ „ 16 „	3d.
Two-year Trainee Cooks—	
First year of training	
Second „ „ „	} 3d.
Four-year Trainee Cooks—	
First year of training	
Second „ „ „	} 3d.
Third „ „ „	3½d.
Fourth „ „ „	5d.

SERVICE WORKERS EMPLOYED UNDER A WRITTEN AGREEMENT RELATING TO GRATUITIES

8. *Where a service worker (as defined in paragraph 2) is employed under a written agreement under which the employer undertakes to pay him in respect of each week of his employment in which he performs some work, a sum not less than the sum (if any) by which the total amount of gratuities from customers received by the workers in connection with his employment during the week falls short of—*

45s. 0d. in the case of a male worker aged 20 years or over

39s. 6d. „ „ „ „ „ „ „ „ 18 years and under 20 years

27s. 6d. „ „ „ „ „ female „ „ 20 years and over

25s. 0d. „ „ „ „ „ „ „ „ 18 years and under 20 years

the minimum remuneration shall be the amount payable under the other provisions of this Schedule REDUCED by—

1s. 0d. per hour in the case of a male worker aged 20 years or over;

10½d. „ „ „ „ „ „ „ „ „ 18 years and under 20 years;

7½d. „ „ „ „ „ „ „ female worker aged 20 years or over;

6½d. „ „ „ „ „ „ „ „ „ 18 years and under 20 years;

for the first 44 hours worked by him in any week.

FULL-TIME WORKERS NOT PROVIDED WITH LAUNDRY

9. Where in the case of a full-time worker, protective clothing or uniform is worn and no provision is made by the employer for laundering or cleaning it free of charge to the worker, the worker shall be paid, in addition to the minimum remuneration to which he is entitled under the other provisions of this Part of this Schedule, an amount of 1s. 0d. per week.

WORKERS REQUIRED TO WEAR UNIFORM OR PROTECTIVE CLOTHING OF A DISTINCTIVE CHARACTER NOT PROVIDED BY THE EMPLOYER

10.—(1) Where the employer requires a worker to wear uniform and does not provide it free of charge to the worker the worker shall be paid, in addition to the minimum remuneration to which he is entitled under the other provisions of this Part of this Schedule, an amount of 5s. 0d. per week.

(2) Where the employer requires a worker to wear protective clothing of a character distinctive to the establishment and does not provide it free of charge to the worker, the worker shall be paid, in addition to the minimum remuneration to which he is entitled under the other provisions of this Part of this Schedule, an amount of 2s. 6d. per week.

EXTRA WAITING STAFF

11. The hourly minimum remuneration payable to the following classes of workers is—

	s.	d.	
In the case of an EXTRA WAITER	3	6	per hour
In the case of an EXTRA WAITRESS	3	0	„ „
In the case of an EXTRA HEAD WAITER	4	6	„ „

Provided that where a worker to whom this paragraph applies works for less than three hours in any day, he shall be paid not less than the minimum remuneration to which he would have been entitled had he worked for three hours.

ADDITIONAL PAYMENT FOR NIGHT WORK

12. Subject to the provisions of this Schedule relating to overtime and to work on customary holidays, the minimum remuneration payable to a worker, other than a night porter, in respect of night work (as defined in paragraph 35), not being emergency duty (as defined in that paragraph), is the remuneration payable to the worker under paragraph 4, 5, 6, 7, 8, 9 or 10, with the addition *per hour* of 25 per cent. of the remuneration set out in *column 3, and columns 4 and 5 as the case may require*, of the appropriate Table in paragraph 4 or 5.

PAYMENT FOR SPREADOVER OF HOURS OF WORK

13.—(1) Subject to the provisions of sub-paragraphs (2) and (3) of this paragraph, where the hours of duty on any day of a worker, other than an extra waiter, extra waitress or extra head waiter, are spread over more than 12 hours calculated from the time at which the worker first commences duty on that day, he shall be paid, in addition to the minimum remuneration to which he is entitled under the other provisions of this Part of this Schedule, remuneration in accordance with the following Table:—

	Where the hours of duty are spread over—			
	more than 12 hours and not more than 13 hours	more than 13 hours and not more than 14 hours	more than 14 hours and not more than 15 hours	more than 15 hours
	Column 1	Column 2	Column 3	Column 4
Male Workers	2d. an hour for all time worked	2d. an hour for all time worked or a payment of 1s. 4d., whichever is the greater	3d. an hour for all time worked or a payment of 2s. 6d., whichever is the greater	6d. an hour for all time worked or a payment of 5s., whichever is the greater
Female Workers	1½d. an hour for all time worked	1½d. an hour for all time worked or a payment of 1s., whichever is the greater	2½d. an hour for all time worked or a payment of 2s. 1d., whichever is the greater	5d. an hour for all time worked or a payment of 4s. 2d., whichever is the greater

(2) Where the worker works for less than eight hours on any day and his hours of duty are spread over more than 13 hours, he shall be paid the minimum remuneration to which he would be entitled under the other provisions of this Part of this Schedule if he had worked for eight hours, and in addition the appropriate remuneration set out in Column 2, 3 or 4 of the foregoing Table:

Provided that, in calculating the remuneration to which the worker would be entitled if he had worked for eight hours, overtime rates shall apply only to overtime worked.

(3) The foregoing provisions of this paragraph shall not apply—

(a) during the off-season to a worker employed in a seasonal establishment; and

(b) to a worker on any day on which his hours of duty are spread over not more than 14 hours who is employed either in a seasonal establishment or in a licensed residential establishment which contains not more than 35 rooms ordinarily available as sleeping accommodation for guests or lodgers.

(4) For the purposes of this paragraph—

(a) where a worker commences a turn of duty on any day before midnight and that turn of duty continues beyond midnight, the hours of duty after midnight shall be treated as hours of duty performed on the day upon which the turn of duty commenced; and

(b) emergency duty (as defined in paragraph 35) shall not be taken into consideration when calculating the hours over which the hours of duty have been spread.

(5) In this paragraph the following expressions have the meanings hereby respectively assigned to them, that is to say:—

"Seasonal establishment" means a licensed residential establishment at which there is posted up a current certificate signed by a qualified auditor certifying that in his opinion more than 50 per cent. of the annual takings at the establishment in respect of the sale of food and drink (other than intoxicating liquor) and the provision of living accommodation is ordinarily earned during the months of June, July, August and September; and for the purposes of this definition—

(a) a certificate shall be treated as current for a period of 12 months from the date thereof; and

(b) "qualified auditor" means a member of one or more of the following bodies:—

The Institute of Chartered Accountants in England and Wales;

The Institute of Chartered Accountants of Scotland;

The Association of Certified and Corporate Accountants;

The Institute of Chartered Accountants in Ireland;

any other body of accountants established in the United Kingdom and for the time being recognised for the purposes of paragraphs (a) and (b) of sub-section (1) of section 161 of the Companies Act 1948, by the Board of Trade;

"Off-season" means the months of a calendar year except the months June, July, August and September.

PAYMENT FOR EMERGENCY DUTY

14. A worker (other than an extra head waiter, an extra waiter or an extra waitress) who is required to perform emergency duty (as defined in paragraph 35), shall be paid for the time so worked—

(1) where the worker works for half an hour or less—1s. 6d.

(2) where the worker works for more than half an hour—3s.

SPECIAL PROVISIONS RELATING TO INTERVALS FOR REST

15. Where an employer does not allow to a worker between the time of finishing duty on any day and the time of commencing the next following turn of duty an interval for rest of

(1) in the case of a worker who is supplied by his employer with full board and lodging, not less than eight consecutive hours;

(2) in the case of any other worker, not less than nine consecutive hours;

the worker shall be paid for all time worked by him which reduces the said interval for rest the minimum remuneration to which he is entitled under the other provisions of this Part of this Schedule with an addition for all such time at the rate of double time (as defined in paragraph 3), provided that the interval for rest shall not be regarded as having been reduced by reason solely of the fact that the worker has performed emergency duty (as defined in paragraph 35).

WORKERS TEMPORARILY TRANSFERRED TO HIGHER GRADE WORK

16. Where a worker is required temporarily to perform the duties of a worker entitled to a higher minimum remuneration than himself for a period of more than—

(1) two hours in a day or seven hours in a week, in the case of a worker who is employed in a licensed residential establishment which contains not more than 35 rooms ordinarily available as sleeping accommodation for guests or lodgers,

or

(2) two hours in any week in the case of a worker other than a worker specified in (1) above,

he shall be paid for the time so worked not less than the minimum remuneration to which he would have been entitled if he had been a worker of that higher grade:

Provided that the foregoing provision shall not apply in respect of time spent in relieving—

(a) any worker who is absent by reason of the fact that it is his weekly day of rest;

(b) for a period not exceeding 12 working days in any 12 months, any worker absent from work with the consent of the employer, but in receipt of not less than the statutory minimum remuneration.

HOURS ON WHICH REMUNERATION IS BASED

17. Subject to the provisions of paragraph 18 (which relates to guaranteed remuneration) the weekly rates specified in this Part of this Schedule relate to a week of *44 hours* and are subject to a proportionate increase or reduction according as the number of hours worked not being overtime is more or less than *44.*

GUARANTEED REMUNERATION

18. A (1) This paragraph applies to workers who ordinarily work for the employer on work to which this Schedule applies for not less than *34 hours* in a week or, in the case of a fortnightly worker (as defined in paragraph 35), for not less than *68 hours* in a fortnight.

(2) Notwithstanding the other provisions of this Schedule, where in respect of any week or fortnight as the case may be, the total remuneration, including any holiday remuneration, payable to a worker under those other provisions is less than the guaranteed remuneration provided under this paragraph, the minimum remuneration payable to that worker for that week or fortnight shall be that guaranteed remuneration.

B (1) The guaranteed remuneration payable in respect of any week to a worker to whom sub-paragraph C does not apply—

(a) who normally works for the employer for not less than *44 hours* in a week on work to which this Schedule applies, is the remuneration to which he would be entitled under paragraph 4, 5, 6, 7 or 8 for *44 hours'* work in his normal occupation;

(b) who normally works for the employer for more than *42 hours* in a week but for less than *44 hours* on work to which this Schedule applies, is the remuneration to which he would be entitled under paragraph 4, 5, 6, 7 or 8 (calculated as in paragraph 17) in respect of the number of hours normally worked by him in a week;

(c) who normally works for the employer for *42 hours* or less in a week, is the remuneration to which he would be entitled under paragraph 4, 5, 6, 7 or 8 (calculated as in paragraph 17) for *42 hours* in a week:

Provided that where the worker normally works for the employer on work to which the Schedule applies for less than *42 hours* in a week by reason only of the fact that he does not hold himself out as normally available for work for more than the number of hours he normally works in the week, and the worker has informed his employer in writing that he does not so hold himself out, the guaranteed remuneration shall be the remuneration (calculated as in paragraph 17) for the number of hours in the week normally worked by the worker for the employer on work to which this Schedule applies.

(2) Guaranteed remuneration is not payable in respect of any week unless the worker throughout his normal working hours in that week (excluding any time allowed to him as a holiday) is

　(*a*) capable of and available for work; and

　(*b*) willing to perform such duties outside his normal occupation as the employer may reasonably require if his normal work is not available in the establishment in which he is employed.

(3) Guaranteed remuneration is not payable in respect of any week if the worker's employment is terminated before the end of that week.

(4) If the employer is unable to provide the worker with work by reason of a strike or other circumstances beyond his control and gives the worker four clear days' notice to that effect, guaranteed remuneration shall not be payable after the expiry of such notice in respect of any week during which, or during part of which, the employer continues to be unable to provide work as aforesaid:

Provided that in respect of the week in which the said notice expires there shall be paid to the worker, in addition to any remuneration payable in respect of time worked in that week, any remuneration that would have been payable if the worker had worked his normal hours of work on any days in the week prior to the expiry of the notice.

C (1) The guaranteed remuneration payable in respect of any fortnight to a fortnightly worker (as defined in paragraph 35)—

　(*a*) who normally works for the employer for not less than *88 hours* in a fortnight on work to which this Schedule applies, is twice the remuneration to which he would be entitled under paragraph 4, 5, 6, 7 or 8 for *44 hours*' work in his normal occupation;

　(*b*) who normally works for the employer for more than *84 hours* in a fortnight but for less than *88 hours* on work to which this Schedule applies, is the remuneration to which he would be entitled under paragraph 4, 5, 6, 7 or 8 (calculated as in paragraph 17) in respect of the number of hours normally worked by him in a fortnight;

　(*c*) who normally works for the employer for *84 hours* or less in a fortnight, is the remuneration to which he would be entitled under paragraph 4, 5, 6, 7 or 8 (calculated as in paragraph 17) for *84 hours* in a fortnight:

Provided that where the worker normally works for the employer on work to which this Schedule applies for less than *84 hours* in a fortnight by reason only of the fact that he does not hold himself out as normally available for work for more than the number of hours he normally works in the fortnight, and the worker has informed his employer in writing that he does not so hold himself out, the guaranteed remuneration shall be the remuneration (calculated as in paragraph 17) for the number of hours in the fortnight normally worked by the worker for the employer on work to which this Schedule applies.

(2) Guaranteed remuneration is not payable in respect of any fortnight unless the worker throughout his normal working hours in that fortnight (excluding any time allowed to him as a holiday) is

　(*a*) capable of and available for work; and

　(*b*) willing to perform such duties outside his normal occupation as the employer may reasonably require if his normal work is not available in the establishment in which he is employed.

(3) Guaranteed remuneration is not payable in respect of any fortnight if the worker's employment is terminated before the end of that fortnight.

(4) If the employer is unable to provide the worker with work by reason of a strike or other circumstances beyond his control and gives the worker four clear days' notice to that effect, guaranteed remuneration shall not be payable after the expiry of such notice in respect of any fortnight during which, or during part of which, the employer continues to be unable to provide work as aforesaid:

Provided that in respect of the fortnight in which the said notice expires there shall be paid to the worker, in addition to any remuneration payable in respect of time worked in that fortnight, any remuneration that would have been payable if the worker had worked his normal hours of work on any days in the fortnight prior to the expiry of the notice.

OVERTIME

19. Subject to the provisions of paragraph 20, minimum overtime rates shall be payable to workers, other than extra head waiters, extra waiters and extra waitresses, as follows:—

(1) in the case of workers other than fortnightly workers:—

(a) on the weekly day of rest for all time worked ... Double time

(b) in any week, exclusive of time worked on a weekly day of rest, for all time worked in excess of *44 hours*—

(i) for the first six hours so worked ... ... Time-and-a-quarter

(ii) thereafter ... ... Time-and-a-half

(2) in the case of fortnightly workers (as defined in paragraph 35):—

(a) on the weekly day of rest for all time worked ... Double time

(b) in any week, exclusive of time worked on a weekly day of rest, for all time worked in excess of *52 hours* ... . Time-and-a-half

(c) in the second week of any fortnight after *88 hours'* work in that fortnight, exclusive of any time in respect of which an overtime rate is payable under (a) or (b) of this sub-paragraph—

(i) for the first 12 hours so worked ... ... Time-and-a-quarter

(ii) thereafter ... . Time-and-a-half

Provided that the provisions of this paragraph shall not apply to emergency duty (as defined in paragraph 35).

SPECIAL PROVISIONS RELATING TO REST DAYS

20.—(1) Where a worker works on one weekly day of rest in any period of two consecutive weeks pursuant to an agreement in writing with his employer that the employer will allow the worker an equivalent time off during the period of the ten following weeks in lieu of time so worked, the worker shall, for the purposes of the provisions of this Schedule relating to remuneration, be treated as though on that day he had performed no work to which this Schedule applies.

(2) Where a worker to whom this paragraph applies is allowed time off pursuant to an agreement as specified in sub-paragraph (1) of this paragraph he shall be treated for the purposes of the provisions of this Schedule relating to remuneration as though in respect of that time he had been employed by the employer in his usual occupation.

SPECIAL PROVISIONS RELATING TO FULL-TIME WORKERS WHO ARE NOT REQUIRED TO WORK ON A CUSTOMARY HOLIDAY

21.—(1) This paragraph applies only to a full-time worker who is not required to work on a customary holiday and who has been in the employer's employment for the six days immediately preceding the customary holiday and (unless excused by the employer or absent by reason of proved sickness) has worked for the employer throughout his normal working hours on the last working day on which work was available to him prior to the holiday and throughout his normal working hours on the next such working day following the holiday.

(2) Where the customary holiday is not a day which has been allowed to the worker and taken by him as a day of annual holiday, he shall be paid for that day one day's holiday pay (as defined in paragraph 35).

(3) Where the customary holiday is a day which has been allowed to a worker and taken by him as a day of annual holiday, and

(a) he is allowed by his employer a day of holiday in lieu of the customary holiday on a day other than the weekly day of rest, within 28 days of the customary holiday, he shall be paid for the holiday given in lieu one day's holiday pay; or

(b) he is not allowed a day in lieu of the customary holiday in accordance with (a) of this sub-paragraph, he shall be paid for the working day next following the 28th day after the customary holiday or for his last working day if he leaves his employment before the said 28th day, the remuneration to which he is entitled under the other provisions of this Schedule for all time worked on that day and in addition one day's holiday pay.

SPECIAL PROVISIONS RELATING TO FULL-TIME WORKERS WHO WORK ON A CUSTOMARY HOLIDAY

22.—(1) Where a full-time worker works on a customary holiday he shall be paid for all time worked on that day the minimum remuneration to which he is entitled under the other provisions of this Part of this Schedule.

(2) Where a full-time worker who has worked on a customary holiday is allowed by his employer, on a day other than the weekly day of rest, a day of holiday in lieu of the customary holiday—

(a) within 28 days of the customary holiday, or

(b) before the end of the holiday season if the customary holiday falls within that season and the last day of that season is more than 28 days after the customary holiday, or

(c) before the end of the next holiday season commencing after the customary holiday if the worker so requests and the employer agrees and the agreement is reduced to writing and sets out the date on which the holiday is to be allowed, he shall be paid for the day so allowed as a holiday one day's holiday pay (as defined in paragraph 35).

(3) Where a full-time worker who has worked on a customary holiday is not allowed a day in lieu of the customary holiday in accordance with sub-paragraph (2) of this paragraph he shall be paid for the working day next following the last day on which the holiday could have been allowed in accordance with that sub-paragraph or for his last working day if he leaves his employment before that day, for all time worked on the said working day the minimum remuneration to which he is entitled under the provisions of this Schedule and in addition one day's holiday pay.

NIGHT WORK IN RELATION TO CUSTOMARY HOLIDAYS

23. For the purposes of paragraphs 21 and 22, where a worker normally works a turn of duty which extends beyond midnight, the whole of the turn of duty worked, or the period which would have been covered by the turn of duty had it been worked, shall be counted as falling on the day upon which it commenced or would have commenced had it been worked.

PART II
ANNUAL HOLIDAY AND HOLIDAY REMUNERATION
DURATION OF ANNUAL HOLIDAY

24. Subject to the provisions of this Part of this Schedule, an employer shall, between the date on which the provisions of this Schedule become effective and 31st October 1969 or, in the case of a worker employed at a seasonal establishment, between the date on which the provisions of this Schedule become effective and 30th November 1969, and during the holiday season (as defined in paragraph 35) in each succeeding year, allow a holiday (in this Schedule referred to as an "annual holiday") to every worker (other than an extra waiter, extra waitress or extra head waiter) for whom statutory minimum remuneration has been fixed, who has been employed by him during the 12 months immediately preceding the commencement of the holiday season (hereinafter referred to as the "qualifying period") for any of the periods of employment (calculated in accordance with the provisions of paragraph 34) set out in the first Column of the Table below and the duration of the annual holiday shall be related to the period of the worker's employment during the qualifying period in accordance with that Table:—

Period of employment during the qualifying period (1)	Duration of annual holiday for a worker whose normal working week is		
	6 days (2)	5 days (3)	4 days or less (4)
At least 8 weeks	2 days	1 day	1 day
„ 12 „	3 „	2 days	2 days
„ 16 „	4 „	3 „	2 „
„ 20 „	5 „	4 „	3 „
„ 24 „	6 „	5 „	4 „
„ 28 „	7 „	6 „	4 „
„ 32 „	8 „	6 „	5 „
„ 36 „	9 „	7 „	5 „
„ 40 „	10 „	8 „	6 „
„ 44 „	11 „	9 „	7 „
„ 48 „	12 „	10 „	8 „

25. Notwithstanding the provisions of paragraph 24:—

(1) the number of days of annual holiday which an employer is required to allow under the provisions of this Schedule shall not exceed the number of days normally worked by the worker in a fortnight;

(2) the worker's annual holiday during the holiday season ending on 31st October 1969 or, in the case of a worker employed at a seasonal establishment, 30th November 1969, shall be reduced by any days of annual holiday duly allowed to him by the employer under the provisions of Order L.R. (38) between 1st April 1969, and the date on which the provisions of this Schedule become effective.

SPELLS OF ANNUAL HOLIDAY

26. An annual holiday shall be allowed on consecutive working days and days of annual holiday shall be treated as consecutive notwithstanding that the worker's weekly day of rest or a customary holiday or a day of holiday in lieu of a customary holiday intervenes:

Provided that where a worker has qualified for more days of annual holiday than the number constituting his normal working week his holiday may be allowed in two separate periods of which one shall consist of at least the number of days constituting his normal working week.

AGREEMENT TO ALLOW ANNUAL HOLIDAY OUTSIDE THE HOLIDAY SEASON

27. Notwithstanding the provisions of paragraph 24, an annual holiday may be allowed—

(1) (a) in the case of a worker employed at a seasonal establishment, during the four months preceding the commencement of the holiday season; or

(*b*) in the case of any other worker, during the five months preceding the commencement of the holiday season;

or (2) in the case of any worker, after the end of the holiday season and before the commencement of the next following holiday season

in the following circumstances, that is to say—

(*a*) in the case of sub-paragraph (1) of this paragraph, where the worker informs his employer not less than one month before the date at which he wishes to take all or part of the annual holiday that he wishes to take it before the commencement of the holiday season and the employer agrees and the said agreement is reduced to writing and sets out the dates on which the annual holiday is to be allowed;

(*b*) in the case of sub-paragraph (2) of this paragraph, where the worker in the course of the holiday season informs his employer that he wishes to take the annual holiday after the end of the holiday season and the employer agrees and the said agreement is reduced to writing and sets out the dates on which the annual holiday is to be allowed.

Where under the provisions of this paragraph an annual holiday is allowed during the four or five month period (as the case may be) preceding the commencement of the holiday season the qualifying period for the purpose of calculating the duration of the said holiday of the worker concerned shall be varied and shall be the 12 months immediately preceding the commencement of the annual holiday, provided that where an annual holiday is allowed to a worker in two separate periods in accordance with the provisions of paragraph 26 the qualifying period as varied referred to in this paragraph shall be the period of 12 months immediately preceding the first holiday period.

APPLICATIONS TO VARY THE HOLIDAY SEASON

28. Notwithstanding the provisions of paragraph 24, the Wages Council may vary the holiday season in respect of any establishment if it receives an application for the purpose from an employer and is satisfied that it is reasonable to do so to meet special circumstances. Such variation may provide for the commencement of the holiday season earlier than 1st April or its extension beyond 30th November in the case of a worker employed at a seasonal establishment or 31st October in the case of any other worker. An application relating to the commencement of the holiday season shall be made to the Wages Council not less than six weeks before the operative date and an application to extend the duration of the holiday season before 15th July. Any such alteration in the holiday season shall not become effective until notice of the decision of the Wages Council has been communicated to the employer concerned.

In the case of any variation of the holiday season under this provision the qualifying period for the purpose of calculating the duration of the annual holiday of the worker or workers concerned shall be varied and shall be the 12 months immediately preceding the commencement of the holiday season as varied.

GENERAL

29. An employer shall give to a worker reasonable notice of the commencing date and duration of his annual holiday and such notice may be given individually to a worker or by the posting of a notice in the place where the worker is employed.

30. Subject to the provisions of paragraph 26, any day of annual holiday under this Schedule may be allowed on a day on which the worker is entitled to a day of holiday or to a half-holiday under any enactment other than the Wages Councils Act 1959(a).

(a) 1959 c. 69.

REMUNERATION FOR ANNUAL HOLIDAY

31.—(1) Subject to the provisions of paragraph 32, a worker qualified to be allowed an annual holiday under this Schedule shall be paid by his employer in respect thereof, on the last pay day preceding such annual holiday, one day's holiday pay (as defined in paragraph 35) in respect of each day thereof.

(2) Where under the provisions of this Schedule an annual holiday is allowed in more than one period the holiday remuneration shall be apportioned accordingly.

32. Where in accordance with the provisions of paragraph 33 or of Order L.R. (38), accrued holiday remuneration has been paid by the employer to the worker in respect of any period of employment in the 12 months immediately preceding the holiday season within which an annual holiday is allowed by the employer to the worker in accordance with the provisions of this Schedule, the amount of holiday remuneration payable by the employer in respect of the said annual holiday under the provisions of paragraph 31 shall be reduced by the amount of the said accrued holiday remuneration, unless that remuneration has been deducted from a previous payment of holiday remuneration made under the provisions of this Schedule or of Order L.R. (38).

ACCRUED HOLIDAY REMUNERATION PAYABLE ON TERMINATION OF EMPLOYMENT

33. Subject to the provisions of this paragraph, where a worker (other than an extra waiter, extra waitress or extra head waiter) ceases to be employed by an employer after the provisions of this Schedule become effective, the employer shall, immediately on the termination of the employment, pay to the worker as accrued holiday remuneration:—

(1) in respect of employment in the 12 months up to the commencing date of the current holiday season, a sum equal to the holiday remuneration for any days of annual holiday for which he has qualified, except days of annual holiday which he has been allowed or has become entitled to be allowed before leaving the employment; and

(2) in respect of any employment since the commencing date of the current holiday season, or if no holiday season is then current, the commencing date of the last holiday season, a sum equal to the holiday remuneration which would have been payable to him if he could have been allowed an annual holiday in respect of that employment at the time of leaving it:

Provided that—

(a) the amount of the accrued holiday remuneration payable to a worker who leaves his employment without the consent of his employer before giving one week's notice of termination of employment or before one week has elapsed from the time of giving such notice, shall be the amount payable under the foregoing provisions of this Schedule less an amount equal to the holiday remuneration which would be payable to him if at the termination of his employment he had been allowed an annual holiday of an equivalent number of days as constituted his normal working week;

(b) accrued holiday remuneration shall not be payable where a worker is dismissed on the ground either of dishonesty or of misconduct involving contravention of the licensing laws and is so informed by the employer at the time of dismissal;

(c) where, during the period or periods in respect of which the said accrued holiday remuneration is payable, the worker has been allowed any day or days of holiday for which he had not qualified under the provisions of this Schedule or of Order L.R. (38), any accrued holiday remuneration payable as aforesaid shall be reduced by the amount of any sum paid by the employer to the worker in respect of such day or days of holiday.

CALCULATION OF EMPLOYMENT

34. For the purpose of calculating any period of employment qualifying a worker for an annual holiday or for any accrued holiday remuneration under this Schedule the worker shall be treated as having been employed—

(1) in the case of a worker other than a fortnightly worker, for a week in respect of any week in which he has worked for the employer for *44 hours* or, where the number of hours normally worked by him for the employer in a week is less than *44*, that number of hours, and in which he has performed some work which entitles him to statutory minimum remuneration;

(2) in the case of a fortnightly worker, for two weeks in respect of any fortnight in which he has worked for the employer for *88 hours* or, where the number of hours normally worked by him for the employer in a fortnight is less than *88*, that number of hours, and in both weeks of which fortnight he has performed some work which entitles him to statutory minimum remuneration;

(3) when absent from work in any of the following circumstances:—

(*a*) on annual holiday allowed under this Schedule, customary holidays or days of holiday in lieu of customary holidays;

(*b*) during proved sickness or accident up to and not exceeding a maximum of 12 weeks in the aggregate during the qualifying period or during the qualifying period as varied in accordance with the provisions of paragraph 27 or 28 or, where under paragraph 33 accrued holiday remuneration is payable on the termination of the employment, in the 12 months immediately preceding the termination of the employment;

(*c*) by leave of the employer.

PART III
GENERAL
DEFINITIONS

35. In this Schedule the following expressions have the meanings hereby respectively assigned to them, that is to say:—

"CATERING CONTRACTING BUSINESS" means a business or part of a business wholly or mainly engaged in supplying food or drink for immediate consumption—

(1) on premises not ordinarily occupied by the person or body of persons carrying on the business; or

(2) in a railway train where the business is carried on otherwise than by a railway company or any Board established by the Transport Act 1962(a) or any subsidiary thereof;
and any activities incidental or ancillary thereto.

"CATERING UNDERTAKING" means any undertaking or any part of an undertaking which consists wholly or mainly in the carrying on (whether for profit or not) of one or more of the following activities, that is to say, the supply of food or drink for immediate consumption, the provision of living accommodation for guests or lodgers or for persons employed in the undertaking and any other activity so far as it is incidental or anciliary to any such activity as aforesaid of the undertaking.

"CENTRAL CATERING ESTABLISHMENT" means an establishment wholly or mainly engaged in the preparation of food or drink for immediate consumption at two or more places of refreshment carried on by the person or body of persons carrying on the establishment but does not include an establishment

---

(a) 1962 c. 46.

wholly or mainly engaged in the preparation of food or drink for consumption on the same premises or in the same building as those on which or as that in which the establishment itself is carried on and for the purpose of this definition a place of refreshment means any place which is used either regularly or occasionally as, or for the purposes of, a restaurant, dining-room, café, tea shop, buffet or similar place or a coffee stall, snack bar or other similar stall or bar.

"CUSTOMARY HOLIDAY" means

(1) in England and Wales—

(a) Christmas Day (or, if Christmas Day falls on a Sunday, such other day as may be prescribed by national proclamation, or if no such day is prescribed, the next following Tuesday), Boxing Day, Good Friday, Easter Monday, Whit Monday (or where another day is substituted therefor by national proclamation, that day), August Bank Holiday and any day proclaimed as an additional Bank Holiday or a general holiday; or

(b) in the case of each of the said days, a day substituted by the employer therefor, being a day recognised by local custom as a day of holiday in substitution for the said day.

(2) In Scotland—

(a) New Year's Day (or the following day if New Year's Day falls on a Sunday), the local Spring Holiday, the local Autumn Holiday and any day proclaimed as an additional Bank Holiday or a general holiday throughout Scotland; and

(b) three other week-days in the course of a calendar year, to be fixed by the employer and notified to the worker not less than three weeks before the holiday- or any other day or days falling within the same calendar year which may be substituted for such day or days by agreement between the employer and the worker or his representative.

"DAY" means a period running from midnight to midnight unless the context otherwise requires.

"EMERGENCY DUTY" means work for not more than one hour performed by a worker involving the interruption of an interval for rest between two turns of duty.

"ESTABLISHMENT" means a licensed residential establishment, licensed restaurant, railway refreshment establishment or licensed workers' hostel.

"FORTNIGHT" means a period of two consecutive weeks of employment and for the purposes of this definition a week that has been treated as consecutive with the week that precedes it shall not be treated as consecutive with the week that follows it.

"FORTNIGHTLY WORKER" is a worker who is employed under a written agreement which provides for his remuneration for overtime to be calculated on a fortnightly basis.

"FULL BOARD" means not less than four meals a day.

"FULL-TIME WORKER" means a worker who normally works for his employer for not less than *68 hours* a fortnight on work to which this Schedule applies.

"HOLIDAY SEASON" means in any year—

(1) in the case of a worker employed at a seasonal establishment the period commencing on 1st April and ending on 30th November in that year, or

(2) in the case of any other worker the period commencing on 1st April and ending on 31st October in that year.

"LICENSED RESIDENTIAL ESTABLISHMENT" means:—

(1) An hotel, inn, boarding house, guest house, hostel or similar establishment, including a holiday camp—

(a) which either contains four or more rooms ordinarily available as sleeping accommodation for guests or lodgers or, if it contains less than four such rooms, which contains sleeping accommodation ordinarily available for not less than eight guests or lodgers; and

(b) at which it is lawful for intoxicating liquor to be sold for consumption on the premises or to be supplied for consumption on the premises by reason of the fact that part of the premises is habitually used for the purposes of a registered club;

but does not include any hostel or similar establishment provided by or by arrangement with an employer wholly or mainly for the purpose of accommodating persons employed by him.

(2) A club—

(a) which either contains four or more rooms ordinarily available as sleeping accommodation for guests or lodgers or, if it contains less than four such rooms, which contains sleeping accommodation ordinarily available for not less than eight guests or lodgers; and

(b) at which is it lawful for intoxicating liquor to be supplied for consumption on the premises.

"LICENSED RESTAURANT" does not include any place which forms part of a licensed residential establishment or which constitutes or forms part of a railway refreshment establishment or any place at which intoxicating liquor can legally be sold or supplied for consumption on the premises by reason only of the fact that in relation to that place an occasional licence is for the time being in force, being a licence granted to some person other than the person carrying on, or a person in the employment of the person carrying on, the activities (other than the supply of intoxicating liquor) of a catering undertaking at that place; but, save as aforesaid, means any place which is used either regularly or occasionally as, or for the purposes of, a restaurant, dining-room, café or similar place at which it is lawful to sell (or supply in the case of a restaurant, dining-room or café of a club) intoxicating liquor for consumption on the premises and includes any bar or other place wholly or mainly used for the sale (or supply in the case of a club) and consumption on the premises of intoxicating liquor if the bar is situate on the same premises as any such restaurant, dining-room, café or similar place as aforesaid and the activities of such restaurant, dining-room, café or similar place constitute the main catering activities carried on at the premises.

"LICENSED WORKERS' HOSTEL" means a hostel or similar establishment provided by or by arrangement with an employer wholly or mainly for the purpose of accommodating persons employed by him otherwise than in a catering undertaking being an establishment at which it is lawful for intoxicating liquor to be sold for consumption on the premises or to be supplied for consumption on the premises by reason of the fact that part of the premises is habitually used for the purpose of a registered club.

"LODGING" means clean and adequate accommodation and facilities for eating, sleeping, washing and leisure.

"MEAL" means a meal of good and sufficient quality and quantity.

"NIGHT WORK" means all time worked on any turn of duty where that turn of duty includes not less than three hours' work between midnight and 6 a.m.

"NORMAL WORKING WEEK" means one half of the number of days on which the worker has most frequently worked in a fortnight in the employment of the employer in the qualifying period or in the qualifying period as varied in accordance with the provisions of paragraph 27 or 28 or, where under paragraph 33 accrued holiday remuneration is payable on the termination of the employment, in the 12 months immediately preceding the date of the termination of the employment: Provided that

(1) part of a day shall count as a day;

(2) no account shall be taken of any week in which the worker did not perform any work for which statutory minimum remuneration has been fixed.

"ONE DAY'S HOLIDAY PAY" means the amount obtained by dividing the appropriate statutory minimum remuneration applicable to the worker for a fortnight's work at the date of the annual holiday or of the termination of his employment as the case may be, by the number of days on which he is normally employed in a fornight.

For the purpose of this definition—

(1) "appropriate statutory minimum remuneration" means the statutory minimum remuneration to which the worker would be entitled if he were working his normal hours of work (exclusive of overtime) and were paid at the single time rate (as defined in paragraph 3), in the case of work for which statutory minimum remuneration is payable, and at the same rate for any work for which statutory minimum remuneration is not payable.

(2) "normal hours of work" means the number of hours which have been most frequently worked by the worker in a normal working week as defined above.

"PROTECTIVE CLOTHING" means any garment other than uniform which protects a worker's normal clothing.

"RAILWAY REFRESHMENT ESTABLISHMENT" means any place of refreshment at a railway station, being a place of refreshment—

(1) at which it is lawful for intoxicating liquor to be sold for consumption on the premises; or

(2) the activities of which are carried on by a railway company or any Board established by the Transport Act 1962 or any subsidiary thereof;

and for the purpose of this definition "place of refreshment" means a place used either regularly or occasionally as, or for the purposes of, a restaurant, dining-room, café, tea shop, canteen or similar place or coffee stall, buffet or bar.

"SEASONAL ESTABLISHMENT" has the meaning assigned to it in paragraph 13.

"STATUTORY MINIMUM REMUNERATION" means minimum remuneration (other than holiday remuneration) which has been fixed by a wages regulation order made by the Secretary of State to give effect to proposals of the Wages Council.

"UNIFORM" means any outer clothing of a character distinctive to the establishment, which replaces the worker's own outer clothing.

"WEEK" means pay week.

"WEEKLY DAY OF REST" means either—

(1) a day in the week fixed by agreement between the employer and the worker as a day of rest for the worker, not being a customary holiday; or

(2) if no such day is fixed the last day of the worker's pay week not being a customary holiday;

and for the purposes of this definition, the word "day" means a period of 24 consecutive hours commencing at the time at which the worker would normally commence his turn of duty.

WORKERS TO WHOM THE SCHEDULE APPLIES

36. Subject to the provisions of paragraph 37, this Schedule applies to all workers employed in Great Britain in a catering undertaking who are employed by the person or body of persons carrying on that undertaking and who are so employed either—

(1) for the purposes of such of the activities of the undertaking as are carried on at a licensed residential establishment or at a licensed restaurant or at a railway refreshment establishment or at a licensed workers' hostel; or

(2) in connection with the provision of food or drink or living accommodation provided wholly or mainly for workers employed for the purposes of any of the activities of the undertaking specified in sub-paragraph (1) of this paragraph;

and who are engaged on any of the following work, that is to say:—

 (*a*) the preparation of food or drink;

 (*b*) the service of food or drink;

 (*c*) work incidental to such preparation or service;

 (*d*) work connected with the provision of living accommodation;

 (*e*) work in connection with any retail sale of goods on premises where the main activity is either the supply of food or drink for immediate consumption or the provision of living accommodation for guests or lodgers or partly the supply of food or drink as aforesaid and partly the provision of living accommodation as aforesaid;

 (*f*) transport work;

 (*g*) work performed at any office or at any store or warehouse or similar place or at any garage or stable or similar place;

 (*h*) any work other than that specified in sub-paragraphs (*a*) to (*g*) hereof performed on or about the premises or place where food or drink is prepared or served or where living accommodation is provided, including work in connection with any service or amenity provided on or about such premises or place.

37. This Schedule does not apply to any of the following workers in respect of their employment in any of the following circumstances, that is to say:—

 (1) workers who are employed by the same employer partly in a catering undertaking and partly in some other undertaking, if their employment in the catering undertaking is confined to work specified either in sub-paragraph (*f*) or sub-paragraph (*g*) of paragraph 36 or partly to work specified in the said sub-paragraph (*f*) and partly to work specified in the said sub-paragraph (*g*), and they are mainly employed on work in or in connection with that other undertaking;

 (2) workers who are employed for the purposes of the activities carried on at any of the following establishments, that is to say:—

 (*a*) any hospital, nursing home or convalescent home or similar establishment providing accomodation for the sick, infirm or mentally defective;

 (*b*) any institution or home where living accommodation is provided for the aged or indigent;

 (*c*) any university, college, school or similar establishment;

 and who are employed by the person or body of persons carrying on the establishment, or, in the case of any of the establishments specified in sub-paragraph (*c*) hereof, by the person or body of persons carrying on any boarding house which forms part of the establishment;

 (3) workers who are employed for the purposes of any of the activities carried on in a railway train;

 (4) workers who are employed for the purposes of any of the activities carried on at a theatre, music-hall or other similar place of entertainment ordinarily used for the public performance of stage plays or variety entertainments;

 (5) workers who are employed for the purposes of any of the activities carried on in the course of a catering contracting business;

 (6) workers who are employed for the purposes of any of the activities of a central catering establishment;

 (7) workers who are employed for the purposes of the activities carried on at a licensed restaurant if the licensed restaurant is situated on premises where the main activity is the sale of intoxicating liquor for consumption on the premises otherwise than with meals supplied on the premises;

(8) workers who are employed by the Crown or by a local authority;

(9) workers in relation to whom the Industrial and Staff Canteen Undertakings Wages Council operates in respect of any employment which is for the time being within the field of operation of that Wages Council;

(10) workers employed in the hotel and catering services of the nationalised railways who are so employed by the British Railways Board or by British Transport Hotels Limited;

(11) workers who are employed as aircraft stewards or aircraft stewardesses;

(12) workers who are employed as managers, manageresses, assistant managers or assistant manageresses;

(13) workers who are the wives of managers and who are required by the employer to assist in the work of an establishment.

38. Nothing in the provisions of this Schedule shall be construed as authorising the making of any deduction or the giving of any remuneration in any manner that is illegal by virtue of the Truck Acts 1831-1940(a), or of any other enactment.

EXPLANATORY NOTE

(This Note is not part of the Order.)

This Order, which has effect from 7th July 1969, sets out the statutory minimum remuneration payable and the holidays to be allowed to workers in substitution for the statutory minimum remuneration and holidays set out in the Wages Regulation (Licensed Residential Establishment and Licensed Restaurant) Order 1968 (Order L.R. (38)) which Order is revoked.

New provisions are printed in italics.

(a) 1831 c. 37; 1887 c. 46; 1896 c. 44; 1940 c. 38.

STATUTORY INSTRUMENTS

1969 No. 756

REPRESENTATION OF THE PEOPLE
The Urban District Council Election Rules 1969

Made - - -	*23rd May* 1969
Laid before Parliament	*5th June* 1969
Coming into Operation	*16th February* 1970

In pursuance of the powers conferred upon me by section 29 and section 165(1) of the Representation of the People Act 1949(**a**), and by section 61 of the Local Government Act 1933(**b**), I hereby make the following Rules for the conduct of an election of urban district councillors and of the chairman of an urban district council, and the following Regulations prescribing the form of declaration of acceptance of office by the chairman of an urban district council and by an urban district councillor :—

1.—(1) These Rules and Regulations may be cited as the Urban District Council Election Rules 1969 and shall come into operation on 16th February 1970 :

Provided that they shall not have effect in relation to an election notice of which has been published before that date.

(2) The Interpretation Act 1889(**c**) shall apply to the interpretation of these Rules and Regulations as it applies to the interpretation of an Act of Parliament.

2.—(1) The Urban District Council Election Rules 1951(**d**), the Urban District-Council Election Rules 1954(**e**) and the Urban District Council Election Rules 1962(**f**) are hereby revoked.

(2) Notwithstanding paragraph (1) of this Rule, the Rules therein mentioned shall apply to any election notice of which has been published before these Rules and Regulations come into operation.

(3) Any reference in any statutory instrument to a rule contained in Schedule 1 to the Urban District Council Election Rules 1951 shall be taken as a reference to the corresponding rule contained in Schedule 1 to these Rules.

3.—(1) For an election of urban district councillors the clerk of the urban district council shall be the returning officer, and if at such election the office of clerk of the urban district council is vacant or the clerk is for any reason unable to act, the chairman of the urban district council shall forthwith appoint another person to be the returning officer for that election :

Provided that, in the case of a first election of urban district councillors for a newly constituted urban district, a person appointed in accordance with the

---

(**a**) 1949 c. 68.
(**c**) 1889 c. 63.
(**e**) S.I. 1954/1485 (1954 II, p. 1920).
(**b**) 1933 c. 51.
(**d**) S.I. 1951/267 (1951 II, p. 385).
(**f**) S.I. 1962/1269 (1962 II, p. 1372).

order constituting the new urban district, or, if the order contains no provision relating to the appointment of a returning officer, a person appointed by the county council, shall be the returning officer.

(2) The returning officer may by writing under his hand appoint a fit person to be his deputy for all or any of the purposes of an election, and any functions which a returning officer is authorised or required to discharge in relation to the election may be discharged by a deputy so appointed.

(3) A deputy acting as returning officer under the provisions of this Rule shall, as respects the election for which he is so acting, follow the instructions of the returning officer.

4. In the application of those provisions of the Representation of the People Act 1949, referred to in section 165(1) of that Act, to an election of the chairman of an urban district council and of urban district councillors the following modification shall have effect :—

In section 119(2)(*b*) of the said Act for the words "such amount not exceeding five hundred pounds" there shall be substituted the words "an amount of fifty pounds or such smaller amount or such larger amount not exceeding three hundred pounds".

5. In the application of the local elections rules contained in Schedule 2 to the Representation of the People Act 1949 to an election of urban district councillors, adaptations, alterations and exceptions shall be made therein so that the said local elections rules shall read as set out in Schedule 1 hereto.

6. The declaration of acceptance of office by the chairman of an urban district council or by an urban district councillor shall be in the form in Schedule 2 hereto, or a form to the like effect.

James Callaghan,
One of Her Majesty's Principal
Secretaries of State.

Home Office,
Whitehall.
23rd May 1969.

SCHEDULE 1

ELECTION RULES

Arrangement of rules

PART I

PROVISIONS AS TO TIME

Rule
1. Timetable.
2. Computation of time.
3. Hours of poll.

PART II

STAGES COMMON TO CONTESTED AND UNCONTESTED ELECTIONS

4. Notice of election.
5. Nomination of candidates.
6. Subscription of nomination paper.
7. Consent to nomination.
8. Place for delivery of nomination papers.
9. Decisions as to validity of nomination papers.
10. Publication of nominations.
11. Withdrawal of candidates.
12. Nomination in more than one ward.
13. Method of election.

PART III

CONTESTED ELECTIONS

General provisions

14. Poll to be taken by ballot.
15. The ballot papers.
16. The official mark.
17. Prohibition of disclosure of vote.
18. Use of schools and public rooms.

Action to be taken before poll

19. Notice of poll.
20. Postal ballot papers.
21. Provision of polling stations.
22. Appointment of presiding officers and clerks.
23. Special lists.
24. Equipment of polling stations.
25. Appointment of polling and counting agents.
26. Declaration of secrecy.

The poll

27. Admission to polling station.
28. Keeping of order in station.
29. Sealing of ballot boxes.
30. Questions to be put to voters.
31. Challenge of voter.
32. Voting procedure.
33. Votes marked by presiding officer.
34. Voting by blind persons.
35. Tendered ballot papers.
36. Spoilt ballot papers.
37. Adjournment of poll in case of riot.
38. Procedure on close of poll.

Counting of votes

39. Attendance at counting of votes.
40. The count.
41. Re-count.
42. Rejected ballot papers.
43. Decisions on ballot papers.
44. Equality of votes.

PART IV
FINAL PROCEEDINGS IN CONTESTED AND UNCONTESTED ELECTIONS

45. Declaration of result.
46. The return.

PART V
DISPOSAL OF DOCUMENTS

47. Sealing of ballot papers.
48. Delivery of documents to clerk of the council.
49. Orders for production of documents.
50. Retention and public inspection of documents.
51. Supplemental provisions as to documents.

PART VI
SUPPLEMENTAL

52. Countermand or abandonment of poll on death of candidate.
53. General duty of returning officer.
54. Notices.
55. Interpretation.

APPENDIX
FORMS

Notice of election.
Nomination paper.
Statement as to persons nominated.
Ballot paper.
Directions for the guidance of the voters in voting.
Certificate of employment.
Declaration to be made by the companion of a blind voter.

PART I
PROVISIONS AS TO TIME
Timetable

1. The proceedings at the election shall be conducted in accordance with the following Table.

TIMETABLE

Proceeding	Time
Publication of notice of election ..	Not later than the twentieth day before the day of election.
Delivery of nomination papers ..	Not later than noon on the fourteenth day before the day of election.
Despatch of notices of decisions on nominations and publication of statement as to persons nominated	Not later than noon on the thirteenth day before the day of election.
Delivery of notices of withdrawals of candidature	Not later than noon on the twelfth day before the day of election.
Notice of poll	Not later than the fifth day before the day of election.
Notice of appointment of polling or counting agents	Not later than the third day before the day of election.
Polling	On the day of election.

Computation of Time

2.—(1) In computing any period of time for the purposes of the Timetable, a Sunday, day of the Christmas break, of the Easter break or of a bank holiday break or day appointed for public thanksgiving or mourning shall be disregarded and any such day shall not be treated as a day for the purpose of any proceedings up to the completion of the poll nor shall the returning officer be obliged to proceed with the counting of the votes thereon:

Provided that where under Part III of these rules a person ought to proceed with the preparation of special lists or the issue of postal ballot papers on the first or last days of the Christmas break, the Easter break or a bank holiday break, or on the Saturday in the Easter break, nothing in this rule shall absolve him from that duty.

(2) In this rule "the Christmas break" means the period beginning with the last week day before Christmas Day and ending with the first week day after Christmas Day which is not a bank holiday, "the Easter break" means the period beginning with the Thursday before and ending with the Tuesday after Easter Day, and "a bank holiday break" means any bank holiday not included in the Christmas break or the Easter break and the period beginning with the last week day before that bank holiday and ending with the next week day which is not a bank holiday.

Hours of poll

3.—(1) The poll shall commence at the hour fixed for the urban district by the county council by any general or special order or, if no such order has been made, at eight o'clock in the morning and be kept open till eight o'clock in the evening of the same day and no longer:

Provided that the poll shall be kept open till nine o'clock in the evening if candidates remaining validly nominated to a number not less than the number of vacancies have, by written notices signed by them and delivered at the place and within the time for delivery of notices of withdrawals of candidature, so requested.

(2) A notice under this rule shall not have effect as respects any candidate if revoked by a further written notice signed by him and delivered as aforesaid.

PART II

STAGES COMMON TO CONTESTED AND UNCONTESTED ELECTIONS

Notice of election

4.—(1) Notice of the election in the form in the Appendix, or a form to the like effect, shall be prepared, signed and published by the returning officer.

(2) The notice shall be published by causing it to be affixed to the offices of the urban district council and, in the case of a ward election, to be exhibited at such conspicuous places in the ward as the returning officer may determine.

(3) The notice of election shall state the date by which application to be treated as an absent voter and other applications and notices about postal or proxy voting must reach the registration officer in order that they may be effective for the election; and in addition the registration officer shall give notice of the date in the electoral area by such means as he thinks best calculated to bring the information to the notice of those concerned.

Nomination of candidates

5.—(1) Each candidate shall be nominated by a separate nomination paper in the form in the Appendix, or a form to the like effect, delivered at the place fixed for the purpose.

(2) The nomination paper shall state the full names, place of residence and (if desired) description of the candidate and the surname shall be placed first in the list of his names.

(3) The description (if any) shall not exceed six words in length, and need not refer to his rank, profession or calling so long as, with the other particulars of the candidate, it is sufficient to identify him.

Subscription of nomination paper

6.—(1) The nomination paper shall be subscribed by two electors for the electoral area as proposer and seconder and by eight other electors for that area as assenting to the nomination.

(2) Where a nomination paper bears the signatures of more than the required number of persons as proposing, seconding or assenting to the nomination of a candidate, the signature or signatures (up to the required number) appearing first on the paper in each category shall be taken into account to the exclusion of any others in that category.

(3) The nomination paper shall give the electoral number of each person subscribing it.

(4) The returning officer shall provide nomination papers and shall supply any elector for the electoral area with as many nomination papers as may be required and shall, at the request of any such elector, prepare for signature a nomination paper.

(5) No person shall—

(a) subscribe more nomination papers than there are vacancies to be filled in the electoral area ; or

(b) subscribe a nomination paper for more than one ward of an urban district divided into wards ; or

(c) subscribe more than one nomination paper in respect of the same candidate:

Provided that a person shall not be prevented from subscribing a nomination paper by reason only of his having subscribed that of a candidate who has died or withdrawn before delivery of the first-mentioned paper.

(6) If any person subscribes nomination papers in contravention of the last foregoing paragraph, his signature shall be inoperative in all but those papers (up to the permitted number) which are first delivered.

(7) In this rule—

the expression "elector for the electoral area" means a person who is registered as a local government elector for the electoral area in the register to be used at the election or who, pending the publication of that register, appears from the electors lists therefor as corrected by the registration officer to be entitled to be so registered (and accordingly includes a person shown in the register or electors lists as below voting age if it appears therefrom that he will be of voting age on the day fixed for the poll, but not otherwise) ;

the expression "electoral number" means the distinctive letter or letters of the parliamentary polling district in which a person is registered together with his number in the said register, or pending the publication of the register, the distinctive letter or letters of the parliamentary polling district in which he is entitled to be registered together with his number (if any) in the electors lists therefor.

Consent to nomination

7.—(1) A person shall not be validly nominated unless his consent to nomination, given in writing on or within one month before the last day for the delivery of nomination papers, and attested by one witness, is delivered at the place and within the time appointed for the delivery of nomination papers:

Provided that if the returning officer is satisfied that owing to the absence of a person from the United Kingdom it has not been reasonably practicable for his consent in writing to be given as aforesaid, a telegram consenting to his nomination and purporting to have been sent by him shall be deemed, for the purpose of this rule, to be consent in writing given by him on the day on which it purports to have been sent, and attestation of his consent shall not be required.

(2) A candidate's consent given under this rule shall contain a statement declaring, with reference to the date of his nomination, that to the best of his belief he will be or is qualified as required by law to be elected to and hold the office in question, and the statement shall give particulars of his qualification.

Place for delivery of nomination papers

8. Every nomination paper shall be delivered at the place fixed by the returning officer.

Decisions as to validity of nomination papers

9.—(1) Where a nomination paper and the candidate's consent thereto are delivered in accordance with these rules the candidate shall be deemed to stand nominated unless and until the returning officer decides that the nomination paper is invalid, or proof is given to the satisfaction of the returning officer of the candidate's death, or the candidate withdraws.

(2) The returning officer shall be entitled to hold a nomination paper invalid only on one of the following grounds, that is to say:—

(a) that the particulars of the candidate or the persons subscribing the paper are not as required by law ; or

(b) that the paper is not subscribed as so required.

(3) The returning officer shall examine the nomination papers, and decide whether the candidates have been validly nominated in accordance with these rules and shall do so as soon as practicable after each paper is delivered.

(4) Where he decides that a nomination paper is invalid, he shall endorse and sign on the paper the fact and the reasons for his decision.

(5) The returning officer shall send notice of his decision to each candidate at his place of residence as stated on his nomination paper.

(6) The decision of the returning officer that a nomination paper is valid shall be final and shall not be questioned in any proceeding whatsoever.

(7) Subject to the last foregoing paragraph, nothing in this rule shall prevent the validity of a nomination being questioned on an election petition.

Publication of nominations

10.—(1) The returning officer shall prepare and publish a statement in the form in the Appendix, or a form to the like effect, showing the persons who have been and stand nominated and any other persons who have been nominated, with the reason why they no longer stand nominated.

(2) The statement shall show the names, addresses and descriptions (if any) of the persons nominated as given in their nomination papers.

(3) The statement shall show the persons standing nominated arranged alphabetically in the order of their surnames, and, if there are two or more of them with the same surname, of their other names.

(4) In the case of a person nominated by more than one nomination paper, the returning officer shall take the particulars required by the foregoing provisions of this rule from such one of the papers as the candidate or the returning officer in default of the candidate may select.

(5) The statement as to persons nominated shall be published by causing it to be affixed to the place appointed for the delivery of nomination papers.

Withdrawal of candidates

11.—(1) A candidate may withdraw from his candidature by notice of withdrawal signed by him and attested by one witness and delivered at the place appointed for the delivery of nomination papers.

(2) In the case of a candidate who is outside the United Kingdom, a notice of withdrawal signed by his proposer and accompanied by a written declaration also so signed of the candidate's absence from the United Kingdom shall be of the same effect as a notice of withdrawal signed by the candidate:

Provided that where the candidate stands nominated by more than one nomination paper a notice of withdrawal under this paragraph shall be effective if, but only if—

(a) it and the accompanying declaration are signed by all the proposers, except any who is, and is stated in the said declaration to be, outside the United Kingdom ; or

(b) it is accompanied, in addition to the said declaration, by a written statement signed by the candidate that the proposer giving the notice is
authorised to do so on the candidate's behalf during his absence from the
United Kingdom.

Nomination in more than one ward

12. A candidate who is validly nominated for more than one ward of an urban
district divided into wards must duly withdraw from his candidature in all those
wards except one, and if he does not so withdraw he shall be deemed to have
withdrawn from his candidature in all those wards.

Method of election

13.—(1) If the number of persons remaining validly nominated for the electoral
area after any withdrawals under these rules exceeds the number of vacancies, the
councillors shall be elected from among them at a poll under Part III of these
rules.

(2) If the said number does not exceed the number of vacancies, the person or
persons (if any) deemed to be elected under the following provisions of this rule
shall be declared elected in accordance with Part IV of these rules.

(3) The person or persons (if any) remaining validly nominated for the electoral
area after any withdrawals under these rules shall be deemed to be elected.

(4) If, at an ordinary election of urban district councillors, no person remains
validly nominated as aforesaid, or the number of persons so remaining validly
nominated is less than the number of vacancies, the retiring councillors for the
electoral area who, if duly nominated, would have been qualified for election or,
if their number is more than that of the vacancies not filled under paragraph (3)
of this rule, such of those councillors as were highest on the poll at the last
ordinary election, or as filled the places of councillors who were highest on the
poll at that election, or if the poll was equal or there was no poll, as may be
determined by the drawing of lots conducted under the direction of the returning
officer, shall be deemed to be elected to fill up the vacancies not filled under
paragraph (3) of this rule.

PART III

CONTESTED ELECTIONS
GENERAL PROVISIONS
Poll to be taken by ballot

14. The votes at the poll shall be given by ballot, the result shall be ascertained by
counting the votes given to each candidate, and the candidate or candidates to whom
the majority of votes have been given shall be declared to have been elected.

The ballot papers

15.—(1) The ballot of every voter shall consist of a ballot paper and the persons
remaining validly nominated for the electoral area after any withdrawals under these
rules, and no others, shall be entitled to have their names inserted in the ballot paper.

(2) Every ballot paper shall be in the form in the Appendix, and shall be printed in
accordance with the directions therein, and—
  (a) shall contain the names and other particulars of the candidates as shown in
      the statement of persons nominated;
  (b) shall be capable of being folded up;
  (c) shall have a number printed on the back;
  (d) shall have attached a counterfoil with the same number printed on the face
      or the back.

(3) The order of the names in the ballot paper shall be the same as in the statement
of persons nominated.

The official mark

16.—(1) Every ballot paper shall be marked with an official mark, which shall be
either embossed or perforated.

(2) The official mark shall be kept secret.

Prohibition of disclosure of vote

17. No person who has voted at the election shall, in any legal proceeding to question the election, be required to state for whom he voted.

Use of schools and public rooms

18.—(1) The returning officer may use, free of charge, for the purpose of taking the poll or counting the votes—

(a) a room in a school maintained or assisted by a local education authority or a school in respect of which grants are made out of moneys provided by Parliament to the person or body of persons responsible for the management of the school;

(b) a room the expense of maintaining which is payable out of any rate.

(2) The returning officer shall make good any damage done to, and defray any expense incurred by the persons having control over, any such room as aforesaid by reason of its being used for the purpose of taking the poll or of counting the votes.

(3) The use of a room in an unoccupied house for the purpose of taking the poll or of counting the votes shall not render that person liable to be rated or to pay any rate for that house.

ACTION TO BE TAKEN BEFORE THE POLL
Notice of poll

19.—(1) Notice of the poll shall be published by the returning officer, and the manner of publication shall be the same as in the case of the notice of election.

(2) Notice of the poll shall specify—

(a) the day and hours fixed for the poll;

(b) the number of councillors to be elected;

(c) the particulars of each candidate remaining validly nominated (the names and other particulars of the candidates, and the order of the names of the candidates, being the same as in the statement of persons nominated);

(d) the names of all persons signing a candidate's nomination paper; and

(e) the situation of each polling station and the description of the persons entitled to vote thereat.

(3) In the case of a candidate nominated by more than one nomination paper, the nomination paper mentioned in sub-paragraph (d) of paragraph (2) of this rule shall be that from which the names and other particulars of the candidate shown in the statement of persons nominated are taken.

(4) The returning officer shall, as soon as practicable after publication of a notice of poll, give to each of the election agents a description in writing of the polling districts, if any.

Postal ballot papers

20. The returning officer shall as soon as practicable send to those entitled to vote by post, at the addresses furnished by them for the purpose, a ballot paper and a declaration of identity in the form set out in the Representation of the People Regulations 1950**(a)**, or a form substantially to the like effect, together with an envelope for their return.

Provision of polling stations

21.—(1) The returning officer shall provide a sufficient number of polling stations and, subject to the following provisions of this rule, shall allot the electors to the polling stations in such manner as he thinks most convenient.

(2) One or more polling stations may be provided in the same room.

(3) The polling station allotted to electors from any parliamentary polling district wholly or partly within the electoral area shall, in the absence of special circumstances, be in the parliamentary polling place for that district, unless the polling place is outside the electoral area.

(4) The returning officer shall provide each polling station with such number of compartments as may be necessary in which the voters can mark their votes screened from observation.

(a) S.I. 1950/1254 (Rev. XX, p. 7: 1950 II, p. 513).

Appointment of presiding officers and clerks

22.—(1) The returning officer shall appoint and pay a presiding officer to attend at each polling station and such clerks as may be necessary for the purposes of the election, but he shall not appoint any person who has been employed by or on behalf of a candidate in or about the election.

(2) The returning officer may, if he thinks fit, preside at a polling station and the provisions of these rules relating to a presiding officer shall apply to a returning officer so presiding with the necessary modifications as to things to be done by the returning officer to the presiding officer or by the presiding officer to the returning officer.

(3) A presiding officer may do, by the clerks appointed to assist him, any act (including the asking of questions) which he is required or authorised by these rules to do at a polling station except order the arrest, exclusion or removal of any person from the polling station.

Special lists

23. The registration officer shall as soon as practicable prepare the following special lists, namely:—

(*a*) a list (in these rules referred to as "the absent voters list") giving the name and number on the register of every person entitled to vote at the election as an absent voter;

(*b*) a list (in these rules referred to as "the list of proxies") giving—

  (i) the names and numbers on the register of the electors for whom proxies have been appointed,

  (ii) the names and addresses of the persons appointed;

(*c*) a list of any persons entitled to vote by post as proxy at the election.

Equipment of polling stations

24.—(1) The returning officer shall provide each presiding officer with such number of ballot boxes and ballot papers as in the opinion of the returning officer may be necessary.

(2) Every ballot box shall be so constructed that the ballot papers can be put therein, but cannot be withdrawn therefrom, without the box being unlocked.

(3) The returning officer shall provide each polling station with—

(*a*) materials to enable voters to mark the ballot papers;

(*b*) instruments for stamping thereon the official mark;

(*c*) copies of the register of electors for the electoral area or such part thereof as contains the names of the electors allotted to the station;

(*d*) the parts of any special lists prepared for the election corresponding to the register of electors for the electoral area or part thereof provided under the last foregoing paragraph.

(4) A notice in the form in the Appendix, giving directions for the guidance of the voters in voting, shall be printed in conspicuous characters and exhibited inside and outside every polling station.

(5) In every compartment of every polling station there shall be exhibited a notice as follows:— "The voter may vote for not more than......candidate(s)".

Appointment of polling and counting agents

25.—(1) Each candidate may, before the commencement of the poll, appoint polling agents to attend at polling stations for the purpose of detecting personation and counting agents to attend at the counting of the votes:
Provided that—

(*a*) the returning officer may limit the number of counting agents, so however that the number shall be the same in the case of each candidate and the number allowed to a candidate shall not (except in special circumstances) be less than the number obtained by dividing the number of clerks employed on the counting by the number of candidates;

(*b*) the appointment of an agent may be on behalf of more than one candidate;

(*c*) not more than three or, if the number of candidates exceeds twenty, four polling agents shall be appointed to attend at any polling station.

(2) If the number of polling agents appointed to attend at a polling station exceeds the permitted number, only those agents, up to the permitted number, whose appointments are signed by or on behalf of the greater number of candidates, or, in the event of an equality in the number of signatures, only such of those agents as may be determined by the returning officer, shall be deemed to have been duly appointed.

(3) Notice in writing of the appointment, stating the names and addresses of the persons appointed, shall be given by the candidate to the returning officer and shall be so given not later than the time appointed for that purpose in the Timetable.

(4) If an agent dies, or becomes incapable of acting, the candidate may appoint another agent in his place, and shall forthwith give to the returning officer notice in writing of the name and address of the agent appointed.

(5) The foregoing provisions of this rule shall be without prejudice to the requirements of section 60(1) of the Representation of the People Act 1949 as to the appointment of paid polling agents, and any appointment authorised by this rule may be made and the notice of appointment given to the returning officer by the candidate's election agent, instead of by the candidate.

(6) In the following provisions of these rules references to polling and counting agents shall be taken as references to agents whose appointments have been duly made and notified and who are within the permitted number.

(7) Any notice required to be given to a counting agent by the returning officer may be delivered at, or sent by post to, the address stated in the notice of appointment.

(8) A candidate may himself do any act or thing which any polling or counting agent of his, if appointed, would have been authorised to do, or may assist his agent in doing any such act or thing.

(9) A candidate's election agent may do or assist in doing anything which a polling or counting agent of his is authorised to do; and anything required or authorised by these rules to be done in the presence of the polling or counting agents may be done in the presence of a candidate's election agent instead of his polling agent or counting agents.

(10) Where by these rules any act or thing is required or authorised to be done in the presence of the polling or counting agents, the non-attendance of any agents or agent at the time and place appointed for the purpose, shall not, if the act or thing is otherwise duly done, invalidate the act or thing done.

Declaration of secrecy

26.—(1) Before the opening of the poll a declaration of secrecy in the form in paragraph (4) of this rule, or in a form as near thereto as circumstances admit, shall be made by—

(*a*) the returning officer and the presiding officers;

(*b*) every clerk authorised to attend at a polling station or the counting of the votes;

(*c*) every candidate attending at a polling station or at the counting of the votes and every election agent so attending;

(*d*) every candidate's wife or husband attending at the counting of the votes;

(*e*) every polling agent and counting agent;

(*f*) every person permitted by the returning officer to attend at the counting of the votes, though not entitled to do so.

(2) Notwithstanding anything in the foregoing paragraph, the following persons attending at the counting of the votes, that is to say:—

(*a*) any candidate;

(*b*) any election agent, or any candidate's wife or husband attending by virtue of the rule authorising election agents and candidates' wives or husbands to attend as such;

(c) any person permitted by the returning officer to attend, though not entitled to do so;

(d) any clerk making the declaration in order to attend at the counting of the votes;

need not make the declaration before the opening of the poll but shall make it before he or she is permitted to attend the counting, and a person becoming obliged to make a declaration by reason of his appointment after the opening of the poll shall make the declaration before acting under the appointment.

(3) The returning officer shall make the declaration in the presence of a Justice of the Peace, and any other person shall make the declaration in the presence either of a Justice of the Peace or of the returning officer, and subsections (1), (2), (3) and (6) of section 53 of the Representation of the People Act 1949 shall be read to the declarant by the person taking the declaration, or shall be read by the declarant in the presence of that person:

Provided that the declaration may be made by the returning officer or any other person before a person who is chairman of the Greater London Council, a county council or a district council or mayor of a borough or rural borough, and may be made by a person other than the returning officer before a person who is clerk of any such council or town clerk of a borough or rural borough.

(4) The declaration shall be as follows:—

"I solemnly promise and declare that I will not at this election for the [Ward of the] Urban District of   do anything forbidden by subsections (1), (2), (3) and (6) of section 53 of the Representation of the People Act 1949 which have been read to [by] me."

The Poll

Admission to polling station

27.—(1) The presiding officer shall regulate the number of voters to be admitted to the polling station at the same time, and shall exclude all other persons except—

(a) the candidates and their election agents;

(b) the polling agents appointed to attend at the polling station;

(c) the clerks appointed to attend at the polling station;

(d) the constables on duty; and

(e) the companions of blind voters.

(2) Not more than one polling agent shall be admitted at the same time to a polling station on behalf of the same candidate.

(3) A constable or person employed by a returning officer shall not be admitted to vote in person elsewhere than at his own polling station under the provisions of the Representation of the People Act 1949 in that behalf, except on production and sur-render of a certificate as to his employment which shall be in the form in the Appendix, or a form to the like effect, and signed by an officer of police of or above the rank of inspector or by the returning officer, as the case may be.

(4) Any certificate surrendered under this rule shall forthwith be cancelled.

Keeping of order in station

28.—(1) It shall be the duty of the presiding officer to keep order at his polling station.

(2) If a person misconducts himself in a polling station, or fails to obey the lawful orders of the presiding officer, he may immediately, by order of the presiding officer, be removed from the polling station by a constable in or near that station or by any other person authorised in writing by the returning officer to remove him, and the person so removed shall not, without the permission of the presiding officer, again enter the polling station during the day.

(3) Any person so removed may, if charged with the commission in the polling station of an offence, be dealt with as a person taken into custody by a constable for an offence without a warrant.

(4) The powers conferred by this rule shall not be exercised so as to prevent a voter who is otherwise entitled to vote at a polling station from having an opportunity of voting at that station.

Sealing of ballot boxes

29. Immediately before the commencement of the poll, the presiding officer shall show the ballot box empty to such persons, if any, as are present in the polling station, so that they may see that it is empty, and shall then lock it up and place his seal on it in such manner as to prevent it being opened without breaking the seal, and shall place it in his view for the receipt of ballot papers, and keep it so locked and sealed.

Questions to be put to voters

30.—(1) The presiding officer may, and if required by a candidate or his election or polling agent shall, put to any person applying for a ballot paper at the time of his application, but not afterwards, the following questions, or either of them, that is to say:—

(*a*) in the case of a person applying as an elector—

  (i) Are you the person registered in the register of local government electors now in force for this urban district [ward] as follows [*read the whole entry from the register*]?

  (ii) Have you already voted at the present election [*adding in the case of an election for several wards*, in this or any other ward] otherwise than as proxy for some other person?

(*b*) in the case of a person applying as proxy—

  (i) Are you the person whose name appears as A.B. in the list of proxies for this election as entitled to vote as proxy on behalf of C.D.?

  (ii) Have you already voted here or elsewhere at the present election as proxy on behalf of C.D.?

(2) A ballot paper shall not be delivered to any person required to answer the above questions or any of them unless he has answered the questions or question satisfactorily.

(3) Save as by this rule authorised, no inquiry shall be permitted as to the right of any person to vote.

Challenge of voter

31.—(1) If at the time a person applies for a ballot paper for the purpose of voting in person, or after he has applied for a ballot paper for that purpose and before he has left the polling station, a candidate or his election or polling agent declares to the presiding officer that he has reasonable cause to believe that the applicant has committed an offence of personation and undertakes to substantiate the charge in a court of law, the presiding officer may order a constable to arrest the applicant, and the order of the presiding officer shall be sufficient authority for the constable so to do.

(2) A person against whom a declaration is made under this rule shall not by reason thereof be prevented from voting.

(3) A person arrested under the provisions of this rule shall be dealt with as a person taken into custody by a constable for an offence without a warrant.

Voting procedure

32.—(1) A ballot paper shall be delivered to a voter who applies therefor, and immediately before delivery—

(*a*) the ballot paper shall be stamped with the official mark, either embossed or perforated;

(*b*) the number, name and description of the elector as stated in the copy of the register of electors shall be called out;

(*c*) the number of the elector shall be marked on the counterfoil;

(*d*) a mark shall be placed in the register of electors against the number of the elector to denote that a ballot paper has been received but without showing the particular ballot paper which has been received; and

(e) in the case of a person applying for a ballot paper as proxy, a mark shall also be placed against his name in the list of proxies.

(2) The voter, on receiving the ballot paper, shall forthwith proceed into one of the compartments in the polling station and there secretly mark his paper and fold it up so as to conceal his vote, and shall then show to the presiding officer the back of the paper, so as to disclose the official mark and put the ballot paper so folded up into the ballot box in the presence of the presiding officer.

(3) The voter shall vote without undue delay, and shall leave the polling station as soon as he has put his ballot paper into the ballot box.

Votes marked by presiding officer

33.—(1) The presiding officer, on the application of—

(a) a voter who is incapacitated by blindness or other physical cause from voting in manner directed by these rules; or

(b) if the poll is taken on a Saturday, a voter who declares that he is a Jew, and objects on religious grounds to vote in manner directed by these rules; or

(c) a voter who declares orally that he is unable to read;

shall, in the presence of the polling agents, cause the vote of the voter to be marked on a ballot paper in manner directed by the voter, and the ballot paper to be placed in the ballot box.

(2) The name and number in the register of electors of every voter whose vote is marked in pursuance of this rule, and the reason why it is so marked, shall be entered on a list (in these rules called "the list of votes marked by the presiding officer").

In the case of a person voting as proxy for an elector, the number to be entered together with the name of the voter shall be the number of the elector.

Voting by blind persons

34.—(1) If a voter makes an application to the presiding officer to be allowed on the ground of blindness to vote with the assistance of another person by whom he is accompanied (in these rules referred to as "the companion"), the presiding officer shall require the voter to declare orally whether he is so incapacitated by his blindness as to be unable to vote without assistance.

(2) If the presiding officer is satisfied that the voter is so incapacitated and is also satisfied by a written declaration made by the companion (in these rules referred to as "the declaration made by the companion of a blind voter") that the companion is a qualified person within the meaning of this rule and has not previously assisted more than one blind person to vote at the election, the presiding officer shall grant the application, and thereupon anything which is by these rules required to be done to or by the said voter in connection with the giving of his vote may be done to, or with the assistance of, the companion.

(3) For the purposes of this rule, a person shall be qualified to assist a blind voter to vote, if that person is either—

(a) a person who is entitled to vote as an elector at the election; or

(b) the father, mother, brother, sister, husband, wife, son or daughter of the blind voter and has attained the age of eighteen years.

(4) The name and number in the register of electors of every voter whose vote is given in accordance with this rule and the name and address of the companion shall be entered on a list (in these rules referred to as "the list of blind voters assisted by companions").

In the case of a person voting as proxy for an elector, the number to be entered together with the name of the voter shall be the number of the elector.

(5) The declaration made by the companion—

(a) shall be in the form in the Appendix;

(b) shall be made before the presiding officer at the time when the voter applies to vote with the assistance of a companion and shall forthwith be given to the presiding officer who shall attest and retain it.

(6) No fee or other payment shall be charged in respect of the declaration.

Tendered ballot papers

35.—(1) If a person, representing himself to be—

(a) a particular elector named in the register and not named in the absent voters list; or

(b) a particular person named in the list of proxies as proxy for an elector and not named in the list of persons entitled to vote by post as proxy,

applies for a ballot paper after another person has voted in person either as the elector or his proxy, the applicant shall, on satisfactorily answering the questions permitted by law to be asked at the poll, be entitled, subject to the following provisions of this rule, to mark a ballot paper (in these rules referred to as "a tendered ballot paper") in the same manner as any other voter.

(2) A tendered ballot paper shall—

(a) be of a colour differing from the other ballot papers;

(b) instead of being put into the ballot box, be given to the presiding officer and endorsed by him with the name of the voter and his number in the register of electors, and set aside in a separate packet.

(3) The name of the voter and his number in the register of electors shall be entered on a list (in these rules referred to as the "tendered votes list").

(4) In the case of a person voting as proxy for an elector, the number to be endorsed or entered together with the name of the voter shall be the number of that elector.

Spoilt ballot papers

36. A voter who has inadvertently dealt with his ballot paper in such manner that it cannot be conveniently used as a ballot paper may, on delivering it to the presiding officer and proving to his satisfaction the fact of the inadvertence, obtain another ballot paper in the place of the ballot paper so delivered (in these rules referred to as "a spoilt ballot paper"), and the spoilt ballot paper shall be immediately cancelled.

Adjournment of poll in case of riot

37. For the purpose of the adjournment of the poll in the event of riot or open violence, a presiding officer shall have the power by law belonging to a presiding officer at a parliamentary election.

Procedure on close of poll

38.—(1) As soon as practicable after the close of the poll, the presiding officer shall, in the presence of the polling agents, make up into separate packets, sealed with his own seal and the seals of such polling agents as desire to affix their seals—

(a) each ballot box in use at the station, sealed so as to prevent the introduction of additional ballot papers and unopened, but with the key attached;

(b) the unused and spoilt ballot papers placed together;

(c) the tendered ballot papers;

(d) the marked copies of the register of electors and of the list of proxies;

(e) the counterfoils of the used ballot papers and the certificates as to employment on duty on the day of the poll;

(f) the tendered votes list, the list of blind voters assisted by companions, the list of votes marked by the presiding officer, a statement of the number of voters whose votes are so marked by the presiding officer under the heads "physical incapacity", "Jews", and "unable to read" and the declarations made by the companions of blind voters;

and shall deliver the packets or cause them to be delivered to the returning officer to be taken charge of by him:

Provided that if the packets are not delivered by the presiding officer personally to the returning officer, the arrangements for their delivery shall require the approval of the returning officer.

(2) The marked copies of the register of electors and of the list of proxies shall be in one packet but shall not be in the same packet as the counterfoils of the used ballot papers and the certificates as to employment on duty on the day of the poll.

(3) The packets shall be accompanied by a statement (in these rules referred to as "the ballot paper account") made by the presiding officer showing the number of ballot papers entrusted to him, and accounting for them under the heads of ballot papers issued and not otherwise accounted for, unused, spoilt and tendered ballot papers.

COUNTING OF VOTES

Attendance at counting of votes

39.—(1) The returning officer shall make arrangements for counting the votes in the presence of the counting agents as soon as practicable after the close of the poll, and shall give to the counting agents notice in writing of the time and place at which he will begin to count the votes.

(2) No person other than—

    (a) the returning officer and his clerks;

    (b) the candidates and their wives or husbands;

    (c) the election agents;

    (d) the counting agents;

may be present at the counting of the votes, unless permitted by the returning officer to attend.

(3) A person not entitled to attend at the counting of the votes shall not be permitted to do so by the returning officer unless the returning officer is satisfied that the efficient counting of the votes will not be impeded, and the returning officer has either consulted the election agents or thought it impracticable to consult them.

(4) The returning officer shall give the counting agents all such reasonable facilities for overseeing the proceedings, and all such information with reference thereto, as he can give them consistently with the orderly conduct of the proceedings and the discharge of his duties in connection therewith.

(5) In particular, where the votes are counted by sorting the ballot papers according to the candidate for whom the vote is given and then counting the number of ballot papers for each candidate, the counting agents shall be entitled to satisfy themselves that the ballot papers are correctly sorted.

The count

40.—(1) Before the returning officer proceeds to count the votes, he shall—

    (a) in the presence of the counting agents open each ballot box and, taking out the ballot papers therein, count and record the number thereof and in the presence of the election agents who are present verify each ballot paper account;

    (b) count such of the postal ballot papers as have been duly returned and record the number counted; and

    (c) then mix together the whole of the ballot papers mentioned in the foregoing sub-paragraphs.

(2) A postal ballot paper shall not be deemed to be duly returned, unless it is returned in the proper envelope so as to reach the returning officer before the close of the poll and is accompanied by the declaration of identity duly signed and authenticated.

(3) The returning officer shall not count any tendered ballot paper.

(4) The returning officer, while counting and recording the number of ballot papers and counting the votes, shall keep the ballot papers with their faces upwards and take all proper precautions for preventing any person from seeing the numbers printed on the back of the papers.

(5) The returning officer shall verify each ballot paper account by comparing it with the number of ballot papers recorded by him, and the unused and spoilt ballot papers in his possession and the tendered votes list (opening and resealing the packets containing the unused and spoilt ballot papers and the tendered votes list) and shall draw up a statement as to the result of the verification which any election agent may copy.

(6) The returning officer shall, so far as practicable, proceed continuously with counting the votes, allowing only time for refreshment:

Provided that he may, in so far as he and the agents agree, exclude the hours between eight o'clock in the evening and nine o'clock on the following morning.

For the purposes of this proviso the agreement of a candidate or his election agent shall be as effective as the agreement of his counting agents, but where a counting agent has been appointed to attend on behalf of more than one candidate jointly, the agreement shall be that of the agent unless each of those candidates or his election agent agrees.

(7) During the excluded time the returning officer shall place the ballot papers and other documents relating to the election under his own seal and the seals of such of the counting agents as desire to affix their seals and shall otherwise take proper precautions for the security of the papers and documents.

Re-count

41.—(1) A candidate or his election agent may, if present when the counting or any re-count of the votes is completed, require the returning officer to have the votes recounted or again re-counted but the returning officer may refuse to do so if in his opinion the request is unreasonable.

(2) No step shall be taken on the completion of the counting or any re-count of votes until the candidates and election agents present at the completion thereof have been given a reasonable opportunity to exercise the right conferred by this rule.

Rejected ballot papers

42.—(1) Any ballot paper—

(*a*) which does not bear the official mark; or

(*b*) on which votes are given for more candidates than the voter is entitled to vote for; or

(*c*) on which anything is written or marked by which the voter can be identified except the printed number on the back; or

(*d*) which is unmarked or void for uncertainty;

shall, subject to the provisions of this rule, be void and not counted.

(2) Where the voter is entitled to vote for more than one candidate, a ballot paper shall not be deemed to be void for uncertainty as respects any vote as to which no uncertainty arises and that vote shall be counted.

(3) A ballot paper on which a vote is marked—

(*a*) elsewhere than in the proper place; or

(*b*) otherwise than by means of a cross; or

(*c*) by more than one mark;

shall not by reason thereof be deemed to be void (either wholly or as respects that vote), if an intention that the vote shall be for one or other of the candidates clearly appears and the way the paper is marked does not of itself identify the voter and it is not shown that he can be identified thereby.

(4) The returning officer shall endorse—

(*a*) the word "rejected" on any ballot paper which under this rule is not to be counted; and

(*b*) in the case of a ballot paper on which any vote is counted under paragraph (2) of this rule, the words "rejected in part" and a memorandum specifying the votes counted;

and shall add to the endorsement the words "rejection objected to" if an objection is made by a counting agent to his decision.

(5) The returning officer shall draw up a statement showing the number of ballot papers rejected, including those rejected in part, under the several heads of—

(*a*) want of official mark;

(*b*) voting for more candidates than voter is entitled to;

(*c*) writing or mark by which voter could be identified;

(*d*) unmarked or wholly void for uncertainty;

(*e*) rejected in part.

Decisions on ballot papers

43. The decision of the returning officer on any question arising in respect of a ballot paper shall be final, but shall be subject to review on an election petition.

Equality of votes

44. Where, after the counting of the votes (including any re-count) is completed, an equality of votes is found to exist between any candidates and the addition of a vote would entitle any of those candidates to be declared elected, the returning officer shall forthwith decide between those candidates by lot, and proceed as if the candidate on whom the lot falls had received an additional vote.

PART IV

FINAL PROCEEDINGS IN CONTESTED AND UNCONTESTED ELECTIONS

Declaration of result

45.—(1) In a contested election, when the result of the poll has been ascertained the returning officer shall forthwith declare to be elected the candidate or candidates for whom the majority of votes have been given, and shall as soon as possible publish the name or names of the candidate or candidates elected and the total number of votes given for each candidate, whether elected or not, together with the number of rejected ballot papers under each head shown in the statement of rejected ballot papers.

(2) In an uncontested election, the returning officer shall, not later than eleven o'clock in the morning on the day of election, publish the name or names of the person or persons elected.

The return

46. The returning officer shall forthwith upon declaration of the result of the election return the name of each person elected to the clerk of the urban district council.

PART V

DISPOSAL OF DOCUMENTS

Sealing of ballot papers

47.—(1) On the completion of the counting at a contested election the returning officer shall seal up in separate packets the counted and rejected ballot papers, including ballot papers rejected in part.

(2) The returning officer shall not open the sealed packets of tendered ballot papers or of counterfoils and certificates as to employment on the day of the poll, or of marked copies of the register of electors and lists of proxies.

Delivery of documents to clerk of the council

48. The returning officer shall then forward to the clerk of the urban district council the following documents, that is to say:—

(a) the packets of ballot papers in his possession;

(b) the ballot paper accounts and the statements of rejected ballot papers and of the result of the verification of the ballot paper accounts;

(c) the tendered votes lists, the lists of blind voters assisted by companions, the lists of votes marked by the presiding officer and the statements relating thereto, and the declarations made by the companions of blind voters;

(d) the packets of counterfoils and certificates as to employment on duty on the day of the poll;

(e) the packets containing marked copies of registers and of lists of proxies, endorsing on each packet a description of its contents, the date of the election to which they relate and the name of the electoral area for which the election was held.

Orders for production of documents

49.—(1) An order for—

(a) the inspection or production of any rejected ballot papers, including ballot papers rejected in part; or (*b*) for the opening of a sealed packet of counterfoils and certificates as to employment on duty on the day of the poll or for the inspection of counted ballot papers,

may be made by either a county court having jurisdiction in the urban district or an election court if the court is satisfied by evidence on oath that the order is required for the purpose of instituting or maintaining a prosecution for an offence in relation to ballot papers, or for the purpose of an election petition.

(2) The order may be made subject to such conditions as to persons, time, place and mode of inspection, production or opening as the court making the order may think expedient and may direct the clerk of the urban district council having custody of the ballot papers and the sealed packets of counterfoils and certificates to retain them intact for such period as may be specified in the order:

Provided that in making and carrying into effect the order, care shall be taken that the way in which the vote of any particular elector has been given shall not be disclosed until it has been proved that his vote was given and the vote has been declared by a competent court to be invalid.

(3) An appeal shall lie to the High Court from any order of a county court made under this rule.

(4) Any power given under this rule to a county court may be exercised by any judge of the court otherwise than in open court.

(5) Where an order is made for the production by the clerk of the urban district council of any document in his possession relating to any specified election, the production by him or his agent of the document ordered in such manner as may be directed by that order shall be conclusive evidence that the document relates to the specified election; and any endorsement on any packet of ballot papers so produced shall be prima facie evidence that the ballot papers are what they are stated to be by the endorsement.

(6) The production from proper custody of a ballot paper purporting to have been used at any election, and of a counterfoil marked with the same printed number and having a number marked thereon in writing, shall be prima facie evidence that the elector whose vote was given by that ballot paper was the person who at the time of the election had affixed to his name in the register of electors the same number as the number written on the counterfoil.

(7) Save as by this rule provided, no person shall be allowed to inspect any rejected or counted ballot papers in the possession of the clerk of the urban district council or to open any sealed packets of counterfoils and certificates.

Retention and public inspection of documents

50.—(1) The clerk of the urban district council shall retain for six months among the records of the urban district all documents relating to an election which are, in pursuance of these rules, forwarded to him by a returning officer or held by him and then, unless otherwise directed by an order under the last foregoing rule, shall cause them to be destroyed.

(2) The said documents, except ballot papers, counterfoils and certificates as to employment on duty on the day of the poll, shall during a period of six months from the day of election be open to public inspection at such time and in such manner as may be determined by the county council.

(3) The clerk of the urban district council shall, on request, supply copies of or extracts from the documents open to public inspection on payment of such fees, and subject to such conditions, as may be determined by the county council.

Supplemental provisions as to documents

51. Subject to the provisions of these rules, the clerk of the urban district council shall, in respect of the custody and destruction of ballot papers and other documents coming into his possession in pursuance of these rules, be subject to the directions of the urban district council.

Part VI

Supplemental

Countermand or abandonment of poll on death of candidate

52.—(1) If at a contested election proof is given to the satisfaction of the returning officer before the result of the election is declared that one of the persons named or to be named as candidate in the ballot papers has died, then the returning officer shall countermand the poll or, if polling has begun, direct that the poll be abandoned, and the provisions of section 36(2) of the Representation of the People Act 1949 shall apply to any further election ordered under the Local Government Act 1933.

(2) Where the poll is abandoned by reason of the death of a candidate, the proceedings at or consequent on that poll shall be interrupted, and the presiding officer at any polling station shall take the like steps (so far as not already taken) for the delivery to the returning officer of ballot boxes and of ballot papers and other documents as he is required to take on the close of the poll in due course, and the returning officer shall dispose of ballot papers and other documents in his possession as he is required to do on the completion in due course of the counting of the votes; but—

(a) it shall not be necessary for any ballot paper account to be prepared or verified; and

(b) the returning officer, without taking any step or further step for the counting of the ballot papers or of the votes, shall seal up all the ballot papers, whether the votes on them have been counted or not, and it shall not be necessary to seal up counted and rejected ballot papers in separate packets.

(3) The foregoing provisions of these rules as to the inspection, production, retention and destruction of ballot papers and other documents relating to a poll at an election shall apply to any such documents relating to a poll abandoned by reason of the death of a candidate, with the following modifications:—

(a) ballot papers on which the votes were neither counted nor rejected shall be treated as counted ballot papers; and

(b) no order shall be made for the production or inspection of any ballot papers or for the opening of a sealed packet of counterfoils or certificates as to employment on duty on the day of the poll unless the order is made by a court with reference to a prosecution.

General duty of returning officer

53. It shall be the general duty of the returning officer to do any act or thing that may be necessary for effectually conducting the election under these rules.

Notices

54. Any notice or other document required under these rules to be affixed to the offices of the urban district council shall be exhibited—

(a) in some conspicuous place on or near the outer door of the offices of the council; or

(b) if the council have no offices, in some conspicuous place in the urban district or in the area to which the document or notice relates.

Interpretation

55.—(1) The expression "electoral area" means the urban district or, if the urban district is divided into wards, a ward.

(2) A reference in this Schedule to a rule shall be construed as a reference to a rule contained in this Schedule.

(3) Any reference in this Schedule to any enactment or statutory instrument shall be taken as a reference to that enactment or statutory instrument as amended or replaced by any other enactment or statutory instrument.

APPENDIX

Note:—The forms contained in this Appendix may be adapted so far as circumstances require.

Rule 4.

NOTICE OF ELECTION

URBAN DISTRICT OF

ELECTION OF URBAN DISTRICT COUNCILLORS for the [Ward of the]
[Wards of the] Urban District.

If the notice relates to more than one election, adapt form accordingly.

1. An election is to be held of Urban District Councillors for the said [ward] [wards] [district].

2. Nomination papers must be delivered at on any day after the date of this notice, but not later than noon on the day of .

3. Forms of nomination paper may be obtained from the returning officer at . The returning officer will at the request of any local government elector for the electoral area prepare for signature a nomination paper.

4. If the election is contested, the poll will take place on the day of .

(Signed).............................
Returning Officer.

day of , 19 .

NOTE 1.—The attention of candidates and electors is drawn to the rules for filling up nomination papers and other provisions relating to nomination contained in the election rules in Schedule 1 to the Urban District Council Election Rules 1969.

NOTE 2.—Every person guilty of a corrupt or illegal practice will, on conviction, be liable to the penalties imposed by the Representation of the People Act 1949.

NOTE 3.—Electors and their proxies should take note that applications to be treated as an absent voter and other applications and notices about postal or proxy voting must reach the electoral registration officer at (*insert address*) by the day of next if they are to be effective for this election.

Rule 5.

NOMINATION PAPER

ELECTION OF URBAN DISTRICT COUNCILLORS for the [Ward of the]
Urban District of .

Date of publication of notice of election...

We, the undersigned, being local government electors for the said [ward] [district], do hereby nominate the undermentioned person as a candidate at the said election.

Candidate's surname	Other names in full	Description (if any)	Home address in full

Signatures	Electoral Number (*see* note 2)	
	Distinctive letter(s)	Number
Proposer..	....	....
Seconder..	....	....
We, the undersigned, being local government electors for the said [ward] [district], do hereby assent to the foregoing nomination.		
1.	....	....
2.	....	....
3.	....	....
4.	....	....
5.	....	....
6.	....	....
7.	....	....
8.	....	....

NOTE 1.—The attention of candidates and local government electors is drawn to the rules for filling up nomination papers and other provisions relating to nomination contained in the election rules in Schedule 1 to the Urban District Council Election Rules 1969.

NOTE 2.—A person's electoral number consists of the distinctive letter or letters of the parliamentary polling district in which he is registered together with his number in the register to be used at the election except that before publication of the register the distinctive letter or letters of the parliamentary polling district in which he is entitled to be registered together with his number (if any) in the electors lists for that register shall be used instead.

NOTE 3.—A local government elector may not—

(*a*) subscribe more nomination papers than there are vacancies to be filled in the electoral area; or

(*b*) subscribe a nomination paper for more than one ward of an urban district divided into wards; or

(*c*) subscribe more than one nomination paper in respect of the same candidate.

NOTE 4.—A person whose name is entered in the register or electors lists may not subscribe a nomination paper if the entry gives as the date on which he will become of voting age a date later than the day fixed for the poll.

Rule 10.   STATEMENT AS TO PERSONS NOMINATED

URBAN DISTRICT OF

The following is a statement as to the persons nominated for election as Urban District Councillors for the [Ward of the] [Wards of the] Urban District.

[Ward] [Wards] [District]	Persons nominated				Pro-poser's name	Decision of returning officer that nomination paper is invalid, or other reason why a person nominated no longer stands nominated
	Sur-name	Other names in full	Home Address in full	Descrip-tion (if any)		
1.	2.	3.	4.	5.	6.	7.

The persons opposite whose names no entry is made in column 7 have been and stand validly nominated.

Dated this   day of   , 19 .

....
Returning Officer.

BALLOT PAPER

Rule 15.

Form of Front of Ballot Paper

Counterfoil
No.

The counterfoil is to have a number to correspond with that on the back of the Ballot Paper.

1 — **BROWN**
(JOHN EDWARD Brown, of 2 The Cottages, Barlington, Grayshire, Labour.)

2 — **BROWN**
(THOMAS WILLIAM Brown, of 15 Barchester Road, Barlington, Grayshire, Liberal.)

3 — **JONES**
(William David Jones, of The Grange, Barlington, Grayshire, Conservative.)

4 — **MERTON**
(Hon. George Travis, commonly called Viscount Merton, of Barlington, Grayshire.

5 — **SMITH**
(Mary Smith, of School House, Barlington, Grayshire, schoolteacher, Progressive.)

6 — **WILLIAMS**
(Elizabeth Williams, of 3 Ivy Lane, Barlington, Grayshire, housewife.)

Form of Back of Ballot Paper

No.

Election for the [Ward of the] Urban District of

day of   , 19   .

Note—The number on the ballot paper is to correspond with that on the counterfoil.

Directions as to printing the ballot paper

1. Nothing is to be printed on the ballot paper except in accordance with these directions.

2. So far as practicable, the following arrangements shall be observed in the printing of the ballot paper:—

   (*a*) no word shall be printed on the face except the particulars of the candidates;

   (*b*) no rule shall be printed on the face except the horizontal rules separating the particulars of the candidates from one another and the vertical rules separating those particulars from the numbers on the left-hand side and the spaces on the right where the vote is to be marked;

   (*c*) the whole space between the top and bottom of the paper shall be equally divided between the candidates by the rules separating their particulars.

3. The surname of each candidate shall in all cases be printed by itself in large capitals, and his full particulars shall be set out below it and shall be printed in ordinary type except that small capitals shall be used—

   (*a*) if his surname is the same as another candidate's, for his other names; and

   (*b*) if his other names are also the same as the other candidate's, either for his residence or for his description unless each of them is the same as that of another candidate with the same surname and other names.

4. The number on the back of the ballot paper shall be printed in ordinary type.

Rule 24.   DIRECTIONS FOR THE GUIDANCE OF THE VOTERS IN VOTING

1. The voter should see that the ballot paper, before it is handed to him, is stamped with the official mark.

2. The voter will go into one of the compartments and, with the pencil provided in the compartment, place a cross on the right-hand side of the ballot paper, opposite the name of each candidate for whom he votes, thus X.

3. The voter will then fold up the ballot paper so as to show the official mark on the back, and leaving the compartment will, without showing the front of the paper to any person, show the official mark on the back to the presiding officer, and then, in the presence of the presiding officer, put the paper into the ballot box, and forthwith leave the polling station.

4. If the voter inadvertently spoils a ballot paper he can return it to the officer, who will, if satisfied of such inadvertence, give him another paper.

5. If the voter votes for more than   candidate(s) or places any mark on the paper by which he may afterwards be identified, his ballot paper will be void, and will not be counted.

6. If the voter fraudulently takes a ballot paper out of a polling station or fraudlently puts into the ballot box any paper other than the one given to him by the officer, he will be liable on conviction to imprisonment for a term not exceeding six months, or to a fine not exceeding twenty pounds or to both such imprisonment and such fine.

CERTIFICATE OF EMPLOYMENT

Rule 27.

Election in the [Ward of the] Urban District of   .

I certify that (name).................................who is numbered...........................
in the register of electors for the electoral area named above, is likely to be unable
to go in person to the polling station allotted to him at the election on (date of
poll)...by reason of the particular circumstances of
his employment on that date—

*(a) as a constable,

*(b) by me for a purpose connected with the election.

Signature ....

*Police rank ....

(Inspector or above)

*Returning Officer.

Date....................................

*Delete whichever is inapplicable.

NOTE.—The person named above is entitled to vote at any polling station of the
above electoral area on production and surrender of this certificate to the presiding
officer.

DECLARATION TO BE MADE BY THE COMPANION OF A BLIND VOTER

Rule 34.

I, A.B., of..., having been requested to assist
C.D., [*in the case of a blind person voting as proxy add* voting as proxy for G.H.]
who is numbered   on the register of local government electors for the
[Ward of the] Urban District of   to record his
vote at the election now being held for the said [ward] [urban district], do hereby
declare that [I am entitled to vote as an elector at the said election] [I am the*   *State the
of the said voter and have attained the age of eighteen   relationship of the
years], and that I have not previously assisted any blind person [except E.F., of   companion to the voter.
], to vote at the said election.

(Signed) A.B.

day of   , 19   .

I, the undersigned, being the presiding officer for the   polling
station for the [Ward of the] Urban District of   ,
do hereby certify that the above declaration, having been first read to the above-
named declarant, was signed by the declarant in my presence.

(Signed) X.Y.

day of   , 19   , at   minutes past   o'clock

[a.m.] [p.m.].

NOTE.—If the person making the above declaration knowingly and wilfully makes
therein a statement false in a material particular, he will be guilty of an offence.

SCHEDULE 2

DECLARATION OF ACCEPTANCE OF OFFICE BY THE CHAIRMAN OF AN URBAN DISTRICT COUNCIL OR BY AN URBAN DISTRICT COUNCILLOR

*Insert description of office.

I, A.B., having been elected to the office of*   , hereby declare that I take the said office upon myself, and will duly and faithfully fulfil the duties thereof according to the best of my judgment and ability.

Dated this   day of   , 19   .

Signature.................................

†If the declaration is made and subscribed before the clerk of the urban district council, or a justice of the peace or magistrate, or a commissioner for oaths, or a British consul, adapt form accordingly.

This declaration was made and subscribed before us

Members of the Urban District Council.†

....
....

EXPLANATORY NOTE

(This Note is not part of the Rules.)

These Rules revoke and replace the Urban District Council Election Rules 1951, as amended, with amendments consequential on the provisions of the Representation of the People Act 1969 (c. 15).

STATUTORY INSTRUMENTS

1969 No. 757

REPRESENTATION OF THE PEOPLE

The Rural District Council Election Rules 1969

Made - - -	23rd May 1969
Laid before Parliament	5th June 1969
Coming into Operation	16th February 1970

In pursuance of the powers conferred upon me by section 29 and section 165(1) of the Representation of the People Act 1949(**a**) and paragraph 31(1) of Schedule 8 to the Local Government Act 1958(**b**), and by section 61 of the Local Government Act 1933(**c**), I hereby make the following Rules for the conduct of an election of rural district councillors and of the chairman of a rural district council, and the following Regulations prescribing the form of declaration of acceptance of office by the chairman of a rural district council and by a rural district councillor :—

1.—(1) These Rules and Regulations may be cited as the Rural District Council Election Rules 1969 and shall come into operation on 16th February 1970 :

Provided that they shall not have effect in relation to an election notice of which has been published before that date.

(2) The Interpretation Act 1889(**d**) shall apply to the interpretation of these Rules and Regulations as it applies to the interpretation of an Act of Parliament.

2.—(1) The Rural District Council Election Rules 1951(**e**), the Rural District Council Election Rules 1954(**f**), the Rural District Council Election Rules 1959(**g**) and the Rural District Council Election Rules 1962(**h**) are hereby revoked.

(2) Notwithstanding paragraph (1) of this Rule, the Rules therein mentioned shall apply to any election notice of which has been published before these Rules and Regulations come into operation.

3.—(1) For an election of rural district councillors the clerk of the rural district council shall be the returning officer, and if at such election the office of clerk of the rural district council is vacant or the clerk is for any reason unable to act, the chairman of the rural district council shall forthwith appoint another person to be the returning officer for that election :

(**a**) 1949 c. 68. (**b**) 1958 c. 55.
(**c**) 1933 c. 51. (**d**) 1889 c. 63.
(**e**) S.I. 1951/266 (1951 II, p. 361). (**f**) S.I. 1954/1484 (1954 II, p. 1919).
(**g**) S.I. 1959/430 (1959 II, p. 2310). (**h**) S.I. 1962/1268 (1962 II, p. 1370).

Provided that, in the case of a first election of rural district councillors for a newly constituted rural district, a person appointed in accordance with the order constituting the new rural district, or, if the order contains no provision relating to the appointment of a returning officer, a person appointed by the county council, shall be the returning officer.

(2) The returning officer may by writing under his hand appoint a fit person to be his deputy for all or any of the purposes of an election, and any functions which a returning officer is authorised or required to discharge in relation to the election may be discharged by a deputy so appointed.

(3) A deputy acting as returning officer under the provisions of this Rule shall, as respects the election for which he is so acting, follow the instructions of the returning officer.

4. Where the poll at an election of rural district councillors is taken together with the poll at an election of rural borough or parish councillors, one ballot box may, if the returning officer thinks fit, be used for the two elections ; but, if separate ballot boxes are used, no vote for any rural district councillor shall be rendered invalid by the ballot paper being placed in the box intended for the reception of ballot papers for rural borough or parish councillors.

5. In the application of those provisions of the Representation of the People Act 1949 referred to in section 165(1) of that Act to an election of the chairman of a rural district council and of rural district councillors the following modification shall have effect :—

In section 119(2)(*b*) of the said Act for the words "such amount not exceeding five hundred pounds" there shall be substituted the words "an amount of fifty pounds or such smaller amount or such larger amount not exceeding three hundred pounds".

6. In the application of the local elections rules contained in Schedule 2 to the Representation of the People Act 1949 to an election of rural district councillors, adaptations, alterations and exceptions shall be made therein so that the said local elections rules shall read as set out in Schedule 1 hereto.

7. The declaration of acceptance of office by the chairman of a rural district council or by a rural district councillor shall be in the form in Schedule 2 hereto, or a form to the like effect.

James Callaghan,
One of Her Majesty's Principal
Secretaries of State.

Home Office,
Whitehall.
23rd May 1969.

SCHEDULE 1

Election Rules

Arrangement of rules

Part I

Provisions as to Time

Rule
1. Timetable.
2. Computation of time.
3. Hours of poll.

Part II

Stages Common to Contested and Uncontested Elections

4. Notice of election.
5. Nomination of candidates.
6. Subscription of nomination paper.
7. Consent to nomination.
8. Place for delivery of nomination papers.
9. Decisions as to validity of nomination papers.
10. Publication of nominations.
11. Withdrawal of candidates.
12. Nomination in more than one electoral area.
13. Method of election.

Part III

Contested Elections

General provisions

14. Poll to be taken by ballot.
15. The ballot papers.
16. The official mark.
17. Prohibition of disclosure of vote.
18. Use of schools and public rooms.

Action to be taken before the poll

19. Notice of poll.
20. Postal ballot papers.
21. Provision of polling stations.
22. Appointment of presiding officers and clerks.
23. Special lists.
24. Equipment of polling stations.
25. Appointment of polling and counting agents.
26. Declaration of secrecy.

The poll

Rule

27. Admission to polling station.
28. Keeping of order in station.
29. Sealing of ballot boxes.
30. Questions to be put to voters.
31. Challenge of voter.
32. Voting procedure.
33. Votes marked by presiding officer.
34. Voting by blind persons.
35. Tendered ballot papers.
36. Spoilt ballot papers.
37. Adjournment of poll in case of riot.
38. Procedure on close of poll.

Counting of votes

39. Attendance at counting of votes.
40. The count.
41. Re-count.
42. Rejected ballot papers.
43. Decisions on ballot papers.
44. Equality of votes.

PART IV

FINAL PROCEEDINGS IN CONTESTED AND UNCONTESTED ELECTIONS

45. Declaration of result.
46. The return.

PART V

DISPOSAL OF DOCUMENTS

47. Sealing of ballot papers.
48. Delivery of documents to clerk of the council.
49. Orders for production of documents.
50. Retention and public inspection of documents.
51. Supplemental provisions as to documents.

PART VI

SUPPLEMENTAL

52. Countermand or abandonment of poll on death of candidate.
53. General duty of returning officer.
54. Notices.
55. Interpretation.

APPENDIX

FORMS

Notice of election.

Nomination paper.

Statement as to persons nominated.

Ballot paper.

Directions for the guidance of the voters in voting.

Certificate of employment.

Declaration to be made by the companion of a blind voter.

PART I

PROVISIONS AS TO TIME

Timetable

1. The proceedings at the election shall be conducted in accordance with the following Table.

TIMETABLE

Proceeding	Time
Publication of notice of election ..	Not later than the twenty-fifth day before the day of election.
Delivery of nomination papers ..	Not later than noon on the nineteenth day before the day of election.
Despatch of notices of decisions on nominations and publication of statement as to persons nominated	Not later than noon on the seventeenth day before the day of election.
Delivery of notices of withdrawals of candidature	Not later than noon on the sixteenth day before the day of election.
Notice of poll	Not later than the fifth day before the day of election.
Notice of appointment of polling or counting agents	Not later than the third day before the day of election.
Polling	On the day of election.

Computation of time

2.—(1) In computing any period of time for the purposes of the Timetable, a Sunday, day of the Christmas break, of the Easter break or of a bank holiday break, or day appointed for public thanksgiving or mourning shall be disregarded and any such day shall not be treated as a day for the purpose of any proceedings up to the completion of the poll nor shall the returning officer be obliged to proceed with the counting of the votes thereon:

Provided that where under Part III of these rules a person ought to proceed with the preparation of special lists or the issue of postal ballot papers on the first or last days of the Christmas break, the Easter break or a bank holiday break, or on the Saturday in the Easter break, nothing in this rule shall absolve him from that duty.

(2) In this rule "the Christmas break" means the period beginning with the last week day before Christmas Day and ending with the first week day after Christmas Day which is not a bank holiday, "the Easter break" means the period beginning

with the Thursday before and ending with the Tuesday after Easter Day, and "a bank holiday break" means any bank holiday not included in the Christmas break or the Easter break and the period beginning with the last week day before that bank holiday and ending with the next week day which is not a bank holiday.

Hours of poll

3.—(1) The poll shall commence at the hour fixed for the electoral area by the county council by any general or special order or, if no such order has been made, at noon and be kept open till eight o'clock in the evening of the same day and no longer :

Provided that the poll shall be kept open till nine o'clock in the evening—

    (i) where the poll is taken together with the poll at an election of rural borough or parish councillors, if the poll at the rural borough or parish election is kept open till nine o'clock in the evening ; or

    (ii) whether or not the poll is so taken, if candidates remaining validly nominated at the election of rural district councillors to a number not less than the number of vacancies at that election have, by written notices signed by them and delivered at the place and within the time for delivery of notices of withdrawals of candidature at that election, so requested.

(2) A notice under this rule shall not have effect as respects any candidate if revoked by a further written notice signed by him and delivered as aforesaid.

PART II

STAGES COMMON TO CONTESTED AND UNCONTESTED ELECTIONS

Notice of election

4.—(1) Notice of the election in the form in the Appendix, or a form to the like effect, shall be prepared, signed and published by the returning officer.

(2) The notice shall be published by causing it to be affixed to the offices of the rural district council and to be exhibited at such conspicuous places in the electoral area as the returning officer may determine.

(3) The notice of election shall state the date by which application to be treated as an absent voter and other applications and notices about postal or proxy voting must reach the registration officer in order that they may be effective for the election ; and in addition the registration officer shall give notice of the date in the electoral area by such means as he thinks best calculated to bring the information to the notice of those concerned.

Nomination of candidates

5.—(1) Each candidate shall be nominated by a separate nomination paper in the form in the Appendix, or a form to the like effect, delivered at the place fixed for the purpose.

(2) The nomination paper shall state the full names, place of residence and (if desired) description of the candidate and the surname shall be placed first in the list of his names.

(3) The description (if any) shall not exceed six words in length, and need not refer to his rank, profession or calling so long as, with the other particulars of the candidate, it is sufficient to identify him.

Subscription of nomination paper

6.—(1) The nomination paper shall be subscribed by two electors for the electoral area as proposer and seconder.

(2) Where a nomination paper bears the signatures of more than the required number of persons as proposing or seconding the nomination of a candidate, the signature appearing first on the paper in each category shall be taken into account to the exclusion of any others in that category.

(3) The nomination paper shall give the electoral number of each person subscribing it.

(4) The returning officer shall provide nomination papers and shall supply any elector for the electoral area with as many nomination papers as may be required and shall, at the request of any such elector, prepare for signature a nomination paper.

(5) No person shall—

(a) subscribe more nomination papers than there are vacancies to be filled in the electoral area ; or

(b) subscribe a nomination paper for more than one electoral area ; or

(c) subscribe more than one nomination paper in respect of the same candidate :

Provided that a person shall not be prevented from subscribing a nomination paper by reason only of his having subscribed that of a candidate who has died or withdrawn before delivery of the first-mentioned paper.

(6) If any person subscribes nomination papers in contravention of the last foregoing paragraph, his signature shall be inoperative in all but those papers (up to the permitted number) which are first delivered.

(7) In this rule—

the expression "elector for the electoral area" means a person who is registered as a local government elector for the electoral area in the register to be used at the election or who, pending the publication of that register, appears from the electors lists therefor as corrected by the registration officer to be entitled to be so registered (and accordingly includes a person shown in the register or electors lists as below voting age if it appears therefrom that he will be of voting age on the day fixed for the poll, but not otherwise) ;

the expression "electoral number" means the distinctive letter or letters of the parliamentary polling district in which a person is registered together with his number in the said register, or pending the publication of the register, the distinctive letter or letters of the parliamentary polling district in which he is entitled to be registered together with his number (if any) in the electors lists therefor.

Consent to nomination

7.—(1) A person shall not be validly nominated unless his consent to nomination, given in writing on or within one month before the last day for the delivery of nomination papers, and attested by one witness, is delivered at the place and within the time appointed for the delivery of nomination papers :

Provided that if the returning officer is satisfied that owing to the absence of a person from the United Kingdom it has not been reasonably practicable for his consent in writing to be given as aforesaid, a telegram consenting to his nomination and purporting to have been sent by him shall be deemed, for the purpose of this rule, to be consent in writing given by him on the day on which it purports to have been sent, and attestation of his consent shall not be required.

(2) A candidate's consent given under this rule shall contain a statement declaring, with reference to the date of his nomination, that to the best of his belief he will be or is qualified as required by law to be elected to and hold the office in question, and the statement shall give particulars of his qualification.

Place for delivery of nomination papers

8. Every nomination paper shall be delivered at the place fixed by the returning officer.

Decisions as to validity of nomination papers

9.—(1) Where a nomination paper and the candidate's consent thereto are delivered in accordance with these rules the candidate shall be deemed to stand nominated unless and until the returning officer decides that the nomination paper is invalid, or proof is given to the satisfaction of the returning officer of the candidate's death, or the candidate withdraws.

(2) The returning officer shall be entitled to hold a nomination paper invalid only on one of the following grounds, that is to say:—

> (a) that the particulars of the candidate or the persons subscribing the paper are not as required by law ; or

> (b) that the paper is not subscribed as so required.

(3) The returning officer shall examine the nomination papers, and decide whether the candidates have been validly nominated in accordance with these rules and shall do so as soon as practicable after each paper is delivered.

(4) Where he decides that a nomination paper is invalid, he shall endorse and sign on the paper the fact and the reasons for his decision.

(5) The returning officer shall send notice of his decision to each candidate at his place of residence as stated on his nomination paper.

(6) The decision of the returning officer that a nomination paper is valid shall be final and shall not be questioned in any proceeding whatsoever.

(7) Subject to the last foregoing paragraph, nothing in this rule shall prevent the validity of a nomination being questioned on an election petition.

Publication of nominations

10.—(1) The returning officer shall prepare and publish a statement in the form in the Appendix, or a form to the like effect, showing the persons who have been and stand nominated and any other persons who have been nominated, with the reason why they no longer stand nominated.

(2) The statement shall show the names, addresses and descriptions (if any) of the persons nominated as given in their nomination papers.

(3) The statement shall show the persons standing nominated arranged alphabetically in the order of their surnames, and, if there are two or more of them with the same surname, of their other names.

(4) In the case of a person nominated by more than one nomination paper, the returning officer shall take the particulars required by the foregoing provisions of this rule from such one of the papers as the candidate or the returning officer in default of the candidate may select.

(5) The statement as to persons nominated shall be published by causing it to be affixed to the place appointed for the delivery of nomination papers.

Withdrawal of candidates

11.—(1) A candidate may withdraw from his candidature by notice of withdrawal signed by him and attested by one witness and delivered at the place appointed for the delivery of nomination papers.

(2) In the case of a candidate who is outside the United Kingdom, a notice of withdrawal signed by his proposer and accompanied by a written declaration also so signed of the candidate's absence from the United Kingdom shall be of the same effect as a notice of withdrawal signed by the candidate:

Provided that where the candidate stands nominated by more than one nomination paper a notice of withdrawal under this paragraph shall be effective if, but only if—

> (a) it and the accompanying declaration are signed by all the proposers, except any who is, and is stated in the said declaration to be, outside the United Kingdom ; or

> (b) it is accompanied, in addition to the said declaration, by a written statement signed by the candidate that the proposer giving the notice is authorised to do so on the candidate's behalf during his absence from the United Kingdom.

Nomination in more than one electoral area

12. A candidate who is validly nominated for more than one electoral area must duly withdraw from his candidature in all those electoral areas except one, and if he does not so withdraw he shall be deemed to have withdrawn from his candidature in all those electoral areas.

Method of election

13.—(1) If the number of persons remaining validly nominated for the electoral area after any withdrawals under these rules exceeds the number of vacancies, the councillors shall be elected from among them at a poll under Part III of these rules.

(2) If the said number does not exceed the number of vacancies, the person or persons (if any) deemed to be elected under the following provisions of this rule shall be declared elected in accordance with Part IV of these rules.

(3) The person or persons (if any) remaining validly nominated for the electoral area after any withdrawals under these rules shall be deemed to be elected.

(4) If, at an ordinary election of rural district councillors, no person remains validly nominated as aforesaid, or the number of persons so remaining validly nominated is less than the number of vacancies, the retiring councillors for the electoral area who, if duly nominated, would have been qualified for election or, if their number is more than that of the vacancies not filled under paragraph (3) of this rule, such of those councillors as were highest on the poll at the last ordinary election, or as filled the places of councillors who were highest on the poll at that election, or if the poll was equal or there was no poll, as may be determined by the drawing of lots conducted under the direction of the returning officer, shall be deemed to be elected to fill up the vacancies not filled under paragraph (3) of this rule.

PART III

CONTESTED ELECTIONS

GENERAL PROVISIONS

Poll to be taken by ballot

14. The votes at the poll shall be given by ballot, the result shall be ascertained by counting the votes given to each candidate, and the candidate or candidates to whom the majority of votes have been given shall be declared to have been elected.

The ballot papers

15.—(1) The ballot of every voter shall consist of a ballot paper and the persons remaining validly nominated for the electoral area after any withdrawals under these rules, and no others, shall be entitled to have their names inserted in the ballot paper.

(2) Every ballot paper shall be in the form in the Appendix, and shall be printed in accordance with the directions therein, and—

   (*a*) shall contain the names and other particulars of the candidates as shown in the statement of persons nominated;

   (*b*) shall be capable of being folded up;

   (*c*) shall have a number printed on the back;

   (*d*) shall have attached a counterfoil with the same number printed on the face or the back;

(*e*) shall be of a different colour from that of any ballot papers used in an election of rural borough or parish councillors held on the same date and for the same area.

(3) The order of the names in the ballot paper shall be the same as in the statement of persons nominated.

The official mark

16.—(1) Every ballot paper shall be marked with an official mark, which shall be either embossed or perforated.

(2) The official mark shall be kept secret.

Prohibition of disclosure of vote

17. No person who has voted at the election shall, in any legal proceeding to question the election, be required to state for whom he voted.

Use of schools and public rooms

18.—(1) The returning officer may use, free of charge, for the purpose of taking the poll or counting the votes—

(*a*) a room in a school maintained or assisted by a local education authority or a school in respect of which grants are made out of moneys provided by Parliament to the person or body of persons responsible for the management of the school;

(*b*) a room the expense of maintaining which is payable out of any rate.

(2) The returning officer shall make good any damage done to, and defray any expense incurred by the persons having control over, any such room as aforesaid by reason of its being used for the purpose of taking the poll or of counting the votes.

(3) The use of a room in an unoccupied house for the purpose of taking the poll or of counting the votes shall not render that person liable to be rated or to pay any rate for that house.

ACTION TO BE TAKEN BEFORE THE POLL

Notice of poll

19.—(1) Notice of the poll shall be published by the returning officer, and the manner of publication shall be the same as in the case of the notice of election.

(2) Notice of the poll shall specify—

(*a*) the day and hours fixed for the poll;

(*b*) the number of councillors to be elected;

(*c*) the particulars of each candidate remaining validly nominated (the names and other particulars of the candidates, and the order of the names of the candidates, being the same as in the statement of persons nominated);

(*d*) the names of the proposer and seconder signing a candidate's nomination paper; and

(*e*) the situation of each polling station and the description of the persons entitled to vote thereat.

(3) In the case of a candidate nominated by more than one nomination paper, the nomination paper mentioned in sub-paragraph (*d*) of paragraph (2) of this rule shall be that from which the names and other particulars of the candidate shown in the statement of persons nominated are taken.

(4) The returning officer shall, as soon as practicable after publication of a notice of poll, give to each of the election agents a description in writing of the polling districts, if any.

Postal ballot papers

20. The returning officer shall as soon as practicable send to those entitled to vote by post, at the addresses furnished by them for the purpose, a ballot paper and a declaration of identity in the form set out in the Representation of the People Regulations 1950(a), or a form substantially to the like effect, together with an envelope for their return.

Provision of polling stations

21.—(1) The returning officer shall provide a sufficient number of polling stations and, subject to the following provisions of this rule, shall allot the electors to the polling stations in such manner as he thinks most convenient.

(2) One or more polling stations may be provided in the same room.

(3) The polling station allotted to electors from any parliamentary polling district wholly or partly within the electoral area shall, in the absence of special circumstances, be in the parliamentary polling place for that district, unless the polling place is outside the electoral area.

(4) The returning officer shall provide each polling station with such number of compartments as may be necessary in which the voters can mark their votes screened from observation.

Appointment of presiding officers and clerks

22.—(1) The returning officer shall appoint and pay a presiding officer to attend at each polling station and such clerks as may be necessary for the purposes of the election, but he shall not appoint any person who has been employed by or on behalf of a candidate in or about the election.

(2) The returning officer may, if he thinks fit, preside at a polling station and the provisions of these rules relating to a presiding officer shall apply to a returning officer so presiding with the necessary modifications as to things to be done by the returning officer to the presiding officer or by the presiding officer to the returning officer.

(3) A presiding officer may do, by the clerks appointed to assist him, any act (including the asking of questions) which he is required or authorised by these rules to do at a polling station except order the arrest, exclusion or removal of any person from the polling station.

Special lists

23. The registration officer shall as soon as practicable prepare the following special lists, namely:—

(a) a list (in these rules referred to as "the absent voters list") giving the name and number on the register of every person entitled to vote at the election as an absent voter;

(b) a list (in these rules referred to as "the list of proxies") giving—

(i) the names and numbers on the register of the electors for whom proxies have been appointed;

(ii) the names and addresses of the persons appointed;

(c) a list of any persons entitled to vote by post as proxy at the election.

(a) S.I. 1950/1254 (Rev. XX, p. 7: 1950 II, p. 513).

Equipment of polling stations

24.—(1) The returning officer shall provide each presiding officer with such number of ballot boxes and ballot papers as in the opinion of the returning officer may be necessary.

(2) Every ballot box shall be so constructed that the ballot papers can be put therein, but cannot be withdrawn therefrom, without the box being unlocked.

(3) The returning officer shall provide each polling station with—

(a) materials to enable voters to mark the ballot papers;

(b) instruments for stamping thereon the official mark;

(c) copies of the register of electors for the electoral area or such part thereof as contains the names of the electors allotted to the station;

(d) the parts of any special lists prepared for the election corresponding to the register of electors for the electoral area or part thereof provided under the last foregoing paragraph.

(4) A notice in the form in the Appendix, giving directions for the guidance of the voters in voting, shall be printed in conspicuous characters and exhibited inside and outside every polling station.

(5) In every compartment of every polling station there shall be exhibited a notice as follows:—"The voter may vote for not more than   candidate(s)"; so however that the notice may be adapted so far as circumstances require.

Appointment of polling and counting agents

25.—(1) Each candidate may, before the commencement of the poll, appoint polling agents to attend at polling stations for the purpose of detecting personation and one or more counting agents up to the number he may be authorised by the returning officer to appoint to attend at the counting of the votes:

Provided that—

(a) the number of counting agents authorised by the returning officer shall be the same in the case of each candidate;

(b) the appointment of an agent may be on behalf of more than one candidate;

(c) not more than three or, if the number of candidates exceeds twenty, four polling agents shall be appointed to attend at any polling station.

(2) If the number of polling agents appointed to attend at a polling station exceeds the permitted number, only those agents, up to the permitted number, whose appointments are signed by or on behalf of the greater number of candidates, or, in the event of an equality in the number of signatures, only such of those agents as may be determined by the returning officer, shall be deemed to have been duly appointed.

(3) Notice in writing of the appointment, stating the names and addresses of the persons appointed, shall be given by the candidate to the returning officer and shall be so given not later than the time appointed for that purpose in the Timetable.

(4) If an agent dies, or becomes incapable of acting, the candidate may appoint another agent in his place, and shall forthwith give to the returning officer notice in writing of the name and address of the agent appointed.

(5) The foregoing provisions of this rule shall be without prejudice to the requirements of section 60(1) of the Representation of the People Act 1949 as to the appointment of paid polling agents, and any appointment authorised by this rule may be made and the notice of appointment given to the returning officer by the candidate's election agent, instead of by the candidate.

(6) In the following provisions of these rules references to polling and counting agents shall be taken as references to agents whose appointments have been duly made and notified and who are within the permitted number.

(7) Any notice required to be given to a counting agent by the returning officer may be delivered at, or sent by post to, the address stated in the notice of appointment.

(8) A candidate may himself do any act or thing which any polling or counting agent of his, if appointed, would have been authorised to do, or may assist his agent in doing any such act or thing.

(9) A candidate's election agent may do or assist in doing anything which a polling or counting agent of his is authorised to do; and anything required or authorised by these rules to be done in the presence of the polling or counting agents may be done in the presence of a candidate's election agent instead of his polling agent or counting agents.

(10) Where by these rules any act or thing is required or authorised to be done in the presence of the polling or counting agents, the non-attendance of any agents or agent at the time and place appointed for the purpose, shall not, if the act or thing is otherwise duly done, invalidate the act or thing done.

Declaration of secrecy

26.—(1) Before the opening of the poll a declaration of secrecy in the form in paragraph (4) of this rule, or in a form as near thereto as circumstances admit, shall be made by—

(a) the returning officer and the presiding officers;

(b) every clerk authorised to attend at a polling station or the counting of the votes;

(c) every candidate attending at a polling station or at the counting of the votes and every election agent so attending;

(d) every candidate's wife or husband attending at the counting of the votes;

(e) every polling agent and counting agent;

(f) every person permitted by the returning officer to attend at the counting of the votes, though not entitled to do so.

(2) Notwithstanding anything in the foregoing paragraph, the following persons attending at the counting of the votes, that is to say:—

(a) any candidate;

(b) any election agent, or any candidate's wife or husband attending by virtue of the rule authorising election agents and candidates' wives or husbands to attend as such;

(c) any person permitted by the returning officer to attend, though not entitled to do so;

(d) any clerk making the declaration in order to attend at the counting of the votes;

need not make the declaration before the opening of the poll but shall make it before he or she is permitted to attend the counting, and a person becoming obliged to make a declaration by reason of his appointment after the opening of the poll shall make the declaration before acting under the appointment.

(3) The returning officer shall make the declaration in the presence of a Justice of the Peace, and any other person shall make the declaration in the presence either of a Justice of the Peace or of the returning officer, and subsections (1), (2), (3) and (6) of section 53 of the Representation of the People Act 1949 shall be read to the declarant by the person taking the declaration, or shall be read by the declarant in the presence of that person:

Provided that the declaration may be made by the returning officer or any other person before a person who is chairman of the Greater London Council, a county council or a district council or mayor of a borough or rural borough, and may be made by a person other than the returning officer before a person who is clerk of any such council or town clerk of a borough or rural borough.

(4) The declaration shall be as follows:—

"I solemnly promise and declare that I will not at this election for the electoral area of   ·   in the Rural District of   do anything forbidden by subsections (1), (2), (3) and (6) of section 53 of the Representation of the People Act 1949, which have been read to [by] me."

THE POLL

Admission to polling station

27.—(1) The presiding officer shall regulate the number of voters to be admitted to the polling station at the same time, and shall exclude all other persons except—

(a) the candidates and their election agents;

(b) the polling agents appointed to attend at the polling station;

(c) the clerks appointed to attend at the polling station;

(d) the constables on duty; and

(e) the companions of blind voters.

(2) Not more than one polling agent shall be admitted at the same time to a polling station on behalf of the same candidate.

(3) A constable or person employed by a returning officer shall not be admitted to vote in person elsewhere than at his own polling station under the provisions of the Representation of the People Act 1949 in that behalf, except on production and surrender of a certificate as to his employment which shall be in the form in the Appendix, or a form to the like effect, and signed by an officer of police of or above the rank of inspector or by the returning officer, as the case may be.

(4) Any certificate surrendered under this rule shall forthwith be cancelled.

Keeping of order in station

28.—(1) It shall be the duty of the presiding officer to keep order at his polling station.

(2) If a person misconducts himself in a polling station, or fails to obey the lawful orders of the presiding officer, he may immediately, by order of the presiding officer, be removed from the polling station by a constable in or near that station or by any other person authorised in writing by the returning officer to remove him, and the person so removed shall not, without the permission of the presiding officer, again enter the polling station during the day.

(3) Any person so removed may, if charged with the commission in the polling station of an offence, be dealt with as a person taken into custody by a constable for an offence without a warrant.

(4) The powers conferred by this rule shall not be exercised so as to prevent a voter who is otherwise entitled to vote at a polling station from having an opportunity of voting at that station.

Sealing of ballot boxes

29. Immediately before the commencement of the poll, the presiding officer shall show the ballot box empty to such persons, if any, as are present in the polling station, so that they may see that it is empty, and shall then lock it up and place his seal on it in such manner as to prevent it being opened without breaking the seal, and shall place it in his view for the receipt of ballot papers, and keep it so locked and sealed.

Questions to be put to voters

30.—(1) The presiding officer may, and if required by a candidate or his election or polling agent shall, put to any person applying for a ballot paper at the time of his application, but not afterwards, the following questions, or either of them, that is to say:—

(*a*) in the case of a person applying as an elector—

    (i) Are you the person registered in the register of local government electors now in force for this electoral area as follows [*read the whole entry from the register*]?

    (ii) Have you already voted at the present election [*adding in the case of an election for several electoral areas*, in this or any other electoral area] otherwise than as proxy for some other person?

(*b*) in the case of a person applying as proxy—

    (i) Are you the person whose name appears as A.B. in the list of proxies for this election as entitled to vote as proxy on behalf of C.D.?

    (ii) Have you already voted here or elsewhere at the present election as proxy on behalf of C.D.?

(2) A ballot paper shall not be delivered to any person required to answer the above questions or any of them unless he has answered the questions or question satisfactorily.

(3) Save as by this rule authorised, no inquiry shall be permitted as to the right of any person to vote.

Challenge of voter

31.—(1) If at the time a person applies for a ballot paper for the purpose of voting in person, or after he has applied for a ballot paper for that purpose and before he has left the polling station, a candidate or his election or polling agent declares to the presiding officer that he has reasonable cause to believe that the applicant has committed an offence of personation and undertakes to substantiate the charge in a court of law, the presiding officer may order a constable to arrest the applicant, and the order of the presiding officer shall be sufficient authority for the constable so to do.

(2) A person against whom a declaration is made under this rule shall not by reason thereof be prevented from voting.

(3) A person arrested under the provisions of this rule shall be dealt with as a person taken into custody by a constable for an offence without a warrant.

Voting procedure

32.—(1) A ballot paper shall be delivered to a voter who applies therefor, and immediately before delivery—

(*a*) the ballot paper shall be stamped with the official mark, either embossed or perforated;

(*b*) the number, name and description of the elector as stated in the copy of the register of electors shall be called out;

(*c*) the number of the elector shall be marked on the counterfoil;

(*d*) a mark shall be placed in the register of electors against the number of the elector to denote that a ballot paper has been received but without showing the particular ballot paper which has been received; and

(*e*) in the case of a person applying for a ballot paper as proxy, a mark shall also be placed against his name in the list of proxies.

(2) The voter, on receiving the ballot paper, shall forthwith proceed into one of the compartments in the polling station and there secretly mark his paper and fold it up so as to conceal his vote, and shall then show to the presiding officer the back of the paper, so as to disclose the official mark and put the ballot paper so folded up into the ballot box in the presence of the presiding officer.

(3) The voter shall vote without undue delay, and shall leave the polling station as soon as he has put his ballot paper into the ballot box.

Votes marked by presiding officer

33.—(1) The presiding officer, on the application of—

(a) a voter who is incapacitated by blindness or other physical cause from voting in manner directed by these rules; or

(b) if the poll is taken on a Saturday, a voter who declares that he is a Jew, and objects on religious grounds to vote in manner directed by these rules; or

(c) a voter who declares orally that he is unable to read;

shall, in the presence of the polling agents, cause the vote of the voter to be marked on a ballot paper in manner directed by the voter, and the ballot paper to be placed in the ballot box.

(2) The name and number in the register of electors of every voter whose vote is marked in pursuance of this rule, and the reason why it is so marked, shall be entered on a list (in these rules called "the list of votes marked by the presiding officer").

In the case of a person voting as proxy for an elector, the number to be entered together with the name of the voter shall be the number of the elector.

Voting by blind persons

34.—(1) If a voter makes an application to the presiding officer to be allowed on the ground of blindness to vote with the assistance of another person by whom he is accompanied (in these rules referred to as "the companion"), the presiding officer shall require the voter to declare orally whether he is so incapacitated by his blindness as to be unable to vote without assistance.

(2) If the presiding officer is satisfied that the voter is so incapacitated and is also satisfied by a written declaration made by the companion (in these rules referred to as "the declaration made by the companion of a blind voter") that the companion is a qualified person within the meaning of this rule and has not previously assisted more than one blind person to vote at the election, the presiding officer shall grant the application, and thereupon anything which is by these rules required to be done to or by the said voter in connection with the giving of his vote may be done to, or with the assistance of, the companion.

(3) For the purposes of this rule, a person shall be qualified to assist a blind voter to vote, if that person is either—

(a) a person who is entitled to vote as an elector at the election ; or

(b) the father, mother, brother, sister, husband, wife, son or daughter of the blind voter and has attained the age of eighteen years.

(4) The name and number in the register of electors of every voter whose vote is given in accordance with this rule and the name and address of the companion shall be entered on a list (in these rules referred to as "the list of blind voters assisted by companions").

In the case of a person voting as proxy for an elector, the number to be entered together with the name of the voter shall be the number of the elector.

(5) The declaration made by the companion—

(a) shall be in the form in the Appendix;

(b) shall be made before the presiding officer at the time when the voter applies to vote with the assistance of a companion and shall forthwith be given to the presiding officer who shall attest and retain it.

(6) No fee or other payment shall be charged in respect of the declaration.

Tendered ballot papers

35.—(1) If a person, representing himself to be—

(a) a particular elector named in the register and not named in the absent voters list; or

(b) a particular person named in the list of proxies as proxy for an elector and not named in the list of persons entitled to vote by post as proxy,

applies for a ballot paper after another person has voted in person either as the elector or his proxy, the applicant shall, on satisfactorily answering the questions permitted by law to be asked at the poll, be entitled, subject to the following provisions of this rule, to mark a ballot paper (in these rules referred to as "a tendered ballot paper") in the same manner as any other voter.

(2) A tendered ballot paper shall—

(a) be of a colour differing from the other ballot papers;

(b) instead of being put into the ballot box, be given to the presiding officer and endorsed by him with the name of the voter and his number in the register of electors, and set aside in a separate packet.

(3) The name of the voter and his number in the register of electors shall be entered on a list (in these rules referred to as the "tendered votes list").

(4) In the case of a person voting as proxy for an elector, the number to be endorsed or entered together with the name of the voter shall be the number of that elector.

Spoilt ballot papers

36. A voter who has inadvertently dealt with his ballot paper in such manner that it cannot be conveniently used as a ballot paper may, on delivering it to the presiding officer and proving to his satisfaction the fact of the inadvertence, obtain another ballot paper in the place of the ballot paper so delivered (in these rules referred to as "a spoilt ballot paper"), and the spoilt ballot paper shall be immediately cancelled.

Adjournment of poll in case of riot

37. For the purpose of the adjournment of the poll in the event of riot or open violence, a presiding officer shall have the power by law belonging to a presiding officer at a parliamentary election.

Procedure on close of poll

38.—(1) As soon as practicable after the close of the poll, the presiding officer shall, in the presence of the polling agents, make up into separate packets, sealed with his own seal and the seals of such polling agents as desire to affix their seals—

(a) each ballot box in use at the station, sealed so as to prevent the introduction of additional ballot papers and unopened, but with the key attached;

(b) the unused and spoilt ballot papers placed together;

(c) the tendered ballot papers;

(d) the marked copies of the register of electors and of the list of proxies;

(e) the counterfoils of the used ballot papers and the certificates as to employment on duty on the day of the poll;

(*f*) the tendered votes list, the list of blind voters assisted by companions, the list of votes marked by the presiding officer, a statement of the number of voters whose votes are so marked by the presiding officer under the heads "physical incapacity", "Jews", and "unable to read" and the declarations made by the companions of blind voters;

and shall deliver the packets or cause them to be delivered to the returning officer to be taken charge of by him:

Provided that if the packets are not delivered by the presiding officer personally to the returning officer, the arrangements for their delivery shall require the approval of the returning officer.

(2) The marked copies of the register of electors and of the list of proxies shall be in one packet but shall not be in the same packet as the counterfoils of the used ballot papers and the certificates as to employment on duty on the day of the poll.

(3) The packets shall be accompanied by a statement (in these rules referred to as "the ballot paper account") made by the presiding officer showing the number of ballot papers entrusted to him, and accounting for them under the heads of ballot papers issued and not otherwise accounted for, unused, spoilt and tendered ballot papers.

COUNTING OF VOTES

Attendance at counting of votes

39.—(1) The returning officer shall make arrangements for counting the votes in the presence of the counting agents as soon as practicable after the close of the poll, and shall give to the counting agents notice in writing of the time and place at which he will begin to count the votes.

(2) No person other than—

(*a*) the returning officer and his clerks;

(*b*) the candidates and their wives or husbands;

(*c*) the election agents;

(*d*) the counting agents;

may be present at the counting of the votes, unless permitted by the returning officer to attend.

(3) A person not entitled to attend at the counting of the votes shall not be permitted to do so by the returning officer unless the returning officer is satisfied that the efficient counting of the votes will not be impeded, and the returning officer has either consulted the election agents or thought it impracticable to consult them.

(4) The returning officer shall give the counting agents all such reasonable facilities for overseeing the proceedings, and all such information with reference thereto, as he can give them consistently with the orderly conduct of the proceedings and the discharge of his duties in connection therewith.

(5) In particular, where the votes are counted by sorting the ballot papers according to the candidate for whom the vote is given and then counting the number of ballot papers for each candidate, the counting agents shall be entitled to satisfy themselves that the ballot papers are correctly sorted.

The count

40.—(1) Before the returning officer proceeds to count the votes, he shall—

(*a*) in the presence of the counting agents open each ballot box and, taking out the ballot papers therein, count and record the number thereof and in the presence of the election agents who are present verify each ballot paper account;

(b) if polls have been taken together for the election of rural district councillors and rural borough or parish councillors, separate the ballot papers relating to the election of rural district councillors from those relating to rural borough or parish councillors and count and record the numbers relating to each election;

(c) count such of the postal ballot papers as have been duly returned and record the number counted; and

(d) then mix together the whole of the ballot papers relating to the election of rural district councillors contained in the ballot boxes.

(2) A postal ballot paper shall not be deemed to be duly returned, unless it is returned in the proper envelope so as to reach the returning officer before the close of the poll and is accompanied by the declaration of identity duly signed and authenticated.

(3) The returning officer shall not count any tendered ballot paper.

(4) The returning officer, while separating, counting and recording the number of ballot papers and counting the votes, shall keep the ballot papers with their faces upwards and take all proper precautions for preventing any person from seeing the numbers printed on the back of the papers.

(5) The returning officer shall verify each ballot paper account by comparing it with the number of ballot papers recorded by him, and the unused and spoilt ballot papers in his possession and the tendered votes list (opening and resealing the packets containing the unused and spoilt ballot papers and the tendered votes list) and shall draw up a statement as to the result of the verification which any election agent may copy.

(6) The returning officer shall, so far as practicable, proceed continuously with counting the votes, allowing only time for refreshment:

Provided that he may, in so far as he thinks necessary, exclude the hours between eight o'clock in the evening and nine o'clock on the following morning.

(7) During the excluded time the returning officer shall place the ballot papers and other documents relating to the election under his own seal and the seals of such of the counting agents as desire to affix their seals and shall otherwise take proper precautions for the security of the papers and documents.

Re-count

41.—(1) A candidate or his election agent may, if present when the counting or any re-count of the votes is completed, require the returning officer to have the votes re-counted or again re-counted but the returning officer may refuse to do so if in his opinion the request is unreasonable.

(2) No step shall be taken on the completion of the counting or any re-count of votes until the candidates and election agents present at the completion thereof have been given a reasonable opportunity to exercise the right conferred by this rule.

Rejected ballot papers

42.—(1) Any ballot paper—

(a) which does not bear the official mark; or

(b) on which votes are given for more candidates than the voter is entitled to vote for; or

(c) on which anything is written or marked by which the voter can be identified except the printed number on the back; or

(d) which is unmarked or void for uncertainty;

shall, subject to the provisions of this rule, be void and not counted.

(2) Where the voter is entitled to vote for more than one candidate, a ballot paper shall not be deemed to be void for uncertainty as respects any vote as to which no uncertainty arises and that vote shall be counted.

(3) A ballot paper on which a vote is marked—

    (*a*) elsewhere than in the proper place; or

    (*b*) otherwise than by means of a cross; or

    (*c*) by more than one mark;

shall not by reason thereof be deemed to be void (either wholly or as respects that vote), if an intention that the vote shall be for one or other of the candidates clearly appears and the way the paper is marked does not of itself identify the voter and it is not shown that he can be identified thereby.

(4) The returning officer shall endorse—

    (*a*) the word "rejected" on any ballot paper which under this rule is not to be counted; and

    (*b*) in the case of a ballot paper on which any vote is counted under paragraph (2) of this rule, the words "rejected in part" and a memorandum specifying the votes counted;

and shall add to the endorsement the words "rejection objected to" if an objection is made by a counting agent to his decision.

(5) The returning officer shall draw up a statement showing the number of ballot papers rejected, including those rejected in part, under the several heads of—

    (*a*) want of official mark;

    (*b*) voting for more candidates than voter is entitled to;

    (*c*) writing or mark by which voter could be identified;

    (*d*) unmarked or wholly void for uncertainty;

    (*e*) rejected in part.

Decisions on ballot papers

43. The decision of the returning officer on any question arising in respect of a ballot paper shall be final, but shall be subject to review on an election petition.

Equality of votes

44. Where, after the counting of the votes (including any re-count) is completed, an equality of votes is found to exist between any candidates and the addition of a vote would entitle any of those candidates to be declared elected, the returning officer shall forthwith decide between those candidates by lot, and proceed as if the candidate on whom the lot falls had received an additional vote.

PART IV

FINAL PROCEEDINGS IN CONTESTED AND UNCONTESTED ELECTIONS

Declaration of result

45.—(1) In a contested election, when the result of the poll has been ascertained the returning officer shall forthwith declare to be elected the candidate or candidates for whom the majority of votes have been given, and shall as soon as possible publish the name or names of the candidate or candidates elected and the total number of votes given for each candidate, whether elected or not, together with the number of rejected ballot papers under each head shown in the statement of rejected ballot papers.

(2) In an uncontested election, the returning officer shall, not later than eleven o'clock in the morning on the day of election, publish the name or names of the person or persons elected.

The return

46. The returning officer shall forthwith upon declaration of the result of the election return the name of each person elected to the clerk of the rural district council.

PART V

DISPOSAL OF DOCUMENTS

Sealing of ballot papers

47.—(1) On the completion of the counting at a contested election the returning officer shall seal up in separate packets the counted and rejected ballot papers, including ballot papers rejected in part.

(2) The returning officer shall not open the sealed packets of tendered ballot papers or of counterfoils and certificates as to employment on the day of the poll, or of marked copies of the register of electors and lists of proxies.

Delivery of documents to clerk of the council

48. The returning officer shall then forward to the clerk of the rural district council the following documents, that is to say:—

(a) the packets of ballot papers in his possession;

(b) the ballot paper accounts and the statements of rejected ballot papers and of the result of the verification of the ballot paper accounts;

(c) the tendered votes lists, the lists of blind voters assisted by companions, the lists of votes marked by the presiding officer and the statements relating thereto, and the declarations made by the companions of blind voters;

(d) the packets of counterfoils and certificates as to employment on duty on the day of the poll;

(e) the packets containing marked copies of registers and of lists of proxies,

endorsing on each packet a description of its contents, the date of the election to which they relate and the name of the electoral area for which the election was held.

Orders for production of documents

49.—(1) An order for—

(a) the inspection or production of any rejected ballot papers, including ballot papers rejected in part; or

(b) for the opening of a sealed packet of counterfoils and certificates as to employment on duty on the day of the poll or for the inspection of counted ballot papers,

may be made by either a county court having jurisdiction in the rural district or an election court if the court is satisfied by evidence on oath that the order is required for the purpose of instituting or maintaining a prosecution for an offence in relation to ballot papers, or for the purpose of an election petition.

(2) The order may be made subject to such conditions as to persons, time, place and mode of inspection, production or opening as the court making the order may think expedient and may direct the clerk of the rural district council having custody of the ballot papers and the sealed packets of counterfoils and certificates to retain them intact for such period as may be specified in the order:

Provided that in making and carrying into effect the order, care shall be taken that the way in which the vote of any particular elector has been given shall not be disclosed until it has been proved that his vote was given and the vote has been declared by a competent court to be invalid.

(3) An appeal shall lie to the High Court from any order of a county court made under this rule.

(4) Any power given under this rule to a county court may be exercised by any judge of the court otherwise than in open court.

(5) Where an order is made for the production by the clerk of the rural district council of any document in his posession relating to any specified election, the production by him or his agent of the document ordered in such manner as may be directed by that order shall be conclusive evidence that the document relates to the specified election; and any endorsement on any packet of ballot papers so produced shall be prima facie evidence that the ballot papers are what they are stated to be by the endorsement.

(6) The production from proper custody of a ballot paper purporting to have been used at any election, and of a counterfoil marked with the same printed number and having a number marked thereon in writing, shall be prima facie evidence that the elector whose vote was given by that ballot paper was the person who at the time of the election had affixed to his name in the register of electors the same number as the number written on the counterfoil.

(7) Save as by this rule provided, no person shall be allowed to inspect any rejected or counted ballot papers in the possession of the clerk of the rural district council or to open any sealed packets of counterfoils and certificates.

Retention and public inspection of documents

50.—(1) The clerk of the rural district council shall retain for six months among the records of the rural district all documents relating to an election which are, in pursuance of these rules, forwarded to him by a returning officer or held by him and then, unless otherwise directed by an order under the last foregoing rule, shall cause them to be destroyed.

(2) The said documents, except ballot papers, counterfoils and certificates as to employment on duty on the day of the poll, shall during a period of six months from the day of election be open to public inspection at such time and in such manner as may be determined by the county council.

(3) The clerk of the rural district council shall, on request, supply copies of or extracts from the documents open to public inspection on payment of such fees, and subject to such conditions, as may be determined by the county council.

Supplemental provisions as to documents

51. Subject to the provisions of these rules, the clerk of the rural district council shall, in respect of the custody and destruction of ballot papers and other documents coming into his possession in pursuance of these rules, be subject to the directions of the rural district council.

PART VI

SUPPLEMENTAL

Countermand or abandonment of poll on death of candidate

52.—(1) If at a contested election proof is given to the satisfaction of the returning officer before the result of the election is declared that one of the persons named or to be named as candidate in the ballot papers has died, then the returning officer shall countermand the poll for the election of rural district councillors or, if polling has begun, direct that the poll be abandoned, and the provisions of section 36(2) of the Representation of the People Act 1949 shall apply to any further election ordered under the Local Government Act 1933.

(2) Where the poll is abandoned by reason of the death of a candidate, the proceedings at or consequent on that poll shall be interrupted, and the presiding officer at any polling station shall take the like steps (so far as not already taken) for the delivery to the returning officer of ballot boxes and of ballot papers and other documents as he is required to take on the close of the poll in due course, and the returning officer shall dispose of ballot papers and other documents in his possession as he is required to do on the completion in due course of the counting of the votes; but—

(a) it shall not be necessary for any ballot paper account to be prepared or verified; and

(b) the returning officer, without taking any step or further step for the counting of the ballot papers or of the votes, shall seal up all the ballot papers, whether the votes on them have been counted or not, and it shall not be necessary to seal up counted and rejected ballot papers in separate packets.

(3) The foregoing provisions of these rules as to the inspection, production, retention and destruction of ballot papers and other documents relating to a poll at an election shall apply to any such documents relating to a poll abandoned by reason of the death of a candidate, with the following modifications:—

(a) ballot papers on which the votes were neither counted nor rejected shall be treated as counted ballot papers; and

(b) no order shall be made for the production or inspection of any ballot papers or for the opening of a sealed packet of counterfoils or certificates as to employment on duty on the day of the poll unless the order is made by a court with reference to a prosecution.

General duty of returning officer

53. It shall be the general duty of the returning officer to do any act or thing that may be necessary for effectually conducting the election under these rules.

Notices

54. Any notice or other document required under these rules to be affixed to the offices of the rural district council shall be exhibited—

(a) in some conspicuous place on or near the outer door of the offices of the council; or

(b) if the council have no offices, in some conspicuous place in the rural district or in the area to which the document or notice relates.

Interpretation

55.—(1) The expression "electoral area" means each ward of a parish, parish or combination of parishes, as the case may be, into which a rural district is divided for the election of rural district councillors: in this paragraph "parish" shall include rural borough.

(2) A reference in this Schedule to a rule shall be construed as a reference to a rule contained in this Schedule.

(3) Any reference in this Schedule to any enactment or statutory instrument shall be taken as a reference to that enactment or statutory instrument as amended or replaced by any other enactment or statutory instrument.

APPENDIX

Note.—The forms contained in this Appendix may be adapted so far as circumstances require.

Rule 4.

NOTICE OF ELECTION

RURAL DISTRICT OF

ELECTION OF RURAL DISTRICT COUNCILLORS for the [Ward of the parish of   ] [Parish of   ] [Combined parishes of   ] [Rural borough of   ] in the Rural District.

If the notice relates to more than one election, adapt form accordingly.

1. An election is to be held of   Rural District Councillors for the said [ward] [parish] [combined parishes] [rural borough].

2. Nomination papers must be delivered at   on any day after the date of this notice, but not later than noon on the   day of   .

3. Forms of nomination paper may be obtained from the returning officer at   . The returning officer will at the request of any local government elector for the electoral area prepare for signature a nomination paper.

4. If the election is contested, the poll will take place on the   day of   .

(Signed)....................................
Returning Officer.

              day of   , 19 .

NOTE 1.—The attention of candidates and electors is drawn to the rules for filling up nomination papers and other provisions relating to nomination contained in the election rules in Schedule 1 to the Rural District Council Election Rules 1969.

NOTE 2.—Every person guilty of a corrupt or illegal practice will, on conviction, be liable to the penalties imposed by the Representation of the People Act 1949.

NOTE 3.—Electors and their proxies should take note that applications to be treated as an absent voter and other applications and notices about postal or proxy voting must reach the electoral registration officer at (*insert address*) by the day of   next if they are to be effective for this election.

NOMINATION PAPER

ELECTION OF RURAL DISTRICT COUNCILLORS for the [Ward of the parish of   ] [Parish of   ] [Combined parishes of   ] [Rural borough of   ] in the Rural District of   .
Date of publication of notice of election...

We, the undersigned, being local government electors for the said [ward] [parish] [combined parishes] [rural borough], do hereby nominate the undermentioned person as a candidate at the said election.

Candidate's surname	Other names in full	Description (if any)	Home address in full

Signatures	Electoral Number (see note 2)	
	Distinctive Letter(s)	Number
Proposer	....	....
Seconder...	....	....

NOTE 1.—The attention of candidates and local government electors is drawn to the rules for filling up nomination papers and other provisions relating to nomination contained in the election rules in Schedule 1 to the Rural District Council Election Rules 1969.

NOTE 2.—A person's electoral number consists of the distinctive letter or letters of the parliamentary polling district in which he is registered together with his number in the register to be used at the election except that before publication of the register the distinctive letter or letters of the parliamentary polling district in which he is entitled to be registered together with his number (if any) in the electors lists for that register shall be used instead.

NOTE 3.—A local government elector may not—

    (a) subscribe more nomination papers than there are vacancies to be filled in the electoral area; or

    (b) subscribe a nomination paper for more than one electoral area of the rural district; or

    (c) subscribe more than one nomination paper in respect of the same candidate.

NOTE 4.—A person whose name is entered in the register or electors lists may not subscribe a nomination paper if the entry gives as the date on which he will become of voting age a date later than the day fixed for the poll.

Rule 10.

STATEMENT AS TO PERSONS NOMINATED

RURAL DISTRICT OF

The following is a statement as to the persons nominated for election as Rural District Councillors for the [Ward of the parish of   ] [Parish of   ] [Combined parishes of   ] [Rural borough of   ] in the Rural District.

[Ward] [Parish] [Combined Parishes] [Rural Borough]	Persons nominated				Proposer's name	Decision of returning officer that nomination paper is invalid, or other reason why a person nominated no longer stands nominated
	Surname	Other names in full	Home address in full	Description (if any)		
1.	2.	3.	4.	5.	6.	7.

The persons opposite whose names no entry is made in column 7 have been and stand validly nominated.

Dated this   day of   , 19   .

....
Returning Officer

BALLOT PAPER   Rule 15.

Form of Front of Ballot Paper

Counterfoil No.		
The counterfoil is to have a number to correspond with that on the back of the Ballot Paper.	**1**	**BROWN** (JOHN EDWARD Brown, of 2 The Cottages, Barlington, Grayshire, Labour.)	
	2	**BROWN** (THOMAS WILLIAM Brown, of 15 Barchester Road, Barlington, Grayshire, Liberal.)	
	3	**JONES** (William David Jones, of The Grange, Barlington, Grayshire, Conservative.)	
	4	**MERTON** (Hon. George Travis, commonly called Viscount Merton, of Barlington, Grayshire.)	
	5	**SMITH** (Mary Smith, of School House, Barlington, Grayshire, schoolteacher, Progressive.)	
	6	**WILLIAMS** (Elizabeth Williams, of 3 Ivy Lane, Barlington, Grayshire, housewife.)	

Form of Back of Ballot Paper

No.

Election for the [Ward of the parish of   ] [Parish of   ]
[Combined parishes of   ] [Rural borough of   ] in the
Rural District of   .
       day of   , 19   .

Note.—The number on the ballot paper is to correspond with that on the counterfoil.

Directions as to printing the ballot paper

1. Nothing is to be printed on the ballot paper except in accordance with these directions.

2. So far as practicable, the following arrangements shall be observed in the printing of the ballot paper:—

   (*a*) no word shall be printed on the face except the particulars of the candidates;

   (*b*) no rule shall be printed on the face except the horizontal rules separating the particulars of the candidates from one another and the vertical rules separating those particulars from the numbers on the left-hand side and the spaces on the right where the vote is to be marked;

   (*c*) the whole space between the top and bottom of the paper shall be equally divided between the candidates by the rules separating their particulars.

3. The surname of each candidate shall in all cases be printed by itself in large capitals, and his full particulars shall be set out below it and shall be printed in ordinary type except that small capitals shall be used—

   (*a*) if his surname is the same as another candidate's for his other names; and

   (*b*) if his other names are also the same as the other candidate's, either for his residence or for his description unless each of them is the same as that of another candidate with the same surname and other names.

4. The number on the back of the ballot paper shall be printed in ordinary type.

Rule 24.

DIRECTIONS FOR THE GUIDANCE OF THE VOTERS IN VOTING

1. The voter should see that the ballot paper, before it is handed to him, is stamped with the official mark.

2. The voter will go into one of the compartments and, with the pencil provided in the compartment, place a cross on the right-hand side of the ballot paper, opposite the name of each candidate for whom he votes, thus X.

3. The voter will then fold up the ballot paper so as to show the official mark on the back, and leaving the compartment will, without showing the front of the paper to any person, show the official mark on the back to the presiding officer, and then, in the presence of the presiding officer, put the paper into the ballot box, and forthwith leave the polling station.

4. If the voter inadvertently spoils a ballot paper he can return it to the officer, who will, if satisfied of such inadvertence, give him another paper.

5. If the voter votes for more than   candidate(s) or places any mark on the paper by which he may afterwards be identified, his ballot paper will be void, and will not be counted.

6. If the voter fraudulently takes a ballot paper out of a polling station or fraudulently puts into the ballot box any paper other than the one given to him by the officer, he will be liable on conviction to imprisonment for a term not exceeding six months, or to a fine not exceeding twenty pounds or to both such imprisonment and such fine.

CERTIFICATE OF EMPLOYMENT   Rule 27.

Election in the [Ward of the parish of   ] [Parish of   ]
[Combined parishes of   ] [Rural Borough of   ] in the Rural
District of

I certify that (name)..who is numbered.....................
in the register of electors for the electoral area named above, is likely to be
unable to go in person to the polling station allotted to him at the election on
(date of poll)...................................by reason of the particular circumstances of
his employment on that date—

*(a) as a constable,
*(b) by me for a purpose connected with the election.

Signature ....

*Police rank..
(Inspector or above)
*Returning Officer.

Date....................................
*Delete whichever is inapplicable.

NOTE.—The person named above is entitled to vote at any polling station of the
above electoral area on production and surrender of this certificate to the presiding
officer.

DECLARATION TO BE MADE BY THE COMPANION OF A BLIND VOTER   Rule 34.

I, A.B., of   , having been requested to
assist C.D., [in the case of a blind person voting as proxy add voting as proxy for
G.H.] who is numbered   on the register of local government electors
for the electoral area of   in the Rural District of
to record his vote at the election now being held for the said electoral area, do hereby
declare that [I am entitled to vote as an elector at the said election] [I am the*   *State the
of the said voter and have attained the age of relationship
eighteen years], and that I have not previously assisted any blind person [except E.F., companion
of   ], to vote at the said election.   to the voter.

(Signed) A.B.
day of   , 19   .

I, the undersigned, being the presiding officer for the   polling station
for the electoral area of   in the Rural District of   ,
do hereby certify that the above declaration, having been first read to the above-
named declarant, was signed by the declarant in my presence.

(Signed) X.Y.
day of   , 19   , at   minutes past   o'clock
[a.m.] [p.m.].

NOTE.—If the person making the above declaration knowingly and wilfully makes
therein a statement false in a material particular, he will be guilty of an offence.

SCHEDULE 2

*Insert description of office.

DECLARATION OF ACCEPTANCE OF OFFICE BY THE CHAIRMAN OF A RURAL DISTRICT COUNCIL OR BY A RURAL DISTRICT COUNCILLOR

I, A.B., having been elected to the office of*   , hereby declare that I take the said office upon myself, and will duly and faithfully fulfil the duties thereof according to the best of my judgment and ability.

Dated this   day of   , 19   .

†If the declaration is made and subscribed before the clerk of the rural district council, or a justice of the peace or magistrate, or a commissioner for oaths, or a British consul, adapt form accordingly.

Signature.............................

This declaration was made and subscribed before us

Members of the Rural District
Council.†

{   ....

....

EXPLANATORY NOTE

(*This Note is not part of the Rules.*)

These Rules revoke and replace the Rural District Council Election Rules 1951, as amended, with amendments consequential on the provisions of the Representation of the People Act 1969 (c. 15). In particular the Rules provide for postal voting.

STATUTORY INSTRUMENTS

1969 No. 758

AGRICULTURE

The Price Stability of Imported Products (Levy Arrangements) (Amendment) Order 1969

Made - - -	*23rd May* 1969
Laid before Parliament	*5th June* 1969
Coming into Operation	*9th June* 1969

The Minister of Agriculture, Fisheries and Food and the Secretaries of State respectively concerned with agriculture in Scotland and Northern Ireland, acting jointly in exercise of the powers conferred on them by section 1(2), (3), (4), (6) and (7) of the Agriculture and Horticulture Act 1964(a) and of all other powers enabling them in that behalf, with the approval of the Treasury, hereby make the following order:—

1. This order may be cited as the Price Stability of Imported Products (Levy Arrangements) (Amendment) Order 1969 ; and shall come into operation on 9th June 1969.

2. The Price Stability of Imported Products (Levy Arrangements) Order 1966(b) shall be amended by inserting in sub-paragraphs (*a*), (*d*), (*e*) and (*f*) of paragraph 8 of Schedule 1 thereto after the word "Antwerp", wherever it appears, the word "Ghent".

In witness whereof the Official Seal of the Minister of Agriculture, Fisheries and Food is hereunto affixed on 15th May 1969.

(L.S.)   *Cledwyn Hughes,*
Minister of Agriculture, Fisheries and Food.

Given under the Seal of the Secretary of State for Scotland on 19th May 1969.

(L.S.)   *William Ross,*
Secretary of State for Scotland.

Given under the hand of the Secretary of State for the Home Department on 21st May 1969.

James Callaghan,
Secretary of State for the Home Department.

Approved 23rd May 1969.

Walter Harrison,
E. Alan Fitch,
Two of the Lords Commissioners of
Her Majesty's Treasury.

(a) 1964 c. 28.   (b) S.I. 1966/936 (1966 II, p. 2271).

EXPLANATORY NOTE

(*This Note is not part of the order.*)

This amending order, which comes into operation on 9th June 1969, extends the provisions in Schedule 1 of the principal order for determining exemption from any general levy for goods from co-operating countries to include wheat from Canada, the United States of America, the Commonwealth of Australia or the Argentine Republic which has been consigned via Ghent.

STATUTORY INSTRUMENTS

1969 No. 759

NATIONAL HEALTH SERVICE, ENGLAND AND WALES

HOSPITAL AND SPECIALIST SERVICES

The National Health Service (Designation of Teaching Hospitals) Order 1969

Made - - -	*22nd May* 1969
Coming into Operation	*1st June* 1969

The Secretary of State, in exercise of the powers conferred upon him by sections 11 and 75 of the National Health Service Act 1946(a) and of all other powers enabling him in that behalf, and after consultation with the University of Wales, hereby orders as follows:—

1. This order may be cited as the National Health Service (Designation of Teaching Hospitals) Order 1969 and shall come into operation on 1st June 1969.

2.—(1) In this order:—

"the Act" means the National Health Service Act 1946;

"the appointed day" means 1st June 1969;

"the Board of Governors" means the Board of Governors of the United Cardiff Hospitals;

"the Hospital Board" means the Welsh Hospital Board;

"the Management Committee" means the Cardiff and District Hospital Management Committee;

"the transferred hospital" means the hospital named in article 3 hereof.

(2) The Interpretation Act 1889(b) shall apply to the interpretation of this order as it applies to the interpretation of an Act of Parliament.

3. In column (2) of Schedule 1 to the National Health Service (Designation of Teaching Hospitals) Order 1959(c) as amended **(d)** (which Schedule lists designated teaching hospitals), after the names of the hospitals listed against the name of the United Cardiff Hospitals in column (1) there shall be added the words "The Royal Hamadryad General and Seamen's Hospital, Cardiff".

4.—(1) All officers of the Hospital Board employed immediately before the appointed day solely at or for the purposes of the transferred hospital shall on that day be transferred to and become officers of the Board of Governors.

(2) All medical and dental officers of the Hospital Board employed immediately before the appointed day partly at and for the purposes of the transferred hospital and partly at and for the purposes of any other hospital shall on that day become officers of the Board of Governors in relation to their

---

(a) 1946 c. 81.   (b) 1889 c. 63.
(c) S.I. 1959/748 (1959 I, p. 1813).
(d) The relevant amending instrument is S.I. 1965/1663 (1965 III, p. 4757).

work at the transferred hospital and all rights and liabilities under their contract in relation thereto with the Hospital Board shall be transferred to the Board of Governors.

(3) Any other officer of the Hospital Board who is employed immediately before the appointed day partly at or for the purposes of the transferred hospital and who does not receive before that day notice in writing from the Hospital Board that he is not to be transferred to the Board of Governors shall on that day be transferred to and become an officer of the Board of Governors.

(4) Any officer who is transferred to the Board of Governors under this article and whose employment was whole-time shall continue to be subject to the remuneration and other conditions of service applicable to a whole-time officer so long as his employment for both the Hospital Board and the Board of Governors amounts in the aggregate to whole-time employment.

5. On the appointed day there shall be transferred to and vest without further conveyance in the Board of Governors:—

(a) any property held immediately before the appointed day by the Hospital Board or the Management Committee—

(i) under section 59 of the Act solely for the purposes of the transferred hospital, and

(ii) under section 60 of the Act solely for the purposes of the transferred hospital; and

(b) any other property held by the Hospital Board or the Management Committee and any rights and liabilities to which either of them were entitled or subject immediately before the appointed day so far as these relate solely to the transferred hospital.

6. On the appointed day capital assets equivalent to assets of the Hospital Endowments Fund with a market value on the 5th July 1948 of such sum as may be determined by agreement between the Hospital Board and the Board of Governors (or in default of agreement such sum, if any, as may be decided by the Secretary of State) shall be transferred from the Fund to the Board of Governors and the respective shares of the Hospital Board and the Management Committee in the net capital sum referred to in the National Health Service (Apportionment of Hospital Endowment Fund) Regulations 1949(a) shall each be reduced by one-half of the assets so transferred.

7. Any action or proceeding or any cause of action or proceeding, pending or existing at the appointed day, by, or against, the Hospital Board or the Management Committee solely in respect of any property, right or liability transferred by this order shall not be prejudicially affected by reason of this order, and may be continued, prosecuted and enforced by, or against, the Board of Governors.

Signed by order of the Secretary of State.

D. G. McPherson,

Assistant Under Secretary of State,
Welsh Office.

22nd May 1969.

(a) S.I. 1949/482 (1949 I, p. 2595).

EXPLANATORY NOTE

(This Note is not part of the Order.)

This Order amends the National Health Service (Designation of Teaching Hospitals) Order 1959 by including The Royal Hamadryad General and Seamen's Hospital, Cardiff, in the group of hospitals designated as The United Cardiff Hospitals and provides for consequential matters relating to officers and property connected with that hospital.

STATUTORY INSTRUMENTS

1969 No. 760

BRITISH NATIONALITY
The British Nationality Regulations 1969

Made - - -		*27th May* 1969
Coming into Operation		*1st June* 1969

ARRANGEMENT OF REGULATIONS

PART I
GENERAL

1. Citation and operation.
2. Interpretation.
3. Revocations and transitional provisions.

PART II
CITIZENSHIP AND NATIONALITY BY REGISTRATION

4. Application for registration under section 6(1) of the Act of 1948.
5. Application for registration under section 6(2) of the Act of 1948.
6. Application for registration under section 7(1) of the Act of 1948.
7. Application for registration under section 12(6) of the Act of 1948.
8. Application for registration under section 1 of the Act of 1964.
9. Application for registration under section 1 of the No. 2 Act of 1964.
10. Application for registration under section 1 of the Act of 1965.
11. Authority to whom application is to be made.
12. Place of registration.

PART III
NATURALISATION AND RESUMPTION OF CITIZENSHIP AND NATIONALITY

13. Application for naturalisation.
14. Certificate of naturalisation.
15. Oath of allegiance for purpose of naturalisation.
16. Declaration of intention to resume nationality made under section 16(2) of the Act of 1948.
17. Declaration of intention to resume citizenship made under section 4(2) of the Cyprus Act 1960.
18. Place of registration of declaration of intention to resume nationality or citizenship.

Part IV

Renunciation and Deprivation of Citizenship and Nationality

19. Declaration of renunciation of citizenship.
20. Notice of proposed deprivation of citizenship or nationality.
21. Cancellation of registration of person deprived of citizenship or nationality.
22. Cancellation and amendment of certificate of naturalisation in case of deprivation of citizenship.

Part V

Supplemental

23. Authorised forms.
24. Certificate of citizenship in case of doubt.
25. Evidence.
26. Fees.
27. Application in relation to associated states.

Schedules

Schedule 1: General requirements as respects applications, etc.

Schedule 2: Application for registration as a citizen of the United Kingdom and Colonies made by a British subject or citizen of the Republic of Ireland on the ground of ordinary residence or Crown service.

Schedule 3: Application for registration as a citizen of the United Kingdom and Colonies made by a British subject or citizen of the Republic of Ireland on the ground of service other than Crown service.

Schedule 4: Application for registration as a citizen of the United Kingdom and Colonies made by a citizen or former citizen of the Republic of South Africa on the ground of ordinary residence or Crown service.

Schedule 5: Application for registration as a citizen of the United Kingdom and Colonies made by a citizen or former citizen of the Republic of South Africa on the ground of service other than Crown service.

Schedule 6: Application for registration as a citizen of the United Kingdom and Colonies made by a woman who has been married to a citizen of the United Kingdom and Colonies.

Schedule 7: Oath of allegiance.

Schedule 8: Application for registration of a minor child of a citizen of the United Kingdom and Colonies as a citizen thereof.

Schedule 9: Application for registration as a citizen of the United Kingdom and Colonies made by a former British subject.

Schedule 10: Application for registration as a citizen of the United Kingdom and Colonies made by a person who has ceased to be a citizen of the United Kingdom and Colonies as a result of a declaration of renunciation for the purpose of remaining or becoming a citizen of a country mentioned in section 1(3) of the Act of 1948.

Schedule 11: Application for registration as a citizen of the United Kingdom and Colonies by certain stateless persons.

Schedule 12: Application for registration as a British subject made by an alien woman who has been married to a British subject.

Schedule 13: Application for a certificate of naturalisation by an alien or British protected person.

Schedule 14: Certificate of naturalisation.

Schedule 15: Declaration of intention to resume British nationality made by a person who has ceased to be a British subject on the loss of British nationality by his father or mother.

Schedule 16: Declaration of intention to resume citizenship of the United Kingdom and Colonies.

Schedule 17: Declaration of renunciation of citizenship.

Schedule 18: Table of fees.

In exercise of the powers conferred upon me by section 29(1) of the British Nationality Act 1948(a), as extended and amended by section 4(7) of the Cyprus Act 1960(b), section 1 of the South Africa Act 1962(c) and Schedule 1 thereto, section 3(2) of the British Nationality Act 1964(d), section 6(2) of the British Nationality (No. 2) Act 1964(e), section 5(2) of the British Nationality Act 1965(f) and section 12 of the West Indies Act 1967(g) and Schedule 3 thereto, I hereby make with the consent, so far as Regulation 26 is concerned, of the Treasury the following Regulations :—

PART I

GENERAL

Citation and operation

1. These Regulations may be cited as the British Nationality Regulations 1969 and shall come into operation on 1st June 1969.

Interpretation

2.—(1) In these Regulations, unless the context otherwise requires, the following expressions have the meanings hereby respectively assigned to them, that is to say :—

"the Act of 1948" means the British Nationality Act 1948 ;

"the Act of 1958" means the British Nationality Act 1958(h) ;

"the Act of 1964" means the British Nationality Act 1964 ;

"the No. 2 Act of 1964" means the British Nationality (No. 2) Act 1964 ;

"the Act of 1965" means the British Nationality Act 1965 ;

"Governor" has, in relation to a protected state to which the provisions of section 8 of the Act of 1948 relating to protectorates are extended by Order in Council made under section 30 of that Act, the same meaning as in the Order ; and in their application to the Channel Islands and the Isle of Man these Regulations shall have effect as if references to the Governor included references to the Lieutenant-Governor ;

"the High Commissioner" means, in relation to a country mentioned in section 1(3) of the Act of 1948, the High Commissioner for Her Majesty's

(a) 1948 c. 56.	(b) 1960 c.52.
(c) 1962 c.23.	(d) 1964 c. 22.
(e) 1964 c.54.	(f) 1965 c.34.
(g) 1967 c.4.	(h) 1958 c.10.

government in the United Kingdom in that country, and includes the acting High Commissioner in that country.

(2) In these Regulations, any reference to a Regulation or Schedule shall be construed as a reference to a Regulation contained in these Regulations or, as the case may be, to a Schedule thereto ; and any reference in a Regulation or Schedule to a paragraph shall be construed as a reference to a paragraph of that Regulation or of that Schedule.

(3) In these Regulations, except where the context otherwise requires, a reference to any enactment shall be construed as a reference to that enactment as amended, extended or applied by any subsequent enactment.

(4) The Interpretation Act 1889(a) shall apply to the interpretation of these Regulations in like manner as it applies to the interpretation of an Act of Parliament.

Revocations and transitional provisions

3.—(1) The British Nationality Regulations 1965(b) and the British Nationality (Amendment) Regulations 1968(c) are hereby revoked.

(2) Section 38 of the Interpretation Act 1889 shall apply in relation to the said Regulations as if these Regulations were an Act of Parliament and the said Regulations were Acts of Parliament repealed by an Act of Parliament.

(3) Without prejudice to paragraph (2), any application, declaration, or direction made or given before the coming into operation of these Regulations in accordance with the provisions of any Regulation revoked by these Regulations by or to any person or authority shall continue to have effect as if made or given in accordance with the corresponding provisions of these Regulations.

PART II

CITIZENSHIP AND NATIONALITY BY REGISTRATION

Application for registration under section 6(1) of the Act of 1948

4.—(1) An application for registration as a citizen of the United Kingdom and Colonies under section 6(1) of the Act of 1948 shall be made to the appropriate authority specified in Regulation 11(1) to (4).

(2) Such an application made by a British subject or a citizen of the Republic of Ireland shall satisfy the requirements of Schedules 1 and 2 unless it is made by virtue of section 3(2) of the Act of 1958, in which case it shall satisfy the requirements of Schedules 1 and 3.

(3) Such an application made by a citizen or former citizen of the Republic of South Africa by virtue of section 1 of the South Africa Act 1962 shall satisfy the requirements of Schedules 1 and 4 unless it is made by virtue of the said section 1 and section 3(2) of the Act of 1958, in which case it shall satisfy the requirements of Schedules 1 and 5.

Application for registration under section 6(2) of the Act of 1948

5.—(1) An application by a woman for registration as a citizen of the United Kingdom and Colonies under section 6(2) of the Act of 1948 shall be made to the appropriate authority specified in Regulation 11(2).

(a) 1889 c.63.   (b) S.I. 1965/1753 (1965 III, p.4956).
(c) S.I. 1968/448 (1968 I, p.1157).

(2) Such an application shall satisfy the requirements of Schedules 1 and 6 and, where the applicant is a British protected person or an alien and is required by the said section 6(2) to take an oath of allegiance, the said oath shall be subscribed and attested in the form set out in Schedule 7 in accordance with the requirements of paragraph 4 of Schedule 1 and, as so subscribed and attested, shall be included in the form of application.

Application for registration under section 7(1) of the Act of 1948

6.—(1) An application for the registration of a minor child of a citizen of the United Kingdom and Colonies as a citizen thereof under section 7(1) of the Act of 1948 shall be made to the appropriate authority specified in Regulation 11(2).

(2) Such an application shall satisfy the requirements of Schedules 1 and 8.

Application for registration under section 12(6) of the Act of 1948

7.—(1) An application for registration as a citizen of the United Kingdom and Colonies under section 12(6) of the Act of 1948 made by virtue of section 3(1)(*b*)(iii) of the Act of 1958 shall be made to the appropriate authority specified in Regulation 11(5).

(2) Such an application shall satisfy the requirements of Schedules 1 and 9.

Application for registration under section 1 of the Act of 1964

8.—(1) An application for registration as a citizen of the United Kingdom and Colonies under section 1 of the Act of 1964 shall be made to the appropriate authority specified in Regulation 11(6).

(2) Such an application shall satisfy the requirements of Schedules 1 and 10.

Application for registration under section 1 of the No. 2 Act of 1964

9.—(1) An application for registration as a citizen of the United Kingdom and Colonies under section 1 of the No. 2 Act of 1964 shall be made to the appropriate authority specified in Regulation 11(2).

(2) Such an application shall satisfy the requirements of Schedules 1 and 11.

Application for registration under section 1 of the Act of 1965

10.—(1) An application by a woman for registration as a British subject under section 1 of the Act of 1965 shall be made to the appropriate authority specified in Regulation 11(2).

(2) Such an application shall satisfy the requirements of Schedules 1 and 12 and the oath of allegiance required by the said section 1 to be taken by an applicant shall be subscribed and attested in the form set out in Schedule 7 in accordance with the requirements of paragraph 4 of Schedule 1 and, as so subscribed and attested, shall be included in the form of application.

Authority to whom application is to be made

11.—(1) Such an application as is mentioned in Regulation 4, made on grounds consisting of, or including, ordinary residence immediately preceding the application, shall be made—

(*a*) in the case of ordinary residence in the United Kingdom, to the Secretary of State at the Home Office ;

(*b*) in the case of ordinary residence in a dependency mentioned in paragraph (7), to the Governor.

(2) Such an application as is mentioned in Regulation 4 (other than an application to which paragraph (1) applies), made on grounds consisting of, or including, Crown service immediately preceding the application under Her Majesty's government in the United Kingdom, or such an application as is mentioned in Regulation 5, 6, 9 or 10 shall be made—

    (a) if the person concerned is resident in a dependency mentioned in paragraph (7), to the Governor ;

    (b) if the person concerned is resident in a commonwealth country mentioned in paragraph (8), to the High Commissioner ;

    (c) in any other case, to the Secretary of State at the Home Office ;
and in this paragraph the expression "the person concerned" means the person making the application.

(3) Such an application as is mentioned in Regulation 4, made on grounds consisting of, or including, service immediately preceding the application in the employment of a society, company or body of persons established as mentioned in section 3(2) of the Act of 1958, shall be made—

    (a) if the society, company or body is established in the United Kingdom and the applicant is serving in its employment in a commonwealth country mentioned in paragraph (8), to the High Commissioner ;

    (b) if the society, company or body is established in the United Kingdom and the applicant is serving otherwise than as aforesaid, to the Secretary of State at the Home Office ;

    (c) if the society, company or body is established in a dependency mentioned in paragraph (7), to the Governor.

(4) Such an application as is mentioned in Regulation 4, made on grounds consisting of, or including, service immediately preceding the application under an international organisation of which Her Majesty's government in the United Kingdom is a member, shall be made—

    (a) if the applicant is serving as aforesaid in a commonwealth country mentioned in paragraph (8), to the High Commissioner ;

    (b) in any other case, to the Secretary of State at the Home Office.

(5) Such an application as is mentioned in Regulation 7 shall be made—

    (a) if the applicant is resident in a dependency mentioned in paragraph (7), to the Governor ;

    (b) in any other case, to the Secretary of State at the Home Office.

(6) Such an application as is mentioned in Regulation 8 shall be made—

    (a) if the applicant is resident in a dependency mentioned in paragraph (7), to the Governor ;

    (b) if the applicant has such a qualifying connection as is mentioned in section 1 of the Act of 1964 and is resident in a commonwealth country mentioned in paragraph (8), to the High Commissioner ;

    (c) in any other case, to the Secretary of State at the Home Office.

(7) The dependencies referred to in this Regulation are the Channel Islands, the Isle of Man, a colony, a protectorate and a protected state to which the provisions of section 8 of the Act of 1948 relating to protectorates are extended by Order in Council made under section 30 thereof.

(8) The commonwealth countries referred to in this Regulation are those countries mentioned in section 1(3) of the Act of 1948 in which there is a High Commissioner.

Place of registration

12.—(1) The registration of a person as a citizen of the United Kingdom and Colonies in pursuance of such an application as is mentioned in Regulation 4, 5, 6, 7, 8 or 9 or as a British subject in pursuance of such an application as is mentioned in Regulation 10 shall be effected at such place as the person to whom the application is made may direct.

(2) If a person is entitled to be registered as a citizen of the United Kingdom and Colonies or as a British subject in pursuance of such an application as aforesaid made to a person other than the Secretary of State and the Secretary of State is satisfied that it is impracticable for the registration to be effected at a place directed by the person to whom the application was made, the registration shall be effected at such place as the Secretary of State may direct.

PART III

NATURALISATION AND RESUMPTION OF CITIZENSHIP AND NATIONALITY

Application for naturalisation

13. An application for a certificate of naturalisation shall satisfy the requirements of Schedules 1 and 13.

Certificate of naturalisation

14.—(1) A certificate of naturalisation granted by the Secretary of State shall be in the form set out in Schedule 14 and shall be signed by an officer of the Home Department not below the rank of Assistant Secretary.

(2) A certificate of naturalisation granted by the Governor of any of the Channel Islands, the Isle of Man or a colony, protectorate or protected state shall be similar to a certificate granted by the Secretary of State and shall be signed by the Governor or by a person authorised by him in that behalf.

(3) Where in accordance with the provisions of section 10(2) of the Act of 1948 the Secretary of State has given his approval to the grant of a certificate of naturalisation by the Governor of a place mentioned in the last foregoing paragraph, the approval of the Secretary of State shall be signified by adding to the certificate a statement to that effect, which shall be signed by a person authorised by him in that behalf.

Oath of allegiance for purpose of naturalisation

15.—(1) The oath of allegiance required by section 10(1) of the Act of 1948 to be taken by a person to whom a certificate of naturalisation has been granted shall be subscribed and attested in the form set out in Schedule 7 in accordance with the requirements of paragraph 4 of Schedule 1 and as so subscribed and attested shall be endorsed on the certificate of naturalisation to which it relates.

(2) The oath of allegiance required as aforesaid shall be taken within one calendar month of the date of the certificate of naturalisation to which it relates, or within such extended time as the Secretary of State (in the case of any certificate) or the Governor of a place mentioned in paragraph (2) of the last foregoing Regulation (in the case of a certificate granted by the Governor of that place) may permit, and if the oath is not taken within the said time the certificate shall have no effect:

Provided that permission shall not be deemed to have been given under this paragraph unless a statement to that effect is endorsed on the certificate and signed by a person authorised by the last foregoing Regulation to sign a certificate of naturalisation.

(3) The oath of allegiance required as aforesaid shall be registered –

(a) if the certificate of naturalisation to which it relates is granted by the Secretary of State, at the Home Office ;

(b) in any other case, in such place as the Governor who grants the certificate may direct or, if no such direction is given, at the Home Office.

(4) Where the oath of allegiance is registered in accordance with the directions of the Governor under the last foregoing paragraph, he shall cause a copy of the oath and of the certificate of naturalisation to which it relates to be sent to the Home Office.

Declaration of intention to resume nationality made under section 16(2) of the Act of 1948

16. A declaration of intention to resume British nationality under section 16(2) of the Act of 1948 shall be made to the Secretary of State and satisfy the requirements of Schedules 1 and 15.

Declaration of intention to resume citizenship made under section 4(2) of the Cyprus Act 1960

17. A declaration of intention to resume citizenship of the United Kingdom and Colonies under section 4(2) of the Cyprus Act 1960 shall be made to the Secretary of State and satisfy the requirements of Schedules 1 and 16.

Place of registration of declaration of intention to resume nationality or citizenship

18. Such a declaration as is mentioned in Regulation 16 or 17 shall be registered at the Home Office.

Part IV

Renunciation and Deprivation of Citizenship and Nationality

Declaration of renunciation of citizenship

19.—(1) A declaration of renunciation of citizenship of the United Kingdom and Colonies under section 19(1) of the Act of 1948 shall satisfy the requirements of Schedules 1 and 17.

(2) Such a declaration as is mentioned in paragraph (1) shall be made—

(a) if the declarant is resident in a country mentioned in section 1(3) of the Act of 1948 in which there is a High Commissioner, to that High Commissioner ;

(b) in any other case, to the Secretary of State at the Home Office.

(3) Such a declaration as is mentioned in paragraph (1) shall, subject to the provisions of the said section 19(1), be registered at such place as the person to whom the declaration is made may direct.

Notice of proposed deprivation of citizenship or nationality

20.—(1) When it is proposed to make an order under section 20 of the Act of 1948 depriving a person of his citizenship of the United Kingdom and Colonies or under section 3 of the Act of 1965 depriving a person of the status of British subject by virtue of section 1 of that Act, the notice required by section 20(6) of the Act of 1948 to be given to that person may be given—

(a) in a case where that person's whereabouts are known, by causing the notice to be delivered to him personally or by sending it to him by post ;

(*b*) in a case where that person's whereabouts are not known, by sending it to his last known address.

(2) Where the Secretary of State has given notice as aforesaid and the person to whom it is given has the right, on making application therefor, to an inquiry under section 20(7) of the Act of 1948, the application shall be made—

(*a*) if that person is in the United Kingdom at the time when the notice is given to him, within twenty-one days from the giving of the notice ;

(*b*) in any other case, within such time, not being less than twenty-one days from the giving of the notice, as the Secretary of State may determine :

Provided that the Secretary of State may in special circumstances at any time extend the time within which the application may be made.

(3) Where the Governor of any of the Channel Islands, the Isle of Man or a colony, protectorate or protected state has given notice as aforesaid, the provisions of the last foregoing paragraph shall apply with the substitution for references to the Secretary of State of references to the Governor and the substitution for the reference to the United Kingdom of a reference to that island, colony, protectorate or state.

(4) Any notice given in accordance with the provisions of this Regulation shall, in a case in which the person to whom it is given has the right, on making application therefor, to an inquiry under section 20(7) of the Act of 1948, include a statement of the time within which such application must be made.

Cancellation of registration of person deprived of citizenship or nationality

21. Where an order has been made depriving a person who is a citizen of the United Kingdom and Colonies by registration of that citizenship or depriving a person who is a British subject by virtue of section 1 of the Act of 1965 of that status, the name of that person shall be removed from the register of citizens of the United Kingdom and Colonies or, as the case may be, from the register of British subjects by virtue of the said section 1.

Cancellation and amendment of certificate of naturalisation in case of deprivation of citizenship

22. Where an order has been made depriving a person naturalised in the United Kingdom and Colonies of his citizenship of the United Kingdom and Colonies, the person so deprived or any other person in possession of the relevant certificate of naturalisation shall, if required by notice in writing given by the Secretary of State or any Governor having power to deprive persons of that citizenship, deliver up the said certificate to such person, and within such time, as may be specified in the notice ; and the said certificate shall thereupon be cancelled or amended.

PART V

SUPPLEMENTAL

Authorised forms

23. Where the preceding provisions of these Regulations require that an application or declaration shall satisfy requirements set out in a Schedule, those requirements shall be treated as satisfied if the application or declaration is made in a form authorised by the Secretary of State or other authority to whom the application or declaration is made, if in the opinion of the Secretary of State or that other authority, as the case may be, the form so authorised is suitable in the circumstances of a particular case.

Certificate of citizenship in case of doubt

24. A certificate of citizenship in case of doubt given under section 25 of the Act of 1948 shall be signed by an officer of the Home Department not below the rank of Assistant Secretary.

Evidence

25. A document may be certified to be a true copy of a document for the purpose of section 27(2) of the Act of 1948 by means of a statement in writing to that effect signed by a person authorised by the Secretary of State, the High Commissioner or the Governor in that behalf.

Fees

26.—(1) Subject to the provisions of this Regulation, the fees specified in Schedule 18 may in the United Kingdom be taken and shall be applied in the manner set out in the said Schedule, and in any country mentioned in section 1(3) of the Act of 1948, the like fees (or fees of the corresponding amounts in the local currency) may be taken and shall be applied in the like manner as fees taken in the United Kingdom :

Provided that no fee shall be taken under this Regulation for witnessing the signing of an application or declaration or for administering the oath of allegiance, in a case where the application or declaration is witnessed, or the oath administered, by a justice of the peace.

(2) Of the fee payable in respect of the grant of a certificate of naturalisation, two pounds (if the applicant is a British protected person) and three pounds (if the applicant is an alien) shall be payable on the submission of the application for a certificate, and the balance shall be payable on the receipt of the decision to grant a certificate :

Provided that where a husband and wife apply at the same time for certificates and are residing together at the time of the applications and the balance is paid in respect of the grant of a certificate to one of them, no balance shall be payable in respect of the grant of a certificate to the other.

Application in relation to associated states

27.—(1) In relation to an associated state a reference in these Regulations to a colony shall be construed as if it included a reference to such a state but in relation to an associated state any reference to the Governor shall be construed as a reference to the Secretary of State or, where he has issued a relevant direction under paragraph 4 of Schedule 3 to the West Indies Act 1967, to the person, or the person for the time being holding the office, specified in the direction.

(2) In accordance with paragraph (1), by reason of the issue of such directions as aforesaid, any reference in these Regulations to the Governor shall be construed—

(*a*) in relation to the associated state of Antigua, of Dominica, of Saint Christopher, Nevis and Anguilla or of Saint Lucia, as a reference to the person holding the office of Secretary to the Cabinet ;

(*b*) in relation to the associated state of Grenada, as a reference to the person holding the office of Permanent Secretary to the Premier.

(3) Regulation 14(3) shall have effect as if the reference therein to section 10(2) of the Act of 1948 included a reference to paragraph 5 of Schedule 3 to the West Indies Act 1967.

James Callaghan,
One of Her Majesty's Principal
Secretaries of State.

21st May 1969.

We consent to Regulation 26 of these Regulations.

Walter Harrison,
E. Alan Fitch,
Two of the Lords Commissioners
of Her Majesty's Treasury.

27th May 1969.

Regulations 4 to 10,　　　　SCHEDULE 1
13, 15 to 17 and 19

GENERAL REQUIREMENTS AS RESPECTS APPLICATIONS, ETC.

1. An application or declaration shall be made in writing and shall state the name, address, age and date of birth of the applicant or declarant.

2. An application, other than such an application as is mentioned in Regulation 6, 7, 8, 9 or 13 shall state whether the applicant has ever renounced or been deprived of citizenship of the United Kingdom and Colonies.

3. An application or declaration shall contain a statutory declaration that the particulars stated therein are true.

4. An application or declaration shall be signed in the presence of, and an oath of allegiance shall be of no effect unless administered by, one of the following persons : —

　(a) in England, Wales or Northern Ireland—
　　　any justice of the peace, commissioner authorised to administer oaths in the Supreme Courts or notary public ;
　(b) in Scotland—
　　　any sheriff, sheriff-substitute, justice of the peace or notary public ;
　(c) in the Channel Islands, the Isle of Man or any colony, protectorate or protected state—
　　　any judge of any court of civil or criminal jurisdiction, any justice of the peace or magistrate, or any person for the time being authorised by the law of the place where the applicant, declarant or deponent is, to administer an oath for any judicial or other legal purpose ;
　(d) in any country mentioned in section 1(3) of the Act of 1948, in the Republic of Ireland or in any territory administered by the government of any such country—
　　　any person for the time being authorised by the law of the place where the applicant, declarant or deponent is, to administer an oath for any judicial or other legal purpose ;
　(e) elsewhere—
　　　any consular officer of Her Majesty's government in the United Kingdom or any person authorised by the Secretary of State in that behalf:

Provided that if the applicant, declarant or deponent is serving in Her Majesty's naval, military or air forces, the application or declaration may be signed in the presence of, or the oath administered by, any officer holding a commission in any of those forces, whether the application, declaration or oath is made or taken in the United Kingdom or elsewhere.

SCHEDULE 2   Regulation 4(2)

BRITISH NATIONALITY ACT 1948, SECTION 6(1)
COMMONWEALTH IMMIGRANTS ACT 1962, SECTION 12(2)

Application for registration as a citizen of the United Kingdom and Colonies made by a British subject or citizen of the Republic of Ireland on the ground of ordinary residence or Crown service.

1. The application shall contain sufficient information to satisfy the authority to whom it is made (hereinafter referred to as "the appropriate authority") that the applicant—

(a) is a British subject or a citizen of the Republic of Ireland ;

(b) is of full age and capacity ;

(c) has been, throughout the period of 5 years (or such shorter period as is specified in accordance with paragraph 2) ending with the date of the application—

(i) ordinarily resident in the United Kingdom or, as the case may be, in a dependency mentioned in Regulation 11(7) and specified in the application, or

(ii) in Crown service under Her Majesty's government in the United Kingdom, or

(iii) partly the one and partly the other.

2. If the applicant desires that a qualifying period shorter than 5 years should be accepted, the application shall specify the shorter period and the special circumstances which the applicant desires should be taken into consideration by the appropriate authority.

SCHEDULE 3   Regulation 4(2)

BRITISH NATIONALITY ACT 1948, SECTION 6(1)
BRITISH NATIONALITY ACT 1958, SECTION 3(2)
COMMONWEALTH IMMIGRANTS ACT 1962, SECTION 12(2)

Application for registration as a citizen of the United Kingdom and Colonies made by a British subject or citizen of the Republic of Ireland on the ground of service other than Crown service.

1. The application shall contain sufficient information to satisfy the authority to whom it is made (hereinafter referred to as "the appropriate authority") that the applicant—

(a) is a British subject or a citizen of the Republic of Ireland ;

(b) is of full age and capacity ;

(c) has been, throughout the period of 5 years (or such shorter period as is specified in accordance with paragraph 2) ending with the date of the application, serving—

(i) under an international organisation of which Her Majesty's government in the United Kingdom is a member ; or

(ii) in the employment of a society, company or body of persons established in the United Kingdom, or, as the case may be, in a dependency mentioned in Regulation 11(7) and specified in the application.

2. If the applicant desires that a qualifying period of service shorter than 5 years should be accepted, the application shall specify the shorter period and the special circumstances which the applicant desires should be taken into consideration by the appropriate authority.

3. The application shall state the nature of the applicant's connection with the United Kingdom and Colonies.

4. The application shall show where the applicant has been ordinarily resident throughout the period of 5 years ending with the date of the application, and shall state whether he has been in Crown service under Her Majesty's government in the United Kingdom during that period or any part of it.

Regulation 4(3)   SCHEDULE 4

BRITISH NATIONALITY ACT 1948, SECTION 6(1)
COMMONWEALTH IMMIGRANTS ACT 1962, SECTION 12(2)
SOUTH AFRICA ACT 1962, SECTION 1

Application for registration as a citizen of the United Kingdom and Colonies made by a citizen or former citizen of the Republic of South Africa on the ground of ordinary residence or Crown service.

1. The application shall contain sufficient information to satisfy the authority to whom it is made (hereinafter referred to as "the appropriate authority") that the applicant—

(a) is a citizen of the Republic of South Africa or has renounced or been deprived of that citizenship on the date specified in the application ;

(b) is of full age and capacity ;

(c) gave notice under paragraph 2 of Schedule 1 to the South Africa Act 1962 on the date specified in the application (being a date not later than 31st December 1965) of his intention to make application for registration as a citizen of the United Kingdom and Colonies ;

(d) has been throughout the period of 5 years (or such shorter period as is specified in accordance with paragraph 2) ending with the date of the application—

(i) ordinarily resident in the United Kingdom or, as the case may be, in a dependency mentioned in Regulation 11(7) and specified in the application ; or

(ii) in Crown service under Her Majesty's government in the United Kingdom ; or

(iii) partly the one and partly the other.

2. If the applicant desires that a qualifying period shorter than 5 years should be accepted, the application shall specify the shorter period and the special circumstances which the applicant desires should be taken into consideration by the appropriate authority.

Regulation 4(3)   SCHEDULE 5

BRITISH NATIONALITY ACT 1948, SECTION 6(1)
BRITISH NATIONALITY ACT 1958, SECTION 3(2)
COMMONWEALTH IMMIGRANTS ACT 1962, SECTION 12(2)
SOUTH AFRICA ACT 1962, SECTION 1

Application for registration as a citizen of the United Kingdom and Colonies made by a citizen or former citizen of the Republic of South Africa on the ground of service other than Crown service.

1. The application shall contain sufficient information to satisfy the authority to whom it is made (hereinafter referred to as "the appropriate authority") that the applicant—

(a) is a citizen of the Republic of South Africa or has renounced or been deprived of that citizenship on the date specified in the application ;

(b) is of full age and capacity ;

(c) gave notice under paragraph 2 of Schedule 1 to the South Africa Act 1962 on the date specified in the application (being a date not later than 31st December 1965) of his intention to make application for registration as a citizen of the United Kingdom and Colonies ;

(d) has been, throughout the period of 5 years (or such shorter period as is specified in accordance with paragraph 2) ending with the date of the application, serving—

(i) under an international organisation of which Her Majesty's government in the United Kingdom is a member ; or

(ii) in the employment of a society, company or body of persons established in the United Kingdom or, as the case may be, in a dependency mentioned in Regulation 11(7) and specified in the application.

2. If the applicant desires that a qualifying period of service shorter than 5 years should be accepted, the application shall specify the shorter period and the special circumstances which the applicant desires should be taken into consideration by the appropriate authority.

3. The application shall state the nature of the applicant's connection with the United Kingdom and Colonies.

4. The application shall show where the applicant has been ordinarily resident throughout the period of 5 years ending with the date of the application, and shall state whether he has been in Crown service under Her Majesty's government in the United Kingdom during that period or any part of it.

SCHEDULE 6　　　　　　Regulation 5(2)

BRITISH NATIONALITY ACT 1948, SECTION 6(2)

Application for registration as a citizen of the United Kingdom and Colonies made by a woman who has been married to a citizen of the United Kingdom and Colonies.

1. The application shall state whether the applicant is a British subject, a citizen of the Republic of Ireland, a British protected person, an alien who is a subject or citizen of a foreign country or a stateless alien.

2. The application shall contain sufficient information to satisfy the authority to whom it is made that the applicant—

(a) has been married to a citizen of the United Kingdom and Colonies, and

(b) is, where it is so stated, a British subject or citizen of the Republic of Ireland.

Regulations 5(2), 10(2)   SCHEDULE 7
       and 15(1)

BRITISH NATIONALITY ACT 1948, SECTION 6(2)
BRITISH NATIONALITY ACT 1948, SECTION 10
BRITISH NATIONALITY ACT 1965, SECTION 1

OATH OF ALLEGIANCE

I, A.B., swear by Almighty God that I will be faithful and bear true allegiance to Her Majesty Queen Elizabeth the Second, Her Heirs and Successors, according to law.

(Signed) A.B.

Sworn and subscribed this   day of   19   before me,

(Signed) X.Y.,

[Justice of the Peace, Commissioner, Notary Public or other official title.]

Regulation 6(2)   SCHEDULE 8

BRITISH NATIONALITY ACT 1948, SECTION 7(1)

Application for registration of a minor child of a citizen of the United Kingdom and Colonies as a citizen thereof.

1. The application shall contain sufficient information to satisfy the authority to whom it is made—
   (a) that the applicant is a parent or guardian of the child and, if he is a guardian, as to how he became such, and
   (b) that the child is a child of a citizen of the United Kingdom and Colonies.

2. The application shall state the reasons for which it is desired that the child should be registered as a citizen of the United Kingdom and Colonies.

Regulation 7(2)   SCHEDULE 9

BRITISH NATIONALITY ACT 1948, SECTION 12(6)
BRITISH NATIONALITY ACT 1958, SECTION 3(1)(b)(iii) AND (c)

Application for registration as a citizen of the United Kingdom and Colonies made by a former British subject.

1. The application shall contain sufficient information to satisfy the authority to whom it is made that the applicant—
   (a) was a British subject immediately before 1st January 1949 ;
   (b) was, on that date, a citizen or potentially a citizen of a country mentioned in section 1(3) of the Act of 1948, as originally enacted and, but for that citizenship or potential citizenship, would have become a citizen of the United Kingdom and Colonies by virtue of section 12(4) of that Act ;
   (c) having been on that date a citizen of such a country, or having subsequently been made one by the coming into operation of a law of that country, lost that citizenship otherwise than by his own act done for the purpose and thereby ceased to be a British subject ;
   (d) is of full age and capacity.

2. The application shall state the nature of the applicant's connection with the United Kingdom and Colonies.

3. If the application is intended to relate to any of the children of the applicant, it shall so state and the names, dates of birth and places of birth of the children in question shall be specified.

SCHEDULE 10   Regulation 8(2)

BRITISH NATIONALITY ACT 1964, SECTION 1

Application for registration as a citizen of the United Kingdom and Colonies made by a person who has ceased to be a citizen of the United Kingdom and Colonies as a result of a declaration of renunciation for the purpose of remaining or becoming a citizen of a country mentioned in section 1(3) *of the Act of* 1948.

1. The application shall contain sufficient information to satisfy the authority to whom it is made (hereinafter referred to as "the appropriate authority") that the applicant—

  (a) has ceased to be a citizen of the United Kingdom and Colonies as a result of a declaration of renunciation made under section 19 of the Act of 1948 ;

  (b) at the time of the declaration was, or was about to become, a citizen of a country mentioned in section 1(3) of the Act of 1948 ;

  (c) either could not have remained or become such a citizen but for the declaration or had reasonable cause to believe that he would be deprived of his citizenship of that country unless he made the declaration ;

  (d) unless he makes such a statement as is mentioned in paragraph 4, has a qualifying connection (as defined in paragraph 2) with the United Kingdom and Colonies or a protectorate or protected state specified in the application, or, if the applicant is a woman, that she has been married to a person who has, or would, if living, have, such a connection ;

  (e) is of full capacity.

2. For the purpose of paragraph 1(d) a person has a qualifying connection—

  (a) in relation to the United Kingdom and Colonies, if he, his father or his father's father—

    (i) was born in the United Kingdom or a colony ; or

    (ii) is or was a person naturalised in the United Kingdom and Colonies ; or

    (iii) was registered as a citizen of the United Kingdom and Colonies ; or

    (iv) became a British subject by reason of the annexation of any territory included in a colony ;

  (b) in relation to a protectorate or protected state, if—

    (i) he was born there ; or

    (ii) his father or his father's father was born there and is or at any time was a British subject.

3. Any reference in paragraph 1 or 2 to any country, or to countries or territories of any description, shall be construed as referring to that country or description as it exists at the date on which the application is made to the appropriate authority ; and paragraph 2(a) does not apply to any person by virtue of any certificate of naturalisation granted or registration effected by the Governor or Government of a country or territory outside the United Kingdom which is not at that date a colony, protectorate or protected state.

4. If the applicant does not have a qualifying connection as defined in paragraph 2 the application shall state the factors which the applicant wishes the appropriate authority to take into account in considering the application.

Regulation 9(2)   **SCHEDULE 11**

BRITISH NATIONALITY (NO. 2) ACT 1964, SECTION 1

Application for registration as a citizen of the United Kingdom and Colonies by certain stateless persons.

1. The application shall contain sufficient information to satisfy the authority to whom it is made that the person in respect of whom it is made is and always has been stateless and is qualified for registration under section 1 of the No. 2 Act of 1964.

2. In the case of an application in respect of a minor by his parent or guardian the application shall state whether the applicant is a parent or guardian of the minor, and if he is a guardian, how he became such.

Regulation 10(2)   **SCHEDULE 12**

BRITISH NATIONALITY ACT 1965, SECTION 1

Application for registration as a British subject made by an alien woman who has been married to a British subject.

1. The application shall contain sufficient information to satisfy the authority to whom it is made that the applicant—

    (*a*) is an alien, and

    (*b*) has been married to a person who at the date of the application is, or but for his death would be, a British subject without citizenship by virtue of section 13 or 16 of the Act of 1948 or a British subject by virtue of section 2(1) of the Act of 1948.

2. The application shall state whether the applicant has ever been deprived of the status of British subject.

Regulation 13   **SCHEDULE 13**

BRITISH NATIONALITY ACT 1948, SECTION 10
COMMONWEALTH IMMIGRANTS ACT 1962, SECTION 12(2)

Application for a certificate of naturalisation by an alien or British protected person.

1. The application shall show whether the applicant is a British protected person or an alien, and, if he is a British protected person, shall state the connection with a protectorate, protected state or other territory by virtue of which he is a British protected person.

2. The application shall contain sufficient evidence to satisfy the Secretary of State or the Governor, as the case may be, that the applicant is of full age and capacity and possesses the requisite qualifications for naturalisation in respect of residence, Crown service, good character, knowledge of the English or other appropriate language and intention with respect to his residence or occupation in the event of a certificate being granted to him, and such further information as the Secretary of State or the Governor may require in order to determine whether the applicant is a fit and proper person to be granted a certificate of naturalisation.

SCHEDULE 14   Regulation 14(1)

BRITISH NATIONALITY ACT 1948, SECTION 10

Certificate of Naturalisation

Whereas A.B., has applied to one of Her Majesty's Principal Secretaries of State for a certificate of naturalisation, alleging with respect to [himself] [herself] the particulars set out below, and has satisfied the Secretary of State that the conditions laid down in the British Nationality Act 1948 [and the Commonwealth Immigrants Act 1962] for the grant of a certificate of naturalisation are fulfilled:

Now, therefore, the Secretary of State, in exercise of the powers conferred upon him by the said Act of 1948, grants to the above named this certificate of naturalisation, and declares that upon taking the oath of allegiance within the time and in the manner required by the regulations made in that behalf [he] [she] is a citizen of the United Kingdom and Colonies as from the date of this certificate.

In witness whereof I have hereto subscribed my name this   day of 19 .

(Signed) C.D.

[Rank]

Home Office,
London.

Particulars relating to applicant

Full name ....

Address ....

Place and date of birth ....

Nationality ....

Single, married, etc. ....

SCHEDULE 15   Regulation 16

BRITISH NATIONALITY ACT 1948, SECTION 16(2)

Declaration of intention to resume British nationality made by a person who has ceased to be a British subject on the loss of British nationality by his father or mother.

1. The declaration shall contain sufficient information to satisfy the Secretary of State—

(a) that the declarant's father or mother, as the case may be, ceased to be a British subject and as to how they ceased to be such ;

(b) that the declarant thereby ceased to be a British subject by virtue of section 12(1) of the British Nationality and Status of Aliens Act 1914(a) ;

(c) that the declarant would, if he had not so ceased to be a British subject, at the time of the application be a citizen of the United Kingdom and Colonies or a British subject without citizenship under section 13 of the Act of 1948.

(a) 4 & 5 Geo. 5. c.17.

Regulation 17

SCHEDULE 16

Cyprus Act 1960, Section 4(2)

Declaration of intention to resume citizenship of the United Kingdom and Colonies.

1. The declaration shall contain sufficient information to satisfy the Secretary of State that the declarant—

   (a) was granted citizenship of the Republic of Cyprus in pursuance of an application made in accordance with section 4 or 5 of Annex D to the Treaty concerning the Establishment of the Republic of Cyprus before he attained the age of 16 years, and

   (b) immediately before being granted such citizenship was a citizen of the United Kingdom and Colonies.

Regulation 19(1)

SCHEDULE 17

British Nationality Act 1948, Section 19
British Nationality Act 1964, Section 2
Declaration of renunciation of citizenship

1. The declaration shall contain sufficient information to satisfy the authority to whom it is made that the declarant—

   (a) is a citizen of the United Kingdom and Colonies ;

   (b) is of full age and capacity ;

   (c) except where paragraph 2 applies, is a citizen or national of another country specified in the declaration.

2. If the declarant is not a citizen or national of another country the declaration shall state that to the best of his knowledge or belief he is about to become such a citizen or national, and shall state the reasons for that belief.

Regulation 26(1)

SCHEDULE 18

Table of Fees

Matter in which fee may be taken	Amount of fee	To whom fee is to be paid
	£ s. d.	
Registration of a woman who is a British protected person or an alien as a citizen under s.6(2) of the British Nationality Act 1948.	2 0 0	Into the Exchequer in accordance with Treasury directions.
Registration of a woman as a British subject under s.1 of the British Nationality Act 1965.	2 0 0	The same.
Registration of a minor who is a British protected person or an alien as a citizen under s.7 of the British Nationality Act 1948—		
Subject as hereinafter provided, where the minor is a British protected person ;	7 10 0	The same.
Subject as hereinafter provided, where the minor is an alien ;	15 0 0	

Matter in which fee may be taken	Amount of fee	To whom fee is to be paid
	£ s. d.	
If the application for the minor's registration was made at the same time as an application by one of his parents for a certificate of naturalisation;	2 0 0	The same.
If the application for the minor's registration was made at the same time as an application for the registration of another minor child of the same parent, except in the case of the first child registered in pursuance of those applications.	2 0 0	
Registration of a stateless person as a citizen under s.1 of the British Nationality (No. 2) Act 1964.	2 0 0	The same.
Grant of a certificate of naturalisation- To a British protected person; To an alien.	15 0 0 30 0 0	The same.
Grant of a certificate of citizenship in case of doubt.	15 0 0	The same.
Witnessing the signing of an application or declaration mentioned in paragraph 4 of Schedule 1 to these Regulations.	5 0	In England or Northern Ireland, if the application or declaration is witnessed, or the oath administered, by a commissioner or notary public to the commissioner or notary public.
Administering the oath of allegiance	5 0	In Scotland, if the application or declaration is witnessed, or the oath administered, by a sheriff or sheriff-substitute, to the sheriff clerk or to any of his deputes, and if by a notary public, to the notary public.
Registration of a declaration of intention to resume British nationality.	2 0 0	Into the Exchequer in accordance with Treasury directions.
Registration of a declaration of renunciation of citizenship other than a declaration made in the circumstances mentioned in s.1(1)(a) of the British Nationality Act 1964.	2 0 0	The same.
Supplying a certified true copy of any notice, certificate, order, declaration or entry given, granted or made by or under the British Nationality Act 1948.	10 0	The same.

For the purposes of this Schedule—

(a) any reference to a child and his parent includes a reference to a step-child and his step-parent, to an illegitimate child and his mother and to an adopted child and his adoptive parent, and

(b) where two or more children of the same parent are registered on the same occasion, the eldest of those children shall be treated as the first child registered on that occasion.

EXPLANATORY NOTE
(*This Note is not part of the Regulations.*)

These Regulations consolidate with amendments the British Nationality Regulations 1965 and the British Nationality (Amendment) Regulations 1968.

The principal changes are that the forms of applications and declarations under the British Nationality Acts are not prescribed ; instead the information which must be contained in applications or declarations to which the Regulations relate is specified. The form of an oath of allegiance and of a certificate of naturalisation, however, continue to be prescribed (in Schedules 7 and 14 respectively).

1969 No. 761

WAGES COUNCILS

The Wages Regulation (General Waste Materials Reclamation) Order 1969

Made - - - -	*28th May* 1969
Coming into Operation	*2nd July* 1969

Whereas the Secretary of State has received from the General Waste Materials Reclamation Wages Council (Great Britain) the wages regulation proposals set out in the Schedule hereto;

Now, therefore, the Secretary of State in exercise of her powers under section 11 of the Wages Councils Act 1959(a), and of all other powers enabling her in that behalf, hereby makes the following Order:—

1. This Order may be cited as the Wages Regulation (General Waste Materials Reclamation) Order 1969.

2.—(1) In this Order the expression "the specified date" means the 2nd July 1969, provided that where, as respects any worker who is paid wages at intervals not exceeding seven days, that date does not correspond with the beginning of the period for which the wages are paid, the expression "the specified date" means, as respects that worker, the beginning of the next such period following that date.

(2) The Interpretation Act 1889(b) shall apply to the interpretation of this Order as it applies to the interpretation of an Act of Parliament and as if this Order and the Order hereby revoked were Acts of Parliament.

3. The wages regulation proposals set out in the Schedule hereto shall have effect as from the specified date and as from that date the Wages Regulation (General Waste Materials Reclamation) Order 1968(c) shall cease to have effect.

Signed by order of the Secretary of State.
28th May 1969.

C. F. Heron,
Deputy Under Secretary of State,
Department of Employment and Productivity.

(a) 1959 c. 69.   (b) 1889 c. 63.
(c) S.I. 1968/8 (1968 I, p. 8).

ARRANGEMENT OF SCHEDULE

Part   Paragraphs
   I.   General   1
  II.   Male workers: general minimum time rates   2
 III.   Female workers: general minimum time rates, piece work basis
        time rates, guaranteed time rate and determination of age rates   3–9
  IV.   Overtime and waiting time   10–12
   V.   Applicability of statutory minimum remuneration   13

Article 3

SCHEDULE

The following minimum remuneration shall be substituted for the statutory minimum remuneration fixed by the Wages Regulation (General Waste Materials Reclamation) Order 1968 (Order D.B. (68)).

STATUTORY MINIMUM REMUNERATION
PART I—GENERAL

1. The minimum remuneration payable to a worker to whom this Schedule applies for all work except work to which a minimum overtime rate applies under Part IV is:—

(1) in the case of a time worker, the general minimum time rate payable to the worker under Part II or Part III of this Schedule;

(2) in the case of a male worker employed on piece work, piece rates each of which would yield, in the circumstances of the case, to an ordinary worker at least the same amount of money as the general minimum time rate which would be payable to the worker under Part II of this Schedule if he were a time worker;

(3) in the case of a female worker employed on piece work, piece rates each of which would yield, in the circumstances of the case, to an ordinary worker at least the same amount of money as the piece work basis time rate applicable to the worker under Part III of this Schedule:

Provided that, where a guaranteed time rate is applicable to a female worker under paragraph 8 and the remuneration calculated on a time work basis at that rate exceeds the remuneration calculated under sub-paragraph (3) of this paragraph on the basis of the said piece rates, the worker shall be paid not less than that guaranteed time rate.

PART II
MALE WORKERS
GENERAL MINIMUM TIME RATES

2. The general minimum time rates payable to male workers employed in any section of the trade are:—

			Per hour
			s. d.
Aged	under 16 years ...	... ...	1 9
„	16 and under 17 years	... ...	2 5
„	17 „ „ 18 „ ...	... ...	2 10
„	18 „ „ 19 „ ...	... ...	3 8
„	19 „ „ 20 „ ...	... ...	4 4
„	20 „ „ 21 „ ...	... ...	5 0
„	21 years or over	... ...	5 2

PART III
FEMALE WORKERS
GENERAL MINIMUM TIME RATES

3. Subject to the provisions of paragraphs 4 and 9, the general minimum time rates payable to female workers employed—

  (1) wholly or mainly on one or more of the operations of the sorting or grading of either woollen rags or woollen and worsted waste materials, or of both such rags and materials, to shade or quality or to both shade and quality, or

  (2) in receiving, stripping, packing, compressing, teagling, craning, despatching or warehousing, when carried on in, or in association with, or in conjunction with, any establishment or department in which the sorting or grading of either woollen rags or woollen and worsted waste materials, or of both such rags and materials, to shade or quality or to both shade and quality, constitutes the sole or main work of the establishment or department,

are as follows:—

	Per hour	
	s.	d.
Aged under 16 years	2	0
„ 16 and under 16½ years	2	8
„ 16½ „ 17 „	3	4
„ 17 „ 17½ „	3	6
„ 17½ „ 18 „	4	1
„ 18 years or over	4	3

4. Notwithstanding the provisions of paragraph 3, where a worker is employed for the first time after reaching the age of 18 years on any work therein mentioned and her employer causes her to be well and sufficiently instructed in the sorting and grading of woollen rags or woollen and worsted waste materials or of both such rags and materials, to shade or quality or to both shade and quality, the general minimum time rate payable during the periods following shall be:—

	Per hour	
	s.	d.
(1) during the first three months of such employment	4	0
(2) during the second three months of such employment	4	1

5. Subject to the provisions of paragraphs 6 and 9, the general minimum time rates payable to female workers other than the workers specified in paragraph 3 or 4 are as follows:—

	Per hour	
	s.	d.
Aged under 16 years	1	11
„ 16 and under 16½ years	2	6
„ 16½ „ 17 „	3	2
„ 17 „ 17½ „,...	3	3
„ 17½ „ 18 „	3	11
„ 18 years or over	4	1

6. Notwithstanding the provisions of paragraph 5, where a worker is employed for the first time after reaching the age of 18 years and her employer causes her to be well and sufficiently instructed in the sorting and grading of waste paper, rags, and paper-making materials, or of paper-making materials, the general minimum time rate payable during the periods following shall be:—

	Per hour	
	s.	d.
during the first six months of such employment	3	11

PIECE WORK BASIS TIME RATES

7. The following piece work basis time rates are applicable to female workers employed on piece work:—

		Per hour
		s. d.
(1) the workers specified in paragraph 3 or 4		4 4
(2) all other workers		4 2

GUARANTEED TIME RATE

8. The guaranteed time rate applicable to a female worker specified in paragraph 4 or 6 when employed on piece work during the period of six months therein mentioned is a rate equal to the general minimum time rate which would be payable to her if she were employed on time work.

DETERMINATION OF AGE RATES

9. The general minimum time rate payable under paragraph 3 or 5 to a female worker aged under 18 years shall be determined (1) during the period 1st January to 30th June in any year by reference to her age or prospective age on 31st March in that year; and (2) during the period 1st July to 31st December in any year by reference to her age or prospective age on 30th September in that year:

Provided that the rate for a female worker aged 17½ and under 18 years having become payable under the provisions of this paragraph shall continue to be payable only until her 18th birthday.

PART IV
OVERTIME AND WAITING TIME
MINIMUM OVERTIME RATES

10. Minimum overtime rates are payable to a worker to whom this Schedule applies as follows:—

(1) On any day other than a Saturday, Sunday or customary holiday—

    (a) for the first 2 hours worked in excess of 7¼ hours on a Monday, Tuesday, Wednesday or Thursday, or in excess of 7¼ hours on a Friday ... ... time-and-a-quarter

    (b) thereafter ... ... time-and-a-half

    Provided that where it is, or may become, the established practice of the employer to require the worker's attendance only on Monday, Tuesday, Wednesday, Thursday and Friday in the week, the foregoing minimum overtime rates of time-and-a-quarter and time-and-a-half shall be payable—

        (i) after 8¼ and 10¼ hours' work respectively on a Monday, Tuesday, Wednesday or Thursday;

        (ii) after 8 and 10 hours' work respectively on a Friday.

(2) On a Saturday, not being a customary holiday—

    (a) for the first 2 hours worked in excess of 3¾ hours time-and-a-quarter

    (b) thereafter ... ... time-and-a-half

(3) On a Sunday or a customary holiday, for all time worked ... ... double time

(4) In any week, for all time worked in excess of 41 hours, exclusive of any time for which a minimum overtime rate is payable under the foregoing provisions of this paragraph ... ... time-and-a-quarter

11. In this Part of this Schedule—

(1) the expression "customary holiday" means—

    (*a*)   (i) In England and Wales—

Christmas Day (or, if Christmas Day falls on a Sunday, such other week day as may be appointed by national proclamation, or, if none is so appointed, the next following Tuesday), Boxing Day, Good Friday, Easter Monday, Whit Monday and August Bank Holiday, and any day proclaimed to be a national holiday;

        (ii) In Scotland—

New Year's Day (or, if New Year's Day falls on a Sunday, the following Monday);

the local Spring holiday;

the local Autumn holiday; and

three other days (being days on which the worker normally works) in the course of a calendar year, to be fixed by the employer and notified to the worker not less than three weeks before the holiday, and any day proclaimed to be a national holiday;

or (*b*) in the case of each of the said days (other than a day fixed by the employer in Scotland and notified to the worker as aforesaid) a day substituted by the employer therefor, being either a day recognised by local custom as a day of holiday in substitution for the said day, or a day agreed between the employer and the worker or his representative.

(2) the expressions "time-and-a-quarter", "time-and-a-half" and "double time" mean respectively:—

    (*a*) in the case of a time worker, one and a quarter times, one and a half times and twice the general minimum time rate otherwise applicable to the worker;

    (*b*) in the case of a female worker employed on piece work:—

        (i) a time rate equal respectively to one quarter, one half and the whole of the piece work basis time rate otherwise applicable to the worker, and, in addition thereto,

        (ii) the minimum remuneration otherwise applicable to the worker under paragraph 1(3);

    (*c*) in the case of a male worker employed on piece work:—

        (i) a time rate equal respectively to one quarter, one half and the whole of the general minimum time rate which would be applicable to the worker if he were a time worker and a minimum overtime rate did not apply, and, in addition thereto,

        (ii) the minimum remuneration otherwise applicable to the worker under paragraph 1(2).

WAITING TIME

12.—(1) A worker is entitled to payment of the minimum remuneration specified in this Schedule for all time during which he is present on the premises of his employer, unless he is present thereon in any of the following circumstances:—

    (*a*) without the employer's consent, express or implied;

    (*b*) for some purpose unconnected with his work and other than that of waiting for work to be given to him to perform;

    (*c*) by reason only of the fact that he is resident thereon;

    (*d*) during normal meal times in a room or place in which no work is being done, and he is not waiting for work to be given to him to perform.

(2) The minimum remuneration payable under sub-paragraph (1) of this paragraph to a piece worker when not engaged on piece work is that which would be payable if he were a time worker.

PART V
APPLICABILITY OF STATUTORY MINIMUM REMUNERATION

13. This Schedule does not apply to male workers engaged in the loading or discharging of water-borne craft in any section of the trade, but, save as aforesaid, this Schedule applies to workers in relation to whom the General Waste Materials Reclamation Wages Council (Great Britain) operates, that is to say, workers employed in Great Britain in the Waste Materials Reclamation Trade (General Waste Branch) specified in the Schedule to the Trade Boards (Waste Materials Reclamation Trade, Great Britain) (General Waste Branch) (Constitution and Proceedings) Regulations 1933(a), which Schedule reads as follows:—

"1. For the purposes of this Schedule:—

The expression 'reclamation' means all operations (including the operations of willowing and garnetting) performed on any waste material or waste article.

The expression 'general waste materials establishment' means an establishment in which the operations specified in paragraph 2(a) hereof and operations connected therewith constitute the principal business carried on.

The expression 'establishment' means any establishment or any branch or department of an establishment.

2. Subject to the provisions of this Schedule the General Waste Branch of the Waste Materials Reclamation trade consists of the following operations:—

(a) reclamation wherever performed of any of the following waste materials or waste articles, that is to say:—rags, waste paper and paper salvage (including paper damaged by fire, newspaper reel-ends, damaged paper reels, outer wrappers of reels and news off-cuts), paper stock, woollen, worsted, flax, or other textile waste (not being jute or cotton waste), textile clippings or cuttings, used bags, used sacks, used sackings, or used tares, scrap rubber, scrap iron or other scrap metals (other than unbroken heavy machinery or plant), fur cuttings, rabbit skins, bones and fat, used tins, used bottles or jars, old ropes or string and broken glass or earthenware;

(b) reclamation of any other waste material or article where performed in or in connection with a general waste materials establishment;

(c) making (whether from new or waste material) or repairing sacks or bags in a general waste materials establishment except where the bags are made or repaired:—

(i) otherwise than for use in the establishment, and

(ii) in an establishment wholly or mainly engaged in the making or repairing of sacks or bags;

and operations connected therewith.

3. Notwithstanding anything in this Schedule the following operations are not operations in the General Waste branch of the Waste Materials Reclamation trade:—

(a) reclamation of any waste material or waste article in an establishment (other than a general waste materials establishment) in which that material or article is produced or is used as material for manufacture or as a container or wrapper for other articles manufactured in the establishment; and operations connected therewith;

(b) reclamation of any waste material or waste article produced in the business of breaking up ships or breaking up or dismantling buildings or machinery or tramway or railway installations or heavy plant when performed in the course of such business; and operations connected therewith;

(c) reclamation of scrap rubber in an establishment in which the scrap rubber is broken down or devulcanised; and operations connected therewith;

(d) reclamation of rabbit skins where performed in an establishment in which such reclamation constitutes the principal business carried on or in connection with an establishment in which the principal business carried on is the manufacture of hatters' fur; and operations connected therewith;

(a) S.R. & O. 1933/833 (Rev. XXIII, p. 497: 1933, p. 2056).

(e) reclamation of bottles or jars preliminary to their use in the same establishment as containers, or when such bottles or jars are the property of a trader and are used by him for the purpose of delivering the contents to a customer and are recovered when empty from the customer by or on behalf of the trader; and operations connected therewith;

(ƒ) reclamation of jute textile cuttings and clippings where carried on in an establishment mainly engaged in operations included in the Trade Boards (Jute) Order, 1919(a), or any amendment thereof;

(g) production of shoddy or mungo or woollen flock or any operations performed in an establishment in which the production of shoddy or mungo or woollen flock is the principal business carried on;

(h) de-tinning of metal or refining of old gold or silver;

(i) repairing or overhauling machinery or plant;

(j) collecting, transporting, packing, warehousing or despatching, when performed by workers in the direct employment of an employer who is not otherwise engaged in the Waste Materials Reclamation trade;

(k) cleaning or washing when performed in an establishment where the cleaning or washing is mainly of articles other than those specified in paragraph 2 hereof;

(l) cleaning of premises by charwomen;

(m) caretaking;

(n) clerical work;

(o) operations performed in or in connection with a cotton waste establishment as defined in the Schedule to the Trade Boards (Waste Materials Reclamation Trade, Great Britain) (Cotton Waste Branch) (Constitution and Proceedings) Regulations, 1929(b)."

EXPLANATORY NOTE

(This Note is not part of the Order.)

This Order, which has effect from 2nd July 1969, sets out the statutory minimum remuneration payable in substitution for that fixed by the Wages Regulation (General Waste Materials Reclamation) Order 1968 (Order D.B. (68)) which Order is revoked.

New provisions are printed in italics.

(a) S.R. & O. 1919/859 (1919 II, p. 517).   (b) S.R. & O. 1929/3 (1929, p. 1378).

STATUTORY INSTRUMENTS

1969 No. 762

WAGES COUNCILS

The Wages Regulation (General Waste Materials Reclamation) (Holidays) Order 1969

Made - - - -	*28th May* 1969
Coming into Operation	*2nd July* 1969

Whereas the Secretary of State has received from the General Waste Materials Reclamation Wages Council (Great Britain) the wages regulation proposals set out in the Schedule hereto:

Now, therefore, the Secretary of State in exercise of her powers under section 11 of the Wages Councils Act 1959(a), and of all other powers enabling her in that behalf, hereby makes the following Order:—

1. This Order may be cited as the Wages Regulation (General Waste Materials Reclamation) (Holidays) Order 1969.

2.—(1) In this Order the expression "the specified date" means the 2nd July 1969, provided that where, as respects any worker who is paid wages at intervals not exceeding seven days, that date does not correspond with the beginning of the period for which the wages are paid, the expression "the specified date" means, as respects that worker, the beginning of the next such period following that date.

(2) The Interpretation Act 1889(b) shall apply to the interpretation of this Order as it applies to the interpretation of an Act of Parliament and as if this Order and the Order hereby revoked were Acts of Parliament.

3. The wages regulation proposals set out in the Schedule hereto shall have effect as from the specified date and as from that date the Wages Regulation (General Waste Materials Reclamation) (Holidays) Order 1963(c), shall cease to have effect.

Signed by order of the Secretary of State.
28th May 1969.

C. F. Heron,
Deputy Under Secretary of State,
Department of Employment and Productivity.

(a) 1959 c. 69.　　　　(b) 1889 c. 63.
(c) S.I. 1963/1658 (1963 III, p. 3171).

SCHEDULE Article 3

The following provisions as to holidays and holiday remuneration shall be substituted for the provisions as to holidays and holiday remuneration set out in the Wages Regulation (General Waste Materials Reclamation) (Holidays) Order 1963, (Order D.B. (62)).

Part I
APPLICATION

1. This Schedule applies to every worker for whom statutory minimum remuneration has been fixed.

Part II
CUSTOMARY HOLIDAYS

2.—(1) An employer shall allow to every worker to whom this Schedule applies a holiday (hereinafter referred to as a "customary holiday") in each year on the days specified in the following sub-paragraph provided that the worker has been in his employment for a period of not less than four weeks immediately preceding the customary holiday and (unless excused by the employer or absent by reason of the proved illness of, or accident to, the worker) has worked for the employer throughout the last working day on which work was available to him immediately preceding the customary holiday.

(2) The said customary holidays are:—

(a) (i) In England and Wales—

Christmas Day (or, if Christmas Day falls on a Sunday, such week day as may be appointed by national proclamation, or, if none is so appointed, the next following Tuesday), Boxing Day, Good Friday, Easter Monday, Whit Monday and August Bank Holiday;

(ii) In Scotland—

New Year's Day (or, if New Year's Day falls on a Sunday, the following Monday);

the local Spring holiday;

the local Autumn holiday; and

three other days (being days on which the worker normally works for the employer) in the course of a calendar year to be fixed by the employer and notified to the worker not less than three weeks before the holiday;

or (b) in the case of each of the said days (other than a day fixed by the employer in Scotland and notified to the worker as aforesaid) a day substituted by the employer therefor, being a day recognised by local custom as a day of holiday in substitution for the said day, or a day substituted therefor by mutual agreement between the employer and the worker or his representative.

Part III
ANNUAL HOLIDAY

3.—(1) Subject to the provisions of paragraph 4, in addition to the holidays specified in Part II of this Schedule an employer shall, between the date on which this Schedule becomes effective, and 30th September 1969, and between 1st May and 30th September in each succeeding year allow a holiday (hereinafter referred to as an "annual holiday") to every worker in his employment to whom this Schedule applies who has been employed by him during the 12 months immediately preceding the commencement of the holiday season for any of the periods of employment (calculated in accordance with the provisions of paragraph 10) set out in the Table below and the duration of the annual holiday shall in the case of each such worker be related to his period of employment during that 12 months as follows:—

Workers with a normal working week of six days		Workers with a normal working week of five days or less	
Period of employment	Duration of annual holiday	Period of employment	Duration of annual holiday
At least 48 weeks	15 days	At least 48 weeks	13 days
„ „ 44 „	11 „	„ „ 43 „	9 „
„ „ 40 „	10 „	„ „ 38 „	8 „
„ „ 36 „	9 „	„ „ 33 „	7 „
„ „ 32 „	8 „	„ „ 28 „	6 „
„ „ 28 „	7 „	„ „ 24 „	5 „
„ „ 24 „	6 „	„ „ 19 „	4 „
„ „ 20 „	5 „	„ „ 14 „	3 „
„ „ 16 „	4 „	„ „ 9 „	2 „
„ „ 12 „	3 „	„ „ 4 „	1 day
„ „ 8 „	2 „		
„ „ 4 „	1 day		

(2) Notwithstanding the provisions of the last foregoing sub-paragraph, the number of days of annual holiday which an employer is required to allow to a worker in any holiday season shall not exceed twice the number of days constituting the worker's normal working week, *plus three days.*

(3) The duration of the worker's annual holiday during the holiday season ending on 30th September 1969, shall be reduced by any days of annual holiday duly allowed to him by the employer under the provisions of Order D.B. (62) between 1st May 1969 and the date on which the provisions of this Schedule become effective.

(4) In this Schedule the expression "holiday season" means in relation to the year 1969 the period commencing on 1st May 1969 and ending on 30th September 1969 and, in each succeeding year, the period commencing on 1st May and ending on 30th September of the same year.

4.—(1) Subject to the provisions of this paragraph, an annual holiday shall be allowed on consecutive working days, being days on which the worker is normally called upon to work for the employer.

(2) (a) Where the number of days of annual holiday for which a worker has qualified exceeds the number of days constituting his normal working week, *but does not exceed twice that number,* the holiday may be allowed in two periods of consecutive working days; so, however, that when a holiday is so allowed, one of the periods shall consist of a number of such days not less than the number of days constituting the worker's normal working week.

(b) *Where the number of days of annual holiday for which a worker has qualified exceeds twice the number of days constituting his normal working week the holiday may be allowed as follows:—*

(i) *as to two periods of consecutive working days, each such period not being less than the period constituting the worker's normal working week, during the holiday season; and*

(ii) *as to the additional days, on working days, to be fixed by agreement between the employer or his representative, and the worker or his representative, either during the holiday season or within the period ending on 30th April immediately following the holiday season.*

(3) For the purposes of this paragraph, days of annual holiday shall be treated as consecutive notwithstanding that a customary holiday or a day upon which the worker does not normally work for the employer intervenes.

(4) Where a customary holiday immediately precedes a period of annual holiday or occurs during such a period and the total number of days of annual holiday required to be allowed in the period under the foregoing provisions of this paragraph, together with any such customary holiday, exceeds the number of days constituting the worker's normal working week then, notwithstanding the foregoing provisions of this paragraph, the duration of that period of annual holiday may be reduced by one day and in such a case one day of annual holiday may be allowed on any working day (not being the worker's weekly short day) in the holiday season.

(5) Subject to the provisions of the foregoing sub-paragraphs of this paragraph, any day of annual holiday under this Schedule may be allowed on a day on which the worker is entitled to a day of holiday or to a half-holiday under any enactment other than the Wages Councils Act 1959.

5. An employer shall give to a worker reasonable notice of the commencing date or dates and duration of the period or periods of his annual holiday. Such notice may be given individually to the worker or by the posting of a notice in the place where the worker is employed.

PART IV

HOLIDAY REMUNERATION

A—CUSTOMARY HOLIDAYS

6.—(1) Subject to the provisions of this paragraph, for each day of customary holiday to which a worker is entitled under Part II of this Schedule he shall be paid by the employer holiday remuneration equal to the appropriate statutory minimum remuneration to which he would have been entitled as a time worker if the day had not been a day of holiday and he had been employed on work for which statutory minimum remuneration is payable for the time usually worked by him on that day of the week:

Provided, however, that payment of the said holiday remuneration is subject to the condition that the worker (unless excused by the employer or absent by reason of the proved illness of, or accident to, the worker) presents himself for employment at the usual starting hour on the first working day following the customary holiday *and works throughout the remainder of that day.*

(2) The holiday remuneration in respect of any customary holiday shall be paid by the employer to the worker on the pay day on which the wages for the week including the first working day following the customary holiday are paid.

B—ANNUAL HOLIDAY

7.—(1) Subject to the provisions of paragraph 8, a worker qualified to be allowed an annual holiday under this Schedule shall be paid by his employer in respect thereof, on the last pay day preceding such annual holiday, *one day's holiday pay* (*as defined in paragraph* 11) *in respect of each day of annual holiday.*

(2) Where under the provisions of paragraph 4 an annual holiday is allowed in more than one period, the holiday remuneration shall be apportioned accordingly.

8. Where any accrued holiday remuneration has been paid by the employer to the worker in accordance with paragraph 9 of this Schedule, or in accordance with the provisions of Order D.B. (62), in respect of employment during any of the periods referred to in that paragraph, or that Order respectively, the amount of holiday remuneration payable by the employer in respect of any annual holiday for which the worker has qualified by reason of employment during the said period shall be reduced by the amount of the said accrued holiday remuneration unless that remuneration has been deducted from a previous payment of holiday remuneration made under the provisions of this Schedule.

ACCRUED HOLIDAY REMUNERATION PAYABLE ON TERMINATION OF EMPLOYMENT

9. Where a worker ceases to be employed by an employer after the provisions of this Schedule become effective the employer shall, immediately on the termination of the employment, pay to the worker as accrued holiday remuneration:—

(1) in respect of employment in the 12 months up to and including the 30th April immediately preceding the date of termination, a sum equal to the holiday remuneration for any days of annual holiday for which he has qualified except days of annual holiday which he has been allowed or has become entitled to be allowed before leaving the employment; and

(2) in respect of any employment since the said 30th April, a sum equal to the holiday remuneration which would have been payable to him if he could have been allowed an annual holiday in respect of that employment at the time of leaving it:
Provided that—

(a) no worker shall be entitled to the payment by his employer of accrued holiday remuneration if he is dismissed on the grounds of misconduct and is so informed in writing by the employer at the time of dismissal;

(b) where a worker is employed under a contract of service under which not less than one week's notice on either side is required to terminate the employment and the worker without the consent of his employer terminates his employment—

(i) without having given not less than one week's notice, or

(ii) before one week has expired from the beginning of such notice,

the amount of accrued holiday remuneration payable to the worker shall be the amount payable under the foregoing provisions of this paragraph, less an amount equal to the holiday remuneration which would be payable to the worker for one day of annual holiday multiplied, in the case of (i) by the number of days constituting the worker's normal working week or, in the case of (ii), by the number of days which at the termination of the employment would complete a normal working week commencing at the beginning of the notice.

PART V

GENERAL

10. For the purposes of calculating any period of employment qualifying a worker for an annual holiday or for any accrued holiday remuneration under this Schedule, the worker shall be treated—

(1) as if he were employed for a week in respect of any week in which—

(a) he has worked for the employer for not less than 24 hours and has performed some work for which statutory minimum remuneration is payable; or

(b) he has been absent throughout the week by reason of the proved illness of, or accident to, the worker, or for a like reason has worked for the employer for less than 24 hours: provided that the number of weeks which may be treated as weeks of employment for such reasons shall not exceed six in the aggregate in the period of 12 months immediately preceding the commencement of the holiday season; or

(c) he has been suspended throughout the week owing to shortage of work: provided that the number of weeks which may be treated as weeks of employment for such reason shall not exceed four in the aggregate in the period of 12 months last mentioned; and

(2) as if he were employed on any day of holiday allowed under the provisions of this Schedule or of Order D.B. (62), and, for the purposes of the provisions of sub-paragraph (1) of this paragraph, a worker who is absent on such a

holiday shall be treated as having worked thereon the number of hours ordinarily worked by him for the employer on that day of the week on work for which statutory minimum remuneration is payable.

11. In this Schedule, unless the context otherwise requires, the following expressions have the meanings hereby respectively assigned to them, that is to say:—

"normal working week" means the number of days on which it has been usual for the worker to work in a week in the employment of the employer in the 12 months immediately preceding the commencement of the holiday season or, where under paragraph 9 accrued holiday remuneration is payable on the termination of the employment, during the 12 months immediately preceding the date of the termination of the employment:

Provided that—

(1) part of a day shall count as a day;

(2) no account shall be taken of any week in which the worker did not perform any work for which statutory minimum remuneration has been fixed.

"one day's holiday pay" means—

the appropriate proportion of the amount which the worker would be entitled to receive from his employer, at the beginning of the holiday or the first period of the holiday, as the case may be, for a week's work, if working his normal working week and the number of daily hours usually worked by him (exclusive of over-time), and if paid—

(a) in the case of a time worker, at the appropriate rate of statutory minimum remuneration for time work, for work to which that rate applies and at the same rate for work (if any) to which that rate does not apply;

(b) in the case of a piece worker, at the appropriate general minimum time rate that would have been applicable to him if he had been employed as a time worker.

In this definition 'appropriate proportion' means—

where the worker's normal working week is six days	*one-sixth*
" " " " " " " five days	
or less	*one-fifth.*

"statutory minimum remuneration" means minimum remuneration (other than holiday remuneration) fixed by a wages regulation order made by the Secretary of State to give effect to proposals submitted to her by the General Waste Materials Reclamation Wages Council (Great Britain).

"week" in paragraphs 3, 6 and 10 means "pay week".

12. The provisions of this Schedule are without prejudice to any agreement for the allowance of any further holidays with pay or for the payment of additional holiday remuneration.

EXPLANATORY NOTE

(This Note is not part of the Order.)

This Order, which has effect from 2nd July 1969, sets out the holidays which an employer is required to allow to workers and the remuneration payable for those holidays, in substitution for the holidays and holiday remuneration fixed by the Wages Regulation (General Waste Materials Reclamation) (Holidays) Order 1963 (Order D.B. (62)) which Order is revoked.

New provisions are printed in italics.

STATUTORY INSTRUMENTS

1969 No. 763 (L.10)

MATRIMONIAL CAUSES
SUPREME COURT OF JUDICATURE, ENGLAND
COUNTY COURTS

The Matrimonial Causes (Amendment) Rules 1969

Made - - -	*23rd May* 1969
Laid before Parliament	*9th June* 1969
Coming into Operation	*16th June* 1969

We, the authority having power to make rules of court for the purposes mentioned in section 7(1) of the Matrimonial Causes Act 1967**(a)**, hereby exercise that power as follows:—

1.—(1) These rules may be cited as the Matrimonial Causes (Amendment) Rules 1969 and shall come into operation on 16th June 1969.

(2) In these rules a rule referred to by number means the rule so numbered in the Matrimonial Causes Rules 1968**(b)** and "Appendix I" means Appendix I to those rules.

(3) The Interpretation Act 1889**(c)** shall apply for the interpretation of these rules as it applies for the interpretation of an Act of Parliament.

2. In rule 44(4) for the words "Lewes or Ryde" and "Brighton and Newport (Isle of Wight)" there shall be substituted the words "or Lewes" and "and Brighton" respectively.

3. In rule 115(1) after the word "provide" there shall be inserted the words "or the court otherwise directs".

4. In Appendix I after the word "Newcastle (A)" there shall be inserted the words "Newport (Isle of Wight)" and the word "Ryde" shall be deleted.

Gardiner, C.,
J. E. S. Simon,
John Latey, J.,
Ifor Lloyd,
Irvon Sunderland,
W. D. S. Caird,
J. L. Williams,
Alan de Piro,
Bryan Anns,
J. D. Clarke,
D. E. Morris.

Dated 23rd May 1969.

(a) 1967 c. 56.   **(b)** S.I. 1968/219 (1968 I, p. 665).   **(c)** 1889 c. 63.

EXPLANATORY NOTE
(This Note is not part of the Rules.)

These rules substitute Newport (Isle of Wight) for Ryde in the list of divorce towns at which matrimonial causes pending in the High Court may be tried, and enable the court to direct that an application for hearing by the judge may be heard otherwise than at a place specified in rule 115 of the Matrimonial Causes Rules 1968.

STATUTORY INSTRUMENTS

1969 No. 767

HOUSING, ENGLAND AND WALES
HOUSING, SCOTLAND
The Assistance for House Purchase and Improvement (Qualifying Lenders) Order 1969

Made	-	-	-	*30th May* 1969
Coming into Operation				*2nd June* 1969

The Minister of Housing and Local Government and the Secretary of State for Scotland, acting jointly in exercise of their powers under sections 27 and 32(2) of the Housing Subsidies Act 1967(a), and after consultation with the Chief Registrar of Friendly Societies as required by section 27(2) of the said Act, hereby order as follows :

1. This order may be cited as the Assistance for House Purchase and Improvement (Qualifying Lenders) Order 1969 and shall come into operation on 2nd June 1969.

2. The Interpretation Act 1889(b) shall apply for the interpretation of this order as it applies for the interpretation of an Act of Parliament.

3. The building societies and friendly society whose names appear respectively in Part I and Part II of the Schedule to this order shall be qualifying lenders for the purposes of all the provisions of Part II of the Housing Subsidies Act 1967.

SCHEDULE
PART I
BUILDING SOCIETIES

The Lincoln Building Society
The Musselburgh Building Society

PART II
FRIENDLY SOCIETY
The Northampton Artisans and Labourers' Friend Society

Given under the official seal of the Minister of Housing and Local Government on 28th May 1969.

(L.S.)

A. Sylvester-Evans,
Under Secretary,
Ministry of Housing and Local Government.

(a) 1967 c. 29.　　　　　　(b) 1889 c. 63.

Given under the Seal of the Secretary of State for Scotland on 30th May 1969.

(L.S.)

                    R. A. Dingwall-Smith,
                       Under-Secretary.

Scottish Development Department,
St. Andrew's House,
Edinburgh 1.

EXPLANATORY NOTE

(This Note is not part of the Order.)

By this order, the Minister of Housing and Local Government and the Secretary of State for Scotland, after appropriate consultation, jointly prescribe further bodies as qualifying lenders for the purpose of operating the Option Mortgage Scheme. These are additional to the bodies already jointly prescribed by previous orders made by the Minister, the Secretary of State for Scotland and the Secretary of State for Wales, and the bodies prescribed by two previous orders made by the Minister ; they are also additional to all local authorities with powers to lend for house purchase and improvement, all building societies designated under section 1 of the House Purchase and Housing Act 1959 (c. 33) (i.e. those with "trustee" status), all development corporations, the Commission for the New Towns and the three Ministers themselves, all these being already designated as qualifying lenders by section 27(1) of the Housing Subsidies Act 1967 itself.

STATUTORY INSTRUMENTS

1969 No. 769

AGRICULTURE

AGRICULTURAL GRANTS, GOODS AND SERVICES

The Ploughing Grants Scheme 1969

Laid before Parliament in draft

Made - - - *30th May* 1969

The Minister of Agriculture, Fisheries and Food and the Secretary of State, acting jointly, in pursuance of sections 1, 2, 3 and 5 of the Agriculture (Ploughing Grants) Act 1952(a), as read with the Transfer of Functions (Wales) Order 1969(b), and all their other enabling powers, with the approval of the Treasury, hereby make the following scheme, a draft of which has been laid before Parliament and has been approved by resolution of each House of Parliament :—

1. This scheme, which may be cited as the Ploughing Grants Scheme 1969, shall apply to England and Wales and Northern Ireland.

2.—(1) In this scheme, unless the context otherwise requires, the following expressions have the meanings hereby respectively assigned to them :—

"the Act" means the Agriculture (Ploughing Grants) Act 1952 ;

"grass" includes clover, lucerne or sainfoin or mixtures of clover, lucerne or sainfoin with grass ;

"land under grass" includes any grazing land ;

"the appropriate Minister", in relation to land in England or Northern Ireland, means the Minister and, in relation to land in Wales, means the Minister and the Secretary of State, acting jointly ;

"the Minister" means the Minister of Agriculture, Fisheries and Food ;

"occupier" in Northern Ireland includes the person who, by virtue of an agreement, whether written or otherwise, has the right to the use of the land at the time of the completion of the operations referred to in this scheme.

(2) For the purposes of this scheme grass shall be regarded as a crop.

(3) The Interpretation Act 1889(c) applies to the interpretation of this scheme as it applies to the interpretation of an Act of Parliament.

(a) 1952 c. 35.   (b) S.I. 1969/388 (1969 I, p. 1070).

(c) 1889 c. 63.

3.—(1) Subject to the provisions of this scheme a grant may be made by the Minister in respect of the following operations—

(*a*) the ploughing up of land under grass ;

(*b*) after ploughing, the carrying out of such further operations on the land as may be required by the appropriate Minister and as are necessary, or form part of the operations necessary, to bring the land into a state of cleanliness, fertility, and fitness for cropping ; and

(*c*) the sowing on that land of a crop, unless the appropriate Minister otherwise determines.

(2) A grant shall not be made under this scheme in respect of any land unless before the commencement of any operations in respect of which such a grant may be made the appropriate Minister has approved those operations in relation to that land and is satisfied that the carrying out thereof on that land, together with any necessary preliminary operations, is likely to involve expenditure which is substantially heavier than normal for operations such as are specified in sub-paragraph (1) of this paragraph.

(3) Where operations in relation to any land have been approved for the purposes of the Ploughing Grants Scheme 1968(a), not being operations deemed to have been so approved by virtue of paragraph 3(3) of that scheme, and any part of the said land has not been ploughed up from grass before 1st June 1969, such operations shall be deemed to have been approved for the purposes of this scheme also.

(4) The person to whom such a grant may be made shall be the occupier of the land on completion of the operations in respect of which the grant is payable.

(5) A grant shall not be made under this scheme in respect of any land which has been the subject of a grant under Part II of any previous scheme made under the Act.

4. The rate of grant to be made in accordance with this scheme shall be £12 per acre :

Provided that in calculating the amount of a grant fractions of an acre less than one quarter of an acre shall be disregarded.

5. A grant under this scheme may only be made where the land ploughed up—

(*a*) is not less than one acre in area ;

(*b*) was ploughed up from grass within the period beginning with 1st June 1969 and ending with 31st May 1970 ; and

(*c*) at the time when such ploughing up was begun was under grass that had been sown not later than 1st June 1957, or had been continuously under grass since before that date.

6. The appropriate Minister may require an applicant for a grant under this scheme to give to any person authorised by the Minister in that behalf, or, in relation to land in Wales, by the Minister and the Secretary of State or either of them, adequate facilities for the inspection of any land to which the application relates.

(a) S.I. 1968/852 (1968 II, p. 2280).

7. Where in the opinion of the appropriate Minister—

(*a*) the ploughing or any other operation in respect of which a grant under this scheme may be made has been inefficiently carried out, or

(*b*) any preliminary operations the expenditure or likely expenditure on which has been taken into account by the appropriate Minister for the purpose of satisfying himself that a grant may be made under this scheme have not been carried out or have been inefficiently carried out, or

(*c*) adequate facilities for the inspection of the land in respect of which any such grant as aforesaid may be made have not been given ;

payment of the grant may be withheld or the amount of the grant may be reduced to such amount as the appropriate Minister considers reasonable.

8. If in respect of any of the operations in respect of which a grant is payable under this scheme payments of moneys provided by Parliament under any enactment other than the Act are available, the Minister in determining the amount of grant payable under this scheme may take into consideration such payments, and may withhold or reduce the amount payable under this scheme accordingly.

9. A grant shall not be made under this scheme in respect of any land which has been the subject of a grassland renovation grant made by virtue of a scheme under section 11 of the Agriculture (Miscellaneous Provisions) Act 1963(**a**).

In Witness whereof the Official Seal of the Minister of Agriculture, Fisheries and Food is hereunto affixed on 22nd May 1969.

(L.S.)
Cledwyn Hughes,

Minister of Agriculture,
Fisheries and Food.

Given under my hand on 22nd May 1969.

George Thomas,
Secretary of State for Wales.

Approved on 30th May 1969.

B. K. O'Malley,

E. Alan Fitch,

Two of the Lords Commissioners
of Her Majesty's Treasury.

(**a**) 1963 c. 11.

EXPLANATORY NOTE

(This Note is not part of the Scheme.)

This scheme, which is made under the Agriculture (Ploughing Grants) Act 1952, provides for the making of grants by the Minister of Agriculture, Fisheries and Food at the rate of £12 per acre in respect of land ploughed up from grass, where after ploughing the operations described in the scheme are carried out. The land must have been under grass since 1st June 1957 and the ploughing must be carried out within the period from 1st June 1969 to 31st May 1970.

Prior approval must be obtained from the appropriate Minister, and this will only be given where he is satisfied that the carrying out of the operations (together with any necessary preliminary operations) is likely to involve expenditure which is substantially heavier than normal for operations of the kind.

Where operations have been expressly approved for the purposes of the 1968 scheme, but any of the ploughing is carried out during the period to which this scheme applies, the approval is to be treated as though it were given for the purposes of this scheme also.

In other respects, except for the advancement of the dates by one year, the scheme is materially the same as the 1968 scheme. It is however made by the Minister and Secretary of State jointly, to take account of devolution to Wales, and there are some minor consequential drafting differences. The appropriate Minister is the Minister of Agriculture, Fisheries and Food in relation to land in England or Northern Ireland, and the Minister and the Secretary of State, acting jointly, in relation to land in Wales.

1969 No. 770

CUSTOMS AND EXCISE

The Anti-Dumping (Provisional Charge to Duty) Order 1969

Made - - - - -		*3rd June* 1969
Laid before the House of Commons		*5th June* 1969
Coming into Operation - -		*6th June* 1969

The Board of Trade, in pursuance of the powers conferred upon them by sections 1, 2, 8 and 9(3) of the Customs Duties (Dumping and Subsidies) Act 1969(a), hereby make the following Order:—

1. This Order may be cited as the Anti-Dumping (Provisional Charge to Duty) Order 1969 and shall come into operation on 6th June 1969.

2. Goods of the description set out in the Schedule hereto (being goods classified in accordance with the Customs Tariff 1959(b) under the heading mentioned in the first column of that Schedule) shall be subject to a provisional charge to duty in respect of a duty of customs at the rate set out in the third column of that Schedule.

3. Section 2 of the Customs Duties (Dumping and Subsidies) Act 1969 (relief where goods are shown not to have been dumped or where the margin of dumping is less than the provisional charge) shall apply in relation to the provisional charge imposed by this Order.

Edmund Dell,

Minister of State,
Board of Trade.

3rd June 1969.

(a) 1969 c. 16.   (b) See S.I. 1968/679 (1968 I, p. 1519).

SCHEDULE

Relevant Tariff Heading	Description of Goods	Relevant Rate
29.35 (G)	Morpholine originating in the Federal Republic of Germany	£23 per ton

EXPLANATORY NOTE

(This Note is not part of the Order.)

This Order makes imports of morpholine originating in the Federal Republic of Germany subject to a provisional charge in respect of an anti-dumping duty.

The making of the Order enables the Commissioners of Customs and Excise to require security for the payment of any anti-dumping duty which may be imposed retrospectively on such imports in accordance with section 8(1) of the Customs Duties (Dumping and Subsidies) Act 1969.

If any duty is imposed retrospectively, it may only be so imposed on goods imported while this Order is in force, and its rate may not exceed the rate mentioned in the Schedule to this Order.

This Order expires automatically after three months unless previously revoked or extended (for not more than three months) by a further Order.

The Order applies section 2 of the Customs Duties (Dumping and Subsidies) Act 1969 in relation to the charge. This section empowers the Board of Trade to grant relief where it is shown that a particular consignment of goods has not been dumped or that the margin of dumping is less than the amount of the provisional charge.

STATUTORY INSTRUMENTS

1969 No. 776

AGRICULTURE

AGRICULTURAL GRANTS, GOODS AND SERVICES

The Fertilisers (United Kingdom) Scheme 1969

Laid before Parliament in draft

Made - - - -	*3rd June* 1969
Coming into Operation	*3rd June* 1969

The Minister of Agriculture, Fisheries and Food, the Secretary of State for Wales and the Secretary of State for Scotland, acting jointly (being the appropriate Ministers as defined in section 6(2) of the Agriculture (Fertilisers) Act 1952(a) as read with Articles 3 and 5 of the Transfer of Functions (Wales) Order 1969(b) in relation to a joint scheme for England and Wales, Scotland and Northern Ireland) in exercise of their powers under sections 1 and 4 of the said Act and sections 4 and 5(1) of the Agriculture (Miscellaneous Provisions) Act 1963(c) (as read with the said Order) and of all other powers enabling them in that behalf, with the approval of the Treasury, hereby make the following scheme of which a draft has been laid before Parliament and has been approved by resolution of each House of Parliament:—

Citation and Application

1. This scheme, which may be cited as the Fertilisers (United Kingdom) Scheme 1969, shall apply to England and Wales, Scotland and Northern Ireland.

Interpretation

2.—(1) In this scheme, unless the context otherwise requires—

"agricultural land" means any land used as arable, meadow or pasture ground, or for the purpose of poultry farming, market gardens, nursery grounds, orchards or allotments, including allotment gardens within the meaning of the Allotments Act 1922(d) or the Allotments (Scotland) Act 1922(e);

"association" means an association of farmers, allotment holders, smallholders, or other occupiers of agricultural land, or an association of mushroom growers, being an association which is registered under the Industrial and Provident Societies Act 1965(f) or the Industrial and Provident Societies Acts (Northern Ireland) 1893 to 1963 or which has written rules governing its constitution and management;

(a) 1952 c. 15.	(b) S.I. 1969/388 (1969 I, p. 1070).
(c) 1963 c. 11.	(d) 1922 c. 51.
(e) 1922 c. 52.	(f) 1965 c. 12.

"delivered" means, where the fertiliser has been purchased by an occupier of agricultural land or a grower of mushrooms, delivered to or at his farm, holding or premises and, where the fertiliser has been purchased by an association, delivered to or at the premises of the association, and "delivery" shall be construed accordingly;

"the Minister" means, in relation to a contribution in respect of a fertiliser delivered in England, Wales or Northern Ireland, the Minister of Agriculture, Fisheries and Food and, in relation to a contribution in respect of a fertiliser delivered in Scotland, the Secretary of State for Scotland.

(2) The Interpretation Act 1889(a) shall apply to the interpretation of this scheme as it applies to the interpretation of an Act of Parliament.

Contributions for Fertilisers

3. Subject to the provisions of this scheme, where any fertiliser containing either nitrogen or phosphoric acid or both nitrogen and phosphoric acid (except where the nitrogen or phosphoric acid or both the nitrogen and phosphoric acid, as the case may be, is or are wholly derived from organic material), not being a fertiliser to which either aldrin or dieldrin has been added, is purchased for use for adding to agricultural land to improve the fertility of the soil or for the growing of mushrooms otherwise than on agricultural land or for application to a crop growing on agricultural land—

(*a*) by the occupier of that agricultural land,

(*b*) by the grower of such mushrooms, or

(*c*) by an association which acquires fertilisers in bulk for redistribution to its members for use for adding to agricultural land in their occupation or for application to crops growing thereon or for use by them for the growing of mushrooms otherwise than on agricultural land

and is delivered to the purchaser during the period beginning with 1st June 1969 and ending with 31st May 1970 the Minister may make a contribution to the purchaser calculated in accordance with the Schedule to this scheme:

Provided that no contribution may be made to any person or association in respect of a fertiliser which has been the subject of a previous application by such person or association for a contribution under this scheme or any earlier scheme made under section 1 of the Agriculture (Fertilisers) Act 1952, where the contribution was refused on the ground that such application was not made within the time allowed by such scheme.

Purchase from Registered Suppliers

4.—(1) Subject as hereinafter provided no contribution shall be made under this scheme in the case of a fertiliser delivered in Great Britain unless the fertiliser shall have been purchased from a person duly registered under section 5 of the Agriculture (Miscellaneous Provisions) Act 1963.

(2) The last foregoing sub-paragraph shall not apply—

(*a*) where the fertiliser is purchased from a person not carrying on within Great Britain the business of supplying fertilisers, or

(*b*) where the fertiliser is purchased from a person carrying on in Great Britain the business of supplying fertilisers who is not registered as mentioned in the said sub-paragraph and the Minister is satisfied that the

---

(a) 1889 c. 63.

purchaser at the time when the contract of sale was made did not know, and could not reasonably have ascertained, that such person was not so registered and that if the contribution were withheld the purchaser would be without any means of recovering his loss.

Manner and Time of Application for Contribution

5.—(1) Any person or association who desires to obtain a contribution in accordance with this scheme shall apply, where the fertiliser is delivered in England or Wales, to the Minister of Agriculture, Fisheries and Food, where the fertiliser is delivered in Scotland, to the Secretary of State and, where the fertiliser is delivered in Northern Ireland, to the Minister of Agriculture for Northern Ireland.

(2) An application for a contribution shall be made in writing, in such form as the Minister may from time to time require, within three months of delivery of the fertiliser, or within such further time as the Minister may in special circumstances allow.

Limitation of Contributions

6.—(1) In calculating the amount of any contribution any fraction of a quarter of a hundredweight of the fertiliser shall be disregarded.

(2) No contribution shall be made in connection with any application unless the total quantity of all the fertilisers to which the application relates is not less than 4 hundredweight.

(3) Where the amount of a contribution calculated at the appropriate rate specified in the Schedule to this scheme in respect of any fertiliser would exceed one half of the cost of the fertiliser when delivered to the purchaser (excluding any charge for credit or spreading and after deducting any rebate or discount allowed or offered), the amount of such contribution shall be reduced to one half of such cost.

(4) If any contribution is payable under any enactment other than the Agriculture (Fertilisers) Act 1952 as extended by section 4 of the Agriculture (Miscellaneous Provisions) Act 1963, or under any other scheme, in respect of fertilisers as regards which a contribution under this scheme may be made, the Minister in determining the amount of contribution payable under this scheme may take into consideration the amount of contribution payable under the other enactment or scheme and may reduce the amount payable under this scheme accordingly.

Verification of Applications

7. The Minister may require an applicant for a contribution to give any person authorised by the Minister in that behalf reasonable facilities for the inspection of any fertiliser to which the application relates, and to produce any accounts, invoices, receipts or other documents and to give all information required by the Minister for the purpose of verifying the application.

Repayment of Contributions

8. An applicant for a contribution shall be required to undertake to repay to the Minister any contribution which may be made in respect of any fertiliser which is not applied or used in accordance with the terms of his application relating thereto.

In Witness whereof the official seal of the Minister of Agriculture, Fisheries and Food is hereunto affixed on 22nd May, 1969.

(L.S.)

Cledwyn Hughes,
Minister of Agriculture, Fisheries and Food.

Given under my hand on 22th May 1969.

George Thomas,
Secretary of State for Wales.

Given under the seal of the Secretary of State for Scotland on 29th May 1969.

(L.S.)

William Ross,
Secretary of State for Scotland.

Approved on 3rd June 1969.

Joseph Harper,
Walter Harrison,
**Two of the Lords Commissioners of
Her Majesty's Treasury.**

SCHEDULE

RATES OF CONTRIBUTION FOR FERTILISERS

	Per ton
	£ s. d.
For each 1 % (and proportionately for each 0.1 %) by weight of nitrogen (N)	5 3
For each 1 % (and proportionately for each 0.1 %) by weight of water-soluble phosphoric acid (P_2O_5)	4 7½
For each 1 % (and proportionately for each 0.1 %) by weight of phosphoric acid (P_2O_5) insoluble in water other than phosphoric acid (P_2O_5) in basic slag or potassic basic slag	2 6

For basic slag or potassic basic slag delivered in Great Britain containing not less (by weight) than:—

					£	s.	d.
6% of phosphoric acid (P_2O_5)	...	...	...	...	1	5	6
7% of phosphoric acid (P_2O_5)	...	...	...	...	1	8	9
8% of phosphoric acid (P_2O_5)	...	...	...	...	1	11	6
9% of phosphoric acid (P_2O_5)	...	...	...	...	1	13	9
10% of phosphoric acid (P_2O_5)	...	...	...	...	1	16	0
11% of phosphoric acid (P_2O_5)	...	...	...	...	1	17	9
12% of phosphoric acid (P_2O_5)	...	...	...	...	1	19	0

and thereafter at rates increased by 3s. 3d. for every additional 1% of phosphoric acid (P_2O_5).

For each 1% by weight of phosphoric acid (P_2O_5) in basic slag or potassic basic slag containing not less than 6% by weight of phosphoric acid (P_2O_5) delivered in Northern Ireland 4 3

For the purposes of this Schedule

(a) "basic slag" means the article defined under that name in Schedule 4 to the Fertilisers and Feeding Stuffs Act 1926(a) as varied in Great Britain by the Fertilisers and Feeding Stuffs Regulations 1968(b) and in Northern Ireland by the Fertilisers and Feeding Stuffs Regulations (Northern Ireland) 1960(c).

(b) "potassic basic slag" means a mixture of basic slag with a potassium salt.

EXPLANATORY NOTE

(*This Note is not part of the Scheme.*)

This Scheme, made under the Agriculture (Fertilisers) Act 1952, as extended by the Agriculture (Miscellaneous Provisions) Act 1963, applies to the United Kingdom and provides for the payment of contributions towards the cost of fertilisers applied to agricultural land or crops thereon or used for the growing of mushrooms. It relates to nitrogenous and phosphatic fertilisers delivered during the year beginning on the 1st June 1969. This Scheme succeeds the Fertilisers (United Kingdom) Scheme 1967 (S.I. 1967/826) as extended by the Fertilisers (United Kingdom) (Extension of Delivery Period) Scheme 1968 (S.I. 1968/851).

(a) 1926 c. 45. (b) S.I. 1968 /218 (1968 I, p. 563).
(c) S.R. & O. (N.I.) 1960/145 p. 508.

STATUTORY INSTRUMENTS

1969 No. 778 (S.61)

AGRICULTURE

AGRICULTURAL GRANTS, GOODS AND SERVICES

The Ploughing Grants (Scotland) Scheme 1969

Laid before Parliament in draft

Made - - - *3rd June* 1969

In exercise of the powers conferred upon me by sections 1, 2, 3 and 5 of the Agriculture (Ploughing Grants) Act 1952(**a**), and of all other powers enabling me in that behalf, and with the approval of the Treasury, I hereby make the following scheme, a draft of which has been laid before Parliament and has been approved by resolution of each House of Parliament :—

1. This scheme may be cited as the Ploughing Grants (Scotland) Scheme 1969.

2.—(1) In this scheme, unless the context otherwise requires, the following expressions have the meanings hereby respectively assigned to them—

"the Act" means the Agriculture (Ploughing Grants) Act 1952 ;

"eligible occupier" means a person who is for the time being an eligible occupier within the meaning of the Crofting Counties Agricultural Grants (Scotland) Scheme 1965(**b**) and, except in the case of a person who is a sub-tenant as is mentioned in section 14(1)(*c*) of the Crofters (Scotland) Act 1961(**c**), who has been offered a grant under the Crofting Counties Agricultural Grants (Scotland) Scheme 1961(**d**), the Crofting Counties Agricultural Grants (Scotland) Scheme 1963(**e**) or the said Scheme of 1965 ;

"grass" includes rye grass and other rotational grasses, clover and permanent grass ;

"land under grass" includes any grazing land ;

"occupier" in relation to any land means the person who has the right to carry out on that land the operations referred to in this scheme.

(2) For the purposes of this scheme grass shall be regarded as a crop.

(3) Any reference in this scheme to any other scheme shall be construed as a reference to that scheme as amended by any subsequent scheme, and if any scheme referred to in this scheme is replaced by a subsequent scheme the reference shall be construed as a reference to that subsequent scheme.

(**a**) 1952 c. 35. (**b**) S.I. 1965/1519 (1965 II, p. 4399).
(**c**) 1961 c. 58. (**d**) S.I. 1961/2266 (1961 III, p. 3973).
(**e**) S.I. 1963/1294 (1963 II, p. 2240).

(4) The Interpretation Act 1889(a) applies for the interpretation of this scheme as it applies for the interpretation of an Act of Parliament.

3.—(1) Subject to the provisions of this scheme a grant may be made by the Secretary of State in respect of the following operations—

(a) the ploughing up of land under grass ;

(b) after ploughing, the carrying out of such further operations on the land as may be required by the Secretary of State and as are necessary, or form part of the operations necessary, to bring the land into a state of cleanliness, fertility, and fitness for cropping ; and

(c) the sowing on that land of a crop, unless in special circumstances the Secretary of State otherwise determines.

(2) A grant shall not be made under this scheme in respect of any land unless before the commencement of any operations in respect of which such a grant may be made the Secretary of State has approved those operations in relation to that land and is satisfied that the carrying out thereof on that land, together with any necessary preliminary operations, is likely to involve expenditure which is substantially heavier than normal for operations such as are specified in sub-paragraph (1) of this paragraph.

(3) Where the Secretary of State has approved operations in relation to any land for the purposes of the Ploughing Grants (Scotland) Scheme 1968(b), not being operations deemed to have been so approved by virtue of paragraph 3(3) of that scheme, and any part of the said land has not been ploughed up from grass before 1st June 1969, such operations shall be deemed to have been approved for the purposes of this scheme also.

(4) A grant shall not be made under this scheme in respect of any land which has been the subject of a grant under Part II of any previous scheme made under the Act.

4. The rate of grant to be made in accordance with this scheme shall be £12 per acre :
Provided that in calculating the amount of a grant fractions of an acre less than one-quarter of an acre shall be disregarded.

5. Subject to the provisions of paragraph 7 of this scheme a grant under this scheme may only be made where the land ploughed up—

(a) is not less than one acre in area ;

(b) was ploughed up from grass within the period beginning with 1st June 1969 and ending with 31st May 1970 ; and

(c) at the time when such ploughing up was begun was under grass that had been sown not later than 1st June 1957, or had been continuously under grass since before that date.

6. The person to whom a grant may be made under this scheme in pursuance of an application made in that behalf shall be the occupier of the land ploughed up as at the date of the completion, on that land, of the operations in respect of which the grant is payable :
Provided that where the occupier is a landholder within the meaning of the Small Landholders (Scotland) Acts 1886 to 1931(c) or a crofter within the

---

(a) 1889 c. 63.   (b) S.I. 1968/860 (1968 II, p. 2283).
(c) 1886 c. 29; 1887 c. 24; 1891 c. 41; 1908 c. 50; 1911 c. 49; 1919 c. 97; 1931 c. 44.

meaning of the Crofters (Scotland) Acts 1955 and 1961(a) or an eligible occupier to whom a grant may be made by virtue of the provisions of the next succeeding paragraph and an application for the grant is made on his behalf as provided by and in the manner specified in head (c) of that paragraph, the grant shall be made to the person making the application.

7. Where land is ploughed up by a landholder within the meaning of the Small Landholders (Scotland) Acts 1886 to 1931 or a crofter within the meaning of the Crofters (Scotland) Acts 1955 and 1961 or an eligible occupier then notwithstanding that the area of that land is less than one acre a grant may be made in respect thereof if—

(a) the area so ploughed up and any areas of land ploughed up by neighbouring landholders or neighbouring crofters or neighbouring eligible occupiers, as the case may be, together in the aggregate amount to or exceed one acre ;

(b) the provisions of this scheme are complied with in relation to all the areas so ploughed up, or in relation to such number of them as, in the aggregate, amount to or exceed one acre ; and

(c) an application for grant in respect of all those areas is made on behalf of those landholders or crofters or eligible occupiers, as the case may be, by the Clerk of the Committee appointed for the management of the common grazings or common pasture in which the landholders or crofters or eligible occupiers, as the case may be, all have shares, or, where there is no such Clerk, or, where they do not all have such shares, by a person who has been duly authorised by the landholders or crofters or eligible occupiers, in a manner satisfactory to the Secretary of State, to make the application.

8. The Secretary of State may require an applicant for a grant under this scheme to give to any person authorised by the Secretary of State in that behalf adequate facilities for the inspection of any land to which the application relates.

9. Where in the opinion of the Secretary of State—

(a) the ploughing or any other operation in respect of which a grant under this scheme may be made has been inefficiently carried out ; or

(b) any preliminary operations the expenditure or likely expenditure on which has been taken into account by the Secretary of State for the purpose of satisfying himself that a grant may be made under this scheme have not been carried out or have been inefficiently carried out ; or

(c) adequate facilities for the inspection of the land in respect of which any such grant as aforesaid may be made have not been given ;

payment of the grant may be withheld or the amount of the grant may be reduced to such amount as the Secretary of State considers reasonable.

10. If in respect of any of the operations in respect of which a grant is payable under this scheme payments of moneys provided by Parliament under any enactment other than the Act are available, the Secretary of State in determining the amount of grant payable under this scheme may take into consideration such payments, and may withhold or reduce the amount payable under this scheme accordingly.

(a) 3 & 4 Eliz. 2. c. 21; 1961 c. 58.

11. A grant shall not be made under this scheme in respect of any land which has been the subject of a grassland renovation grant made by virtue of a scheme under section 11 of the Agriculture (Miscellaneous Provisions) Act 1963(**a**).

William Ross,
One of Her Majesty's Principal
Secretaries of State.

St. Andrew's House,
   Edinburgh.
30th May 1969.
We approve.

Joseph Harper,
Walter Harrison,
Two of the Lords Commissioners
of Her Majesty's Treasury.

3rd June 1969.

EXPLANATORY NOTE
(This Note is not part of the Scheme.)

This Scheme, which is made under the Agriculture (Ploughing Grants) Act 1952, provides for the making of grants by the Secretary of State at the rate of £12 per acre in respect of land ploughed up from grass, where after ploughing the operations described in the Scheme are carried out. The land must have been under grass since 1st June 1957 and the ploughing must be carried out within the period from 1st June 1969 to 31st May 1970.

Prior approval must be obtained from the Secretary of State, and this will only be given where he is satisfied that the carrying out of the operations (together with any necessary preliminary operations) is likely to involve expenditure which is substantially heavier than normal for operations of the kind.

Where operations have been expressly approved for the purposes of the 1968 scheme, but any of the ploughing is carried out during the period to which this Scheme applies, the approval is to be treated as though it were given for the purposes of this Scheme also. In other respects, except for the advancement of the dates by one year, the Scheme is materially the same as the 1968 scheme.

(**a**) 1963 c. 11.

STATUTORY INSTRUMENTS

1969 No. 779

AGRICULTURE

The Price Stability of Imported Products (Rates of Levy No. 12) Order 1969

Made - - - - *4th June* 1969
Coming into Operation 5th June 1969

The Minister of Agriculture, Fisheries and Food, in exercise of the powers conferred upon him by section 1(2), (4), (5), (6) and (7) of the Agriculture and Horticulture Act 1964(a) and of all other powers enabling him in that behalf, hereby makes the following order:—

1. This order may be cited as the Price Stability of Imported Products (Rates of Levy No. 12) Order 1969; and shall come into operation on 5th June 1969.

2.—(1) In this order—

"the Principal Order" means the Price Stability of Imported Products (Levy Arrangements) Order 1966(b), as amended by any subsequent order and if any such order is replaced by any subsequent order the expression shall be construed as a reference to such subsequent order;

AND other expressions have the same meaning as in the Principal Order.

(2) The Interpretation Act 1889(c) shall apply to the interpretation of this order as it applies to the interpretation of an Act of Parliament and as if this order and the orders hereby revoked were Acts of Parliament.

3. In accordance with and subject to the provisions of Part II of the Principal Order (which provides for the charging of levies on imports of certain specified commodities)—

(*a*) the rate of general levy for such imports into the United Kingdom of any specified commodity as are described in column 2 of Part I of the Schedule to this order in relation to a tariff heading indicated in column 1 of that Part shall be the rate set forth in relation thereto in column 3 of that Part;

(*b*) the rate of country levy for such imports into the United Kingdom of any specified commodity as are described in column 2 of Part II of the Schedule to this order in relation to a tariff heading indicated in column 1 of that Part shall be the rate set forth in relation thereto in column 3 of that Part.

4. The Price Stability of Imported Products (Rates of Levy No. 10) Order 1969(d) and the Price Stability of Imported Products (Rates of Levy No. 11) Order 1969(e) are hereby revoked.

In Witness whereof the Official Seal of the Minister of Agriculture, Fisheries and Food is hereunto affixed on 4th June 1969.

(L.S.)

A. C. Sparks,
Authorised by the Minister.

(a) 1964 c. 28.   (b) S.I. 1966/936 (1966 II, p. 2271).   (c) 1889 c. 63.
(d) S.I. 1969/664 (1969 II, p. 1824).   (e) S.I. 1969/676 (1969 II, p. 1847).

SCHEDULE

PART I

1. Tariff Heading	2. Description of Imports	3. Rate of General Levy
	Imports of:—	per ton £ s. d.
10.01	Denatured wheat	10 0
10.01	Any wheat (other than seed wheat the value of which is not less than £34 per ton, denatured wheat and durum wheat) for which a minimum import price level is prescribed	5 0
10.03	Barley	1 10 0
11.02	Cereal meals— of barley .. .. of maize	7 5 0 10 0
11.02	Rolled, flaked, crushed or bruised cereals— barley	5 15 0

PART II

1. Tariff Heading	2. Description of Imports	3. Rate of Country Levy
	Imports of:—	per ton £ s. d.
10.01	Denatured wheat which has been grown in and consigned to the United Kingdom from— Belgium, the French Republic or the Kingdom of the Netherlands.. .. .. the Kingdom of Sweden	10 0 5 0
10.01	Any wheat (other than seed wheat the value of which is not less than £34 per ton, denatured wheat and durum wheat) for which a minimum import price level is prescribed and which is grown in and consigned to the United Kingdom from the French Republic or the Kingdom of the Netherlands ..	5 0
10.03	Barley which has been grown in and consigned to the United Kingdom from Canada	1 10 0

EXPLANATORY NOTE

(This Note is not part of the Order.)

This order, which comes into operation on 5th June 1969, re-enacts with amendments the Price Stability of Imported Products (Rates of Levy No. 10) Order 1969 and the Price Stability of Imported Products (Rates of Levy No. 11) Order 1969.

It:—

(*a*) increases to 10*s*. per ton the general levy on imports of denatured wheat;

(*b*) increases to 10*s*. per ton the country levy on imports of denatured wheat which has been grown in and consigned to the United Kingdom from Belgium, France or the Netherlands;

(*c*) reduces to 10*s*. per ton the general levy on maize meal; and

(*d*) reimposes unchanged the other rates of general and country levy prescribed by the above-mentioned orders.

1969 No. 783

POST OFFICE

The British Commonwealth and Foreign Post Amendment (No. 4) Regulations 1969

Made - - -	*5th June* 1969
Laid before Parliament	*13th June* 1969
Coming into Operation	*1st July* 1969

I, the Right Honourable John Thomson Stonehouse, M.P., Her Majesty's Postmaster General, by virtue of the powers conferred on me by sections 5, 15 and 81 of the Post Office Act 1953(**a**), as amended or substituted by section 28 of and the Schedule to the Post Office Act 1961(**b**), and of all other powers enabling me in this behalf, do hereby make the following Regulations:—

Commencement, citation and interpretation

1.—(1) These Regulations shall come into operation on the 1st July 1969, and may be cited as the British Commonwealth and Foreign Post Amendment (No. 4) Regulations 1969.

(2) These Regulations shall be read as one with the British Commonwealth and Foreign Post Regulations 1965(**c**) (hereinafter called "the principal Regulations"), as amended (**d**).

(3) The Interpretation Act 1889(**e**) applies for the interpretation of these Regulations as it applies for the interpretation of an Act of Parliament.

Specified countries or places

2. In Part 1 of Schedule 2 to the principal Regulations, as amended (which Schedule specifies the countries or places in which certain rates of postage and limits of weight and size apply)—

(*a*) in the description of the territories comprising Australia and its overseas and Trust Territories there shall be deleted the words "and Nauru";

(*b*) the words "Basutoland" and "Bechuanaland Protectorate" shall be deleted; and

(*c*) the words "Botswana", "Lesotho" and "Nauru" shall be inserted in their appropriate places in alphabetical order.

(**a**) 1953 c. 36.   (**b**) 1961 c. 15.
(**c**) S.I. 1965/1735 (1965 III, p. 4878).
(**d**) S.I. 1965/2173, S.I. 1966/912, S.I. 1968/1254 (1965 III, p. 6371; 1966 II, p. 2185 1968 II, p. 3440).
(**e**) 1889 c. 63.

Certain outgoing packets

3. In Part 2 of Schedule 3 to the principal Regulations (which Part specifies the rates of postage under regulation 5(1)) for item 1 there shall be substituted the following:—

1.   Printed packet:

    (*a*)   not exceeding 2 oz. in weight   ...   .   2d.

    (*b*)   exceeding 2 oz. in weight:
        for the first 2 oz.   ...   .   2d.

        for the next 2 oz. or fractional part thereof   ...   ...   1d.

        for each additional 4 oz. or fractional part thereof   ...   3d.

John Stonehouse,
Her Majesty's Postmaster General.

Dated 5th June 1969.

EXPLANATORY NOTE

(This Note is not part of the Regulations.)

These Regulations, which come into operation on the 1st July 1969, amend the regulations relating to postal packets (other than parcels) sent to or received from British Commonwealth or foreign countries (except the Republic of Ireland).

The Schedule of specified countries or places is amended to take account of recent changes of status of the countries concerned.

The rates of postage for printed packets sent to Her Majesty's Forces overseas are revised so as to eliminate any charge containing an odd halfpenny. The effect of the changes is as follows:—

					Old rate	New rate
First 2 oz.	...	...	...	...	2d.	2d.
Next 2 oz.	...	...	...	...	1½d.	1d.
Subsequent weight steps		...	...	1½d. per 2 oz.	3d. per 4 oz.

STATUTORY INSTRUMENTS

1969 No. 784

POST OFFICE

The British Commonwealth and Foreign Parcel Post Amendment (No. 4) Regulations 1969

Made - - -	*5th June* 1969
Laid before Parliament	*13th June* 1969
Coming into Operation	*1st July* 1969

I, The Right Honourable John Thomson Stonehouse, M.P., Her Majesty's Postmaster General, by virtue of the powers conferred on me by sections 5, 10, 15 and 81 of the Post Office Act 1953(a), as amended or substituted by section 28 of and the Schedule to the Post Office Act 1961(b), and of all other powers enabling me in this behalf, do hereby make the following Regulations:—

Commencement, citation and interpretation

1.—(1) These Regulations shall come into operation on the 1st July 1969, and may be cited as the British Commonwealth and Foreign Parcel Post Amendment (No. 4) Regulations 1969.

(2) These Regulations shall be read as one with the British Commonwealth and Foreign Parcel Post Regulations 1965(c) (hereinafter called "the principal Regulations"), as amended (d).

(3) The Interpretation Act 1889(e) applies for the interpretation of these Regulations as it applies for the interpretation of an Act of Parliament.

Cash on delivery parcels

2. For Schedule 1 to the principal Regulations (which sets out the scale of fees to be charged and paid at the time of posting of outgoing cash on delivery parcels in addition to the postage and any other charges payable thereon) there shall be substituted the following:—

(a) 1953 c. 36.   (b) 1961 c. 15.
(c) S.I. 1965/1734 (1965 III, p. 4859).
(d) There is no amendment which relates expressly to the subject matter of these regulations.   (e) 1889 c.63.

"Regulation 18

SCHEDULE 1

CASH ON DELIVERY PARCELS

SCALE OF FEES

Trade Charge		Fee s.	d.
Not exceeding £1			4
Exceeding £1 but not exceeding £2			7
,, £2 ,, ,, ,, £3			9
,, £3 ,, ,, ,, £4		1	0
,, £4 ,, ,, ,, £5		1	2
,, £5 ,, ,, ,, £6		1	5
,, £6 ,, ,, ,, £7		1	7
,, £7 ,, ,, ,, £8		1	10
,, £8 ,, ,, ,, £9		2	0
,, £9 ,, ,, ,, £10		2	3
,, £10 ,, ,, ,, £11		2	5
,, £11 ,, ,, ,, £12		2	8
,, £12 ,, ,, ,, £13		2	10
,, £13 ,, ,, ,, £14		3	1
,, £14 ,, ,, ,, £15		3	3
,, £15 ,, ,, ,, £16		3	6
,, £16 ,, ,, ,, £17		3	8
,, £17 ,, ,, ,, £18		3	11
,, £18 ,, ,, ,, £19		4	1
,, £19 ,, ,, ,, £20		4	4
,, £20 ,, ,, ,, £21		4	6
,, £21 ,, ,, ,, £22		4	9
,, £22 ,, ,, ,, £23		4	11
,, £23 ,, ,, ,, £24		5	2
,, £24 ,, ,, ,, £25		5	4
,, £25 ,, ,, ,, £26		5	7
,, £26 ,, ,, ,, £27		5	9
,, £27 ,, ,, ,, £28		6	0
,, £28 ,, ,, ,, £29		6	2
,, £29 ,, ,, ,, £30		6	5
,, £30 ,, ,, ,, £31		6	7
,, £31 ,, ,, ,, £32		6	10
,, £32 ,, ,, ,, £33		7	0
,, £33 ,, ,, ,, £34		7	3
,, £34 ,, ,, ,, £35		7	5
,, £35 ,, ,, ,, £36		7	8
,, £36 ,, ,, ,, £37		7	10
,, £37 ,, ,, ,, £38		8	1
,, £38 ,, ,, ,, £39		8	3
,, £39 ,, ,, ,, £40		8	6"

John Stonehouse,

Her Majesty's Postmaster General.

Dated 5th June 1969.

EXPLANATORY NOTE
(This Note is not part of the Regulations.)

These Regulations, which come into operation on the 1st July 1969, further amend the British Commonwealth and Foreign Parcel Post Regulations 1965 by rounding down to the next penny the fees payable on outgoing cash on delivery parcels which include an odd halfpenny.

STATUTORY INSTRUMENTS

1969 No. 785 (S. 62)

EDUCATION, SCOTLAND

The Teachers Superannuation Account (Rates of Interest) (Scotland) Regulations 1969

Made - - -	*3rd June* 1969
Laid before Parliament	*16th June* 1969
Coming into Operation	*1st July* 1969

In exercise of the powers conferred upon me by section 18 of and paragraph 3(*d*) of Schedule 1 to the Teachers Superannuation (Scotland) Act 1968(**a**) as read with the Minister for the Civil Service Order 1968(**b**) and of all other powers enabling me in that behalf and after consultation with representatives of education authorities, teachers and other bodies appearing to me to be likely to be affected as required by section 18(5) of the said Act, and with the consent of the Minister for the Civil Service I hereby make the following regulations:—

Citation and Commencement

1. These regulations may be cited as the Teachers Superannuation Account (Rates of Interest) (Scotland) Regulations 1969 and shall come into operation on 1st July 1969.

Interpretation

2.—(1) In these regulations, unless the context otherwise requires—

"accounting period" means, in relation to the teachers superannuation account, the period of twelve months beginning on 1st April in each year;

"security" means a redeemable security issued by Her Majesty's Government in the United Kingdom;

"the teachers superannuation account" means the account required to be kept or treated as having been kept under section 5(1) of the Teachers Superannuation (Scotland) Act 1968.

(2) For the purposes of these regulations—

   (*a*)   the price of a security shall be the price half-way between the highest and lowest prices shown in the quotations therefor in the Official Daily List of the London Stock Exchange for the relevant date or, if that Exchange is or was closed on that date, the latest previous date on which it is or was open; and

   (*b*)   the rate of interest on an investment in a security shall be the rate equivalent to the gross annual yield therefrom expressed as a percentage of the sum deemed to be invested therein.

(3) The Interpretation Act 1889(**c**) shall apply for the interpretation of these regulations as it applies for the interpretation of an Act of Parliament.

(**a**) 1968 c. 12. (**b**) S.I. 1968/1656 (1968 III, p. 4485).

(**c**) 1889 c. 63.

Rates of Interest

3.—(1) Subject to the provisions of regulations 4 and 5 hereof, the sum representing interest which, under the terms of paragraph 3(d) of Schedule 1 to the Teachers Superannuation (Scotland) Act 1968, is to be treated as having been paid into the revenue of the teachers superannuation account shall be calculated in accordance with the following provisions of this regulation.

(2) The rate of interest on each of the sums specified in column (1) of the following table (being sums together making up the balance of revenue over expenditure remaining at the end of the accounting period beginning on 1st April 1960 and also forming part of the balance of revenue over expenditure remaining at the end of each subsequent accounting period) shall for the accounting period beginning on 1st April 1961 and for each subsequent accounting period be that specified opposite thereto in column (2):—

TABLE

(1) Sum	(2) Rate of Interest
£	
41,427,918	$3\frac{1}{2}$ per cent.
44,504,981	The rate of interest on an investment deemed to have been made on 1st April 1961 in Treasury $5\frac{1}{2}$ per cent. Stock, 2008-12
2,960,983	The rate of interest on an investment deemed to have been made on 1st October 1956 in $3\frac{1}{2}$ per cent. Funding Stock, 1999-2004
3,435,546	The rate of interest on an investment deemed to have been made on 1st October 1957 in $3\frac{1}{2}$ per cent. Funding Stock, 1999-2004
3,311,174	The rate of interest on an investment deemed to have been made on 1st October 1958 in $3\frac{1}{2}$ per cent. Funding Stock, 1999-2004
3,601,355	The rate of interest on an investment deemed to have been made on 1st October 1959 in $3\frac{1}{2}$ per cent. Funding Stock, 1999-2004
3,677,994	The rate of interest on an investment deemed to have been made on 1st October 1960 in $3\frac{1}{2}$ per cent. Funding Stock, 1999-2004

(3) The rate of interest on the balance of revenue (exclusive of interest thereon) over expenditure during the accounting period beginning on 1st April 1961 and each subsequent accounting period shall for that period be one-half of the rate of interest on the investment of an amount equal to such balance deemed to have been made on 1st October in that period in a security selected by the Secretary of State after consultation with the Government Actuary.

(4) The rate of interest on any part of the balance of revenue over expenditure remaining at the end of any accounting period beginning on 1st April 1961 or subsequently, being a part which accrued during that period, shall for the next succeeding and each subsequent accounting period be the rate of interest on the investment deemed to have been made in accordance with paragraph (3) of this regulation in the accounting period in which such part accrued.

Redemption of Securities

4.—(1) Subject to paragraph (3) of this regulation, on the date of redemption of a security in which an investment is deemed to have been made for the purposes of these regulations—

(*a*) the sum representing interest which, in accordance with regulation 3, is treated as having been paid into the revenue of the teachers superannuation account in respect of that investment shall be increased by the amount by which the notional proceeds of the redemption thereof exceeds the sum deemed to have been invested therein or, as the case may be, reduced by the amount by which those proceeds fall short of that sum; and

(*b*) a sum equivalent to the sum deemed to have been invested therein shall be deemed to be re-invested in a security selected by the Secretary of State after consultation with the Government Actuary.

(2) The re-investment made in pursuance of paragraph (1)(*b*) of this regulation shall be deemed to be in substitution for the investment in the redeemed security and any rate of interest determined by reference to that investment shall be varied accordingly.

(3) The notional proceeds of redemption referred to in paragraph (1) of this regulation shall be the amount which would be received in respect of an investment on the redemption of the security in which it is deemed to have been made, less any capital gains tax deemed to be payable in accordance with regulation 5.

(4) For the purposes of this regulation the date of redemption of a security shall be the last date on which it may be redeemed in accordance with the terms on which it was issued.

Income Tax and Capital Gains Tax

5.—(1) In relation to any investment deemed to have been made for the purposes of these regulations—

(*a*) income tax in respect of interest, and

(*b*) capital gains tax in respect of any capital gains accruing on the redemption of the security in which it was made

shall be deemed to be payable to the same extent as they would be payable if the investment belonged to a superannuation fund approved for the purposes of section 379 of the Income Tax Act 1952(**a**) and providing benefits similar to those provided from the teachers superannuation account.

(2) The rates of income tax and capital gains tax, if any, deemed to be payable in any year under paragraph (1) of this regulation shall be the rates of those taxes charged for that year under the relevant Finance Act.

(3) Any question arising under this regulation as to the extent to which income tax and capital gains tax shall be deemed to be payable under paragraph (1) of this regulation shall be decided by the Secretary of State and his decision thereon shall be final.

(**a**) 1952 c. 10.

William Ross,
One of Her Majesty's
Principal Secretaries of State.

St. Andrew's House,
Edinburgh, 1.
27th May 1969.

Consent of the Minister for the Civil Service given under his Official Seal on
3rd June 1969.

J. E. Herbecq,
(L.S.)   Authorised by the Minister
for the Civil Service.

EXPLANATORY NOTE
(This Note is not part of the Regulations.)

These Regulations prescribe the method of calculating the sums representing
interest which, in each accounting period from that beginning on 1st April 1961,
are to be deemed to be added to the Teachers Superannuation Account.

The amount of interest added to the credit balance in the Teachers Superannuation Account has been calculated at $3\frac{1}{2}$ per cent. per annum since the
account was started in 1926. Under these Regulations for the accounting period
beginning on 1st April 1961 and subsequent accounting periods interest will
continue at that rate on the part of the balance that accrued before 1st April 1956,
but in respect of balances accruing subsequently it will be at rates determined by
reference to the notional yield from investment in redeemable Government
securities.

The Regulations have retrospective effect by virtue of section 18(7) of the
Teachers Superannuation (Scotland) Act 1968.

STATUTORY INSTRUMENTS

1969 No. 790

PENSIONS

The Superannuation (Scottish Teaching and English Local Government) Interchange Rules 1969

Made - - - -		*4th June* 1969
Laid before Parliament		*20th June* 1969
Coming into Operation		*23rd June* 1969

ARRANGEMENT OF RULES

PART I

GENERAL

1. Citation and Commencement.
2. Interpretation.
3. Prescribed Period.

PART II

TRANSFER FROM TEACHING SERVICE TO LOCAL GOVERNMENT EMPLOYMENT

4. Application.
5. Excepted Cases.
6. Transfer Value.
7. Reckoning of Service.
8. Voluntary Contributions.
9. Computation of Contributions.
10. Benefits under Teachers Regulations of 1969.
11. Modification of Contributions and Benefits by reason of National Insurance.
12. Questions and Appeals.
13. Application of Section 11(3) of Act of 1953.

PART III

TRANSFER FROM LOCAL GOVERNMENT EMPLOYMENT TO TEACHING SERVICE

14. Application.
15. Excepted Cases.

16. Discretionary Increase of Benefits.
17. Transfer Value.
18. Supplementary Provisions as to Transfer Values.
19. Reckoning of Service.
20. Voluntary Contributions.
21. Commencement of Employment.
22. Computation of Contributions.
23. Benefits under Acts or Scheme.
24. Modification of Contributions and Benefits by reason of National Insurance.

The Secretary of State, with the consent of the Minister for the Civil Service, and the Minister of Housing and Local Government, acting jointly, in exercise of the powers conferred on them by sections 2 and 15 of the Superannuation (Miscellaneous Provisions) Act 1948(a) as amended by section 11 of the Superannuation (Miscellaneous Provisions) Act 1967(b) and as read with the Minister for the Civil Service Order 1968(c), and of all other powers enabling them in that behalf, hereby make the following rules:—

PART I

GENERAL

Citation and Commencement

1. These rules may be cited as the Superannuation (Scottish Teaching and English Local Government) Interchange Rules 1969 and shall come into operation on 23rd June 1969.

Interpretation

2.—(1) In these rules, unless the context otherwise requires—

"the Act" means the Superannuation (Miscellaneous Provisions) Act 1948;

"the Act of 1909" means the Asylums Officers' Superannuation Act 1909(d);

"the Act of 1937" means the Local Government Superannuation Act 1937(e);

"the Act of 1953" means the Local Government Superannuation Act 1953(f);

"the Acts of 1937 to 1953" means the Local Government Superannuation Acts 1937 to 1953(g);

"added years" means, in relation to local government employment, any additional years of service reckonable under regulation 12 of the Benefits Regulations or any corresponding provision of a local Act scheme and includes any additional years of service which, having been granted under any such provision or under any similar provision contained in any other enactment or scheme, have subsequently become and are reckonable under or by virtue of rules made under sections 2 and 15 of the Act or any other enactment;

(a) 1948 c. 33.
(b) 1967 c. 28.
(c) S.I. 1968/1656 (1968 III, p. 4485).
(d) 1909 c. 48.
(e) 1937 c. 68.
(f) 1953 c. 25.
(g) 1937 c. 68; 1939 c. 94; 1953 c. 25.

"the Benefits Regulations" means the Local Government Superannuation (Benefits) Regulations 1954(a);

"fund authority" means a local authority maintaining a superannuation fund to which a person either becomes a contributor after ceasing to be employed in teaching service or, as the case may be, was last a contributor before he became employed in teaching service;

"local authority" has the same meaning as in the Act of 1937;

"local government employment" means employment by virtue of which the person employed is or is deemed to be a contributory employee or local Act contributor;

"Local Government Modification Regulations" means the National Insurance (Modification of Local Government Superannuation Schemes) Regulations 1947(b) and any provisions contained in the Benefits Regulations or in a local Act scheme or in a scheme made in relation to a local Act replacing wholly or in part the provisions of the first-mentioned regulations;

"national service", in relation to any person, means service which is relevant service within the meaning of the Reserve and Auxiliary Forces (Protection of Civil Interests) Act 1951(c) and any similar service immediately following relevant service entered into with the consent of the authority or person by whom he was last employed or, as the case may be, appointed to an office before undertaking that service;

"operative date" means the date of the coming into operation of these rules;

"pension" has the meaning assigned to it by the Act;

"prescribed period" has the meaning assigned to that expression by rule 3;

"reckonable service" means such service as is by virtue of the Teachers Regulations of 1969 reckonable service for all the purposes of Part I of the Teachers Superannuation (Scotland) Act 1968(d);

"repaid contributions" means any sum paid to a person under the Teachers Schemes, the Teachers Regulations of 1957, the Teachers Regulations of 1969, the Acts of 1937 to 1953 or a local Act scheme by way of repayment of contributions (other than voluntary contributions and contributions made or deemed to be made for the purpose of securing benefits for a widow, children or other dependants); and includes both any interest included in such sum and any amount deducted therefrom in respect of liability to income tax arising by reason of the payment;

"the Teachers Regulations of 1957" means the Teachers (Superannuation) (Scotland) Regulations 1957(e) as amended(f);

"the Teachers Regulations of 1969" means the Teachers Superannuation (Scotland) Regulations 1969(g) as amended (h);

"the Teachers Schemes" means the Superannuation Scheme for Teachers in Scotland dated 5th June 1919(i), the Superannuation Scheme for Teachers (Scotland) 1926(j) and the Superannuation Scheme for Teachers (Scotland) 1952(k);

"teaching service" means—

(a) reckonable service; or

(a) S.I. 1954/1048 (1954 II, p. 1595).
(b) S.R. & O. 1947/1245 (Rev. XVI, p. 273: 1947 I, p. 1498).
(c) 1951 c. 65.   (d) 1968 c. 12.
(e) S.I. 1957/356 (1957 I, p. 733).
(f) S.I. 1958/1595, 1963/2111, 1965/1166, 1966/1229, 1967/1736 (1958 I, p. 1077; 1963 III, p. 4685; 1965 II, p. 3284; 1966 III, p. 3295; 1967 III, p. 4657).
(g) S.I. 1969/77 (1969 I, p. 133).   (h) S.I. 1969/659).
(i) S.R. & O. 1919/1105 (1919 I, p. 688). (j) S.R. & O. 1926/363 (1926 p. 449).
(k) S.I. 1952/464 (1952 I, p. 873).

(*b*) service which for the purposes of the Teachers Regulations of 1969 is service as an organiser;

"the Transfer Value Regulations" means the Local Government Superannuation (Transfer Value) Regulations 1954(**a**);

"voluntary contributions" means—

(*a*) in relation to employment in teaching service, additional contributions being paid under regulation 9 of the Teachers Regulations of 1957 or regulation 31 of the Teachers Regulations of 1969 in respect of a period of previous employment and any contributions being paid as a condition of any other period (not being a period of war service within the meaning of the Education (Scotland) (War Service Superannuation) Act 1939(**b**) or of national service) being reckoned as reckonable service; and

(*b*) in relation to local government employment, payments (other than completed payments, that is to say, payments made in respect of a liability which has been wholly discharged) of any of the following categories—

(i) additional contributory payments of the kind referred to in section 2(3) and (4) of the Act of 1953;

(ii) any similar payments made under a local Act scheme as a condition of reckoning any period of employment as service or as a period of contribution for the purposes of the scheme, or, where the local Act scheme provides for the reckoning of non-contributing service, as contributing service for the purposes of the scheme;

(iii) any payments made for the purpose of increasing the length at which any period of service or of contribution would be reckonable for the purpose of calculating a benefit under a local Act scheme; and

(iv) any payments made in respect of added years.

(2) For the purposes of these rules a justices' clerk shall be deemed to be in the employment of the magistrates' courts committee or committee of magistrates by whom he is, or under the provisions of any enactment is deemed to have been, appointed, and in relation to any such person references to "employment" shall be construed accordingly.

(3) Other expressions which have meanings assigned to them by the Acts of 1937 to 1953 or the Teachers Regulations of 1969 have, unless the context otherwise requires, the same respective meanings for the purposes of these rules.

(4) Any reference in these rules to the provisions of any enactment, rules, regulations or other instrument shall, unless the context otherwise requires, be construed as a reference to those provisions as amended, modified, affected or re-enacted by any subsequent enactment, rules, regulations or instrument.

(5) References in these rules to a rule or to a Part shall, unless the context otherwise requires, be construed as references to a rule or to a Part of these rules, as the case may be.

(6) The Interpretation Act 1889(**c**) shall apply for the interpretation of these rules as it applies for the interpretation of an Act of Parliament.

(a) S.I. 1954/1212 (1954 II, p. 1723).　　　　(b) 1939 c. 96.
(c) 1889 c. 63.

Prescribed Period

3.—(1) For the purposes of these rules, subject as hereafter in this rule provided, the expression "prescribed period" shall mean—

(a) in the case of a person who, immediately after ceasing to be employed in teaching service or local government employment, became engaged in national service, a period of six months after the date of termination of the national service;

(b) in the case of a person to whom section 6 of the Act has become applicable, a period of five years after the date on which he ceased to be employed in local government employment or such longer period as the Minister of Housing and Local Government may in any particular case allow; and

(c) in the case of any other person, a period of twelve months after the date on which he ceased to be employed in teaching service or local government employment.

(2) The Secretary of State in the case of a person entering teaching service and the fund authority in the case of a person entering local government employment may, with the agreement of the other, extend the period of six months or twelve months, whichever is appropriate, specified in paragraph (1) of this rule.

(3) Subject as in paragraph (4) of this rule provided—

(a) in reckoning the periods of six months and twelve months specified in paragraph (1) of this rule no account shall be taken of any period spent by a person on a course of study or training which he undertook after leaving his former employment; and

(b) if a person left his former employment in order to undertake a course of study or training and on completion of that course became engaged in national service, he shall be deemed for the purposes of paragraph (1) of this rule to have left his former employment at the time when he completed the said course of study or training.

(4) The provisions of paragraph (3) of this rule shall not apply to a person who in his new employment is in local government employment unless the authority employing him are satisfied, or to a person who in his new employment is in teaching service unless the Secretary of State is satisfied, that by reason of his having undertaken the said course of study or training he is better fitted for the duties of his new employment.

PART II

TRANSFER FROM TEACHING SERVICE TO LOCAL GOVERNMENT EMPLOYMENT

Application

4.—(1) Except as hereinafter provided, this Part shall apply to a person who—

(a) enters, or before the operative date entered, local government employment within the prescribed period after ceasing to be employed in teaching service;

(b) before or within three months after entering local government employment or within six months after the operative date, whichever period shall last expire, or within such longer period as the fund authority may with the agreement of the Secretary of State in any particular case allow, notifies that authority in writing that he desires this Part to apply to him and furnishes that authority with particulars in writing of any national service in which he has been engaged since ceasing to be employed in teaching service; and (*c*) within three months after entering local government employment or within six months after the operative date, whichever period shall last expire, or within such longer period as the fund authority may in any particular case allow, pays to that authority an amount equal to any repaid contributions paid to him after he last ceased to be employed in teaching service, together with any compound interest thereon payable in accordance with paragraph (2) of this rule.

(2) For the purposes of paragraph (1)(*c*) of this rule—

(*a*) compound interest shall not be payable unless the period between a person's ceasing to be employed in teaching service and entering local government employment exceeds one year;

(*b*) compound interest shall be calculated on the amount of the repaid contributions at three per cent per annum with half-yearly rests from the day one year after that on which the person ceased to be employed in teaching service or from the day on which repaid contributions were paid to him, whichever shall be the later, to the day on which he notified the fund authority as required by paragraph (1)(*b*) of this rule; and

(*c*) if the amount of compound interest calculated as aforesaid exceeds a sum equal to one half of the difference between the amount of the transfer value payable under rule 6 and the amount of the transfer value which would have been so payable if calculated by reference to the person's age on ceasing to be employed in teaching service, it shall be reduced to that sum.

Excepted Cases

5. This Part shall not apply to a person who—

(*a*) has received payment of any pension (other than repayment of contributions) under the Teachers Schemes, the Teachers Regulations of 1957 or the Teachers Regulations of 1969;

(*b*) is a person in respect of whom a transfer value has been paid otherwise than under these rules by the Secretary of State since he last ceased to be employed in teaching service;

(*c*) last ceased to be employed in teaching service before 4th February 1948; or

(*d*) last ceased to be employed in teaching service on or after 4th February 1948 but before the operative date, unless—

(i) he has been employed in local government employment without a break of twelve months or more at any one time from the date when he ceased to be employed in teaching service until the operative date or, if he ceased to be employed in local government employment before the operative date, until the date when he so ceased; and

(ii) if he ceased to be employed in local government employment before the operative date, the Secretary of State and the local authority maintaining the fund to which he was last a contributor agree that this Part shall apply to him.

Transfer Value

6.—(1) In respect of a person to whom this Part applies the Secretary of State shall, out of moneys provided by Parliament, pay to the fund authority a transfer value of an amount calculated in accordance with the following provisions of this rule.

(2) Subject as hereafter in this rule provided, the transfer value shall be an amount equal to the transfer value which would have been payable under the Transfer Value Regulations if the person, at the date when he ceased to be

employed in teaching service, had ceased to be a contributory employee under one local authority and had become such an employee under another local authority in the circumstances described in section 29 of the Act of 1937 and had been entitled to reckon as contributing service his reckonable service and his service reckonable for the purposes of Part VII of the Teachers Regulations of 1969.

(3) For the purpose of calculating the amount of a transfer value any period of service which, having originally been non-contributing service or non-contributing service for the purposes of regulations made under section 67 of the National Health Service Act 1946(a) or section 66 of the National Health Service (Scotland) Act 1947(b), became reckonable as reckonable service by virtue of such regulations or of rules made under section 2 of the Act shall be treated as non-contributing service.

(4) For the purposes of paragraph (2) of this rule service which is reckoned as contributing service shall be deemed to have been affected or modified in accordance with regulations applicable to contributing service made under section 110 of the National Insurance Act 1965(c), or under any provision corresponding thereto contained in an enactment repealed by that Act, in like manner and to the like extent, as nearly as may be, as it was affected or modified by other such regulations.

(5) In calculating the amount of a transfer value there shall be excluded—
   (a) any period of war service within the meaning of the Education (Scotland) (War Service Superannuation) Act 1939 and of national service within the meaning of the Teachers' Pensions (National Service) (Scotland) Rules 1952(d) in respect of which, at the time the transfer value is paid, the contributions remain unpaid; and
   (b) any period of previous employment and any period additional to actual service in respect of which the person was immediately before ceasing to be employed in teaching service paying voluntary contributions and in respect of which, at the time the transfer value is paid, he has not elected to continue to pay such contributions.

(6) In respect of a person who ceased to be employed in teaching service more than one year before the operative date the amount of the transfer value shall, except in a case to which paragraph (7) of this rule applies, be—
   (a) calculated by reference to his age on the operative date; and
   (b) where either paragraph (2) or paragraph (3) of rule 3 applies, reduced by the amount of any compound interest payable by him in accordance with rule 4(2).

(7) In respect of a person who became employed in local government employment on or after the operative date and where either paragraph (2) or paragraph (3) of rule 3 applies the amount of the transfer value shall be—
   (a) calculated by reference to his age on the date on which he became employed in local government employment; and
   (b) reduced by the amount of any compound interest payable by him in accordance with rule 4(2).

Reckoning of Service

7.—(1) Subject as hereafter in this rule provided, so much service as is taken into account under rule 6 for the purpose of calculating the amount of the transfer value payable in respect of a person shall be reckoned as contributing

(a) 1946 c. 81.   (b) 1947 c. 27.
(c) 1965 c. 51.   (d) S.I. 1952/518 (1952 I, p. 928).

service or as service under a local Act scheme or a period of contribution for the purposes of such a scheme.

(2) So much service as is taken into account as non-contributing service under rule 6 for the purpose of calculating the amount of the transfer value payable in respect of a person shall be reckoned as non-contributing service.

(3) Any service of a person to whom this Part applies which under the Teachers Regulations of 1969 is reckonable only for the purpose of calculating the amount of any pension payable to or in respect of him or only for the purpose of determining whether he is entitled to any pension shall be reckoned only for the corresponding like purpose under the Acts of 1937 to 1953 or a local Act scheme.

(4) Except as in this rule before provided, a person to whom this Part applies shall not be entitled under section 12(2) of the Act of 1937 or any corresponding provision of a local Act scheme to reckon as service any local government employment prior to the date on which he became employed in teaching service if,

(a) a transfer value has been paid in respect of that local government employment under rule 17 or under any corresponding provision contained in other rules made under section 2 of the Act, or

(b) a transfer of assets in respect of his accrued pension rights has been made out of a local authority's superannuation fund under any enactment.

Voluntary Contributions

8.—(1) A person to whom this Part applies may elect to continue to pay voluntary contributions being paid by him immediately before ceasing to be employed in teaching service.

(2) If a person elects as aforesaid and—

(a) within three months of becoming employed in local government employment, or within such longer period as the fund authority may in any particular case allow, pays to that authority a sum equal to the aggregate of any sum paid to him by way of return of voluntary contributions on or after ceasing to be employed in teaching service, any interest added thereto and any amount deducted therefrom in respect of liability to income tax by reason of the payment, and

(b) thereafter pays to that authority any amounts outstanding in respect of those voluntary contributions at the times at which and in the manner in which they would have been payable if he had remained in teaching service,

his local government employment shall be affected in the manner prescribed by the following provisions of this rule.

(3) In respect of voluntary contributions made in respect of any period of previous employment and any period additional to actual service, the person shall enjoy rights and be subject to liabilities as if those years were added years in respect of which payments are being made in his local government employment under regulation 12 of the Benefits Regulations or, if in his local government employment he is subject to a local Act scheme, under such provisions corresponding to the said regulation 12 or to regulation 5 of the Local Government Superannuation (Reckoning of Service on Transfer) Regulations 1954(a) as are contained in that scheme.

(4) In respect of voluntary contributions other than those to which paragraph (3) of this rule applies, the person shall be treated as if those contributions had been completed immediately before he ceased to be employed in teaching service.

(a) S.I. 1954/1211 (1954 II, p. 1676).

Computation of Contributions

9.—(1) Where a person to whom this Part applies ceases to be employed in local government employment or dies, then, in calculating any amount payable to or in respect of him by way of return of contributions, the amount of his contributions in respect of service reckonable in accordance with rule 7(1) shall be taken to include such amount as would have been payable by way of return of contributions under the Teachers Schemes or the Teachers Regulations of 1957 or the Teachers Regulations of 1969 if, on his ceasing to be employed in teaching service, he had been entitled to be repaid his contributions without interest.

(2) Where an amount payable by way of return of contributions or by way of benefit is a sum equal to, or which falls to be calculated by reference to, the amount of a person's contributions with compound interest thereon, compound interest shall also be payable in respect of the amount by which those contributions are increased under the last preceding paragraph, calculated—

(a) as respects the period ending immediately before the day on which he entered local government employment, at the rate at which it would have been calculated under the Teachers Schemes or the Teachers Regulations of 1957 or the Teachers Regulations of 1969, as the case may be, if on ceasing to be employed in teaching service he had been entitled to a return of contributions together with compound interest thereon; and

(b) as respects the period beginning with the date on which he entered local government employment, in accordance with the provisions of section 10 of the Act of 1937 or, as the case may be, the corresponding provisions of the relevant local Act scheme.

(3) Notwithstanding anything in this rule previously contained, the sum by which contributions are increased by virtue of paragraph (1) or (2) of this rule shall not include—

(a) any sum in respect of contributions which, on or after the person's ceasing to be employed in teaching service, were returned to and retained by him; or

(b) any amount in respect of voluntary contributions which are not continued in pursuance of rule 8 of these rules.

Benefits under Teachers Regulations of 1969

10. Subject to the provisions of Part III and of other rules made under section 2 of the Act, no payment of any pension shall be made under the Teachers Regulations of 1969 to any person or his personal representatives in respect of any service which is taken into account in calculating the amount of a transfer value under rule 6.

Modification of Contributions and Benefits by reason of National Insurance

11.—(1) The modifications for which the Local Government Modification Regulations provide shall not apply to a person to whom this Part applies if either—

(a) he ceased to be employed in teaching service before 1st February 1969 and at the time of so ceasing was not subject to the national insurance modifications; or

(b) he ceased to be employed in teaching service on or after 1st February 1969 and at the time of so ceasing was not subject to paragraph 3 of Schedule 5 to the Teachers Regulations of 1969.

(2) Without prejudice to the operation of the National Insurance (Modification of Local Government Superannuation Schemes) No. 2 Regulations 1961(a), the modifications for which the Local Government Modification Regulations provide shall apply to any other person to whom this Part applies as if any service reckonable in accordance with rule 7(1) were service for the purposes of the Acts of 1937 to 1953 or service for the purposes of a local Act scheme, as the case may be, rendered on or after 5th July 1948.

(3) Where any pension which might have become payable under the Teachers Schemes or the Teachers Regulations of 1957 to a person to whom this Part applies would have been subject to the national insurance modifications by reference to a table and his age at a given date, the provisions of the Local Government Modification Regulations modifying pensions in similar manner shall apply to that person and for that purpose the relevant date shall be that which was relevant for the purposes of the national insurance modifications of those Schemes or Regulations.

(4) Where any pension which might have become payable under the Teachers Regulations of 1969 to a person to whom this Part applies would have been subject to modification under Part IV of Schedule 5 to those regulations by reference to a table and his age at a given date, the provisions of the Local Government Modification Regulations modifying pensions in similar manner shall apply to that person and for that purpose the relevant date shall be that which was relevant for the purposes of the said Schedule 5.

(5) In this rule "the national insurance modifications" means the reduction in contributions and pensions in consequence of National Insurance prescribed respectively in section 105(3) of the Education (Scotland) Act 1962(b) and in regulations 22 and 42 of the Teachers Regulations of 1957.

(6) Nothing in this rule shall affect the application of regulation 18 of the National Insurance (Modification of Local Government Superannuation Schemes) Regulations 1963(c) (which provides for reduction of local government pensions in respect of certain former employments).

Questions and Appeals

12. The provisions of section 35 of the Act of 1937 (which section relates to the decision of questions and appeals) shall have effect in relation to a person (not being a local Act contributor), to whom this Part applies as if the reference therein to regulations made under that Act included a reference to these rules.

Application of Section 11(3) of Act of 1953

13.—(1) Section 11(3) of the Act of 1953 (which subsection enables certain persons who would otherwise be debarred on grounds of age from becoming contributory employees or local Act contributors to become such employees or such contributors and to reckon previous pensionable employment) shall apply to a person who before the operative date entered the employment of a local authority after ceasing to be employed in teaching service on or after 4th February 1948.

(2) For the purposes of paragraph (1) of this rule section 11(3) of the Act of 1953 shall have effect as if for the references therein to the passing of that Act there were substituted references to the coming into operation of these rules.

(a) S.I. 1961/405 (1961 I, p. 1031).
(c) S.I. 1963/2060 (1963 III, p. 4363).

(b) 1962 c. 47.

PART III

TRANSFER FROM LOCAL GOVERNMENT EMPLOYMENT TO TEACHING SERVICE

Application

14.—(1) Except as hereinafter provided, this Part shall apply to a person who—

(a) becomes, or before the operative date became, employed in teaching service within the prescribed period after ceasing to be employed in local government employment;

(b) before or within three months after becoming employed in teaching service or within six months after the operative date, whichever period shall last expire, or within such longer period as the Secretary of State may with the agreement of the fund authority in any particular case allow, notifies the Secretary of State in writing that he desires this Part to apply to him and furnishes the Secretary of State with particulars in writing of any national service in which he has been engaged since ceasing to be employed in local government employment; and

(c) within three months after becoming employed in teaching service or within six months after the operative date, whichever period shall last expire, or within such longer period as the Secretary of State may in any particular case allow, pays to the Secretary of State an amount equal to any repaid contributions paid to him after he last ceased to be employed in local government employment, together with any compound interest thereon payable in accordance with paragraph (2) of this rule.

(2) For the purposes of paragraph (1)(c) of this rule—

(a) compound interest shall not be payable unless—
  (i) the period between the person's ceasing to be employed in local government employment and his becoming employed in teaching service exceeds one year; and
  (ii) the fund authority requires that it be paid;

(b) compound interest shall be calculated on the amount of the repaid contributions at three per cent per annum with half-yearly rests from the day one year after that on which the person ceased to be employed in local government employment or from the day on which repaid contributions were paid to him, whichever shall be the later, to the day on which he notified the Secretary of State as required by paragraph (1)(b) of this rule; and

(c) if the amount of compound interest calculated as aforesaid exceeds a sum equal to one half of the difference between the amount of the transfer value payable under rule 17 and the amount of the transfer value which would have been so payable if calculated by reference to the person's age on ceasing to be employed in local government employment, it shall be reduced to that sum.

Excepted Cases

15. This Part shall not apply to a person who—

(a) has received payment of any pension (other than repayment of contributions) under the Acts of 1937 to 1953 or a local Act scheme;

(b) is a person in respect of whom a transfer value has been paid otherwise than under these rules, by a fund authority since he last ceased to be employed in local government employment;

(*c*) last ceased to be employed in local government employment before 4th February 1948; or

(*d*) last ceased to be employed in local government employment on or after 4th February 1948 but before the operative date, unless—
  (i) he is employed in teaching service on the operative date, or, if he is not so employed on that date, the Secretary of State agrees that this Part shall apply to him; and
  (ii) the fund authority agrees that this Part shall apply to him.

Discretionary Increase of Benefits

16.—(1) The local authority by whom a person to whom this Part applies was last employed may, within six months after the date on which they are notified by the Secretary of State of such application, exercise in relation to that person any discretion which, with a view to increasing the pension payable to him, it would have been open to them to exercise at the time when he left their employment if he had then retired and had been entitled to a retirement pension under regulation 5 of the Benefits Regulations or, if that regulation was not applicable to him, to any corresponding benefit provided under the superannuation provisions which were applicable to him in his former employment.

(2) A decision made in the exercise of any discretion under paragraph (1) of this rule shall be subject to the limitations and restrictions (if any) and to the right of appeal (if any) to which it would have been subject if the discretion had been exercised on the person's retirement in the circumstances aforesaid.

(3) Where a discretion has been exercised under paragraph (1) of this rule the service reckonable, immediately before he ceased to be employed in local government employment, by the person in whose favour the discretion has been exercised shall be deemed to have been correspondingly increased.

(4) Any increase in service, if attributable to a decision under this rule to increase the pension payable to the person otherwise than by any notional increase or extension of the service reckonable for the purpose of calculating that pension or by treating any specified period of non-contributing service as contributing service, or, under a local Act scheme, by similarly converting service of one category to service of another category, shall be ascertained by converting the service in respect of which the higher rate of benefit is payable into contributing service or service for the purposes of the relevant local Act scheme in the manner in which non-contributing service is converted into contributing service under section 2(4) of the Act of 1953.

Transfer Value

17.—(1) In respect of a person to whom this Part applies the fund authority shall, out of the superannuation fund maintained by them, pay to the Secretary of State a transfer value of an amount calculated in accordance with the following provisions of this rule.

(2) Subject as hereafter in this rule provided, the transfer value shall be an amount equal to the transfer value which would have been payable under the Transfer Value Regulations if the person, at the date when he ceased to be a contributory employee or local Act contributor, had become such an employee or contributor under another local authority in the circumstances described in section 29 of the Act of 1937.

(3) In calculating the amount of a transfer value—
  (*a*) there shall be included any increase of service of the person by reason of the exercise under rule 16 of a discretion in his favour;

(b) there shall be excluded any added years in respect of which the person was immediately before ceasing to be employed in local government employment paying voluntary contributions and in respect of which, at the time the transfer value is paid, he has not elected to continue to pay such contributions; and

(c) the Transfer Value Regulations shall be deemed to be modified—

(i) by the omission from sub-paragraph (a) of the definition of "service" in paragraph 1 of Schedule 1 thereto of the words "not being such service as is mentioned in proviso (a) to that subsection"; and

(ii) by the omission, in respect of a person who was an established officer or servant within the meaning of the Act of 1909, of sub-paragraph (c) of the said definition.

(4) In respect of a person who ceased to be employed in local government employment more than one year before the operative date the amount of the transfer value shall, except in a case to which paragraph (5) of this rule applies, be—

(a) calculated by reference to his age on the operative date; and

(b) where either paragraph (2) or paragraph (3) of rule 3 applies, reduced by the amount of any compound interest payable by him in accordance with rule 14(2).

(5) In respect of a person who became employed in teaching service on or after the operative date and where either paragraph (2) or paragraph (3) of rule 3 applies the amount of the transfer value shall be—

(a) calculated by reference to his age on the date on which he became employed in teaching service; and

(b) reduced by the amount of any compound interest payable by him in accordance with rule 14(2).

(6) The amount of the transfer value shall be reduced by an amount equal to any sum payable by the fund authority by way of income tax by reason of its payment.

Supplementary Provisions as to Transfer Values

18.—(1) Where the amount of a transfer value payable under rule 17 is increased by reason of the exercise under rule 16 of a discretion by a local authority, that authority shall pay the amount of the increase to the superannuation fund out of which the transfer value is payable.

(2) When paying a transfer value under rule 17 a fund authority shall furnish to the Secretary of State and to the person in respect of whom it is paid the like particulars relating to that person's pensionable service as would have been given to him if instead of becoming employed in teaching service he had re-entered local government employment.

(3) Where—

(a) a transfer value is payable under rule 17 by a fund authority in respect of a person who before entering local government employment has been subject to the Act of 1909 ; and

(b) the body by whom he was last employed while subject to that Act would, if he had become entitled to a superannuation allowance on leaving local government employment, have been liable to contribute to that allowance that body shall pay to the fund authority a sum equal to the transfer value which that body would have been liable to pay to the Secretary of State for Social Services under regulation 56(4) of the National Health Service (Superannuation) Regulations 1950(a) if that regulation had become applicable to the person on the date on which he became employed in teaching service ; and where that body would have had in respect of any such contribution a right of contribution from any other body, that other body shall pay to the fund authority a sum equal to the transfer value which that other body would have been liable to pay to the Secretary of State for Social Services under paragraph (5) of the said regulation 56 if that regulation had become applicable to the person when he became employed in teaching service.

(4) Where any body referred to in the last preceding paragraph has been dissolved or has ceased to exercise functions as such, references to that body shall be construed as references to the appropriate authority as defined in paragraph (15) of the regulation mentioned therein.

Reckoning of Service

19.—(1) Subject as hereafter in this rule provided, in respect of a person to whom this Part applies—

(*a*) there shall be reckoned as reckonable service—

    (i) any period of service which, at the time of his ceasing to be employed in local government employment, is reckonable as contributing service or as service or a period of contribution for the purposes of a local Act scheme ;

    (ii) any period of national service after ceasing to be employed in local government employment which would have been reckonable as aforesaid if he had again become employed in local government employment after the termination thereof ; and

    (iii) one half of any period of service which, at the time of his ceasing to be employed in local government employment, is reckonable as non-contributing service ; and

(*b*) there shall be reckoned as class C external service for the purposes of the Teachers Regulations of 1969 any period of service which, at the time of his ceasing to be employed in local government employment, is reckonable as non-contributing service, except in so far as that service is reckoned under this rule or those regulations as reckonable service or as class A or class B external service for the purposes of those regulations.

(2) Where a person to whom this Part applies has, during his local government employment, been employed as a part-time employee, the period of his part-time service shall be treated—

(*a*) for the purpose of determining whether he has served for any minimum period prescribed by the Teachers Regulations of 1969 as necessary for any pension to be paid to or in respect of him as if it were whole-time service ; and

(*b*) for the purpose of calculating the amount of any pension payable under the Teachers Regulations of 1969, as if it were whole-time service for a proportionately reduced period.

(3) Where by virtue of a scheme modifying the Act of 1937 any period of service of a person to whom this Part applies is reckoned at a fraction of its actual length for the purpose of calculating the amount of the transfer value payable under rule 17, then, for the purpose of calculating the amount of any

---

(a) S.I. 1950/497 (1950 I, p. 1327).

pension payable to or in respect of him under the Teachers Regulations, only that fraction of that period of service shall be reckoned as reckonable service.

(4) In respect of a person to whom this Part applies there shall not by virtue of this Part be reckoned as reckonable service—

(*a*) any service which he is or was entitled to reckon as contributing or non-contributing service by virtue of section 17 of the Act of 1937 or the corresponding provisions of a local Act scheme if that service is reckonable service under the Teachers' Superannuation Regulations 1967(**a**) ; or

(*b*) any service which in his case is deemed to be service to which the said section 17 applies by virtue of the Local Government Superannuation (England and Scotland) Regulations 1948(**b**), if that service is reckonable as reckonable service otherwise than by virtue of these rules ; or

(*c*) any service which is the subject of a direction under section 17(3) of the Act of 1953 that all rights enjoyed by or in respect of the person with respect to that service shall be forfeited.

(5) The whole of any period of service to which paragraph (1) of this rule applies shall, for the purpose of calculating under section 4(3) of the Teachers Superannuation (Scotland) Act 1968 the average salary of a person to whom this Part applies, be reckoned as a period of employment in reckonable service and his salary during any period so reckoned shall be such amount as would under the Benefits Regulations be taken into account for the purpose of determining the annual average of his remuneration during that period.

(6) Notwithstanding anything in this rule before contained, any service of a person to whom this Part applies which under the Acts of 1937 to 1953 or a local Act scheme was at the time he ceased to be employed in local government employment reckonable only for the purpose of calculating the amount of any pension payable to or in respect of him or only for the purpose of determining whether he was entitled to any pension shall be reckoned only for the corresponding like purpose under the Teachers Regulations of 1969.

Voluntary Contributions

20.—(1) A person to whom this Part applies may elect to continue to pay voluntary contributions of any category being paid by him immediately before ceasing to be employed in local government employment.

(2) If a person elects as aforesaid and—

(*a*) within three months of becoming employed in teaching service, or within such longer period as the Secretary of State may in any particular case allow, pays to the Secretary of State a sum equal to the aggregate of any sum paid to him on or after ceasing to be employed in local government employment by way of return of voluntary contributions of any category he has elected to continue to pay, any interest added thereto and any amount deducted therefrom in respect of liability to income tax arising by reason of the payment, and

(*b*) thereafter pays to the Secretary of State any amounts outstanding in respect of voluntary contributions of any category he has elected to continue to pay at the times at which they would have been payable if he remained in local government employment,

his teaching service shall be affected in the manner prescribed by the following provisions of this rule.

_____

(**a**) S.I. 1967/489 (1967 I, p. 1562).
(**b**) S.I. 1948/1131 (Rev. XVII, p. 813: 1948 I, p. 3304).

(3) In respect of voluntary contributions paid in respect of added years, those years shall be reckoned as reckonable service.

(4) In respect of voluntary contributions paid otherwise than in respect of added years, the service in respect of which they are paid shall be reckoned for the purposes of the Teachers Regulations of 1969 in the manner in which it would under rule 19 have been so reckoned if the payment of the contributions had been completed immediately before the person ceased to be employed in local government employment.

(5) The provisions of paragraphs (5)(*b*), (6), (7) and (10) of regulation 31 and of regulation 37 of the Teachers Regulations of 1969 shall apply to voluntary contributions payable under this rule as if they were additional contributions payable in respect of previous employment within the meaning of those regulations.

(6) If a person does not elect as aforesaid or if voluntary contributions are repaid to him under regulation 37 of the Teachers Regulations of 1969, as applied by this rule, the period in respect of which such contributions were paid shall be reckoned for the purposes of the Teachers Regulations of 1969 only to the extent, if any, to which it would have been so reckoned if no such payments or contributions had been made in respect thereof.

Commencement of Employment

21. For the purposes of regulation 40(1)(*a*)(ii) of the Teachers Regulations of 1969 the date on which a person to whom this Part applies entered local government employment shall be deemed to be a date on which he became employed in teaching service.

Computation of Contributions

22.—(1) Where a person to whom this Part applies ceases to be employed in teaching service or dies, then, in computing the sum to which he or his personal representatives shall be entitled under the Teachers Regulations of 1969, there shall be included a sum in respect of contributions paid by him in respect of service which by virtue of these rules is reckoned as reckonable service and, in the case of a person who has elected in pursuance of rule 20 to continue paying voluntary contributions, in respect also of voluntary contributions paid by him before becoming employed in teaching service which have either not been returned to him or, if returned, have been paid to the Secretary of State under rule 20 and have not subsequently been again returned.

(2) In computing the amount of the sum so included for the purposes of this rule compound interest shall be calculated—

(*a*) as respects the period ending immediately before the date on which the person became employed in teaching service, in the manner in which such interest, if any, would have been calculated if the occasion for making the calculation had occurred immediately before that date ; and

(*b*) as respects the period beginning with that date, in accordance with the provisions of Part IV of the Teachers Regulations of 1969.

Benefits under Acts or Scheme

23. Subject as in Part II provided, no payment of any pension shall be made under the Acts of 1937 to 1953, the Benefits Regulations or a local Act scheme to or in respect of any person in respect of any local government employment which is reckoned as reckonable service under this Part.

Modification of Contributions and Benefits by reason of National Insurance

24.—(1) In relation to a person to whom this Part applies—

(a) the following paragraphs of Schedule 5 to the Teachers Regulations of 1969, that is to say—

paragraph 3 (which provides for the reduction of contributions),

paragraph 5 (which provides for the reduction of pensions by fixed annual amounts specified therein), and

paragraph 6 (which provides for the reduction of pensions by annual amounts ascertained by reference to a table and age at a given date) shall not apply if, on the date on which he ceased to be employed in local government employment, the contributions payable by him as a contributory employee or local Act contributor were not subject to reduction by virtue of the Local Government Modification Regulations ;

(b) paragraphs 3 and 5 of the said Schedule 5 shall apply if any pension payable to him under the Acts of 1937 to 1953 or a local Act scheme would, apart from the National Insurance (Modification of Local Government Superannuation Schemes) No. 2 Regulations 1961, have been subject to reduction by virtue of paragraph 3(3) of Schedule 3 to the Benefits Regulations ; and

(c) paragraphs 3 and 6 of the said Schedule 5 shall apply if any pension payable to him under the Acts of 1937 to 1953 or a local Act scheme would, apart from the National Insurance (Modification of Local Government Superannuation Schemes) No. 2 Regulations 1961, have been subject to reduction by virtue of paragraph 2(2) of Schedule 3 to the Benefits Regulations.

(2) Where, by virtue of paragraph (1)(c) of this rule, paragraph 6 of Schedule 5 to the Teachers Regulations of 1969 applies to a person the date of modification for the purposes of the latter paragraph shall be the date which was in relation to him the material date for the purposes of Schedule 3 to the Benefits Regulations.

Given under the seal of the Secretary of State for Scotland on 30th May 1969.

(L.S.)

William Ross,
Secretary of State for Scotland.

Given under the Official Seal of the Minister of Housing and Local Government on 3rd June 1969.

(L.S.)

Anthony Greenwood,
Minister of Housing and Local Government.

Consent of the Minister for the Civil Service given under his Official Seal on 4th June 1969.

(L.S.)

J. E. Herbecq,
Authorised by the Minister for the Civil Service.

EXPLANATORY NOTE
(This Note is not part of the Rules.)

These Rules provide for preservation of the superannuation rights of persons who change their employment in either direction between pensionable teaching service in Scotland and pensionable local government employment in England and Wales.

Since provision for this purpose has not previously existed, the Rules apply subject to certain conditions, under powers conferred by section 2(5) of the Superannuation (Miscellaneous Provisions) Act 1948, to changes of employment before the date of their coming into operation but not earlier than 4th February 1948. The effect is thus that the Rules can be applied to changes of employment at any time during the period already covered by similar Rules now in force both in Scotland and in England and Wales.

1969 No. 791

PENSIONS

The Increase of Pensions (Extension) Regulations 1969

Made - - - -	*9th June* 1969
Laid before Parliament	*16th June* 1969
Coming into Operation	*17th June* 1969

The Minister for the Civil Service, in exercise of the powers conferred upon him by section 1(4) of the Pensions (Increase) Act 1969(a) and paragraphs 13*(a)* and 14 of Schedule 2 to that Act, and of all other powers enabling him in that behalf, hereby makes the following Regulations:—

1. These Regulations may be cited as the Increase of Pensions (Extension) Regulations 1969, and shall come into operation on 17th June 1969.

2. The Interpretation Act 1889(b) shall apply for the interpretation of these Regulations as it applies for the interpretation of an Act of Parliament.

3.—(1) The persons specified in the first column of the Schedule hereto are hereby empowered to pay increases of the pensions specified in the second column of that Schedule not exceeding the increases authorised by section 1 of the Pensions (Increase) Act 1969 which would be payable if those pensions were specified in Schedule 1 thereto.

(2) Any increase authorised by these Regulations may take effect as from 1st April 1969.

Given under the Official Seal of the Minister for the Civil Service on 9th June 1969.

(L.S.)

J. E. Herbecq,

Authorised by the Minister
for the Civil Service.

9th June 1969.

(a) 1969 c. 7.   (b) 1889 c. 63.

SCHEDULE

Persons empowered to pay increases	Pensions which may be increased
1. The Greater London Council and the mayor, aldermen and burgesses of the London Boroughs of Bexley, Croydon, Newham, Redbridge and Waltham Forest.	A pension payable under subsections (9) to (11) of section 80 of the London Passenger Transport Act 1933(a).
2. The mayor, aldermen and burgesses of the London Borough of Southwark.	A pension payable by them in respect of employment in the Borough Market, Southwark.

EXPLANATORY NOTE

(This note is not part of the Regulations.)

These Regulations authorise the local authorities mentioned in paragraph 1 of the Schedule to grant increases, not exceeding those for which section 1 of the Pensions (Increase) Act 1969 provides, to those pensioners who were formerly employed in tramway undertakings and who elected to continue to be members of local authority Superannuation Funds after the undertakings were taken over under the London Passenger Transport Act 1933.

The Regulations also empower the London Borough of Southwark to grant similar increases to those receiving pensions from their Superannuation Fund in respect of former employment in the Borough Market, Southwark.

In accordance with paragraph 14 of Schedule 2 to the Pensions (Increase) Act 1969, the increases may take effect from 1st April 1969.

(a) 1933 c. 14.

1969 No. 793

SOCIAL SECURITY

The National Insurance (Modification of Local Government Superannuation Schemes) Regulations 1969

Made -	-	-	-	*6th June* 1969
Laid before Parliament				*20th June* 1969
Coming into Operation				*1st July* 1969

ARRANGEMENT OF REGULATIONS

PART I

INTRODUCTORY

1. Title and commencement
2. Interpretation
3. Definition of enactments
4. Purport of Parts II, III and IV
5. Equivalent pension benefits
6. Local Act schemes
7. Retained local Act rights

PART II

FLAT-RATE REDUCTION

8. Persons subject to flat-rate reduction
9. Definition of "material date"
10. Reduction of contributions
11. Reduction in payments for added years and additional contributory payments
12. Reduction of pensions
13. Persons transferring from the National Health Service or Scottish local government
14. Persons subject to old modification schemes
15. Persons transferring from fire brigade
16. Persons in part-time employment
17. Extensions of time for national service, etc.

Part III

Combined and Graduated Reduction

18. Persons subject to combined or graduated reduction
19. Reduction of contributions
20. Reduction of payments for added years and additional contributory payments
21. Reduction of pensions
22. Reduction of short service and death grants
23. Reduction of benefit attributable to added years, etc.
24. Calculation of disability pension
25. Calculation of additional compensatory benefit
26. Persons in part-time employment

Part IV

Miscellaneous and Consequential

27. Contributions deemed to have been made under the Act of 1937
28. Reduction of transfer values
29. Adjustments following payment in lieu of contributions
30. Adjustments between authorities
31. Modification of certain interchange rules
32. Reduction of pension in respect of other reckonable service
33. Payments for added years and additional contributory payments continued from a former employment
34. Amendments to actuarial valuation and administration regulations

Part V

Equivalent Pension Benefits

35. Equivalent pension benefits
36. Commencement of benefits not later than insured pensionable age
37. Limitations on surrender, termination, etc., of pensions

Part VI

Local Act Schemes

38. General modification of local Act schemes
39. Modification, etc., of particular regulations

Part VII

Revocations, Etc.

40. Revocations
41. Enactments ceasing to apply, etc.

SCHEDULES

Schedule 1   Flat-rate reduction of pensions

Schedule 2   Flat-rate reduction of voluntary payments

Schedule 3   Combined and graduated reduction of certain voluntary payments

Schedule 4   Combined and graduated reduction of pensions

Schedule 5   Reduction of transfer values

Schedule 6   Interchange rules affected by regulation 31

Schedule 7   Amendments to the actuarial valuation regulations

Schedule 8   Amendments to the administration regulations

Schedule 9   Reduction of benefits under regulation 36

Schedule 10 Revocations

The Minister of Housing and Local Government, having been determined to be the appropriate Minister for the purposes of section 110 of the National Insurance Act 1965(a) in relation to the schemes for the provision of pensions and other benefits established under the Local Government Superannuation Acts 1937 to 1953(b) and similar local Acts, in exercise of his powers under the said section 110, and under sections 22(3), 29, 30(3), 36(6) and 40(1) of the Local Government Superannuation Act 1937, and of all other powers enabling him in that behalf, hereby makes the following regulations:—

PART I

INTRODUCTORY

Title and commencement

1. These regulations may be cited as the National Insurance (Modification of Local Government Superannuation Schemes) Regulations 1969, and shall come into operation on 1st July 1969.

Interpretation

2.—(1) For the purposes of these regulations, any enactment or group of enactments referred to in regulation 3 has the meaning assigned to it thereby, and unless the context otherwise requires—

"contributing service" and "non-contributing service" have the same respective meanings as in the Act of 1937;

"contributory employee" has the same meaning as in the Act of 1937, and for the purposes of these regulations includes additionally a person deemed to be a contributory employee;

"disqualifying break of service" has the same meaning as in the Act of 1937;

"early retirement classes" means persons of any of the following descriptions—

(*a*) a female nurse, female physiotherapist, midwife or health visitor to whom regulation 21 of the Benefits Regulations applies; or

(*b*) a person to whom the Benefits Regulations apply with the modifications provided in regulation 23 thereof;

(a) 1965 c.51.   (b) 1937 c. 68; 1939 c. 18; 1953 c. 25.

"employing authority" has the same meaning as in the Act of 1937;

"enactment" includes any instrument made under an Act;

"established officer or servant" has the meaning which was assigned to it by the Asylums Officers' Superannuation Act 1909(a);

"general Act scheme" means the local government superannuation Acts and the rules and regulations for the time being in force thereunder so far as they relate to contributory employees, and includes the provisions of any local enactment relating to the contributory employees of any local authority who are not a local Act authority;

"insured person" means an insured person for the purposes of the Insurance Acts;

"local Act authority" has the same meaning as in the Act of 1937;

"local Act contributor" has the same meaning as in the Act of 1937 and for the purposes of these regulations includes additionally—

(a) a person deemed to be a local Act contributor, and

(b) a person entitled to participate in any of the benefits of a superannuation fund maintained under a local Act scheme;

"local Act scheme" has the same meaning as in the Act of 1937, and includes any such scheme which is applied to any particular class of employees by regulations made under the Act of 1953;

"local authority" has the same meaning as in the Act of 1937;

"material date" has the meaning assigned to it by regulation 9;

"maximum graduated remuneration" means for any period or part of a period of employment occurring—

(a) before 5th October 1966, the maximum annual amount on which, during that period or part, graduated contributions were payable for any one employment under section 1(1)(b) of the National Insurance Act 1959(b) or section 4(1) of the Insurance Act (which sections relate to graduated contributions under those Acts), and

(b) after 4th October 1966, the maximum annual amount on which such contributions would have been payable under the said section 4(1) before any amendment thereof by section 1 of the National Insurance Act 1966(c) (which increased graduated contributions, to enable payment of earnings-related benefit);

"the Minister" means the Minister of Housing and Local Government;

"modification provision" means any provision of a pension scheme which secures the reduction of pensions under the scheme in connection with the operation of any insurance code;

"national service", in relation to any person, means service which is relevant service within the meaning of the Reserve and Auxiliary Forces (Protection of Civil Interests) Act 1951(d), and any similar service immediately following relevant service entered into with the consent of the authority or person by whom he was employed before entering that service or in the case of a person who holds an appointment to an office and is not employed under a contract of employment, with the consent of the authority by whom he was appointed;

(a) 1909 c. 48.   (b) 1959 c. 47.
(c) 1966 c. 6.   (d) 1951 c. 65.

"non-participating employment" has the same meaning as in section 56(1) of the Insurance Act;

"old modification scheme" means a scheme made pursuant to section 28(3) of the Widows', Orphans' and Old Age Contributory Pensions Act 1936(a);

"participating employment" means, in relation to any period which is reckonable as service for the purposes of the local government superannuation Acts, any employment in which a person—

(a) is required to pay graduated contributions under section 4(1)(c) of the Insurance Act as amended by section 1 of the National Insurance Act 1966, or

(b) would be required to pay such contributions if the amount which was paid in any income tax week on account of his remuneration (or which would have been paid but for any suspension of remuneration due to leave of absence) exceeded the amount first mentioned in section 4(1) of the Insurance Act as so amended,

and includes any similar period of employment in which a person is, or would be, required to pay graduated contributions under the Northern Ireland Act or the Isle of Man Act; but the expression does not include any period of national service in respect of which contributions are paid under the Superannuation (Local Government Staffs) (National Service) Rules 1949 to 1954(b) if immediately prior to entering national service the person was in non-participating employment;

"payment in lieu of contributions" means a payment in lieu of contributions under Part III of the Insurance Act;

"pension" means a retirement pension or a benefit under the Benefits Regulations corresponding to a superannuation allowance under Part I of the Act of 1937, and includes a pension to which a person has become entitled prospectively, on attaining some greater age;

"person entitled to 1937 benefits" means a person entitled to a benefit under the Benefits Regulations corresponding to a superannuation allowance under Part I of the Act of 1937, and "1937 benefits" shall be construed accordingly;

"person entitled to 1954 benefits" means a person (other than a person entitled to 1937 benefits) entitled to benefits under the Benefits Regulations, and "1954 benefits" shall be construed accordingly;

"person subject to flat-rate reduction", "person subject to graduated reduction" and "person subject to combined reduction" have the respective meanings assigned by regulation 4, and "flat-rate reduction", "graduated reduction" and "combined reduction" mean the appropriate reduction required to be made in relation to such a person by Part II or III, as the case may be, of these regulations;

"person entitled to the optant's rate" means a person who—

(a) was a contributory employee, a local Act contributor or an established officer or servant at some time within 12 months before the material date, and

(b) gave notice pursuant to regulation 10 of the 1947 regulations, and

(a) 1936 c. 33.
(b) S.I. 1949/545; 1951/2145; 1954/1228 (1949 I, p.3105; 1951 II, p. 164; 1954 II, p. 1760).

(c) becomes entitled to a pension without having had a break of more than 12 months since that time (except as permitted by regulation 17),

and "entitled to the optant's rate" shall be construed accordingly;

"person who retains unmodified status" means—

(a) a person whose contributions and pension were, by virtue of the 1947 regulations or of interchange rules, not subject immediately before the commencement of these regulations to reduction to take into account his entitlement to a state flat-rate pension, or

(b) a person in respect of whom there is received, on or after the commencement of these regulations, pursuant to interchange rules, a transfer value which has been calculated by reference to the transfer value regulations and which has not been reduced under any modification provision,

and who in either case remains a contributory employee or local Act contributor without a disqualifying break of service (except as permitted by regulation 17);

"reckonable", in relation to service, means reckonable or otherwise entitled to be taken into account in calculating the amount of a pension;

"retirement pension" means a retirement pension under regulation 5 of the Benefits Regulations;

"retiring remuneration", in relation to a retirement pension, means the remuneration on which that benefit is calculated, or if that benefit is not calculated by reference to remuneration, the annual average of the person's remuneration for the purposes of the relevant superannuation scheme during the period of 3 years ending with the last day of his service;

"Stage I" means the period from 3rd April 1961 to 5th January 1964;

"Stage II" means the period from 6th January 1964;

"state flat-rate pension" means a retirement pension referred to in section 30 of the Insurance Act;

"state graduated pension" means a graduated retirement benefit referred to in section 36 of the Insurance Act;

"war service" has the same meaning as in the Local Government Staffs (War Service) Act 1939(a).

(2) For the purposes of regulations 28(2)(b) and 32(1), any reference to a period of employment at the end of which a payment in lieu of contributions has been made or is required to be made shall include a reference to a period of employment which has become reckonable by virtue of interchange rules and in respect of which equivalent pension benefits have been assured for the purposes of Part III of the Insurance Act.

(3) In these regulations, any reference to any benefit assured or payable, payment made or other thing whatsoever done under the Insurance Act or Insurance Acts shall be deemed to include a reference to a corresponding benefit, payment or thing assured, payable, made or done under the National Insurance Act 1959.

(4) In these regulations, any reference to a payment in lieu of contributions made under any insurance code shall be construed as a reference to a payment in lieu of contributions or a corresponding payment made under the Northern Ireland Act or the Isle of Man Act.

(a) 1939 c. 94.

(5) In these regulations, unless the context otherwise requires, references to any enactment shall be construed as references to that enactment as amended, modified, extended, applied or re-enacted by or under any subsequent enactment, including these regulations.

(6) Any reference in these regulations to a regulation, schedule or paragraph which is not otherwise identified is a reference to that regulation or schedule of these regulations or to that paragraph of the regulation in which the reference occurs, as the case may be.

(7) For the purposes of these regulations, no account shall be taken, where any amount of money falls to be paid, of fractions of a penny less than a halfpenny, and fractions of a penny of a halfpenny or more shall be treated as a penny.

(8) As from the first payment of remuneration or of retirement pension made in the new currency on or after 15th February 1971 (the day appointed under section 1 of the Decimal Currency Act 1967(a)) references in paragraph (7) to a penny and to a halfpenny shall be read as referring to a new penny and to a new halfpenny respectively.

(9) The Interpretation Act 1889(b) shall apply for the interpretation of these regulations as it applies for the interpretation of an Act of Parliament, and as if these regulations and the regulations revoked by regulation 40 were Acts of Parliament.

Definition of enactments

3. In these regulations—

"the Act of 1937" means the Local Government Superannuation Act 1937;

"the 1947 regulations" means the National Insurance (Modification of Local Government Superannuation Schemes) Regulations 1947(c);

"the Act of 1948" means the Superannuation (Miscellaneous Provisions) Act 1948(d);

"the Act of 1953" means the Local Government Superannuation Act 1953;

"the actuarial valuation regulations" means the Local Government Superannuation (Actuarial Valuations) Regulations 1954(e);

"the administration regulations" means the Local Government Superannuation (Administration) Regulations 1954(f);

"the Benefits Regulations" means the Local Government Superannuation (Benefits) Regulations 1954(g);

"the Firemen's Pension Scheme" means the scheme for the time being in force under section 26 of the Fire Services Act 1947(h);

"the Insurance Act" means the National Insurance Act 1965;

"the Insurance Acts" means the National Insurance Acts 1965 to 1969(i);

"insurance code" means the Insurance Act, the Northern Ireland Act or the Isle of Man Act;

(a) 1967 c. 47.   (b) 1889 c. 63.
(c) S.R. & O. 1947/1245 (Rev. XVI, p. 273; 1947 I, p. 1498).
(d) 1948 c. 33.   (e) S.I. 1954/1224 (1954 II, p. 1537).
(f) S.I. 1954/1192 (1954 II, p. 1570).   (g) S.I. 1954/1048 (1954 II, p. 1595).
(h) 1947 c. 41.
(i) 1965 c. 51; 1966 c. 6; 1967 c. 73; 1969 c. 4.

"interchange rules" means rules made under section 2 of the Act of 1948 (which provides for the pensions of persons transferring to different employment) and includes any similar instrument made, or having effect as if made, under any other Act which makes similar provision;

"the Isle of Man Act" means the National Insurance (Isle of Man) Act 1961 (an Act of Tynwald);

"the local government superannuation Acts" means the Local Government Superannuation Acts 1937 to 1953;

"the Northern Ireland Act" means the National Insurance Act (Northern Ireland 1959(a);

"the old Insurance Acts" means the National Health Insurance Acts 1936 to 1941(b) or the Widows', Orphans' and Old Age Contributory Pensions Act 1936;

"the transfer value regulations" means the Local Government Superannuation (Transfer Value) Regulation 1954(c).

Purport of Parts II, III and IV

4.—(1) The provisions of Parts II and III of these regulations shall have effect for modifying the general Act scheme in relation to the contributions and other superannuation payments payable by and the benefits payable to contributory employees who are or have been insured persons, in connection with the operation of the enactments relating to state flat-rate and graduated pensions; and in these regulations, subject to the provisions of paragraph (2)—

(a) "person subject to flat-rate reduction" means such a person to whom the said Part II applies;

(b) "person subject to graduated reduction" means such a person who retains unmodified status and to whom the said Part III applies in respect of any period of participating employment; and

(c) "person subject to combined reduction" means any other such person to whom the said Part III so applies.

(2) The provisions of Part II of these regulations shall not apply for the flat-rate reduction of the contributions or other superannuation payments payable by or the benefits payable to any person in respect of any period during which the provisions of Part III of these regulations apply for the combined reduction thereof:

Provided that this paragraph shall not affect regulation 13 or 14 so far as either regulation enables a person to retain the benefit of any modifications referred to therein.

(3) The provisions of Part IV of these regulations shall have effect for modifying the general Act scheme consequent upon the other provisions of these regulations.

Equivalent pension benefits

5. The provisions of Part V of these regulations shall have effect for modifying the general Act scheme in order to ensure that the benefits secured thereby are equivalent pension benefits for the purpose of the Insurance Acts.

(a) 1959 c. 21. (N.I.)
(b) 1936 c. 32; 1937 (1 & 2 Geo. 6) c. 3; 1938 c. 14; 1939 c. 84; 1941 c. 39.
(c) S.I. 1954/1212 (1954 II, p. 1723).

Local Act schemes

6. So far as the provisions of these regulations can (with the modifications hereinafter referred to) apply to a local Act scheme, they shall so apply; and for this purpose they shall have effect subject to the modifications set out in Part VI hereof.

Retained local Act rights

7. Where a contributory employee retains by virtue of any enactment rights corresponding to those which he formerly enjoyed as a local Act contributor, Parts II to V of these regulations shall apply to him subject to any modifications necessary to give effect to his retained rights.

PART II

FLAT-RATE REDUCTION

Persons subject to flat-rate reduction

8.—(1) The provisions of this Part of these regulations shall apply to any insured person who is, or immediately before becoming entitled to a pension was, a contributory employee, unless he is a person described in paragraph (3).

(2) The provisions of this Part of these regulations shall apply to any such person referred to in regulation 13, 14 or 15 subject to any modifications effected thereby, and to any such person in part-time employment to the extent specified in regulation 16.

(3) The persons referred to in paragraph (1) are—

(*a*) any person who retains unmodified status;

(*b*) any person who entered the employment in which he is a contributory employee after leaving other employment in which he was a contributory employee or a local Act contributor or in respect of which he was super-annuable out of public funds, having become (otherwise than in consequence of permanent ill-health or infirmity of mind or body) entitled to immediate payment of a pension or a corresponding benefit payable under any enactment;

(*c*) any person who—

(i) being a person to whom section 6(1) of the Act of 1953 applies (which section relates to re-employed pensioners), entered employment in which he was a contributory employee or a local Act contributor within 12 months after leaving employment in respect of which he became entitled to immediate payment of a pension or injury allowance, payable out of public funds, other than a pension or benefit to which sub-paragraph (*b*) above applies; and

(ii) immediately before he left the last-mentioned employment retained unmodified status; and

(iii) has not had a disqualifying break of service since the said section 6(1) first applied to him.

Definition of "material date"

9. In this Part of these regulations, the expression "material date", in relation to a person described in column (1) of the following table, means the date specified in column (2) in respect of such person:—

TABLE

(1)	(2)

1. An insured person who on 1st September 1947—
   (i) was insured under the old Insurance Acts and
   (ii) was a contributory employee, a local Act contributor or an established officer or servant—
	1st September 1947

2. An insured person who first at any time between 1st September 1947 and 30th September 1954—
   (i) was insured under the old Insurance Acts or an insured person and
   (ii) was such in the capacity of contributory employee, local Act contributor or established officer or servant—
	The date on which he was first after 1st September 1947 insured under the old Insurance Acts or an insured person

3. Any other insured person—	The date on which he was first an insured person in the capacity of contributory employee or local Act contributor

Reduction of contributions

10. Subject to the provisions of this Part of these regulations, the amount of the contributions payable under the general Act scheme by a person subject to flat-rate reduction shall be reduced as from the material date at a rate per annum of—

(a) £3 0s. 8d. in the case of a man or of a woman in the early retirement classes or

(b) £3 5s. 0d. in the case of a woman serving in any other capacity;

and the amount of the contributions payable in respect of that person by the employing authority shall be reduced at the same rate.

Reduction in payments for added years and additional contributory payments

11.—(1) Any amount payable by a person subject to flat-rate reduction—

(a) by way of additional contributions in respect of years added under regulation 12 of the Benefits Regulations, or

(b) in accordance with schedule 2 to the Benefits Regulations in respect of a period of non-contributing service of which account may be taken in calculating the amount of the reduction of any pension to which the person may become entitled,

shall be reduced, in the case of the additional contributions mentioned in paragraph (a) by the annual amount, and in the case of any amount to which paragraph (b) applies by the lump sum, obtained by—

(i) ascertaining the sum by which, in respect of the years so added or the period of non-contributing service which may be so taken into account, any pension to which the person may become entitled is liable to be reduced under paragraph 1 of schedule 1; and

(ii) taking for each pound of the sum so ascertained (and proportionately for any fraction of a pound) the sum shown in the appropriate column of table I or II, as the case may be, in schedule 2 in relation to the age which corresponds with his age on the date on which consent was given under regulation 12 of, or notice was given under schedule 2 to, the Benefits Regulations, as the case may be.

(2) In reckoning the amount of the equivalent contributions payable by an employing authority in respect of years added as aforesaid, account shall be taken of any reduction under this regulation of the person's additional contributions.

Reduction of pensions

12.—(1) Subject to the provisions of this Part of these regulations, where a pension becomes payable to a person subject to flat-rate reduction, by reason of his ceasing to hold employment under an authority which was treated as his employer for purposes of section 3 of the Insurance Act (which relates to flat-rate contributions), the pension shall be reduced in accordance with the provisions of schedule 1.

(2) The reduction referred to in paragraph (1) shall take effect on the date on which the pension becomes payable unless the person has not then reached pensionable age within the meaning of the Insurance Act, in which case the reduction shall take effect on the date on which he reaches that age.

Persons transferring from the National Health Service or Scottish local government

13.—(1) This regulation applies to any person who became or becomes a contributory employee or local Act contributor within 12 months after leaving employment in relation to which—

(*a*) he was entitled to participate in superannuation benefits provided by regulations made under section 67(1) of the National Health Service Act 1946**(a)** or section 66(1) of the National Health Service (Scotland) Act 1947**(b)**, or

(*b*) he was a contributory employee or local Act contributor within the meaning of the Local Government Superannuation (Scotland) Act 1937**(c)**,

having left that employment on or after 5th July 1948, or if he left that employment on or after that date in order to undertake national service, within 6 months after the termination of that service, so long as he remains a contributory employee without a disqualifying break of service (except as permitted by regulation 17).

(2) The provisions of the Act of 1937 with respect to the payment of contributions shall apply, or continue to apply, in relation to any person to whom this regulation applies subject, as nearly as may be, to modifications corresponding to any which, by virtue of his having been an insured person, were applicable in relation to him in the former employment referred to in paragraph (1).

(a) 1946 c. 81.   (b) 1947 c.27.
(c) 1937 c.69.

(3) Where this regulation applies to any person immediately before he becomes entitled to a pension, that pension shall be subject to modifications corresponding to those which were applicable in relation to him in the former employment referred to in paragraph (1).

(4) For the purposes of this regulation no account shall be taken of any modification applicable in relation to a person solely by virtue of his having been a person of a special class, unless he was a person of that class on becoming a contributory employee or local Act contributor.

Persons subject to old modification schemes

14.—(1) This regulation applies to any person in relation to whom an old modification scheme was in force, or by virtue of regulation 12(3) of the 1947 regulations was deemed to be in force, immediately before 1st September 1947, and who did not give notice pursuant to regulation 10 of those regulations, so long as he remains a contributory employee without a break of more than 12 months (except as permitted by regulation 17).

(2) The provisions of the Act of 1937 with respect to the payment of contributions shall continue to apply in relation to any person to whom this regulation applies subject to modifications corresponding to any which were applicable in relation to him by virtue of the old modification scheme.

(3) Where this regulation applies to any person immediately before he becomes entitled to a pension, that pension shall be subject to modifications corresponding to those which were applicable in relation to him by virtue of the old modification scheme; and if he is entitled to a retirement grant under the Benefits Regulations the amount thereof shall be reduced by the amount ascertained by—

(a) multiplying 3/80ths of the amount which, by the said scheme, was required to be deducted from the annual average of his remuneration in calculating his superannuation allowance by the number of years of contributing service in respect of which his pension is by virtue of the said modifications reduced;

(b) multiplying 3/160ths of the amount which was required to be deducted as aforesaid by the number of years of non-contributing service in respect of which his pension is so reduced; and

(c) increasing the sum of the products by ½ per cent. for any such year of contributing service, and by ¼ per cent. for any such year of non-contributing service, in respect of which his retirement grant is increased under regulation 14 of the Benefits Regulations:

Provided that—

(i) where a person's pension is by virtue of regulation 5(3) of the Benefits Regulations at the rate of 20/80ths of his average remuneration, he shall be treated as having had, and as having paid reduced contributions in respect of, additional contributing service equal to the difference between the period of his service (non-contributing service being reckoned in calculating that period at half its full length) and 20 years;

(ii) where the old modification scheme contained provision that the superannuation allowance should not be reduced below a sum calculated by reference to a fraction of a person's average remuneration, that provision shall apply to the reduction of a retirement pension as if the reference were to 60/80ths of the said fraction;

(iii) so much of this paragraph as relates to the reduction of a retirement grant shall not apply to any person unless under the said scheme the amount of the reduction of benefit was calculated by reference to the annual average of his remuneration;

(iv) where under the said scheme the reduction was subject to a maximum amount in respect of each year or other shorter period of payment, the retirement grant shall not be reduced by any greater amount than the amount by which the capital value of the said maximum amount (or, as the case may be, of the annual equivalent of the maximum amount) exceeds the capital value of the amount by which the pension is reduced.

Persons transferring from fire brigade

15.—(1) This regulation applies to any person who—

(*a*) becomes or became a contributory employee or a local Act contributor having left employment which is or is treated as employment as a member of a fire brigade of a class prescribed by the Firemen's Pension Scheme for the purposes of section 2 of the Fire Services Act 1951**(a)** (which provides for the application of that Scheme to the exclusion of other pension enactments), and

(*b*) immediately before leaving that employment was an insured person in relation thereto, and

(*c*) by virtue of that employment became entitled, under regulations made by the Secretary of State under section 28 of the Fire Services Act 1947 (which contains supplementary provisions for the preservation of pensions), to reckon a period as contributing service or service for the purposes of a local Act scheme.

(2) If a person to whom this regulation applies was not subject to the operation of the provisions of the Firemen's Pension Scheme requiring the reduction of ordinary, short service and ill-health pensions in relation to any insured person, this Part of these regulations shall not apply to him so long as he remains a contributory employee or local Act contributor without a disqualifying break of service (except as permitted by regulation 17).

(3) If a person to whom this regulation applies was subject to the operation of the provisions referred to in paragraph (2)—

(*a*) this Part of these regulations in their application to him shall have effect as if, when he became a contributory employee or local Act contributor, the period referred to in paragraph (1)(*c*) became contributing service or service for the purposes of the local Act scheme, as the case may be, rendered after 5th July 1948; and

(*b*) if he was so subject by virtue of the making of an election or the giving of a notice and has not had a break of more than 12 months (except as permitted by regulation 17) the provisions of schedule 1 shall apply in relation to him as if the period referred to in paragraph (1)(*c*) were contributing service to which paragraph 1(3) of that schedule applied, with the substitution for the reference to age on the material date of a reference to age at the date on which the said election or notice became effective.

(a) 1951 c. 27.

(4) No account shall be taken for the purposes of this regulation of any period which a person became entitled to reckon as contributing service or service for the purposes of the local Act scheme, as the case may be, unless it is attributable to service which would have been taken into account for the purposes of the provisions of the Firemen's Pension Scheme referred to in paragraph (2).

Persons in part-time employment

16.—(1) Where a person subject to flat-rate reduction is during any period a contributory employee in the part-time employment of one or more local authorities and is also in other employment in which he is not a contributory employee, then if his employer in that other employment is treated as his employer for the purposes of section 3 of the Insurance Act no account shall be taken for the purposes of this Part of these regulations of his service during that period.

(2) Where an insured person is a contributory employee in the part-time employment of two or more employing authorities, this Part of these regulations shall only apply in relation to him in his employment under the authority (if any) which is treated as his employer for the purposes of section 3 of the Insurance Act.

(3) Where an insured person is a contributory employee in each of two or more separate employments under the same employing authority, then, subject to the provisions of paragraphs (1) and (2), this Part of these regulations shall apply in relation to him only in whichever of those employments occupies the greater part of his time or, if this cannot readily be ascertained, in whichever the authority may determine.

(4) Notwithstanding anything contained in this Part of these regulations, where two or more pensions are payable in respect of employments which had been held concurrently under the same employing authority, this Part shall only apply for the reduction of whichever of those pensions is attributable to the employment which occupied the greater part of his time or, if this cannot readily be ascertained, whichever the authority may determine.

Extensions of time for national service, etc.

17. Notwithstanding any provision of this Part of these regulations—

(*a*) a person engaged in war service within 12 months before the material date shall be deemed to have been a contributory employee or local Act contributor or an established officer or servant within 12 months before that date if he undertook that service on ceasing to be employed in one of those capacities;

(*b*) a person shall not be treated as having had a break of more than 12 months or a disqualifying break of service if at any time he ceased to be a contributory employee or local Act contributor or an established officer or servant in order to undertake war service or immediately after so ceasing became engaged in national service, but re-entered employment in one of those capacities within 12 months of the termination of his war service or 6 months of the termination of his national service, as the case may be;

(*c*) any reference (however expressed) to a period of more than 12 months from the date on which a person left local government employment or to a break of more than 12 months shall be construed, in relation to a person to whom section 6 of the Act of 1948 (which makes special provision as to periods of emergency) has become applicable, as a reference to a period of 5 years from the date of leaving that employment, or such longer period as the Minister may in any particular case allow.

PART III

COMBINED AND GRADUATED REDUCTION

Persons subject to combined or graduated reduction

18. This Part of these regulations shall apply to any contributory employee who is or has been an insured person in respect of any period of participating employment.

Reduction of contributions

19. Subject to the provisions of this Part of these regulations, the amount of the contributions payable under the general Act scheme by a person subject to combined or graduated reduction shall be reduced by the appropriate rate per annum specified in the following table:—

TABLE

Case	Rate per annum
A. A person subject to combined reduction	The greater of— (a) 1 per cent. of so much of his remuneration as ascertained for the purposes of the general Act scheme as does not exceed the maximum graduated remuneration for the time being or (b) £3 0s. 8d. in the case of a man or of a woman in the early retirement classes or £3 5s. in the case of a woman serving in any other capacity;
B. A person subject to graduated reduction	A rate calculated as for Case A, *minus*— £3 0s. 8d. in the case of a man or a woman in the early retirement classes or £3 5s. in the case of a woman serving in any other capacity;
C. A person subject to combined reduction to whom regulation 13 or 14 applies	A rate calculated as for Case B, *plus*— the amount by which his contributions are required to be reduced under that regulation;

and the contributions payable in respect of that person by the employing authority shall be reduced at the same rate.

Reduction of payments for added years and additional contributory payments

20.—(1) Any amounts payable by or in respect of a person subject to combined or graduated reduction by way of additional contributions in respect of years added under regulation 12 of the Benefits Regulations shall be reduced throughout the period for which they are payable in accordance with the provisions of paragraph 1 of schedule 3.

(2) Where in respect of any period of participating employment, or any period of non-participating employment in respect of which a payment in lieu of contributions is required to be made, additional contributory payments of the kind referred to in section 2(3) of the Act of 1953 are made by a person subject to combined or graduated reduction, those payments shall be reduced in accordance with the provisions of paragraphs 2 and 3 of schedule 3.

Reduction of pensions

21.—(1) Subject to the provisions of these regulations, where a pension becomes payable to a person subject to combined or graduated reduction, on his ceasing to hold employment under an authority which was treated as his employer for the purposes of section 3 of the Insurance Act, and any period of service reckonable in calculating the amount of the pension was in participating employment, the part of the pension which is attributable to any such period of service shall be reduced in accordance with the provisions of schedule 4.

(2) The provisions of regulation 12(2) as to the date on which a reduction under regulation 12(1) takes effect shall apply to a reduction under paragraph (1).

(3) No account shall be taken under paragraph (1) of any part of a period of service in respect of which a reduction of pension is required to be made under regulation 32.

(4) For the purposes of this Part of these regulations no account shall be taken of any period of participating employment as a contributory employee or local Act contributor occurring during an income tax year if no graduated contributions have been paid under the Insurance Acts in respect of any such period during that year.

(5) Notwithstanding anything in paragraph (4), a period of employment as a contributory employee or local Act contributor at the end of which a payment in lieu of contributions is required to be made shall be treated as a period of participating employment.

Reduction of short service and death grants

22.—(1) The benefits to which this regulation applies are short service grants under regulation 9 of the Benefits Regulations, death grants under regulation 10 of those Regulations, and lump sum grants or similar benefits payable to or in respect of a person to whom regulation 7 applies in circumstances where no pension is payable.

(2) Subject to the provisions of this regulation, if there is payable to or in respect of a contributory employee a benefit to which this regulation applies and either—

> (*a*) a payment in lieu of contributions is required to be made by reason of the cessation of his employment, or such a payment has previously been made in respect of him as a contributory employee or local Act contributor in circumstances not involving a return of contributions, or
>
> (*b*) a payment in lieu of contributions had been made under any insurance code upon the termination of any period of employment which, by virtue of interchange rules, is reckonable in any manner and to any extent as service as a contributory employee, and—
>
>> (i) the transfer value payable in respect of that employment has been adjusted to take account of the payment in lieu of contributions, and
>>
>> (ii) where superannuation contributions had been made by him in that employment, the payment in lieu of contributions was made in circumstances not involving the return of those superannuation contributions,

the employing authority may resolve that the relevant benefit shall be reduced by a sum not exceeding one half of the payment in lieu of contributions, or the aggregate of such payments if more than one has been made, and in that case the amount of the benefit shall be calculated accordingly.

(3) No payment in lieu of contributions shall be taken into account for the purposes of this regulation—

(*a*) on more than one occasion, or

(*b*) if the payment is one which has been reduced under regulation 13 of the National Insurance (Non-participation—Assurance of Equivalent Pension Benefits) Regulations 1960(**a**) or any corresponding enactment in force in Northern Ireland or the Isle of Man.

(4) Where any benefit to which this regulation applies is payable on the cessation of two or more concurrently held employments, the power conferred by this regulation shall be exercisable—

(*a*) in relation to any payment in lieu of contributions then required to be made, by the authority making that payment, and

(*b*) in relation to any such payment previously made, by whichever of the authorities lately employing the person as they may agree, or in default of agreement, as may be determined by the Minister, and when the said employments were held under the same employing authority, the power shall be exercised in relation to such one only of the benefits as the authority may determine.

Reduction of benefit attributable to added years, etc.

23. In any case where a payment referred to in regulation 20 has been reduced in accordance with the provisions of schedule 3, the period in respect of which any such payment has been made shall be treated as a period of service (rendered, if any requisite consent was given during Stage II, during that Stage) in participating employment in respect of which graduated contributions have been paid; and the part of the pension to which the person concerned subsequently becomes entitled which is attributable to that period shall be reduced in accordance with the provisions of this Part of these regulations.

Calculation of disability pension

24. Where a retirement pension granted on the grounds of incapacity to perform the duties of an employment by reason of permanent ill-health or infirmity of mind or body is, under regulation 5(3)(*a*) of the Benefits Regulations, payable at a minimum rate, the amount (if any) by which such minimum rate exceeds the amount which would have been payable apart from that regulation shall not be subject to combined or graduated reduction; but if any part of the pension is subject to flat-rate reduction, the first-mentioned amount shall likewise be subject to flat-rate reduction.

Calculation of additional compensatory benefit

25.—(1) In reckoning the amount of any retirement pension for the purpose of estimating the maximum additional benefit which an employing authority may grant under regulation 13(1) of the Benefits Regulations, no account shall be taken of any reduction required to be made under these regulations.

(**a**) S.I. 1960/1103 (1960 II, p.2244).

(2) Where any additional benefit referred to in paragraph (1) supplements a retirement pension which is subject to flat-rate reduction, the additional benefit shall likewise be subject to flat-rate reduction; and for this purpose the additional benefit shall be deemed to be paid in respect of a period of service which is subsequent to any material date, and which at the relevant rate of retiring remuneration would have created entitlement to a retirement pension equivalent to the additional benefit.

Persons in part-time employment

26.—(1) Where a person in the part-time employment of one or more employing authorities is also in other employment in which he is not a contributory employee, then if his employer in that other employment is treated as his employer for the purposes of section 3 of the Insurance Act, this Part of these regulations shall not apply to him.

(2) The provisions of regulation 16(2), (3) and (4) shall have effect as if set out in terms in this regulation, subject only to the modification that references to Part II of these regulations shall be construed as references to Part III.

PART IV

MISCELLANEOUS AND CONSEQUENTIAL

Contributions deemed to have been made under the Act of 1937

27. If in respect of any period a contributory employee pays no contributions under the Act of 1937 because the amount of the reduction in his contributions provided for by Part II or III of these regulations equals or exceeds the amount of his contributions, he shall nevertheless be deemed for the purposes of section 12(1)(*a*) of the Act of 1937 (which relates to the reckoning of service in respect of which a person is required to contribute) to have made the contributions required in respect of that period.

Reduction of transfer values

28.—(1) Subject to the provisions of paragraph (2), where under the transfer value regulations a transfer value is payable in respect of a person subject to flat-rate reduction, the amount of the transfer value shall be reduced by the sum shown in the appropriate column of the table in schedule 5 in relation to an age which corresponds to that of the person on the date on which he ceased to be employed or, if he is a person to whom section 6 of the Act of 1948 (which makes special provision as to periods of emergency) has become applicable, the date on which he enters his new employment, in respect of each one pound of the amount by which any benefit by way of annual amounts to which he may become entitled as a contributory employee may be reduced under schedule 1 in respect of any service of which account is taken in the calculation of the transfer value, and by a proportionate sum in respect of any fraction of a pound included in the said amount.

(2) Where under the transfer value regulations a transfer value is payable for a period of service of one month or more which is or which includes—

  (*a*) service in participating employment or

  (*b*) service in non-participating employment at the end of which a payment in lieu of contributions had been made under any insurance code, being service which is reckonable for the purpose of calculating reductions of pension under Part III of these regulations or under regulation 32, the amount of the transfer value (or such part of it as is attributable to the period of such employment) shall be reduced in accordance with paragraph (3); and if the person is subject to combined reduction the remainder (if any) of the transfer value shall be reduced as it would be in respect of a person subject to flat-rate reduction.

(3) The transfer value (or such part of it as is attributable to the period of any such employment as is mentioned in paragraph (2)) shall be reduced by an amount equal to one quarter of the aggregate of sums calculated in accordance with paragraphs 4 and 5 of schedule 1 to the transfer value regulations—

(a) in respect of any such period or part of such period during Stage I, on so much of the person's remuneration as does not exceed £780 per annum, and

(b) in respect of any such period or part of such period during Stage II, on so much of the person's remuneration as does not exceed the maximum graduated remuneration for that period or part:

Provided that—

(i) where a transfer value becomes payable in respect of any person subject to graduated reduction, and either the contributions payable by him in his former employment have been subject to such reduction or a payment in lieu of contributions has been made on his ceasing to hold that employment, there shall be added to the transfer value or part as reduced the amount by which the transfer value or part would have been reduced under paragraph (1) if the benefit referred to therein had fallen to be reduced in pursuance of paragraph 1(2) of schedule 1, but the transfer value shall not thereby be increased to an amount greater than would have been the case if it had not been subject to modification under this regulation;

(ii) where a transfer value becomes payable in respect of any person subject to combined reduction who is also subject to an old modification scheme, and either the contributions payable by him in his former employment have been subject to such reduction, or a payment in lieu of contributions has been made on his ceasing to hold that employment, no account shall be taken in calculating the amount of the transfer value or part, or of the reduction required to be made hereunder, of any reduction of remuneration required to be made pursuant to proviso (iii) to the definition of "remuneration" in paragraph 1 of schedule 1 to the transfer value regulations;

(iii) the reduction in respect of any period of non-participating employment at the end of which a payment in lieu of contributions had been made under any insurance code shall be calculated as if the person's remuneration had been £780 per annum during any period or part of a period during Stage I, and the maximum graduated remuneration during any period or part of a period during Stage II; and

(iv) no account shall be taken of any amount attributable to a period of employment mentioned in paragraph (1) if the period is of less than one month's duration.

(4) If because of this regulation no sum is payable in respect of any transfer value, payment of the transfer value shall, for the purposes of any enactment requiring such payment, be deemed to have been made.

Adjustments following payment in lieu of contributions

29.—(1) In this regulation "returned contributions" means an amount payable under the general Act scheme to or in respect of a contributory employee by way of return of contributions, and includes any contributions deemed to have been made during any period of former employment which has become reckonable by virtue of interchange rules.

(2) Subject to the provisions of this regulation, where a contributory employee leaves employment, or dies, in circumstances in which returned contributions are due, and a payment in lieu of contributions has previously been made in respect of him in circumstances in which returned contributions were not due, those returned contributions shall be reduced by a sum equal to the amount, or the aggregate of the amounts, by which under section 60(5) of the Insurance Act (which defines an employer's rights against an insured person in respect of payments in lieu of contributions) they could have been reduced if returned at the time when the previous payment in lieu of contributions was made.

(3) Paragraph (2) shall also apply for the reduction of returned contributions where a payment in lieu of contributions has been made under any insurance code in respect of any period of former employment which is reckonable as service as a contributory employee if—

(a) that payment in lieu was made in circumstances not involving the return of any superannuation contributions made by him in that employment, and

(b) the transfer value payable in respect of that employment has been adjusted to take account of that payment in lieu;

and where no superannuation contributions were payable in that employment, any amount returnable in respect of contributions deemed to have been made therein shall be reduced by a sum equal to one half of that payment in lieu.

(4) No payment in lieu of contributions shall be taken into account for the purposes of this regulation—

(a) on more than one occasion, or

(b) if the payment is one which has been reduced under regulation 13 of the National Insurance (Non-participation—Assurance of Equivalent Pension Benefits) Regulations 1960 or any corresponding enactment in force in Northern Ireland or the Isle of Man.

(5) Where returned contributions are due in the circumstances mentioned in paragraph (2) on the cessation of two or more concurrently held employments, the reduction required by that paragraph shall be made by such one of the authorities paying the returned contributions as they may agree, or as in default of agreement the Minister may determine, and where those employments were held under the same employing authority, the reduction shall be made in relation to such one only of the employments as the authority may determine.

(6) Where returned contributions are reduced under paragraph (2) or under section 60(5) of the Insurance Act or any corresponding provision of the Northern Ireland Act or the Isle of Man Act, any sum so deducted shall not form part of any amount payable to or in respect of him, either as returned contributions or as a benefit ascertained by reference to the amount of the contributions paid by him, on the occasion of any later cessation of his employment.

Adjustments between authorities

30. Where a payment in lieu of contributions is made in respect of any contributory employee, the authority responsible for making the payment shall be entitled to recover out of the superannuation fund to which the person was last a contributor or, if the authority themselves maintain that fund, shall be entitled to retain out of that fund a sum not exceeding the lesser of the following amounts—

(*a*) the amount of the payment in lieu of contributions, less the amount (if any) which the authority could recover or retain under section 60 of the Insurance Act in respect of that payment or, in the case of a person to whom regulation 22 applies but the power conferred by that regulation is not invoked, the amount of the payment in lieu of contributions less the amount by which the short service grant or death grant or similar benefit could have been reduced under that regulation; and

(*b*) the amount paid into the fund in respect of the person (less any sum returnable to him as contributions) together with compound interest at the rate of 3 per cent. per annum with half-yearly rests.

Modification of certain interchange rules

31. Where any of the interchange rules referred to in schedule 6 provide, in relation to any person, that regulations made by the Minister under section 110 of the Insurance Act or any earlier enactment corresponding thereto shall not apply to him (either in whole or in part) on entering local government employment, those rules shall be read as providing that these regulations shall apply to him as a person who retains unmodified status.

Reduction of pension in respect of other reckonable service

32.—(1) Where a person has entered local government employment after having been employed in other employment (in this regulation referred to as "his former employment") and, by virtue of interchange rules, any service reckonable by him in his former employment is to be reckoned in any manner and to any extent as service as a contributory employee, then if his reckonable service in his former employment included any period of participating employment or non-participating employment at the end of which a payment in lieu of contributions had been made under any insurance code, so much of any pension payable to him at the termination of his local government employment as is attributable to any such period shall, in lieu of any reduction for which Part III of these regulations provides, be reduced—

(*a*) in the like manner as if—

(i) he had continued in his former employment and retired from it on the day on which he left local government employment, and

(ii) any modification provision applicable to him immediately before he left his former employment had been applied in relation to the period of his service before that date, or

(*b*) if no modification provision was applicable to him at that time and the transfer value payable in respect of that employment had been adjusted to take account of the payment in lieu of contributions, by the amount of the graduated retirement benefit payable under any insurance code in respect of the payment in lieu of contributions.

(2) Nothing in paragraph (1) shall affect any provision in interchange rules with regard to the modification of superannuation benefits in connection with the state flat-rate pension or to the right of any person to be excepted from such modification.

(3) A local authority, in determining any question arising under paragraph (1) relating to the service of any person in his former employment and the operation of any modification provision applicable to him in that employment, shall be entitled to treat as conclusive any relevant certificate issued by his employer in that employment or by the body administering the superannuation scheme to which he was subject therein.

Payments for added years and additional contributory payments continued from a former employment

33. Where in pursuance of interchange rules a contributory employee continues to make the like payments in respect of added years or additional contributory payments as he had been entitled to make in his former employment (as defined in regulation 32), and those payments are reduced in accordance with any provision corresponding with regulation 20, then, unless the payments commenced while he was a contributory employee or local Act contributor, the part of any pension to which he subsequently becomes entitled which is attributable to those payments shall be reduced in the manner provided in regulation 32(1), as if that part of the pension had been attributable to a period of such former employment.

Amendments to actuarial valuation and administration regulations

34.—(1) The actuarial valuation regulations and the administration regulations shall continue to have effect subject to the modifications set out in schedules 7 and 8 respectively, which repeat the effect of modifications made by the National Insurance (Modification of Local Government Superannuation Schemes) No 2 Regulations 1961(a), subject only to further modifications consequential on amendment or re-enactment of the enactments referred to therein.

(2) In schedules 7 and 8, "regulation" means a regulation contained in the regulations to which the schedule relates.

Part V

Equivalent Pension Benefits

Equivalent pension benefits

35. The general Act scheme shall have effect subject to the modifications contained in this Part of the Regulations, being modifications required to ensure that the benefits secured by that scheme are equivalent pension benefits for the purposes of the Insurance Acts.

Commencement of benefits not later than insured pensionable age

36.—(1) Notwithstanding any provision contained in the general Act scheme to the effect that a benefit is not payable to an employee who attains the age of 60 years unless the employee has completed 40 years' service, a female contributory employee not otherwise entitled to receive a pension under that

(a) S.I. 1961/405 (1961 I, p. 1031).

scheme shall upon retirement be entitled, in lieu of any other benefit receivable by her thereunder, to receive the benefits mentioned in paragraph (2) on ceasing to hold an employment in which she was a contributory employee if she has attained the age of 60 years and has completed 10 years' service.

(2) The benefits referred to in paragraph (1) are such benefits as would have been payable to a female contributory employee under the general Act scheme in respect of the service actually reckonable by her immediately before she ceased to hold her employment if—

    (a) she had then reached pensionable age as defined in paragraph (5), and

    (b) the amount of any benefit so calculated had been reduced according to the age at which she ceased to hold her employment by the percentage shown in the column appropriate to her pensionable age in the table in schedule 9:

Provided that an annual pension so payable in respect of any period of service shall not be less than the minimum rate of equivalent pension benefits applicable in respect of that period under the Insurance Acts.

(3) For the purposes of the proviso to paragraph (2) "service" means service in a non-participating employment which is reckonable by the employee for the purpose of calculating the amount of any benefit payable to her, except any earlier period of such service in respect of which—

    (a) a payment in lieu of contributions had been made, or

    (b) equivalent pension benefits satisfying the requirements of the Insurance Acts had already been assured to her.

(4) In calculating benefit for the purposes of—

    (i) paragraph (2),

    (ii) regulation 7 of the Local Government Superannuation (Benefits) (New Towns Staffs) Regulations 1958(a), or

    (iii) rule 4(2) of the Superannuation (Local Government and Overseas Employment) Interchange Rules 1958(b),

no account shall be taken of any reduction required by the provisions of Part II or III of these regulations; but those provisions shall apply for the reduction of benefit when the person attains or has attained pensionable age within the meaning of the Insurance Act.

(5) In paragraph (2), "pensionable age" means the earliest age at which, if the person were to remain a contributory employee without any break in service, she would become entitled, on ceasing to be employed, to a pension other than a pension payable in consequence of her being incapable of discharging efficiently the duties of her employment by reason of permanent ill-health or infirmity of mind or body.

Limitations on surrender, termination, etc., of pensions

37. No provision in the general Act scheme—

    (a) for the surrender, commutation or assignment of a pension, or

    (b) for the reduction, termination or suspension of a pension, where the provision is invoked for any cause other than one prescribed by

---

(a) S.I. 1958/1273 (1958 II, p. 1806).   (b) S.I. 1958/1416 (1958 II, p. 1845).

regulations made or deemed to have been made under section 57(1)(c) of the Insurance Act (which section describes equivalent pension benefits),

shall operate so as to reduce a pension payable in respect of any period of service to an employee who attains the age of 65 years in the case of a man, or 60 years in the case of a woman, below the minimum rate of equivalent pension benefits applicable in respect of that period under the Insurance Acts; and for this purpose "service" has the meaning assigned to it by regulation 36(3).

PART VI

LOCAL ACT SCHEMES

General modification of local Act schemes

38. For the purpose of modifying these regulations to apply to a local Act scheme, any reference to an expression appearing in column (1) of the table below (which lists expressions used in the general Act scheme) shall be deemed to include a reference to the expression appearing opposite thereto in column (2) (which lists corresponding or similar expressions appropriate to a local Act scheme):—

TABLE

	(1)	(2)
1.	contributory employee	local Act contributor
2.	contributing service	service or a period of contribution for purposes of a local Act scheme
3.	employing authority local authority	local Act authority
4.	the local government superannuation Acts, or the regulations thereunder	a local Act under which a superannuation fund is maintained or a local Act scheme, or any enactment referred to in item 4 of column (1) as applied by such an Act or scheme
5.	a provision (including any complete Part) in the local government superannuation Acts or the regulations thereunder, or in these regulations	the corresponding or similar provision in a local Act or local Act scheme, or the provision referred to in item 5 of column (1) as applied by such an Act or scheme
6.	a superannuation benefit under the Benefits Regulations	a corresponding or similar superannuation benefit under the local Act or local Act scheme;

and the provisions of these regulations referred to in regulation 39 shall have effect in their application to a local Act scheme subject to the further modifications specified in that regulation.

Modification, etc., of particular regulations

39.—(1) In regulation 2(1), in the definition of "early retirement classes", for the reference to regulation 21 of the Benefits Regulations there shall be substituted a reference to regulation 22 thereof.

(2) Regulation 14 shall not apply to a local Act contributor.

(3) In regulation 20, for the reference to additional contributory payments of the kind referred to in section 2(3) of the Act of 1953, there shall be substituted a reference to—

(*a*) payments made under a local Act scheme as a condition of reckoning any period of employment as service or as a period of contribution for the purposes of the scheme or, where the local Act scheme provides for the reckoning of non-contributing service, as contributing service for the purposes of the scheme; and

(*b*) payments made for the purpose of increasing the length at which any period of service or of contribution would be reckonable for the purpose of calculating a benefit under a local Act scheme.

(4) For the purposes of paragraphs 1 and 2 of schedule 3, the additional contributions and payments required in the case of a local Act contributor shall be at the appropriate rate specified in the paragraph in question or at such rate as an actuary shall certify to be necessary in order to secure, as nearly as may be, a similar proportionate reduction in the amount of the contributions or payments, as the case may be, to that provided for therein.

Part VII

Revocations, Etc.

Revocations

40. The regulations referred to in schedule 10 are hereby revoked.

Enactments ceasing to apply, etc.

41.—(1) The following enactments, which provide for the modification of retirement benefits and other payments under the general Act scheme and certain local Act schemes, namely—

(*a*) Part III of and Schedule 3 to the Benefits Regulations,

(*b*) Part IV of the City of London Superannuation Scheme 1955(a),

(*c*) Part IV of the Manchester Superannuation (Benefits) Scheme 1955(b), and

(*d*) article 9 of the Manchester Superannuation (Service) Scheme 1957(c), shall cease to apply; and instead the provisions of these regulations shall apply for such modification.

(2) In regulation 5(3)(*b*) (as amended by regulation 20(1) of the National Insurance (Modification of Local Government Superannuation Schemes) Regulations 1963(d)) and regulation 8(4) of the Benefits Regulations, references to Part III of those regulations or to Part III of the National Insurance (Modification of Local Government Superannuation Schemes) No. 2 Regulations 1961 shall be read as referring to the National Insurance (Modification of Local Government Superannuation Schemes) Regulations 1969.

(**a**) Approved by S.I. 1955/476.   (**b**) Approved by S.I. 1955/1347.
(**c**) Approved by S.I. 1957/1685.   (**d**) S.I. 1963/2060 (1963 III, p. 4363).

Regulation 12

SCHEDULE 1

Flat-Rate Reduction of Pensions

Reductions to be made under this schedule

1.—(1) Subject to the provisions of this schedule, the pension payable to a person subject to flat-rate reduction shall be reduced—

(*a*) for each year which is reckonable as contributing service, by the basic reduction specified in respect of him in sub-paragraph (2) or (3), as the case may be, of this paragraph;

(*b*) for each year which is reckonable as non-contributing service, by one half of that sum;

(*c*) for any fraction of a year which is reckonable under a local Act scheme, by an equivalent fraction of that sum.

(2) Except in the case of a person entitled to the optant's rate, the basic reduction shall be £1 14s. in respect of service on and after the material date or 5th July 1948, whichever is the earlier.

(3) In the case of a person entitled to the optant's rate, the basic reduction shall be the sum shown in the relevant column of table I or II in this schedule in relation to the age which corresponds with his age on the material date in respect of—

(*a*) service on and after the material date or 5th July 1948, whichever is the earlier, and

(*b*) service before the material date during which he paid reduced contributions under an old modification scheme to which he was subject immediately before, or when he was last a contributory employee before, the material date.

Mode of reckoning service

2. For the purpose of calculating the amount of the reduction under this schedule—

(*a*) all periods of service in respect of which the reduction is required to be made shall be aggregated;

(*b*) the period reckonable as contributing service in calculating the amount of the reduction for the aggregate period shall be the number of completed years of all periods of such service comprised in that period;

(*c*) the period so reckonable as non-contributing service shall be the remainder of the aggregate period after deducting the completed years of contributing service, but if such remainder amounts to a period of less than a year or to a number of years and a period of less than a year, the period of less than a year shall, if it amounts to or exceeds 6 months, be treated as a year and in any other case be disregarded;

(*d*) where in pursuance of section 12(5) of the Act of 1937 a period of part-time service is treated as though it were whole-time service for a proportionately reduced period for the purposes of calculating a pension, paragraph 1 of this schedule shall apply as if the part-time service in question had been reckonable at its full length (but so that the reduction thus made shall not exceed the amount of the pension attributable to that service); and

(*e*) any service in excess of 40 years' contributing service or 40 years' contributing service and non-contributing service, the non-contributing service being reckoned at half its full length, shall be disregarded.

Added years

3.—(1) For the purposes of this schedule, any added years shall be deemed to be contributing service rendered after 5th July 1948; but any added years which before 5th July 1948 had become reckonable under a local Act or local Act scheme shall be reckoned accordingly as service before that date.

(2) In this paragraph "added years" means any additional years of service reckonable under regulation 12 of the Benefits Regulations or under a local Act or local Act scheme or under regulations made under the Act of 1937.

Pension subject to minimum pension provision

4. For the purposes of this schedule, where a retirement pension is, by virtue of regulation 5(3) of the Benefits Regulations, at the rate of 20/80ths of a person's average remuneration, he shall be treated as having reckonable as contributing service, and as having paid reduced contributions in respect of, an additional period equal to the difference between the aggregate of his contributing and non-contributing service (non-contributing service being reckoned for that purpose at half its full length) and 20 years.

Persons subject to old modification schemes

5. If a person, having paid reduced contributions for any period under an old modification scheme, or an earlier enactment corresponding thereto, had paid thereunder a sum representing the difference between those contributions and the sum he would have contributed if both contributions had not been reduced, his service during that period shall not be treated as service in respect of which reduced contributions were paid.

Service in respect of which reduced transfer value has been paid

6. Where after the commencement of these regulations a person becomes entitled to reckon service by virtue of interchange rules, and there has been paid a transfer value which is in part reduced, by reason of modification provisions in the pension scheme concerned, and in part unreduced, the service to which the unreduced part relates shall be treated as service before 1st September 1947.

Maximum flat-rate reduction

7. No pension shall be reduced under this schedule by more than £67 15s. 0d. per annum.

TABLE I

Optant's rate—male officers and servants

(1) Age									(2) Annual sum		
									£	s.	d.
Under 20 ...	...	...	...	...	...	...	...	...	1	14	0
20 and under 21	...	...	...	...	...	...	...	...	1	14	0
21 ,, ,, 22	...	...	...	...	...	...	...	...	1	13	0
22 ,, ,, 23	...	...	...	...	...	...	...	...	1	12	6
23 ,, ,, 24	...	...	...	...	...	...	...	...	1	12	0
24 ,, ,, 25	...	...	...	...	...	...	...	...	1	11	0
25 ,, ,, 26	...	...	...	...	...	...	...	...	1	10	6
26 ,, ,, 27	...	...	...	...	...	...	...	...	1	10	0
27 ,, ,, 28	...	...	...	...	...	...	...	...	1	9	6
28 ,, ,, 29	...	...	...	...	...	...	...	...	1	9	0
29 ,, ,, 30	...	...	...	...	...	...	...	...	1	8	6
30 ,, ,, 31	...	...	...	...	...	...	...	...	1	8	0
31 ,, ,, 32	...	...	...	...	...	...	...	...	1	7	6
32 ,, ,, 33	...	...	...	...	...	...	...	...	1	7	0
33 ,, ,, 34	...	...	...	...	...	...	...	...	1	6	0
34 ,, ,, 35	...	...	...	...	...	...	...	...	1	5	6
35 ,, ,, 36	...	...	...	...	...	...	...	...	1	5	0
36 ,, ,, 37	...	...	...	...	...	...	...	...	1	4	6
37 ,, ,, 38	...	...	...	...	...	...	...	...	1	4	0
38 ,, ,, 39	...	...	...	...	...	...	...	...	1	3	6
39 ,, ,, 40	...	...	...	...	...	...	...	...	1	3	0
40 ,, ,, 41	...	...	...	...	...	...	...	...	1	2	6
41 ,, ,, 42	...	...	...	...	...	...	...	...	1	2	0
42 ,, ,, 43	...	...	...	...	...	...	...	...	1	1	6
43 ,, ,, 44	...	...	...	...	...	...	...	...	1	1	0
44 ,, ,, 45	...	...	...	...	...	...	...	...	1	0	6
45 ,, ,, 46	...	...	...	...	...	...	...	...	1	0	0
46 ,, ,, 47	...	...	...	...	...	...	...	...		19	6
47 ,, ,, 48	...	...	...	...	...	...	...	...		19	0
48 ,, ,, 49	...	...	...	...	...	...	...	...		18	6
49 ,, ,, 50	...	...	...	...	...	...	...	...		18	0
50 ,, ,, 51	...	...	...	...	...	...	...	...		17	6
51 ,, ,, 52	...	...	...	...	...	...	...	...		17	0
52 ,, ,, 53	...	...	...	...	...	...	...	...		17	0
53 ,, ,, 54	...	...	...	...	...	...	...	...		16	6
54 ,, ,, 55	...	...	...	...	...	...	...	...		16	0
55 and over	...	...	...	...	...	...	...	...		15	6

TABLE II

Optant's rate—female officers and servants

(1) Age	Annual sum	
	(2) Those in early retirement classes	(3) Others
	£ s. d.	£ s. d.
Under 20 ...	1 14 0	1 14 0
20 and under 21 ...	1 14 0	1 14 0
21 „ „ 22 ...	1 11 0	1 11 6
22 „ „ 23 ...	1 8 0	1 9 6
23 „ „ 24 ...	1 5 6	1 7 6
24 „ „ 25 ...	1 3 0	1 5 6
25 „ „ 26 ...	1 1 0	1 4 0
26 „ „ 27 ...	19 6	1 2 6
27 „ „ 28 ...	18 0	1 1 0
28 „ „ 29 ...	17 0	1 0 0
29 „ „ 30 ...	16 0	19 0
30 „ „ 31 ...	15 6	18 0
31 „ „ 32 ...	15 0	17 6
32 „ „ 33 ...	14 6	17 0
33 „ „ 34 ...	14 0	16 6
34 „ „ 35 ...	13 6	16 0
35 „ „ 36 ...	13 0	15 6
36 „ „ 37 ...	13 0	15 0
37 „ „ 38 ...	12 6	14 6
38 „ „ 39 ...	12 6	14 0
39 „ „ 40 ...	12 6	13 6
40 „ „ 41 ...	12 0	13 6
41 „ „ 42 ...	12 0	13 0
42 „ „ 43 ...	12 0	13 0
43 „ „ 44 ...	11 6	12 6
44 „ „ 45 ...	11 6	12 6
45 „ „ 46 ...	11 0	12 0
46 „ „ 47 ...	11 0	12 0
47 „ „ 48 ...	11 0	12 0
48 „ „ 49 ...	11 0	11 6
49 „ „ 50 ...	11 0	11 6
50 and over ...	11 0	11 0

Regulation 11

SCHEDULE 2

Flat-Rate Reduction of Voluntary Payments

Table I

Payments in respect of added years

(1) Age at date of giving consent	(2) Men	(3) Women
	s. d.	s. d.
27 and under 28 ...	1 4	2 1
28 „ „ 29 ...	1 5	2 3
29 „ „ 30 ...	1 6	2 6
30 „ „ 31 ...	1 7	2 8
31 „ „ 32 ...	1 8	2 11
32 „ „ 33 ...	1 9	3 1
33 „ „ 34 ...	1 10	3 4
34 „ „ 35 ...	1 11	3 7
35 „ „ 36 ...	2 1	3 10
36 „ „ 37 ...	2 2	4 1
37 „ „ 38 ...	2 4	4 5
38 „ „ 39 ...	2 6	4 9
39 „ „ 40 ...	2 8	5 1
40 „ „ 41 ...	2 10	5 6
41 „ „ 42 ...	3 0	5 11
42 „ „ 43 ...	3 3	6 5
43 „ „ 44 ...	3 6	6 11
44 „ „ 45 ...	3 10	7 6
45 „ „ 46 ...	4 3	8 2
46 „ „ 47 ...	4 8	9 0
47 „ „ 48 ...	5 1	9 11
48 „ „ 49 ...	5 8	10 11
49 „ „ 50 ...	6 4	12 2
50 „ „ 51 ...	7 1	13 8
51 „ „ 52 ...	8 1	15 7
52 „ „ 53 ...	9 4	17 11
53 „ „ 54 ...	11 0	21 0
54 „ „ 55 ...	13 3	25 2

TABLE II

ADDITIONAL CONTRIBUTORY PAYMENTS

(1) Age at date of giving notice	(2) Male officers and servants	(3) Female officers and servants (other than those mentioned in column (4))	(4) Female officers and servants in the early retirement classes
	£ s. d.	£ s. d.	£ s. d.
Under 20	2 0 0	1 0 0	15 0
20 and under 21 ...	2 1 0	1 2 0	17 0
21 „ „ 22 ...	2 3 0	1 4 0	19 0
22 „ „ 23 ...	2 5 0	1 7 0	1 2 0
23 „ „ 24 ...	2 6 0	1 10 0	1 5 0
24 „ „ 25 ...	2 8 0	1 13 0	1 9 0
25 „ „ 26 ...	2 10 0	1 17 0	1 14 0
26 „ „ 27 ...	2 12 0	2 2 0	2 1 0
27 „ „ 28 ...	2 14 0	2 8 0	2 9 0
28 „ „ 29 ...	2 16 0	2 15 0	2 17 0
29 „ „ 30 ...	2 18 0	3 2 0	3 6 0
30 „ „ 31 ...	3 0 0	3 9 0	3 17 0
31 „ „ 32 ...	3 2 0	3 17 0	4 8 0
32 „ „ 33 ...	3 4 0	4 5 0	4 19 0
33 „ „ 34 ...	3 6 0	4 12 0	5 9 0
34 „ „ 35 ...	3 9 0	5 0 0	5 19 0
35 „ „ 36 ...	3 11 0	5 8 0	6 8 0
36 „ „ 37 ...	3 13 0	5 15 0	6 15 0
37 „ „ 38 ...	3 15 0	6 3 0	7 1 0
38 „ „ 39 ...	3 17 0	6 11 0	7 7 0
39 „ „ 40 ...	4 0 0	6 18 0	7 12 0
40 „ „ 41 ...	4 2 0	7 5 0	7 17 0
41 „ „ 42 ...	4 4 0	7 13 0	8 2 0
42 „ „ 43 ...	4 7 0	8 0 0	8 6 0
43 „ „ 44 ...	4 10 0	8 7 0	8 11 0
44 „ „ 45 ...	4 13 0	8 13 0	8 16 0
45 „ „ 46 ...	4 16 0	8 19 0	9 1 0
46 „ „ 47 ...	4 19 0	9 5 0	9 6 0
47 „ „ 48 ...	5 2 0	9 11 0	9 12 0
48 „ „ 49 ...	5 5 0	9 17 0	9 18 0
49 „ „ 50 ...	5 9 0	10 4 0	10 4 0
50 „ „ 51 ...	5 13 0	10 11 0	10 10 0
51 „ „ 52 ...	5 17 0	10 18 0	10 16 0
52 „ „ 53 ...	6 1 0	11 5 0	11 2 0
53 „ „ 54 ...	6 5 0	11 12 0	11 9 0
54 „ „ 55 ...	6 10 0	12 0 0	11 16 0
55 „ „ 56 ...	6 15 0	12 8 0	12 4 0
56 „ „ 57 ...	7 0 0	12 16 0	12 13 0
57 „ „ 58 ...	7 6 0	13 5 0	13 2 0
58 „ „ 59 ...	7 12 0	13 14 0	13 12 0
59 „ „ 60 ...	7 18 0	14 3 0	14 2 0
60 „ „ 61 ...	8 4 0		
61 „ „ 62 ...	8 11 0		
62 „ „ 63 ...	8 19 0		
63 „ „ 64 ...	9 8 0		
64 „ „ 65 ...	9 17 0		

Regulation 20

SCHEDULE 3

Combined and Graduated Reduction of Certain Voluntary Payments

1. The additional contributions referred to in regulation 20(1) shall be—

  (i) where consent to the making of the payments was given during Stage I, at the rate of three-quarters of the appropriate percentage of remuneration specified in column 2 of schedule 1 to the Benefits Regulations for so much of the remuneration as does not exceed £780 per annum, and at the appropriate percentage so specified for so much of the remuneration (if any) as exceeds that amount; or

  (ii) where such consent was given during Stage II, at the like rate so specified for so much of the remuneration as does not exceed the maximum graduated remuneration in force at the time when such consent was given, and at the appropriate percentage so specified for so much of the remuneration (if any) as exceeds that amount.

2.—(1) The payments referred to in regulation 20(2) shall be—

  (*a*) at the rate of three-quarters of the appropriate percentage of remuneration specified in column 2, 3 or 4 of the table in schedule 2 to the Benefits Regulations, in respect of the specified remuneration, and

  (*b*) at the full rate so specified, in respect of any part of the remuneration which exceeds the specified remuneration.

(2) In this paragraph the expression "specified remuneration" means—

  (*a*) in respect of any period of employment during Stage I, the remuneration received, up to a maximum of £780;

  (*b*) in respect of any period of employment during Stage II, the remuneration received, up to the maximum graduated remuneration;

but where the payments are begun during Stage II in respect of any period of employment at the end of which a payment in lieu of contributions is or was required to be made, the expression means—

  (i) in respect of any period of employment during Stage I, £780 per annum;

  (ii) in respect of any period of employment during Stage II, the maximum graduated remuneration taken into account in calculating the payment in lieu of contributions.

3. In the case of a person subject to combined reduction, the reduction required by this schedule shall not be less than any reduction which would, but for regulation 4(2), have been required by regulation 11.

Regulation 21

SCHEDULE 4

Combined and Graduated Reduction of Pensions

Reductions to be made under this schedule

1.—(1) So much of any pension as is attributable to any period of participating employment (excluding any period referred to in regulation 21(5)) shall be treated in accordance with the paragraph of the table in this schedule which is appropriate to the case:

Provided that in no case shall the reduction effected thereunder exceed the combined reduction.

(2) For the purposes of this schedule, periods of service shall be computed in the same manner as they are computed under paragraph 2(*a*), (*b*), (*c*) and (*d*) of schedule 1 for the purposes of that schedule.

Definitions

2. In this schedule—

"relevant remuneration", in relation to a person, means—

    (i) in respect of any period or part of a period of participating employment during Stage I, so much of his retiring remuneration as does not exceed £780, and

    (ii) in respect of any such period or part during Stage II, so much of his retiring remuneration as does not exceed the maximum graduated remuneration;

"combined reduction" means—

    (i) for each year of participating employment which is reckonable as contributing service, a sum equal to 1/240th of relevant remuneration;

    (ii) for each such year which is reckonable as non-contributing service, a sum equal to 1/480th of relevant remuneration; and

    (iii) for any fraction of such a year which is reckonable under a local Act scheme, by an equivalent fraction of a sum equal to 1/240th of relevant remuneration; and

"sum to be added back" means the aggregate of—

    (i) £1 14s. for each year of contributing service,

    (ii) 17s. for each year of non-contributing service, and

    (iii) an equivalent fraction of £1 14s. for any fraction of a year which is reckonable under a local Act scheme,

comprised in the period of participating employment.

Only 40 years' contributing service to be taken into account

3. There shall be deducted from the amount of the combined reduction, in respect of any service in excess of 40 years' contributing service or 40 years' contributing and non-contributing service, the non-contributing service being reckoned at half its full length—

    (*a*) in the case of a person other than a person entitled to the optant's rate, the sum of £1 14s. in respect of each completed year comprised in such service, or

    (*b*) in the case of a person entitled to the optant's rate, a sum in respect of each such year equal to that by which the retirement benefit would have been reduced if the year had been reckonable as contributing service and if paragraph 1(3) of schedule 1 had applied.

Minimum reduction

4. In relation to a person who would, but for regulation 4(2), have been subject to flat-rate reduction, the combined reduction shall not be less than the reduction which would have been required by Part II of these regulations if he had been subject thereto.

Retirement from non-participating employment

5. For the purposes of this schedule, where a person becomes entitled to a pension on ceasing to be employed in a non-participating employment, or would have become entitled to a pension in those circumstances had he not continued in employment for more than five years after attaining pensionable age within the meaning of the Insurance Act, no account shall be taken, in respect of any period of participating employment, of retiring remuneration in excess of that specified during the period in a certificate of non-participation issued under section 56 of the Insurance Act as the level of his remuneration at which his employment would have become non-participating employment.

Treatment of period at the end of which payment in lieu of contributions is made

6. Paragraphs 1 to 4 of this schedule shall apply for the reduction of so much of any pension as is attributable to any period of employment referred to in regulation 21(5) as if the relevant remuneration had been—

(*a*) in relation to any period or part of a period during Stage I, £780, and

(*b*) in relation to any period or part of a period during Stage II, the maximum graduated remuneration taken into account in calculating the payment in lieu of contributions.

TABLE

	Case	Treatment of pension
A	Person subject to combined reduction	Reduce by the combined reduction
B	Person subject to graduated reduction	Reduce by the combined reduction and then— Increase by the sum to be added back
C	Person subject to combined reduction who is also entitled to the optant's rate	Treat as for Case B, and then— Reduce further by the amount of the reduction specified in paragraph 1(3) of schedule 1
D	Person subject to combined reduction who is also subject to an old modification scheme	Treat as for Case B, and then— Reduce further by the amount of the modification referred to in regulation 14(3)

Provided that where an old modification scheme postpones reduction until the pensioner attains an age greater than pensionable age within the meaning of the Insurance Acts, the pensioner shall, until he attains that greater age, be treated as a person subject to graduated reduction.

SCHEDULE 5   *Regulation* 28
REDUCTION OF TRANSFER VALUES

(1) Age	(2) Male officers and servants			(3) Female officers and servants (other than those mentioned in column (4))			(4) Female officers and servants in the early retirement classes		
	£	s.	d.	£	s.	d.	£	s.	d.
Under 20	2	0	0	1	0	0		15	0
20 and under 21	2	1	0	1	2	0		17	0
21 ,, ,, 22	2	3	0	1	4	0		19	0
22 ,, ,, 23	2	5	0	1	7	0	1	2	0
23 ,, ,, 24	2	6	0	1	10	0	1	5	0
24 ,, ,, 25	2	8	0	1	13	0	1	9	0
25 ,, ,, 26	2	10	0	1	17	0	1	14	0
26 ,, ,, 27	2	12	0	2	2	0	2	1	0
27 ,, ,, 28	2	14	0	2	8	0	2	9	0
28 ,, ,, 29	2	16	0	2	15	0	2	17	0
29 ,, ,, 30	2	18	0	3	2	0	3	6	0
30 ,, ,, 31	3	0	0	3	9	0	3	17	0
31 ,, ,, 32	3	2	0	3	17	0	4	8	0
32 ,, ,, 33	3	4	0	4	5	0	4	19	0
33 ,, ,, 34	3	6	0	4	12	0	5	9	0
34 ,, ,, 35	3	9	0	5	0	0	5	19	0
35 ,, ,, 36	3	11	0	5	8	0	6	8	0
36 ,, ,, 37	3	13	0	5	15	0	6	15	0
37 ,, ,, 38	3	15	0	6	3	0	7	1	0
38 ,, ,, 39	3	17	0	6	11	0	7	7	0
39 ,, ,, 40	4	0	0	6	18	0	7	12	0
40 ,, ,, 41	4	2	0	7	5	0	7	17	0
41 ,, ,, 42	4	4	0	7	13	0	8	2	0
42 ,, ,, 43	4	7	0	8	0	0	8	6	0
43 ,, ,, 44	4	10	0	8	7	0	8	11	0
44 ,, ,, 45	4	13	0	8	13	0	8	16	0
45 ,, ,, 46	4	16	0	8	19	0	9	1	0
46 ,, ,, 47	4	19	0	9	5	0	9	6	0
47 ,, ,, 48	5	2	0	9	11	0	9	12	0
48 ,, ,, 49	5	5	0	9	17	0	9	18	0
49 ,, ,, 50	5	9	0	10	4	0	10	4	0
50 ,, ,, 51	5	13	0	10	11	0	10	10	0
51 ,, ,, 52	5	17	0	10	18	0	10	16	0
52 ,, ,, 53	6	1	0	11	5	0	11	2	0
53 ,, ,, 54	6	5	0	11	12	0	11	9	0
54 ,, ,, 55	6	10	0	12	0	0	11	16	0
55 ,, ,, 56	6	15	0	12	8	0	12	4	0
56 ,, ,, 57	7	0	0	12	16	0	12	13	0
57 ,, ,, 58	7	6	0	13	5	0	13	2	0
58 ,, ,, 59	7	12	0	13	14	0	13	12	0
59 ,, ,, 60	7	18	0	14	3	0	14	2	0
60 ,, ,, 61	8	4	0	14	3	0	14	3	0
61 ,, ,, 62	8	11	0	13	13	0	13	13	0
62 ,, ,, 63	8	19	0	13	4	0	13	4	0
63 ,, ,, 64	9	8	0	12	15	0	12	15	0
64 ,, ,, 65	9	17	0	12	6	0	12	6	0
65 ,, ,, 66	9	18	0	11	16	0	11	16	0
66 ,, ,, 67	9	9	0	11	6	0	11	6	0
67 ,, ,, 68	9	1	0	10	17	0	10	17	0
68 ,, ,, 69	8	13	0	10	8	0	10	8	0
69 ,, ,, 70	8	5	0	9	18	0	9	18	0
70 ,, ,, 71	7	17	0	9	9	0	9	9	0

Regulation 31

SCHEDULE 6

INTERCHANGE RULES AFFECTED BY REGULATION 31

The Superannuation (Local Government and Public Boards) Interchange Rules 1949 and 1955(a)

The Superannuation (English Local Government and Isle of Man) Interchange Rules 1951(b)

The Superannuation (English Local Government and Northern Ireland) Interchange Rules 1952 and 1958(c)

The Superannuation (English Local Government and Northern Ireland Health Service) Interchange Rules 1957(d)

The Superannuation (English Local Government and Northern Ireland Civil Service) Interchange Rules 1957(e)

The Superannuation (English Local Government and Jersey) Interchange Rules 1961(f)

The Superannuation (Teaching and Local Government) Interchange Rules 1961(g)

The Superannuation (Civil Service and Local Government) Interchange Rules 1968(h)

The Superannuation (Local Government and National and Local Government Officers Association) Interchange Rules 1969(i)

The Superannuation (Scottish Teaching and English Local Government) Interchange Rules 1969(j)

(a) S.I. 1949/1464; 1955/1546 (1949 I, p. 3075; 1955 II, p. 1782).
(b) S.I. 1951/309 (1951 II, p. 148).
(c) S.I. 1952/937; 1958/2136 (1952 II, p. 2354; 1958 II, p. 1822).
(d) S.I. 1957/2197 (1957 II, p. 1783).   (e) S.I. 1957/1155 (1957 II, p. 1774).
(f) S.I. 1961/316 (1961 I, p. 501).   (g) S.I. 1961/1895 (1961 III, p. 3556).
(h) S.I. 1968/72 (1968 I, p. 182).   (i) S.I. 1969/456 (1969 I, p. 1300).
(j) S.I. 1969/790 (1969 II, p. 2207).

SCHEDULE 7

AMENDMENTS TO THE ACTUARIAL VALUATION REGULATIONS

PART I

1. In regulation 5(3)(*a*) (which regulation relates to the form of report upon actuarial valuation), for category (ii) there shall be substituted the following—

"(ii) all other persons whose rights or liabilities with respect to the payment of superannuation contributions, or the receipt of superannuation benefits, are subject to modification in connection with the National Insurance Act 1965;".

2. In regulation 7(1) (which provides for an estimate of liabilities), for sub-paragraph (*e*) there shall be substituted the following—

"(*e*) contributory employees of that authority whose rights or liabilities with respect to the payment of superannuation contributions, or the receipt of superannuation benefits, are subject to modification in connection with the National Insurance Act 1965, showing separately the persons whose liabilities are for the time being subject to modification only in connection with retirement pension under section 30 of that Act;".

3.—(1) References in the actuarial valuation regulations to any form set out in schedule 2 thereto shall be construed as including a reference to a form which is substantially to the like effect as the form so set out.

(2) For Form A (Consolidated Revenue Account) set out in the said schedule 2 there shall be substituted the form set out in Part II of this schedule.

(3) In Form H (Valuation Balance Sheet) set out in the said schedule 2—

(*a*) after the item relating to the value of pensions to spouses or other dependants there shall be inserted the following further item—

"Value of net cost to the fund of future payments under regulation 30 of the National Insurance (Modification of Local Government Superannuation Schemes) Regulations 1969"; and

(*b*) at the foot of the form there shall be added the following note—

"The item 'Value of net cost to the fund of future payments under regulation 30 of the National Insurance (Modification of Local Government Super-annuation Schemes) Regulations 1969' corresponds with paragraph (ii) of the item 'Payments under regulation 30 of the National Insurance (Modification of Local Government Superannuation Schemes) Regulations 1969' in the Consolidated Revenue Account (Form A)".

Part II

"Form A"

Consolidated Revenue Account

for the period from.................................... to....................................

	£		£
Amount of the superannuation fund at the beginning of the period		Superannuation benefits:—	
Contributions by employees		(i) pensions to retired employees...	
Equivalent contributions by authorities interested in the fund less reductions under schemes made under section 22 (6) of the Act for disposing of a surplus		(ii) widows' pensions	
		(iii) pensions to widows and dependants under an allocation scheme	
Annual charges		(iv) retirement grants	
Transfer values		(v) death grants	
Additional contributory payments (including payments made in pursuance of regulations made under section 13 (1) (b) of the Act in respect of service reckonable under those regulations)		(a) payments in respect of employees	
		(b) reduction under regulation 22 of the National Insurance (Modification of Local Government Superannuation Schemes) Regulations 1969	
Payments in respect of additional years of service reckonable under section 2 (1) of the Local Government Superannuation Act 1953, and payments made in pursuance of regulations made under section 13 (1) (b) of the Act in respect of additional years of service reckonable under those regulations		(vi) short service grants	
		(a) payments to employees	
		(b) reduction under regulation 22 of the National Insurance (Modification of Local Government Superannuation Schemes) Regulations 1969	
		(vii) payments on cessation of widows' pensions (regulation 8 (7) of the Local Government Superannuation (Benefits) Regulations 1954) ...	
Interest (including income tax refunds)		Returns of contributions on withdrawal:—	
		(i) payments to employees	
		(ii) payments to employing authorities under section 60 of the National Insurance Act 1965	
		Transfer values	

Other income (to be specified) ... ...

Income tax:—
   (i) on returns of contributions ... ...
   (ii) on transfer values ... ...
   (iii) on interest income ... ...
Payments under regulation 30 of the National Insurance (Modification of Local Government Superannuation Schemes) Regulations 1969:—
   (i) in respect of persons for whom a transfer value reduced under regulation 28 of those regulations is payable
   (ii) in respect of any other persons, less the amount of any reduction in death grants or short service grants made under regulation 22 of those regulations ...
Other expenditure (to be specified) ... ...
Amount of the superannuation fund at the end of the period

NOTES.—(i) The item "Annual charges" comprises amounts payable under the following provisions of the Act:—
  (a) section 21 (1);
  (b) section 22 (1);
  (c) section 22 (2);
  (d) section 22 (6);
  (e) combination schemes under section 2 (1) and (2);
  (f) admission agreements made or deemed to be made under section 15 (1) and (2) of the Local Government Superannuation Act 1953 or made under section 7 of the Superannuation (Miscellaneous Provisions) Act 1948.

(ii) "Contributions" includes payments which under any regulations are treated as contributions; and the item "Returns of contributions on withdrawal" is to include the amount reserved to meet any liabilities that may subsequently accrue in respect of employees who ceased to hold their employment in the last year of the accounting period and in respect of whom payments by way either of transfer value or return of contributions were not due to be made during that period. The amount reserved should be stated separately. An appropriate adjustment in respect of the amounts paid should be made in the next succeeding account.

(iii) All items in the above account must include any amounts (such as accrued interest, transfer values, etc.) which are appropriate to the period but which were not received or paid (as the case may be) during the period.

Certified correct.

Dated .... Signed .... Chief Financial Officer."

Regulation 34

SCHEDULE 8

AMENDMENTS TO THE ADMINISTRATION REGULATIONS

1. After paragraph (2) of regulation 2 (which relates to interpretation) there shall be inserted the following paragraph:—

"(2A) Any reference in these regulations to an enactment relating to national insurance shall be construed as including a reference to any earlier enactment corresponding thereto.".

2. In regulation 6 (which relates to questions to be decided by an employing authority)—

(i) for sub-paragraph (*d*) of paragraph (4) there shall be substituted the following—

"(*d*) what rate of contribution he is liable to pay to the appropriate superannuation fund; whether that rate of contribution is, by virtue of regulations made under section 110 of the National Insurance Act 1965, a reduced rate, and if so, the amount of the reduction and the date from which the reduction has effect;"

(ii) for sub-paragraph (*g*) of paragraph (4) there shall be substituted the following—

"(*g*) what previous service, if any, he is entitled to reckon, whether that service counts as contributing service, non-contributing service, qualifying service or as a period of contribution; whether any (and, if so, what period or periods) of that service was part-time service, and if it was, what proportion of whole-time service it represents; what period or periods of that service were in participating employment or non-participating employment for the purposes of Part III of the National Insurance (Modification of Local Government Superannuation Schemes) Regulations 1969; whether any such period of participating employment falls to be disregarded under regulation 21(4) of the said regulations of 1969; and whether a payment in lieu of contributions has been made or equivalent pension benefits have been assured under Part III of the National Insurance Act 1965 in respect of any such period of non-participating employment, and the amount of any payment in lieu of contributions;".

3. After regulation 13 (which relates to the transmission of information by employing authorities to administering authorities) the following regulation shall be inserted:—

"13A.—(1) Every employing authority not being an administering authority shall, from time to time, notify the appropriate administering authority of—

(*a*) the amount of any payment in lieu of contributions which becomes payable under the National Insurance Act 1965 in respect of a contributory employee, and the period to which such payment relates;

(*b*) details of the amount, if any, by which the employing authority have resolved under regulation 22 of the National Insurance (Modification of Local Government Superannuation Schemes) Regulations 1969 to reduce the amount of any benefit payable to, or in respect of, a contributory employee;

(*c*) details of any amount which the employing authority are entitled to recover under section 60(1) of the National Insurance Act 1965 or under regulation 30 of the National Insurance (Modification of Local Government Superannuation Schemes) Regulations 1969 in respect of any payment in lieu of contributions made under that Act.

(2) The payment by an administering authority of any amounts referred to in paragraph (1)(c) of this regulation shall be accompanied by a statement showing—

(a) the names of the contributory employees in relation to whom the payment is made;

(b) the amounts which have been deducted from superannuation benefits pursuant to any resolution referred to in paragraph (1)(b) of this regulation.".

4. In regulation 16(1) (which relates to the exchange of information between local authorities in cases of transfer)—

(a) for sub-paragraph (e) there shall be substituted the following sub-paragraph—

"(e) the rate of his contribution and if, by virtue of regulations made under section 110 of the National Insurance Act 1965, that rate is, or has been, a reduced rate, the amount of the reduction and the date from which, or, as the case may be, the period during which, the reduction had effect;";

(b) in sub-paragraph (f) the following item shall be added—

"(vi) whether the employment was participating employment or non-participating employment for the purposes of Part III of the National Insurance (Modification of Local Government Superannuation Schemes) Regulations 1969, the dates of commencement and termination of any such employment and of any participating employment which falls to be disregarded under regulation 21(4) of the said regulations of 1969 and such information about temporary interruptions occurring in any period of non-participating employment as may be required for the purposes of regulation 3 of the National Insurance (Non-Participation—Assurance of Equivalent Pension Benefits) Regulations 1960;";

(c) after sub-paragraph (j) the following paragraph shall be added—

"(k) details of the amount, showing the period to which it related, of any payment in lieu of contributions made under the National Insurance Act 1965, the National Insurance Act (Northern Ireland) 1959 or the National Insurance (Isle of Man) Act 1961 (an Act of Tynwald) with respect to the person.".

Regulation 36

SCHEDULE 9

REDUCTION OF BENEFITS UNDER REGULATION 36

PART I

PENSION

Age of woman on ceasing to be employed	Percentage reduction to be made under regulation 36(2)(*b*) by reference to the under-mentioned pensionable age				
	61	62	63	64	65
60	7	15	21	28	33
61	—	8	15	22	28
62	—	—	8	16	23
63	—	—	—	9	17
64	—	—	—	—	9

PART II

RETIREMENT GRANT OR EQUIVALENT LUMP SUM BENEFIT

Age of woman on ceasing to be employed	Percentage reduction to be made under regulation 36(2)(*b*) by reference to the under-mentioned pensionable age				
	61	62	63	64	65
60	4	9	13	16	20
61	—	5	9	13	17
62	—	—	5	9	14
63	—	—	—	5	10
64	—	—	—	—	5

SCHEDULE 10
REVOCATIONS

Column 1 Regulations revoked	Column 2 References	Column 3 Extent of revocation
The National Insurance (Modification of Local Government Superannuation Schemes) Regulations 1947	S.R. & O. 1947/1245 (Rev. XVI, p. 273: 1947 I, p. 1498).	The whole regulations
The National Insurance (Modification of Local Government Superannuation Schemes) Amendment Regulations 1947	S.R. & O. 1947/1675 (1947 I, p. 1507).	The whole regulations
The National Insurance (Modification of Local Government Superannuation Schemes) Amendment Regulations 1948	S.R. & O. 1948/1225 (Rev. XIV, p. 284: 1948 I, p. 2861).	The whole regulations
The National Insurance (Modification of Local Government Superannuation Schemes) (Amendment) Regulations 1949	S.I. 1949/632 (1949 I, p. 2750).	The whole regulations
The National Insurance (Modification of Local Government Superannuation Schemes) (Amendment No. 2) Regulations 1949	S.I. 1949/1466 (1949 I, p. 2752).	The whole regulations
The National Insurance (Modification of Local Government Superannuation Schemes) (Amendment) Regulations 1952	S.I. 1952/938 (1952 II, p. 2192).	The whole regulations
The National Insurance (Modification of Local Government Superannuation Schemes) (Amendment) Regulations 1954	S.I. 1954/1207 (1954 I, p. 1408).	The whole regulations
The Local Government Superannuation (Transfer Value) Regulations 1954	S.I. 1954/1212 (1954 II, p. 1723).	Part IV and Schedule 5
The National Insurance (Modification of Local Government Superannuation Schemes) Regulations 1961	S.I. 1961/21 (1961 I, p. 46).	The whole regulations
The National Insurance (Modification of Local Government Superannuation Schemes) No. 2 Regulations 1961	S.I. 1961/405 (1961 I, p. 1031).	The whole regulations
The National Insurance (Modification of Local Government Superannuation Schemes) Regulations 1963	S.I. 1963/2060 (1963 III, p. 4363).	The whole regulations
The National Insurance (Modification of Local Government Superannuation Schemes) (Amendment) Regulations 1966	S.I. 1966/1129 (1966 III, p. 2727).	The whole regulations

Given under the official seal of the Minister of Housing and Local Government on 6th June 1969.

(L.S.)

Anthony Greenwood,
Minister of Housing and
Local Government.

EXPLANATORY NOTE

(This Note is not part of the Regulations.)

These regulations consolidate the National Insurance (Modification of Local Government Superannuation Schemes) Regulations 1947 to 1954 and the National Insurance (Modification of Local Government Superannuation Schemes) Regulations 1961 to 1966, which modify the enactments relating to the superannuation of local government employees to take account of the contributions payable and the benefits receivable under the National Insurance Act 1965. The modifications take the form of reductions both of contribution and of benefit under the local government enactments. The regulations also supersede those provisions of the Local Government Superannuation (Benefits) Regulations 1954 which provide directly for modification of benefits.

The relevant provisions of the National Insurance Act 1965 are (a) those relating to flat-rate pension and (b) those relating to graduated pension. Local government employees whose remuneration does not exceed a certain level are within the graduated pension scheme; the remainder are not within the scheme or have been contracted out (except for purposes of the earnings-related short-term benefit scheme introduced by the National Insurance Act 1966).

Persons subject to the local government superannuation scheme are all placed into one of the following four classes:—

1. Those subject to no reduction—i.e. those who (a) enjoy "unmodified" status, by being within the National Insurance scheme before 1st September 1947, as local government employees, and by subsequently retaining that status (which can be lost by certain breaks or changes in employment) and (b) are contracted out of the graduated pension scheme;

2. Those subject to flat-rate reduction—i.e. those who (a) do not enjoy, or have lost, "unmodified" status and (b) are contracted out of the graduated pension scheme;

3. Those subject to graduated reduction—i.e. those who (a) enjoy "unmodified" status and (b) are within the graduated pension scheme;

4. Those subject to combined reduction—i.e. those who (a) do not enjoy, or have lost, "unmodified" status and (b) are within the graduated pension scheme.

The maximum reductions applicable to each class are as follows:—

(a) for those subject to flat-rate reduction: a reduction in contribution of £3 5s. 0d. or £3 0s. 8d. per year, and a reduction in pension of £1 14s. 0d. per year of contributing service (or 17s. 0d. per year of non-contributing service) to a maximum of £67 15s. 0d. per year;

(b) for those subject to graduated reduction: reductions as for a person subject to combined reduction *less* the amount of the reductions which would have been applicable had they been subject to flat-rate reduction;

(c) for those subject to combined reduction: a reduction in contribution of 1 per cent. per year on the maximum annual amount on which contributions are payable towards the graduated pension scheme, and a reduction in pension of 1/240 per year of contributing service (or 1/480 per year of non-contributing service).

Provision is made to prevent anomalies as between classes and to preserve rights of certain special categories of employee. Corresponding reductions are made in relation to all forms of additional contributions and short service and death grants.

The substance of these modifications is contained in Parts II and III of the Regulations. Part IV contains consequential provisions in relation to transfer values, to adjustments necessitated by payments in lieu of contributions (which assure rights under the graduated scheme where there is a transfer to employment which is not contracted out) and to other regulations relating to the administration of local government superannuation. Part V assures to local government employees pension benefits not less favourable than those available under the graduated pension scheme (thus enabling them to be contracted out). Part VI deals with local Act schemes. Part VII provides for revocations.

Considerable drafting changes have been made from the revoked regulations; but the changes of substance are minor. These include—

(i) provision for treatment of service on transfer to local government employment from other employment with a transfer value modified in part only;

(ii) a revised definition of national service;

(iii) the supersession by these regulations of modification provisions in local Act schemes;

(iv) a clarification of the point of time (namely, upon retirement) when a female employee who has attained 60 becomes entitled to a local government pension under the equivalent pension benefit provisions of Part V.

STATUTORY INSTRUMENTS

1969 No. 794 (S.63)

ANIMALS

DEER

The Sale of Venison (Forms etc.) (Scotland) Regulations 1969

Made - - -	6th *June* 1969
Laid before Parliament	17th *June* 1969
Coming into Operation	3rd *July* 1969

In exercise of the powers conferred upon me by sections 1(3) and 2(1) of the Sale of Venison (Scotland) Act 1968(**a**) and of all other powers enabling me in that behalf I hereby make the following regulations :—

Citation, commencement and interpretation

1.—(1) These regulations may be cited as the Sale of Venison (Forms etc.) (Scotland) Regulations 1969 and shall come into operation on 3rd July 1969.

(2) In these regulations the expression "the Act" means the Sale of Venison (Scotland) Act 1968.

(3) The Interpretation Act 1889(**b**) shall apply for the interpretation of these regulations as it applies for the interpretation of an Act of Parliament.

Forms

2. The form contained in Schedule 1 to these regulations or a form substantially to the like effect shall be the form to be used for the purposes of making a return under section 1(3) of the Act.

3. The form contained in Schedule 2 to these regulations or a form substantially to the like effect shall be the form to be used for the purpose of entering records of all purchases and receipts of venison in the book required to be kept under section 2(1) of the Act and the particulars specified in the form contained in the said Schedule 2 shall be the particulars to be entered in such book.

William Ross,
One of Her Majesty's Principal
Secretaries of State.

St. Andrew's House,
Edinburgh.
6th June 1969.

(**a**) 1968 c. 38.   (**b**) 1889 c. 63.

SCHEDULE 1

Regulation 2

SALE OF VENISON (SCOTLAND) ACT 1968

.....................................Local Authority

RETURN TO THE RED DEER COMMISSION OF PERSONS REGISTERED AS DEALERS IN VENISON AT 1ST JANUARY 197 .

Date of Registration (1)	Full name of person registered (2)	Address of person registered (3)	Present address of person registered if different from (3) (4)

Regulation 3

SCHEDULE 2

SALE OF VENISON (SCOTLAND) ACT 1968

FORM OF RECORD OF PURCHASES AND RECEIPTS OF VENISON TO BE KEPT BY REGISTERED VENISON DEALERS

Date of purchase or receipt†	Species*	Particulars of carcases purchased or received						Particulars of parts of carcases purchased or received			Particulars of seller or in the case of a receipt the source‡ from which receipt obtained
		Male*		Female*		Total					
		No.	Weight	No.	Weight	No.	Weight	No. (of parts)	Description (of parts)	Weight	

†Where the source of the venison is deer killed by the dealer, enter date of killing

*Where it is not possible to obtain particulars to complete these columns, insert "not known"

‡Where the source of the venison is deer killed by the dealer, enter the name of the Estate on which killed.

EXPLANATORY NOTE

(This Note is not part of the Regulations.)

These Regulations prescribe the forms in which returns by local authorities of persons registered as venison dealers should be made to the Red Deer Commission, the form in which registered venison dealers should keep records of purchases and receipts of venison and the particulars to be entered in the book of records of such purchases and receipts.

STATUTORY INSTRUMENTS

1969 No. 804 (C.17)

MINES AND QUARRIES
The Mines and Quarries (Tips) Act 1969 (Commencement No. 1) Order 1969

Made - - - 12*th June* 1969

The Minister of Power in exercise of his powers under section 38(3) of the Mines and Quarries (Tips) Act 1969(a) hereby makes the following Order :—

1. This Order may be cited as the Mines and Quarries (Tips) Act 1969 (Commencement No. 1) Order 1969.

2. Part I of the Mines and Quarries (Tips) Act 1969 shall come into operation on 30th June 1969.

Dated 12th June 1969.

Roy Mason,

Minister of Power.

EXPLANATORY NOTE
(This Note is not part of the Order.)

This Order brings into operation on 30th June 1969 Part I of the Mines and Quarries (Tips) Act 1969, which provides for the security of tips associated with mines and quarries which have not been abandoned.

(a) 1969 c. 10.

STATUTORY INSTRUMENTS

1969 No. 805 (C.18)

MINES AND QUARRIES

The Mines and Quarries (Tips) Act 1969 (Commencement No. 2) Order 1969

Made - - - *12th June* 1969

The Minister of Housing and Local Government and the Secretary of State for Wales, in exercise of the powers conferred on them jointly by section 38(3) of the Mines and Quarries (Tips) Act 1969(a), and of all other powers enabling them in that behalf, hereby order as follows :—

1. This order may be cited as the Mines and Quarries (Tips) Act 1969 (Commencement No. 2) Order 1969.

2. Part II of the Mines and Quarries (Tips) Act 1969, in its application to England and Wales, shall come into operation on 30th June 1969.

Given under the official seal of the Minister of Housing and Local Government on 12th June 1969.

(L.S.)

Anthony Greenwood,
Minister of Housing and Local Government.

Given under my hand on 12th June 1969.

George Thomas,
Secretary of State for Wales.

EXPLANATORY NOTE

(This Note is not part of the Order.)

This Order brings into operation on 30th June 1969, in England and Wales, Part II of the Mines and Quarries (Tips) Act 1969, which provides for the prevention of public danger from disused tips.

(a) 1969 c. 10.

STATUTORY INSTRUMENTS

1969 No. 806

MINES AND QUARRIES
The Mines and Quarries (Tips) (Rate of Interest) Order 1969

Made - - -	*12th June* 1969
Laid before Parliament	*23rd June* 1969
Coming into Operation	*30th June* 1969

The Minister of Housing and Local Government, the Secretary of State for Wales and the Secretary of State for Scotland, in exercise of the powers conferred on them jointly by section 23(5) of the Mines and Quarries (Tips) Act 1969**(a)** and of all other powers enabling them in that behalf, hereby order as follows:—

1. This order may be cited as the Mines and Quarries (Tips) (Rate of Interest) Order 1969 and shall come into operation on 30th June 1969.

2. The Interpretation Act 1889**(b)** shall apply for the interpretation of this order as it applies for the interpretation of an Act of Parliament.

3. The rate of interest recoverable by a local authority under section 23(5) of the Mines and Quarries (Tips) Act 1969 (which provides for the recovery by local authorities of certain sums with interest from the date of the demand therefor under subsection (4) of the said section) shall be seven per cent. per annum.

Given under the official seal of the Minister of Housing and Local Government on 12th June 1969.

(L.S.)

Anthony Greenwood,
Minister of Housing and Local
Government.

Given under my hand on 12th June 1969.

George Thomas,
Secretary of State for Wales.

Given under the seal of the Secretary of State for Scotland on 12th June 1969.

(L.S.)

William Ross,
Secretary of State for Scotland.

(a) 1969 c. 10.   **(b)** 1889 c. 63.

EXPLANATORY NOTE

(This Note is not part of the Order.)

This Order, which applies throughout England, Wales and Scotland, specifies seven per cent. as the rate of interest recoverable by local authorities under section 23 of the Mines and Quarries (Tips) Act 1969 in respect of remedial operations on disused mine or quarry tips from owners and contributories.

STATUTORY INSTRUMENTS

1969 No. 807

MINES AND QUARRIES

The Disused Mine and Quarry Tips (Prescribed Forms) Regulations 1969

Made - - -	12*th June* 1969
Laid before Parliament	23*rd June* 1969
Coming into Operation	30*th June* 1969

The Minister of Housing and Local Government (as respects England, except Monmouthshire) and the Secretary of State for Wales (as respects Wales and Monmouthshire), in exercise of their powers under sections 14, 16, 17, and 36(1) of, and paragraph 2 of Schedule 2 to, the Mines and Quarries (Tips) Act 1969(**a**), and of all other powers enabling them in that behalf, hereby make the following regulations :—

Title and commencement

1. These regulations may be cited as the Disused Mine and Quarry Tips (Prescribed Forms) Regulations 1969, and shall come into operation on 30th June 1969.

Interpretation

2.—(1) The Interpretation Act 1889(**b**) shall apply for the interpretation of these regulations as it applies for the interpretation of an Act of Parliament.

(2) In these regulations, any reference to a numbered form is a reference to the form bearing that number in the schedule hereto, or a form substantially to the like effect.

Prescribed forms for purposes of remedial operations on disused tips

3. The prescribed forms for the undermentioned provisions of Part II of the Mines and Quarries (Tips) Act 1969 (which provide for the carrying out of remedial operations on disused mine and quarry tips constituting a public danger) shall be as follows :—

(*a*) for the purposes of section 14(1), the form of notice by a local authority requiring the owner of a disused tip to carry out remedial operations shall be form 1 ;

(*b*) for the purposes of section 14(5), the form of counter-notice by an owner requiring the local authority to exercise its powers under section 17 shall be form 2 ;

(**a**) 1969 c.10.   (**b**) 1889 c.63.

(c) for the purposes of section 16(1), the form of notice by a local authority cancelling a notice given under section 14 shall be form 3 ;

(d) for the purposes of section 17(2), the form of notice by a local authority to the owner of its intention to carry out remedial operations shall be form 4 ;

(e) for the purposes of section 17(3), the form of notice by a local authority to the owner where possible danger to the public requires it to proceed before serving a notice under section 17(2) shall be form 5 ;

(f) for the purposes of paragraph 2 of Schedule 2, the form of notice by a local authority specifying remedial operations which it proposes to carry out on a disused tip of which it is the owner shall be form 6.

SCHEDULE

FORM 1

MINES AND QUARRIES (TIPS) ACT 1969
SECTION 14(1)

REMEDIAL OPERATIONS ON DISUSED TIP

NOTICE TO OWNER

To:

The council of ....("the council") hereby gives you notice under section 14(1) of the above-mentioned Act as follows:—

1. It appears to the council that the disused mine or quarry refuse tip at ...., which is situated wholly or partly within its area, is unstable and, by reason of that instability, constitutes or is likely to constitute a danger to members of the public.

2. The council requires you, as owner of the tip, to carry out the remedial operations specified in the schedule below.

3. The remedial operations should be carried out within a period beginning ....* days after the date of service of this notice and ending on..............

4. The council proposes, in accordance with section 14(4) of the Act, to serve a copy of this notice on the following persons:—

OR

The council does not propose to serve copies of this notice in accordance with section 14(4) of the Act.

If you consider that any [other] person comes within the terms of section 14(4) (Note 1), you are asked to notify the council immediately, as copies have to be served within seven days of service of this notice. (Your interests may be affected.)

5. Section 14(6) of the Act gives you the right to enter on to any land referred to in the notice which is not in your occupation but in which you have an estate or interest superior to that of the occupier, and the right to take with you such other persons and such equipment as may be necessary, in order to carry out remedial operations and works of reinstatement.

6. Section 15 of the Act gives you [and any person referred to in paragraph 4] the right, within 21 days beginning with the date of service of this notice, to appeal to the court (Note 2) for an order varying or cancelling the notice on certain grounds (Note 3).

7. Under section 19 of the Act you may apply to the court for an order that a contribution towards your expenses shall be made by certain persons (Note 4). If you do not appeal to the court under section 15, you may apply for a contribution order within three months beginning with the date of service of this notice ; or if you do appeal you may apply within a period ending three months after the date on which your appeal has been finally determined (or withdrawn).

8. If, without reasonable excuse, an owner fails to carry out specified remedial operations within the specified period (or any extended period granted in the course of an application to the court) he commits an offence under the Act.

9. Under section 23(2) of the Act, the council has certain powers for the recovery of the expenses of carrying out exploratory tests. Any account for such expenses will be submitted separately.

---

* Insert a figure. The period must, however, begin not less than 21 days after the date of service—see section 14(1).

10. Section 14(5) of the Act gives you the right, within 21 days beginning with the day on which this notice was served, to serve a counter-notice in the prescribed form (Note 5). Where such a counter-notice is served—

    (*a*) the council must serve a copy on the persons (if any) on whom it served a copy of this notice ;

    (*b*) this notice is deemed never to have been served ;

    (*c*) the council must, as soon as is reasonably practicable, exercise its powers under section 17 in relation to the tip described in paragraph 1.

Section 17 empowers the council to carry out remedial operations itself. Section 23 would then entitle the council to recover its expenses from you ; but both you and the council would be entitled to apply to the court for a contribution order. (A government grant might, however, be payable towards the council's expenses, and this would reduce the amount payable by all concerned.)

(Signed)..............................

Date........................   Clerk of the..........................

SCHEDULE

Remedial operations

NOTES

1. Persons on whom a copy of this notice must be served are:—

    (*a*) any other person who is in occupation of the whole or part of the land on which any remedial operations specified in the notice are required to be carried out and any other person who, to the knowledge of the local authority, has an estate or interest, otherwise than as a mortgagee, in that land; and

    (*b*) any other person who, to the knowledge of the local authority, either has an estate or interest, otherwise than as a mortgagee, in the land on which the tip is situated, or had such an estate or interest at any time within the period of twelve years immediately preceding the date of the service of the notice on the owner of the tip; and

    (*c*) any other person who, to the knowledge of the local authority, has an interest in (including a right to acquire) all or any of the material comprised in the tip; and

    (*d*) any other person who, to the knowledge of the local authority, has at any time within the period referred to in paragraph (*b*) above used the tip for the purpose of the deposit of refuse from a mine or quarry; and

    (*e*) any other person who the local authority has reason to believe has, at any time within that period, caused or contributed to the instability of the tip by the carrying out of any operations on the tip, on the land on which it is situated or on neighbouring land or by failing to take any steps which he might reasonably have taken to prevent the tip from becoming unstable.

Their position in relation to the notice is very similar to the owner's: in particular, they have rights of appeal to the court, and are liable to a contribution order.

2. The court is the High Court or, in the circumstances described in section 28, the county court.

3. The grounds on which application may be made to the court are:—

(*a*) that there is no reasonable ground for believing that the tip is unstable or that, by reason of instability, the tip constitutes or is likely to constitute a danger to members of the public;

(*b*) that the remedial operations specified in the notice are more extensive that is necessary to secure the safety of members of the public;

(*c*) that the stability of the tip could be ensured by the carrying out of operations different, in whole or in part, from the remedial operations specified in the notice and that the owner is prepared to undertake those alternative operations;

(*d*) that the owner or some other person has already begun, or has entered into a contract with a third party to begin, operations different, in whole or in part, from the remedial operations specified in the notice and those alternative operations will ensure the stability of the tip;

(*e*) that the time within which the remedial operations are to be carried out is not reasonably sufficient for the purpose;

(*f*) that there is some defect or error in, or in connection with the notice.

4. The persons liable to a contribution order are:—

(*a*) any person who at the date of the service of the notice under section 14 had an estate or interest, otherwise than as a mortgagee, in the land on which the tip is situated and any person who had such an estate or interest at any time within the period of twelve years immediately preceding that date;

(*b*) any other person who has, at any time within that period, used the tip for the purpose of the deposit of refuse from a mine or quarry; and

(*c*) any other person who, in the opinion of the court, has at any time within that period caused or contributed to the instability of the tip by the carrying out of any operations on the tip, on the land on which it is situated or on neighbouring land or by failing to take any steps which he might reasonably have taken to prevent the tip from becoming unstable;

and circumstances to which the court must have particular regard are:—

(*a*) the extent to which it appears to the court that that person has, by any act or omission, caused or contributed to the instability of the tip;

(*b*) the extent to which that person has used the tip for the deposit of refuse;

(*c*) the nature and extent of any estate or interest which that person had, at the date of the service of the notice under section 14, in the land on which the tip is situated;

(*d*) in the case of a person who had an estate or interest in that land but disposed of it before that date, whether, in the opinion of the court, he disposed of his estate or interest for the purpose of evading any liability (whether under this Part of this Act or otherwise) in connection with the disused tip; and

(*e*) the terms of any covenant, agreement or statutory provision affecting the rights and obligations in relation to the tip of that person and the owner thereof.

5. The form of counter-notice is set out as form 2 in the Disused Mine and Quarry Tips (Prescribed Forms) Regulations 1969, obtainable through Her Majesty's Stationery Office or any bookseller. [If the council prefers to offer the owner a copy of the prescribed form of counter-notice, it should say so at this point, and the reference to the regulations may be omitted.]

FORM 2

MINES AND QUARRIES (TIPS) ACT 1969
SECTION 14(5)

REMEDIAL OPERATIONS ON DISUSED TIP

OWNER'S COUNTER-NOTICE

To the council of

I, ..., having been served with a notice under section 14(1) of the above-mentioned Act requiring me to carry out remedial operation at ...., hereby give notice under section 14(5) that I require the council to exercise its powers under section 17.

Signature.............................

Address.............................

Date.............................

FORM 3

MINES AND QUARRIES (TIPS) ACT 1969
SECTION 16(1)

REMEDIAL OPERATIONS ON DISUSED TIP

CANCELLATION OF NOTICE TO OWNER

To:

The council of .... ("the council") hereby gives you notice under section 16(1) of the above-mentioned Act as follows:

1. The notice dated .... requiring you to carry out remedial operations on the disused mine or quarry refuse tip at................ ....is hereby cancelled ; and you are no longer required to carry out these operations.

2. The council proposes to serve you with another notice specifying different operations from those previously specified.

OR

2. The council proposes to carry out remedial operations itself and a notice under section 17 will be served in due course.

OR

2. The council does not propose to take any further action.

OR

2. The council has not yet decided what (if any) further action should be taken.

3. If you have incurred expenditure in compliance with the cancelled notice, you may apply to the court (namely, the High Court, or in the circumstances described in section 28 the county court) for an order directing the council to reimburse to you the whole, or such part as the court thinks fit, of any expenditure incurred by you in consequence of the cancelled notice and of any expenditure attributable to its cancellation (i.e. on the reinstatement of any land or on the cancellation of any contract or otherwise). The court would have regard to all the circumstances of the case and particular regard to the grounds of cancellation and to the future intentions of the council.

4. If you have carried out any work under the notice and a contribution order has been or is made by the court, your rights of recovery from a contributory will be curtailed by Schedule 4 to the Act, having regard to your right to seek compensation from the council.

Signed.............................

Date........................   Clerk of the...........................

FORM 4

MINES AND QUARRIES (TIPS) ACT 1969
SECTION 17(2)

REMEDIAL OPERATIONS ON DISUSED TIP

NOTICE TO OWNER

To:

The council of ....("the council") hereby gives you notice under section 17(2) of the above-mentioned Act as follows:

1. It appears to the council that the disused mine or quarry refuse tip at ...., which is situated wholly or partly within its area, and of which you are the owner, is unstable and, by reason of that instability, constitutes or is likely to constitute a danger to members of the public.

2. Instead of requiring you to carry out remedial operations yourself, the council proposes itself to carry out the remedial operations specified in the schedule below and works of reinstatement.

3. The remedial operations will be begun not less than 21 days after the day on which this notice is served, unless an earlier start is made because of possible danger to members of the public.

4. In accordance with sections 14(4) and 17(5) of the Act a copy of this notice has been or will be served on the following persons:—

OR

The council does not propose to serve copies of this notice in accordance with sections 14(4) and 17(5) of the Act.

If you consider that any [other] person comes within the terms of section 14(4) (Note 1), you are asked to notify the council as soon as possible. (Your interests may be affected.)

5. Section 18(1) gives any person authorised in writing by the council the right at any reasonable time to enter upon the land upon which the disused tip is situated or upon any neighbouring land for any purpose connected with the carrying out of remedial operations or works of reinstatement; but twenty-four hours' notice in writing has to be given to the occupier except in case of urgency. Obstruction of or interference with the carrying out of remedial operations is an offence under the Act.

6. Under section 19 of the Act you may apply to the court (Note 2) for an order that a contribution towards the expenses otherwise falling on you (see paragraph 7) shall be made by certain persons (Note 3). You may apply for a contribution order within three months beginning with the date of service of this notice.

7. Section 23 gives the council the right to recover from you—

(a) expenses reasonably incurred on any exploratory tests which gave rise to the remedial operations;

(b) expenses reasonably incurred on the remedial operations and consequential works of reinstatement ;

(c) establishment charges not exceeding 5 per cent. of (a) and (b) ; and

(d) any compensation payable by the council to persons other than yourself for damage and disturbance.

8. If the court makes a contribution order under section 19 (on application by yourself or by the council), the council will recover the specified percentage of its expenses direct from the contributory. (A government grant might, however, be payable towards the council's expenses, and this would reduce the amount payable by all concerned.)

9. You will be entitled, within six weeks beginning with the date of service of a demand for expenses, to appeal against it to the court on any of certain grounds (Note 4).

(Signed)...............................

Date......................... Clerk of the...........................

NOTES

1. Persons on whom a copy of this notice must be served are—

(a) any other person who is in occupation of the whole or part of the land on which any remedial operations specified in the notice are required to be carried out and any other person who, to the knowledge of the local authority, has an estate or interest, otherwise than as a mortgagee, in that land; and

(b) any other person who, to the knowledge of the local authority, either has an estate or interest, otherwise than as a mortgagee, in the land on which the tip is situated, or had such an estate or interest at any time within the period of twelve years immediately preceding the date of the service of the notice on the owner of the tip; and

(c) any other person who, to the knowledge of the local authority, has an interest in (including a right to acquire) all or any of the material comprised in the tip; and

(d) any other person who, to the knowledge of the local authority, has at any time within the period referred to in paragraph (b) above used the tip for the purpose of the deposit of refuse from a mine or quarry; and

(e) any other person who the local authority has reason to believe has, at any time within that period, caused or contributed to the instability of the tip by the carrying out of any operations on the tip, on the land on which it is situated or on neighbouring land or by failing to take any steps which he might reasonably have taken to prevent the tip from becoming unstable.

They are liable to a contribution order, as referred to in this notice.

2. The court is the High Court or, in the circumstances described in section 28, the county court.

3. The persons liable to a contribution order are:—

(a) any person who at the date of the service of the notice under section 17 had an estate or interest, otherwise than as a mortgagee, in the land on which the tip is situated and any person who had such an estate or interest at any time within the period of twelve years immediately preceding that date;

(b) any other person who has, at any time within that period, used the tip for the purpose of the deposit of refuse from a mine or quarry; and

(c) any other person who, in the opinion of the court, has at any time within that period caused or contributed to the instability of the tip by the carrying out of any operations on the tip, on the land on which it is situated or on neighbouring land or by failing to take any steps which he might reasonably have taken to prevent the tip from becoming unstable;

and circumstances to which the court must have particular regard are:—

(a) the extent to which it appears to the court that that person has, by any act or omission, caused or contributed to the instability of the tip;

(b) the extent to which that person has used the tip for the deposit of refuse;

(c) the nature and extent of any estate or interest which that person had, at the date of the service of the notice under section 17, in the land on which the tip is situated;

(d) in the case of a person who had an estate or interest in that land but disposed of it before that date, whether, in the opinion of the court, he disposed of his estate or interest for the purpose of evading any liability (whether under this Part of this Act or otherwise) in connection with the disused tip; and

(e) the terms of any covenant, agreement or statutory provision affecting the rights and obligations in relation to the tip of that person and the owner thereof.

4. Grounds of appeal against a demand for expenses are:—

(a) that the amount of the expenses incurred by the local authority in carrying out exploratory tests or remedial operations was greater than was reasonable;

(b) that the amount of the expenses incurred by the local authority in carrying out works of reinstatement was greater than was reasonably necessary to reinstate the land in consequence of the remedial operations;

(c) that, at the time the remedial operations were begun, there was no reasonable ground for believing that the disused tip concerned was unstable or that, by reason of instability, the tip constituted or was likely to constitute a danger to members of the public;

(d) that the remedial operations carried out by the local authority were more extensive than was necessary to secure the safety of members of the public;

(e) that, because the time taken by the local authority to carry out the exploratory tests or the remedial operations or any consequential works of reinstatement was unreasonably long, the compensation paid or payable to any person in pursuance of a claim under section 20 in respect of damage or disturbance is greater than it would otherwise have been;

(f) that the amount of the compensation paid or payable to any person in pursuance of a claim under section 20 is greater than is necessary to compensate him in respect of any damage or disturbance suffered;

(g) that, in the case of a demand served on a contributory, the amount claimed in the demand is greater than the specified percentage of the total amount recoverable by the local authority under section 23(1);

(h) that, in the case of a demand served on the owner of the disused tip concerned, the amount claimed in the demand does not give proper allowance for any sum or sums which the local authority is entitled to recover from any contributory or contributories.

FORM 5

MINES AND QUARRIES (TIPS) ACT 1969
SECTION 17(3)

REMEDIAL OPERATIONS ON DISUSED TIP

NOTICE TO OWNER

To:

The council of ....("the council") hereby
gives you notice under section 17(3) of the above-mentioned Act as follows:—

1. The council has reasonable ground for believing that the disused mine or
quarry tip at ...., which is
situated wholly or partly within its area, and of which you are the owner, is
unstable and that possible danger to members of the public requires the immediate
carrying out of remedial operations.

2. Accordingly the council has commenced operations, and in the schedule
below there are specified the nature and extent of the operations and of the consequential works of reinstatement which it proposes to carry out.

3. In accordance with sections 14(4) and 17(5) of the Act a copy of this notice
has been or will be served on the following persons:—

OR

The council does not propose to serve copies of this notice in accordance with
sections 14(4) and 17(5) of the Act.

If you consider that any [other] person comes within the terms of section 14(4)
(Note 1), you are asked to notify the council as soon as possible. (Your interests
may be affected.)

4. Section 18(1) and (4) gives any person authorised in writing by the council the
right at any reasonable time to enter upon the land upon which the disused tip is
situated or upon any neighbouring land for any purpose connected with the
carrying out of remedial operations or works of reinstatement without notice.
Obstruction of or interference with the carrying out of remedial operations is an
offence under the Act.

5. Under section 19 of the Act you may apply to the court (Note 2) for an order
that a contribution towards the expenses otherwise falling on you (see paragraph 6)
shall be made by certain persons (Note 3).   You may apply for a contribution
order within three months beginning with the date of service of this notice.

6. Section 23 gives the council the right to recover from you—

   (a) expenses reasonably incurred on any exploratory tests which gave rise to
       the remedial operations ;

   (b) expenses reasonably incurred on the remedial operations and consequential
       works of reinstatement ;

   (c) establishment charges not exceeding 5 per cent. of (a) and (b) ; and

   (d) any compensation payable by the council to persons other than yourself
       for damage and disturbance.

7. If the court makes a contribution order under section 19 (on application by yourself or by the council), the council will recover the specified percentage of its expenses direct from the contributory. (A government grant might, however, be payable towards the council's expenses, and this would reduce the amount payable by all concerned.)

8. You will be entitled, within six weeks beginning with the date of service of a demand for expenses, to appeal against it to the court on any of certain grounds (Note 4).

Signed..........................

Date........................   Clerk of the..........................

SCHEDULE

NOTES

1. Persons on whom a copy of this notice must be served are:—

(*a*) any other person who is in occupation of the whole or part of the land on which any remedial operations specified in the notice are required to be carried out and any other person who, to the knowledge of the local authority, has an estate or interest, otherwise than as a mortgagee, in that land; and

(*b*) any other person who, to the knowledge of the local authority, either has an estate or interest, otherwise than as a mortgagee, in the land on which the tip is situated, or had such an estate or interest at any time within the period of twelve years immediately preceding the date of the service of the notice on the owner of the tip; and

(*c*) any other person who, to the knowledge of the local authority, has an interest in (including a right to acquire) all or any of the material comprised in the tip; and

(*d*) any other person who, to the knowledge of the local authority, has at any time within the period referred to in paragraph (*b*) above used the tip for the purpose of the deposit of refuse from a mine or quarry; and

(*e*) any other person who the local authority has reason to believe has, at any time within that period, caused or contributed to the instability of the tip by the carrying out of any operations on the tip, on the land on which it is situated or on neighbouring land or by failing to take any steps which he might reasonably have taken to prevent the tip from becoming unstable.

They are liable to a contribution order, as referred to in this notice.

2. The court is the High Court, or, in the circumstances described in section 28, the county court.

3. The persons liable to a contribution order are:—

(*a*) any person who at the date of the service of the notice under section 17 had an estate or interest, otherwise than as a mortgagee, in the land on which the tip is situated and any person who had such an estate or interest at any time within the period of twelve years immediately preceding that date;

(*b*) any other person who has, at any time within that period, used the tip for the purpose of the deposit of refuse from a mine or quarry; and

(*c*) any other person who, in the opinion of the court, has at any time within that period caused or contributed to the instability of the tip by the carrying out of any operations on the tip, on the land on which it is situated or on neighbouring land or by failing to take any steps which he might reasonably have taken to prevent the tip from becoming unstable;

and circumstances to which the court must have particular regard are:—

    (a) the extent to which it appears to the court that that person has, by any act or omission, caused or contributed to the instability of the tip;

    (b) the extent to which that person has used the tip for the deposit of refuse;

    (c) the nature and extent of any estate or interest which that person had, at the date of the service of the notice under section 17, in the land on which the tip is situated;

    (d) in the case of a person who had an estate or interest in that land but disposed of it before that date, whether, in the opinion of the court, he disposed of his estate or interest for the purpose of evading any liability (whether under this Part of this Act or otherwise) in connection with the disused tip; and

    (e) the terms of any covenant, agreement or statutory provision affecting the rights and obligations in relation to the tip of that person and the owner thereof.

4. Grounds of appeal against a demand for expenses are:—

    (a) that the amount of the expenses incurred by the local authority in carrying out exploratory tests or remedial operations was greater than was reasonable;

    (b) that the amount of the expenses incurred by the local authority in carrying out works of reinstatement was greater than was reasonably necessary to reinstate the land in consequence of the remedial operations;

    (c) that, at the time the remedial operations were begun, there was no reasonable ground for believing that the disused tip concerned was unstable or that, by reason of instability, the tip constituted or was likely to constitute a danger to members of the public;

    (d) that the remedial operations carried out by the local authority were more extensive than was necessary to secure the safety of members of the public;

    (e) that, because the time taken by the local authority to carry out the exploratory tests or the remedial operations or any consequential works of reinstatement was unreasonably long, the compensation paid or payable to any person in pursuance of a claim under section 20 in respect of damage or disturbance is greater than it would otherwise have been;

    (f) that the amount of the compensation paid or payable to any person in pursuance of a claim under section 20 is greater than is necessary to compensate him in respect of any damage or disturbance suffered;

    (g) that, in the case of a demand served on a contributory, the amount claimed in the demand is greater than the specified percentage of the total amount recoverable by the local authority under section 23(1);

    (h) that, in the case of a demand served on the owner of the disused tip concerned, the amount claimed in the demand does not give proper allowance for any sum or sums which the local authority is entitled to recover from any contributory or contributories.

FORM 6

MINES AND QUARRIES (TIPS) ACT 1969
SCHEDULE 2, PARAGRAPH 2

REMEDIAL OPERATIONS ON DISUSED TIP

The council of ....("the council") hereby gives you, ...being—

    (a)

notice under paragraph 2 of Schedule 2 to the above-mentioned Act as follows:—

1. The council, as owner of a disused mine or quarry refuse tip at...........
........................, and situated wholly or partly in its area—

    (i) considers that the tip is unstable and, by reason of that instability, constitutes or is likely to constitute a danger to members of the public ;

    (ii) has determined to carry out remedial operations in relation to that tip ;

    (iii)(b) requires to enter on land at....................................
        in order to carry out those operations or works of reinstatement ;

    (iv)(b) considers that it may be entitled to claim a contribution from some person.

2. The remedial operations proposed are specified in the schedule below.

3. Section 18(1) gives any person authorised in writing by the council the right at any reasonable time to enter upon the land upon which the disused tip is situated or upon any neighbouring land for any purpose connected with the carrying out of remedial operations or works of reinstatement ; but twenty-four hours' notice in writing has to be given to the occupier except in case of urgency. Obstruction of or interference with the carrying out of remedial operations is an offence under the Act.

4. At any time within three months of starting remedial operations, the council may apply to the court under section 19 for an order requiring a contribution to be made towards its expenses (Note 1). It must give prior notice of any such application.

5. If the court makes a contribution order under section 19, the council will recover the specified percentage of its expenses direct from the contributory. (A government grant might, however, be payable towards the council's expenses, and this would reduce the amount payable by all concerned.)

6. You will be entitled, within 6 weeks beginning with the date of service of a demand for expenses, to appeal against it to the court on any of certain grounds (Note 2).

Signed............................

Date........................   Clerk of the.........................

(a)   Indicate capacity in which the person is being served: see section 14(a) to (e)

(b)   (iii) or (iv) should be deleted where it is not appropriate. The council should note carefully that paragraph 1(c) of Schedule 2 presents alternatives, which have been separated in this form.

SCHEDULE

NOTES

1. The persons liable to a contribution order are:—

(a) any person who at the date of the commencement of the remedial operations had an estate or interest, otherwise than as a mortgagee, in the land on which the tip is situated and any person who had such an estate or interest at any time within the period of twelve years immediately preceding that date;

(b) any other person who has, at any time within that period used the tip for the purpose of the deposit of refuse from a mine or quarry; and

(c) any other person who, in the opinion of the court, has at any time within that period caused or contributed to the instability of the tip by the carrying out of any operations on the tip, on the land on which it is situated or on neighbouring land or by failing to take any steps which he might reasonably have taken to prevent the tip from becoming unstable;

and circumstances to which the court must have particular regard are:—

(a) the extent to which it appears to the court that that person has, by any act or omission, caused or contributed to the instability of the tip;

(b) the extent to which that person has used the tip for the deposit of refuse;

(c) the nature and extent of any estate or interest which that person had, at the date of the commencement of remedial operations, in the land on which the tip is situated;

(d) in the case of a person who had an estate or interest in that land but disposed of it before that date, whether, in the opinion of the court, he disposed of his estate or interest for the purpose of evading any liability (whether under this Part of this Act or otherwise) in connection with the disused tip; and

(e) the terms of any covenant, agreement or statutory provision affecting the rights and obligations in relation to the tip of that person and the owner thereof.

2. Grounds of appeal against a demand for expenses are:—

(a) that the amount of the expenses incurred by the local authority in carrying out exploratory tests or remedial operations was greater than was reasonable;

(b) that the amount of the expenses incurred by the local authority in carrying out works of reinstatement was greater than was reasonably necessary to reinstate the land in consequence of the remedial operations;

(c) that, at the time the remedial operations were begun, there was no reasonable ground for believing that the disused tip concerned was unstable or that, by reason of instability, the tip constituted or was likely to constitute a danger to members of the public;

(d) that the remedial operations carried out by the local authority were more extensive than was necessary to secure the safety of members of the public;

(e) that, because the time taken by the local authority to carry out the exploratory tests or the remedial operations or any consequential works of reinstatement was unreasonably long, the compensation paid or payable to any person in pursuance of a claim under section 20 in respect of damage or disturbance is greater than it would otherwise have been;

(f) that the amount of the compensation paid or payable to any person in pursuance of a claim under section 20 is greater than is necessary to compensate him in respect of any damage or disturbance suffered;

(g) that, in the case of a demand served on a contributory, the amount claimed in the demand is greater than the specified percentage of the total amount recoverable by the local authority under section 23(1);

(h) that, in the case of a demand served on the owner of the disused tip concerned, the amount claimed in the demand does not give proper allowance for any sum or sums which the local authority is entitled to recover from any contributory or contributories.

Given under the official seal of the Minister of Housing and Local Government on 12th June 1969.

(L.S.)

Anthony Greenwood,
Minister of Housing and
Local Government.

Given under my hand on 12th June 1969.

George Thomas,
Secretary of State for Wales.

EXPLANATORY NOTE

(This Note is not part of the Regulations.)

Part II of the Mines and Quarries (Tips) Act 1969 gives local authorities functions in relation to disused tips which, by reason of instability, constitute a public danger. They may require the owner of the tip to carry out remedial operations ; or they may carry out remedial operations themselves. Also, an owner who is required to carry out such operations may require the local authority to carry out those operations itself. These Regulations prescribe the form of the notices which are required to be served in connection with these procedures.

STATUTORY INSTRUMENTS

1969 No. 808

FACTORIES

The Ionising Radiations (Sealed Sources) Regulations 1969

Made - - - -	12*th June* 1969
Laid before Parliament	25 *th June* 1969

Coming into Operation—

Regulations 32, 46 *and* 47	13th December 1969
Remainder - - -	13th July 1969

ARRANGEMENTS OF REGULATIONS

			Reg.
PART I	—	Interpretation and General	1—4
PART II	—	Administration, Notifications and Records	5—10
PART III	—	Basic Principles of Protection	11—15
PART IV	—	Radiological Supervision	16—22
PART V	—	Medical Supervision	23—31
PART VI	—	Organisation of Work	32—38
PART VII	—	Monitoring	39
PART VIII	—	Radiography and Other Processes	40—44
PART IX	—	X-ray Crystallography and Spectrometry	45
PART X	—	Measuring and Detecting Devices and Static Eliminators	46 and 47
SCHEDULE	—	Maximum permissible radiation doses	

REGULATIONS

The Secretary of State—

(*a*) by virtue of her powers under sections 76 and 180(6) and (7) of the Factories Act 1961(**a**) and of all other powers enabling her in that behalf; and

(*b*) after publishing, pursuant to Schedule 4 to the said Act of 1961, notice of the proposal to make the Regulations and not having received any objection to the draft in regard to which she is required by the said Schedule to direct an inquiry to be held,

hereby makes the following special Regulations:—

PART I

INTERPRETATION AND GENERAL

Citation, commencement and revocation

1.—(1) These Regulations may be cited as the Ionising Radiations (Sealed Sources) Regulations 1969. Regulations 32, 46 and 47 shall come into operation on 13th December 1969 and the remainder of these Regulations on 13th July 1969.

(2) The Ionising Radiations (Sealed Sources) Regulations 1961(**b**) are hereby revoked.

(**a**) 1961 c. 34. (**b**) S.I. 1961/1470 (1961 II, p. 2975).

Interpretation

2.—(1) The Interpretation Act 1889(a) shall apply to the interpretation of these Regulations as it applies to the interpretation of an Act of Parliament, and as if these Regulations and the Regulations hereby revoked were Acts of Parliament.

(2) For the purposes of these Regulations, unless the context otherwise requires, the following expressions have the meanings hereby assigned to them respectively, that is to say—

"adequate shielding" means shielding or a demarcating barrier outside which the radiation dose rate averaged over any one minute does not exceed 0·75 millirems per hour or where only classified workers are affected 2·5 millirems per hour, and cognate expressions shall be construed accordingly;

"appointed doctor" means—

(a) (i) as respects any factory to which Regulation 3(2) applies;

(ii) for the purposes of implementing any arrangements made thereunder with employers of classified workers, as respects any factory to which Regulation 3(3) applies; and

(iii) for the purposes of any medical examination in pursuance of Regulation 25(1)(a),

any fully registered medical practitioner appointed to be a factory doctor for any of the purposes of the principal Act; and

(b) as respects any other factory and any other medical examination, a fully registered medical practitioner specially appointed under section 151 of the principal Act to be appointed factory doctor for the factory for the purposes of these Regulations or of the Ionising Radiations (Sealed Sources) Regulations 1961 or the appointed factory doctor for the district in which the factory is situated;

"approved" means approved for the time being for the purposes of these Regulations or of the Ionising Radiations (Sealed Sources) Regulations 1961 by certificate of the Chief Inspector;

"atomic energy" means the energy released from atomic nuclei as the result of any process, including the fission process, but does not include energy released in any process of natural transmutation or radioactive decay which is not accelerated or influenced by external means;

"authorised person" in any of these Regulations means a person for the time being authorised in writing by the occupier for the purposes of that Regulation;

"calendar quarter" means the period of three calendar months beginning with 1st January, 1st April, 1st July or 1st October;

"classified worker" has the meaning assigned to it in Regulation 16(1);

"competent person" means a person appointed in pursuance of Regulation 7;

"factory" means any factory and any premises, places, processes, operations and works to which the provisions of Part IV of the principal Act with respect to special regulations for safety and health are applied by any of the following provisions of that Act, namely, section 123 (which relates to electrical stations), section 124 (which relates to institutions), so much of section 125 as relates to warehouses other than warehouses belonging to the owners, trustees or conservators of any dock, wharf or quay, section 126 (which relates to ships) and section 127 (which relates to building operations and works of engineering construction);

(a) 1889 c. 63.

"health register" means the register referred to in Regulation 31;

"ionising radiations" means electromagnetic radiation (that is to say, X-rays and gamma rays) or corpuscular radiation (that is to say, alpha particles, beta particles, electrons, positrons, protons, neutrons, or heavy particles) being electromagnetic radiation or corpuscular radiation capable of producing ions and emitted from a radioactive substance or from a machine or apparatus that is intended to produce ionising radiations or from a machine or apparatus in which charged particles are accelerated by a voltage of not less than five kilovolts;

"monitoring" means measuring in accordance with Regulation 39 and "monitor" shall be construed accordingly;

"nuclear reactor" means any plant (including any machinery, equipment or appliance, whether affixed to land or not) designed or adapted for the production of atomic energy by a fission process in which a controlled chain reaction can be maintained without an additional source of neutrons;

"the principal Act" means the Factories Act 1961;

"protected employment" means employment as respects which requirements are for the time being imposed under the principal Act (including the requirements of these Regulations) for recording the radiation doses received by the persons employed;

"radiation area" means a part of a factory in which any person is exposed to a radiation dose rate which when averaged over any one minute exceeds or is liable to exceed 0·75 millirems per hour, otherwise than infrequently and transiently;

"radiation dose record" means the record referred to in Regulation 19(1);

"radioactive substance" means any substance which consists of or contains radionuclides, whether natural or artificial, and of which the activity exceeds 0·002 of a microcurie per gramme of substance; in the case of a chain of radionuclides, consisting of a parent and daughters, the only nuclide to be taken into consideration being that having the highest activity of those present;

"sealed source" means any radioactive substance sealed in a container (otherwise than solely for the purpose of storage, transport or disposal) or bonded wholly within material and includes the immediate container or the bonding, but does not include any nuclear fuel element or any radioactive substance inside a nuclear reactor;

"transfer record" means a record prepared on the termination of any person's employment of radiation doses received by him being a record prepared in accordance with requirements for the time being imposed under the principal Act (including the requirements of these Regulations);

"useful beam" means, in the case of X-rays, that part of the radiation from an X-ray tube that passes through the aperture, cone or other device for collimating the X-ray beam; and, in other cases, any ionising radiations from a sealed source that can be employed for the purposes for which the sealed source is used.

(3) References in these Regulations to any enactment shall be construed as references to that enactment as amended by or under any other enactment.

Application of Regulations

3.—(1) Except as provided in paragraphs (4) and (5) of this Regulation, these Regulations shall apply to all factories in which any sealed source is, or is proposed to be, stored, manipulated, maintained, operated, used or installed, or in which there is operated or used, or proposed to be operated or used, any machine or apparatus that is intended to produce ionising radiations or any machine or apparatus (being a machine or apparatus which emits ionising radiations) in which charged particles are accelerated by a voltage of not less than five kilovolts.

(2) Where in any factory the occupier is neither the owner nor the hirer of a sealed source or of such a machine or apparatus as is referred to in paragraph (1) of this Regulation being a sealed source, machine or apparatus which is used by or under the direction of some person other than the occupier or a person in the employment of the occupier, that other person or (if he is in the employment of the owner or hirer) the employer of that other person, shall in relation to that sealed source, machine or apparatus be deemed to be the occupier of the factory for the purposes of these Regulations.

(3) Where in any factory (other than a factory to which the last foregoing paragraph applies) any classified worker is employed by some person other than the occupier, the occupier shall be deemed to have complied in respect of any such worker so employed with any requirement imposed on him by Part IV or Part V of these Regulations, if he has made effective arrangements which secure that the employer of the worker complies as respects that worker with that requirement as if the employer were the occupier.

(4) Nothing in these Regulations shall apply with respect to any apparatus exclusively used in a room specially set apart for the purpose, for the prevention, diagnosis or treatment of illness or injury.

(5) Nothing in these Regulations shall apply with respect to—

(a) any sealed source at or near the surface of which the dose rate of ionising radiations does not exceed ten millirems per hour not being one of a number of sealed sources placed together and whose collective dose rate at or near the surface exceeds ten millirems per hour; or

(b) any ionising radiations that do not arise from a sealed source or from such a machine or apparatus as is referred to in paragraph (1) of this Regulation; or

(c) any installation of a class or description which is on the date of the making of these Regulations prescribed for the purposes of section 1 (1) (b) of the Nuclear Installations Act 1965(a), and situate on a site in respect of which a nuclear site licence granted under the said Act is in force; or

(d) any apparatus intended only for the purpose of receiving visual images sent by television—

(i) when operated at a voltage of not more than 20 kilovolts in the course of its manufacture, repair, maintenance or testing; or

(ii) in any other circumstances, when the dose rate at or near the surface of the apparatus does not exceed 0·5 millirems per hour.

In sub-paragraph (a) and (d) of this paragraph the expression "at or near the surface" means as near the surface as is practicable for the purpose of measuring the dose rate of ionising radiations.

(6) The provisions of these Regulations shall be in addition to and not in substitution for or in diminution of other requirements imposed by or under the principal Act.

(a) 1965 c. 57.

Exemption certificates

4.—(1) The Chief Inspector may (subject to such conditions as may be specified therein) by certificate in writing (which he may in his discretion revoke at any time) exempt from all or any of the requirements of these Regulations—

(a) any factory or part of any factory; or

(b) any class or description of factories or parts thereof; or

(c) any machine, plant, apparatus, process, article or substance or any class or description of machines, plant, apparatus, processes, articles or substances; or

(d) the employment of any person or any class or description of persons,

if he is satisfied that the requirements in respect of which the exemption is granted are not necessary for the protection of persons employed. Where such exemption is granted a legible copy of the certificate, showing the conditions (if any) subject to which it has been granted, shall be kept posted in any factory where the exemption applies in a position where it may be conveniently read by the persons employed.

(2) Exemptions granted under Regulation 4 of the Ionising Radiations (Sealed Sources) Regulations 1961 from requirements of those Regulations shall continue in force and shall have effect as if they were exemptions granted under this Regulation from the corresponding requirements of these Regulations.

PART II

ADMINISTRATION, NOTIFICATIONS AND RECORDS

Notification of use and disuse of sealed sources, etc.

5.—(1) The occupier shall give previous notice in writing to the inspector for the district (which, except in cases of emergency, shall be not less than one month's notice or such shorter notice as the inspector may agree to accept) before undertaking in a factory for the first time after the date of commencement of these Regulations or for the first time after a notice under paragraph (2) of this Regulation given in respect of the factory has expired, work to which this Regulation applies:

Provided that an occupier who is at the date of the commencement of these Regulations undertaking work to which this Regulation applies (or who would at that date but for a merely temporary cessation be undertaking such work) shall not be required under this paragraph to give notice to the inspector for the district in respect of that work if notice has been given in respect of it under Regulation 6(1) or (2) of the Ionising Radiations (Sealed Sources) Regulations 1961.

(2) The occupier shall either before or within seven days after ceasing to use the factory (otherwise than merely temporarily) for work to which this Regulation applies give notice in writing to that effect to the inspector for the district.

(3) In this Regulation the expression "work to which this Regulation applies" means work involving the storage, manipulation, maintenance, operation, use or installation of sealed sources or the operation or use of any machine or apparatus of the kind referred to in Regulation 3(1).

Notification of accidents, etc.

6. The inspector for the district shall be notified in writing—

(a) in the circumstances specified in Regulation 36, if any sealed source is lost or mislaid; and

(*b*) as soon as possible after it is discovered—
  (i) of any breakage of the immediate container or the bonding of a sealed source; and
  (ii) of any leakage of any radioactive substance beyond the approved extent from the immediate container or the bonding of a sealed source.

Appointment of a competent person

7.—(1) The occupier shall appoint one or more competent persons to exercise special supervision with regard to the requirements of these Regulations and to assist in enforcing the observance of them.

(2) The name or names of the competent person or competent persons shall be kept posted in the factory where it or they can be conveniently read by the persons employed. Where different persons are appointed under this Regulation for different parts of the factory or for different processes the names shall be posted in such a manner that the persons employed can readily identify the competent person or competent persons appointed under this Regulation for the part of the factory or for the processes in which they are employed.

(3) Where in any factory more than one competent person is appointed under this Regulation, any reference in these Regulations to the competent person appointed in accordance with this Regulation shall be deemed to include a reference to any one of those persons or, as the case may be, to the person appointed, or to any one of the persons appointed, for the part of the factory or for the processes concerned.

Notifications to the competent person

8. The competent person appointed in accordance with Regulation 7 shall be informed of every matter which is required to be notified to the inspector for the district under Regulation 6.

Investigations by the competent person

9. In addition to his other duties, the competent person appointed in accordance with Regulation 7 shall investigate the circumstances of every occurrence notified to him under Regulation 8 and report thereon to the occupier with a recommendation as to the action to be taken.

Preservation of records

10. Every register, certificate or record kept in pursuance of these Regulations or of the Ionising Radiations (Sealed Sources) Regulations 1961 and every transfer record and copy transfer record received by an employer in pursuance of Regulation 22 of these Regulations or of Regulation 31 of the said Regulations of 1961 shall be preserved in the factory or in such place outside the factory as may be approved and kept available for inspection by any inspector or by the appointed doctor for at least the following periods after the last entry therein, that is to say, thirty years in the cases of the health register, the radiation dose records, the transfer records and the copy transfer records, three years in the case of the register kept in pursuance of Regulation 34(5) of these Regulations or of Regulation 15(5) of the said Regulations of 1961 and two years in all other cases: Provided that where a copy of or an extract from or a summary of any such document or documents as aforesaid has been approved, the provisions of this Regulation may be complied with as respects the said copy or extract or summary (as the case may be) in place of the document or documents from which the extract, or of which the copy or the summary, has been made.

Part III

Basic Principles of Protection

Restriction of exposure to ionising radiations

11.—(1) Without prejudice to the other requirements of these Regulations, the occupier shall do all that is reasonably practicable to restrict the extent to which the persons employed are exposed to ionising radiations; and no person employed shall expose himself to ionising radiations to a greater extent than is reasonably necessary for the purposes of his work.

(2) Without prejudice to any approved arrangements under Regulation 15 for the time being in force and applicable to him, no person shall receive any radiation dose in excess of those permitted under the Schedule to these Regulations.

Provision of shielding against ionising radiations

12. Without prejudice to the other requirements of these Regulations as to adequate shielding, all sources of ionising radiations shall, where reasonably practicable, be adequately shielded.

Direction and size of useful beam

13.—(1) Wherever practicable the useful beam shall be directed away from adjacent occupied areas.

(2) The useful beam shall be limited by appropriate means to the minimum size reasonably necessary for the work.

(3) Where appropriate, suitable measures shall be taken to limit scattered radiation.

Instruction of persons employed

14. No person employed shall be exposed to ionising radiations unless he has received appropriate instruction (to the extent that this is necessary having regard to the circumstances of his employment) concerning the hazards involved and the precautions to be observed.

Arrangements for protection of workers

15.—(1) Without prejudice to the other requirements of these Regulations, where the Chief Inspector has reasonable cause to believe as respects any factory that any person employed may have received, or is likely to receive, in any calendar year or in any calendar quarter, as the case may be, a sum of radiation doses greater than three-tenths of the appropriate dose permitted under the Schedule to these Regulations, the Chief Inspector may serve on the occupier a written notice requiring him to make approved arrangements as respects all or any of the following matters, that is to say—

(*a*) for the wearing by any person employed of a photographic film or an appropriate radiation dosemeter, and for the keeping and preserving of records of doses received;

(*b*) for the monitoring of any part of the factory, and for the keeping and preserving of records of measurements obtained by such monitoring;

(*c*) for determining in the case of any person employed the amount of radioactive substances in his body, for estimating, when practicable, the radiation dose therefrom, and for the keeping and preserving of records of any determination and estimation so made;

(*d*) for the suspension of any person from work in which he will be exposed to ionising radiations or for imposing special conditions on his continued employment on any such work;

(*e*) for the medical examination of any person employed; and

(*f*) for the making of a special entry in the radiation dose record in respect of any person employed.

(2) It shall be the duty of every person employed to comply with the requirements of any such approved arrangements in so far as they require the wearing by him of photographic film or a radiation dosemeter or require him to be medically examined.

Part IV

Radiological Supervision

Classified workers

16.—(1) The following persons shall for the purposes of these Regulations be designated by the occupier as classified workers, that is to say, persons who are employed for any of their time in radiation areas in work involving the storage, manipulation, maintenance, operation, use or installation of sealed sources or the operation or use of any machine or apparatus of the kind referred to in Regulation 3(1), not being persons employed in accordance with an approved scheme of work within the meaning of the next following paragraph; and in these Regulations the expression "classified worker" shall be construed accordingly.

(2) In the foregoing paragraph of this Regulation "approved scheme of work" means an approved scheme of work as respects which the Chief Inspector is satisfied that the operating and working conditions and the system of control and instruction are such that a person working in accordance with the scheme is not likely to receive in any calendar year a sum of radiation doses exceeding three-tenths of the appropriate dose permitted in any calendar year under the Schedule to these Regulations.

(3) No person under the age of eighteen shall be employed on work which requires him to be designated as a classified worker.

(4) The names of all persons designated as classified workers shall be kept entered in the health register.

Current employment in more than one factory

17. Where any person is or is to be currently employed as a classified worker in more than one factory by the same employer—

(*a*) all the factories in which that person is or is to be so currently employed shall in relation to that person be deemed, for the purposes of these Regulations, to constitute one factory;

(*b*) except in the cases referred to in paragraph (*a*) of the definition of the expression "appointed doctor" in Regulation 2(2), references in these Regulations to the appointed doctor shall be construed as references to the appointed doctor for any one of those factories;

(*c*) the references to the health register in Regulations 25, 30 and 31, shall be taken as references to the health register for any one of those factories, so, however, that as respects any period only one health register shall be used in respect of that person; and (*d*) the reference in Regulation 28(1) to the factory shall be taken as a reference to any one of those factories.

Film badges and dosemeters

18.—(1) The occupier shall make suitable arrangements for the wearing on an appropiate part or parts of his person by every classified worker of either a suitable photographic film or films in an appropriate holder or holders or a suitable dosemeter or suitable dosemeters, being a dosemeter or dosemeters of an approved type, during any working period in which that worker is liable to be exposed to ionising radiations. It shall be the duty of every classified worker to wear in a proper manner any film or dosemeter provided for him in pursuance of this Regulation, and at intervals specified by the occupier to return every such film or dosemeter to the occupier for the purposes of the examination mentioned in paragraph (2) of this Regulation.

(2) The occupier shall obtain the said films, film holders and dosemeters from an approved laboratory and arrange for the films and dosemeters, identified by reference to the particular wearer, to be returned at appropriate intervals to that laboratory for examination and for the issue to the occupier, by the director or other responsible person at the laboratory, of certificates containing the approved particulars of the results of the examination of each film and dosemeter.

Radiation dose records

19.—(1) Subject to the provisions of paragraph (2) of this Regulation, a radiation dose record shall be kept containing as respects each classified worker the approved particulars of the maximum radiation doses permitted under the Schedule to these Regulations and of the radiation doses received by him and, as respects any person employed (whether or not he is a classified worker), any special entry required in accordance with Regulation 15 or 21.

(2) Where it appears to an occupier that any person employed or engaged for employment by him as a classified worker, either

    (*a*) was previously engaged—

        (i) in work in a factory being work done before the imposition of requirements under the principal Act (including these Regulations) for recording the radiation doses received by the persons employed in such work, but which, if, after the date of coming into operation of these Regulations, it had been done by a person employed would have been protected employment; or

        (ii) in work not done in a factory but which if, after the date of the coming into operation of these Regulations, it had been done in a factory by a person employed, would have been protected employment; or

    (*b*) at times other than the hours during which he is employed by him is engaged in work of a kind specified in sub-paragraph (*a*) (ii) of this paragraph,

and such person produces to the occupier any document purporting to be a record of radiation doses received by that person whilst performing the work, the occupier shall, so far as practicable, enter in the radiation dose record kept as respects that person in pursuance of the foregoing paragraph of this Regulation, the particulars contained in the said document of the radiation doses received by him whilst performing that work.

(3) The radiation dose record as respects any person shall be kept up to date and shall be open to the inspection of that person at all reasonable times.

(4) For the purposes of the radiation dose record, a dose received during any period as indicated by a certificate issued in pursuance of Regulation 18(2) which did not fall wholly within one calendar quarter shall be deemed to have been received at a uniform rate on all the days (whether working days or not) throughout the period.

Excessive exposure of persons employed

20.—(1) Whenever any person has reasonable cause to believe as respects himself (if employed) or any other person employed that he has received any radiation dose in excess of that permitted under the Schedule to these Regulations, he shall report the circumstances to the occupier who shall forthwith make an investigation or arrange for an investigation to be made.

(2) Where any such investigation as aforesaid confirms a report made under the foregoing paragraph of this Regulation or the occupier has other reason to believe that any person employed has received a radiation dose in excess of that permitted under the Schedule to these Regulations, the occupier shall forthwith—

(a) notify the appointed doctor;

(b) notify the inspector for the district; and

(c) keep a record of the circumstances as respects that person.

(3) Whenever it appears from the radiation dose record that any worker has received a radiation dose in excess of that permitted under the Schedule to these Regulations, the occupier shall forthwith—

(a) make an investigation or arrange for an investigation to be made;

(b) notify the appointed doctor; and

(c) notify the inspector for the district.

Radiation doses greater or less than shown by the film badge or dosemeter

21.—(1) Whenever the occupier has reasonable cause to believe that any person has received during any period during which a film or dosemeter is required to be worn by that person in pursuance of these Regulations a radiation dose which is much greater or much less than the dose indicated by any certificate issued in accordance with these Regulations as respects the films or dosemeters worn by him during that period, the occupier shall make an investigation or arrange for an investigation to be made and where any such investigation confirms his belief, the occupier shall apply to the Chief Inspector for approval of a special entry and such special entry so approved shall be made in that person's radiation dose record.

(2) Whenever the Chief Inspector has reason to believe that any person has received during any period during which a film or dosemeter is required to be worn by that person in pursuance of these Regulations a radiation dose which is much greater or much less than the dose indicated by any certificate issued in accordance with these Regulations as respect the films or dosemeters worn by him during that period, the Chief Inspector may approve a special entry and any such special entry so approved shall be made in that person's radiation dose record.

Transfer records

22.—(1) Where any person as respects whom an employer is or has been required to keep a radiation dose record ceases to be employed by that employer, that employer shall forthwith prepare a transfer record in the approved form and containing the approved particulars. The employer, if he knows the whereabouts of that person, shall forthwith supply him with the transfer record and shall in any case forthwith send a copy of it to the inspector for the district.

(2) Before any person who was previously in protected employment with another employer is employed, or engaged for employment, as a classified worker, that person shall notify his employer or, as the case may be, prospective employer, of the said previous protected employment; and shall, if he has received from his employer in that previous employment a transfer record and that record is still in his possession, produce it to his employer or, as the case may be, prospective employer, and make it available to the appointed doctor. In the event of that person being employed, or engaged for employment, as a classified worker the transfer record shall be handed to and retained by the employer.

(3) When the occupier is aware that any person employed, or engaged for employment, as a classified worker was previously in protected employment with another employer and that person does not produce a transfer record in pursuance of the last foregoing paragraph of this Regulation, the occupier shall forthwith apply to the inspector for the district for a copy of that record.

PART V

MEDICAL SUPERVISION

Arrangements for supervision

23. The occupier shall make arrangements for medical supervision by the appointed doctor of all classified workers, including specific arrangements as provided in this Part of these Regulations.

Facilities for appointed doctor

24.—(1) For the purpose of examinations conducted at a factory to which these Regulations apply, the occupier shall provide for the exclusive use of the appointed doctor on the occasion of the examination a room properly cleaned and adequately warmed and lighted and furnished with a screen, a table with writing materials, chairs, an examination couch and a wash basin with a supply of clean, running hot and cold or warm water.

(2) The occupier shall afford to the appointed doctor adequate facilities for inspecting any process, operation or work in which a person having been, being or to be examined by the appointed doctor has been, is or is proposed to be, employed.

Medical examination of persons before employment as classified workers

25.—(1) No person shall be employed in a factory as a classified worker unless—

    (*a*) within the period of fourteen months immediately preceding his first employment in that factory, he has been examined by an appointed doctor and, by signed entry by the said doctor in the health register, certified fit for employment as a classified worker; and

    (*b*) he has at any time undergone a suitable blood examination, an adequate report of the results of which is available and known to the said doctor.

(2) In this Regulation, the expression "first employment in that factory" means first employment in that factory as a classified worker or re-employment

in that factory as a classified worker following any cessation of employment as a classified worker in that factory for a period exceeding fourteen months.

Periodic medical examination of persons employed

26. The occupier shall arrange for medical examinations by the appointed doctor of every worker who is a classified worker once in every calendar year so long as his employment as a classified worker continues, if it appears from his radiation dose record that during the immediately preceding calendar year he has received a sum of radiation doses which is greater than three-tenths of the appropriate doses permitted in any calendar year under the Schedule to these Regulations.

Special medical examination of persons employed

27. Where the occupier has notified the appointed doctor in accordance with Regulation 20 that any person employed has received a radiation dose in excess of that permitted under the Schedule to these Regulations, the occupier shall arrange for the person concerned to undergo without delay a medical examination by the appointed doctor in any case where the excessive radiation dose either—

(a) exceeds 10 rems in the case of a dose to parts of the body other than the hands, forearms, feet and ankles from all or any one or more of the following, that is to say, X-rays, gamma rays and neutrons; or

(b) in any other case exceeds the doses permitted under the Schedule to these Regulations.

Place of medical examinations and duty of persons concerned

28.—(1) Except where otherwise authorised or directed in writing by the inspector for the district, any medical examination by the appointed doctor (being an appointed doctor appointed by virtue of paragraph (b) of the definition of the expression "appointed doctor" in Regulation 2(2)) for the purposes of these Regulations shall take place at the factory.

(2) Due notice of every medical examination for the purposes of these Regulations shall be given by the occupier to those concerned and it shall be the duty of the persons employed as classified workers to submit themselves for examination by the appointed doctor in accordance with these Regulations as required by such notice and for any special examination required under Regulation 29(1) and to submit to the taking of samples for every blood examination the results of which are used for the purposes of these Regulations, being an examination made after the coming into operation of these Regulations.

Blood and other special examinations

29.—(1) As respects any medical examination for the purposes of these Regulations the appointed doctor may at his discretion require an examination of the blood or any other special examination. Any such special examination may be carried out at a place other than the factory.

(2) Every blood examination for the purposes of these Regulations, being an examination made after the coming into operation of these Regulations, shall be made by an approved laboratory or an approved person.

(3) The report of every such blood examination as aforesaid shall be sent to the appointed doctor.

Suspension from employment as a classified worker or in radiation areas

30.—(1) The appointed doctor shall have power, to be exercised by written certificate in the health register signed by him, to suspend from employment as a classified worker or from work in a radiation area any worker examined by him under these Regulations.

(2) No person so suspended shall again be employed as a classified worker or in a radiation area without the written approval of the appointed doctor entered in the health register.

(3) The occupier shall forthwith notify the inspector for the district whenever any worker is suspended from employment in accordance with these Regulations.

Health register

31.—(1) A health register shall be kept containing the approved particulars of all classified workers and the appointed doctor shall enter in the health register the dates and results of examinations of those persons.

(2) The appointed doctor shall enter in the health register the date and result of any medical examination under Regulation 27 of any worker other than a classified worker.

PART VI
ORGANISATION OF WORK

Marking of radiation area boundaries

32.—(1) There shall where reasonably practicable be a barrier or barriers marking the boundaries of every radiation area or where the use of such barrier or barriers is not reasonably practicable the said boundaries shall be marked by other suitable means.

(2) Suitable notices warning persons in the vicinity shall be displayed at a sufficient number of suitable places on or near to the boundaries of all radiation areas.

Handling of sealed sources

33. No sealed source shall be handled by direct contact with the bare hand.

Construction and maintenance of sealed sources

34.—(1) The immediate container or the bonding of every sealed source shall be of adequate mechanical strength and free from patent defect.

(2) A distinguishing number or other identifying mark shall be on or attached to every sealed source.

(3) The immediate container or the bonding of every sealed source shall be protected as far as practicable against accidental damage.

(4) An approved test for leakage of radioactive substance shall be made by a qualified person at least once in every period of twenty-six months of—

    (*a*) every immediate container or bonding which forms part of a sealed source ; or

    (*b*) every container in which a sealed source is permanently installed but which does not form part of the sealed source.

(5) A register shall be kept containing the approved particulars of every test carried out in pursuance of paragraph (4) of this Regulation.

Leakage or breakage of a sealed source

35. Where there are reasonable grounds to believe that any radioactive substance is leaking, or is likely to leak, beyond the approved extent from the immediate container or the bonding which forms part of a sealed source, and in the event of the immediate container or the bonding which forms part of a sealed source being broken—

(a) all practicable measures shall be taken forthwith to safeguard the persons employed, including, where necessary, the immediate vacation of all appropriate areas ;

(b) the immediate container or bonding shall be placed in a leak-proof container forthwith and shall not be brought into use until any necessary repairs have been effected ; and

(c) effective steps shall be taken as soon as practicable by or under the supervision of an authorised person to decontaminate areas affected by the radioactive substance. Any person taking part in such work shall be properly equipped for the purpose.

Accounting for sealed sources

36.—(1) Subject to the provisions of paragraph (2) of this Regulation, an authorised person shall keep a record of the following particulars in respect of every sealed source received into the factory, that is to say—

(a) the distinguishing number or other identifying mark ;

(b) the date of receipt into the factory ;

(c) the nature of the radioactive substance in the sealed source at the date referred to in sub-paragraph (b) ;

(d) the activity expressed in curies of the radioactive substance in the sealed source at a date specified by the authorised person in the record ;

(e) the whereabouts of the sealed source, kept up to date on each working day ; and

(f) the date, and manner of disposal of the sealed source, when it leaves the factory.

Whenever a sealed source is reactivated or, as the case may be, received back into the factory after reactivation, it shall for the purposes of this paragraph be treated as a sealed source received into the factory at the date of reactivation or of receipt back into the factory after reactivation, as the case may be.

(2) Nothing in this Regulation shall apply to sealed sources—

(a) in the course of their being manufactured ; or

(b) while stored, without having been used, on the premises in which they were manufactured or in which their manufacture was completed.

(3) It shall be the duty of every person employed to notify the competent person forthwith if he has reasonable grounds for believing that any sealed source has been lost or mislaid. The competent person shall take immediate steps with a view to finding the sealed source and if the sealed source is not accounted for within twenty-four hours, the occupier shall notify the inspector for the district forthwith in accordance with Regulation 6.

Storage of sealed sources

37.—(1) Sealed sources when not in use shall be kept securely in a suitable store reserved for the storage of radioactive substances and, where reasonably practicable, shall be kept in appropriate protective receptacles.

(2) Where necessary to protect the persons employed from gaseous radioactive substances, adequate and suitable arrangements shall be made for ventilating every such store to the open air by mechanical means.

(3) A suitable notice warning persons in the vicinity shall be kept prominently displayed outside every store which contains a sealed source.

Transport within a factory of sealed sources

38.—(1) No sealed source shall be transported within a factory unless it is transported—

(a) in a suitable container or by other appropriate methods ;

(b) by or under the immediate supervision of an authorised person ; and

(c) in such a way that the person receiving it is made aware that what he is receiving is a sealed source.

(2) Every container containing any sealed source shall be kept marked with a suitable warning notice to indicate that its contents are radioactive.

PART VII

MONITORING

Provision, maintenance and use of monitoring instruments

39.—(1) The occupier shall ensure that there is provided and properly maintained an appropriate and efficient radiation dosemeter or dose rate meter by means of which appropriate measurements shall be made at such intervals as are necessary for the purpose of ascertaining the efficiency of methods for the restriction of exposure to, and for shielding against, ionising radiations.

(2) Any dosemeter or dose rate meter provided under this Regulation may be provided for use in more than one factory.

(3) The occupier shall ensure that every such radiation dosemeter and dose rate meter when first taken into use in the factory or as the case may be, in the first of the factories for which it is provided, has been tested by a qualified person, and that it is subsequently re-tested by a qualified person at least once in every period of fourteen months and also after any repair of a defect which could affect its accuracy. There shall be kept a register containing the approved particulars of every test carried out in pursuance of this paragraph.

(4) All measurements under this Regulation shall be made by the competent person or by an authorised person.

PART VIII

RADIOGRAPHY AND OTHER PROCESSES

Application of Part VIII of these Regulations

40. The processes to which this Part of these Regulations applies are :—

(a) the use of ionising radiations in radiography or fluoroscopy ;

(b) the testing of machines and apparatus intended to produce ionising radiations, not being machines or apparatus to which Regulation 45 or 47 applies ;

(c) the use of ionising radiations in the irradiation of materials for the purpose of inducing chemical, physical or biological changes, including the irradiation of materials for the purpose of sterilisation, disinfection or disinfestation or for the purpose of preserving food, but not including changes induced solely for the purpose of measuring ionising radiations.

Provision of enclosure for ionising radiations

41. The processes to which this Part of these Regulations applies shall be carried on only—

(*a*) within a walled enclosure or a cabinet, being an enclosure or cabinet set apart for the purpose which provides adequate shielding and from which are effectively excluded all persons while any machine or apparatus therein which is intended to produce ionising radiations is energised and all persons other than authorised persons when a sealed source is exposed ; or

(*b*) in accordance with an approved scheme of work as respects which the Chief Inspector is satisfied that the operating and working conditions and the system of control and instruction are such that the radiation doses received by a person working in accordance with the scheme will not exceed the doses permitted in the case of that person under the Schedule to these Regulations :

Provided that (except in cases to which sub-paragraph (*b*) applies) where ionising radiations are being used in radiography and the provision of such a walled enclosure or such a cabinet is not reasonably practicable, effective steps shall be taken to isolate the radiography from other work and to exclude all except authorised persons from a suitable enclosure or, where the provision of such an enclosure is not reasonably practicable, from a suitably marked area round the work.

Design of walled enclosure or cabinet

42.—(1) Where a walled enclosure or a cabinet is provided—

(*a*) effective devices shall be provided and maintained—

    (i) to ensure that if any door or part of the walled enclosure or of the cabinet is opened while any machine or apparatus therein is energised the machine or apparatus is automatically de-energised and cannot be energised so long as that door or part is open ; and

    (ii) where the walled enclosure or the cabinet is an enclosure or cabinet to which no person is authorised to have access while a sealed source contained therein is exposed, to ensure that no door or part of the enclosure or of the cabinet can be opened while the sealed source is exposed and that the sealed source cannot be exposed while any such door or part is open ; and

(*b*) the control panel for any machine or apparatus therein which is intended to produce ionising radiations shall be situated outside the walled enclosure or cabinet.

(2) Where necessary for the protection of persons who may be accidentally shut inside a walled enclosure or a cabinet, there shall be provided and properly maintained one or more of the following, that is to say—

(*a*) means of exit so constructed that those persons can leave the enclosure or cabinet without delay ;

(*b*) means whereby those persons can quickly control all the sources of ionising radiations within the enclosure or cabinet ;

(c) shielding for such persons within the enclosure or cabinet appropriate to the circumstances.

(3) Where necessary suitable means of communication shall be provided and maintained to enable persons shut inside a walled enclosure or a cabinet to summon help from outside the enclosure or cabinet.

Warning signals

43.—(1) Adequate warning to all persons in the vicinity shall be given by appropriate light or audible signals or both—

(a) when a sealed source is about to be exposed or when a machine or apparatus is about to be energised ; and

(b) while a sealed source is exposed or a machine or apparatus is energised, and the signals given for the purposes of sub-paragraph (a) of this paragraph shall be distinguishable from those given for the purposes of sub-paragraph (b).

(2) In the case of X-ray machines or apparatus the warning signals shall be arranged to operate automatically.

(3) Suitable warning notices capable of being easily read by persons in the vicinity shall be displayed when ionising radiations are about to be used in, and while they are being used in, an enclosure or marked area in pursuance of the proviso to Regulation 41.

Operational precautions

44.—(1) Every sealed source shall be moved only by the use of a handling rod or tool or an automatic or mechanical method or some other suitable method of remote control.

(2) In all the processes (other than radiography) which are carried on within a walled enclosure or a cabinet, while a sealed source is exposed or a machine or apparatus is energised, no material shall be brought into the beam of radiation except by the use of mechanisms operated from outside the walled enclosure or the cabinet.

(3) In radiography, the radiographic set-up shall be completed before the machine or apparatus is energised or before the sealed source is exposed and no changes in the set-up shall be made while the machine or apparatus is energised or otherwise than by the use of remote controls while the sealed source is exposed.

(4) Whenever practicable, fluorescent screens shall be viewed indirectly by the use of inclined mirrors or other means.

Part IX

X-ray Crystallography and Spectrometry

Requirements as to X-ray crystallography and spectrometry

45.—(1) This Regulation applies to X-ray crystallographic apparatus and apparatus used for X-ray spectrometry.

(2) Apparatus to which this Regulation applies shall be adequately shielded.

(3) Effective arrangements shall be provided, maintained and used to prevent insertion of any part of the body into a useful beam.

(4) Where an X-ray diffraction camera or slit collimating system is in use the useful beam passing between the X-ray tube aperture and the camera or collimating system shall be completely enclosed so as to provide adequate shielding.

(5) Adequate warning to all persons in the vicinity shall be given by appropriate light or audible signals or both while the X-ray tube or apparatus to which this Regulation applies is energised. The warning signals shall be arranged to operate automatically.

Part X

Measuring and Detecting Devices and Static Eliminators

Requirements as to sealed sources used in gauges, etc.

46.—(1) This Regulation applies to sealed sources used in thickness gauges, density gauges, package monitors, level gauges, static eliminators, analysers or other analytical, inspection or gauging equipment.

(2) The sealed source shall be provided with an adequate and efficient cover plate, shutter or shield which—
> (a) shall be capable of being easily, securely and quickly placed or moved so as to attenuate the useful beam as far as is reasonably practicable ;
> (b) shall be used whenever practicable to attenuate the useful beam and whenever reasonably practicable shall be arranged to operate automatically,

and a means shall be provided to indicate clearly whether or not the said cover plate, shutter or shield is in the closed position.

(3) The housing of each sealed source shall be legibly engraved, stamped or otherwise permanently marked to give a warning that it contains radioactive material.

Requirements as to machines and apparatus used in gauges, monitors, etc.

47.—(1) This Regulation applies to machines or apparatus designed to produce ionising radiations (other than machines or apparatus to which Part VIII or IX of these Regulations applies) used in thickness gauges, density gauges, package monitors, level gauges, analysers or other analytical, inspection or gauging equipment.

(2) The machine or apparatus shall be adequately shielded.

(3) Adequate warning to all persons in the vicinity shall be given by appropriate light or audible signals or by both, arranged to operate automatically—
> (a) when a machine or apparatus is about to be energised ;
> (b) while a machine or apparatus is energised ;
> (c) when any shutter used for the purpose of attenuating the useful beam is about to be opened ; and
> (d) while any shutter used for the purpose of attenuating the useful beam is open,

and the signals given for the purposes of sub-paragraphs (a) to (d) of this paragraph shall be distinguishable from each other.

(4) Effective arrangement shall be provided, maintained and used to prevent insertion of any part of the body into a useful beam.

12th June 1969.

Barbara Castle,
First Secretary of State and Secretary
of State for Employment and Productivity.

Regulations 11(2), 15(1), 16(2), 19(1), 20,
        26, 27 and 41

SCHEDULE

Maximum Permissible Radiation Doses

Application of Schedule

1. The doses specified in this Schedule relate to ionising radiations (other than alpha particles emitted by radioactive substances) that originate (otherwise than from radioactive substances within the human body) either in a factory or in a place outside a factory in which any work of a kind specified in Regulation 19(2)(*a*)(ii) is carried on—

   (*a*) from any radioactive substance ; or

   (*b*) from any machine or apparatus that is intended to produce ionising radiations or in which charged particles are accelerated by a voltage of not less than five kilovolts not being apparatus exclusively used (in a room specially set apart for the purpose) for the prevention, diagnosis or treatment of illness or injury,

and for the purposes of this Schedule other ionising radiations shall not be taken into account.

Maximum permissible doses

2.—(1) Except as provided in paragraph 3 of this Schedule, in any calendar year the maximum permissible sum of doses for persons employed in a factory from any ionising radiations shall be—

   (*a*) 75 rems to the hands, forearms, feet and ankles of which not more than 40 shall be received in any calendar quarter ;

   (*b*) 15 rems to the lenses of the eyes of which not more than 8 shall be received in any calendar quarter ; and

   (*c*) 30 rems to other parts of the body of which not more than 15 shall be received in any calendar quarter.

The provisions of (*c*) of this sub-paragraph shall be without prejudice to the provisions of sub-paragraph (2) of this paragraph.

(2) Except as provided in paragraph 3 of this Schedule, the sum of doses received in any calendar quarter by any person to parts of the body other than the eyes, hands, forearms, feet and ankles from all or any one or more of the following, that is to say, X-rays, gamma rays and neutrons shall not exceed 3 rems (or in the case of women 1.3 rems), and the number of rems in the total cumulative dose received therefrom to those parts of the body shall not at any time exceed five times the number of years from the first day of January of the year in which that worker attained the age of eighteen. For the purpose of calculating the said doses a part of a year shall be counted as a year. For the purposes of Regulations 15, 16 and 26 the maximum permissible dose in any one year from X-rays, gamma rays and neutrons to parts of the body other than the eyes, hands, forearms, feet and ankles shall be taken to be 5 rems.

(3) If the occupier is aware that any person employed was during any period—

   (*a*) in protected employment ; or

   (*b*) in employment which, if it had occurred after the coming into operation of any Regulations under the principal Act, would have been protected employment ; or

   (*c*) in any other work involving exposure to ionising radiations,

for which no information is available to the occupier as to the doses that person received during that period of the kinds, and to the parts of the body, specified in sub-paragraph (2) of this paragraph, that person shall, for the purpose of calculating his total cumulative dose referred to in the said sub-paragraph, be deemed to have received doses at the rate of five rems a year during that period.

Maximum permissible doses for pregnant female persons

3. In the case of any female person whom the occupier knows, or has reasonable cause to believe, to be pregnant the maximum permissible sum of doses from all or any one or more of the following, that is to say, X-rays, gamma rays and neutrons during the remaining period of her pregnancy shall be one rem.

EXPLANATORY NOTE

(This Note is not part of the Regulations.)

These Regulations impose requirements for the protection of persons employed in factories and other places to which the Factories Act 1961 applies against ionising radiations arising from radioactive substances sealed in a container or bonded wholly within material or from any machine or apparatus that is intended to produce ionising radiations or in which charged particles are accelerated by a voltage of not less than five kilovolts. These Regulations supersede the Ionising Radiations (Sealed Sources) Regulations 1961 which are revoked.

STATUTORY INSTRUMENTS

1969 No. 813

FACTORIES

The Fees of Appointed Factory Doctors (Amendment) Order 1969

Made - - - -	13*th June* 1969
Coming into Operation	13*th July* 1969

The Secretary of State by virtue of her powers under section 152 of the Factories Act 1961(a) and of all other powers enabling her in that behalf, hereby makes the following Order:—

1.—(1) This Order may be cited as the Fees of Appointed Factory Doctors (Amendment) Order 1969 and shall come into operation on 13th July 1969.

(2) The Interpretation Act 1889(b) shall apply to the interpretation of this Order as it applies to the interpretation of an Act of Parliament.

2. The Fees of Appointed Factory Doctors Order 1968(c), as amended, **(d)** shall have effect as if—

    (*a*) for the reference in Article 4(3)(*c*) to the Ionising Radiations (Sealed Sources) Regulations 1961(e) there were substituted a reference to the Ionising Radiations (Sealed Sources) Regulations 1969(f); and

    (*b*) for the reference in Article 5(*d*) to Regulation 27(2) of the Ionising Radiations (Sealed Sources) Regulations 1961 there were substituted a reference to Regulation 29(1) of the Ionising Radiations (Sealed Sources) Regulations 1969.

Signed by order of the Secretary of State.

13th June 1969.

K. Barnes,
Deputy Under Secretary of State,
Department of Employment and Productivity.

EXPLANATORY NOTE

(This Note is not part of the Order.)

This Order further amends the Fees of Appointed Factory Doctors Order 1968 by substituting for the references in that Order to the Ionising Radiations (Sealed Sources) Regulations 1961 references to the Ionising Radiations (Sealed Sources) Regulations 1969 which supersede the 1961 Regulations.

(a) 1961 c.34.   (b) 1889 c.63.
(c) S.I. 1968/937 (1968 II, p.2445).   (d) S.I. 1968/1771 (1968 III, p.4799).
(e) S.I. 1961/1470 (1961 II, p.2975).   (f) S.I. 1969/808(1969 II, p. 2296).

STATUTORY INSTRUMENTS

1969 No. 820

INDUSTRIAL TRAINING

The Industrial Training Levy (Furniture and Timber) Order 1969

Made - - - -	16*th June* 1969
Laid before Parliament	25*th June* 1969
Coming into Operation	2*nd July* 1969

The Secretary of State after approving proposals submitted by the Furniture and Timber Industry Training Board for the imposition of a further levy on employers in the furniture and timber industry and in exercise of her powers under section 4 of the Industrial Training Act 1964(a) and of all other powers enabling her in that behalf hereby makes the following Order:—

Title and commencement

1. This Order may be cited as the Industrial Training Levy (Furniture and Timber) Order 1969 and shall come into operation on 2nd July 1969.

Interpretation

2.—(1) In this Order unless the context otherwise requires:—

(a) "an appeal tribunal" means an industrial tribunal established under section 12 of the Industrial Training Act 1964;

(b) "assessment" means an assessment of an employer to the levy;

(c) "the Board" means the Furniture and Timber Industry Training Board;

(d) "business" means any activities of industry or commerce;

(e) "dock work" and "registered dock worker" have the same meanings as in the Docks and Harbours Act 1966(b);

(f) "emoluments" means all emoluments assessable to income tax under Schedule E (other than pensions), being emoluments from which tax under that Schedule is deductible, whether or not tax in fact falls to be deducted from any particular payment thereof;

(g) "employer" means a person who is an employer in the furniture and timber industry at any time in the third levy period, but does not include a person in whose case the sum of the emoluments paid or payable to all the persons employed by him at or from a furniture and timber establishment in the third base period is less than £5,000;

(h) "furniture and timber establishment" means an establishment in Great Britain engaged in the third base period wholly or mainly in the furniture and timber industry for a total of twenty-seven or more weeks or,

---

(a) 1964 c. 16.   (b) 1966 c. 28.

being an establishment that commenced to carry on business in the third base period, for a total number of weeks exceeding one half of the number of weeks in the part of the said period commencing with the day on which business was commenced and ending on the last day thereof;

(*i*) "the furniture and timber industry" means any one or more of the activities which, subject to the provisions of paragraph 2 of Schedule 1 to the industrial training order, are specified on paragraph 1 of that Schedule as the activities of the furniture and timber industry;

(*j*) "the industrial training order" means the Industrial Training (Furniture and Timber Industry Board) Order 1965(a);

(*k*) "the levy" means the levy imposed by the Board in respect of the third levy period;

(*l*) "notice" means a notice in writing;

(*m*) "the third base period" means the period of twelve months that commenced on 6th April 1968;

(*n*) "the third levy period" means the period commencing with the day upon which this Order comes into operation and ending on 5th April 1970.

(2) In the case where a furniture and timber establishment is taken over (whether directly or indirectly) by an employer in succession to, or jointly with, another person, a person employed at any time in the third base period at or from the establishment shall be deemed, for the purposes of this Order, to have been so employed by the employer carrying on the said establishment on the day upon which this Order comes into operation, and any reference in this Order to persons employed by an employer at or from a furniture and timber establishment in the third base period shall be construed accordingly.

(3) For the purposes of this Order no regard shall be had to the emoluments of any person wholly engaged either in the supply of food or drink for immediate consumption or, being a registered dock worker, in dock work.

(4) Any reference in this Order to an establishment that commences to carry on business or that ceases to carry on business shall not be taken to apply where the location of the establishment is changed but its business is continued wholly or mainly at or from the new location, or where the suspension of activities is of a temporary or seasonal nature.

(5) The Interpretation Act 1889(b) shall apply to the interpretation of this Order as it applies to the Interpretation of an Act of Parliament.

Imposition of the Levy

3.—(1) The levy to be imposed by the Board on employers in respect of the third levy period shall be assessed in accordance with the provisions of this Article.

(2) The levy shall be assessed by the Board separately in respect of each furniture and timber establishment of an employer but in agreement with the employer one assessment may be made in respect of any number of such establishments, in which case those establishments shall be deemed for the purposes of that assessment to constitute one establishment.

(a) S.I. 1965/2028 (1965 III, p. 5998).   (b) 1889 c. 63.

(3) Subject to the provisions of this Article, the levy assessed in respect of a furniture and timber establishment shall be an amount equal to 1.4 per cent. of the sum of the emoluments of all persons employed by the employer at or from that establishment in the third base period.

(4) The amount of the levy imposed in respect of an establishment that ceases to carry on business in the third levy period shall be in the same proportion to the amount that would otherwise be due under paragraph (3) of this Article as the number of days between the commencement of the said levy period and the date of cessation of business (both dates inclusive) bears to the number of days in the said levy period.

Assessment Notices

4.—(1) The Board shall serve an assessment notice on every employer assessed to the levy, but one notice may comprise two or more assessments.

(2) The amount of any assessment payable under an assessment notice shall be rounded down to the nearest £2 or multiple thereof.

(3) An assessment notice shall state the Board's address for the service of a notice of appeal or of an application for an extension of time for appealing.

(4) An assessment notice may be served on the person assessed to the levy either by delivering it to him personally or by leaving it, or sending it to him by post, at his last known address or place of business in the United Kingdom or, if that person is a corporation, by leaving it, or sending it by post to the corporation, at such address or place of business or at its registered or principal office.

Payment of the Levy

5.—(1) Subject to the provisions of this Article and of Articles 6 and 7, the amount of each assessment appearing in an assessment notice served by the Board shall be payable to the Board in two equal instalments, and the first such instalment shall be due one month after the date of the notice and the second on 1st December 1969 except where the date of the assessment notice is later than 30th September 1969 in which case the second instalment shall be due three months after the date of the notice.

(2) An instalment of an assessment shall not be recoverable by the Board until there has expired the time allowed for appealing against the assessment by Article 7(1) of this Order and any further period or periods of time that the Board or an appeal tribunal may have allowed for appealing under paragraph (2) or (3) of that Article or, where an appeal is brought, until the appeal is decided or withdrawn.

Withdrawal of Assessment

6.—(1) The Board may, by a notice served on the person assessed to the levy in the same manner as an assessment notice, withdraw an assessment if that person has appealed against that assessment under the provisions of Article 7 of this Order and the appeal has not been entered in the Register of Appeals kept under the appropriate Regulations specified in paragraph (5) of that Article.

(2) The withdrawal of an assessment shall be without prejudice to the power of the Board to serve a further assessment notice in respect of any establishment to which that assessment related and, where the withdrawal is made by reason

of the fact that an establishment has ceased to carry on business in the third levy period, the said notice may provide that the whole amount payable thereunder in respect of the establishment shall be due one month after the date of the notice.

Appeals

7.—(1) A person assessed to the levy may appeal to an appeal tribunal against the assessment within one month from the date of the service of the assessment notice or within any further period or periods of time that may be allowed by the Board or an appeal tribunal under the following provisions of this Article.

(2) The Board by notice may for good cause allow a person assessed to the levy to appeal to an appeal tribunal against the assessment at any time within the period of four months from the date of the service of the assessment notice or within such further period or periods as the Board may allow before such time as may then be limited for appealing has expired.

(3) If the Board shall not allow an application for extension of time for appealing, an appeal tribunal shall upon application made to the tribunal by the person assessed to the levy have the like powers as the Board under the foregoing paragraph.

(4) In the case of an establishment that ceases to carry on business in the third levy period on any day after the date of the service of the relevant assessment notice the foregoing provisions of this Article shall have effect as if for the period of four months from the date of the service of the assessment notice mentioned in paragraph (2) of this Article there were substituted the period of six months from the date of the cessation of business.

(5) An appeal or an application to an appeal tribunal under this Article shall be made in accordance with the Industrial Tribunals (England and Wales) Regulations 1965(a) as amended by the Industrial Tribunals (England and Wales) (Amendment) Regulations 1967(b) except where the establishment to which the relevant assessment relates is wholly in Scotland in which case the appeal or application shall be made in accordance with the Industrial Tribunals (Scotland) Regulations 1965(c) as amended by the Industrial Tribunals (Scotland) (Amendment) Regulations 1967(d).

(6) The powers of an appeal tribunal under paragraph (3) of this Article may be exercised by the President of the Industrial Tribunals (England and Wales) or by the President of the Industrial Tribunals (Scotland) as the case may be.

Evidence

8.—(1) Upon the discharge by a person assessed to the levy of his liability under an assessment the Board shall if so requested issue to him a certificate to that effect.

(2) The production in any proceedings of a document purporting to be certified by the Secretary of the Board to be a true copy of an assessment or other notice issued by the Board or purporting to be a certificate such as is

(a) S.I. 1965/1101 (1965 II, p. 2805).   (b) S.I. 1967/301 (1967 I, p. 1040).
(c) S.I. 1965/1157 (1965 II, p. 3266).   (d) S.I. 1967/302 (1967 I, p. 1050).

mentioned in the foregoing paragraph of this Article shall, unless the contrary is proved, be sufficient evidence of the document and of the facts stated therein.

Signed by order of the Secretary of State.
16th June 1969.

Roy Hattersley,
Joint Parliamentary Under Secretary of State,
Department of Employment and Productivity.

EXPLANATORY NOTE

(*This Note is not part of the Order.*)

This Order gives effect to proposals submitted by the Furniture and Timber Industry Training Board to the Secretary of State for Employment and Productivity for the imposition of a further levy on employers in the furniture and timber industry for the purpose of raising money towards the expenses of the Board.

The levy is to be imposed in respect of the third levy period commencing with the date upon which this Order comes into operation and ending on 5th April 1970. The levy will be assessed by the Board and there will be a right of appeal against an assessment to an industrial tribunal.

1969 No. 822

AGRICULTURE

The Price Stability of Imported Products (Rates of Levy No. 13) Order 1969

Made - - - - 16*th June* 1969
Coming into Operation 17*th June* 1969

The Minister of Agriculture, Fisheries and Food, in exercise of the powers conferred upon him by section 1(2), (4), (5), (6) and (7) of the Agriculture and Horticulture Act 1964(**a**) and of all other powers enabling him in that behalf, hereby makes the following order:—

1. This order may be cited as the Price Stability of Imported Products (Rates of Levy No. 13) Order 1969; and shall come into operation on 17th June 1969.

2.—(1) In this order—

"the Principal Order" means the Price Stability of Imported Products (Levy Arrangements) Order 1966(**b**) as amended (**c**), and as amended by any subsequent order and if any such order is replaced by any subsequent order the expression shall be construed as a reference to such subsequent order;

AND other expressions have the same meaning as in the Principal Order.

(2) The Interpretation Act 1889(**d**) shall apply to the interpretation of this order as it applies to the interpretation of an Act of Parliament.

3. In accordance with and subject to the provisions of Part II of the Principal Order (which provides for the charging of levies on imports of certain specified commodities), and notwithstanding the provisions of Article 3 of the Price Stability of Imported Products (Rates of Levy No. 12) Order 1969(**e**),—

(*a*) the rate of general levy for such imports into the United Kingdom of any specified commodity as are described in column 2 of Part I of the Schedule to this order in relation to a tariff heading indicated in column 1 of that Part shall be the rate set forth in relation thereto in column 3 of that Part;

(*b*) the rate of country levy for such imports into the United Kingdom of any specified commodity as are described in column 2 of Part II of the Schedule to this order in relation to a tariff heading indicated in column 1 of that Part shall be the rate set forth in relation thereto in column 3 of that Part.

In Witness whereof the Official Seal of the Minister of Agriculture, Fisheries and Food is hereunto affixed on 16th June 1969.

(L.S.)

A. C. Sparks,
Authorised by the Minister.

(**a**) 1964 c. 28.   (**b**) S.I. 1966/936 (1966 II. p. 2271).   (**c**) S.I. 1969/758(1969 II, p. 2137).
(**d**) 1889 c. 63   (**e**) S.I. 1969/779(1969 II, p. 2322).

SCHEDULE

PART I

1. Tariff Heading	2. Description of Imports	3. Rate of General Levy
		per ton £ s. d.
10.01	Imports of:— Any wheat (other than seed wheat the value of which is not less than £34 per ton, denatured wheat and durum wheat) for which a minimum import price level is prescribed	10 0

PART II

1. Tariff Heading	2. Description of Imports	3. Rate of Country Levy
		per ton £ s. d.
10.01	Imports of:— Any wheat (other than seed wheat the value of which is not less than £34 per ton, denatured wheat and durum wheat) for which a minimum import price level is prescribed and which is grown in and consigned to the United Kingdom from— the French Republic .. .. the Kingdom of the Netherlands	 10 0 5 0

EXPLANATORY NOTE

(This Note is not part of the Order.)

This order, which comes into operation on 17th June 1969, increases on and after that date to 10*s*. per ton in each case, the general levy on imports of wheat (other than seed wheat the value of which is not less than £34 per ton, denatured wheat and durum wheat) and the country levy on such wheat which is grown in and consigned to the United Kingdom from France.

STATUTORY INSTRUMENTS

1969 No. 826 (C.19)

ROAD TRAFFIC

The Road Safety Act 1967 (Commencement No. 3) Order 1969

Made - - - 17*th June* 1969

The Minister of Transport, in exercise of his powers under section 33(3) of the Road Safety Act 1967(**a**) and of all other enabling powers, hereby makes the following Order :—

1. Section 17(1) of the Road Safety Act 1967 and so much of paragraph 9 of Schedule 1 to that Act as provides that in section 232(1)(*a*) of the Road Traffic Act 1960 the reference to Part 1 of the principal Act shall include a reference to section 17(1) of the Road Safety Act 1967 shall come into operation on the 8th July 1969.

2. This Order may be cited as the Road Safety Act 1967 (Commencement No. 3) Order 1969.

Given under the Official Seal of the Minister of Transport the 17th June 1969.

(L.S.)

G. R. W. Brigstocke,
An Under Secretary of the
Ministry of Transport.

EXPLANATORY NOTE

(This Note is not part of the Order.)

This Order brings into operation on 8th July 1969 section 17(1) of the Road Safety Act 1967 whereby a person in charge of a stationary goods vehicle on a road may be required by a goods vehicle examiner or a police constable in uniform to take the vehicle to a suitable place not more than one mile away for the purpose of having it inspected.

(**a**) 1967 c. 30.

STATUTORY INSTRUMENTS

1969 No. 833

CIVIL AVIATION

The Civil Aviation (Investigation of Accidents) Regulations 1969

Made - - -		*17th June* 1969
Coming into Operation		*1st July* 1969

The Board of Trade, in exercise of their powers under section 10 of the Civil Aviation Act 1949(a), as amended (b), as having effect by virtue of the Transfer of Functions (Civil Aviation) Order 1966(c) and of all other powers enabling them in that behalf, hereby make the following Regulations :—

Interpretation and Application

1. These Regulations shall come into operation on 1st July 1969 and may be cited as the Civil Aviation (Investigation of Accidents) Regulations 1969.

2.—(1) The Interpretation Act 1889(d) shall apply for the interpretation of these Regulations as it applies for the interpretation of an Act of Parliament and as if these Regulations and the Regulations hereby revoked were Acts of Parliament.

(2) In these Regulations, unless the context otherwise requires—

"the Board" means the Board of Trade ;

"commander" in relation to an aircraft means the member of the crew designated as commander of that aircraft by the operator thereof, or failing such a person, the person who is for the time being the pilot in command of the aircraft ;

"Inspector" means a person appointed as an Inspector of Accidents under these Regulations ;

"operator" in relation to an aircraft means the person for the time being having the management of that aircraft ;

"owner" means, where an aircraft is registered, the registered owner ;

"pilot in command" in relation to an aircraft means a person who for the time being is in charge of the piloting of the aircraft without being under the direction of any other pilot in the aircraft ;

"substantial damage" includes any damage or structural failure which adversely affects the structural strength, performance or flight characteristics of the aircraft and which would normally require the major repair or replacement of the affected component.

(a) 1949 c. 67.
(b) The relevant amendment is Sect. 23 of the Civil Aviation Act 1968 c.61.
(c) S.I. 1966/741 (1966 II, p.1732).   (d) 1889 c.63.

(3) For the purposes of these Regulations, and of section 26 of the Interpretation Act 1889 in its application to these Regulations, a document may be served on any person by sending it by post in a letter addressed to that person at his last or usual place of abode or place of business.

3. These Regulations relate only to civil aviation and shall apply to accidents arising out of or in the course of air navigation which occur to civil aircraft in or over the United Kingdom, or elsewhere to civil aircraft registered in the United Kingdom :

Provided that they shall not apply to any accident in respect of which a direction has been given under any Regulations made by the Secretary of State and the Board of Trade acting jointly under section 10 of the Civil Aviation Act 1949, as amended.

Purpose of Accident Investigation

4. The main purpose of investigating accidents under these Regulations shall be to determine the circumstances and causes of the accident with a view to avoiding accidents in the future, rather than to ascribe blame to any person.

Duty to furnish information relating to accidents

5. An accident shall be notified in accordance with the provisions of Regulation 6 if, between the time when any person boards an aircraft with the intention of flight and such time as all persons have disembarked therefrom—

(a) any person suffers death or serious injury while in or upon the aircraft or by direct contact with the aircraft or anything attached thereto ; or

(b) the aircraft receives substantial damage.

6.—(1) Where an accident occurs of which notification is required to be given under Regulation 5 the commander of the aircraft involved at the time of the accident or if he be killed or incapacitated then the operator of the aircraft shall forthwith give notice thereof to the Board by the quickest means of communication available and in the case of an accident occurring in or over the United Kingdom shall also notify forthwith the local police authorities of the accident and of the place where it occurred.

(2) The notice to the Board referred to in paragraph (1) of this Regulation shall commence with the identifying abbreviation ACCID, and shall state as far as possible—

(a) the type, model and the nationality and registration marks of the aircraft ;

(b) the name of the owner, operator and hirer, if any, of the aircraft ;

(c) the name of the commander of the aircraft ;

(d) the date and Greenwich mean time of the accident ;

(e) the last point of departure and the next point of intended landing of the aircraft ;

(f) the position of the aircraft with reference to some easily defined geographical point ;

(g) (i) the number of persons on board the aircraft at the time of the accident,

(ii) the number of those persons killed as a result of the accident,

(iii) the number of those persons seriously injured as the result of the accident,

(iv) the number of persons killed or seriously injured elsewhere than on the aircraft ;

(h) the nature of the accident and brief particulars of damage to the aircraft as far as is known.

(3) Where an accident to which these Regulations apply occurs, whether in or over the United Kingdom or elsewhere, the owner, operator, commander or hirer of the aircraft shall, if so required by notice in writing from the Board, send to the Board within such time as may be specified in the notice, such information as is in his possession or control with respect to the accident in such form as the Board may require.

Removal of damaged aircraft

7.—(1) Where an accident occurs in or over the United Kingdom, of which notification is required to be given under Regulation 5, no person other than an authorised person shall have access to the aircraft involved in the accident and the aircraft shall not except under the authority of the Board be removed or otherwise interfered with :

Provided that, subject to the provisions of section 15(3) of the Customs and Excise Act 1952(a)—

(i) the aircraft may be removed or interfered with so far as may be necessary for the purpose of extricating persons or animals, removing any mails carried by the aircraft, preventing destruction by fire or other cause, or preventing any danger or obstruction to the public or to air navigation or to other transport or, under the supervision of a constable, for the purpose of removing any other property from the aircraft ;

(ii) if an aircraft is wrecked on the water, the aircraft or any of its contents may be removed to such extent as may be necessary for bringing it or them to a place of safety.

(2) In this Regulation the expression "authorised person" means any person authorised by the Board either generally or specially to have access to any aircraft involved in an accident and includes any constable or any officer of Customs and Excise.

Inspectors of Accidents

8.—(1) For the purpose of carrying out investigation into the circumstances and causes of accidents to which these Regulations apply the Board shall appoint persons as Inspectors of Accidents, one of whom shall be appointed by the Board as Chief Inspector of Accidents.

(2) In the case of any accident, whether or not such accident is one of which notification is required to be given under Regulation 5, the Chief Inspector shall determine whether or not an investigation is to be carried out.

(3) Without prejudice to the power of an Inspector to seek such advice or assistance as he may deem necessary in making an investigation, the Board may at the request of the Chief Inspector appoint persons to assist any Inspector in a particular investigation and such persons shall for the purpose of so doing have such of the powers of an Inspector under these Regulations as may be specified in their appointment.

Powers of Inspectors

9. For the purpose of the investigation of any accident to which these Regulations apply, an Inspector shall have power—

(a) by summons under his hand to call before him and examine all such persons as he thinks fit, to require such persons to answer any question

(a) 1952 c.44.

or furnish any information or produce any books, papers, documents and articles which the Inspector may consider relevant, and to retain any such books, papers, documents and articles until the completion of the investigation or any inquiry held pursuant to Regulation 16 of these Regulations ;

(b) to take statements from all such persons as he thinks fit and to require any such person to make and sign a declaration of the truth of the statement made by him ;

(c) to have access to and examine any aircraft involved in the accident and the place where the accident occurred, and for that purpose to require any such aircraft or any part or equipment thereof to be preserved unaltered pending examination ;

(d) to examine, remove, test, take measures for the preservation of, or otherwise deal with the aircraft or any part thereof or anything contained therein ;

(e) to enter and inspect any place or building the entry or inspection whereof appears to the Inspector to be requisite for the purposes of the investigation or of any inquiry held as aforesaid ;

(f) to take measures for the preservation of evidence.

Inspector's Investigation

10.—(1) Public notice that an Inspector's investigation is taking place shall be given in such manner as the Chief Inspector may think fit and shall invite any persons who desire to make representations concerning the circumstances or causes of the accident to do so in writing within a time to be specified in the notice.

(2) An Inspector's investigation shall be held in private.

(3) Where it appears to the Inspector that in order to resolve any conflict of evidence or that for any other reason it is expedient so to do, he may permit any person to appear before him and to call evidence and examine witnesses.

(4) Every person summoned by the Inspector as a witness in accordance with these Regulations shall be allowed such expenses as the Board, with the approval of the Treasury, may determine.

(5) Subject to the provisions of Regulation 11 of these Regulations, upon completion of an Inspector's investigation the Chief Inspector or such other Inspector as may be authorised by the Board shall make a report to the Board. The report shall state the circumstances of the accident and conclusions as to the cause together with any observations and recommendations which the person making the report thinks fit to make with a view to the preservation of life and the avoidance of similar accidents in the future.

Notice and Representations

11.—(1) No report shall be made to the Board under Regulation 10(5) of these Regulations in respect of an accident until the Inspector has—

(a) served a notice under this Regulation upon the operator and commander of the aircraft involved in that accident and on any other person, including the Board, whose reputation is, in the Inspector's opinion, likely to be adversely affected by the report, and

(b) considered any representations which may be made to him in accordance with paragraph (3) of this Regulation by or on behalf of the persons served with such notice.

(2) The notice referred to in paragraph (1) of this Regulation shall include particulars of any of those proposed findings and conclusions as to the circumstances and causes of the accident which may affect the person on whom the notice is served.

(3) Any representations made pursuant to paragraph (1) of this Regulation shall be in writing and shall be served on the Inspector within 28 days of service of the notice referred to in that paragraph.

(4) Any person who has been served with a notice pursuant to paragraph (1) of this Regulation shall be served with a copy of the report made to the Board.

Review Board

12.—(1) Any person, other than the Board, who has been served with a notice pursuant to Regulation 11(1) of these Regulations may, at any time before the expiration of the period of 21 days from the day on which he has been served with a copy of the report to the Board, serve on the Board written notice (hereinafter called "the notice of review") that he wishes those findings and conclusions in the report from which it appears that any degree of blame for the accident may be attributed to him, or to any deceased person whose executor, administrator or other personal representative he is, to be reviewed by a Review Board.

(2) The Review Board shall consist of a person to be appointed for the purpose by the Lord Chancellor, sitting with such technical Assessors, if any, as may be so appointed.

(3) The notice of review shall state concisely the grounds on which the findings and conclusions in the report are challenged. A copy of the notice of review shall, at the same time as it is served on the Board, be served on the Treasury Solicitor and the person requesting the review shall inform the Treasury Solicitor whether or not he proposes to be legally represented at the hearing of the review and of the name and address of the solicitor, if any, acting for him, or of any other person who will be representing him at the review.

(4) A copy of the notice of review shall also be served by the person requesting the review on each of the persons on whom the Inspector has served a notice under Regulation 11 of these Regulations ; and for this purpose the person requesting the review may require the Inspector to furnish him with the names and addresses of those persons.

(5) In a case where the Board having made representations pursuant to Regulation 11(1) of these Regulations wish those findings and conclusions in the report from which it appears that any degree of blame for the accident may be attributed to the Board to be reviewed by a Review Board appointed under this Regulation, the Board shall, before the expiration of the period of 14 days from the day of receipt by the Board of the Inspector's report, serve a notice of review on the Treasury Solicitor. The Board shall serve a copy of the notice on each of the persons on whom the Inspector has served a notice under Regulation 11 of these Regulations.

13.—(1) Where notice of review has been served under Regulation 12 of these Regulations, the Board shall forthwith entrust the review to the appointed Review Board.

(2) The Board shall serve on the person requesting the review and all persons on whom the Inspector has served a notice under Regulation 11 of these Regu-

lations, not less than 21 days' notice of the date, time and place of the hearing of the review (hereinafter called "the notice of hearing").

(3) The hearing shall be in public unless the Review Board determines, in relation to the whole or part of the review, that it is to be held in private in the interest of justice or in the public interest :

Provided that a decision by the Review Board that the hearing, or part of it, shall be held in private shall not preclude a member of the Council on Tribunals, or in the case of a Review Board sitting in Scotland, any member of the Scottish Committee of that Council, from being present at the hearing.

(4) The Review Board shall be assisted by the Treasury Solicitor, or by Counsel instructed by him, who shall present any evidence required by the Review Board and may examine any witnesses giving evidence at the review.

(5) The person requesting the review shall be heard by the Review Board and shall have the right to produce witnesses and examine any other witnesses giving evidence at the review.

(6) Before the date fixed for the hearing of the review the Review Board shall hold a preliminary meeting at which any directions may be given or any preliminary or interlocutory order as to the procedure may be made. Notice of the date, time and place of the preliminary meeting shall be given by the Treasury Solicitor to all persons on whom the notice of hearing has been served and any person intending to make any application to the Review Board at the meeting shall give notice thereof to the Treasury Solicitor.

(7) Any person, including the Board, who in the opinion of the Review Board may be affected by the review may be granted leave to appear and to produce witnesses and examine any other witnesses giving evidence at the review. Any application for such leave may be made to the Review Board at the preliminary meeting.

(8) In any proceedings of the Review Board the person requesting the review and any other person appearing pursuant to leave granted under paragraph (7) of this Regulation may appear in person or be represented by any other person whom he may have authorised to represent him.

(9) In addition to all the powers of an Inspector under these Regulations the Review Board may administer the oath to any witness, or require any witness to make and sign a declaration of the truth of the statements made by him in his examination.

(10) Every person summoned by the Review Board as a witness in accordance with this Regulation shall be allowed such expenses as the Board, with the approval of the Treasury, may determine.

(11) (a) The Review Board may, if it thinks fit, order any person who appears or is represented as mentioned in paragraph (8) above to pay in respect of the costs of the Review Board such sum as may be specified in the order, or the taxed amount of those costs or such part thereof as may be so specified, and, without prejudice to the generality of the foregoing, the Review Board shall, in determining whether to make an order as to costs against any person, have regard to whether or not that person took advantage of such opportunities as were open to him to make representations under Regulation 11 of these Regulations.

(b) Any costs required by an order under the foregoing sub-paragraph to be taxed may be taxed on the common fund basis by the Supreme Court Taxing Office.

(c) Any sum payable by virtue of an order under sub-paragraph (a) of this paragraph shall, if the county court so orders, be recoverable by execution issued from the county court or otherwise as if payable under an order of that court.

(12) Upon completion of the review the Review Board shall make a report to the Board containing a summary of the proceedings at the hearing and either confirming or rejecting in whole or in part those findings and conclusions of the Inspector which were the subject of the review, together with its reasons therefor, and the Board shall serve a copy of the report on all persons who appeared or were represented before the Review Board.

Publication of Reports

14. The Board shall, unless in their opinion there are good reasons to the contrary, cause the Inspector's report and, where a Review Board has been held, the report of the Review Board, to be made public wholly or in part in such manner as they think fit :

Provided that—

(i) in any case where notice has been given under Regulation 11(1) of these Regulations, the Inspector's report shall not be published before the expiry of the time for service of a notice of review under Regulation 12(1) of these Regulations ;

(ii) in any case where a Review Board is held, the Inspector's report shall not be published until the completion of the review.

Reopening of Investigation or Review

15.—(1) In the case of any Inspector's investigation which has not been the subject of a review, the Chief Inspector may cause the investigation to be reopened, and in the case of a review the Board may direct the review to be reheard, in both cases either generally or as to any part thereof, and the Chief Inspector or the Board, as the case may be, shall do so—

(a) if new and important evidence has been discovered, or

(b) if for any other reason there is in his or their opinion ground for suspecting that a miscarriage of justice has occurred.

(2) If the Board direct any review to be reheard, the Lord Chancellor may direct that the review shall be reheard either by the Review Board by whom it was heard in the first instance or by some other Review Board appointed by him to hold the rehearing.

(3) Any investigation reopened or review reheard shall be subject to and conducted in accordance with the provisions of these Regulations relating to an Inspector's investigation or review thereof as the case may be.

Public Inquiries

16.—(1) Where it appears to the Board that it is expedient in the public interest to hold a Public Inquiry into the circumstances and causes of or into any particular matter relating to an accident to which these Regulations apply, they may direct that a Public Inquiry be held by a Commissioner appointed by the Lord Chancellor. In any such case any Inspector's investigation relating to the accident or to the particular matter, as the case may be, shall be discontinued except for the purpose of rendering assistance as required by paragraph (3) of this Regulation.

(2) The Commissioner (hereinafter called "the Court") shall be a barrister of not less than ten years standing and shall be assisted by not less than two

Assessors possessing aeronautical, engineering or other special skill or know-ledge. The Assessors shall be appointed by the Lord Chancellor.

(3) Where the Board have directed a Public Inquiry to be held, they shall remit the case to the Attorney-General, and thereafter the preparation and presentation of the case shall be conducted by the Treasury Solicitor under the direction of the Attorney-General ; the Chief Inspector of Accidents shall render such assistance to the Court and to the Attorney-General as is in his power.

(4) When a Public Inquiry has been ordered the Attorney-General may cause a notice, to be called a notice of inquiry, to be served upon the owner, operator, hirer and commander of any aircraft involved in the accident, as well as upon any person who in his opinion ought to be served with such notice. The notice shall contain a statement of the questions which on the information then in the possession of the Attorney-General he intends to raise on the hearing of the inquiry and he may by subsequent notice amend, add to, or omit any of the questions specified in the notice of inquiry.

(5) The Attorney-General, the owner, the operator, the hirer, the commander and any other person upon whom a notice of inquiry has been served, shall be deemed to be parties to the proceedings.

(6) Any other person, including the Board, may, by leave of the Court appear, and any person who so appears shall thereupon become a party to the proceed-ings. Any application for such leave may be made to the Court at a pre-liminary meeting.

(7) At any time before the date appointed for holding the inquiry, the Court may hold a preliminary meeting at which any directions may be given or any preliminary or interlocutory order as to the procedure may be made. Any persons making any application to the Court at a preliminary meeting shall give notice thereof to the Treasury Solicitor.

(8) (i) The Court shall have, for the purposes of the inquiry, all the powers of a Magistrates' Court, and without prejudice to those powers, the Court may—

(a) enter and inspect, or authorise any person to enter and inspect, any place or building entry or inspection whereof appears to the Court requisite for the purposes of the inquiry ;

(b) by summons require the attendance as witnesses of all such persons as the Court thinks fit to call and examine, and require such persons to answer any questions or furnish any information or produce any books, papers, documents and articles which the Court may consider relevant ;

(c) administer the oath to any such witness, or require any witness to make and sign a declaration of the truth of the statement made by him in his examination ;

(ii) the Assessors shall have the same power of entry and inspection as the Court.

(9) Affidavits and statutory declarations may, by permission of the Court and saving all just exceptions, be used as evidence at the hearing.

(10) At the time and place appointed for holding the inquiry the Court may proceed with the inquiry whether the parties, upon whom a notice of inquiry has been served, or any of them are present or not.

(11) The Court shall hold the inquiry in open Court save to the extent to which the Court is of opinion that in the interest of justice or in the public interest any part of the evidence, or any argument relating thereto, should be heard in camera.

(12) The proceedings on the inquiry shall commence with the production and examination of witnesses on behalf of the Attorney-General. These witnesses, after being examined on behalf of the Attorney-General, may be cross-examined by the parties in such order as the Court may direct, and may then be re-examined on behalf of the Attorney-General. Questions asked and documents tendered as evidence in the course of the examination of these witnesses shall not be open to objection merely on the ground that they do or may raise questions which are not contained in or which vary from the questions specified in the notice of inquiry or subsequent notices referred to in paragraph (4) of this Regulation.

(13) When the examination of the witnesses produced on behalf of the Attorney-General has been concluded, the Attorney-General shall state the questions in reference to the accident and to the conduct of persons connected with the accident upon which the opinion of the Court is desired. In framing the questions for the opinion of the Court, the Attorney-General shall make such modifications in, additions to or omissions from the questions in the notice of inquiry or subsequent notices referred to in paragraph (4) of this Regulation as, having regard to the evidence which has been given, the Attorney-General or the Court may think fit.

(14) After the questions for the opinion of the Court have been stated, the Court shall proceed to hear the parties to the proceedings and determine the questions so stated. Each party to the proceedings shall be entitled to address the Court and produce witnesses or recall any of the witnesses who have already been examined for further examination and generally adduce evidence. The parties shall be heard and their witnesses examined, cross-examined and re-examined in such order as the Court shall direct. Further witnesses may also be produced and examined on behalf of the Attorney-General and may be cross-examined by the parties and re-examined on behalf of the Attorney-General.

(15) When the whole of the evidence in relation to the questions for the opinion of the Court has been concluded any of the parties who desires so to do may address the Court upon the evidence and the Court may be addressed in reply upon the whole case on behalf of the Attorney-General.

(16) The Court may adjourn the inquiry from time to time and from place to place, and where an adjournment is asked for by any party to the inquiry the Court may impose such terms as to payment of costs or otherwise as it may think just as a condition of granting the adjournment.

(17) The Court shall make a report to the Board stating fully the circumstances of the case and the opinion of the Court touching the causes of the accident or on the particular matter referred to the Court and adding any observations and recommendations which the Court thinks fit to make with a view to the preservation of life and the avoidance of similar accidents in future.

(18) Each Assessor shall either sign the report with or without reservations, or state in writing his dissent therefrom and his reasons for such dissent, and such reservations or dissent and reasons (if any) shall be forwarded to the Board with the report. The Board shall unless in their opinion there are good

reasons to the contrary cause any such report and reservations or dissent and reasons (if any) to be made public wholly or in part in such a manner as they think fit.

(19) Every person attending as a witness before the Court shall be allowed such expenses as would be allowed to a witness attending before a Court of Record, and in case of dispute as to the amount to be allowed, the same shall be referred by the Court to a Master of the Supreme Court Taxing Office who on request signed by the Court shall ascertain and certify the proper amount of the expenses ; provided that in the case of any party to the proceedings or of any person in the employment of such a party, any such expenses may be disallowed if the Court in its discretion so directs.

Rehearing of Public Inquiries

17.—(1) The Board may, in any case where a Public Inquiry has been held, direct a rehearing of the inquiry either generally or as to any part thereof and shall do so—

  (a) if new and important evidence has been discovered, or
  (b) if for any other reason there is in their opinion ground for suspecting that a miscarriage of justice has occurred.

(2) If the Board direct any inquiry to be reheard, the Lord Chancellor may direct that the inquiry shall be reheard either by the Court by whom the inquiry was heard in the first instance or by some other person appointed by him to hold the rehearing.

(3) Any rehearing shall be subject to and conducted in accordance with the provisions of these Regulations relating to the holding of Public Inquiries.

General

18.—(1) Where an accident has occurred in or over the United Kingdom to an aircraft registered in any country or territory other than the United Kingdom, the Board may authorise an investigator appointed by the duly competent authority of that other country or territory to carry out an investigation in the United Kingdom and in that event the Board shall so far as they are able facilitate inquiries by the investigator so appointed.

(2) In any Inspector's investigation or any Public Inquiry an accredited representative of the country or territory in which the aircraft is registered, or of any country or territory in which the aircraft was manufactured or which has, on request, furnished information in connection with the accident, may take part in the investigation or in the Inquiry as the case may be, that is to say he shall be permitted to visit the scene of the accident, examine the wreckage, question witnesses, receive copies of all pertinent documents (saving all just exceptions), have access to all relevant evidence and make submissions; and he may be accompanied by such technical and other advisers as may be considered necessary by the authorities of the country or territory by which he is appointed.

(3) The Inspector, in the case of the period of 28 days prescribed in Regulation 11(3) of these Regulations, and the Board, in the case of the period of 21 days prescribed in Regulation 12(1) thereof, shall have power to extend the said period, and this power shall be exercisable notwithstanding that the period so prescribed has expired.

19.—(1) A person shall not obstruct or impede the Court or the Review Board or an Inspector of Accidents or an Assessor or any person acting under the authority of the Board in the exercise of any powers or duties under these Regulations.

(2) A person shall not without reasonable excuse (proof whereof shall lie on him) fail, after having had the expenses (if any) to which he is entitled tendered to him, to comply with any summons or requisition of the Court holding a Public Inquiry or a Review Board or an Inspector of Accidents holding an Inspector's investigation under these Regulations.

Provisions as to Scotland

20.—(1) In the case of any accident occurring in or over Scotland any review of an Inspector's investigation and any Public Inquiry, or rehearing of a review or a Public Inquiry, shall be held in Scotland unless the Board after consulting with the Lord Advocate otherwise determine.

(2) In the application of the Regulations to Scotland and to any review or Public Inquiry held there—

(a) for any reference to the Lord Chancellor there shall be substituted a reference to the Lord President of the Court of Session ;

(b) for any reference to the Attorney-General there shall be substituted a reference to the Lord Advocate ;

(c) for any reference to the Treasury Solicitor there shall be substituted a reference to the Crown Agent ;

(d) for any reference to a barrister there shall be substituted a reference to an advocate ;

(e) for any reference to a summons there shall be substituted a reference to an order ;

(f) for any reference to a Magistrates' Court there shall be substituted a reference to a Court of Summary Jurisdiction ;

(g) for any reference to a witness attending before a Court of Record there shall be substituted a reference to a witness attending an inquiry under the Fatal Accidents Inquiry (Scotland) Act 1895(a) ;

(h) for any reference to costs there shall be substituted a reference to expenses ;

(i) for sub-paragraphs (b) and (c) of Regulation 13(11) there shall be substituted the following sub-paragraphs :

"(b) Any expenses required by an order under the foregoing sub-paragraph to be taxed shall be taxed by the Auditor of the Court of Session as if between solicitor and client on the basis that a reasonable amount in respect of all expenses reasonably incurred shall be allowable ; and the Auditor shall endorse on the order a docquet stating the amount of the expenses as so taxed.

(c) Any order under sub-paragraph (a) above, together with any docquet endorsed thereon under the last foregoing sub-paragraph, may be recorded for execution in the Books of Council and Session, and shall be enforceable accordingly" ;

(j) in Regulation 16(3) the words "by the Treasury Solicitor" shall be omitted.

Provisions as to Northern Ireland

21.—(1) In the case of any accident occurring in or over Northern Ireland any review of an Inspector's investigation and any Public Inquiry or rehearing of a review or a Public Inquiry, shall be held in Northern Ireland unless the

---

(a) 1895 c. 36.

Board after consulting with the Minister of Home Affairs of Northern Ireland otherwise determine.

(2) In the application of these Regulations to Northern Ireland and to any review or Public Inquiry held there—

> (a) for any reference to the Lord Chancellor, there shall be substituted a reference to the Lord Chief Justice of Northern Ireland ;
>
> (b) for any reference to the Attorney-General, there shall be substituted a reference to the Attorney-General for Northern Ireland ;
>
> (c) for any reference to the Treasury Solicitor, there shall be substituted a reference to the Chief Crown Solicitor for Northern Ireland ;
>
> (d) for any reference to a barrister, there shall be substituted a reference to a barrister practising in Northern Ireland ;
>
> (e) for any reference to a Court of Record, there shall be substituted a reference to the High Court of Justice in Northern Ireland or any judge thereof ;
>
> (f) for any reference to the Supreme Court Taxing Office, there shall be substituted a reference to the Taxing Office of the Supreme Court of Judicature of Northern Ireland ;
>
> (g) for any reference to a Magistrates' Court there shall be substituted a reference to a Court of Summary Jurisdiction ;
>
> (h) for any reference to local police authorities, there shall be substituted a reference to a district inspector or head constable of the Royal Ulster Constabulary having authority in the district, or in a district contiguous to that, in or over which an accident occurs.

Revocation

22. The Civil Aviation (Investigation of Accidents) Regulations 1951(a) are hereby revoked :

Provided that, without prejudice to Regulation 2(1) of these Regulations, the revocation shall not affect any investigation or Inquiry commenced under those Regulations and any such investigation or Inquiry may be continued as if these Regulations had not been made.

Robert Burns,
A Second Secretary
of the Board of Trade.

June 17th, 1969.

(a) S.I. 1951/1653 (1951 I, p.234).

EXPLANATORY NOTE

(This Note is not part of the Regulations.)

These Regulations, made under section 10 of the Civil Aviation Act 1949, as amended, provide for the holding of investigations by Inspectors of accidents appointed by the Board of Trade and of Public Inquiries into the circumstances and causes of accidents to civil aircraft.

They also prescribe the procedures governing such investigations and Inquiries. The Regulations revoke and replace with modifications the Civil Aviation (Investigation of Accidents) Regulations 1951. The principal modifications are as follows: —

(a) A new regulation now provides that the main purpose of accident investigation shall be to determine the circumstances and causes of the accident with a view to avoiding accidents in the future (Regulation 4).

(b) The Board of Trade may now appoint persons to assist an Inspector of Accidents in the investigation of a particular accident and confer on such persons such of the powers of an Inspector as may be specified in their appointment (Regulation 8(3)).

(c) A new procedure is introduced in relation to Inspectors' investigations requiring the Inspector to give notice of his findings and conclusions to persons affected by them and to consider any representations by those persons. Provision is also made for those persons to challenge the findings and conclusions of the Inspector prior to publication of his report before a Review Board appointed for the purpose by the Lord Chancellor and in accordance with procedure set out in the Regulations (Regulations 11, 12 and 13).

(d) In relation to Public Inquiries a new provision is made for the Court to hold a preliminary meeting to deal with preliminary or interlocutory matters (Regulation 16(7)).

(e) Provision is made for the holding of Review Boards and Public Inquiries in Scotland or Northern Ireland in respect of accidents occurring there, unless the Board of Trade determine otherwise after consultation with the Lord Advocate or the Minister of Home Affairs of Northern Ireland (Regulations 20 and 21).

STATUTORY INSTRUMENTS

1969 No. 834

CIVIL AVIATION

The Air Corporations (General Staff, Pilots and Officers Pensions) (Amendment) Regulations 1969

Made	-	-	-	18*th June* 1969
Coming into Operation				1*st July* 1969

The Board of Trade, in exercise of their powers under section 24 of the Air Corporations Act 1967(**a**) and of all other powers enabling them in that behalf, after consulting with each of the Corporations and with such organisations representative of the employees to whom the Regulations will relate as appear to the Board to be appropriate, hereby make the following Regulations:—

1.—(1) These Regulations shall come into operation on 1st July 1969 and may be cited as the Air Corporations (General Staff, Pilots and Officers Pensions) (Amendment) Regulations 1969.

(2) These Regulations—

(*a*) shall be construed as one with the Air Corporations (General Staff Pensions) Regulations 1948(**b**);

(*b*) may be cited together with the Air Corporations (Pensions) Regulations 1948 to 1968(**c**) as the Air Corporations (Pensions) Regulations 1948 to 1969.

(3) The Interpretation Act 1889(**d**) shall apply for the purpose of the interpretation of these Regulations as it applies for the purpose of the interpretation of an Act of Parliament.

2.—(1) The Joint Pension Scheme established and maintained by virtue of the Air Corporations (Pensions) Regulations 1948 to 1968 shall be in accordance with the provisions of the Trust Deed and amending Deeds, copies of which are set out in the Schedules to those Regulations as further amended by a Deed dated 19th May 1969 a copy of which is set out in the Schedule to these Regulations.

(2) The said Deed dated 19th May 1969 is accordingly confirmed and shall come into operation on 1st July 1969.

Geoffrey Parker,
An Under Secretary
of the Board of Trade.

18th June 1969.

(**a**) 1967 c. 33.
(**b**) S.I. 1948/2361 (Rev. I, p. 1275; 1948 I, p. 437).
(**c**) See S.I. 1948/2361 (Rev. I, p. 1275: 1948 I, p. 437) and amending instruments down to S.I. 1968/1577 (1968 III, p. 4378).
(**d**) 1889 c. 63.

SCHEDULE

THIS DEED is made the nineteenth day of May One thousand nine hundred and sixty nine BETWEEN BRITISH OVERSEAS AIRWAYS CORPORATION whose principal office is situated at Speedbird House, Heathrow Airport (London), Hounslow in the County of Middlesex and BRITISH EUROPEAN AIRWAYS CORPORATION whose principal office is situated at Bealine House Ruislip in the County of Middlesex BOAC RESTAURANTS LIMITED AND B.E.A. HELICOPTERS LIMITED (hereinafter called "the Employers") of the first part Rankin Lorimer Weir Derek Harding Glover Angus John Dore Betts Robert Gilchrist Cunningham Ralph Arthur Fuller Charles Victor Green Cyril Alfred Herring Oliver James Hinch Reginald Banwell Johnson Charles George Klimcke Thomas Nisbete and John Charles William Springbett the Management Trustees for the time being of the Airways Corporations Joint Pension Scheme (hereinafter called "The Management Trustees") of the second part and AIRWAYS CORPORATIONS JOINT PENSION FUND TRUSTEES LIMITED (hereinafter called "the Custodian Trustees" which expression shall include the Custodian Trustees for the time being) of the third part AND IS supplemental to the various Deeds set out in the Air Corporations Pensions Regulations 1948 to 1968.

WHEREAS

(1) The parties hereto are desirous of effecting certain amendments to the Trust Deed of the Airways Corporations Joint Pension Scheme.

(2) At a meeting of the Management Trustees held on the twelfth day of March 1969 the said Rankin Lorimer Weir and the said Charles George Klimcke were appointed to execute this Deed in accordance with the provisions of Clause 18 of the said Trust Deed

NOW IT IS HEREBY AGREED AND DECLARED BY AND BETWEEN THE PARTIES HERETO AS FOLLOWS:—

1. Clause 6 of the TRUST DEED shall be amended by deleting sub-paragraph (ii) of paragraph (a) thereof and substituting therefore the following sub-paragraph:
    "(ii) The purchase of or the advance of money upon the security of any immovable property either solely or jointly with others on such terms as the Management Trustees shall approve such property being of any tenure or kind in the United Kingdom the Isle of Man or the Channel Islands.
    If the Management Trustees shall think fit having regard to the special circumstances of any particular case the making of loans to contributors upon the security of any dwelling houses of such amounts and upon such terms as may be approved by the Management Trustees."

2. Save as expressly altered amended or varied hereby the Trust Deed as heretofore amended shall continue and remain in force and shall have effect as if the alterations amendments or variations herein set out were where applicable inserted therein.

3. This Deed is conditional on its being confirmed by Regulations made by the Board of Trade under Section 24 of the Air Corporations Act ,1967 and if so confirmed shall come into force on such date as may be specified in that behalf in such Regulations.

IN WITNESS WHEREOF the Corporations, B.R.L., Helicopters and the Custodian Trustees have caused their respective Common Seals to be hereunto affixed and the Management Trustees have hereunto set their hands and seals the day and year first before written.

THE COMMON SEAL OF BRITISH OVERSEAS AIRWAYS ⎫
CORPORATION was hereunto affixed in the ⎬ (L.S.)
presence of: ⎭

    KEITH GRANVILLE
    Member

    R. M. FORREST
    Secretary

THE COMMON SEAL OF BRITISH EUROPEAN AIRWAYS
CORPORATION was hereunto affixed in the presence   }   (L.S.)
of:

        M. J. LESTER
         Secretary

THE COMMON SEAL of BOAC RESTAURANTS
LIMITED was hereunto affixed in the presence of: }   (L.S.)

        T. J. GLOVER
         Director
        D. G. DODSON
         Secretary

THE COMMON SEAL of B.E.A. HELICOPTERS LIMITED
was hereunto affixed in the presence of: }   (L.S.)

        J. A. Cameron
         Director
        R. D. KEEFE
         Secretary

SIGNED SEALED AND DELIVERED by the said RANKIN
LORIMER WEIR in the presence of: }   R. L. WEIR

        CHRISTINE LOOSEN (Secy)
        21, Windsor Road,
        Bray, Berks.

SIGNED SEALED AND DELIVERED by the said CHARLES
GEORGE KLIMCKE in the presence of: }   C. G. KLIMCKE

        T. NISBET
        B.O.A.C.,
        LONDON AIRPORT.

THE COMMON SEAL of AIRWAYS CORPORATIONS
JOINT PENSION FUND TRUSTEES LIMITED was   }   (L.S.)
hereunto affixed in the presence of:
        R. L. WIER
         Director
        H. BROMAGE
         Secretary

EXPLANATORY NOTE

(This Note is not part of the Regulations.)

These Regulations amend the investment clause of the Airways Corporations
Joint Pensions Scheme by extending the power of the Management Trustees to
make direct investments in immovable property so as to permit them to do so
jointly with others.

1969 No. 839

CUSTOMS AND EXCISE

The Import Duties (Temporary Exemptions) (No. 4) Order 1969

Made - - - -	*23rd June* 1969
Laid before the House of Commons -	*27th June* 1969
Coming into Operation	*3rd July* 1969

The Lords Commissioners of Her Majesty's Treasury, by virtue of the powers conferred on them by sections 3(6) and 13 of the Import Duties Act 1958(a), and of all other powers enabling them in that behalf, on the recommendation of the Board of Trade hereby make the following Order:—

1.—(1) This Order may be cited as the Import Duties (Temporary Exemptions) (No. 4) Order 1969.

(2) The Interpretation Act 1889(b) shall apply for the interpretation of this Order as it applies for the interpretation of an Act of Parliament.

(3) This Order shall come into operation on 3rd July 1969.

2.—(1) Until the beginning of 1st January 1970 or, in the case of goods in relation to which an earlier day is specified in Schedule 1 to this order, until the beginning of that day, any import duty which is for the time being chargeable on goods of a heading of the Customs Tariff 1959 specified in that Schedule shall not be chargeable in respect of goods of any description there specified in relation to that heading.

(2) The period for which the goods of the headings of the Customs Tariff 1959 and descriptions specified in Schedule 2 to this Order are exempt from import duty shall be extended until the beginning of 1st January 1970 or, in the case of goods in relation to which an earlier day is specified in that Schedule, until the beginning of that day.

(3) Any entry in column 2 in Schedule 1 or 2 to this Order is to be taken to comprise all goods which would be classified under an entry in the same terms constituting a subheading (other than the final subheading) in the relevant heading in the Customs Tariff 1959.

(4) For the purposes of classification under the Customs Tariff 1959, in so far as that depends on the rate of duty, any goods to which paragraph (1) or (2) above applies shall be treated as chargeable with the same duty as if this Order had not been made.

E. Alan Fitch,
Joseph Harper,
Two of the Lords Commissioners
of Her Majesty's Treasury.

23rd June 1969

(a) 1958 c. 6.   (b) 1889 c. 63.

SCHEDULE 1
Goods temporarily exempt from Import Duty

Tariff Heading	*Description*
05.15	Norway Pout (Trisopterus (Gadus) Esmarkii)
15.04	Sperm oil, unrefined
27.07	Anthracene
29.01	Anthracene
	Octa-1,7-diene (until 4th September 1969)
29.02	1-Chloro-*n*-dodecane
	Trichlorobenzene, mixed isomers
	Vinyl chloride (until 4th September 1969)
29.04	2,3-Dibromopropan-1-ol containing not more than 0·1 per cent. by weight of 1,2,3-tribromopropane (until 4th September 1969)
29.06	3,5-Di*tert*butyl-4-hydroxybenzyl alcohol
	Resorcinol (until 4th September 1969)
29.09	3,4-Epoxytricyclo[5,2,1,0^{2,6}]decanol
29.12	2-Chlorobenzaldehyde
29.13	17α-Hydroxypregn-4-ene-3,11,20-trione
29.14	*tert*Decanoic acid, mixed isomers (until 4th September 1969)
29.16	Sodium dihydrogen citrate
29.22	1,6-Diaminohexane adipate (until 4th September 1969)
	NN'-Di-2-naphthyl-*p*-phenylenediamine (until 4th September 1969)
	N-Methyl-4-nitroaniline
29.26	3-Dimethylaminomethyleneaminophenyl methylcarbamate hydrochloride
29.35	N-*tert*Butylbenzothiazole-2-sulphenamide (until 6th November 1969)
	Cytosine-1 β-D-arabinoside hydrochloride
	OO-Diethyl O-3,5,6-trichloro-2-pyridyl phosphorothioate
	Diphenoxarsin-10-yl oxide
	*meso*Inositol hexanicotinate (until 4th September 1969)
	2-(Methoxycarbonylhydrazonomethyl)quinoxaline 1,4-dioxide
29.44	Clindamycin hydrochloride
29.45	Ferrous sulphate-glycine complex
	Sodium dihydridodi-(2-methoxyethoxy)aluminate
39.01	Nylon 66 in the forms covered by Note 3(*b*) of Chapter 39, which on ignition yields not less than 0·02 per cent. and not more than 2·0 per cent. by weight of ash consisting mainly of titanium dioxide and which, when dissolved in aqueous formic acid containing 90 per cent. by weight of formic acid to give a solution containing 8·4 per cent. by weight of nylon 66 polymer, increases the dynamic viscosity of the solvent by a ratio not greater than 50·0, both viscosities being measured at 25° ± 0·05° centigrade in a U-tube capillary viscometer by the method described in British Standard 188:1957 (as amended up to and including September 1964) (until 4th September 1969)

SCHEDULE 2
Goods for which exemption from Import Duty extended

Tariff Heading	*Description*
25.19	Magnesite, dead-burned, containing (*a*) not less than 94 per cent. by weight of magnesium compounds expressed as MgO, (*b*) a total of not more than 1·0 per cent. by weight of aluminium compounds and iron compounds expressed as Al_2O_3 and Fe_2O_3, (*c*) a total of not less than 2·5 per cent. by weight and not more than 5·0 per cent. by weight of calcium compounds and silicon compounds expressed as CaO and SiO_2, and in which the weight of calcium compounds expressed as CaO is not less than 1·5 times the weight of silicon compounds expressed as SiO_2 (until 4th September 1969)

Tariff Heading	Description

28.18   Barium oxide

Magnesium oxide, dead-burned but not fused, of a purity not less than 96 per cent., containing (a) a total of not more than $1\cdot0$ per cent. by weight of aluminium compounds and iron compounds expressed as Al_2O_3 and Fe_2O_3, (b) a total of not more than $3\cdot5$ per cent. by weight of calcium compounds and silicon compounds expressed as CaO and SiO_2, the weight of silicon compounds being not less than $1\cdot5$ times and not more than $3\cdot0$ times the weight of calcium compounds; and (c) of which not less than 50 per cent. by weight is retained by a sieve having a nominal width of aperture of 3/16 inch (until 4th September 1969)

Magnesium oxide, dead-burned but not fused, of a purity not less than 96 per cent., which contains (a) not more than $0\cdot05$ per cent. by weight of boron compounds expressed as B_2O_3, (b) a total of not more than $0\cdot5$ per cent. by weight of aluminium compounds and iron compounds expressed as Al_2O_3 and Fe_2O_3, (c) a total of not less than $1\cdot0$ per cent. by weight and not more than $3\cdot5$ per cent. by weight of calcium compounds and silicon compounds expressed as CaO and SiO_2, the weight of calcium compounds being not less than $1\cdot5$ times and not more than $2\cdot5$ times the weight of silicon compounds; and (d) of which not less than 35 per cent. by weight is retained by a sieve having a nominal width of aperture of 3/16 inch (until 4th September 1969)

29.02   Vinyl bromide (until 4th September 1969)

29.04   Tridecyl alcohol, mixed isomers (until 4th September 1969)

29.06   2,6-Ditertbutylphenol

29.07   2,4,5-Trichlorophenol (until 4th September 1969)

29.13   Cyclo-octanone

29.14   Chloroacetyl chloride
2,4-Dichlorobenzoyl chloride
Glycidyl methacrylate
n-Octanoic acid

29.22   N-n-Butylaniline
1,2-Diaminoethane (until 4th September 1969)
Diethylenetriamine (until 4th September 1969)
Tetraethylenepentamine (until 4th September 1969)
Triethylenetetramine (until 4th September 1969)

29.23   4-Chloro-2,5-dimethoxyaniline
2,5-Dimethoxyaniline
2-Dimethylaminoethyl methacrylate

29.24   N-2,3-Epoxypropyltrimethylammonium chloride

29.35   Quinoline (until 4th September 1969)
5-Vinyl-2-picoline

29.44   Natamycin

38.19   Prepared catalysts, in the form of spheres, containing silver or silver oxide dispersed in, or deposited on, aluminium oxide or silica or other compounds of silicon, and which contain not less than 7 per cent. by weight and not more than 25 per cent. by weight of total silver calculated as Ag

49.11   Identification kits, consisting essentially of a series of transparent slides or foils printed to depict individual characteristics of the human face or head; parts of such kits

51.02   Monofil wholly of fluorocarbon polymer (until 4th September 1969)

Tariff Heading	Description

68.13 Asbestos paper, rubber impregnated, in rolls, being not less than 0·75 millimetre and not more than 0·85 millimetre in thickness, weighing not less than 0·71 kilogramme and not more than 0·78 kilogramme per square metre, and which, when heated to a temperature of 1,000° centigrade, has a loss in weight of not less than 28 per cent. and not more than 32 per cent.

70.03 Amber-coloured tubing of soda glass, not being glass containing 0·25 per cent. or more of cadmium, free or combined, calculated as Cd (until 4th September 1969)

Tubing of neutral glass, in straight lengths and capable of passing a test corresponding with the test for limit of alkalinity of glass prescribed by British Pharmacopoeia, 1953, not including (a) glass with a content of more than 85 per cent. of silica and boric oxide together, or (b) glass of fused silica or fused quartz (until 4th September 1969)

70.10 Carboys having a capacity of not less than 5 gallons

73.06 Iron or steel ingots, blocks, lumps and similar forms, other than those manufactured entirely from pig iron smelted wholly with charcoal (until 6th November 1969)

73.07 Iron or steel blooms, billets, slabs and sheet bars (until 6th November 1969)

73.08 Iron or steel coils for re-rolling (until 6th November 1969)

73.14 Iron or steel wire of a diameter not less than 0·019 inch nor more than 0·200 inch, and having a coating of nickel of not less than 0·0001 inch in thickness

Iron-nickel alloy wire, copper-clad and nickel-plated, having an overall diameter of not less than 400 microns and not more than 450 microns, the nickel plating being not less than 5 microns and not more than 30 microns in thickness; the whole containing not less than 20 per cent. by weight of copper, not less than 25 per cent. by weight of nickel and not less than 40 per cent. by weight of iron, and having, when measured on an 0·20 metre length, a percentage elongation not less than 18 and not more than 25, and a tensile strength not less than 430 newtons per square millimetre and not more than 530 newtons per square millimetre, the rate of straining being 50 millimetres per minute (until 4th September 1969)

73.15 Cold-rolled steel strip, with dressed edges, in coils, the strip being not less than 0·002 inch nor more than 0·007 inch in thickness and not less than ¼ inch nor more than 4 inches in width, containing not less than 16 per cent. by weight nor more than 18 per cent. by weight of chromium, and not less than 6 per cent. by weight nor more than 8 per cent. by weight of nickel and being of a tensile strength of not less than 115 tons per square inch

Cold-rolled steel strip, with dressed edges, in coils, the strip being not less than 0·002 inch nor more than 0·040 inch in thickness and not less than $\frac{1}{16}$ inch nor more than 4 inches in width, containing not less than 16 per cent. by weight nor more than 18 per cent. by weight of chromium, and not less than 6 per cent. by weight nor more than 8 per cent. by weight of nickel, and being of a tensile strength of not less than 120 tons per square inch

Single strand alloy steel wire coated with niobium alloy containing tin and with an outer coating of silver (until 4th September 1969)

Steel wire containing not less than 23 per cent. by weight of chromium, not less than 18 per cent. by weight of nickel and not less than 0·35 per cent. by weight of total carbon, and weighing not less than 8·0 grammes and not more than 33·0 grammes per metre (until 4th September 1969)

Tariff Heading	Description

74.05   Tape consisting of a layer of niobium alloy containing tin, laminated between two layers of copper foil whether or not coated with tin, and being (a) not less than 0·25 inch nor more than 0·75 inch in width and (b) not more than 0·005 inch in thickness

83.13   Tinplate caps for sealing jars, of an internal diameter on the rim of not less than 1·580 inches and not more than 1·610 inches and a maximum depth of not less than 0·415 inch and not more than 0·425 inch stamped from tinplate of nominal thickness of 0·0055 inch or of 0·0066 inch, with an internal curl, a vinyl coating applied to the internal surface and a plasticised lining compound deposited on the internal side wall and top sealing panel to form a sealing gasket (until 4th September 1969)

85.14   Microphones, of a kind for incorporation in deaf aids, approximately rectangular in shape, with a maximum thickness not exceeding 0·165 inch and a total of the length and width not exceeding 0·675 inch, exclusive of sound tube (until 4th September 1969)

85.18   Tantalum capacitors greater than 10 microfarads in capacitance, of a kind for incorporation in deaf aids, with a maximum length not exceeding 7 millimetres exclusive of leads and with a transverse cross section having a circumference not exceeding 14 millimetres (until 4th September 1969)

Tantalum capacitors, of a kind for incorporation in deaf aids, with a maximum length not exceeding 7 millimetres exclusive of leads and with a transverse cross section having a circumference not exceeding 10 millimetres (until 4th September 1969)

85.19   Carbon track volume controls of a kind for incorporation in deaf aids, being of drum type with a cylindrical drum not exceeding 12 millimetres in diameter and 4 millimetres in thickness (until 4th September 1969)

85.23   Insulated tape incorporating a layer of niobium alloy containing tin laminated between two layers of copper foil, whether or not coated with tin and being (a) not less than 0·25 inch nor more than 0·75 inch in width and (b) not more than 0·005 inch in thickness

90.01   Lenses, Fresnel, converging, being composite sheets of artificial plastics, bearing a concentric system of grooves of a uniform density, not less than 18 grooves per centimetre; the lenses being not more than 1·0 centimetres in thickness, not less than 27 centimetres and not more than 29 centimetres square, with chamfered corners and having a focal length not greater than 16 centimetres

Lenses, prisms, mirrors and other optical elements, not optically worked, of thallium bromide-iodide

Photographic process screens of the contact type, consisting of a base of cellulose acetate or of poly(ethylene terephthalate) on which is a regularly spaced pattern of grey-coloured or magenta-coloured dots (until 4th September 1969)

90.17   Ampoule injectors consisting of a glass reservoir connected to a flexible plastic tube in which is inserted a hypodermic needle protected by a removable plastic sheath, of a total length not exceeding 10 centimetres (until 4th September 1969)

Endoradiosondes for the measurement of pH; and specialised receiving and recording apparatus therefor

90.19   Aortic heart valves (until 4th September 1969)

Earphones, of a kind for incorporation in deaf aids, approximately rectangular in shape, with a maximum thickness not exceeding 0·165 inch and a total of the length and width not exceeding 0·675 inch exclusive of sound tube (until 4th September 1969)

Mitral heart valves (until 4th September 1969)

EXPLANATORY NOTE

(This Note is not part of the Order.)

This Order provides that the goods listed in Schedule 1 shall be temporarily exempt from import duty, and those listed in Schedule 2 shall continue to be exempt from import duty, both until 1st January 1970, except for items for which an earlier day is specified.

1969 No. 840

ALIENS

The Aliens (Approved Ports) Order 1969

Made   -   -   -   -   *20th June* 1969
Coming into Operation   *1st July* 1969

In pursuance of the power conferred upon me by Articles 1(3) and 29 of the Aliens Order 1953(**a**), I hereby make the following Order:—

1. This Order may be cited as the Aliens (Approved Ports) Order 1969 and shall come into operation on 1st July 1969.

2. The ports specified in the Schedule hereto shall be approved ports for the purposes of the Aliens Order 1953.

3. The Aliens (Approved Ports) Order 1959(**b**), the Aliens (Approved Ports) Order 1963(**c**) and the Aliens (Approved Ports) Order 1966(**d**) are hereby revoked.

James Callaghan,

One of Her Majesty's Principal
Secretaries of State.

Home Office,
   Whitehall.

20th June, 1969.

SCHEDULE

APPROVED PORTS

Seaports

Belfast	Leith and Granton
Bristol	Liverpool
Cardiff	London
Dover	Middlesbrough
Falmouth	Newhaven
Folkestone	Newport (Monmouth)
Glasgow	Plymouth
Grimsby	Ramsgate Hoverport
Harwich	Southampton
Hull	Swansea
Immingham	Tyne Ports

(**a**) S.I. 1953/1671 (1953 I, p. 94).   (**b**) S.I. 1959/2108 (1959 I, p. 225).
(**c**) S.I. 1963/1871 (1963 III, p. 3461).   (**d**) S.I. 1966/431 (1966 I, p. 934).

Airports

Ashford	Liverpool
Belfast	Luton
Birmingham	Lydd (Ferryfield)
Bournemouth (Hurn)	Manchester
Bristol	Manston
Edinburgh (Turnhouse)	Newcastle (Woolsington)
Gatwick-London	Prestwick
Glamorgan (Rhoose)	Southampton
Glasgow	Southend
Heathrow-London	Stansted-London

EXPLANATORY NOTE

(This Note is not part of the Order.)

This Order consolidates with amendments the Orders revoked by Article 3. Ramsgate Hoverport is added to the list of seaports approved for the purposes of the Aliens Order 1953. Stansted-London is added to the list of airports approved for those purposes and certain changes of nomenclature are made in that list.

STATUTORY INSTRUMENTS

1969 No. 841 (S. 66)

EDUCATION, SCOTLAND

The Education Authority Bursaries
(Scotland) Regulations 1969

Made - - - -		*23rd June* 1969
Laid before Parliament		*30th June* 1969
Coming into Operation		*1st July* 1969

In exercise of the powers conferred upon me by section 49 of the Education (Scotland) Act 1962(a), and of all other powers enabling me in that behalf, and after causing a draft of the regulations to be published and sending a copy thereof to every education authority in accordance with the provisions of section 144(2) of the said Act of 1962 and having had regard to the representations made by education authorities and other persons interested, I hereby make the following regulations:—

Citation and commencement

1. These regulations may be cited as the Education Authority Bursaries (Scotland) Regulations 1969 and shall come into operation on 1st July 1969.

Interpretation

2.—(1) In these regulations, unless the context otherwise requires:—

    (*a*)   "Act" means the Education (Scotland) Act 1962;

    (*b*)   "bursary" means a bursary, scholarship or other allowance granted under section 49 of the Act and "holder" shall be construed accordingly;

    (*c*)   "course of study" includes a series of periods of related study which are separated by periods of employment;

    (*d*)   "income" for the purpose of the Schedules has the same meaning as in the Income Tax Acts;

    (*e*)   "payment period" means a period in respect of which a sum is payable to or for behoof of the holder and shall be a period of twelve months:

Provided that where a bursary is granted in respect of a period of study of less than three academic terms, the payment period may be less than twelve months;

    (*f*)   "Regulations of 1963" and "Regulations of 1965" mean respectively the Education Authority Bursaries (Scotland) Regulations 1963(b), and the Education Authority Bursaries (Scotland) (Amendment No. 1) Regulations 1965(c).

(2) Other expressions used in these regulations to which meanings are assigned by the Act shall, unless the context otherwise requires, have the same respective meanings in these regulations as in the Act.

(3) The Interpretation Act 1889(d) applies for the interpretation of these regulations as it applies for the interpretation of an Act of Parliament.

(a) 1962 c. 47.   (b) S.I. 1963/1132 (1963 II, p. 1914).   (c) S.I. 1965/1298 (1965 II, p. 3703).
(d) 1889 c. 63.

(4) References in these regulations to any enactment, regulation or other instrument shall, except where the context otherwise requires, be construed as references to the said enactment, regulation or other instrument as amended by or under any other enactment, regulation or instrument.

(5) References in these regulations to a Regulation or to a Schedule or to a Part shall, unless the context otherwise requires, be construed as references to a Regulation of these regulations or to a Schedule or to a Part of a Schedule annexed to these regulations, as the case may be.

Revocation

3. Subject to Regulation 12, the Regulations of 1963 and the Regulations of 1965 shall cease to have effect.

Requirements for the granting of bursaries

4.—(1) The power conferred on an education authority by section 49 of the Act shall, subject to the proviso to this paragraph, be exercised only in relation to persons who fulfil the requirement as to residence specified in the next following paragraph:

Provided that an education authority may, in relation to a person who does not fulfil the said requirement, exercise the said power if the person has such connection with the area of the authority as to make it reasonable for them to do so.

(2) The requirement as to residence is that, in the case of a bursary granted under section 49(1) of the Act, the person, or in the case of a bursary granted under section 49(2) of the Act, the parent of the person, is, or was, ordinarily resident in the area of the authority on:—

    (*a*) where the payment period commences on any date during the period from the first day of August to the last day of December, the last day of June preceding that date; or

    (*b*) where the payment period commences on any date during the period from the first day of January to the last day of March, the last day of November preceding that date; or

    (*c*) where the payment period commences on any date during the period from the first day of April to the last day of July, the last day of February preceding that date:

Provided that for the purposes of this paragraph:—

    (i) a person who becomes resident in the area of an education authority wholly or mainly for the purpose of attending a course of study in respect of which a bursary may be granted under section 49 of the Act shall be deemed to be ordinarily resident not in that area but in the area of the education authority in which he, or his parent, as the case may be, is, or was, ordinarily resident on the date specified, as the case may be, under (a), (b) or (c) of this paragraph; and

    (ii) a person who on the said last day of June, last day of November, or last day of February, as the case may be, is in the care of a local authority under the Children Act 1948**(a)**, or is committed to the care of a local authority as a fit person under the Children and Young Persons (Scotland) Act 1937**(b)**, shall be deemed to be ordinarily resident, or shall be deemed to be the child of a parent who is ordinarily resident, as the case may be, in the area which includes the area of that local authority or, if that local authority are entitled to recover expenses duly incurred by them in respect of the person from another local authority, in the area which includes the area of the other local authority.

    (a) 1948 c. 43.   **(b)** 1937 c. 37.

(3) Any question which may arise as to whether any requirement of this regulation is fulfilled in any particular case shall be determined by the Secretary of State whose decision shall be final.

Period of tenure of bursaries

5. Subject to the conditions of tenure specified in the next following regulation, any bursary granted shall be tenable for the payment period in respect of which the bursary was granted.

Conditions of tenure of bursaries

6. Every bursary granted shall be subject to the following conditions:—

(1) that the holder shall attend regularly the course of study in respect of which the bursary was granted;

(2) that the holder or any person acting on his behalf shall, at such times as the education authority who granted the bursary require, provide to that education authority such information and such documents as they may require to enable them to exercise their functions for the purposes of these regulations; and

(3) that the education authority shall be satisfied as to the holder's conduct and progress.

When intimating the granting of the bursary to the holder or to a person acting on his behalf, the education authority shall give notice to him of these conditions and shall inform him that if the holder or any person acting on his behalf does not comply with these conditions or if the education authority are not satisfied as to the holder's conduct or progress, either payment of the bursary may be suspended for a period to be fixed by them or the bursary may be withdrawn, without further warning. If, after such intimation and notice have been given, the holder or any person acting on his behalf does not comply with these conditions or if the education authority are not satisfied as to the holder's conduct or progress, the education authority may warn the holder or the person acting on his behalf, or may suspend payment for a period to be fixed by them, or may withdraw the bursary:

Provided that nothing in this regulation shall prevent the education authority from granting another bursary in respect of the same or another course of study to a person whose bursary has been withdrawn.

Assessment of higher school bursaries

7. The sum to be paid in any payment period in respect of a bursary granted under section 49(2)(*c*) of the Act shall be the sum, if any, assessed in accordance with the provisions of Schedule 1.

Assessment of full-time further education bursaries

8. Subject to the provisions of Regulation 9 and Regulation 10, the sum to be paid in any payment period in respect of a bursary granted under section 49(1) of the Act for a course of full-time further education shall be the sum, if any, whereby the estimated expenditure assessed in accordance with the provisions of Part 1 of Schedule 2 exceeds the aggregate of:—

(*a*) the contribution, if any, assessed in accordance with the provisions of Part 2 of Schedule 2;

(*b*) where any property is held in trust for the education or maintenance of the holder or of persons of whom the holder is one, such sum as may be made available from the said property in accordance with the conditions of trust; and

(*c*) where during any payment period the holder is or is likely to be entitled to income from any source other than from employment during vacations from his studies, such sum as the holder can, in the opinion of the education authority, be expected to contribute without hardship out of the said income towards the estimated expenditure.

Re-assessment of sums to be paid

9. The holder of a bursary or any person acting on his behalf may at any time during, or within one month following the end of, a payment period submit to the education authority an application for the reassessment of the sum to be paid in relation to that payment period. If the education authority are satisfied that a change has occurred in the financial or other circumstances of the holder or of any person whose income was taken into account, or in any of the sums taken into account, in assessing the sum to be paid, and that the holder or any person whose income was taken into account has suffered or is likely to suffer hardship by reason of the said change, they shall re-assess the sum to be paid in accordance with the provisions of these regulations.

Suspension of bursaries where other awards are held

10. If at any time the holder is in receipt of any other scholarship or other similar allowance for education which is paid out of moneys provided by Parliament or out of any funds aided by grants from the said moneys, payments on account of any bursary granted under these Regulations shall be suspended while the holder continues to hold the said scholarship or other allowance.

Method of payment

11.—(1) The sum to be paid in respect of any bursary granted under these regulations may be paid to the holder of the bursary or to another person for his behoof, or in part to the holder and in part to the said other person, and, where the estimated expenditure assessed in accordance with the provisions of Part 1 of Schedule 2 includes fees payable by the holder to an educational institution, the amount of the said fees may be paid to the institution on his behalf.

(2) Any payment under these regulations may be made in a lump sum or by instalments as the education authority may think fit:

Provided that:—

(i) no payment shall be made before the holder has been accepted for admission to the course of study in respect of which the bursary was granted; and

(ii) the education authority shall make payments at such time as will enable expenditure to be met by or on behalf of the holder as and when necessary.

Transitory provisions

12. In relation to any bursary granted before the day on which these regulations come into operation:—

(1) the Regulations of 1963 and 1965 shall have effect for the purposes of any payment period current on the said day (including any re-assessment under Regulation 8(4) of the Regulations of 1963) but for no other purposes; and

(2) the sum to be paid in respect of any payment period commencing after the said day in the case of any person who at any time during the period of twelve months ending on 30th June 1969, was the holder of a bursary under the Regulations of 1963 and 1965, shall be not less than the sum which would have been paid had these regulations not come into operation; and

(3) these regulations shall have effect for all other purposes, subject to any necessary modifications.

William Ross,
One of Her Majesty's Principal
Secretaries of State.

St. Andrews House,
    Edinburgh.
23rd June 1969.

SCHEDULE 1

Higher School Bursaries

The sum to be paid

1. The sum to be paid in respect of any bursary granted under section 49(2)(*c*) of the Act which is tenable in respect of the fifth or any subsequent year of an approved course of secondary education or tenable by a person over the age of 16 years attending a special school shall be ascertained by applying the balance of income, determined in accordance with the provisions of this Schedule and set out in column (1) of the following Table, to the scale which is set out in column (2) of the said Table; and the sum to be paid in respect of any other bursary granted under section 49(2)(*c*) of the Act shall be ascertained by applying the said balance of income to the scale which is set out in column (3) of the following Table:—

Balance of Income Column (1)	Rate of the sum to be paid Column (2)	Rate of the sum to be paid Column (3)
£500 and under	£120 a year	£85 a year
£501–£550	£105 "	£75 "
£551–£600	£90 "	£65 "
£601–£650	£75 "	£55 "
£651–£700	£60 "	£45 "
£701–£750	£45 "	£35 "
£751–£800	£30 "	£25 "
£801–£850	£15 "	£15 "
£851 and over	Nil	Nil

Provided that:—

(i) where the education authority accommodate the holder at a boarding school or in a hostel, home or other institution under section 50(2)(*b*) of the Act or make other provision of board and lodging for him under section 50(2)(*c*) of the Act, the sum to be awarded in accordance with the said Table shall be reduced by not less than one half;

(ii) where in any particular case the education authority consider that it would be reasonable to determine that the amount of the balance of income should be nil, they may so determine.

Persons whose balance of income is assessable

2. The education authority shall assess the balance of income of the parents of the holder or, if both parents are dead, or the parents are unable to maintain the holder, of any person legally liable to maintain the holder.

Assessment of total income

3.—(1) The total income of any person the balance of whose income is to be assessed under the last foregoing paragraph shall be assessed by the education authority in relation to a period of twelve months ending on a date to be fixed by the education authority being, save in exceptional circumstances, a date not later than the beginning of the payment period.

(2) Where the total income of a husband and wife in their capacity as parents is being assessed under the last foregoing sub-paragraph, their income shall be aggregated and the total aggregated income shall be taken into account for the purposes of this Schedule:

Provided that where the husband and wife have been divorced or are living apart the education authority shall have regard to any financial arrangements subsisting between the parties and to the whole circumstances, and shall decide whether the total income of one or both of the parties shall be taken into account for the purposes of this Schedule.

(3) Where the total income of a person, other than a parent of the holder, legally liable to maintain the holder is being assessed under sub-paragraph (1) of this paragraph and the said person is married, the income of the husband or wife, as the case may be, of the said person shall not be taken into account.

Assessment of charges upon income

4. The education authority shall assess in relation to a period of twelve months being, unless the authority decide otherwise, the same period of twelve months as is used for the purposes of the last foregoing paragraph the aggregate of the following charges upon the income of any person whose total income is assessed under the said paragraph, that is to say:—

(1) the amount of any sums paid by way of interest allowed for income tax purposes and, as the case may be, paid by way of interest on any loan in respect of a repayment contract under any scheme made under Part II of the Housing Subsidies Act 1967(a);

(2) the amount of an allowance of £120 each towards the maintenance of any dependants of the said person other than the holder and the wife or husband, as the case may be, of the said person:

> Provided that:—
> (i) the said allowance shall be reduced by the amount of the estimated income during the said period of the dependant in respect of whom it is allowed;
> (ii) where the dependant is also the holder of a scholarship or other similar allowance in respect of full-time further education which is paid out of moneys provided by Parliament or out of any fund aided by grants from the said moneys, the allowance under this sub-paragraph shall be the amount of any parental contribution taken into account in the assessment of the said scholarship or other allowance or £120, whichever is less;
> (iii) where there are in the same family two or more holders of bursaries granted under section 49(2)(c) of the Act, no allowance under this sub-paragraph shall be taken into account in respect of any of these holders but the balance of income shall be reduced by twenty-five per cent. in respect of each such holder other than the holder in respect of whom a bursary is being assessed;

(3) the amount of any expenditure upon contributions under a superannuation scheme, premiums under a retirement annuity contract and premiums under a life insurance policy which, in the opinion of the education authority, is reasonably incurred, provided that the amount so assessed shall not exceed one-tenth of the said total income; and

(4) the amount of any exceptional item of expenditure which in the opinion of the education authority is reasonably incurred.

The balance of income

5. The balance of income shall be the sum, if any, whereby the total income assessed under paragraphs 2 and 3 of this Schedule exceeds the charges assessed under paragraph 4 of this Schedule.

Provided that where, in the opinion of the education authority, insufficient information is available to enable them to ascertain the balance of income, they may assess the balance of income at such sum as they consider reasonable.

(a) 1967 c. 29.

SCHEDULE 2

Full-time Further Education Bursaries   Regulation 8

Part 1—Estimated Expenditure

1. In assessing the estimated expenditure in relation to bursaries for full-time further education granted under section 49(1) of the Act, the education authority shall take into account the sums required for:—

(1) the payment of fees, including matriculation, class, tuition, examination and laboratory fees, necessarily incurred by the holder (whether such fees are included in a comprehensive fee or are charged as separate fees) and any other fees which, in the opinion of the education authority, are reasonably incurred;

(2) the acquisition of books, instruments, tools and materials and of any special clothing which, in the opinion of the education authority, are necessary to the holder's course of study;

(3) the payment of expenses arising out of the membership of clubs or societies connected with the educational institution at which the bursary is tenable, where, in the opinion of the education authority, such membership is necessary to enable the holder to take a proper part in the corporate life of the institution;

(4) the payment of travelling expenses which, in the opinion of the education authority are necessarily incurred by the holder in connection with his attendance at his course of study, except in so far as allowances or facilities are provided under section 51(1) of the Act;

(5) an allowance towards the cost of maintaining the holder (during periods other than vacations) of 65s. a week in respect of residence at home or 105s. a week in respect of residence elsewhere than at home, until he attains the age of 18 years:

Provided that where the holder resides in a college hostel or college residence, the allowance shall be the actual charge for such residence;

(6) an allowance towards the cost of maintaining the holder (during periods other than vacations) of 75s. a week in respect of residence at home or 115s. a week in respect of residence elsewhere than at home, after he has attained the age of 18 years:

Provided that where the holder resides in a college hostel or college residence, the allowance shall be the actual charge for such residence;

(7) an allowance of 75s. a week towards the cost of maintaining the holder, after he has attained the age of 18 years, during the Christmas and Easter vacations and the first two weeks of the summer vacation:

Provided that if the holder is required for the purposes of his course of study to attend regularly at an educational institution for less than three academic terms in a payment period, the allowance shall be paid only in respect of those weeks of vacation which fall within the period between the first date and the last date of the period of attendance or six weeks, whichever is less;

(8) an allowance of 35s. a week towards the personal expenses of the holder during periods in respect of which an allowance under either or both sub-paragraphs (6) and (7) is payable;

(9) an allowance to be made at the discretion of the education authority towards the maintenance of any person who is dependent upon the holder;

(10) an allowance to be made at the discretion of the education authority to any holder who has attained the age of 26 years before the start of the course of study for which the bursary is granted.

2. For the purposes of sub-paragraphs (5) and (6) of the foregoing paragraph, the holder shall be deemed to be residing at home if he is residing in the same household as the person or one of the persons whose balance of income is assessed under paragraph 2 of Part 2 of this Schedule.

Part 2—The Contribution

Classification of bursaries

1. For the purposes of this Part, bursaries granted under section 49(1) of the Act to persons until they have attained the age of 18 years shall be classed as category A bursaries; and bursaries granted under section 49(1) of the Act to persons after they have attained the age of 18 years shall be classed as category B bursaries.

Persons whose balance of income is assessable

2. The education authority shall assess the balance of income of the parents of the holder or, if both parents are dead, or the parents are unable to maintain the holder, of any person legally liable to maintain the holder.

Assessment of total income

3.—(1) The total income of any person the balance of whose income is to be assessed under the last foregoing paragraph shall be assessed by the education authority in relation to a period of twelve months ending on a date to be fixed by the education authority being, save in exceptional circumstances, a date not later than the beginning of the payment period.

(2) Where the total income of a husband and wife in their capacity as parents is being assessed under the last foregoing sub-paragraph, their income shall be aggregated and the total aggregated income shall be taken into account for the purposes of this Part:

Provided that where the husband and wife have been divorced or are living apart the education authority shall have regard to any financial arrangements subsisting between the parties and to the whole circumstances, and shall decide whether the total income of one or both of the parties shall be taken into account for the purposes of this Part.

(3) Where the total income of a person, other than a parent of the holder, legally liable to maintain the holder is being assessed under sub-paragraph (1) of this paragraph and the said person is married, the income of the husband or wife, as the case may be, of the said person shall not be taken into account.

Assessment of charges upon income

4. The education authority shall assess in relation to a period of twelve months being, unless the authority decide otherwise, the same period of twelve months as is used for the purposes of the last foregoing paragraph the aggregate of the following charges upon the income of any person whose total income is assessed under the said paragraph, that is to say—

(1) the amount of any sums paid by way of interest allowed for income tax purposes and, as the case may be, paid by way of interest on any loan in respect of a repayment contract under any scheme made under Part II of the Housing Subsidies Act 1967(a);

(2) the amount of an allowance of £120 each in the assessment of a category A bursary or of £200 each in the assessment of a category B bursary, towards the maintenance of any dependants of the said person other than the holder and any dependant who is the holder of a scholarship or other similar allowance for education which is paid out of moneys provided by Parliament or out of any fund aided by grants from the said moneys and the wife or husband, as the case may be, of the said person:

Provided that the said allowance shall be reduced by the amount of the income during the said period of the dependant in respect of whom it is allowed;

(3) the amount of any expenditure which, in the opinion of the education authority, is reasonably incurred upon the education of members of the said person's family, other than the holder and any member who is the holder of a scholarship or other similar allowance for education which is paid out of moneys provided by Parliament or out of any fund aided by grants from the said moneys;

(4) the amount of any expenditure upon contributions under a superannuation scheme, premiums under a retirement annuity contract and premiums under a life insurance policy which, in the opinion of the education authority is reasonably incurred, provided that the amount so assessed shall not exceed one-tenth of the said total income; and

(5) the amount of any exceptional item of expenditure which in the opinion of the education authority is reasonably incurred.

(a) 1967 c. 29.

Balance of income

5. The balance of income shall be the amount, if any, whereby the total income assessed under paragraph 3 of this Part exceeds the total charges upon the said total income assessed under the last foregoing paragraph:

Provided that where, in the opinion of the education authority, insufficient information is available to enable them to ascertain the balance of income, they may assess the balance of income at such sum as they consider reasonable.

The contribution

6. Subject to the provisions of paragraphs 7 and 8 of this Part, the contribution to be taken into account shall be as follows:—

    (*a*) in the assessment of a category A bursary, if the balance of income is not less than £501 the contribution shall be £15 with the addition of £15 for every complete £50 by which the balance of income exceeds £501; and

    (*b*) in the assessment of a category B bursary, if the balance of income is not less than £900 the contribution shall be £20 with the addition of £1 for every complete £10 by which the balance of income exceeds £900.

Reduced contributions

7.—(1) The contribution or the sum of the contributions ascertained under this Part shall be reduced by the amount of any contribution by the same person which has been taken into account in the assessment of the amount of any allowance granted by the Secretary of State under section 75(4)(*g*) of the Act.

(2) If in any payment period the holder is required for the purposes of his course of study to attend regularly at the educational institution for less than three academic terms, the contribution so ascertained shall be reduced by such sum as the education authority consider reasonable.

(3) Where in any particular case the education authority are satisfied that it would be unreasonable to expect the parents of the holder or the person legally liable to maintain him to make the contribution so ascertained, no contribution shall be taken into account.

Combined assessments

8. Where there are in the same family two or more holders, the foregoing provisions of this Part shall be modified as the case may be as follows:—

(1) Where the bursaries are all of category A, or are all of category B, the references in paragraphs 4(2) and (3) to "the holder" where second occurring shall be construed as references to the said two or more holders, and the contribution shall be attributed to each of the bursaries in such proportion as the education authority consider reasonable.

(2) Where one or more of the bursaries is of category A and one or more of the bursaries is of category B, the contributions to be assessed for the purpose of Regulation 8(*a*) shall be assessed as follows:—

    (*a*) the contribution in respect of the category B bursary or bursaries shall be assessed in accordance with the foregoing paragraphs of this Part, the references in paragraphs 4(2) and (3) to "the holder" where second occurring being construed as references to the holders of category B bursaries and holders of allowances under section 75(4) (g) of the Act, as the case may be. Where more than one of the bursaries is of category B, the contribution shall be attributed to each of the category B bursaries in such proportion as the education authority consider reasonable;

    (*b*) the contribution in respect of the category A bursary or bursaries shall be assessed in accordance with the foregoing paragraphs of this Part, the references in paragraphs 4(2) and (3) to "the holder" where second occurring being construed as references to the holders of category A bursaries, category B bursaries and holders of allowances under section 75(4) (g) of the Act, as the case may be, and shall be reduced by the amount of the contribution in respect of the category B bursary or bursaries ascertained as in the immediately foregoing sub-paragraph. Where more than one of the bursaries is of category A, the contribution shall be attributed to each of the category A bursaries, in such proportion as the education authority consider reasonable.

EXPLANATORY NOTE
(*This Note is not part of the Regulations.*)

These Regulations replace the Education Authority Bursaries (Scotland) Regulations 1963 and 1965 and prescribe how education authorities are to calculate the value of higher school bursaries and bursaries for full-time further education which they decide to grant under section 49 of the Education (Scotland) Act 1962.

The main changes are:—

All applications for bursaries are now to be considered and assessed on a year-to-year basis and eligibility is to be considered by reference to the place of ordinary residence on certain specified dates.

Higher school bursaries are dealt with in Schedule 1 and are presented in simplified form as a table of bursaries payable at certain levels of parents' "balance of income". The maximum bursary for a person in the fourth year of a secondary course is increased from £70 to £85 a year, and for a person in a fifth or subsequent year it is increased from £100 to £120 a year.

The assessment of bursaries for full-time further education is dealt with in Schedule 2. There are two scales. The scale for students who have not yet attained the age of 18 years, is comparable to that for higher school bursaries. The rates are 65s. a week for students living at home and 105s. a week for students living away from home. The parental contribution applicable to the assessment of these bursaries is £15 at a balance of income of £501 with the addition of £15 for every complete £50 by which the balance of income exceeds £501.

The following table shows the changes in the weekly rates of bursaries for students of 18 years and over:—

Item	Regulations of 1963	New Regulations
Maintenance during term-time—		
At Home	60s.	75s.
Away from Home	Minimum of 95s.	115s.
Maintenance during vacations (Christmas and Easter vacations and the first two weeks of the summer vacation)...	60s.	75s.
Personal expenses allowance	30s.	35s.

The parental contribution scale applicable to the assessment of bursaries for students of 18 years of age and over is £20 at a balance of income of £900 with the addition of £1 for every complete £10 by which the balance of income exceeds £900.

Education authorities may, at their discretion, give additional allowances to students who have dependants and to certain students who have attained the age of 26 years at the start of their courses.

STATUTORY INSTRUMENTS

1969 No. 842

FOREIGN COMPENSATION

The Foreign Compensation Commission (Union of Soviet Socialist Republics) Rules Approval Instrument 1969

Made - - - -	*23rd June* 1969
Laid before Parliament	*30th June* 1969
Coming into Operation	*1st July* 1969

Whereas the Foreign Compensation Commission have, in the exercise of their powers under section 4 of the Foreign Compensation Act 1950(a), made rules of procedure and submitted them to the Lord Chancellor for his approval:

Now, therefore, the Lord Chancellor, in exercise of the powers conferred on him by sections 4 and 8 of the said Act hereby approves the said rules in the form set out in the Schedule hereto.

This instrument may be cited as the Foreign Compensation Commission (Union of Soviet Socialist Republics) Rules Approval Instrument 1969 and shall come into operation on 1st July 1969.

Dated 23rd June 1969.

Gardiner, C.

SCHEDULE

The Foreign Compensation Commission in exercise of their powers under section 4 of the Foreign Compensation Act 1950, hereby make the following Rules:—

Citation and extent

1.—(1) These Rules may be cited as the Foreign Compensation Commission (Union of Soviet Socialist Republics) Rules 1969.

(2) The Interpretation Act 1889(b) shall apply to the interpretation of these Rules as it applies to the interpretation of an Act of Parliament.

(3) These Rules shall apply to all applications under the Foreign Compensation (Union of Soviet Socialist Republics) Order 1969(c), and the Foreign Compensation Commission Rules 1956(d), shall not apply to such applications.

(a) 1950 c. 12.   (b) 1889 c. 63.
(c) S.I. 1969/735(1969 II, p. 1978).   (d) S.I. 1956/962 (1956 I, p. 1021).

2.—(1) In these Rules, unless the context otherwise requires, the following expressions have the meanings hereby assigned to them respectively, that is to say:—

"The Act of 1950" means the Foreign Compensation Act 1950;

"The Act of 1969" means the Foreign Compensation Act 1969(a);

"Chief Examiner" means the Chief Examiner appointed by the Commission and any person authorised by the Commission to act as such;

"The Commission" means the Foreign Compensation Commission;

"Commissioner" means the Chairman or a member of the Commission;

"Fund" means any fund into which any sums are paid pursuant to an Order in Council made under the Act of 1950 as amended by the Act of 1969;

"Legal Officer" means the Legal Officer appointed by the Commission to represent the interests of the Fund and any person authorised by the Commission to act on his behalf;

"Pleading" means the Application (or any document accepted by the Commission in lieu thereof), the Answer (if any), the Reply (if any), a Written Argument (if any); and any amendment of or particulars delivered in respect of the above documents;

"Registrar" means the Registrar appointed by the Commission and includes an Assistant Registrar so appointed;

"The Order in Council" means the Foreign Compensation (Union of Soviet Socialist Republics) Order 1969.

(2) Expressions defined in the Order in Council shall have the meanings therein assigned to them.

Language of proceedings and translations

3.—(1) All Applications to and the proceedings of the Commission shall be in the English language.

(2) The Commission may at any time order that an English translation shall be made of any measure or other document, and any copy of a translation so made or submitted by the Applicant may be certified by the Registrar to be a true translation and shall thereafter be accepted without challenge in any proceedings.

(3) The Commission may appoint interpreters to interpret oral evidence in any proceedings or translate documents for the use of the Commission and the Legal Officer.

(4) The Commission may appoint language arbiters to whom any disputed question of translation or interpretation shall be referred, and the decision of any language arbiter shall be accepted as final.

Power to receive evidence

4. The Commission shall not be bound by rules of evidence and may admit in evidence any document or any statement whether on oath or not which they deem to have probative value, but no such document or statement may without leave of the Commission be used unless it has been disclosed to the Applicant or the Legal Officer, as the case may be, not more than 21 days after the delivery

---

(a) 1969 c. 20.

of a Reply in accordance with Rule 18, or, if none has been so delivered, after the expiry of the time limited therefor, and in the case of such a statement the Commission may direct that it shall not be used unless the maker thereof is produced for cross-examination.

Public hearing

5. Subject to any direction given by the Commission every oral hearing shall be in public.

Claims for compensation

6. Unless the Commission otherwise order, compensation shall be claimed by an application in the appropriate form issued or approved by the Commission and shall be signed by the Applicant or in the case of a corporation by its Secretary or a Director. Applications shall be addressed to the Commission and delivered by post or otherwise and their receipt shall be acknowledged.

Time and form of applications

7.—(1) No application shall be entertained unless it has reached the Commission on or before the 31st December 1969:

Provided that—

(a) if the Applicant shall have delivered on or before the said date Part I of the application form issued by the Commission, or such other document as the Commission may accept as giving sufficient notice of the claim, he shall be deemed to have complied with this Rule;

(b) if the application shall not have been made on the form issued by the Commission, the Commission may as a condition of entertaining the application require the Applicant to complete and deliver to the Commission an application in such form not later than one month after the said date;

(c) Part II of the application form issued by the Commission and any relevant appendices thereto shall be completed and delivered to the Commission not later than one month after the said date.

(2) Save with the leave of not less than two Commissioners no claim shall be entertained which has been withdrawn by or on behalf of an Applicant either in writing or at an oral hearing.

Claims on behalf of deceased persons

8. Where no grant of representation has been made in the United Kingdom, an application may be made on behalf of an estate of a deceased person—

(a) by any person claiming to be entitled to represent the estate of the deceased; or

(b) by any person appearing to the Commission to be the widower, widow, child, parent, brother or sister of the deceased.

Provided that:

(i) the Commission shall not entertain more than one application on behalf of the same estate;

(ii) the Commission may at any time as regards any applicant set a time limit within which a grant of representation in the United Kingdom shall be obtained and produced to the Commission;

(iii) upon the obtaining of such a grant the person to whom it is made, if not already the applicant, shall be substituted as applicant and shall sign or countersign all relevant appropriate forms;

(iv) if no such grant of representation shall have been obtained within any time limit so set by the Commission or if the person to whom it has been made shall fail within any time limit set by the Commission to sign or countersign any appropriate form, any such application shall not be further entertained by the Commission;

(v) no determination of a claim in any such case shall be made unless and until a grant of representation in the United Kingdom shall have been obtained and produced as aforesaid.

Infants

9.—(1) Application may be made on behalf of an infant by his next friend.

(2) Any such application may be carried on—

(*a*) by his father or guardian, or

(*b*) by any person appointed for the purpose by his father or guardian, or

(*c*) by a person appointed by the Commission.

(3) Upon any such infant attaining full age, the application shall be carried on in his name unless he shall repudiate it in writing upon or within three months after his attaining full age.

Unincorporated associations

10.—(1) Where a claim under the Order in Council is made in respect of any property of an unincorporated association, charitable or otherwise, the Commission may appoint any two or more persons who appear to them to be suitable to represent the interests of the association to make or continue an Application on its behalf.

(2) The Commission may at any time discharge any appointment so made or appoint any other person in addition to, or in substitution for, any person previously so appointed.

(3) No person shall be appointed under the preceding paragraphs of this Rule without his consent in writing.

(4) The persons for the time being so appointed shall for all the purposes of these Rules be deemed to be the Applicant.

Joinder of claims

11. Several distinct claims under the Order in Council may be made in one application, but if it appears that they cannot conveniently be disposed of together the Commission may give directions for their separate disposal.

Register of applicants

12.—(1) The Chief Examiner shall enter in a Register short particulars of each application and of any amendment thereto.

(2) The Register shall be in such form as the Commission may direct and shall be available for inspection by all Applicants claiming under the Order in Council during usual office hours.

(3) Any Applicant may inform the Legal Officer of any objection he may have to the claim of any other Applicant and the grounds thereof, and in that event the Legal Officer shall report the objection and the grounds therefor to the Commission.

Preliminary assessment of loss

13.—(1) Where it appears to a Commissioner that the application form has been properly completed and that the only issue or issues to be determined under the Application relate to the amount of a loss sustained, then after any directions to the Applicant as to the production of evidence required have been complied with, two Commissioners of whom the first aforementioned Commissioner may be one shall, after such consultations, if any, with the Legal Officer, as they think fit, make a preliminary assessment of the amount to which the Applicant is entitled on his claim on the evidence submitted in the Application and on any other information made available to them; provided that one Commissioner shall have power to make a preliminary assessment under this paragraph where the aggregate of all amounts claimed by an Applicant under Parts IV and VI of the Order in Council does not exceed £10,000.

(2) The Applicant and the Legal Officer shall be sent a statement in writing of the preliminary assessment together with a notice informing them that if, within a period of 21 days from the date of the notice, the Applicant consents in writing to the amount assessed and the Legal Officer does not object, specifying the grounds of his objection, the Commission may make a determination in accordance with such preliminary assessment.

(3) If an Applicant does not accept the assessment, or the Legal Officer objects to it, or if the Commission decide for any other reason not to make a determination in accordance with it, they shall give directions as to all subsequent proceedings in accordance with the procedure in these Rules.

Determination of issues

14. Where it appears to a Commissioner that the application form has been properly completed and that there are issues to be determined under the Application which do not relate solely to the amount of the loss sustained, the Commissioner may give such directions as appear to him to be expedient for a speedy determination of the issues (including the amount of the loss) in accordance with the procedure in these Rules.

Unopposed applications

15.—(1) In any case where directions shall have been given under paragraph (3) of Rule 13 or under Rule 14, the Legal Officer may file with the Registrar a Statement recommending the Commission to admit a claim at the sum claimed or agreed in writing by the Applicant to be the amount of his loss, and the Commission may determine the matter accordingly by admitting the claim at a sum not less than the sum so recommended. A recommendation may be filed at any time before determination notwithstanding that an Answer has been filed under Rule 17.

(2) Before making a determination under this Rule the Commission may require the Applicant to make a statutory declaration of the statements by which he has supported his claim.

Summary dismissal

16.—(1) In any case where directions shall have been given under Rule 14, if it appears to the Legal Officer that as regards any claim or claims made by the Applicant the facts alleged by the Applicant are such that the Applicant cannot satisfy the Commission of the matters requisite for the establishment of such claim or claims under the Order, the Legal Officer may apply to the Commission for an order that any such claim or claims be summarily dismissed. Not less than 21 days' notice of his intention so to apply shall be served upon the Applicant. Any such notice shall state the grounds for the said application and shall be in Form E of the Appendix to these Rules.

(2) An application by the Legal Officer under this Rule shall be heard orally by the Commission who may after taking into consideration any oral or written submissions made by the Legal Officer and the Applicant make an order dismissing such claim or claims wholly or in part or give such directions in the matter as may be thought proper, provided that the Commission may at any time thereafter on reasonable cause shown by the Applicant revoke any such order or dismissal wholly or in part, and any such revocation shall not be deemed to be a review within the meaning of Rule 43.

(3) Any order made by the Commission under this Rule shall be made by not less than two Commissioners and shall not be subject to review.

Answer

17. If the Legal Officer does not make a recommendation under Rule 15, or the Commission do not accept it, if made, then, subject to any order of summary dismissal that may be made and to any further directions that may be given on the hearing of an application made under Rule 15, the Legal Officer shall file an Answer setting out any matters affecting the Application which in his view the Commission should consider. A copy of the Answer shall be served on the Applicant.

Reply

18. The Applicant shall have the right within 21 days after service of the Answer to deliver to the Registrar a Reply, together with any further particulars, and a copy thereof for service on the Legal Officer.

Further and better particulars

19. Where the Applicant or the Legal Officer refuses or fails to supply further and better particulars when requested to do so in writing, the Commission may, upon a request being made, give directions for the delivery of such particulars. If the Applicant refuse or fail to comply with any such directions within the time specified therein the Commission may treat his claim as withdrawn.

Oral hearing

20.—(1) The Applicant may, at any time within 21 days after service of the Answer or with his Reply, make a demand in writing to the Commission for a determination of his application by way of oral hearing.

(2) If the Applicant elects or the Commission decide that there shall be an oral hearing, the Applicant may apply at any time for a date and place to be fixed or the Commission may of their own motion fix the same. Notice shall be given to the Applicant by the Registrar of the date and place and of any adjournment of the hearing.

Preliminary determinations

21. One Commissioner may at any time order a preliminary determination upon any question of fact or law.

Written arguments

22. If the Applicant does not demand an oral hearing he may submit a written argument within 21 days of the service of the Answer or with his Reply, whichever is the later, not containing allegations of fact other than those which he has already pleaded, and thereupon the Commission may, without further reference to him, make a determination after considering any submissions which the Legal Officer may make.

Amendments

23.—(1) Subject to the provisions of the next following Rule, a pleading may be amended only with the leave of the Commission which shall be granted only in special circumstances.

(2) A copy of the amendment shall be delivered to the Registrar with a copy for service on the Applicant or the Legal Officer, as the case may be.

Change of applicant

24.—(1) Subject to the provisions of Rule 25 no Applicant shall be removed with or without the substitution of a new Applicant in his place, nor shall any new Applicant be added, without an application to, and an order of, the Commission. Any such application shall be accompanied by full reasons therefor and shall contain the full name, age, nationality and address of the proposed new Applicant. It shall be served on the Legal Officer and all existing Applicants.

(2) If the Legal Officer or any existing Applicant desires to oppose such application he must so inform the Commission and the proposed new Applicant within 21 days of the service on him of such application.

(3) Any order by the Commission granting such application shall contain any directions necessary to carry such order into effect.

Death of applicant

25.—(1) On the death of an Applicant his application is abated as regards any claim not determined before his death unless the claim survives to a joint Applicant.

(2) Subject as hereinafter provided an abated application may be revived by the personal representative of the deceased Applicant (being the person to whom a grant of probate or confirmation or letters of administration shall have been made in any part of the United Kingdom) by producing such grant to the Commission and signing the application form filed by the deceased Applicant with the Commission:

Provided that after the expiration of 6 months from the date of the death of the deceased Applicant an application may be revived only with the leave of not less than two Commissioners, who may grant or refuse leave at their absolute discretion.

Associated applications

26. Where there are pending at the same time two or more applications which could, in the opinion of the Commission, be conveniently taken together, the Commission may, on the request of an Applicant or the Legal Officer or of their own motion, order that such several applications or parts thereof shall be adjudicated at the same time. Upon making such order the Commission shall give any consequential directions that may be required.

Oaths

27. Any member of the Commission shall have power to administer an oath to or take the affirmation of any Applicant or witness and to require any such person to take such oath or make such affirmation and to answer any question to which the Commission may legally require an answer.

Expert witnesses and reports

28.—(1) Unless the Commission otherwise direct, not more than one expert witness in respect of each technical aspect of the application shall be called by the Applicant or the Legal Officer.

(2) The Commission may at any time, on the request of the Applicant or the Legal Officer or of their own motion, order that a report be provided by any person nominated by the Commission on any matter which they are to consider, and a copy thereof shall be supplied to the Applicant and the Legal Officer to enable them to comment thereon or to apply to the Commission for leave to cross-examine the maker thereof.

Summonses to witnesses and orders to forward documents

29.—(1) A summons for any person to attend to give evidence and to produce documents shall be in Form A of the Appendix to these Rules and an order to forward documents shall be in Form B, with such variations as circumstances may require.

(2) Where any Applicant or the Legal Officer desires a summons or order to issue, the Registrar shall issue the same and shall, in the case of a summons in Form A, specify therein a sum to be tendered to the person to be summoned to attend which shall be reasonably sufficient to cover his expenses in travelling to and from the place of hearing.

(3) The Applicant or Legal Officer, as the case may be, shall serve with the summons an undertaking, in Form D of the Appendix, to pay to the person summoned to attend compensation for loss of time and any additional expenses which are certified by the Registrar to have been reasonably incurred.

(4) Each summons or order shall contain the name of one person only and shall be served personally a reasonable time before the date fixed for hearing.

(5) No summons or order issued pursuant to this Rule shall be valid, unless it is served upon the person named therein within 12 weeks from the date of signature by the Registrar and unless the conditions contained therein with regard to the payment of expenses and loss of time are complied with.

(6) A person served with a summons to attend to give evidence may apply to the Commission to set aside the same, whereupon notice shall be sent by the Registrar to the person at whose instance the summons was issued.

Orders to furnish information

30. The Applicant or the Legal Officer may at any time apply to the Commission for, or the Commission may of their own motion issue, an order in Form C of the Appendix to these Rules, with such variations as circumstances may require, addressed to any person to furnish such written information as may be specified in the order.

Power to inspect

31. Where in response to an order under Rule 29 or Rule 30 the person to whom it is addressed forwards to the Commission any document or a statement, the Registrar shall forthwith inform the Applicant and the Legal Officer, who shall be entitled to inspect and take copies thereof. If any such document or statement is used by the Applicant or the Legal Officer it shall be treated as though it has been disclosed in accordance with the provisions of Rule 4.

Taking evidence abroad

32. The Commission may give such directions for the taking of evidence abroad and of the manner thereof as may be deemed expedient.

Time

33. Subject to the provisions of Article 6(1) of the Order in Council, the time appointed by these Rules for doing any act or taking any step in proceedings:—

(*a*) shall, if the act is to be done or the step taken by a person normally resident outside the United Kingdom of Great Britain and Northern Ireland, be extended by 21 days; and

(*b*) may be extended, if the Commission so order, for any period in their discretion notwithstanding that the time appointed has already expired;

Provided that the time for completing and delivering to the Commission any relevant application form or appendix thereto referred to in either of the provisoes (*b*) and (*c*) to paragraph (1) of Rule 7 shall in no circumstances be extended so as to expire more than two months after the 31st December 1969.

Applications in the course of proceedings

34.—(1) Save as otherwise provided in these Rules, any Commissioner may, if an Applicant or the Legal Officer requests it or the Commission so order, give directions of an interlocutory nature in connection with any proceedings.

(2) If notice of appeal is delivered to the Registrar within 7 days by an Applicant or the Legal Officer, and the Commissioner gives leave, an appeal shall lie from his decision to two other Commissioners.

Service by post

35. Save as otherwise provided in these Rules, any notice or other document required or authorised to be served on any person for the purpose of these Rules may be sent by pre-paid post to that person at his last ordinary or permanent address notified to the Commission or other address for service specified in any notice given under these Rules, and if so sent it shall be deemed to have been duly served on the date of such posting. The address of a solicitor instructed by the Applicant to act generally in relation to his claim shall be deemed to be an address for service specified as aforesaid.

Copies of notices and requests

36. All notices and requests to the Commission or to the Registrar shall be in writing and a copy thereof shall at the same time be served on the Applicant or the Legal Officer, as the case may be.

Right of audience

37.—(1) Save as provided in sub-paragraph (2) hereof the following persons only may address the Commission:—

> (*a*) an Applicant, other than a corporation. A corporation shall be represented by a barrister or solicitor retained on its behalf or with leave of the Commission in case of hardship by a member of the Board of Directors or by its Secretary;
>
> (*b*) the Legal Officer;
>
> (*c*) a barrister retained by or on behalf of an Applicant or the Legal Officer;
>
> (*d*) a solicitor acting generally in the proceedings for an Applicant or a solicitor acting as agent for that solicitor, but not a solicitor retained as an advocate by a solicitor so acting.

(2) At any hearing before one Commissioner and on the hearing of any appeal therefrom the right of audience shall extend to any person in the regular employment of a solicitor.

(3) A person having in Scotland, Northern Ireland or any part of the Commonwealth qualifications and rights of audience similar to those of a barrister or solicitor in England shall have the same right before the Commission.

Non-compliance with rules

38. Non-compliance with any of these Rules shall not render void any proceedings unless the Commission shall so direct.

Determination and notice thereof

39.—(1) The determination by the Commission of all matters save as otherwise provided by these Rules shall be made by not less than two Commissioners and a notice in writing thereof shall be given to the Applicant and the Legal Officer, and it shall not be necessary for the Commission to meet for the purpose of announcing their determination:

Provided that a provisional determination, not by way of an oral hearing, of an application in respect of any claim may be made by one Commissioner if the aggregate of all amounts claimed by an Applicant under Parts IV and VI of the Order in Council does not exceed £10,000.

(2) Every determination under Part VI of the Order in Council that any claim is established shall state the serial number or numbers of every Bond or State Note in respect of which a claim is established.

(3) Every such determination in regard to a claim in respect of a State Note shall be conditional upon the production to the Commission, within such time as the Commission shall direct, of each State Note in respect of which a claim is established, and the Chief Examiner shall stamp every State Note so produced with the appropriate stamp approved by the Commission and attach to or endorse upon such determination a certificate signed by the Chief Examiner that the State Note has been so produced and stamped.

(4) A determination to or upon which any such certificate shall have been attached or endorsed shall, subject to Rule 43, thereupon become unconditional, and a notice in writing to that effect shall be given to the Applicant, to whom the State Note so stamped shall if he so requests in writing and at his risk and expense be returned.

Selection of commissioners

40.—(1) The Chairman, or in his absence the Vice-Chairman, may select the Commissioners required to hear and determine any particular application or group of applications or any matter arising therein, and may from time to time vary the Commissioners selected, and where more than one Commissioner is required shall appoint the Commissioner who is to preside.

(2) If in the course of any hearing one or more of the Commissioners so appointed becomes unable to attend, another Commissioner may, with the consent of the Applicant, in like manner be appointed.

Majority decision

41. In case of disagreement the majority decision of the Commissioners sitting shall prevail. If equally divided the determination of the presiding Commissioner shall be decisive.

Admissions by Legal Officer

42. In determining any application the Commission shall not be bound by any admission or concession by the Legal Officer on any question of fact or of law.

Provisional determinations and reviews

43.—(1) Save as provided in Rule 16, all determinations of the Commission shall be provisional and subject to review. Subject as hereinafter provided, the time for and procedure upon review shall be at the discretion of the Commission.

(2) Before reviewing any provisional determination the Commission shall serve upon the Applicant notice of intention to review.

(3) The Commission may invite the Applicant and the Legal Officer to submit additional evidence or written arguments or to attend an oral hearing on review, or may give leave to them respectively so to do if application for such leave is made before the expiration of 21 days after service of notice of intention to review, but, unless so invited or given leave and subject as hereinafter provided, neither the Applicant nor the Legal Officer shall be entitled to have an oral hearing on review or to submit any additional evidence or arguments.

(4) The Applicant shall be entitled to submit additional written evidence and arguments or to have an oral hearing if the Commission propose on review to disallow or reduce the amount of any claim provisionally allowed, and the Legal Officer shall be so entitled if the Commission propose on review to increase the amount of a claim provisionally allowed or to allow a claim provisionally disallowed.

(5) The Commission shall serve upon the Applicant and the Legal Officer respectively (as the case may require) notice in writing of any such proposal as is referred to in paragraph (4) of this Rule, and any written evidence and arguments and demand for an oral hearing on review shall be served upon the Commission before the expiration of 21 days from the service of the notice of such proposal.

(6) There shall not be more than one review of any determination.

(7) If it appears to the Commission that an Applicant has died and no grant of representation to his estate has been produced to them, the Commission may review the provisional determination of a claim made by the deceased Applicant

without serving any notice of intention to review, or may, if they think fit, by order appoint such person as they think proper to represent the estate of the deceased Applicant for the purpose of such review, and in that case the foregoing provisions of this Rule shall apply to the person so appointed as they apply to an Applicant and notice of intention to review shall be served upon that person.

(8) Where the Commission receive no acknowledgement within 21 days from the date of posting of the notice of intention to review, or such further period as may be specified therein for replying thereto, the provisions of paragraph (7) of this Rule shall apply as if the Applicant had died.

Amendment of determinations and orders

44. Clerical mistakes in determinations or orders or errors arising from any accidental slip or omission may at any time be corrected by the Commission of its own motion after giving notice to the Applicant and the Legal Officer or on the application of the Applicant or the Legal Officer after giving notice to the other of them, without review.

APPENDIX

FORM A

FOREIGN COMPENSATION ACT 1950

SUMMONS TO ATTEND TO GIVE EVIDENCE

FOREIGN COMPENSATION COMMISSION

IN THE MATTER OF AN APPLICATION pending before the Foreign Compensation Commission
       by

                                Applicant

To

      of

You are hereby summoned to attend at
on the   day of   19   at   in
the   noon and so from day to day until the above Matter has been heard to give evidence in the above application.

And also to bring with you and produce at the time and place aforesaid (specify documents to be produced)

Dated   day of   19 .

                                             Registrar.

This summons is issued at the request of*

You are not obliged to attend unless on the service of this summons the said*
                    tenders to you the sum of £   on account of your expenses, and gives you a written undertaking to pay to you such further sum in respect of expenses and loss of time as the Registrar to the Commission may certify to be reasonable.

If you fail to attend as aforesaid the Chairman of the Commission may certify your offence to the High Court which may if it thinks fit punish you as for a contempt of Court.

You may if you think fit apply in writing to the Commission, for just cause, particulars whereof must be stated, to set aside this summons. Any such request must be sent by registered post addressed to the Registrar of the Commission at Alexandra House, Kingsway, London, W.C.2, within three days after service of this summons. If the cause alleged is ill-health a medical certificate must be enclosed with the request.

This summons is of no validity unless served upon you within twelve weeks from the date of its signature as above.

Receipt of Expenses

I hereby acknowledge the receipt of the sum of £   on account of my expenses and of the required written undertaking.

                        Signed†.....................................

---

*Fill in name of person making request for Summons.
†To be signed by person to whom summons is directed.

FORM B

FOREIGN COMPENSATION ACT 1950

ORDER TO FORWARD DOCUMENTS

FOREIGN COMPENSATION COMMISSION

IN THE MATTER OF AN APPLICATION pending before the Foreign Compensation Commission

by

Applicant

To

of

You are hereby required to forward by registered post to the Commission at Alexandra House, Kingsway, London, W.C.2, on or before the   day of   19   , the following documents:—

If the said documents or any of them are not in your possession, custody or power or if you claim to have legal objection to the production of the documents or any of them you must on or before the last-mentioned date forward as above directed a declaration signed by yourself giving the reasons for your inability or objection to forward each of the documents to which such reasons apply.

If you know the name and/or address of the person in whose possession, custody or power the said documents or any of them now are or have been you must give it.

Dated   day of   19   .

Registrar.

This Order is issued at the request of*

If you fail to comply with this Order the Chairman of the Commission may certify your offence to the High Court which may if it thinks fit punish you as for a contempt of Court.

This Order is of no validity unless served upon you within twelve weeks from the date of its signature as above.

The Commission will refund to you the cost of forwarding the said documents.

*Fill in name of person making request for summons.

FORM C

FOREIGN COMPENSATION ACT 1950

ORDER TO FURNISH INFORMATION

FOREIGN COMPENSATION COMMISSION

IN THE MATTER OF AN APPLICATION pending before the Foreign Compensation Commission
by

                     Applicant

To

       of

You are hereby required to furnish the information specified in the Schedule hereto which must be forwarded by registered post addressed to the Registrar, Foreign Compensation Commission, Alexandra House, Kingsway, London, W.C.2, before the   day of   19 .

Dated   day of   19 .

                                     Registrar,
                         By order of the Commission.

If you fail to comply with this Order the Chairman of the Commission may certify your offence to the High Court which may if it thinks fit punish you as for a contempt of Court.

If in addition to furnishing the information as above directed you wish to give oral evidence at your own expense please so indicate in order that you may be notified of the date of hearing.

The Commission will refund to you the postage incurred in complying with this Order.

Schedule

FORM D

FOREIGN COMPENSATION ACT 1950

FORM OF UNDERTAKING TO PAY EXPENSES AND COMPENSATION FOR LOSS OF TIME
FOREIGN COMPENSATION COMMISSION

In addition to the sum of £   paid to the said*
in respect of expenses I hereby undertake to pay to the said*
such further sum in respect of expenses and/or loss of time as the Registrar of the Commission may certify to be reasonable.

                         ....
                         Signature of the person applying
                            for summons in Form A

*Insert name of witness

FORM E
FOREIGN COMPENSATION ACT 1950
APPLICATION FOR SUMMARY DISMISSAL
FOREIGN COMPENSATION COMMISSION
IN THE MATTER OF THE FOREIGN COMPENSATION (UNION OF SOVIET SOCIALIST REPUBLICS) ORDER 1969

AND

IN THE MATTER OF THE APPLICATION OF

TAKE NOTICE that the Legal Officer intends to apply to the Commission under Rule 16 of the Foreign Compensation Commission (Union of Soviet Socialist Republics) Rules 1969 at
on   day the   day of   19   at 10.15 a.m.
for an order that the application of the above-named Applicant so far as regards the under-mentioned claims be dismissed on the grounds hereinafter stated that is to say

The claims in respect of

The grounds for this application are that the requirements of the above Order cannot be satisfied, in that

And further take notice that the said application will be heard orally by the Commission and that you may attend such hearing and that the Commission will take into consideration submissions (if any) made by you or on your behalf orally at the hearing or in writing.

Dated this   day of   19   .

Registrar.

The Seal of the Foreign Compensation Commission was hereunto affixed this 23rd day of June 1969.

(L.S.)   *C. Montgomery White,*
                                              Chairman of the Commission.

                                              H. Walsh,
                                              Secretary.

EXPLANATORY NOTE
(*This Note is not part of the Order.*)

These Rules prescribe the procedure to be followed in proceedings before the Foreign Compensation Commission relating to applications made under the Foreign Compensation (Union of Soviet Socialist Republics) Order 1969.

The Rules are intended to enable claims to be disposed of more speedily than they could under the Commission's usual rules of procedure and are similar to the Foreign Compensation Commission (Egyptian Claims) Rules 1959 (S.I. 1959/640).

1969 No. 843

AGRICULTURAL EMPLOYMENT

SAFETY, HEALTH AND WELFARE

The Agriculture (Poisonous Substances) (Amendment) Regulations 1969

Made	- - -	*23rd June* 1969
Laid before Parliament		*1st July* 1969
Coming into Operation		*2nd July* 1969

The Minister of Agriculture, Fisheries and Food and the Secretary of State, acting jointly, in exercise of the powers conferred on them by section 1 of the Agriculture (Poisonous Substances) Act 1952(a), (as extended by the Agriculture (Poisonous Substances) (Extension) Orders 1960 to 1966(b)), and of all other powers enabling them in that behalf and after consultation with such organisations as appear to them to represent the interests concerned, hereby make the following regulations :—

Citation, extent and commencement

1. These regulations, which may be cited as the Agriculture (Poisonous Substances) (Amendment) Regulations 1969, shall apply to Great Britain and shall come into operation on 2nd July 1969.

Interpretation

2. These regulations shall be construed as one with the Agriculture (Poisonous Substances) Regulations 1966 to 1967(c), and may be cited together with those Regulations as the Agriculture (Poisonous Substances) Regulations 1966 to 1969.

Amendment of the Agriculture (Poisonous Substances) Regulations 1966

3. On the coming into operation of these regulations the Agriculture (Poisonous Substances) Regulations 1966 shall have effect as if—

    (*a*) In Regulation 3(1) of the said regulations there were inserted after the definition of "smoke generator" the following definition. viz.

        " "smoke shreds" means shreds of combustible material. chemically treated to promote burning and impregnated with a specified substance" ;

    (*b*) in sub-paragraph (*c*) of the definition of "specified substance" in Regulation 3(1) of the said regulations there were substituted for the reference to 0.4 per cent by weight of dichlorvos. a reference to 0.5 per

---

(a) 1952 c. 60. For change of title of the Minister, see S.I. 1955/554 (1955 I, p. 1200).
(b) S.I. 1960/398, 1965/1395, 1966/645 (1960 I, p. 83; 1965 II, p. 4115; 1966 II, p. 1452).
(c) S.I. 1966/1063, 1967/1860 (1966 II, p. 2600; 1967 III, p. 4998).

cent by weight of dichlorvos and in sub-paragraph (*d*) of the said definition there were inserted after the word "strip" the words "or an impregnated pellet of polyvinyl chloride";

(*c*) in Regulation 5(2) there were inserted after the words "smoke generator" the words "or where smoke shreds have been used";

(*d*) there were included in Part II of Schedule 1 to the said regulations the entry contained in Part I of the Schedule hereto;

(*e*) in Part II of Schedule 1, column 1, paragraph 1 there were inserted after "3" the words "or 3A"; and

(*f*) there were included in Part III of Schedule 2 to the said regulations the entry contained in Part II of the Schedule hereto.

In Witness whereof the Official Seal of the Minister of Agriculture, Fisheries and Food is hereunto affixed on 19th June 1969.

(L.S.)

Cledwyn Hughes,

Minister of Agriculture, Fisheries and Food.
Given under the Seal of the Secretary of State for Scotland on 23rd June 1969.

(L.S.)

William Ross,
Secretary of State for Scotland.

Regulation 3

SCHEDULE
PART I

Column 1	Column 2	Column 3
Operations prohibited except when protective clothing is worn	Substances in relation to which operations are carried out	Protective clothing required to be worn
3A. Opening a container containing smoke shreds which contain not more than 40 per cent by weight of the substance specified in Column 2 or transferring the contents from one container to another.	Nicotine	Rubber gloves

PART II

Column 1 Common Name and Classification	Column 2 Substance
(*a*) demephion (b)	Any mixture of demephion-0 [dimethyl 2-(methylthio) ethyl phosphorothionate] and demephion-S [dimethyl *S*-[2-(methylthio) ethyl] phosphorothiolate]
(*b*) demeton-S-methyl sulphone (b)	*S*-[2-(ethyl-sulphonyl) ethyl] dimethyl phosphorothiolate

EXPLANATORY NOTE

(This Note is not part of the Regulations.)

These regulations amend the Agriculture (Poisonous Substances) Regulations 1966. Workers to whom these regulations apply may not, and their employers may not cause or permit them to, carry out certain operations with specified poisonous substances unless the prescribed safety measures, including the wearing of protective clothing, are observed.

The effect of these regulations is to require that workers who enter a greenhouse in which smoke shreds as herein defined have been used shall wear the same protective clothing as is specified by the principal regulations in cases where the greenhouse has been sprayed by means of an aerosol or a smoke generator with a specified substance. Workers opening a container of smoke shreds which contain not more than 40 per cent by weight of nicotine, or transferring the contents need no longer wear a face shield ; rubber gloves are the only protective clothing now required for this operation.

In addition, the definition of a specified substance is amended so that an aerosol which contains 0.5 per cent by weight of dichlorvos (instead of 0.4 per cent) and an impregnated pellet of polyvinyl chloride containing not more than 20 per cent by weight of dichlorvos and, in both cases, no other specified substance, are now exempted from the definition. Two further substances, demephion (b) and demeton-S-methyl sulphone (b) are added to the list of poisonous substances.

STATUTORY INSTRUMENTS

1969 No. 844

PUBLIC HEALTH, ENGLAND AND WALES

The Public Health (Infectious Diseases) (Amendment) Regulations 1969

Made - - -	*23rd June* 1969
Laid before Parliament	*1st July* 1969
Coming into Operation	*7th July* 1969

The Secretary of State for Social Services, in exercise of his powers under section 143 (as extended by section 56 of the Health Services and Public Health Act 1968(**a**)) and section 283(2) of, and paragraph 1 of Schedule 1 to, the Public Health Act 1936(**b**) and section 108 of the Local Government Act 1933(**c**), and of all other powers enabling him in that behalf, hereby makes the following regulations :—

Title and commencement

1. These regulations may be cited as the Public Health (Infectious Diseases) (Amendment) Regulations 1969 and shall come into operation on 7th July 1969.

Interpretation

2.—(1) In these regulations "the principal regulations" mean the Public Health (Infectious Diseases) Regulations 1968(**d**).

(2) The Interpretation Act 1889(**e**) shall apply to the interpretation of these regulations as it applies to the interpretation of an Act of Parliament.

Amendment of the principal regulations

3.—(1) The regulation of the principal regulations mentioned in column 1 of the Schedule to these regulations shall be amended as provided for in column 2 thereof against that regulation.

(2) After regulation 2(1) of the principal regulations there shall be added the following paragraph—

"(1A) In regulations 6 and 10 references to Wales include Monmouthshire and references to England do not include Monmouthshire".

(**a**) 1968 c. 46. (**b**) 1936 c. 49.
(**c**) 1933 c. 51. (**d**) S.I. 1968/1366 (1968 II, p. 3800).
(**e**) 1889 c. 63.

SCHEDULE   Regulation 3

1	2
Regulation 2 (which defines expressions for the purposes of the regulations)	For the definition of "Chief Medical Officer" there shall be substituted the following definitions:— "Chief Medical Officer for England" means the Chief Medical Officer to the Department of Health and Social Security; "Chief Medical Officer for Wales" means The Chief Medical Officer to the Welsh Office;
Regulation 6 (which requires cases of certain infectious diseases to be reported to the Chief Medical Officer)	In paragraph (2) for the words "shall immediately inform the Chief Medical Officer" there shall be substituted the words "shall, if his district or port health district is in England immediately inform the Chief Medical Officer for England, or, if his district or port health district is in Wales immediately inform the Chief Medical Officer for Wales" In paragraph (3) for the words "to the Chief Medical Officer" there shall be substituted the words "to the Chief Medical Officer for England if the address of the patient in the certificate is in England or to the Chief Medical Officer for Wales if such address is in Wales".
Regulation 10 (which requires the presence of infected rats to be reported to the Chief Medical Officer)	For the words "shall report the matter to the Chief Medical Officer" there shall be substituted the words "shall if the district or port health district is in England report the matter to the Chief Medical Officer for England or if such district is in Wales to the Chief Medical Officer for Wales"

R. H. S. Crossman,
Secretary of State for Social Services.

23rd June 1969.

EXPLANATORY NOTE
(This Note is not part of the Regulations.)

These Regulations amend the Public Health (Infectious Diseases) Regulations 1968 to require the Chief Medical Officer for Wales instead of the Chief Medical Officer for England to be informed of cases of certain infectious diseases occurring in Wales or Monmouthshire and the existence in Wales or Monmouthshire of infected rats.

STATUTORY INSTRUMENTS

1969 No. 848

EDUCATION, ENGLAND AND WALES

LOCAL GOVERNMENT, ENGLAND AND WALES

The Training of Teachers (Amendment) Regulations 1969

Made - - - -	24*th June* 1969
Laid before Parliament	30*th June* 1969
Coming into Operation	1*st July* 1969

The Secretary of State for Education and Science, in exercise of the powers conferred upon him by Section 4(2) of the Local Government Act 1966(**a**), hereby makes the following regulations : —

Citation, commencement and interpretation

1.—(1) These regulations may be cited as the Training of Teachers (Amendment) Regulations 1969 and shall come into operation on 1st July 1969.

(2) The Interpretation Act 1889(**b**) shall apply for the interpretation of these regulations as it applies for the interpretation of an Act of Parliament.

Amendment of Regulations

2. Regulation 12 (government of colleges) of the Training of Teachers Regulations 1967(**c**) shall cease to apply to maintained colleges of education and accordingly there shall be inserted immediately after the word " Every " at the beginning of that regulation the word " voluntary ".

Given under the Official Seal of the Secretary of State for Education and Science on 24th June 1969.

(L.S.)

Edward Short,
Secretary of State for Education and Science.

EXPLANATORY NOTE

(*This Note is not part of the Regulations.*)

These Regulations revoke the requirement that colleges of education maintained by local education authorities shall be conducted in accordance with articles of government made with the approval of the Secretary of State, provision to this effect having been made by the Education (No. 2) Act 1968 (c. 37).

(**a**) 1966 c. 42.   (**b**) 1889 c. 63.   (**c**) S.I. 1967/792 (1967 II, p. 2319).

1969 No. 849 (S.67)

NURSES AND MIDWIVES

The Nurses (Regional Nurse-Training Committees) (Scotland) Amendment Order 1969

Made - - - -	*16th June* 1969
Laid before Parliament	*3rd July* 1969
Coming into Operation	*7th July* 1969

In exercise of the powers conferred on me by section 19(1) of and Schedule 4 to the Nurses (Scotland) Act 1951(a) and of all other powers enabling me in that behalf, and after consultation with the General Nursing Council for Scotland, I hereby make the following order:—

1. This order may be cited as the Nurses (Regional Nurse-Training Committees) (Scotland) Amendment Order 1969 and shall come into operation on 7th July 1969.

2. The Interpretation Act 1889(b) applies for the interpretation of this order as it applies for the interpretation of an Act of Parliament.

3. Part II of Schedule 2 to the Nurses (Regional Nurse-Training Committees) (Scotland) Order 1963(c) as amended (d) shall be further amended as follows:—

For paragraph 3 (which prescribes maximum rates of payment for travel by private motor vehicle by a member of a Regional Nurse-Training Committee) there shall be substituted the following:—

"**3.**—(1) The rate for travel by a member's own private motor vehicle shall not, subject as hereinafter mentioned, exceed 4d. a mile, and where this rate would exceed the appropriate rate for the vehicle otherwise payable under sub-paragraph (2) the lower rate of 2¾d. a mile shall be paid.

(2) The rate for travel by a member's own private motor vehicle in circumstances which involve a substantial saving in his time or are otherwise reasonable or where it is in the interests of the Committee that he should so travel rather than by public service shall not exceed:—

    (*a*) in the case of a motor car or tri-car exceeding 500, but not exceeding 1199, cubic centimetres cylinder capacity, 9d. a mile for the first 2,000 miles for which in any financial year the member uses a private motor car or tri-car for any official journeys, 7¼d. a mile for the next 5,000 miles in the same year, and thereafter in the same year 5¼d. a mile;

    (*b*) in the case of a motor car or tri-car exceeding 1199 cubic centimetres cylinder capacity, 10½d. a mile for the first 2,000 miles for which in any financial year the member uses a private motor car or tri-car for any official journeys, 9d. a mile for the next 5,000 miles in the same year, and thereafter in the same year 6¾d. a mile;

(a) 1951 c. 55.   **(b)** 1889 c. 63.   (c) S.I. 1963/1342 (1963 II, p. 2325).

(d) The relevant amending orders are S.I. 1964/1990, 1965/2176, 1967/1615, 1968/1448 (1964 III, p. 5052; 1965 III, p. 6376; 1967 III, p. 4455; 1968 III, p. 4184).

(c) in the case of a motor car or tri-car exceeding 150, but not exceeding 500, cubic centimetres cylinder capacity, or of a motor cycle or motor cycle combination exceeding 150 cubic centimetres cylinder capacity, 4½d. a mile for the first 7,000 miles for which in any financial year the member uses a private motor car or tri-car or motor cycle or motor cycle combination for any official journeys, and thereafter in the same year 2¾d. a mile;

(d) in the case of a motor vehicle not exceeding 150 cubic centimetres cylinder capacity, 2¾d. a mile.

(3) The rates mentioned in sub-paragraphs (1) and (2) may be increased:

(a) by not more than ½d. a mile for the carriage otherwise than by motor cycle, autocycle or motor assisted pedal cycle, of each additional passenger to whom an allowance would otherwise be payable under this order:

Provided that where the mileage rate does not exceed 4d. an increase of 1d. may be allowed for the carriage of each additional passenger, subject to a limit of 4d. a mile for four or more passengers;

(b) by not more than the amount of any expenditure incurred on tolls, ferries or parking fees; and

(c) in the case of an absence overnight from the usual place of residence the amount of any expenditure incurred on garaging a motor vehicle.

(4) (a) for the purpose of calculating mileage under (a), (b) and (c) of sub-paragraph (2) no account shall be taken of mileage for which the rate, excluding any allowance for passengers, does not exceed 4d. a mile.

(b) for the purpose of this paragraph:

'cubic centimetres cylinder capacity' shall be calculated in the manner prescribed by regulation 46 of the Road Vehicles (Registration and Licensing) Regulations 1964(a):

Provided that where the engine of a car has been rebored, the calculation shall be based on the engine as it was when new;

'official journeys' means journeys undertaken by a member of a Committee or sub-committee, being journeys in respect of which the member is paid his travelling expenses (whether in his capacity as member or in his capacity as officer) by the Committee, the General Nursing Council for Scotland, the Central Midwives Board for Scotland, or any authority subject to the provisions of the National Health Service (Travelling Allowances etc.) (Scotland) Determination 1968;

'motor cycle' means a motor cycle without a side-car.''

4. Part III of Schedule 2 to the Nurses (Regional Nurse-Training Committees) (Scotland) Order 1963(b) as amended (c) shall be further amended as follows:—

For paragraphs 1, 3 and 4 (which prescribe maximum rates of overnight and day subsistence allowances payable to a member of a Regional Nurse-Training Committee) there shall be substituted the following:—

"**1.**—(1) When a member is necessarily absent overnight from his home or from his place of business, on the business of the Committee or sub-committee, there shall be payable to him for each night up to a total of 21 successive nights—

(a) when such night is spent within a four-mile radius of the King Charles I statue at Charing Cross, London, an allowance of 104s. and

---

(a) S.I. 1964/1178 (1964 II, p. 2722). (b) S. I. 1963/1342 (1963 II, p. 2325).
(c) The relevant amending orders are S.I. 1964/1990, 1967/968, 1968/1448 (1964 III, p. 5052; 1967 II, p. 2929; 1968 III, p. 4184).

(*b*) when such night is spent elsewhere than within such radius, an allowance of 95s.

(2) When a member is so absent for more than 21 successive nights there shall be paid to him such allowance as the Secretary of State shall on application determine."

"**3.** A day allowance in respect of duties not involving a night's absence shall be payable at the rate of 8s. when a member is necessarily absent from his home or place of business for more than five hours but for not more than eight hours, and at the rate of 17s. 6d. when his absence exceeds eight hours; and where the member orders lunch or dinner (costing 15s. or more) on a train or boat, or high tea (costing 11s. or more) on any train where it is offered instead of dinner, the said rates shall respectively be 12s. 3d. and 21s. 9d. or, where lunch and dinner (or high tea) are both so ordered during an absence exceeding eight hours, 24s. 6d.

4. Where the member's absence exceeds twelve hours and he had to commence his journey before he could reasonably be expected to have taken breakfast at home, the day allowance rate mentioned in the preceding paragraph may, at the discretion of the Committee, be increased to 25s. 6d. or, where the member orders one meal on a train or a boat, to 29s. 9d., or where two or more meals are so ordered, to 32s. 6d.

For the purposes of this paragraph a meal means breakfast (costing 11s. 6d. or more) or high tea (costing 11s. or more) or lunch or dinner (costing 15s. or more)."

William Ross,
One of Her Majesty's
Principal Secretaries of State.

St. Andrew's House,
   Edinburgh.
16th June 1969.

EXPLANATORY NOTE

(*This Note is not part of the Order.*)

This Order increases the rates of allowances payable to members of Regional Nurse-Training Committees and their sub-committees for day and night subsistence and for travel by private motor vehicle.

1969 No. 850 (S.68)

ROAD TRAFFIC

The Cycle Racing on Highways (Special Authorisation) (Scotland) Regulations 1969

Made - - - -	20*th June*, 1969
Laid before Parliament	8*th July*, 1969
Coming into Operation	10*th July*, 1969

In exercise of the powers conferred on me by section 12 of the Road Traffic Act 1960(a) and of all other powers enabling me in that behalf, and after consultation with representative organisations in accordance with the provisions of section 260(2) of that Act, I hereby make the following regulations:—

1.—(1) These regulations may be cited as the Cycle Racing on Highways (Special Authorisation) (Scotland) Regulations 1969 and shall come into operation on 10th July, 1969.

(2) In these regulations—

(*a*) " specified events " means the cycle racing events it is proposed to hold on or between 12th and 26th July 1969, particulars of which are specified in the Schedule to these regulations ;

(*b*) " the principal regulations " means the Cycle Racing on Highways (Scotland) Regulations 1960(b), as amended by the Cycle Racing on Highways (Amendment) (Scotland) Regulations 1963(c) ;

(*c*) expressions to which a meaning is assigned by the principal regulations shall continue to have that meaning.

(3) The Interpretation Act 1889(d) shall apply for the interpretation of these regulations as it applies for the interpretation of an Act of Parliament.

2.—(1) The principal regulations shall have effect in their application to any bicycle race comprised in any of the specified events as if in regulation 5(1)(*a*)(i) for the condition that the number of competitors must not exceed forty there were substituted the condition that the number of competitors must not exceed sixty.

(2) The foregoing provisions of this regulation shall have effect in relation to any bicycle race comprised in any of the specified events notwithstanding that after the coming into operation of these regulations the title of that event is changed from that specified in column 1 of the Schedule to these regulations or that some person other than the person specified in column 3 of the said Schedule becomes the promoter of that event.

(3) Save as otherwise provided by the foregoing provisions of these regulations, the principal regulations shall apply to a bicycle race comprised in any of the specified events as they apply to any other bicycle race.

William Ross,
One of Her Majesty's Principal
Secretaries of State.

St. Andrew's House,
Edinburgh.
20th June, 1969.

(a) 1960 c. 16.   (b) S.I. 1960/270 (1960 III, p. 3053).
(c) S.I. 1963/1071 (1963 II, p. 1848).   (d) 1889 c. 63.

SCHEDULE

Cycle Racing Events in Scotland 1969

1. Title of event	2. Proposed time for the holding of the event	3. Name and address of the promoter of the event
1. The Journal Trophy 2-Day Cycle Road Race	12th to 13th July 1969 (inclusive)	C. Stamp, Esq., 50 Mountfield Gardens, Kenton, Newcastle-upon-Tyne.
2. The Scottish Milk for Energy Cycle Race	22nd to 26th July 1969 (inclusive)	A. Campbell, Esq., 7 Beaufort Drive, Kirkintilloch, Dunbartonshire.

EXPLANATORY NOTE

(*This Note is not part of the Regulations.*)

The Cycle Racing on Highways (Scotland) Regulations 1960 authorise certain races or trials of speed between bicycles or tricycles, not being motor vehicles (described in those regulations as bicycle races), to be held on public highways subject to certain conditions including the condition that the number of competitors taking part must not exceed 40. These Regulations provide for varying this condition in the case of the two bicycle races (as defined in the 1960 regulations) specified in the Schedule, by increasing to 60 the maximum number of competitors who may take part in the said events.

1969 No. 851

LANDLORD AND TENANT

The Irish Land (Finance) (Amendment) Rules 1969

Made - - -	*24th June* 1969
Laid before Parliament	*30th June* 1969
Coming into Operation	*1st July* 1969

The Treasury, in exercise of the powers conferred upon them by sections 41, 45 and 46 of the Irish Land Act 1903**(a)** and section 14 of the Irish Land Act 1909**(b)** and of all other powers enabling them in that behalf, hereby make the following Rules:—

1. These Rules may be cited as the Irish Land (Finance) (Amendment) Rules 1969, and shall come into operation on 1st July 1969.

2. The Interpretation Act 1889**(c)** shall apply for the interpretation of these Rules as it applies for the interpretation of an Act of Parliament.

3. The Irish Land (Finance) Rules 1912**(d)**, as amended **(e)**, shall be further amended by substituting for paragraph (2) of Rule 16 thereof the following paragraph:—

"(2) The aggregate of—

(*a*) the total amount accumulated at any date in accordance with the foregoing paragraph, and

(*b*) in the case of an advance repayable by means of a three and a quarter per cent. annuity, a sum equal to fifty-six per cent. of such amount, or, in the case of an advance repayable by means of a three and a half per cent. annuity, a sum equal to seventy per cent. of such amount,

shall be taken to be the amount of the advance repaid up to that date."

4. Rule 1(*a*) of the Irish Land (Finance) (Amendment) Rules 1961**(f)**, and the Irish Land (Finance) (Amendment) Rules 1968**(g)**, are hereby revoked.

Walter Harrison,
Joseph Harper,
Two of the Lords Commissioners
of Her Majesty's Treasury.

24th June 1969.

(a) 1903 c. 37. **(b)** 1909 c. 42.
(c) 1889 c. 63. **(d)** S.R. & O. 1912/69 (1912, p. 405).
(e) See S.R. & O. 1913, p. 349; S.I. 1961/1012, 1968/991 (1961 II, p. 1958; 1968 II, p. 2646).
(f) S.I. 1961/1012 (1961 II, p. 1958). **(g)** S.I. 1968/991 (1968 II, p. 2646).

EXPLANATORY NOTE

(This Note is not part of the Rules.)

These Rules further amend the Irish Land (Finance) Rules 1912 by substituting a new Rule 16(2) which, in sub-paragraph (*b*), specifies a new and higher percentage rate for the purpose of ascertaining the amount repaid in the case of an advance under the Irish Land Acts 1903 and 1909 repayable by means of a $3\frac{1}{2}$ per cent. annuity.

STATUTORY INSTRUMENTS

1969 No. 854

ANTARCTICA

The Antarctic Treaty (Specially Protected Area) Order 1969

Made - - - -	*25th June* 1969
Laid before Parliament	*1st July* 1969
Coming into Operation	*2nd July* 1969

At the Court at Buckingham Palace, the 25th day of June 1969

Present,

The Queen's Most Excellent Majesty in Council

Her Majesty, in exercise of the powers conferred upon Her by section 7(2)(*b*) of the Antarctic Treaty Act 1967(**a**), is pleased, by and with the advice of Her Privy Council, to order, and it is hereby ordered, as follows:—

1. This Order may be cited as the Antarctic Treaty (Specially Protected Area) Order 1969 and shall come into operation on 2nd July 1969.

2. For the purposes of the Antarctic Treaty Act 1967, the following area, being one of the areas listed in Annex B to Schedule 2 to the said Act, is designated as a Specially Protected Area:

SPECIALLY PROTECTED AREA No. 12

FILDES PENINSULA, KING GEORGE ISLAND,
SOUTH SHETLAND ISLANDS

Lat. 62° 11′ S., Long. 58° 52′ W.

This area, the location of which is shown on the map in the Schedule hereto, consists of the fresh-water lake, including the surrounding land within 100 metres of the shore, situated about 500 metres north of Suffield Point and 2·5 kilometres east-north-east of Bellingshausen Station on Fildes Peninsula.

W. G. Agnew.

(**a**) 1967 c. 65.

SCHEDULE

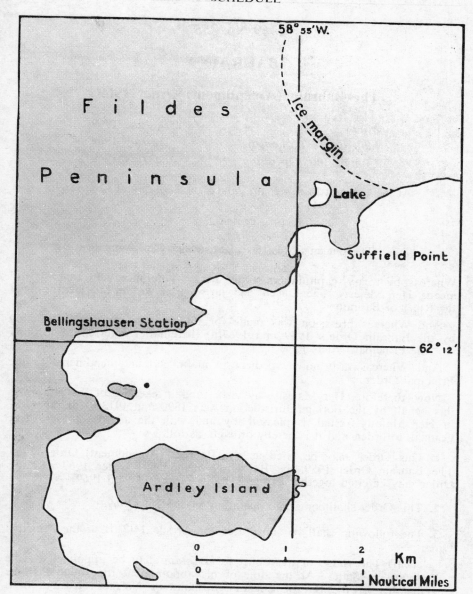

EXPLANATORY NOTE

(This Note is not part of the Order.)

This Order designates as a Specially Protected Area for the purposes of the Antarctic Treaty Act 1967 a further area in the Antarctic which has been recommended for inclusion in Annex B to the Agreed Measures for the Conservation of Antarctic Fauna and Flora (Schedule 2 to the Act) in pursuance of Article IX(1) of the Antarctic Treaty.

STATUTORY INSTRUMENTS

1969 No. 855

BAHRAIN

The Bahrain (Amendment) Order 1969

Made - - - -	25*th June* 1969
Laid before Parliament	1*st July* 1969
Coming into Operation	2*nd July* 1969

At the Court at Buckingham Palace, the 25th day of June 1969

Present,

The Queen's Most Excellent Majesty in Council

Whereas by treaty, capitulation, grant, usage, sufferance, and other lawful means Her Majesty The Queen has jurisdiction within the territories of the Ruler of Bahrain:

And Whereas provision was made for the exercise of such jurisdiction by the Bahrain Orders 1959 and 1967(a) (hereinafter referred to together as " the Principal Order "):

And Whereas it is now expedient to make certain amendments to the Principal Order:

Now, therefore, Her Majesty, by virtue and in exercise of the powers in this behalf by the Foreign Jurisdiction Acts 1890 and 1913(b) or otherwise in Her Majesty vested, is pleased, by and with the advice of Her Privy Council, to order, and it is hereby ordered, as follows:—

1. This Order may be cited as the Bahrain (Amendment) Order 1969. The Bahrain Order 1959, the Bahrain (Amendment) Order 1967 and this Order may be cited together as the Bahrain Orders 1959 to 1969.

2. This Order shall come into operation on 2nd July 1969.

3. The following shall be substituted for Article 14(2)(i) of the Principal Order:—

" (2)(i) The Judge of the Court for Bahrain shall be appointed by the Secretary of State. At the time of his appointment the Judge shall be a member of the Bar of England, Scotland or Northern Ireland, or a solicitor of the Supreme Court in England or Northern Ireland, or a Writer to Her Majesty's Signet or a solicitor in the Supreme Courts of Scotland or shall be a person who has held a judicial office which, in the opinion of the Secretary of State, makes him a fit person to hold office as a Judge of the Court for Bahrain. Persons similarly qualified may be appointed as Assistant Judges from time to time by the Secretary of State. Each Judge or Assistant Judge may exercise all the powers and jurisdiction of the Court."

(a) S.I. 1959/1035, 1967/24 (1959 I, p. 250; 1967 I, p. 53).   (b) 1890 c. 37 ; 1913 c. 16.

4. The following shall be substituted for Article 14(3)(i) of the Principal Order: —

" (3)(i) The Judge of the Chief Court shall be appointed by Her Majesty by Warrant under Her Royal Sign Manual. He shall be a member of the Bar of England, Scotland or Northern Ireland of not less than nine years' standing or a person who has held a judicial office which, in the opinion of the Secretary of State, makes him a fit person to hold office as a Judge of the Chief Court. The Secretary of State may appoint from persons similarly qualified for such periods as he thinks fit such Assistant Judges of the Chief Court as may from time to time be required. Each Judge or Assistant Judge of the Chief Court may exercise all the powers and jurisdiction of the Court."

5. The following shall be substituted for Article 15(4)(ii) of the Principal Order: —

" (ii) The Political Resident may appoint any fit person to act for the Registrar of the Court for Bahrain for such period as he may consider advisable or until the appointment is revoked and the person so appointed may act during a vacancy in the office of Registrar or whenever the Registrar is absent or ill or on any other occasion at the request of the Registrar."

6. The amendments to the Principal Order shall not affect the past operation of the Principal Order or any right, title, obligation or liability accrued or the validity or invalidity of anything done or suffered under the Principal Order before the coming into operation of this Order.

W. G. Agnew.

EXPLANATORY NOTE

(This Note is not part of the Order.)

This Order amends the Bahrain Orders 1959 and 1967 to provide that the Judge and Assistant Judges of the Chief Court for the Persian Gulf and of the Court for Bahrain may be appointed from persons who have held appropriate judicial office and to provide for the appointment of a person to act for the Registrar of the Court for Bahrain in case of need.

STATUTORY INSTRUMENTS

1969 No. 856

QATAR

The Qatar (Amendment) Order 1969

Made - - - -	*25th June* 1969
Laid before Parliament	*1st July* 1969
Coming into Operation	*2nd July* 1969

At the Court at Buckingham Palace, the 25th day of June 1969

Present,

The Queen's Most Excellent Majesty in Council

Whereas by treaty, capitulation, grant, usage, sufferance, and other lawful means Her Majesty The Queen has jurisdiction within the territories of the Ruler of Qatar:

And Whereas provision was made for the exercise of such jurisdiction by the Qatar Orders 1959 to 1963(a) (hereinafter referred to together as "the Principal Order"):

And Whereas it is now expedient to make certain amendments to the Principal Order:

Now, therefore, Her Majesty, by virtue and in exercise of the powers in this behalf by the Foreign Jurisdiction Acts 1890 and 1913(b) or otherwise in Her Majesty vested, is pleased, by and with the advice of Her Privy Council, to order, and it is hereby ordered, as follows:—

1. This Order may be cited as the Qatar (Amendment) Order 1969. The Qatar Order 1959, the Qatar (Amendment) Order 1962, the Qatar (Amendment) Order 1963 and this Order may be cited together as the Qatar Orders 1959 to 1969.

2. This Order shall come into operation on 2nd July 1969.

3. The following shall be substituted for Article 14(2)(i) of the Principal Order:—

"(2)(i) The Judge of the Court for Qatar shall be appointed by the Secretary of State. At the time of his appointment the Judge shall be a member of the Bar of England, Scotland or Northern Ireland, or a solicitor of the Supreme Court in England or Northern Ireland, or a Writer to Her Majesty's Signet or a solicitor in the Supreme Courts of Scotland or shall be a person who has held a judicial office which, in the opinion of the Secretary of State, makes him a fit person to hold office as a Judge of the Court for Qatar. Persons similarly qualified may be appointed as Assistant Judges from time to time by the Secretary of State. Each Judge or Assistant Judge may exercise all the powers and jurisdiction of the Court."

(a) S.I. 1959/1038, 1962/406, 1963/2093 (1959 II, p. 2252; 1962 I, p. 470; 1963 III, p. 4614).
(b) 1890 c. 37; 1913 c. 16.

4. The following shall be substituted for Article 14(3)(i) of the Principal Order:—

"(3)(i) The Judge of the Chief Court shall be appointed by Her Majesty under Her Royal Sign Manual. He shall be a member of the Bar of England, Scotland or Northern Ireland of not less than nine years' standing or a person who has held a judicial office which, in the opinion of the Secretary of State, makes him a fit person to hold office as a Judge of the Chief Court. The Secretary of State may appoint from persons similarly qualified for such periods as he thinks fit such Assistant Judges of the Chief Court as may from time to time be required. Each Judge or Assistant Judge of the Chief Court may exercise all the powers and jurisdiction of the Court."

5. The following shall be substituted for Article 15(4)(ii) of the Principal Order:—

"(ii) The Political Resident may appoint any fit person to act for the Registrar of the Court for Qatar for such period as he may consider advisable or until the appointment is revoked and the person so appointed may act during a vacancy in the office of Registrar or whenever the Registrar is absent or ill or on any other occasion at the request of the Registrar."

6. The amendments to the Principal Order shall not affect the past operation of the Principal Order or any right, title, obligation or liability accrued or the validity or invalidity of anything done or suffered under the Principal Order before the coming into operation of this Order.

W. G. Agnew.

EXPLANATORY NOTE

(This Note is not part of the Order.)

This Order amends the Qatar Orders 1959 to 1963 to provide that the Judge and Assistant Judges of the Chief Court for the Persian Gulf and of the Court for Qatar may be appointed from persons who have held appropriate judicial office and to provide for the appointment of a person to act for the Registrar of the Court for Qatar in case of need.

1969 No. 857

SOUTH ATLANTIC TERRITORIES

The St. Helena Supreme Court Order 1969

Made - - - -	25th June 1969
Laid before Parliament	1st July 1969
Coming into Operation	On a day to be appointed under section 1(2)

At the Court at Buckingham Palace, the 25th day of June 1969

Present,

The Queen's Most Excellent Majesty in Council

Her Majesty, by virtue and in exercise of the powers in that behalf conferred by section 112 of the Government of India Act 1833(a), the British Settlements Acts 1887 and 1945(b) or otherwise in Her Majesty vested, is pleased, by and with the advice of Her Privy Council, to order, and it is hereby ordered, as follows :—

PART I: PRELIMINARY

Citation and commence- ment.

1.—(1) This Order may be cited as the St. Helena Supreme Court Order 1969.

(2) This Order shall come into operation on such day as the Governor may by proclamation published in the St. Helena Government Gazette appoint.

Inter- pretation.

2.—(1) In this Order, unless the context otherwise requires :—

" Chief Justice " means the Chief Justice of St. Helena and includes any person appointed to act as Chief Justice ;

" existing Court " means the Court established by the existing Order ;

" existing Order " means the Order in Council providing for the administration of justice in St. Helena made on the 13th February 1839(c) ;

" Supreme Court " means the Supreme Court of St. Helena established by this Order.

(2) Sections 47, 48 and 49(1) of the Constitution set out in Schedule 1 to the St. Helena (Constitution) Order 1966(d) and, subject thereto and to the necessary adaptations, the Interpretation Act 1889(e) shall apply for the purpose of interpreting this Order and otherwise in relation thereto, as they apply for the purpose of interpreting and in relation to the said Constitution ; and for the purposes of the said sections 47 and 48 a person appointed under subsection (2) of section 7 of this Order to hold the Supreme Court shall be deemed to be appointed to an office.

(a) 1833 c. 85.   (b) 1887 c. 54; 9 & 10 Geo. 6 c. 7.
(c) Rev. XX, p. 559.   (d) S.I. 1966/1458 (1966 III, p. 3937).   (e) 1889 c. 63.

3.—(1) The Orders in Council specified in the Schedule to this Order are revoked with effect from the commencement of this Order.

Revocation of existing Order and certain other Orders, and transitional.

(2) The existing laws shall have effect in respect of any time, or any period commencing, after the commencement of this Order as if references to the existing Court or to any judge thereof were references to the Supreme Court or the Chief Justice as the case may be.

(3) Notwithstanding the provisions of subsection (1) of this section—

(a) any cause or matter pending before the existing Court immediately prior to the commencement of this Order may be continued thereafter before the Supreme Court as if such cause or matter had been instituted in the Supreme Court ;

(b) any decree or order of the existing Court given or made before the commencement of this Order may, in so far as it has not been fully executed or enforced, be executed or enforced as if it were a decree or order of the Supreme Court ; and

(c) any appeal from the existing Court pending immediately before the commencement of this Order may be continued and determined thereafter as if it were an appeal from the Supreme Court.

(4) Where any office has been established by or under the existing Order and any provision of this Order establishes a similar or an equivalent office, any person who immediately before the commencement of this Order held or was acting in the former office shall be deemed to have been appointed, as from the commencement of this Order, to hold or act in the latter office in accordance with the provisions of this Order and to have taken any necessary oath :

Provided that any person who under and by virtue of the provisions of the existing Order would have been required to vacate his office at the expiration of any period shall vacate his office at the end of that period.

(5) For the purposes of this section, the expression " existing laws " means all Orders in Council made by virtue and in exercise of the powers, or any of them, by virtue and in exercise of which this Order is made, all Ordinances, and all rules, regulations, orders and other instruments made under such Orders in Council or Ordinances, which have been made for, or have effect as part of the law of, St. Helena or its Dependencies immediately before the commencement of this Order.

Part II: The Court

4.—(1) There shall be a Supreme Court in and for St. Helena and its Dependencies which shall be styled the Supreme Court of St. Helena and shall be a superior court of record.

Establishment of Supreme Court.

(2) The Supreme Court shall have such jurisdiction in and in relation to St. Helena and its Dependencies as is conferred by this Order and as may be conferred by or under any law for the time being in force in St. Helena or any of its Dependencies.

(3) Subject to the provisions of this Order and to any law for the time being in force in St. Helena or any of its Dependencies, the Supreme Court shall possess and may exercise all the jurisdiction which is vested in, or is capable of being exercised by, Her Majesty's High Court of Justice in England.

Exercise of jurisdiction of High Court.

5.—(1) It shall be lawful for the Supreme Court to be held by and before—

(*a*) the Chief Justice ;

(*b*) a person empowered by, or appointed under, section 7 to hold the Court ; or

(*c*) for the purposes mentioned in subsection (2) of this section, a person empowered by that subsection to continue to sit and hold the Court.

(2) Any person appointed to act as Chief Justice under subsection (3) of section 6 or empowered by or appointed under section 7 to hold the Court may, notwithstanding that his appointment has expired or been revoked or, as the case may be, that the circumstances in which he is empowered to hold the Court cease to obtain, continue to sit and hold the Court for the purposes of giving judgment or otherwise in relation to any proceeding commenced before him while his appointment was subsisting or, as the case may be, such circumstances obtained.

(3) Subject, in the case of a person appointed under subsection (2) of section 7, to any restriction contained in the instrument of appointment, a person by and before whom the Supreme Court may be held shall, in the exercise of the jurisdiction of the Supreme Court, have all the powers and authority of the Court and, save as provided in subsection (5) of this section, the jurisdiction, powers, authority, privileges and immunities conferred on the Chief Justice.

(4) Where, at any time, there are two or more persons by and before whom the Supreme Court may be held, sittings of the Court may be held simultaneously by each person.

(5) A person appointed under subsection (2) of section 7 shall not exercise

(*a*) any power to make rules of court ;

(*b*) any other power which, by any other law in force in St. Helena or its Dependencies, he is specifically excluded from exercising.

Appointment of Chief Justice and acting Chief Justice.

6.—(1) The Governor shall, on instructions given by Her Majesty through a Secretary of State, appoint a judge of the Supreme Court who shall be styled the Chief Justice of St. Helena.

(2) An appointment under subsection (1) of this section shall be made by letters patent under the public seal and a person so appointed shall hold office on such terms and conditions as the Governor shall, in accordance with such instructions aforesaid, prescribe.

(3) If—

(*a*) there is no subsisting appointment under subsection (1) of this section ; or

(*b*) the Chief Justice has not assumed, or is, for any reason, unable to perform the functions of, his office ; or

(*c*) the Chief Justice is absent from St. Helena and its Dependencies (and is not in passage between one part and another),

the Governor may appoint a fit and proper person to act as Chief Justice.

(4) An appointment under subsection (3) of this section—

(*a*) shall expire—

    (i) on the assumption, or the resumption, of the functions of his office by the Chief Justice, or on the return of the Chief Justice to St. Helena and its Dependencies, as the case may be ;

    (ii) at the end of the period, if any, for which it was made,

whichever first occurs ; and

(*b*) if not made for any specific period, may be revoked by the Governor.

7.—(1) If—

Persons empowered to hold Supreme Court.

(*a*) at a time when an appointment may be made under subsection (3) of section 6 of a person to act as Chief Justice, there is no subsisting appointment under that subsection, the Governor may himself hold the Supreme Court ;

(*b*) the Chief Justice or, if there is a subsisting appointment under subsection (3) of section 6, the person appointed to act as Chief Justice, is absent from St. Helena, the Governor may himself hold the Supreme Court in St. Helena.

(2) If, at any time, the Governor considers that the state or distribution of business of the Supreme Court makes it desirable that an additional person be appointed by and before whom the Supreme Court may be held, he may appoint a fit and proper person to hold the Court, either generally or for any special purpose.

(3) An appointment under subsection (2) of this section shall expire at the end of the period, if any, for which it was made and, if not made for any specific period, may be revoked by the Governor.

8. There shall be—

Registry and local registries.

(*a*) a registry of the Supreme Court in St. Helena ; and

(*b*) such local registries, subordinate to such Registry, in such of the Dependencies as may be necessary for the administration of justice and as may be established by the Governor.

9.—(1) There shall be—

Officers of the Court.

(*a*) A Registrar and Clerk of the Peace (hereinafter referred to as " the Registrar ") ; and

(*b*) such deputy registrars and other officers of the Supreme Court as shall be necessary for the administration of justice and for the due execution of the powers and authorities granted or committed to the Supreme Court,

and the Registrar and such deputy registrars and other officers shall perform such functions and discharge such duties as may be prescribed by law or as may be directed by the Chief Justice or, subject to any directions of the Chief Justice, by any other person by and before whom the Court may be held.

(2) Subsections (2) and (3) of section 46 of the Constitution set out in Schedule 1 to the St. Helena (Constitution) Order 1966 shall apply to the offices to which and the officers to whom this section refers :

Provided that, at any time when there is a subsisting appointment under subsection (1) or (3) of section 6 of this Order, the Governor shall, before exercising any of his powers under subsection (2) of the said section 46, consult the Chief Justice.

Powers and privileges of Supreme Court and Officers.

10. The Supreme Court and a person by and before whom the Court is held shall have in all respects the same powers in respect of contempt of Court, and any such person aforesaid and all officers of the Supreme Court shall have and enjoy the same immunities from legal proceedings as, by the law of England, are for the time being had and enjoyed by the Supreme Court of Judicature in England or the Judges and corresponding officers thereof.

Seal of Supreme Court.

11. The Supreme Court shall have, and as occasion arises use, a seal bearing a device and impression of the Royal Arms within a border bearing the words " Seal of the Supreme Court of St. Helena " which seal shall be kept in the custody of the Registrar.

W. G. Agnew.

SCHEDULE

Section 3.

The Order in Council for establishing the due administration of justice in St. Helena made on the 13th day of February 1839.

The Order in Council empowering the Governor of St. Helena to act in certain cases in place of the Chief Justice made on the 5th day of April 1852(**a**).

The Order in Council relating to trials in St. Helena with the aid of assessors made on the 29th day of June 1878(**b**).

The Order in Council relating to trials in St. Helena with the aid of assessors made on the 10th day of January 1910(**c**).

The Order in Council making further provision for the administration of justice in St. Helena made on the 3rd day of October 1935(**d**).

EXPLANATORY NOTE

(This Note is not part of the Order.)

This Order reconstitutes the Supreme Court of St. Helena and its Dependencies.

(**a**) Rev. XX, p. 570.   (**b**) Rev. XX, p. 571.
(**c**) Rev. XX, p. 572.   (**d**) Rev. XX, p. 568.

STATUTORY   INSTRUMENTS

1969 No. 858

OVERSEAS TERRITORIES

The Admiralty Jurisdiction (St. Helena and its Dependencies) Order 1969

Made - - - -	*25th June* 1969
Coming into Operation	*On the day appointed for the commencement of the St. Helena Supreme Court Order* 1969

At the Court at Buckingham Palace, the 25th day of June 1969

Present,

The Queen's Most Excellent Majesty in Council

Her Majesty, by virtue and in exercise of the power vested in Her by section 56 of the Administration of Justice Act 1956(a) and of all other powers enabling Her in that behalf, is pleased, by and with the advice of Her Privy Council to order, and it is hereby ordered, as follows: —

1.—(1) This Order may be cited as the Admiralty Jurisdiction (St. Helena and its Dependencies) Order 1969.

(2) This Order shall come into operation on the date appointed by the Governor of St. Helena and its Dependencies for the commencement of the St. Helena Supreme Court Order 1969(b).

Citation and commencement.

2. The Colonial Courts of Admiralty Act 1890(c) shall, in relation to the Supreme Court of St. Helena, have effect as if for the reference in subsection (2) of section 2 thereof to the Admiralty jurisdiction of the High Court in England there were substituted a reference to the Admiralty jurisdiction of that court as defined by section 1 of the Administration of Justice Act 1956 subject to the adaptations and modifications of the said section 1 that are specified in the First Schedule to this Order.

Admiralty jurisdiction of Supreme Court of St. Helena.

3. The provisions of sections 3, 4, 6, 7 and 8 of Part I of the Administration of Justice Act 1956 shall extend to St. Helena and its Dependencies with the adaptations and modifications that are specified in the Second Schedule to this Order.

Application of provisions of Administration of Justice Act 1956.

4. The Admiralty Jurisdiction (St. Helena) Order 1964(d) is hereby revoked.

Revocation of existing Order.

W. G. Agnew.

(a) 1956 c. 46.   (b) S.I. 1969/857(1969 II, p. 2394).
(c) 1890 c. 27.   (d) S.I. 1964/1664 (1964 III, p. 3775).

Article 2.

FIRST SCHEDULE

ADAPTATIONS AND MODIFICATIONS OF SECTION 1 OF THE ADMINISTRATION OF JUSTICE ACT 1956

In subsection (1) the words " and any other jurisdiction connected with ships or aircraft vested in the High Court apart from this section which is for the time being assigned by rules of court to the Probate, Divorce and Admiralty Division " shall be deleted ;

In subsection (3) the words and figures " under sections five hundred and forty-four to five hundred and forty-six of the Merchant Shipping Act 1894(a) " shall be deleted and the words " under sections twenty-one and twenty-two of the Wrecks Ordinance of St. Helena(b) " shall be substituted ;

In subsection (4) after the words and figures " Merchant Shipping Acts 1894 to 1954 " there shall be inserted the words " or of the Wrecks Ordinance of St. Helena ".

Article 3.

SECOND SCHEDULE

PROVISIONS OF PART I OF THE ADMINISTRATION OF JUSTICE ACT 1956 EXTENDED TO ST. HELENA AND ITS DEPENDENCIES AND ADAPTATIONS AND MODIFICATIONS THERETO.

SECTION 3

In subsections (1), (3), (5), (6) and (7), the words " the High Court, the Liverpool Court of Passage, and any county court " shall be deleted and the words " the Supreme Court of St. Helena " shall be substituted ;

In subsection (2) the words " the High Court " shall be deleted and the words " the Supreme Court of St. Helena " shall be substituted ;

In subsection (4) the words " High Court and (where there is such jurisdiction) the Admiralty jurisdiction of the Liverpool Court of Passage or any county court " shall be deleted and the words " Supreme Court of St. Helena " shall be substituted ;

In subsection (8) the words " England and Wales " shall be deleted and the words " St. Helena and its Dependencies " shall be substituted.

SECTION 4

Subsection (1) shall be deleted and the following subsection shall be substituted : —

" (1) No court in St. Helena or its Dependencies shall entertain an action in personam to enforce a claim to which this section applies unless—

(a) the defendant has his habitual residence or a place of business in St. Helena or its Dependencies ; or

(b) the cause of action arose within the territorial waters of St. Helena or its Dependencies ; or

(c) an action arising out of the same incident or series of incidents is proceeding in the court or has been heard and determined in the court.

In this subsection " territorial waters of St. Helena or its Dependencies " includes any port, dock or harbour in St. Helena or its Dependencies ".

In subsection (2) the words " in England and Wales " shall be deleted and the words " in St. Helena and its Dependencies " shall be substituted, and the words " outside England and Wales " shall be deleted and the words " outside St. Helena and its Dependencies " shall be substituted.

In subsection (5) the words " the High Court " shall be deleted and the words " the Supreme Court of St. Helena " shall be substituted.

Subsection (6) shall be omitted.

(a) 1894 c. 60.   (b) Laws of St. Helena, Rev. 1950, Cap. 134.

SECTION 6

The words "England and Wales" shall be deleted and the words "St. Helena and its Dependencies" shall be substituted.

SECTION 7

Subsection (1) shall be deleted and the following subsection shall be substituted:—

"(1) Section six hundred and eighty-eight of the Merchant Shipping Act 1894 (which relates to the detention of ships by customs officers in certain cases) shall cease to have effect, but nothing in this Part of the Act affects the provisions of section twenty-eight of the Wrecks Ordinance of St. Helena (which relates to the power of a receiver of wrecks to detain a ship in respect of a salvage claim).";

Subsection (2) shall be omitted.

EXPLANATORY NOTE

(This Note is not part of the Order.)

This Order provides that the Supreme Court of St. Helena, which is a Colonial Court of Admiralty, shall have the Admiralty jurisdiction of the High Court of England, as defined in section 1 of the Administration of Justice Act 1956, with certain modifications. It also extends certain of the provisions contained in Part I of that Act to St. Helena and its Dependencies.

STATUTORY INSTRUMENTS

1969 No. 859

TRUCIAL STATES

The Trucial States (Amendment) Order 1969

Made - - - -	*25th June* 1969
Laid before Parliament	*1st July* 1969
Coming into Operation	*2nd July* 1969

At the Court at Buckingham Palace, the 25th day of June 1969

Present,

The Queen's Most Excellent Majesty in Council

Whereas by treaty, capitulation, grant, usage, sufferance, and other lawful means Her Majesty The Queen has jurisdiction within the territories of the Rulers of Dubai, Sharjah, Ras-al-Khaimah, Ajman, Umm al Qaiwain, Abu Dhabi and Fujairah:

And Whereas provision was made for the exercise of such jurisdiction by the Trucial States Orders 1959 and 1963(a) (hereinafter referred to together as "the Principal Order"):

And Whereas it is now expedient to make certain amendments to the Principal Order:

Now, therefore, Her Majesty, by virtue and in exercise of the powers in this behalf by the Foreign Jurisdiction Acts 1890 and 1913(b) or otherwise in Her Majesty vested, is pleased, by and with the advice of Her Privy Council, to order, and it is hereby ordered, as follows:—

1. This Order may be cited as the Trucial States (Amendment) Order 1969. The Trucial States Order 1959, the Trucial States (Amendment) Order 1963 and this Order may be cited together as the Trucial States Orders 1959 to 1969.

2. This Order shall come into operation on 2nd July 1969.

3. In Article 4 of the Principal Order, for the meaning assigned to the expression "Political Agent" there shall be substituted the following:—

"'Political Agent' means Her Majesty's Political Agent in the Trucial States resident at Dubai or Her Majesty's Political Agent in the Trucial States resident at Abu Dhabi."

4. The following shall be substituted for Article 14(2)(i) of the Principal Order:

"(2)(i) The Judge of the Court for the Trucial States shall be appointed by the Secretary of State. At the time of his appointment the Judge shall be a member of the Bar of England, Scotland or Northern Ireland, or a solicitor of the Supreme Court in England or Northern Ireland, or a Writer to Her Majesty's Signet or a solicitor in the Supreme Courts of Scotland or shall be a person who has held a judicial office which, in the opinion of the Secretary of State, makes him a fit person to hold

---

(a) S.I. 1959/1039, 1963/2095 (1959 II, p. 2676; 1963 III, p. 4666).
(b) 1890 c. 37; 1913 c. 16.

office as a Judge of the Court for the Trucial States. Persons similarly qualified may be appointed as Assistant Judges from time to time by the Secretary of State. Each Judge or Assistant Judge may exercise all the powers and jurisdiction of the Court."

5. The following shall be substituted for Article 14(3)(i) of the Principal Order:—

" (3)(i) The Judge of the Chief Court shall be appointed by Her Majesty by Warrant under Her Royal Sign Manual. He shall be a member of the Bar of England, Scotland or Northern Ireland of not less than nine years' standing or a person who has held a judicial office which, in the opinion of the Secretary of State, makes him a fit person to hold office as a Judge of the Chief Court. The Secretary of State may appoint from persons similarly qualified for such periods as he thinks fit such Assistant Judges of the Chief Court as may from time to time be required. Each Judge or Assistant Judge of the Chief Court may exercise all the powers and jurisdiction of the Court."

6. The following shall be substituted for Article 15(4) of the Principal Order:—

" (4)(i) The Registrar of the Court for the Trucial States shall be appointed by the Secretary of State and the other officers shall be appointed by the Political Agent with the approval of the Political Resident.

(ii) The Political Resident may appoint any fit person to act for the Registrar of the Court for the Trucial States for such period as he may consider advisable or until the appointment is revoked and the person so appointed may act during a vacancy in the office of Registrar or whenever the Registrar is absent or ill or on any other occasion at the request of the Registrar."

7. The following paragraph shall be added to Article 17 of the Principal Order:—

" (3) In case of the absence or illness of the Judge of the Court for the Trucial States the Registrar of the Court for the Trucial States shall have all the power and authority of an Assistant Judge of the Court; provided that such power and authority shall not extend to the hearing of criminal cases committed for trial, or to civil matters other than those which may be assigned to a Registrar under the preceding paragraph of this Article, or to the hearing of appeals."

8. The following paragraph shall be added to Article 25 of the Principal Order:—

" (6) Where a person who is a member of a levy force referred to in Article 8(1)(ii) is accused of an offence alleged to have been committed when he was outside the Trucial States in the course of his service with that levy force, such person may be tried and punished under this Order as if the offence had been committed within the Trucial States. In this paragraph an offence means any act or omission which would be an offence if done within the Trucial States."

9. The amendments to the Principal Order shall not affect the past operation of the Principal Order or any right, title, obligation or liability accrued or the validity or invalidity of anything done or suffered under the Principal Order before the coming into operation of this Order.

W. G. Agnew.

EXPLANATORY NOTE

(This Note is not part of the Order.)

This Order amends the Trucial States Orders 1959 and 1963:

(i) to change the definition of " Political Agent ";

(ii) to provide that the Judge and Assistant Judges of the Chief Court may be appointed from persons who have held appropriate judicial office and that the Judge of the Court for the Trucial States should be a person having legal qualifications rather than, as hitherto, the Political Agent *ex officio*;

(iii) to provide for persons to act in case of need for the Judge or Registrar of the Court for the Trucial States;

(iv) to make express provision for the exercise of jurisdiction within the Trucial States over offences committed by members of a levy force (such as the Trucial Oman Scouts) when outside the Trucial States in the course of their service.

1969 No. 860

UNITED NATIONS

The Southern Rhodesia (United Nations Sanctions) (Channel Islands) Order 1969

Made - - - -	*25th June* 1969
Laid before Parliament	*1st July* 1969
Coming into Operation	*2nd July* 1969

At the Court at Buckingham Palace, the 25th day of June 1969

Present,

The Queen's Most Excellent Majesty in Council

Whereas under Article 41 of the Charter of the United Nations the Security Council of the United Nations has, by a resolution passed on 29th May 1968, called upon Her Majesty's Government in the United Kingdom and other Members of the United Nations to take certain measures in relation to Southern Rhodesia including measures relating to trade and dealing in, and the carriage of, goods, the operation of airlines and aircraft, entry into their territories of persons connected with Southern Rhodesia and the promotion of emigration to Southern Rhodesia:

And whereas the said resolution reaffirmed, to the extent that it did not supersede, the resolution passed on 16th December 1966 by which the Security Council of the United Nations so called upon Her Majesty's Government in the United Kingdom and other Members of the United Nations to take certain measures in relation to Southern Rhodesia, including measures relating to undertakings in Southern Rhodesia for the manufacture or assembly of aircraft and motor vehicles:

Now, therefore, Her Majesty, in exercise of the powers conferred on Her by section 1 of the United Nations Act 1946(a), is pleased, by and with the advice of Her Privy Council, to order, and it is hereby ordered, as follows:—

Citation, commencement and extent

1.—(1) This Order may be cited as the Southern Rhodesia (United Nations Sanctions) (Channel Islands) Order 1969 and shall come into operation on 2nd July 1969.

(2) This Order shall extend to the Channel Islands so as to be law, respectively, in the Bailiwick of Guernsey and in the Bailiwick of Jersey only.

(a) 1946 c. 45.

Interpretation

2.—(1) In this Order the following expressions have the meanings hereby respectively assigned to them, that is to say:—

"the Bailiff" means, in the application of this Order to the Bailiwick of Guernsey, the Bailiff of Guernsey and, in its application to the Bailiwick of Jersey, the Bailiff of Jersey and, in either case, includes a person lawfully performing the functions of the Bailiff;

"commander", in relation to an aircraft, means the person designated as commander of the aircraft by the operator thereof, and includes any person who is for the time being in charge or command of the aircraft;

"land transport vehicle" includes a barge;

"master", in relation to a ship, includes any person (other than a pilot) for the time being in charge of the ship;

"operator", in relation to an aircraft or to a land transport vehicle, means the person for the time being having the management of the aircraft or the vehicle;

"owner", in relation to a ship, includes any person for the time being having the management of the ship and any person to whom it is chartered; and

"person in Southern Rhodesia" includes any body constituted or incorporated under the law of Southern Rhodesia and any body carrying on business (whether within Southern Rhodesia or not) which is controlled by persons or bodies resident in Southern Rhodesia or constituted or incorporated as aforesaid.

(2) Any provision of this Order which relates to goods exported from Southern Rhodesia (or to the exportation of goods from Southern Rhodesia) shall not have effect in respect of goods exported (or the exportation of goods) which have only passed through Southern Rhodesia in transit and have not been the subject of any transaction there other than a transaction relating solely to their transportation; and any provision of this Order which relates to the exportation of goods to Southern Rhodesia, the supply or delivery of goods to or to the order of any person in Southern Rhodesia or the importation of goods into Southern Rhodesia shall not have effect in relation to goods which are intended only to pass through Southern Rhodesia in transit and not to be the subject of any transaction there other than a transaction relating solely to their transportation.

(3) For the purposes of this Order, the entry into Southern Rhodesia of a vehicle shall not be regarded as constituting the supply or delivery of that vehicle to or to the order of any person in Southern Rhodesia or as constituting its importation into Southern Rhodesia if the entry is merely for the purpose of the vehicle transporting persons into, out of or across Southern Rhodesia or transporting goods across Southern Rhodesia and is not part of or associated with a transaction involving a transfer of the ownership of the vehicle or of any interest therein.

(4) This Order applies to or in relation to any ship or aircraft or any body corporate that purports to be registered in any particular place or, as the case may be, that purports to be incorporated or constituted under the law of that place as it applies to or in relation to any ship or aircraft that is so registered or any body corporate that is so incorporated or constituted.

(5) For the purposes of this Order a reference to a country or territory specified in this paragraph is a reference to a country or territory hereinafter mentioned, that is to say to—

(a) the United Kingdom;

(b) any of the Channel Islands;

(c) the Isle of Man;

(d) an associated state within the meaning of the West Indies Act 1967(a);

(e) a colony or protectorate within the meaning of the British Nationality Act 1948(b); or

(f) any foreign country in which for the time being Her Majesty has jurisdiction;

and a reference to a British ship or aircraft registered as mentioned in this paragraph is a reference to such a ship or aircraft registered in any of the said countries and territories.

(6) Any provision of this Order which prohibits the doing of a thing except under the authority of a licence shall not have effect in relation to the doing of that thing outside the Bailiwick of Guernsey or, as the case may be, the Bailiwick of Jersey under the authority of a licence granted—

(a) under this Order, otherwise than in its application to the Bailiwick in question, where the thing is done elsewhere in the Channel Islands;

(b) under the corresponding law of a country or territory specified in paragraph (5) (c), (d), (e) or (f) of this Article, where the thing is done in that country or territory, or

(c) under the corresponding law of the United Kingdom, wherever the thing is done;

and, for the purposes of this paragraph, any reference to the corresponding law of a country or territory is a reference to any provision of law, for the time being in force therein, which substantially corresponds to the relevant provision of this Order.

(7) The Interpretation Act 1889(c) shall apply, with the necessary adaptations, for the purpose of interpreting this Order and otherwise in relation thereto as it applies for the purpose of interpreting and in relation to Acts of Parliament.

Revocation and transitional provisions

3.—(1) The Southern Rhodesia (Prohibited Trade and Dealings) (Channel Islands) Order 1967(d) (hereinafter referred to as "the existing Order") is hereby revoked.

(2) Without prejudice to the provisions of section 38 of the Interpretation Act 1889 as applied by Article 2 of this Order, references to this Order, or to a particular provision thereof, in Articles 10 and 16 (together with Schedule 2) of this Order shall be construed as including references to the existing Order or, as the case may require, to the corresponding provision of the existing Order.

(a) 1967 c. 4.   (b) 1948 c. 56.
(c) 1889 c. 63.   (d) S.I. 1967/19 (1967 I, p. 25).

(3) The references in Articles 5(3) and 8 of this Order to goods that have been exported from Southern Rhodesia in contravention of Article 5(1) of this Order shall be deemed to include references to goods which have been exported from Southern Rhodesia in contravention of Article 2(1) of the existing Order.

Importation of certain goods into the Channel Islands

4.—(1) All goods that are exported from Southern Rhodesia after the commencement of this Order are prohibited to be imported into any of the Channel Islands except under the authority of a licence granted by the Board of Administration of the States of Guernsey or, as the case may be, by the Finance Committee of the States of Jersey.

(2) Nothing in this Article shall be construed so as to prejudice any other provision of law prohibiting or restricting the importation of goods into any of the Channel Islands.

Exportation of goods from Southern Rhodesia

5.—(1) No person shall export any goods from Southern Rhodesia except under the authority of a licence granted by the Board of Administration of the States of Guernsey or, as the case may be, by the Finance Committee of the States of Jersey.

(2) Except under such authority as aforesaid, no person shall—

(*a*) make or carry out any contract for the exportation of any goods from Southern Rhodesia after the commencement of this Order; or

(*b*) make or carry out any contract for the sale of any goods which he intends or has reason to believe that another person intends to export from Southern Rhodesia after the commencement of this Order; or

(*c*) do any act calculated to promote the exportation of any goods from Southern Rhodesia.

(3) Except under such authority as aforesaid, no person shall deal in any goods that have been exported from Southern Rhodesia in contravention of paragraph (1) of this Article, that is to say, shall, by way of trade or otherwise for gain, acquire or dispose of such goods or of any property or interest in them or any right to or charge upon them or process them or do any act calculated to promote any such acquisition, disposal or processing by himself or any other person.

(4) Any person who contravenes the foregoing provisions of this Article shall be guilty of an offence against this Order and, in the case of a person who—

(*a*) is a citizen of the United Kingdom and Colonies or a British subject without citizenship or a British protected person and is ordinarily resident in the Bailiwick of Guernsey or, as the case may be, the Bailiwick of Jersey; or

(*b*) is a body incorporated or constituted under the law of the Bailiwick of Guernsey or, as the case may be, the Bailiwick of Jersey,

shall, in the Bailiwick in question, be guilty of such an offence wherever the contravention takes place.

(5) Nothing in this Article shall be construed so as to prejudice any other provision of law prohibiting or restricting the exportation of goods from Southern Rhodesia or acts incidental or related thereto.

Exportation of certain goods from the Channel Islands

6.—(1) All goods are prohibited to be exported from any of the Channel Islands to Southern Rhodesia except under the authority of a licence granted by the Board of Administration of the States of Guernsey or, as the case may be, by the Finance Committee of the States of Jersey.

(2) Nothing in this Article shall be construed so as to prejudice any other provision of law prohibiting or restricting the exportation of goods from any of the Channel Islands.

Supply of goods to Southern Rhodesia

7.—(1) No person shall—

(*a*) supply or deliver or agree to supply or deliver to or to the order of any person in Southern Rhodesia any goods that are not in that country;

(*b*) supply or deliver or agree to supply or deliver any such goods to any person, knowing or having reasonable cause to believe that they will be supplied or delivered to or to the order of a person in Southern Rhodesia or that they will be used for the purposes of any business carried on in or operated from Southern Rhodesia; or

(*c*) do any act calculated to promote the supply or delivery of any goods in contravention of the foregoing provisions of this paragraph,

except under the authority of a licence granted by the Board of Administration of the States of Guernsey or, as the case may be, by the Finance Committee of the States of Jersey.

(2) Any person who contravenes the foregoing provisions of this Article shall be guilty of an offence against this Order and, in the case of a person who—

(*a*) is a citizen of the United Kingdom and Colonies or a British subject without citizenship or a British protected person and is ordinarily resident in the Bailiwick of Guernsey or, as the case may be, the Bailiwick of Jersey; or

(*b*) is a body incorporated or constituted under the law of the Bailiwick of Guernsey or, as the case may be, the Bailiwick of Jersey,

shall, in the Bailiwick in question, be guilty of such an offence wherever the contravention takes place.

Carriage of certain goods exported from or destined for Southern Rhodesia

8.—(1) Without prejudice to the generality of Article 5 of this Order, no ship or aircraft to which this Article applies and no land transport vehicle within any of the Channel Islands shall be used for the carriage of any goods if those goods are being or have been exported from Southern Rhodesia in contravention of Article 5(1) of this Order.

(2) Without prejudice to the generality of Articles 6 and 7 of this Order, no ship or aircraft to which this Article applies and no land transport vehicle within any of the Channel Islands shall be used for the carriage of any goods if the carriage is, or forms part of, carriage from any place outside Southern Rhodesia to any destination therein or to any person for the purposes of any business carried on in or operated from Southern Rhodesia.

(3) This Article applies to British ships and aircraft registered as mentioned in Article 2(5) of this Order and to any other ship or aircraft that is for the time being chartered to any person who is—

(a) a citizen of the United Kingdom and Colonies or a British subject without citizenship or a British protected person and is ordinarily resident in the Bailiwick of Guernsey or, as the case may be, the Bailiwick of Jersey; or

(b) a body incorporated or constituted under the law of the Bailiwick of Guernsey or, as the case may be, the Bailiwick of Jersey.

(4) If any ship, aircraft or land transport vehicle is used in contravention of paragraph (1) of this Article, then—

(a) in the case of a British ship or aircraft registered as mentioned in Article 2(5) of this Order, the owner and the master of the ship or, as the case may be, the operator and the commander of the aircraft; or

(b) in the case of any other ship or aircraft, the person to whom the ship or aircraft is for the time being chartered and, if he is such a person as is referred to in sub-paragraph (a) or sub-paragraph (b) of paragraph (3) of this Article, the manager or the master of the ship or, as the case may be, the operator or the commander of the aircraft; or

(c) in the case of a land transport vehicle, the operator of the vehicle,

shall be guilty of an offence against this Order unless he proves that he did not know and had no reason to suppose that the goods were being or had been exported from Southern Rhodesia in contravention of Article 5(1) of this Order.

(5) If any ship, aircraft or land transport vehicle is used in contravention of paragraph (2) of this Article, then—

(a) in the case of a British ship or aircraft registered as mentioned in Article 2(5) of this Order, the owner and the master of the ship or, as the case may be, the operator and the commander of the aircraft; or

(b) in the case of any other ship or aircraft, the person to whom the ship or aircraft is for the time being chartered and, if he is such a person as is referred to in sub-paragraph (a) or sub-paragraph (b) of paragraph (3) of this Article, the manager or the master of the ship or, as the case may be, the operator or the commander of the aircraft; or

(c) in the case of a land transport vehicle, the operator of the vehicle,

shall be guilty of an offence against this Order unless he proves that he did not know and had no reason to suppose that the carriage of the goods in question was, or formed part of, carriage from any place outside Southern Rhodesia to any destination therein or to any person for the purposes of any business carried on in or operated from Southern Rhodesia.

(6) Nothing in this Article applies to any goods in so far as those goods are being carried for the purposes of the doing of any thing which, by virtue of the grant of any licence or permission, is not prohibited by this Order.

(7) Nothing in this Article shall be construed so as to prejudice any other provision of law prohibiting or restricting the use of ships, aircraft or land transport vehicles.

Manufacture or assembly in Southern Rhodesia of aircraft or motor vehicles

9.—(1) No person shall—

(*a*) operate or use any undertaking in Southern Rhodesia, whether established before or after the commencement of this Order, as an undertaking to which this Article applies; or

(*b*) authorise any undertaking in Southern Rhodesia to be operated or used by any other person as an undertaking to which this Article applies or give his consent to or connive in or by his neglect contribute to such operation or use,

except under the authority of a licence granted by the Board of Administration of the States of Guernsey or, as the case may be, by the Finance Committee of the States of Jersey.

(2) Except under such authority as aforesaid, no person shall—

(*a*) establish in Southern Rhodesia any undertaking to which this Article applies; or

(*b*) convert any undertaking in Southern Rhodesia into an undertaking to which this Article applies; or

(*c*) dispose (whether absolutely or for any lesser interest) of any undertaking in Southern Rhodesia to any other person if he knows or has reasonable cause to believe that that other person intends to use it as an undertaking to which this Article applies; or

(*d*) acquire (whether absolutely or for any lesser interest) any undertaking in Southern Rhodesia with the intention of using it as an undertaking to which this Article applies; or

(*e*) dispose (whether absolutely or for any lesser interest) of any property or assets of or forming part of any undertaking in Southern Rhodesia to which this Article applies to any other person otherwise than in the ordinary course of the business of that undertaking or acquire any such property or assets disposed of as aforesaid.

(3) No person shall—

(*a*) make or carry out any contract for any of the following transactions, that is to say:—

(i) the use or operation of any undertaking or the authorisation of, or the giving of consent to, the use or operation of any undertaking; or

(ii) the establishment, conversion, disposal or acquisition of any undertaking; or

(iii) the disposal or acquisition of the property or assets of or forming part of any undertaking,

if that transaction would be in contravention of the foregoing provisions of this Article; or

(*b*) do any other act calculated to promote any such transaction.

(4) The undertakings to which this Article applies are undertakings for the manufacture or assembly of aircraft or motor vehicles.

(5) Any person who contravenes the foregoing provisions of this Article shall be guilty of an offence against this Order and, in the case of a person who—

(*a*) is a citizen of the United Kingdom and Colonies or a British subject without citizenship or a British protected person and is ordinarily resident in the Bailiwick of Guernsey or, as the case may be, the Bailiwick of Jersey; or

(*b*) is a body incorporated or constituted under the law of the Bailiwick of Guernsey or, as the case may be, the Bailiwick of Jersey,

shall, in the Bailiwick in question, be guilty of such an offence wherever the contravention takes place.

Investigation, etc. of suspected British ships and aircraft

10.—(1) Where any authorised officer, that is to say, any such officer as is referred to in section 692(1) of the Merchant Shipping Act 1894(a), has reason to suspect that any British ship registered as mentioned in Article 2(5) of this Order has been or is being or is about to be used in contravention of paragraph (1) or paragraph (2) of Article 8 of this Order, he may (either alone or accompanied and assisted by persons under his authority) board the ship and search her and, for that purpose, may use or authorise the use of reasonable force, and he may request the master of the ship to furnish such information relating to the ship and her cargo and produce for his inspection such documents so relating and such cargo as he may specify; and an authorised officer (either there and then or upon consideration of any information furnished or document or cargo produced in pursuance of such a request) may, in the case of a ship that is reasonably suspected of being or of being about to be used in contravention of Article 8(2) of this Order, exercise the following further powers with a view to the prevention of the commission (or the continued commission) of any such contravention or in order that enquiries into the matter may be pursued, that is to say, he may either direct the master to refrain, except with the consent of an authorised officer, from landing at any port specified by the officer any part of the ship's cargo that is so specified or request the master to take any one or more of the following steps:—

(*a*) to cause the ship not to proceed with the voyage on which she is then engaged or about to engage until the master is notified by any authorised officer that the ship may so proceed;

(*b*) if the ship is then in a port in any of the Channel Islands, to cause her to remain there until the master is notified by any authorised officer that the ship may depart; and

(*c*) to take her to any other destination that may be specified by the officer in agreement with the master;

and the master shall comply with any such request or direction.

(2) Without prejudice to the provisions of paragraph (8) of this Article, where a master refuses or fails to comply with a request made under this Article that his ship shall or shall not proceed to or from any place or where an authorised officer otherwise has reason to suspect that such a request that has been so made may not be complied with, any such officer may take such

---

(a) 1894 c. 60.

steps as appear to him to be necessary to secure compliance with that request and, without prejudice to the generality of the foregoing, may for that purpose enter upon, or authorise entry upon, that ship and use, or authorise the use of, reasonable force.

(3) Where the Bailiff has reason to suspect that any aircraft registered as mentioned in Article 2(5) of this Order has been or is being or is about to be used in contravention of paragraph (1) or paragraph (2) of Article 8 of this Order or Article 12 of this Order, the Bailiff may request the operator and the commander of the aircraft or either of them to furnish such information relating to the aircraft and its cargo and produce for his inspection such documents so relating and such cargo as he may specify, and the Bailiff may (either alone or accompanied and assisted by persons under his authority) board the aircraft and search it and, for that purpose, may use or authorise the use of reasonable force; and, if the aircraft is then in any of the Channel Islands, the Bailiff (either there and then or upon consideration of any information furnished or document or cargo produced in pursuance of such a request) may further request the operator and the commander or either of them to cause the aircraft to remain in the Bailiwick of Guernsey or, as the case may be, the Bailiwick of Jersey until notified that the aircraft may depart; and the operator and the commander shall comply with any such request.

(4) Without prejudice to the provisions of paragraph (8) of this Article, where the Bailiff has reason to suspect that any request that an aircraft should remain in the Bailiwick of Guernsey or, as the case may be, the Bailiwick of Jersey that has been made under paragraph (3) of this Article may not be complied with, the Bailiff may take such steps as appear to him to be necessary to secure compliance with that request and, without prejudice to the generality of the foregoing, may for that purpose—

(a) enter, or authorise entry, upon any land and upon that aircraft;

(b) detain, or authorise the detention of, that aircraft; and

(c) use, or authorise the use of, reasonable force.

(5) Without prejudice to Article 18(1) of this Order, any reference in this Article to the Bailiff shall be construed as including a reference to any person authorised by him for the purposes thereof, either generally or in a particular case; and a person so authorised shall, if requested to do so, produce evidence of his authority before exercising any power thereunder.

(6) No information furnished or document produced by any person in pursuance of a request made under this Article shall be disclosed except—

(a) with the consent of the person by whom the information was furnished or the document was produced:

Provided that a person who has obtained information or is in possession of a document only in his capacity as servant or agent of another person may not give consent for the purposes of this sub-paragraph but such consent may instead be given by any person who is entitled to that information or to the possession of that document in his own right; or

(b) to any person who would have been empowered under this Article to request that it be furnished or produced or to any person holding or acting in any office under or in the service of the Crown in respect of the Government of the United Kingdom or under or in the service of the Government of any other country or territory specified in Article 2(5) of this Order; or

(c) on the authority of the Secretary of State, to any organ of the United Nations or to any person in the service of the United Nations or of the Government of any other country for the purpose of assisting the United Nations or that Government in securing compliance with or detecting evasion of measures in relation to Southern Rhodesia decided upon by the Security Council of the United Nations; or

(d) with a view to the institution of, or otherwise for the purposes of, any proceedings for an offence against this Order or, with respect to any of the matters regulated by this Order, for an offence against any enactment relating to customs or for an offence against any provision of law with respect to similar matters that is for the time being in force in any country or territory specified in Article 2(5) of this Order.

(7) Any power conferred by this Article to request the furnishing of information or the production of a document or of cargo for inspection shall include a power to specify whether the information should be furnished orally or in writing and in what form and to specify the time by which and the place in which the information should be furnished or the document or cargo produced for inspection.

(8) The following persons shall be guilty of an offence against this Order, that is to say:—

(a) a master of a ship who disobeys any direction given under paragraph (1) of this Article with respect to the landing of any cargo; or

(b) a master of a ship or an operator or a commander of an aircraft who, without reasonable excuse, refuses or fails within a reasonable time to comply with any request made under this Article by any person empowered to make it or who wilfully furnishes false information or produces false documents to such a person in response to such a request; or

(c) a master or a member of the crew of a ship or an operator or a commander or a member of the crew of an aircraft who wilfully obstructs any such person (or any person acting under the authority of any such person) in the exercise of his powers under this Article.

(9) Nothing in this Article shall be construed so as to prejudice any other provision of law conferring powers or imposing restrictions or enabling restrictions to be imposed with respect to ships or aircraft.

Transfer of certain property overseas

11.—(1) The property to which this Article applies is property of any description situated outside the United Kindgom, the Channel Islands and the Isle of Man in which a person to whom this Article applies has any such interest as is hereinafter described, that is to say, that he owns it or that the ownership of it can be transferred only with his consent or concurrence or that there is vested in him any power (whether alone or when used together with a power vested in any other person) to determine whether the ownership of it should be tranferred; and, for the purposes of this Article, the expression "property" includes any interest in or right over any property (whether that interest or right be present or future and whether it be vested or contingent).

(2) The persons to whom this Article applies are all persons who are citizens of the United Kingdom and Colonies, British subjects without citizenship or British protected persons and are ordinarily resident in the Bailiwick of Guernsey

or, as the case may be, the Bailiwick of Jersey and all bodies incorporated or constituted under the law of the Bailiwick of Guernsey or, as the case may be, the Bailiwick of Jersey.

(3) If it appears to the Bailiff that the transfer of the ownership of any property to which this Article applies may facilitate the contravention or evasion of this Order, he may, for the purpose of preventing or restricting the transfer of the ownership of that property, give to any person to whom this Article applies and who has such an interest in it as aforesaid directions in writing requiring him to take or, as the case may require, to refrain from taking such action in relation to that property as the directions may specify; and any person to whom directions are given under this Article shall comply with them.

(4) Any directions given under this Article may be either general or special, may be subject to or without conditions and may be revoked or varied by subsequent such directions.

(5) Any person who contravenes paragraph (3) of this Article shall be guilty of an offence against this Order.

Restrictions on the use of certain aircraft

12.—(1) Except under the authority of a licence granted by the Board of Trade, no aircraft to which this Article applies shall fly on any flight between any place that is within Southern Rhodesia and any place, whether within or outside any of the Channel Islands, that is outside Southern Rhodesia for the purpose of carrying passengers or cargo between those places.

(2) The aircraft to which this Article applies are—

  (a) aircraft registered as mentioned in Article 2(5) of this Order;

  (b) aircraft that are not so registered but that are operated by or on behalf of a body incorporated or constituted under the law of the Bailiwick of Guernsey or, as the case may be, the Bailiwick of Jersey; and

  (c) any other aircraft that is for the time being chartered to any person who is—

    (i) a citizen of the United Kingdom and Colonies or a British subject without citizenship or a British protected person and is ordinarily resident in the Bailiwick of Guernsey or, as the case may be, the Bailiwick of Jersey; or

    (ii) a body incorporated or constituted under the law of the Bailiwick of Guernsey or, as the case may be, the Bailiwick of Jersey.

(3) If any aircraft is flown in contravention of paragraph (1) of this Article then the operator and the commander of the aircraft, and, when it is chartered as mentioned in paragraph (2)(c) of this Article, the person to whom it is for the time being chartered, shall be guilty of an offence against this Order and, in the case of such a person as is mentioned in the said paragraph (2)(c), shall, in the Bailiwick in question, be guilty of such an offence wherever the contravention takes place.

Restrictions on certain air service linking arrangements

13.—(1) Except under the authority of a licence granted by the Board of Trade, no person shall, whether alone or together with any other person or body, make or carry out any arrangement or agreement to which this Article applies.

(2) This Article applies to any arrangement or agreement—

(*a*) for co-ordinating any air transport service provided by means of an air-craft to which Article 12 of this Order applies and which is not a Southern Rhodesian aircraft with any air transport service provided by means of a Southern Rhodesian aircraft; or

(*b*) whereby a person operating an air transport service by means of an aircraft to which Article 12 of this Order applies and which is not a Southern Rhodesian aircraft provides any civil aviation facility for or on behalf of, or in collaboration or association with, a person operating an air transport service by means of a Southern Rhodesian aircraft, or for the purposes of or in connection with a civil aviation facility provided by any such last-mentioned person.

(3) In this Article—

(*a*) "air transport service" means any carriage of passengers or cargo by air, whether or not for reward, and whether organised on regular schedules or for one or more specific occasions;

(*b*) "civil aviation facility" means any facility or service provided for the purposes of or in connection with the carriage of passengers or cargo by air or for the purposes of or in connection with the operation of aircraft therefor; and

(*c*) an aircraft is deemed to be a Southern Rhodesian aircraft if, and only if, it is an aircraft to which Article 12 of this Order applies and—

  (i) it is registered in Southern Rhodesia; or

  (ii) it is operated by or on behalf of a body incorporated or constituted under the law of Southern Rhodesia; or

  (iii) it is for the time being chartered to such a body.

(4) Any person who contravenes paragraph (1) of this Article shall be guilty of an offence against this Order and, in the case of a person who—

(*a*) is a citizen of the United Kingdom and Colonies or a British subject without citizenship or a British protected person and is ordinarily resident in the Bailiwick of Guernsey or, as the case may be, the Bailiwick of Jersey; or

(*b*) is a body incorporated or constituted under the law of the Bailiwick of Guernsey or, as the case may be, the Bailiwick of Jersey,

shall, in the Bailiwick in question, be guilty of such an offence wherever the contravention takes place.

Restrictions on entry into the Channel Islands

14.—(1) This Article applies to the following persons, that is to say—

(*a*) any Commonwealth citizen to whom section 1 of the Commonwealth Immigrants Act 1962(**a**) applies (not being a person for the time being exempt by virtue of section 17 of that Act from control under Part I thereof or from deportation under Part II thereof) who, on seeking entry into any of the Channel Islands—

  (i) does not satisfy an immigration officer or, as the case may be, an aliens officer that he is a citizen of the United Kingdom and Colonies, and

  (ii) tenders to such an officer a document being or purporting to be a current passport or other document establishing a person's identity

---

(**a**) 1962 c. 21.

or nationality issued by, in the name of, on behalf of, or under the authority of the Government of Southern Rhodesia, or the Governor or any Minister or any other officer of the Government of Southern Rhodesia, or any person or body of persons in Southern Rhodesia exercising or claiming to exercise any governmental functions in relation to that country, by whatever name described (including any person or body of persons claiming to be the Government of that country or to be a Minister or Ministers or any officer of such a Government or otherwise to exercise authority on behalf of such a Government); and

(b) any Commonwealth citizen whom the Secretary of State has reason to believe—

    (i) to be ordinarily resident in Southern Rhodesia; and

    (ii) to have furthered or encouraged or to be likely to further or encourage any unconstitutional action in Southern Rhodesia or any action calculated to evade or contravene or to facilitate the evasion or contravention of this Order or of the Order revoked by this Order or of any provision of law with respect to similar matters from time to time in force in any country or territory specified in Article 2(5) of this Order.

(2) Subject to the next following paragraph, an immigration officer or, as the case may be, an aliens officer may, on the examination under Part I of the Commonwealth Immigrants Act 1962 of any person to whom this Article applies, under this Article—

(a) refuse him admission into the Bailiwick of Guernsey or, as the case may be, the Bailiwick of Jersey, or

(b) admit him into the Bailiwick of Guernsey or, as the case may be, the Bailiwick of Jersey subject to conditions.

(3) The power to refuse admission or to admit subject to conditions under the preceding paragraph shall not be exercised on any occasion in respect of any person, whether or not he is a Commonwealth citizen to whom section 1 of the Commonwealth Immigrants Act 1962 applies, save in so far as the person could have been refused admission or, as the case may be, admitted subject to the like condition, under section 2 of that Act—

(a) had subsection (3) thereof been omitted, and

(b) where he is not a Commonwealth citizen to whom the said section 1 applies, had he been such a citizen.

(4) Subject to the next following paragraph, where a person is convicted of an offence under this Article, the court by or before which he is convicted, or any court to which his case is brought by way of appeal against conviction or sentence, may, under this Article, recommend that a deportation order be made in respect of him; and where such a recommendation for deportation is in force in respect of a person the Lieutenant Governor may, if he thinks fit, make an order requiring him to leave the Bailiwick of Guernsey or, as the case may be, the Bailiwick of Jersey.

(5) A court shall not recommend, under the preceding paragraph, the making of a deportation order in respect of a person save in so far as it could have recommended, under section 7 of the Commonwealth Immigrants Act 1962, the making of such an order in respect of him or could have so recommended had he been a Commonwealth citizen to whom section 6 of that Act applies.

(6) The provisions of Schedule 1 to this Order shall have effect for the purposes of this Article.

(7) Nothing in this Article shall be construed as derogating from any powers conferred by the Commonwealth Immigrants Act 1962 in relation to a person to whom this Article applies.

(8) Any reference in this Article to an immigration officer or, as the case may be, an aliens officer shall be construed as a reference to such an officer within the meaning of the Commonwealth Immigrants Act 1962 and any reference, in this Article or in Schedule 1 to this Order, to that Act shall be construed as a reference thereto (as modified, amended or extended by or under any enactment) as it has effect as part of the law of the Bailiwick of Guernsey or, as the case may be, the Bailiwick of Jersey.

Restrictions on certain activities promoting emigration to Southern Rhodesia

15.—(1) Except under the authority of a licence granted by the Bailiff, no person shall—

    (a) publish, or be a party to the publication of, any advertisement or any public notice or announcement soliciting or encouraging other persons to take up employment or residence in Southern Rhodesia; or

    (b) do any other act calculated to solicit or encourage members of the public generally or members of any particular class of the public to take up such employment or residence.

(2) Any person who contravenes paragraph (1) of this Article shall be guilty of an offence against this Order unless, in the case of a person who publishes, or is a party to the publication of, an advertisement or a public notice or announcement of such a character as is described in sub-paragraph (a) of that paragraph, he proves that he did not know and could not with reasonable diligence have ascertained that the advertisement, notice or announcement was of that character.

(3) Nothing in paragraph (1)(b) of this Article shall be construed as prohibiting the publication of factual accounts of actions. events, places or things.

Obtaining of evidence and information

16. The provisions of Schedule 2 to this Order shall have effect in order to facilitate the obtaining, by or on behalf of the Bailiff, of evidence and information for the purpose of securing compliance with or detecting evasion of this Order and in order to facilitate the obtaining of evidence of the commission of an offence against this Order.

Penalties and proceedings

17.—(1) Any person guilty of an offence against this Order shall be liable on conviction to imprisonment for a term not exceeding two years or to a fine or to both.

(2) Where any body corporate is guilty of an offence against this Order and that offence is proved to have been committed with the consent or connivance of, or to be attributable to any neglect on the part of, any director, manager, secretary or other similar officer of the body corporate or any person who was purporting to act in any such capacity, he, as well as the body corporate, shall be guilty of that offence and shall be liable to be proceeded against and punished accordingly.

(3) In any proceedings against any person for a contravention of Article 11(3) of this Order, if it is proved that, notwithstanding any directions given to him under that Article in relation to any property, the ownership of that property or of any interest in or right over that property has been transferred, the burden of proving that he complied with those directions shall lie on him.

(4) Proceedings for an offence against this Order may be taken, and the offence may for all incidental purposes be treated as having been committed, in any place in the Channel Islands where any person charged with that offence is for the time being.

(5) Proceedings for an offence against this Order, in its application to the Bailiwick of Jersey, shall not be instituted except by, or with the consent of, the Attorney-General for Jersey:

Provided that this paragraph shall not prevent the arrest, or the issue or execution of a warrant for the arrest, of any person in respect of such an offence, or the remanding in custody or on bail, of any person charged with such an offence, notwithstanding that the necessary consent to the institution of proceedings for the offence has not been obtained.

Exercise of powers

18.—(1) An authority specified in paragraph (2) of this Article may, to such extent and subject to such restrictions and conditions as they may think proper, delegate or authorise the delegation of any of their powers under this Order (other than the power to grant a search warrant under paragraph 2 of Schedule 2 to this Order) to any person, or class or description of persons, approved by them, and references in this Order to such an authority shall be construed accordingly.

(2) The authorities referred to in paragraph (1) of this Article are the Lieutenant Governor, the Bailiff and the Board of Trade.

(3) Any licences granted under this Order may be either general or special, may be subject to or without conditions, may be limited so as to expire on a specified date unless renewed and may be varied or revoked by the authority that granted them.

W. G. Agnew.

SCHEDULE 1   Article 14

SUPPLEMENTARY PROVISIONS CONNECTED WITH RESTRICTIONS OF ENTRY

1. The provisions of the Commonwealth Immigrants Act 1962 set out in the first column of the table contained in this Schedule (which relate to the matters described in the second column thereof) shall have effect for the purposes of Article 14 of this Order as if they were set out in that Article subject, however, to the general modifications set out in the next following paragraph and the particular modifications set out in the third column of the said table.

2. Any such provision shall have effect, as aforesaid, as if—

(a) any reference therein to a Commonwealth citizen to whom section 1 applies or who is subject to control under Part I of the Act were a reference to a person to whom Article 14 of this Order applies ;

(b) any reference therein to refusal of admission or admission subject to conditions under section 2 were a reference to refusal of admission or admission subject to conditions under Article 14 of this Order, and

(c) any reference therein to any other provision of the Act, or to the Act, were a reference to that provision, or to the provisions of the Act, as it has effect for the purposes of Article 14 of this Order.

TABLE

Provision	Subject Matter	Particular Modifications
S. 3(1), (2) and (3)	Supplementary provisions as to control of immigration	—
S. 4	Offences	—
S.8	Procedure and appeals in respect of deportation recommendations	Subs. (1)(b) shall be omitted.
S. 9(2) and (3)	Deportation orders	—
S.10	Supplementary provisions as to deportation	—
S. 11	Offences in connection with deportation orders	—
S. 13	General provisions as to detained persons	—
S. 14	Penalties, proceedings, etc.	—
S. 15	General provisions as to orders, etc.	—
S. 16(3) and (4)	Exercise of functions by officers	—
S. 18(4)	Expenses	—
S. 21(2), (3) and (4)	Interpretation	—
Schedule 1, except paras. 5, 6 and 7	Supplementary provisions as to control of immigration	The second reference in para. 1(1) to Pt. I shall be construed as including a reference to Article 11 of this Order.
Schedule 2	Supplementary provisions as to deportation	—

SCHEDULE 2

Article 16

EVIDENCE AND INFORMATION

1.—(1) Without prejudice to any other provision of this Order, or any provision of any other law, the Bailiff may request any person in or resident in the Bailiwick of Guernsey or, as the case may be, the Bailiwick of Jersey to furnish to him any information in his possession or control, or to produce to him any document in his possession or control, which he may require for the purpose of securing compliance with or detecting evasion of this Order ; and any person to whom such a request is made shall comply with it within such time and in such manner as may be specified in the request.

(2) Nothing in the foregoing sub-paragraph shall be taken to require any person who has acted as advocate or solicitor for any person to disclose any privileged communication made to him in that capacity.

(3) Where a person is convicted for failing to furnish information or produce a document when requested so to do under this paragraph, the court may make an order requiring him, within such period as may be specified in the order, to furnish the information or produce the document.

(4) The power conferred by this paragraph to request any person to produce documents shall include power to take copies of or extracts from any document so produced and to request that person, or, where that person is a body corporate, any other person who is a present or past officer of, or is employed by, the body corporate, to provide an explanation of any of them.

(5) Without prejudice to Article 18(1) of this Order, any reference in this paragraph to the Bailiff shall be construed as including a reference to any person authorised by him for the purposes thereof, either generally or in a particular case ; and a person so authorised shall, if requested to do so, produce evidence of his authority before exercising any power thereunder.

2.—(1) If the appropriate officer mentioned in sub-paragraph (5) of this paragraph is satisfied by information given on oath—

(a) that there is reasonable ground for suspecting that an offence against this Order has been or is being committed and that evidence of the commission of the offence is to be found on any premises specified in the information, or in any vehicle, vessel or aircraft so specified ; or

(b) that any documents which ought to have been produced under paragraph 1 of this Schedule and have not been produced are to be found on any such premises or in any such vehicle, vessel or aircraft,

he may grant a search warrant authorising any police officer, together with any other persons named in the warrant and any other police officers, to enter the premises specified in the information or, as the case may be, any premises upon which the vehicle, vessel or aircraft so specified may be, at any time within one month from the date of the warrant and to search the premises, or, as the case may be, the vehicle, vessel or aircraft.

(2) A person authorised by any such warrant as aforesaid to search any premises or any vehicle, vessel or aircraft may search every person who is found in, or whom he has reasonable ground to believe to have recently left or to be about to enter, those premises or that vehicle, vessel or aircraft and may seize any document or article found on the premises or in the vehicle, vessel or aircraft or on such person which he has reasonable ground to believe to be evidence of the commission of any such offence as aforesaid or any documents which he has reasonable ground to believe ought to have been produced under paragraph 1 of this Schedule or to take in relation to any such article or document any other steps which may appear necessary for preserving it and preventing interference with it :

Provided that no female shall, in pursuance of any warrant issued under this paragraph, be searched except by a female.

(3) Where, by virtue of this paragraph, a person is empowered to enter any premises, vehicle, vessel or aircraft, he may use such force as is reasonably necessary for that purpose.

(4) Any documents or articles of which possession is taken under this paragraph may be retained for a period of three months or, if within that period there are commenced any proceedings for such an offence as aforesaid to which they are relevant, until the conclusion of those proceedings.

(5) In the application of this paragraph to the Bailiwick of Guernsey, the reference in sub-paragraph (1) to the appropriate officer shall be construed—

(a) in relation to the Islands of Guernsey, Herm and Jethou, as a reference to the Bailiff ;

(b) in relation to the Island of Alderney, as a reference to the Chairman of the Court of Alderney ; and

(c) in relation to the Island of Sark, as a reference to the Seneschal of Sark,

and, in the application of this paragraph to the Bailiwick of Jersey, that reference shall be construed as a reference to the Bailiff.

(6) In the application of this paragraph to the Bailiwick of Guernsey any reference in sub-paragraph (1) to a police officer shall be construed as a reference to a member of the salaried police force of the Island of Guernsey, and—

(a) in relation to the Islands of Guernsey, Herm and Jethou, within the limits of his jurisdiction, as a reference to a member of the special constabulary of the Island of Guernsey ;

(b) in relation to the Island of Alderney, as a reference to a member of any police force which may be established by the States of Alderney ; and

(c) in relation to the Island of Sark, as a reference to the Constable and to the Vingtenier.

3. No information furnished or document produced (including any copy or extract made of any document produced) by any person in pursuance of a request made under this Schedule and no document seized under paragraph 2(2) of this Schedule shall be disclosed except—

(a) with the consent of the person by whom the information was furnished or the document was produced or the person from whom the document was seized :

Provided that a person who has obtained information or is in possession of a document only in his capacity as servant or agent of another person may not give consent for the purposes of this sub-paragraph but such consent may instead be given by any person who is entitled to that information or to the possession of that document in his own right ; or

(b) to any person who would have been empowered under this Schedule to request that it be furnished or produced or to any person holding or acting in any office under or in the service of the Crown in respect of the Government of the United Kingdom or under or in the service of the Government of any other country or territory specified in Article 2(5) of this Order ; or

(c) on the authority of the Secretary of State, to any organ of the United Nations or to any person in the service of the United Nations or of the Government of any other country for the purpose of assisting the United Nations or that Government in securing compliance with or detecting evasion of measures in relation to Southern Rhodesia decided upon by the Security Council of the United Nations ; or

(d) with a view to the institution of, or otherwise for the purposes of, any proceedings for an offence against this Order (in its application to either the Bailiwick of Guernsey or the Bailiwick of Jersey) or for an offence against any provision of law with respect to similar matters that is for the time being in force in any country or territory specified in Article 2(5) of this Order.

4. Any person who—

(a) without reasonable excuse, refuses or fails within the time and in the manner specified (or, if no time has been specified, within a reasonable time) to comply with any request made under this Schedule by any person who is empowered to make it ; or

(b) wilfully furnishes false information or a false explanation or otherwise wilfully obstructs any person in the exercise of his powers under this Schedule ; or

(c) with intent to evade the provisions of this Schedule, destroys, mutilates, defaces, secretes or removes any document,

shall be guilty of an offence against this Order.

EXPLANATORY NOTE

(This Note is not part of the Order.)

This Order, made under the United Nations Act 1946, applies to the Channel Islands.

The Order revokes and replaces, in some cases with modifications, the Southern Rhodesia (Prohibited Trade and Dealings) (Channel Islands) Order 1967, which restricted trade and dealings in or in connection with Southern Rhodesia. It also introduces certain further restrictions and confers certain further powers in connection with Southern Rhodesia.

The Order restricts the importation into the Channel Islands of goods exported from Southern Rhodesia and the exportation from the Channel Islands of goods intended for Southern Rhodesia. It also imposes restrictions, in the law of the Channel Islands, on the exportation from Southern Rhodesia of the former goods and the supply to Southern Rhodesia of the latter goods, as well as certain related activities and dealings, including the carriage of these goods in British ships or aircraft. The Order imposes restrictions with respect to undertakings in Southern Rhodesia for the manufacture or assembly of aircraft or motor vehicles. It authorises the imposition of restrictions on the transfer of certain property if this might facilitate an evasion of the Order. It restricts the use of certain aircraft operating to or from Southern Rhodesia and certain related civil aviation transactions. It authorises restrictions upon the entry into the Channel Islands of certain persons connected with Southern Rhodesia and it prohibits certain advertisements and similar activities aimed at encouraging emigration to Southern Rhodesia.

The Order also makes provision for the investigation of ships and aircraft that are suspected of contravening the Order and it confers powers to obtain evidence and information for the purposes of the Order.

STATUTORY INSTRUMENTS

1969 No. 861

UNITED NATIONS

The Southern Rhodesia (United Nations Sanctions) (Isle of Man) Order 1969

Made - - -	*25th June* 1969
Laid before Parliament	*1st July* 1969
Coming into Operation	*2nd July* 1969

At the Court at Buckingham Palace, the 25th day of June 1969

Present,

The Queen's Most Excellent Majesty in Council

Whereas under Article 41 of the Charter of the United Nations the Security Council of the United Nations has, by a resolution passed on 29th May 1968, called upon Her Majesty's Government in the United Kingdom and other Members of the United Nations to take certain measures in relation to Southern Rhodesia, including measures relating to trade and dealing in, and the carriage of, goods, the operation of airlines and aircraft, entry into their territories of persons connected with Southern Rhodesia and the promotion of emigration to Southern Rhodesia:

And whereas the said resolution reaffirmed, to the extent that it did not supersede, the resolution passed on 16th December 1966 by which the Security Council of the United Nations so called upon Her Majesty's Government in the United Kingdom and other Members of the United Nations to take certain measures in relation to Southern Rhodesia, including measures relating to undertakings in Southern Rhodesia for the manufacture or assembly of aircraft and motor vehicles:

Now, therefore, Her Majesty, in exercise of the powers conferred on Her by section 1 of the United Nations Act 1946(a), is pleased, by and with the advice of Her Privy Council, to order, and it is hereby ordered, as follows:—

Citation, commencement and extent

1.—(1) This Order may be cited as the Southern Rhodesia (United Nations Sanctions) (Isle of Man) Order 1969 and shall come into operation on 2nd July 1969.

(2) This Order shall extend to the Isle of Man so as to be law in that Island only.

(a) 1946 c. 45.

Interpretation

2.—(1) In this Order the following expressions have the meanings hereby respectively assigned to them, that is to say:—

"commander", in relation to an aircraft, means the person designated as commander of the aircraft by the operator thereof, and includes any person who is for the time being in charge or command of the aircraft;

"land transport vehicle "includes a barge;

"master", in relation to a ship, includes any person (other than a pilot) for the time being in charge of the ship;

"operator", in relation to an aircraft or to a land transport vehicle, means the person for the time being having the management of the aircraft or the vehicle;

"owner", in relation to a ship, includes any person for the time being having the management of the ship and any person to whom it is chartered; and

"person in Southern Rhodesia" includes any body constituted or incorporated under the law of Southern Rhodesia and any body carrying on business (whether within Southern Rhodesia or not) which is controlled by persons or bodies resident in Southern Rhodesia or constituted or incorporated as aforesaid.

(2) Any provision of this Order which relates to goods exported from Southern Rhodesia (or to the exportation of goods from Southern Rhodesia) shall not have effect in respect of goods exported (or the exportation of goods) which have only passed through Southern Rhodesia in transit and have not been the subject of any transaction there other than a transaction relating solely to their transportation; and any provision of this Order which relates to the exportation of goods to Southern Rhodesia, the supply or delivery of goods to or to the order of any person in Southern Rhodesia or the importation of goods into Southern Rhodesia shall not have effect in relation to goods which are intended only to pass through Southern Rhodesia in transit and not to be the subject of any transaction there other than a transaction relating solely to their transportation.

(3) For the purposes of this Order, the entry into Southern Rhodesia of a vehicle shall not be regarded as constituting the supply or delivery of that vehicle to or to the order of any person in Southern Rhodesia or as constituting its importation into Southern Rhodesia if the entry is merely for the purpose of the vehicle transporting persons into, out of or across Southern Rhodesia or transporting goods across Southern Rhodesia and is not part of or associated with a transaction involving a transfer of the ownership of the vehicle or of any interest therein.

(4) This Order applies to or in relation to any ship or aircraft or any body corporate that purports to be registered in any particular place or, as the case may be, that purports to be incorporated or constituted under the law of that place as it applies to or in relation to any ship or aircraft that is so registered or any body corporate that is so incorporated or constituted.

(5) For the purposes of this Order a reference to a country or territory specified in this paragraph is a reference to a country or territory hereinafter mentioned, that is to say to—

(*a*) the United Kingdom;

(*b*) any of the Channel Islands;

(*c*) the Isle of Man;

(*d*) an associated state within the meaning of the West Indies Act 1967**(a)**;

(*e*) a colony or protectorate within the meaning of the British Nationality Act 1948**(b)**; or

(*f*) any foreign country in which for the time being Her Majesty has jurisdiction;

and a reference to a British ship or aircraft registered as mentioned in this paragraph is a reference to such a ship or aircraft registered in any of the said countries and territories.

(6) Any provision of this Order which prohibits the doing of a thing except under the authority of a licence shall not have effect in relation to the doing of that thing outside the Isle of Man under the authority of a licence granted—

(*a*) under the corresponding law of a country or territory specified in paragraph (5) (*b*), (*d*), (*e*) or (*f*) of this Article, where the thing is done in that country or territory, or

(*b*) under the corresponding law of the United Kingdom, wherever the thing is done;

and, for the purposes of this paragraph, any reference to the corresponding law of a country or territory is a reference to any provision of law, for the time being in force therein, which substantially corresponds to the relevant provision of this Order.

(7) The Interpretation Act 1889**(c)** shall apply, with the necessary adaptations, for the purpose of interpreting this Order and otherwise in relation thereto as it applies for the purpose of interpreting and in relation to Acts of Parliament.

Revocation and transitional provisions

3.—(1) The Southern Rhodesia (Prohibited Trade and Dealings) (Isle of Man) Order 1967**(d)** (hereinafter referred to as "the existing Order") is hereby revoked.

(2) Without prejudice to the provisions of section 38 of the Interpretation Act 1889 as applied by Article 2 of this Order, references to this Order, or to a particular provision thereof, in Articles 10 and 16 (together with Schedule 2) of this Order shall be construed as including references to the existing Order or, as the case may require, to the corresponding provision of the existing Order.

(3) The references in Articles 5(3) and 8 of this Order to goods that have been exported from Southern Rhodesia in contravention of Article 5(1) of this Order shall be deemed to include references to goods which have been exported from Southern Rhodesia in contravention of Article 2(1) of the existing Order.

(a) 1967 c. 4. (b) 1948 c. 56.
(c) 1889 c. 63. (d) S.I. 1967/20 (1967 I, p. 39).

Importation of certain goods into the Isle of Man

4.—(1) Except under the authority of a licence granted—

(*a*) under this Order by the Lieutenant Governor, or

(*b*) under the Import of Goods (Control) Order 1954(**a**) by the Board of Trade,

all goods that are exported from Southern Rhodesia after the commencement of this Order are prohibited to be imported into the Isle of Man.

(2) This Article shall have effect for the purposes of the Customs and Excise Act 1952(**b**), as continued in force in the Isle of Man by the Customs (Isle of Man) Act 1958 (an Act of Tynwald), as an enactment relating to customs and as an enactment with respect to the importation of goods, and the provisions of the said Act of 1952 shall apply accordingly.

(3) Nothing in this Article shall be construed so as to prejudice any other provision of law prohibiting or restricting the importation of goods into the Isle of Man.

Exportation of goods from Southern Rhodesia

5.—(1) Except under the authority of a licence granted by the Lieutenant Governor no person shall export any goods from Southern Rhodesia.

(2) Except under such authority as aforesaid, no person shall—

(*a*) make or carry out any contract for the exportation of any goods from Southern Rhodesia after the commencement of this Order ; or

(*b*) make or carry out any contract for the sale of any goods which he intends or has reason to believe that another person intends to export from Southern Rhodesia after the commencement of this Order ; or

(*c*) do any act calculated to promote the exportation of any goods from Southern Rhodesia.

(3) Except under such authority as aforesaid, no person shall deal in any goods that have been exported from Southern Rhodesia in contravention of paragraph (1) of this Article, that is to say, shall, by way of trade or otherwise for gain, acquire or dispose of such goods or of any property or interest in them or any right to or charge upon them or process them or do any act calculated to promote any such acquisition, disposal or processing by himself or any other person.

(4) Any person who contravenes the foregoing provisions of this Article shall be guilty of an offence against this Order and, in the case of a person who—

(*a*) is a citizen of the United Kingdom and Colonies or a British subject without citizenship or a British protected person and is ordinarily resident in the Isle of Man ; or

(*b*) is a body incorporated or constituted under the law of the Isle of Man, shall be guilty of such an offence wherever the contravention takes place.

(5) Nothing in this Article shall be construed so as to prejudice any other provision of law prohibiting or restricting the exportation of goods from Southern Rhodesia or acts incidental or related thereto.

(**a**) S.I. 1954/23 (1954 I, p. 640). (**b**) 1952 c. 44.

Exportation of certain goods from the Isle of Man

6.—(1) Except under the authority of a licence granted—

(*a*) under this Order by the Lieutenant Governor, or

(*b*) under the Export of Goods (Control) Order 1967(**a**) by the Board of Trade,

all goods are prohibited to be exported from the Isle of Man to Southern Rhodesia.

(2) This Article shall have effect for the purposes of the Customs and Excise Act 1952, as continued in force in the Isle of Man by the Customs (Isle of Man) Act 1958 (an Act of Tynwald), as an enactment relating to customs and as an enactment with respect to the exportation of goods, and the provisions of the said Act of 1958 shall apply accordingly.

(3) Nothing in this Article shall be construed so as to prejudice any other provision of law prohibiting or restricting the exportation of goods from the Isle of Man.

Supply of goods to Southern Rhodesia

7.—(1) Except under the authority of a licence granted by the Lieutenant Governor no person shall—

(*a*) supply or deliver or agree to supply or deliver to or to the order of any person in Southern Rhodesia any goods that are not in that country ;

(*b*) supply or deliver or agree to supply or deliver any such goods to any person, knowing or having reasonable cause to believe that they will be supplied or delivered to or to the order of a person in Southern Rhodesia or that they will be used for the purposes of any business carried on in or operated from Southern Rhodesia ; or

(*c*) do any act calculated to promote the supply or delivery of any goods in contravention of the foregoing provisions of this paragraph.

(2) Any person who contravenes the foregoing provisions of this Article shall be guilty of an offence against this Order and, in the case of a person who—

(*a*) is a citizen of the United Kingdom and Colonies or a British subject without citizenship or a British protected person and is ordinarily resident in the Isle of Man ; or

(*b*) is a body incorporated or constituted under the law of the Isle of Man,

shall be guilty of such an offence wherever the contravention takes place.

Carriage of certain goods exported from or destined for Southern Rhodesia

8.—(1) Without prejudice to the generality of Article 5 of this Order, no ship or aircraft to which this Article applies and no land transport vehicle within the Isle of Man shall be used for the carriage of any goods if those goods are being or have been exported from Southern Rhodesia in contravention of Article 5(1) of this Order.

(**a**) S.I. 1967/675 (1967 I, p. 2080).

(2) Without prejudice to the generality of Articles 6 and 7 of this Order, no ship or aircraft to which this Article applies and no land transport vehicle within the Isle of Man shall be used for the carriage of any goods if the carriage is, or forms part of, carriage from any place outside Southern Rhodesia to any destination therein or to any person for the purposes of any business carried on in or operated from Southern Rhodesia.

(3) This Article applies to British ships and aircraft registered as mentioned in Article 2(5) of this Order and to any other ship or aircraft that is for the time being chartered to any person who is—

(a) a citizen of the United Kingdom and Colonies or a British subject without citizenship or a British protected person and is ordinarily resident in the Isle of Man ; or

(b) a body incorporated or constituted under the law of the Isle of Man.

(4) If any ship, aircraft or land transport vehicle is used in contravention of paragraph (1) of this Article, then—

(a) in the case of a British ship or aircraft registered as mentioned in Article 2(5) of this Order, the owner and the master of the ship or, as the case may be, the operator and the commander of the aircraft ; or

(b) in the case of any other ship or aircraft, the person to whom the ship or aircraft is for the time being chartered and, if he is such a person as is referred to in sub-paragraph (a) or sub-paragraph (b) of paragraph (3) of this Article, the manager or the master of the ship or, as the case may be, the operator or the commander of the aircraft ; or

(c) in the case of a land transport vehicle, the operator of the vehicle,

shall be guilty of an offence against this Order unless he proves that he did not know and had no reason to suppose that the goods were being or had been exported from Southern Rhodesia in contravention of Article 5(1) of this Order.

(5) If any ship, aircraft or land transport vehicle is used in contravention of paragraph (2) of this Article, then—

(a) in the case of a British ship or aircraft registered as mentioned in Article 2(5) of this Order, the owner and the master of the ship or, as the case may be, the operator and the commander of the aircraft ; or

(b) in the case of any other ship or aircraft, the person to whom the ship or aircraft is for the time being chartered and, if he is such a person as is referred to in sub-paragraph (a) or sub-paragraph (b) of paragraph (3) of this Article, the manager or the master of the ship or, as the case may be, the operator or the commander of the aircraft ; or

(c) in the case of a land transport vehicle, the operator of the vehicle,

shall be guilty of an offence against this Order unless he proves that he did not know and had no reason to suppose that the carriage of the goods in question was, or formed part of, carriage from any place outside Southern Rhodesia to any destination therein or to any person for the purposes of any business carried on in or operated from Southern Rhodesia.

(6) Nothing in this Article applies to any goods in so far as those goods are being carried for the purposes of the doing of any thing which, by virtue of the grant of any licence or permission, is not prohibited by this Order.

(7) Nothing in this Article shall be construed so as to prejudice any other provision of law prohibiting or restricting the use of ships, aircraft or land transport vehicles.

Manufacture or assembly in Southern Rhodesia of aircraft or motor vehicles

9.—(1) Except under the authority of a licence granted by the Lieutenant Governor, no person shall—

(*a*) operate or use any undertaking in Southern Rhodesia, whether established before or after the commencement of this Order, as an undertaking to which this Article applies ; or

(*b*) authorise any undertaking in Southern Rhodesia to be operated or used by any other person as an undertaking to which this Article applies or give his consent to or connive in or by his neglect contribute to such operation or use.

(2) Except under such authority as aforesaid, no person shall—

(*a*) establish in Southern Rhodesia any undertaking to which this Article applies ; or

(*b*) convert any undertaking in Southern Rhodesia into an undertaking to which this Article applies ; or

(*c*) dispose (whether absolutely or for any lesser interest) of any undertaking in Southern Rhodesia to any other person if he knows or has reasonable cause to believe that that other person intends to use it as an undertaking to which this Article applies ; or

(*d*) acquire (whether absolutely or for any lesser interest) any undertaking in Southern Rhodesia with the intention of using it as an undertaking to which this Article applies ; or

(*e*) dispose (whether absolutely or for any lesser interest) of any property or assets of or forming part of any undertaking in Southern Rhodesia to which this Article applies to any other person otherwise than in the ordinary course of the business of that undertaking or acquire any such property or assets disposed of as aforesaid.

(3) No person shall—

(*a*) make or carry out any contract for any of the following transactions, that is to say :—

(i) the use or operation of any undertaking or the authorisation of, or the giving of consent to, the use or operation of any undertaking ; or

(ii) the establishment, conversion, disposal or acquisition of any undertaking ; or

(iii) the disposal or acquisition of the property or assets of or forming part of any undertaking,

if that transaction would be in contravention of the foregoing provisions of this Article ; or

(*b*) do any other act calculated to promote any such transaction.

(4) The undertakings to which this Article applies are undertakings for the manufacture or assembly of aircraft or motor vehicles.

(5) Any person who contravenes the foregoing provisions of this Article shall be guilty of an offence against this Order and, in the case of a person who—

(*a*) is a citizen of the United Kingdom and Colonies or a British subject without citizenship or a British protected person and is ordinarily resident in the Isle of Man ; or

(*b*) is a body incorporated or constituted under the law of the Isle of Man.

shall be guilty of such an offence wherever the contravention takes place.

Investigation, etc. of suspected British ships and aircraft   •

10.—(1) Where an authorised officer, that is to say, any such officer as is referred to in section 692(1) of the Merchant Shipping Act 1894(**a**), has reason to suspect that any British ship registered as mentioned in Article 2(5) of this Order has been or is being or is about to be used in contravention of paragraph (1) or paragraph (2) of Article 8 of this Order, he may (either alone or accompanied and assisted by persons under his authority) board the ship and search her and, for that purpose, may use or authorise the use of reasonable force, and he may request the master of the ship to furnish such information relating to the ship and her cargo and produce for his inspection such documents so relating and such cargo as he may specify ; and an authorised officer (either there and then or upon consideration of any information furnished or document or cargo produced in pursuance of such a request) may, in the case of a ship that is reasonably suspected of being or of being about to be used in contravention of Article 8(2) of this Order, exercise the following further powers with a view to the prevention of the commission (or the continued commission) of any such contravention or in order that enquiries into the matter may be pursued, that is to say, he may either direct the master to refrain, except with the consent of an authorised officer, from landing at any port specified by the officer any part of the ship's cargo that is so specified or request the master to take any one or more of the following steps :—

(*a*) to cause the ship not to proceed with the voyage on which she is then engaged or about to engage until the master is notified by any authorised officer that the ship may so proceed ;

(*b*) if the ship is then in a port in the Isle of Man, to cause her to remain there until the master is notified by any authorised officer that the ship may depart ; and

(*c*) to take her to any other destination that may be specified by the officer in agreement with the master ;

and the master shall comply with any such request or direction.

(2) Without prejudice to the provisions of paragraph (8) of this Article, where a master refuses or fails to comply with a request made under this Article that his ship shall or shall not proceed to or from any place or where an authorised officer otherwise has reason to suspect that such a request that has been so made may not be complied with, any such officer may take such steps as appear to him to be necessary to secure compliance with that request and, without prejudice to the generality of the foregoing, may for that purpose enter upon, or authorise entry upon, that ship and use, or authorise the use of, reasonable force.

(**a**) 1894 c. 60.

(3) Where a competent authority or competent officer specified in paragraph (5) of this Article has reason to suspect that any aircraft registered as mentioned in Article 2(5) of this Order has been or is being or is about to be used in contravention of paragraph (1) or paragraph (2) of Article 8 of this Order or Article 12 of this Order, that authority or officer may request the operator and the commander of the aircraft or either of them to furnish such information relating to the aircraft and its cargo and produce for their or his inspection such documents so relating and such cargo as they or he may specify, and that officer may (either alone or accompanied and assisted by persons under his authority) board the aircraft and search it and, for that purpose, may use or authorise the use of reasonable force ; and, if the aircraft is then in the Isle of Man, such a competent authority or competent officer (either there and then or upon consideration of any information furnished or document or cargo produced in pursuance of such a request) may further request the operator and the commander or either of them to cause the aircraft to remain in the Isle of Man until notified that the aircraft may depart ; and the operator and the commander shall comply with any such request.

(4) Without prejudice to the provisions of paragraph (8) of this Article, where a competent authority or competent officer specified in paragraph (5) of this Article has reason to suspect that any request that an aircraft should remain in the Isle of Man that has been made under paragraph (3) of this Article may not be complied with, that authority or officer may take such steps as appear to them or him to be necessary to secure compliance with that request and, without prejudice to the generality of the foregoing, may for that purpose—

(a) enter, or authorise entry, upon any land and upon that aircraft ;

(b) detain, or authorise the detention of, that aircraft ; and

(c) use, or authorise the use of, reasonable force.

(5) For the purposes of this Article—

(a) any reference to a competent authority is a reference to the Lieutenant Governor or to the Board of Trade, and

(b) any reference to a competent officer is a reference to a person authorised for the relevant purpose, either generally or in a particular case, by a competent authority or to an officer of customs and excise,

but a person authorised as aforesaid to exercise any power for the purposes of paragraph (3) or paragraph (4) of this Article shall, if requested to do so, produce evidence of his authority before exercising that power.

(6) No information furnished or document produced by any person in pursuance of a request made under this Article shall be disclosed except—

(a) with the consent of the person by whom the information was furnished or the document was produced :

  Provided that a person who has obtained information or is in possession of a document only in his capacity as servant or agent of another person may not give consent for the purposes of this sub-paragraph but such consent may instead be given by any person who is entitled to that information or to the possession of that document in his own right ; or

(b) to any person who would have been empowered under this Article to request that it be furnished or produced or to any person holding or acting in any office under or in the service of the Crown in respect of the Government of the United Kingdom or under or in the service of the Government of any other country or territory specified in Article 2(5) of this Order ; or

(c) on the authority of the Secretary of State, to any organ of the United Nations or to any person in the service of the United Nations or of the Government of any other country for the purpose of assisting the United Nations or that Government in securing compliance with or detecting evasion of measures in relation to Southern Rhodesia decided upon by the Security Council of the United Nations ; or

(d) with a view to the institution of, or otherwise for the purposes of, any proceedings for an offence against this Order or, with respect to any of the matters regulated by this Order, for an offence against any enactment relating to customs or for an offence against any provision of law with respect to similar matters that is for the time being in force in any country or territory specified in Article 2(5) of this Order.

(7) Any power conferred by this Article to request the furnishing of information or the production of a document or of cargo for inspection shall include a power to specify whether the information should be furnished orally or in writing and in what form and to specify the time by which and the place in which the information should be furnished or the document or cargo produced for inspection.

(8) The following persons shall be guilty of an offence against this Order, that is to say :—

(a) a master of a ship who disobeys any direction given under paragraph (1) of this Article with respect to the landing of any cargo ; or

(b) a master of a ship or an operator or a commander of an aircraft who, without reasonable excuse, refuses or fails within a reasonable time to comply with any request made under this Article by any person empowered to make it or who wilfully furnishes false information or produces false documents to such a person in response to such a request ; or

(c) a master or a member of the crew of a ship or an operator or a commander or a member of the crew of an aircraft who wilfully obstructs any such person (or any person acting under the authority of any such person) in the exercise of his powers under this Article.

(9) Nothing in this Article shall be construed so as to prejudice any other provision of law conferring powers or imposing restrictions or enabling restrictions to be imposed with respect to ships or aircraft.

Transfer of certain property overseas

11.—(1) The property to which this Article applies is property of any description situated outside the United Kingdom, the Channel Islands and the Isle of Man in which a person to whom this Article applies has any such interest as is hereinafter described, that is to say, that he owns it or that the ownership of it can be transferred only with his consent or concurrence or that there is vested in him any power (whether alone or when used together with a power vested in any other person) to determine whether the ownership of it should be transferred ; and, for the purposes of this Article, the expression "property" includes any interest in or right over any property (whether that interest or right be present or future and whether it be vested or contingent).

(2) The persons to whom this Article applies are all persons who are citizens of the United Kingdom and Colonies, British subjects without citizenship or British protected persons and are ordinarily resident in the Isle of Man and all bodies incorporated or constituted under the law of the Isle of Man.

(3) If it appears to the Lieutenant Governor that the transfer of the ownership of any property to which this Article applies may facilitate the contravention or evasion of this Order, he may, for the purpose of preventing or restricting the transfer of the ownership of that property, give to any person to whom this Article applies and who has such an interest in it as aforesaid directions in writing requiring him to take or, as the case may require, to refrain from taking such action in relation to that property as the directions may specify ; and any person to whom directions are given under this Article shall comply with them.

(4) Any directions given under this Article may be either general or special, may be subject to or without conditions and may be revoked or varied by subsequent such directions.

(5) Any person who contravenes paragraph (3) of this Article shall be guilty of an offence against this Order.

Restrictions on the use of certain aircraft

12.—(1) Except under the authority of a licence granted by the Board of Trade, no aircraft to which this Article applies shall fly on any flight between any place that is within Southern Rhodesia and any place, whether within or outside the Isle of Man, that is outside Southern Rhodesia for the purpose of carrying passengers or cargo between those places.

(2) The aircraft to which this Article applies are—

(a) aircraft registered as mentioned in Article 2(5) of this Order ;

(b) aircraft that are not so registered but that are operated by or on behalf of a body incorporated or constituted under the law of the Isle of Man ; and

(c) any other aircraft that is for the time being chartered to any person who is—

(i) a citizen of the United Kingdom and Colonies or a British subject without citizenship or a British protected person and is ordinarily resident in the Isle of Man ; or

(ii) a body incorporated or constituted under the law of the Isle of Man.

(3) If any aircraft is flown in contravention of paragraph (1) of this Article, then the operator and the commander of the aircraft, and, when it is chartered as mentioned in paragraph (2)(c) of this Article, the person to whom it is for the time being chartered, shall be guilty of an offence against this Order and, in the case of such a person as is mentioned in the said paragraph (2)(c), shall be guilty of such an offence wherever the contravention takes place.

Restrictions on certain air service linking arrangements

13.—(1) Except under the authority of a licence granted by the Board of Trade, no person shall, whether alone or together with any other person or body, make or carry out any arrangement or agreement to which this Article applies.

(2) This Article applies to any arrangement or agreement—

(*a*) for co-ordinating any air transport service provided by means of an aircraft to which Article 12 of this Order applies and which is not a Southern Rhodesian aircraft with any air transport service provided by means of a Southern Rhodesian aircraft ; or

(*b*) whereby a person operating an air transport service by means of an aircraft to which Article 12 of this Order applies and which is not a Southern Rhodesian aircraft provides any civil aviation facility for or on behalf of, or in collaboration or association with, a person operating an air transport service by means of a Southern Rhodesian aircraft, or for the purposes of or in connection with a civil aviation facility provided by any such last-mentioned person.

(3) In this Article—

(*a*) "air transport service" means any carriage of passengers or cargo by air, whether or not for reward, and whether organised on regular schedules or for one or more specific occasions ;

(*b*) "civil aviation facility" means any facility or service provided for the purposes of or in connection with the carriage of passengers or cargo by air or for the purposes of or in connection with the operation of aircraft therefor ; and

(*c*) an aircraft is deemed to be a Southern Rhodesian aircraft if, and only if, it is an aircraft to which Article 12 of this Order applies and—

(i) it is registered in Southern Rhodesia ; or

(ii) it is operated by or on behalf of a body incorporated or constituted under the law of Southern Rhodesia ; or

(iii) it is for the time being chartered to such a body.

(4) Any person who contravenes paragraph (1) of this Article shall be guilty of an offence against this Order and, in the case of a person who—

(*a*) is a citizen of the United Kingdom and Colonies or a British subject without citizenship or a British protected person and is ordinarily resident in the Isle of Man ; or

(*b*) is a body incorporated or constituted under the law of the Isle of Man,

shall be guilty of such an offence wherever the contravention takes place.

Restrictions on entry into the Isle of Man

14.—(1) This Article applies to the following persons, that is to say—

(*a*) any Commonwealth citizen to whom section 1 of the Commonwealth Immigrants Act 1962(**a**) applies (not being a person for the time being exempt by virtue of section 17 of that Act from control under Part I thereof or from deportation under Part II thereof) who, on seeking entry into the Isle of Man—

(i) does not satisfy an immigration officer that he is a citizen of the United Kingdom and Colonies, and

---

(a) 1962 c. 21.

(ii) tenders to such an officer a document being or purporting to be a current passport or other document establishing a person's identity or nationality issued by, in the name of, on behalf of, or under the authority of the Government of Southern Rhodesia, or the Governor or any Minister or any other officer of the Government of Southern Rhodesia, or any person or body of persons in Southern Rhodesia exercising or claiming to exercise any governmental functions in relation to that country, by whatever name described (including any person or body of persons claiming to be the Government of that country or to be a Minister or Ministers or any officer of such a Government or otherwise to exercise authority on behalf of such a Government); and

(b) any Commonwealth citizen whom the Secretary of State has reason to believe—

(i) to be ordinarily resident in Southern Rhodesia; and

(ii) to have furthered or encouraged or to be likely to further or encourage any unconstitutional action in Southern Rhodesia or any action calculated to evade or contravene or to facilitate the evasion or contravention of this Order or of the Order revoked by this Order or of any provision of law with respect to similar matters from time to time in force in any country or territory specified in Article 2(5) of this Order.

(2) Subject to the next following paragraph, an immigration officer may, on the examination under Part I of the Commonwealth Immigrants Act 1962 of any person to whom this Article applies, under this Article—

(a) refuse him admission into the Isle of Man, or

(b) admit him into the Isle of Man subject to conditions.

(3) The power to refuse admission or to admit subject to conditions under the preceding paragraph shall not be exercised on any occasion in respect of any person, whether or not he is a Commonwealth citizen to whom section 1 of the Commonwealth Immigrants Act 1962 applies, save in so far as the person could have been refused admission or, as the case may be, admitted subject to the like condition, under section 2 of that Act—

(a) had subsection (3) thereof been omitted, and

(b) where he is not a Commonwealth citizen to whom the said section 1 applies, had he been such a citizen.

(4) Subject to the next following paragraph, where a person is convicted of an offence under this Article, the court by or before which he is convicted, or any court to which his case is brought by way of appeal against conviction or sentence, may, under this Article, recommend that a deportation order be made in respect of him; and where such a recommendation for deportation is in force in respect of a person the Lieutenant Governor may, if he thinks fit, make an order requiring him to leave the Isle of Man.

(5) A court shall not recommend, under the preceding paragraph, the making of a deportation order in respect of a person save in so far as it could have recommended, under section 7 of the Commonwealth Immigrants Act 1962, the making of such an order in respect of him or could have so recommended had he been a Commonwealth citizen to whom section 6 of that Act applies.

(6) The provisions of Schedule 1 to this Order shall have effect for the purposes of this Article.

(7) Nothing in this Article shall be construed as derogating from any powers conferred by the Commonwealth Immigrants Act 1962 in relation to a person to whom this Article applies.

(8) Any reference in this Article to an immigration officer shall be construed as a reference to such an officer within the meaning of the Commonwealth Immigrants Act 1962 and any reference, in this Article or in Schedule 1 to this Order, to that Act shall be construed as a reference thereto (as modified, amended or extended by or under any enactment) as it has effect as part of the law of the Isle of Man.

Restrictions on certain activities promoting emigration to Southern Rhodesia

15.—(1) Except under the authority of a licence granted by the Lieutenant Governor, no person shall—

(a) publish, or be a party to the publication of, any advertisement or any public notice or announcement soliciting or encouraging other persons to take up employment or residence in Southern Rhodesia; or

(b) do any other act calculated to solicit or encourage members of the public generally or members of any particular class of the public to take up such employment or residence.

(2) Any person who contravenes paragraph (1) of this Article shall be guilty of an offence against this Order unless, in the case of a person who publishes, or is a party to the publication of, an advertisement or a public notice or announcement of such a character as is described in sub-paragraph (a) of that paragraph, he proves that he did not know and could not with reasonable diligence have ascertained that the advertisement, notice or announcement was of that character.

(3) Nothing in paragraph (1)(b) of this Article shall be construed as prohibiting the publication of factual accounts of actions, events, places or things.

Obtaining of evidence and information

16. The provisions of Schedule 2 to this Order shall have effect in order to facilitate the obtaining, by or on behalf of the Lieutenant Governor or the Board of Trade or the Commissioners of Customs and Excise, of evidence and information for the purpose of securing compliance with or detecting evasion of this Order and in order to facilitate the obtaining, by or on behalf of the Lieutenant Governor or the Board of Trade or the Commissioners of Customs and Excise, of evidence of the commission of an offence against this Order or, with respect to any of the matters regulated by this Order, of an offence relating to customs.

Penalties and proceedings

17.—(1) Any person guilty of an offence against this Order shall be liable—

(a) on conviction on information to imprisonment for a term not exceeding two years or to a fine or to both; or

(b) on summary conviction to imprisonment for a term not exceeding six months or to a fine not exceeding £500 or to both.

(2) Where any body corporate is guilty of an offence against this Order and that offence is proved to have been committed with the consent or connivance of, or to be attributable to any neglect on the part of, any director, manager, secretary or other similar officer of the body corporate or any person who was purporting to act in any such capacity, he, as well as the body corporate, shall be guilty of that offence and shall be liable to be proceeded against and punished accordingly.

(3) In any proceedings against any person for a contravention of Article 11(3) of this Order, if it is proved that, notwithstanding any directions given to him under that Article in relation to any property, the ownership of that property or of any interest in or right over that property has been transferred, the burden of proving that he complied with those directions shall lie on him.

(4) Summary proceedings for an offence against this Order, being an offence alleged to have been committed outside the Isle of Man, may be commenced at any time not later than twelve months from the date on which the person charged first enters the Isle of Man after committing the offence.

(5) Proceedings for an offence against this Order may be taken, and the offence may for all incidental purposes be treated as having been committed, in any place in the Isle of Man where any person charged with that offence is for the time being.

(6) Proceedings for an offence against this Order shall not be instituted except by, or with the consent of, the Attorney-General for the Isle of Man or the Board of Trade:

Provided that this paragraph shall not prevent the arrest, or the issue or execution of a warrant for the arrest, of any person in respect of such an offence, or the remanding in custody or on bail, of any person charged with such an offence, notwithstanding that the necessary consent to the institution of proceedings for the offence has not been obtained.

Excercise of powers

18.—(1) An authority specified in paragraph (2) of this Article may, to such extent and subject to such restrictions and conditions as they may think proper, delegate or authorise the delegation of any of their powers under this Order (other than the power to give authority under paragraph 2 of Schedule 2 to this Order to apply for a search warrant) to any person, or class or description of persons, approved by them, and references in this Order to such an authority shall be construed accordingly.

(2) The authorities referred to in paragraph (1) of this Article are the Lieutenant Governor and the Board of Trade.

(3) Any licences granted under this Order may be either general or special, may be subject to or without conditions, may be limited so as to expire on a specified date unless renewed and may be varied or revoked by the authority that granted them.

W. G. Agnew,

SCHEDULE 1   Article 14

SUPPLEMENTARY PROVISIONS CONNECTED WITH RESTRICTIONS OF ENTRY

1. The provisions of the Commonwealth Immigrants Act 1962 set out in the first column of the table contained in this Schedule (which relate to the matters described in the second column thereof) shall have effect for the purposes of Article 14 of this Order as if they were set out in that Article subject, however, to the general modifications set out in the next following paragraph and the particular modifications set out in the third column of the said table.

2. Any such provision shall have effect, as aforesaid, as if—

(a) any reference therein to a Commonwealth citizen to whom section 1 applies or who is subject to control under Part I of the Act were a reference to a person to whom Article 14 of this Order applies;

(b) any reference therein to refusal of admission or admission subject to conditions under section 2 were a reference to refusal of admission or admission subject to conditions under Article 14 of this Order, and

(c) any reference therein to any other provision of the Act, or to the Act, were a reference to that provision, or to the provisions of the Act, as it has effect for the purposes of Article 14 of this Order.

TABLE

Provision	Subject Matter	Particular Modifications
S. 3(1), (2) and (3)	Supplementary provisions as to control of immigration	—
S.4	Offences	—
S.8	Procedure and appeals in respect of deportation recommendations	Subs. (1)(*b*) shall be omitted.
S. 9(2) and (3)	Deportation orders	—
S. 10	Supplementary provisions as to deportation	—
S. 11	Offences in connection with deportation orders	—
S. 13	General provisions as to detained persons	—
S. 14	Penalties, proceedings, etc.	—
S. 15	General provisions as to orders, etc.	—
S. 16(3) and (4)	Exercise of functions by officers	—
S. 18(4)	Expenses	—
S. 21(2), (3) and (4)	Interpretation	—
Schedule 1, except paras. 5, 6 and 7	Supplementary provisions as to control of immigration	The second reference in para. 1(1) to Pt. I shall be construed as including a reference to Article 11 of this Order.
Schedule 2	Supplementary provisions as to deportation	—

SCHEDULE 2   Article 16

EVIDENCE AND INFORMATION

1.—(1) Without prejudice to any other provision of this Order, or any provision of any other law, the Lieutenant Governor or the Board of Trade (or any person authorised by him or them for that purpose either generally or in a particular case) or the Commissioners of Customs and Excise may request any person in or resident in the Isle of Man to furnish to him or them (or to that authorised person) any information in his possession or control, or to produce to him or them (or to that authorised person) any document in his possession or control, which he or they (or that authorised person) may require for the purpose of securing compliance with or detecting evasion of this Order; and any person to whom such a request is made shall comply with it within such time and in such manner as may be specified in the request.

(2) Nothing in the foregoing sub-paragraph shall be taken to require any person who has acted as counsel or solicitor for any person to disclose any privileged communication made to him in that capacity.

(3) Where a person is convicted on information for failing to furnish information or produce a document when requested so to do under this paragraph, the court may make an order requiring him, within such period as may be specified in the order, to furnish the information or produce the document.

(4) The power conferred by this paragraph to request any person to produce documents shall include power to take copies of or extracts from any document so produced and to request that person, or, where that person is a body corporate, any other person who is a present or past officer of, or is employed by, the body corporate, to provide an explanation of any of them.

2.—(1) If any justice of the peace is satisfied by information on oath given by a person authorised by the Lieutenant Governor or the Board of Trade or the Commissioners of Customs and Excise to act for the purposes of this paragraph either generally or in a particular case—

(a) that there is reasonable ground for suspecting that an offence against this Order or, with respect to any of the matters regulated by this Order, an offence against any enactment relating to customs has been or is being committed and that evidence of the commission of the offence is to be found on any premises specified in the information, or in any vehicle, vessel or aircraft so specified; or

(b) that any documents which ought to have been produced under paragraph 1 of this Schedule and have not been produced are to be found on any such premises or in any such vehicle, vessel or aircraft,

he may grant a search warrant authorising any constable, together with any other persons named in the warrant and any other constables, to enter the premises specified in the information or, as the case may be, any premises upon which the vehicle, vessel or aircraft so specified may be, at any time within one month from the date of the warrant and to search the premises, or, as the case may be, the vehicle, vessel or aircraft.

(2) A person authorised by any such warrant as aforesaid to search any premises or any vehicle, vessel or aircraft may search every person who is found in, or whom he has reasonable ground to believe to have recently left or to be about to enter, those premises or that vehicle, vessel or aircraft and may seize any document or article found on the premises or in the vehicle, vessel or aircraft or on such person which he has reasonable ground to believe to be evidence of the commission of any

such offence as aforesaid or any documents which he has reasonable ground to believe ought to have been produced under paragraph 1 of this Schedule or to take in relation to any such article or document any other steps which may appear necessary for preserving it and preventing interference with it:

Provided that no female shall, in pursuance of any warrant issued under this paragraph, be searched except by a female.

(3) Where, by virtue of this paragraph, a person is empowered to enter any premises, vehicle, vessel or aircraft, he may use such force as is reasonably necessary for that purpose.

(4) Any documents or articles of which possession is taken under this paragraph may be retained for a period of three months or, if within that period there are commenced any proceedings for such an offence as aforesaid to which they are relevant, until the conclusion of those proceedings.

3. A person authorised by the Lieutenant Governor or the Board of Trade to exercise any power for the purposes of this Schedule shall, if requested to do so, produce evidence of his authority before exercising that power.

4. No information furnished or document produced (including any copy or extract made of any document produced) by any person in pursuance of a request made under this Schedule and no document seized under paragraph 2(2) of this Schedule shall be disclosed except—

(*a*) with the consent of the person by whom the information was furnished or the document was produced or the person from whom the document was seized:

Provided that a person who has obtained information or is in possession of a document only in his capacity as servant or agent of another person may not give consent for the purposes of this sub-paragraph but such consent may instead be given by any person who is entitled to that information or to the possession of that document in his own right; or

(*b*) to any person who would have been empowered under this Schedule to request that it be furnished or produced or to any person holding or acting in any office under or in the service of the Crown in respect of the Government of the United Kingdom or under or in the service of the Government of any other country or territory specified in Article 2(5) of this Order; or

(*c*) on the authority of the Secretary of State, to any organ of the United Nations or to any person in the service of the United Nations or of the Government of any other country for the purpose of assisting the United Nations or that Government in securing compliance with or detecting evasion of measures in relation to Southern Rhodesia decided upon by the Security Council of the United Nations; or

(*d*) with a view to the institution of, or otherwise for the purposes of, any proceedings for an offence against this Order or, with respect to any of the matters regulated by this Order, for an offence against any enactment relating to customs or for an offence against any provision of law with respect to similar matters that is for the time being in force in any country or territory specified in Article 2(5) of this Order.

5. Any person who—

(*a*) without reasonable excuse, refuses or fails within the time and in the manner specified (or, if no time has been specified, within a reasonable time) to comply with any request made under this Schedule by any person who is empowered to make it; or

(*b*) wilfully furnishes false information or a false explanation or otherwise wilfully obstructs any person in the exercise of his powers under this Schedule; or

(*c*) with intent to evade the provisions of this Schedule, destroys, mutilates, defaces, secretes or removes any document,

shall be guilty of an offence against this Order.

EXPLANATORY NOTE

(This Note is not part of the Order.)

This Order, made under the United Nations Act 1946, applies to the Isle of Man.

The Order revokes and replaces, in some cases with modifications, the Southern Rhodesia (Prohibited Trade and Dealings) (Isle of Man) Order 1967, which restricted trade and dealings in or in connection with Southern Rhodesia. It also introduces certain further restrictions and confers certain further powers in connection with Southern Rhodesia.

The Order restricts the importation into the Isle of Man of goods exported from Southern Rhodesia and the exportation from the Isle of Man of goods intended for Southern Rhodesia. It also imposes restrictions, in the law of the Isle of Man, on the exportation from Southern Rhodesia of the former goods and the supply to Southern Rhodesia of the latter goods, as well as certain related activities and dealings, including the carriage of these goods in British ships or aircraft. The Order imposes restrictions with respect to undertakings in Southern Rhodesia for the manufacture or assembly of aircraft or motor vehicles. It authorises the imposition of restrictions on the transfer of certain property if this might facilitate an evasion of the Order. It restricts the use of certain aircraft operating to or from Southern Rhodesia and certain related civil aviation transactions. It authorises restrictions upon the entry into the Isle of Man of certain persons connected with Southern Rhodesia and it prohibits certain advertisements and similar activities aimed at encouraging emigration to Southern Rhodesia.

The Order also makes provision for the investigation of ships and aircraft that are suspected of contravening the Order and it confers powers to obtain evidence and information for the purposes of the Order.

STATUTORY INSTRUMENTS

1969 No. 862

JUDGES

The County Court Judges (Maximum Number) Order 1969

Laid before Parliament in draft

Made - - -	*25th June* 1969
Coming into Operation	*1st July* 1969

At the Court at Buckingham Palace, the 25th day of June 1969.

Present,

The Queen's Most Excellent Majesty in Council

Whereas a draft of the following Order was laid before Parliament and approved by resolution of each House of Parliament:

Now, therefore, Her Majesty, in exercise of the powers conferred on Her by section 1(2) of the Administration of Justice Act 1968(a), is pleased, by and with the advice of Her Privy Council, to order, and it is hereby ordered, as follows:—

1.—(1) This Order may be cited as the County Court Judges (Maximum Number) Order 1969 and shall come into operation on 1st July 1969.

(2) The Interpretation Act 1889(b) shall apply to the interpretation of this Order as it applies to the interpretation of an Act of Parliament.

2. In section 1(1)(*b*)(iii) of the Administration of Justice Act 1968, which prescribes the maximum number of county court judges, for the words "ninety-seven" there shall be substituted the words "one hundred and five".

W. G. Agnew.

EXPLANATORY NOTE
(*This Note is not part of the Order.*)

This Order increases from 97 to 105 the maximum number of county court judges authorised by the Administration of Justice Act 1968.

(a) 1968 c. 5.   (b) 1889 c. 63.

STATUTORY INSTRUMENTS

1969 No. 863

LAND REGISTRATION

The Registration of Title Order 1969

Made - - - -		*25th June* 1969
Coming into Operation		
Article 2(*a*) - -		*1st October* 1969
Article 2(*b*) - -		*1st December* 1969

At the Court at Buckingham Palace, the 25th day of June 1969

Present,

The Queen's Most Excellent Majesty in Council

Her Majesty, in exercise of the powers conferred upon Her by section 120(1) of the Land Registration Act 1925(**a**), is pleased, by and with the advice of Her Privy Council, to order and declare, and it is hereby ordered and declared, as follows:—

1. This Order may be cited as the Registration of Title Order 1969, and Article 2(*a*) shall come into operation on 1st October 1969 and Article 2(*b*) shall come into operation on 1st December 1969.

2. Registration of title to land is to be compulsory on sale—

(*a*) in the county boroughs of Luton and Plymouth, the municipal boroughs of Bedford and Dunstable and the urban district of Kempston, on and after 1st October 1969; and

(*b*) in the county boroughs of Liverpool, Newcastle upon Tyne and Nottingham, and the urban districts of Beeston and Stapleford, Carlton, Long Eaton and West Bridgford, on and after 1st December 1969.

W. G. Agnew.

EXPLANATORY NOTE

(*This Note is not part of the Order.*)

This Order extends the system of compulsory registration of title on sale of land to the county boroughs of Luton and Plymouth, the municipal boroughs of Bedford and Dunstable and the urban district of Kempston, with effect from 1st October 1969; and to the county boroughs of Liverpool, Newcastle upon Tyne and Nottingham and the urban districts of Beeston and Stapleford, Carlton, Long Eaton and West Bridgford, with effect from 1st December 1969.

(a) 1925 c. 21.

STATUTORY INSTRUMENTS

1969 No. 864

INCOME TAX

The Double Taxation Relief (Taxes on Income) (South Africa) Order 1969

Laid before the House of Commons in draft

Made - - - - 25th June 1969

At the Court at Buckingham Palace, the 25th day of June 1969

Present,

The Queen's Most Excellent Majesty in Council

Whereas a draft of this Order was laid before the Commons House of Parliament in accordance with the provisions of section 347(6) of the Income Tax Act 1952(a), and an Address has been presented to Her Majesty by that House praying that an Order may be made in the terms of this Order:

Now, therefore, Her Majesty, in exercise of the powers conferred upon Her by section 347(1) of the said Income Tax Act 1952, as amended by section 39 and section 64 of the Finance Act 1965(b), and of all other powers enabling Her in that behalf, is pleased, by and with the advice of Her Privy Council, to order, and it is hereby ordered, as follows:—

1. This Order may be cited as the Double Taxation Relief (Taxes on Income) (South Africa) Order 1969.

2. It is hereby declared—

(*a*) that the arrangements specified in the Convention set out in the Schedule to this Order have been made with the Government of the Republic of South Africa with a view to affording relief from double taxation in relation to income tax, corporation tax or capital gains tax and taxes of a similar character imposed by the laws of South Africa; and

(*b*) that it is expedient that those arrangements should have effect.

W. G. Agnew.

(a) 15 & 16 Geo. 6 & 1 Eliz. 2. c. 10.   (b) 1965 c. 25.

SCHEDULE

CONVENTION BETWEEN THE GOVERNMENT OF THE UNITED KINGDOM OF GREAT BRITAIN AND NORTHERN IRELAND AND THE GOVERNMENT OF THE REPUBLIC OF SOUTH AFRICA FOR THE AVOIDANCE OF DOUBLE TAXATION AND THE PREVENTION OF FISCAL EVASION WITH RESPECT TO TAXES ON INCOME AND CAPITAL GAINS

The Government of the United Kingdom of Great Britain and Northern Ireland and the Government of the Republic of South Africa;

Desiring to conclude a Convention for the avoidance of double taxation and the prevention of fiscal evasion with respect to taxes on income and capital gains;

Have agreed as follows:—

ARTICLE 1

(1) The taxes which are the subject of this Convention are:

(a) in South Africa:

(i) the normal tax;

(ii) the non-resident shareholders' tax;

(iii) the undistributed profits tax;

(iv) the non-residents tax on interest; and

(v) the provincial income and personal taxes

(hereinafter referred to as "South African tax");

(b) in the United Kingdom of Great Britain and Northern Ireland:

(i) the income tax (including surtax);

(ii) the corporation tax; and

(iii) the capital gains tax

(hereinafter referred to as "United Kingdom tax").

(2) This Convention shall also apply to any identical or substantially similar taxes which are subsequently imposed in addition to, or in place of, the existing taxes.

ARTICLE 2

(1) In this Convention, unless the context otherwise requires:

(a) the term "United Kingdom" means Great Britain and Northern Ireland;

(b) the term "South Africa" means the Republic of South Africa;

(c) the terms "a Contracting State" and "the other Contracting State" mean the United Kingdom or South Africa, as the context requires;

(d) the term "taxation authorities" means, in the case of the United Kingdom, the Commissioners of Inland Revenue or their authorised representative; in the case of South Africa, the Secretary for Inland Revenue or his authorised representative; and in the case of any territory to which this Convention is extended under Article 26, the competent authority for the administration in such territory of the taxes to which this Convention applies;

(e) the term "tax" means United Kingdom tax or South African tax, as the context requires;

(f) the term "person" includes any body of persons, corporate or not corporate;

(g) the term "company" means any body corporate;

(*h*) the terms "United Kingdom enterprise" and "South African enterprise" mean respectively an industrial or commercial enterprise or undertaking carried on by a resident of the United Kingdom and an industrial or commercial enterprise or undertaking carried on by a resident of South Africa, and the terms "enterprise of a Contracting State" and "enterprise of the other Contracting State" mean a United Kingdom enterprise or a South African enterprise, as the context requires;

(*i*) the term "international traffic" includes traffic between places in one country in the course of a voyage which extends over more than one country.

(2) Where under this Convention any income is exempt from tax, or is to be granted relief from tax, in a Contracting State if (with or without other conditions) it is subject to tax in the other Contracting State and that income is subject to tax in that other Contracting State by reference to the amount thereof which is remitted to or received in that other Contracting State, the exemption or relief to be allowed under this Convention in the first-mentioned Contracting State shall apply only to the amount so remitted or received.

(3) In the application of the provisions of this Convention by a Contracting State any term not otherwise defined shall, unless the context otherwise requires, have the meaning which it has under the laws in force in the territory of that Contracting State relating to the taxes which are the subject of this Convention.

ARTICLE 3

(1) For the purposes of this Convention the term "resident of a Contracting State" means any person who, under the law of that State, is liable to taxation therein by reason of his domicile, residence, place of management or any other criterion of a similar nature. The terms "resident of the United Kingdom" and "resident of South Africa" shall be construed accordingly.

(2) Where by reason of the provisions of paragraph (1) of this Article an individual is a resident of both Contracting States, then his status shall be determined in accordance with the following rules:

(*a*) He shall be deemed to be a resident of the Contracting State in which he has a permanent home available to him; if he has a permanent home available to him in both Contracting States, he shall be deemed to be a resident of the Contracting State with which his personal and economic relations are closest (hereinafter referred to as "his centre of vital interests").

(*b*) If the Contracting State in which he has his centre of vital interests cannot be determined, or if he has not a permanent home available to him in either Contracting State, he shall be deemed to be a resident of the Contracting State in which he has an habitual abode.

(*c*) If he has an habitual abode in both Contracting States or in neither of them, he shall be deemed to be a resident of the Contracting State of which he is a national.

(*d*) If he is a national of both Contracting States or of neither of them, the taxation authorities of the Contracting States shall determine the question by mutual agreement.

(3) Where by reason of the provisions of paragraph (1) of this Article, a person other than an individual is a resident of both Contracting States, then it shall be deemed to be a resident of the Contracting State in which its place of effective management is situated.

ARTICLE 4

(1) For the purposes of this Convention, the term "permanent establishment" means a fixed place of business in which the business of the enterprise is wholly or partly carried on.

(2) The term "permanent establishment" shall include especially:

(a) a place of management;

(b) a branch;

(c) an office;

(d) a factory;

(e) a workshop;

(f) a mine, quarry or other place of extraction of natural resources;

(g) a building site or construction or assembly project which exists for more than twelve months.

(3) The term "permanent establishment" shall not be deemed to include:

(a) the use of facilities solely for the purpose of storage, display or delivery of goods or merchandise belonging to the enterprise;

(b) the maintenance of a stock of goods or merchandise belonging to the enterprise solely for the purpose of storage, display or delivery;

(c) the maintenance of a stock of goods or merchandise belonging to the enterprise solely for the purpose of processing by another enterprise;

(d) the maintenance of a fixed place of business solely for the purpose of purchasing goods or merchandise, or for collecting information, for the enterprise;

(e) the maintenance of a fixed place of business solely for the purpose of advertising, for the supply of information, for scientific research or for similar activities which have a preparatory or auxiliary character, for the enterprise.

(4) An enterprise of a Contracting State shall be deemed to have a permanent establishment in the other Contracting State if it carries on the activity of providing the services of public entertainers or of athletes referred to in Article 15, in that other Contracting State.

(5) A person acting in a Contracting State on behalf of an enterprise of the other Contracting State—other than an agent of an independent status to whom paragraph (6) of this Article applies—shall be deemed to be a permanent establishment in the first-mentioned State if he has, and habitually exercises in that State, an authority to conclude contracts in the name of the enterprise, unless his activities are limited to the purchase of goods or merchandise for the enterprise.

(6) An enterprise of a Contracting State shall not be deemed to have a permanent establishment in the other Contracting State merely because it carries on business in that other State through a broker, general commission agent or any other agent of independent status, where such persons are acting in the ordinary course of their business.

(7) The fact that a company which is a resident of a Contracting State controls or is controlled by a company which is a resident of the other Contracting State, or which carries on business in that other State (whether through a permanent establishment or otherwise), shall not of itself constitute either company a permanent establishment of the other.

ARTICLE 5

(1) Income from immovable property may be taxed in the Contracting State in which such property is situated.

(2) (a) The term "immovable property" shall, subject to sub-paragraph (b) below, be defined in accordance with the law of the Contracting State in which the property in question is situated.

(*b*) The term "immovable property" shall in any case include property accessory to immovable property, livestock and equipment used in agriculture and forestry, rights to which the provisions of general law respecting landed property apply, usufruct of immovable property and rights to variable or fixed payments as consideration for the working of, or the right to work, mineral deposits, sources and other natural resources; ships, boats and aircraft shall not be regarded as immovable property.

(3) The provisions of paragraph (1) of this Article shall apply to income derived from the direct use, letting, or use in any other form of immovable property.

(4) The provisions of paragraphs (1) and (3) of this Article shall also apply to the income from immovable property of an enterprise and to income from immovable property used for the performance of professional services.

ARTICLE 6

(1) The industrial or commercial profits of a United Kingdom enterprise shall not be subject to South African tax unless the enterprise carries on a trade or business in South Africa through a permanent establishment situated therein. If it carries on a trade or business as aforesaid, tax may be imposed on those profits by South Africa, but only on so much of them as is attributable to that permanent establishment.

(2) The industrial or commercial profits of a South African enterprise shall not be subject to United Kingdom tax unless the enterprise carries on a trade or business in the United Kingdom through a permanent establishment situated therein. If it carries on a trade or business as aforesaid, tax may be imposed on those profits by the United Kingdom, but only on so much of them as is attributable to that permanent establishment.

(3) Where an enterprise of a Contracting State carries on a trade or business in the other Contracting State through a permanent establishment situated therein, there shall be attributed to that permanent establishment the industrial or commercial profits which it might be expected to derive in that other Contracting State if it were an independent enterprise engaged in the same or similar activities under the same or similar conditions and dealing at arm's length with the enterprise of which it is a permanent establishment.

(4) In the determination of the profits of a permanent establishment, there shall be allowed as deductions expenses of the enterprise (other than expenses which would not be deductible if the permanent establishment were a separate enterprise) which are incurred for the purposes of the permanent establishment including executive and general administrative expenses so incurred, whether in the Contracting State in which the permanent establishment is situated or elsewhere.

(5) No profits shall be attributed to a permanent establishment by reason of the mere purchase by that permanent establishment of goods or merchandise for the enterprise.

(6) The term "industrial or commercial profits" means income derived by an enterprise from the conduct of a trade or business, including income derived by an enterprise from the furnishing of services of employees or other personnel, but it does not include dividends, interest, royalties (as defined in Articles 9, 10 and 11) or rents other than dividends, interest, royalties or rents effectively connected with a trade or business carried on through a permanent establishment which an enterprise of one of the Contracting States has in the other Contracting State; nor does the term include remuneration for personal (including professional) services.

(7) Nothing in the foregoing provisions of this Article shall affect any of the provisions of the law of the United Kingdom relating to the liability to tax of a life assurance company not having its head office in the United Kingdom in respect of income from the investments of its life assurance fund, being provisions which (except in so far as they were rendered ineffective by virtue of Article III of the Convention between the

Government of the United Kingdom and the Government of South Africa for the Avoidance of Double Taxation and the Prevention of Fiscal Evasion with respect to Taxes on Income signed at Cape Town on 28th May, 1962(a)) were in force on the date of signature of this Convention, or which, if they have been modified since that date, have been modified only in minor respects so as not to affect their general character.

ARTICLE 7

A resident of a Contracting State shall be exempt from tax in the other Contracting State on profits from the operation of ships or aircraft other than profits from voyages of ships or aircraft confined solely to places in the other Contracting State.

ARTICLE 8

Where

(a) an enterprise of a Contracting State participates directly or indirectly in the management, control or capital of an enterprise of the other Contracting State; or

(b) the same persons participate directly or indirectly in the management, control or capital of an enterprise of a Contracting State and an enterprise of the other Contracting State;

and in either case, conditions are made or imposed between the two enterprises, in their commercial or financial relations, which differ from those which would be made between independent enterprises, then any profits which would, but for those conditions, have accrued to one of the enterprises, but, by reason of those conditions, have not so accrued, may be included in the profits of that enterprise and taxed accordingly.

ARTICLE 9

(1) Dividends paid by a company which is a resident of a Contracting State to a resident of the other Contracting State may be taxed in that other Contracting State.

(2) However, such dividends may be taxed in the Contracting State of which the company paying the dividends is a resident, and according to the law of that Contracting State, but the tax so charged shall not exceed:

(a) 5 per cent of the gross amount of the dividends if those dividends are beneficially owned by a company which is a resident of the other Contracting State and which controls directly or indirectly at least 25 per cent of the voting power of the company paying the dividends;

(b) in other cases 15 per cent of the gross amount of the dividends if those dividends are either

(i) beneficially owned by a company which is a resident of the other Contracting State, or

(ii) paid to a resident of the other Contracting State who is subject to tax there in respect thereof.

This paragraph shall not affect the taxation of the company in respect of the profits out of which the dividends are paid.

(3) The term "dividends" as used in this Article means income from shares or other rights, not being debt-claims, participating in profits, as well as income from other corporate rights assimilated to income from shares by the taxation law of the Contracting State of which the company making the distribution is a resident and also includes any other item of income (other than royalties exempt from tax under Article 11 of this Convention) which, under the law of the Contracting State of which the company paying the dividends is a resident, is treated as a dividend or distribution of a company.

(a) S.I. 1962/2352 (1962 III, p. 3264).

(4) If the beneficial owner of dividends being a resident of a Contracting State owns 10 per cent or more of the class of shares in respect of which the dividends are paid and does not suffer tax thereon in that State then paragraph (2) of this Article shall not apply to the dividends to the extent that they can have been paid only out of profits which the company paying the dividends earned or other income which it received in a period ending twelve months or more before the relevant date. For the purposes of this paragraph the term "relevant date" means the date on which the beneficial owner of the dividends became the owner of 10 per cent or more of the class of shares in question. Provided that this paragraph shall apply only if the shares were acquired primarily for the purpose of securing the benefit of this Article and not for bona fide commercial reasons.

(5) The provisions of paragraphs (1) and (2) of this Article shall not apply if the recipient of the dividends, being a resident of a Contracting State, has in the other Contracting State, of which the company paying the dividends is a resident, a permanent establishment and the holding by virtue of which the dividends are paid is effectively connected with the business carried on through such permanent establishment.

(6) Where a company which is a resident of a Contracting State derives profits or income from the other Contracting State, that other Contracting State may not impose any tax on the dividends paid by the company to persons who are not residents of that other Contracting State, or subject the company's undistributed profits to a tax on undistributed profits, even if the dividends paid or the undistributed profits consist wholly or partly of profits or income arising in such other State.

ARTICLE 10

(1) Interest arising in one of the Contracting States and paid to a resident of the other Contracting State may be taxed in that other State.

(2) However, such interest may be taxed in the Contracting State in which it arises, and according to the law of that Contracting State, but the tax so charged shall not exceed 10 per cent of the gross amount of the interest if the recipient is subject to tax thereon in the other Contracting State.

(3) The term "interest" as used in this Article means income from Government securities, from bonds or debentures, whether or not secured by mortgage and whether or not carrying a right to participate in profits, and from other debt-claims of every kind as well as all other income assimilated to income from money lent by the taxation law of the Contracting State in which the income arises.

(4) The provisions of paragraph (2) of this Article shall not apply if the recipient of the interest, being a resident of a Contracting State, has in the other Contracting State a permanent establishment and the debt-claim giving rise to the interest is effectively connected with a trade or business carried on through such permanent establishment.

(5) Any provision in the law of a Contracting State which relates only to interest paid to a non-resident company with or without any further requirement, or which relates only to interest payments between interconnected companies, with or without any further requirement, shall not operate so as to require such interest paid to a company which is a resident of the other Contracting State to be left out of account as a deduction in computing the taxable profits of the company paying the interest as being a dividend or distribution. The preceding sentence shall not apply to interest paid to a company which is a resident of a Contracting State in which more than 50 per cent of the voting power is controlled directly or indirectly by a person or persons resident in the other Contracting State.

(6) Interest shall be deemed to arise in a Contracting State when the payer is that State itself, a political sub-division, a local authority, or a resident of that State. Where, however, the person paying the interest, whether he is a resident of a Contracting State or not, has in a Contracting State a permanent establishment in connection with which the indebtedness on which the interest is paid was incurred, and such interest is borne by such permanent establishment, then such interest shall be deemed to arise in the Contracting State in which the permanent establishment is situated.

(7) Where, owing to a special relationship between the payer and the recipient or between both of them and some other person, the amount of the interest paid, having regard to the debt-claim for which it is paid, exceeds the amount which would have been agreed upon by the payer and the recipient in the absence of such relationship, the provisions of this Article shall apply only to the last-mentioned amount.

ARTICLE 11

(1) Royalties arising in a Contracting State and paid to a resident of the other Contracting State who is subject to tax there in respect thereof shall be exempt from tax in the first-mentioned Contracting State.

(2) The term "royalties" as used in this Article:

(a) means payments of any kind received as a consideration for the use of, or the right to use, any copyright of literary, artistic or scientific work (including cinematograph films and films or tapes for radio or television broadcasting), any patent, trade mark, design or model, plan, secret formula or process, or for the use of, or the right to use, industrial, commercial or scientific equipment, or for information concerning industrial, commercial or scientific experience, but

(b) does not include any amount paid in respect of the operation of a mine, oil well or quarry or of any other extraction of natural resources.

(3) The provisions of paragraph (1) of this Article shall not apply if the recipient of the royalties, being a resident of a Contracting State has in the other Contracting State a permanent establishment and the right or property giving rise to the royalties is effectively connected with a trade or business carried on through such permanent establishment.

(4) (a) Any provision of the law of a Contracting State which requires royalties paid by a company to be left out of account as a deduction in computing the company's taxable profits as being a distribution shall not operate in relation to royalties paid to a resident of the other Contracting State.

(b) The provisions of sub-paragraph (a) of this paragraph shall not apply to royalties paid to a company which is a resident of that other Contracting State where:

(i) the same persons participate directly or indirectly in the management or control of the company paying the royalties and the company deriving the royalties, and

(ii) more than 50 per cent of the voting power in the company deriving the royalties is controlled directly or indirectly by a person or persons resident in the Contracting State in which the company paying the royalties is resident.

(5) Where, owing to a special relationship between the payer and the recipient or between both of them and some other person, the amount of the royalties paid, having regard to the use, right or information for which they are paid, exceeds the amount which would have been agreed upon by the payer and the recipient in the absence of such relationship, the provisions of this Article shall apply only to the last-mentioned amount.

ARTICLE 12

(1) Capital gains from the alienation of any property forming part of the business property of a permanent establishment which an enterprise of a Contracting State has in the other Contracting State or of any property pertaining to a fixed base available to a resident of a Contracting State in the other Contracting State for the purpose of performing professional services, including such gains from the alienation of such a permanent establishment (alone or together with the whole enterprise) or of such a fixed base, may be taxed in the other Contracting State.

(2) Notwithstanding paragraph (1) of this Article, capital gains derived by a resident of a Contracting State from the alienation of ships and aircraft operated in international traffic and movable property pertaining to the operation of such ships and aircraft shall be taxable only in that Contracting State.

(3) Capital gains from the alienation of any property other than those mentioned in paragraph (1) of this Article shall be taxable only in the Contracting State of which the alienator is a resident.

(4) The provisions of paragraph (3) of this Article shall not affect the right of a Contracting State to levy according to its own law a tax on capital gains from the alienation of any property derived by an individual who is a resident of the other Contracting State and has been a resident of the first-mentioned Contracting State at any time during the five years immediately preceding the alienation of the property.

ARTICLE 13

Income derived by a resident of a Contracting State in respect of professional services or other independent activities of a similar character shall be subjected to tax only in that Contracting State unless he has a fixed base regularly available to him in the other Contracting State for the purpose of performing his activities. If he has such a fixed base, such part of that income as is attributable to that base may be taxed in the other Contracting State.

ARTICLE 14

(1) Subject to the provisions of Articles 16, 17 and 18, salaries, wages and other similar remuneration derived by a resident of a Contracting State in respect of an employment shall be subjected to tax only in that State unless the employment is exercised in the other Contracting State. If the employment is so exercised, such remuneration as is derived therefrom may be taxed in that other State.

(2) Notwithstanding the provisions of paragraph (1) of this Article, remuneration derived by a resident of a Contracting State in respect of an employment exercised in the other Contracting State shall be subjected to tax only in the first-mentioned State if:

(a) the recipient is present in the other State for a period or periods not exceeding in the aggregate 183 days in the fiscal year concerned, and

(b) the remuneration is paid by or on behalf of an employer who is not a resident of the other State, and

(c) the remuneration is not deducted from the profits of a permanent establishment or a fixed base which the employer has in the other State.

(3) In relation to remuneration of a director of a company derived from the company the preceding provisions of this Article shall apply as if the remuneration were remuneration of an employee in respect of an employment, and as if references to employers were references to the company.

(4) Notwithstanding the preceding provisions of this Article, remuneration for personal services performed aboard a ship or aircraft in international traffic may be taxed in the Contracting State of which the person deriving the profits from the operation of the ship or aircraft is a resident.

ARTICLE 15

Notwithstanding anything contained in this Convention, income derived by public entertainers, such as theatre, motion picture, radio or television artistes, and musicians, and by athletes, from their personal activities as such may be taxed in the Contracting State in which these activities are exercised.

ARTICLE 16

(1) Any pension (other than a pension of the kind referred to in paragraph (2) of Article 17) and any annuity, derived from sources within South Africa by an individual who is a resident of the United Kingdom and subject to United Kingdom tax in respect thereof, shall be exempt from South African tax.

(2) Any pension (other than a pension of the kind referred to in paragraph (2) of Article 17) and any annuity, derived from sources within the United Kingdom by an individual who is a resident of South Africa and subject to South African tax in respect thereof, shall be exempt from United Kingdom tax.

(3) The term "annuity" means a stated sum payable periodically at stated times, during life or during a specified or ascertainable period of time, under an obligation to make the payments in return for adequate and full consideration in money or money's worth.

ARTICLE 17

(1) Remuneration (other than pensions) paid by a Contracting State to any individual for services rendered to that Contracting State in the discharge of governmental functions shall be exempt from tax in the other Contracting State if the individual is not ordinarily resident in that State or is ordinarily resident in that State solely for the purpose of rendering those services.

(2) Any pension paid by a Contracting State to any individual for services rendered to that Contracting State in the discharge of governmental functions shall be exempt from tax in the other Contracting State, in so far as the remuneration for those services was exempt from tax in that State under paragraph (1) of this Article or would have been so exempt if this Convention had been in force at the time when the remuneration was paid.

(3) The provisions of this Article shall not apply to payments in respect of services rendered in connection with any trade or business carried on by either of the Contracting States for purposes of profit.

(4) For the purposes of this Article, the term "Contracting State", in the case of South Africa, includes the Administrations of the Provinces of South Africa.

ARTICLE 18

A professor or teacher who visits one of the Contracting States for a period not exceeding two years for the purpose of teaching at a university, college, school or other educational institution in that Contracting State and who is, or was immediately before that visit, a resident of the other Contracting State shall be exempt from tax in the first-mentioned Contracting State on any remuneration for such teaching in respect of which he is subject to tax in the other Contracting State.

ARTICLE 19

Payments which a student or business apprentice from a Contracting State who is present in the other Contracting State solely for the purpose of his education or training receives for the purpose of his maintenance, education or training, shall not be taxed in that other State, provided that such payments are made to him from sources outside that other State.

ARTICLE 20

Any income not dealt with in the foregoing provisions of this Convention derived by a resident of a Contracting State who is subject to tax there in respect thereof shall be subjected to tax only in that State.

ARTICLE 21

(1) Subject to the provisions of paragraph (3) of this Article, individuals who are residents of South Africa shall be entitled to the same personal allowances, reliefs and reductions for the purposes of United Kingdom taxation as British subjects not resident in the United Kingdom.

(2) Subject to the provisions of paragraph (3) of this Article, individuals who are residents of the United Kingdom shall be entitled to the same personal allowances, reliefs and reductions for the purposes of South African tax as South African citizens not resident in South Africa.

(3) Nothing in this Convention shall entitle an individual who is a resident of a Contracting State and whose income from the other Contracting State consists solely of dividends, interest or royalties (or solely of any combination thereof) to the personal allowances, reliefs and reductions of the kind referred to in this Article for the purposes of taxation in that other State.

ARTICLE 22

(1) Subject to the provisions of the law of the United Kingdom regarding the allowance as a credit against United Kingdom tax of tax payable in a territory outside the United Kingdom (which shall not affect the general principle hereof):

(a) South African tax payable under the laws of South Africa and in accordance with this Convention, whether directly or by deduction, on profits, income or chargeable gains from sources within South Africa (excluding in the case of a dividend, tax payable in respect of the profits out of which the dividend is paid) shall be allowed as a credit against any United Kingdom tax computed by reference to the same profits, income or chargeable gains by reference to which the South African tax is computed;

(b) in the case of a dividend paid by a company which is a resident of South Africa to a company which is resident in the United Kingdom and which controls directly or indirectly at least 10 per cent of the voting power in the South African company, the credit shall take into account (in addition to any South African tax creditable under sub-paragraph (a) above) the South African tax payable by the company in respect of the profits out of which such dividend is paid.

(2) Where United Kingdom tax is payable under the laws of the United Kingdom and in accordance with this Convention, whether directly or by deduction, on profits, income or chargeable gains derived from sources within the United Kingdom by a resident of South Africa, and that tax is borne by him, South Africa shall either impose no tax on such profits, income or chargeable gains or shall, subject to such provisions (which shall not affect the general principle hereof) as may be enacted in South Africa, allow as a credit against any South African tax payable in respect of such profits, income or chargeable gains so much of the United Kingdom tax as does not exceed the South African tax. In the case of a dividend paid by a company which is a resident of the United Kingdom to a company which is resident in South Africa and which controls directly or indirectly at least 10 per cent of the voting power in the United Kingdom company, any such credit shall take into account (in addition to any United Kingdom tax creditable under the preceding provisions of this paragraph) the United Kingdom tax payable by the company in respect of the profits out of which such dividend is paid.

(3) Paragraphs (1) and (2) of this Article shall have no application in relation to any tax which is repayable.

(4) For the purposes of this Article, remuneration for personal (including professional) services performed in a Contracting State shall be deemed to be income from sources within that State, and the services of an individual whose services are wholly or mainly performed in ships or aircraft operated in international traffic by a resident of a Contracting State shall be deemed to be performed in that State.

(5) Where profits on which an enterprise of a Contracting State has been charged to tax in that State are also included in the profits of an enterprise of the other State and the profits so included are profits which would have accrued to that enterprise of the other State if conditions operative between each of the enterprises had been those which might be expected to operate between independent enterprises dealing at arm's length, the amount of such profits included in the profits of both enterprises shall be treated for the purposes of this Article as income from a source in the other State of the enterprise of the first-mentioned State and relief shall be given accordingly under paragraph (1) or paragraph (2) of this Article.

ARTICLE 23

(1) The nationals of a Contracting State shall not be subjected in the territory of the other Contracting State to any taxation or any requirement connected therewith which is other or more burdensome than the taxation and connected requirements to which the nationals of the other State in the same circumstances are or may be subjected.

(2) In this Article the term "nationals" means:

(a) in relation to South Africa:

all South African citizens and all legal persons, partnerships and associations deriving their status as such from the law in force in South Africa.

(b) in relation to the United Kingdom:

all British subjects and British protected persons

(i) residing in the United Kingdom or any territory to which this Convention is extended under Article 26, or

(ii) deriving their status as such from connection with the United Kingdom or any territory to which this Convention is extended under Article 26,

and all legal persons, partnerships and associations deriving their status as such from the law in force in the United Kingdom or in any territory to which the Convention is extended under Article 26.

(3) The taxation on a permanent establishment which an enterprise of a Contracting State has in the other Contracting State shall not be less favourably levied in that other State than the taxation levied on enterprises of that other State carrying on the same activities.

(4) Enterprises of a Contracting State, the capital of which is wholly or partly owned or controlled, directly or indirectly, by one or more residents of the other Contracting State, shall not be subjected in the first-mentioned Contracting State to any taxation or any requirement connected therewith which is other or more burdensome than the taxation and connected requirements to which other similar enterprises of that first-mentioned State are or may be subjected.

(5) Nothing contained in this Article shall be construed as obliging either Contracting State to grant to individuals not resident in that State any of the personal allowances and reliefs for tax purposes which are granted to individuals so resident, nor as conferring any exemption from tax in a State in respect of dividends paid to a company which is a resident of the other State.

(6) In determining for the purpose of United Kingdom tax whether a company is a close company, the term "recognised stock exchange" shall include the Johannesburg Stock Exchange.

(7) In this Article the term "taxation" means the taxes which are the subject of this Convention.

ARTICLE 24

The taxation authorities of the Contracting States may communicate with each other directly for the purpose of giving effect to the provisions of this Convention and for resolving any difficulty or doubt as to the application or interpretation of this Convention.

ARTICLE 25

The taxation authorities of the Contracting States shall exchange such information (being information which is at their disposal under their respective taxation laws in the normal course of administration) as is necessary for carrying out the provisions of this Convention or for the prevention of fraud or for the administration of statutory provisions against legal avoidance in relation to the taxes which are the subject of this Convention. Any information so exchanged shall be treated as secret but may be disclosed to persons (including a court or administrative body) concerned with assessment, collection, enforcement or prosecution in respect of taxes which are the subject of this Convention. No information shall be exchanged which would disclose any trade, business, industrial or professional secret or any trade process.

ARTICLE 26

(1) This Convention may be extended either in its entirety or with modifications, by agreement between the Contracting States, to all or any of the territories for whose international relations either Contracting State is responsible and which impose taxes substantially similar in character to those which are the subject of this Convention, and any such extension shall take effect from such date and subject to such modification and conditions (including conditions as to termination) as may be specified and agreed between the Contracting States in Notes to be exchanged for this purpose.

(2) The termination in respect of the United Kingdom or South Africa of this Convention shall, unless otherwise expressly agreed by both Contracting States, terminate the application of this Convention to any territory to which the Convention has been extended under this Article.

ARTICLE 27

(1) This Convention shall be ratified and the instruments of ratification shall be exchanged in South Africa as soon as possible.

(2) This Convention shall enter into force after the expiration of thirty days following the date on which the instruments of ratification are exchanged(a) and shall thereupon have effect:

(a) in the United Kingdom:

(i) as respects income tax (including surtax) and capital gains tax, for any year of assessment beginning on or after 6th April, 1968; and

(ii) as respects corporation tax, for any financial year beginning on or after 1st April, 1968;

(b) in South Africa:

(i) as respects taxes on income, for any year of assessment beginning on or after 1st March, 1968;

(ii) as respects non-resident shareholders' tax, on dividends declared on or after 1st March, 1968; and

(iii) as respects non-residents tax on interest, on interest payable on or after 1st March, 1968.

(3) Subject to paragraph (4) of this Article the Convention between the Government of the United Kingdom and the Government of South Africa for the Avoidance of Double Taxation and the Prevention of Fiscal Evasion with respect to Taxes on Income signed at Cape Town on 28th May, 1962, together with the Protocol amending that Convention signed at Cape Town on 14th June, 1967(b), shall terminate and cease to be effective as respects taxes to which this Convention in accordance with paragraph (2) of this Article applies.

(a) Instruments of ratification were exchanged on 29th May 1969.
(b) S.I. 1967/1489 (1967 III, p. 4199).

(4) Where any greater relief from tax in a Contracting State would have been afforded by any provision of the Convention signed at Cape Town on 28th May, 1962, as amended by the Protocol signed at Cape Town on 14th June, 1967, than is due under this Convention, any such provision as aforesaid shall continue to have effect in that State:

(a) in the case of the United Kingdom:

for any year of assessment or financial year beginning before the entry into force of this Convention;

(b) in the case of South Africa:

(i) as respects taxes on income, for any year of assessment beginning before the entry into force of this Convention;

(ii) as respects non-resident shareholders' tax, on dividends declared before the entry into force of this Convention; and

(iii) as respects non-residents tax on interest, on interest payable before the entry into force of this Convention.

(5) This Convention shall not affect any agreement in force which, in accordance with Article XXIV of the Convention signed at Cape Town on 28th May, 1962, extends that Convention to any territory.

ARTICLE 28

This Convention shall continue in effect indefinitely but either of the Contracting States may, on or before the thirtieth day of June in any calendar year after the year 1972 give, through diplomatic channels, notice of termination to the other Contracting State and, in such event, this Convention shall cease to have effect:

(a) in the United Kindom:

(i) as respects income tax (including surtax) and capital gains tax, for any year of assessment beginning on or after 6th April in the calendar year next following that in which the notice is given;

(ii) as respects corporation tax, for any financial year beginning on or after 1st April in the calendar year next following that in which the notice is given;

(b) in South Africa:

(i) as respects taxes on income, for any year of assessment beginning on or after 1st March in the calendar year next following that in which the notice is given;

(ii) as respects non-residents shareholders' tax, on dividends declared on or after 1st March in the calendar year next following that in which the notice is given; and

(iii) as respects non-residents tax on interest, on interest payable on or after 1st March in the calendar year next following that in which the notice is given.

In witness whereof the undersigned, duly authorised thereto by their respective Governments, have signed this Convention.

Done in duplicate at London this 21st day of November, 1968, in the English and Afrikaans languages, both texts being equally authoritative.

For the Government of the United Kingdom of Great Britain and Northern Ireland:

MAURICE FOLEY

For the Government of the Republic of South Africa:

H. G. LUTTIG

EXPLANATORY NOTE
(This Note is not part of the Order.)

Under the Convention with South Africa scheduled to this Order (which is to replace the Convention signed in Cape Town on 28th May, 1962, as amended by the Protocol signed in Cape Town on 14th June, 1967) shipping and air transport profits, certain trading profits not arising through a permanent establishment, royalties, pensions (other than Government pensions) and the earnings of temporary business visitors are (subject to certain conditions) to be taxed only in the country of the taxpayer's residence. Government salaries and pensions are normally to be taxed by the paying Government only. Remuneration of visiting teachers and professors and payments made for the maintenance of visiting students are (subject to certain conditions) to be exempt in the country visited. Capital gains are normally to be taxed only in the country of the taxpayer's residence unless they arise from the disposal of the assets of a permanent establishment which the taxpayer has in the other country.

The rate of tax in the source country on dividends paid to residents of the other country is, in general, not to exceed 5 per cent if the recipient is a company which controls at least 25 per cent of the voting power in the paying company, or 15 per cent in other cases. The rate of tax in the source country on interest paid to residents of the other country is, in general, not to exceed 10 per cent.

Where income continues to be taxable in both countries, relief from double taxation is to be given by the country of the taxpayer's residence. In the case of dividends, credit for South African tax on the profits out of which the dividend is paid is to be given for United Kingdom tax purposes where the recipient of the dividend is a company which controls at least 10 per cent of the voting power in the paying company. There are provisions safeguarding nationals and enterprises of one country against discriminatory taxation in the other country, and for the exchange of information and consultation between the taxation authorities of the two countries.

The Convention is in general to take effect in the United Kingdom for 1968/69 and subsequent years.

STATUTORY INSTRUMENTS

1969 No. 865

PATENTS
DESIGNS
TRADE MARKS

The Patents Etc. (Laos) (Convention) Order 1969

Made - - -		*25th June* 1969
Coming into Operation		*8th July* 1969

At the Court at Buckingham Palace, the 25th day of June 1969.

Present,

The Queen's Most Excellent Majesty in Council

Her Majesty, in exercise of the powers conferred upon Her by section 95 of the Patents Act 1949(a), section 37 of the Registered Designs Act 1949(b) and section 88 of the Patents and Designs Act 1907(c), as amended (d), is pleased, by and with the advice of Her Privy Council, to order, and it is hereby ordered, as follows:—

1. This Order may be cited as the Patents Etc. (Laos) (Convention) Order 1969, and shall come into operation on 8th July 1969.

2. The Interpretation Act 1889(e) shall apply to the interpretation of this Order as it applies to the interpretation of an Act of Parliament.

3. The Patents Etc. (Central African Republic, Chad, Laos, Upper Volta and Roumania) (Convention) Order 1963(f) shall have effect as if the reference in article 1 thereof to the Kingdom of Laos were omitted.

W. G. Agnew.

EXPLANATORY NOTE

(*This Note is not part of the Order.*)

This Order takes account of the denunciation by the Kingdom of Laos of the International Convention for the Protection of Industrial Property (as revised in Lisbon in 1958). It provides that Laos is no longer to be a Convention Country for any of the purposes of the Acts relating to Patents, Designs and Trade Marks.

(a) 1949 c. 87.   (b) 1949 c. 88.   (c) 1907 c. 29.
(d) The amendments are not directly relevant to this Order.
(e) 1889 c. 63.   (f) S.I. 1963/1919 (1963 III, p. 3765).

STATUTORY INSTRUMENTS

1969 No. 866 (C. 20)

ROAD TRAFFIC

The Vehicle and Driving Licences Act 1969 (Commencement No. 1) Order 1969

Made - - - -	*25th June* 1969
Laid before Parliament	*27th June* 1969
Coming into Operation	*30th June* 1969

The Minister of Transport hereby makes this Order in exercise of his powers under section 38(2) of the Vehicle and Driving Licences Act 1969(a) and of all other enabling powers.

1. This Order may be cited as the Vehicle and Driving Licences Act 1969 (Commencement No. 1) Order 1969.

2. Sections 16(2), in so far as it relates to paragraph 13 of Schedule 2, 16(5), 33, 34 and 38 of the Vehicle and Driving Licences Act 1969 shall come into operation on 30th June 1969.

Given under the Official Seal of the Minister of Transport the 25th June 1969.

(L.S.)

Richard Marsh,
Minister of Transport.

EXPLANATORY NOTE

(This Note is not part of the Order.)

This Order brings into operation on the 30th June 1969 the following provisions of the Vehicle and Driving Licences Act 1969:—

Section 16(2), in so far as it relates to Schedule 2, paragraph 13, which amends paragraph 1 of Schedule 15 to the Road Traffic Act 1960. The amendment will permit the Minister of Transport to prescribe heavy goods vehicles the driving of which will not entitle a person to claim a driver's licence for heavy goods vehicles under the transitional provisions in Schedule 15.

Section 16(5), which reduces from 10 to 5 years the period within which a person is entitled to be granted a driver's licence for heavy goods vehicles from the time he passed the driving test or held a full licence.

Section 33, which relates to interpretation.

Section 34, which relates to orders and regulations.

Section 38, which relates to the short title, commencement and extent.

(a) 1969 c. 27.

STATUTORY INSTRUMENTS

1969 No. 867

TAXES

The Selective Employment Payments Variation Order 1969

Laid before Parliament in draft
Made - - - *25th June* 1969
Coming into Operation *7th July* 1969

The Secretary of State with the consent of the Treasury in exercise of her powers under section 9(1) of the Selective Employment Payments Act 1966(a) (hereinafter referred to as "the principal Act") and of all other powers enabling her in that behalf hereby makes the following Order, a draft of which has been approved by resolution of each House of Parliament.

Citation, commencement and interpretation

1.—(1) This Order may be cited as the Selective Employment Payments Variation Order 1969 and shall come into operation on 7th July 1969.

(2) The Interpretation Act 1889(b) shall apply to the interpretation of this Order as it applies to the interpretation of an Act of Parliament.

(3) The references in this Order to sections are references to sections of the principal Act.

Additions to employments to which section 1 applies

2.—(1) Section 1 (which, subject to the provisions of the Revenue Act 1968(c) specifies employments as respects which an employer is entitled to selective employment premium) shall have effect as if to subsection (2) (*a*) thereof there were added the following:—

"(vii) the conversion, by using machinery to remove deleterious material or by using machinery to alter the size or shape, of scrap metal to a recognised trade specification for making new metal or for use in the manufacture of chemicals; or

(viii) the production of waste paper or waste paper board in bales to a recognised trade specification for making pulp, by the use of machinery, both to remove deleterious material and to produce the said bales; or

(ix) the production of cinematograph films for public exhibition including television presentation; or

(x) industrial photoprinting, that is to say, so much of the activities falling under sub-head 2 of minimum list heading 899 (which relates to photography) as consists of the photographic reproduction of technical drawings and the production for exhibition, display or publicity, in each case for the purpose of another's business (including the purposes of a Government Department, a local authority or a public body), of prints of photographic enlargements."

(a) 1966 c. 32.   (b) 1889 c. 63.   (c) 1968 c. 11.

(2) The Selective Employment Payments Variation Order 1968(a) (Article 2 of which specifies additional employments to which section 1 applies) shall have effect subject to the following amendments (being amendments designed to include in the said section 1 certain further additional employments):—

    (*a*) in sub-paragraph (*a*) and in sub-paragraph (*b*) of Article 1(5) there shall be added at the end of each sub-paragraph the words "or a slaughter-house provided by a local authority"

    (*b*) in Article 2 there shall be substituted for the words "slaughtering animals in a knacker's yard or slaughterhouse" the words "slaughter-ing animals in or from a knacker's yard or in a slaughterhouse".

Additions to employments to which section 2 applies

3. Section 2 (which specifies employments as respects which an employer is entitled to selective employment refund) shall have effect as if to subsection (3) (*a*) thereof there were added the following:—

"(v) heading 601 (which relates to gas);".

Signed by order of the Secretary of State.

Roy Hattersley,
Joint Parliamentary Under Secretary of State,
Department of Employment and Productivity.

25th June 1969.

We consent.

Walter Harrison,
B. K. O'Malley,
Two of the Lords Commissioners
of Her Majesty's Treasury.

25th June 1969.

EXPLANATORY NOTE
(*This Note is not part of the Order.*)

This Order adds to the employments which may be eligible for payments under section 1 of the Selective Employment Payments Act 1966, employments in establishments engaged in certain activities relating to processing of scrap metal and waste paper, the production of cinematograph films and industrial photo-printing, establishments engaged in slaughtering animals in a local authority slaughterhouse, and establishments which include a knacker's yard where most of the slaughtering of animals takes place otherwise than at the yard, and also to employments which may be eligible for refund under section 2, employments in establishments engaged in processing natural gas.

(a) S.I. 1968/1147 (1968 II, p. 3133).

STATUTORY INSTRUMENTS

1969 No. 868

WAGES COUNCILS

The Wages Regulation (Linen and Cotton Handkerchief etc.) Order 1969

Made - - - -	*25th June* 1969
Coming into Operation	*23rd July* 1969

Whereas the Secretary of State has received from the Linen and Cotton Handkerchief and Household Goods and Linen Piece Goods Wages Council (Great Britain) the wages regulation proposals set out in the Schedule hereto ;

Now, therefore, the Secretary of State in exercise of her powers under section 11 of the Wages Councils Act 1959(a), and of all other powers enabling her in that behalf, hereby makes the following Order:—

1. This Order may be cited as the Wages Regulation (Linen and Cotton Handkerchief etc.) Order 1969.

2.—(1) In this Order the expression " the specified date " means the 23rd July 1969, provided that where, as respects any worker who is paid wages at intervals not exceeding seven days, that date does not correspond with the beginning of the period for which the wages are paid, the expression " the specified date " means, as respects that worker, the beginning of the next such period following that date.

(2) The Interpretation Act 1889(b) shall apply to the interpretation of this Order as it applies to the interpretation of an Act of Parliament and as if this Order and the Order hereby revoked were Acts of Parliament.

3. The wages regulation proposals set out in the Schedule hereto shall have effect as from the specified date and as from that date the Wages Regulation (Linen and Cotton Handkerchief etc.) Order 1967(c), shall cease to have effect.

Signed by order of the Secretary of State.

25th June 1969.

A. A. Jarratt,
Deputy Under Secretary of State,
Department of Employment and Productivity.

SCHEDULE

Article 3

The following minimum remuneration shall be substituted for the statutory minimum remuneration fixed by the Wages Regulation (Linen and Cotton Handkerchief etc.) Order 1967 (Order H.L. (68)).

(a) 1959 c. 69.   (b) 1889 c. 63.   (c) S.I. 1967/1513 (1967 III, p. 4220).

STATUTORY MINIMUM REMUNERATION

PART I

GENERAL

1. The minimum remuneration payable to a worker to whom this Schedule applies for all work except work to which a minimum overtime rate applies under Part IV of this Schedule is : —

(1) in the case of a time worker, the hourly general minimum time rate payable to the worker under Part II or Part III of this Schedule ;

(2) in the case of a male worker employed on piece work, piece rates each of which would yield, in the circumstances of the case, to an ordinary worker at least the same amount of money as the hourly general minimum time rate which would be payable to the worker under Part III of this Schedule if he were a time worker ;

(3) in the case of a female worker employed on piece work, piece rates each of which would yield, in the circumstances of the case, to an ordinary worker at least the same amount of money as the hourly piece work basis time rate applicable to the worker under Part II of this Schedule.

PART II

FEMALE WORKERS

GENERAL MINIMUM TIME RATES

2. The general minimum time rates payable to female workers are as follows :—

	Per hour		Per week of 41½ hours	
	s.	d.	s.	d.
Aged 18 years or over	3	7·08	149	0
„ 17 and under 18 years	2	9·11	114	6
„ 16 „ „ 17 „	2	3·33	94	6
„ under 16 years	1	8·60	71	3

Provided that the general minimum time rate payable, during her first year's employment in the trade, to a worker who enters, or has entered, the trade for the first time at or over the age of 18 years shall be : —

	Per hour		Per week of 41½ hours	
During the 1st three months of such employment	2	3·98	96	9
„ „ 2nd „ „ „ „ „	2	6·36	105	0
„ „ 3rd „ „ „ „ „	2	9·69	116	6
„ „ 4th „ „ „ „ „	3	0·72	127	0

PIECE WORK BASIS TIME RATE

	Per hour		Per week of 41½ hours	
	s.	d.	s.	d.
3. The piece work basis time rate applicable to female workers of any age employed on piece work is ...	3	9·47	157	3

Part III

MALE WORKERS

GENERAL MINMUM TIME RATES

4. The general minimum time rates payable to male workers are as follows:—

	Per hour		Per week of 41½ hours	
	s.	d.	s.	d.
Aged 19 years or over	5	1·23	211	9
„ 18½ and under 19 years	4	6·14	187	3
„ 18 „ „ 18½ „	3	11·93	165	9
„ 17½ „ „ 18 „	3	4·19	139	0
„ 17 „ „ 17½ „	2	11·57	123	0
„ 16½ „ „ 17 „	2	6·94	107	0
„ 16 „ „ 16½ „	2	2·31	91	0
„ 15½ „ „ 16 „	1	11·20	80	3
„ under 15½ years	1	8·39	70	6

Part IV

OVERTIME AND WAITING TIME

MINIMUM OVERTIME RATES

5.—(1) Minimum overtime rates are payable to any worker to whom this Schedule applies as follows:—

    (a) on any day other than a Saturday or Sunday—

        (i) for the first two hours worked in excess of 8 hours and 18 minutes ... ...   time-and-a-quarter

        (ii) thereafter ... ...   time-and-a-half

        Provided that where the employer and the worker by agreement in writing fix in respect of each weekday the number of hours after which a minimum overtime rate shall be payable and the total number of such hours amounts to 41½ weekly, the following minimum overtime rates shall be payable in substitution for those set out above—

        (i) for the first two hours worked in excess of the agreed number of hours ... ...   time-and-a-quarter

        (ii) thereafter ... ...   time-and-a-half

    (b) on a Saturday—

        (i) for the first two hours worked ... ...   time-and-a-quarter

        (ii) thereafter ... ...   time-and-a-half

    (c) on a Sunday—

        for all time worked ... ...   double time

(2) In this Part of this Schedule the expressions " time-and-a-quarter ", " time-and-a-half " and " double time " mean, respectively, one and a quarter times, one and a half times and twice the minimum remuneration otherwise payable to the worker.

WAITING TIME

6.—(1) A worker is entitled to payment of the minimum remuneration specified in this Schedule for all time during which he is present on the premises of his employer, unless he is present thereon in any of the following circumstances:—

    (a) without the employer's consent, express or implied;

    (b) for some purpose unconnected with his work and other than that of waiting for work to be given to him to perform;

(c) by reason only of the fact that he is resident thereon ;

(d) during normal meal times in a room or place in which no work is being done, and he is not waiting for work to be given to him to perform.

(2) The minimum remuneration payable under sub-paragraph (1) of this paragraph to a piece worker when not engaged on piece work is that which would be payable if he were a time worker.

PART V

APPLICABILITY OF STATUTORY MINIMUM REMUNERATION

7. Subject to the provisions of paragraph 8, this Schedule applies to workers in relation to whom the Linen and Cotton Handkerchief and Household Goods and Linen Piece Goods Wages Council (Great Britain) operates, that is to say, workers employed in Great Britain in the trade specified in the Regulations made by the Minister and dated 28th May 1920(a), with respect to the Constitution and Proceedings of the Trade Board for the Linen and Cotton Handkerchief and Household Goods and Linen Piece Goods Trade (Great Britain) namely : —

(1) The making of such articles as are specified in (a) and (b) below, from linen or cotton or mixed linen and cotton fabrics (excepting knitted fabrics), or from other textile fabrics when the work is carried on in establishments mainly engaged in the making of such articles from the before-mentioned fabrics, viz. : —

(a) Handkerchiefs (including mufflers or flags when made in association or conjunction with handkerchiefs) ;

(b) Bed-linen, towels, dusters, table-napery, bed-spreads, tea-cloths, table-centres, sideboard-covers, cushion-covers, or similar household articles ;

including all or any of the following operations : —

(i) Hooking, cutting or tearing the material ;

(ii) Vice-folding ;

(iii) Machine hemming, hem-stitching, spoking, over-locking, tambouring, button-holing, and other plain or fancy machine stitching ;

(iv) All processes of embroidery or decorative needlework done by machine, whether before or after the making of the articles of the description specified above ;

(v) The following processes if done by machine—thread-drawing, thread-clipping, top-sewing, scalloping, nickelling and paring ;

(vi) All processes of laundering, smoothing, folding, ornamenting, boxing, finishing, warehousing, packing and other similar operations incidental to or appertaining to the making of the articles of the description specified above.

(2) The making up in linen warehouses or in establishments mainly engaged in linen lapping, of linen or mixed linen and cotton or other textile fabrics in the piece, or of linen or mixed linen and cotton or other textile articles cut from the piece, including—

Measuring, cutting, lapping, ornamenting, boxing, warehousing, packing and similar operations.

8. Notwithstanding the provisions of paragraph 7, this Schedule does not apply to workers who are persons registered as handicapped by disablement in pursuance of the Disabled Persons (Employment) Acts 1944 and 1958(b), in respect of their employment by Remploy Limited.

(a) S.R. & O. 1920/854 (1920 II, p. 854). (b) 1944 c. 10; 1958 c. 33.

EXPLANATORY NOTE

(This Note is not part of the Order.)

This Order, which has effect from 23rd July 1969, sets out the statutory minimum remuneration payable in substitution for that fixed by the Wages Regulation (Linen and Cotton Handkerchief etc.) Order 1967 (Order H.L.(68)), which Order is revoked.

New provisions are printed in italics.

STATUTORY INSTRUMENTS

1969 No. 869
WAGES COUNCILS
The Wages Regulation (Linen and Cotton Handkerchief etc.) (Holidays) Order 1969

Made - - -	*25th June* 1969
Coming into Operation	*23rd July* 1969

Whereas the Secretary of State has received from the Linen and Cotton Handkerchief and Household Goods and Linen Piece Goods Wages Council (Great Britain) the wages regulation proposals set out in the Schedule hereto ;

Now, therefore, the Secretary of State in exercise of her powers under section 11 of the Wages Councils Act 1959(a), and of all other powers enabling her in that behalf, hereby makes the following Order :—

1. This Order may be cited as the Wages Regulation (Linen and Cotton Handkerchief etc.) (Holidays) Order 1969.

2.—(1) In this Order the expression "the specified date" means the 23rd July 1969, provided that where, as respects any worker who is paid wages at intervals not exceeding seven days, that date does not correspond with the beginning of the period for which the wages are paid, the expression "the specified date" means, as respects that worker, the beginning of the next such period following that date.

(2) The Interpretation Act 1889(b) shall apply to the interpretation of this Order as it applies to the interpretation of an Act of Parliament and as if this Order and the Order hereby revoked were Acts of Parliament.

3. The wages regulation proposals set out in the Schedule hereto shall have effect as from the specified date and as from that date the Wages Regulation (Linen and Cotton Handkerchief etc.) (Holidays) Order 1967(c) shall cease to have effect.

Signed by order of the Secretary of State.

25th June 1969.

A. A. Jarratt,
Deputy Under Secretary of State,
Department of Employment and Productivity.

Article 3   SCHEDULE

The following provisions as to holidays and holiday remuneration shall be substituted for the provisions as to holidays and holiday remuneration set out in the Wages Regulation (Linen and Cotton Handkerchief etc.) (Holidays) Order 1967 (hereinafter referred to as "Order H.L.(69)").

PART I
APPLICATION

1. This Schedule applies to every worker (other than an outworker) for whom statutory minimum remuneration has been fixed.

(a) 1959 c. 69.   (b) 1889 c. 63.
(c) S.I. 1967/1514 (1967 III, p. 4225).

Part II

CUSTOMARY HOLIDAYS

2.—(1) Subject to the provisions of sub-paragraph (3) of this paragraph an employer shall allow a day of holiday (hereinafter referred to as a "customary holiday") in each year on each of the days specified in the next following sub-paragraph to every worker in his employment to whom this Schedule applies who:—

(a) has been in his employment throughout the 8 weeks immediately preceding the said day; and

(b) has worked for the employer during the whole or part of that period; and

(c) is in his employment on the day of the customary holiday.

(2) The said customary holidays are:—

(a) (i) in England and Wales—

Christmas Day (or, if Christmas Day falls on a Sunday, such week day as may be appointed by national proclamation, or, if none is so appointed, the next following Tuesday), Boxing Day, New Year's Day, Good Friday, Easter Monday and Whit Monday (or where another day is substituted therefor by national proclamation, that day);

(ii) in Scotland—

New Year's Day and the day following or, if New Year's Day falls on a Sunday, the following Monday and Tuesday, or, if New Year's Day falls on a Saturday, New Year's Day and the following Monday, the local Spring holiday, the local Autumn holiday, and two other days (being days on which the worker normally works for the employer) in the course of each calender year, to be fixed by the employer in consultation with the worker or his representative and notified to the worker not less than three weeks in advance;

or (b) in the case of each of the said days (other than a day fixed by the employer in Scotland and notified to the worker as aforesaid) a day substituted therefor by agreement between the employer and the worker to be allowed within the period of six weeks next ensuing.

(3) Notwithstanding the preceding provisions of this paragraph an employer may (except where in the case of a woman or young person such requirement would be unlawful) require a worker who is otherwise entitled to any customary holiday under the foregoing provisions of this Schedule to work thereon and, in lieu of any customary holiday on which he so works, the employer shall allow the worker a day's holiday (hereinafter referred to as "a holiday in lieu of a customary holiday") on a weekday on which he would normally work for the employer within the period of six weeks next ensuing.

Part III

ANNUAL HOLIDAY

3.—(1) Subject to the provisions of paragraph 4, in addition to the holidays specified in Part II of this Schedule an employer shall, between the date on which the provisions of this Schedule become effective and 5th April 1970 and in each succeeding period of 12 months commencing on 6th April allow a holiday (hereinafter referred to as an "annual holiday") to every worker in his employment to whom this Schedule applies who has been employed by him during the 12 months ending on 5th April immediately preceding the commencement of the holiday season (hereinafter referred to as the "qualifying period") for any of the periods of employment (calculated in accordance with the provisions of paragraph 10) specified below and the duration of the annual holiday shall, in the case of each such worker, be related to his period of employment during that 12 months as follows:—

Period of employment					Duration of annual holiday in 12 months commencing 6th April		
					1969	1970	1971 and thereafter
At least 48 weeks				...	13 *days*	14 *days*	15 *days*
,, ,, 43 ,, ...				...	9 ,,	9 ,,	9 ,,
,, ,, 38 ,, ...				...	8 ,,	8 ,,	8 ,,
,, ,, 33 ,, ...				...	7 ,,	7 ,,	7 ,,
,, ,, 28 ,, ...				...	6 ,,	6 ,,	6 ,,
,, ,, 24 ,, ...				...	5 ,,	5 ,,	5 ,,
,, ,, 19 ,, ...				...	4 ,,	4 ,,	4 ,,
,, ,, 14 ,, ...				...	3 ,,	3 ,,	3 ,,
,, ,, 9 ,, ...				...	2 ,,	2 ,,	2 ,,
,, ,, 4 ,, ...				...	1 day	1 day	1 day

(2) Notwithstanding the provisions of the foregoing sub-paragraph the number of days of annual holiday which an employer is required to allow to a worker—

(*a*) in the holiday season commencing 1st May 1969 shall not exceed in the aggregate—

in the case of a worker with a normal working week of four days or more, twice the number of days constituting the worker's normal working week, *plus three days;* and

in the case of a worker with a normal working week of less than four days, *three times the number of days constituting the worker's normal working week;*

(*b*) in the holiday season commencing *6th April 1970* shall not exceed in the aggregate—

in the case of a worker with a normal working week of four days or more, twice the number of days constituting the worker's normal working week, *plus four days;* and

in the case of a worker with a normal working week of less than four days, *three times the number of days constituting the worker's normal working week;* and

(*c*) in the holiday season commencing *6th April 1971* and in each succeeding holiday season commencing on *6th April*, shall not exceed in the aggregate *three times the number of days constituting the worker's normal working week.*

(3) In this Schedule the expression "holiday season" means in relation to the year 1969 the period commencing on 1st May 1969 and ending on *5th April 1970* and in relation to the year 1970 and each succeeding year, the period commencing on *6th April* and ending on the next following *5th April.*

(4) The duration of the worker's annual holiday in the holiday season ending on *5th April 1970* shall be reduced by any days of annual holiday duly allowed to him by the employer under the provisions of Order H.L. (69) between 1st May 1969 and the date on which the provisions of this Schedule become effective.

4.—(1) Subject to the provisions of this paragraph an annual holiday under this Schedule shall be allowed *in accordance with an agreement between the employer and the worker or his representative* on consecutive working days being days on which the worker normally works for the employer, and days of annual holiday shall be treated as consecutive notwithstanding that a holiday under the provisions of Part II of this Schedule intervenes.

(2)(*a*) Where the number of days of annual holiday for which a worker has qualified exceeds the number of days constituting his normal working week, but does not exceed twice that number, the holiday may be allowed in two periods of consecutive working days; so, however, that when a holiday is so allowed, one of the periods shall consist of a number of such days not less than the number of days constituting the worker's normal working week.

(b) Where the number of days of annual holiday for which a worker has qualified exceeds twice the number of days constituting his normal working week the holiday may be allowed *in the holiday season* as follows:—

    (i) as to two periods of consecutive working days, each such period not being less than the period constituting the worker's normal working week; and

    (ii) as to any additional days, on working days being days on which the worker normally works for the employer.

(3) Subject to the provisions of sub-paragraph (1) of this paragraph, any day of annual holiday under this Schedule may be allowed on a day on which the worker is entitled to a day of holiday or to a half-holiday under any enactment other than the Wages Councils Act 1959.

5. The employer shall give to the worker notice of the commencing date and duration of his annual holiday either individually or by a notice which the worker has reasonable opportunities of reading in the course of his employment or which is reasonably accessible to him in some other way. Such notice shall be given not later than the 31st December immediately preceding the annual holiday or when the worker commences employment with the employer, whichever is the later.

PART IV

HOLIDAY REMUNERATION

A.—CUSTOMARY HOLIDAYS AND HOLIDAYS IN LIEU OF CUSTOMARY HOLIDAYS

6.—(1) Subject to the provisions of this paragraph, for each day allowed as a holiday under Part II of this Schedule the worker shall be paid by his employer the following remuneration:—

    (a) in respect of days allowed in the holiday season commencing on 1st May 1969, in the case of a worker who has been in the employment of the employer for the whole of the 12 months ending on 5th April 1969, an amount equal to *one-thirteenth of 5 per cent* of his total remuneration (determined in accordance with paragraph 11) during that period;

    (b) in respect of days allowed in the holiday season commencing on 6th April 1970, in the case of a worker who has been in the employment of the employer for the whole of the 12 months immediately preceding, an amount equal to *one-fourteenth of 5.4 per cent* of his total remuneration (determined in accordance with paragraph 11) during that period; and

    (c) in respect of days allowed in the holiday season commencing on 6th April 1971 and each succeeding holiday season, in the case of a worker who has been in the employment of the employer for the whole of the 12 months ending on 5th April immediately preceding, an amount equal to *one-fifteenth of 5.8 per cent* of his total remuneration (determined in accordance with paragraph 11) during that period;

    (d) in the case of a worker who has been in the employment of the employer for any lesser period, one-fifth of his average weekly earnings, such average weekly earnings to be determined by dividing the worker's total remuneration (determined in accordance with paragraph 11) by the number of weeks of employment (calculated in accordance with paragraph 10).

(2) Subject to the provisions of sub-paragraphs (3) and (4) of this paragraph, the holiday remuneration in respect of any holiday allowed under Part II of this Schedule shall be paid by the employer to the worker on the pay day on which wages are paid for the week including the holiday.

(3) Where a worker ceases to be employed before being allowed a holiday in lieu of a customary holiday to which he has become entitled he shall be paid the holiday remuneration for that day immediately on the termination of his employment and in such a case sub-paragraph (4) of this paragraph shall not apply.

(4) Payment of remuneration in respect of the said holiday is subject to the condition that the worker (unless excused by the employer or absent by reason of proved incapacity due to sickness or injury) works for the employer the number of hours ordinarily worked by him or such lesser number of hours as may be required by the employer, on the first working day on which work is available to him following the holiday.

B.—ANNUAL HOLIDAY

7.—(1) Subject to the provisions of this paragraph and of paragraph 8, a worker qualified to be allowed an annual holiday under Part III of this Schedule shall be paid as holiday remuneration by his employer in respect thereof, on the last pay day preceding such annual holiday—

(a) in relation to the holiday season commencing 1st May 1969, an amount equal to 5 per cent of his total remuneration (determined in accordance with paragraph 11) during the qualifying period;

(b) in relation to the holiday season commencing 6th April 1970, an amount equal to 5.4 per cent of his total remuneration (determined in accordance with paragraph 11) during the qualifying period; and

(c) in relation to the holiday season commencing 6th April 1971, and to each succeeding holiday season, an amount equal to 5.8 per cent of his total remuneration (determined in accordance with paragraph 11) during the qualifying period.

(2) Where under the provisions of paragraph 4 an annual holiday is allowed in more than one period, the holiday remuneration shall be apportioned accordingly.

8. Where any accrued holiday remuneration has been paid by the employer to the worker (in accordance with paragraph 9 of this Schedule or with Order H.L. (69)) in respect of employment during any of the periods referred to in that paragraph or that Order, the amount of holiday remuneration payable by the employer in respect of any annual holiday for which the worker has qualified by reason of employment during the said period shall be reduced by the amount of the said accrued holiday remuneration unless that remuneration has been deducted from a previous payment of holiday remuneration made under the provisions of this Schedule or of Order H.L. (69).

ACCRUED HOLIDAY REMUNERATION PAYABLE ON TERMINATION OF EMPLOYMENT

9. Where a worker ceases to be employed by an employer after the provisions of this Schedule become effective, the employer shall, immediately on the termination of the employment (hereinafter called "the termination date"), pay to the worker as accrued holiday remuneration:—

(1) in respect of employment in the 12 months up to and including the 5th April immediately preceding the termination date, a sum equal to the holiday remuneration for any days of annual holiday for which he has qualified except days of annual holiday which he has been allowed or has become entitled to be allowed before leaving the employment; and

(2) in respect of any employment of at least four weeks duration since the said 5th April, a sum equal to the holiday remuneration which would have been payable to him if he could have been allowed an annual holiday in respect of that employment at the time of leaving it.

PART V
GENERAL

10. For the purposes of calculating any period of employment qualifying a worker for a holiday under this Schedule, the worker shall be treated:—

(1) as if he were employed for a week in respect of any week during the qualifying period in which—

(a) he has worked for the employer on at least three days and has performed some work for which statutory minimum remuneration is payable and any absence from work on the other days of the week is with the consent of the employer;

(b) he has been absent throughout the week or worked less than three days by reason of proved incapacity due to sickness or injury and has returned to the employment of the employer on the termination of the period of absence:

Provided that the number of weeks which may be so treated as weeks of employment shall not exceed:—

(i) 26 weeks in the case of proved incapacity in respect of which the worker is entitled to injury benefit under the National Insurance (Industrial Injuries) Act 1965(a);

and (ii) 8 weeks in the case of any other proved incapacity;

(2) as if he were employed on any day of holiday allowed under the provisions of this Schedule.

11. A worker's total remuneration shall include:—

(1) all payments paid or payable to the worker by the employer in respect of his employment except:—

(a) payments by way of annual holiday remuneration;

(b) payments by way of accrued holiday remuneration; and

(c) payments in respect of any period of absence from work by reason of incapacity due to sickness or injury; and

(2) in respect of any period of absence which under the provisions of sub-paragraph (1)(b) of paragraph 10 is to be treated as a period of employment, the amount to which he would have been entitled if he had worked during that period as a time worker for the number of daily hours normally worked by him.

12. In this Schedule, unless the context otherwise requires, the following expressions have the meanings hereby respectively assigned to them, that is to say:—

"NORMAL WORKING WEEK" means the number of days on which it has been usual for the worker to work in a week in the employment of the employer during the qualifying period or, where under paragraph 9 accrued holiday remuneration is payable on the termination of the employment, in the 12 months immediately preceding the termination date:

Provided that—

(1) part of a day shall count as a day;

(2) no account shall be taken of any week in which the worker did not perform any work for which statutory minimum remuneration has been fixed.

"OUTWORKER" means a worker who works in his own home or in any other place not under the control or management of the employer.

"STATUTORY MINIMUM REMUNERATION" means minimum remuneration (other than holiday remuneration) fixed by a wages regulation order made by the Secretary of State to give effect to proposals submitted to her by the Linen and Cotton Handkerchief and Household Goods and Linen Piece Goods Wages Council (Great Britain).

"WEEK" means "pay week".

13. The provisions of this Schedule are without prejudice to any agreement for the allowance of any further holidays with pay or for the payment of additional holiday remuneration.

_____

(a) 1965 c. 52.

EXPLANATORY NOTE

(This Note is not part of the Order.)

This Order, which has effect from 23rd July 1969, sets out the holidays which an employer is required to allow to workers and the remuneration payable for those holidays in substitution for the holidays and holiday remuneration fixed by the Wages Regulation (Linen and Cotton Handkerchief etc.) (Holidays) Order 1967 (Order H.L.(69)), which Order is revoked.

New provisions are printed in italics.

STATUTORY INSTRUMENTS

1969 No. 870 (C.21) (S.69)

MINES AND QUARRIES

The Mines and Quarries (Tips) Act 1969 (Commencement No. 3) Order 1969

Made - - - *26th June* 1969

In exercise of the powers conferred on me by section 38(3) of the Mines and Quarries (Tips) Act 1969(**a**), I hereby make the following Order :—

1. This Order may be cited as the Mines and Quarries (Tips) Act 1969 (Commencement No. 3) Order 1969.

2. Part II of the Mines and Quarries (Tips) Act 1969 in its application to Scotland, shall come into operation on 30th June 1969.

William Ross,
One of Her Majesty's Principal
Secretaries of State.

St. Andrew's House,
Edinburgh.
26th June 1969.

EXPLANATORY NOTE

(This Note is not part of the Order.)

This Order brings into operation on 30th June 1969 the provisions—relating to the prevention of public danger—of Part II of the Mines and Quarries (Tips) Act 1969 which are applicable to Scotland.

(**a**) 1969 c.10.

STATUTORY INSTRUMENTS

1969 No. 871

FOOD AND DRUGS

FOOD HYGIENE

The Meat (Sterilization) Regulations 1969

Made - - - -	*24th June* 1969
Laid before Parliament	*4th July* 1969
Coming into Operation	*1st November* 1969

The Minister of Agriculture, Fisheries and Food and the Secretary of State for Social Services, acting jointly, in exercise of the powers conferred on them by sections 13 and 123 of the Food and Drugs Act 1955(a), as read with the Secretary of State for Social Services Order 1968(b), and of all other powers enabling them in that behalf, hereby make the following regulations, after consultation with such organisations as appear to them to be representative of interests substantially affected by the regulations and reference to the Food Hygiene Advisory Council under section 82 of the said Act:—

PART I

PRELIMINARY

Citation and commencement

1. These regulations may be cited as the Meat (Sterilization) Regulations 1969; and shall come into operation on 1st November 1969.

Interpretation

2.—(1) In these regulations, unless the context otherwise requires—

"the Act" means the Food and Drugs Act 1955;

"authorised officer" means an authorised officer of a council and for the purposes of these regulations has the meaning assigned to it by section 86 of the Act;

"butchers' meat" means meat from any animal slaughtered in the United Kingdom for sale for human consumption;

"carcase" includes part of a carcase;

"competent authority" means an authority having power under the laws in force in any country to examine food and to certify as to its fitness for human consumption;

"contravention" in relation to any provision of these regulations includes a failure to comply with that provision;

"imported meat" means meat originating outside the United Kingdom;

"knacker meat" means meat from any animal slaughtered in, or from any carcase brought into, a knacker's yard in the United Kingdom;

(a) 4 & 5 Eliz. 2. c. 16.   (b) S.I. 1968/1699 (1968 III, p. 4585).

"local authority" has the meaning assigned to it by section 85 of the Act;

"meat" does not include bones, blood, whalemeat or a whole dead animal, but does include offal and fat and any product of which a principal ingredient is meat;

"the Minister" means the Minister of Agriculture, Fisheries and Food;

"processor" means any person who in the course of his processing business sterilizes meat;

"sale by retail" means any sale to a person buying otherwise than for the purpose of re-sale but does not include any sale of meat direct from a slaughterhouse or knacker's yard, or, being imported meat, direct from its port of entry, to any hospital, medical or veterinary school or similar institution for instructional or diagnostic purposes or to any processor for sterilization by him or to any manufacturing chemist for the purpose of the manufacture by him of pharmaceutical products or to any zoological garden, menagerie, mink farm or trout farm or to any person for preparation for sale by him to a processor or manufacturing chemist; and "sell by retail" shall be construed accordingly;

"sterilized" means treated by boiling or by steam under pressure until every piece of meat is cooked throughout; or dry-rendered, digested or solvent-processed into technical tallow, greases, glues, feeding meals or fertilizers:

AND other expressions have the same meaning as in the Act.

(2) The Interpretation Act 1889(a) shall apply to the interpretation of these regulations as it applies to the interpretation of an Act of Parliament and as if these regulations and the regulations hereby revoked were Acts of Parliament.

Saving

3. Nothing in these regulations shall affect the operation of any Act, or any order made under the Diseases of Animals Act 1950(b), relating to the sterilization of waste food for feeding to animals.

PART II

UNFIT BUTCHERS' MEAT AND KNACKER MEAT

Unfit meat to be sterilized before removal from slaughterhouse

4. Subject to the provisions of these regulations, the occupier of a slaughterhouse shall not cause or permit to be removed from the slaughterhouse any meat which is unfit for human consumption, and no person shall so remove any such meat, unless it has first been sterilized:

Provided that it shall be a defence in any proceedings for any contravention of this regulation for the defendant to prove that he did not know, and could not with reasonable diligence have ascertained, that the meat was unfit for human consumption.

Meat to be sterilized before removal from knacker's yard

5. Subject to the provisions of these regulations, the occupier of a knacker's yard shall not cause or permit to be removed from the knacker's yard any meat, and no person shall so remove any meat, unless it has first been sterilized.

(a) 1889 c. 63.   (b) 1950 c. 36.

Exemptions from regulations 4 *and* 5

6. Nothing in regulations 4 and 5 of these regulations shall apply to the removal from any slaughterhouse or knacker's yard of any meat—

(*a*) to any hospital, medical or veterinary school or similar institution for instructional or diagnostic purposes or to any manufacturing chemist for the manufacture by him of pharmaceutical products;

(*b*) to any processor for sterilization by him, or to any zoological garden, menagerie, mink farm or trout farm, or to any person by arrangement in writing with an authorised officer for preparation before further removal to any processor or manufacturing chemist or for storage if such meat is in each case removed in a vehicle or impervious container which is kept closed and locked at all times except when necessary for the loading or unloading of the contents or their examination by an authorised officer and which bears a notice of adequate size and conspicuously visible containing a distinct, legible and unambiguous statement to the effect that the meat is not for human consumption.

No knacker meat or unfit butchers' meat to be in possession for sale unless sterilized

7.—(1) Subject to the provisions of these regulations, no person shall have in his possession for the purpose of sale or preparation for sale any butchers' meat which is unfit for human consumption or any knacker meat unless, in each case, it is sterilized:

Provided that it shall be a defence in any proceedings for any contravention of this regulation for the defendant to prove either—

(*a*) that he did not know and could not with reasonable diligence have ascertained, that the meat was unfit for human consumption or, as the case may be, was knacker meat, or

(*b*) that he had made arrangements for it to be sterilized without any unnecessary delay.

(2) Nothing in this regulation shall apply as respects any meat in any slaughterhouse or knacker's yard or as respects any meat—

(*a*) in the possession of any person while in transit, in a vehicle or impervious container which is kept closed and locked at all times except when necessary for the loading or unloading of the contents or their examination by an authorised officer and which bears a notice of adequate size and conspicuously visible containing a distinct, legible and unambiguous statement to the effect that the meat is not for human consumption, from a slaughterhouse or knacker's yard to—

(i) any processor;

(ii) any zoological garden, menagerie, mink farm or trout farm;

(iii) any person by arrangement in writing with an authorised officer for preparation before removal to any processor or manufacturing chemist or for storage;

(*b*) in the possession of any person while in transit from a slaughterhouse or knacker's yard to any hospital, medical or veterinary school or similar institution for instructional or diagnostic purposes or to any manufacturing chemist for the manufacture by him of pharmaceutical products;

(*c*) on the premises—

(i) of any processor for sterilization by him on those premises;

(ii) of any manufacturing chemist for the manufacture by him on those premises of pharmaceutical products;

(iii) of any zoological garden, menagerie, mink farm or trout farm;

(iv) of any person by arrangement in writing with an authorised officer for preparation before removal to any processor or manufacturing chemist or for storage on those premises if that person's arrangements are suitable and sufficient for ensuring that the meat is kept segregated from other meat and he does not part with possession of the meat otherwise than on its destruction or its delivery or consignment to a processor or manufacturing chemist in a vehicle or impervious container which is kept closed and locked at all times except when necessary for the loading or unloading of the contents or their examination by an authorised officer and which bears a notice of adequate size and conspicuously visible containing a distinct, legible and unambiguous statement to the effect that the meat is not for human consumption;

(d) in transit to the premises of any processor or manufacturing chemist in a vehicle or container in accordance with sub-paragraph (c)(iv) above.

Exemptions

8.—(1) Where there are no facilities for sterilization in a slaughterhouse or knacker's yard the provisions of this Part of these regulations shall not apply as respects any meat removed from that slaughterhouse or knacker's yard by arrangement in writing with an authorised officer to a place where it will be sterilized or destroyed.

(2) Nothing in this Part of these regulations shall apply in relation to imported meat.

PART III

IMPORTED MEAT UNFIT FOR, OR NOT INTENDED FOR, HUMAN CONSUMPTION

Requirements when imported meat which is unfit for, or not intended for, human consumption is stored in, or removed from, the port of entry

9. No person shall remove or cause to be removed from its port of entry or place or cause to be placed in storage at its port of entry—

(a) any imported meat which is unfit for human consumption,

(b) any meat, other than the meat of a rabbit or hare, imported from the Republic of Ireland or the Channel Islands for the purpose of sale otherwise than for human consumption which does not bear a meat inspection stamp of a competent authority in the Republic of Ireland or the Channel Islands, as the case may be,

(c) any imported meat, other than the meat of a rabbit or hare, which has been imported from any place elsewhere than the Republic of Ireland or the Channel Islands without an official certificate for the time being recognised by the Minister in accordance with the provisions of the Imported Food Regulations 1968(a),

unless, in each case, that meat is sterilized or unless every piece thereof or every package containing any of that meat bears a notice of adequate size and conspicuously visible containing a distinct, legible and unambiguous statement to

(a) S.I. 1968/97 (1968 I, p. 272).

the effect that the meat is unfit for human consumption or that it is not for human consumption.

Imported meat which is unfit for, or not intended for, human consumption not to be in possession for sale unless sterilized

10.—(1) Subject to the provisions of these regulations, no person shall have in his possession for the purpose of sale or preparation for sale—

(*a*) any imported meat which is unfit for human consumption,

(*b*) any meat, other than the meat of a rabbit or hare, imported from the Republic of Ireland or the Channel Islands for the purpose of sale otherwise than for human consumption which, at the time of importation, did not bear a meat inspection stamp of a competent authority in the Republic of Ireland or the Channel Islands, as the case may be,

(*c*) any imported meat, other than the meat of a rabbit or hare, which has been imported from any place elsewhere than the Republic of Ireland or the Channel Islands without an official certificate for the time being recognised by the Minister in accordance with the provisions of the Imported Food Regulations 1968,

unless, in each case, that meat is sterilized:

Provided that it shall be a defence in any proceedings for any contravention of this regulation for the defendant to prove either—

(i) that he did not know, and could not with reasonable diligence have ascertained, that that meat was meat to which the foregoing provisions of this regulation apply; or

(ii) that he had made arrangements for it to be sterilized without any unnecessary delay.

(2) Nothing in this regulation shall apply as respects any meat—

(*a*) in the possession of any person while in transit, in a vehicle or impervious container which is kept closed and locked at all times except when necessary for the loading or unloading of the contents or their examination by an authorised officer and which bears a notice of adequate size and conspicuously visible containing a distinct, legible and unambiguous statement to the effect that the meat is not for human consumption, from its port of entry to—

(i) any processor;

(ii) any zoological garden, menagerie, mink farm or trout farm;

(iii) any person by arrangement in writing with an authorised officer for preparation before removal to any processor or manufacturing chemist or for storage;

(*b*) in the possession of any person while in transit from its port of entry to any hospital, medical or veterinary school or similar institution for instructional or diagnostic purposes or to any manufacturing chemist for the manufacture by him of pharmaceutical products;

(*c*) on the premises—

(i) of any processor for sterilization by him on those premises;

(ii) of any manufacturing chemist for the manufacture by him on those premises of pharmaceutical products;

(iii) of any zoological garden, menagerie, mink farm or trout farm;

(iv) of any person by arrangement in writing with an authorised officer for preparation before removal to any processor or manufacturing chemist or for storage on those premises if that person's arrangements are suitable and sufficient for ensuring that the meat is kept segregated from other meat and he does not part with possession of the meat otherwise than on its destruction or its delivery or consignment to a processor or manufacturing chemist in a vehicle or impervious container which is kept closed and locked at all times except when necessary for the loading or unloading of the contents or their examination by an authorised officer and which bears a notice of adequate size and conspicuously visible containing a distinct, legible and unambiguous statement to the effect that the meat is not for human consumption;

(d) in transit to the premises of any processor or manufacturing chemist in a vehicle or container in accordance with sub-paragraph (c)(iv) above.

Part IV

Sales

Meat unfit for, or not intended for, human consumption and knacker meat not to be sold by retail unless sterilized

11. No person shall sell, or offer or expose for sale, by retail—

(a) any butchers' meat or imported meat which in either case is unfit for human consumption or any knacker meat,

(b) any meat, other than the meat of a rabbit or hare, imported from the Republic of Ireland or the Channel Islands for the purpose of sale otherwise than for human consumption which, at the time of importation, did not bear a meat inspection stamp of a competent authority in the Republic of Ireland or the Channel Islands, as the case may be,

(c) any imported meat, other than the meat of a rabbit or hare, which has been imported from any place elsewhere than the Republic of Ireland or the Channel Islands without an official certificate for the time being recognised by the Minister in accordance with the provisions of the Imported Food Regulations 1968,

unless, in each case, that meat is sterilized:

Provided that it shall be a defence in any proceedings for any contravention of this regulation for the defendant to prove that he did not know, and could not with reasonable diligence have ascertained, that that meat was meat to which the foregoing provisions of this regulation apply.

Part V

Administration and General

Record of consignment or delivery of meat

12.—(1) Any person responsible for the consignment or delivery, in any of the circumstances described in these regulations, of—

(a) any meat which is unfit for human consumption,

(b) any knacker meat,

(c) any meat, other than the meat of a rabbit or hare, which has been imported from the Republic of Ireland or the Channel Islands for the purpose of sale otherwise than for human consumption and which, at the time of importation, did not bear a meat inspection stamp of a competent authority in the Republic of Ireland or the Channel Islands, as the case may be, or (*d*) any imported meat, other than the meat of a rabbit or hare, which has been imported from any place elsewhere than the Republic of Ireland or the Channel Islands without an official certificate for the time being recognised by the Minister in accordance with the provisions of the Imported Food Regulations 1968,

shall give or send with the said meat to the person by whom or on whose behalf the meat is to be received a notice bearing information relating to the said meat including particulars of the date of its consignment or delivery, the quantity and the description thereof and the respective names and addresses of the person responsible for its consignment or delivery, as the case may be, and of the person by whom or on whose behalf it is to be received.

(2) The person responsible for the consignment or delivery of meat as mentioned in the last preceding paragraph shall retain a copy of the said notice, and the person by whom or on whose behalf the notice is received shall retain the original thereof, as a record in each case for a period of 3 months after the date of the said consignment or delivery and each shall on request by an authorised officer produce the same for inspection by him at any time during that period.

Right of seizure

13.—(1) An authorised officer may at all reasonable times examine any meat not intended for human consumption which has been sold, or is offered or exposed for sale or is in the possession of, or has been deposited with or consigned to, any person for the purpose of sale or preparation for sale; and if it appears to him that the meat, being meat to which the requirements of Part II, III or IV of these regulations apply—

(*a*) is required to be but has not been sterilized, or, as the case may be,

(*b*) is required to bear but does not bear a notice,

in accordance with those requirements, he may seize it and remove it in order to have it dealt with by a justice of the peace.

(2) An officer who seizes any meat under paragraph (1) of this regulation shall inform the person in whose possession the meat was found of his intention to have it dealt with by a justice of the peace, and any person who under Part II, III or IV of these regulations might be liable to a prosecution in respect of the meat shall, if he attends before the justice of the peace, be entitled to be heard and to call witnesses.

(3) If it appears to a justice of the peace that any meat brought before him, whether seized under the provisions of this regulation or not, is meat to which the requirements of Part II, III or IV of these regulations apply and is required to be but has not been dealt with in accordance with those requirements, he shall condemn it and order it to be destroyed or to be so dealt with.

(4) If a justice of the peace refuses to condemn any meat seized under this regulation by an authorised officer, the council shall compensate the owner of the meat for any depreciation in its value resulting from its seizure and removal.

Right of examination

14.—(1) Subject to the provisions of this regulation, if an authorised officer has reason to suspect that any vehicle or container contains any meat to which the requirements of Part II, III or IV of these regulations apply, and which is intended for sale or is in the course of delivery after sale, he may examine the contents of the vehicle or container and for that purpose may, if necessary, detain the vehicle or container; and if the officer finds any meat, being meat to which the requirements of Part II, III or IV of these regulations apply and which is required to be but has not been dealt with in accordance with those requirements, he may deal with it as meat falling within paragraph (1) of regulation 13 of these regulations and paragraphs (2) to (4) of that regulation shall apply accordingly.

(2) Nothing in this regulation shall authorise the detention of—

(a) any vehicle belonging to the British Railways Board, the London Transport Board or the National Freight Corporation and used by any of them for the purposes of their undertaking;

(b) any vehicle belonging to a railway company and used by them for the purposes of their undertaking; or

(c) any authorised vehicle used for the purpose of his business as a carrier of goods by a person holding an A licence or a B licence under Part IV of the Road Traffic Act 1960(a).

Penalties and enforcement

15.—(1) If any person contravenes or fails to comply with any of the foregoing provisions of these regulations he shall be guilty of an offence and shall be liable to a fine not exceeding one hundred pounds or to imprisonment for a term not exceeding three months, or to both, and, in the case of a continuing offence, to a further fine not exceeding five pounds for each day during which the offence continues after conviction.

(2) Each local authority shall enforce and execute such provisions in their district:

Provided that each port health authority shall enforce and execute such provisions in their district.

Application of various sections of the Act

16.—(1) Sections 113 (which relates to a contravention due to some person other than the person charged), 115(2) (which relates to the conditions under which a warranty may be pleaded as a defence) and 116 (which relates to offences in relation to warranties and certificates of analysis) of the Act shall apply for the purposes of these regulations as if references therein to proceedings, or a prosecution, under or taken or brought under the Act included references to proceedings, or a prosecution as the case may be, taken or brought for an offence under these regulations.

(2) Paragraph (b) of the proviso to section 108 (1) of the Act shall apply for the purposes of these regulations as if the reference therein to section 116 of the Act included a reference to that section as applied by these regulations.

Revocation

17.—(1) The Meat (Staining and Sterilization) Regulations 1960(b) are hereby revoked.

(2) The Food and Drugs (Legal Proceedings) Regulations 1962(c), as amended (d), shall be further amended by deleting therefrom regulation 5 thereof.

(a) 1960 c. 16.   (b) S.I. 1960/1268 (1960 II, p. 1523).
(c) S.I. 1962/1287 (1962 II, p. 1378).
(d) There is no amendment which relates expressly to the subject matter of these regulations.

In Witness whereof the Official Seal of the Minister of Agriculture, Fisheries and Food is hereunto affixed on 19th June 1969.

(L.S.)   *Cledwyn Hughes*,
                                                   Minister of Agriculture,
                                                   Fisheries and Food.

                                                   R. H. S. Crossman,
                                    Secretary of State for Social Services.

24th June 1969.

EXPLANATORY NOTE

(This Note is not part of the Regulations.)

These regulations, which apply to England and Wales only, supersede the Meat (Staining and Sterilization) Regulations 1960, as amended, and come into operation on 1st November 1969.

The regulations require all knacker meat and meat (other than the meat of a rabbit or hare) which is imported otherwise than for human consumption, as well as all butchers' meat or imported meat which in either case is unfit for human consumption, to be sterilized before entering the chain of distribution. They also require that imported meat which is unfit for human consumption or imported otherwise than for human consumption and without an official certificate or meat inspection stamp and which is stored in or removed from the port of entry shall be sterilized or shall bear a notice to the effect that the meat is not fit for human consumption. The different categories of meat to which the regulations relate are defined in regulation 2(1).

Provision is made whereby zoos, menageries, mink farms, trout farms and processors may obtain such meat unsterilized if it is transported in locked containers or vehicles. Supplies of meat to hospitals, medical or veterinary schools or similar institutions for instructional or diagnostic purposes and to manufacturing chemists for the manufacture of pharmaceutical products are unaffected by the regulations.

The regulations also require that on consignment or delivery of specified meat a notice be given or sent therewith giving particulars of the meat and the names and addresses of the persons from and to whom it is being conveyed (regulation 12).

The regulations are to be enforced by local authorities and port health authorities and prescribe the maximum penalties provided for in section 106 of the Food and Drugs Act 1955.

STATUTORY INSTRUMENTS

1969 No. 873

FOOD AND DRUGS
The Welfare Foods (Northern Ireland) Order 1969

Made - - - *26th June* 1969

In exercise of the powers conferred on me by section 20(4) of the Emergency Laws (Re-enactments and Repeals) Act 1964(a), I hereby order as follows :—

1. This Order may be cited as the Welfare Foods (Northern Ireland) Order 1969.

2. 1st July 1969 is appointed as the date as from which orders made under section 4 of the Emergency Laws (Re-enactments and Repeals) Act 1964 shall not extend to Northern Ireland.

James Callaghan,
One of Her Majesty's Principal
Secretaries of State.

Home Office,
 Whitehall.
26th June 1969.

EXPLANATORY NOTE

(This Note is not part of the Order.)

Section 4 of the Emergency Laws (Re-enactments and Repeals) Act 1964 provides for the making of orders for the administration of welfare food schemes. Section 20(4) provides that, as from such date as the Secretary of State may by order appoint, orders made under section 4 shall not extend to Northern Ireland. This Order appoints 1st July 1969 for this purpose (the date when the Welfare Foods Act (Northern Ireland) 1968 (c. 26) comes into operation). Accordingly the Welfare Foods (Northern Ireland) Order 1968 (S.I. 1968/427), which is the order under section 4 of the 1964 Act now in force in Northern Ireland, will cease to have effect.

(a) 1964 c.60.

STATUTORY INSTRUMENTS

1969 No. 875

TELEVISION

The Television Act 1964 (Additional Payments) Order 1969

Laid before Parliament in draft

Made - - -	*26th June* 1969
Coming into operation	*1st July* 1969

I, The Right Honourable John Thomson Stonehouse, M.P., Her Majesty's Postmaster General, with the approval of the Treasury and after consultation with the Independent Television Authority, by virtue of the powers conferred on me by Section 13(6) of the Television Act 1964(**a**), do hereby order as follows:—

1.—(1) This Order may be cited as the Television Act 1964 (Additional Payments) Order 1969, and shall come into operation on 1st July 1969.

(2) The Interpretation Act 1889(**b**) shall apply for the interpretation of this Order as it applies for the interpretation of an Act of Parliament.

2. Subsection (4) of Section 13 of the Television Act 1964 (which contains a Table giving the amount of the additional payments to be made by the programme contractors to the Independent Television Authority if the accounting period is a period of 12 months) shall be amended by substituting the following Table for the Table contained in the said subsection:—

" TABLE

RATES FOR A 12-MONTH PERIOD

	Appropriate rate for determining amount of additional payment
For the first half a million pounds of the advertising receipts of the programme contractor for the 12-month accounting period	Nil
For the next one million pounds of those advertising receipts	7 per cent.
For the next two-and-a-half million pounds of those advertising receipts..	25 per cent.
For the next six million pounds of those advertising receipts	35 per cent.
For the amount by which those advertising receipts exceed the aggregate of the said sums of half a million pounds, one million pounds, two-and-a-half million pounds and six million pounds	47$\frac{1}{2}$ per cent."

(**a**) 1964 c. 21.   (**b**) 1889 c. 63.

Dated 26th June 1969

> *John Stonehouse,*
> Her Majesty's Postmaster General.

We approve of this Order.

> *Wally Harrison,*
> *Joseph Harper,*
> Two of the Lords Commissioners of
> Her Majesty's Treasury.

26th June 1969.

EXPLANATORY NOTE

(*This Note is not part of the Order.*)

This Order amends the Table in Section 13(4) of the Television Act 1964, which gives the amount of the additional payments to be made by the programme contractors to the Independent Television Authority if the accounting period is 12 months. By Section 13(2) of the Act the additional payments are to be paid into the Exchequer of the United Kingdom or of Northern Ireland as provided by Section 14(3).

STATUTORY INSTRUMENTS

1969 No. 876 (S. 70)

ANIMALS

PREVENTION OF CRUELTY

The Agriculture (Spring Traps) (Scotland) Order 1969

Made - - - *25th June* 1969

In exercise of the powers conferred upon me by section 50(4) of the Agriculture (Scotland) Act 1948(a), as amended by section 10 of the Pests Act 1954(b) and as read with section 2 of the Agriculture (Spring Traps) (Scotland) Act 1969(c) and of all other powers enabling me in that behalf, I hereby make the following order:—

Citation and interpretation

1.—(1) This order may be cited as the Agriculture (Spring Traps) (Scotland) Order 1969.

(2) The Interpretation Act 1889(d) shall apply for the interpretation of this order as it applies for the interpretation of an Act of Parliament.

Use of unapproved spring traps

2. As from 1st July 1969, the use, for the purpose of killing foxes, of spring traps other than traps of a type and make approved by the Secretary of State in terms of section 50(3) of the Agriculture (Scotland) Act 1948 as amended by section 10 of the Pests Act 1954, is as respects all land in Scotland hereby authorised.

William Ross,
One of Her Majesty's Principal
Secretaries of State.

St. Andrew's House,
Edinburgh.
25th June 1969.

(a) 1948 c. 45.   (b) 1954 c. 68.
(c) 1969 c. 26.   (d) 1889 c. 63.

EXPLANATORY NOTE

(This Note is not part of the Order.)

Under section 50 of the Agriculture (Scotland) Act 1948, as amended by section 10 of the Pests Act 1954, it is an offence to use, for the purpose of killing or taking animals, any spring trap other than one of a type and make approved by the Secretary of State. The Secretary of State is, however, empowered to authorise the use of unapproved traps and in the Agriculture (Spring Traps) (Scotland) Order 1958 (S.I. 1958/1778) he authorised the use of unapproved traps for the purpose of killing foxes and otters. By section 2 of the Agriculture (Spring Traps) (Scotland) Act 1969 the existing order authorising the use of unapproved traps will cease to have effect as from 1st July 1969.

By this Order the Secretary of State authorises as from 1st July 1969 the continued use of unapproved traps against foxes only.

1969 No. 878

AGRICULTURE

The Price Stability of Imported Products (Rates of Levy No. 14) Order 1969

Made - - - - 27th June 1969
Coming into Operation 28th June 1969

The Minister of Agriculture, Fisheries and Food, in exercise of the powers conferred upon him by section 1(2), (4), (5), (6) and (7) of the Agriculture and Horticulture Act 1964(a) and of all other powers enabling him in that behalf, hereby makes the following order:—

1. This order may be cited as the Price Stability of Imported Products (Rates of Levy No. 14) Order 1969; and shall come into operation on 28th June 1969.

2.—(1) In this order—

"the Principal Order" means the Price Stability of Imported Products (Levy Arrangements) Order 1966(b) as amended (c) and as amended by any subsequent order, and if any such order is replaced by any subsequent order the expression shall be construed as a reference to such subsequent order;

AND other expressions have the same meaning as in the Principal Order.

(2) The Interpretation Act 1889(d) shall apply to the interpretation of this order as it applies to the interpretation of an Act of Parliament and as if this order and the orders hereby revoked were Acts of Parliament.

3. In accordance with and subject to the provisions of Part II of the Principal Order (which provides for the charging of levies on imports of certain specified commodities)—

(a) the rate of general levy for such imports into the United Kingdom of any specified commodity as are described in column 2 of Part I of the Schedule to this order in relation to a tariff heading indicated in column 1 of that Part shall be the rate set forth in relation thereto in column 3 of that Part;

(b) the rate of country levy for such imports into the United Kingdom of any specified commodity as are described in column 2 of Part II of the Schedule to this order in relation to a tariff heading indicated in column 1 of that Part shall be the rate set forth in relation thereto in column 3 of that Part.

4. The Price Stability of Imported Products (Rates of Levy No. 12) Order 1969(e) and the Price Stability of Imported Products (Rates of Levy No. 13) Order 1969(f) are hereby revoked.

In Witness whereof the Official Seal of the Minister of Agriculture, Fisheries and Food is hereunto affixed on 27th June 1969.

(L.S.)

R. J. E. Taylor,
Assistant Secretary.

(a) 1964 c. 28.   (b) S.I. 1966/936 (1966 II. p. 2271).   (c) S.I. 1969/758 (1969 II, p. 2137).
(d) 1889 c. 63.   (e) S.I. 1969/779 (1969 II, p. 2195).   (f) S.I. 1969/822 (1969 II, p. 2322).

SCHEDULE

PART I

1. Tariff Heading	2. Description of Imports	3. Rate of General Levy
		per ton £ s. d.
10.01	Imports of:— Denatured wheat	10 0
10.01	Any wheat (other than seed wheat the value of which is not less than £34 per ton, denatured wheat and durum wheat) for which a minimum import price level is prescribed	10 0
10.03	Barley	1 10 0
11.02	Cereal meals— of barley .. .. of maize	7 5 0 15 0
11.02	Rolled, flaked, crushed or bruised cereals— barley	5 15 0

PART II

1. Tariff Heading	2. Description of Imports	3. Rate of Country Levy
		per ton £ s. d.
10.01	Imports of:— Denatured wheat which has been grown in and consigned to the United Kingdom from— Belgium, the French Republic or the Kingdom of the Netherlands .. .. the Kingdom of Sweden	 10 0 5 0
10.01	Any wheat (other than seed wheat the value of which is not less than £34 per ton, denatured wheat and durum wheat) for which a minimum import price level is prescribed and which is grown in and consigned to the United Kingdom from— Belgium or the French Republic .. .. the Kingdom of the Netherlands	 10 0 5 0
10.03	Barley which has been grown in and consigned to the United Kingdom from Canada	1 10 0

EXPLANATORY NOTE

(This Note is not part of the Order.)

This order, which comes into operation on 28th June 1969, re-enacts with amendments the Price Stability of Imported Products (Rates of Levy No. 12) Order 1969 and the Price Stability of Imported Products (Rates of Levy No. 13) Order 1969.   It:—

(a) increases to 15s. per ton the general levy on imports of maize meal;

(b) fixes a country levy of 10s. per ton on imports of wheat (other than seed wheat the value of which is not less than £34 per ton, denatured wheat and durum wheat) which has been grown in and consigned to the United Kingdom from Belgium; and

(c) reimposes unchanged the other rates of general and country levy pre-scribed by the above-mentioned orders.

STATUTORY INSTRUMENTS

1969 No. 879

INDUSTRIAL TRAINING

The Industrial Training (Road Transport Board) Order 1969

Made	- - -	*26th June* 1969
Laid before Parliament		*7th July* 1969
Coming into Operation		*16th July* 1969

The Secretary of State after consultation with the Road Transport Industry Training Board and with organisations and associations of organisations appearing to be representative respectively of substantial numbers of employers engaging in the activities hereinafter mentioned and of substantial numbers of persons employed in those activities and with the bodies established for the purpose of carrying on under national ownership industries in which the said activities are carried on to a substantial extent and in exercise of her powers under section 9 of the Industrial Training Act 1964(a) and of all other powers enabling her in that behalf hereby makes the following Order : —

Citation, commencement and interpretation

1.—(1) This Order may be cited as the Industrial Training (Road Transport Board) Order 1969 and shall come into operation on 16th July 1969.

(2) In this Order—

(*a*) "the Act" means the Industrial Training Act 1964 ;

(*b*) "the Board" means the Road Transport Industry Training Board ;

(*c*) "Levy Order" means the Industrial Training Levy (Road Transport) Order 1967(b) and the Industrial Training Levy (Road Transport) Order 1968(c) ;

(*d*) "the principal Order" means the Industrial Training (Road Transport Board) Order 1966(d) ;

(3) The Interpretation Act 1889(e) shall apply to the interpretation of this Order as it applies to the interpretation of an Act of Parliament and as if this Order and the principal Order were Acts of Parliament.

Activities of the Board

2. The activities in relation to which the Board exercises the functions conferred by the Act upon industrial training boards shall, in lieu of the activities specified in Schedule 1 to the principal Order, be the activities specified in the Schedule to this Order, and accordingly in the principal Order the latter Schedule shall be substituted for the former Schedule.

(a) 1964 c. 16.
(c) S.I. 1968/1835 (1968 III, p. 4841).
(e) 1889 c. 63.

(b) S.I. 1967/1309 (1967 III, p. 3939).
(d) S.I. 1966/1112 (1966 III, p. 2712).

INDUSTRIAL TRAINING

Transitional provisions

3.—(1) The chairman and other members of the Board on the day upon which this Order comes into operation shall continue to be members of the Board and to hold and vacate their offices in accordance with the terms of the instruments appointing them to be members.

(2) The provisions of this Order shall not—

(*a*) extend the operation of either Levy Order ;

(*b*) affect the operation of either Levy Order in relation to the assessment of an employer within the meaning of that Order in respect of an establishment that was engaged in the relevant levy period wholly or mainly in activities included in the Schedule to this Order ;

(*c*) affect the operation of any assessment notice served by the Board under the provisions of either Levy Order before the date upon which this Order comes into operation or any appeal or other proceedings arising out of any such notice.

26th June 1969.

Barbara Castle,
First Secretary of State and Secretary
of State for Employment and Productivity.

Article 2

SCHEDULE
The Road Transport Industry

1. Subject to the provisions of this Schedule, the activities of the road transport industry are the following activities in so far as they are carried out in Great Britain : —

(*a*) the carriage of passengers by motor vehicles on roads for hire or reward ;

(*b*) the carriage or haulage of goods by goods vehicles on roads for hire or reward ;

(*c*) the letting out on hire (with or without the services of the drivers) of motor vehicles for the conveyance of persons or of goods vehicles for the carriage or haulage of goods ;

(*d*) arranging by way of business the transport of goods by goods vehicles on roads ;

(*e*) the repair of motor vehicles or goods vehicles ;

(*f*) the collection of motor vehicles or goods vehicles and their delivery by road by way of business ;

(*g*) giving instruction by way of business in the driving of motor vehicles or goods vehicles ;

(*h*) dealing in motor vehicles or goods vehicles ;

(*i*) selling by retail, motor spirit, diesel fuel or lubricating or other oils for use in motor vehicles or goods vehicles ;

(*j*) dealing (not being selling by retail) in components, replacements, spare parts or accessories (not being tyres) for motor vehicles or goods vehicles ;

(*k*) dealing in, or letting out on hire, transport service equipment ;

(*l*) dealing in, letting out on hire or the repair by way of business of, agricultural or horticultural machinery and equipment ;

(*m*) the removal of furniture by way of business ;

(*n*) public warehousing ;

(*o*) any activities (other than those above mentioned), being—

    (i) related activities incidental or ancillary to principal activities of the road transport industry ; or

    (ii) activities undertaken in the administration, control or direction of one or more establishments, being establishments engaged wholly or mainly in principal activities of that industry, in related activities incidental or ancillary thereto, or in the administration, control or direction of one or more other establishments engaged in such principal or related activities ;

and carried out, in either case, by the employer engaged in those principal activities or, where that employer is a company, by the company or by an associated company of the company ;

(*p*) any activities of industry or commerce (other than road transport activities) carried out at or from an establishment mainly engaged—

    (i) in road transport activities ; or

    (ii) in road transport activities and in activities described in the Appendix to this Schedule, but to a greater extent in road transport activities than in activities described in that Appendix in relation to any one industry.

2. Notwithstanding anything contained in this Schedule, there shall not be included in the activities of the road transport industry : —

(*a*) the activities of any establishment engaged—

    (i) mainly in activities not being road transport activities or activities described in the Appendix to this Schedule ; or

    (ii) to a less extent in road transport activities than in activities described in that Appendix in relation to any one industry ;

(*b*) the activities of any establishment engaged wholly or mainly in related activities, being activities—

    (i) incidental or ancillary to the activities of one or more establishments (in this sub-paragraph hereafter referred to as "the principal establishment") engaged wholly or mainly in any activities not being principal activities of the road transport industry ; and

    (ii) carried out by the employer carrying on the principal establishment or, where that employer is a company, by the company or by an associated company of the company ;

(*c*) the activities of any establishment engaged wholly or mainly in business as follows—

    (i) in banking, finance or insurance ;

    (ii) as exporters, not being activities to which paragraph 1(*o*)(i) of this Schedule applies ; or

    (iii) in funeral undertaking ;

(*d*) the activities of any establishment (other than an establishment of the London Transport Board) engaged wholly or mainly in the repair of vehicle bodies, not being activities of a kind specified in paragraph 3(*p*)(v) of this Schedule ;

(*e*) the activities of—

    (i) the Electricity Council, the Central Electricity Generating Board, an Area Electricity Board, the North of Scotland Hydro-Electric Board or the South of Scotland Electricity Board ;

    (ii) the Gas Council or an Area Gas Board ;

    (iii) the Home-Grown Cereals Authority ;

    (iv) a harbour authority when acting in that capacity ;

    (v) a marketing board ;

    (vi) statutory water undertakers within the meaning of the Water Act 1945(**a**) or regional water boards or water development boards within the meaning of the Water (Scotland) Act 1967(**b**), being the activities of such undertakers or boards in the exercise of their powers or duties as such ; or

    (vii) the United Kingdom Atomic Energy Authority ;

(*f*) when carried out by the London Transport Board any activities that are specified in paragraph 1(*o*) of this Schedule, not being activities that are specified in head (ii), (v) or (vi) of paragraph 3(*p*) and are incidental or ancillary to principal activities of the road transport industry ;

(*g*) any activities of a local authority or of a joint board or joint committee of such authorities, not being activities carried out for the purposes of a passenger road transport service provided by the authority, board or committee ;

(*h*) the activities of any company, association or body that is required by its constitution to apply its profits, if any, or other income in promoting its objects and is prohibited thereby from paying any dividend to its members, and that has for its sole or principal object or among its principal objects the provision of facilities for any of the purposes mentioned in section 15(1) of the Disabled Persons (Employment) Act 1944(**c**) (which relates to the provision for registered persons who are seriously disabled of work or training) ;

(*i*) any work, occupation or training that is provided in accordance with arrangements made by a local authority under the Disabled Persons (Employment) Act 1958(**d**) or any other enactment that authorises or requires the provision of arrangements for persons suffering from illness, severe physical defect or disability or from mental disorder, or for persons who have been suffering from illness or whose care is undertaken with a view to preventing them from becoming ill, or for old people ;

(*j*) dock work performed by a registered dock worker ; or

(*k*) the supply of food or drink for immediate consumption.

3. In this Schedule unless the context otherwise requires : —

(*a*) "agricultural or horticultural machinery and equipment" means any machinery, plant, equipment or appliance designed primarily or adapted for use in agriculture or horticulture ;

(*b*) "business" means a trade or business carried on for the purposes of gain ;

(*c*) "company" includes any body corporate, and "subsidiary" has the same meaning as by virtue of section 154 of the Companies Act 1948(**e**) it has for the purpose of that Act ;

(*d*) "dealing" means by way of business and in the capacity of principal, agent or broker—

    (i) in relation to products situate in Great Britain, buying or selling such products ;

    (ii) in relation to products situate elsewhere, importing such products into Great Britain ;

but does not include any transaction in the nature of an auction ;

(*e*) "dock work" and "registered dock worker" have the same meanings as in the Docks and Harbours Act 1966(**f**) ;

(*f*) "goods" includes goods or burden of any description ;

(*g*) "goods vehicles" mean motor vehicles constructed or adapted for use for the carriage of goods, or trailers so constructed or adapted, and "trailers" means vehicles drawn by motor vehicles ;

(a) 1945 c. 42.   (b) 1967 c. 78.
(c) 1944 c. 10.   (d) 1958 c. 33.
(e) 1948 c. 38.   (f) 1966 c. 28.

(h) "harbour authority" means a harbour authority within the meaning of the Harbours Act 1964(a);

(i) "letting out on hire" does not include a letting under a hire-purchase agreement;

(j) "marketing board" means the Aberdeen and District Milk Marketing Board, the British Egg Marketing Board, the British Wool Marketing Board, the Hops Marketing Board, the Milk Marketing Board, the North of Scotland Milk Marketing Board, the Potato Marketing Board or the Scottish Milk Marketing Board;

(k) "motor vehicles" means mechanically propelled vehicles intended or adapted for use on roads, and includes tram-cars and trolley vehicles, but does not include implements for cutting grass that are not capable of being used or adapted for any other purpose, or contractors' plant; and for the purposes of this definition "contractors' plant" means machinery, plant or equipment of a kind intended for use in operations on the site of any building work or civil engineering work, but does not include lorries, ready-mixed concrete vehicles or other mechanically propelled vehicles mainly used for the carriage of goods on roads;

(l) "office premises" has the same meaning as in section 1(2) of the Offices, Shops and Railway Premises Act 1963(b);

(m) "petroleum" means crude oil, liquefied petroleum gas, aviation fuel, motor spirit, kerosene, white spirit, diesel fuel, fuel oil, gas oil, lubricating oil or any similar product;

(n) "principal activities of the road transport industry" means activities which, subject to the provisions of paragraph 2 of this Schedule, are specified in paragraph 1, other than sub-paragraphs (o) and (p) thereof, as activities of the road transport industry;

(o) "public warehousing" means keeping any premises (not being a public garage or parking place, a caravan site, or a place where boats are anchored, laid up or moored) wholly or mainly for the purpose of the storage of goods for reward for persons other than the occupier or, where the occupier is a company, for persons other than the company or an associated company of the company, but does not include keeping any premises wholly or mainly for the storage of petroleum, or for the custody of animals or other living creatures or as a cloakroom or safe depository;

(p) "related activities" means any of the following activities, that is to say—

   (i) research or development;

   (ii) design or drawing;

   (iii) buying, selling, letting out on hire, testing, advertising, packing, distribution, transport or any similar operations;

   (iv) operations of a kind performed at office premises or laboratories, or at stores, warehouses, or similar places;

   (v) cleaning, washing or garaging vehicles, or carrying out running repairs or minor adjustments thereto;

   (vi) training of employees or apprentices;

(q) "repair" (except in relation to the expression "running repairs") means all or any of the operations of repair, reconditioning, modification, alteration, conversion, maintenance, cleaning, washing or carrying out running repairs or minor adjustments;

(r) "road" means a highway or any other road to which the public has access;

(s) "road transport activities" means any one or more of the principal activities of the road transport industry and the activities included in that industry by virtue of paragraph 1(o) of this Schedule;

(a) 1964 c. 40.   (b) 1963 c. 41.

(*t*) "selling by retail" in relation to any products means selling such products by way of business to a person buying otherwise than for the purpose of re-sale, use in manufacture or processing ;

(*u*) "transport service equipment" means plant or equipment of a kind used in the testing or analysis of performance of motor vehicles or goods vehicles, in their repair or in their recovery when damaged ;

(*v*) "vehicle bodies" includes motor cycle sidecars, invalid carriages and bodies for caravans.

4.—(1) References in this Schedule to the provisions of any enactment shall be construed as references to those provisions as amended by or under any subsequent enactment.

(2) For the purposes of this Schedule two companies shall be taken to be associated companies if one is a subsidiary of the other or both are subsidiaries of a third company, and "associated company" shall be construed accordingly.

(3) For the purposes of this Schedule, goods shall not be deemed to be carried or hauled for hire or reward if—

(*a*) they are goods sold, used or let on hire or hire-purchase in the course of a business carried on by the carrier or haulier thereof and are being delivered or collected by him ; or

(*b*) they are goods which have been, or are to be, subjected to a process or treatment in the course of a business carried on by the carrier or haulier thereof, and are being delivered or collected by him ; or

(*c*) they are carried by a person engaged in agriculture in any locality, for or in connection with the business of agriculture carried on by another person in that locality, and the goods vehicle in which they are carried is used by the carrier or haulier for the carriage of goods for or in connection with his agricultural business ;

and for the purposes of this sub-paragraph the references to the carrier or haulier shall be taken to include an associated company of the carrier or haulier, being a company.

APPENDIX

The activities that would be included in an industry specified in Column 1 hereof by virtue of the industrial training order specified in the corresponding entry in Column 2, if the provisions specified in Column 3 were omitted from that order.

Column 1	Column 2	Column 3
The wool, jute and flax industry	The Industrial Training (Wool Industry Board) Order 1964 as amended by the Industrial Training (Wool, Jute and Flax Board) Order 1968(a)	Schedule 1 Paragraph 1(*s*)
The iron and steel industry	The Industrial Training (Iron and Steel Board) Order 1964(b)	Schedule 1 Paragraph 1(*j*)
The construction industry	The Industrial Training (Construction Board) Order 1964 as amended by the Industrial Training (Construction Board) Order 1967(c)	Schedule 1 Paragraph 1(*l*)

(a) S.I. 1964/907, 1968/898 (1964 II, p. 1928; 1968 II, p. 2376).
(b) S.I. 1964/949 (1964 II, p. 2127).
(c) S.I. 1964/1079, 1967/924 (1964 II, p. 2384; 1967 II, p. 2757).

APPENDIX *(cont.)*

Column 1	Column 2	Column 3
The engineering industry	The Industrial Training (Engineering Board) Order 1964 as amended by the Industrial Training (Engineering Board) Order 1968(a)	Schedule 1 Paragraph 1(m)
The shipbuilding industry	The Industrial Training (Shipbuilding Board) Order 1964 as amended by the Industrial Training (Shipbuilding Board) Order 1968(b)	Schedule 1 Paragraph 1(g)
The ceramics, glass and mineral products industry	The Industrial Training (Ceramics, Glass and Mineral Products Board) Order 1965 as amended by the Industrial Training (Ceramics, Glass and Mineral Products Board) Order 1969(c)	Schedule 1 Paragraph 1(p)
The furniture and timber industry	The Industrial Training (Furniture and Timber Industry Board) Order 1965(d)	Schedule 1 Paragraph 1(r)
The man-made fibres producing industry	The Industrial Training (Man-made Fibres Producing Industry Board) Order 1966(e)	Schedule 1 Paragraph 1(d)
The carpet industry	The Industrial Training (Carpet Board) Order 1966 as amended by the Industrial Training (Carpet Board) Order 1968(f)	Schedule 1 Paragraph 1(f)
The knitting, lace and net industry	The Industrial Training (Knitting, Lace and Net Industry Board) Order 1966(g)	Schedule 1 Paragraph 1(j)
The cotton and allied textiles industry	The Industrial Training (Cotton and Allied Textiles Board) Order 1966(h)	Schedule 1 Paragraph 1(p)
The agricultural, horticultural and forestry industry	The Industrial Training (Agricultural, Horticultural and Forestry Board) Order 1966(i)	Schedule 1 Paragraph 1(m)
The hotel and catering industry	The Industrial Training (Hotel and Catering Board) Order 1966(j)	Schedule 1 Paragraph 1(e)
The civil air transport industry	The Industrial Training (Civil Air Transport Board) Order 1967(k)	Schedule 1 Paragraph 1(h)
The petroleum industry	The Industrial Training (Petroleum Board) Order 1967(l)	Schedule 1 Paragraph 1(h)
The rubber and plastics processing industry	The Industrial Training (Rubber and Plastics Processing Board) Order 1967(m)	Schedule 1 Paragraph 1(k)
The chemical and allied products industry	The Industrial Training (Chemical and Allied Products Board) Order 1967(n)	Schedule 1 Paragraph 1(s)
The paper and paper products industry	The Industrial Training (Paper and Paper Products Board) Order 1968(o)	Schedule 1 Paragraph 1(j)

(a) S.I. 1964/1086, 1968/1333 (1964 II, p. 2402; 1968 II, p. 3694).
(b) S.I. 1964/1782, 1968/1614 (1964 III, p. 3928; 1968 III, p. 4432).
(c) S.I. 1965/1391, 1969/689 (1965 II, p. 4062; 1969 II, p. 1858).
(d) S.I. 1965/2028 (1965 III, p. 5998).
(e) S.I. 1966/143 (1966 I, p. 257).
(f) S.I. 1966/245, 1968/1882 (1966 I, p. 499; 1968 III, p. 5017).
(g) S.I. 1966/246 (1966 I, p. 506).   (h) S.I. 1966/823 (1966 II, p. 1907).
(i) S.I. 1966/969 (1966 II, p. 2333).   (j) S.I. 1966/1347 (1966 III, p. 3669).
(k) S.I. 1967/263 (1967 I, p. 968).   (l) S.I. 1967/648 (1967 I, p. 2032).
(m) S.I. 1967/1062 (1967 II, p. 3151).   (n) S.I. 1967/1386 (1967 III, p. 4049).
(o) S.I. 1968/787 (1968 II, p. 2194).

APPENDIX (*cont.*)

Column 1	Column 2	Column 3
The printing and publishing industry	The Industrial Training (Printing and Publishing Board) Order 1968(**a**)	Schedule 1 Paragraph 1(*n*)
The distributive industry	The Industrial Training (Distributive Board) Order 1968(**b**)	Schedule 1 Paragraph 1(*h*)
The food, drink and tobacco industry	The Industrial Training (Food, Drink and Tobacco Board) Order 1968(**c**)	Schedule 1 Paragraph 1(*q*)
The footwear, leather and fur skin industry	The Industrial Training (Footwear, Leather and Fur Skin Board) Order 1968(**d**)	Schedule 1 Paragraph 1(*v*)

EXPLANATORY NOTE

(*This Note is not part of the Order.*)

This Order re-defines the activities in relation to which the Road Transport Industry Training Board exercises its functions. The Board was established on 15th September 1966 by the Industrial Training (Road Transport Board) Order 1966.

Amongst the activities henceforth to be included in the road transport industry are dealing in, letting out on hire or repairing agricultural or horticultural machinery and equipment.

There will henceforth be excluded from the industry—

(*a*) the activities of an establishment engaged wholly or mainly in selling by wholesale tyres or in the public warehousing of petroleum products ;

(*b*) the activities of a local authority other than the provision of a passenger road transport service.

(**a**) S.I. 1968/786 (1968 II, p. 2185).   (**b**) S.I. 1968/1032 (1968 II, p. 2709).
(**c**) S.I. 1968/1033 (1968 II, p. 2721).   (**d**) S.I. 1968/1763 (1968 III, p. 4785).

1969 No. 880

INDUSTRIAL TRAINING

The Industrial Training Levy (Road Transport) Order 1969

Made - - -		*26th June* 1969
Laid before Parliament		*7th July* 1969
Coming into Operation		*16th July* 1969

The Secretary of State after approving proposals submitted by the Road Transport Industry Training Board for the imposition of a further levy on employers in the road transport industry and in exercise of her powers under section 4 of the Industrial Training Act 1964(a) and of all other powers enabling her in that behalf hereby makes the following Order :—

Title and commencement

1. This Order may be cited as the Industrial Training Levy (Road Transport) Order 1969 and shall come into operation on 16th July 1969.

Interpretation

2.—(1) In this Order unless the context otherwise requires :—

(*a*) "an appeal tribunal" means an industrial tribunal established under section 12 of the Industrial Training Act 1964 ;

(*b*) "assessment" means an assessment of an employer to the levy ;

(*c*) "the Board" means the Road Transport Industry Training Board ;

(*d*) "business" means any activities of industry or commerce ;

(*e*) "emoluments" means all emoluments assessable to income tax under Schedule E (other than pensions), being emoluments from which tax under that Schedule is deductible, whether or not tax in fact falls to be deducted from any particular payment thereof ;

(*f*) "employer" means a person who is an employer in the road transport industry at any time in the third levy period ;

(*g*) "the industrial training order" means the Industrial Training (Road Transport Board) Order 1969(b) ;

(*h*) "the levy" means the levy imposed by the Board in respect of the third levy period ;

(*i*) "notice" means a notice in writing ;

(a) 1964 c. 16.   (b) S.I. 1969/879 (1969 II, p. 2495).

(j) "road transport establishment" means an establishment in Great Britain engaged in the third base period wholly or mainly in the road transport industry for a total of twenty-seven or more weeks or, being an establishment that commenced to carry on business in the third base period, for a total number of weeks exceeding one half of the number of weeks in the part of the said period commencing with the day on which business was commenced and ending on the last day thereof ;

(k) "the road transport industry" means any one or more of the activities which, subject to the provisions of paragraph 2 of the Schedule to the industrial training order, are specified in paragraph 1 of that Schedule as the activities of the road transport industry ;

(l) "the third base period" means the period of twelve months that commenced on 6th April 1968 ;

(m) "the third levy period" means the period commencing with the day upon which this Order comes into operation and ending on 5th April 1970 ;

(n) other expressions have the same meanings as in the industrial training order.

(2) Any reference in this Order to a person employed at or from a road transport establishment shall in any case where the employer is a company be construed as including a reference to any director of the company (or any person occupying the position of director by whatever name he is called) who devotes substantially the whole of his time to the service the company.

(3) In the case where a road transport establishment is taken over (whether directly or indirectly) by an employer in succession to, or jointly with, another person, a person employed at any time in the third base period at or from the establishment shall be deemed, for the purposes of this Order, to have been so employed by the employer carrying on the said establishment on the day upon which this Order comes into operation, and any reference in this Order to persons employed by the employer at or from a road transport establishment in the third base period shall be construed accordingly.

(4) Any reference in this Order to an establishment that commences to carry on business or that ceases to carry on business shall not be taken to apply where the location of the establishment is changed but its business is continued wholly or mainly at or from the new location, or where the suspension of activities is of a temporary or seasonal nature.

(5) The Interpretation Act 1889(a) shall apply to the interpretation of this Order as it applies to the interpretation of an Act of Parliament.

Imposition of the Levy

3.—(1) The levy to be imposed by the Board on employers in respect of the third levy period shall be assessed in accordance with the provisions of this Article.

(2) The levy shall be assessed by the Board in respect of each employer and, subject to the provisions of this Article, the amount thereof shall be the following percentage of the sum of the emoluments of all the persons employed by

---

(a) 1889. c. 63.

the employer at or from a road transport establishment in the third base period, that is to say—

(a) where the said sum did not exceed £5,000, 0·75 per cent.;

(b) where the said sum exceeded £5,000, but did not exceed £15,000, 1·5 per cent.;

(c) in any other case, 2·2 per cent.

(3) Where any persons whose emoluments are taken into account for the purposes of paragraph (2) of this Article were employed at or from an establishment that ceases to carry on business in the third levy period, the sum of the emoluments of those persons shall, for the purposes of the assessment, be reduced in the same proportion as the number of days between the commencement of the said levy period and the date of cessation of business (both dates inclusive) bears to the number of days in the said levy period, but the appropriate percentage shall be determined in accordance with the provisions of the said paragraph as if the provisions of this paragraph did not apply.

(4) For the purposes of this Article no regard shall be had to the emoluments of any person employed as follows:—

(a) by the London Transport Board wholly in any activities specified in paragraph 1(o) of the Schedule to the industrial training order, not being activities that are specified in head (ii), (v) or (vi) of paragraph 3(p) of that Schedule and are incidental or ancillary to principal activities of the road transport industry ;

(b) by a local authority or a joint board or joint committee of such authorities in any activities, not being activities carried out for the purposes of a passenger road transport service provided by the authority, board or committee ;

(c) wholly as a registered dock worker on dock work ; or

(d) wholly in the supply of food or drink for immediate consumption.

Assessment Notices

4.—(1) The Board shall serve an assessment notice on every employer assessed to the levy.

(2) The amount payable under an assessment notice shall be rounded down to the nearest £1.

(3) An assessment notice shall state the Board's address for the service of a notice of appeal or of an application for an extension of time for appealing.

(4) An assessment notice may be served on the person assessed to the levy either by delivering it to him personally or by leaving it, or sending it to him by post, at his last known address or place of business in the United Kingdom or, if that person is a corporation, by leaving it, or sending it by post to the corporation, at such address or place of business or at its registered or principal office.

Payment of Levy

5.—(1) Subject to the provisions of this Article and of Articles 6 and 7, the amount of the assessment appearing in an assessment notice served by the Board shall be payable to the Board as follows—

(a) where paragraph (2)(a) of Article 3 of this Order applies, by one payment due one month after the date of the assessment notice ;

(*b*) where paragraph (2)(*b*) of that Article applies, by two instalments equal respectively to two-thirds and one-third of the amount of the assessment, which instalments shall be due respectively one month and four months after the date of the assessment notice ; or

(*c*) where paragraph (2)(*c*) of the said Article applies, by two instalments equal respectively to six-elevenths and five-elevenths of the amount of the assessment, which instalments shall be due respectively one month and four months after the date of the assessment notice.

(2) No part of an assessment shall be recoverable by the Board until there has expired the time allowed for appealing against the assessment by Article 7(1) of this Order and any further period or periods of time that the Board or an appeal tribunal may have allowed for appealing under paragraph (2) or (3) of that Article or, where an appeal is brought, until the appeal is decided or withdrawn.

Withdrawal of Assessment

6.—(1) The Board may, by a notice served on the person assessed to the levy in the same manner as an assessment notice, withdraw an assessment if that person has appealed against that assessment under the provisions of Article 7 of this Order and the appeal has not been entered in the Register of Appeals kept under the appropriate Regulations specified in paragraph (5) of that Article.

(2) The withdrawal of an assessment shall be without prejudice to the power of the Board to serve a further assessment notice on the employer, and where the withdrawal is made by reason of the fact that an establishment has ceased to carry on business in the third levy period, the said notice may provide that the whole amount payable thereunder shall be due one month after the date of the notice.

Appeals

7.—(1) A person assessed to the levy may appeal to an appeal tribunal against the assessment within one month from the date of the service of the assessment notice or within any further period or periods of time that may be allowed by the Board or an appeal tribunal under the following provisions of this Article.

(2) The Board by notice may for good cause allow a person assessed to the levy to appeal to an appeal tribunal against the assessment at any time within the period of four months from the date of the service of the assessment notice or within such further period or periods as the Board may allow before such time as may then be limited for appealing has expired.

(3) If the Board shall not allow an application for extension of time for appealing, an appeal tribunal shall upon application made to the tribunal by the person assessed to the levy have the like powers as the Board under the foregoing paragraph.

(4) In the case of an assessment that has reference to an establishment that ceases to carry on business in the third levy period on any day after the date of the service of the assessment notice, the foregoing provisions of this Article shall have effect as if for the period of four months from the date of the service of the assessment notice mentioned in paragraph (2) of this Article there were substituted the period of six months from the date of the cessation of business.

(5) An appeal or an application to an appeal tribunal under this Article shall be made in accordance with the Industrial Tribunals (England and Wales) Regulations 1965(**a**) as amended by the Industrial Tribunals (England and Wales) (Amendment) Regulations 1967(**b**) except where the assessment relates to persons employed at or from an establishment which is wholly in Scotland and to no other persons in which case the appeal or application shall be made in accordance with the Industrial Tribunals (Scotland) Regulations 1965(**c**) as amended by the Industrial Tribunals (Scotland) (Amendment) Regulations 1967(**d**).

(6) The powers of an appeal tribunal under paragraph (3) of this Article may be exercised by the President of the Industrial Tribunals (England and Wales) or by the President of the Industrial Tribunals (Scotland) as the case may be.

Evidence

8.—(1) Upon the discharge by a person assessed to the levy of his liability under an assessment the Board shall if so requested issue to him a certificate to that effect.

(2) The production in any proceedings of a document purporting to be certified by the Secretary of the Board to be a true copy of an assessment or other notice issued by the Board or purporting to be a certificate such as is mentioned in the foregoing paragraph of this Article shall, unless the contrary is proved, be sufficient evidence of the document and of the facts stated therein.

26th June 1969.

Barbara Castle,
First Secretary of State and Secretary
of State for Employment and Productivity.

(**a**) S.I. 1965/1101 (1965 II, p. 2805).   (**b**) S.I. 1967/301 (1967 I, p. 1040).
(**c**) S.I. 1965/1157 (1965 II, p. 3266).   (**d**) S.I. 1967/302 (1967 I, p. 1050).

EXPLANATORY NOTE

(This Note is not part of the Order.)

This Order gives effect to proposals submitted to the Secretary of State for Employment and Productivity by the Road Transport Industry Training Board for the imposition of a further levy upon employers in the road transport industry for the purpose of raising money towards the expenses of the Board.

The levy is to be imposed in respect of the third levy period commencing with the day upon which this Order comes into operation and ending on 5th April 1970. The levy will be assessed by the Board and there will be a right of appeal against an assessment to an industrial tribunal.

STATUTORY INSTRUMENTS

1969 No. 881

DEFENCE

Military Pensions (Ministry of Overseas Development) Regulations 1969

Made - - - -	24th June 1969
Coming into Operation	25th June 1969

In exercise of the powers conferred on me by section 4 of the Pensions and Yeomanry Pay Act 1884(a) and Article 2(1)(a) of the Transfer of Functions (Overseas Pensions) Order 1965(b), I hereby make the following Regulations:—

1. These Regulations may be cited as the Military Pensions (Ministry of Overseas Development) Regulations 1969.

2. Where any part of the personal estate of a person referred to in section 4 of the aforesaid Act to whom a pension is payable by virtue of section 1 of the Pensions (India, Pakistan and Burma) Act 1955(c) or any order made thereunder is held by or under the control of the Minister of Overseas Development, and the amount thereof does not exceed £40, payment may be made—

(a) if there is an unrevoked will which it is not proposed to prove, to the person or persons who appear to the Minister to be beneficially entitled under the terms of the will;

(b) if no person appears to the Minister to be entitled to payment under the terms of the will, or if there is no will and Letters of Administration are not being taken out,

   (i) to the widow absolutely if the deceased left a widow or a widow and children;

   (ii) if the deceased left children only, to such of them as they may jointly agree upon and in the absence of any such agreement to such of them in such manner as appears to the Minister to be proper having regard to the laws applicable on an intestacy or to the payment of the funeral expenses of the deceased by any of them;

(c) in any other case, to such persons as the Minister may direct.

3. Notwithstanding the provisions of regulation 2 of these Regulations the production of Probate or Letters of Administration may be required if such a course seems desirable to the Minister.

R. E. Prentice,
Minister of Overseas Development.

24th June 1969.

(a) 1884 c. 55.   (b) S.I. 1965/1528 (1965 II, p. 4435).   (c) 1955 c. 22.

EXPLANATORY NOTE

(This Note is not part of the Regulations.)

These Regulations enable amounts not exceeding £40, held by the Minister of Overseas Development and forming part of the personal estate of certain deceased military pensioners who served in the former Indian forces or their widows or relatives, to be distributed without receipt of a declaration in the form set out in the schedule to the Military Pensions Commonwealth Relations Office Regulations 1959 (S.I. 1959/735).

1969 No. 882

INDUSTRIAL ORGANISATION AND DEVELOPMENT

The Hosiery and Knitwear Industry (Scientific Research Levy) Order 1969

Laid before Parliament in draft

Made - - -	*27th June* 1969
Coming into Operation	1st *July* 1969

Whereas it appears to the Board of Trade that it is expedient that funds be made available for the purpose of scientific research in connection with the hosiery and knitwear industry:

And Whereas it further appears to the Board of Trade that there is a body, called the Hosiery and Allied Trades Research Association, capable of carrying out such scientific research satisfactorily:

And Whereas the Board of Trade have consulted the organisations appearing to them to be representative of substantial numbers of persons carrying on business in the industry and the organisations representative of persons employed in the industry appearing to the Board of Trade to be appropriate:

And Whereas a draft of this Order has been approved by a resolution of each House of Parliament:

Now, therefore, the Board of Trade in pursuance of the powers conferred upon them by section 9 of the Industrial Organisation and Development Act 1947(a), hereby order as follows:—

Citation, commencement and interpretation

1.—(1) This Order may be cited as the Hosiery and Knitwear Industry (Scientific Research Levy) Order 1969 and shall come into operation on 1st July 1969.

(2) In this Order—

(*a*) "carrying out on commission" means in relation to any process the carrying out in pursuance of a contract of work and labour (with or without the provision of materials) of that process wholly or mainly upon or from materials owned in the course of his business by another person;

(*b*) "the industry" means the hosiery and knitwear industry;

(a) 1947 c. 40.

(c) "the designated activities" means the activities designated in the Schedule hereto.

(3) The Interpretation Act 1889(a) shall apply to the interpretation of this Order as it applies to the interpretation of an Act of Parliament.

Extent of the Industry

2. For the purposes of this Order the hosiery and knitwear industry shall consist of the activities designated in the Schedule hereto.

Persons to whom the Order applies

3. The persons to whom this Order applies are every person who on 1st July 1969 is carrying on, or who thereafter commences to carry on, business in the industry.

Levy Periods

4. The levy periods shall be the periods of six months ending on 30th June and 31st December respectively in each year and the base period in relation to any levy period shall be the period of six months immediately preceding that levy period.

Payment of Levies

5. Every person to whom this Order applies who has carried on business in the industry at any time during the first seven days of a levy period shall pay in respect of that levy period a charge calculated—

(a) in the case of a person carrying on any of the activities specified in paragraph 2(1) or 2(2) of the Schedule hereto, in accordance with the provisions of Article 6(1), (2), (3) and (5) hereof ;

(b) in the case of a person carrying on the activity specified in paragraph 2(3) of the Schedule hereto, in accordance with the provisions of Article 6(4) and (5) :

Provided that a person shall not be liable to pay any charge in respect of a levy period if the total amount on which that charge is to be calculated under Article 6 does not exceed £5,000.

Computation of Levies

6.—(1) The charge to be paid by any person by virtue of the provisions of Article 5(a) hereof in respect of any levy period shall be calculated at the rate of 6s. 8d. for every £1,000 of—

(a) the net aggregate value of the products supplied by him during the base period in pursuance of contracts of sale (being products of the designated activities carried on by him) ; and

(b) the aggregate of the amounts received by him during the base period in respect of the carrying out on commission of any process specified in paragraph 2(1) or (2) of the Schedule hereto for any person other than a person carrying on the activity specified in paragraph 2(1)(a).

(a) 1889. c. 63.

(2) The net aggregate value of the products supplied by a person during a base period shall be calculated by aggregating the prices received or receivable for such products before any deduction by way of discount, commission or allowance but excluding any sum in respect of purchase tax, and deducting therefrom—

(a) the aggregate of the prices paid or payable by that person for products of the designated activities supplied to him in pursuance of contracts of sale during that period being products acquired by him for the purpose of subjecting them to any process specified in paragraph 2(1)(b) or 2(2)(b) of the Schedule hereto, before any deduction by way of discount, commission or allowance but excluding any sum in respect of purchase tax ;

(b) the aggregate of the amounts paid by that person during that period in respect of the carrying out at any time for him of any process specified in paragraph 2(3) of the Schedule hereto (being a process carried out in Great Britain) by any person therein specified ;

(c) the aggregate of the expenditure shown to the satisfaction of the Board of Trade to have been reasonably incurred by that person during that period—

   (i) in respect of the maintaining and staffing of premises outside the United Kingdom in connection with the export therefrom of the products of the designated activities carried on by him ;

   (ii) for—

      (a) the advertising of the products of the designated activities carried on by him ; and

      (b) the procuring of contracts of sale of the products of the designated activities carried on by him ;
      being expenditure consisting of payment made or to be made to persons other than his employees ;

   (iii) in respect of the remuneration and expenses of his employees wholly engaged in the procuring of contracts of sale of the products of the designated activities carried on by him.

(3) There shall be deducted from the aggregate amount specified in paragraph (1)(b) of this Article the aggregate of the amounts paid by that person during that period in respect of the carrying out at any time for him of any process specified in paragraph 2(3) of the Schedule hereto (being a process carried out in Great Britain) by any person therein specified.

(4) The charge to be paid by any person by virtue of the provisions of Article 5(b) hereof in respect of any levy period shall be calculated at the rate of 6s. 8d. for every £1,000 of the aggregate of the amounts received by him during the base period in respect of the carrying out at any time of any process comprised in the activity specified in paragraph 2(3) of the Schedule hereto.

(5) The amount of the charge payable by any person in respect of any levy period shall, where necessary, be rounded to the nearest multiple of 6s. 8d.

Time for payment of levies

7.—(1) As soon as may be after the commencement of each levy period the Board of Trade will by notice, given in such manner as they think best adapted for informing the persons affected, require payment of the charges imposed by this Order in respect of that levy period.

(2) Every person liable to pay a charge imposed by this Order in respect of any levy period shall pay that charge within 30 days of the date on which the notice referred to in paragraph (1) of this Article is given in respect of that period.

(3) Every such charge shall be paid direct to the Board of Trade.

(4) The amount of any such charge shall be recoverable by the Board of Trade as a debt.

(5) All monies received by the Board of Trade in respect of any such charge shall be paid by them into the Hosiery and Knitwear Industry (Levy) Deposit Account, being an account opened by Her Majesty's Paymaster General on behalf of the Board of Trade, and shall be issued thereout to the Hosiery and Allied Trades Research Association to meet any expenses incurred by it in respect of scientific research in connection with the industry.

Furnishing of Information

8.—(1) Every person to whom this Order applies shall, within 30 days of the commencement of the first levy period in respect of which he is liable to pay a charge by virtue of the provisions of Article 5 hereof, furnish to the Board of Trade the following information—

(a) his name and address;

(b) the business name (if any) under which he carries on a business comprising any of the designated activities;

(c) the principal place of such business; and

(d) a description of such business.

(2) The Board of Trade may by notice in writing require any person to whom this Order applies:—

(a) to furnish such returns and other information;

(b) to keep such records; and

(c) to produce for examination such books and other documents and records

as may appear to the Board of Trade to be reasonably requisite for the purpose of the recovery of any charge imposed by this Order.

Enforcement

9. Any person who is required by notice in writing by the Board of Trade under the provisions of paragraph (2) of Article 8 hereof to furnish returns or other information, to keep records, or to produce for examination books or other documents or records, shall furnish in such form and manner and within such time such returns or other information as may be specified in the notice, or, as the case may be, keep such records or produce at such time such books or other documents or records in his custody or under his control as may be so specified.

Penalties

10.—(1) If any person required by or under the provisions of Article 8 hereof to furnish returns or other information, to keep records or to produce for examination books or other documents or records fails to furnish, keep or produce them in accordance with the requirement he shall, unless he proves that he had reasonable excuse for the failure, be liable on summary conviction to a fine not exceeding five pounds for every day during which the failure continues.

(2) If any person, in purporting to fulfil any requirement imposed by or under the provisions of Article 8 hereof to furnish returns or other information, knowingly or recklessly makes any statement which is false in a material particular he shall be liable on summary conviction to a fine not exceeding fifty pounds, or on conviction on indictment to imprisonment for a term not exceeding two years or to a fine not exceeding one hundred pounds or to both such imprisonment and such fine.

Edmund Dell,
Minister of State,
Board of Trade.

27th June 1969.

SCHEDULE

1. In this Schedule—

   (a) "narrow fabrics" means fabrics not exceeding 18″ in width with two selvedges ;

   (b) "knitted articles" means articles produced by the carrying on of the activities specified in sub-paragraphs (1)(a), (2)(a) or (2)(b) of paragraph 2 ;

   (c) "making up" means any process of examining, laying, cutting, seaming, binding, embroidery, button-holing, button-sewing and other sewing, heat welding or adhesive processes, and "made-up" shall be construed accordingly ;

   (d) "finishing" means any of the processes commonly known as dyeing, scouring, bleaching, shrink resisting, preboarding, post boarding, softening, milling, brushing, raising, cropping, weighting, decatising, stentering, setting, boarding, pressing, calendering, stabilising, bulking, relaxing, stoving, solvent scouring, water-resisting, flame-resisting, sizing and other similar processes ;

   (e) "packaging" means any process of inspecting, sorting, grading, packing, and packaging for dispatch.

2. The hosiery and knitwear industry shall consist of the following activities so far as carried on in Great Britain :—

   (1) (a) the knitting (whether on commission or not) on a weft-knitting machine of articles including garments, garment lengths, footwear or shaped pieces or other fabrics (not being narrow fabrics) ;

   (b) when carried out (whether on commission or not) by a person engaged in the activity specified in head (a) of this sub-paragraph,

   (i) the subjection of yarn to any of the processes commonly known as reeling, warping, beaming, winding, rewinding, cleaning and lubricating so far as the treatment of yarn by that process is performed on machinery which forms a subsidiary part of plant used for the production of knitted articles, and such treatment is ancillary to the main operations conducted on such plant ;

   (ii) the making up of knitted articles or of goods from knitted articles ;

    (iii) the application to knitted articles or goods made up from knitted articles of any of the processes commonly known as heat setting, steam pressing, straightening, folding, mending and any other similar process ;

    (iv) the finishing of knitted articles or of goods made up from knitted articles ;

    (v) the packaging of knitted articles or of goods made up from knitted articles ;

(2) the procurement by a person engaged in the activity specified in sub-paragraph (1)(a) of the carrying out on commission (whether in Great Britain or not) of—

    (a) the activity specified in sub-paragraph (1)(a), or

    (b) any process specified in heads (i) to (v) of sub-paragraph (1)(b) by any person ;

(3) the carrying out on commission for a person engaged in the activity specified in sub-paragraph (1)(a) by a person not so engaged of any process specified in head (iv) of sub-paragraph (1)(b).

EXPLANATORY NOTE

(This Note is not part of the Order.)

This Order which is made under the Industrial Organisation and Development Act 1947, imposes levies on persons carrying on business in the hosiery and knitwear industry. The proceeds of the levies will be used to finance scientific research to be carried out in connection with the industry by the Hosiery and Allied Trades Research Association.

1969 No. 884

INDUSTRIAL TRAINING

The Industrial Training (Iron and Steel Board) Order 1969

Made	-	-	-	27*th June* 1969
Laid before Parliament				7*th July* 1969
Coming into Operation				16*th July* 1969

The Secretary of State after consultation with the Iron and Steel Industry Training Board and with organisations and associations of organisations appearing to be representative respectively of substantial numbers of employers engaging in the activities hereinafter mentioned and of substantial numbers of persons employed in those activities and with a body established for the purpose of carrying on under national ownership an industry in which the said activities are carried on to a substantial extent and in exercise of her powers under section 9 of the Industrial Training Act 1964(a) and of all other powers enabling her in that behalf hereby makes the following Order:—

Citation, commencement and interpretation

1.—(1) This Order may be cited as the Industrial Training (Iron and Steel Board) Order 1969 and shall come into operation on 16th July 1969.

(2) In this Order—

(*a*) " the Act " means the Industrial Training Act 1964 ;

(*b*) " the Board " means the Iron and Steel Industry Training Board ;

(*c*) " Levy Order " includes the Industrial Training Levy (Iron and Steel) Order 1965(b), the Industrial Training Levy (Iron and Steel) Order 1966(c), the Industrial Training Levy (Iron and Steel) Order 1967(d) and the Industrial Training Levy (Iron and Steel) Order 1969(e) ;

(*d*) " the principal Order " means the Industrial Training (Iron and Steel Board) Order 1964(f).

(3) The Interpretation Act 1889(g) shall apply to the interpretation of this Order as it applies to the interpretation of an Act of Parliament and as if this Order and the principal Order were Acts of Parliament.

Activities of the Board

2. The activities in relation to which the Board exercises the functions conferred by the Act upon industrial training boards shall, in lieu of the activities specified in Schedule 1 to the principal Order, be the activities specified in the Schedule to this Order, and accordingly in the principal Order the latter Schedule shall be substituted for the former Schedule.

Transitional provisions

3.—(1) The chairman and other members of the Board on the day upon which this Order comes into operation shall continue to be members of the

---

(a) 1964 c. 16.

(b) S.I. 1965/1204 (1965 II, p. 3427).

(c) S.I. 1966/932 (1966 II, p. 2262).

(d) S.I. 1967/1334 (1967 III, p. 3980).

(e) S.I. 1969/1 (1969 I, p. 1).

(f) S.I. 1964/949 (1964 II, p. 2127).

(g) 1889 c. 63.

Board and to hold and vacate their offices in accordance with the terms of the instruments appointing them to be members.

(2) The provisions of this Order shall not—

(*a*) extend the operation of a Levy Order ;

(*b*) affect the operation of a Levy Order in relation to the assessment of an employer within the meaning of that Order in respect of an establishment that was engaged in the relevant levy period wholly or mainly in activities included in the Schedule to this Order ;

(*c*) affect the operation of any assessment notice served by the Board under the provisions of a Levy Order before the date upon which this Order comes into operation or any appeal or other proceedings arising out of any such notice.

Signed by order of the Secretary of State.

27th June 1969.

Roy Hattersley,
Joint Parliamentary Under Secretary of State,
Department of Employment and Productivity.

Article 2   SCHEDULE

THE IRON AND STEEL INDUSTRY

1. Subject to the provisions of this Schedule, the activities of the iron and steel industry are the following activities in so far as they are carried out in Great Britain : —

(*a*) the quarrying or mining of iron ore or the treatment or preparation of iron ore for smelting ;

(*b*) the smelting of iron ore in a blast furnace with or without other metalliferous materials, or the production of iron by any other process ;

(*c*) the production of steel by any process ;

(*d*) when carried out in association with any of the foregoing activities—

(i) the quarrying of limestone ;

(ii) the production of coke ;

(iii) the casting of iron or steel by any process ;

(iv) the production with or without heat of any iron or steel forgings ;

(v) the annealing or heat treatment of steel ;

(*e*) the rolling, with or without heat, of iron or steel products for the purpose of reducing the cross-sectional area thereof ;

(*f*) the production from iron or steel of bright bars, hot finished tubes or hot finished pipes ;

(*g*) when carried out by an employer (or an associated company of the employer, being a company) mainly engaged in the production of iron or steel and in the production from iron or steel of hot finished tubes or hot finished pipes—

(i) the production of cold finished tubes or cold finished pipes ;

(ii) the manipulation or fabrication of any tubes or pipes ;

(*h*) the production of tinplate, terneplate, iron or steel wire, or steel wire ropes ;

(i) when carried out in association with any of the foregoing activities the production of galvanised or other coated steel sheets ;

(j) any activities, being—

    (i) related activities incidental or ancillary to principal activities of the iron and steel industry ; or

    (ii) activities undertaken in the administration, control or direction of one or more establishments, being establishments engaged wholly or mainly in principal activities of that industry, in related activities incidental or ancillary thereto, or in the administration, control or direction of one or more other establishments engaged in such principal or related activities ;

and carried out, in either case, by the employer engaged in those principal activities or, where that employer is a company, by the company or by an associated company of the company ;

(k) any activities of industry or commerce (other than iron and steel activities) carried out at or from an establishment mainly engaged—

    (i) in iron and steel activities ; or

    (ii) in iron and steel activities and in activities described in the Appendix to this Schedule but to a greater extent in iron and steel activities than in activities described in that Appendix in relation to any one industry.

2. Notwithstanding anything contained in this Schedule, there shall not be included in the activities of the iron and steel industry—

(a) the activities of any establishment engaged—

    (i) mainly in activities not being iron and steel activities or activities described in the Appendix to this Schedule ; or

    (ii) to a less extent in iron and steel activities than in activities described in that Appendix in relation to any one industry ;

(b) the activities of any establishment engaged wholly or mainly in related activities, being activities—

    (i) incidental or ancillary to the activities of one or more establishments (in this sub-paragraph hereafter referred to as " the principal establishment ") engaged wholly or mainly in any activities not being principal activities of the iron and steel industry ; and

    (ii) carried out by the employer carrying on the principal establishment or, where that employer is a company, by the company or by an associated company of the company ;

(c) the supply of food or drink for immediate consumption.

3. In this Schedule unless the context otherwise requires—

(a) " company " includes any body corporate, and " subsidiary " has the same meaning as by virtue of section 154 of the Companies Act 1948(a) it has for the purposes of that Act ;

(b) " iron " and " steel " include respectively alloy iron and alloy steel containing in each case more than fifty-five per cent. of pure iron by weight ;

(c) " iron and steel activities " means any one or more of the principal activities of the iron and steel industry and the activities included in that industry by virtue of paragraph 1(j) of this Schedule ;

(d) " office premises " has the same meaning as in section 1(2) of the Offices, Shops and Railway Premises Act 1963(b) ;

(e) " principal activities of the iron and steel industry " means activities which, subject to the provisions of paragraph 2 of this Schedule, are specified in paragraph 1, other than sub-paragraphs (j) and (k) thereof, as activities of the iron and steel industry ;

(f) " production " includes any process or operation incidental or appertaining to production ;

(a) 1948 c. 38.   (b) 1963 c. 41.

(g) " related activities " means any of the following activities, that is to say —

   (i) research, development, design or drawing ;

   (ii) buying, selling, testing, advertising, packing, distribution, transport or any similar operations ;

   (iii) operations of a kind performed at office premises or laboratories, or at stores, warehouses or similar places ;

   (iv) cleaning, washing or garaging vehicles or carrying out running repairs or minor adjustments thereto ;

   (v) training of employees or apprentices.

4. For the purposes of this Schedule two companies shall be taken to be associated companies if one is a subsidiary of the other or both are subsidiaries of a third company, and " associated company " shall be construed accordingly.

APPENDIX

The activities that would be included in an industry specified in Column 1 hereof by virtue of the industrial training order specified in the corresponding entry in Column 2, if the provisions specified in Column 3 were omitted from that order.

Column 1	Column 2	Column 3
The wool, jute and flax industry	The Industrial Training (Wool Industry Board) Order 1964 as amended by the Industrial Training (Wool, Jute and Flax Board) Order 1968(a)	Schedule 1 Paragraph 1(s)
The construction industry	The Industrial Training (Construction Board) Order 1964 as amended by the Industrial Training (Construction Board) Order 1967(b)	Schedule 1 Paragraph 1(l)
The engineering industry	The Industrial Training (Engineering Board) Order 1964 as amended by the Industrial Training (Engineering Board) Order 1968(c)	Schedule 1 Paragraph1(m)
The shipbuilding industry	The Industrial Training (Shipbuilding Board) Order 1964 as amended by the Industrial Training (Shipbuilding Board) Order 1968(d)	Schedule 1 Paragraph 1(g)
The ceramics, glass and mineral products industry	The Industrial Training (Ceramics, Glass and Mineral Products Board) Order 1965 as amended by the Industrial Training (Ceramics, Glass and Mineral Products Board) Order 1969(e)	Schedule 1 Paragraph 1(p)
The furniture and timber industry	The Industrial Training (Furniture and Timber Industry Board) Order 1965(f)	Schedule 1 Paragraph 1(r)
The man-made fibres producing industry	The Industrial Training (Man-made Fibres Producing Industry Board) Order 1966(g)	Schedule 1 Paragraph 1(d)

(a) S.I. 1964/907, 1968/898 (1964 II, p. 1928; 1968 II, p. 2376).
(b) S.I. 1964/1079, 1967/924 (1964 II, p. 2384; 1967 II, p. 2757).
(c) S.I. 1964/1086, 1968/1333 (1964 II, p. 2402; 1968 II, p. 3694).
(d) S.I. 1964/1782, 1968/1614 (1964 III, p. 3928; 1968 III, p. 4432).
(e) S.I. 1965/1391, 1969/689 (1965 II, p. 4062; 1969 II, p. 1858).
(f) S.I. 1965/2028 (1965 III, p. 5998).
(g) S.I. 1966/143 (1966 I, p. 257).

APPENDIX (*contd.*)

Column 1	Column 2	Column 3
The carpet industry	The Industrial Training (Carpet Board) Order 1966 as amended by the Industrial Training (Carpet Board) Order 1968(a)	Schedule 1 Paragraph 1(*f*)
The knitting, lace and net industry	The Industrial Training (Knitting, Lace and Net Industry Board) Order 1966(b)	Schedule 1 Paragraph 1(*j*)
The cotton and allied textiles industry	The Industrial Training (Cotton and Allied Textiles Board) Order 1966(c)	Schedule 1 Paragraph 1(*p*)
The agricultural, horticultural and forestry industry	The Industrial Training (Agricultural, Horticultural and Forestry Board) Order 1966(d)	Schedule 1 Paragraph 1(*m*)
The road transport industry	The Industrial Training (Road Transport Board) Order 1966 as amended by the Industrial Training (Road Transport Board) Order 1969(e)	Schedule 1 Paragraph 1(*p*)
The hotel and catering industry	The Industrial Training (Hotel and Catering Board) Order 1966(f)	Schedule 1 Paragraph 1(*e*)
The civil air transport industry	The Industrial Training (Civil Air Transport Board) Order 1967(g)	Schedule 1 Paragraph 1(*h*)
The petroleum industry	The Industrial Training (Petroleum Board) Order 1967(h)	Schedule 1 Paragraph 1(*h*)
The rubber and plastics processing industry	The Industrial Training (Rubber and Plastics Processing Board) Order 1967(i)	Schedule 1 Paragraph 1(*k*)
The chemical and allied products industry	The Industrial Training (Chemical and Allied Products Board) Order 1967(j)	Schedule 1 Paragraph 1(*s*)
The paper and paper products industry	The Industrial Training (Paper and Paper Products Board) Order 1968(k)	Schedule 1 Paragraph 1(*j*)
The printing and publishing industry	The Industrial Training (Printing and Publishing Board) Order 1968(l)	Schedule 1 Paragraph 1(*n*)
The distributive industry	The Industrial Training (Distributive Board) Order 1968(m)	Schedule 1 Paragraph 1(*h*)
The food, drink and tobacco industry	The Industrial Training (Food, Drink and Tobacco Board) Order 1968(n)	Schedule 1 Paragraph 1(*q*)
The footwear, leather and fur skin industry	The Industrial Training (Footwear, Leather and Fur Skin Board) Order 1968(o)	Schedule 1 Paragraph 1(*v*)

(a) S.I. 1966/245, 1968/1882 (1966 I, p. 499; 1968 III, p. 5017).
(b) S.I. 1966/246 (1966 I, p. 506).
(c) S.I. 1966/823 (1966 II, p. 1907).
(d) S.I. 1966/969 (1966 II, p. 2333).
(e) S.I. 1966/1112, 1969/879 (1966 III, p. 2712).
(f) S.I. 1966/1347 (1966 III, p. 3669).
(g) S.I. 1967/263 (1967 I, p. 506).
(h) S.I. 1967/648 (1967 I, p. 2032).
(i) S.I. 1967/1062 (1967 II, p. 3151).
(j) S.I. 1967/1386 (1967 III, p. 4049).
(k) S.I. 1968/787 (1968 II, p. 2194).
(l) S.I. 1968/786 (1968 II, p. 2185).
(m) S.I. 1968/1032 (1968 II, p. 2709).
(n) S.I. 1968/1033 (1968 II, p. 2721).
(o) S.I. 1968/1763 (1968 III, p. 4785).

EXPLANATORY NOTE
(This Note is not part of the Order.)

The Iron and Steel Industry Training Board was established on 3rd July 1964 by the Industrial Training (Iron and Steel Board) Order 1964 which defined the iron and steel industry in relation to which the Board exercises its functions. This Order re-defines that industry.

The principal changes in the definition of the industry are the inclusion therein of—

(*a*) the production of cold finished tubes or cold finished pipes ;

(*b*) the manipulation or fabrication of any tubes or pipes ;

when carried out by an employer (or associated company) mainly engaged in the production of iron or steel and in the production from iron or steel of hot finished tubes or pipes.

STATUTORY INSTRUMENTS

1969 No. 886

FRIENDLY SOCIETIES

DECIMAL CURRENCY

The Friendly Societies (Halfpenny) Regulations 1969

Made - - -	*30th June* 1969
Laid before Parliament	*9th July* 1969
Coming into Operation	*10th July* 1969

The Chief Registrar of Friendly Societies pursuant to the powers conferred upon him by section 6(6) of the Decimal Currency Act 1969(a) and of all other powers enabling him in that behalf hereby makes the following Regulations:—

1.—(1) These Regulations may be cited as the Friendly Societies (Halfpenny) Regulations 1969 and shall come into operation on 10th July 1969.

(2) The Interpretation Act 1889(b) shall apply to the interpretation of these Regulations as it applies to the interpretation of an Act of Parliament.

(3) In these Regulations—

"registered friendly society" and "society" mean a friendly society registered under the Friendly Societies Act 1896(c) or a branch so registered of such a friendly society;

"collecting society" has the meaning assigned to it by section 1 of the Industrial Assurance Act 1923(d) as amended by Schedule 6 to the Companies Act 1967(e).

2.—(1) This regulation applies to a payment payable to a registered friendly society, not being a collecting society, under a contract made by the society with a member of the society in the course of its business in Great Britain, whether contained in the society's rules or not, which is one of a series of payments payable periodically of an amount which, apart from this regulation, would be or include a halfpenny.

(2) Successive payments in a series, being each a payment to which this regulation applies and beginning with the first of such successive payments which falls due on or after 1st August 1969, shall be alternately reduced and increased in that order by the amount of a halfpenny and accordingly when such successive payments would be, but for this regulation, each of an amount of a halfpenny no amount shall be payable in respect of the first payment of every two such successive payments in the series beginning as aforesaid.

S. D. Musson,
Chief Registrar of Friendly Societies.

30th June 1969.

(a) 1969 c. 19.　　(b) 1889 c. 63.　　(c) 1896 c. 25.
(d) 1923 c. 8.　　(e) 1967 c. 81.

EXPLANATORY NOTE

(This Note is not part of the Regulations.)

These Regulations are consequent upon the halfpenny ceasing to be legal tender on the 1st August 1969 and provide that periodical payments payable by a member to a registered friendly society which are of or include a halfpenny shall as from that date be reduced and increased alternately by a halfpenny.

1969 No. 887

INDUSTRIAL ASSURANCE

DECIMAL CURRENCY

The Industrial Assurance (Halfpenny) Regulations 1969

Made - - -	*30th June* 1969
Laid before Parliament	*9th July* 1969
Coming into Operation	*10th July* 1969

The Industrial Assurance Commissioner pursuant to the powers conferred upon him by section 6(6) of the Decimal Currency Act 1969(a) and of all other powers enabling him in that behalf hereby makes the following Regulations:—

1.—(1) These Regulations may be cited as the Industrial Assurance (Halfpenny) Regulations 1969 and shall come into operation on 10th July 1969.

(2) The Interpretation Act 1889(b) shall apply to the interpretation of these Regulations as it applies to the interpretation of an Act of Parliament.

(3) In these Regulations—

"industrial assurance company", "industrial assurance business" and "collecting society" have the meaning assigned to them by section 1 of the Industrial Assurance Act 1923(c) as amended by Schedule 6 to the Companies Act 1967(d).

2.—(1) This regulation applies to a payment payable to an industrial assurance company under a contract of assurance made by the company in the course of its industrial assurance business in Great Britain or to a collecting society under a contract made by the society with a member of the society in the course of its business in Great Britain, whether contained in the society's rules or not, which is one of a series of payments payable periodically of an amount which, apart from this regulation, would be or include a halfpenny.

(2) Successive payments in a series, being each a payment to which this regulation applies and beginning with the first of such successive payments which falls due on or after 1st August 1969, shall be alternately reduced and increased in that order by the amount of a halfpenny and accordingly when such successive payments would be, but for this regulation, each of an amount of a halfpenny no amount shall be payable in respect of the first payment of every two such successive payments in the series beginning as aforesaid.

S. D. Musson,
Industrial Assurance Commissioner.

30th June 1969.

(a) 1969 c. 19.   (b) 1889 c. 63.   (c) 1923 c. 8.   (d) 1967 c. 81.

EXPLANATORY NOTE

(This Note is not part of the Regulations.)

These Regulations are consequent upon the halfpenny ceasing to be legal tender on the 1st August 1969 and provide that periodical payments payable to an industrial assurance company or collecting society under an industrial assurance contract which are of or include a halfpenny shall as from that date be reduced and increased alternately by a halfpenny.

STATUTORY INSTRUMENTS

1969 No. 888

ROAD TRAFFIC

The 'Pelican' Pedestrian Crossings Regulations and General Directions 1969

Made - - -	30*th June* 1969
Laid before Parliament	8*th July* 1969
Coming into Operation	11*th July* 1969

ARRANGEMENT

PART I—GENERAL

	Paragraph
Citation and commencement	1
Revocation	2
Interpretation	3

PART II—REGULATIONS

	Regulation
Citation	1
Amendment of Pedestrian Crossings Regulations 1954 ...	2
'Pelican' crossings	3
Variations in dimensions	4
Significance of traffic signs	5
Significance of the vehicular traffic light signals	6
Significance of the traffic signs for pedestrians	7
Movement of traffic and precedence of pedestrians	8
Requirements with respect to the stopping of vehicles on the approach to a 'Pelican' crossing	9
Prohibition against the proceeding of vehicles across a 'Pelican' crossing	10
Precedence of pedestrians over vehicles on a 'Pelican' crossing	11
Prohibitions against the waiting of vehicles and pedestrians on a 'Pelican' crossing	12

SCHEDULES

		Page
1.	The size, colour and type of traffic signs at a 'Pelican' crossing	2536
2.	The manner of indicating the presence and limits of a 'Pelican' crossing	2538

PART III—GENERAL DIRECTIONS

	Paragraph
Citation	1
Number of traffic signals	2
Manner of placing traffic signals	3
Additional traffic signals	4
Colouring of containers and posts	5
Approval of sites and mechanisms	6
Special cases	7

The following Regulations

(a) in so far as they contain provisions prescribing traffic signs to be used in connection with crossings for foot passengers, are made by the Secretary of State and the Minister of Transport acting jointly in exercise of their powers under section 54 of the Road Traffic Regulation Act 1967(a) (hereinafter referred to as "the Act of 1967") and of all other enabling powers, and after consultation with representative organisations in accordance with the provisions of section 107(2) of the Act of 1967 :

(b) in so far as they contain other provisions relating to crossings for foot passengers, are made by the Secretary of State (as respects such of those provisions as relate to crossings for foot passengers on roads in Scotland, Wales and Monmouthshire) and the Minister of Transport (as respects such of those provisions as relate to crossings for foot passengers on roads in England excluding Monmouthshire) respectively, each acting in exercise of his powers under section 23 of the Act of 1967, and of all other enabling powers, and after such consultation as aforesaid.

The following General Directions are given by the Secretary of State and the Minister of Transport acting jointly in exercise of their powers under section 55 of the Act of 1967, and of all other enabling powers.

PART I—GENERAL

Citation and commencement

1. This Instrument may be cited as the 'Pelican' Pedestrian Crossings Regulations and General Directions 1969, and shall come into operation on the 11th July 1969.

Revocation

2. The Pedestrian Crossings (Push Button Control) Regulations and General Directions 1967(b) are hereby revoked as from 10th July 1971.

Interpretation

3.—(1) In this Instrument unless the context otherwise requires the following expressions have the meanings hereby respectively assigned to them :—

"the appropriate Minister" means, in relation to a crossing established on a road in Scotland Wales or Monmouthshire, the Secretary of State, and in relation to a crossing established on a road in England excluding Monmouthshire, the Minister of Transport ;

(a) 1967 c. 76. (b) S.I. 1967/178 (1967 I, p. 309).

"carriageway" does not include that part of any road which consists of a street refuge or central reservation, whether within the limits of a crossing or not ;

"central reservation" means any provision, not consisting of a street refuge, made in a road for separating one part of the carriageway of that road from another part of that carriageway for the safety or guidance of vehicular traffic using that road ;

"crossing" means a crossing for foot passengers established either—

(a) by a local authority in accordance with the provisions for the time being in force of a scheme submitted and approved under section 21 of the Act of 1967, or

(b) in the case of a trunk road, by the Secretary of State or the Minister in the discharge of the duty imposed on him by section 22 of the Act of 1967 ;

"one-way street" means any road on which the driving of vehicles otherwise than in one direction is prohibited at all times ;

" 'Pelican' crossing" means a crossing—

(a) at which there are traffic signs of the size, colour and type prescribed by Regulation 3(1) of and Schedule 1 to the Regulations contained in Part II of this Instrument, and

(b) the presence and limits of which are indicated in accordance with Regulation 3(2) of and Schedule 2 to the Regulations contained in Part II of this Instrument ;

"stop line" in relation to the driver of a motor vehicle approaching a 'Pelican' crossing means the white line indicating the approach to the crossing in accordance with paragraph 3 of Schedule 2 to the Regulations contained in Part II of this Instrument, which is parallel to the limits of the crossing and on the same side of the crossing as the driver ;

"stud" means any mark or device on the carriageway, whether or not projecting above the surface thereof ;

"vehicular traffic light signal", "pedestrian light signal" and "indicator for pedestrians" mean respectively the traffic signals of those descriptions prescribed by Regulation 3(1) of and Schedule 1 to the Regulations contained in Part II of this Instrument.

(2) Any reference in this Instrument to a light shown by a signal or indicator is a reference to a light of constant intensity unless the contrary intention appears.

(3) Any reference in this Instrument to any enactment or instrument shall be construed, unless the context otherwise requires, as a reference to that enactment or instrument as amended, re-enacted or replaced by any subsequent enactment or instrument.

(4) The Interpretation Act 1889(a) shall apply for the interpretation of this Instrument as it applies for the interpretation of an Act of Parliament, and as if for the purposes of section 38 of that Act this Instrument were an Act of Parliament and the Instrument revoked by paragraph 2 of this Part of this Instrument were an Act of Parliament thereby repealed.

(a) 52 & 53 Vict. c. 63.

PART II—REGULATIONS

Citation

1. The Regulations contained in this Part of this Instrument may be cited as the 'Pelican' Pedestrian Crossings Regulations 1969.

Amendment of Pedestrian Crossings Regulations 1954

2. The Pedestrian Crossings Regulations 1954(**a**) as amended by the Pedestrian Crossings (Push Button Control) Regulations 1962(**b**) and the Pedestrian Crossings (Push Button Control) Regulations 1967(**c**) shall have effect as if there were added to the end of the definition of the expression "crossing" in Regulation 2(1) the words "or the 'Pelican' Pedestrian Crossings Regulations 1969", but as from 10th July 1971 the said definition shall have effect as if the words "the Pedestrian Crossings (Push Button Control) Regulations 1967 or" were deleted.

'Pelican' crossings

3.—(1) The provisions of Schedule 1 to these Regulations shall have effect as respects the size, colour and type of the traffic signs which are to be placed at or near a crossing for the purpose of constituting it a 'Pelican' crossing.

(2) The provisions of Schedule 2 to these Regulations shall have effect for regulating the manner in which the presence and limits of a crossing are to be indicated for the purpose of constituting it a 'Pelican' crossing.

Variations in dimensions

4.—(1) Any variation in a dimension (other than as to the height of a letter) specified in any of the diagrams in Parts II and III of Schedule 1 to these Regulations shall be treated as permitted by these Regulations if the variation—

(*a*) in the case of a dimension of less than 50 millimetres, does not exceed 10% of that dimension ;

(*b*) in the case of a dimension of 50 millimetres or more but less than 300 millimetres, does not exceed 5% of that dimension ; or

(*c*) in the case of a dimension of 300 millimetres or more, does not exceed $2\frac{1}{2}$% of that dimension.

(2) Any variation in a dimension as to the height of a letter specified in either of the diagrams in Part III of Schedule 1 to these Regulations shall be treated as permitted by these Regulations if the variation does not exceed 5% of that dimension.

(3) Any variation in a dimension of a white line or gap specified in Schedule 2 to these Regulations shall be treated as permitted by these Regulations if the variation—

(*a*) in the case of a dimension of 3 metres or more, does not exceed 15% of that dimension ;

(*b*) in the case of a dimension of 300 millimetres or more but less than 3 metres, does not exceed 20% of that dimension ; or

(*c*) in the case of a dimension of less than 300 millimetres, where the actual dimension exceeds the dimension so specified, does not exceed 20% of the dimension so specified, and where the actual dimension is less than the dimension so specified, does not exceed 10% of the dimension so specified.

(**a**) S.I. 1954/370 (1954 II, p. 1948).   (**b**) S.I. 1962/425 (1962 I, p. 479).
(**c**) S.I. 1967/178 (1967 I. p. 309).

(4) Any variation in the angle between a row of studs and the edge of a carriageway or longitudinal broken line specified in Schedule 2 shall be treated as permitted by these Regulations if the variation does not exceed 20 degrees.

Significance of traffic signs

5. Regulations 6 and 7 of these Regulations are made under section 54 of the Act of 1967 and shall have effect for the purpose of prescribing the warnings, information, requirements and prohibitions which are to be conveyed to traffic by the traffic signs of the size, colour and type prescribed by Regulation 3(1) of and Schedule 1 to these Regulations.

Significance of the vehicular traffic light signals

6.—(1) The vehicular traffic light signal at a 'Pelican' crossing shall convey the following information, requirements and prohibitions :—

(*a*) the green light shall convey the information that vehicular traffic may proceed across the crossing ;

(*b*) the amber light shall convey the prohibition that vehicular traffic shall not proceed beyond the stop line, or, if the stop line is not for the time being visible, beyond the vehicular traffic light signal facing such traffic on the side of the carriageway on which vehicles approach the crossing, except in the case of any vehicle which when the amber light is first shown is so close to the said line or signal that it cannot safely be stopped before passing the line or signal ;

(*c*) the red light shall convey the prohibition that vehicular traffic shall not proceed beyond the stop line, or, if the stop line is not for the time being visible, beyond the vehicular traffic light signal facing such traffic on the side of the carriageway on which vehicles approach the crossing ; and

(*d*) the flashing amber light shall convey the information that vehicular traffic may proceed across the crossing but that every foot passenger, if the foot passenger is on the carriageway within the limits of that crossing before any part of a vehicle has entered those limits, has the right of precedence within those limits over that vehicle, and the requirement that the driver of a vehicle shall accord such precedence to any such foot passenger.

(2) Vehicular traffic passing the vehicular traffic light signal in accordance with the foregoing provisions of this Regulation shall proceed with due regard to the safety of other users of the road and subject to the direction of any police constable or traffic warden in uniform who may be engaged in the regulation of traffic.

Significance of the traffic signs for pedestrians

7.—(1) The traffic signs for pedestrians at a 'Pelican' crossing shall convey to foot passengers the warnings and information mentioned in the following paragraphs of this Regulation.

(2) The pedestrian light signal shall convey to foot passengers the following warnings and information :—

(*a*) the red light shown by the pedestrian light signal shall convey to a foot passenger the warning that he should not in the interests of safety use the crossing ;

(*b*) the green light shown by the pedestrian light signal shall convey to a foot passenger the information that he may use the crossing and drivers of vehicles may not cause their vehicles to enter the limits of the crossing ; and

(c) the flashing green light shown by the pedestrian light signal shall convey—

   (i) to a foot passenger who is already on the crossing when the flashing green light is first shown the information that he may continue to use the crossing, that vehicular traffic may proceed across the crossing, and that if he is on the carriageway within the limits of the crossing before any part of a vehicle has entered those limits he has the right of precedence within those limits over that vehicle, and

   (ii) to a foot passenger who is not already on the crossing when the flashing green light is first shown the warning that he should not in the interests of safety start to cross the carriageway.

(3) When the word "WAIT" shown by the indicator for pedestrians is illuminated it shall convey to a foot passenger the same warning as that conveyed by the red light shown by the pedestrian light signal.

(4) Any audible signal emitted by any device for emitting audible signals provided in conjunction with the indicator for pedestrians shall convey to a foot passenger the information that he may use the crossing and drivers of vehicles may not cause their vehicle to enter the limits of the crossing.

Movement of traffic and precedence of pedestrians

8. Regulations 9, 10, 11 and 12 of these Regulations are made under section 23 of the Act of 1967 and shall have effect with respect to the movement of traffic (including foot passengers) and the precedence of the foot passengers over vehicles at and in the vicinity of a 'Pelican' crossing.

Requirements with respect to the stopping of vehicles on the approach to a 'Pelican' crossing

9.—(1) Subject to the provisions of paragraph (2) of this Regulation, the driver of a vehicle shall not cause the vehicle or any part thereof to stop on the carriageway between—

(a) a 'Pelican' crossing, the approach to which is indicated by a pattern of studs as provided in paragraph 3 of Schedule 2 to these Regulations, and

(b) the line of studs in that pattern situated furthest from the crossing, on the side of the road on which the pattern of studs is placed, or, if the road is a one-way street, on either side of the road.

(2) Nothing in paragraph (1) of this Regulation shall apply—

(a) so as to prevent a vehicle stopping on any length of road or any side thereof so long as may be necessary to enable the vehicle, if it cannot be used for such purpose without stopping on that length of road or side thereof, to be used in connection with any building operation or demolition, the removal of any obstruction to traffic, the maintenance, improvement or reconstruction of that length of road or side thereof, or the laying, erection, alteration or repair in or near to that length of road of any sewer or of any main, pipe or apparatus for the supply of gas, water or electricity, or of any telegraphic line as defined in the Telegraph Act 1878(a) ;

(a) 41 & 42 Vict. c. 76.

SCHEDULE 2 (See Regulation 3)

THE MANNER OF INDICATING THE PRESENCE AND LIMITS OF A 'PELICAN' CROSSING

Manner of indicating the limits of the crossing

1.—(1) Every crossing which is a 'Pelican' crossing and its limits shall be indicated by two lines of studs placed across the carriageway or between the edge of the carriageway and a street refuge or central reservation in accordance with the following provisions of this paragraph.

(2) Each line formed by the outside edges of the studs shall be so separated from the other line so formed that the distance between any point on one of those lines and the nearest point on the other line shall not be less than 2·4 metres nor more than 5 metres or such greater distance (not being more than 10 metres) as may be authorised in writing by the appropriate Minister in the case of any particular crossing;

Provided that the foregoing provisions of this sub-paragraph shall be regarded as having been complied with in the case of any crossing which for the most part complies with those provisions notwithstanding that those provisions may not be so complied with as respects the distance from one or more points on one line to the nearest point on the other line, so long as the general indication of the lines is not thereby materially impaired.

(3) The studs of which each line is constituted shall be so placed that the distance from the centre of any one stud to the centre of the next stud in the line is not less than 500 millimetres nor more than 720 millimetres, and a distance of not more than 1·3 metres is left between the edge of the carriageway central reservation or street refuge at either end of the line and the centre of the stud nearest thereto:

Provided that the foregoing provisions of this sub-paragraph shall be regarded as having been complied with in the case of any line where most of the studs constituting it comply with those provisions notwithstanding that those provisions may not be complied with as respects one or more such studs, so long as the general indication of the line is not thereby materially impaired.

(4) Studs shall not be fitted with reflecting lenses and shall be—

(*a*) white, silver or light grey in colour;

(*b*) square or circular in plan, the sides of a square stud and the diameter of a circular stud not being less than 95 millimetres nor more than 110 millimetres in length; and

(*c*) so fixed that they do not project more than 15 millimetres above the carriageway at their highest points nor more than 6 millimetres at their edges.

2. A crossing or its limits shall not be deemed to have ceased to be indicated in accordance with the provisions of the foregoing paragraph by reason only of the discoloration or temporary removal or displacement of one or more studs in any line so long as the general indication of the line is not thereby materially impaired.

Manner of indicating the vehicular approach to the crossing

3.—(1) Subject to the following provisions of this paragraph, the approach for vehicular traffic to a 'Pelican' crossing shall be indicated by a pattern of studs placed and white lines marked on the carriageway in accordance with the following provisions of this paragraph.

(2) On a road, not being a one-way street, and where the crossing is not a crossing which extends only between the edge of the carriageway and a street refuge or a central reservation, the pattern of studs and white lines shall be indicated on each side of the crossing and shall comply with the following requirements, the relevant dimensions being those shown without brackets:—

(*a*) There shall be a transverse stop line 200 millimetres (300 millimetres) wide from the edge of the carriageway to the centre of the carriageway on the side of the carriageway on which vehicles approach the crossing, parallel to the line of studs indicating the limits of the crossing on the side of the crossing nearer to the approaching vehicles, and not less than 1·7 metres nor more than 2·0 metres from such line of studs.

(b) There shall be a longitudinal broken line 100 millimetres wide along the centre of the carriageway extending from the end of the transverse stop line away from the crossing and consisting of three (five) strips 4·0 metres (6·0 metres) long and two (four) gaps 2·0 metres (3·0 metres) long arranged alternately in such a manner that the first strip adjoins the transverse stop line.

(c) There shall be two rows of studs from the edge of the carriageway to the centre of the carriageway on the side of the carriageway on which vehicles approach the crossing, complying with the following requirements:—

  (i) The two rows shall be parallel to each other.

  (ii) The row of studs further from the crossing shall be not less than 14·0 metres (23·5 metres) nor more than 16·0 metres (26·5 metres) from the line of studs indicating the limits of the crossing on the side of the crossing nearer to the approaching vehicles except where such distances would be inappropriate having regard to the layout and conditions at the place where the crossing is situated.

  (iii) If the edge of the carriageway and the longitudinal broken line are parallel at the places where the two rows of studs meet them the two rows of studs shall be straight and at right angles to the edge of the carriageway and in any other case the two rows of studs shall be curved as appropriate so as to meet the edge of the carriageway or the longitudinal broken line at a right angle.

  (iv) Each row of studs shall have the same number of studs.

  (v) The two rows of studs shall be not less than 300 millimetres nor more than 410 millimetres apart, measured between the centres of the studs.

  (vi) There shall be not more than 1·3 metres between the edge of the carriageway and the centre of the nearest stud thereto in each row.

  (vii) There shall be not less than 500 millimetres nor more than 720 millimetres between the centre of any stud in a row and the centre of the next stud thereto in that row.

  (viii) There shall be not less than 500 millimetres nor more than 720 millimetres between the centre of the longitudinal broken line and the centre of the nearest stud thereto in each row.

(3) On a road, being a one-way street, or where a crossing extends only between the edge of the carriageway and a street refuge or a central reservation, the pattern of studs and white lines shall be indicated on the side of the crossing on which vehicles approach the crossing and shall comply with the following requirements, the relevant dimensions being those shown without brackets:—

(a) There shall be a transverse stop line 200 millimetres (300 millimetres) wide from one edge of the carriageway to the other, in the case of a crossing on a one-way street, or, in the case of a crossing which extends only between the edge of the carriageway and a street refuge or a central reservation, from that edge of the carriageway to the centre of the carriageway or to the edge of the central reservation, as the case may be, in each case parallel to the nearer line of studs indicating the limits of the crossing and not less than 1·7 metres nor more than 2·0 metres from such line of studs.

(b) There shall be a longitudinal broken line 100 millimetres wide along the centre of the carriageway extending from the centre of the transverse stop line in the case of a crossing on a one-way street, or, in the case of a crossing which extends only between the edge of the carriageway and a central refuge from the end of the transverse stop line away from the crossing and consisting of three (five) strips 4·0 metres (6·0 metres) long and two (four) gaps 2·0 metres (3·0 metres) long arranged alternately in such a manner that the first strip adjoins the transverse stop line.

(c) There shall be two rows of studs from one edge of the carriageway to the other, in the case of a crossing on a one-way street, or, in the case of a crossing which extends only between the edge of the carriageway and a street refuge or a central reservation, from that edge of the carriageway to the centre of the carriageway, or to the edge of the central reservation, as the case may be, in each case complying with the following requirements:—

(i) The two rows shall be parallel to each other.

(ii) The row of studs further from the crossing shall be not less than 14·0 metres (23·5 metres) nor more than 16·0 metres (26·5 metres) from the nearer line of studs indicating the limits of the crossing except where such distances would be inappropriate having regard to the layout and conditions at the place where the crossing is situate.

(iii) If the two edges of the carriageway and the longitudinal broken line, or the edge of the carriageway and the edge of the central reservation, are parallel at the places where the two rows meet them, the two rows of studs shall be straight and at right angles to the edge of the carriageway and in any other case the two rows of studs shall be curved as appropriate so as to meet the edge of the carriageway, or the edge of the central reservation, or the longitudinal broken line, as the case may be, at a right angle.

(iv) Each row of studs shall have the same number of studs.

(v) The two rows of studs shall be not less than 300 millimetres apart nor more than 410 millimetres apart, measured between the centres of the studs.

(vi) There shall be not more than 1·3 metres between the edge or centre of the carriageway, or the edge of the central reservation, as the case may be, and the centre of the nearest stud thereto in each row.

(vii) Except in the case of the two studs in each row which lie one on each side of the longitudinal centre line, there shall be not less than 500 millimetres nor more than 720 millimetres between the centre or any stud in a row and the centre of the next stud thereto in that row.

(viii) There shall be not less than 500 millimetres nor more than 720 millimetres between the centre of the longitudinal centre line and the centre of the nearest stud thereto in each row on each side thereof.

(4) In the case of a road on which a speed limit on the driving of motor vehicles is not in force by virtue of any enactment—

(a) of 30 miles per hour or less, where figures appear in the last two preceding sub-paragraphs in brackets alongside other figures in relation to the dimensions of the pattern of studs, the figures in brackets shall apply in substitution for the said other figures;

(b) of 40 miles per hour or less, where figures appear in the last two preceding sub-paragraphs in brackets alongside other figures in relation to the dimensions of the pattern of white lines, the figures in brackets shall apply in substitution for the said other figures.

(5) The transverse stop line may be omitted or its angle in relation to and its distance from the crossing varied and the longitudinal broken line may be omitted having regard to the layout and conditions at the place where the crossing is situate.

(6) The requirements of this paragraph shall be regarded as having been complied with in the case of any pattern of studs or white lines if most of the studs or the lengths of white lines comply with those requirements notwithstanding that one or more studs or some of the lengths of white line may not comply with those requirements so long as the general appearance of the pattern of studs or white lines is not thereby materially impaired.

(7) The approach to a crossing shall not be regarded as having ceased to be indicated by a pattern of studs or white lines in accordance with the foregoing provisions by reason only of the discoloration, temporary removal or displacement of one or more studs in the pattern of studs or a length of white line in the pattern of white lines so

long as the general appearance of the pattern of studs or white lines is not thereby materially impaired.

(8) The provisions of sub-paragraph (4) of paragraph 1 of this Schedule shall apply to the studs mentioned in this paragraph as they apply to the studs mentioned in that sub-paragraph.

(9) Where the appropriate authority is satisfied in relation to a particular approach to a crossing that by reason of the existence at or near that crossing of a road junction which is on the same side of that crossing and on the same side of the road as that approach—

(a) the application of Regulation 9 of the Regulations contained in Part II of this Instrument in relation to that approach will not be appropriate unless the pattern of studs by which that approach is to be indicated is varied as hereinafter provided, or

(b) that the application of the said Regulation 9 in relation to that approach would be inappropriate even if the pattern of studs were varied as aforesaid,

then, in the case mentioned in (a) of this sub-paragraph, that approach shall be indicated in accordance with the foregoing provisions of this paragraph varied by the substitution for the distance of not less than 14·0 metres nor more than 16·0 metres specified in paragraph 3 (2) of this Schedule, or for the said distance of not less than 23·5 metres nor more than 26·5 metres, as the case may be, of such shorter distance (not being less than 9 metres) as the appropriate authority may think fit, and, in the case mentioned in (b) of this sub-paragraph, it shall not be necessary for that approach to be indicated in accordance with this paragraph:

Provided that for the purpose of the application of this sub-paragraph to a crossing which is on a road which is a one-way street the foregoing provisions of this sub-paragraph shall have effect as if the words "and on the same side of the road" were omitted.

In this sub-paragraph the expression "appropriate authority" means, in relation to an approach to a crossing which is on a trunk road in England, the Minister, and in relation to an approach to a crossing which is on a trunk road in Scotland, or Wales, the Secretary of State, and, in relation to an approach to any other crossing, the Council in whose scheme under section 21 of the Act of 1967 the crossing is for the time being included.

PART III

GENERAL DIRECTIONS

Citation

1. The Directions contained in this Part of this Instrument may be cited as the 'Pelican' Pedestrian Crossings General Directions 1969.

Number of traffic signals

2.—(1) The vehicular traffic light signals, pedestrian light signals and indicators for pedestrians placed at or near a 'Pelican' crossing which extends from one edge of the carriageway to the opposite edge of the carriageway on a road which is not a one-way street shall be placed so that there are two vehicular traffic light signals, one pedestrian light signal and one indicator for pedestrians on each side of the carriageway:

Provided that—

(a) where there is a street refuge or central reservation on the crossing, the said vehicular traffic light signals shall be so placed that there is one on each side of the carriageway and two on the refuge or reservation;

(b) one or more additional indicators for pedestrians shall be placed on the refuge or reservation; and

(c) if vehicular traffic light signals are placed at or near a crossing in accordance with this paragraph additional vehicular traffic light signals may be placed over the carriageway.

(2) The said light signals and indicators placed at or near a 'Pelican' crossing which extends only between the edge of the carriageway and a street refuge or a central reservation or a 'Pelican' crossing on a road which is a one-way street shall be placed so that one vehicular traffic light signal, one pedestrian light signal and one indicator for pedestrians are on each end of the crossing on the side of the carriageway on which vehicles approach the crossing:

Provided that—

(a) where there is a street refuge or central reservation on a 'Pelican' crossing on a road which is a one-way street an additional vehicular traffic light signal shall be placed on the refuge or central reservation;

(b) one or more additional indicators for pedestrians shall be placed on the refuge or reservation; and

(c) if vehicular traffic light signals are placed at or near a crossing in accordance with this paragraph additional vehicular traffic light signals may be placed over the carriageway.

Manner of placing traffic signals

3. Subject to the following provisions of these Directions the light signals and indicators placed at or near any 'Pelican' crossing in accordance with the foregoing provisions of these Directions shall be so arranged that—

(a) each vehicular traffic light signal shall face the stream of traffic it is intended to control,

(b) each pedestrian light signal at either end of the crossing shall be so placed as to be clearly visible to any person who is about to use the crossing at the other end of the crossing, and

(c) each indicator for pedestrians shall be so placed that the push button in the indicator is readily accessible to foot passengers who wish to press it.

Additional traffic signals

4. Subject to the following provisions of these Directions, one or more additional vehicular traffic light signals, pedestrian light signals or indicators for pedestrians may be placed at or near any 'Pelican' crossing with the prior approval in writing of the appropriate Minister.

Colouring of containers and posts

5.—(1) The containers of the vehicular traffic light signals and of the pedestrian light signals shall be coloured black and may be mounted on a black backing board with a white border not less than 45 millimetres nor more than 55 millimetres in width.

(2) Where a vehicular traffic light signal, a pedestrian light signal or an indicator for pedestrians is mounted on a post specially provided for the purposes, that part of the post which extends above ground level shall be coloured grey and may have one white band not less than 140 millimetres nor more than 160 millimetres in depth, the lower edge of the band being not less than 1·5 metres nor more than 1·7 metres above the level of the surface of the ground in the immediate vicinity.

Approval of sites and mechanisms

6. Vehicular traffic light signals, pedestrian light signals and indicators for pedestrians, may be placed at or near any 'Pelican' crossing only—

(a) at sites approved in writing by or on behalf of the appropriate Minister after consideration of such plans for the sites, particulars of the apparatus to be used and information as to the volume and character of traffic affected as the appropriate Minister may require and the approval will specify the position of the signals and the number of signal aspects, and

(b) if the apparatus is of a type which has been approved in writing by or on behalf of the appropriate Minister.

Special cases

7. Nothing in these Directions shall be taken to limit the power of the appropriate Minister by any special Direction to dispense with, add to or modify any of the requirements of these Directions in relation to any particular case.

Dated the 30th June 1969.

William Ross,
One of Her Majesty's Principal
Secretaries of State.

Dated the 30th June 1969.

George Thomas,
One of Her Majesty's Principal
Secretaries of State.

Given under the Official Seal of the Minister of Transport the 30th June 1969.

(L.S.)

Richard Marsh,
Minister of Transport.

EXPLANATORY NOTE

(This Note is not part of the Instrument.)

In Part I of this Instrument, paragraph 2 revokes the Pedestrian Crossings (Push Button Control) Regulations and General Directions 1967, which relate to push button controlled pedestrian crossings commonly known as "X-Ways", as from the 10th July 1971.

Part II of this Instrument provides a new method of regulating traffic at pedestrian crossings by means of light signals and indicators for pedestrians which can be made to work by pedestrians pressing a push button in the indicators. Pedestrian crossings at or near which such light signals are placed and the presence and limits of which are marked in accordance with the provisions of these Regulations are intended to be known as and are defined as " 'Pelican' crossings" (see Part I, paragraph 3(1)).

Regulation 3(1) and Schedule 1 prescribe the nature of the traffic signs which are to be placed at or near a 'Pelican' crossing. Schedule 1 provides amongst other things—

(*a*) that such traffic signs shall consist of a combination of vehicular traffic light signals, pedestrian light signals and indicators for pedestrians (paragraph 1),

(*b*) that the vehicular traffic light signals shall comprise three lamps, one red, one amber and one green (paragraph 2),

(*c*) that the pedestrian light signals shall be of the size, colour and type shown either in Diagram 1 or 2 in Part II of Schedule 1 (paragraph 3),

(*d*) that the indicators for pedestrians shall be of the size, colour and type shown either in Diagram 1 or 2 in Part III of Schedule 1 and shall incorporate a push button which may be used by foot passengers (paragraph 4),

(*e*) that (except when the light signals and indicators are working by remote control) the use of the push button shall cause the light signals and indicators to show lights in the manner and sequence set out in Part IV of Schedule 1, which will include—

(i) the showing by the vehicular traffic light signals of an amber light followed by a red light followed by a flashing amber light followed by a green light which will be shown until the use of the push button causes the same sequence of lights to be shown;

(ii) the showing by the pedestrian light signals of a red light while the vehicular traffic light signals are showing a green light or an amber light, a green light while the vehicular traffic light signals are showing a red light and a flashing green light while the vehicular traffic light signals are showing a flashing amber light;

(iii) the emission of a regular pulsed audible signal, where provided, while the pedestrian light signals are showing a green light;

(f) for authorising the light signals and indicators to be so designed and constructed as to be capable of working by remote control or for their operation to be suspended (Schedule 1 paragraph 6).

Regulation 3(2) and Schedule 2 provide for the manner in which the presence and limits of a 'Pelican' crossing are to be indicated. Schedule 2 (paragraph 3) includes provision for marking the carriageway on the approach to a crossing with a pattern of studs and transverse and longitudinal white lines.

Regulation 4 provides that slight variations from the prescribed dimensions of the traffic signs, indicators, etc. placed at a 'Pelican' crossing are permissible.

Regulations 5, 6 and 7 prescribe the warnings, information, requirements and prohibitions conveyed by the vehicular and pedestrian light signals. These signals are given the following meanings—

(a) when the vehicular traffic light signal is showing a steady green light vehicular traffic may proceed across the crossing (Regulation 6(1));

(b) when the signal is showing a steady amber light vehicular traffic is prohibited from proceeding beyond the stop line marked on the carriageway, or, if that line is not for the time being visible, beyond the vehicular traffic light signal unless the vehicle is so close to the stop line or signal that it cannot safely be stopped before passing the line or signal (Regulation 6(1));

(c) when the signal is showing a steady red light vehicular traffic is prohibited from proceeding beyond the stop line marked on the carriageway or, if that line is not for the time being visible, beyond the vehicular traffic light signal (Regulation 6(1));

(d) when the signal is showing a flashing amber light vehicular traffic may proceed across the crossing but must accord precedence to any foot passenger who is on the carriageway within the limits of that crossing (Regulation 6(1));

(e) when the pedestrian light signal is showing a steady red light it shall convey the warning that foot passengers should not in the interest of safety use the crossing (Regulation 7(2));

(f) when the pedestrian light signal is showing a green light it shall convey the information that foot passengers may use the crossing and vehicular traffic is stopped;

(g) when the pedestrian light signal is showing a flashing green light it shall convey the information that foot passengers already on the crossing shall have precedence over any vehicle and the warning that foot passengers not already on the crossing should not in the interest of safety start to cross.

Regulations 8 to 12 make provision as to the precedence of foot passengers over vehicles on a 'Pelican' crossing and the movement of traffic at and in the vicinity of a 'Pelican' crossing.

Part III of this Instrument provides for the number, placing and arrangement of vehicular traffic light signals, pedestrian light signals and indicators for pedestrians at a 'Pelican' crossing.

1969 No. 889

SUGAR

The Sugar (Rates of Surcharge and Surcharge Repayments) (No. 5) Order 1969

Made - - -	*30th June* 1969
Laid before Parliament	1*st July* 1969
Coming into Operation	2*nd July* 1969

The Minister of Agriculture, Fisheries and Food, in exercise of the powers conferred on him by sections 7(4), 8(6) and 33(4) of the Sugar Act 1956(a) having effect subject to the provisions of section 3 of, and Part II of Schedule 5 to, the Finance Act 1962(b), and section 58 of the Finance Act 1968 (c) and of all other powers enabling him in that behalf, with the concurrence of the Treasury, on the advice of the Sugar Board, hereby makes the following order:—

1.—(1) This order may be cited as the Sugar (Rates of Surcharge and Surcharge Repayments) (No. 5) Order 1969; and shall come into operation on 2nd July 1969.

(2) The Interpretation Act 1889(d) shall apply for the interpretation of this order as it applies for the interpretation of an Act of Parliament.

2. Notwithstanding the provisions of Article 2 of the Sugar (Rates of Surcharge and Surcharge Repayments) (No. 4) Order 1969(e), the rates of surcharge payable under and in accordance with the provisions of section 7 of the Sugar Act 1956, having effect as aforesaid, in respect of sugar and invert sugar imported or home produced or used in the manufacture of imported composite sugar products shall on and after 2nd July 1969 be those rates specified in Schedule 1 to this order.

3. For the purpose of section 8(3)(*b*) of the Sugar Act 1956, having effect as aforesaid, the rates of surcharge repayments in respect of invert sugar produced in the United Kingdom from materials on which on or after 2nd July 1969 sugar duty has been paid or, by virtue of paragraph 1 of Part II of Schedule 5 to the Finance Act 1962, is treated as having been paid shall, notwithstanding the provisions of Article 3 of the Sugar (Rates of Surcharge and Surcharge Repayments) (No. 4) Order 1969 be those specified in Schedule 2 to this order.

(a) 1956 c. 48.   (b) 1962 c. 44.
(c) 1968 c. 44.   (d) 1889 c. 63.
(e) S.I. 1969/588 (1969 I, p. 1560).

In Witness whereof the Official Seal of the Minister of Agriculture, Fisheries and Food is hereunto affixed on 30th June 1969.

(L.S.)

R. G. R. Wall,

Authorised by the Minister.

We concur.

30th June 1969.

Joseph Harper,
Walter Harrison,

Two of the Lords Commissioners of
Her Majesty's Treasury.

SCHEDULE 1

PART I

SURCHARGE RATES FOR SUGAR

Polarisation	Rate of Surcharge per cwt.	
	s.	d.
Exceeding—		
99°	18	8·0
98° but not exceeding 99°	17	7·2
97° ,, ,, ,, 98°	17	2·0
96° ,, ,, ,, 97°	16	8·7
95° ,, ,, ,, 96°	16	3·3
94° ,, ,, ,, 95°	15	9·9
93° ,, ,, ,, 94°	15	4·5
92° ,, ,, ,, 93°	14	11·2
91° ,, ,, ,, 92°	14	5·8
90° ,, ,, ,, 91°	14	0·4
89° ,, ,, ,, 90°	13	7·0
88° ,, ,, ,, 89°	13	1·6
87° ,, ,, ,, 88°	12	9·2
86° ,, ,, ,, 87°	12	4·7
85° ,, , ,, 86°	12	0·7
84° ,, ,, ,, 85°	11	8·6
83° ,, ,, ,, 84°	11	4·6
82° ,, ,, ,, 83°	11	0·6
81° ,, ,, ,, 82°	10	9·0
80° ,, ,, ,, 81°	10	5·4
79° ,, ,, ,, 80°	10	1·8
78° ,, ,, ,, 79°	9	10·2
77° ,, ,, ,, 78°	9	6·6
76° ,, ,, ,, 77°	9	3·1
Not exceeding 76°	9	0·0

PART II
SURCHARGE RATES FOR INVERT SUGAR

Sweetening matter content by weight	Rate of Surcharge per cwt.
	s. d.
70 per cent. or more	11 10
Less than 70 per cent. and more than 50 per cent.	8 6
Not more than 50 per cent.	4 2

SCHEDULE 2
SURCHARGE REPAYMENT RATES FOR INVERT SUGAR

Sweetening matter content by weight	Rate of Surcharge Repayment per cwt.
	s. d.
More than 80 per cent.	14 0
More than 70 per cent. but not more than 80 per cent.	11 10
More than 60 per cent. but not more than 70 per cent.	8 6
More than 50 per cent. but not more than 60 per cent.	6 9
Not more than 50 per cent. and the invert sugar not being less in weight than 14 lb. per gallon	4 2

EXPLANATORY NOTE
(This Note is not part of the Order.)

This order prescribes—

(a) increases equivalent to 2s. 4d. per cwt. of refined sugar in the rates of surcharge payable on sugar and invert sugar which become chargeable with surcharge on or after 2nd July 1969;

(b) correspondingly increased rates of surcharge repayment in respect of invert sugar produced in the United Kingdom from materials on which surcharge has been paid.

STATUTORY INSTRUMENTS

1969 No. 890

SUGAR

The Composite Sugar Products (Surcharge and Surcharge Repayments—Average Rates) (No. 5) Order 1969

Made - - - -	30th June 1969
Laid before Parliament	1st July 1969
Coming into Operation	2nd July 1969

Whereas the Minister of Agriculture, Fisheries and Food (hereinafter called " the Minister ") has on the recommendation of the Commissioners of Customs and Excise (hereinafter called " the Commissioners ") made an order(a) pursuant to the powers conferred upon him by sections 9(1) and 9(4) of the Sugar Act 1956(b), having effect subject to the provisions of section 3 of, and Part II of Schedule 5 to, the Finance Act 1962(c), to the provisions of section 52(2) of the Finance Act 1966(d), and to the provisions of Section 58 of the Finance Act 1968(e), providing that in the case of certain descriptions of composite sugar products surcharge shall be calculated on the basis of an average quantity of sugar or invert sugar taken to have been used in the manufacture of the products, and that certain other descriptions of composite sugar products shall be treated as not containing any sugar or invert sugar, and that in the case of certain descriptions of goods in the manufacture of which sugar or invert sugar is used, surcharge repayments shall be calculated on the basis of an average quantity of sugar or invert sugar taken to have been so used:

Now, therefore, the Minister, on the recommendation of the Commissioners and in exercise of the powers conferred upon him by sections 9(1), 9(4) and 33(4) of the Sugar Act 1956, having effect as aforesaid, and of all other powers enabling him in that behalf, hereby makes the following order:—

1.—(1) This order may be cited as the Composite Sugar Products (Surcharge and Surcharge Repayments—Average Rates) (No. 5) Order 1969; and shall come into operation on 2nd July 1969.

(2) The Interpretation Act 1889(f) shall apply for the interpretation of this order as it applies for the interpretation of an Act of Parliament.

2. Surcharge payable on or after 2nd July 1969 under and in accordance with the Sugar Act 1956, having effect as aforesaid, in respect of sugar and invert sugar used in the manufacture of the descriptions of imported composite sugar products specified in column 2 of Schedule 1 to this order shall, notwithstanding the provisions of the Sugar (Rates of Surcharge and Surcharge Repayments) (No. 5) Order 1969(g) and the Composite Sugar Products (Surcharge and Surcharge Repayments—Average Rates) (No. 4) Order 1969(a), be calculated by reference to the weight or value, as the case may be, of the products at the rates specified in relation thereto in column 3 of the said Schedule.

(a) S.I. 1969/589 (1969 I, p. 1563).   (b) 1956 c. 48.   (c) 1962 c. 44.
(d) 1966 c. 18.   (e) 1968 c. 44.   (f) 1889 c. 63.
(g) S.I. 1969/889 (1969 II, p. 2549).

3. Imported composite sugar products other than those of a description specified in Schedules 1 and 2 to this order shall be treated as not containing any sugar or invert sugar for the purposes of surcharge payable on or after 2nd July 1969.

4. Surcharge repayments payable on and after 2nd July 1969 under and in accordance with the provisions of section 8 of the Sugar Act 1956, having effect as aforesaid, in respect of sugar and invert sugar used in the manufacture of the descriptions of goods specified in column 1 of Schedule 3 to this order shall, notwithstanding the provisions of the Sugar (Rates of Surcharge and Surcharge Repayments) (No. 5) Order 1969(a) and the Composite Sugar Products (Surcharge and Surcharge Repayments—Average Rates) (No. 4) Order 1969(b), be calculated by reference to the quantity of the goods at the rates specified in relation thereto in column 2 of the said Schedule.

In Witness whereof the Official Seal of the Minister of Agriculture, Fisheries and Food is hereunto affixed on 30th June 1969.

(L.S.)

R. G. R. Wall,
Authorised by the Minister.

SCHEDULE 1

In this Schedule:—

" Tariff heading " means a heading or, where the context so requires, a subheading of the Customs Tariff 1959 (see paragraph (1) of Article 1 of the Import Duties (General) (No. 4) Order 1968(c)).

" Per cent." means, where it occurs in relation to any rate of surcharge, per cent. of the value for customs duty purposes of the product to which it relates.

Tariff heading	Description of Imported Composite Sugar Products	Rate of Surcharge
		per cwt. s. d.
04.02	Milk and cream, preserved, concentrated or sweetened, containing more than 10 per cent. by weight of added sweetening matter	8 3
17.02 (B) (2) and 17.05 (B)	Syrups containing sucrose sugar, whether or not flavoured or coloured, but not including fruit juices containing added sugar in any proportion:—	
	containing 70 per cent. or more by weight of sweetening matter	11 10
	containing less than 70 per cent., and more than 50 per cent., by weight of sweetening matter...	8 6
	containing not more than 50 per cent. by weight of sweetening matter	4 2

(a) S.I. 1969/889 (1969 II, p. 2549).   (b) S.I. 1969/589 (1969 I, p. 1563).
(c) S.I. 1968/679 (1968 I, p. 1519).

Tariff heading	Description of Imported Composite Sugar Products	Rate of Surcharge
		per cwt. s. d.
17.02 (F) ...	Caramel:—	
	Solid	18 8
	Liquid	13 1
17.04	Sugar confectionery, not containing cocoa	15 2
18.06	Chocolate and other food preparations containing cocoa:—	
	Chocolate couverture not prepared for retail sale; chocolate milk crumb, liquid	8 3
	Chocolate milk crumb, solid	10 3
	Solid chocolate bars or blocks, milk or plain, with or without fruit or nuts; other chocolate confectionery consisting wholly of chocolate or of chocolate and other ingredients not containing added sugar, but not including such goods when packed together in retail packages with goods liable to surcharge at a higher rate	8 5
	Other	10 10
		per cent.
19.08	Pastry, biscuits, cakes and other fine bakers' wares containing added sweetening matter:—	
	Biscuits	4
	Other	$2\frac{2}{5}$
20.01	Vegetables and fruit, prepared or preserved by vinegar or acetic acid, containing added sweetening matter	$5\frac{3}{5}$
20.03	Fruit preserved by freezing, containing added sugar	2
		per cwt. s. d.
20.04	Fruit, fruit-peel and parts of plants, preserved by sugar (drained, glacé or crystallised)	12 3
20.05	Jams, fruit jellies, marmalades, fruit purée and fruit pastes, being cooked preparations, containing added sweetening matter	11 9
		per cent.
20.06	Fruit otherwise prepared or preserved, containing added sweetening matter:—	
	Ginger	8
	Other	2

SCHEDULE 2

Tariff heading	Description of Imported Composite Sugar Products
17.05 (A) and (B)	Sugar and invert sugar, flavoured or coloured.

SCHEDULE 3

Description of goods	Rate of surcharge repayment per bulk barrel of 36 gallons
Lager	9·3d.
All beer other than lager	8·3d.

EXPLANATORY NOTE

(*This Note is not part of the Order.*)

This order provides for increases on and after 2nd July 1969 in the average rates of surcharge payable on imported composite sugar products of the descriptions specified in Schedule 1 and in the average rates of surcharge repayment in respect of exported goods of the descriptions specified in Schedule 3. These correspond to the increases in surcharge rates effected by the Sugar (Rates of Surcharge and Surcharge Repayments) (No. 5) Order 1969 (S.I. 1969/889). Provision is also made for certain imported composite sugar products to be treated as not containing any sugar or invert sugar.

STATUTORY INSTRUMENTS

1969 No. 894

WAGES COUNCILS

The Wages Regulation (Button Manufacturing) Order 1969

Made - - - -	*1st July* 1969
Coming into Operation	*23rd July* 1969

Whereas the Secretary of State has received from the Button Manufacturing Wages Council (Great Britain) the wages regulation proposals set out in the Schedule hereto ;

Now, therefore, the Secretary of State in exercise of her powers under section 11 of the Wages Councils Act 1959(a), and of all other powers enabling her in that behalf, hereby makes the following Order:—

1. This Order may be cited as the Wages Regulation (Button Manufacturing) Order 1969.

2.—(1) In this Order the expression " the specified date " means the 23rd July 1969, provided that where, as respects any worker who is paid wages at intervals not exceeding seven days, that date does not correspond with the beginning of the period for which the wages are paid, the expression " the specified date " means, as respects that worker, the beginning of the next such period following that date.

(2) The Interpretation Act 1889(b) shall apply to the interpretation of this Order as it applies to the interpretation of an Act of Parliament and as if this Order and the Order hereby revoked were Acts of Parliament.

3. The wages regulation proposals set out in the Schedule hereto shall have effect as from the specified date and as from that date the Wages Regulation (Button Manufacturing) Order 1968(c), shall cease to have effect.

Signed by order of the Secretary of State.

A. A. Jarratt,
Deputy Under Secretary of State.
Department of Employment and
Productivity.

1st July 1969.

(a) 1959 c. 69.   (b) 1889 c. 63.   (c) S.I. 1968/742 (1968 II, p. 2112).

SCHEDULE Article 3

The following minimum remuneration shall be substituted for the statutory minimum remuneration fixed by the Wages Regulation (Button Manufacturing) Order 1968 (Order V.(65)).

STATUTORY MINIMUM REMUNERATION

PART I

GENERAL

1.—(1) The minimum remuneration payable to a worker to whom this Schedule applies for all work except work to which a minimum overtime rate applies under Part V is—

    (a) in the case of a worker other than an outworker,

        (i) where the worker is employed on time work, the general minimum time rate payable to the worker under Part II or Part III of this Schedule ;

        (ii) where the worker is employed on piece work, piece rates each of which would yield, in the circumstances of the case, to an ordinary worker at least the same amount of money as the piece work basis time rate applicable to the worker under Part II or Part III of this Schedule ;

    (b) in the case of an outworker,

        (i) where a general minimum piece rate applies under Part IV of this Schedule, that rate ;

        (ii) where no general minimum piece rate applies, piece rates each of which would yield, in the circumstances of the case, to an ordinary worker at least the same amount of money as the piece work basis time rate applicable to the worker under Part IV of this Schedule.

(2) In this Schedule the expression " outworker " means a worker who works in his own home or in any other place that is not under the control or management of the employer.

PART II

MALE WORKERS OTHER THAN OUTWORKERS

GENERAL MINIMUM TIME RATES

2. The general minimum time rates payable to male workers (other than out-workers) are as follows :—

	Per hour	
	s.	d.
Aged 21 years or over	5	2¼
„ 20 and under 21 years	4	9¼
„ 19 „ „ 20 „	4	4¾
„ 18 „ „ 19 „	4	1
„ 17 „ „ 18 „	3	4¾
„ 16 „ „ 17 „	3	0¾
„ under 16 years	2	9½

PIECE WORK BASIS TIME RATE

	Per hour
	s. d.
3. The piece work basis time rate applicable to a male worker of any age (other than an outworker) employed on piece work is ...	5 9¼

PART III

FEMALE WORKERS OTHER THAN OUTWORKERS

GENERAL MINIMUM TIME RATES

4. The general minimum time rates payable to female workers (other than outworkers) are as follows:—

	Per hour
	s. d.
Aged 18 years or over	4 3
„ 17 and under 18 years	3 7½
„ 16 „ „ 17 „	3 2¾
„ under 16 years	2 9

PIECE WORK BASIS TIME RATE

	Per hour
	s. d.
5. The piece work basis time rate applicable to a female worker of any age employed on piece work (other than an outworker) is ...	4 5

PART IV

OUTWORKERS

GENERAL MINIMUM PIECE RATES

6. The following general minimum piece rates are payable to an outworker where the materials for sewing the buttons by hand are provided by the employer and the worker actually performs the work:—

The carding of buttons—

	Per gross of buttons	
	Sew through	Shanks
	s. d.	s. d.
12 buttons or over per card	10	1 0
5–11 buttons per card	1 0	1 1
3–4 „ „ „	1 3	1 4
1–2 „ „ „	1 6	1 8

Provided that where perforated or sectional cards are used the above rates shall apply to each section or knotting off or fastening off.

PIECE WORK BASIS TIME RATE

	Per hour
	s. d.
7. The piece work basis time rate applicable to all outworkers employed on piece work, other than those to whom the general minimum piece rates set out in paragraph 6 apply is	2 11

Part V

OVERTIME AND WAITING TIME

MINIMUM OVERTIME RATES

TIME WORKERS

8.—(1) Subject to the provisions of this paragraph, the following minimum overtime rates are payable to male or female workers (other than outworkers) employed on time work:—

(a) on a Saturday, not being a customary holiday—

for all time worked in excess of five hours   ...   time-and-a-quarter

(b) on a Sunday or a customary holiday—

for all time worked   ...   . double time

(c) in any week exclusive of any time in respect of which a minimum overtime rate is payable under the provisions of (a) or (b) above—

for all time worked in excess of

40 hours   ...   . time-and-a-quarter

(2) Where the employer normally requires attendance on Sunday instead of Saturday, for the purposes of this paragraph (except where in the case of a woman or young person such substitution is unlawful) Saturday shall be treated as a Sunday and Sunday as a Saturday.

FEMALE PIECE WORKERS

9. The following minimum overtime rates are payable to female workers (other than outworkers) employed on piece work for all time worked in excess of 40 hours in any week:—

(1) Piece rates each of which would yield, in the circumstances of the case, at least 4s. 5d. per hour to an ordinary worker and in addition thereto,

(2) a time rate of 1d. per hour.

10. In this Part of this Schedule,

(1) the expression " customary holiday " means:—

(a) (i) in England and Wales—

Christmas Day (or, if Christmas Day falls on a Sunday, such weekday as may be appointed by national proclamation, or, if none is so appointed, the next following Tuesday), Boxing Day, Good Friday, Easter Monday, Whit Monday and August Bank Holiday ;

(ii) In Scotland—

New Year's Day (or, if New Year's Day falls on a Sunday, the following Monday) ;

the local Spring holiday ;

the local Autumn holiday ; and

three other days (being days on which the worker normally works) in the course of a calendar year, to be fixed by the employer and notified to the worker not less than three weeks before the holiday ;

or (b) in the case of each of the said days (other than a day fixed by the employer in Scotland and notified to the worker as aforesaid) a day substituted by the employer therefor, being a day recognised by local custom as a day of holiday in substitution for the said day ;

(2) the expressions " time-and-a-quarter " and " double time " mean, respectively, one and a quarter times and twice the general minimum time rate otherwise payable to the worker.

WAITING TIME

11.—(1) A worker is entitled to payment of the minimum remuneration specified in this Schedule for all time during which he is present on the premises of his employer unless he is present thereon in any of the following circumstances : —

(a) without the employer's consent, express or implied ;

(b) for some purpose unconnected with his work and other than that of waiting for work to be given to him to perform ;

(c) by reason only of the fact that he is resident thereon ;

(d) during normal meal times in a room or place in which no work is being done, and he is not waiting for work to be given to him to perform.

(2) The minimum remuneration payable under sub-paragraph (1) of this paragraph to a piece worker when not engaged on piece work is that which would be payable if the worker were a time worker.

Part VI

APPLICABILITY OF STATUTORY MINIMUM REMUNERATION

12. This Schedule applies to workers in relation to whom the Button Manufacturing Wages Council (Great Britain) operates, that is to say, workers employed in Great Britain in the trade specified in the Schedule to the Trade Boards (Button Manufacturing Trade, Great Britain) (Constitution and Proceedings) Regulations 1938(a), which reads as follows : —

" Schedule

1. Subject to the provisions of this Schedule the following operations and processes shall constitute the Button Manufacturing Trade : —

(a) all processes and operations in the making from any material other than precious metals and precious stones of buttons, button-moulds, metal fancy buttons, button-headed studs, upholsterers' buttons or upholsterers' button-headed nails (excluding in all cases, except as hereinafter provided, the making of the shanks), or in the covering of button-moulds ;

(b) All processes and operations in the making of the following articles when done in association with or in conjunction with the work specified in sub-paragraph (a) above—

(i) shanks ;

(ii) studs, links or parts thereof from any material other than metal ;

(iii) clasps, slides, ornaments and similar articles used on wearing apparel when such articles are made—

(1) wholly or mainly from any material other than metal, and

(2) in a branch or department in which articles mentioned in sub-paragraph (a) are made or carded ;

(c) (i) the carding wherever carried on of any of the articles specified in sub-paragraph (a) above ;

(a) S.R. & O. 1938/1497 (1938 II, p. 3238).

(ii) the carding of any of the articles specified in sub-paragraph (b) above, except when done apart from any of the making which is included in the trade herein specified and from the carding of articles specified in sub-paragraph (a) ;

(d) The manufacture of metal small-wares as specified in Paragraphs (1) to (6) of the Appendix to the Trade Boards (Stamped or Pressed Metal-Wares) Order 1924(a)*, when carried on in an establishment mainly engaged in any of the processes or operations mentioned above ;

(e) All processes and operations in the (i) assembling, or (ii) finishing of articles specified above when done in association with or in conjunction with any of the above-mentioned processes or operations ;

(f) All processes and operations in the warehousing, packing or despatching of any of the articles specified above when done in association with or in conjunction with any of the above-mentioned processes or operations.

2. Notwithstanding anything in this Schedule the following processes or operations shall not be processes or operations of the Button Manufacturing Trade : —

(a) The manufacture of wooden button-moulds where not carried on in association with or in conjunction with button-making ;

(b) the making of buttons or the covering of button-moulds in an establishment in which (i) such work is performed in association with or in conjunction with the making of wearing apparel and (ii) the majority of the buttons made or of the button-moulds covered are for use on such wearing apparel ;

(c) The making of buttons or the covering of button-moulds when done in association with or in conjunction with the manufacture of embroidery and trimmings, unless such making of buttons or covering of button-moulds is done (i) by machine process and (ii) in a separate department by workers exclusively engaged thereon ;

(d) The processes or operations specified in Paragraph 1 above when performed in an establishment mainly engaged in the manufacture of articles of real or imitation jewellery except when performed by a worker who during the whole time that he works in any week in such establishment is wholly or mainly employed on such processes or operations ;

(e) Any work which by Paragraph (7) of the Appendix to the Trade Boards (Stamped or Pressed Metal-Wares) Order, 1924*, is included in the Stamped or Pressed Metal-Wares Trade."

* (Paragraphs (1) to (7) of the Appendix to the Trade Boards (Stamped or Pressed Metal-Wares) Order 1924, referred to in the Schedule to the Trade Boards (Button Manufacturing Trade, Great Britain) (Constitution and Proceedings) Regulations 1938, set out above are as follows : —

(1) The manufacture from metal in sheet or strip form by cold stamping or cold pressing of articles known in the trade as metal small wares ;

(2) the cutting, shearing, annealing and hardening of metal in an establishment in which the metal is used for such manufacture ;

(3) the covering of corset steels prior to capping or tipping in an establishment in which the steels are capped or tipped ;

(4) finishing (including dipping, nickelling, plating, tinning, japanning, stove-enamelling, lacquering, bronzing, colouring, painting, varnishing, barrelling, burnishing, grinding, planishing, polishing, and the capping, counting, lopping, studding, or tipping of corset busks or

(a) S.R. & O. 1924/832 (1924, p. 1753).

steels) and similar operations when done in conjunction with such manufacture ;

(5) viewing, inspecting, testing, sorting, boxing, carding, carrying, delivering, despatching, labelling, packeting, packing, portering, warehousing, weighing and similar processes or operations when done in conjunction with such manufacture ;

(6) the assembling of the above-mentioned wares or parts thereof, whether the things assembled are made inside or outside Great Britain ; and

(7) any process or operation which is included in the Button-making Trade, as defined for the purposes of the Trade Boards Acts, when carried on in an establishment mainly engaged in any of the processes or operations defined in the preceding paragraphs hereof.)

EXPLANATORY NOTE

(*This Note is not part of the Order.*)

This Order, which has effect from 23rd July 1969, sets out the statutory minimum remuneration payable in substitution for that fixed by the Wages Regulation (Button Manufacturing) Order 1968 (Order V.(65)) which Order is revoked.

New provisions are printed in italics.

STATUTORY INSTRUMENTS

1969 No. 895

CUSTOMS AND EXCISE

The Anti-Dumping Duty (No. 1) Order 1969

Made - - - - -	*2nd July* 1969
Laid before the House of Commons	*3rd July* 1969
Coming into Operation - -	*4th July* 1969

The Board of Trade, in pursuance of the powers conferred upon them by sections 1 and 2 of the Customs Duties (Dumping and Subsidies) Act 1969(a) (hereinafter referred to as " the Act "), hereby make the following Order:—

1. This Order may be cited as the Anti-Dumping Duty (No. 1) Order 1969 and shall come into operation on 4th July 1969.

2. There shall be charged upon the import into the United Kingdom of goods of the description set out in the second column of the Schedule to this Order (being goods classified in accordance with the Customs Tariff 1959(b) under the heading mentioned in the first column of that Schedule) a duty of customs at the rate mentioned in the third column.

3. Section 2 of the Act (which provides for the giving of relief where goods are shown not to have been dumped or where the margin of dumping is shown to be less than the duty payable on them) shall apply in relation to the duty imposed by this Order.

Edmund Dell,
Minister of State,
Board of Trade.

2nd July 1969.

(a) 1969 c. 16.   (b) S.I. 1968/679 (1968 I, p. 1519).

SCHEDULE

Relevant Tariff Heading	Description of Goods	Rate of Duty
91.04 (A) (2)	Mechanical alarm clocks of a value less than 12s. 0d. each originating in the People's Republic of China	2s. 0d. each

EXPLANATORY NOTE

(This Note is not part of the Order.)

This Order imposes an anti-dumping duty on mechanical alarm clocks of a value less than twelve shillings originating in the People's Republic of China. The rate of the duty is 2s. 0d. per clock.

Article 3 of the Order applies section 2 of the Customs Duties (Dumping and Subsidies) Act 1969. This section enables the Board of Trade to grant relief where goods are shown not to have been dumped or where the margin of dumping is shown to be less than the duty payable.

1969 No. 896

ACQUISITION OF LAND

COMPENSATION

The Acquisition of Land (Rate of Interest after Entry) (No. 2) Regulations 1969

Made - - -	*1st July* 1969
Laid before Parliament	*9th July* 1969
Coming into Operation	*10th July* 1969

The Treasury, in exercise of the powers conferred upon them by section 32(1) of the Land Compensation Act 1961(a), and of all other powers enabling them in that behalf, hereby make the following Regulations:—

1. These Regulations may be cited as the Acquisition of Land (Rate of Interest after Entry) (No. 2) Regulations 1969, and shall come into operation on 10th July 1969.

2. The Interpretation Act 1889(b) shall apply for the interpretation of these Regulations as it applies for the interpretation of an Act of Parliament.

3. The rate of interest on any compensation in respect of the compulsory acquisition of an interest in any land on which entry has been made before the payment of the compensation shall be 9½ per cent. per annum.

4. The Acquisition of Land (Rate of Interest after Entry) Regulations 1969(c) are hereby revoked.

Joseph Harper,
Walter Harrison,
Two of the Lords Commissioners
of Her Majesty's Treasury.

1st July 1969.

EXPLANATORY NOTE

(This Note is not part of the Regulations.)

These Regulations increase from 9 per cent. to 9½ per cent. per annum the rate of interest payable where entry is made, before payment of compensation, on land in England and Wales which is being purchased compulsorily, and revoke the Acquisition of Land (Rate of Interest after Entry) Regulations 1969.

(a) 1961 c. 33.   (b) 1889 c. 63.   (c) S.I. 1969/458 (1969 I, p. 1315).

STATUTORY INSTRUMENTS

1969 No. 897

ACQUISITION OF LAND

COMPENSATION

The Acquisition of Land (Rate of Interest after Entry) (Scotland) (No. 2) Regulations 1969

Made - - -	*1st July* 1969
Laid before Parliament	*9th July* 1969
Coming into Operation	*10th July* 1969

The Treasury, in exercise of the powers conferred upon them by section 40(1) of the Land Compensation (Scotland) Act 1963(a), and of all other powers enabling them in that behalf, hereby make the following Regulations:—

1.—(1) These Regulations may be cited as the Acquisition of Land (Rate of Interest after Entry) (Scotland) (No. 2) Regulations 1969, and shall come into operation on 10th July 1969.

(2) These Regulations shall extend to Scotland only.

2. The Interpretation Act 1889(b) shall apply for the interpretation of these Regulations as it applies for the interpretation of an Act of Parliament.

3. The rate of interest on any compensation in respect of the compulsory acquisition of an interest in any land on which entry has been made before the payment of the compensation shall be $9\frac{1}{2}$ per cent. per annum.

4. The Acquisition of Land (Rate of Interest after Entry) (Scotland) Regulations 1969(c) are hereby revoked.

Joseph Harper,

Walter Harrison,

Two of the Lords Commissioners
of Her Majesty's Treasury.

1st July 1969.

EXPLANATORY NOTE

(This note is not part of the Regulations.)

These Regulations increase from 9 per cent. to $9\frac{1}{2}$ per cent. per annum the rate of interest payable where entry is made, before payment of compensation, on land in Scotland which is being purchased compulsorily, and revoke the Acquisition of Land (Rate of Interest after Entry) (Scotland) Regulations 1969.

(a) 1963 c. 51.   (b) 1889 c. 63.   (c) S.I. 1969/459 (1969 I, p. 1316).

STATUTORY INSTRUMENTS

1969 No. 901

WAGES COUNCILS

The Wages Regulation (Baking) (England and Wales) Order 1969

Made - - -	*2nd July* 1969
Coming into Operation	*6th August* 1969

Whereas the Secretary of State has received from the Baking Wages Council (England and Wales) the wages regulation proposals set out in the Schedule hereto ;

Now, therefore, the Secretary of State in exercise of her powers under section 11 of the Wages Councils Act 1959(**a**), and of all other powers enabling her in that behalf, hereby makes the following Order :—

1. This Order may be cited as the Wages Regulation (Baking) (England and Wales) Order 1969.

2.—(1) In this Order the expression "the specified date" means the 6th August 1969, provided that where, as respects any worker who is paid wages at intervals not exceeding seven days, that date does not correspond with the beginning of the period for which the wages are paid, the expression "the specified date" means, as respects that worker, the beginning of the next such period following that date.

(2) The Interpretation Act 1889(**b**) shall apply to the interpretation of this Order as it applies to the interpretation of an Act of Parliament and as if this Order and the Orders hereby revoked were Acts of Parliament.

3. The wages regulation proposals set out in the Schedule hereto shall have effect as from the specified date and as from that date the Wages Regulation (Baking) (England and Wales) Order 1965(**c**) and the Wages Regulation (Baking) (England and Wales) (Amendment) Order 1968(**d**) shall cease to have effect.

Signed by order of the Secretary of State.
2nd July 1969.

A. A. Jarratt,
Deputy Under Secretary of State,
Department of Employment and Productivity.

(**a**) 1959 c. 69.   (**b**) 1889 c. 63.
(**c**) S.I. 1965/2169 (1965 III, p. 6344).   (**d**) S.I. 1968/327 (1968 I, p. 957).

ARRANGEMENT OF SCHEDULE

Part   Paragraphs
   I. General   1
  II. Male and female workers: general minimum time rates and
      rates for workers on special classes of work...   2–6
 III. Overtime, work on a customary holiday and waiting time ...   7–9
 IV. Guaranteed weekly remuneration   10
  V. Classes of workers, Areas and other definitions 11–13
 VI. Workers to whom the Schedule applies   14

Article 3

SCHEDULE

The following minimum remuneration shall be substituted for the statutory minimum remuneration fixed by the Wages Regulation (Baking) (England and Wales) Order 1965 (Order BK (75)), as amended by the Wages Regulation (Baking) (England and Wales) (Amendment) Order 1968 (Order BK (78)).

STATUTORY MINIMUM REMUNERATION

PART I

GENERAL

1.—(1) Subject to the provisions of Part IV of this Schedule relating to guaranteed weekly remuneration, the minimum remuneration payable to a worker to whom this Schedule applies is as follows:—

(a) for all work except work on a customary holiday and work to which a minimum overtime rate applies under Part III of this Schedule—

(i) in the case of a time worker, the hourly general minimum time rate payable to the worker under Part II of this Schedule;

(ii) in the case of a worker employed on piece work, piece rates each of which would yield, in the circumstances of the case, to an ordinary worker at least the same amount of money as the hourly general minimum time rate which would be payable to the worker under Part II of this Schedule if he were a time worker:

Provided that, where the remuneration of a worker calculated on a time-work basis at the hourly general minimum time rate which would be payable to him under Part II of this Schedule if he were a time worker exceeds the remuneration calculated under sub-paragraph (a) (ii) of this paragraph on the basis of the said piece rates, the worker shall be paid not less than that hourly general minimum time rate;

(b) for any work to which a minimum overtime rate applies under Part III of this Schedule, that minimum overtime rate;

(c) for any work on a customary holiday the remuneration specified in Part III of this Schedule.

(2) In this Schedule the expression "hourly general minimum time rate" means the general minimum time rate applicable to the worker under Part II of this Schedule divided by 40.

Part II

GENERAL MINIMUM TIME RATES
MALE WORKERS (NOT BEING NIGHT WORKERS) AND FEMALE WORKERS (NOT BEING WORKERS SPECIFIED IN PARAGRAPH 3)

2. Subject to the provisions of this Part of this Schedule, the general minimum time rates set out in the next following Table apply to male workers (not being night workers) and to female workers (not being workers specified in paragraph 3):

Provided that the general minimum time rate applicable to a male or female certificated worker aged under 21 years who performs the work of any one of the descriptions of workers appearing in the next following Table shall be that of an adult worker of that description in the same area who is aged 21 and under 23 years.

DESCRIPTION OF WORKERS	Column 1		Column 2		Column 3	
	The respective areas are defined in paragraph 12					
	All workers in LONDON AREA		All workers in PROVINCIAL AREA A and workers in wholesale cake and flour confectionery branch in PROVINCIAL AREA B		All workers in PROVINCIAL AREA B except those in wholesale cake and flour confectionery branch	
	Per week of 40 hours s. d.	Per hour s. d.	Per week of 40 hours s. d.	Per hour s. d.	Per week of 40 hours s. d.	Per hour s. d.
(1) MALE WORKERS (not being night workers)						
(*a*) FOREMAN CONFECTIONER	*248 4*	*6 2½*	*246 8*	*6 2*	*241 8*	*6 0½*
(*b*) FOREMAN BAKER	*248 4*	*6 2½*	*246 8*	*6 2*	*241 8*	*6 0½*
(*c*) FIRST HAND	*235 0*	*5 10½*	*233 4*	*5 10*	*230 0*	*5 9*
(*d*) SINGLE HAND	*233 4*	*5 10*	*231 8*	*5 9½*	*228 4*	*5 8½*
(*e*) SECOND HAND	*230 0*	*5 9*	*228 4*	*5 8½*	*225 0*	*5 7½*
(*f*) DOUGHMAKER	*230 0*	*5 9*	*228 4*	*5 8½*	*225 0*	*5 7½*
(*g*) CONFECTIONERY MIXER	*230 0*	*5 9*	*228 4*	*5 8½*	*225 0*	*5 7½*
(*h*) OVENMAN	*230 0*	*5 9*	*228 4*	*5 8½*	*225 0*	*5 7½*
(*i*) CONFECTIONER or TABLE HAND, aged 21 years or over, other than a worker to whom (1)(*j*) applies	*223 4*	*5 7*	*221 8*	*5 6½*	*218 4*	*5 5½*
(*j*) CONFECTIONER or TABLE HAND, aged 21 and under 23 years who is employed, wholly or mainly, in making bread and flour confectionery, or either of them, without the use of power machinery other than one doughkneader or one cake mixer, or both, and has completed less than five years' employment in the trade	*215 0*	*5 4½*	*213 4*	*5 4*	*210 0*	*5 3*
(*k*) STOKER	*220 0*	*5 6*	*216 8*	*5 5*	*213 4*	*5 4*
(*l*) CHARGE HAND (packing and despatch department)	1½d. per hour in addition to the rate appropriate to his age as specified in Column 1, 2 or 3 of (1)(*m*)					

(m) OTHER MALE WORKERS, being aged—						
21 years or over	216 8	5 5	215 0	5 4½	211 8	5 3½
20½ and under 21 years	195 0	4 10½	193 4	4 10	190 0	4 9
20 " " 20½ "	183 4	4 7	180 0	4 6	176 8	4 5
19½ " " 20 "	176 8	4 5	175 0	4 4½	168 4	4 2½
19 " " 19½ "	168 4	4 2½	166 8	4 2	163 4	4 1
18½ " " 19 "	160 0	4 0	158 4	3 11½	155 0	3 10½
18 " " 18½ "	153 4	3 10	151 8	3 9½	148 4	3 8½
17½ " " 18 "	130 0	3 3	126 8	3 2	123 4	3 1
17 " " 17½ "	120 0	3 0	118 4	2 11½	115 0	2 10½
16½ " " 17 "	116 8	2 11	115 0	2 10½	111 8	2 9½
16 " " 16½ "	115 0	2 10½	113 4	2 10	108 4	2 8½
Under 16 years	105 0	2 7½	103 4	2 7	100 0	2 6
(n) Workers employed as JOBBERS	2d. per hour in addition to the rate otherwise payable under (1)(a) to (m)					
(2) FEMALE WORKERS (not being workers specified in paragraph 3)						
(a) FOREWOMAN	191 8	4 9½	190 0	4 9	185 0	4 7½
(b) CHARGE HAND other than a charge hand (packing and despatch department)	181 8	4 6½	180 0	4 6	176 8	4 5
(c) CHARGE HAND (packing and despatch department)	1½. per hour in addition to the rate appropriate to her age as specified in Column 1, 2 or 3 of (2)(f)					
(d) SINGLE HAND	176 8	4 5	175 0	4 4½	170 0	4 3
(e) CONFECTIONER, being aged—						
21 years or over	173 4	4 4	171 8	4 3½	165 0	4 1½
20½ and under 21 years	156 8	3 11	155 0	3 10½	150 0	3 9
20 " " 20½ "	148 4	3 8½	145 0	3 7½	141 8	3 6½
19½ " " 20 "	145 0	3 7½	143 4	3 7	138 4	3 5½
19 " " 19½ "	141 8	3 6½	140 0	3 6	135 0	3 4½
(f) OTHER FEMALE WORKERS being aged—						
21 years or over	163 4	4 1	161 8	4 0½	158 4	3 11½
20½ and under 21 years	150 0	3 9	148 4	3 8½	145 0	3 7½
20 " " 20½ "	145 0	3 7½	143 4	3 7	140 0	3 6
19½ " " 20 "	141 8	3 6½	140 0	3 6	136 8	3 5
19 " " 19½ "	138 4	3 5½	136 8	3 5	133 4	3 4
18½ " " 19 "	136 8	3 5	135 0	3 4½	128 4	3 2½
18 " " 18½ "	135 0	3 4½	133 4	3 4	128 4	3 2½
17½ " " 18 "	116 8	2 11	115 0	2 10½	111 8	2 9½
17 " " 17½ "	111 8	2 9½	110 0	2 9	105 0	2 7½
16½ " " 17 "	110 0	2 9	108 4	2 8½	103 4	2 7
16 " " 16½ "	108 4	2 8½	105 0	2 7½	101 8	2 6½
Under 16 years	100 0	2 6	98 4	2 5½	95 0	2 4½
(g) Workers employed as JOBBERS	1½d. per hour in addition to the rate otherwise payable under (2)(a) to (f).					

FEMALE WORKERS EMPLOYED AS SUBSTITUTES FOR MALE WORKERS IN MAKING BREAD

3.—(1) The general minimum time rate applicable to a female worker who is employed on a class of work which before the war was normally undertaken by men and who is engaged, wholly or mainly, on one or more of the operations of the making of bread (including the operations mentioned as part of "making" in the definition of the baking trade set out in paragraph 14), is

(a) in the case of a female worker who performs the full duties which before the war were performed by a male worker, the general minimum time rate which would be applicable to a male worker of her age employed on the work; or

(b) in the case of a female worker who does not perform the full duties which before the war were performed by a male worker, three quarters of the general minimum time rate which would be applicable to a male worker of her age employed on the work.

(2) For the purposes of this paragraph the expression "before the war" means "during the six months immediately preceding 3rd September 1939".

MALE LATE ENTRANTS

4. Notwithstanding the provisions of paragraph 2, where a male worker specified in (1)(l) or (1)(m) of the Table in the said paragraph (including such a worker when employed as a jobber but not as a night worker), enters or has entered the trade for the first time between the ages of 17 and 20 years, the general minimum time rate applicable to him until he completes 12 months' employment in the trade or until he reaches the age of 20 years, whichever period is the less, shall be that applicable to a male worker one year his junior employed on the same work.

NIGHT WORKERS

5.—(1) For the purposes of this Schedule:—

(a) a night worker is a worker who is employed for not less than a total of three hours between the hours of 6 p.m. on one day and 6 a.m. on the next following day and the night worker's rate shall apply to such a worker in respect of that spell of duty or those spells of duty which include some period or periods between the said hours;

(b) "night worker's rate" means the general minimum time rate applicable to a night worker;

(c) "corresponding day rate" means as respects any night worker the general minimum time rate which would be payable to that worker under the provisions of paragraph 2 in respect of the same work in the same area.

(2) Subject to the provisions of this sub-paragraph, the night worker's rate is the corresponding day rate increased by 15 per cent.:

Provided that—

(a) in the case of a male night worker aged 18 and under 21 years, other than a certificated worker, the night worker's rate shall be the corresponding day rate increased by 2s. 6d. per week of 40 hours, such increased rate being further increased by 15 per cent.;

(b) in the case of a night worker whose corresponding day rate is that specified in (1)(j) of the Table in paragraph 2, the night worker's rate shall be the rate under (1)(i) of the said Table for a day worker in the same area increased by 15 per cent.

WORKER IN DIFFERENT AREAS

6. In the case of a worker whose duties take him into more than one area, the appropriate rate shall be that applicable to workers in the area where the bakehouse is situated.

PART III

OVERTIME, WORK ON A CUSTOMARY HOLIDAY AND WAITING TIME

MINIMUM OVERTIME RATES

7.—(1) Subject to the provisions of this paragraph, overtime is payable at the following minimum rates:—

(a) on any day other than a Sunday or customary holiday—

    (i) for the first 2 hours worked in excess of 9 hours   time-and-a-quarter

    (ii) thereafter ...   .   time-and-a-half

(b) on a Sunday—

    for all time worked between midnight of the preceding day and midnight of the Sunday   ...   double time

    Provided that where in accordance with his usual practice a worker (other than a night worker) works for one hour or less on Sunday afternoon or evening on a preliminary doughing operation he shall be paid the appropriate general minimum time rate.

(c) in any week (exclusive of any time in respect of which any minimum overtime rate is payable under the foregoing provisions of this sub-paragraph and any time worked on a customary holiday)—

    (i) in the case of a worker who works for less than 20 hours in the bakehouse and for the remainder of his time on delivery—

        for all time worked in excess of 48 hours   ...   time-and-a-quarter

    (ii) in the case of any other worker—

        for the first 4 hours worked in excess of 40 hours ...   .   time-and-a-quarter

        thereafter ...   .   time-and-a-half

(2) Notwithstanding the provisions of (a)(i) and (c)(ii) of sub-paragraph (1) of this paragraph, overtime at the rate of time-and-a-quarter shall not be paid for more than an aggregate of four hours worked in any week and any overtime so worked in excess of four hours in the aggregate shall be paid for at the overtime rate of time-and-a-half.

(3) In calculating the time worked in any week for the purposes of this Part of this Schedule a worker who has been allowed, and has taken, a customary holiday or a holiday in lieu of a customary holiday in that week under a wages regulation (holidays) order shall be treated as having worked 6 hours 40 minutes on any such customary holiday or holiday in lieu of a customary holiday.

WORK ON A CUSTOMARY HOLIDAY

8. The remuneration payable to a worker for work on a customary holiday shall be not less than the amount calculated as follows:—

Circumstances	Calculation of Remuneration
(1) where, under the provisions of a wages regulation (holidays) order, the worker is entitled to and is to be allowed a holiday in lieu of a customary holiday on a day other than a Sunday	time-and-a-half for all time worked;
(2) where, under the provisions of a wages regulation (holidays) order, it is mutually agreed between the employer and the worker that a holiday in lieu of a customary holiday shall not be allowed to the worker	time-and-a-half for all time worked on the customary holiday to which such agreement relates and, in addition, an amount equal to the holiday remuneration to which the worker would have been entitled under the provisions of a wages regulation (holidays) order had he been allowed a holiday on that day;
(3) where a worker who is ordinarily employed on a spell of duty which starts before and ends after midnight has been allowed a holiday for the period of 24 hours commencing at noon on the day prior to a customary holiday	double time for all time worked up to midnight of the spell of duty commencing on the customary holiday;
(4) in any other circumstances	double time for all time worked:

Provided that in the case of a worker who is ordinarily employed on a spell of duty which starts before and ends after midnight the provisions of (1), (2) and (4) of this paragraph shall be applicable to time worked during the period of 24 hours commencing at noon on the day prior to the customary holiday.

WAITING TIME

9.—(1) A worker is entitled to payment of the minimum remuneration specified in this Schedule for all time during which he is present on the premises of his employer, unless he is present thereon in any of the following circumstances:—

(a) without the employer's consent, express or implied;

(b) for some purpose unconnected with his work and other than that of waiting for work to be given to him to perform;

(c) by reason only of the fact that he is resident thereon;

(d) during normal meal times in a room or place in which no work is being done, and he is not waiting for work to be given to him to perform.

(2) The minimum remuneration payable under sub-paragraph (1) of this paragraph to a piece worker when not engaged on piece work is that which would be payable to him if he were a time worker.

Part IV

GUARANTEED WEEKLY REMUNERATION

10.—(1) Notwithstanding the foregoing provisions of this Schedule, where in any week the total amount of the minimum remuneration payable to any worker—

(a) under those provisions; and

(b) by way of holiday remuneration under any wages regulation (holidays) order;

would be less than the guaranteed weekly remuneration provided for by this paragraph, the minimum remuneration payable to that worker for that week shall, in lieu of the minimum remuneration which would otherwise be payable under those provisions and that order, be the guaranteed weekly remuneration provided for by this paragraph.

(2) Subject to the provisions of this paragraph, a worker (other than a jobber) who ordinarily works for the employer for at least 36 hours weekly on work to which this Schedule applies shall be entitled to be paid in respect of any week not less than the guaranteed weekly remuneration for 40 hours:

Provided that where the worker normally works for the employer on work to which this Schedule applies for less than 40 hours in the week by reason only of the fact that he does not hold himself out as normally available for work for more than the number of hours he normally works in the week, the guaranteed weekly remuneration shall be for the number of hours in the week normally worked by the worker for the employer on work to which this Schedule applies.

(3) Guaranteed weekly remuneration shall be calculated at the minimum rate or rates ordinarily applicable to the worker in respect of time ordinarily worked by him (excluding overtime, except on Sunday) on work to which this Schedule applies in the following manner, that is to say—

(a) at double time in respect of Sunday work in excess of 4 hours; and

(b) at the night worker's rate in respect of work to which that rate is ordinarily applicable; and

(c) as to any other time, at the hourly general minimum time rate ordinarily applicable to the worker:

Provided that where the ordinary working week of a night worker or of a worker (including a night worker) who ordinarily works overtime on Sunday is less than 40 hours and the worker is not a worker to whom the proviso to sub-paragraph (2) of this paragraph applies, the guaranteed weekly remuneration in respect of a week shall be whichever of the two following amounts is the greater, that is to say—

(i) the amount due in respect of the worker's ordinary weekly working hours calculated in accordance with the foregoing provisions of this sub-paragraph; or

(ii) an amount equal to 40 hours' pay calculated at the minimum rate or rates applicable to a worker of the corresponding class and area who is solely employed on day work other than overtime.

(4) Guaranteed weekly remuneration is not payable in respect of any week unless the worker throughout his normal working hours in that week, excluding any day allowed to him as a holiday, is—

(a) capable of and available for work, and

(b) willing to perform such duties outside his normal occupation as the employer may reasonably require if his normal work is not available in the establishment in which he is employed.

(5) If the employer is unable to provide the worker with work during the worker's normal working hours by reason of a strike, failure of supplies, or any cause beyond the employer's control and gives the worker four clear days' notice that work will not be available, guaranteed weekly remuneration shall not be payable after the expiry of such notice in respect of any week during which or part of which the employer continues to be unable to provide work as aforesaid:

Provided that the guaranteed weekly remuneration payable to a worker in respect of the week in which the said notice expires shall be such proportion of the guaranteed weekly remuneration payable to the worker under the foregoing provisions of this paragraph as the number of the worker's normal working hours on work to which this Schedule applies, falling in that week up to the expiry of the notice, bears to the number of hours in the week normally worked by the worker for the employer on work to which this Schedule applies.

(6) The guaranteed weekly remuneration applicable to a piece worker shall be the sum to which he would be entitled if he were a time worker.

(7) In this paragraph the expression "week" means "pay week"

Part V

INTERPRETATION

CLASSES OF WORKERS

11.—(1) In this Schedule, unless the context otherwise requires, the following expressions have the meanings hereby respectively assigned to them, that is to say—

(a) in the case of a male worker:

A FOREMAN is an adult worker with four or more workers under him.

A FIRST HAND is an adult worker in charge of a department, working under the instruction of a foreman, or in charge of a bakery where less than five workers including himself are employed.

A SECOND HAND is an adult worker who takes charge in the absence of the foreman or first hand, where four or more workers are employed.

A DOUGHMAKER is an adult worker wholly or mainly engaged in dough-making in the making of bread.

A CONFECTIONERY MIXER is an adult worker wholly or mainly engaged in the mixing of dough for flour confectionery and in the mixing of flour confectionery or either of those operations.

An OVENMAN is an adult worker responsible for, and wholly or mainly engaged in, the baking of bread and flour confectionery, or either of them, including the regulating of an oven.

A TABLE HAND is a worker wholly or mainly engaged in one or more of the operations of moulding, scaling and handling of dough, or in feeding an oven or ovens with full or empty tins or in clearing an oven or ovens.

A STOKER is an adult worker wholly or mainly engaged in the firing and regulating of ovens.

(b) in the case of a female worker:

A FOREWOMAN is an adult worker with four or more workers under her.

A CHARGE HAND, other than a charge hand (packing and despatch department), is an adult worker in charge of a department, working under the instruction of a foreman or forewoman, or in charge of a bakery where less than five workers including herself are employed.

(c) in the case of a male or female worker:

A SINGLE HAND is an adult worker in charge of production with no other adult worker or certificated worker.

A CHARGE HAND (packing and despatch department) is a worker who is wholly or mainly employed in, and is in charge of, a packing or despatch department, having not less than two workers (excluding vanmen) under him and working under the instruction of a foreman or manager.

A CONFECTIONER is a worker wholly or mainly engaged in the manufacture, including mixing, moulding, scaling and handling, of unbaked flour confectionery, cake mixings or paste, or in decorating, or finishing, flour confectionery.

A JOBBER is a member of the class of worker, known in the trade as jobbers, who undertake short engagements on a day to day basis.

A CERTIFICATED WORKER is a worker who has received from the National Joint Apprenticeship Council for the Baking Industry (England and Wales) a certificate of completion of satisfactory apprenticeship.

(d) in the case of a male or female worker, ADULT WORKER means a worker aged 21 years or over.

(2) For the purpose of the definition of first hand, single hand (male or female), second hand or charge hand, including a charge hand (packing and despatch department), account shall be taken in the calculation of the numbers of workers employed only of workers who are working during the hours of work of the worker in question, provided that the temporary absence of a worker shall not be regarded as reducing the number of workers employed at any time.

(3) The wholesale cake and flour confectionery branch of the Baking Trade is that branch of the trade in which the production of cake and other flour confectionery is carried on in an undertaking supplying six or more retail establishments and employing ten or more workers on such work.

AREAS

12. In this Schedule—

(1) "London Area" comprises the Metropolitan Police District, as defined on 1st April 1965, the City of London, the Inner Temple and the Middle Temple.

(2) In England (other than the London Area and Monmouthshire)

    (a) "Provincial A Area" comprises all areas other than those in "Provincial B Area";

    (b) "Provincial B Area" comprises all areas which according to the Registrar General's Census of Population 1961 were administered by Rural District Councils.

(3) In Wales and Monmouthshire

    (a) "Provincial A Area" comprises

        (i) The county boroughs of Cardiff, Methyr, Newport and Swansea.

        (ii) The municipal boroughs of Abergavenny, Aberystwyth, Bangor, Barry, Carmarthen, Colwyn Bay, Conway, Flint, Haverfordwest, Llanelly, Neath, Pembroke, Port Talbot, Rhondda and Wrexham.

        (iii) The urban districts of Abercarn, Aberdare, Abertillery, Bedwas and Machen, Bedwellty, Blaenavon, Bridgend, Brynmawr, Caerphilly, Connah's Quay, Cwmbran, Ebbw Vale, Gelligaer, Glyncorrwg, Holyhead, Llandudno, Llwchwr, Maesteg, Milford Haven, Moutain Ash, Mynyddislwyn, Nantyglo and Blaina, Ogmore and Garw, Penarth, Pontypool, Pontypridd, Porthcawl, Prestatyn, Rhyl, Rhymney, Risca, and Tredegar.

        (iv) The rural districts of Cardiff, Cowbridge, Gower, Hawarden, Llantrisant and Llantwit-Fardre, Neath, Penybont, Pontardawe, Pontypool and Wrexham.

    (b) "Provincial B Area" comprises all other areas.

OTHER DEFINITIONS

13. In this Schedule—

(1) "time-and-a-quarter", "time-and-a-half" and "double time" mean respectively—

(a) in the case of a time worker, one and a quarter times, one and a half times and twice the hourly general minimum time rate otherwise payable to the worker;

(b) in the case of a worker employed on piece work, a time rate equal respectively to one quarter, one half and the whole of the hourly general minimum time rate which would be payable to the worker if he were a time worker and neither a minimum overtime rate nor a rate for work on a customary holiday applied and, in addition thereto, the minimum remuneration otherwise payable to the worker under paragraph 1(1)(a)(ii);

(2) "customary holiday" means—

Christmas Day (or, if Christmas Day falls on a Sunday, such week day as may be appointed by national proclamation, or, if none is so appointed, the next following Tuesday), Boxing Day, Good Friday, Easter Monday, Whit Monday (or where another day is substituted therefor by proclamation, that day), August Bank Holiday and any day proclaimed as an additional Bank Holday or as a public holiday, or, in the case of each of the said days, such week day (other than a weekly short day) as may be substituted therefor, being a day on which the worker normally works and which is by local custom recognised as a day of holiday;

(3) "spell of duty" means a period of work broken only by intervals for meals;

(4) "wages regulation (holidays) order" means a wages regulation order made by the Secretary of State to give effect to proposals relating to holidays and holiday remuneration submitted to her by the Baking Wages Council (England and Wales).

PART VI

APPLICABILITY OF STATUTORY MINIMUM REMUNERATION

14. This Schedule applies to workers in relation to whom the Baking Wages Council (England and Wales) operates, that is to say, workers employed in England and Wales in the Baking Trade as defined in the Schedule to the Baking Wages Council, England and Wales (Constitution) Order 1947(a), which Schedule reads as follows:—

"1. Subject to the provisions of this Schedule the Baking Trade consists of the following operations:—

(1) the making of bread, pastry, and flour confectionery and work incidental thereto;

(2) the making of other articles of food and work incidental thereto in an undertaking, or branch or department thereof, mainly engaged on one or more of the operations specified in paragraph 1 (1);

(3) the sale and distribution of any of the articles of food referred to in the preceding sub-paragraphs by a worker who in the same week is also engaged in any of the work specified in those sub-paragraphs.

2. Notwithstanding anything in this Schedule the following operations are not operations in the Baking Trade:—

(1) the making of biscuits in an undertaking, or a branch or department of an undertaking, mainly engaged in the making of biscuits, and the making of any other article of food therein by workers mainly engaged in the making of biscuits;

(a) S.R. & O. 1947/887 (Rev. XXIII, p. 456: 1947 I, p. 2215).

(2) the making of any of the articles of food referred to in paragraph 1 hereof:—

    (a) in an hotel, boarding house, restaurant, café or similar establishment:—

        (i) for consumption on the premises; or

        (ii) for consumption off the premises at meals served by persons ordinarily employed on the premises;

    (b) by a railway undertaking for consumption on its trains, restaurant cars, ships or premises;

(3) the making of:—

    (a) meat pies, sausage rolls or similar articles of pastry (including bread for use therein); or

    (b) bread for use in sausages or similar articles of food

in an undertaking where no bread, pastry or flour confectionery is made other than that specified in this sub-paragraph;

(4) operations included in:—

    (a) the Trade Boards (Milk Distributive) Order, 1928(a);

    (b) the Trade Boards (Sugar Confectionery and Food Preserving) Order, 1913(b);

    (c) the Trade Boards (Grocery and Provisions) Order, 1920(c);

or any amendments or variations of the aforesaid Orders.

3. For the purpose of this Schedule 'pastry' and 'articles of pastry' include articles of food made wholly or partly of pastry; 'meat' includes game, poultry, egg or fish; 'flour confectionery' includes cakes, oatcakes, shortbread and biscuits; 'biscuits' do not include oatcakes or shortbread; and 'making' includes the packing, wrapping and other handling of the articles of food when made before their first despatch for sale or distribution."

EXPLANATORY NOTE

(This Note is not part of the Order.)

This Order, which has effect from 6th August 1969, sets out the statutory minimum remuneration payable in substitution for that fixed by the Wages Regulation (Baking) (England and Wales) Order 1965 (Order BK (75)) as amended by the Wages Regulation (Baking) (England and Wales) (Amendment) Order 1968 (Order BK (78)) which Orders are revoked.

New provisions are printed in italics.

(a) S.R. & O. 1928/475 (1928 p. 1262). (b) Confirmed by 3 & 4 Geo. 5. c. clxii. (c) S.R. & O. 1920/958 (1920 II, p. 774).

STATUTORY INSTRUMENTS

1969 No. 902 (C. 22)

ROAD TRAFFIC

The Heavy Goods Vehicles (Drivers' Licences) (Commencement) Order 1969

Made - - - -	*1st July* 1969
Laid before Parliament	*16th July* 1969
Coming into Operation	*4th August* 1969

The Minister of Transport in exercise of his powers under section 192(1) of the Road Traffic Act 1960(**a**) as substituted by section 19(1) of the Road Safety Act 1967(**b**) and under section 199 of the said Act of 1960 hereby makes the following Order:—

1. The day specified for the purposes of paragraph 1 of Schedule 15 to the Road Traffic Act 1960 as amended by section 32(1) of and Schedule 1 to the Road Safety Act 1967 shall be the 1st February 1970.

2. The day appointed for the purposes of section 192(1) of the Road Traffic Act 1960 as amended by section 19(1) of the Road Safety Act 1967 shall be the 2nd February 1970.

3. This Order may be cited as the Heavy Goods Vehicles (Drivers' Licences) (Commencement) Order 1969, and shall come into operation on the 4th August 1969.

Given under the Official Seal of the Minister of Transport the 1st July 1969.

(L.S.)

Richard Marsh,
Minister of Transport.

EXPLANATORY NOTE

(This Note is not part of the Order.)

Under the Heavy Goods Vehicles (Drivers' Licences) Regulations 1969 (S.I. 1969/903) heavy goods vehicle drivers' licences may be applied for and issued, on a voluntary basis, on and after the 4th August 1969. Generally, existing drivers who have not less than six months' experience of driving such vehicles in the year ending on a specified date are eligible for such a licence without passing a test. Article 1 provides that the date on which the year ends is the 1st February 1970.

Article 2 of this Order provides that section 192(1) of the Road Traffic Act 1960 shall come into force on the 2nd February 1970. On and after that day it will be an offence under Part V of the Road Traffic Act 1960

(**a**) 1960. c. 16.   (**b**) 1967 c. 30.

for any person to drive, or to employ another person to drive, most types of heavy goods vehicles on a road, unless the driver holds a heavy goods vehicle driver's licence authorising him to drive a heavy goods vehicle of that class.

STATUTORY INSTRUMENTS

1969 No. 903

ROAD TRAFFIC

The Heavy Goods Vehicles (Drivers' Licences) Regulations 1969

Made - - - -	*1st July* 1969
Laid before Parliament	*16th July* 1969
Coming into Operation	*4th August* 1969

ARRANGEMENT OF REGULATIONS

PART I—GENERAL

	Regulation
Commencement and citation	1
Interpretation	2

PART II—LICENCES

Applications for licences	3
Qualifications of applicants	4
Issue of licences	5
Form of licences	6
Signature of licences	7
Fees for licences	8
Provisional licences	9
Suspension or revocation	10
Removal of disqualification	11
Withdrawal of licence under Part II of the Act of 1960	12
Lost, defaced and exchanged licences	13
Production of licences	14

PART III—TESTS

Applications for tests	15
Qualifications of applicants for a test of competence	16
Persons who may conduct tests	17
Nature of tests	18
Results of tests	19
Evidence of results of tests	20
Production of vehicle for test, etc.	21

Fees for tests 22
Refund of fees 23
Additional qualification... 24

PART IV—SUPPLEMENTARY

Service personnel 25
Northern Irish licences 26
Offences 27
Exemptions 28
Transitional licences 29
Revocations 30

SCHEDULES

                                                               Page

1.   Classes of heavy goods vehicles 16

2. Part I   Form of heavy goods vehicle full driver's licence... ... 17

   Part II   Form of heavy goods vehicle provisional driver's licence 17

3.   Diagram of distinguishing mark to be displayed on a
                vehicle driven under a provisional licence 18

4.   Nature of tests—operations... 19

5. Part I   Form of certificate of passing a test of competence to
                drive a heavy goods vehicle 19

   Part II   Form of statement of failure to pass a test of competence
                to drive a heavy goods vehicle 19

   Part III   Form of certificate of being treated as having passed a
                Part II test of competence to drive 20

The Minister of Transport in exercise of his powers under sections 20, 21 and 29 of, and paragraph 20(3) of Schedule 1 to, the Road Safety Act 1967(a) and section 19 of the said Act of 1967 as amended by section 16(5) of the Vehicle and Driving Licences Act 1969(b), and sections 194 and 196 of the Road Traffic Act 1960(c) and paragraph 1 of Schedule 15 to the said Act of 1960 as amended by section 16(2) of, and paragraph 13 of Schedule 2 to, the said Act of 1969, and of all other powers enabling him in that behalf, and after consultation with representative organisations in accordance with the provisions of section 29(6) of the said Act of 1967 and section 260(2) of the said Act of 1960, hereby makes the following Regulations:—

(a) 1967 c. 30.   (b) 1969 c. 27.
(c) 8 & 9 Eliz. 2. c. 16.

Part I—Preliminary

Commencement and citation

1. These Regulations shall come into operation on the 4th August 1969 and may be cited as the Heavy Goods Vehicles (Drivers' Licences) Regulations 1969.

Interpretation

2.—(1) In these Regulations, unless the context otherwise requires, the following expressions have the meanings hereby respectively assigned to them, that is to say:—

"the Act of 1960" means the Road Traffic Act 1960 as amended by the Act of 1967 and by the Vehicle and Driving Licences Act 1969;

"the Act of 1967" means the Road Safety Act 1967 as amended by the Vehicle and Driving Licences Act 1969;

"articulated vehicle" means a motor car or heavy motor car as defined in section 253(2) and (3) of the Act of 1960 so constructed that a trailer may by partial superimposition be attached thereto in such a manner as to cause a substantial part of the weight of the trailer to be borne thereby and which has a trailer so attached;

"clerk to the traffic commissioners" means the clerk to the traffic commissioner for the Metropolitan Traffic Area or the clerk to the traffic commissioners for any other traffic area;

"full licence" means a hgv driver's licence other than a provisional hgv driver's licence;

"hgv driver's licence" means a heavy goods vehicle driver's licence;

"licensing authority" has the same meaning as in section 193(1) of the Act of 1960;

"test" means a test of competence to drive heavy goods vehicles of any class conducted under section 19(2) of the Road Safety Act 1967.

"vehicle with automatic transmission" shall mean a vehicle in which the driver is not provided with any means whereby he may, independently of the use of the accelerator or the brakes, vary gradually the proportion of the power being produced by the engine which is transmitted to the road wheels of the vehicle.

(2) In these Regulations, unless the context otherwise requires—

(*a*) any reference to a class or classes of heavy goods vehicles is a reference to one of the classes or to the classes of heavy goods vehicles specified in Schedule 1 to these Regulations;

(*b*) any reference to a numbered class of such vehicles is a reference to the class of that number specified in that Schedule; and

(*c*) any reference to additional classes, in relation to a class of heavy goods vehicles, is a reference to the classes specified in the column in that Schedule headed "additional classes" in relation to that class.

(3) In these Regulations any reference to any enactment or instrument shall be construed, unless the context otherwise requires, as a reference to that enactment or instrument as amended, re-enacted or replaced by any subsequent enactment or instrument.

(4) The Interpretation Act 1889(a) shall apply for the interpretation of these Regulations as it applies for the interpretation of an Act of Parliament.

(a) 52 & 53 Vict. c. 63.

PART II—LICENCES

Applications for licences

3.—(1) A person who desires to obtain the grant of a hgv driver's licence shall—

(a) furnish to the appropriate licensing authority all relevant particulars and make any relevant declaration specified in such form as the Minister of Transport may require,

(b) submit his application not more than two months before the date on which the licence is to have effect,

(c) if he is a person to whom paragraph 3(a) of Schedule 15 to the Act of 1960 applies, submit his application not more than six months prior to the time of expiry of his licence granted under Part II of the Act of 1960 which, at the beginning of the appointed day, authorised him to drive a heavy goods vehicle, and

(d) send with his application—

(i) if required by the licensing authority, a certificate in such form as the Minister of Transport may require signed by a registered medical practitioner as that expression is construed by section 5(2) of the Medical Act 1956**(a)** not more than three months prior to the date on which the licence is to have effect,

(ii) if he is an applicant for a hgv driver's licence under paragraph 1 of Schedule 15 to the Act of 1960, a certificate in such form as the Minister of Transport may require,

(iii) his licence granted under Part II of the Act of 1960,

(iv) the fee for the hgv driver's licence, and

(v) a pass certificate showing that he has passed the test within the relevant period for the class of heavy goods vehicles which the hgv driver's licence applied for will authorise him to drive except in the case of an application for a provisional licence or a hgv driver's licence under paragraph 1 of Schedule 15 to the Act of 1960 or where he has held a full hgv driver's licence authorising him to drive such vehicles within the relevant period.

In this sub-sub-paragraph "relevant period" means the period specified in section 19(2) of the Act of 1967 ending on the date of the coming into force of the hgv driver's licence applied for.

(2) Any application for a hgv driver's licence which does not comply with the foregoing paragraph may be treated by the licensing authority as of no effect, but where the licensing authority so treats such an application or refuses the grant of a licence any fee and any documents required by sub-paragraph (d) of that paragraph to be sent with the application shall be returned to the applicant.

(3) A person shall not apply for a hgv driver's licence if—

(a) he holds a hgv driver's licence which has been suspended,

(b) he is disqualified for holding or obtaining a hgv driver's licence,

(c) he is disqualified by a court for holding or obtaining a licence to drive a motor vehicle granted under Part II of the Act of 1960, or

(d) in the event of the application being granted he would hold more than one hgv driver's licence.

(a) 4 & 5 Eliz. 2. c. 76.

(4) In this Regulation "appropriate licensing authority" means the licensing authority to whom the application for a licence is required to be made in accordance with section 193 of the Act of 1960 or Regulation 25 of these Regulations, as the case may be.

Qualifications of applicants

4. An applicant for a hgv driver's licence shall have the following qualifications, experience and knowledge:—

(*a*) he must not be a person to whom paragraph (3) of the last preceding Regulation applies;

(*b*) he shall not suffer from any disease or physical disability likely to cause the driving by him of a heavy goods vehicle to be a source of danger to the public;

(*c*) he shall on the date of commencement of the hgv driver's licence applied for be aged 21 years or over in the case of an applicant for a hgv driver's licence for class 1, 1A, 2, 2A, 3, or 3A, of heavy goods vehicles (except in the case of an applicant for a hgv driver's licence to drive motor vehicles, owned by the Secretary of State for Defence and used for naval, military or air force purposes, or motor vehicles so used while being driven by persons for the time being subject to the orders of a member of the armed forces of the Crown) or 17 years or over in the case of an applicant for a hgv driver's licence for class 4 or 4A of such vehicles; and

(*d*) he shall hold a licence granted under Part II of the Act of 1960 authorising him to drive a vehicle or vehicles in the class of heavy goods vehicles in respect of which he desires to obtain the grant of a licence.

Issue of licences

5. If the licence held by the applicant under Part II of the Act of 1960 contains a provision under section 100(4) of that Act limiting the applicant to the driving of vehicles of a particular construction or design only, any full licence granted to the applicant to drive a heavy goods vehicle shall contain a corresponding limitation.

Form of licences

6.—(1) hgv drivers' licences shall be issued in the form of a book containing:—

(*a*) in the case of a full licence, particulars in the form set out in Part I of Schedule 2 to these Regulations,

(*b*) in the case of a provisional licence, particulars in the form set out in Part II of that Schedule.

(2) Where an applicant for a hgv driver's licence is already a holder of a hgv driver's licence the licensing authority may, instead of issuing him with a new book, issue the appropriate hgv driver's licence by affixing in the book already held a page or pages containing such particulars as would fall to be included in any new book issued to the applicant.

Signature of licences

7. Every person to whom a hgv driver's licence is granted shall forthwith sign it in ink with his usual signature.

Fees for licences

8. The fee for the grant of a full licence shall be £1 and the fee for the grant of a provisional licence shall be 10s. 0d.:

Provided that the fee for a full licence granted for a period less than three years by virtue of paragraph 4 of Schedule 15 to the Act of 1960 shall be reduced proportionately.

Provisional licences

9.—(1) A full licence to drive any class of heavy goods vehicles shall also be treated for the purposes of Part V of the Act of 1960 as a provisional licence to drive heavy goods vehicles of any other class which the holder is not prohibited under section 97 of the Act of 1960 by reason of his age from driving.

(2) Subject to paragraph (3) of this Regulation, a provisional licence, including a full licence which is treated as a provisional licence under the foregoing paragraph, shall be subject to the following conditions, that is to say the holder shall not drive a heavy goods vehicle of any class which he may drive by virtue of the provisional licence—

(a) otherwise than under the supervision of a person who is present with him in the vehicle and who either holds a full licence to drive that class of vehicle or is a person who by virtue of paragraph 3(a) of Schedule 15 to the Act of 1960 is the holder of a licence issued under Part II of that Act, other than a provisional licence, authorising him to drive heavy goods vehicles of that class;

(b) unless there is clearly displayed in a conspicuous manner on the front and on the back of the vehicle a distinguishing mark in the form set out in Schedule 3 to these Regulations;

(c) which is being used to draw a trailer, except where the trailer is part of an articulated vehicle being driven by the holder.

(3) The condition specified in paragraph 2(a) of this Regulation shall not apply whilst the holder of a provisional licence is undergoing a test.

Suspension or revocation

10.—(1) The holder of a hgv driver's licence which has been suspended or revoked by a licensing authority shall on receipt of notice either delivered to the holder personally or sent by the recorded delivery service to the holder's last known address of the decision of the licensing authority to suspend or revoke the licence forthwith deliver it to the licensing authority for endorsement or cancellation.

(2) A licensing authority who suspends a hgv driver's licence shall endorse particulars of the suspension on the hgv driver's licence and shall return it to the holder at the end of the period of suspension on a demand in writing being made by that person.

Removal of disqualification

11.—(1) A licensing authority may remove a disqualification under paragraph (a) of section 19(3) of the Act of 1967 if the application for the removal of the disqualification is made after the expiration of whichever is relevant of the following periods from the commencement of the disqualification, that is to say—

(a) two years, if the disqualification is for less than four years;

(b) one half of the period of the disqualification, if it is for less than ten years but not less than four years;

(c) five years in any other case, including disqualification for an indefinite period.

(2) Where an application under section 19(4) of the Act of 1967 and the preceding paragraph for the removal of a disqualification is refused, a further such application in respect of the same person shall not be entertained if made within three months after the date of refusal.

Withdrawal of licence under Part II of the Act of 1960

12.—(1) If the holder of a hgv driver's licence is disqualified for holding or obtaining a licence under Part II of the Act of 1960, or if such a licence is refused or revoked under section 100 of the Act of 1960, he shall forthwith—

(a) notify the licensing authority in whose area he resides of the particulars of the disqualification refusal or revocation, and

(b) deliver his hgv driver's licence to that licensing authority.

(2) Where a person who has delivered his hgv driver's licence to a licensing authority in accordance with the foregoing paragraph ceases to be disqualified, unless the hgv driver's licence has been revoked or a period of suspension is still current, the licensing authority on production of that person's licence granted under the said Part II shall return the hgv driver's licence to him if it has not expired.

Lost, defaced and exchanged licences

13.—(1) If the holder of a hgv driver's licence satisfies the licensing authority by whom it was granted that the hgv driver's licence has been lost or defaced the licensing authority shall, on payment of a fee of 5s. 0d. and in the case of a defaced hgv driver's licence on surrender to the licensing authority of the licence, issue to him a duplicate hgv driver's licence and shall endorse thereon particulars of any suspension endorsed upon the original hgv driver's licence and the duplicate so issued shall have the same effect as the original.

(2) If at any time while a duplicate, which was issued in the place of a lost hgv driver's licence, is in force the original hgv driver's licence is found and the person to whom the original hgv driver's licence was issued becomes aware of that fact he shall forthwith inform the licensing authority and, if it is not in his possession, take all reasonable steps to obtain possession of it, and if it is in his possession or he obtains possession of it shall return it as soon as may be to the licensing authority by whom it was issued.

(3) If the holder of a hgv driver's licence surrenders it and applies for a new hgv driver's licence he shall, if he so requires, on payment of a fee of 5s. 0d. be granted a hgv driver's licence to continue in force only for the period for which the surrendered licence would have continued if not surrendered.

Production of licences

14.—(1) Subject to paragraph (5) of this Regulation, any such person as follows, that is to say,—

(a) the driver of a heavy goods vehicle on a road, or

(*b*) a person who accompanies the holder of a provisional licence while the holder is driving a heavy goods vehicle on a road,

shall, on being so required by a police constable or an examiner appointed under section 183 of the Act of 1960, produce his hgv driver's licence for examination, so as to enable the constable or examiner to ascertain the name and address of the holder of the hgv driver's licence, the date of issue, and the authority by which it was issued, and shall, on being so required by an examiner as aforesaid, give his name and address and acknowledge that such information as recorded by the examiner on the examiner's record sheet is correct by signing the said record sheet.

(2) Subject to paragraph (5) of this Regulation, any such person as follows, that is to say,—

(*a*) a person whom a police constable has reasonable cause to believe to have been the driver of a heavy goods vehicle at a time when an accident occurred owing to its presence on a road, or

(*b*) a person whom a police constable has reasonable cause to believe to have committed an offence in relation to the use of a heavy goods vehicle on a road,

shall, on being so required by a police constable, produce his hgv driver's licence for examination so as to enable the constable to ascertain the name and address of the holder of the hgv driver's licence, the date of issue, and the authority by whom it was issued.

(3) Subject to paragraph (5) of this Regulation, where a hgv driver's licence has been suspended or revoked by a licensing authority, then if the holder of the hgv driver's licence fails to deliver it to that authority for endorsement or cancellation as required by Regulation 10(1) of these Regulations, a police constable or an examiner appointed under section 183 of the Act of 1960 may require him to produce it, and upon its being produced may seize it and deliver it for endorsement or cancellation to that authority.

(4) Subject to paragraph (5) of this Regulation, where a police constable or an examiner appointed under section 183 of the Act of 1960 has reasonable cause to believe that the person to whom a licence has been granted, or any other person, has knowingly made a false statement for the purpose of obtaining the grant of the hgv driver's licence, the police constable or examiner may require the holder of the hgv driver's licence to produce it to him.

(5) If any person is unable to produce his hgv driver's licence when required to do so in accordance with any of the foregoing paragraphs of this Regulation, it shall be a sufficient compliance with that paragraph if—

(*a*) in a case where the hgv driver's licence was required by a police constable to be produced, within five days after the production of his hgv driver's licence was so required he produces the hgv driver's licence in person for examination for the same purposes at such police station as may have been specified by him at the time its production was required, or

(*b*) in a case where the hgv driver's licence was required by an examiner appointed under section 183 of the Act of 1960 to be produced, within ten days after the production of his hgv driver's licence was so required it is produced for examination for the same purposes at the office of such examiner appointed under section 183 of the Act of 1960 or such licensing authority as may have been specified by him at the time its production was required.

(6) The holder of a hgv driver's licence shall, upon being required to do so by a licensing authority cause his hgv driver's licence or his licence granted under Part II of the Act of 1960 to be produced to that authority within ten days after the day on which the requirement was made.

PART III—TESTS

Applications for tests

15.—(1) A person who desires to take a test to be conducted by an examiner appointed under Regulation 17(1)(*a*) of these Regulations shall apply for an appointment for a test to the clerk to the traffic commissioners for the area in which the driving test centre at which the applicant wishes to be tested is situated.

(2) An applicant for such an appointment shall, when making the application, specify the class of goods vehicles in respect of which he desires to take the test and pay to the said clerk the fee for the test prescribed by Regulation 22.

(3) Upon receipt of an application and fee for a test in accordance with this Regulation from a person qualified in accordance with the next following Regulation to take the test applied for the said clerk shall make arrangements for the taking of the test and offer the applicant an appointment.

(4) A person who has previously submitted himself for a test and failed to pass shall not submit himself for a test before the expiration of one month from the date of the previous test, except under an order of a court or sheriff under section 20(3) of the Act of 1967.

Qualifications of applicants for a test of competence

16. An applicant for a test shall hold licences granted under Part II and Part V of the Act of 1960 entitling him to drive a vehicle or vehicles in the class of heavy goods vehicles in respect of which he desires to take the test:

Provided that this Regulation shall not require an applicant to hold a licence under Part V of the Act of 1960 if he is a person to whom paragraph 3(*a*) of Schedule 15 to the Act of 1960 applies.

Persons who may conduct tests

17.—(1) Tests may be conducted by—

(*a*) examiners appointed for that purpose by the Minister of Transport,

(*b*) examiners appointed for that purpose by the Secretary of State, in so far as concerns the testing of persons subject to the Naval Discipline Act 1957**(a)**, to military law or to air force law, or of persons employed in the driving of motor vehicles for the purposes of the naval, military or air forces of Her Majesty raised in the United Kingdom,

(*c*) in England and Wales, by the chief officer of any fire brigade maintained in pursuance of the Fire Services Act 1947**(b)** or, in Scotland by the fire-master of such a brigade, in so far as concerns the testing of members of any such brigade or of persons employed in the driving of motor vehicles for the purposes of any such brigade,

---

(a) 1957 c. 53.   **(b)** 10 & 11 Geo. 6. c. 41.

    (*d*) any chief officer of police in so far as concerns the testing—

        (i) of members of a police force, or

        (ii) of persons employed in the driving of vehicles for police purposes by a police authority, or by the Receiver for the Metropolitan Police District or by the Commissioner of Police for the Metropolis.

    (2) Any person authorised by virtue of sub-paragraph (*c*) or (*d*) of the preceding paragraph of this Regulation to conduct tests may, subject to the approval of the Minister of Transport, authorise suitable persons to act as examiners of those who submit themselves for a test.

Nature of tests

    18. The nature of the test shall be that the candidate shall satisfy the examiner that—

    (*a*) he is fully conversant with the contents of the Highway Code,

    (*b*) he has sufficient knowledge of the mechanical operation of the vehicle on which he is tested, including at the discretion of the examiner the effect of distribution of load on the performance of the vehicle, to enable him to drive it safely,

    (*c*) he is competent to drive without danger to and with due consideration for other users of the road, the vehicle on which he is tested,

    (*d*) he is able to perform safely and competently the operations specified in Schedule 4 to these Regulations.

Results of tests

    19. A person who has passed a test to drive a class of heavy goods vehicles shall be deemed for the purposes of Part V of the Act of 1960 to have passed in addition the test for any additional classes of heavy goods vehicles relating to that class.

Evidence of results of tests

    20.—(1) A person who passes a test shall be furnished with a certificate to that effect in the form (adapted as the case may require) set out in Part I of Schedule 5 to these Regulations.

    (2) A person who fails to pass a test shall be furnished with a statement to that effect in the form (adapted as the case may require) set out in Part II of Schedule 5 to these Regulations.

Production of vehicle for test, etc.

    21.—(1) A person submitting himself for a test shall—

    (*a*) provide for the purpose of the test a vehicle which:—

        (i) is a vehicle of the class in respect of which he requires to be tested and in the case of a test in respect of class 2, 2A, 3 or 3A not be an articulated vehicle or the tractive unit thereof;

        (ii) is suitable for the purpose of the test;

        (iii) is not carrying any goods or burden of any description;

(iv) is fitted with a seat which is firmly secured to the vehicle and in such a position that the examiner may properly conduct the test from it and afford adequate protection from bad weather to the examiner when conducting the test;

(v) is not a vehicle in respect of which any person is required to be employed as a driver or attendant in addition to the applicant under section 72 of the Act of 1960; and

(vi) is not fitted with a device designed to permit a person other than the driver to operate the accelerator, unless any pedal or lever by which the device is operated and any other parts which it may be necessary to remove to make the device inoperable by such a person during the test have been removed; and

(b) produce to the examiner who is to conduct the test his driving licence granted under Part II of the Act of 1960 and his licence granted under Part V of that Act and shall sign the examiner's attendance record:

Provided that this sub-paragraph shall not require him to produce a licence under Part V of the Act of 1960 if he is a person to whom paragraph 3(a) of Schedule 15 to the Act of 1960 applies.

(2) Where a person submitting himself for a test provides a vehicle which does not comply with the foregoing paragraph or fails to produce his licences as aforesaid or fails to sign the examiner's attendance record the examiner may refuse to conduct the test.

Fees for tests

22. The fee payable in respect of a test to be conducted by an examiner appointed under Regulation 17(1)(a) of these Regulations shall be £6.

Refund of fees

23. The fee paid in pursuance of Regulations 15 and 22 on application for an appointment for a test may be repaid in the following cases and not otherwise, that is to say:—

(a) if no such appointment is made, or an appointment made is subsequently cancelled by or on behalf of the Minister of Transport;

(b) if the person for whom the appointment is made gives notice cancelling the appointment to the clerk to the traffic commissioners by whom the appointment was made of not less than three clear days (excluding Saturdays, Sundays, any bank holiday, Christmas Day or Good Friday) before the date of the appointment.

For the purposes of this Regulation "bank holiday" means a day which is, or is to be observed as, a bank holiday, or a holiday, under the Bank Holidays Act 1871(a) or the Holidays Extension Act 1875(b), either generally or in the locality in which is situated the office of the clerk to the traffic commissioners to whom notice cancelling an appointment for a test falls to be given;

(c) if the person for whom the appointment is made keeps the appointment but the test does not take place, or is not completed, for reasons attributable neither to him nor to any vehicle provided by him for the purposes of the test; or

---

(a) 34 & 35 Vict. c. 17. **(b)** 38 & 39 Vict. c. 13.

(d) if an order for repayment of the fee is made by a court or sheriff under section 20(3) of the Act of 1967 pursuant to a finding that the test was not properly conducted in accordance with these Regulations.

Additional qualification

24.—(1) A person who passes a test shall be treated as having passed the test of competence prescribed under section 99(2) of Part II of the Act of 1960 to drive:—

(a) if he is under the age of 21 years:—

    (i) motor cars, if the vehicle on which he passes the test is not a vehicle with automatic transmission, or

    (ii) motor cars with automatic transmission, if the vehicle on which he passes the test is a vehicle with automatic transmission; or

(b) if he is 21 years of age or over:—

    (i) vehicles in group 1A of Schedule 5 to the Motor Vehicles (Driving Licences) Regulations 1963**(a)**, as amended by the Motor Vehicles (Driving Licences) (Amendment) Regulations 1969**(b)**, if the vehicle on which he passes the test is not a vehicle with automatic transmission, or

    (ii) vehicles in group 1B of Schedule 5 to the said Regulations of 1963, as so amended, if the vehicle on which he passes the test is a vehicle with automatic transmission;

if-(a) at the time he takes the test he is the holder of a provisional licence granted under the said Part II, and

(b) at that time he does not hold and is not entitled to be granted a full licence under the said Part II in respect of any such vehicle:

Provided that if the test proves his competence to drive vehicles of a particular construction or design only he shall be treated as having passed the said test of competence to drive such vehicles in that group only.

(2) A person who is treated as having passed the test of competence prescribed under section 99(2) of Part II of the Act of 1960 under paragraph (1) of this Regulation shall be furnished with a certificate to that effect in the form (adapted as the case may require) set out in Part III of Schedule 5 to these Regulations.

PART IV—SUPPLEMENTARY

Service personnel

25. The function of issuing licences under Part V of the Act of 1960 to persons subject to the Naval Discipline Act 1957, to military law or to air force law to drive such vehicles and of revoking and suspending such licences shall be exercisable by the licensing authority for the South Eastern Traffic Area.

Northern Irish licences

26.—(1) The licensing authority for the North Western Traffic Area is hereby prescribed for the purposes of section 19(8) and (9) of the Act of 1967 (suspension, revocation and disqualification in respect of Northern Ireland licences as respects Great Britain).

(a) S.I. 1963/1026 (1963 II, p. 1730).   **(b)** S.I. 1969/252 (1969 I, p. 640).

(2) For the purposes of section 19(9) of the Act of 1967 (appeals in respect of a Northern Ireland licence against suspension, revocation or disqualification) the holder of a Northern Ireland licence may appeal for a reconsideration of his case to:—

(i) a magistrates' court which he may nominate at the time he puts down his appeal, or

(ii) in the absence of a nomination of a particular court under (i), the magistrates' court in whose area the office of the licensing authority for the North Western Traffic Area is located.

Offences

27. It is hereby declared that a contravention of or failure to comply with Regulation 3(3), 7, 9(2), 10(1), 12(1), 13(2), 14 or 15(4) is an offence, and accordingly by virtue of section 20(2) of the Act of 1967 a person who contravenes or fails to comply with such a Regulation is liable on summary conviction to a fine not exceeding £20.

Exemptions

28.—(1) Part V of, and paragraph 1 of Schedule 15 to, the Act of 1960 shall not apply to heavy goods vehicles of the following classes:—

(*a*) track laying vehicles;

(*b*) vehicles propelled by steam;

(*c*) road rollers;

(*d*) road construction vehicles used or kept on the road solely for the conveyance of built-in road construction machinery (with or without articles or materials used for the purpose of that machinery);

(*e*) engineering plant;

(*f*) works trucks;

(*g*) an industrial tractor, that is to say a tractor, not being a land tractor, having an unladen weight not exceeding $3\frac{1}{2}$ tons, designed and used primarily for work off roads, or for work on roads in connection only with road construction or maintenance (including any such tractor when fitted with an implement or implements designed primarily for use in connection with such work, whether or not any such implement is of itself designed to carry a load), and which is so constructed as to be incapable of exceeding a speed of 20 miles per hour on the level under its own power.

(*h*) land locomotives and land tractors;

(*i*) digging machines;

(*j*) vehicles exempted from excise duty by virtue of section 6(6) of the Vehicles (Excise) Act 1962(a) (vehicles used less than a certain distance on public roads);

(*k*) any motor car as defined in section 253(2) of the Act of 1960 so constructed that a trailer may by partial superimposition be attached thereto in such a manner as to cause a substantial part of the weight of the trailer to be borne thereby, but which has no trailer attached;

(*l*) vehicles used as public service vehicles as defined in sections 117 and 118 of the Act of 1960;

(a) 10 & 11 Eliz. 2. c. 13.

(m) vehicles used for no other purpose than the haulage of lifeboats and the conveyance of the necessary gear of the lifeboats which are being hauled;

(n) vehicles registered before 1st January 1940 used unladen and not drawing a laden trailer;

(o) vehicles in the service of a visiting force or headquarters;

(p) wheeled armoured vehicles being the property of, or for the time being under the control of, the Secretary of State for Defence;

(q) a vehicle driven by a police constable for the purpose of removing or avoiding obstruction to other road users or danger to other road users or members of the public, for the purpose of safeguarding property, including the heavy goods vehicle and its load, or for other similar purposes; and

(r) any articulated vehicle, the tractive unit of which does not exceed 15 cwt unladen weight.

(2) Paragraph 1 of Schedule 15 to the Act of 1960 shall not apply in a case to which section 192(3) of that Act applies, or to heavy goods vehicles to which section 192(4) of that Act applies.

(3) In this Regulation:—

(a) "track laying", in relation to a vehicle, means that the vehicle is so designed and constructed that the weight thereof is transmitted to the road surface either by means of continuous tracks or by a combination of wheels and continuous tracks in such circumstances that the weight transmitted to the road surface by the tracks is not less than half the weight of the vehicle;

(b) "road construction vehicle" and "road construction machinery" have the meanings given thereto by section 6(8) of the Vehicles (Excise) Act 1962;

(c) "works truck" has the meaning given thereto in Schedule 2 to the Goods Vehicles (Plating and Testing) Regulations 1968(a);

(d) "engineering plant," "land locomotive" and "land tractor" have the meanings given thereto in Regulation 3(1) of the Motor Vehicles (Construction and Use) Regulations 1969(b);

(e) "digging machine" has the meaning given thereto in Schedule 3 to the Vehicles (Excise) Act 1962;

(f) expressions used in sub-paragraph (n) of paragraph (1) have the same meaning as in the Visiting Forces and International Headquarters (Application of Law Order) 1965(c).

Transitional licences

29.—(1) Any hgv driver's licence granted under paragraph 1 of Schedule 15 to the Act of 1960 to an applicant who has been in the habit of driving, during any period or periods referred to in the said paragraph 1, a heavy goods vehicle or vehicles of any class shall be granted in respect of each class of heavy goods vehicles which he has been in the habit of driving during the said period or periods and in respect of such additional classes relating to that class.

(2) Any hgv driver's licence granted under paragraph 1 of the said Schedule 15 to an applicant, who is unable to satisfy the licensing authority that he qualifies under the preceding paragraph but who can satisfy the licensing authority

(a) S.I. 1968/601 (1968 I, p. 1372).   (b) S.I. 1969/321 (1969 I, p. 829).
(c) S.I. 1965/1536 (1965 II, p. 4462).

that during periods referred to in the said paragraph 1 and amounting in aggregate to six months he has been in the habit of driving heavy goods vehicles of a combination of classes, shall be restricted to the lowest class of heavy goods vehicles comprised in that combination and such additional classes (if any) relating to that class.

In construing for the purposes of this paragraph the reference to the lowest class of heavy goods vehicles, class 1 in column 1 of Schedule 1 to these Regulations shall be treated as the highest class and each succeeding class in that column shall be treated as lower than any preceding class.

Revocations

30. The Heavy Goods Vehicles (Drivers' Licences) Regulations 1936**(a)** and the Heavy Goods Vehicles (Drivers' Licences) (Amendment) Regulations 1938**(b)**, each as having effect by virtue of section 267(2) of, and paragraph 1 of Schedule 19 to, the Road Traffic Act 1960, are hereby revoked.

Given under the Official Seal of the Minister of Transport the 1st July 1969.

(L.S.) *Richard Marsh,*
Minister of Transport.

(a) S.R. & O. 1936/1244 (Rev. XX, p. 478: 1936 II, p. 2185).
(b) S.R. & O. 1938/451 (Rev. XX, p. 478, 1938 II, p. 3017).

(See Regulations 2, 3,
4, 9, 19, 21 and 29)

SCHEDULE 1

Classes of heavy goods vehicles

1 Class	2 Definition	3 Additional Classes
Class 1	an articulated vehicle not with automatic transmission, other than a vehicle coming within class 4.	Classes 1A, 2, 2A, 3, 3A, 4 and 4A
Class 1A	an articulated vehicle with automatic transmission, other than a vehicle coming within class 4A.	Classes 2A, 3A and 4A
Class 2	a heavy goods vehicle not with automatic transmission, other than an articulated vehicle, designed and constructed to have more than four wheels in contact with the road surface.	Classes 2A, 3 and 3A
Class 2A	a heavy goods vehicle with automatic transmission, other than an articulated vehicle, designed and constructed to have more than four wheels in contact with the road surface.	Class 3A
Class 3	a heavy goods vehicle not with automatic transmission, other than an articulated vehicle, designed and constructed to have not more than four wheels in contact with the road surface.	Class 3A
Class 3A	a heavy goods vehicle with automatic transmission, other than an articulated vehicle, designed and constructed to have not more than four wheels in contact with the road surface.	
Class 4	an articulated vehicle not with automatic transmission, the tractive unit of which does not exceed two tons unladen weight.	Class 4A
Class 4A	an articulated vehicle with automatic transmission, the tractive unit of which does not exceed two tons unladen weight.	

For the purposes of the above definitions where a vehicle is fitted with two wheels in line transversely and the distance between the centres of their respective areas of contact with the road is less than 18 inches they shall be regarded as only one wheel,

(See Regulation 6)

SCHEDULE 2

PART I

Form of heavy goods vehicle full driver's licence.

Road Traffic Act 1960
Road Safety Act 1967
**HEAVY GOODS VEHICLE
DRIVER'S LICENCE**

Issued by the Licensing Authority for
[

Space for name and address
of holder

]

    is hereby authorised to drive heavy goods vehicles of Classes
       1, 1A, 2, 2A, 3, 3A, 4, 4A

         ....
         ....
         ....

from ....until ....inclusive.

PROVISIONAL LICENCE

This licence has effect as a provisional licence in respect of the classes of heavy goods
vehicles for which it is not a full licence. Such heavy goods vehicles may be driven
subject to the conditions applying to provisional licence holders and the minimum age
requirements being satisfied.

Usual signature of licensee...

PART II

Form of heavy goods vehicle provisional driver's licence.

Road Traffic Act 1960
Road Safety Act 1967
**HEAVY GOODS VEHICLE
PROVISIONAL DRIVER'S LICENCE**

Issued by the Licensing Authority for
[

Space for name and address
of holder

]

is hereby authorised to drive heavy goods vehicles of [all Classes] [Classes 4 and 4A]
subject to the conditions prescribed in Regulation 9 of the Heavy Goods Vehicles
(Drivers' Licences) Regulations 1969

from ....until ....inclusive.

Usual signature of licensee...

SCHEDULE 3

Diagram of distinguishing mark to be displayed on a vehicle driven under a provisional licence

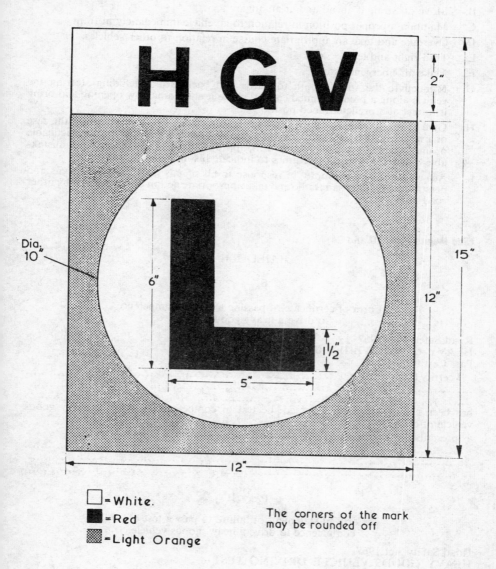

The corners of the mark
may be rounded off

(See Regulation 18)

SCHEDULE 4

Nature of tests—operations

A.　Start the engine of the vehicle.

B.　Move off straight ahead and at an angle.

C.　Maintain a proper position in relation to a vehicle immediately in front.

D.　Overtake and take an appropriate course in relation to other vehicles.

E.　Turn right and left.

F.　Make an emergency stop.

G.　Manoeuvre the vehicle both forwards and backwards, including steering the vehicle along a predetermined course; make it enter a narrow opening and bring it to rest at a predetermined position.

H.　Give by mechanical means, if fitted to the vehicle, and by arm, except in the case of a vehicle with a left-hand drive or a disabled driver for whom it is impracticable or undesirable to give signals by arm, appropriate signals in clear and unmistakable manner at appropriate times to indicate his intended actions.

I.　Act correctly and promptly in response to all signals given by traffic signs and persons regulating road traffic and take appropriate action on signs given by other road users.

(See Regulations 20 and 24)

SCHEDULE 5

Part I

Form of certificate of passing a test of competence to drive a heavy goods vehicle

Road Safety Act 1967
HEAVY GOODS VEHICLE DRIVING TEST
Pass Certificate

I certify that..

....

....

has been examined and has passed the test of competence to drive a heavy goods vehicle of class

as prescribed for the purposes of section 19(2) of the Road Safety Act 1967.

....

....

....

Part II

Form of statement of failure to pass a test of competence to drive a heavy goods vehicle.

Road Safety Act 1967
HEAVY GOODS VEHICLE DRIVING TEST
Statement of Failure

Name ....

Address ....

....

has this day been examined on a heavy goods vehicle of Class.........and has failed to pass the test of competence to drive prescribed for the purposes of section 19(2) of the Road Safety Act 1967.

Part III

Form of certificate of being treated as having passed
a Part II test of competence to drive

Road Traffic Act 1960
Road Safety Act 1967
HEAVY GOODS VEHICLE DRIVING TEST
Pass certificate for ordinary driving test

....
has been examined and has passed a test of competence conducted under section 19(2)
of the Road Safety Act 1967, and shall be treated under Regulation 24 of the Heavy
Goods Vehicles (Drivers' Licences) Regulations 1969 as having passed the test of
competence prescribed under section 99(2) of the Road Traffic Act 1960 to drive
....
....
....
prescribed for the purposes of section 99(2) of the Road Traffic Act 1960.

EXPLANATORY NOTE

(This Note is not part of the Regulations.)

On or after 2nd February 1970, the day appointed by the Minister of Transport in the Heavy Goods Vehicles (Drivers' Licences) (Commencement) Order
1969 (S.I. 1969/902) for the purposes of section 192(1) of the Road Traffic Act
1960 as substituted by section 19(1) of the Road Safety Act 1967 it will generally—subject to the transitional provisions of para. 3(*a*) of Schedule 15 to the
Road Traffic Act 1960—be an offence to drive a heavy goods vehicle, or to
employ another person to drive a heavy goods vehicle, unless the driver has a
heavy goods vehicle driver's licence authorising him to drive heavy goods
vehicles of that class.

These Regulations make provision for the issue of licences to drive heavy
goods vehicles, and for the conduct of tests of competence to drive such vehicles.

Regulation 2(2) and Schedule 1 define the classes of heavy goods vehicles.

Part II of the Regulations deals with heavy goods vehicle drivers' licences.
Regulations 3 to 8 and Schedule 2 deal with applications for licences, their issue,
their form, and the fee for them. Regulation 9 deals with provisional licences,
and Schedule 3 prescribes the distinguishing mark to be displayed on a vehicle
driven under a provisional licence. Regulations 10 to 14 deal with licences which
have been suspended, revoked, lost, defaced or exchanged, disqualification of
holders of licences, and the production of licences.

Part III of the Regulations deals with tests of competence to drive heavy goods
vehicles. The Regulations in this Part deal with applications for tests, appointment of examiners, nature of tests, production of a vehicle for the test and the
fee for a test. Regulation 20 and Schedule 5 prescribe the form of the 'pass' and
'fail' certificates.

Part IV of the Regulations deals with various supplementary matters including the appointment of licensing authorities for Navy, Army and Air Force
personnel, and for Northern Irish licences, a declaration of the Regulations
contravention of which is to be an offence, and a list of certain heavy goods
vehicles, drivers of which are exempt from any need for a heavy goods vehicle
driver's licence.

STATUTORY INSTRUMENTS

1969 No. 904

REPRESENTATION OF THE PEOPLE

The Representation of the People Regulations 1969

Made - - -	*2nd June* 1969
Laid before Parliament	*12th June* 1969
Coming into Operation—	
Regulations 21, 22, 28, 29-58, 68, 69, 74	*16th February* 1970
Regulation 70(2) *and Schedules*	*In accordance with Regulation 2*
Remainder	*16th July* 1969

ARRANGEMENT OF REGULATIONS

PART I

GENERAL

1. Citation and extent.
2. Commencement.
3. Revocation and savings.
4. Interpretation.

PART II

REGISTRATION

The Register

5. Separate part of register for each registration unit.
6. Separate letter for each parliamentary polling district.
7. Order of names.
8. Marking of names to indicate at which elections person entitled to vote.
9. Marking of names to indicate manner of voting.

The Electors Lists

10. Form of electors lists.
11. Publication of the electors lists.

Claims and Objections

12. Notice of claims and objections.
13. Time for making claims and objections.
14. Form of claims and objections.
15. Entry and preliminary disposal of claims and objections.
16. Hearing of claims and objections.
17. Corrections to the electors lists.
18. Other corrections to the electors lists.

Publication and Sale of the Register

19. Publication of register.
20. Registration officer to furnish copies of register.
21. Free copies of register.
22. Sale of register.

Supplementary

23. Declaration as to age and nationality.
24. Power of registration officer to delegate his duties.
25. Information from householders.
26. Adaptation of electors lists and register in consequence of altered polling districts.

Corrupt and Illegal Practices List

27. Corrupt and illegal practices list.

Correction of Register

28. Correction of register.

PART III

ABSENT VOTERS, PROXIES AND POSTAL PROXIES

29. Application to be treated as an absent voter.
30. Record and list of absent voters.
31. Application to vote by proxy.
32. Appointment of proxy.
33. Proxy paper.
34. Cancellation and disregard of proxy appointment.
35. Record and list of proxies.
36. Application by proxy to vote by post.
37. Record and list of postal proxies.
38. Certificate of employment.

PART IV

ISSUE AND RECEIPT OF POSTAL BALLOT PAPERS

Interpretation

39. Interpretation of Part IV.

Issue of Postal Ballot Papers

40. Form of postal ballot paper.
41. Form of declaration of identity.
42. Persons entitled to be present at issue and receipt of postal ballot papers.
43. Declaration of secrecy.
44. Notice of issue of postal ballot papers.
45. Marking of postal ballot paper.
46. Refusal to issue postal ballot paper.
47. Ballot paper envelope.
48. Delivery of postal ballot papers to post office.
49. Provision of postal voters' ballot box.
50. Sealing up of special lists and counterfoils.
51. Spoilt postal ballot paper.

Receipt of Postal Ballot Papers

52. Receipt of covering envelope.
53. Opening of postal voters' ballot box.
54. Opening of covering envelopes.
55. Sealing up of rejected votes and declarations of identity.
56. Opening of ballot paper envelopes.
57. Abandoned poll.
58. Forwarding of documents.

Part V

Service Voters

59. Service declaration by members of the forces and spouses.
60. Qualification for Crown servant.
61. Service declaration by Crown servants, British Council employees and spouses.
62. Transmission of service declaration by Crown servants, British Council employees and spouses.
63. Service declaration by person about to leave the United Kingdom.
64. Proceedings by registration officer on receipt of service declaration.
65. Invalid service declaration.
66. Evidence as to service declaration.

Part VI

Supplementary

67. Appeals.
68. Official poll card.
69. Return and declaration of election expenses.
70. Forms.
71. Sending of notices, etc.
72. Publication of documents.
73. Misnomers.
74. Time.
75. Penalties.

SCHEDULES

SCHEDULE 1: Forms.

Forms for use by registration officers

Form A: Return by occupier as to residents.
Form B: Notice as to publication of a draft register of electors and making of claims and objections.
Form C: Notice as to publication of the electors lists and making of claims and objections.
Form D: Proxy paper.

Forms for use by returning officers

Form E: Elector's official poll card.
Form F: Proxy's official poll card.
Form G: Certificate of employment.
Form H: Declaration of identity.

Forms for use by service voters

Form J: Service declaration and application for appointment of proxy by a member of the forces.
Form K: Service declaration and application for appointment of proxy by the spouse of a member of the forces.
Form L: Service declaration and application for appointment of proxy by a Crown servant or by a person employed by the British Council.
Form M: Service declaration and application for appointment of proxy by the spouse of a Crown servant or of a person employed by the British Council.
Form N: Application by a service voter in the United Kingdom to vote by post.

Forms for use by other persons

Form O: Form of claim to be registered as an elector.
Form P: Form of objection to an entry in the electors lists.
Form Q: Application to be treated as an absent voter for an indefinite period owing to occupation or physical incapacity.
Form R: Application to vote by post owing to change of residence.
Form S: Application to be treated as an absent voter for a particular election.
Form T: Application to be treated as an absent voter for an indefinite period owing to air or sea journey.
Form U: Application for appointment of proxy.
Form V: Application by a proxy to vote by post.
Form W: Application by service voter's spouse for appointment of proxy.
Form X: Return of expenses required by section 63 of the Representation of the People Act 1949 to be authorised by an election agent.
Form Y: Declaration as to expenses required by section 63 of the Representation of the People Act 1949 to be authorised by an election agent.

SCHEDULE 2: Table of comparison of election rules.

In exercise of the powers conferred on me by sections 42 and 171(5) of the Representation of the People Act 1949(**a**), I hereby make the following Regulations :—

PART I

GENERAL

Citation and extent

1.—(1) These Regulations may be cited as the Representation of the People Regulations 1969.

(2) These Regulations shall not extend to Scotland or Northern Ireland.

Commencement

2.—(1) The following provisions of these Regulations, namely, Regulations 21, 22, 28, 29 to 58 (inclusive), 68, 69, Regulation 70(2) except in so far as Regulation 70(2) relates to form O or P, and Regulation 74 and so much of the Schedules as relates to those provisions, shall come into operation on 16th February 1970 :

Provided that Regulations 29 to 58 (inclusive), 68, 69, 70(2) and 74 shall not have effect in relation to an election notice of which has been published before 16th February 1970.

(2) Except as otherwise provided by paragraph (1) of this Regulation, these Regulations shall come into operation fourteen days after they have been approved by both Houses of Parliament.

Revocation and savings

3.—(1) The following provisions of the Representation of the People Regulations 1950(**b**), as amended (**c**), namely, Regulations 18, 19, 25 to 52 (inclusive), 64, 65(2) except so far as Regulation 65(2) relates to form O or P, Regulations 65(3) and 69, and so much of the Schedules to those Regulations and of the Greater London (Elections) Order 1964(**d**) as relates to those provisions, shall be revoked as from 16th February 1970 :

Provided that Regulations 25 to 52 (inclusive), 64, 65(2), 65(3) and 69, and so much of the Schedules to the Regulations of 1950 as relates to the said Regulations, shall continue to have effect in relation to an election notice of which has been published before 16th February 1970.

(2) Except as otherwise provided by paragraph (1) of this Regulation, the Representation of the People Regulations 1950, the Representation of the People Regulations 1953(**e**), the Representation of the People Regulations 1954(**f**) and so much of the Greater London (Elections) Order 1964 as relates to those Regulations are hereby revoked.

(**a**) 1949 c.68. (**b**) S.I. 1950/1254 (Rev. XX, p.7: 1950 II, p. 513).
(**c**) The amending instruments are S.I. 1953/1107, 1954/498, 1964/346 (1953 II, p.1757; 1954 II, p.1921; 1964 I, p.540).
(**d**) S.I. 1964/346 (1964 I, p.540). (**e**) S.I. 1953/1107 (1953 II, p.1757).
(**f**) S.I. 1954/498 (1954 II, p.1921).

(3) Section 38 of the Interpretation Act 1889(**a**) shall apply as if these Regulations were an Act of Parliament and as if any Regulations revoked by these Regulations were Acts of Parliament repealed by an Act of Parliament.

(4) Without prejudice to the said section 38 any register, list or record prepared, any application, appointment or declaration made, any proceedings initiated or other thing done under any Regulations revoked by these Regulations shall not be invalidated by the revocation effected by paragraph (1) or (2) of this Regulation and shall, in so far as it could have been prepared, made, initiated or done under any provision of these Regulations, have effect as if it had been prepared, made, initiated or done under that provision.

(5) Any reference in any statutory instrument to a Regulation revoked by these Regulations shall be taken as a reference to the corresponding Regulation contained in these Regulations.

Interpretation

4.—(1) For the purpose of these Regulations, unless the context otherwise requires—

the expression "the Act of 1949" means the Representation of the People Act 1949 ;

the expression "the Act of 1969" means the Representation of the People Act 1969(**b**) ;

the expression "postal proxy" means a person entitled to vote by post as proxy at an election ;

the expression "registration officer" means an electoral registration officer.

(2) Any act or thing which is required by these Regulations to be done by, to or before the mayor of a borough may, in any case in which the office of mayor is vacant or the mayor is for any reason unable to act, be done by, to or before the deputy mayor of the borough or, if there is no deputy mayor, or the deputy mayor is for any reason unable to act, by, to or before such alderman of the borough as the council of the borough may choose for that purpose.

(3) A claim or objection includes a claim or objection that a letter or date should or should not be placed against a person's name in the electors lists and the register in accordance with Regulation 8 or Regulation 9(*a*) or (*b*).

(4) A reference in these Regulations to any enactment or statutory instrument shall be construed as including a reference to that enactment or statutory instrument as amended or replaced by any other enactment or statutory instrument.

(5) A reference in these Regulations to a Regulation shall be construed as a reference to a Regulation contained in these Regulations.

(6) A reference in these Regulations to a form identified by means of a letter shall be construed as a reference to the form so identified in Schedule 1 to these Regulations.

(7) A reference in these Regulations to the record and list of absent voters, proxies or postal proxies shall be taken as referring to the records and lists prepared for parliamentary and local government elections.

(8) The Interpretation Act 1889 shall apply to the interpretation of these Regulations as it applies to the interpretation of an Act of Parliament.

(**a**) 1889 c.63.   (**b**) 1969 c. 15.

PART II

REGISTRATION

The Register

Separate part of register for each registration unit

5.—(1) The register shall be framed in separate parts for each registration unit in the constituency.

(2) The registration unit shall be each parliamentary polling district if wholly contained in an electoral area or, where a parliamentary polling district is contained in more than one electoral area, each part of the polling district contained in a separate electoral area.

Separate letter for each parliamentary polling district

6. There shall be a separate letter or letters in the register for each parliamentary polling district and such letter or letters shall be deemed to form part of an elector's number in the register.

Order of names

7.—(1) Subject to paragraph (2) of this Regulation, the names in each registration unit shall be arranged in street order unless the local authority whose clerk is registration officer determine for any unit that street order is not reasonably practicable in which case the names shall be arranged in alphabetical order or partly in street order and partly in alphabetical order, as the local authority may determine.

(2) The names of every service voter in any registration unit who in his service declaration has given an address at which the declarant has resided in the United Kingdom, not being an address at which he would have been residing but for the circumstances entitling him to make the declaration, shall be grouped in alphabetical order at the end of the registration unit beneath a heading indicating that the service voters have so declared.

(3) The names in the register shall be numbered so far as is reasonably practicable consecutively ; and there shall be a separate series of numbers (beginning with the number one) for each parliamentary polling district.

Marking of names to indicate at which elections person entitled to vote

8.—(1) To indicate that an elector is not entitled to vote at a parliamentary election the letter "L" shall be placed against his name in the electors lists and the register.

(2) If an elector will attain voting age before the end of the twelve months following the day by which a register is required to be published but will not be of voting age on the first day of those twelve months, the date on which he will attain that age shall be placed against his name in the electors lists as well as in the register.

Marking of names to indicate manner of voting

9. To indicate the manner in which an elector is entitled to vote at an election there shall be placed—

(*a*) in the electors lists and the register against the name of any elector who is a service voter the letter "S" ;

(*b*) in the electors lists and the register against the name of any elector who is a merchant seaman the letter "M" ;

(*c*) in any copy of the register or part thereof provided for a polling station—

(i) against the name of any elector who is, or whose proxy is, entitled to vote by post the letter "A",

(ii) against the name of any elector on behalf of whom a proxy is entitled to vote the letter "P".

The Electors Lists

Form of electors lists

10.—(1) The electors lists shall be framed in separate parts for each registration unit in the constituency.

(2) The electors lists for a registration unit shall consist of—

List A—a copy of the register in force for the unit,

List B—a list of newly qualified electors, that is to say, persons who are qualified for registration as parliamentary or as local government electors in respect of qualifying addresses for which they are not registered in the register in force or who, since the qualifying date of the register in force, have become entitled to be registered as residents instead of as service voters, or vice versa, in respect of those addresses, and

List C—a list of persons who have ceased to be qualified as electors or whose qualification has been altered, that is to say, persons who, being registered in respect of qualifying addresses in the register in force, have ceased to be qualified for registration as parliamentary or as local government electors in respect of those addresses or who, since the qualifying date for the register in force, have become entitled to be registered as residents instead of as service voters, or vice versa, in respect of those addresses :

Provided that where the area of a registration unit differs from the area of that unit as constituted for the purposes of the register in force, the registration unit may be treated as having the same area as it had for the purposes of the register in force.

(3) The names in List B need not be numbered.

(4) The names in List C shall have opposite them their numbers in the register in force.

(5) Notwithstanding the provisions of paragraphs (2), (3) and (4) of this Regulation, the electors lists for a registration unit may, with the consent of the Secretary of State, be prepared as a draft register so as to show only the persons appearing to the registration officer to be entitled to be registered, together with their qualifying addresses, and to comply with the provisions of the preceding Regulations :

Provided that the names in the draft register need not be numbered.

Publication of the electors lists

11.—(1) The registration officer shall publish the electors lists by—

(*a*) making a copy thereof available for inspection at his office ;

(*b*) as soon as practicable making copies of the part of the electors lists relating to each electoral area available for inspection at a specified place in or near that electoral area to which the public have access ;

(*c*) publishing a notice (to be combined with the notice of claims and objections referred to in Regulation 12) specifying the said place.

(2) The electors lists shall be published on or before the twenty-eighth day of November and shall be kept published till the publication of the register prepared from those lists.

Claims and Objections

Notice of claims and objections

12.—(1) The registration officer shall at the time of publishing the electors lists publish a notice in Form C or, in the case of electors lists to which Regulation 10(5) applies, in Form B specifying the manner in which and the time within which claims and objections in respect of the electors lists may be made.

(2) The said notice shall be published in the way the registration officer thinks best calculated to bring the said notice to the attention of the electors.

Time for making claims and objections

13.—(1) A claim or objection in respect of the electors lists which is delivered to the registration officer after the sixteenth day of December shall be disregarded :

Provided that an objection to a claim shall not be disregarded if it is delivered to the registration officer within three days after the claim has been entered in the list of claims.

(2) A service declaration made with reference to a qualifying date and made during the twelve months ending with that date, but received too late for inclusion of the declarant's name in the electors lists, shall, if it is received by the registration officer—

(*a*) not later than the last day for making claims, be treated as a claim,

(*b*) after the said last day, be disregarded.

Form of claims and objections

14.—(1) A claim shall be in Form O and may be made by a person either on his own behalf or on behalf of another person.

(2) An objection shall be in Form P.

(3) Claims and objections shall be made available for inspection in the registration officer's office till completion of the hearing of claims and objections.

Entry and preliminary disposal of claims and objections

15.—(1) The registration officer shall keep separate lists of claims and objections and shall, on receipt of a claim or objection, forthwith enter in the appropriate list the name and qualifying address of the claimant or the person in respect of whom the objection is made.

(2) If the registration officer is of opinion—

(a) that the particulars given in a claim or objection are insufficient, he may ask for further information and take no further action until such information is supplied ;

(b) that a claim may be allowed without a hearing, he may allow the claim, provided that no objection is made thereto, and shall so inform the person making the claim ;

(c) that the objector is not entitled to object, he may disallow the objection and shall so inform the objector ;

(d) that a claim or objection cannot be allowed because—

(i) the matter has been concluded by the decision of a court, or

(ii) the particulars given in a claim or objection do not entitle the claimant or objector to succeed,

he may send to the person making the claim or objection a notice stating his opinion and the grounds thereof and that he intends to disallow the claim or objection unless that person gives the registration officer notice within three days from the date of the first mentioned notice that he requires the claim or objection to be heard, and, if he receives no such notice within the said time, he may disallow the claim or objection.

(3) The registration officer shall, unless he allows or disallows the claim or objection under paragraph (2) of this Regulation, send a notice, in the case of a claim, to the person making the claim and, in the case of an objection, to the objector and the person objected to, stating the time and place at which he proposes to hear the claim or objection ; and the notice sent to a person objected to shall also state the name and address of the objector and the grounds of the objection.

(4) The time fixed for the hearing of a claim or objection shall not be earlier than the third day after the date of the notice referred to in paragraph (3) of this Regulation.

(5) The registration officer shall make available for inspection at his office till completion of the hearing of claims and objections the lists of claims and objections together with the time and place at which he proposes to hear any claim or objection.

Hearing of claims and objections

16.—(1) On the hearing of a claim, the person making the claim and any person who has duly made an objection and, on the hearing of an objection, the objector and the person objected to and, on the hearing of either, any other person who appears to the registration officer to be interested shall be entitled to appear and be heard.

(2) The right to appear and be heard includes the right to make written representations.

(3) Any person entitled to appear and be heard may do so either in person or by any other person on his behalf.

(4) The registration officer may, at the request of any person entitled to appear and be heard or, if he thinks fit, without such a request, require that the evidence tendered by any person shall be given on oath and may administer an oath for the purpose.

Corrections to the electors lists

17. Any alteration to the electors lists which is required—

(*a*) to carry out the registration officer's decision with respect to any claim or objection,

(*b*) to correct any clerical error,

(*c*) to correct any misnomer or inaccurate description,

(*d*) to delete the name of any person who the registration officer is satisfied is dead,

shall be made by the registration officer.

Other corrections to the electors lists

18.—(1) Where it appears to the registration officer that it is necessary to make any alteration (other than an alteration under Regulation 17) to the electors lists in order to ensure that no person shall be incorrectly registered, or registered when not entitled, he shall send to the person affected by the alteration a notice stating the proposed alteration and shall give him an opportunity within five days from the date of such notice of objecting to the alteration and, if necessary, of appearing and being heard in accordance with the provisions of Regulation 16.

(2) After the said five days the registration officer shall make such alteration (if any) as seems to him to be necessary.

Publication and Sale of the Register

Publication of register

19.—(1) The registration officer shall publish the register by making a copy available for inspection at his office and by making copies of the part of the register relating to each electoral area available for inspection as soon as practicable at the place at which copies of the part of the electors lists relating to that electoral area have been made available for inspection.

(2) The register shall be kept published until the coming into force of the next register.

Registration officer to furnish copies of register

20.—(1) A copy of the register shall, on publication, be furnished by the registration officer to the Secretary of State and the British Museum.

(2) An abstract of the contents of the register shall be furnished by the registration officer to the Secretary of State at such times and in such form and giving such particulars as the Secretary of State may require.

Free copies of register

21. The registration officer shall on request supply without fee—

(*a*) four copies of the register for the constituency (which may be printed on one side only) and four copies of Lists B and C of the electors lists therefor, or, in the case of electors lists to which Regulation 10(5) applies, of the draft register therefor, so long as the lists are kept published, to any person who satisfies the registration officer that he requires them for use in connection with his own or some other person's prospective candidature at a parliamentary election for that constituency:

Provided that not more than one person in respect of the same candidature shall be so supplied;

(b) two copies of the register for the constituency to each candidate at a parliamentary election for that constituency or his election agent;

(c) one copy of the register for any electoral area to each candidate at a local government election for that area or his election agent.

Sale of register

22. The registration officer shall supply to any person copies of any part or parts of the register in force or of any electors lists therefor so long as there are sufficient copies available after allowing for the number which may be required for the purposes of any election (including the purposes of Regulation 21) on payment—

(a) in the case of a person who has been supplied in pursuance of Regulation 21 with a copy of the register or the electors lists or who is a returning officer or a local authority, of a fee at the rate of one shilling for each one thousand (or part of one thousand) names in such copy;

(b) in the case of any other person, of a fee at the rate of five shillings for each one thousand (or part of one thousand) names in such copy.

Supplementary

Declaration as to age and nationality

23.—(1) The registration officer before registering any person (other than a service voter) may, if he thinks it necessary—

(a) require that person either to produce a birth certificate or to make a statutory declaration as to the date of his birth,

(b) require that person either to produce a certificate of naturalisation or a document showing that he has become a British subject by virtue of registration, or to make a statutory declaration that he was a British subject or citizen of the Republic of Ireland on the qualifying date.

(2) Where a declaration is so made, any fee payable in connection therewith shall be paid by the registration officer as part of his registration expenses.

(3) Any such declaration shall be made available for inspection in the registration officer's office till completion of the hearing of claims and objections.

Power of registration officer to delegate his duties

24. The registration officer may require the clerk of the authority of any county borough, London borough or county district wholly or partly within the area for which he acts (or an officer designated for the purpose by the council of any such borough or district) to perform on his behalf all or any of his registration duties so far as they relate to the preparation and publication of the electors lists for any registration unit within the area of that borough or district, including the duty of carrying out a house to house or other sufficient inquiry as to the persons entitled to be registered (excluding persons entitled to be registered in pursuance of a service declaration), and to give information required for the purposes of his registration duties.

Information from householders

25. The registration officer may require any householder or person owning or occupying any premises within the area for which he acts or the agent or factor of any such person to give information required for the purposes of his registration duties.

Adaptation of electors lists and register in consequence of altered polling districts

26.—(1) Where the Secretary of State directs a local authority to make or himself makes any alteration of parliamentary polling districts, he may also direct that—

(*a*) the register in force be adapted to the alteration ;

(*b*) if the alteration takes place between the publication of any electors lists and the coming into force of the register prepared from those lists, the form of that register be framed in accordance with the alterations.

(2) Where any alteration of parliamentary polling districts is made otherwise than by virtue of section 11(4) of the Act of 1949 (which relates to powers exercisable by the Secretary of State), the local authority whose clerk is registration officer may direct the registration officer to make the adaptations set out in paragraph (1) of this Regulation.

(3) Except as otherwise provided by this Regulation an alteration of parliamentary polling districts shall not be effective until the coming into force of the first register prepared from the electors lists published after the alteration is made.

Corrupt and Illegal Practices List

Corrupt and illegal practices list

27.—(1) The registration officer shall, at the same time as he publishes the electors lists, prepare and publish the corrupt and illegal practices list (if any) required by section 40(1) of the Act of 1949 by making a copy thereof available for inspection at the same places as he makes available copies of the electors lists or any part thereof.

(2) A person named in the corrupt and illegal practices list may claim to be omitted therefrom and any person may object to the omission of any person from such list, and paragraph (1) of Regulation 13, paragraph (3) of Regulation 14 and Regulations 15 and 16 shall apply to any such claim and objection as they apply to a claim or objection in respect of the electors lists.

(3) A claim may be made by a person either on his own behalf or on behalf of another person and shall give particulars of the grounds on which the person concerned should be omitted, and an objection to the omission of any person shall give the name and address of the objector and the person in respect of whom the objection is made and the grounds on which such person should be entered in the corrupt and illegal practices list including particulars of the alleged conviction by a court or of the alleged report of any election court.

(4) The registration officer shall make such alterations to the corrupt and illegal practices list as are required to carry out his decisions on any claims or objections or to correct any clerical error, misnomer or inaccurate description.

(5) Where it appears to the registration officer that a person not named in the corrupt and illegal practices list should be entered therein, he shall send to that person a notice that he intends to enter him therein and shall give him an opportunity within five days from the date of such notice of objecting and being heard in accordance with the provisions of Regulation 16, and after the said five days he shall make such alteration as seems to him to be necessary.

(6) The registration officer shall publish the corrected corrupt and illegal practices list (if any) at the same time as he publishes the register and in the same manner as he publishes each part of the register.

(7) A copy of the corrected corrupt and illegal practices list shall, on publication, be furnished by the registration officer to the Secretary of State and the British Museum.

(8) The clerk of the authority of each local government area who is required under section 40(2) of the Act of 1949 to make out a corrupt and illegal practices list shall, not later than fourteen days before the date for the publication of the electors lists, send to the registration officer of each constituency wholly or partly within that local government area a copy of such list (if any).

(9) From the corrected list or lists, as the case may be, described in paragraph (6) of this Regulation the said clerk shall make out a revised corrupt and illegal practices list and shall publish it by making a copy thereof available for inspection at his office.

(10) The corrupt and illegal practices list as first published and as corrected or revised shall be kept published for the same length of time as the electors lists and the register.

Correction of Register

Correction of register

28.—(1) When a registration officer makes an alteration in a register pursuant to section 7(2) of the Act of 1969, he shall—

(a) send to the person affected by the alteration and, if he gives effect to a decision on an objection made with respect to the electors lists, to the objector a notice stating the alteration;

(b) make a copy of the alteration available for inspection at his office;

(c) make copies of the alteration available for inspection at the place at which copies of the part of the register to which the alteration relates have been made available for inspection;

(d) furnish a copy of the alteration to the Secretary of State and the British Museum;

(e) supply without a fee a copy of the alteration to each person to whom he has supplied copies of the register or part thereof to which the alteration relates in pursuance of Regulation 21 or 22(a).

(2) Copies of alterations made available for inspection under this Regulation shall be kept available for the same length of time as the register is kept published.

Part III

Absent Voters, Proxies and Postal Proxies

Application to be treated as an absent voter

29.—(1) An application to be treated as an absent voter shall be made in respect of each qualifying address and shall—

(*a*) be in Form S in any case where the application is made for a particular election only,

(*b*) be in Form R in any case where the application is based on the ground that the applicant no longer resides at his qualifying address,

(*c*) be in Form N in any case where the applicant is a service voter,

(*d*) be in Form W in any case where the applicant is the spouse of a service voter, has made a service declaration, but has not yet been registered as a service voter in pursuance of that declaration,

(*e*) be in Form T in any case where the application is based on the ground that the applicant is unable or likely to be unable to go in person from his qualifying address to the polling station without making a journey by air or sea,

(*f*) be in Form Q in any other case.

(2) (*a*) An application to be treated as an absent voter based on the ground of religious observance shall not be allowed by the registration officer unless it is accompanied by a certificate signed by a minister of the applicant's religious denomination certifying the nature and times of the religious observances and that the applicant is bound to observe them.

(*b*) An application to be treated as an absent voter based on the ground of physical incapacity shall be allowed by the registration officer if—

(i) the applicant has been registered as a blind person by a local authority under section 29(4)(*g*) of the National Assistance Act 1948(**a**) ; or

(ii) the application is accompanied by a certificate signed by a registered medical practitioner or a Christian Science practitioner certifying that the applicant is unable, or likely to be unable, by reason either of blindness or any other physical incapacity to go in person to the polling station or, if able to go, to vote unaided and estimating the probable duration of the period during which the applicant is likely to be so unable.

(3) An application to be treated as an absent voter shall be disregarded—

(*a*) for the purposes of a parliamentary election if it is received by the registration officer after the twelfth day before the day of the poll at that election ;

(*b*) for the purposes of a local government election if it is received by the registration officer after the fourteenth day before the day of the poll at that election:

Provided that an application on the grounds of the applicant's employment on the day of the poll by a returning officer or mayor or as a constable may be allowed after the said twelfth or fourteenth day as the case may be.

(a) 1948 c. 29.

(4) An application to be no longer treated as an absent voter may be disregarded—

(*a*) for the purposes of a parliamentary election if it is received by the registration officer after the twelfth day before the day of the poll at that election ;

(*b*) for the purposes of a local government election if it is received by the registration officer after the fourteenth day before the day of the poll at that election.

(5) The registration officer on disallowing a person's application to be treated as an absent voter shall notify the applicant of the fact.

(6) Where under section 13(3)(*c*) or 24(3)(*c*) of the Act of 1949 the registration officer gives notice to an absent voter that he has reason to believe there has been a material change of circumstances, that person shall cease to be treated as an absent voter seven days after the date on which the registration officer sends such notice.

Record and list of absent voters

30.—(1) Subject to the provisions of this Regulation, the record and list of absent voters shall be in such a form as appears to the registration officer to be convenient.

(2) The address to which a ballot paper is to be sent shall be placed opposite the name and number in the register of each absent voter in the absent voters list unless a proxy (other than a service voter's proxy) has been appointed to vote on his behalf, in which case the letter "P" shall be placed opposite his name.

(3) As soon as the absent voters list has been prepared, the registration officer shall publish it by making a copy thereof available for inspection at his office.

(4) The registration officer shall make a copy of the record of absent voters available for inspection at his office.

(5) As soon as practicable after the preparation of the absent voters list, the registration officer shall, on request and without fee, supply to each candidate or his election agent a copy of the absent voters list :

Provided that if such a request is made before any issue of ballot papers to those entitled to vote by post, the registration officer shall supply a copy of the said list, or a copy of so much of the said list as relates to that issue, before that issue.

Application to vote by proxy

31.—(1) An application by a service voter for the appointment of a proxy to vote on his behalf shall be in the form of Part 2 of Form J, K, L or M, as the case may be.

(2) An application by an absent voter who is not a service voter for the appointment of a proxy to vote on his behalf shall be in Form U or W, as the case may be.

Appointment of proxy

32.—(1) For the purpose of ascertaining in pursuance of section 14(4) of the Act of 1949 and of that subsection as applied by section 25(6) of that Act that a proxy is capable of being and willing to be appointed, the registration officer shall, unless he is satisfied that the person nominated in the application as first choice is not capable of being and willing to be appointed, notify him that a proxy paper will be issued to him unless within five days from the date of such notice the registration officer receives notice from him that he is not capable of being and willing to be appointed.

(2) If the person nominated as first choice is not capable of being and willing to be appointed, the registration officer shall, if another person is nominated as second choice, deal in like manner with such person:

Provided that if the application is received by the registration officer after publication of notice of an election, the registration officer need not do so until after the day of the poll for that election.

(3) If for any reason the registration officer does not issue a proxy paper in pursuance of an application made to him, he shall notify the person making the application why he has not done so.

Proxy paper

33.—(1) The proxy paper to be issued by the registration officer shall be in Form D.

(2) As soon as may be after issue of the proxy paper the registration officer shall send a notice of the fact to the elector stating the name of the person to whom the paper has been issued.

Cancellation and disregard of proxy appointment

34.—(1) Where the appointment of a proxy is cancelled by notice given to the registration officer or ceases to be or no longer remains in force under section 14(5) of the Act of 1949 or that subsection as applied by section 25(6) of that Act, the registration officer shall forthwith notify the person whose appointment as proxy has been cancelled or is no longer in force of the fact and remove his name from the record of proxies.

(2) Where a service voter is entitled to vote by post at an election, the registration officer shall forthwith notify his proxy (if any) of the fact and that his appointment will not have effect for that election.

(3) An application for the issue of a proxy paper shall be disregarded—

   (*a*) for the purposes of a parliamentary election if it is received by the registration officer after the twelfth day before the day of the poll at that election;

   (*b*) for the purposes of a local government election if it is received by the registration officer after the fourteenth day before the day of the poll at that election.

(4) A notice cancelling the appointment of a proxy may be disregarded—

   (*a*) for the purposes of a parliamentary election if it is received by the registration officer after the twelfth day before the day of the poll at that election;

   (*b*) for the purposes of a local government election if it is received by the registration officer after the fourteenth day before the day of the poll at that election.

Record and list of proxies.

35.—(1) The record and list of proxies shall be in such a form as appears to the registration officer to be convenient.

(2) As soon as the list of proxies has been prepared, the registration officer shall publish it by making a copy thereof available for inspection at his office.

(3) The registration officer shall make a copy of the record of proxies available for inspection at his office.

(4) As soon as practicable after the preparation of the list of proxies, the registration officer shall, on request and without fee, supply to each candidate or his election agent a copy of the list of proxies.

Application by proxy to vote by post

36.—(1) An application by a proxy to vote by post shall be in Form V.

(2) Such an application shall be disregarded—

(a) for the purposes of a parliamentary election if it is received by the registration officer after the twelfth day before the day of the poll at that election ;

(b) for the purposes of a local government election if it is received by the registration officer after the fourteenth day before the day of the poll at that election :

Provided that if under the proviso to Regulation 29(3) the applicant becomes entitled to vote by post as an absent voter at a parliamentary or local government election after the said twelfth or fourteenth day as the case may be, such an application may be allowed after the said twelfth or fourteenth day as the case may be.

(3) The registration officer on disallowing such an application shall notify the applicant of the fact.

(4) An application under section 15(7)(a) of the Act of 1949 whereby a proxy ceases to be entitled to vote by post may be disregarded for the purposes of a parliamentary election if it is received by the registration officer after the twelfth day before the day of the poll at that election.

Record and list of postal proxies

37.—(1) Subject to the provisions of this Regulation, the record and list of postal proxies shall be in such a form as appears to the registration officer to be convenient.

(2) The list of postal proxies shall give the name and number in the register of the elector and opposite them the name of the proxy and the address to which the ballot paper is to be sent.

(3) As soon as the postal proxies list has been prepared, the registration officer shall publish it by making a copy thereof available for inspection at his office.

(4) The registration officer shall make a copy of the record of postal proxies available for inspection at his office.

(5) As soon as practicable after the preparation of the postal proxies list, the registration officer shall, on request and without fee, supply to each candidate or his election agent a copy of the postal proxies list:

Provided that if such a request is made before any issue of ballot papers to those entitled to vote by post, the registration officer shall supply a copy of the said list or a copy of so much of the said list as relates to that issue, before that issue.

Certificate of employment

38. The certificate as to the employment of constables and persons employed by the returning officer or mayor on the day of the poll (to enable such a constable or person to vote elsewhere than at his own polling station) shall be in Form G and signed, in the case of a constable, by a member of a police force of or above the rank of inspector.

PART IV

ISSUE AND RECEIPT OF POSTAL BALLOT PAPERS

Interpretation

Interpretation of Part IV

39.—(1) For the purpose of this Part of these Regulations, unless the context otherwise requires—

the expression "agent" includes the election agent and a person appointed to attend in the election agent's place;

the expression "issue" includes the original and any subsequent issue;

the expression "postal ballot paper" means a ballot paper issued to a postal voter;

the expression "postal voter" means a person entitled to vote by post at an election as an absent voter or as a proxy.

(2) For the purpose of this Part of these Regulations, so far as it relates to the issue of postal ballot papers in an election of a borough councillor for a borough which is not a London borough, references to the returning officer shall be taken as references to the mayor.

(3)(*a*) For the purpose of this Part of these Regulations, unless the context otherwise requires, the expression "election rules" means the local elections rules in Schedule 2 to the Act of 1949, the rules in Schedule 1 to the Urban District Council Election Rules 1969(**a**), the rules in Schedule 1 to the Rural District Council Election Rules 1969(**b**) and the parliamentary elections rules in Schedule 2 to the Act of 1949.

(*b*) The table of comparison set out in Schedule 2 to these Regulations shows (so far as is necessary for the construction of these Regulations) the provisions of the rules there mentioned which correspond to one another and, except in so far as the context otherwise requires, any reference in these Regulations to a specified provision of the election rules shall be taken as a reference both to—

    (i) the provision specified in the first column of that Schedule, and

    (ii) the corresponding provisions in the second, third and fourth columns thereof.

Issue of Postal Ballot Papers

Form of postal ballot paper

40. The ballot papers to be sent to postal voters shall be in the same form as, and indistinguishable from, the ballot papers delivered to other voters.

(**a**) S.I. 1969/756 (1969 II, p. 2080).   (**b**) S.I. 1969/757 (1969 II, p. 2107).

Form of declaration of identity

41. The declaration of identity sent with the ballot paper to a postal voter shall be in Form H.

Persons entitled to be present at issue and receipt of postal ballot papers

42.—(1) No person other than—

(*a*) the returning officer and his clerks,

(*b*) a candidate,

(*c*) an election agent or any person appointed by a candidate to attend in his election agent's place,

(*d*) any agents appointed under paragraph (2) of this Regulation,

may be present at the proceedings on the issue or receipt of postal ballot papers.

(2) Where postal ballot papers are to be issued, or the envelopes contained in the postal voters' ballot boxes are to be opened, simultaneously in two or more batches, each candidate may appoint one or more agents up to the number he may be authorised by the returning officer to appoint not exceeding the number of such batches so, however, that the number authorised shall be the same in the case of each candidate.

(3) Notice of the appointment stating the names and addresses of the persons appointed shall be given by the candidate to the returning officer before the time fixed for the issue of the postal ballot papers or the opening of the said postal voters' ballot boxes, as the case may be.

(4) If an agent dies or becomes incapable of acting, the candidate may appoint another agent in his place and shall forthwith give to the returning officer notice in writing of the name and address of the agent appointed.

(5) Agents may be appointed and notice of appointment given to the returning officer by the candidate's election agent instead of by the candidate.

(6) In this Part of these Regulations references to agents shall be taken as references to agents whose appointments have been duly made and notified and, in the case of agents appointed under paragraph (2) of this Regulation, who are within the number authorised by the returning officer.

(7) A candidate may himself do any act or thing which any agent of his, if appointed, would have been authorised to do, or may assist his agent in doing any such act or thing.

(8) Where in this Part of these Regulations any act or thing is required or authorised to be done in the presence of the candidates or their agents, the non-attendance of any such persons or person at the time and place appointed for the purpose shall not, if the act or thing is otherwise duly done, invalidate the act or thing done.

Declaration of secrecy

43.—(1) Every person attending the proceedings on the issue or receipt of postal ballot papers shall make a declaration of secrecy in the form in paragraph (3) of this Regulation, or in a form as near thereto as circumstances admit, before the issue of postal ballot papers:

Provided that if any person attends only the proceedings on the receipt of postal ballot papers, he need not make the declaration before the issue but shall make it before he is permitted to attend the proceedings on the receipt of postal ballot papers.

(2) The returning officer shall make the declaration in the presence of a justice of the peace or a person who is chairman of the Greater London Council, a county council or a district council or mayor of a borough or rural borough and any other person shall make the declaration in the presence either of a justice of the peace or of the returning officer or of a person who is chairman or clerk of the Greater London Council, a county council or a district council or mayor or town clerk of a borough or rural borough and subsections (4) and (6) of section 53 of the Act of 1949 shall be read to the declarant by the person taking the declaration or shall be read by the declarant in the presence of that person.

(3) The declaration shall be as follows:—

"I solemnly promise and declare that I will not do anything forbidden by subsections (4) and (6) of section 53 of the Representation of the People Act 1949, which have been read to [by] me."

(4) Any person before whom a declaration is authorised to be made under this Regulation may take the declaration.

Notice of issue of postal ballot papers

44.—(1) The returning officer shall give each candidate not less than two days' notice in writing of the time and place at which he will issue postal ballot papers and of the number of agents he may appoint under Regulation 42(2) to attend the said issue.

(2) Where any subsequent issue of postal ballot papers is made, the returning officer shall notify each candidate as soon as practicable of the time and place at which he will make such subsequent issue and of the number of agents he may appoint under Regulation 42(2) to attend such issue.

Marking of postal ballot paper

45.—(1) Each postal ballot paper issued shall be stamped with the official mark either embossed or perforated, and the name and number in the register of the elector shall be called out, and such number shall be marked on the counterfoil, and a mark shall be placed in the absent voters list or the list of postal proxies against the number of the elector to denote that a ballot paper has been issued to the elector or his proxy but without showing the particular ballot paper issued.

(2) The number of a postal ballot paper shall be marked on the declaration of identity sent with that paper.

Refusal to issue postal ballot paper

46. Where a returning officer is satisfied that two or more entries in either the absent voters list or the list of postal proxies relate to the same elector or that a postal proxy has been appointed for a person entered in the absent voters list, he shall not issue more than one ballot paper in respect of the same elector.

Ballot paper envelope

47. The returning officer shall, in addition to the ballot paper, declaration of identity and envelope for their return (hereinafter referred to as a "covering envelope") which he is required by rule 21 of the election rules to send to a postal voter, send a smaller envelope marked "ballot paper envelope" bearing the number of the ballot paper.

Delivery of postal ballot papers to post office

48.—(1) Envelopes addressed to postal voters shall be counted and forthwith delivered by the returning officer to the nearest head post office, or such other office as may be arranged with the head postmaster, and the postmaster shall stamp with the post office date stamp a form of receipt to be presented by the returning officer stating the number of envelopes so delivered, and shall immediately forward such envelopes for delivery to the persons to whom they are addressed.

(2) At local government elections first-class postage of all such envelopes and all covering envelopes shall be prepaid by the returning officer.

Provision of postal voters' ballot box

49.—(1) The returning officer shall, at the proceedings on the original issue of postal ballot papers, provide a ballot box or ballot boxes for the reception of the covering envelopes when returned by the postal voters.

(2) Every such ballot box shall be shown open and empty to the agents present and shall then be locked by the returning officer and sealed with the seal of the returning officer and the seals of such of the agents as desire to affix their seals in such manner as to prevent its being opened without breaking the seal.

(3) Every such ballot box shall be marked "postal voters' ballot box" and with the name of the constituency or the electoral area for which the election is held.

(4) The returning officer shall make provision for the safe custody of every such ballot box.

Sealing up of special lists and counterfoils

50.—(1) The returning officer, as soon as practicable after the completion of the issue of the postal ballot papers, and in the presence of the agents, shall make up in separate packets—

(*a*) the marked copies of the absent voters list and of the list of postal proxies, and

(*b*) the counterfoils of those ballot papers which were issued,

and shall seal such packets.

(2) The sealed packet containing the marked copies of the absent voters list and of the list of postal proxies may be opened by the returning officer for the purposes of a subsequent issue, and on completion of that issue the copies shall be again made up and sealed in accordance with the last foregoing paragraph.

Spoilt postal ballot paper

51.—(1) If a postal voter has inadvertently dealt with his postal ballot paper in such manner that it cannot be conveniently used as a ballot paper (in these Regulations referred to as "a spoilt postal ballot paper") he may return (either by hand or by post) to the returning officer the spoilt postal ballot paper, the declaration of identity, the ballot paper envelope and the covering envelope.

(2) The returning officer, on receipt of the said documents, shall, unless the documents are received too late for another postal ballot paper to be returned

before the close of the poll, issue another postal ballot paper and the fore-going provisions of this Part of these Regulations, but not sub-paragraph (*b*), (*c*) or (*d*) of paragraph (1) or paragraphs (2) to (8) of Regulation 42 or Regulation 44, shall apply accordingly.

(3) The spoilt postal ballot paper, the declaration of identity and the ballot paper envelope shall be immediately cancelled.

(4) The returning officer, as soon as practicable after cancelling the said documents, shall make up the said documents in a separate packet and shall seal the packet ; and if on any subsequent occasion documents are cancelled as aforesaid, the sealed packet shall be opened and the additional cancelled documents included therein and the packet shall thereupon be again made up and sealed.

Receipt of Postal Ballot Papers

Receipt of covering envelope

52. The returning officer shall, immediately on receipt (whether by hand or by post) of a covering envelope before the close of the poll, place it unopened in a postal voters' ballot box locked and sealed in accordance with Regulation 49.

Opening of postal voters' ballot box

53.—(1) Each postal voters' ballot box shall be opened by the returning officer in the presence of the agents.

(2) So long as the returning officer secures that there is at least one postal voters' ballot box for the reception of covering envelopes up to the time of the close of the poll the other postal voters' ballot boxes may previously be opened by him.

(3) The returning officer shall give each candidate at least forty-eight hours' notice in writing of the time and place of his opening of each postal voters' ballot box and the envelopes contained therein and of the number of agents the candidate may appoint under Regulation 42(2) to be present at each opening.

Opening of covering envelopes

54.—(1) When a postal voters' ballot box has been opened, the returning officer shall count and note the number of covering envelopes, and shall then open each covering envelope separately.

(2) Where a covering envelope does not contain both a declaration of identity and a ballot paper envelope or, there being no ballot paper envelope, a ballot paper, he shall mark the covering envelope "rejected", attach thereto the contents (if any) of the covering envelope and place it in a separate receptacle (hereinafter referred to as "the receptacle for votes rejected") ; and if the covering envelope does not contain the declaration separately, the returning officer shall open the ballot paper envelope to ascertain if the declaration is inside that envelope.

(3) On opening a covering envelope, other than one to which paragraph (2) of this Regulation applies, he shall first satisfy himself that the declaration of identity has been duly signed and authenticated and, if he is not so satisfied, he

shall mark the declaration "rejected", attach thereto the ballot paper envelope or, if there is no such envelope, the ballot paper, and place it in the receptacle for votes rejected :

Provided that before so doing he shall show the declaration to the agents and, if any objection is made by any agent to his decision, he shall add the words "rejection objected to".

(4) Where the number on the declaration of identity duly signed and authenticated agrees with the number on the ballot paper envelope, he shall place the declaration in a separate receptacle (hereinafter referred to as "the receptacle for declarations of identity") and the ballot paper envelope in another separate receptacle (hereinafter referred to as "the receptacle for ballot paper envelopes").

(5) Where there is no ballot paper envelope or the ballot paper envelope has been opened under paragraph (2) of this Regulation, he shall—

(a) where the number on the declaration of identity duly signed and authenticated agrees with the number on the ballot paper, place the declaration in the receptacle for declarations of identity and the ballot paper in a ballot box previously shown open and empty to the agents present and locked by the returning officer and sealed with the seal of the returning officer and the seals of such of the agents as desire to affix their seals in such manner as to prevent its being opened without breaking the seal, which shall be subsequently treated as a ballot box for the purpose of rule 41 of the election rules, and

(b) where the number on the said declaration does not agree with the number on the ballot paper, mark the declaration "rejected", attach thereto the ballot paper and place it in the receptacle for votes rejected.

(6) Where the number on the declaration of identity duly signed and authenticated does not agree with the number on the ballot paper envelope or that envelope has no number on it, he shall open the envelope and shall—

(a) where the number on the declaration agrees with the number on the ballot paper, place the declaration in the receptacle for declarations of identity and the ballot paper in the ballot box referred to in paragraph (5) of this Regulation, and

(b) where the number on the declaration does not agree with the number on the ballot paper or there is no ballot paper, mark the declaration "rejected", attach thereto the ballot paper (if any) and place it in the receptacle for votes rejected.

(7) Except for the purposes of ascertaining under paragraph (2) of this Regulation whether a ballot paper envelope contains a declaration of identity or under paragraph (6) of this Regulation whether the number on the declaration agrees with the number on the ballot paper, the returning officer shall not open the ballot paper envelopes before they are opened under Regulation 56.

Sealing up of rejected votes and declarations of identity

55. On the conclusion of the proceedings under Regulation 54 the returning officer shall put the contents of the receptacle for votes rejected and the contents of the receptacle for declarations of identity into two separate packets and shall seal up such packets.

Opening of ballot paper envelopes

56.—(1) After sealing up the said packets the returning officer shall open separately each ballot paper envelope placed in the receptacle for ballot paper envelopes.

(2) Where a ballot paper envelope does not contain a ballot paper, he shall mark the envelope "rejected".

(3) Where the number on the ballot paper envelope agrees with the number on the ballot paper contained therein, he shall place the ballot paper in the ballot box referred to in Regulation 54(5).

(4) Where the number on the ballot paper envelope does not agree with the number on the ballot paper contained therein, he shall mark the ballot paper "rejected" and attach the ballot paper envelope thereto.

(5) He shall put into a separate packet the envelopes and the ballot papers marked "rejected" under the provisions of this Regulation and shall seal up such packet.

Abandoned poll

57. Where a poll is abandoned, or countermanded after postal ballot papers have been issued, by reason of the death of a candidate, the returning officer—

(a) shall not take any step or further step to open covering envelopes or deal with their contents in accordance with the provisions of this Part of these Regulations, and

(b) shall, notwithstanding Regulation 55 or 56, treat all unopened covering envelopes and the contents of those which have been opened as if they were counted ballot papers.

Forwarding of documents

58.—(1) The returning officer shall forward, in the case of a parliamentary election, to the Clerk of the Crown in Chancery and, in the case of a local government election, to the clerk of the authority to which councillors are to be elected, at the same time as he forwards the documents mentioned in rule 49 of the election rules—

(a) any packets referred to in Regulation 50, 51, 55 or 56, subject to the provisions of Regulation 57, endorsing on each packet a description of its contents, the date of the election to which it relates and the name of the constituency or electoral area for which the election was held, and

(b) a statement of the number of postal ballot papers issued in such form and giving such other particulars with respect to such papers as the Secretary of State may require.

(2) Where any covering envelopes are received by the returning officer after the close of the poll or any envelopes addressed to postal voters are returned as undelivered too late to be readdressed, or any spoilt postal ballot papers are returned too late to enable other postal ballot papers to be issued, he shall put them unopened into a separate packet, seal up such packet and forward it at a subsequent date in the manner described in paragraph (1) of this Regulation.

(3) Any packet or statement forwarded under this Regulation shall be deemed to have been forwarded in pursuance of the election rules.

(4) A copy of the statement referred to in paragraph (1) of this Regulation shall, in the case of a parliamentary election, be furnished by the returning officer to the Secretary of State.

PART V

SERVICE VOTERS

Service declaration by members of the forces and spouses

59.—(1) A service declaration made by a member of the forces shall be in Form J.

(2) A service declaration made by the spouse of a member of the forces shall be in Form K.

(3) A service declaration made by either a member of the forces or his or her spouse shall be attested by a commissioned officer who is a member of the forces or by an officer of a Government department and shall be transmitted by or on behalf of the declarant to the appropriate registration officer.

Qualification for Crown servant

60. A person employed in the service of the Crown in a post outside the United Kingdom the occupant of which is required to devote his whole time to the duties of that post and the remuneration of which is paid wholly out of moneys provided by Parliament (hereinafter referred to as "a Crown servant") shall have a service qualification.

Service declaration by Crown servants, British Council employees and spouses

61.—(1) A service declaration made by a Crown servant or by a person who is employed by the British Council in a post outside the United Kingdom (hereinafter referred to as "a British Council employee") shall be in Form L.

(2) A service declaration made by the spouse of a Crown servant or of a British Council employee shall be in Form M.

(3) A service declaration made by a person who is or will be a Crown servant or by his or her spouse shall be attested by an officer of or designated by the Government department under which that person or his or her spouse is or will be employed or by another person himself having a service qualification through being employed in the service of the Crown in a post outside the United Kingdom.

(4) A service declaration made by a person who is or will be a British Council employee or by his or her spouse shall be attested by an officer of the British Council or by another person himself having a service qualification through being employed in the service of the Crown in a post outside the United Kingdom.

Transmission of service declaration by Crown servants, British Council employees and spouses

62.—(1) A service declaration made by a person who is or will be a Crown servant or by his or her spouse shall be transmitted by the declarant to the Government department under which that person or his or her spouse is or will be employed or to an officer designated by that department and transmitted by that department or officer to the appropriate registration officer.

(2) A service declaration made by a person who is or will be a British Council employee or by his or her spouse shall be transmitted by the declarant to the British Council and transmitted by the British Council to the appropriate registration officer.

Service declaration by person about to leave the United Kingdom

63. A service declaration made by a person about to leave the United Kingdom in such circumstances as to acquire a service qualification shall be made not more than six weeks before the date on which he expects to leave the United Kingdom.

Proceedings by registration officer on receipt of service declaration

64. Subject to Regulation 65, the registration officer on receipt of a service declaration shall notify the declarant that his declaration has been received.

Invalid service declaration

65.—(1) Where a service declaration does not appear—
  (*a*) to be properly made out and attested, or
  (*b*) to have been transmitted in the proper manner to the registration officer,
the registration officer shall return the declaration to the declarant and explain his reasons for so doing.

(2) Where the registration officer has been notified by the appropriate Government department or an officer designated by that department or has been notified by the British Council that a person is not entitled to make a service declaration, he shall not enter that person's name in the electors lists and shall notify that person that he has not done so but that that person may make a claim to be so entered.

Evidence as to service declaration

66. The registration officer shall treat a notice from the appropriate Government department or an officer designated by that department or a notice from the British Council that a person is not entitled to make a service declaration or that a person's service declaration has ceased to be in force as conclusive evidence thereof.

PART VI

SUPPLEMENTARY

Appeals

67.—(1) A person desiring to appeal against the decision of a registration officer must give notice of appeal to the registration officer and to the opposite party (if any) when the decision is given, or within fourteen days thereafter, specifying the grounds of appeal.

(2) The registration officer shall forward any such notice to the county court in the manner directed by rules of court together in each case with a statement of the material facts which in his opinion have been established in the case and of his decision upon the whole case and on any point which may be specified as a ground of appeal, and shall also furnish to the court any further information which the court may require and which he is able to furnish.

(3) Where it appears to the registration officer that any notices of appeal given to him are based on similar grounds, he shall inform the county court of the fact for the purpose of enabling the court (if it thinks fit) to consolidate the appeals or select a case as a test case.

(4) Where under section 45(4) and (7) of the Act of 1949 the registration officer makes any alteration in the corrected corrupt and illegal practices list prepared by him which affects the revised list prepared by the clerk of the authority of a local government area, he shall notify the clerk of the alteration and the clerk shall make a similar alteration in the said revised list prepared by him.

Official poll card

68.—(1) The official poll card issued to an elector shall be in Form E.

(2) The official poll card issued to the proxy of an elector shall be in Form F.

Return and declaration of election expenses

69.—(1) The return and declaration of expenses required by section 63 of the Act of 1949 to be authorised by an election agent shall be in Forms X and Y.

(2) The fee for inspecting a return or declaration (including any accompanying documents) specified in section 77(1) of, or paragraph 8(1) of Schedule 6 to, the Act of 1949 (which relate to returns and declarations of election expenses) shall be five shillings.

(3) The price of a copy of any such return, declaration or document shall be at the rate of one shilling for the contents of each side of each page.

Forms

70.—(1) Form A shall be used for the purpose for which it is expressed to be applicable.

(2) The registration officer shall without fee supply a reasonable number of copies of Forms N to W to any person.

(3) The forms set out in Schedule 1 to these Regulations or forms substantially to the like effect may be used with such variations as the circumstances may require.

Sending of notices, etc.

71.—(1) Any application, notice, claim or objection which is required by these Regulations to be made to the registration officer, returning officer or mayor shall be in writing and sent by post or delivered to his office or to the address specified by him for the purpose.

(2) Where the registration officer, returning officer or mayor is required by these Regulations to notify any person, such notification shall be in writing and may be sent by post—

    (a) in the case of a person other than a service voter, to the address furnished by that person for the purpose of such notification or of any record or, if there is no such address, to the last known place of abode of that person ;

    (b) in the case of a service voter, to any address provided by him for the purpose of such notification or of any record or to the address provided for the purpose by the appropriate Government department or, as the case may be, the British Council.

Publication of documents

72.—(1) Any failure to publish a document in accordance with these Regulations shall not invalidate the document, but this provision shall not relieve the registration officer from any penalty for such a failure.

(2) A document which is made available for inspection in pursuance of these Regulations shall be made available during ordinary business hours.

(3) Where a document is made available for inspection, any person may make a copy of, or take extracts from, such document.

Misnomers

73. No misnomer or inaccurate description of any person or place in any notice, electors list, list of claims or objections, corrupt and illegal practices list, special list or register shall prejudice the operation of that document with respect to that person or place in any case where the description of the person or place is such as to be commonly understood.

Time

74.—(1) Subject to the provisions of the following paragraphs of this Regulation, where the last day of the time allowed by these Regulations for any matter falls on a Sunday, or a day of the Christmas break, of the Easter break or of a bank holiday break, that time shall be extended until the end of the next following day which is not one of the days before mentioned.

(2) In computing for the purposes of Regulations 29, 34 and 36 the period of twelve or fourteen days before the day of the poll at a parliamentary or local government election, as the case may be, a Sunday, or a day of the Christmas break, of the Easter break or of a bank holiday break shall be disregarded.

(3) In this Regulation "the Christmas break", "the Easter break" and "a bank holiday break" have the same meanings as in rule 2 of the parliamentary or local elections rules, as the case may be, except that in paragraph (1) of this Regulation a bank holiday means a day which is a bank holiday under the Bank Holidays Act 1871(**a**) in England and Wales.

Penalties

75.—(1) If any person fails to comply with or gives false information in pursuance of any such requisition of the registration officer as is mentioned in Regulation 25, he shall be liable on summary conviction to a fine not exceeding £50.

(2) If any person without lawful authority destroys, mutilates, defaces or removes any notice published by the registration officer in connection with his registration duties or any copies of a document which have been made available for inspection in pursuance of those duties, he shall be liable on summary conviction to a fine not exceeding £20.

James Callaghan,
One of Her Majesty's Principal
Secretaries of State.

Home Office,
Whitehall.
2nd June 1969.

(**a**) 1871 c. 17.

SCHEDULE 1

Forms

Forms for use by registration officers

FORM A: RETURN BY OCCUPIER AS TO RESIDENTS

Representation of the People Acts

Register of Electors 19

Qualifying date: 10th October 19   . Register in force for twelve months from 16th February 19   .

I have to compile and publish an up-to-date Register of Electors for 19   . To do so, I need information which you, as Occupier, are obliged by law to supply. Please complete this form accurately and return it to me now—there is no need to wait until the qualifying date before doing so. You should also complete the form even though you intend to move house some time after the qualifying date.

Registers of Electors are needed so that everyone who is entitled to vote at parliamentary or local elections may do so. A person whose name does not appear in the Register cannot vote.

The notes within tell you how to fill up the form, but if you need any further help, I shall be glad to give it.

The Electoral Registration Officer.

Please complete parts 1, 2 and 3 and sign the declaration (part 4)

Part 1. Address

No. of flat, room or floor (where applicable)	No. of house (or name if it is not numbered)	Name of street or road	Parish or town: postal district or postcode (if any)

Part 2. Residents eligible to be included (*see* Notes 1 and 2)

If there are none, please write "None"

Surname and title (Mr., Mrs., etc.) (BLOCK LETTERS) Occupier's name first	Full Christian names or forenames (BLOCK LETTERS)	If aged 18 on or before 16th February 19 enter a √ in this column.	If 18th birthday is after 16th February 19 and on or before the following 15th February give date of birth (see note 1)	If a merchant seaman enter "M." (see note 1(e))

Part 3. Other residents

Is any part of your house/flat separately occupied by persons not entered above? Answer Yes or No

Part 4. Declaration

I declare that to the best of my knowledge and belief—

    (*a*) the particulars given above are true and accurate;

    (*b*) all those whose names are entered above are British subjects or citizens of the Irish Republic and are over 18 or will attain their 18th birthday on or before 15th February 19 .

Signature................................... Date...

NOTES

1. You should enter every British subject (Commonwealth citizens are British subjects) or citizen of the Irish Republic who will be resident at your address on 10th October 19   and who is 18 years of age or over on 16th February next or whose 18th birthday is after 16th February next and on or before the following 15th February (people in this age-group can vote at elections held on or after the date of their 18th birthday).

You should include—

    (a) Those who normally live at your address but are temporarily away, e.g. on holiday, as a student or in hospital (including informal patients in psychiatric hospitals);

    (b) Resident guests, other than short-stay visitors;

    (c) Lodgers and resident domestics;

    (d) Any person who is away working, unless his absence will be for more than six months;

    (e) Merchant seamen. Enter "M." against the name of a merchant seaman. He will then be invited to appoint a proxy to vote for him, or to vote by post. A merchant seaman may be included if he would have been resident at an address (including a hostel or club for merchant seamen) but for the nature of his occupation;

    (f) Reservists called up for service or training.

2. Do not enter—

    (a) Members of H.M. Forces

    (b) Crown servants employed outside the United Kingdom

    (c) Persons employed by the British Council in posts outside the United Kingdom

    (d) Wives or husbands of members of H.M. Forces, of Crown servants or of British Council Staff employed outside the United Kingdom if they are living abroad to be with their husbands or wives, as the case may be

Their names will be included in the Register if they have made the necessary service declaration; to do this they should apply to their Service or Department or the British Council

    (e) Aliens.

Regulation 12

FORM B: NOTICE AS TO PUBLICATION OF A DRAFT REGISTER OF ELECTORS AND MAKING OF CLAIMS AND OBJECTIONS

REPRESENTATION OF THE PEOPLE ACTS

DRAFT REGISTER OF ELECTORS

WHAT THE DRAFT REGISTER IS FOR

1. The register of electors for the twelve months beginning on 16th February next will be based on the draft register. Unless your name is on the register of electors you will not be able to vote at parliamentary or local government elections. To make sure that you will be on the new register and able to vote you should therefore look at the draft register to see that your name is included on it.

HOW TO FIND YOUR NAME IN THE DRAFT REGISTER

2. Before you can trace your name in the draft register you must know in which polling district you live. If you do not know, ask whether an index of streets is available showing where your address appears in the register.

WHAT TO DO IF YOU FIND THAT YOUR NAME IS NOT ON THE DRAFT REGISTER

3. If your name is not on the draft register and you think it ought to be, you should submit a claim to the electoral registration officer before 16th December on a form which he will give you.

4. Your name ought to be on the register if you are over 18 now, or your 18th birthday is not later than 15th February in the year after next, and

either (i) you were resident at an address in the constituency on 10th October last,

or (ii) you had, as a service voter, made a service declaration on or before 10th October last in respect of an address in the constituency.

OBJECTIONS TO OR ALTERATION OF ENTRIES

5. A request for the alteration of any entry, or an objection to the inclusion of any other person's name, should be submitted to the electoral registration officer before 16th December on a form which he will give you.

JURY SERVICE

6. Some names in the draft register have the letter J printed against them. This relates to jury service. An explanation is given in the headnotes to the draft register.

Signature   ....
                       Electoral Registration Officer

Address   ....

                 ....

                 ....

Date.....................................

FORM C: NOTICE AS TO PUBLICATION OF THE ELECTORS LISTS ^{Regulation 12}
AND MAKING OF CLAIMS AND OBJECTIONS

REPRESENTATION OF THE PEOPLE ACTS

ELECTORS LISTS

WHAT THE LISTS ARE FOR

1. The register of electors for the twelve months beginning on 16th February next will be based on these electors lists. Unless your name is on the register of electors you will not be able to vote at parliamentary or local government elections. To make sure that you will be on the new register and able to vote you should therefore look at these lists.

HOW TO FIND YOUR NAME IN THE LISTS

2. Before you can trace your name in the lists you must know in which polling district you live. If you do not know, ask whether an index of streets is available showing where your address appears in the register.

3. There are three lists, marked A, B and C.

   List A is the register for the present year.

   List B shows the names which will be added to it next year.

   List C shows the names which will be removed from it next year.

   (i) Look at List A first.

   (ii) If your name is in List A, look at List C. If your name is not in List C, then it will be included in the new register, and you will be able to vote.

   (iii) If your name is not in List A, look at List B. If your name is in List B, then it will be included in the new register, and you will be able to vote.

WHAT TO DO IF YOU FIND THAT YOUR NAME WILL NOT BE ON THE REGISTER

4. If you think your name ought to be on the register, you should submit a claim to the electoral registration officer before 16th December on a form which he will give you.

5. Your name ought to be on the register if you are over 18 now, or your 18th birthday is not later than 15th February in the year after next, and

either (i) you were resident at an address in the constituency on 10th October last,

   or (ii) you had, as a service voter, made a service declaration on or before 10th October last in respect of an address in the constituency.

OBJECTIONS TO OR ALTERATION OF ENTRIES

6. A request for the alteration of any entry, or an objection to the inclusion of any other person's name, should be submitted to the electoral registration officer before 16th December on a form which he will give you.

JURY SERVICE

7. Some names in the lists have the letter J printed against them. This relates to jury service. An explanation is given in the headnotes to the lists.

Signature ....
                                Electoral Registration Officer

Address ....
         ....
         ....

Date ....

Regulation 33

FORM D: PROXY PAPER

REPRESENTATION OF THE PEOPLE ACTS

Constituency...

Polling District..

Local government electoral area(s)...

....

    (Name of proxy)..

    (Address) ....

    ....

    ....

is hereby appointed as proxy for

    (Name of elector)...

              *service voter

who is qualified as a ——————— to be registered for

               resident

(Qualifying address)..

....

            *the parliamentary election for the above constituency

*Delete
whichever is   on ....
inapplicable to vote for *him/her at ———————————————————————

            *any election for the above parliamentary constituency
            or local government electoral area(s) (*see* Note 1)

This proxy appointment is not valid until...

                  Signature ....
                        Electoral Registration Officer

                  Address...
                      ....
                      ....

Date.................................

NOTES

1. If your appointment as proxy is for a particular parliamentary election, it will be valid for that election only. In other cases your appointment will continue in force until the electoral registration officer informs you to the contrary (e.g. because the elector cancels it).

If the elector is shown on this form as a resident, your appointment will be valid for all parliamentary and local government elections for the constituency and local government electoral area(s) named above, but not for rural borough or parish council elections.

If the elector is shown on this form as a service voter, your appointment will be valid for all parliamentary and local government elections for the constituency and local government electoral area(s) named above (including rural borough and parish council elections) unless the elector applies to vote by post at a particular parliamentary election. If he does this, your appointment will be suspended for that election only and you will be so informed.

If a ballot paper is issued to the elector at the polling station before you apply for a ballot paper on his behalf, you will not be entitled to vote as proxy.

2. To vote as proxy at an election you must go in person to the polling station for the elector's qualifying address, except that you may apply to vote by post as proxy if either—

(a) you are entitled to vote by post in respect of your own vote at the election, or

(b) in the case of a parliamentary election only, your address is not in the same borough and constituency as the address for which the elector is registered, or is not within the same urban district, rural borough or parish as that address.

Any application to vote by post as proxy should be made on Form V which may be obtained from the electoral registration officer.

3. It is an offence to vote, whether in person or by post, as proxy for some other person if you know that that person is subject to a legal incapacity to vote, e.g. if that person has been convicted and is detained in a penal institution in pursuance of his sentence.

Forms for use by returning officers

Regulation 68.

FORM E: ELECTOR'S OFFICIAL POLL CARD

REPRESENTATION OF THE PEOPLE ACTS

Front of card

OFFICIAL POLL CARD

Constituency

....

Polling Day.....................................

Your polling station will be

....

Number on Register ....

Name ....

Address ....

....

....

....

Back of card

PARLIAMENTARY ELECTION

The poll will be open from 7 a.m. to 10 p.m.

The address of your polling station is shown on the front of this card.

When you go to the polling station tell the clerk your name and address, as shown on the front of this card. The presiding officer will give you a ballot paper; see that he stamps the official mark on it before he gives it to you.

Mark your vote on the ballot paper secretly in one of the voting compartments. Put one X in the space to the right opposite the name of the candidate for whom you wish to vote. You may vote for only one candidate. If you put any other mark on the ballot paper, your vote may not be counted.

Then fold the ballot paper so as to conceal your vote, show the official mark on the back to the presiding officer and put the paper into the ballot box.

If you spoil the ballot paper by mistake do not destroy it; give it back to the presiding officer and ask for another.

ISSUED BY THE RETURNING OFFICER

FORM F: PROXY'S OFFICIAL POLL CARD   Regulation 68

REPRESENTATION OF THE PEOPLE ACTS

Front of card

PROXY'S OFFICIAL POLL CARD

Proxy's name ....

Proxy's address...

....

Back of card

PARLIAMENTARY ELECTION

....CONSTITUENCY

Polling day ....

The poll will be open from 7 a.m. to 10 p.m.

The elector named below whose proxy you are is entitled to vote at the polling station—

....

....

To vote as proxy you must go to that polling station. Tell the clerk that you wish to vote as proxy; give the name and qualifying address of the elector, as follows:—

Number on Register..

Name..

Address ....

....

The presiding officer will give you the elector's ballot paper. The method of voting as proxy is the same as for casting your own vote.

It is an offence to vote as proxy for some other person if you know that that person is subject to a legal incapacity to vote, e.g. if that person has been convicted and is detained in a penal institution in pursuance of his sentence.

ISSUED BY THE RETURNING OFFICER

Regulation 38.

FORM G: CERTIFICATE OF EMPLOYMENT

REPRESENTATION OF THE PEOPLE ACTS

ELECTION IN THE

....

CONSTITUENCY/LOCAL GOVERNMENT ELECTORAL AREA

I certify that (name)...

who is numbered.....................................in the register of electors for the

constituency/electoral area named above, is likely to be unable to go in person

to the polling station allotted to him at the election on (date of poll).................

...............by reason of the particular circumstances of his employment on that

date—

*Delete
whichever is
inapplicable.

*(a) as a constable,

*(b) by me for a purpose connected with the election.

Signature ....
*Mayor/Returning Officer/Police Officer (Inspector or above)

Date.............................

Note.—The person named above is entitled to vote at any polling station of
the above constituency/electoral area on production and surrender of this
certificate to the presiding officer.

FORM H: DECLARATION OF IDENTITY

REPRESENTATION OF THE PEOPLE ACTS

Front of form

Ballot Paper No...............................

I hereby declare that I am the person to whom the ballot paper numbered as above was sent.

Voter's signature (or mark)..

The voter, who is personally known to me, has signed (or marked) this declaration in my presence.

Witness's signature.....................................

SEE INSTRUCTIONS ON THE BACK OF THIS FORM

Back of form

INSTRUCTIONS TO THE VOTER

1. You must sign (or mark) the declaration of identity in the presence of a person known to you.

2. You may vote for not more than...........candidate[s].

3. Place a cross (X) on the right-hand side of the ballot paper opposite the name[s] of the candidate[s] for whom you vote. Do this secretly: if you cannot vote without assistance, the person assisting you must not disclose how you have voted.

4. Put the ballot paper in the small envelope marked "A" and seal it. Then put the envelope marked "A", together with this declaration of identity, in the larger envelope marked "B". Return it without delay. The ballot paper, in order to be counted, must be received by the returning officer not later than the close of the poll.

5. If you receive more than one ballot paper, remember that it is illegal to vote more than once (otherwise than as proxy) at the same election.

6. At this election you cannot vote in person at a polling station, even if you receive an official poll card.

7. If you inadvertently spoil your postal ballot paper, you can apply to the returning officer for another one. With your application you must return, in a fresh envelope, the spoilt ballot paper, the declaration of identity and the envelopes marked "A" and "B". Remember that there is little time available if a fresh postal ballot paper is to be counted.

Forms for use by service voters

Regulation 59.

FORM J: SERVICE DECLARATION AND APPLICATION FOR APPOINTMENT OF PROXY BY A MEMBER OF THE FORCES

REPRESENTATION OF THE PEOPLE ACTS

REGISTER OF ELECTORS 19

Qualifying date: 10th October 19 .

Register in force for twelve months from 16th February 19 .

Part 1.

Surname ....
    (BLOCK LETTERS)

Other names...
    (BLOCK LETTERS)

Service (R.N., Army,   Regiment
R.A.F., etc.) ....or Corps................................

Rank or Rating...........................Service No....................................

Present Service address...

....

I HEREBY DECLARE—

    (1) that I am a British subject or citizen of the Republic of Ireland;

    (2) that—

        *(a) I shall be 18 years of age or over on 16th February 19 ;

        OR

*Delete
whichever is
inapplicable.

        *(b) (*if 18th birthday is after* 16th February 19 *and on or before the following* 15th February)

my 18th birthday is on

Day	Month	Year
:	:	

    (3) that I reside, or but for my service would reside, in the United Kingdom, and—

        *(a) reside, or but for my service would reside, at (full postal address in block letters)...

           ....

           ....

        OR

        *(b) (*if the declarant cannot give any such address*) have resided in the United Kingdom at (full postal address in block letters)

           ....

           ....

           ....

I HEREBY CANCEL any previous declaration made by me.

Signature of declarant................................Date...........................

Signature and Rank of attesting officer (*see* Note 3)...............................

NOTES

1. This declaration is to be made with a view to registration in the register of electors which will be in force for twelve months from 16th February 19   and with reference to your circumstances on the qualifying date for that register, i.e. 10th October 19 .

2. The declaration is to be made during the twelve months ending with the qualifying date.

3. The declaration must be attested by a commissioned officer or by an officer of a Government Department.

4. When completed and attested, this form should be sent to the Electoral Registration Officer.

Part 2.

Regulation 31.

PROXY APPOINTMENT

(While you are outside the United Kingdom you can vote only by proxy.)

I HEREBY CANCEL ANY PREVIOUS PROXY APPOINTMENT AND APPLY FOR THE APPOINTMENT AS MY PROXY OF—

Names of first choice...
(BLOCK LETTERS)

Postal address...
(BLOCK LETTERS)

....

Relationship, if any, to elector..

OR IF HE OR SHE IS UNWILLING OR UNABLE TO BE APPOINTED

Names of second choice...
(BLOCK LETTERS)

Postal address...
(BLOCK LETTERS)

....

Relationship, if any, to elector..

Signature.....................   Date.......................

NOTES

1. A person to vote as proxy must be a British subject or citizen of the Republic of Ireland, of voting age and not subject to any legal incapacity to vote. A proxy appointed in consequence of this application will be entitled to vote for you at all parliamentary and local government elections.

2. If the address in paragraph (3) of Part 1 is the same as that in your previous declaration (if any), you need not apply for the appointment of a proxy unless you want to appoint a different one; the previous appointment will remain valid. If, however, the address is different, you will need to apply afresh for the appointment of a proxy.

3. If at any time you wish to cancel the appointment of your proxy, you should notify the Electoral Registration Officer.

Regulation 59

FORM K: SERVICE DECLARATION AND APPLICATION FOR APPOINTMENT OF PROXY BY THE SPOUSE OF A MEMBER OF THE FORCES

REPRESENTATION OF THE PEOPLE ACTS

REGISTER OF ELECTORS 19

Qualifying date: 10th October 19 .

Register in force for twelve months from 16th February 19 .

Part 1.

Surname ....
(BLOCK LETTERS)

Other names..
(BLOCK LETTERS)

Other names of *husband/wife..

Service (R.N., Army,   Regiment
R.A.F., etc.)...............................or Corps..................................

Rank or Rating...........................Service No................................

Present address of *husband/wife...
....

I HEREBY DECLARE

   (1) that I am a British subject or citizen of the Republic of Ireland;

   (2) that—

     *(a) I shall be 18 years of age or over on 16th February 19 ;

     OR

     *(b) (if 18th birthday is after 16th February 19 and on or before the following 15th February)

	Day	Month	Year
my 18th birthday is on	:		:

*Delete whichever is inapplicable.

   (3) that I reside, or expect to go abroad within six weeks (see Note 2) to reside, outside the United Kingdom to be with my *husband/wife who is a member of the forces;

   (4) that but for my *husband's/wife's service I would be residing in the United Kingdom, and—

     *(a) would be residing at (full postal address in block letters)
....
....

     OR

     *(b) (if the declarant cannot give any such address) have resided in the United Kingdom at (full postal address in block letters)
....
....
....

I HEREBY CANCEL any previous declaration made by me.

Signature of declarant...Date........................

Signature and Rank of attesting officer (see Note 3)....................................

NOTES

1. This declaration is to be made with a view to registration in the register of electors which will be in force for twelve months from 16th February 19   and with reference to your circumstances on the qualifying date for that register, i.e. 10th October 19 .

2. The declaration is to be made during the twelve months ending with the qualifying date, but a person about to leave the United Kingdom must not make it more than six weeks before the expected date of departure.

3. The declaration must be attested by a commissioned officer or by an officer of a Government Department.

4. When completed and attested this form should be sent to the Electoral Registration Officer.

Part 2.

Regulation 31.

PROXY APPOINTMENT

(While you are outside the United Kingdom you can vote only by proxy.)

I HEREBY CANCEL ANY PREVIOUS PROXY APPOINTMENT AND APPLY FOR THE APPOINTMENT AS MY PROXY OF—

Names of first choice...
　　(BLOCK LETTERS)

Postal address..
　　(BLOCK LETTERS)

　　...

Relationship, if any, to elector...

OR IF HE OR SHE IS UNWILLING OR UNABLE TO BE APPOINTED

Names of second choice..
　　(BLOCK LETTERS)

Postal address..
　　(BLOCK LETTERS)

　　...

Relationship, if any, to elector...

Signature.. Date......................

NOTES

1. A person to vote as proxy must be a British subject or citizen of the Republic of Ireland, of voting age and not subject to any legal incapacity to vote. A proxy appointed in consequence of this application will be entitled to vote for you at all parliamentary and local government elections.

2. If the address in paragraph (4) of Part 1 is the same as that in your previous declaration (if any) you need not apply for the appointment of a proxy unless you want to appoint a different one; the previous appointment will remain valid. If, however, the address is different, you will need to apply afresh for the appointment of a proxy.

3. If at any time you wish to cancel the appointment of your proxy, you should notify the Electoral Registration Officer.

Regulation 61.

FORM L: SERVICE DECLARATION AND APPLICATION FOR APPOINTMENT OF PROXY BY A CROWN SERVANT OR BY A PERSON EMPLOYED BY THE BRITISH COUNCIL

REPRESENTATION OF THE PEOPLE ACTS

REGISTER OF ELECTORS 19 .

Qualifying date: 10th October 19 .

Register in force for twelve months from 16th February 19 .

Part 1.

Surname ....
     (BLOCK LETTERS)

Other names...
     (BLOCK LETTERS)

I HEREBY DECLARE—

    (1) that I am a British subject or citizen of the Republic of Ireland;

    (2) that—

      *(a) I shall be 18 years of age or over on 16th February 19   ;

      OR

      *(b) (if 18th birthday is after 16th February 19   and on or before the following 15th February)

Day	Month	Year
:	:	

      my 18th birthday is on

*Delete whichever is inapplicable.

    (3) that I am employed, or leaving the United Kingdom to take up employment (see Note 2), in the service of the *Crown/British Council—

      Description of post...

      Name of Government Department under which you are employed (if applicable)..

      Present address..

      ....

    (4) that but for my service abroad I would be residing in the United Kingdom, and—

      *(a) would be residing at (full postal address in block letters).............

      ....

      ....

      OR

      *(b) (if the declarant cannot give any such address) have resided in the United Kingdom at (full postal address in block letters)

      ....

      ....

      ....

I HEREBY CANCEL any previous declaration made by me.

Signature of declarant..Date.....................

Signature of person attesting (see Note 3).......................................

Rank or official position..

NOTES

1. This declaration is to be made with a view to registration in the register of electors which will be in force for twelve months from 16th February 19 and with reference to your circumstances on the qualifying date for that register, i.e. 10th October 19 .

2. The declaration is to be made during the twelve months ending with the qualifying date, but a person about to leave the United Kingdom must not make it more than six weeks before the expected date of departure.

3. The declaration must be attested by an officer of, or designated by, the Government Department under which you are employed, or, as the case may be, by an officer of the British Council, or by another person who has a service qualification through being employed in the service of the Crown in a post outside the United Kingdom.

4. This form when completed and attested should be returned to the Government Department under which you are employed or to an officer designated by that Department or to the British Council as the case may be.

Part 2.   Regulation 31.

PROXY APPOINTMENT

(While you are outside the United Kingdom you can vote only by proxy.)

I HEREBY CANCEL ANY PREVIOUS PROXY APPOINTMENT AND APPLY FOR THE APPOINTMENT AS MY PROXY OF—

Names of first choice...
    (BLOCK LETTERS)

Postal address..
    (BLOCK LETTERS)

....

Relationship, if any, to elector...

OR IF HE OR SHE IS UNWILLING OR UNABLE TO BE APPOINTED

Names of second choice...
    (BLOCK LETTERS)

Postal address..
    (BLOCK LETTERS)

....

Relationship, if any, to elector...

Signature.. Date.......................

NOTES

1. A person to vote as proxy must be a British subject or citizen of the Republic of Ireland, of voting age and not subject to any legal incapacity to vote. A proxy appointed in consequence of this application will be entitled to vote for you at all parliamentary and local government elections.

2. If the address in paragraph (4) of Part 1 is the same as that in your previous declaration (if any) you need not apply for the appointment of a proxy unless you want to appoint a different one; the previous appointment will remain valid. If, however, the address is different, you will need to apply afresh for the appointment of a proxy.

3. If at any time you wish to cancel the appointment of your proxy, you should notify the Electoral Registration Officer.

Regulation 61.

FORM M: SERVICE DECLARATION AND APPLICATION FOR APPOINTMENT OF PROXY BY THE SPOUSE OF A CROWN SERVANT OR OF A PERSON EMPLOYED BY THE BRITISH COUNCIL

REPRESENTATION OF THE PEOPLE ACTS

REGISTER OF ELECTORS 19 .

Qualifying date: 10th October 19 .
Register in force for twelve months from 16th February 19 .

Part 1.

Surname ....
    (BLOCK LETTERS)
Other names..
    (BLOCK LETTERS)
Other names of *husband/wife..

I HEREBY DECLARE—

(1) that I am a British subject or citizen of the Republic of Ireland;
(2) that—
    *(a) I shall be 18 years of age or over on 16th February 19 ;
    OR
    *(b) (if 18th birthday is after 16th February 19 and on or before the following 15th February)

Day	Month	Year
my 18th birthday is on	:	:

*Delete whichever is is inapplicable.

(3) that I reside, or expect to go abroad within six weeks (see Note 2) to reside, outside the United Kingdom to be with my *husband/wife, who is employed, or is leaving the United Kingdom to take up employment, in the service of the *Crown/British Council—

Description of *husband's/wife's post...
Name of Government Department under which *husband/wife employed (if applicable)..
Present address of *husband/wife..
....

(4) that but for my *husband's/wife's service I would be residing in the United Kingdom, and—
    *(a) would be residing at (full postal address in block letters)
    ....
    ....

    OR

    *(b) (if the declarant cannot give any such address) have resided in the United Kingdom at (full postal address in block letters)
    ....
    ....
    ....

I HEREBY CANCEL any previous declaration made by me.

Signature of declarant..Date........................
Signature of person attesting (see Note 3)..
Rank or official position..

Notes

1. This declaration is to be made with a view to registration in the register of electors which will be in force for twelve months from 16th February 19   and with reference to your circumstances on the qualifying date for that register, i.e. 10th October 19 .

2. The declaration is to be made during the twelve months ending with the qualifying date, but a person about to leave the United Kingdom must not make it more than six weeks before the expected date of departure.

3. The declaration must be attested by an officer of, or designated by, the Government Department under which your husband or wife is employed, or, as the case may be, by an officer of the British Council, or by another person who has a service qualification through being employed in the service of the Crown in a post outside the United Kingdom.

4. This form when completed and attested should be returned to the Government Department under which your husband or wife is employed or to an officer designated by that Department or to the British Council as the case may be.

Part 2.

Regulation 31.

Proxy Appointment

(While you are outside the United Kingdom you can vote only by proxy.)

I HEREBY CANCEL ANY PREVIOUS PROXY APPOINTMENT AND APPLY FOR THE APPOINTMENT AS MY PROXY OF—

Names of first choice...
(BLOCK LETTERS)

Postal address...
(BLOCK LETTERS)
....

Relationship, if any, to elector..

OR IF HE OR SHE IS UNWILLING OR UNABLE TO BE APPOINTED

Names of second choice...
(BLOCK LETTERS)

Postal address...
(BLOCK LETTERS)
....

Relationship, if any, to elector..

Signature...Date ....

Notes

1. A person to vote as proxy must be a British subject or citizen of the Republic of Ireland, of voting age and not subject to any legal incapacity to vote. A proxy appointed in consequence of this application will be entitled to vote for you at all parliamentary and local government elections.

2. If the address in paragraph (4) of Part 1 is the same as that in your previous declaration (if any), you need not apply for the appointment of a proxy unless you want to appoint a different one; the previous appointment will remain valid. If, however, the address is different, you will need to apply afresh for the appointment of a proxy.

3. If at any time you wish to cancel the appointment of your proxy, you should notify the Electoral Registration Officer.

Regulation 29.

FORM N: APPLICATION BY A SERVICE VOTER IN THE UNITED KINGDOM TO VOTE BY POST

REPRESENTATION OF THE PEOPLE ACTS

I, (Surname)..
    (BLOCK LETTERS)

(Other names) ....
    (BLOCK LETTERS)

(Rank or   (Service
Rating) ....No.).................................

am registered as a service voter for

....

(Give the qualifying address which you gave on your service declaration)

and I apply for a ballot paper for the coming parliamentary election to be sent to me at

....

....

(Give full postal address in block letters)

Signature...............................   Date........................

NOTES

1. If you have changed your name since completing your service declaration, put your former name in brackets after your present name.

2. You should send this application to the Electoral Registration Officer at the address stated on his acknowledgment of your service declaration.

Forms for use by other persons

FORM O: FORM OF CLAIM TO BE REGISTERED AS AN ELECTOR

Regulation 14.

REPRESENTATION OF THE PEOPLE ACTS

(If this form is sent to the Electoral Registration Officer by post, postage must be prepaid.)

Constituency of..

To the Electoral Registration Officer

Qualifications for Registration

For parliamentary and local government electors, residence on 10th October last; a service voter must have made a service declaration on or before that date.

The person must be a British subject or citizen of the Republic of Ireland; and he must be 18 years of age or over on 16th February next, or after 16th February next and on or before the following 15th February (people in this latter age group can vote at elections held on or after the date of their 18th birthday).

Note. Any false declaration made by a person for the purpose of this claim will render such person liable to a penalty.

1. Surname and...Other ....
   title (Mr., Mrs., etc.)   names
   (BLOCK LETTERS)   (BLOCK LETTERS)

2. Full postal address (in BLOCK LETTERS) of premises for which claimant claims to be qualified to be registered

   No. or Name...

   Street or road...

   Parish or town: postal district or postcode (if any)............................
   ....

3. (a) Will the claimant be 18 years of age or over on 16th February next? (Yes or No)...

   (b) If not, give date of birth...

4. (a) Was claimant resident at the said address on 10th October last? (Yes or No)...

   (b) Had claimant made a service declaration by 10th October last? (Yes or No)...

   (c) Was claimant a merchant seaman on 10th October last? (Yes or No)...

DECLARATION

The particulars above are true and correct in all respects. The claimant is a British subject or citizen of the Republic of Ireland; and he claims the parliamentary and/or local government franchise to which such particulars entitle him.

Signature of claimant or person making claim on behalf of claimant
....

Address of person making claim (if not the claimant)
....
....

Date..

Regulation 14.

FORM P: FORM OF OBJECTION TO AN ENTRY IN THE ELECTORS LISTS

REPRESENTATION OF THE PEOPLE ACTS

(If this form is sent to the Electoral Registration Officer by post, postage must be prepaid.)

*Here insert extract from printed electors lists, stating registration unit, or name and address as given in claim.

1. *Form of objection* (*parliamentary electors*)

To the Electoral Registration Officer for the constituency of....................

I hereby give you notice that I object to the entry of*.............................

....

....

....

†Delete if inapplicable.

as a parliamentary elector [in accordance with the claim made in that behalf]†

The grounds of my objection are..

....

....

....

‡Here insert extract from printed electors lists, stating registration unit.

I am entered in the electors lists as a parliamentary elector for the above constituency as follows‡:—

....

....

Signature ....

Address ....

Date...

*Here insert extract from printed electors lists, stating registration unit, or name and address as given in claim.

2. *Form of objection* (*local government electors*)

To the Electoral Registration Officer for..

I hereby give notice that I object to the entry of*.......................................

....

....

†Delete if inapplicable

as a local government elector for [all] [the following] local government area[s] [in accordance with the claim made in that behalf]†.............................

....

The grounds of my objection are..

....

....

‡Here insert extract from printed electors lists, stating registration unit.

I am entered in the lists of local government electors for the above area[s] as follows‡...

....

Signature ....

Address ....

Date.....................................

FORM Q: APPLICATION TO BE TREATED AS AN ABSENT VOTER FOR AN INDEFINITE PERIOD OWING TO OCCUPATION OR PHYSICAL INCAPACITY   Regulation 29.

REPRESENTATION OF THE PEOPLE ACTS

(1) I, (Surname)...
    (BLOCK LETTERS)

    (Other names)...
    (BLOCK LETTERS)

am qualified to be registered as an elector for (address in full in block letters)
....
....

(2) I apply to be treated as an absent voter at parliamentary and local government elections because I am likely to be unable to go in person to the polling station (or, where (c) or (d) below applies, to vote unaided)—

*(a) by reason of the general nature of my occupation, service or employment as   *Delete whichever is inapplicable.
....
              (Give full reasons for application)

*(b) by reason of the general nature of the occupation, service or employment of my *husband/wife as
....
    and my resulting absence from my qualifying address until...............
    (insert likely date of return) to be with my *husband/wife

*(c) by reason of blindness† (in respect of which I have been registered as a blind person by the..   †If the applicant is not registered as a blind person delete the words in brackets and ask a medical practitioner to complete the certificate below.
..............................Council)

*(d) by reason of physical incapacity (see Note 2).

Signature.. Date...........................

Address in the United Kingdom (in block letters) to which ballot paper is to be sent (if different from address given above)
....
....

MEDICAL CERTIFICATE

I certify—

(a) that the statement at (2) above is correct;

(b) that the applicant's inablility is likely to continue for....................
months/indefinitely*.

    *It is important to indicate which alternative applies.

Signature ....

Address...
....

Date..

Notes

1. This application, if allowed, will continue in force until you cancel it or cease to be registered for your present qualifying address or become registered in a different capacity or until the Electoral Registration Officer gives you notice to the contrary. This application will be valid for all parliamentary and local government elections at which you are entitled to vote except rural borough and parish council elections. A separate application should be made for each qualifying address.

2. Where the ground of the application is blindness or other physical incapacity, the certificate above should be completed by a doctor (or by a Christian Science practitioner), unless you are registered as a blind person.

3. If the ground of the application is the nature of your occupation, service or employment (or that of your husband or wife) and you are likely to be at sea or out of the United Kingdom at the time of an election, you may apply to have a proxy appointed to vote for you. If so, apply on Form U which may be obtained from the Electoral Registration Officer.

4. If you have been appointed proxy for an elector in the same parliamentary constituency or local government electoral area, you may apply on Form V to vote as such by post, but not if you yourself have a proxy appointed for you.

Form V may be obtained from the Electoral Registration Officer.

5. Any change of the address to which ballot papers are to be sent should be notified promptly to the Electoral Registration Officer. If you wait until an election occurs, you may be too late.

FORM R: APPLICATION TO VOTE BY POST OWING TO CHANGE OF RESIDENCE

Regulation 29.

REPRESENTATION OF THE PEOPLE ACTS

I, (Surname)..
(BLOCK LETTERS)

(Other names)...
(BLOCK LETTERS)

am qualified to be registered as an elector for (old address in full in block letters)

....

....

....

I apply to be treated as an absent voter at parliamentary elections because I no longer reside there.   My new address is (new address in full in block letters)

....

....

....

Signature.. Date.........................

NOTES

1. This application, if allowed, will continue in force for all parliamentary elections so long as you remain registered for your old address.

2. Temporary absence, e.g. on holiday, does NOT constitute a change of residence.

3. This application cannot be allowed if the address at which you now reside is in the same borough and constituency as the address for which you are registered, or within the same urban district, rural borough or parish.

4. If you have been appointed proxy for an elector you may apply on Form V to vote as such by post at parliamentary elections.   Form V may be obtained from the Electoral Registration Officer.

Regulation 29. **FORM S: APPLICATION TO BE TREATED AS AN ABSENT VOTER FOR A PARTICULAR ELECTION**

REPRESENTATION OF THE PEOPLE ACTS

I, (Surname)..
(BLOCK LETTERS)

(Other names)...
(BLOCK LETTERS)

am qualified to be registered as an elector for (address in full in block letters)
....
....

and I apply to be treated as an absent voter at the coming parliamentary/local government election (*see* Note 1)
in ....
constituency/local government electoral area because I am likely to be unable to go in person to the polling station allotted to me, owing to—

*(a) my service in one of Her Majesty's reserve or auxiliary forces (*see* Note 2)
....;

*(b) my employment on polling day
* (i) as a constable;
*(ii) by the returning officer or mayor in connection with the election in..
constituency/local government electoral area;

*Delete whichever is inapplicable.

*(c) my being bound to the following religious observances (*see* Note 3)
....;

*(d) my acting as returning officer for..
constituency/local government electoral area;

*(e) my/my husband's/my wife's candidature
in ....constituency.

Signature.................................... Date................................

Address in the United Kingdom (in block letters) to which ballot paper is to be sent (if different from address given above)
....
....

CERTIFICATE

To be completed where (c) above applies

I certify that the statement at (*c*) above is correct.

Signature...
(Minister of the elector's religious denomination)

Address ....
....

Date...

NOTES

1. Where (*a*), (*b*) or (*c*) applies, the application may be made for any parliamentary or local government election except a rural borough or parish council election. Where (*d*) applies, the application may be made for a parliamentary general election or ordinary local government election (with the same exceptions). Where (*e*) applies, the application may be made only for a parliamentary general election.

2. Where (*a*) applies, the application must state the name of the reserve or auxiliary force concerned. If the application is for a particular parliamentary election and you are likely to be at sea or out of the United Kingdom on polling day, you may apply on Form U to have a proxy appointed to vote for you.

3. Where (*c*) applies, the application must state the nature and times of the religious observances. The certificate above must be completed by a minister of your religious denomination.

4. If you have been appointed proxy for an elector in the same constituency or local government electoral area, you may apply on Form V to vote as such by post, but not if you yourself have a proxy appointed for you.

The forms referred to may be obtained from the Electoral Registration Officer.

Regulation 29.

FORM T: APPLICATION TO BE TREATED AS AN ABSENT VOTER FOR AN INDEFINITE PERIOD OWING TO AIR OR SEA JOURNEY

REPRESENTATION OF THE PEOPLE ACTS

I, (Surname)...
    (BLOCK LETTERS)

(Other names)...
    (BLOCK LETTERS)

am qualified to be registered as an elector for (address in full in block letters)

....

....

and I apply to be treated as an absent voter at parliamentary and local government elections (*see* Note 1) because I am likely to be unable to go in person from the above address to the polling station without making a journey by air or sea.

Signature... Date.................................

Address in the United Kingdom (in block letters) to which ballot paper is to be sent (if different from address given above)

....

....

NOTES

1. The journey in question is the journey necessary to go to the polling station from your qualifying address, not from where you may happen to be at the time of an election.

2. This application, if allowed, will continue in force until you cancel it or cease to be registered for your present qualifying address or become registered in a different capacity or until the Electoral Registration Officer gives you notice to the contrary. It will be valid for all parliamentary and local government elections at which you are entitled to vote except rural borough and parish council elections. A separate application should be made for each qualifying address.

3. If you have been appointed proxy for an elector in the same parliamentary constituency or local government electoral area, you may apply on Form V to vote as such by post, but not if you yourself have a proxy appointed for you.
Form V may be obtained from the Electoral Registration Officer.

4. Any change of the address to which ballot papers are to be sent should be notified promptly to the Electoral Registration Officer. If you wait until an election occurs, you may be too late.

FORM U: APPLICATION FOR APPOINTMENT OF PROXY

Regulation 31.

REPRESENTATION OF THE PEOPLE ACTS

(*Not to be used by service voters*)

I, (Surname)...
    (BLOCK LETTERS)

(Other names)...
    (BLOCK LETTERS)

am qualified to be registered as an elector for (address in full in block letters)

....

....

....

I have applied to be treated as an absent voter—

    (*a*)   at parliamentary and local government elections owing to—

        * (i)   the general nature of my occupation, service or employment;

        *(ii) the general nature of the occupation, service, or employment of my *husband/wife and my resulting absence from my qualifying address to be with *him/her;

  *(*b*) at the coming parliamentary election in...
        constituency owing to my service in Her Majesty's reserve or auxiliary forces;

*Delete whichever is inapplicable.

and I declare that I am likely to be at sea or outside the United Kingdom on polling day.

I therefore apply for the person named below as first choice (or, if he or she is unwilling or unable to be appointed, the person named as second choice) to be appointed as proxy to vote for me.

PROXY APPOINTMENT

1. First choice (the elector must fill this up)

Full names...
   (BLOCK LETTERS)

Postal address..
   (BLOCK LETTERS)

....

Relationship, if any, to elector

....

2. Second choice (the elector should fill this up as the first choice may be unwilling or unable to be appointed)

Full names...
   (BLOCK LETTERS)

Postal address..
   (BLOCK LETTERS)

....

Relationship, if any, to elector

....

Signature..   Date...................................

1. A person to vote as proxy must be a British subject or citizen of the Republic of Ireland, of voting age and not subject to any legal incapacity to vote.

2. Where (*a*) applies, a proxy appointed in consequence of your application to be treated as an absent voter will be entitled to vote for you at all parliamentary and local government elections except rural borough and parish council elections. You can cancel the appointment by giving notice to the Electoral Registration Officer.

3. Where (*b*) applies, the proxy's appointment will be for a particular parliamentary election only.

FORM V: APPLICATION BY A PROXY TO VOTE BY POST

Regulation 36.

REPRESENTATION OF THE PEOPLE ACTS

I, (Surname)...
    (BLOCK LETTERS)

(Other names)...
    (BLOCK LETTERS)

have been appointed proxy for

(†Name) ....
    (BLOCK LETTERS)

†As shown on proxy paper.

who is registered as an elector for

(†Qualifying address)...
    (BLOCK LETTERS)

....

and I apply to vote by post as proxy for the above-named elector because—

*(a) I am entitled to vote by post as an absent voter: the address for which I am registered as an elector is
(address in full in block letters)

*Delete whichever is inapplicable.

....

....

*(b) the address entered below is in a different area from the address for which the above-named elector is registered (*see* Note 2).

A ballot paper should be sent to me at the following address (block letters) in the United Kingdom

....

....

....

Signature.. Date...............................

NOTES

1. Where (a) applies, this application, if allowed, will be valid for all parliamentary and local government elections (except rural borough and parish council elections) for which your application to be treated as an absent voter is valid so long as your appointment as proxy continues. Where (b) applies, the application will be valid only for parliamentary elections and will remain in force until you cancel it or cease to be proxy for the elector.

2. Where (b) applies, the application cannot be allowed if your address is in the same area as the address for which the elector is registered, i.e. within the same borough and constituency, or within the same urban district, rural borough or parish.

Regulations,
29, 31.

FORM W: APPLICATION BY SERVICE VOTER'S SPOUSE FOR APPOINTMENT OF PROXY

REPRESENTATION OF THE PEOPLE ACTS

Part 1.

Surname ....
    (BLOCK LETTERS)

Other names..
    (BLOCK LETTERS)

Other names of *husband/wife...

    *(a)   Service (R.N.,   Regiment
            Army, R.A.F., etc.).......................or Corps............................

            Rank or Rating...........................Service No............................

            OR

*Delete
whichever is
inapplicable.
    *(b)   Name of Government Department under   Description
            which *husband/wife employed ....of post........................

            OR

    *(c)   British Council   Description
                                of post.................................

Present address of *husband/wife

        ....
        ....

    (1)   I am qualified to be registered as an elector for (address in full in block letters)

        ....
        ....

(2) I have made a service declaration on Form K/Form M that I reside, or expect to go abroad within six weeks to reside, outside the United Kingdom to be with my *husband/wife.

(3) I therefore apply to be treated as an absent voter and for the person named below as first choice (or, if he or she is unwilling or unable to be appointed, the person named as second choice) to be appointed to vote as proxy for me at parliamentary and local government elections.

Part 2.

PROXY APPOINTMENT

   1. First choice (the elector must fill this up)

Full names...
    (BLOCK LETTERS)

Postal address...
    (BLOCK LETTERS)
    ....

Relationship, if any, to elector
    ....

2. Second choice (the elector should fill this up as the first choice may be unwiiling or unable to be appointed)

Full names ....
    (BLOCK LETTERS)

Postal address..
    (BLOCK LETTERS)
....

Relationship, if any, to elector
....

Signature... Date...................................

NOTE

A person to vote as proxy must be a British subject or citizen of the Republic of Ireland, of voting age and not subject to any legal incapacity to vote. A proxy appointed in consequence of this application will be entitled to vote for you at all parliamentary and local government elections, except rural borough and parish council elections, until your service declaration on Form K/Form M takes effect.

FORM X: RETURN OF EXPENSES REQUIRED BY SECTION 63 OF THE REPRESENTATION OF THE PEOPLE ACT 1949 TO BE AUTHORISED BY AN ELECTION AGENT

Regulation 69.

REPRESENTATION OF THE PEOPLE ACTS

ELECTION IN THE

....
CONSTITUENCY/LOCAL GOVERNMENT ELECTORAL AREA

Date of publication of notice of election...

The expenses incurred at the above election in support of...............................

..............................a candidate thereat, by...

....
(*insert name of person or association or body of persons incurring the expenses*) being expenses required by section 63 of the Representation of the People Act

1949 to be authorised by the election agent, amounted to £....................

The written authority of the election agent is annexed hereto.

Signature... Date...................................

Regulation 69 **FORM Y: DECLARATION AS TO EXPENSES REQUIRED BY SECTION 63 OF THE REPRESENTATION OF THE PEOPLE ACT 1949 TO BE AUTHORISED BY AN ELECTION AGENT**

REPRESENTATION OF THE PEOPLE ACTS

ELECTION IN THE

....
CONSTITUENCY/LOCAL GOVERNMENT ELECTORAL AREA

Date of publication of notice of election...

I hereby declare that—

1. I am the person *or* a director, general manager, secretary or similar officer of the association or body of persons named as incurring expenses in the accompanying return, marked..................., of expenses required by section 63 of the Representation of the People Act 1949 to be authorised by an election agent.

2. To the best of my knowledge and belief the said return is complete and correct.

3. The matters for which the expenses referred to in the said return were incurred were as follows..
....
....

Signature ....

Office held..
(In the case of an association or body of persons)

Date.....................................

Regulation 39

SCHEDULE 2

TABLE OF COMPARISON OF ELECTION RULES

Local elections rules	Schedule 1 to the Urban District Council Election Rules 1969	Schedule 1 to the Rural District Council Election Rules 1969	Parliamentary elections rules
Rule 21	Rule 20	Rule 20	Rule 25
„ 41	„ 40	„ 40	„ 46
„ 49	„ 48	„ 48	„ 56

EXPLANATORY NOTE

(This Note is not part of the Regulations.)

These Regulations revoke and replace the Representation of the People Regulations 1950 as amended. Amendments have been made in consequence of the passing of the Representation of the People Act 1969 (c.15). In particular provision is made for marking the names of persons coming of voting age during the currency of the register and of merchant seamen (Regulations 8 and 9) ; for correcting the published register (Regulation 28) ; for applications to be treated as absent voters based on the ground of religious observance (Regulation 29(2)(*a*)) ; for service declarations by British Council employees (Part V of the Regulations) ; prescribing the fees for inspection and copies of the return and declaration of election expenses (Regulation 69) ; and for the computation of time (Regulation 74).

Other amendments have also been made. In particular the fee for the sale of the register (Regulation 22) and the penalties for certain offences (Regulation 75) have been varied : spoilt postal ballot papers may be replaced (Regulation 51) ; and the procedure for dealing with postal ballot papers where a candidate has died has been specified (Regulation 57).

1969 No. 905

REPRESENTATION OF THE PEOPLE

The Representation of the People (Northern Ireland) Regulations 1969

Made - - - -	*2nd June* 1969
Laid before Parliament	*12th June* 1969
Coming into Operation—	
Regulations 8, 9, 15, 16-45, 55, 56, 57(2), 61	*16th February* 1970
Schedule	*In accordance with Regulation* 2
Remainder	*16th July* 1969

ARRANGEMENT OF REGULATIONS

PART I

GENERAL

1. Citation and extent.
2. Commencement.
3. Revocation and savings.
4. Interpretation.

PART II

REGISTRATION
The Register

5. Preparation of the register.
6. Marking of names to indicate manner of voting or persons not of voting age.
7. Registration officer to furnish copies of register.
8. Free copies of register.
9. Sale of register.

Supplementary

10. Declaration as to age and nationality.
11. Power of registration officer to delegate his duties.
12. Information from householders.
13. Adaptation of electors list and register in consequence of altered polling districts.

Corrupt and Illegal Practices List

14. Corrupt and illegal practices list.

Correction of Register

15. Correction of register.

PART III

ABSENT VOTERS, PROXIES AND POSTAL PROXIES

16. Application to be treated as an absent voter.
17. Record and list of absent voters.
18. Application to vote by proxy.
19. Appointment of proxy.
20. Proxy paper.
21. Cancellation and disregard of proxy appointment.
22. Record and list of proxies.
23. Application by proxy to vote by post.
24. Record and list of postal proxies.
25. Certificate of employment.

PART IV

ISSUE AND RECEIPT OF POSTAL BALLOT PAPERS

Interpretation

26. Interpretation of Part IV.

Issue of Postal Ballot Papers

27. Form of postal ballot paper.
28. Form of declaration of identity.
29. Persons entitled to be present at issue and receipt of postal ballot papers.
30. Declaration of secrecy.
31. Notice of issue of postal ballot papers.
32. Marking of postal ballot paper.
33. Refusal to issue postal ballot paper.
34. Ballot paper envelope.
35. Delivery of postal ballot papers to post office.
36. Provision of postal voters' ballot box.
37. Sealing up of special lists and counterfoils.
38. Spoilt postal ballot paper.

Receipt of Postal Ballot Papers·

39. Receipt of covering envelope.
40. Opening of postal voters' ballot box.
41. Opening of covering envelopes.
42. Sealing up of rejected votes and declarations of identity.
43. Opening of ballot paper envelopes.
44. Abandoned poll.
45. Forwarding of documents.

PART V

SERVICE VOTERS

46. Service declaration by members of the forces and spouses.
47. Qualification for Crown servant.
48. Service declaration by Crown servants, British Council employees and spouses.
49. Transmission of service declaration by Crown servants, British Council employees and spouses.
50. Service declaration by person about to leave the United Kingdom.
51. Proceedings by registration officer on receipt of service declaration.
52. Invalid service declaration.
53. Evidence as to service declaration.

PART VI

SUPPLEMENTARY

54. Appeals.
55. Official poll card.
56. Return and declaration of election expenses.
57. Forms.
58. Sending of notices, etc.
59. Publication of documents.
60. Misnomers.
61. Time.
62. Penalties.

SCHEDULE: FORMS.

Forms for use by registration officers

Form A: Return by occupier as to residents.
Form B: Proxy paper.

Forms for use by returning officers

Form C: Elector's official poll card.
Form D: Proxy's official poll card.
Form E: Certificate of employment.
Form F: Declaration of identity.

Forms for use by service voters

Form G: Service declaration and application for appointment of proxy by a member of the forces.

Form H: Service declaration and application for appointment of proxy by the spouse of a member of the forces.

Form I: Service declaration and application for appointment of proxy by a Crown servant or by a person employed by the British Council.

Form J: Service declaration and application for appointment of proxy by the spouse of a Crown servant or of a person employed by the British Council.

Form K: Application by a service voter in the United Kingdom to vote by post.

Forms for use by other persons

Form L: Application to be treated as an absent voter for an indefinite period owing to occupation or physical incapacity.

Form M: Application to vote by post owing to change of residence.

Form N: Application to be treated as an absent voter for a particular election.

Form O: Application to be treated as an absent voter for an indefinite period owing to air or sea journey.

Form P: Application for appointment of proxy.

Form Q: Application by a proxy to vote by post.

Form R: Application by service voter's spouse for appointment of proxy.

Form S: Return of expenses required by section 63 of the Representation of the People Act 1949 to be authorised by an election agent.

Form T: Declaration as to expenses required by section 63 of the Representation of the People Act 1949 to be authorised by an election agent.

In exercise of the powers conferred on me by sections 42 and 171(5) of the Representation of the People Act 1949(a), I hereby make the following Regulations:—

PART I

GENERAL

Citation and extent

1.—(1) These Regulations may be cited as the Representation of the People (Northern Ireland) Regulations 1969.

(2) These Regulations shall apply only to Northern Ireland.

Commencement

2.—(1) The following provisions of these Regulations, namely, Regulations 8, 9, 15, 16 to 45 (inclusive), 55, 56, 57(2) and 61, and so much of the Schedule as relates to those provisions, shall come into operation on 16th February 1970:

Provided that Regulations 16 to 45 (inclusive), 55, 56, 57(2) and 61 shall not have effect in relation to an election notice of which has been published before 16th February 1970.

(2) Except as otherwise provided by paragraph (1) of this Regulation, these Regulations shall come into operation fourteen days after they have been approved by both Houses of Parliament.

Revocation and savings

3.—(1) The following provisions of the Representation of the People (Northern Ireland) Regulations 1950(b), as amended (c), namely, Regulations 18, 19, 25 to 52 (inclusive), 64, 65(2) and (3) and 69 and so much of the Schedule to those Regulations as relates to those provisions, shall be revoked as from 16th February 1970:

Provided that Regulations 25 to 52 (inclusive), 64, 65(2) and (3) and 69 and so much of the Schedule to the Regulations of 1950 as relates to the said Regulations, shall continue to have effect in relation to an election notice of which has been published before 16th February 1970.

(2) Except as otherwise provided by paragraph (1) of this Regulation, the Representation of the People (Northern Ireland) Regulations 1950, the Representation of the People (Northern Ireland) Regulations 1952(d), the Representation of the People (Northern Ireland) Regulations 1953(e), the Representation of the People (Northern Ireland) Regulations 1954(f), and the Representation of the People (Northern Ireland) Regulations 1962(g) are hereby revoked.

(3) Section 38 of the Interpretation Act 1889(h) shall apply as if these Regulations were an Act of Parliament and as if any Regulations revoked by these Regulations were Acts of Parliament repealed by an Act of Parliament.

(4) Without prejudice to the said section 38 any register, list or record prepared, any application, appointment or declaration made, any proceedings initiated or other thing done under any Regulations revoked by these Regulations shall not be invalid by the revocation effected by paragraph (1) of this Regulation and shall, in so far as it could have been prepared, made, initiated or done under

---

(a) 1949 c.68. (b) S.I. 1950/1255 (Rev. XX, p.105: 1950 II, p.609).
(c) The amending instruments are S.I. 1952/1894, 1953/1108, 1954/499, 1962/1633 (1952 III, p.2821; 1953 II, p.1760; 1954 II, p.1923; 1962 II, p.1900).
(d) S.I. 1952/1894 (1952 III, p.2821). (e) S.I. 1953/1108 (1953 II, p.1760).
(f) S.I. 1954/499 (1954 II, p.1923). (g) S.I. 1962/1633 (1962 II, p.1900).
(h) 1889 c.63.

any provision of these Regulations, have effect as if it had been prepared, made, initiated or done under that provision.

Interpretation

4.—(1) For the purpose of these Regulations, unless the context otherwise requires—

the expression "the Act of 1949" means the Representation of the People Act 1949;

the expression "postal proxy" means a person entitled to vote by post as proxy at an election;

the expression "registration officer" means an electoral registration officer.

(2) Unless the context otherwise requires a claim or objection includes a claim or objection that a letter or date should or should not be placed against a person's name in the electors list and the register in accordance with Regulation 6(1)(*a*) or (*b*) or (2).

(3) A reference in these Regulations to any enactment or statutory instrument shall be construed as including a reference to that enactment or statutory instrument as amended or replaced by any other enactment or statutory instrument.

(4) A reference in these Regulations to a Regulation shall be construed as a reference to a Regulation contained in these Regulations.

(5) A reference in these Regulations to a form identified by means of a letter shall be construed as a reference to the form so identified in the Schedule to these Regulations.

(6) The Interpretation Act 1889 shall apply to the interpretation of these Regulations as it applies to the interpretation of an Act of Parliament.

PART II

REGISTRATION

The Register

Preparation of the register

5.—(1) The register shall, so far as practicable, be combined with the register of parliamentary electors or, as the case may be, the register of parliamentary and local electors prepared and published under section 28 of the Electoral Law Act (Northern Ireland) 1962(**a**), the names of persons registered only as parliamentary or local electors, or both, under that Act being marked to indicate that fact.

(2) All claims for registration and all objections to any person's registration shall be made within the time and in the manner prescribed by, and shall be dealt with in accordance with the provisions of, the said Act of 1962, so however that nothing in this paragraph shall apply to any appeal under section 45 of the Act of 1949 (which relates to registration appeals).

(3) Without prejudice to the provisions of the foregoing paragraph the register and electors list shall be prepared and published in the manner and for the time laid down by or under the said Act of 1962.

Marking of names to indicate manner of voting or persons not of voting age

6.—(1) To indicate the manner in which an elector is entitled to vote at an election there shall be placed—

(*a*) in the electors list and the register against the name of any elector who is a service voter the letter "S";

(*b*) in the electors list and the register against the name of any elector who is a merchant seaman the letter "M";

(**a**) 1962 c. 14 (N.I.).

(c) in any copy of the register or part thereof provided for a polling station—

   (i) against the name of any elector who is, or whose proxy is, entitled to vote by post the letter "A",

   (ii) against the name of any elector on behalf of whom a proxy is entitled to vote the letter "P".

(2) If an elector will attain voting age before the end of the twelve months following the day by which a register is required to be published but will not be of voting age on the first day of those twelve months, the date on which he will attain that age shall be placed against his name in the electors list as well as in the register.

Registration officer to furnish copies of register

7.—(1) A copy of the register shall, on publication, be furnished by the registration officer to the Secretary of State and the British Museum.

(2) An abstract of the contents of the register shall be furnished by, or on behalf of, the registration officer to the Secretary of State at such times and in such form and giving such particulars as the Secretary of State may require.

Free copies of register

8. The registration officer shall on request supply without fee—

(a) four copies of the register for the constituency (which may be printed on one side only) and four copies of the electors list therefor so long as the list is kept published, to any person who satisfies the registration officer that he requires them for use in connection with his own or some other person's prospective candidature at a parliamentary election for that constituency:

   Provided that not more than one person in respect of the same candidature shall be so supplied;

(b) two copies of the register for the constituency to each candidate at a parliamentary election for that constituency or his election agent.

Sale of register

9. The registration officer shall supply to any person copies of any part or parts of the register in force or of any electors list therefor, so long as there are sufficient copies available after allowing for the number which may be required for the purposes of any election (including the purposes of Regulation 8) on payment—

(a) in the case of a person who has been supplied in pursuance of Regulation 8 with a copy of the register or the electors list or who is a returning officer, of a fee at the rate of one shilling for each one thousand (or part of one thousand) names in such copy;

(b) in the case of any other person, of a fee at the rate of five shillings for each one thousand (or part of one thousand) names in such copy.

Supplementary

Declaration as to age and nationality

10.—(1) The registration officer before registering any person (other than a service voter) may, if he thinks it necessary—

(a) require that person either to produce a birth certificate or to make a statutory declaration as to the date of his birth;

(*b*) require that person either to produce a certificate of naturalisation or a document showing that he has become a British subject by virtue of registration, or to make a statutory declaration that he was a British subject or citizen of the Republic of Ireland on the qualifying date.

(2) Where a declaration is so made, any fee payable in connection therewith shall be paid by the registration officer as part of his registration expenses.

(3) Any such declaration shall be made available for inspection in the registration officer's office till completion of the hearing of claims and objections.

Power of registration officer to delegate his duties

11. The registration officer may require the town clerk of a borough or the clerk of the council of an urban district wholly or partly within the area for which he acts to perform on his behalf all or any of his registration duties so far as they relate to the preparation and publication of the electors list for any registration unit within the area of that borough or district, including the duty of carrying out a house to house or other sufficient inquiry as to the persons entitled to be registered (excluding persons entitled to be registered in pursuance of a service declaration), and to give information required for the purposes of his registration duties.

Information from householders

12. The registration officer may require any householder or person owning or occupying any premises within the area for which he acts or the agent or factor of any such person to give information required for the purposes of his registration duties.

Adaptation of electors list and register in consequence of altered polling districts

13. Where an alteration of parliamentary polling districts is made, the registration officer may—

(*a*) adapt the register to the alteration;

(*b*) if the alteration is made between the publication of any electors list and the coming into force of the register prepared from that list, frame the form of that register in accordance with the altered polling districts,

but except in cases where he does so an alteration of polling districts shall not be effective until the coming into force of the first register prepared from the electors list published after the alteration is made.

Corrupt and Illegal Practices List

Corrupt and illegal practices list

14.—(1) The corrupt and illegal practices list shall, so far as practicable, be combined with the corrupt and illegal practices list prepared and published under section 32 of the Electoral Law Act (Northern Ireland) 1962.

(2) Any person named in the corrupt and illegal practices list may claim to have his name omitted therefrom and any registration officer and any person named in the electors list for the register may object to the omission of the name of any person from such corrupt and illegal practices list: such claims and objections shall be sent to the same person and within the same time and be dealt with by the registration officer and the revising officer in like manner as nearly as circumstances permit as claims and objections relating to the electors list are to be sent and dealt with.

(3) Where, whether or not an objection to the omission has been made, it appears to the revising officer that a person not named in the corrupt and illegal

practices list ought to be so named, he shall, after giving such person an opportunity of appearing before him to show cause to the contrary, insert his name in such list and remove his name from the electors list.

(4) The corrupt and illegal practices list shall be published in the manner and for the time laid down by the Electoral Law Act (Northern Ireland) 1962.

(5) A copy of the corrupt and illegal practices list shall on publication be furnished by the registration officer to the Secretary of State and the British Museum.

Correction of Register

Correction of register

15.—(1) When a registration officer makes an alteration in a register pursuant to section 7(2) of the Representation of the People Act 1969, he shall—

(a) send to the person affected by the alteration and, if he gives effect to a decision on an objection made with respect to the electors list, to the objector a notice stating the alteration;

(b) make a copy of the alteration available for inspection at his office;

(c) make copies of the alteration available for inspection at the place at which copies of the part of the register to which the alteration relates have been made available for inspection;

(d) furnish a copy of the alteration to the Secretary of State and the British Museum;

(e) supply without fee a copy of the alteration to each person to whom he has supplied copies of the register or part thereof to which the alteration relates in pursuance of Regulation 8 or 9(a).

(2) Copies of alterations made available for inspection under this Regulation shall be kept available for the same length of time as the register is kept published.

PART III

ABSENT VOTERS, PROXIES AND POSTAL PROXIES

Application to be treated as an absent voter

16.—(1) An application to be treated as an absent voter shall be made in respect of each qualifying address and shall—

(a) be in Form N in any case where the application is made for a particular election only,

(b) be in Form M in any case where the application is based on the ground that the applicant no longer resides at his qualifying address,

(c) be in Form K in any case where the applicant is a service voter,

(d) be in Form R in any case where the applicant is the spouse of a service voter, has made a service declaration, but has not yet been registered as a service voter in pursuance of that declaration,

(e) be in Form O in any case where the application is based on the ground that the applicant is unable or likely to be unable to go in person from his qualifying address to the polling station without making a journey by air or sea,

(f) be in Form L in any other case.

(2) (a) An application to be treated as an absent voter based on the ground of religious observance shall not be allowed by the registration officer unless it

is accompanied by a certificate signed by a minister of the applicant's religious denomination certifying the nature and times of the religious observances and that the applicant is bound to observe them.

(b) An application to be treated as an absent voter based on the ground of physical incapacity shall be allowed by the registration officer if—

(i) the applicant has been registered as a blind person by a local authority under section 14(3)(h) of the Welfare Services Act (Northern Ireland) 1949(a); or

(ii) the application is accompanied by a certificate signed by a registered medical practitioner or a Christian Science practitioner certifying that the applicant is unable, or likely to be unable, by reason either of blindness or any other physical incapacity to go in person to the polling station or, if able to go, to vote unaided and estimating the probable duration of the period during which the applicant is likely to be so unable.

(3) An application to be treated as an absent voter shall be disregarded for the purposes of an election if it is received by the registration officer after the twelfth day before the day of the poll at that election:

Provided that an application on the grounds of the applicant's employment on the day of the poll by a returning officer or as a constable may be allowed after the said day.

(4) An application to be no longer treated as an absent voter may be disregarded for the purposes of an election if it is received by the registration officer after the twelfth day before the day of the poll at that election.

(5) The registration officer on disallowing a person's application to be treated as an absent voter shall notify the applicant of the fact.

(6) Where under section 13(3)(c) of the Act of 1949 the registration officer gives notice to an absent voter that he has reason to believe there has been a material change of circumstances, that person shall cease to be treated as an absent voter seven days after the date on which the registration officer sends such notice.

Record and list of absent voters

17.—(1) Subject to the provisions of this Regulation, the record and list of absent voters shall be in such a form as appears to the registration officer to be convenient.

(2) The address to which a ballot paper is to be sent shall be placed opposite the name and number in the register of each absent voter in the absent voters list unless a proxy (other than a service voter's proxy) has been appointed to vote on his behalf, in which case the letter "P" shall be placed opposite his name.

(3) As soon as the absent voters list has been prepared the registration officer shall publish it by making a copy thereof available for inspection at his office.

(4) The registration officer shall make a copy of the record of absent voters available for inspection at his office.

(5) As soon as practicable after the preparation of the absent voters list, the registration officer shall, on request and without fee, supply to each candidate or his election agent a copy of the absent voters list:

Provided that if such a request is made before any issue of ballot papers to

---

(a) 1949 c. 1 (N.I.).

those entitled to vote by post, the registration officer shall supply a copy of the said list, or a copy of so much of the said list as relates to that issue, before that issue.

Application to vote by proxy

18.—(1) An application by a service voter for the appointment of a proxy to vote on his behalf shall be in the form of Part 2 of Form G, H, I or J, as the case may be.

(2) An application by an absent voter who is not a service voter for the appointment of a proxy to vote on his behalf shall be in Form P or R, as the case may be.

Appointment of proxy

19.—(1) For the purpose of ascertaining in pursuance of section 14(4) of the Act of 1949 that a proxy is capable of being and willing to be appointed, the registration officer shall, unless he is satisfied that the person nominated in the application as first choice is not capable of being and willing to be appointed, notify him that a proxy paper will be issued to him unless within five days from the date of such notice the registration officer receives notice from him that he is not capable of being and willing to be appointed.

(2) If the person nominated as first choice is not capable of being and willing to be appointed, the registration officer shall, if another person is nominated as second choice, deal in like manner with such person:

Provided that if the application is received by the registration officer after publication of notice of an election, the registration officer need not do so until after the day of the poll for that election.

(3) If for any reason the registration officer does not issue a proxy paper in pursuance of an application made to him, he shall notify the person making the application why he has not done so.

Proxy paper

20.—(1) The proxy paper to be issued by the registration officer shall be in Form B.

(2) As soon as may be after issue of the proxy paper the registration officer shall send a notice of the fact to the elector stating the name of the person to whom the paper has been issued.

Cancellation and disregard of proxy appointment

21.—(1) Where the appointment of a proxy is cancelled by notice given to the registration officer or ceases to be or no longer remains in force under section 14(5) of the Act of 1949, the registration officer shall forthwith notify the person whose appointment as proxy has been cancelled or is no longer in force of the fact and remove his name from the record of proxies.

(2) Where a service voter is entitled to vote by post at an election, the registration officer shall forthwith notify his proxy (if any) of the fact and that his appointment will not have effect for that election.

(3) An application for the issue of a proxy paper shall be disregarded for the purposes of an election if it is received by the registration officer after the twelfth day before the day of the poll at that election.

(4) A notice cancelling the appointment of a proxy may be disregarded for the purposes of an election if it is received by the registration officer after the twelfth day before the day of the poll at that election.

Record and list of proxies

22.—(1) The record and list of proxies shall be in such a form as appears to the registration officer to be convenient.

(2) As soon as the list of proxies has been prepared, the registration officer shall publish it by making a copy thereof available for inspection at his office.

(3) The registration officer shall make a copy of the record of proxies available for inspection at his office.

(4) As soon as practicable after the preparation of the list of proxies, the registration officer shall, on request and without fee, supply to each candidate or his election agent a copy of the list of proxies.

Application by proxy to vote by post

23.—(1) An application by a proxy to vote by post shall be in Form Q.

(2) Such an application shall be disregarded for the purposes of an election if it is received by the registration officer after the twelfth day before the day of the poll at that election:

Provided that if under the proviso to Regulation 16(3) the applicant becomes entitled to vote by post as an absent voter after the said twelfth day, such an application may be allowed after the said twelfth day.

(3) The registration officer on disallowing such an application shall notify the applicant of the fact.

(4) An application under section 15(7)(*a*) of the Act of 1949 whereby a proxy ceases to be entitled to vote by post may be disregarded for the purposes of an election if it is received by the registration officer after the twelfth day before the day of the poll at that election.

Record and list of postal proxies

24.—(1) Subject to the provisions of this Regulation, the record and list of postal proxies shall be in such a form as appears to the registration officer to be convenient.

(2) The list of postal proxies shall give the name and number in the register of the elector and opposite them the name of the proxy and the address to which the ballot paper is to be sent.

(3) As soon as the postal proxies list has been prepared, the registration officer shall publish it by making a copy thereof available for inspection at his office.

(4) The registration officer shall make a copy of the record of postal proxies available for inspection at his office.

(5) As soon as practicable after the preparation of the postal proxies list, the registration officer shall, on request and without fee, supply to each candidate or his election agent a copy of the postal proxies list:

Provided that if such a request is made before any issue of ballot papers to those entitled to vote by post, the registration officer shall supply a copy of the said list or a copy of so much of the said list as relates to that issue, before that issue.

Certificate of employment

25. The certificate as to the employment of constables and persons employed by the returning officer on the day of the poll (to enable such a constable or person to vote elsewhere than at his own polling station) shall be in Form E and signed, in the case of a constable, by an officer of the Royal Ulster Constabulary of or above the rank of District Inspector.

PART IV

ISSUE AND RECEIPT OF POSTAL BALLOT PAPERS

Interpretation

Interpretation of Part IV

26. For the purpose of this Part of these Regulations, unless the context otherwise requires—

the expression "agent" includes the election agent and a person appointed to attend in the election agent's place;

the expression "issue" includes the original and any subsequent issue;

the expression "postal ballot paper" means a ballot paper issued to a postal voter;

the expression "postal voter" means a person entitled to vote by post at an election as an absent voter or as a proxy.

Issue of Postal Ballot Papers

Form of postal ballot paper

27. The ballot papers to be sent to postal voters shall be in the same form as, and indistinguishable from, the ballot papers delivered to other voters.

Form of declaration of identity

28. The declaration of identity sent with the ballot paper to a postal voter shall be in Form F.

Persons entitled to be present at issue and receipt of postal ballot papers

29.—(1) No person other than—

(*a*) the returning officer and his clerks,

(*b*) a candidate,

(*c*) an election agent or any person appointed by a candidate to attend in his election agent's place,

(*d*) any agents appointed under paragraph (2) of this Regulation,

may be present at the proceedings on the issue or receipt of postal ballot papers.

(2) Where postal ballot papers are to be issued, or the envelopes contained in the postal voters' ballot boxes are to be opened, simultaneously in two or more batches, each candidate may appoint one or more agents up to the number he may be authorised by the returning officer to appoint not exceeding the number of such batches so, however, that the number authorised shall be the same in the case of each candidate.

(3) Notice of the appointment stating the names and addresses of the persons appointed shall be given by the candidate to the returning officer before the time fixed for the issue of the postal ballot papers or the opening of the said postal voters' ballot boxes, as the case may be.

(4) If an agent dies or becomes incapable of acting, the candidate may appoint another agent in his place and shall forthwith give to the returning officer notice in writing of the name and address of the agent appointed.

(5) Agents may be appointed and notice of appointment given to the returning officer by the candidate's election agent instead of by the candidate.

(6) In this Part of these Regulations references to agents shall be taken as references to agents whose appointments have been duly made and notified

and, in the case of agents appointed under paragraph (2) of this Regulation, who are within the number authorised by the returning officer.

(7) A candidate may himself do any act or thing which any agent of his, if appointed, would have been authorised to do, or may assist his agent in doing any such act or thing.

(8) Where in this Part of these Regulations any act or thing is required or authorised to be done in the presence of the candidates or their agents, the non-attendance of any such persons or person at the time and place appointed for the purpose shall not, if the act or thing is otherwise duly done, invalidate the act or thing done.

Declaration of secrecy

30.—(1) Every person attending the proceedings on the issue or receipt of postal ballot papers shall make a declaration of secrecy in the form in paragraph (3) of this Regulation, or in a form as near thereto as circumstances admit, before the issue of postal ballot papers:

Provided that if any person attends only the proceedings on the receipt of postal ballot papers, he need not make the declaration before the issue but shall make it before he is permitted to attend the proceedings on the receipt of postal ballot papers.

(2) The returning officer shall make the declaration in the presence of a justice of the peace and any other person shall make the declaration in the presence either of a justice of the peace or of the returning officer or of a person who is the secretary of a county council or the town clerk of a borough and subsections (4) and (6) of section 53 of the Act of 1949 shall be read to the declarant by the person taking the declaration or shall be read by the declarant in the presence of that person.

(3) The declaration shall be as follows:—

"I solemnly promise and declare that I will not do anything forbidden by subsections (4) and (6) of section 53 of the Representation of the People Act 1949, which have been read to [by] me."

(4) Any person before whom a declaration is authorised to be made under this Regulation may take the declaration.

Notice of issue of postal ballot papers

31.—(1) The returning officer shall give each candidate not less than two days' notice in writing of the time and place at which he will issue postal ballot papers and of the number of agents he may appoint under Regulation 29(2) to attend the said issue.

(2) Where any subsequent issue of postal ballot papers is made, the returning officer shall notify each candidate as soon as practicable of the time and place at which he will make such subsequent issue and of the number of agents he may appoint under Regulation 29(2) to attend such issue.

Marking of postal ballot paper

32.—(1) Each postal ballot paper issued shall be stamped with the official mark either embossed or perforated, and the name and number in the register of the elector shall be called out, and such number shall be marked on the counterfoil, and a mark shall be placed in the absent voters list or the list of postal proxies against the number of the elector to denote that a ballot paper has been issued to the elector or his proxy but without showing the particular ballot paper issued.

(2) The number of a postal ballot paper shall be marked on the declaration of identity sent with that paper.

Refusal to issue postal ballot papers

33. Where a returning officer is satisfied that two or more entries in either the absent voters list or the list of postal proxies relate to the same elector or that a postal proxy has been appointed for a person entered in the absent voters list, he shall not issue more than one ballot paper in respect of the same elector.

Ballot paper envelope

34. The returning officer shall, in addition to the ballot paper, declaration of identity and envelope for their return (hereinafter referred to as a "covering envelope") which he is required by rule 25 of the parliamentary elections rules to send to a postal voter, send a smaller envelope marked "ballot paper envelope" bearing the number of the ballot paper.

Delivery of postal ballot papers to post office

35. Envelopes addressed to postal voters shall be counted and forthwith delivered by the returning officer to the nearest head post office, or such other office as may be arranged with the head postmaster, and the postmaster shall stamp with the post office date stamp a form of receipt to be presented by the returning officer stating the number of envelopes so delivered, and shall immediately forward such envelopes for delivery to the persons to whom they are addressed.

Provision of postal voters' ballot box

36.—(1) The returning officer shall, at the proceedings on the original issue of postal ballot papers, provide a ballot box or ballot boxes for the reception of the covering envelopes when returned by the postal voters.

(2) Every such ballot box shall be shown open and empty to the agents present and shall then be locked by the returning officer and sealed with the seal of the returning officer and the seals of such of the agents as desire to affix their seals in such manner as to prevent its being opened without breaking the seal.

(3) Every such ballot box shall be marked "postal voters' ballot box" and with the name of the constituency for which the election is held.

(4) The returning officer shall make provision for the safe custody of every such ballot box.

Sealing up of special lists and counterfoils

37.—(1) The returning officer, as soon as practicable after the completion of the issue of the postal ballot papers, and in the presence of the agents, shall make up in separate packets—

(a) the marked copies of the absent voters list and of the list of postal proxies, and
(b) the counterfoils of those ballot papers which were issued,
and shall seal such packets.

(2) The sealed packet containing the marked copies of the absent voters list and of the list of postal proxies may be opened by the returning officer for the purposes of a subsequent issue, and on completion of that issue the copies shall be again made up and sealed in accordance with the last foregoing paragraph.

Spoilt postal ballot paper

38.—(1) If a postal voter has inadvertently dealt with his postal ballot paper in such manner that it cannot be conveniently used as a ballot paper (in these

Regulations referred to as "a spoilt postal ballot paper") he may return (either by hand or by post) to the returning officer the spoilt postal ballot paper, the declaration of identity, the ballot paper envelope and the covering envelope.

(2) The returning officer, on receipt of the said documents, shall, unless the documents are received too late for another postal ballot paper to be returned before the close of the poll, issue another postal ballot paper and the foregoing provisions of this Part of these Regulations, but not sub-paragraph (*b*), (*c*) or (*d*) of paragraph (1) or paragraphs (2) to (8) of Regulation 29 or Regulation 31, shall apply accordingly.

(3) The spoilt postal ballot paper, the declaration of identity and the ballot paper envelope shall be immediately cancelled.

(4) The returning officer, as soon as practicable after cancelling the said documents, shall make up the said documents in a separate packet and shall seal the packet; and if on any subsequent occasion documents are cancelled as aforesaid, the sealed packet shall be opened and the additional cancelled documents included therein and the packet shall thereupon be again made up and sealed.

Receipt of Postal Ballot Papers

Receipt of covering envelope

39. The returning officer shall, immediately on receipt (whether by hand or by post) of a covering envelope before the close of the poll, place it unopened in a postal voters' ballot box locked and sealed in accordance with Regulation 36.

Opening of postal voters' ballot box

40.—(1) Each postal voters' ballot box shall be opened by the returning officer in the presence of the agents.

(2) So long as the returning officer secures that there is at least one postal voters' ballot box for the reception of covering envelopes up to the time of the close of the poll the other postal voters' ballot boxes may previously be opened by him.

(3) The returning officer shall give each candidate at least forty-eight hours' notice in writing of the time and place of his opening of each postal voters' ballot box and the envelopes contained therein and of the number of agents the candidate may appoint under Regulation 29(2) to be present at each opening.

Opening of covering envelopes

41.—(1) When a postal voters' ballot box has been opened, the returning officer shall count and note the number of covering envelopes, and shall then open each covering envelope separately.

(2) Where a covering envelope does not contain both a declaration of identity and a ballot paper envelope or, there being no ballot paper envelope, a ballot paper, he shall mark the covering envelope "rejected", attach thereto the contents (if any) of the covering envelope and place it in a separate receptacle (hereinafter referred to as "the receptacle for votes rejected"); and if the covering envelope does not contain the declaration separately, the returning officer shall open the ballot paper envelope to ascertain if the declaration is inside that envelope.

(3) On opening a covering envelope, other than one to which paragraph (2) of this Regulation applies, he shall first satisfy himself that the declaration of identity has been duly signed and authenticated and, if he is not so satisfied, he shall mark the declaration "rejected", attach thereto the ballot paper envelope

or, if there is no such envelope, the ballot paper, and place it in the receptacle for votes rejected:

Provided that before so doing he shall show the declaration to the agents and, if any objection is made by any agent to his decision, he shall add the words "rejection objected to".

(4) Where the number on the declaration of identity duly signed and authenticated agrees with the number on the ballot paper envelope, he shall place the declaration in a separate receptacle (hereinafter referred to as "the receptacle for declarations of identity") and the ballot paper envelope in another separate receptacle (hereinafter referred to as "the receptacle for ballot paper envelopes").

(5) Where there is no ballot paper envelope or the ballot paper envelope has been opened under paragraph (2) of this Regulation, he shall—

(*a*) where the number on the declaration of identity duly signed and authenticated agrees with the number on the ballot paper, place the declaration in the receptacle for declarations of identity and the ballot paper in a ballot box previously shown open and empty to the agents present and locked by the returning officer and sealed with the seal of the returning officer and the seals of such of the agents as desire to affix their seals in such manner as to prevent its being opened without breaking the seal, which shall be subsequently treated as a ballot box for the purpose of rule 46 of the parliamentary elections rules, and

(*b*) where the number on the said declaration does not agree with the number on the ballot paper, mark the declaration "rejected", attach thereto the ballot paper and place it in the receptacle for votes rejected.

(6) Where the number on the declaration of identity duly signed and authenticated does not agree with the number on the ballot paper envelope or that envelope has no number on it, he shall open the envelope and shall—

(*a*) where the number on the declaration agrees with the number on the ballot paper, place the declaration in the receptacle for declarations of identity and the ballot paper in the ballot box referred to in paragraph (5) of this Regulation, and

(*b*) where the number on the declaration does not agree with the number on the ballot paper or there is no ballot paper, mark the declaration "rejected", attach thereto the ballot paper (if any) and place it in the receptacle for votes rejected.

(7) Except for the purposes of ascertaining under paragraph (2) of this Regulation whether a ballot paper envelope contains a declaration of identity or under paragraph (6) of this Regulation whether the number on the declaration agrees with the number on the ballot paper, the returning officer shall not open the ballot paper envelopes before they are opened under Regulation 43.

Sealing up of rejected votes and declarations of identity

42. On the conclusion of the proceedings under Regulation 41 the returning officer shall put the contents of the receptacle for votes rejected and the contents of the receptacle for declarations of identity into two separate packets and shall seal up such packets.

Opening of ballot paper envelopes

43.—(1) After sealing up the said packets the returning officer shall open separately each ballot paper envelope placed in the receptacle for ballot paper envelopes.

(2) Where a ballot paper envelope does not contain a ballot paper, he shall mark the envelope "rejected".

(3) Where the number on a ballot paper envelope agrees with the number on the ballot paper contained therein, he shall place the ballot paper in the ballot box referred to in Regulation 41(5).

(4) Where the number on the ballot paper envelope does not agree with the number on the ballot paper contained therein, he shall mark the ballot paper "rejected" and attach the ballot paper envelope thereto.

(5) He shall put into a separate·packet the envelopes and the ballot papers marked "rejected" under the provisions of this Regulation and shall seal up such packet.

Abandoned poll

44. Where a poll is abandoned, or countermanded after postal ballot papers have been issued, by reason of the death of a candidate, the returning officer—

    (a) shall not take any step or further step to open covering envelopes or deal with their contents in accordance with the provisions of this Part of these Regulations, and

    (b) shall, notwithstanding Regulation 42 or 43, treat all unopened covering envelopes and the contents of those which have been opened as if they were counted ballot papers.

Forwarding of documents

45.—(1) The returning officer shall forward to the Clerk of the Crown for Northern Ireland at the same time as he forwards the documents mentioned in rule 56 of the parliamentary elections rules—

    (a) any packets referred to in Regulation 37, 38, 42 or 43, subject to the provisions of Regulation 44, endorsing on each packet a description of its contents, the date of the election to which it relates and the name of the constituency, and

    (b) a statement of the number of postal ballot papers issued in such form and giving such other particulars with respect to such papers as the Secretary of State may require.

(2) Where any covering envelopes are received by the returning officer after the close of the poll or any envelopes addressed to postal voters are returned as undelivered too late to be readdressed, or any spoilt postal ballot papers are returned too late to enable other postal ballot papers to be issued, he shall put them unopened into a separate packet, seal up such packet and forward it at a subsequent date in the manner described in paragraph (1) of this Regulation.

(3) Any packet or statement forwarded under this Regulation shall be deemed to have been forwarded in pursuance of the parliamentary elections rules.

(4) A copy of the statement referred to in paragraph (1) of this Regulation shall be furnished by the returning officer to the Secretary of State.

PART V

SERVICE VOTERS

Service declaration by members of the forces and spouses

46.—(1) A service declaration made by a member of the forces shall be in Form G.

(2) A service declaration made by the spouse of a member of the forces shall be in Form H.

(3) A service declaration made by either a member of the forces or his or her spouse shall be attested by a commissioned officer who is a member of the forces or by an officer of Her Majesty's Government in the United Kingdom or of Her Majesty's Government in Northern Ireland and shall be transmitted by or on behalf of the declarant to the appropriate registration officer.

Qualification for Crown servant

47. A person employed in the service of the Crown in a post outside the United Kingdom the occupant of which is required to devote his whole time to the duties of that post and the remuneration of which is paid wholly out of moneys provided by Parliament (hereinafter referred to as "a Crown servant") shall have a service qualification.

Service declaration by Crown servants, British Council employees and spouses

48.—(1) A service declaration made by a Crown servant or by a person who is employed by the British Council in a post outside the United Kingdom (hereinafter referred to as "a British Council employee") shall be in Form I.

(2) A service declaration made by the spouse of a Crown servant or of a British Council employee shall be in Form J.

(3) A service declaration made by a person who is or will be a Crown servant or by his or her spouse shall be attested by an officer of or designated by the Government department under which that person or his or her spouse is or will be employed or by another person himself having a service qualification through being employed in the service of the Crown in a post outside the United Kingdom.

(4) A service declaration made by a person who is or will be a British Council employee or by his or her spouse shall be attested by an officer of the British Council or by another person himself having a service qualification through being employed in the service of the Crown in a post outside the United Kingdom.

Transmission of service declaration by Crown servants, British Council employees and spouses

49.—(1) A service declaration made by a person who is or will be a Crown servant or by his or her spouse shall be transmitted by the declarant to the Government department under which that person or his or her spouse is or will be employed or to an officer designated by that department and transmitted by that department or officer to the appropriate registration officer.

(2) A service declaration made by a person who is or will be a British Council employee or by his or her spouse shall be transmitted by the declarant to the British Council and transmitted by the British Council to the appropriate registration officer.

Service declaration by person about to leave the United Kingdom

50. A service declaration made by a person about to leave the United Kingdom in such circumstances as to acquire a service qualification shall be made not more than six weeks before the date on which he expects to leave the United Kingdom.

Proceedings by registration officer on receipt of service declaration

51. Subject to Regulation 52, the registration officer on receipt of a service declaration shall notify the declarant that his declaration has been received.

Invalid service declaration

52.—(1) Where a service declaration does not appear—

(*a*) to be properly made out and attested, or

(*b*) to have been transmitted in the proper manner to the registration officer, the registration officer shall return the declaration to the declarant and explain his reasons for so doing.

(2) Where the registration officer has been notified by the appropriate Government department or an officer designated by that department or has been notified by the British Council that a person is not entitled to make a service declaration, he shall not enter that person's name in the electors list and shall notify that person that he has not done so but that that person may make a claim to be so entered.

Evidence as to service declaration

53. The registration officer shall treat a notice from the appropriate Government department or an officer designated by that department or a notice from the British Council that a person is not entitled to make a service declaration or that a person's service declaration has ceased to be in force as conclusive evidence thereof.

PART VI

SUPPLEMENTARY

Appeals

54.—(1) A person desiring to appeal against the decision of a registration officer must give notice of appeal to the registration officer and to the opposite party (if any) when the decision is given, or within fourteen days thereafter, specifying the grounds of appeal.

(2) The registration officer shall forward any such notice to the county court in the manner directed by rules of court together in each case with a statement of the material facts which in his opinion have been established in the case and of his decision upon the whole case and on any point which may be specified as a ground of appeal, and shall also furnish to the court any further information which the court may require and which he is able to furnish.

(3) Where it appears to the registration officer that any notices of appeal given to him are based on similar grounds, he shall inform the county court of the fact for the purpose of enabling the court (if it thinks fit) to consolidate the appeals or select a case as a test case.

(4) In relation to the determination of claims and objections with respect to registration any reference in this Regulation to the registration officer shall be construed as a reference to the revising officer.

Official poll card

55.—(1) The official poll card issued to an elector shall be in Form C.

(2) The official poll card issued to the proxy of an elector shall be in Form D.

Return and declaration of election expenses

56.—(1) The return and declaration of expenses required by section 63 of the Act of 1949 to be authorised by an election agent shall be in Forms S and T.

(2) The fee for inspecting a return or declaration (including any accompanying documents) specified in section 77(1) of the Act of 1949 (which relate to returns and declarations of election expenses) shall be five shillings.

(3) The price of a copy of any such return, declaration or document shall be at the rate of one shilling for the contents of each side of each page.

Forms

57.—(1) Form A may be used for the purpose for which it is expressed to be applicable.

(2) The registration officer shall without fee supply a reasonable number of copies of Forms K to R to any person.

(3) The forms set out in the Schedule to these Regulations or forms substantially to the like effect may be used with such variations as the circumstances may require.

Sending of notices, etc.

58.—(1) Any application, notice, claim or objection which is required by these Regulations to be made to the registration officer, revising officer or returning officer shall be in writing and sent by post or delivered to his office or to the address specified by him for the purpose.

(2) Where the registration officer, revising officer or returning officer is required by these Regulations to notify any person, such notification shall be in writing and may be sent by post—

(*a*) in the case of a person other than a service voter, to the address furnished by that person for the purpose of such notification or of any record or, if there is no such address, to the last known place of abode of that person;

(*b*) in the case of a service voter, to any address provided by him for the purpose of such notification or of any record or to the address provided for the purpose by the appropriate Government department or, as the case may be, the British Council.

Publication of documents

59.—(1) Any failure to publish a document in accordance with these Regulations shall not invalidate the document, but this provision shall not relieve the registration officer from any penalty for such a failure.

(2) A document which is made available for inspection in pursuance of these Regulations shall be made available during ordinary business hours.

(3) Where a document is made available for inspection, any person may make a copy of, or take extracts from, such document.

Misnomers

60. No misnomer or inaccurate description of any person or place in any notice, electors list, list of claims or objections, corrupt and illegal practices list, special list or register shall prejudice the operation of that document with respect to that person or place in any case where the description of the person or place is such as to be commonly understood.

Time

61.—(1) In computing for the purposes of Regulations 16, 21 and 23 the period of twelve days before the day of the poll at an election a Sunday, or a day of the Christmas break, of the Easter break or of a bank holiday break shall be disregarded.

(2) In this Regulation "the Christmas break", "the Easter break" and "a bank holiday break" have the same meanings as in rule 2 of the parliamentary elections rules.

Penalties

62.—(1) If any person fails to comply with or gives false information in pursuance of any such requisition of the registration officer as is mentioned in Regulation 12, he shall be liable on summary conviction to a fine not exceeding £50.

(2) If any person without lawful authority destroys, mutilates, defaces or removes any notice published by the registration officer in connection with his registration duties or any copies of a document which have been made available for inspection in pursuance of those duties, he shall be liable on summary conviction to a fine not exceeding £20.

> *James Callaghan,*
> One of Her Majesty's Principal
> Secretaries of State.

Home Office,
    Whitehall.
2nd June 1969.

SCHEDULE

FORMS

Forms for use by registration officers

FORM A: RETURN BY OCCUPIER AS TO RESIDENTS

Regulation 57.

REPRESENTATION OF THE PEOPLE ACTS

REGISTER OF ELECTORS 19

Qualifying date: 15th September 19 .
Qualifying period; the three months ending on 15th September 19 .

Register in force for twelve months from 16th February 19 .

I have to compile and publish an up-to-date Register of Electors for 19 . To do so, I need information which you, as Occupier, are obliged by law to supply. Please complete this form accurately and return it to me now—there is no need to wait until the qualifying date before doing so. You should also complete the form even though you intend to move house some time after the qualifying date.

Registers of Electors are needed so that everyone who is entitled to vote at parliamentary elections may do so. A person whose name does not appear in the Register cannot vote.

The notes within tell you how to fill up the form, but if you need any further help, I shall be glad to give it.

The Electoral Registration Officer

Please complete parts 1, 2 and 3 and sign the declaration (part 4)

Part 1. Address

No. of flat, room or floor (where applicable)	No. of house (or name, if it is not numbered)	Name of Street or Road	Town or townland: postal district or postcode (if any)

Part 2. Residents eligible to be included (*see* Notes 1 and 2)

If there are none, please write "None"

Surname and title (Mr., Mrs., etc.) (BLOCK LETTERS) Occupier's name first	Full Christian names or fore-names (BLOCK LETTERS)	If aged 18 on or before 16th February 19 enter a √ in this column	If 18th birthday is after 16th February 19 and on or before the following 15th February give date of birth (see note 1)	If a merchant seaman enter "M." (see note 1(e))

Part 3. Other residents

Is any part of your house/flat separately occupied by persons not entered above? Answer Yes or No

Part 4. Declaration

I declare that to the best of my knowledge and belief—

    (*a*) the particulars given above are true and accurate;

    (*b*) all those whose names are entered above are British subjects or citizens of the Irish Republic and are over 18 or will attain their 18th birthday on or before 15th February 19 .

Signature... Date........................

NOTES

1. You should enter every British subject (Commonwealth citizens are British subjects) or citizen of the Irish Republic who will be resident at your address on 15th September 19 , who has been residing there or elsewhere in Northern Ireland during the whole of the period of three months before that date, and who is 18 years of age or over on 16th February next, or whose 18th birthday is after 16th February next and on or before the following 15th February (people in this age-group can vote at elections held on or after the date of their 18th birthday).

You should include—

(a) Those who normally live at your address but are temporarily away, e.g. on holiday, as a student or in hospital (including informal patients in psychiatric hospitals);

(b) Resident guests, other than short-stay visitors;

(c) Lodgers and resident domestics;

(d) Any person who is away working, unless his absence will be for more than six months;

(e) Merchant seamen. Enter "M." against the name of a merchant seaman. He will then be invited to appoint a proxy to vote for him, or to vote by post. A merchant seaman may be included if he would have been resident at an address (including a hostel or club for merchant seamen) but for the nature of his occupation;

(f) Reservists called up for service or training.

2. Do not enter—

(a) Members of H.M. Forces

(b) Crown servants employed outside the United Kingdom

(c) Persons employed by the British Council in posts outside the United Kingdom

(d) Wives or husbands of members of H.M. Forces, of Crown Servants or of British Council staff employed outside the United Kingdom if they are living abroad to be with their husbands or wives as the case may be

Their names will be included in the Register if they have made the necessary service declaration; to do this they should apply to their Service or Department or the British Council.

(e) Aliens.

Regulation 20.

FORM B: PROXY PAPER

——————

REPRESENTATION OF THE PEOPLE ACTS

——————

Constituency..

Polling district..
    (Name of proxy)..
    (Address)...
    ....
    ....

is hereby appointed as proxy for
    (Name of elector)...

*Delete which-
ever is
inapplicable.

who is qualified as a $\frac{\text{*service voter}}{\text{resident}}$ to be registered for

(Qualifying address)..
....   *the parliamentary election for the above constituency
    on ....

to vote for *him/her at $\overline{}$
    *any parliamentary election for the above constituency
    (*see* Note 1)

This proxy appointment is not valid until..

Signature... Date.....................
(Electoral Registration Officer)
Address ....
    ....

NOTES

1. If your appointment as proxy is for a particular parliamentary election, it will be valid for that election only. In other cases your appointment will continue in force until the electoral registration officer informs you to the contrary (e.g. because the elector cancels it).

If the elector is shown on this form as a resident, your appointment will be valid for all elections for the constituency named above.

If the elector is shown on this form as a service voter, your appointment will be valid for all such elections unless the elector applies to vote by post at a particular election. If he does this, your appointment will be suspended for that election only and you will be so informed.

If a ballot paper is issued to the elector at the polling station before you apply for a ballot paper on his behalf, you will not be entitled to vote as proxy.

2. To vote as proxy at an election you must go in person to the polling station for the elector's qualifying address, except that you may apply to vote by post as proxy if either—

    (*a*) you are entitled to vote by post in respect of your own vote at the election
    or
    (*b*) your address is not in the same borough and constituency as the address for which the elector is registered, or is not within the same urban or rural district as that address.

Any application to vote by post as proxy should be made on Form Q which may be obtained from the electoral registration officer.

3. It is an offence to vote, whether in person or by post, as proxy for some other person if you know that that person is subject to a legal incapacity to vote, e.g. if that person has been convicted and is detained in a penal institution in pursuance of his sentence.

Forms for use by returning officers

FORM C: ELECTOR'S OFFICIAL POLL CARD

Regulation 55.

REPRESENTATION OF THE PEOPLE ACTS

Front of card

OFFICIAL POLL CARD

Constituency

....

Polling Day...

Your polling station will be

....

Number on Register....................

Name ....

Address ....

....

....

....

Back of card

PARLIAMENTARY ELECTION

The poll will be open from 7 a.m. to 10 p.m.

The address of your polling station is shown on the front of this card.

When you go to the polling station tell the clerk your name and address, as shown on the front of this card. The presiding officer will give you a ballot paper; see that he stamps the official mark on it before he gives it to you.

Mark your vote on the ballot paper secretly in one of the voting compartments. Put one X in the space to the right opposite the name of the candidate for whom you wish to vote. You may vote for only one candidate. If you put any other mark on the ballot paper, your vote may not be counted.

Then fold the ballot paper so as to conceal your vote, show the official mark on the back to the presiding officer and put the paper into the ballot box.

If you spoil the ballot paper by mistake do not destroy it; give it back to the presiding officer and ask for another.

ISSUED BY THE RETURNING OFFICER

Regulation 55.

FORM D: PROXY'S OFFICIAL POLL CARD

REPRESENTATION OF THE PEOPLE ACTS

Front of card

PROXY'S OFFICIAL POLL CARD

Proxy's name...

Proxy's address...

....

Back of card

PARLIAMENTARY ELECTION

.... CONSTITUENCY

Polling day...

The poll will be open from 7 a.m. to 10 p.m.

The elector named below whose proxy you are is entitled to vote at the polling station—

....

....

To vote as proxy you must go to that polling station. Tell the clerk that you wish to vote as proxy; give the name and qualifying address of the elector, as follows:—

Number on Register..

Name..

Address..

....

The presiding officer will give you the elector's ballot paper. The method of voting as proxy is the same as for casting your own vote.

It is an offence to vote as proxy for some other person if you know that that person is subject to a legal incapacity to vote, e.g. if that person has been convicted and is detained in a penal institution in pursuance of his sentence.

ISSUED BY THE RETURNING OFFICER

FORM E: CERTIFICATE OF EMPLOYMENT

REPRESENTATION OF THE PEOPLE ACTS

ELECTION IN THE

....CONSTITUENCY

I certify that (name)..who
is numbered........................in the register of electors for the constituency
named above, is likely to be unable to go in person to the polling station allotted
to him at the election on (date of poll)...
by reason of the particular circumstances of his employment on that date—

    *(a) as a constable,

    *(b) by me for a purpose connected with the election.

               Signature ....

               *Police Officer
                   (District Inspector or above)

               *Returning officer.

*Delete whichever is inapplicable.

Date................................

Note.—The person named above is entitled to vote at any polling station of
the above constituency on production and surrender of this certificate to the
presiding officer.

Regulation 28.

FORM F: DECLARATION OF IDENTITY

REPRESENTATION OF THE PEOPLE ACTS

Front of Form

Ballot Paper No......................................

I hereby declare that I am the person to whom the ballot paper numbered as above was sent.

Voter's signature (or mark)..

The voter, who is personally known to me, has signed (or marked) this declaration in my presence.

Witness's Signature...

SEE INSTRUCTIONS ON THE BACK OF THIS FORM

Back of form

INSTRUCTIONS TO THE VOTER

1. You must sign (or mark) the declaration of identity in the presence of a person known to you.

2. You may vote for not more than one candidate.

3. Place a cross (X) on the right-hand side of the ballot paper opposite the name of the candidate for whom you vote. Do this secretly: if you cannot vote without assistance, the person assisting you must not disclose how you have voted.

4. Put the ballot paper in the small envelope marked "A" and seal it. Then put the envelope marked "A", together with this declaration of identity, in the larger envelope marked "B". Return it without delay. The ballot paper, in order to be counted, must be received by the returning officer not later than the close of the poll.

5. If you receive more than one ballot paper, remember that it is illegal to vote more than once (otherwise than as proxy) at the same election.

6. At this election you cannot vote in person at a polling station, even if you receive an official poll card.

7. If you inadvertently spoil your postal ballot paper, you can apply to the returning officer for another one. With your application you must return, in a fresh envelope, the spoilt ballot paper, the declaration of identity and the envelopes marked "A" and "B". Remember that there is little time available if a fresh postal ballot paper is to be counted.

Forms for use by service voters

FORM G: SERVICE DECLARATION AND APPLICATION FOR APPOINTMENT OF PROXY BY A MEMBER OF THE FORCES

Regulation 46.

REPRESENTATION OF THE PEOPLE ACTS

REGISTER OF ELECTORS 19 .

Qualifying date: 15th September 19 .

Register in force for twelve months from 16th February 19 .

Part 1.

Surname ....
     (BLOCK LETTERS)

Other names...
     (BLOCK LETTERS)

Service (R.N., Army,
R.A.F., etc.)...............................Regiment or Corps..........................

Rank or Rating.........................Service No.......................................

Present service address...

       ....

I HEREBY DECLARE—

    (1) that I am a British subject or citizen of the Republic of Ireland;

    (2) that—

        *(a) I shall be 18 years of age or over on 16th February 19 ;
    OR

        *(b) (*if 18th birthday is after* 16*th February* 19 *and on or before the* *Delete which-
        following 15*th February*) my 18th birthday is on   ever is
                                     inapplicable.

Day	Month	Year
:	:	:

    (3) that I reside, or but for my service would reside, in the United Kingdom, and—

        *(a) reside, or but for my service would reside, at (full postal address in block letters)..

        ....

        ....

    OR

        *(b) (*if the declarant cannot give any such address*) have resided in the United Kingdom at (full postal address in block letters)

        ....

        ....

        ....

I HEREBY CANCEL any previous declaration made by me.

Signature of declarant....................................... Date........................

Signature and Rank of attesting officer (*see* Note 3).................................

NOTES

1. This declaration is to be made with a view to registration in the register of electors which will be in force for twelve months from 16th February 19   and with reference to your circumstances on the qualifying date for that register, i.e. 15th September 19   . A person whose service declaration is in force on the qualifying date is treated as resident in Northern Ireland during the qualifying period of three months before that date.

2. The declaration is to be made during the twelve months ending with the qualifying date.

3. The declaration must be attested by a commissioned officer or by an officer of a Government Department.

4. When completed and attested, this form should be sent to the Electoral Registration Officer.

Part 2.

Regulation 18.

PROXY APPOINTMENT

(While you are outside the United Kingdom you can vote only by proxy.)

I HEREBY CANCEL ANY PREVIOUS PROXY APPOINTMENT AND APPLY FOR THE APPOINTMENT AS MY PROXY OF—

Names of first choice..
  (BLOCK LETTERS)

Postal address...
  (BLOCK LETTERS)

Relationship, if any, to elector..

OR IF HE OR SHE IS UNWILLING OR UNABLE TO BE APPOINTED

Names of second choice...
  (BLOCK LETTERS)

Postal Address...
  (BLOCK LETTERS)

Relationship, if any, to elector..

Signature.. Date......................

NOTES

1. A person to vote as proxy must be a British subject or citizen of the Republic of Ireland, of voting age and not subject to any legal incapacity to vote.

A proxy appointed in consequence of this application will be entitled to vote for you at all parliamentary elections.

2. If the address in paragraph (3) of Part 1 is the same as that in your previous declaration (if any), you need not apply for the appointment of a proxy unless you want to appoint a different one; the previous appointment will remain valid. If, however, the address is different, you will need to apply afresh for the appointment of a proxy.

3. If at any time you wish to cancel the appointment of your proxy, you should notify the Electoral Registration Officer.

FORM H: SERVICE DECLARATION AND APPLICATION FOR APPOINTMENT OF PROXY BY THE SPOUSE OF A MEMBER OF THE FORCES

Regulation 46.

REPRESENTATION OF THE PEOPLE ACTS

REGISTER OF ELECTORS 19 .

Qualifying date: 15th September 19 .

Register in force for twelve months from 16th February 19 .

Part 1.

Surname ....
  (BLOCK LETTERS)

Other names..
  (BLOCK LETTERS)

Other names of *husband/wife...

Service (R.N., Army,
R.A.F., etc.).....................................Regiment or Corps.........................

Rank or Rating........................Service No......................................

Present address of *husband/wife..

....

I HEREBY DECLARE—

(1) that I am a British subject or citizen of the Republic of Ireland;

(2) that—

  *(a) I shall be 18 years of age or over on 16th February 19 ;
  OR
  *(b) (if 18th birthday is after 16th February 19 and on or before the following 15th February) my 18th birthday is on

Day	Month	Year
:	:	

*Delete whichever is inapplicable.

(3) that I reside, or expect to go abroad within six weeks (see Note 2) to reside, outside the United Kingdom to be with my *husband/wife who is a member of the forces;

(4) that but for my *husband's/wife's service I would be residing in the United Kingdom, and—

  *(a) would be residing at (full postal address in block letters)

  ....

  ....

  OR

  *(b) (if the declarant cannot give any such address) have resided in the United Kingdom at (full postal address in block letters)

  ....

  ....

  ....

I HEREBY CANCEL any previous declaration made by me.

Signature of declarant.................................... Date......................

Signature and Rank of attesting officer (see Note 3) ....

Notes

1. This declaration is to be made with a view to registration in the register of electors which will be in force for twelve months from 16th February 19   and with reference to your circumstances on the qualifying date for that register, i.e. 15th September 19 . A person whose service declaration is in force on the qualifying date is treated as resident in Northern Ireland during the qualifying period of three months before that date.

2. The declaration is to be made during the twelve months ending with the qualifying date, but a person about to leave the United Kingdom must not make it more than six weeks before the expected date of departure.

3. The declaration must be attested by a commissioned officer or by an officer of a Government Department.

4. When completed and attested this form should be sent to the Electoral Registration Officer.

Regulation 18. Part 2.

PROXY APPOINTMENT

(While you are outside the United Kingdom you can vote only by proxy.)

I HEREBY CANCEL ANY PREVIOUS PROXY APPOINTMENT AND APPLY FOR THE APPOINTMENT AS MY PROXY OF—

Names of first choice...
   (BLOCK LETTERS)

Postal address...
   (BLOCK LETTERS)

....

Relationship, if any, to elector...

OR IF HE OR SHE IS UNWILLING OR UNABLE TO BE APPOINTED

Names of second choice...
   (BLOCK LETTERS)

Postal address...
   (BLOCK LETTERS)

....

Relationship, if any, to elector...

Signature.. Date.........................

Notes

1. A person to vote as proxy must be a British subject or citizen of the Republic of Ireland, of voting age and not subject to any legal incapacity to vote. A proxy appointed in consequence of this application will be entitled to vote for you at all parliamentary elections.

2. If the address in paragraph (4) of Part 1 is the same as that in your previous declaration (if any) you need not apply for the appointment of a proxy unless you want to appoint a different one; the previous appointment will remain valid. If, however, the address is different, you will need to apply afresh for the appointment of a proxy.

3. If at any time you wish to cancel the appointment of your proxy, you should notify the Electoral Registration Officer.

FORM I: SERVICE DECLARATION AND APPLICATION FOR APPOINTMENT OF PROXY BY A CROWN SERVANT OR BY A PERSON EMPLOYED BY THE BRITISH COUNCIL

Regulation 48.

REPRESENTATION OF THE PEOPLE ACTS

REGISTER OF ELECTORS 19   .

Qualifying date: 15th September 19   .

Register in force for twelve months from 16th February 19   .

Part 1.

Surname ....
    (BLOCK LETTERS)

Other names...
    (BLOCK LETTERS)

I HEREBY DECLARE—

(1) that I am a British subject or citizen of the Republic of Ireland;

(2) that—

*(a) I shall be 18 years of age or over on 16th February 19   ;
OR

*(b) (*if 18th birthday is after 16th February 19   and on or before the following 15th February*) my 18th birthday is on

Day	Month	Year
:	.	:

(3) that I am employed, or leaving the United Kingdom to take up employment (*see* Note 2), in the service of the *Crown/British Council—

Description of post..

Name of Government Department under which you are employed (if applicable)...

Present address...

....

*Delete whichever is inapplicable.

(4) that but for my service abroad I would be residing in the United Kingdom, and—

*(a) would be residing at (full postal address in block letters)

....

....

OR

*(b) (*if the declarant cannot give any such address*) have resided in the United Kingdom at (full postal address in block letters)

....

....

....

I HEREBY CANCEL any previous declaration made by me.

Signature of declarant.................................Date..................

Signature of person attesting (*see* Note 3)..............................

Rank or official position..

NOTES

1. This declaration is to be made with a view to registration in the register of electors which will be in force for twelve months from 16th February 19   and with reference to your circumstances on the qualifying date for that register, i.e. 15th September 19   . A person whose service declaration is in force on the qualifying date is treated as resident in Northern Ireland during the qualifying period of three months before that date.

2. The declaration is to be made during the twelve months ending with the qualifying date, but a person about to leave the United Kingdom must not make it more than six weeks before the expected date of departure.

3. The declaration must be attested by an officer of, or designated by, the Government Department under which you are employed, or, as the case may be, by an officer of the British Council, or by another person who has a service qualification through being employed in the service of the Crown in a post outside the United Kingdom.

4. This form when completed and attested should be returned to the Government Department under which you are employed or to an officer designated by that Department or to the British Council as the case may be.

Regulation 18. Part 2.

PROXY APPOINTMENT

(While you are outside the United Kingdom you can vote only by proxy.)

I HEREBY CANCEL ANY PREVIOUS PROXY APPOINTMENT AND APPLY FOR THE APPOINTMENT AS MY PROXY OF—

Names of first choice..
    (BLOCK LETTERS)

Postal address ....
    (BLOCK LETTERS)

....

Relationship, if any, to elector..

OR IF HE OR SHE IS UNWILLING OR UNABLE TO BE APPOINTED

Names of second choice..
    (BLOCK LETTERS)

Postal address ....
    (BLOCK LETTERS)

....

Relationship, if any, to elector..

Signature... Date...............................

NOTES

1. A person to vote as proxy must be a British subject or citizen of the Republic of Ireland, of voting age and not subject to any legal incapacity to vote. A proxy appointed in consequence of this application will be entitled to vote for you at all parliamentary elections.

2. If the address in paragraph (4) of Part 1 is the same as that in your previous declaration (if any) you need not apply for the appointment of a proxy unless you want to appoint a different one; the previous appointment will remain valid. If, however, the address is different, you will need to apply afresh for the appointment of a proxy.

3. If at any time you wish to cancel the appointment of your proxy, you should notify the Electoral Registration Officer.

FORM J: SERVICE DECLARATION AND APPLICATION FOR Regulation 48. APPOINTMENT OF PROXY BY THE SPOUSE OF A CROWN SERVANT OR OF A PERSON EMPLOYED BY THE BRITISH COUNCIL

REPRESENTATION OF THE PEOPLE ACTS

REGISTER OF ELECTORS 19

Qualifying date: 15th September 19 .

Register in force for twelve months from 16th February 19 .

Part 1.

Surname ....

    (BLOCK LETTERS)

Other names...

    (BLOCK LETTERS)

Other names of *husband/wife...

I HEREBY DECLARE—

    (1) that I am a British subject or citizen of the Republic of Ireland;

    (2) that—

        *(a) I shall be 18 years of age or over on 16th February 19 .

    OR

        *(b) (if 18th birthday is after 16th February 19 and on or before the following 15th February) my 18th birthday is on

Day	Month	Year
:	:	:

    (3) that I reside, or expect to go abroad within six weeks (see Note 2) to reside, outside the United Kingdom to be with my *husband/wife, who is employed, or is leaving the United Kingdom to take up employment, in the service of the *Crown/British Council—

    Description of *husband's/wife's post... *Delete which-
ever is inappli-
cable.

    Name of Government Department under which employed (if applicable)

    ....

    Present address of *husband/wife...

    ....

    (4) that but for my *husband's/wife's service I would be residing in the United Kingdom, and—

        *(a) would be residing at (full postal address in block letters)

        ....

        ....

    OR

        *(b) (if the declarant cannot give any such address) have resided in the United Kingdom at (full postal address in block letters)

        ....

        ....

        ....

I HEREBY CANCEL any previous declaration made by me.

Signature of declarant...Date......................

Signature of person attesting (see Note 3)......................................

Rank or official position...

NOTES

1. This declaration is to be made with a view to registration in the register of electors which will be in force for twelve months from 16th February 19 and with reference to your circumstances on the qualifying date for that register, i.e. 15th September 19   . A person whose service declaration is in force on the qualifying date is treated as resident in Northern Ireland during the qualifying period of three months before that date.

2. The declaration is to be made during the twelve months ending with the qualifying date, but a person about to leave the United Kingdom must not make it more than six weeks before the expected date of departure.

3. The declaration must be attested by an officer of, or designated by, the Government Department under which your husband or wife is employed, or, as the case may be, by an officer of the British Council, or by another person who has a service qualification through being employed in the service of the Crown in a post outside the United Kingdom.

4. This form when completed and attested should be returned to the Government Department under which your husband or wife is employed or to an officer designated by that Department or to the British Council as the case may be.

Regulation 18.   **Part 2.**

PROXY APPOINTMENT

(While you are outside the United Kingdom you can vote only by proxy.)

I HEREBY CANCEL ANY PREVIOUS PROXY APPOINTMENT AND APPLY FOR THE APPOINTMENT AS MY PROXY OF—

Names of first choice..
    (BLOCK LETTERS)

Postal address ....
    (BLOCK LETTERS)

....

Relationship, if any, to elector...

OR IF HE OR SHE IS UNWILLING OR UNABLE TO BE APPOINTED

Names of second choice...
    (BLOCK LETTERS)

Postal address ....
    (BLOCK LETTERS)

....

Relationship, if any, to elector...

Signature.. Date............................

NOTES

1. A person to vote as proxy must be a British subject or citizen of the Republic of Ireland, of voting age and not subject to any legal incapacity to vote. A proxy appointed in consequence of this application will be entitled to vote for you at all parliamentary elections.

2. If the address in paragraph (4) of Part 1 is the same as that in your previous declaration (if any), you need not apply for the appointment of a proxy unless you want to appoint a different one; the previous appointment will remain valid. If, however, the address is different, you will need to apply afresh for the appointment of a proxy.

3. If at any time you wish to cancel the appointment of your proxy, you should notify the Electoral Registration Officer.

FORM K: APPLICATION BY A SERVICE VOTER IN THE UNITED KINGDOM TO VOTE BY POST

Regulation 16.

REPRESENTATION OF THE PEOPLE ACTS

I, (Surname)..
    (BLOCK LETTERS)

(Other names)..
    (BLOCK LETTERS)

(Rank or   (Service
Rating) .... No.)..

am registered as a service voter for

....

(Give the qualifying address which you gave on your service declaration)

and I apply for a ballot paper for the coming parliamentary election to be sent to me at

....

....

(Give full postal address in block letters)

Signature .... Date...........................

NOTES

1. If you have changed your name since completing your service declaration, put your former name in brackets after your present name.

2. You should send this application to the Electoral Registration Officer at the address stated on his acknowledgment of your service declaration.

Forms for use by other persons

Regulation 16. **FORM L: APPLICATION TO BE TREATED AS AN ABSENT VOTER FOR AN INDEFINITE PERIOD OWING TO OCCUPATION OR PHYSICAL INCAPACITY**

REPRESENTATION OF THE PEOPLE ACTS

(1) I, (Surname)...
    (BLOCK LETTERS)

(Other names)...
    (BLOCK LETTERS)

am qualified to be registered as an elector for (address in full in block letters)

....

....

....

(2) I apply to be treated as an absent voter at parliamentary elections because I am likely to be unable to go in person to the polling station (or, where (c) or (d) below applies, to vote unaided):

*Delete which-ever is inapplicable.

*(a) by reason of the general nature of my occupation, service or employment as

....
        (Give full reasons for application)

*(b) by reason of the general nature of the occupation, service or employment of my *husband/wife as

....

and my resulting absence from my qualifying address until...............
(insert likely date of return) to be with my *husband/wife

*(c) by reason of blindness† (in respect of which I have been registered as a blind person by the...
....Welfare Authority)

†If the applicant is not registered as a blind person delete the words and ask a medical practitioner to complete the certificate below.

*(d) by reason of physical incapacity (*see* Note 2)

Signature..   Date...................................

Address in the United Kingdom (in block letters) to which ballot paper is to be sent (if different from address given above)

....

....

MEDICAL CERTIFICATE

I certify—

(a) that the statement at (2) above is correct;

(b) that the applicant's inability is likely to continue for.....................
months/indefinitely*.

*It is important to indicate which alternative applies.

Signature ....

Address ....

....

....

Date..

NOTES

1. This application, if allowed, will continue in force until you cancel it or cease to be registered for your present qualifying address or become registered in a different capacity or until the Electoral Registration Officer gives you notice to the contrary. This application will be valid for all parliamentary elections at which you are entitled to vote. A separate application should be made for each qualifying address.

2. Where the ground of the application is blindness or other physical incapacity, the certificate above should be completed by a doctor (or by a Christian Science practitioner), unless you are registered as a blind person.

3. If the ground of the application is the nature of your occupation, service or employment (or that of your husband or wife) and you are likely to be at sea or out of the United Kingdom at the time of an election, you may apply to have a proxy appointed to vote for you. If so, apply on Form P which may be obtained from the Electoral Registration Officer.

4. If you have been appointed proxy for an elector in the same parliamentary constituency you may apply on Form Q to vote as such by post, but not if you yourself have a proxy appointed for you. Form Q may be obtained from the Electoral Registration Officer.

5. Any change of the address to which ballot papers are to be sent should be notified promptly to the Electoral Registration Officer. If you wait until an election occurs, you may be too late.

Regulation 16. FORM M: APPLICATION TO VOTE BY POST OWING TO CHANGE OF RESIDENCE

REPRESENTATION OF THE PEOPLE ACTS

I, (Surname)..
 (BLOCK LETTERS)

 (Other names) ....
 (BLOCK LETTERS)

am qualified to be registered as an elector for (old address in full in block letters)

....

....

....

I apply to be treated as an absent voter at parliamentary elections because I no longer reside there. My new address is (new address in full in block letters)

....

Signature.. Date...................................

NOTES

1. This application, if allowed, will continue in force for all parliamentary elections so long as you remain registered for your old address.

2. Temporary absence, e.g. on holiday, does NOT constitute a change of residence.

3. This application cannot be allowed if the address at which you now reside is in the same borough and constituency as the address for which you are registered, or within the same urban or rural district.

4. If you have been appointed proxy for an elector you may apply on Form Q to vote as such by post at parliamentary elections. Form Q may be obtained from the Electoral Registration Officer.

FORM N: APPLICATION TO BE TREATED AS AN ABSENT VOTER FOR A PARTICULAR ELECTION

Regulation 16.

REPRESENTATION OF THE PEOPLE ACTS

I, (Surname)..
     (BLOCK LETTERS)
     (Other names)..
     (BLOCK LETTERS)
am qualified to be registered as an elector for (address in full in block letters)
....
....
and I apply to be treated as an absent voter at the coming parliamentary election
(*see* Note 1)
in ....
constituency because I am likely to be unable to go in person to the polling
station allotted to me, owing to—

    (a) my service in one of Her Majesty's reserve or auxiliary forces
        (*see* Note 2)...;

    (b) my employment on polling day
        (i) as a constable;
        (ii) by the returning officer in connection with the election in
        ....constituency;

    (c) my being bound to the following religious observances (*see* Note 3)
        ....;

    (d) my acting as returning officer for...........................constituency;

    (e) my/my husband's/my wife's candidature
        in ....constituency;

*Delete whichever is inapplicable.

Signature .... Date.......................
  Address in the United Kingdom (in block letters) to which ballot paper is
to be sent (if different from address given above)
....
....

CERTIFICATE

To be completed where (c) above applies

I certify that the statement at (*c*) above is correct.
Signature ....
(Minister of the elector's religious denomination)
Address ....
....
Date.......................................

NOTES

1. Where (*a*), (*b*), or (*c*) applies, the application may be made for any parliamentary election. Where (*d*) or (*e*) applies, the application may be made for any parliamentary general election.

2. Where (*a*) applies, the application must state the name of the reserve or auxiliary force concerned. If the application is for a particular parliamentary election and you are likely to be at sea or out of the United Kingdom on polling day, you may apply on Form P to have a proxy appointed to vote for you.

3. Where (*c*) applies, the application must state the nature and times of the religious observances. The certificate above must be completed by a minister of your religious denomination.

4. If you have been appointed proxy for an elector in the same constituency, you may apply on Form Q to vote as such by post, but not if you yourself have a proxy appointed for you.

The forms referred to may be obtained from the Electoral Registration Officer.

FORM O: APPLICATION TO BE TREATED AS AN ABSENT VOTER FOR AN INDEFINITE PERIOD OWING TO AIR OR SEA JOURNEY

Regulation 16.

REPRESENTATION OF THE PEOPLE ACTS

I, (Surname)..
    (BLOCK LETTERS)

(Other names)..
    (BLOCK LETTERS)

am qualified to be registered as an elector for (address in full in block letters)

....

....

and I apply to be treated as an absent voter at parliamentary elections (*see* Note 1) because I am likely to be unable to go in person from the above address to the polling station without making a journey by air or sea.

Signature... Date..............................
    Address in the United Kingdom (in block letters) to which ballot paper is to be sent (if different from address given above)

....

....

NOTES

1. The journey in question is the journey necessary to go to the polling station from your qualifying address, not from where you may happen to be at the time of an election.

2. This application, if allowed, will continue in force until you cancel it or cease to be registered for your present qualifying address or become registered in a different capacity or until the Electoral Registration Officer gives you notice to the contrary. It will be valid for all parliamentary elections at which you are entitled to vote. A separate application should be made for each qualifying address.

3. If you have been appointed proxy for an elector in the same parliamentary constituency, you may apply on Form Q to vote as such by post, but not if you yourself have a proxy appointed for you. Form Q may be obtained from the Electoral Registration Officer.

4. Any change of the address to which ballot papers are to be sent should be notified promptly to the Electoral Registration Officer. If you wait until an election occurs, you may be too late.

FORM P: APPLICATION FOR APPOINTMENT OF PROXY

Regulation 18.

REPRESENTATION OF THE PEOPLE ACTS

(*Not to be used by service voters*)

I, (Surname)...
       (BLOCK LETTERS)
      (Other names)...
       (BLOCK LETTERS)
am qualified to be registered as an elector for (address in full in block letters)
....
....
....

I have applied to be treated as an absent voter—
    (*a*) at parliamentary and local government elections owing to—
      *(i) the general nature of my occupation, service or employment;
      *(ii) the general nature of the occupation, service, or employment
        of my *husband/wife and my resulting absence from my qualifying
        address to be with *him/her;

*Delete whichever is inapplicable.

    *(*b*) at the coming parliamentary election in.....................................
      constituency owing to my service in Her Majesty's reserve or auxiliary
      forces;
and I declare that I am likely to be at sea or outside the United Kingdom on
polling day.

I therefore apply for the person named below as first choice (or, if he or she is
unwilling or unable to be appointed, the person named as second choice) to be
appointed as proxy to vote for me.

PROXY APPOINTMENT

1. First choice (the elector must fill this up)

Full names..
    (BLOCK LETTERS)
Postal address..
    (BLOCK LETTERS)
....
Relationship, if any, to elector

....

2. Second choice (the elector should fill this up as the first choice may be
unwilling or unable to be appointed)

Full names..
    (BLOCK LETTERS)
....
Postal address..
    (BLOCK LETTERS)
....
Relationship, if any, to elector

....

Signature................................... Date...................

NOTES

1. A person to vote as proxy must be a British subject or citizen of the Republic of Ireland, of voting age and not subject to any legal incapacity to vote.

2. Where (*a*) applies, a proxy appointed in consequence of your application to be treated as an absent voter will be entitled to vote for you at all parliamentary elections. You can cancel the appointment by giving notice to the Electoral Registration Officer.

3. Where (*b*) applies, the proxy's appointment will be for a particular parliamentary election only.

Regulation 23.   ## FORM Q: APPLICATION BY A PROXY TO VOTE BY POST

REPRESENTATION OF THE PEOPLE ACTS

I, (Surname)..
    (BLOCK LETTERS)

(Other names)..
    (BLOCK LETTERS)

have been appointed proxy for

†As shown on proxy paper.

(†Name)...
    (BLOCK LETTERS)

who is registered as an elector for

(†Qualifying address)..
    (BLOCK LETTERS)

....

and I apply to vote by post as proxy for the above-named elector because

*Delete whichever is inapplicable.

    *(a) I am entitled to vote by post as an absent voter: the address for which I am registered as an elector is
    (address in full in block letters)

      ....

      ....

    *(b) the address entered below is in a different area from the address for which the above-named elector is registered (see Note 2).

A ballot paper should be sent to me at the following address (block letters) in the United Kingdom

....

....

....

Signature...................................... Date................................

NOTES

1. Where (a) applies, this application, if allowed, will be valid for all parliamentary elections for which your application to be treated as an absent voter is valid so long as your appointment as proxy continues. Where (b) applies, the application will remain in force until you cancel it or cease to be proxy for the elector.

2. Where (b) applies, the application cannot be allowed if your address is in the same area as the address for which the elector is registered, i.e. within the same borough and constituency or within the same urban or rural district.

FORM R: APPLICATION BY SERVICE VOTER'S SPOUSE FOR APPOINTMENT OF PROXY

Regulations 16, 18.

REPRESENTATION OF THE PEOPLE ACTS

Part 1.

Surname ....
(BLOCK LETTERS)
Other names..
(BLOCK LETTERS)
Other names of *husband/wife...
    *(a) Service (R.N.,   Regiment
    Army, R.A.F., etc.).....................or Corps..................
    Rank or Rating.......................Service No....................
    OR
    *(b) Name of Government Department under   Description
    which *husband/wife employed....................of post.................
    OR
    *(c) British Council   Description
      of post...............................

*Delete whichever is inapplicable.

Present address of *husband/wife
....
....

(1) I am qualified to be registered as an elector for (address in full in block letters)
....
....

(2) I have made a service declaration on Form H/Form J that I reside, or expect to go abroad within six weeks to reside, outside the United Kingdom to be with my *husband/wife.

(3) I therefore apply to be treated as an absent voter and for the person named below as first choice (or, if he or she is unwilling or unable to be appointed, the person named as second choice) to be appointed to vote as proxy for me at parliamentary elections.

Part 2.

PROXY APPOINTMENT

1. First choice (the elector must fill this up)
Full names...
(BLOCK LETTERS)
Postal address...
(BLOCK LETTERS)
....
Relationship, if any, to elector
....

2. Second choice (the elector should fill this up as the first choice may be unwilling or unable to be appointed)
Full names...
(BLOCK LETTERS)
Postal address...
(BLOCK LETTERS)
....
Relationship, if any, to elector
....

Signature............................ Date...............................

NOTE

1. A person to vote as proxy must be a British subject or citizen of the Republic of Ireland, of voting age and not subject to any legal incapacity to vote. A proxy appointed in consequence of this application will be entitled to vote for you at all parliamentary elections.

Regulation 56. **FORM S: RETURN OF EXPENSES REQUIRED BY SECTION 63 OF THE REPRESENTATION OF THE PEOPLE ACT 1949 TO BE AUTHORISED BY AN ELECTION AGENT**

———

REPRESENTATION OF THE PEOPLE ACTS

———

ELECTION IN THE

.... CONSTITUENCY

Date of publication of notice of election..

The expenses incurred at the above election in support of............................

....a candidate thereat, by.............................

....

(*insert name of person or association or body of persons incurring the expenses*) being expenses required by section 63 of the Representation of the People Act 1949 to be authorised by the election agent, amounted to £..........................

The written authority of the election agent is annexed hereto.

Signature... Date....................................

FORM T: DECLARATION AS TO EXPENSES REQUIRED BY SECTION 63 OF THE REPRESENTATION OF THE PEOPLE ACT 1949 TO BE AUTHORISED BY AN ELECTION AGENT _{Regulation 56.}

REPRESENTATION OF THE PEOPLE ACTS

ELECTION IN THE

.... CONSTITUENCY

Date of publication of notice of election..
I hereby declare that—

1. I am the person *or* a director, general manger, secretary or similar officer of the association or body of persons named as incurring expenses in the accompanying return, marked................, of expenses required by section 63 of the Representation of the People Act 1949 to be authorised by an election agent.

2. To the best of my knowledge and belief the said return is complete and correct.

3. The matters for which the following expenses referred to in the said return were incurred were as follows..

....

....

Signature ....

Office held..:..................
(In the case of an association or body of persons)

Date.......................................

EXPLANATORY NOTE

(This Note is not part of the Regulations.)

These Regulations revoke and replace the Representation of the People (Northern Ireland) Regulations 1950, as amended. Amendments have been made in consequence of the passing of the Representation of the People Act 1969 (c.15). In particular provision is made for marking the names of persons coming of voting age during the currency of the register and of merchant seamen (Regulation 6); for correcting the published register (Regulation 15); for applications to be treated as absent voters based on the ground of religious observance (Regulation 16(2)(*a*)); for service declarations by British Council employees (Part V of the Regulations); prescribing the fees for inspection and copies of the return and declaration of election expenses (Regulation 56); and for the computation of time (Regulation 61).

Other amendments have also been made. In particular the fees for the sale of the register (Regulation 9) and the penalties for certain offences (Regulation 62) have been varied: spoilt postal ballot papers may be replaced (Regulation 38); and the procedure for dealing with postal ballot papers where a candidate has died has been specified (Regulation 44).

STATUTORY INSTRUMENTS

1969 No. 906

NATIONAL HEALTH SERVICE, ENGLAND AND WALES

The National Health Service (Charges for Appliances) Regulations 1969

Made - - - -	*3rd July* 1969	
Laid before Parliament	*8th July* 1969	
Coming into Operation	*11th August* 1969	

The Secretary of State for Social Services, in exercise of his powers under sections 41 and 74 of the National Health Service Act 1946(a), section 1 of, and the Schedule to, the National Health Service Act 1951(b), section 7 of the National Health Service Act 1952(c) and section 2 of the National Health Service Act 1961(d), and of all other powers enabling him in that behalf, hereby makes the following regulations:—

1.—(1) These regulations may be cited as the National Health Service (Charges for Appliances) Regulations 1969 and shall come into operation on 11th August 1969.

(2) The Interpretation Act 1889(e) applies to the interpretation of these regulations as it applies to the interpretation of an Act of Parliament.

2. The authorised charge per lens (specified in the Schedule to the National Health Service Act 1951 for glasses other than children's glasses) which was increased by section 1(2) of the National Health Service Act 1961 to 12s. 6d., or in the case of a bifocal or multifocal lens to 20s. 0d., is hereby increased to 16s. 0d., or in the case of a bifocal or multifocal lens to 25s. 0d.

3. The authorised charges specified in the Schedule to the National Health Service Act 1951 for one denture with the number of teeth specified in Column 1 of the table below shall, instead of being the amount specified in relation thereto in Column 2 (being the amount specified in section 1(1) of the National Health Service Act 1961), be the amount specified in relation thereto in Column 3.

TABLE

Column 1				*Column 2*			*Column 3*		
				£	s.	d.	£	s.	d.
1, 2 or 3 teeth	..	..	..	2	5	0	2	16	0
4 to 8 teeth ..	..	..	..	2	10	0	3	2	0
More than 8 teeth ..	..	..		2	15	0	3	9	0

4. The maximum charge specified in section 2(2) of the National Health Service Act 1952 (maximum charge for services some of which are chargeable under the Act of 1951), which was increased to £5 by section 1(1) of the National Health Service Act 1961, shall be increased to £6 5s. 0d.

5. No charge, which would otherwise be payable under section 1 of the National Health Service Act 1951, shall be payable in respect of the supply (including the replacement) of a dental appliance as part of hospital and specialist services to a person who has undergone operative procedures affecting the mandible, the maxilla, or the soft tissues of the mouth as part of treatment for invasive tumours.

(a) 1946 c. 81.   (b) 1951 c. 31.   (c) 1952 c. 25.   (d) 1961 c. 19.   (e) 1889 c. 63.

6. The National Health Service (Supplementary Ophthalmic Services) Regulations 1956(a), as amended(b), shall be further amended as follows:—

(1) For regulation 14(1) (making and recovery by opticians of charges for the supply of optical appliances), as substituted by regulation 3(3) of the National Health Service (Supplementary Ophthalmic Services) (No. 1) Regulations 1961(c), there shall be substituted the following paragraph:—

" **14.**—(1) Subject to the provisions of this regulation, an optician shall, in respect of the supply under these regulations of such optical appliances as are described in the Schedule to the National Health Service Act 1951 be entitled to make and recover the appropriate charge specified in the said Schedule, as varied by section 1 of the National Health Service Act 1961 or by regulations made under section 2 of the said Act."

(2) In Part VII of Form No. 1 of Schedule 3, as substituted by regulation 3(6) of the said regulations of 1961, for the expression " 12s. 6d." there shall be substituted the expression " 16s. 0d." and for the expression " 20s. 0d." there shall be substituted the expression " 25s. 0d.".

7. In the National Health Service (Charges for Appliances) Regulations 1951(d), as amended by the National Health Service (Charges for Appliances) Regulations 1961(e), for regulation 3 there shall be substituted the following regulation:—

" **3.** These regulations relate to the charges authorised by the National Health Service Act 1951, as varied by section 1 of the National Health Service Act 1961 or by regulations made under section 2 of the said Act, to be made and recovered in respect of the supply of dental and optical appliances under Part II of the National Health Service Act 1946."

8. These regulations shall not have effect—

(*a*) in relation to a dental appliance supplied under Part II of the National Health Service Act 1946 or to an optical appliance supplied under Part II or Part IV thereof, if the examination or testing of sight leading to the supply of the appliance, or the first such examination or testing, took place before the commencement of these regulations; or

(*b*) in relation to a dental appliance supplied under Part IV of the said Act of 1946 or in relation to services provided as part of the general dental services under Part IV thereof, if the contract or arrangement in pursuance of which the appliance is supplied or the services are provided was made before the commencement of these regulations.

R. H. S. Crossman,

Secretary of State for Social Services.

3rd July 1969.

(a) S.I. 1956/1078 (1956 I, p. 1524).
(b) The relevant amending instrument is S.I. 1961/908 (1961 II, p. 1752).
(c) S.I. 1961/908 (1961 II, p. 1752).   (d) S.I. 1951/843 (1951 I, p. 1389).
(e) S.I. 1961/909 (1961 II, p. 1757).

EXPLANATORY NOTE

(This Note is not part of the Regulations.)

These Regulations increase the authorised charge for glasses supplied under the National Health Service by increasing the charge per lens from 12*s*. 6*d*. to 16*s*. 0*d*. for single-vision lenses and from 20*s*. 0*d*. to 25*s*. 0*d*. for bifocal or multi-focal lenses. They also increase the authorised charges for the supply of dentures and the maximum charge for a course of dental treatment including the provision of dentures, and make consequential amendments to the regulations dealing with the recovery of charges.

The regulations also exempt from charges for dentures supplied by hospitals persons who have undergone operative procedures affecting the mouth as part of treatment for invasive tumours.

STATUTORY INSTRUMENTS

1969 No. 909

WAGES COUNCILS

The Wages Regulation (Brush and Broom) (Amendment) (No. 2) Order 1969

Made - - -	*3rd July* 1969
Coming into Operation	*25th July* 1969

Whereas the Secretary of State has received from the Brush and Broom Wages Council (Great Britain) the wages regulation proposals set out in the Schedule hereto;

Now, therefore, the Secretary of State in exercise of her powers under section 11 of the Wages Councils Act 1959(a), and of all other powers enabling her in that behalf, hereby makes the following Order:—

1. This Order may be cited as the Wages Regulation (Brush and Broom) (Amendment) (No. 2) Order 1969.

2.—(1) In this Order the expression "the specified date" means the 25th July 1969, provided that where, as respects any worker who is paid wages at intervals not exceeding seven days, that date does not correspond with the beginning of the period for which the wages are paid, the expression "the specified date" means, as respects that worker, the beginning of the next such period following that date.

(2) The Interpretation Act 1889(b) shall apply to the interpretation of this Order as it applies to the interpretation of an Act of Parliament.

3. The wages regulation proposals set out in the Schedule hereto shall have effect as from the specified date and as from that date the Wages Regulation (Brush and Broom) (Amendment) Order 1969(c) shall cease to have effect.

Signed by order of the Secretary of State.
3rd July 1969.

A. A. Jarratt,

Deputy Under Secretary of State,
Department of Employment and Productivity.

(a) 1959 c. 69.   (b) 1889 c. 63.   (c) S.I. 1969/208 (1969 I, p. 528).

SCHEDULE   Article 3

STATUTORY MINIMUM REMUNERATION

The Wages Regulation (Brush and Broom) Order 1967 (a) (Order M. (105)) shall have effect as if in Schedule 1 thereto:—

1   for Parts II and III there were substituted the following Parts:—

"PART II
GENERAL MINIMUM TIME RATES AND PIECE WORK BASIS TIME RATE FOR MALE WORKERS
GENERAL MINIMUM TIME RATES

4.—(1) The general minimum time rates payable to male workers other than the apprentices to whom Part IV of this Schedule applies are as follows:—

	Per hour s. d.
(a) Workers (of any age) who have completed an apprenticeship of not less than three years in one or more of the operations or branches of work specified in (a) of sub-paragraph (2) of this paragraph ...	6 2½
(b) Workers (other than those specified at (a) of this sub-paragraph) who are employed in any of the operations or branches of work specified in (a) or (b) of sub-paragraph (2) of this paragraph and have had not less than three years' experience in one or more of them, being aged:—	
(i) 19 years or over	6 2½
(ii) 18 years and under 19 years	5 3½
(c) Workers who are wholly or mainly employed in any of the operations specified in (c) of sub-paragraph (2) of this paragraph and have had not less than three years' experience in one or more of them, being aged:—	
21 years or over	6 2½
(d) All other workers, being aged:—	
21 years or over	5 9
20 ,, and under 21 years	5 1
19 ,, ,, ,, 20 ,, ...	4 6
18 ,, ,, ,, 19 ,, ...	4 0
17½ ,, ,, ,, 18 ,, ...	3 4
17 ,, ,, ,, 17½ ,, ...	3 0½
16½ ,, ,, ,, 17 ,, ...	2 10
16 ,, ,, ,, 16½ ,, ...	2 7½
15½ ,, ,, ,, 16 ,, ...	2 5½
under 15½ years	2 3½

Provided that where the worker is employed on any of the operations specified in (b) or (c) of sub-paragraph (2) of this paragraph, and has had more than six months' but less than three years' experience on one or more of such operations, the general minimum time rate otherwise payable to the worker shall be increased as follows but so as in no case to exceed 6s. 2½d. per hour:—

	Per hour d.
During the 2nd six months of such experience	1½
During the 3rd six months of such experience	2½
During the 4th six months of such experience	3½
During the 5th six months of such experience	4½
During the 6th six months of such experience	5½

(a) S.I. 1967/1759 (1967 III, p. 4669).

(2) The operations or branches of work referred to in the last foregoing sub-paragraph are as follows:—

(a) 'Pan' (hair and bass), 'Hairs,' 'Finishing' (that is, the work of all wood-workers employed in finishing or part-finishing brushes or brooms by hand or machine), 'Boring or Drilling' (hand and machine), 'Drawing', 'Bone brush cutting,' 'Bone brush fashioning,' 'Bone brush drilling,' 'Bone brush profiling', the manufacture of artists', medical, painting, whitewash and tar brushes, and brushes not otherwise specified; and (i) the drafting, dressing (including cutting), or mixing of animal hair, bass, whisk or other fibre where the operative performs the aforesaid operations singly or in combination by hand or partly by hand and partly by machine; (ii) the working of ivory or celluloid; (iii) the turning of bone; where all or any of the operations specified in (i), (ii) or (iii) are carried on in association with or in conjunction with the manufacture of brushes (other than feather brushes) or brooms.

(b) The dressing of bass or fibre by hand or by machine; the cutting and preparation of material for toilet or tooth-brush manufacture; the shaping (including the setting-up of knives and other incidental work) of wooden or plastic boards or handles by spindle moulding or automatic shaping machine or by both such machines; boring; hand finishing; hand drawing; machine filling; the flirting, brushing, trimming, examining of brushes; polishing or hand polishing, dipping and cellulose spraying; sand-papering and buffing, the making of twisted wire brushes; the making of artists' brushes.

(c) The receiving, keeping and storing of stock including raw materials; the packing and despatching of the finished products.

PIECE WORK BASIS TIME RATE

5.   The piece work basis time rate applicable to workers specified in (a) or (b) of sub-paragraph (1) of paragraph 4 is 6s. 9d. per hour.

PART III
GENERAL MINIMUM TIME RATES AND PIECE WORK BASIS TIME RATES FOR FEMALE WORKERS

6.—(1) The following rates apply to female workers other than the apprentices to pan setting to whom paragraph 7 applies:—

	General minimum time rates Per hour s. d.	Piece work basis time rates Per hour s. d.
(a) Pan Hands of any age employed on:—		
(i) Coco or any other fibre brooms or banisters of any length (except bass and bassine heads on stocks over 12 in. in length and more than 30 knots round, and whisk brooms and banisters). Bass heads up to 12 in. stock, 30 knots round.	4 10	5 0
(ii) Broom heads up to 11½ in. stock, or banisters up to 8¼ in. blade, middles being made of all fibre or fibre and drafts mixed up to 3½ in., and outsides of any material up to and including 3½ in. Banisters (whisk) up to 7½ in. blade made with common Venetian tops (imported as tops); sweeps' hand brushes up to and including 5 in. blade, or toy hearth brushes up to and including 3½ in., both made with fibre, fibre and drafts, drafts only or china below 3 in. But excluding any brushes provided for in (a) (i) of this sub-paragraph.	5 3½	5 5½
(iii) Work other than that provided for in (a) (i) and (ii) of this sub-paragraph	6 2½	6 6½

(b) Drawing Hands employed on drawing wire brushes (with or without the operation of trimming) of:—
 (i) 38 gauge wire or finer 4 11   5 1
 (ii) thicker than 38 gauge wire 5 2½   5 4½
(c) Workers employed on any of the operations specified in sub-paragraph (2) of this paragraph who have had not less than three years' experience in one or more of such operations 4 2   4 5
(d) All other workers, being aged:—
 19 years or over 4 0
 18 years and under 19 years 3 8
 17½ ,, ,, ,, 18 ,, ...   3 4
 17 ,, ,, ,, 17½ ,, ...   3 0½   4 5
 16½ ,, ,, ,, 17 ,, ...   2 10
 16 ,, ,, ,, 16½ ,, ...   2 7½
 15½ ,, ,, ,, 16 ,, ...   2 5½
 under 15½ years 2 3½

Provided that where the worker is employed on any of the operations specified in sub-paragraph (2) of this paragraph and has had more than six months' but less than three years' experience on one or more of such operations, the general minimum time rate otherwise payable to the worker shall be increased as follows but so as in no case to exceed 4s. 2d. per hour.

Per hour
d.
During the 2nd six months of such experience 1
During the 3rd six months of such experience 1½
During the 4th six months of such experience 2
During the 5th six months of such experience 2½
During the 6th six months of such experience 3

(2) The operations referred to in (c) and (d) of the last foregoing sub-paragraphs are as follows:—

The dressing of bass or fibre by hand or by machine; the cutting and preparation of material for toilet or tooth-brush manufacture; the shaping (including the setting-up of knives and other incidental work) of wooden or plastic boards or handles by spindle moulding or automatic shaping machine or by both such machines; boring; hand finishing; hand drawing (other than the hand drawing of wire brushes); machine filling; the flirting, brushing, trimming, examining of brushes; polishing or hand polishing, dipping and cellulose spraying; sand-papering and buffing, the making of twisted wire brushes; the making of artists' brushes; making painting brushes by sectional methods; finishing painting brushes by sectional methods; making shaving brushes by sectional methods; finishing shaving brushes by sectional methods."

2. for Part VI there were substituted the following part:—

"PART VI
GENERAL MINIMUM PIECE RATES FOR MALE OR FEMALE WORKERS

15. The general minimum piece rates payable to the workers to whom this Schedule applies, other than the female apprentices to pan setting and the male apprentices to whom the minimum rates specified in Part IV respectively apply, are the piece rates specified in Part VII or Part VIII of the Schedule increased by 170 per cent."

3. for sub-paragraph (3) of paragraph 16 there were substituted the following sub-paragraph:—

"(3) EXTRAS TO COLUMN 2 ARE AS FOLLOWS:—

Knots less
per penny
Banisters and dust (sweeps) with handles (excluding blade), 20 inches long or over ... ... ½

Setting with Gumati	$\frac{1}{2}$
Setting with Kitool	$\frac{1}{4}$
Setting all work with a mixture of another material with Kitool, Gumati, bone or bassine	$\frac{1}{2}$
Setting all work with used hair	1
Setting all work with riflings, drafts, rough undressed hair or shake-up	1
Setting all work except stipplers with China 3 in. and up to and including 3¼ in.	$\frac{1}{2}$
Setting all work, except stipplers, with China under 3 in.	1
Setting all work, except stipplers, with any material (dressed or undressed) under 3 in., other than China	$\frac{1}{2}$
Cutting off toilet banisters...	1
Setting with glue	1
Cement prepared by operator	$\frac{1}{2}$
Cutting off carpet banisters and brooms...	$\frac{1}{2}$
Cutting coco 2d. per doz. brushes.	
Boring and setting banisters of over ⅝-in. and not exceeding ⅞-in. diam. ...	$\frac{1}{2}$
Boring and setting banisters ⅝-in. diam. and under	1
Setting brushes containing only 5 knots	$\frac{1}{2}$
Setting brushes containing only 4 knots	$\frac{1}{2}$
Setting brushes containing only 3 knots	1
Setting brushes containing only 2 knots	$1\frac{1}{2}$
Setting brushes containing only 1 knot	2
Work with synthetic monofilaments up to and including ·008-in. gauge ...	1
Work with synthetic monofilaments gauges ·009 to ·019-in. inclusive	$\frac{3}{4}$
Work with synthetic monofilaments gauges ·020-in. and over	1
Work with mixtures containing more than one-third synthetic monofilaments and materials other than Kitool, Gumati, bone or bassine	$\frac{3}{4}$
Provided that not more than three of these extras on one job shall be counted being three giving the maximum yield to the worker."	

4. for sub-paragraph (4) of paragraph 16 there were substituted the following sub-paragraph:—

"(4) EXTRAS TO COLUMN 3 ARE AS FOLLOWS:—

	Knots less per penny
Setting banisters with seconds or riflings	$\frac{1}{2}$
Setting banisters with used bass	1
Setting banisters with whalebone	$\frac{1}{4}$
Setting brooms with seconds or riflings	$\frac{1}{2}$
Setting brooms with used bass	1
Setting brooms with monkey bass	$\frac{1}{4}$
Setting brooms with cane	$1\frac{1}{4}$
Setting brooms with whalebone	$\frac{1}{2}$
Setting brooms with Union (mixture of bass with cane and/or whalebone) ...	$\frac{1}{2}$
Setting brooms and road sweeping machine rollers with monofilament with forged, barbed end	$1\frac{1}{4}$
Setting bass and bassine above 3 ins. to 3½ ins....	$\frac{1}{4}$
Setting bass and bassine 3 ins. and under	$\frac{1}{2}$
If a ⅝-in. or larger bit is used in item 18 or items 44 to 50	$\frac{1}{2}$
Cutting off banisters	$\frac{3}{4}$
Putting wire in bass or cane—each wire 4d. in 1s. extra.	
Putting wire in bass or cane if wire bent by pan hand—each wire 5d. in 1s. extra."	

EXPLANATORY NOTE

(This Note is not part of the Order.)

This Order, which has effect from 25th July 1969, amends Schedule 1 to the Wages Regulation (Brush and Broom) Order 1967 (Order M (105)) by changing some of the minimum piece rates for male workers and repeats without alteration the increases in statutory minimum remuneration contained in the Wages Regulation (Brush and Broom) (Amendment) Order 1969 (Order M (108)) which Order is revoked.

New provisions are printed in italics.

1969 No. 911

POLICE

The Police (Amendment) (No. 2) Regulations 1969

Made - - - -		*3rd July* 1969
Laid before Parliament		*11th July* 1969
Coming into Operation		*17th July* 1969

In exercise of the powers conferred on me by section 33 of the Police Act 1964**(a)**, and after consulting the Police Council for Great Britain in accordance with section 45(4) of that Act, I hereby make the following Regulations:—

1.—(1) These Regulations may be cited as the Police (Amendment) (No. 2) Regulations 1969.

(2) These Regulations shall come into operation on 17th July 1969 and shall have effect as respects the year ending 30th April 1969 as provided in Regulation 4 thereof but, subject as aforesaid, shall have effect as from 1st May 1969.

2. In these Regulations any reference to the principal Regulations is a reference to the Police Regulations 1968**(b)**, as amended**(c)**.

3. In Schedule 6 to the principal Regulations (which, as set out in the Appendix to the Police (Amendment) (No. 2) Regulations 1968**(d)** and amended by Regulation 2 of the Police (Amendment) (No. 4) Regulations 1968**(e)**, relates to motor vehicle allowances)—

(*a*) for the Table in paragraph 1 there shall be substituted the following Table:—

"TABLE

Cylinder capacity	Annual rate of fixed element	Mileage element	
		Basic rate per mile	Reduced rate per mile
1,200 c.c. or more but less than 1,700 c.c.	£86	8d.	5d.
1,000 c.c. or more but less than 1,200 c.c.	£77	7d.	4½d.
Less than 1,000 c.c.	£69	6¼d.	4d."

(a) 1964 c. 48.
(b) S.I. 1968/26 (1968 I, p. 38).
(c) The relevant amending instruments are S.I. 1968/766, 1761 (1968 II, p. 2142; III, p. 4774).
(d) S.I. 1968/766 (1968 II, p. 2142).
(e) S.I. 1968/1761 (1968 III, p. 4774).

(b) for the Table in paragraph 2 there shall be substituted the following Table:—

"TABLE

Cylinder capacity	Rate per mile
1,200 c.c. or more but less than 1,700 c.c.	1s. 2¼d.
1,000 c.c. or more but less than 1,200 c.c.	1s. 0¾d.
Less than 1,000 c.c.	11¼d."

4.—(1) As respects the year ending 30th April 1969 a motor vehicle allowance payable under Regulation 48 of the principal Regulations shall be calculated as hereinafter provided.

(2) So far as the motor vehicle allowance falls to be calculated by reference to completed months of authorised use ending, or mileage of authorised use performed, on or after 1st March 1969, it shall be calculated in accordance with the principal Regulations as amended by Regulation 3 of these Regulations, which shall have effect accordingly.

(3) Nothing in Regulation 3 of these Regulations shall affect the calculation of the motor vehicle allowance so far as it falls to be calculated by reference to completed months of authorised use ending, or mileage of authorised use performed, before 1st March 1969.

James Callaghan,
One of Her Majesty's Principal
Secretaries of State.

Home Office,
Whitehall.
3rd July 1969.

EXPLANATORY NOTE
(This Note is not part of the Regulations.)

These Regulations amend the Police Regulations 1968.

Regulation 3 increases the rates at which motor vehicle allowances are payable. These allowances are payable on an annual basis and, for the purposes thereof, a year is taken as a period of 12 months beginning on 1st May. They are calculated by reference to completed months of authorised use and mileage performed in the year in question.

Regulation 4 makes transitory provision for the calculation of these allowances in the year ending 30th April 1969 and provides that Regulation 3 shall have effect as from 1st March 1969 as respects the calculation of motor vehicle allowances by reference to months of use completed or mileage performed on or after that date. Subject to Regulation 4, Regulation 1 (2) provides that the Regulations shall have effect as from 1st May 1969. This provision for retrospective effect is made in exercise of the power conferred by section 33(4) of the Police Act 1964.

STATUTORY INSTRUMENTS

1969 No. 912 (S.72)

REPRESENTATION OF THE PEOPLE

The Representation of the People (Scotland) Regulations 1969

Made - - -	*3rd June* 1969
Laid before Parliament	*12th June* 1969
Coming into Operation—	
Regulations 21-23, 28-57, 67, 68, 73	*16th February* 1970
Regulation 69(2) *and Schedules*	*In accordance with Regulation 2*
Remainder	*16th July* 1969

ARRANGEMENT OF REGULATIONS

PART I

GENERAL

1. Citation.
2. Commencement.
3. Revocation and savings.
4. Interpretation.

PART II

REGISTRATION

The Register and Electors Lists

5. Separate part of electors lists and register for each registration unit.
6. Order of names in register.
7. Registration number in register.
8. Marking of names to indicate at which elections person entitled to vote.
9. Marking of names to indicate manner of voting.
10. Form of the electors lists.
11. Publication of the electors lists.

Claims and Objections

12. Notice of claims and objections.
13. Time for making claims and objections.
14. Form of claims and objections.

15. Entry and preliminary disposal of claims and objections.
16. Hearing of claims and objections.
17. Corrections to the electors lists.
18. Other corrections to the electors lists.

Publication and Sale of the Register

19. Publication of register.
20. Registration officer to furnish copies of register.
21. Free copies of register.
22. Sale of register.

Correction of Register

23. Correction of register.

Supplementary

24. Declaration as to age and nationality.
25. Information from householders.
26. Adaptation of electors lists and register in consequence of altered polling districts.

Corrupt and Illegal Practices Lists

27. Corrupt and illegal practices lists.

PART III
ABSENT VOTERS, PROXIES AND POSTAL PROXIES

28. Application to be treated as an absent voter.
29. Record and list of absent voters.
30. Application to vote by proxy.
31. Appointment of proxy.
32. Proxy paper.
33. Cancellation and disregard of proxy appointment.
34. Record and list of proxies.
35. Application by proxy to vote by post.
36. Record and list of postal proxies.
37. Certificate of employment.

PART IV
ISSUE AND RECEIPT OF POSTAL BALLOT PAPERS
Interpretation

38. Interpretation of Part IV.

Issue of Postal Ballot Papers

39. Form of postal ballot paper.
40. Form of declaration of identity.
41. Persons entitled to be present at issue and receipt of postal ballot papers.
42. Declaration of secrecy.
43. Notice of issue of postal ballot papers.
44. Marking of postal ballot paper.
45. Refusal to issue postal ballot paper.
46. Ballot paper envelope.
47. Delivery of postal ballot papers to post office.
48. Provision of postal voters ballot box.
49. Sealing up of special lists and counterfoils.
50. Spoilt postal ballot paper.

Receipt of Postal Ballot Papers

51. Receipt of covering envelope.
52. Opening of postal voters ballot box.
53. Opening of covering envelopes.
54. Sealing up of rejected votes and declarations of identity.
55. Opening of ballot paper envelopes.
56. Abandoned poll.
57. Forwarding or retention of documents.

Part V
Service Voters

58. Service declaration by members of the forces and spouses.
59. Qualification for Crown servant.
60. Service declaration by Crown servants, British Council employees and spouses.
61. Transmission of service declaration by Crown servants, British Council employees and spouses.
62. Service declaration by person about to leave the United Kingdom.
63. Proceedings by registration officer on receipt of service declaration.
64. Invalid service declaration.
65. Evidence as to service declaration.

Part VI
Supplementary

66. Appeals.
67. Official poll card.
68. Return and declaration of election expenses.
69. Forms.

70. Sending of notices, etc.
71. Publication of documents.
72. Misnomers.
73. Time.
74. Penalties.

SCHEDULES

SCHEDULE 1: Forms.

Forms for use by registration officers

Form A: Return by householder as to residents.
Form B: Notice as to publication of a draft register of electors and making of claims and objections.
Form C: Notice as to publication of the electors lists and making of claims and objections.
Form D: Proxy paper.

Forms for use by returning officers

Form E: Elector's official poll card.
Form F: Proxy's official poll card.
Form G: Certificate of employment.
Form H: Declaration of identity.

Forms for use by service voters

Form J: Service declaration and application for appointment of proxy by a member of the forces.
Form K: Service declaration and application for appointment of proxy by the spouse of a member of the forces.
Form L: Service declaration and application for appointment of proxy by a Crown servant or by a person employed by the British Council.
Form M: Service declaration and application for appointment of proxy by the spouse of a Crown servant or of a person employed by the British Council.
Form N: Application by a service voter in the United Kingdom to vote by post.

Forms for use by other persons

Form O: Claim to be registered as an elector.
Form P: Form of objection to an entry in the electors lists.
Form Q: Application to be treated as an absent voter for an indefinite period owing to occupation or physical incapacity.
Form R: Application to vote by post owing to change of residence.
Form S: Application to be treated as an absent voter for a particular election.

Form T : Application to be treated as an absent voter for an indefinite period owing to air or sea journey necessary from qualifying address.

Form U : Application by absent voter for appointment of proxy.

Form V : Application by a proxy to vote by post.

Form W : Application by service voter's spouse for appointment of proxy.

Form X : Return of expenses required by section 63 of the Representation of the People Act 1949 to be authorised by an election agent.

Form Y : Declaration as to expenses required by section 63 of the Representation of the People Act 1949 to be authorised by an election agent.

SCHEDULE 2 : Table of comparison of election rules.

In exercise of the powers conferred on me by sections 42 and 171(5) of the Representation of the People Act 1949(**a**), I hereby make the following regulations :—

PART I
GENERAL

Citation

1. These regulations may be cited as the Representation of the People (Scotland) Regulations 1969.

Commencement

2.—(1) The following provisions of these regulations, namely, regulations 21 to 23 (inclusive), 28 to 57 (inclusive), 67, 68, regulation 69(2) except in so far as regulation 69(2) relates to form O or P, and regulation 73 and so much of the Schedules as relates to those provisions, shall come into operation on 16th February 1970 :

Provided that regulations 28 to 57 (inclusive), 67, 68, 69(2) and 73 shall not have effect in relation to an election notice of which has been published before 16th February 1970.

(2) Except as otherwise provided by paragraph (1) of this regulation, these regulations shall come into operation fourteen days after they have been approved by both Houses of Parliament.

Revocation and savings

3.—(1) The following provisions of the Representation of the People (Scotland) Regulations 1950(**b**), as amended (**c**), namely regulations 18, 19, 24 to 51 (inclusive), 63, 64(2) except so far as regulation 64(2) relates to form O or P, regulations 64(3) and 68, and so much of the Schedules to those regulations as relates to those provisions shall be revoked as from 16th February 1970 :

Provided that regulations 24 to 51 (inclusive), 63, 64(2), 64(3) and 68, and so much of the Schedules to the regulations of 1950 as relates to the said regulations shall continue to have effect in relation to an election notice of which has been published before 16th February 1970.

(**a**) 1949 c.68.   (**b**) S.I. 1950/1250 (Rev. XX p. 56: 1950 II, p. 560).
(**c**) The amending instruments are S.I. 1953/1109, 1954/515, 1957/777 (1953 II, p. 1763; 1954 II, p. 1922; 1957 II, p. 1949).

(2) Except as otherwise provided by paragraph (1) of this regulation, the Representation of the People (Scotland) Regulations 1950, the Representation of the People ((Scotland) Regulations 1953(a), the Representation of the People (Scotland) Regulations 1954(b), and the Representation of the People (Scotland) Regulations 1957(c), are hereby revoked.

(3) Section 38 of the Interpretation Act 1889(d), shall apply as if these regulations were an Act of Parliament and as if any regulations revoked by these regulations were Acts of Parliament repealed by an Act of Parliament.

(4) Without prejudice to the said section 38, any register, list or record prepared, any application, appointment or declaration made, any proceedings initiated or other thing done under any regulations revoked by these regulations shall not be invalidated by the revocations effected by paragraph (1) or (2) of this regulation and shall, in so far as it could have been prepared, made, initiated or done under any provision of these regulations, have effect as if it had been prepared, made, initiated or done under that provision.

(5) Any reference in any statutory instrument to a regulation revoked by these regulations shall be taken as a reference to the corresponding regulation contained in these regulations.

Interpretation

4.—(1) For the purpose of these regulations, unless the context otherwise requires—

the expression "the Act of 1949" means the Representation of the People Act 1949 ;

the expression "the Act of 1969" means the Representation of the People Act 1969(e) ;

the expression "postal proxy" means a person entitled to vote by post as proxy at an election ;

the expression "registration area" means a county or county of a city ;

the expression "registration officer" means an electoral registration officer.

(2) A claim or objection includes a claim or objection that a letter or date should or should not be placed against a person's name in the electors lists and the register in accordance with regulation 8 or regulation 9(a).

(3) A reference in these regulations to any enactment or statutory instrument shall be construed as including a reference to the enactment or statutory instrument as amended or replaced by any other enactment or statutory instrument.

(4) A reference in these regulations to a regulation shall be construed as a reference to a regulation contained in these regulations.

(5) A reference in these regulations to a form identified by means of a letter shall be construed as a reference to the form so identified in Schedule 1 to these regulations.

(6) A reference in these regulations to the record and list of absent voters, proxies or postal proxies shall be taken as referring to the records and lists prepared for parliamentary and local government elections.

(7) The Interpretation Act 1889 shall apply to the interpretation of these regulations as it applies to the interpretation of an Act of Parliament.

(a) S.I.1953/1109 (1953 II, p. 1763).   (b) S.I. 1954/515 (1954 II, p. 1922).
(c) S.I. 1957/777 (1957 II, p. 1949).   (d) 1889 c.63.
(e) 1969 c. 15.

PART II

REGISTRATION

The Register and Electors Lists

Separate part of electors lists and register for each registration unit

5.—(1) Both the electors lists and the register shall be framed in separate parts for each registration unit.

(2) The registration unit shall be each parliamentary polling district if wholly contained in an electoral area or, where a parliamentary polling district is contained in more than one electoral area, each part of the polling district contained in a separate electoral area.

Order of names in register

6.—(1) Subject to paragraph (2) of this regulation, the names in each registration unit in the register shall be arranged in street order unless the local authority appointing the registration officer determine for any unit that street order is not reasonably practicable in which case the names shall be arranged in alphabetical order or partly in street order and partly in alphabetical order, as the local authority may determine.

(2) The names of every service voter in any registration unit who in his service declaration has given an address at which the declarant has resided in the United Kingdom, not being an address at which he would have been residing but for the circumstances entitling him to make the declaration, shall be grouped in alphabetical order at the end of the registration unit beneath a heading indicating that the service voters have so declared.

Registration number in register

7.—(1) The names in each parliamentary polling district in the register shall be numbered consecutively so far as is reasonably practicable with a separate series of numbers (beginning with the number one) for each parliamentary polling district or, where a parliamentary polling district is partly in one registration area and partly in another, for each part of a parliamentary polling district contained in a separate registration area.

(2) There shall be a separate letter or letters in the register for each parliamentary polling district or, where a parliamentary polling district is partly in one registration area and partly in another, for each part of a parliamentary polling district contained in a separate registration area, and such letter or letters shall be deemed to form part of an elector's number on the register.

Marking of names to indicate at which elections person entitled to vote

8.—(1) To indicate that an elector is not entitled to vote at a parliamentary election the letter "L" shall be placed against his name in the electors lists and the register.

(2) If an elector will attain voting age before the end of twelve months following the day by which a register is required to be published but will not be of voting age on the first day of those twelve months, the date on which he will attain that age shall be placed against his name in the electors lists as well as in the register.

Marking of names to indicate manner of voting

9. To indicate the manner in which an elector is entitled to vote at an election there shall be placed—

(*a*) in the electors lists and the register—

   (i) against the name of any elector who is a service voter the letter "S",

   (ii) against the name of any elector who is a merchant seaman the letter "M" ;

(*b*) in any copy of the register or part thereof provided for a polling station—

   (i) against the name of any elector who is, or whose proxy is, entitled to vote by post the letter "A",

   (ii) against the name of any elector on behalf of whom a proxy is entitled to vote the letter "P".

Form of the electors lists

10.—(1) The electors lists for a registration unit shall consist of—

List A—a copy of the register in force for the unit.

List B—a list of newly qualified electors, that is to say, persons who are qualified for registration as parliamentary or as local government electors in respect of qualifying addresses for which they are not registered in the register in force or who, since the qualifying date of the register in force, have become entitled to be registered as residents instead of as service voters, or vice versa, in respect of those addresses, and

List C—a list of persons who have ceased to be qualified as electors or whose qualification has been altered, that is to say, persons who, being registered in respect of qualifying addresses in the register in force, have ceased to be qualified for registration as parliamentary or as local government electors in respect of those addresses or who, since the qualifying date for the register in force, have become entitled to be registered as residents instead of as service voters, or vice versa, in respect of those addresses :

Provided that where the area of a registration unit differs from the area of that unit as constituted for the purposes of the register in force, the registration unit may be treated as having the same area as it had for the purposes of the register in force.

(2) The names in List B need not be numbered.

(3) The names in List C shall have opposite them their numbers in the register in force.

(4) Notwithstanding the provisions of paragraphs (1), (2) and (3) of this regulation, the electors lists for a registration unit may, with the consent of the Secretary of State, be prepared as a draft register so as to show only the persons appearing to the registration officer to be entitled to be registered, together with their qualifying addresses, and to comply with the provisions of the preceding regulations :

Provided that the names in the draft register need not be numbered.

Publication of the electors lists

11.—(1) The registration officer shall publish the electors lists by—

(*a*) making a copy thereof available for inspection at his office ;

(*b*) as soon as practicable making copies of the part of the electors lists relating to each electoral area available for inspection at a specified place in or near that electoral area to which the public have access ;

(*c*) publishing a notice, to be combined with the notice of claims and objections referred to in regulation 12, specifying the said place.

(2) The electors lists shall be published on or before the twenty-eighth day of November and shall be kept published till the publication of the register prepared from those lists.

Claims and Objections

Notice of claims and objections

12.—(1) The registration officer shall at the time of publishing the electors lists publish a notice in Form C or, in the case of electors lists to which regulation 10(4) applies, in Form B specifying the manner in which and the time within which claims and objections in respect of the electors lists may be made.

(2) The said notice shall be published in the way the registration officer thinks best calculated to bring the said notice to the attention of the electors.

Time for making claims and objections

13.—(1) A claim or objection in respect of the electors lists which is delivered to the registration officer after the sixteenth day of December shall be disregarded :

Provided that an objection to a claim shall not be disregarded if it is delivered to the registration officer within three days after the claim has been entered in the list of claims.

(2) A service declaration made with reference to a qualifying date and made during the twelve months ending with that date, but received too late for inclusion of the declarant's name in the electors lists, shall, if it is received by the registration officer—

(*a*) not later than the last day for making claims, be treated as a claim,

(*b*) after the said last day, be disregarded.

Form of claims and objections

14.—(1) A claim shall be in Form O and may be made by a person either on his own behalf or on behalf of another person.

(2) An objection shall be in Form P.

(3) Claims and objections shall be made available for inspection in the registration officer's office till completion of the hearing of claims and objections.

Entry and preliminary disposal of claims and objections

15.—(1) The registration officer shall keep separate lists of claims and objections and shall, on receipt of a claim or objection, forthwith enter in the appropriate list the name and qualifying address of the claimant or the person in respect of whom the objection is made.

(2) If the registration officer is of opinion—

(a) that the particulars given in a claim or objection are insufficient, he may ask for further information and take no further action until such information is supplied ;

(b) that a claim may be allowed without a hearing, he may allow the claim, provided that no objection is made thereto, and shall so inform the person making the claim ;

(c) that the objector is not entitled to object, he may disallow the objection and shall so inform the objector ;

(d) that a claim or objection cannot be allowed because—

(i) the matter has been concluded by the decision of a court, or

(ii) the particulars given in a claim or objection do not entitle the claimant or objector to succeed,

he may send to the person making the claim or objection a notice stating his opinion and the grounds thereof and that he intends to disallow the claim or objection unless that person gives the registration officer notice within three days from the date of the first mentioned notice that he requires the claim or objection to be heard, and, if he receives no such notice within the said time, he may disallow the claim or objection.

(3) The registration officer shall, unless he allows or disallows the claim or objection under paragraph (2) of this regulation, send a notice, in the case of a claim, to the person making the claim and, in the case of an objection, to the objector and the person objected to, stating the time and place at which he proposes to hear the claim or objection ; and the notice sent to a person objected to shall also state the name and address of the objector and the grounds of the objection.

(4) The time fixed for the hearing of a claim or objection shall not be earlier than the third day after the date of the notice referred to in paragraph (3) of this regulation.

(5) The registration officer shall make available for inspection at his office till completion of the hearing of claims and objections the lists of claims and objections together with the time and place at which he proposes to hear any claim or objection.

Hearing of claims and objections

16.—(1) On the hearing of a claim, the person making the claim and any person who has duly made an objection and, on the hearing of an objection, the objector and the person objected to and, on the hearing of either, any other person who appears to the registration officer to be interested shall be entitled to appear and be heard.

(2) The right to appear and be heard includes the right to make written representations.

(3) Any person entitled to appear and be heard may do so either in person or by any other person on his behalf.

(4) The registration officer may, at the request of any person entitled to appear and be heard or, if he thinks fit, without such a request, require that the evidence tendered by any person shall be given on oath and may administer an oath for the purpose.

Corrections to the electors lists

17. Any alteration to the electors lists which is required :—

(*a*) to carry out the registration officer's decision with respect to any claim or objection,

(*b*) to correct any clerical error,

(*c*) to correct any misnomer or inaccurate description,

shall be made by the registration officer.

Other corrections to the electors lists

18.—(1) Where it appears to the registration officer that it is necessary to make any alteration (other than an alteration under regulation 17) to the electors lists in order to ensure that no person shall be incorrectly registered, or registered when not entitled, he shall send to the person affected by the alteration a notice stating the proposed alteration and shall give him an opportunity within five days from the date of such notice of objecting to the alteration and if necessary of appearing and being heard in accordance with the provisions of regulation 16.

(2) After the said five days the registration officer shall make such alteration (if any) as seems to him to be necessary.

Publication and Sale of the Register

Publication of register

19.—(1) The registration officer shall publish the register by making a copy available for inspection at his office and by making copies of the part of the register relating to each electoral area available for inspection as soon as practicable at the place at which copies of the part of the electors lists relating to that electoral area have been made available for inspection.

(2) The register shall be kept published until the coming into force of the next register.

Registration officer to furnish copies of register

20.—(1) A copy of the register shall, on publication, be furnished by the registration officer to the returning officer for parliamentary elections, to the British Museum and to the National Library of Scotland.

(2) An abstract of the contents of the register shall be furnished by the registration officer to the Secretary of State at such times and in such form and giving such particulars as the Secretary of State may require.

Free copies of register

21. The registration officer shall on request supply without fee—

(*a*) four copies of the register (which may be printed on one side only) for any constituency or part of a constituency included in the registration area and four copies of Lists B and C of the electors lists therefor, or, in the case of electors lists to which regulation 10(4) applies, of the draft register therefor. so long as the lists are kept published. to any person who satisfies the registration officer that he requires them for use in connection with his own or some other person's prospective candidature at a parliamentary election for that constituency :

Provided that not more than one person in respect of the same candidature shall be so supplied ;

(b) two copies of the register for any constituency or part of a constituency included in the registration area to each candidate at a parliamentary election for that constituency or his election agent ;

(c) one copy of the register for any electoral area to each candidate at a local government election for that area or his election agent.

Sale of register

22. The registration officer shall supply to any person copies of any part or parts of the register in force or of any electors lists therefor so long as there are sufficient copies available after allowing for the number which may be required for the purposes of any election (including the purposes of regulation 21) on payment—

(a) in the case of a person who has been supplied in pursuance of regulation 21 with a copy of the register or electors lists or who is a returning officer or a local authority, of a fee at the rate of one shilling for each one thousand (or part of one thousand) names in such copy ;

(b) in the case of any other person, of a fee at the rate of five shillings for each one thousand (or part of one thousand) names in such copy.

Correction of Register

Correction of register

23.—(1) When a registration officer makes an alteration in a register pursuant to section 7(2) of the Act of 1969, he shall—

(a) send to the person affected by the alteration and. if he gives effect to a decision on an objection made with respect to the electors lists, to the objector a notice stating the alteration ;

(b) make a copy of the alteration available for inspection at his office ;

(c) make copies of the alteration available for inspection at the place at which copies of the part of the register to which the alteration relates have been made available for inspection ;

(d) furnish a copy of the alteration to the returning officer for parliamentary elections, to the British Museum and to the National Library of Scotland ;

(e) supply without fee a copy of the alteration to each person to whom he has supplied copies of the register or part thereof to which the alteration relates in pursuance of regulation 21 or 22(a).

(2) Copies of alterations made available for inspection under this regulation shall be kept available for the same length of time as the register is kept published.

Supplementary

Declaration as to age and nationality

24.—(1) The registration officer before registering any person (other than a service voter) may, if he thinks it necessary—

(a) require that person either to produce a birth certificate or to make a statutory declaration as to the date of his birth ;

(b) require that person either to produce a certificate of naturalisation or a document showing that he has become a British subject by virtue of registration, or to make a statutory declaration that he was a British subject or citizen of the Republic of Ireland on the qualifying date.

(2) Where a declaration is so made, any fee payable in connection therewith shall be paid by the registration officer as part of his registration expenses.

(3) Any such declaration shall be made available for inspection in the registration officer's office till completion of the hearing of claims and objections.

Information from householders

25. The registration officer may require any householder or person owning or occupying any premises within the area for which he acts or the agent or factor of any such person to give information required for the purposes of his registration duties.

Adaptation of electors lists and register in consequence of altered polling districts

26.—(1) Where the Secretary of State directs a returning officer to make or himself makes any alteration of parliamentary polling districts, he may also direct that—

(a) the register in force be adapted to the alteration ;

(b) if the alteration takes place between the publication of any electors lists and the coming into force of the register prepared from those lists, the form of that register be framed in accordance with the alterations.

(2) Where any alteration of parliamentary polling districts is made otherwise than by virtue of section 11(4) of the Act of 1949 (which relates to powers exercisable by the Secretary of State), the registration officer shall, if required by the returning officer, make the adaptations set out in paragraph (1) of this regulation.

(3) Except as otherwise provided by this regulation an alteration of parliamentary polling districts shall not be effective until the coming into force of the first register prepared from the electors lists published after the alteration is made.

Corrupt and Illegal Practices Lists

Corrupt and illegal practices lists

27.—(1) The registration officer shall, at the same time as he publishes the electors lists, prepare and publish the corrupt and illegal practices lists (if any) required by section 40(1) and (2) of the Act of 1949 by making a copy thereof available for inspection at the same places as he makes available copies of the electors lists or any part thereof.

(2) A person named in either of the said corrupt and illegal practices lists may claim to be omitted therefrom and any person may object to the omission of any person from such list, and paragraph (1) of regulation 13, paragraph (3) of regulation 14 and regulations 15 and 16 shall apply to any such claim or objection as they apply to a claim or objection in respect of the electors lists.

(3) A claim may be made by a person either on his own behalf or on behalf of another person and shall give particulars of the grounds on which the person concerned should be omitted, and an objection to the omission of any person shall give the name and address of the objector and the person in respect of whom the objection is made and the grounds on which such person should be entered in the corrupt and illegal practices list including particulars of the alleged conviction by a court or of the alleged report of any election court.

(4) The registration officer shall make such alterations to the corrupt and illegal practices lists as are required to carry out his decisions on any claims or objections or to correct any clerical error, misnomer or inaccurate description.

(5) Where it appears to the registration officer that a person not named in the said corrupt and illegal practices lists or either of them should be entered in one or both of those lists, he shall send to that person a notice that he intends to enter him therein and shall give him an opportunity within five days from the date of such notice of objecting and being heard in accordance with the provisions of regulation 16 and after the said five days he shall make such alteration as seems to him to be necessary.

(6) The registration officer shall publish the corrected corrupt and illegal practices lists (if any) at the same time as he publishes the register and in the same manner as he publishes each part of the register.

(7) A copy of each of the corrected corrupt and illegal practices lists shall, on publication, be furnished by the registration officer to the returning officer for parliamentary elections, to the British Museum and to the National Library of Scotland.

(8) The corrupt and illegal practices lists as first published and as corrected shall be kept published for the same length of time as the electors lists and the register.

Part III

Absent Voters, Proxies and Postal Proxies

Application to be treated as an absent voter

28.—(1) An application to be treated as an absent voter shall be made in respect of each qualifying address and shall :—

(a) be in Form S in any case where the application is made for a particular election only,

(b) be in Form R in any case where the application is based on the ground that the applicant no longer resides at his qualifying address,

(c) be in Form N in any case where the applicant is a service voter,

(d) be in Form W in any case where the applicant is the spouse of a service voter, has made a service declaration, but has not yet been registered as a service voter in pursuance of that declaration, (*c*) be in Form T in any case where the application is based on the ground that the applicant is unable or likely to be unable to go in person from his qualifying address to the polling station without making a journey by air or sea,

(*f*) be in Form Q in any other case.

(2) (*a*) An application to be treated as an absent voter based on the ground of religious observance shall not be allowed by the registration officer unless it is accompanied by a certificate signed by a minister of the applicant's religious denomination certifyng the nature and times of the religious observances and that the applicant is bound to observe them.

(*b*) An application to be treated as an absent voter based on the ground of physical incapacity shall be allowed by the registration officer if—

  (i) the applicant has been registered as a blind person by a local authority under section 29(4)(*g*) of the National Assistance Act 1948(**a**) ; or

  (ii) the application is accompanied by a certificate signed by a registered medical practitioner or a Christian Science practitioner certifying that the person is unable, or likely to be unable, by reason either of blindness or of any other physical incapacity to go in person to the polling station or, if able to go, to vote unaided, and estimating the probable duration of the period during which the applicant is likely to be so unable.

(3) An application to be treated as an absent voter shall be disregarded—

  (*a*) for the purposes of a parliamentary election if it is received by the registration officer after the twelfth day before the day of the poll at that election ;

  (*b*) for the purposes of a local government election if it is received by the registration officer after the last day for the delivery of nomination papers at that election:

Provided that an application on the grounds of the applicant's employment on the day of the poll by a returning officer or as a constable may be allowed after the said twelfth or last day as the case may be.

(4) An application to be no longer treated as an absent voter may be disregarded—

  (*a*) for the purposes of a parliamentary election if it is received by the registration officer after the twelfth day before the day of the poll at that election ;

  (*b*) for the purposes of a local government election if it is received by the registration officer after the last day for the delivery of nomination papers at that election.

(5) The registration officer on disallowing a person's application to be treated as an absent voter shall notify the applicant of the fact.

(6) Where under section 13(3)(*c*) or 24(3)(*c*) of the Act of 1949 the registration officer gives notice to an absent voter that he has reason to believe there has been a material change of circumstances, that person shall cease to be treated as an absent voter seven days after the date on which the registration officer sends such notice.

(**a**) 1948 c. 29.

Record and list of absent voters

29.—(1) Subject to the provisions of this regulation, the record and list of absent voters shall be in such a form as appears to the registration officer to be convenient.

(2) The address to which a ballot paper is to be sent shall be placed opposite the name and number on the register of each absent voter in the absent voters list unless a proxy (other than a service voter's proxy) has been appointed to vote on his behalf, in which case the letter "P" shall be placed opposite his name.

(3) As soon as the absent voters list has been prepared, the registration officer shall publish it by making a copy thereof available for inspection at his office.

(4) The registration officer shall make a copy of the record of absent voters available for inspection at his office.

(5) As soon as practicable after the preparation of the absent voters list, the registration officer shall, on request and without fee, supply to each candidate or his election agent a copy of the absent voters list :

Provided that if such a request is made before any issue of ballot papers to those entitled to vote by post, the registration officer shall supply a copy of the said list, or a copy of so much of the said list as relates to that issue, before that issue.

Application to vote by proxy

30.—(1) An application by a service voter for the appointment of a proxy to vote on his behalf shall be in the form of Part 2 of Form J, K, L or M, as the case may be.

(2) An application by an absent voter who is not a service voter for the appointment of a proxy to vote on his behalf shall be in Form U or W, as the case may be.

Appointment of proxy

31.—(1) For the purpose of ascertaining in pursuance of section 14(4) of the Act of 1949 and of that subsection as applied by section 25(6) of that Act that a proxy is capable of being and willing to be appointed, the registration officer shall, unless he is satisfied that the person nominated in the application as first choice is not capable of being and willing to be appointed, notify him that a proxy paper will be issued to him unless within five days from the date of such notice the registration officer receives notice from him that he is not capable of being and willing to be appointed.

(2) If the person nominated as first choice is not capable of being and willing to be appointed, the registration officer shall, if another person is nominated as second choice, deal in like manner with such person :

Provided that if the application is received by the registration officer after publication of notice of an election, the registration officer need not do so until after the day of the poll for that election.

(3) If for any reason the registration officer does not issue a proxy paper in pursuance of an application made to him, he shall notify the person making the application why he has not done so.

Proxy Paper

32.—(1) The proxy paper to be issued by the registration officer shall be in Form D.

(2) As soon as may be after issue of the proxy paper the registration officer shall send a notice of the fact to the elector stating the name of the person to whom the paper has been issued.

Cancellation and disregard of proxy appointment

33.—(1) Where the appointment of a proxy is cancelled by notice given to the registration officer or ceases to be in force under section 14(5) of the Act of 1949 or that subsection as applied by section 25(6) of that Act, the registration officer shall forthwith notify the person whose appointment as proxy has been cancelled or is no longer in force of the fact and remove his name from the record of proxies.

(2) Where a service voter is entitled to vote by post at an election, the registration officer shall forthwith notify his proxy (if any) of the fact and that his appointment will not have effect for that election.

(3) An application for the issue of a proxy paper shall be disregarded—

(a) for the purposes of a parliamentary election if it is received by the registration officer after the twelfth day before the day of the poll at that election ;

(b) for the purposes of a local government election if it is received by the registration officer after the last day for the delivery of nomination papers at that election.

(4) A notice cancelling the appointment of a proxy may be disregarded—

(a) for the purposes of a parliamentary election if it is received by the registration officer after the twelfth day before the day of the poll at that election ;

(b) for the purposes of a local government election if it is received by the registration officer after the last day for the delivery of nomination papers at that election.

Record and list of proxies

34.—(1) The record and list of proxies shall be in such form as appears to the registration officer to be convenient.

(2) As soon as the list of proxies has been prepared, the registration officer shall publish it by making a copy thereof available for inspection at his office.

(3) The registration officer shall make a copy of the record of proxies available for inspection at his office.

(4) As soon as practicable after the preparation of the list of proxies, the registration officer shall, on request and without fee, supply to each candidate or his election agent a copy of the list of proxies.

Application by proxy to vote by post

35.—(1) An application by a proxy to vote by post shall be in Form V.

(2) Such an application shall be disregarded—

(a) for the purposes of a parliamentary election if it is received by the registration officer after the twelfth day before the day of the poll at that election;

(*b*) for the purposes of a local government election if it is received by the registration officer after the last day for the delivery of nomination papers at that election:

Provided that if under the proviso to regulation 28(3) the applicant becomes entitled to vote by post as an absent voter at a parliamentary or local government election after the said twelfth or last day as the case may be, such an application may be allowed after the said twelfth or last day as the case may be.

(3) The registration officer on disallowing such an application shall notify the applicant of the fact.

(4) An application under section 15(7)(*a*) of the Act of 1949 whereby a proxy ceases to be entitled to vote by post may be disregarded for the purposes of a parliamentary election if it is received by the registration officer after the twelfth day before the day of the poll at that election.

Record and list of postal proxies

36.—(1) Subject to the provisions of this regulation, the record and list of postal proxies shall be in such a form as appears to the registration officer to be convenient.

(2) The list of postal proxies shall give the name and number on the register of the elector and opposite them the name of the proxy and the address to which the ballot paper is to be sent.

(3) As soon as the postal proxies list has been prepared, the registration officer shall publish it by making a copy thereof available for inspection at his office.

(4) The registration officer shall make a copy of the record of postal proxies available for inspection at his office.

(5) As soon as practicable after the preparation of the postal proxies list, the registration officer shall, on request and without fee, supply to each candidate or his election agent a copy of the postal proxies list:

Provided that if such a request is made before any issue of ballot papers to those entitled to vote by post, the registration officer shall supply a copy of the said list, or a copy of so much of the said list as related to that issue, before that issue.

Certificate of employment

37. The certificate as to the employment of constables and persons employed by the returning officer on the day of the poll (to enable such a constable or person to vote elsewhere than at his own polling station) shall be in Form G and signed, in the case of a constable, by a member of a police force of or above the rank of inspector.

PART IV
ISSUE AND RECEIPT OF POSTAL BALLOT PAPERS
Interpretation

Interpretation of Part IV

38.—(1) For the purpose of this Part of these regulations, unless the context otherwise requires—

the expression "agent" includes the election agent and a person appointed to attend in the election agent's place;

the expression "issue" includes the original and any subsequent issue;

the expression "postal ballot paper" means a ballot paper issued to a postal voter;

the expression "postal voter" means a person entitled to vote by post at an election as an absent voter or as a proxy.

(2) (*a*) For the purpose of this Part of these regulations, unless the context otherwise requires, the expression "election rules" means the parliamentary elections rules in Schedule 2 to the Act of 1949 and the Scottish local elections rules in Schedule 3 to that Act.

(*b*) The table of comparison set out in the Schedule 2 to these regulations shows (so far as is necessary for the construction of these regulations) the provisions of the rules there mentioned which correspond to one another and, except in so far as the context otherwise requires, any reference in these regulations to a specified provision of the election rules shall be taken as a reference both to—

(i) the provision specified in the first column of that Schedule, and

(ii) the corresponding provision in the second column thereof.

Issue of Postal Ballot Papers

Form of postal ballot paper

39. The ballot papers to be sent to postal voters shall be in the same form as, and indistinguishable from, the ballot papers delivered to other voters.

Form of declaration of identity

40. The declaration of identity sent with the ballot paper to a postal voter shall be in Form H.

Persons entitled to be present at issue and receipt of postal ballot papers

41.—(1) No person other than—

(*a*) the returning officer and his clerks,

(*b*) a candidate,

(*c*) an election agent or any person appointed by a candidate to attend in his election agent's place,

(*d*) any agents appointed under paragraph (2) of this regulation,

may be present at the proceedings on the issue or receipt of postal ballot papers.

(2) Where postal ballot papers are to be issued, or the envelopes contained in the postal voters ballot boxes are to be opened, simultaneously in two or more batches, each candidate may appoint one or more agents up to the number he may be authorised by the returning officer to appoint not exceeding the number of such batches so, however, that the number authorised shall be the same in the case of each candidate.

(3) Notice of the appointment stating the names and addresses of the persons appointed shall be given by the candidate to the returning officer before the time fixed for the issue of the postal ballot papers or the opening of the said postal voters ballot boxes, as the case may be.

(4) If an agent dies or becomes incapable of acting, the candidate may appoint another agent in his place and shall forthwith give to the returning officer notice in writing of the name and address of the agent appointed.

(5) Agents may be appointed and notice of appointment given to the returning officer by the candidate's election agent instead of by the candidate.

(6) In this Part of these regulations references to agents shall be taken as references to agents whose appointments have been duly made and notified and, in the case of agents appointed under paragraph (2) of this regulation, who are within the number authorised by the returning officer.

(7) A candidate may himself do any act or thing which any agent of his, if appointed, would have been authorised to do, or may assist his agent in doing any such act or thing.

(8) Where in this Part of these regulations any act or thing is required or authorised to be done in the presence of the candidates or their agents, the non-attendance of any such persons or person at the time and place appointed for the purpose shall not, if the act or thing is otherwise duly done, invalidate the act or thing done.

Declaration of secrecy

42.—(1) Every person attending the proceedings on the issue or receipt of postal ballot papers shall make a declaration of secrecy in the form in paragraph (3) of this regulation, or in a form as near thereto as circumstances admit, before the issue of postal ballot papers:

Provided that if any person only attends the proceedings on the receipt of postal ballot papers, he need not make the declaration before the issue but shall make it before he is permitted to attend the proceedings on the receipt of postal ballot papers.

(2) The returning officer shall make the declaration in the presence of a justice of the peace, and any other person shall make the declaration in the presence either of a justice of the peace or of the returning officer or of a person who is a county clerk or a town clerk and section 53(4) and (6) of the Act of 1949 shall be read to the declarant by the person taking the declaration, or shall be read by the declarant in the presence of that person.

(3) The declaration shall be as follows:—

"I solemnly promise and declare that I will not do anything forbidden by subsections (4) and (6) of section fifty-three of the Representation of the People Act 1949, which have been read to [by] me."

(4) Any person before whom a declaration is authorised to be made under this regulation may take the declaration.

Notice of issue of postal ballot papers

43.—(1) The returning officer shall give each candidate not less than two days' notice in writing of the time and place at which he will issue the postal ballot papers and of the number of agents he may appoint under regulation 41(2) of these regulations to attend the said issue.

(2) Where any subsequent issue of postal ballot papers is made, the returning officer shall notify each candidate as soon as practicable of the time and place at which he will make such subsequent issue and of the number of agents he may appoint under regulation 41(2) to attend such issue.

Marking of postal ballot paper

44.—(1) Each postal ballot paper issued shall be stamped with the official mark either embossed or perforated, and the name and number on the register of the elector shall be called out, and such number shall be marked on the counterfoil, and a mark shall be placed in the absent voters list or the list of postal proxies against the number of the elector to denote that a ballot paper has been issued to the elector or his proxy but without showing the particular ballot paper issued.

(2) The number of a postal ballot paper shall be marked on the declaration of identity sent with that paper.

Refusal to issue postal ballot paper

45. Where a returning officer is satisfied that two or more entries in either the absent voters list or the list of postal proxies relate to the same elector or that a postal proxy has been appointed for a person entered in the absent voters list, he shall not issue more than one ballot paper in respect of the same elector.

Ballot paper envelope

46. The returning officer shall, in addition to the ballot paper, declaration of identity and envelope for their return, marked "B", (hereinafter referred to as a "covering envelope") which he is required by rule 25 of the election rules to send to a postal voter, send a smaller envelope marked "A" and "ballot paper envelope" bearing the number of the ballot paper.

Delivery of postal ballot papers to post office

47.—(1) Envelopes addressed to postal voters shall be counted and forthwith delivered by the returning officer to the nearest head post office, or such other office as may be arranged with the head postmaster, and the postmaster shall stamp with the post office date stamp a form of receipt to be presented by the returning officer stating the number of envelopes so delivered, and shall immediately forward such envelopes for delivery to the persons to whom they are addressed.

(2) At local government elections first-class postage of all such envelopes and all covering envelopes shall be prepaid by the returning officer.

Provision of postal voters ballot box

48.—(1) The returning officer shall, at the proceedings on the original issue of postal ballot papers, provide a ballot box or ballot boxes for the reception of the covering envelopes when returned by the postal voters.

(2) Every such ballot box shall be shown open and empty to the agents present and shall then be locked by the returning officer and sealed with the seal of the returning officer and the seals of such of the agents as desire to affix their seals in such manner as to prevent its being opened without breaking the seal.

(3) Every such ballot box shall be marked "postal voters ballot box".

(4) The returning officer shall make provision for the safe custody of every such ballot box.

Sealing up of special lists and counterfoils

49.—(1) The returning officer, as soon as practicable after the completion of the issue of the postal ballot papers, and in the presence of the agents, shall make up in separate packets—

　　(a) the marked copies of the absent voters list and of the list of postal proxies, and

(b) the counterfeits of those ballot papers which were issued,
and shall seal such packets.

(2) The sealed packet containing the marked copies of the absent voters list and of the list of postal proxies may be opened by the returning officer for the purposes of a subsequent issue, and on completion of that issue the copies shall again be made up and sealed in accordance with the last foregoing paragraph.

Spoilt postal ballot paper

50.—(1) If a postal voter has inadvertently dealt with his postal ballot paper in such a manner that it cannot be conveniently used as a ballot paper (in these regulations referred to as "a spoilt postal ballot paper") he may return (either by hand or by post) to the returning officer the spoilt postal ballot paper, the declaration of identity, the ballot paper envelope and the covering envelope.

(2) The returning officer, on receipt of the said documents, shall, unless the documents are received too late for another postal ballot paper to be returned before the close of the poll, issue another postal ballot paper and the foregoing provisions of this Part of these regulations, but not sub-paragraph (b), (c) or (d) of paragraph (1) or paragraphs (2) to (8) of regulation 41 or regulation 43, shall apply accordingly.

(3) The spoilt postal ballot paper, the declaration of identity and the ballot paper envelope shall be immediately cancelled.

(4) The returning officer, as soon as practicable after cancelling the said documents, shall make up the said documents in a separate packet and shall seal the packet; and if on any subsequent occasion documents are cancelled as aforesaid, the sealed packet shall be opened and the additional cancelled documents included therein and the packet shall thereupon be again made up and sealed.

Receipt of Postal Ballot Papers

Receipt of covering envelope

51. The returning officer shall, immediately on receipt (whether by hand or by post) of a covering envelope before the close of the poll, place it unopened in a postal voters ballot box locked and sealed in accordance with regulation 48.

Opening of postal voters ballot box

52.—(1) Each postal voters ballot box shall be opened by the returning officer in the presence of the agents.

(2) So long as the returning officer secures that there is at least one postal voters ballot box for the reception of covering envelopes up to the time of the close of the poll, the other postal voters ballot boxes may previously be opened by him.

(3) The returning officer shall give each candidate at least forty-eight hours' notice in writing of the time and place of his opening of each postal voters ballot box and the envelopes contained therein and of the number of agents the candidate may appoint under regulation 41(2) to be present at each opening.

Opening of covering envelopes

53.—(1) When a postal voters ballot box has been opened, the returning officer shall count and note the number of covering envelopes, and shall then open each covering envelope separately.

(2) Where a covering envelope does not contain both a declaration of identity and a ballot paper envelope or, there being no ballot paper envelope, a ballot paper, he shall mark the covering envelope "rejected", attach thereto the contents (if any) of the covering envelope and place it in a separate receptacle (hereinafter referred to as "the receptacle for votes rejected"); and if the covering evvelope does not contain the declaration separately, the returning officer shall open the ballot paper envelope to ascertain if the declaration is inside that envelope.

(3) On opening a covering envelope, other than one to which paragraph (2) of this regulation applies, he shall first satisfy himself that the declaration of identity has been duly signed and authenticated and, if he is not so satisfied, he shall mark the declaration "rejected", attach thereto the ballot paper envelope or, if there is no such envelope, the ballot paper, and place it in the receptacle for votes rejected:

Provided that before so doing he shall show the declaration to the agents and, if any objection is made by any agent to his decision, he shall add the words "rejection objected to".

(4) Where the number on the declaration of identity duly signed and authenticated agrees with the number on the ballot paper envelope, he shall place the declaration in a separate receptacle (hereinafter referred to as "the receptacle for declarations of identity") and the ballot paper envelope in another separate receptacle (hereinafter referred to as "the receptacle for ballot paper envelopes").

(5) Where there is no ballot paper envelope or the ballot paper envelope has been opened under paragraph (2) of this regulation, he shall—

(a) where the number on the declaration of identity duly signed and authenticated agrees with the number on the ballot paper, place the declaration in the receptacle for declarations of identity and the ballot paper in a ballot box previously shown open and empty to the agents present and locked by the returning officer and sealed with the seal of the returning officer and the seals of such of the agents as desire to affix their seals in such manner as to prevent its being opened without breaking the seal, which shall be subsequently treated as a ballot box for the purpose of rule 46 of the election rules, and

(b) where the number on the said declaration does not agree with the number on the ballot paper, mark the declaration "rejected", attach thereto the ballot paper and place it in the receptacle for votes rejected.

(6) Where the number on the declaration of identity duly signed and authenticated does not agree with the number on the ballot paper envelope or that envelope has no number on it, he shall open the envelope and shall—

(a) where the number on the declaration agrees with the number on the ballot paper, place the declaration in the receptacle for declarations of identity and the ballot paper in the ballot box referred to in paragraph (5) of this regulation, and

(b) where the number on the declaration does not agree with the number on the ballot paper or there is no ballot paper, mark the declaration "rejected", attach thereto the ballot paper (if any) and place it in the receptacle for votes rejected.

(7) Except for the purposes of ascertaining under paragraph (2) of this regulation whether a ballot paper envelope contains a declaration of identity or under paragraph (6) of this regulation whether the number on the declaration agrees with the number on the ballot paper, the returning officer shall not open the ballot paper envelopes before they are opened under regulation 55.

Sealing up of rejected votes and declarations of identity

54. On the conclusion of the proceedings under regulation 53 the returning officer shall put the contents of the receptacle for votes rejected and the contents of the receptacle for declarations of identity into two separate packets and shall seal up such packets.

Opening of ballot paper envelopes

55.—(1) After sealing up the said packets the returning officer shall open separately each ballot paper envelope placed in the receptacle for ballot paper envelopes.

(2) Where a ballot paper envelope does not contain a ballot paper, he shall mark the envelope "rejected".

(3) Where the number on a ballot paper envelope agrees with the number on the ballot paper contained therein, he shall place the ballot paper in the ballot box referred to in regulation 53(5).

(4) Where the number on the ballot paper envelope does not agree with the number on the ballot paper contained therein, he shall mark the ballot paper "rejected" and attach the ballot paper envelope thereto.

(5) He shall put into a separate packet the envelopes and the ballot papers marked "rejected" under the provisions of this regulation and shall seal up such packet.

Abandoned poll

56. Where a poll is abandoned, or countermanded after postal ballot papers have been issued, by reason of the death of a candidate, the returning officer—

(a) shall not take any step or further step to open covering envelopes or deal with their contents in accordance with the provisions of this Part of these regulations, and

(b) shall, notwithstanding regulation 54 or 55, treat all unopened covering envelopes and the contents of those which have been opened as if they were counted ballot papers.

Forwarding or retention of documents

57.—(1) The returning officer, in the case of a parliamentary election, shall forward to the sheriff clerk and, in the case of a local government election, shall forward to the county clerk or the town clerk or retain as the case may be, at the same time as he so forwards or retains the documents mentioned in rule 56 of the election rules—

(a) any packets referred to in regulation 49, 50, 54 or 55, subject to the provisions of regulation 56, endorsing on each packet a description of its contents, the date of the election to which it relates and the name of the constituency or electoral area for which the election was held, and (*b*) a statement of the number of postal ballot papers issued in such form and giving such other particulars with respect to such papers as the Secretary of State may require.

(2) Where any covering envelopes are received by the returning officer after the close of the poll or any envelopes addressed to postal voters are returned as undelivered too late to be readdressed, or any spoilt postal ballot papers are returned too late to enable other postal ballot papers to be issued, he shall put them unopened into a separate packet, seal up such packet and forward or retain it at a subsequent date in the manner described in paragraph (1) of this regulation.

(3) Any packet or statement forwarded or retained under this regulation shall be deemed to have been forwarded or retained in pursuance of the election rules.

(4) A copy of the statement referred to in paragraph (1) of this regulation shall, in the case of a parliamentary election, be furnished by the returning officer to the Secretary of State.

PART V

SERVICE VOTERS

Service declaration by member of the forces and spouses

58.—(1) A service declaration made by a member of the forces shall be in Form J.

(2) A service declaration made by the spouse of a member of the forces shall be in Form K.

(3) A service declaration made by either a member of the forces or his or her spouse shall be attested by a commissioned officer who is a member of the forces or by an officer of a Government department and shall be transmitted by or on behalf of the declarant to the appropriate registration officer.

Qualification for Crown servant

59. A person employed in the service of the Crown in a post outside the United Kingdom the occupant of which is required to devote his whole time to the duties of that post and the remuneration of which is paid wholly out of moneys provided by Parliament (hereinafter referred to as "a Crown servant") shall have a service qualification.

Service declaration by Crown servants, British Council employees and spouses

60.—(1) A service declaration made by a Crown servant or a person who is employed by the British Council in a post outside the United Kingdom (hereinafter referred to as "a. British Council employee") shall be in Form L.

(2) A service declaration made by the spouse of a Crown servant or of a British Council employee shall be in Form M.

(3) A service declaration made by a person who is or will be a Crown servant or by his or her spouse shall be attested by an officer of or designated by the Government department under which that person or his or her spouse is or will be employed or by another person himself having a service qualification through being employed in the service of the Crown in a post outside the United Kingdom.

(4) A service declaration made by a person who is or will be a British Council employee or by his or her spouse shall be attested by an officer of the British Council or by another person himself having a service qualification through being employed in the service of the Crown in a post outside the United Kingdom.

Transmission of service declaration by Crown servants, British Council employees and spouses

61.—(1) A service declaration made by a person who is or will be a Crown servant or by his or her spouse shall be transmitted by the declarant to the Government department under which that person or his or her spouse is or will be employed or to an officer designated by that department and transmitted by that department or officer to the appropriate registration officer.

(2) A service declaration made by a person who is or will be a British Council employee or by his or her spouse shall be transmitted by the declarant to the British Council and transmitted by the British Council to the appropriate registration officer.

Service declaration by person about to leave the United Kingdom

62. A service declaration made by a person about to leave the United Kingdom in such circumstances as to acquire a service qualification shall be made not more than six weeks before the date on which he expects to leave the United Kingdom.

Proceedings by registration officer on receipt of service declaration

63. Subject to regulation 64, the registration officer on receipt of a service declaration shall notify to the declarant that his declaration has been received.

Invalid service declaration

64.—(1) Where a service declaration does not appear—

(a) to be properly made out and attested, or

(b) to have been transmitted in the proper manner to the registration officer,

the registration officer shall return the declaration to the declarant and explain his reasons for so doing.

(2) Where the registration officer has been notified by the appropriate Government department or an officer designated by that department or, has been notified by the British Council that a person is not entitled to make a service declaration, he shall not enter that person's name in the electors lists and shall notify that person that he has not done so but that that person may make a claim to be so entered.

Evidence as to service declaration

65. The registration officer shall treat a notice from the appropriate Government department or an officer designated by that department or a notice from the British Council that a person is not entitled to make a service declaration or that a person's service declaration has ceased to be in force as conclusive evidence thereof.

Part VI

Supplementary

Appeals

66.—(1) A person desiring to appeal against the decision of a registration officer must give notice of appeal to the registration officer and to the opposite party (if any) when the decision is given, or within fourteen days thereafter, specifying the grounds of appeal.

(2) The registration officer shall forward any such notice to the sheriff in the manner directed by rules of court together in each case with a statement of the material facts which in his opinion have been established in the case and of his decision upon the whole case and on any point which may be specified as a ground of appeal, and shall also furnish to the sheriff any further information which the sheriff may require and which he is able to furnish.

(3) Where it appears to the registration officer that any notices of appeal given to him are based on similar grounds, he shall inform the sheriff of the fact for the purpose of enabling the sheriff (if he thinks fit) to consolidate the appeals or select a case as a test case.

Official poll card

67.—(1) The official poll card issued to an elector shall be in Form E.

(2) The official poll card issued to the proxy of an elector shall be in Form F.

Return and declaration of election expenses

68.—(1) The return and declaration of expenses required by section 63 of the Act of 1949 to be authorised by an election agent shall be in Forms X and Y.

(2) The fee for inspecting a return or declaration (including any accompanying documents) specified in section 77(1) of paragraph 8(1) of Schedule 6 to, the Act of 1949 (which relate to returns and declarations of election expenses) shall be five shillings.

(3) The price of a copy of any such return, declaration or document shall be at the rate of one shilling for the contents of each side of each page.

Forms

69.—(1) Form A shall be used for the purpose for which it is expressed to be applicable.

(2) The registration officer shall without fee supply a reasonable number of copies of Forms N to W to any person.

(3) The forms set out in Schedule 1 to these regulations or forms substantially to the like effect may be used with such variations as the circumstances may require.

Sending of notices, etc.

70.—(1) Any application, notice, claim or objection which is required by these regulations to be made to the registration officer or returning officer shall be in writing and sent by post or delivered to his office or to the address specified by him for the purpose.

(2) Where the registration officer or returning officer is required by these regulations to notify any person, such notification shall be in writing and may be sent by post—

(*a*) in the case of a person other than a service voter, to the address furnished by that person for the purpose of such notification or of any record or, if there is no such address, to the last known place of abode of that person;

(*b*) in the case of a service voter, to the address provided by him for the purpose of such notification or of any record or to the address provided for the purpose by the appropriate Government department or, as the case may be, the British Council.

Publication of documents

71.—(1) Any failure to publish a document in accordance with these regulations shall not invalidate the document, but this provision shall not relieve the registration officer from any penalty for such a failure.

(2) A document which is made available for inspection in pursuance of these regulations shall be made available during ordinary business hours.

(3) Where a document is made available for inspection, any person may make a copy of, or take extracts from, such document.

Misnomers

72. No misnomer or inaccurate description of any person or place in any notice, electors list, list of claims or objections, corrupt and illegal practices list, special list or register shall prejudice the operation of that document with respect to that person or place in any case where the description of the person or place is such as to be commonly understood.

Time

73.—(1) Subject to the provisions of the following paragraphs of this regulation, where the last day of the time allowed by these regulations for any matter falls on a Sunday, Christmas Day, Good Friday, bank holiday or day appointed for public thanksgiving or mourning, that time shall be extended until the end of the next following day which is not one of the days before mentioned.

(2) In computing for the purposes of regulations 28, 33 and 35 the period of twelve days before the day of the poll at a parliamentary election a Sunday, or a day of the Christmas break, of the Easter break or of a bank holiday break shall be disregarded.

(3) In this regulation "the Christmas break", "the Easter break" and "a bank holiday break" have the same meanings as in rule 2 of the parliamentary elections rules; and in paragraph (1) of this regulation "bank holiday" means a bank holiday in Scotland under the Bank Holidays Act 1871(**a**).

Penalties

74.—(1) If any person fails to comply with or gives false information in pursuance of any such requisitions of the registration officer as is mentioned in regulation 25 he shall be liable on summary conviction to a fine not exceeding £50.

(a) 1871 c. 17.

(2) If any person without lawful authority destroys, mutilates, defaces or removes any notice published by the registration officer in connection with his registration duties or any copies of a document which have been made available for inspection in pursuance of those duties, he shall be liable on summary conviction to a fine not exceeding £20.

William Ross,
One of Her Majesty's Principal
Secretaries of State.

St. Andrew's House,
Edinburgh.
3rd June 1969.

SCHEDULE 1

FORMS

Forms for use by registration officers

FORM A: RETURN BY HOUSEHOLDER AS TO RESIDENTS Regulation 69

REPRESENTATION OF THE PEOPLE ACTS

REGISTER OF ELECTORS 19

Qualifying date: 10th October 19 . Register in force for twelve months from 16th February 19 .

I have to compile and publish an up-to-date Register of Electors for 19 . To do so, I need information which you, as Householder, are obliged by law to supply. Please complete this form accurately and return it to me now—there is no need to wait until the qualifying date before doing so. You should also complete the form even though you intend to move house some time after the qualifying date.

Registers of Electors are needed so that everyone who is entitled to vote at parliamentary or local elections may do so. A person whose name does not appear in the Register cannot vote.

The notes within tell you how to fill up the form, but if you need any further help, I shall be glad to give it.

The Electoral Registration Officer

Please complete Parts 1, 2 and 3 and sign the declaration (Part 4)

Part 1.

Name and Address:—

(a) Full name of Householder..

(b) Full postal address (where applicable state street, name and number of

house and postcode)...

....

Part 2. Residents eligible to be included (see Notes 1 and 2)

If there are none, please write "None"

Surname (BLOCK LETTERS) (Enter House-holder's name first, if resident)	Full Christian names or forenames (BLOCK LETTERS)	AGE		If a merchant seaman enter "M" (see note 1(e))
		If aged 18 on or before 16th February 19 enter a √ in this column	If 18th birthday is after 16th February 19 and on or before the following 15th February give date of birth (see note 1)	
....	....	....	....	....
....	....	....	....	....
....	....	....	....	....
....	....	....	....	....
....	....	....	....	....
....	....	....	....	....
....	....	....	....	....
....	....	....	....	....
....	....	....	....	....
....	....	....	....	....

Part 3. Other residents

(1) Is any part of your house/flat separately occupied by persons whose names are not entered in Part 2? State "YES" or "NO"....................

(2) If "YES" give names of separate occupiers................................

....

....

Part 4. Declaration

I declare to the best of my knowledge and belief—

(a) the particulars given above are true and accurate;

(b) all those whose names are entered in Part 2 above are British subjects or citizens of the Irish Republic and are over 18 or will attain their 18th birthday on or before 15th February, 19 .

Signature.. Date.......................

NOTES

1. You should enter every British subject (Commonwealth citizens are British subjects) or citizen of the Irish Republic who will be resident at your address on 10th October 19 and who is 18 years of age or over on 16th February next or whose 18th birthday is after 16th February next and on or before the following 15th February (people in this age-group can vote at elections held on or after the date of their 18th birthday).

You should include—

(a) Those who normally live at your address but are temporarily away, e.g. on holiday, as a student or in hospital (including informal patients in mental hospitals);

(b) Resident guests, other than short-stay visitors;

(c) Lodgers and resident domestics;

(d) Any person who is away working, unless his absence will be for more than six months;

(e) Merchant seamen. Enter "M" against the name of a merchant seaman. He will then be invited to appoint a proxy to vote for him, or to vote by post. A merchant seaman may be included if he would have been resident at an address (including a hostel or club for merchant seamen) but for the nature of his occupation;

(f) Reservists called up for service or training.

2. Do not enter—

(a) Members of H.M. Forces

(b) Crown servants employed outside the United Kingdom

(c) Persons employed by the British Council in posts outside the United Kingdom

(d) Wives or husbands of members of H.M. Forces, of Crown servants or of British Council staff employed outside the United Kingdom if they are living abroad to be with their husbands or wives, as the case may be

Their names will be included in the Register if they have made the necessary service declaration; to do this they should apply to their Service or Department or the British Council

(e) Aliens.

FORM B: NOTICE AS TO PUBLICATION OF A DRAFT REGISTER OF ELECTORS AND MAKING OF CLAIMS AND OBJECTIONS

————

REPRESENTATION OF THE PEOPLE ACTS

————

DRAFT REGISTER OF ELECTORS

WHAT THE DRAFT REGISTER IS FOR

1. The register of electors for the twelve months beginning on 16th February next will be based on the draft register. Unless your name is on the register of electors you will not be able to vote at parliamentary or local government elections. To make sure that you will be on the new register and able to vote you should therefore look at the draft register to see that your name is included on it.

HOW TO FIND YOUR NAME IN THE DRAFT REGISTER

2. Before you can trace your name in the draft register you must know in which polling district you live. If you do not know, ask whether an index of streets is available showing where your address appears in the register.

WHAT TO DO IF YOU FIND THAT YOUR NAME IS NOT ON THE DRAFT REGISTER

3. If your name is not on the draft register and you think it ought to be, you should submit a claim to the electoral registration officer before 16th December on a form which he will give you.

4. Your name ought to be on the register if you are over 18 now, or your 18th birthday is not later than 15th February in the year after next, and

either (i) you were resident at an address in the constituency on 10th October last,

    or (ii) you had, as a service voter, made a service declaration on or before 10th October last in respect of an address in the constituency.

OBJECTIONS TO OR ALTERATION OF ENTRIES

5. A request for the alteration of any entry, or an objection to the inclusion of any other person's name, should be submitted to the electoral registration officer before 16th December on a form which he will give you.

Signature ....
             Electoral Registration Officer

Address ....

....

Date...........................

FORM C: NOTICE AS TO PUBLICATION OF THE ELECTORS LISTS Regulation 12 AND MAKING OF CLAIMS AND OBJECTIONS

REPRESENTATION OF THE PEOPLE ACTS

ELECTORS LISTS

WHAT THE LISTS ARE FOR

1. The register of electors for the twelve months beginning on 16th February next will be based on these electors lists. Unless your name is on the register of electors you will not be able to vote at parliamentary or local government elections. To make sure that you will be on the new register and able to vote you should therefore look at these lists.

HOW TO FIND YOUR NAME IN THE LISTS

2. Before you can trace your name in the lists you must know in which polling district you live. If you do not know, ask whether an index of streets is available showing where your address appears in the register.

3. There are three lists, marked A, B and C.

List A is the register for the present year.

List B shows the names which will be added to it next year.

List C shows the names which will be removed from it next year.

  (i) Look at List A first.

  (ii) If your name is in List A, look at List C. If your name is not in List C, then it will be included in the new register, and you will be able to vote.

  (iii) If your name is not in List A, look at List B. If your name is in List B, then it will be included in the new register, and you will be able to vote.

WHAT TO DO IF YOU FIND THAT YOUR NAME WILL NOT BE ON THE REGISTER

4. If you think your name ought to be on the register, you should submit a claim to the electoral registration officer before 16th December on a form which he will give you.

5. Your name ought to be on the register if you are over 18 now, or your 18th birthday is not later than 15th February in the year after next, and

either (i) you were resident at an address in the constituency on 10th October last,

  or (ii) you had, as a service voter, made a service declaration on or before 10th October last in respect of an address in the constituency.

OBJECTIONS TO OR ALTERATION OF ENTRIES

6. A request for the alteration of any entry, or an objection to the inclusion of any other person's name, should be submitted to the electoral registration officer before 16th December on a form which he will give you.

Signature ....
  Electoral Registration Officer

Address ....

  ....

Date...............................

FORM D: PROXY PAPER

REPRESENTATION OF THE PEOPLE ACTS

Constituency..

Polling district..

Local government electoral area(s)...

(Name of proxy)...

(Address)...

....

is hereby appointed as proxy for

(Name of elector)...

who is qualified as a *$\frac{\text{service voter}}{\text{resident}}$ to be registered for

(Qualifying address)..

*Delete which-
ever is inappli-
cable.

....

to vote for *him/her at

*the parliamentary election for the above constituency

on ....

*any election for the above parliamentary constituency
or local government electoral area(s) (*see* Note 1)

This proxy appointment is not valid until...

Signature.. Date.........................
(Electoral Registration Officer)

Address ....

....

NOTES

1. If your appointment as proxy is for a particular parliamentary election, it will be valid for that election only. In other cases your appointment will continue in force until the electoral registration officer informs you to the contrary (e.g. because the elector cancels it).

If the elector is shown on this form as a resident, your appointment will be valid for all parliamentary and local government elections for the constituency and local government electoral area(s) named above.

If the elector is shown on this form as a service voter, your appointment will be valid for all parliamentary and local government elections for the constituency and local government electoral area(s) named above unless the elector applies to vote by post at a particular parliamentary election. If he does this, your appointment will be suspended for that election only and you will be so informed.

If a ballot paper is issued to the elector at the polling station before you apply for a ballot paper on his behalf, you will not be entitled to vote as proxy.

2. To vote as proxy at an election you must go in person to the polling station for the elector's qualifying address, except that you may apply to vote by post as proxy if either—

(a) you are entitled to vote by post in respect of your own vote at the election, or

(b) in the case of a parliamentary election only, your address is not in the same burgh and constituency as the address for which the elector is registered, or is not within the same county electoral division.

Any application to vote by post as proxy should be made on Form V which may be obtained from the electoral registration officer.

3. It is an offence to vote, whether in person or by post, as proxy for some other person if you know that that person is subject to a legal incapacity to vote, e.g. if that person has been convicted and is detained in a penal institution in pursuance of his sentence.

Forms for use by returning officers

Regulation 67   FORM E: ELECTOR'S OFFICIAL POLL CARD

REPRESENTATION OF THE PEOPLE ACTS

Front of card

OFFICIAL POLL CARD

Constituency

....

Polling Day..

Your polling station will be

....

Number on Register ....

Name ....

Address ....

....

....

....

Back of card

PARLIAMENTARY ELECTION

The poll will be open from 7 a.m. to 10 p.m.

The address of your polling station is shown on the front of this card.

When you go to the polling station tell the clerk your name and address as shown on the front of this card. The presiding officer will give you a ballot paper; see that he stamps the official mark on it before he gives it to you.

Mark your vote on the ballot paper secretly in one of the voting compartments. Put one X in the space to the right opposite the name of the candidate for whom you wish to vote. You may vote for only one candidate. If you put any other mark on the ballot paper, your vote may not be counted.

Then fold the ballot paper in two to conceal your vote, show the official mark on the back to the presiding officer and put the paper into the ballot box.

If you spoil the ballot paper by mistake do not destroy it; give it back to the presiding officer and ask for another.

ISSUED BY THE RETURNING OFFICER

FORM F: PROXY'S OFFICIAL POLL CARD   Regulation 67

REPRESENTATION OF THE PEOPLE ACTS

Front of card

PROXY'S OFFICIAL POLL CARD

Proxy's name...

Proxy's address..

....

Back of card

PARLIAMENTARY ELECTION

CONSTITUENCY

....

Polling day...

The poll will be open from 7 a.m. to 10 p.m.

The elector named below whose proxy you are is entitled to vote at the polling station—

....

....

To vote as proxy you must go to that polling station. Tell the clerk that you wish to vote as proxy; give the name and qualifying address of the elector, as follows:—

Number on Register...

Name...

Address ....

....

The presiding officer will give you the elector's ballot paper. The method of voting as proxy is the same as for casting your own vote.

It is an offence to vote as proxy for some other person if you know that that person is subject to a legal incapacity to vote, e.g. if that person has been convicted and is detained in a penal institution in pursuance of his sentence.

ISSUED BY THE RETURNING OFFICER

Regulation 37

FORM G: CERTIFICATE OF EMPLOYMENT

_____

REPRESENTATION OF THE PEOPLE ACTS

_____

ELECTION IN THE

....

CONSTITUENCY/LOCAL GOVERNMENT ELECTORAL AREA

_____

I certify that (name)..
who is numbered..............................in the register of electors for the constituency/electoral area named above, is likely to be unable to go in person to the polling station allotted to him at the election on (date of poll).................
by reason of the particular circumstances of his employment on that date—

*Delete whichever is inapplicable.

*(a) as a constable,

*(b) by me for a purpose connected with the election.

Signature ....
*Returning Officer/Police Officer (Inspector or above)

Date.................................

NOTE: The person named above is entitled to vote at any polling station of the above constituency/electoral area on production and surrender of this certificate to the presiding officer.

FORM H: DECLARATION OF IDENTITY

REPRESENTATION OF THE PEOPLE ACTS

Front of form

Ballot Paper No.........................

I hereby declare that I am the person to whom the ballot paper numbered as above was sent.

Voter's signature (or mark)..

The voter, who is personally known to me, has signed (or marked) this declaration in my presence.

Witness's Signature...

Witness's Address...

SEE INSTRUCTIONS ON THE BACK OF THIS FORM

Back of form

INSTRUCTIONS TO THE VOTER

1. You must sign (or mark) the declaration of identity in the presence of a person known to you, who will then add his signature and address.

2. You may vote for not more than   candidate[s].

3. Place a cross (X) on the right-hand side of the ballot paper opposite the name[s] of the candidate[s] for whom you vote. Do this secretly: if you cannot vote without assistance, the person assisting you must not disclose how you have voted.

4. Put the ballot paper in the small envelope marked "A" and seal it. Then put the envelope marked "A", together with this declaration of identity, in the larger envelope marked "B". Return it without delay. The ballot paper, in order to be counted, must be received by the returning officer not later than the close of the poll.

5. If you receive more than one ballot paper, remember that it is illegal to vote more than once (otherwise than as proxy) at the same election.

6. At this election you cannot vote in person at a polling station, even if you receive an official poll card.

7. If you inadvertently spoil your postal ballot paper, you can apply to the returning officer for another one. With your application you must return, in a fresh envelope, the spoilt ballot paper, the declaration of identity and the envelopes marked "A" and "B". Remember that there is little time available if a fresh postal ballot paper is to be counted.

Forms for use by service voters

Regulation 58   FORM J: SERVICE DECLARATION AND APPLICATION FOR APPOINT-
MENT OF PROXY BY A MEMBER OF THE FORCES

REPRESENTATION OF THE PEOPLE ACTS

REGISTER OF ELECTORS 19

Qualifying date: 10th October 19

Register in force for twelve months from 16th February 19 .

Part 1.

Surname ....

            (BLOCK LETTERS)

Other names..

            (BLOCK LETTERS)

Service (R.N., Army,

R.A.F., etc.).................................Regiment or Corps.............................

Rank or Rating...........................Service No..

Present service address...

....

I HEREBY DECLARE—

     (1) that I am a British subject or citizen of the Republic of Ireland

     (2) that—

         *(*a*) I shall be 18 years of age or over on 16th February 19

         OR

         *(*b*) (if 18th birthday is after 16th February 19   and on or before the following 15th February)*

            my 18th birthday is on

Day	Month	Year
:		:

*Delete which-
ever is inappli-
cable.

     (3) that I reside, or but for my service would reside, in the United Kingdom, and—

         *(*a*) reside, or but for my service would reside, at (full postal address in block letters)...

....

....

         OR

         *(*b*) (if the declarant cannot give any such address)* have resided in the United Kingdom at (full postal address in block letters)

....

....

....

I HEREBY CANCEL any previous declaration made by me.

Signature of declarant...Date........................

Signature and Rank of attesting officer (*see* Note 3)................................

NOTES

1. This declaration is to be made with a view to registration in the register of electors which will be in force for twelve months from 16th February 19   and with reference to your circumstances on the qualifying date for that register, i.e. 10th October 19 .

2. The declaration is to be made during the twelve months ending with the qualifying date.

3. The declaration must be attested by a commissioned officer or by an officer of a Government Department.

4. When completed and attested, this form should be sent to the Electoral Registration Officer.

Part 2.

Regulation 30

PROXY APPOINTMENT

(While you are outside the United Kingdom you can vote only by proxy.)

I HEREBY CANCEL ANY PREVIOUS PROXY APPOINTMENT AND APPLY FOR THE APPOINTMENT AS MY PROXY OF—

Names of first choice...
(BLOCK LETTERS)

Postal Address...
(BLOCK LETTERS)

....

Relationship, if any, to elector...

OR IF HE OR SHE IS UNWILLING OR UNABLE TO BE APPOINTED

Names of second choice..
(BLOCK LETTERS)

Postal Address...
(BLOCK LETTERS)

....

Relationship, if any, to elector...

Signature.. Date....................

NOTES

1. A person to vote as proxy must be a British subject or citizen of the Republic of Ireland, of voting age and not subject to any legal incapacity to vote. A proxy appointed in consequence of this application will be entitled to vote for you at all parliamentary and local government elections.

2. If the address in paragraph (3) of Part 1 is the same as that in your previous declaration (if any) you need not apply for the appointment of a proxy unless you want to appoint a different one; the previous appointment will remain valid. If, however, the address is different, you will need to apply afresh for the appointment of a proxy.

3. If at any time you wish to cancel the appointment of your proxy, you should notify the Electoral Registration Officer.

Regulation 58 **FORM K: SERVICE DECLARATION AND APPLICATION FOR APPOINTMENT OF PROXY BY THE SPOUSE OF A MEMBER OF THE FORCES**

REPRESENTATION OF THE PEOPLE ACTS

REGISTER OF ELECTORS 19

Qualifying date: 10th October 19 .

Register in force for twelve months from 16th February 19

Part 1.

Surname ....
    (BLOCK LETTERS)

Other names...
    (BLOCK LETTERS)

Other names of *husband/wife...

Service (R.N., Army,
R.A.F., etc.)...............................Regiment or Corps............................

Rank or Rating...........................Service No...................................

Present address of *husband/wife..

....

I HEREBY DECLARE—

    (1) that I am a British subject or citizen of the Republic of Ireland

    (2) that—

        *(a) I shall be 18 years of age or over on 16th February 19

        OR

        *(b) (if 18th birthday is after 16th February 19 and on or before the following 15th February)

	Day	Month	Year
my 18th birthday is on	:		:

*Delete whichever is inapplicable.

    (3) that I reside, or expect to go abroad within six weeks (see Note 2) to reside, outside the United Kingdom to be with my *husband/wife who is a member of the forces.

    (4) that but for my *husband/wife's service I would be residing in the United Kingdom, and—

        *(a) would be residing at (full postal address in block letters)

        ....

        ....

        OR

        *(b) (if the declarant cannot give any such address) have resided in the United Kingdom at (full postal address in block letters)

        ....

        ....

        ....

I HEREBY CANCEL any previous declaration made by me.

Signature of
declarant.. Date........................

Signature and Rank of attesting officer (see Note 3)

NOTES

1. This declaration is to be made with a view to registration in the register of electors which will be in force for twelve months from 16th February 19   and with reference to your circumstances on the qualifying date for that register, i.e. 10th October 19 .

2. The declaration is to be made during the twelve months ending with the qualifying date, but a person about to leave the United Kingdom must not make it more than six weeks before the expected date of departure.

3. The declaration must be attested by a commissioned officer or by an officer of a Government Department.

4. When completed and attested this form should be sent to the Electoral Registration Officer.

Part 2.   **Regulation 30**

Part 2 of this form shall be the same as Part 2 of Form J in this Schedule except that in paragraph 2 of the notes thereto for the reference to "paragraph (3) of Part 1" there shall be substituted a reference to "paragraph (4) of Part 1".

Regulation 60

FORM L: SERVICE DECLARATION AND APPLICATION FOR APPOINTMENT OF PROXY BY A CROWN SERVANT OR BY A PERSON EMPLOYED BY THE BRITISH COUNCIL

REPRESENTATION OF THE PEOPLE ACTS

REGISTER OF ELECTORS 19

Qualifying date: 10th October 19 .

Register in force for twelve months from 16th February 19 .

Part 1.

Surname ....
(BLOCK LETTERS)

Other names...
(BLOCK LETTERS)

I HEREBY DECLARE—

(1) that I am a British subject or citizen of the Republic of Ireland

(2) that—

*(a) I shall be 18 years of age or over on 16th February 19

OR

*(b) (if 18th birthday is after 16th February 19 and on or before the following 15th February)

	Day	Month	Year
my 18th birthday is on	:		:

(3) that I am employed, or leaving the United Kingdom to take up employment (see Note 2), in the service of the *Crown/British Council—

*Delete whichever is inapplicable.

Description of post...

Name of Government Department
under which you are employed (if applicable)................................

Present address..
....

(4) that but for my service abroad I would be residing in the United Kingdom, and

*(c) would be residing at (full postal address in block letters)...............
....
....

OR

*(b) (if the declarant cannot give any such address) have resided in the United Kingdom at (full postal address in block letters)
....
....
....

I HEREBY CANCEL any previous declaration made by me

Signature of
declarant.. Date........................

Signature of person attesting (see Note 3)...

Rank or official position...

NOTES

1. This declaration is to be made with a view to registration in the register of electors which will be in force for twelve months from 16th February 19   and with reference to your circumstances on the qualifying date for that register, i.e. 10th October 19 .

2. The declaration is to be made during the twelve months ending with the qualifying date, but a person about to leave the United Kingdom must not make it more than six weeks before the expected date of departure.

3. The declaration must be attested by an officer of, or designated by, the Government Department under which you are employed, or, as the case may be, by an officer of the British Council, or by another person who has a service qualification through being employed in the service of the Crown in a post outside the United Kingdom.

4. This form when completed and attested should be returned to the Government Department under which you are employed or to an officer designated by that Department or to the British Council as the case may be.

Part 2.

Regulation 30

Part 2 of this form shall be the same as Part 2 of Form J in this Schedule except that in paragraph 2 of the notes thereto for the reference to "paragraph (3) of Part 1" there shall be substituted a reference to "paragraph (4) of Part 1".

Regulation 60

FORM M: SERVICE DECLARATION AND APPLICATION FOR APPOINTMENT OF PROXY BY THE SPOUSE OF A CROWN SERVANT OR OF A PERSON EMPLOYED BY THE BRITISH COUNCIL

REPRESENTATION OF THE PEOPLE ACTS

REGISTER OF ELECTORS 19 .

Qualifying date: 10th October 19 .

Register in force for twelve months from 16th February 19 .

Part 1.

Surname ....
(BLOCK LETTERS)

Other names...
(BLOCK LETTERS)

Other names of *husband/wife

I HEREBY DECLARE—

(1) that I am a British subject or citizen of the Republic of Ireland

(2) that—

   *(a) I shall be 18 years of age or over on 16th February 19

   OR

   *(b) (if 18th birthday is after 16th February 19   and on or before the following 15th February)

my 18th birthday is on

Day	Month	Year
:		:

*Delete whichever is inapplicable.

(3) that I reside, or expect to go abroad within six weeks (see Note 2) to reside, outside the United Kingdom to be with my *husband/wife, who is employed, or is leaving the United Kingdom to take up employment, in the service of the *Crown/British Council.

Description of *husband/wife's post...

Name of Government Department
under which *husband/wife employed (if applicable).......................

Present address of *husband/wife..
....

(4) that but for my *husband/wife's service I would be residing in the United Kingdom, and—

   *(a) would be residing at (full postal address in block letters)...............
....
....

   OR

   *(b) (if the declarant cannot give any such address) have resided in the United Kingdom at (full postal address in block letters)..................
....
....
....

I HEREBY CANCEL any previous declaration made by me

Signature of
declarant... Date.......................

Signature of person attesting (see Note 3)...

Rank or official position...

NOTES

1. This declaration is to be made with a view to registration in the register of electors which will be in force for twelve months from 16th February 19   and with reference to your circumstances on the qualifying date for that register, i.e. 10th October 19 .

2. The declaration is to be made during the twelve months ending with the qualifying date, but a person about to leave the United Kingdom must not make it more than six weeks before the expected date of departure.

3. The declaration must be attested by an officer of, or designated by, the Government Department under which your husband or wife is employed, or, as the case may be, an officer of the British Council, or by another person who has a service qualification through being employed in the service of the Crown in a post outside the United Kingdom.

4. This form when completed and attested should be returned to the Government Department under which your husband or wife is employed or to an officer designated by that Department or to the British Council as the case may be.

Part 2. Regulation 30

Part 2 of this form shall be the same as Part 2 of Form J in this Schedule except that in paragraph 2 of the notes thereto for the reference to "paragraph (3) of Part 1" there shall be substituted a reference to "paragraph (4) of Part 1"

FORM N: APPLICATION BY A SERVICE VOTER IN THE UNITED
KINGDOM TO VOTE BY POST

_____

REPRESENTATION OF THE PEOPLE ACTS

_____

I, (Surname...
(BLOCK LETTERS)

(Other names)...
(BLOCK LETTERS)

(Rank or   (Service
Rating).. No.)..........................

am registered as a Service voter for

....

....

(Give the qualifying address which you gave on your service declaration)

and I apply for a ballot paper for the coming parliamentary election to be sent
to me at

....

....

(Give full postal address in block letters)

Signature ....Date ....

NOTES

1. If you have changed your name since completing your service declaration,
put your former name in brackets after your present name.

2. You should send this application to the Electoral Registration Officer
at the address stated on his ackowledgement of your service declaration.

Forms for use by other persons

FORM O: CLAIM TO BE REGISTERED AS AN ELECTOR

Regulation 14

REPRESENTATION OF THE PEOPLE ACTS

(If this form in sent to the Electoral Registration Officer by post, postage must be prepaid)

The last day for lodging a claim is 16th December

Constituency of...

To the Electoral Registration Officer

1. Surname (BLOCK LETTERS)..

2. Other names (BLOCK LETTERS) ....

3. (a) Will claimant be 18 years of age or over on 16th February next? (Yes or No)..

   (b) If not, give date of birth of claimant...

4. Full postal address of claimant's usual residence as at 10th October last

....

5. (a) Was claimant resident at the said address on 10th October last? (Yes or No) ....

   (b) Had claimant made a service declaration by 10th October last? (Yes or No) ....

   (c) Was claimant a merchant seaman on 10th October last? (Yes or No)

....

DECLARATION

The above particulars are true and correct in all respects, and in accordance with them the claimant, who is a British subject or citizen of the Republic of Ireland, claims to be registered as a parliamentary and local government elector.

Signature of claimant or person signing on behalf of claimant.....................

Address of person signing (if not the claimant)..

....

Date..............................

The qualifications for registration are:

For parliamentary and local government elections, residence on 10th October last; a service voter must have made a service declaration on or before the date.

The person must be a British subject or citizen of the Republic of Ireland; and he must be 18 years of age or over on 16th February next or after 16th February next and on or before the following 15th February (people in this latter age group can vote at elections held on or after the date of their 18th birthday).

Note.—Any false declaration made by a person for the purpose of this claim will render such person liable to a penalty.

Regulation 14   **FORM P: FORM OF OBJECTION TO AN ENTRY IN THE ELECTORS LISTS**

———

REPRESENTATION OF THE PEOPLE ACTS

———

(If this form is sent to the Electoral Registration Officer by post, postage must be prepaid.)

1. *Form of objection* (*parliamentary electors*)

To the Electoral Registration Officer for the constituency of..........................

*Here insert extract from printed electors lists, stating registration unit, or name and address as given in claim.

I hereby give you notice that I object to the entry of*................................

....

....

....

†Delete if inapplicable.

as a parliamentary elector [in accordance with the claim made in that behalf]†
The grounds of my objection are

....

....

....

‡Here insert extract from printed electors lists, stating registration unit.

I am entered in the electors list as a parliamentary elector for the above constituency as follows‡ ....

....

....

Signature ....

Address ....

Date ....

2. *Form of objection* (*local government electors*)

To the Electoral Registration Officer for...

*Here insert extract from printed electors lists, stating registration unit, or name and address as given in claim.

I hereby give you notice that I object to the entry of*................................

....

....

†Delete if inapplicable.

as a local government elector for [all] [the following] local government area[s] [in accordance with the claim made in that behalf]†

....

The grounds of my objection are...

....

....

‡Here insert extract from printed electors lists, stating registration unit.

I am entered in the lists of local government electors for the above area[s] as follows‡

....

....

Signature ....

Address ....

....

Date...

FORM Q: APPLICATION TO BE TREATED AS AN ABSENT VOTER FOR AN INDEFINITE PERIOD OWING TO OCCUPATION OR PHYSICAL INCAPACITY

Regulation 28

REPRESENTATION OF THE PEOPLE ACTS

I, (Surname)...
(BLOCK LETTERS)

(Other names)...
(BLOCK LETTERS)

am qualified to be registered as an elector for (address in full in block letters)

....

....

....

I apply to be treated as an absent voter at parliamentary and local government elections because I am likely to be unable to go in person to the polling station (or, where (c) or (d) below applies, to vote unaided)—

*(a) by reason of the general nature of my occupation, service or employment as

....

(Give full reasons for application)

*(b) by reason of the general nature of the occupation, service or employment of my *husband/wife as

*Delete whichever is inapplicable.

....

and my resulting absence from my qualifying address until............

...............(insert likely date of return) to be with my *husband/wife

*(c) by reason of blindness† (in respect of which I have been registered as a blind person by the..

....Council)

†If the applicant is not registered as a blind person delete the words in brackets and ask a medical practitioner to complete the certificate below

*(d) by reason of physical incapacity (see Note 2)

Signature... Date ....

Address in the United Kingdom (in block letters) to which ballot paper is to be sent (if different from address given above)

....

....

Medical Certificate

I certify—

(*a*) that the statement at (2) above is correct;

(*b*) that the applicant's inability is likely to continue for.........months/indefinitely*

*It is important to indicate which alternative applies.

Signature ....

Address ....

....

....

Date...................................

Notes

1. This application, if allowed, will continue in force until you cancel it or cease to be registered for your present qualifying address or become registered in a different capacity or until the Electoral Registration Officer gives you notice to the contrary. This application will be valid for all parliamentary and local government elections at which you are entitled to vote. A separate application should be made for each qualifying address.

2. Where the ground of the application is blindness or other physical incapacity, the certificate above must be completed by a doctor (or by a Christian Science practitioner), unless you are registered as a blind person.

3. If the ground of the application is the nature of your occupation, service or employment (or that of your husband or wife) and you are likely to be at sea or out of the United Kingdom at the time of an election, you may apply to have a proxy appointed to vote for you. If so, apply on Form U which may be obtained from the Electoral Registration Officer.

4. If you have been appointed proxy for an elector in the same parliamentary constituency or local government electoral area, you may apply on Form V to vote as such by post, but not if you yourself have a proxy appointed for you.

Form V may be obtained from the Electoral Registration Officer.

5. Any change of address to which ballot papers are to be sent should be notified promptly to the Electoral Registration Officer. If you wait until an election occurs, you may be too late.

FORM R: APPLICATION TO VOTE BY POST OWING TO CHANGE OF RESIDENCE

Regulation 28

REPRESENTATION OF THE PEOPLE ACTS

I, (Surname)..
(BLOCK LETTERS)

(Other names)..
(BLOCK LETTERS)

am qualified to be registered as an elector for (old address in full in block letters)

....

....

....

I apply to be treated as an absent voter at parliamentary elections because I no longer reside there.   My new address is (new address in full in block letters)

....

....

....

Signature... Date.....................

NOTES

1. This application, if allowed, will continue in force for all parliamentary elections so long as you remain registered for your old address.

2. Temporary absence, e.g. on holiday, does NOT constitute a change of residence.

3. This application cannot be allowed if the address at which you now reside is in the same burgh and constituency as the address for which you are registered, or within the same county electoral division.

4. If you have been appointed proxy for an elector you may apply on Form V to vote as such by post at parliamentary elections.   Form V may be obtained from the Electoral Registration Officer.

Regulation 28   **FORM S: APPLICATION TO BE TREATED AS AN ABSENT VOTER FOR A PARTICULAR ELECTION**

REPRESENTATION OF THE PEOPLE ACTS

I, (Surname)..
    (BLOCK LETTERS)

(Other names)..
    (BLOCK LETTERS)

am qualified to be registered as an elector for (address in full in block letters)

....

....

and I apply to be treated as an absent voter at the coming parliamentary/ local government election (*see* Note 1)

in ....

constituency/local government electoral area because I am likely to be unable to go in person to the polling station allotted to me, owing to—

*(a) my service in one of Her Majesty's reserve or auxiliary forces

(*see* Note 2)...;

*(b) my employment on polling day

*(i) as a constable;

*(ii) by the returning officer in connection with the election in .... constituency/local government electoral area;

*(c) my being bound to the following religious observances (*see* Note 3)

....

....;

*(d) my acting as returning officer for....................................... constituency/local government electoral area;

*(e) my/my husband's/my wife's candidature

in ....constituency.

Signature.. Date........................

Address in the United Kingdom (in block letters) to which ballot paper is to be sent (if different from address given above)

....

....

CERTIFICATE

To be completed where (c) above applies

I certify that the statement at (c) above is correct.

Signature..

(Minister of the elector's religious denomination)

Address ....

....

Date...

NOTES

1. Where (a), (b) or (c) applies, the application may be made for any parliamentary or local government election. Where (d) applies, the application may be made for any parliamentary general election or ordinary local government election. Where (e) applies, the application may be made only for a parliamentary general election.

2. Where (a) applies, the application must state the name of the reserve or auxiliary force concerned. If the application is for a particular parliamentary election and you are likely to be at sea or out of the United Kingdom on polling day, you may apply on Form U to have a proxy appointed to vote for you.

3. Where (c) applies, the application must state the nature and times of the religious observances. The certificate above must be completed by a minister of your religious denomination.

4. If you have been appointed proxy for an elector in the same constituency or local government electoral area, you may apply on Form V to vote as such by post, but not if you yourself have a proxy appointed for you.

The forms referred to may be obtained from the Electoral Registration Officer.

Regulation 28   **FORM T: APPLICATION TO BE TREATED AS AN ABSENT VOTER FOR AN INDEFINITE PERIOD OWING TO AIR OR SEA JOURNEY NECESSARY FROM QUALIFYING ADDRESS**

REPRESENTATION OF THE PEOPLE ACTS

I, (Surname)...
    (BLOCK LETTERS)

(Other names)..
    (BLOCK LETTERS)

am qualified to be registered as an elector for (address in full in block letters)

....

....

and I apply to be treated as an absent voter at parliamentary and local government elections (*see* Note 1) because I am likely to be unable to go in person from the above address to the polling station without making a journey by air or sea.

Signature.. Date.......................

Address in the United Kingdom (in block letters) to which ballot paper is to be sent (if different from address given above)

....

....

NOTES

1. The journey in question is the journey necessary to go to the polling station from your qualifying address, not from where you may happen to be at the time of an election.

2. This application, if allowed, will continue in force until you cancel it or cease to be registered for your present qualifying address or become registered in a different capacity or until the Electoral Registration Officer gives you notice to the contrary. It will be valid for all parliamentary and local government elections at which you are entitled to vote. A separate application should be made for each qualifying address.

3. If you have been appointed proxy for an elector in the same parliamentary constituency or local government electoral area, you may apply on Form V to vote as such by post, but not if you yourself have a proxy appointed for you. Form V may be obtained from the Electoral Registration Officer.

4. Any change of the address to which ballot papers are to be sent should be notified promptly to the Electoral Registration Officer; if you wait until an election occurs, you may be too late.

FORM U: APPLICATION BY ABSENT VOTER FOR APPOINTMENT OF PROXY
Regulation 30

REPRESENTATION OF THE PEOPLE ACTS

(*Not to be used by service voters*)

I, Surname..
    (BLOCK LETTERS)

(Other names)...
    (BLOCK LETTERS)

am qualified to be registered as an elector for (address in full in block letters)

....

....

....

I have applied to be treated as an absent voter—

    *(a) at parliamentary and local government elections owing to—

        *(i) the general nature of my occupation, service or employment;

        *(ii) the general nature of the occupation, service or employment of my *husband/wife and my resulting absence from my qualifying address to be with *him/her

    *(b) at the coming parliamentary election in................................... constituency owing to my service in Her Majesty's reserve or auxiliary forces;

*Delete whichever is inapplicable.

and I declare that I am likely to be at sea or outside the United Kingdom on polling day.

I therefore apply for the person named below as first choice (or, if he or she is unwilling or unable to be appointed, the person named as second choice) to be appointed as proxy to vote for me.

PROXY APPOINTMENT

1. First choice (The elector must fill this up)

Full names..
    (BLOCK LETTERS)

....

Postal address..
    (BLOCK LETTERS)

....

Relationship, if any, to elector

....

2. Second choice (the elector should fill this up as the first choice may be unwilling or unable to be appointed)

Full names..
    (BLOCK LETTERS)

....

Postal address..
    (BLOCK LETTERS)

....

Relationship, if any, to elector

....

Signature... Date.............................

NOTES

1. A person to vote as proxy must be a British subject or citizen of the Republic of Ireland, of voting age and not subject to any legal incapacity to vote.

2. Where (*a*) applies a proxy appointed in consequence of your application to be treated as an absent voter will be entitled to vote for you at all parliamentary and local government elections. You can cancel the appointment by giving notice to the Electoral Registration Officer

3. Where (*b*) above applies the proxy's appointment will be for a particular parliamentary election only.

FORM V: APPLICATION BY A PROXY TO VOTE BY POST   Regulation 35

REPRESENTATION OF THE PEOPLE ACTS

I, (Surname)..
  (BLOCK LETTERS)

(Other names)..
  (BLOCK LETTERS)

have been appointed proxy for

(†Name) .... †As shown on
  (BLOCK LETTERS)   proxy paper.

who is registered as an elector for

(†Qualifying address)...
  (BLOCK LETTERS)

....

and I apply to vote by post as proxy for the above-named elector because—

  *(a) I am entitled to vote by post as an absent voter: the address for
       which I am registered as an elector is
       (address in full, in block letters)

       .... *Delete which-
       .... ever is inappli-
                                                                                    cable.

  *(b) the address entered below is in a different area from the address
       for which the above-named elector is registered (see Note 2).

       A ballot paper should be sent to me at the following address (block
       letters) in the United Kingdom

       ....
       ....
       ....

Signature.. Date......................

NOTES

1. Where (a) applies, this application, if allowed, will be valid for any parliamentary or local government election for which your application to be treated as an absent voter is valid so long as your appointment as proxy continues. Where (b) applies, the application will be valid only for parliamentary elections and will remain in force until you cancel it or cease to be a proxy for the elector.

2. Where (b) applies, the application cannot be allowed if your address is in the same area as the address for which the elector is registered, i.e. within the same burgh and constituency, or within the same county electoral division.

Regulations
28, 30
FORM W: APPLICATION BY SERVICE VOTER'S SPOUSE FOR APPOINTMENT OF PROXY

REPRESENTATION OF THE PEOPLE ACTS

Part 1

Surname ....
      (BLOCK LETTERS)

Other names ....
      (BLOCK LETTERS)

Other names of *husband/wife..

    *(a) Service (R.N.,   Regiment
         Army, R.A.F., etc.)....................................or Corps.................

    Rank or Rating....................................Service No...............

*Delete whichever is inapplicable.

    OR

    *(b) Name of Government Department under   Description

         which *husband/wife employed........................of post..............

    OR

    *(c) British Council   Description
                                     of post..............

    Present address of *husband/wife

    ....

    ....

    ....

(1) I am qualified to be registered as an elector for (address in full in block letters)

    ....

    ....

(2) I have made a service declaration on Form K/Form M that I reside, or expect to go abroad within six weeks to reside, outside the United Kingdom to be with my *husband/wife.

(3) I therefore apply to be treated as an absent voter and for the person named below as first choice (or, if he or she is unwilling or unable to be appointed, the person named as second choice) to be appointed to vote as proxy for me at parliamentary and local government elections.

Part 2

PROXY APPOINTMENT

1. First choice (The elector must fill this up)

Full names...
(BLOCK LETTERS)

Postal address..
(BLOCK LETTERS)

....

Relationship, if any, to elector

....

2. Second choice (the elector should fill this up as the first choice may be unwilling or unable to be appointed)

Full names...
(BLOCK LETTERS)

Postal address..
(BLOCK LETTERS)

....

Relationship, if any, to elector

....

Signature... Date.....................

NOTE

A person to vote as proxy must be a British Subject or citizen of the Republic of Ireland, of voting age and not subject to any legal incapacity to vote. A proxy appointed in consequence of your application to be treated as an absent voter will be entitled to vote for you at all parliamentary and local government elections until your service declaration on Form K/Form M takes effect.

FORM X: RETURN OF EXPENSES REQUIRED BY SECTION 63 OF THE REPRESENTATION OF THE PEOPLE ACT 1949 TO BE AUTHORISED BY AN ELECTION AGENT

Regulation 68

REPRESENTATION OF THE PEOPLE ACTS

ELECTION IN THE

....

CONSTITUENCY/LOCAL GOVERNMENT ELECTORAL AREA

Date of publication of notice of election..

The expenses incurred at the above election in support of.....................

....a candidate thereat, by.............................

....

(*insert name of person or association or body of persons incurring the expenses*) being expenses required by section 63 of the Representation of the People Act 1949, to be authorised by the election agent, amounted to £.....................

The written authority of the election agent is annexed hereto.

Signature... Date.....................

Regulation 68   FORM Y: DECLARATION AS TO EXPENSES REQUIRED BY SECTION 63 OF THE REPRESENTATION OF THE PEOPLE ACT 1949 TO BE AUTHORISED BY AN ELECTION AGENT

REPRESENTATION OF THE PEOPLE ACTS

ELECTION IN THE

....

CONSTITUENCY/LOCAL GOVERNMENT ELECTORAL AREA

Date of publication of notice of election...

I hereby declare that—

1. I am the person or a director, general manager, secretary or similar officer of the association or body of persons named as incurring expenses in the accompanying return, marked......., of expenses required by section 63 of the Representation of the People Act 1949, to be authorised by an election agent.

2. To the best of my knowledge and belief the said return is complete and correct.

3. The matters for which the expenses referred to in the said return were incurred were as follows...

....

....

Signature ....

Office held...
(In the case of an association or body of persons)

Date...................................

Regulation 38   SCHEDULE 2

TABLE OF COMPARISON OF ELECTION RULES

Parliamentary elections rules	Scottish local elections rules
Rule 25	Rule 18
,, 46	,, 39
,, 56	,, 47

EXPLANATORY NOTE

(This Note is not part of the Regulations.)

These Regulations revoke and replace the Representations of the People (Scotland) Regulations 1950 as amended. Amendments have been made in consequence of the passing of the Representation of the People Act 1969 (c.15). In particular provision is made for marking the names of persons coming of voting age during the currency of the register and of merchant seamen (Regulations 8 and 9); for correcting the published register (Regulation 23); for applications to be treated as absent voters based on the ground of religious observance (Regulations 28(2)(*a*)); for service declarations by British Council employees (Part V of the Regulations); prescribing the fees for inspection and copies of the return and declaration of election expenses (Regulation 68); and for the computation of time (Regulation 73).

Other amendments have also been made. In particular the fee for the sale of the register (Regulation 22) and the penalties for certain offences (Regulation 74) have been varied: spoilt postal ballot papers may be replaced (Regulation 50); and the procedure for dealing with postal ballot papers where a candidate has died has been specified (Regulation 56).

STATUTORY INSTRUMENTS

1969 No. 913 (C. 23)

ROAD TRAFFIC

The Vehicle and Driving Licences Act 1969 (Commencement No. 2) Order 1969

Made - - -	*4th July* 1969
Laid before Parliament	11*th July* 1969
Coming into Operation	14*th July* 1969

The Minister of Transport, in exercise of his powers under section 38(2) of the Vehicle and Driving Licences Act 1969(a) and of all other enabling powers, hereby makes the following Order:—

1. This Order may be cited as the Vehicle and Driving Licences Act 1969 (Commencement No. 2) Order 1969.

2. Section 18(2) of the Vehicle and Driving Licences Act 1969 shall come into operation on the 14th July 1969.

Given under the Official Seal of the Minister of Transport the 4th July 1969.

(L.S.)

Richard Marsh,
Minister of Transport.

EXPLANATORY NOTE

(*This Note is not part of the Order.*)

This Order brings into operation on 14th July 1969, section 18(2) of the Vehicle and Driving Licences Act 1969, which extends the powers of the Minister of Transport under section 14(9) of the Road Safety Act 1967 to make regulations, *inter alia*, providing that licences under the Vehicles (Excise) Act 1962 shall not be granted for goods vehicles to which section 14(2) of the 1967 Act applies unless evidence is produced that test certificates are in force for the vehicles, so that the regulations may be made so as to apply to such classes only of those vehicles as may be specified in the regulations.

(a) 1969 c. 27.

1969 No. 915

ANIMALS

DISEASES OF ANIMALS

The Equine Animals (Importation) Order 1969

Made - - -		*3rd July* 1969
Laid before Parliament		*16th July* 1969
Coming into Operation		*16th August* 1969

The Minister of Agriculture, Fisheries and Food and the Secretary of State, acting jointly, in exercise of the powers vested in them under sections 1, 24, 33, 84 and 85 of the Diseases of Animals Act 1950(a) (as extended by the Diseases of Animals (Extensions of Definitions) Order 1952(b) and adapted to air transport by section 11 of the Agriculture (Miscellaneous Provisions) Act 1954(c) and as read with the Transfer of Functions (Animal Health) Order 1955(d)) and all other powers enabling them in that behalf, hereby order as follows :—

Citation, extent and commencement

1. This Order, which may be cited as the Equine Animals (Importation) Order 1969, applies to Great Britain and shall come into operation on 16th August 1969.

Interpretation

2.—(1) In this order unless the context otherwise requires the following expressions have the meanings hereby respectively assigned to them :—

"the Act" means the Diseases of Animals Act 1950 ;

"equine animal" means a horse, ass, mule (which includes hinny) or zebra ;

"inspector" has the meaning assigned to it by section 84(4) of the Act ;

"the Minister" means the Minister of Agriculture, Fisheries and Food ;

"specified country" means any of the countries (or other places) specified in Schedule 1 to this order, being countries (or other places) in relation to which the Minister and the Secretary of State are satisfied that equine animals therein are affected with African horse sickness (*Pestis equorum*), or that there is risk of their being so affected.

(2) The Interpretation Act 1889(e) applies to the interpretation of this order as it applies to the interpretation of an Act of Parliament, and as if this order and the orders hereby revoked were Acts of Parliament.

(a) 1950 c. 36. For change of title of the Minister see S.I. 1955/554 (1955 I, p. 1200).
(b) S.I. 1952/1236 (1952 I, p. 128).
(c) 1954 c. 39.
(d) S.I. 1955/958 (1955 I, p. 1184).
(e) 1889 c. 63.

Extension of definitions

3. For the purposes of this order, and for the purposes of sections 1, 24, 33 and Part III of the Act, in so far as they may be applicable to the making, administration and enforcement of this order—

> (*a*) the definition of the expression "animals" contained in section 84(1) of the Act (as extended to specified equine animals by the Diseases of Animals (Extension of Definitions) Order 1952) shall continue to be extended so as to comprise zebras, and

> (*b*) the definition of the expression "disease" in section 84(3) of the Act shall continue to be extended so as to comprise infectious equine anaemia, encephalomyelitis, equine virus abortion and African horse sickness (*Pestis equorum*).

Regulation of importation of equine animals into Great Britain

4.—(1) The landing or unloading in Great Britain of any equine animal brought from a specified country is hereby prohibited.

(2) The landing or unloading in Great Britain of any equine animal brought from any country (not being a specified country) outside Great Britain, except Northern Ireland, the Republic of Ireland, the Channel Islands or the Isle of Man, is hereby prohibited unless it is accompanied by a certificate as mentioned in article 5 below of a veterinary surgeon duly authorised by the government of the country from which the equine animal was brought.

(3) For the purposes of paragraph (1) above an equine animal is brought from a specified country if its journey to Great Britain started in a specified country, or any vehicle, vessel or aircraft carrying the animal in the course of its journey to Great Britain passed through, called at or landed in a specified country ; and for the purposes of paragraph (2) above the country from which an equine animal is brought to Great Britain means the country in which its journey to Great Britain started but does not include any country (other than a specified country) through which the animal passed in transit on its way to a port or aerodrome for shipment to Great Britain without any break of journey except such as may be necessary for feeding watering or rest or incidental to transhipment or the working of traffic.

Provisions as to certificates

5.—(1) Any certificate required by this order shall be in the form set forth in Schedule 2 to this order, or to the like effect.

(2) A certificate may refer to more than one equine animal, but the full particulars required thereon shall be separately given in respect of each animal referred to in the certificate.

(3) In the case of—

> (*a*) a racehorse, or

> (*b*) a horse entered for the purposes of exhibition or competition at any show, parade or event,

travelling with a permanent identity document approved under international arrangements the certificate required by this order may be incorporated with that document and shall contain such minor modifications as are appropriate to the circumstances of the case.

(4) Any certificate required by this order shall be delivered up (or, where paragraph (3) of this article applies, produced) on the landing or unloading of any equine animal referred to in the certificate by the person in charge of the animal to an officer of Customs and Excise at the place of landing or unloading.

Power to require mallein test on arrival in Great Britain

6. For the purpose of preventing the introduction or spread of glanders (or farcy), the Minister may cause any equine animal imported into Great Britain from any country (not being a specified country) outside Great Britain except Northern Ireland, the Republic of Ireland, the Channel Islands or the Isle of Man to be tested with mallein by a veterinary inspector at any time within twenty-eight days after the arrival of the animal, and the owner of the animal and occupier of the premises where the animal is located shall give all necessary facilities for such testing.

Detention of equine animals illegally imported

7.—(1) If any equine animal is imported into Great Britain in contravention of this order, the Minister in respect of an equine animal landed or unloaded in England or Wales, or the Secretary of State in respect of an equine animal landed or unloaded in Scotland, may serve on any person having the control or custody of the animal a notice in writing requiring him at the expense of the owner of the animal or the person on whom the notice was served to detain or isolate the animal subject to any conditions imposed by the notice and to subject it, or to permit it to be subjected to, such examinations and tests as the Minister or Secretary of State may determine ; and the person on whom such a notice is served shall comply with the requirements thereof.

(2) If any person on whom such a notice is served fails to comply with the requirements thereof it shall be lawful for an inspector, without prejudice to any proceedings for an offence arising out of such default, to seize the animal in respect of which the notice was served, and to detain or isolate it and subject it to such examinations and tests as he may determine.

(3) A person who has failed to comply with the terms of any such notice shall give all necessary facilities to an inspector to enable him to exercise the power conferred on him by paragraph (2) of this article, and the reasonable expenses incurred by such an inspector in exercising the said power shall be recoverable as a civil debt from the owner of the animal or the person on whom the notice was served.

Revocation and saving

8.—(1) The orders set forth in Schedule 3 to this order are hereby revoked.

(2) Any certificate given (whether or not accompanied by a declaration), or notice served, under any provision of the orders revoked by this order and in force immediately before the coming into operation of this order shall not be invalidated by such revocation but shall have effect as if given or served under the corresponding provision of this order.

Enforcement

9. This order shall, except where it is otherwise provided, be executed and enforced by the Local Authority.

In Witness whereof the Official Seal of the Minister of Agriculture, Fisheries and Food is hereunto affixed on 3rd July 1969.

(L.S.)   *Cledwyn Hughes,*
                                              Minister of Agriculture,
                                                  Fisheries and Food.

Given under the Seal of the Secretary of State for Scotland on 3rd July 1969.

(L.S.)   *William Ross,*
                                                  Secretary of State
                                                      for Scotland.

SCHEDULE 1

Countries (or other places) from which the landing or unloading in Great Britain of equine animals is prohibited

1. The Kingdom of Afghanistan
    Bahrain
    The Republic of Cyprus
    The Republic of India
    The Empire of Iran
    The Republic of Iraq
    The State of Israel
    The Hashemite Kingdom of Jordan
    The State of Kuwait
    The Lebanese Republic

    The Sultanate of Muscat and Oman
    The Republic of Pakistan
    Qatar
    The Kingdom of Saudi Arabia
    The Peoples' Republic of Southern
              Yemen
    The Syrian Arab Republic
    Any of the Trucial States
    The Republic of Turkey
    The Yemen

2. Any country or other place in Africa.

SCHEDULE 2

Veterinary Certificate for Importation of Equine Animals into Great Britain
Description of Animal

Type and Breed..Age...........Sex...........

I, the undersigned, being a Veterinary Surgeon duly authorised by the Government of.....................................(A) hereby certify, in respect of the animal described above, that:—

(1) The owner or person in charge of the animal has made a written declaration to me that to the best of his knowledge and belief the animal has not, during the 24 months immediately preceding the present exportation been in or called at Afghanistan, Bahrain, Cyprus, India, Iran, Iraq, Israel, Jordan, Kuwait, Lebanon, Muscat and Oman, Pakistan, Qatar, Saudi Arabia, South Yemen, Syria, any of the Trucial States, Turkey, Yemen, any country or place in Africa or any country where African Horse Sickness has existed at any time during the past 24 months.

Notes
(A) Insert name of country from which animal was exported.

(2) (*a*) In the 24 months immediately preceding the present exportation no case of African Horse Sickness has occurred in............................(A)

(B) Insert date of importation.

(*b*) The animal has, within 48 hours before its exportation, been examined by me and showed no symptoms of any communicable disease.

(C) Insert date of test.

(*c*) After making enquiries, to the best of my knowledge and belief, during the 3 months immediately preceding the present exportation since entering..............................(A) on................................(B) the animal has not suffered from nor been on any premises in which infectious equine anaemia, or encephalomyelitis, or any clinical case of equine virus abortion, or any notifiable disease of equines has existed during the past 3 months, and the animal has not otherwise been exposed to the risk of infection by these diseases.

Alternatives: one to be completed and the other deleted.

(*d*) (i) During the 6 months immediately preceding the present exportation no case of glanders has occurred in.....................................(A)

or

(ii) The animal was tested with mallein on................................(C) (not more than 10 days before export), and showed a negative result

Alternatives: one to be completed and others deleted.

or

(iii) The animal was subjected to a complement fixation test for glanders on.......................................(C) (not more than 10 days before export) with a negative result.

....Signature of
duly authorised Veterinary Surgeon

....Date

Article 8

SCHEDULE 3

Orders revoked	References
The Importation of Horses, Asses and Mules Order 1957	S.I. 1957/467 (1957 I, p. 159).
The Importation of Horses, Asses and Mules (Amendment) (No. 2) Order 1966	S.I. 1966/1327 (1966 III, p. 3657).
The Importation of Horses, Asses and Mules (African Horse Sickness) (Prohibition) Order 1961	S.I. 1961/260 (1961 I, p. 436).
The Importation of Horses, Asses and Mules (African Horse Sickness) (Amendment) Order 1966	S.I. 1966/1349 (1966 III, p. 3679).
The Zebras (Control of Importation) Order 1963	S.I. 1963/1004 (1963 II, p. 1662).

EXPLANATORY NOTE

(This Note is not part of the Order.)

This Order consolidates with amendments the Importation of Horses, Asses and Mules Order 1957 as amended, and as extended to zebras by the Zebras (Control of Importation) Order 1963.

The Order continues the absolute prohibition on importing equine animals from specified countries in relation to which a risk of African Horse Sickness is considered to exist (but Spain, Portugal and Gibraltar are no longer specified), and provides for the substitution of a new form of veterinary certificate applicable to the importation of equine animals from all other countries outside Great Britain except Northern Ireland, the Republic of Ireland, the Channel Islands and the Isle of Man.

STATUTORY   INSTRUMENTS

1969 No. 918 (S.73)

NATIONAL HEALTH SERVICE, SCOTLAND

The National Health Service (Charges for Appliances) (Scotland) Regulations 1969

Made - - - - *7th July* 1969
Laid before Parliament 8th *July* 1969
Coming into Operation 11*th August* 1969

In exercise of the powers conferred on me by section 42 of the National Health Service (Scotland) Act 1947(a), section 1 of, and the Schedule to, the National Health Service Act 1951(b), section 7 of the National Health Service Act 1952(c) and section 2 of the National Health Service Act 1961(d), and of all other powers enabling me in that behalf, I hereby make the following regulations:—

1.—(1) These regulations may be cited as the National Health Service (Charges for Appliances) (Scotland) Regulations 1969 and shall come into operation on 11th August 1969.

(2) The Interpretation Act 1889(e) applies for the interpretation of these regulations as it applies for the interpretation of an Act of Parliament.

2. The authorised charge per lens (specified in the Schedule to the National Health Service Act 1951 for glasses other than children's glasses), which was increased by section 1(2) of the National Health Service Act 1961 to 12*s*. 6*d*., or in the case of a bifocal or multifocal lens to 20*s*. is hereby increased to 16*s*., or in the case of a bifocal or multifocal lens to 25*s*.

3. The authorised charges specified in the Schedule to the National Health Service Act 1951 for one denture with the number of teeth specified in Column 1 of the table below shall, instead of being the amount specified in relation thereto in Column 2 (being the amount specified in section 1(1) of the National Health Service Act 1961), be the amount specified in relation thereto in Column 3.

TABLE

Column 1					*Column* 2	*Column* 3
					£ *s. d.*	£ *s. d.*
1, 2 or 3 teeth	..	..	..	..	2 5 0	2 16 0
4 to 8 teeth	..	..	..	..	2 10 0	3 2 0
More than 8 teeth	..	..	..	..	2 15 0	3 9 0

4. The maximum charge specified in section 2(2) of the National Health Service Act 1952 (maximum charge for services some of which are chargeable under the Act of 1951), which was increased to £5 by section 1(1) of the National Health Service Act 1961, shall be increased to £6 5*s*.

5. No charge, which would otherwise be payable under section 1 of the National Health Service Act 1951, shall be payable in respect of the supply (including the replacement) of a dental appliance as part of hospital and specialist services to a person who has undergone operative procedures affecting the mandible, the maxilla, or the soft tissues of the mouth as part of treatment for invasive tumours.

(a) 1947 c. 27.   (b) 1951 c. 31.   (c) 1952 c. 25.   (d) 1961 c. 19.   (e) 1889 c. 63.

6. In the National Health Service (General Dental and Supplementary Ophthalmic Services) (Scotland) Regulations 1951(a), as amended(b) for paragraph (1) of regulation 5 (Making of charges for the supply of optical appliances) as substituted by regulation 4 of the National Health Service (Supplementary Ophthalmic Services) (Scotland) Amendment Regulations 1961(c) there shall be substituted the following paragraph:—

" **5.**—(1) Subject to the provisions of this regulation, an optician shall, in respect of the supply under Part IV of the Act of 1947 of such optical appliances as are described in the Schedule to the National Health Service Act 1951 be entitled to make and recover the appropriate charge specified in the said schedule, as varied by section 1 of the National Health Service Act 1961 or by regulations made under section 2 of the said Act."

7. In the National Health Service (Charges for Appliances) (Scotland) Regulations 1951(d), as amended by the National Health Service (Charges for Appliances) (Scotland) Amendment Regulations 1961(e), for regulation 2 there shall be substituted the following regulation:—

" **2.** These regulations relate to the charges authorised by the National Health Service Act 1951, as varied by section 1 of the National Health Service Act 1961 or by regulations made under section 2 of the said Act, to be made and recovered in respect of the supply of dental and optical appliances under Part II of the National Health Service (Scotland) Act 1947."

8. These regulations shall not have effect—

(*a*) in relation to a dental appliance supplied under Part II of the National Health Service (Scotland) Act 1947 or to optical appliances supplied under Part II or Part IV thereof, if the examination or testing of sight leading to the supply of the appliance, or the first such examination or testing, took place before the commencement of these regulations; or

(*b*) in relation to a dental appliance supplied under Part IV of the said Act of 1947 or in relation to services provided as part of the general dental services under Part IV thereof, if the contract or arrangement in pursuance of which the appliance is supplied or the services are provided was made before the commencement of these regulations.

St. Andrew's House,
  Edinburgh.
7th July 1969.

William Ross,
One of Her Majesty's Principal
Secretaries of State.

(a) S.I. 1951/861 (1951 I, p. 1412).   (b) S.I. 1956/41, 1961/915 (1956 I, p. 1612, 1961 II, p. 1761).
(c) S.I. 1961/915 (1961 II, p. 1761).   (d) S.I. 1951/862 (1951 I, p. 1411).
(e) S.I. 1961/917 (1961 II, p. 1771).

EXPLANATORY NOTE

(*This Note is not part of the Regulations.*)

These regulations increase the authorised charge for glasses supplied under the National Health Service by increasing the charge per lens from 12*s*. 6*d*. to 16*s*. for single vision lenses and from 20*s*. to 25*s*. for bifocal or multifocal lenses. They also increase the authorised charges for the supply of dentures and the maximum charge for a course of dental treatment including the provision of dentures, and make consequential amendments to the regulations dealing with the recovery of charges. The regulations also exempt from charges for dentures supplied by hospitals persons who have undergone operative procedures affecting the mouth as part of treatment for invasive tumours.

1969 No. 921 (L. 11)

LEGAL AID AND ADVICE, ENGLAND

The Legal Aid (Extension of Proceedings) Regulations 1969

Made - - - - -	21st May 1969
Laid before Parliament	16th June 1969
Coming into Operation	1st August 1969

The Lord Chancellor, in exercise of the powers conferred on him by sections 1 and 12 of the Legal Aid and Advice Act 1949(a), hereby makes the following Regulations :—

1.—(1) These Regulations may be cited as the Legal Aid (Extension of Proceedings) Regulations 1969 and shall come into operation on 1st August 1969.

(2) The Interpretation Act 1889(b) shall apply to the interpretation of these Regulations as it applies to the interpretation of an Act of Parliament.

2. Notwithstanding anything in paragraph 1 of Part II of the First Schedule to the Legal Aid and Advice Act 1949, the making of a counter-claim for defamation in proceedings for which legal aid may be given shall not of itself affect any right of the defendant to the counterclaim to legal aid in the proceedings and legal aid may be granted to enable him to defend such counterclaim.

3. The proceedings in which legal aid may be given shall include the proceedings contained in the Schedule to these Regulations.

Dated 21st May 1969.

Gardiner, C.

SCHEDULE

PROCEEDINGS IN CONNECTION WITH WHICH LEGAL AID MAY BE GIVEN

1. Proceedings in a magistrates' court or a court of quarter sessions under sections 62, 63, 65, 66, 84, 85(1) and 102(1)(*a*) and (*b*) of the Children and Young Persons Act 1933(c), section 40 of the Education Act 1944(d), and section 33 of the Children and Young Persons Act 1963(e).

2. Proceedings in a magistrates' court under sections 2 and 4 of the Children Act 1948(f), section 43 of the National Assistance Act 1948(g), section 22 of the Maintenance Orders Act 1950(h), section 4 of the Maintenance Orders Act 1958(i), section 3 of the Children and Young Persons Act 1963, and section 23 of the Ministry of Social Security Act 1966(j).

(a) 1949 c. 51.	(b) 1889 c. 63.	(c) 1933 c. 12.	(d) 1944 c. 31.	(e) 1963 c. 37.
(f) 1948 c. 43.	(g) 1948 c. 29.	(h) 1950 c. 37.	(i) 1958 c. 39.	(j) 1966 c. 20.

3. Proceedings in a magistrates' court in which a parent or guardian opposes the making of an adoption order and the court is asked to dispense with his consent under section 5 of the Adoption Act 1958(a).

EXPLANATORY NOTE

(*This Note is not part of the Regulations.*)

These Regulations make legal aid available for proceedings to vary a maintenance order registered in a magistrates' court, proceedings relating to a resolution by a local authority assuming parental rights over a child, opposed adoption proceedings in a magistrates' court and for proceedings by the Supplementary Benefits Commission or a local authority in respect of a person's failure to maintain or accommodate dependants. They also make legal aid available in certain proceedings which are partly in respect of defamation, and re-enact those provisions of the Legal Aid (General) Regulations 1962 (S.I. 1962/148 as amended by the Legal Aid (General) (Amendment) Regulations 1964, S.I. 1964/1893) relating to the extension of legal aid to cases in which a child or young person is brought before a court as being in need of care, protection or control.

(a) 7 & 8 Eliz. 2. c. 5.

STATUTORY INSTRUMENTS

1969 No. 922 (L.12)

LEGAL AID AND ADVICE, ENGLAND

The Legal Aid (Assessment of Resources) (Amendment) Regulations 1969

Made - - -	10*th June*, 1969
Laid before Parliament	14*th July*, 1969
Coming into Operation	1*st August*, 1969

The Lord Chancellor, in exercise of the powers conferred on him by sections 4 and 12 of the Legal Aid and Advice Act 1949(**a**), and with the concurrence of the Treasury, hereby makes the following Regulations:—

1.—(1) These Regulations may be cited as the Legal Aid (Assessment of Resources) (Amendment) Regulations 1969 and shall come into operation on 1st August, 1969.

(2) The Interpretation Act 1889(**b**) shall apply to the interpretation of these Regulations as it applies to the interpretation of an Act of Parliament.

(3) In these Regulations, a regulation referred to by number means the regulation so numbered in the Legal Aid (Assessment of Resources) Regulations 1960(**c**) as amended(**d**).

2. Regulation 1(2) (which relates to the interpretation of expressions used in the Regulations) shall be further amended in the definition of "authorised summary proceedings" as follows:—

(*a*) in sub-paragraph (iv) by deleting the word "and" where it occurs after the words "of the Education Act 1944" and by the addition of the following words at the end:—

"section 22 of the Maintenance Orders Act 1950(**e**), section 4 of the Maintenance Orders Act 1958(**f**), sections 2 and 4 of the Children Act 1948(**g**), section 43 of the National Assistance Act 1948(**h**) and section 23 of the Ministry of Social Security Act 1966(**i**), and"

(*b*) by adding the following sub-paragraph (v):—

"(v) Proceedings in a magistrates' court in which a parent or guardian opposes the making of an adoption order and the court is asked to dispense with his consent under section 5 of the Adoption Act 1958(**j**)".

Dated 21st May, 1969.

We concur,

Gardiner, C.

E. Alan Fitch,
J. McCann,
Two of the Lords Commissioners of
Dated 10th June, 1969.　　　　　　　Her Majesty's Treasury.

(**a**) 1949 c. 51.　　　　(**b**) 1889 c. 63.　　　　(**c**) S.I.1960/1471 (1960 II, p. 1749).
(**d**) The relevant amending instruments are S.I.1961/555, 1964/1907 (1961 I, p. 1220; 1964 III, p. 4239).　　(**e**) 1950 c. 37　　　(**f**) 1958 c. 39.　　　(**g**) 1948 c. 43.
(**h**) 1948 c. 29.　　　　(**i**) 1966 c. 20.　　　　(**j**) 7 & 8 Eliz. 2. c. 5.

EXPLANATORY NOTE

(This Note is not part of the Regulations.)

These Regulations provide for the determination of the resources of a person who applies for legal aid in respect of proceedings to vary a maintenance order registered in a magistrates' court, proceedings relating to a resolution by a local authority assuming parental rights over a child, opposed adoption proceedings in a magistrates' court or for proceedings by the Supplementary Benefits Commission or a local authority in respect of his refusal to maintain his dependants.

STATUTORY INSTRUMENTS

1969 No. 923 (L. 13)

LEGAL AID AND ADVICE, ENGLAND

The Legal Aid (General) (Amendment) Regulations 1969

Made - - - -	21*st May* 1969
Laid before Parliament	14*th July* 1969
Coming into Operation	1*st August* 1969

The Lord Chancellor, in exercise of the powers conferred on him by sections 1 and 12 of the Legal Aid and Advice Act 1949(**a**), hereby makes the following Regulations:—

1.—(1) These Regulations may be cited as the Legal Aid (General) (Amendment) Regulations 1969 and shall come into operation on 1st August 1969.

(2) The Interpretation Act 1889(**b**) shall apply to the interpretation of these Regulations as it applies to the interpretation of an Act of Parliament.

(3) In these Regulations, a regulation referred to by number means the regulation so numbered in the Legal Aid (General) Regulations 1962(**c**) as amended(**d**).

2. For the words "Regulation 1A" in the definition of "authorised summary proceedings" in regulation 1(3)(*d*) there shall be substituted the words "the schedule to the Legal Aid (Extension of Proceedings) Regulations 1969".

3. Regulation 1A is hereby revoked.

Dated 21st May 1969.

Gardiner, C.

EXPLANATORY NOTE

(*This Note is not part of the Regulations.*)

These Regulations amend the definition of "authorised summary proceedings" so as to include the proceedings to which legal aid has been extended by the Legal Aid (Extension of Proceedings) Regulations 1969 and revoke Regulation 1A which was replaced by those Regulations.

(**a**) 1949 c. 51.   (**b**) 1889 c. 63.   (**c**) S.I. 1962/148 (1962 I, p. 117).
(**d**) The relevant amending instrument is S.I. 1964/1893 (1964 III, p. 4218).

STATUTORY INSTRUMENTS

1969 No. 927 (S. 74)

POLICE

The Police (Scotland) Amendment (No. 3) Regulations 1969

Made - - -	*3rd July* 1969
Laid before Parliament	*17th July* 1969
Coming into Operation	*18th July* 1969

In exercise of the powers conferred on me by section 26 of the Police (Scotland) Act 1967(**a**), and of all other powers enabling me in that behalf, and after consulting the Police Council for Great Britain in accordance with section 26(8) of the said Act of 1967, I hereby make the following regulations :—

1.—(1) These regulations may be cited as the Police (Scotland) Amendment (No. 3) Regulations 1969.

(2) These regulations shall come into operation on 18th July 1969 and shall have effect as from 1st May 1969 but in the year ended 30th April 1969 they shall have effect as provided for in regulation 4 hereof.

2. In these regulations any reference to the principal regulations is a reference to the Police (Scotland) Regulations 1968(**b**), as amended (**c**).

3. In Schedule 6 of the principal regulations (which relates to motor vehicle allowances)—

(*a*) for the table in sub-paragraph (1) of paragraph 1 there shall be substituted the following table :—

TABLE

Cylinder capacity	Annual rate of fixed element	Mileage element	
		Basic rate per mile	Reduced rate per mile
1,200 c.c. or more but less than 1,700 c.c.	£86	8d.	5d.
1,000 c.c. or more but less than 1,200 c.c.	£77	7d.	4½d.
Less than 1,000 c.c.	£69	6¼d.	4d.

(**a**) 1967 c. 77.
(**b**) S.I. 1968/716 (1968 II, p. 2024).
(**c**) The relevant amending instrument is S.I. 1968/1963 (1968 III, p. 5363).

(*b*) for the table in paragraph 2 there shall be substituted the following table:—

TABLE

Cylinder capacity	Rate per mile
1,200 c.c. or more but less than 1,700 c.c.	1s. 2¼d.
1,000 c.c. or more but less than 1,200 c.c.	1s. 0¾d.
Less than 1,000 c.c.	11¼d.

4.—(1) As respects the year ended 30th April 1969 a motor vehicle allowance payable under regulation 50 of the principal regulations shall be calculated as hereinafter provided.

(2) So far as the motor vehicle allowance falls to be calculated by reference to completed months of authorised use ending, or mileage of authorised use performed, on or after 1st March 1969, it shall be calculated in accordance with the principal regulations as amended by regulation 3 of these regulations, which shall have effect accordingly.

(3) Nothing in regulation 3 of these regulations shall affect the calculation of the motor vehicle allowance so far as it falls to be calculated by reference to completed months of authorised use ending, or mileage of authorised use performed, before 1st March 1969.

William Ross,
One of Her Majesty's Principal
Secretaries of State.

St. Andrew's House,
Edinburgh.
3rd July 1969.

EXPLANATORY NOTE
(This Note is not part of the Regulations.)

These Regulations amend the Police (Scotland) Regulations 1968.

Regulation 3 increases the rates at which motor vehicle allowances are payable. These allowances are payable on an annual basis and, for the purposes thereof, a year is taken as a period of 12 months beginning on 1st May. They are calculated by reference to completed months of authorised use and mileage performed in the year in question.

Regulation 4 makes transitory provision for the calculation of these allowances in the year ending 30th April 1969 and provides that regulation 3 shall have effect as from 1st March 1969 as respects the calculation of motor vehicle allowances by reference to months of use completed or mileage performed on or after that date. Subject to regulation 4, regulation 1(2) provides that the regulations shall have effect as from 1st May 1969. This provision for retrospective effect is made in exercise of the power conferred by section 26(3) of the Police (Scotland) Act 1967.

STATUTORY INSTRUMENTS

1969 No. 929

WAGES COUNCILS
The Wages Regulation (Hollow-ware) (Holidays) Order 1969

Made - - -		*9th July* 1969
Coming into Operation		*4th August* 1969

Whereas the Secretary of State has received from the Hollow-ware Wages Council (Great Britain) the wages regulation proposals set out in the Schedule hereto ;

Now, therefore, the Secretary of State in exercise of her powers under section 11 of the Wages Councils Act 1959(**a**), and of all other powers enabling her in that behalf, hereby makes the following Order :—

1. This Order may be cited as the Wages Regulation (Hollow-ware) (Holidays) Order 1969.

2.—(1) In this Order the expression "the specified date" means the 4th August 1969, provided that where, as respects any worker who is paid wages at intervals not exceeding seven days, that date does not correspond with the beginning of the period for which the wages are paid, the expression "the specified date" means, as respects that worker, the beginning of the next such period following that date.

(2) The Interpretation Act 1889(**b**) shall apply to the interpretation of this Order as it applies to the interpretation of an Act of Parliament and as if this Order and the Order hereby revoked were Acts of Parliament.

3. The wages regulation proposals set out in the Schedule hereto shall have effect as from the specified date and as from that date the Wages Regulation (Hollow-ware) (Holidays) Order 1966(**c**) as amended by Schedule 2 to the Wages Regulation (Hollow-ware) Order 1968(**d**) shall cease to have effect.

Signed by order of the Secretary of State.

9th July 1969.

A. A. Jarratt,
Deputy Under Secretary of State,
Department of Employment and Productivity.

SCHEDULE
Article 3

The following provisions as to holidays and holiday remuneration shall be substituted for the provisions as to holidays and holiday remuneration set out in the Wages Regulation (Hollow-ware) (Holidays) Order 1966 (Order H. (92)) as amended by Schedule 2 to the Wages Regulation (Hollow-ware) Order 1968 (Order H.(96)).

(**a**) 1959 c. 69.
(**c**) S.I. 1966/669 (1966 II, p. 1506).

(**b**) 1889 c. 63.
(**d**) S.I. 1968/626 (1968 I, p. 1464).

PART I

APPLICATION

1. This Schedule applies to every worker for whom statutory minimum remuneration has been fixed.

PART II

CUSTOMARY HOLIDAYS

2.—(1) An employer shall allow to every worker in his employment to whom this Schedule applies a holiday (hereinafter referred to as a "customary holiday") in each year on the days specified in the next following sub-paragraph, provided that the worker:—

    (a) was in his employment on the day immediately preceding the customary holiday;

    (b) has performed some work for the employer during the period of 12 weeks immediately preceding the customary holiday; and

    (c) (unless excused by the employer or absent by reason of the proved illness of the worker) has worked throughout the last working day on which work was available to him before the customary holiday.

(2) The said customary holidays are:—

    (a) (i) in England and Wales—

        Christmas Day (or, if Christmas Day falls on a Sunday, such weekday as may be appointed by national proclamation, or, if none is so appointed, the next following Tuesday), Boxing Day, Good Friday, Easter Monday, Whit Monday, (or where another day is substituted therefor by national proclamation, that day) August Bank Holiday and two other days (being days on which the worker normally works) in the course of a calendar year, to be fixed by the employer and notified to the worker not less than three weeks before the holiday;

      (ii) in Scotland—

        New Year's Day (or, if New Year's Day falls on a Sunday, the following Monday);
        the local Spring holiday;
        the local Autumn holiday; and
        five other days (being days on which the worker normally works) in the course of a calendar year, to be fixed by the employer and notified to the worker not less than three weeks before the holiday;

  or (b) in the case of each of the said days (other than a day fixed by the employer and notified to the worker as aforesaid), a day substituted therefor, being either a day recognised by local custom as a day of holiday in substitution for the said day, or a day fixed by agreement between the employer and the worker or his agent.

(3) Notwithstanding the preceding provisions of this paragraph, an employer may (except where in the case of a woman or young person such a requirement would be unlawful) require a worker who is otherwise entitled to any customary holiday under the foregoing provisions of this Schedule to work thereon, and, in lieu of any customary holiday on which he so works, the employer shall allow to the worker a day's holiday (hereinafter referred to as a "holiday in lieu of a customary holiday") on a weekday on which he would normally work for the employer within the period of four weeks next ensuing.

(4) A worker who is required to work on a customary holiday shall be paid:—

    (a) for all time worked thereon at the minimum rate then appropriate to the worker for work on a customary holiday; and

    (b) in respect of the holiday in lieu of the customary holiday, holiday remuneration in accordance with paragraph 6.

Part III

ANNUAL HOLIDAY

3.—(1) In addition to the holidays specified in Part II of this Schedule, and subject to the provisions of paragraph 4, an employer shall—

(a) between the date on which the provisions of this Schedule become effective and 31st October 1969, allow a holiday (hereinafter referred to as an "annual holiday") to every worker in his employment to whom this Schedule applies who has been employed by him during the 12 months immediately preceding the commencement of the holiday season for any of the periods of employment (calculated in accordance with the provisions of paragraph 10) set out in the appropriate table below and the duration of the annual holiday shall, in the case of each such worker, be related to his period of employment during that 12 months as follows:—

Workers with a normal working week of six days

Column 1 Period of employment	Column 2 Duration of annual holiday
Not less than 48 weeks	13 days
Not less than 44 weeks but less than 48 weeks ...	11 "
" " 40 " " " " 44 weeks ...	10 "
" " 36 " " " " 40 " ...	9 "
" " 32 " " " " 36 " ...	8 "
" " 28 " " " " 32 " ...	7 "
" " 24 " " " " 28 " ...	6 "
" " 20 " " " " 24 " ...	5 "
" " 16 " " " " 20 " ...	4 "
" " 12 " " " " 16 " ...	3 "
" " 8 " " " " 12 " ...	2 "
" " 4 " " " " 8 " ...	1 day

Workers with a normal working week of five days or less

Column 1 Period of employment	Column 2 Duration of annual holiday
Not less than 48 weeks	11 days
Not less than 43 weeks but less than 48 weeks ...	9 "
" " 38 " " " " 43 weeks ...	8 "
" " 33 " " " " 38 " ...	7 "
" " 28 " " " " 33 " ...	6 "
" " 24 " " " " 28 " ...	5 "
" " 19 " " " " 24 " ...	4 "
" " 14 " " " " 19 " ...	3 "
" " 9 " " " " 14 " ...	2 "
" " 4 " " " " 9 " ...	1 day

(b) between 1st April 1970 and 31st October 1970, and in each succeeding year between 1st April and 31st October, allow a holiday (hereinafter referred to as an "annual holiday") to every worker in his employment to whom this Schedule applies who has been employed by him during the 12 months immediately preceding the commencement of the holiday season for any of the periods of employment (calculated in accordance with the provisions of paragraph 10) set out in the appropriate table below and the duration of the annual holiday shall, in the case of each such worker, be related to his period of employment during that 12 months as follows:—

Workers with a normal working week of six days

Column 1 Period of employment		Column 2 Duration of annual holiday
Not less than 48 weeks	...	14 days
Not less than 44 weeks but less than 48 weeks	...	11 ,,
,, ,, 40 ,, ,, ,, ,, 44 ,,	...	10 ,,
,, ,, 36 ,, ,, ,, ,, 40 ,,	...	9 ,,
,, ,, 32 ,, ,, ,, ,, 36 ,,	...	8 ,,
,, ,, 28 ,, ,, ,, ,, 32 ,,	...	7 ,,
,, ,, 24 ,, ,, ,, ,, 28 ,,	...	6 ,,
,, ,, 20 ,, ,, ,, ,, 24 ,,	...	5 ,,
,, ,, 16 ,, ,, ,, ,, 20 ,,	...	4 ,,
,, ,, 12 ,, ,, ,, ,, 16 ,,	...	3 ,,
,, ,, 8 ,, ,, ,, ,, 12 ,,	...	2 ,,
,, ,, 4 ,, ,, ,, ,, 8 ,,	...	1 day

Workers with a normal working week of five days or less

Column 1 Period of employment		Column 2 Duration of annual holiday
Not less than 48 weeks	...	12 days
Not less than 43 weeks but less than 48 weeks	...	9 ,,
,, ,, 38 ,, ,, ,, ,, 43 ,,	...	8 ,,
,, ,, 33 ,, ,, ,, ,, 38 ,,	...	7 ,,
,, ,, 28 ,, ,, ,, ,, 33 ,,	...	6 ,,
,, ,, 24 ,, ,, ,, ,, 28 ,,	...	5 ,,
,, ,, 19 ,, ,, ,, ,, 24 ,,	...	4 ,,
,, ,, 14 ,, ,, ,, ,, 19 ,,	...	3 ,,
,, ,, 9 ,, ,, ,, ,, 14 ,,	...	2 ,,
,, ,, 4 ,, ,, ,, ,, 9 ,,	...	1 day

(2) Notwithstanding the provisions of the last foregoing sub-paragraph:—

    (a) the number of days of annual holiday which an employer is required to allow to a worker in respect of a period of employment during the 12 months immediately preceding 1st April 1969 shall not exceed in the aggregate twice the number of days constituting the worker's normal working week *plus one day;*

    (b) the number of days of annual holiday which an employer is required to allow to a worker in respect of a period of employment during the 12 months immediately preceding 1st April 1970 and during the 12 months immediately preceding 1st April in any succeeding year shall not exceed in the aggregate twice the number of days constituting the worker's normal working week *plus two days.*

(3) the duration of the worker's annual holiday during the holiday season ending on 31st October 1969 shall be reduced by any days of annual holiday duly allowed to him by the employer under the provisions of Order H. (92) between 1st April 1969 and the date on which the provisions of this Schedule become effective.

(4) In this Schedule the expression "holiday season" means in relation to an annual holiday during the year 1969 the period commencing on 1st April 1969, and ending on 31st October 1969, and in relation to each subsequent year, the period commencing on 1st April and ending on 31st October in that year.

4.—(1) *Subject to the provisions of this paragraph,* an annual holiday under this Schedule shall be allowed on consecutive working days, being days on which the worker is normally called upon to work for the employer, and days of annual holiday shall be treated as consecutive notwithstanding that a customary holiday on which the worker is not required to work for the employer or a holiday in lieu of a customary holiday intervenes:

(2)   (a) Where the number of days of annual holiday for which a worker has qualified exceeds the number of days constituting his normal working week but does not exceed twice that number, the holiday may be allowed in two separate periods of consecutive working days; so, however, that when a holiday is so allowed, one of the periods shall consist of a number of such days not less than the number of days constituting the worker's normal working week;

    (b) *Where the number of days of annual holiday for which a worker has qualified exceeds twice the number of days constituting his normal working week the holiday may be allowed as follows:—*

        (i) *as to two periods of consecutive working days, each such period not being less than the period constituting the worker's normal working week during the holiday season; and*

        (ii) *as to any additional days, on working days which need not be consecutive, to be fixed by the employer after consultation with the worker, either during the holiday season or before the beginning of the next following holiday season.*

(3) *Where a day of holiday allowed to a worker under Part II of this Schedule immediately precedes a period of annual holiday or occurs during such a period then, notwithstanding the foregoing provisions of this paragraph, the duration of that period of annual holiday may be reduced by one day and in such a case one day of annual holiday may be allowed on any working day in the holiday season, or by agreement between the employer and the worker or his representative, on any working day before the beginning of the next following holiday season.*

(4) Subject to the foregoing provisions of this paragraph, any day of annual holiday under this Schedule may be allowed on a day on which the worker is entitled to a day of holiday or to a half-holiday under any enactment other than the Wages Councils Act 1959.

5. An employer shall give to a worker reasonable notice of the commencing date or dates and duration of the period or periods of his annual holiday. Such notice may be given individually to the worker or by the posting of a notice in the place where the worker is employed.

Part IV

HOLIDAY REMUNERATION

A—CUSTOMARY HOLIDAYS AND HOLIDAYS IN LIEU OF CUSTOMARY HOLIDAYS

6.—(1) For each day of holiday which a worker is allowed under Part II of this Schedule he shall be paid by the employer holiday remuneration equal to the amount to which he would have been entitled, calculated at the general minimum time rate applicable to the worker (or which would be applicable if he were a time worker) increased by 17½ per cent., if the day had not been a day of holiday and he had been employed on work entitling him to statutory minimum remuneration for the time normally worked by him on that day of the week:

Provided, however, that payment of the said holiday remuneration is subject to the condition that the worker presents himself for employment at the usual starting hour on the first working day following the holiday and works throughout that day or, if he fails to do so, failure is by reason of his proved illness or with the consent of the employer.

(2) The holiday remuneration in respect of any customary holiday shall be paid by the employer to the worker on the pay day on which the wages for the pay week including the first working day following the customary holiday are paid.

(3) The holiday remuneration in respect of any holiday in lieu of a customary holiday shall be paid on the pay day on which the wages for the pay week including the first working day following that holiday in lieu of a customary holiday are paid:

Provided that the said payment shall be made immediately upon the termination of the worker's employment in the case where he ceases to be employed before being allowed a holiday in lieu of a customary holiday to which he is entitled, and in that case the proviso contained in sub-paragraph (1) of this paragraph shall not apply.

B—ANNUAL HOLIDAY

7.—(1) Subject to the provisions of paragraph 8, a worker qualified to be allowed an annual holiday under this Schedule shall be paid by the employer in respect thereof, on the last pay day preceding such annual holiday, one day's holiday pay (as defined in paragraph 11) in respect of each day thereof.

(2) Where under the provisions of paragraph 4 an annual holiday is allowed in more than one period, the holiday remuneration shall be apportioned accordingly.

8. Where any accrued holiday remuneration has been paid by the employer to the worker in accordance with paragraph 9 or with Order H. (92) in respect of employment during any of the periods referred to in that paragraph or that Order, the amount of holiday remuneration payable by the employer in respect of any annual holiday for which the worker has qualified by reason of employment during the said period shall be reduced by the amount of the said accrued holiday remuneration unless that remuneration has been deducted from a previous payment of holiday remuneration made under the provisions of this Schedule or of Order H. (92).

ACCRUED HOLIDAY REMUNERATION PAYABLE ON TERMINATION OF EMPLOYMENT

9. Where a worker ceases to be employed by an employer after the provisions of this Schedule become effective the employer shall, immediately on the termination of the employment (hereinafter referred to as the "termination date") pay to the worker as accrued holiday remuneration:—

(1) in respect of employment in the 12 months up to the preceding 31st March, a sum equal to the holiday remuneration for any days of annual holiday for which he has qualified, except days of annual holiday which he has been allowed or has become entitled to be allowed before leaving the employment; and

(2) in respect of any employment since the preceding 31st March, a sum equal to the holiday remuneration which would have been payable to him if he could have been allowed an annual holiday in respect of that employment at the time of leaving it.

PART V

GENERAL

10. For the purposes of calculating any period of employment qualifying a worker for an annual holiday or for any accrued holiday remuneration under this Schedule, the worker shall be treated—

(1) as if he were employed for a week in respect of any week in which—

    (a) he has worked for the employer for not less than eight hours and has performed some work for which statutory minimum remuneration is payable;

    (b) he has been absent throughout the week or has worked for the employer for less than eight hours by reason of the proved illness of, or accident to, the worker, provided that the number of weeks which may be treated as weeks of employment for such reasons shall not exceed eight weeks at any one time in the period of 12 months immediately preceding the commencement of the holiday season;

    (c) he has been suspended throughout the week owing to shortage of work in the period of 12 months last mentioned; and

(2) as if he were employed on any day of holiday allowed under the provisions of this Schedule, or of Order H. (92), and for the purposes of the provisions of sub-paragraph (1) of this paragraph, a worker who is absent on such a holiday shall be treated as having worked thereon the number of hours ordinarily worked by him on that day of the week for the employer on work for which statutory minimum remuneration is payable.

11. In this Schedule, unless the context otherwise requires, the following expressions have the meanings hereby respectively assigned to them, that is to say:—

"normal working week" means the number of days on which it has been usual for the worker to work in a week in the employment of the employer in the 12 months immediately preceding the worker's first period of annual holiday or immediately preceding 17th October if no part of the annual holiday has been allowed before that date or, where under paragraph 9 accrued holiday remuneration is payable on the termination of the employment, in the 12 months immediately preceding the date of the termination of the employment:

Provided that—

(1) part of a day shall count as a day;

(2) no account shall be taken of any week in which the worker did not perform any work for which statutory minimum remuneration has been fixed.

"one day's holiday pay" means the appropriate proportion of the remuneration which the worker would be entitled to receive from his employer at the date of the annual holiday (or where the holiday is allowed in more than one period at the date of the first period) or at the termination date, as the case may require, for one week's work if working his normal working week and the number of daily hours normally worked by him (exclusive of overtime) and if paid at the general minimum time rate applicable to the worker (or which would be applicable if he were a time worker), increased by $17\frac{1}{2}$ per cent., for work for which statutory minimum remuneration is payable and at the same rate (increased as aforesaid) for any work for which such remuneration is not payable, and in this definition "appropriate proportion" means—

where the worker's normal working week is six days ... one-sixth
where the worker's normal working week is five days ... one-fifth
where the worker's normal working week is four days or less one-quarter

"statutory minimum remuneration" means minimum remuneration (other than holiday remuneration) fixed by a wages regulation order made by the Secretary of State to give effect to the proposals submitted to her by the Council.

"week" in paragraphs 3 and 10 means "pay week".

12. The provisions of this Schedule are without prejudice to any agreement for the allowance of any further holidays with pay or for the payment of additional holiday remuneration.

EXPLANATORY NOTE

(*This Note is not part of the Order.*)

This Order, which has effect from 4th August 1969, sets out the holidays which an employer is required to allow to workers and the remuneration payable to such workers for those holidays, in substitution for the holidays and holiday remuneration fixed by the Wages Regulation (Hollow-ware) (Holidays) Order 1966 (Order H. (92)), as amended by Schedule 2 to the Wages Regulation (Hollow-ware) Order 1968 (Order H. (96)). Order H.92 is revoked.

New provisions are printed in italics.

1969 No. 930

WAGES COUNCILS

The Wages Regulation (Hollow-ware) Order 1969

Made - - -		*9th July* 1969
Coming into Operation		*4th August* 1969

Whereas the Secretary of State has received from the Hollow-ware Wages Council (Great Britain) the wages regulation proposals set out in the Schedule hereto ;

Now, therefore, the Secretary of State in exercise of her powers under section 11 of the Wages Councils Act 1959(**a**), and of all other powers enabling her in that behalf, hereby makes the following Order :—

1. This Order may be cited as the Wages Regulation (Hollow-ware) Order 1969.

2.—(1) In this Order the expression "the specified date" means the 4th August 1969, provided that where, as respects any worker who is paid wages at intervals not exceeding seven days, that date does not correspond with the beginning of the period for which the wages are paid, the expression "the specified date" means, as respects that worker, the beginning of the next such period following that date.

(2) The Interpretation Act 1889(**b**) shall apply to the interpretation of this Order as it applies to the interpretation of an Act of Parliament and as if this Order and the Order hereby revoked were Acts of Parliament.

3. The wages regulation proposals set out in the Schedule hereto shall have effect as from the specified date and as from that date the Wages Regulation (Hollow-ware) Order 1968(**c**) shall cease to have effect.

Signed by order of the Secretary of State.

A. A. Jarratt,
Deputy Under Secretary of State,
Department of Employment and Productivity.

9th July 1969.

(**a**) 1959 c. 69.　　　　　　　　　　　　(**b**) 1889 c. 63.
(**c**) S.I. 1968/626 (1968 I, p. 1464).

Article 3   SCHEDULE

The following minimum remuneration shall be substituted for the statutory minimum remuneration fixed by the Wages Regulation (Hollow-ware) Order 1968 (Order H.(96)).

STATUTORY MINIMUM REMUNERATION
PART I
GENERAL

1. The minimum remuneration payable to a worker to whom this Schedule applies for all work except work to which a minimum overtime rate applies under Part IV is:—

(1) in the case of a time worker, the general minimum time rate payable to the worker under Part II or Part III of this Schedule;

(2) in the case of a worker employed on piece work, piece rates each of which would yield, in the circumstances of the case, to an ordinary worker at least the same amount of money as the piece work basis time rate applicable to the worker under Part II or Part III of this Schedule.

PART II
MALE WORKERS
TIME WORKERS

2. The general minimum time rates payable to male time workers are as follows:—

	General minimum time rates per hour
	s. d.
(1) Workers aged 21 years or over and employed in the enamel ware section of the trade as—	
(a) Fusers' helpers who work in association with fusers	⎫
(b) Annealers, or	⎬ 5 10½
(c) Scalers	⎭
(2) All other workers except learners	5 8
(3) Learners, being aged—	
20 and under 21 years	4 8⅜
19 „ „ 20 „	3 10¼
18 „ „ 19 „	3 5¼
17 „ „ 18 „	2 10⅜
16 „ „ 17 „	2 4⅞
under 16 years	2 0⅜

Provided that the general minimum time rate otherwise payable to a learner who enters, or has entered, the trade for the first time when aged not less than 17 but less than 21 years shall, during his first 12 months' employment in the trade or until he attains the age of 21 years, whichever period is the lesser, be reduced as follows:—

(a) during the first six months of such employment or until he attains the age of 21 years, whichever period is the lesser, by 1d. per hour;

(b) during the second six months of such employment or until he attains the age of 21 years, whichever period is the lesser, by ½d. per hour.

PIECE WORKERS

3. The piece work basis time rates applicable to male piece workers are as follows:—

	Piece work basis time rates per hour
	s. d.

(1) Workers (other than learners) employed—

(a) as fusers' helpers or dippers in the enamel ware section of the trade   ..   .. }
(b) otherwise than as such fusers' helpers or dippers   ..   .. }   5 $10\frac{1}{2}$

(2) Learners employed—

(a) as fusers' helpers or dippers in the enamel ware section of the trade, being aged—

20 and under 21 years	..	..	..	..	..	4 $10\frac{1}{2}$
19 ,, ,, 20 ,,	..	..	..	..	..	4 $0\frac{5}{8}$
18 ,, ,, 19 ,,	..	..	..	..	..	3 $6\frac{7}{8}$
17 ,, ,, 18 ,,	..	..	..	..	..	2 $11\frac{7}{8}$
16 ,, ,, 17 ,,	..	..	..	..	..	2 $6\frac{1}{8}$
under 16 years	..	..	..	..	..	2 $0\frac{7}{8}$

(b) otherwise than as such fusers' helpers or dippers, being aged—

20 and under 21 years	..	..	..	..	..	4 $10\frac{1}{2}$
19 ,, ,, 20 ,,	..	..	..	..	..	4 $0\frac{5}{8}$
18 ,, ,, 19 ,,	..	..	..	..	..	3 $6\frac{1}{2}$
17 ,, ,, 18 ,,	..	..	..	..	..	2 $11\frac{3}{4}$
16 ,, ,, 17 ,,	..	..	..	..	..	2 $6\frac{1}{8}$
under 16 years	..	..	..	..	..	1 $11\frac{1}{2}$

PART III

FEMALE WORKERS

TIME WORKERS

4. The general minimum time rates payable to female time workers are as follows:—

	General minimum time rates per hour
	s. d.
(1) Workers other than learners	4 9
(2) Learners, being aged—	
17 and under 18 years	3 11⅜
16 „ „ 17 „	2 10¼
under 16 years	2 4⅞

Provided that the general minimum time rates payable during her first 12 months' employment in the trade to a learner who enters, or has entered, the trade for the first time at or over the age of 16 years shall be—

during the first six months of such employment	2 4⅛
during the second six months of such employment	2 4⅞

PIECE WORKERS

5. The piece work basis time rates applicable to female piece workers are as follows:—

	Piece work basis time rates per hour
	s. d.
(1) Workers other than learners	4 10¼
(2) Learners, being aged—	
17 and under 18 years	4 0⅝
16 „ „ 17 „	3 1⅛
under 16 years	2 5½

Provided that the piece work basis time rates applicable during her first 12 months' employment in the trade to a learner who enters, or has entered, the trade for the first time at or over the age of 16 years shall be—

during the first six months of such employment	2 4¾
during the second six months of such employment	2 5⅝

PART IV

OVERTIME AND WAITING TIME

MINIMUM OVERTIME RATES

6.—(1) The following minimum overtime rates are payable to all workers other than male workers employed as fusers' helpers, dippers, annealers or scalers in the enamel ware section of the trade:—

(a) on a Sunday or a customary holiday—
for all time worked ..   ..   **double time**

(b) on a Saturday, not being a customary holiday—
for all time worked in excess of 4 hours ..   ..   **time-and-a-half**

(c) in any week exclusive of any time in respect of which a minimum overtime rate is payable under the foregoing provisions of this sub-paragraph—
for all time worked in excess of 40 hours..   ...   **time-and-a-quarter**

(2) The following minimum overtime rates are payable to male workers employed as fusers' helpers, dippers, annealers or scalers in the enamel ware section of the trade:—

(a) on a Sunday or a customary holiday—
for all time worked in excess of 2 hours ..   ..   **double time**

(b) in any week exclusive of any time in respect of which double time is payable under (a) of this sub-paragraph—
for all time worked in excess of 40 hours..   ..   **time-and-a-quarter**

7. In this Part of this Schedule,

(1) the expression "customary holiday" means:—

(a) (i) in England and Wales—
Christmas Day (or, if Christmas Day falls on a Sunday, such week-day as may be appointed by national proclamation, or, if none is so appointed, the next following Tuesday), Boxing Day, Good Friday, Easter Monday, Whit Monday (or where another day is substituted therefor by national proclamation, that day), August Bank Holiday and two other days (being days on which the worker normally works) in the course of a calendar year, to be fixed by the employer and notified to the worker not less than three weeks before the holiday;

(ii) in Scotland—
New Year's Day (or, if New Year's Day falls on a Sunday, the following Monday); the local Spring holiday, the local Autumn holiday; and five other days (being days on which the worker normally works) in the course of a calendar year, to be fixed by the employer and notified to the worker not less than three weeks before the holiday;

or (b) in the case of each of the said days (other than a day fixed by the employer and notified to the worker as aforesaid), a day substituted therefor, being either a day recognised by local custom as a day of holiday in substitution for the said day, or a day fixed by agreement between the employer and the worker or his agent.

(2) the expressions "time-and-a-quarter", "time-and-a-half" and "double time" mean respectively—

(a) in the case of a time worker, one and a quarter times, one and a half times and twice the general minimum time rate otherwise payable to the worker;

(*b*) in the case of a piece worker, such piece rates as would each yield respectively, in the circumstances of the case, to an ordinary worker at least the same amount of money as one and a quarter times, one and a half times and twice the piece work basis time rate otherwise applicable to the worker.

WAITING TIME

8.—(1) A worker is entitled to payment of the minimum remuneration specified in this Schedule for all time during which he is present on the premises of his employer, unless he is present thereon in any of the following circumstances:—

(*a*) without the employer's consent, express or implied;

(*b*) for some purpose unconnected with his work and other than that of waiting for work to be given to him to perform;

(*c*) by reason only of the fact that he is resident thereon;

(*d*) during normal meal times in a room or place in which no work is being done and he is not waiting for work to be given to him to perform.

(2) The minimum remuneration payable under sub-paragraph (1) of this paragraph to a piece worker when not engaged in piece work, is that which would be payable if the worker were a time worker.

PART V

INTERPRETATION

9. In this Schedule the expression "learner" means:—

(1) in the case of a male worker, a worker aged under 21 years and employed under conditions which, in the circumstances of the case, afford a reasonable prospect of advancement to the position of a worker other than a learner;

(2) in the case of a female worker, a worker aged under 18 years, or a worker aged 18 years or over having less than 12 months' experience in the trade, the worker being employed in either case under conditions which, in the circumstances of the case, afford a reasonable prospect of advancement to the position of a worker other than a learner.

APPLICABILITY OF STATUTORY MINIMUM REMUNERATION

10.—(1) This Schedule does not apply to workers employed as watchmen, but save as aforesaid applies to workers in relation to whom the Hollow-ware Wages Council (Great Britain) operates, that is to say, workers employed in Great Britain in the operations in the Hollow-ware Branch of the Hollow-ware Making trade specified in the Schedule to the Trade Boards (Hollow-ware Trade, Great Britain) (Constitution and Proceedings) Regulations 1937(**a**), namely:—

(*a*) all work in connection with—

(i) the manufacture from sheet iron or sheet steel (hereinafter called black plate) of articles of hollow-ware or parts thereof;

(ii) the manufacture of baths and dustbins from black plate or from black plate coated with any metal, of an average thickness not exceeding ·0392 of an inch (20 Birmingham Gauge);

(iii) the manufacture from any iron or steel of forged, stamped or pressed mountings or fittings or parts thereof, for articles specified in (*a*) (i) and (ii) of this sub-paragraph when done by workers wholly or mainly so engaged, or in association or conjunction with the manufacture specified in (*a*) (i) and (ii) of this sub-paragraph;

(**a**) S.R. & O. 1937/325 (1937, p. 2335).

(b) all work in connection with—

  (i) the manufacture of kegs, drums, tapers, taper-necked cans and painters' pots, or parts thereof;

    from black plate of an average thickness less than ·125 of an inch (10 Birmingham Gauge), or

    from black plate coated with any metal and of an average thickness exceeding ·01745 of an inch (27 Birmingham Gauge) but less than ·125 of an inch (10 Birmingham Gauge),

    and the repair thereof;

    when done in a department mainly engaged on work specified in (a) of this sub-paragraph;

  (ii) the manufacture from any iron or steel of forged, stamped or pressed mountings or fittings, or parts thereof, for the articles to the manufacture or repair of which (b) (i) of this sub-paragraph applies.

(2) Work in connection with the manufacture specified in sub-paragraph (1) of this paragraph includes—

  (a) finishing;

  (b) the work of persons employed in the factory or workshop in counting or weighing materials handed to workers and articles or parts thereof received from workers;

  (c) packing, warehousing, despatching, the work of inside messengers, yard-workers and stokers and work of a similar nature.

(3) Notwithstanding anything in this paragraph the following operations are not operations in the Hollow-ware branch of the Hollow-ware making trade:—

  (a) work specified in sub-paragraph (1) of this paragraph when performed in an establishment, branch or department mainly engaged on other work and in which the jointing and finishing of the articles or parts of articles specified in sub-paragraph (1) of this paragraph are done by workers mainly employed in jointing and finishing other articles;

  (b) finishing (other than enamelling) when performed in a department mainly engaged in the finishing of articles other than articles specified in sub-paragraph (1) of this paragraph and in which no manufacture specified in sub-paragraph (1) of this paragraph is carried on;

  (c) packing, warehousing, despatching, the work of inside messengers, yard-workers and stokers, and work of a similar nature when performed in an establishment not otherwise engaged in operations in the hollow-ware branch of the hollow-ware making trade;

  (d) the manufacture of baths or dustbins from black plate or from black plate coated with any metal, of an average thickness exceeding ·0392 of an inch (20 Birmingham Gauge);

  (e) the manufacture referred to in (a) (ii) of sub-paragraph (1) of this paragraph in an establishment, branch or department mainly engaged in the operations specified in (d) of this sub-paragraph or in operations other than those specified in sub-paragraph (1) of this paragraph or both in such operations and such manufacture;

  (f) the manufacture of component parts of motor vehicles, motor plants, aircraft, cycles or motor cycles;

  (g) the manufacture of any article or part of any article when made in an establishment mainly engaged in the manufacture of motor vehicles, motor plants, aircraft, cycles or motor cycles or of component parts thereof;

  (h) all clerical work other than work specified in (b) of sub-paragraph (2) of this paragraph;

(*i*) the manufacture of tin rollers, tin roller drums, card cases, coiler cans and other articles for use with textile or other machinery;

(*j*) all work in connection with the maintenance or upkeep of premises, machinery or plant;

(*k*) all work included under the Trade Boards (Keg and Drum Trade, Great Britain) (Constitution and Proceedings) Regulations 1928**(a)**;

(*l*) all work included under the Trade Boards (Tin Box Trade, Great Britain) (Constitution and Proceedings) Regulations 1928**(b)**.

(4) The expression "finishing" includes operations of coating (including the processes of galvanising, tinning, enamelling, painting, japanning, lacquering and varnishing), polishing and cleaning articles.

EXPLANATORY NOTE

(This Note is not part of the Order.)

This Order, which has effect from 4th August 1969, sets out the statutory minimum remuneration payable in substitution for that fixed by the Wages Regulation (Hollow-ware) Order 1968 (Order H.(96)), which Order is revoked.

New provisions are printed in italics.

(a) S.R. & O. 1928/844 (1928, p. 1276).   **(b)** S.R. & O. 1928/847 (1928, p. 1289).

STATUTORY INSTRUMENTS

1969 No. 931 (L. 14)

PENSIONS

The Pensions Appeal Tribunals (England and Wales) (Amendment) Rules 1969

Made - - -	*8th July* 1969
Laid before Parliament	*17th July* 1969
Coming into Operation	*21st July* 1969

The Lord Chancellor, in exercise of the powers conferred on him by paragraph 5(4) of the Schedule to the Pensions Appeal Tribunals Act 1943(a) and after consultation with the Council on Tribunals in accordance with section 8 of the Tribunals and Inquiries Act 1958(b), hereby makes the following Rules :—

1. These Rules may be cited as the Pensions Appeal Tribunals (England and Wales) (Amendment) Rules 1969 and shall come into operation on 21st July 1969.

2. The Pensions Appeal Tribunals (England and Wales) (Amendment) Rules 1946(c) as amended (d) shall be further amended as follows :—

For Part I of the Schedule 2 (which relates to subsistence allowances payable to appellants etc.,) there shall be substituted the following :—

" PART I

SUBSISTENCE ALLOWANCES TO APPELLANTS, ETC.

1. The maximum allowance payable under paragraph (1) of Rule 27 to an appellant or other person absent from home for the purpose of attending the Tribunal or undergoing a medical examination shall be—

   (*a*) for a period of two and a half hours or more but less than five hours consecutively, 3s. 0d., or for a period of five hours or more but less than ten hours consecutively, 5s. 6d., or for a period of ten hours or more consecutively, 11s. 6d.;

   (*b*) in addition to any sum payable under paragraph (*a*),

   (i) for each night spent within 4 miles of Charing Cross, 40s. 0d.;

   (ii) for each night·spent elsewhere, 36s. 0d.

(a) 1943 c. 39.   (b) 1958 c. 66.
(c) S.R. & O. 1946/1708 (Rev. XVII, p. 733; 1946 I, p. 1313).
(d) The relevant amending instruments are: S.I. 1957/1827, 1965/273 (1957 II, p. 1833; 1965 I, p. 687).

2. When the appellant or other person is absent from home for more than twenty-four hours he shall be entitled to a further allowance calculated in accordance with the foregoing provisions for periods of absence during each successive period of twenty-four hours. "

Dated 8th July 1969.

Gardiner, C.

EXPLANATORY NOTE

(This Note is not part of the Rules.)

These Rules further amend the Pensions Appeal Tribunals (England and Wales) (Amendment) Rules 1946, so as to increase the subsistence allowances payable to appellants and their attendants.

1969 No. 936

HORTICULTURE

GRADING AND TRANSPORT OF PRODUCE

The Grading of Produce (Apples) (Amendment) Regulations 1969

Made - - - -	10*th July* 1969
Laid before Parliament	18*th July* 1969
Coming into Operation	21*st July* 1969

The Minister of Agriculture, Fisheries and Food and the Secretary of State, acting jointly in exercise of the powers conferred upon them by sections 11, 13 and 23 of the Agriculture and Horticulture Act 1964(a) and of all other powers enabling them in that behalf, hereby make the following regulations after consultation with such organisations as appear to either of them to be representative of interests affected by the regulations:—

Citation, commencement and interpretation

1.—(1) These regulations may be cited as the Grading of Produce (Apples) (Amendment) Regulations 1969; and shall come into operation on 21st July 1969.

(2) The Interpretation Act 1889(b) shall apply to the interpretation of these regulations as it applies to the interpretation of an Act of Parliament.

Amendment of the Grading of Produce (Apples) Regulations 1967

2. The Grading of Produce (Apples) Regulations 1967(c), as amended (d), shall be further amended as follows:—

(*a*) by substituting in Schedule 2 thereto (which contains the definition of the grade of quality—CLASS 1) for the final sentence of the paragraph headed "Development and ripeness" the following sentence:—

"Each apple of a dessert variety shall be sufficiently developed to ensure the proper completion of the ripening process and the state of development and ripeness of each apple of any variety shall be such as to allow it to remain in good condition during the normal period of distribution.";

(*b*) by substituting in Schedule 3 thereto (which contains the definition of the grade of quality—CLASS 2) for the final sentence of the paragraph headed "Development and ripeness" the following sentence:—

"Each apple of a dessert variety shall be reasonably well developed and the state of development and ripeness of each apple of any variety shall be such as to allow it to remain in reasonably good condition during the normal period of distribution.".

(a) 1964 c.28.
(c) S.I. 1967/1020 (1967 II, p.3083).
(b) 1889 c.63.
(d) S.I. 1968/1040 (1968 II, p.2745).

In Witness whereof the Official Seal of the Minister of Agriculture, Fisheries and Food is hereunto affixed on 8th July 1969.

(L.S.)   *Cledwyn Hughes,*
Minister of Agriculture, Fisheries and Food.

Given under the Seal of the Secretary of State for Scotland on 10th July 1969.

(L.S.)   *William Ross,*
Secretary of State for Scotland.

EXPLANATORY NOTE

(This Note is not part of the Regulations.)

These regulations, which come into operation on 21st July 1969, amend the requirements in the Grading of Produce (Apples) Regulations 1967, as amended, as to the state of development of apples falling within Class 1 and Class 2 respectively.

STATUTORY INSTRUMENTS

1969 No. 937

HORTICULTURE

GRADING AND TRANSPORT OF PRODUCE

The Grading of Produce (Pears) (Amendment) Regulations 1969

Made - - - -	10*th July* 1969
Laid before Parliament	18*th July* 1969
Coming into Operation	21*st July* 1969

The Minister of Agriculture, Fisheries and Food and the Secretary of State, acting jointly in exercise of the powers conferred upon them by sections 11, 13 and 23 of the Agriculture and Horticulture Act 1964(a) and of all other powers enabling them in that behalf, hereby make the following regulations after consultation with such organisations as appear to either of them to be representative of interests affected by the regulations:—

Citation, commencement and interpretation

1.—(1) These regulations may be cited as the Grading of Produce (Pears) (Amendment) Regulations 1969; and shall come into operation on 21st July 1969.

(2) The Interpretation Act 1889(b) shall apply to the interpretation of these regulations as it applies to the interpretation of an Act of Parliament.

Amendment of the Grading of Produce (Pears) Regulations 1967

2. The Grading of Produce (Pears) Regulations 1967(c), as amended (d), shall be further amended as follows:—

(*a*) by substituting in Schedule 2 thereto (which contains the definition of the grade of quality—CLASS 1) for the final sentence of the paragraph headed "Development and ripeness" the following sentence:—

"It shall be sufficiently developed to ensure the proper completion of the ripening process and its state of development and ripeness shall be such as to allow it to remain in good condition during the normal period of distribution.";

(*b*) by substituting in Schedule 3 thereto (which contains the definition of the grade of quality—CLASS 2) for the final sentence of the paragraph headed "Development and ripeness" the following sentence:—

"It shall be reasonably well developed and its state of development and ripeness shall be such as to allow it to remain in reasonably good condition during the normal period of distribution.".

(a) 1964 c.28.   (b) 1889 c.63.
(c) S.I. 1967/1019 (1967 II, p.3077).   (d) S.I. 1968/1041 (1968 II, p.2748).

In Witness whereof the Official Seal of the Minister of Agriculture, Fisheries and Food is hereunto affixed on 8th July 1969.

(L.S.)
Cledwyn Hughes,
Minister of Agriculture, Fisheries and Food.

Given under the Seal of the Secretary of State for Scotland on 10th July 1969.

(L.S.)
William Ross,
Secretary of State for Scotland.

EXPLANATORY NOTE

(This Note is not part of the Regulations.)

These regulations, which come into operation on 21st July 1969, amend the requirements in the Grading of Produce (Pears) Regulations 1967, as amended, as to the state of development of pears falling within Class 1 and Class 2 respectively.

1969 No. 939

SAVINGS BANKS

The Savings Banks (Ordinary Deposits) (Limits) Order 1969

Laid before Parliament in draft

Made - - -	11*th July* 1969
Coming into Operation	14*th July* 1969

The Treasury, in exercise of the powers conferred upon them by section 4 of the Post Office Savings Bank Act 1954(**a**), section 12 of the Trustee Savings Banks Act 1954(**b**), section 16 of the Trustee Investments Act 1961(**c**) and paragraph 5 of Schedule 4 to that Act, and section 7(1) of the Post Office Savings Bank Act 1966(**d**), and of all other powers enabling them in that behalf, hereby make the following Order :—

1. This Order may be cited as the Savings Banks (Ordinary Deposits) (Limits) Order 1969, and shall come into operation on 14th July 1969.

2. The Interpretation Act 1889(**e**) shall apply for the interpretation of this Order as it applies for the interpretation of an Act of Parliament.

3.—(1) Subject to the provisions of this Order, it shall not be lawful for the Postmaster General to receive a deposit from, or make a credit to an account of, any person by way of ordinary deposit, or for a trustee savings bank to receive a deposit from, or make a credit to an account of, any person by way of savings account deposit (as defined by section 1(3) of the Trustee Savings Banks Act 1964(**f**)), in any case where the amount standing to the credit of that person by way of ordinary deposit in the Post Office Savings Bank or by way of savings account deposit in the trustee savings bank, whether solely or jointly with any other person, and whether the depositor has or has not more than one account by way of ordinary deposit in the Post Office Savings Bank or by way of savings account deposit in the trustee savings bank, as the case may be, exceeds, or would as a result of the receipt of the said deposit or the making of the said credit exceed, £10,000.

(2) The foregoing paragraph shall not operate to prevent—

(*a*) the transfer of an account from one trustee savings bank to another trustee savings bank ; or

(**a**) 1954 c. 62.	(**b**) 1954 c. 63.
(**c**) 1961 c. 62.	(**d**) 1966 c. 12.
(**e**) 1889 c. 63.	(**f**) 1964 c. 4.

(*b*) the crediting to a depositor's account in any savings bank of—

(i) interest on deposits in any such account,

(ii) dividends on any Government stock or bonds held by him on the Post Office Register,

(iii) any sum accruing to him in respect of any savings bank annuity or insurance,

(iv) any sum transferred from the account of another depositor who has died.

(3) In computing for the purposes of this Order the amount standing to the credit of any person, whether solely or jointly with any other person and whether the depositor has or has not more than one account as aforesaid, there shall not be taken into account deposits made for the purpose of an immediate—

(*a*) investment in any Government stock or bonds, or

(*b*) loan, free of interest, to Her Majesty's Government.

(4) For the purposes of this Order, a person who is a trustee shall be treated separately in his personal capacity and in his capacity as trustee, and in the latter capacity separately in respect of each separate trust fund ; and so much of the property in the hands of a trustee shall be treated as a separate trust fund as is held on trusts which (as respects the beneficiaries or their respective interests or the purposes of the trust or as respects the powers of the trustee) are not identical with those on which other property in his hands is held.

(5) In computing for the purposes of this Order the amount standing to the credit of any person, there shall not be taken into account any amounts received from a trustee on behalf of that person for an account in the joint names of the trustee and that person.

4.—(1) The limits on the amounts of deposits imposed by this Order shall not apply to deposits made—

(*a*) with the approval of the National Debt Commissioners,

(i) by a friendly society being a registered society within the meaning of the Friendly Societies Act 1896(**a**) or by a registered branch of such a society ;

(ii) by a society being a building society within the meaning of the Building Societies Act 1962(**b**) ;

(iii) by a society registered or deemed to be registered under the Industrial and Provident Societies Act 1965(**c**) ;

(iv) by a charitable or provident institution or society ;

(v) by any person in respect of donations or bequests for the maintenance, education or benefit of the poor ;

(vi) by a savings club ; or

(vii) by a penny savings bank ; or

(**a**) 1896 c. 25. (**b**) 1962 c. 37.
(**c**) 1965 c. 12.

(b) in the Post Office Savings Bank. with the approval of the Postmaster General. by a Government Department or Office : or

(c) by virtue or in pursuance of any enactment in that behalf. by a sheriff clerk in Scotland or a clerk of the Crown and Peace in Northern Ireland.

(2) The National Debt Commissioners and the Postmaster General may attach to their approval referred to in this article such conditions as may seem to them appropriate and may at any time revoke or vary an approval given by them or revise the conditions attached thereto.

5.—(1) The Savings Banks (Deposits) (Limits) Order 1960(**a**) and the Savings Banks (Deposits) (Limits) (Amendment) Order 1961(**b**) are hereby revoked.

(2) In so far as any approval given by the National Debt Commissioners or the Postmaster General before the date on which this Order comes into operation could be given under article 4 of this Order, it shall have effect as if it had been given under that Article.

Joseph Harper,
B. K. O'Malley,

Two of the Lords Commissioners
of Her Majesty's Treasury.

11th July 1969.

EXPLANATORY NOTE

(This Note is not part of the Order.)

This Order consolidates, with amendments, the Savings Banks (Deposits) (Limits) Order 1960, the Savings Banks (Deposits) (Limits) (Amendment) Order 1961, and article 2 of the Savings Banks (Deposits) (Limits) Order 1966. It applies to deposits in ordinary accounts in the Post Office Savings Bank and savings accounts in the Ordinary Department of a Trustee Savings Bank and its main purposes are :

(a) To increase from £5,000 to £10,000 the limit on the aggregate amount standing to the credit of a Savings Bank account.

(b) To define the conditions under which the limit shall not prevent the making of certain classes of deposit.

(c) To define the conditions under which a depositor will be allowed, for the purpose of calculating his maximum permitted deposits, to count the deposits he has made in his personal capacity separately from those he has made as a trustee or those a trustee has made on his behalf for an account in their joint names, and his deposits in respect of different trust funds. separately from each other.

(d) To define certain kinds of deposit which are ignored in computing the amount of the account for the purposes of the limit.

(e) To define the terms and conditions under which the limit may be waived in favour of certain classes of depositor.

(a) S.I. 1960/779 (1960 III, p. 3062).   (b) S.I. 1961/2412 (1961 III, p. 4454).

1969 No. 940

SAVINGS BANKS

The Post Office Savings Bank (Investment Deposits) (Limits) Order 1969

Laid before Parliament in draft

Made - - -	11*th July* 1969
Coming into Operation	14*th July* 1969

The Treasury, in exercise of the powers conferred upon them by section 4 of the Post Office Savings Bank Act 1954(**a**), section 12 of the Trustee Savings Banks Act 1954(**b**), section 16 of the Trustee Investments Act 1961(**c**) and paragraph 5 of schedule 4 to that Act, and section 7(1) of the Post Office Savings Bank Act 1966(**d**), and of all other powers enabling them in that behalf, hereby make the following Order:—

1. This Order may be cited as the Post Office Savings Bank (Investment Deposits) (Limits) Order 1969, and shall come into operation on 14th July 1969.

2. The Interpretation Act 1889(**e**) shall apply for the interpretation of this Order as it applies for the interpretation of an Act of Parliament.

3.—(1) Subject to the provisions of this Order, it shall not be lawful for the Postmaster General to receive a deposit from, or make a credit to an account of, any person by way of investment deposit in any case where the amount standing to the credit of that person by way of investment deposit in the Post Office Savings Bank, whether solely or jointly with any other person, and whether in one or more accounts, exceeds, or would as a result of the receipt of the said deposit or the making of the said credit exceed, £10,000.

(2) The foregoing paragraph shall not operate to prevent the receipt of or the crediting of—

(*a*) any amount allowed by the Post Office Savings Bank to a depositor by way of interest in respect of his investment deposit account; or

(*b*) any amount transferred from the investment deposit account of another depositor in the Post Office Savings Bank who has died.

(3) For the purposes of this Order, a person who is a trustee shall be treated separately in his personal capacity and in his capacity as trustee and in the latter capacity separately in respect of each separate trust fund; and so much of the property in the hands of a trustee shall be treated as a separate trust

---

(**a**) 1954 c. 62.	(**b**) 1954 c. 63.
(**c**) 1961 c. 62.	(**d**) 1966 c. 12.
(**e**) 1889 c. 63.	

fund as is held on trusts which (as respects the beneficiaries or their respective interests or the purposes of the trust or as respects the powers of the trustee) are not identical with those on which other property in his hands is held.

(4) In computing for the purposes of this Order the amount standing to the credit of any person, there shall not be taken into account any amounts received from a trustee on behalf of that person for an account in the joint names of the trustee and that person.

4. The Savings Banks (Deposits) (Limits) Order 1966(**a**) is hereby revoked.

Joseph Harper,
B. K. O'Malley,
Two of the Lords Commissioners
of Her Majesty's Treasury.

11th July 1969.

EXPLANATORY NOTE
(This Note is not part of the Order.)

This Order revokes the Savings Banks (Deposits) (Limits) Order 1966.

This Order reproduces the provisions of article 1 of the Order of 1966 (imposing, with certain exceptions, a limit on the aggregate amount which can be accepted by the Postmaster General from any person by way of investment deposit in the Post Office Savings Bank), but substitutes a limit of £10,000 for the limit of £5,000 specified in the Order of 1966.

The provisions of article 2 of the Order of 1966 (relating to ordinary deposits and savings account deposits in Savings Banks) are reproduced in the Savings Banks (Ordinary Deposits) (Limits) Order 1969 (S.I. 1969/939), and not in this Order.

(**a**) S.I.1966/734 (1966 II, p. 1710).

STATUTORY INSTRUMENTS

1969 No. 941

SAVINGS BANKS

The Trustee Savings Banks (Special Investments) (Limits) (Amendment) Order 1969

Laid before Parliament in draft

Made - - -	11*th July* 1969
Coming into Operation	14*th July* 1969

The Treasury, in exercise of the powers conferred upon them by section 15 of the Trustee Savings Banks Act 1954(**a**) and of all other powers enabling them in that behalf, hereby make the following Order:—

1. This Order may be cited as the Trustee Savings Banks (Special Investments) (Limits) (Amendment) Order 1969, and shall come into operation on 14th July 1969.

2. The Interpretation Act 1889(**b**) shall apply for the interpretation of this Order as it applies for the interpretation of an Act of Parliament.

3. The Trustee Savings Banks (Special Investments) (Limits) Order 1960(**c**), as amended (**d**), shall be further amended by substituting in article 1 thereof' for the figures "£5,000", the figures "£10,000".

4. The Trustee Savings Banks (Special Investments) (Limits) (Amendment) Order 1966(**e**) is hereby revoked.

Joseph Harper,
B. K. O'Malley,

Two of the Lords Commissioners
of Her Majesty's Treasury.

11th July 1969.

(**a**) 1954 c. 63.
(**b**) 1889 c. 63.
(**c**) S.I. 1960/1322 (1960 III, p. 3067).
(**d**) S.I. 1961/2413 (1961 III, p. 4456) and S.I. 1966/750 (1966 II, p. 1744).
(**e**) S.I. 1966/750 (1966 II, p. 1744).

EXPLANATORY NOTE

(This Note is not part of the Order.)

The Trustee Savings Banks (Special Investments) (Limits) Order 1960 as amended, imposed, with certain exceptions, a limit of £5,000 as the aggregate amount which could be accepted from any person for special investment by a Trustee Savings Bank. This Order increases the limit to £10,000.

STATUTORY INSTRUMENTS

1969 No. 942

SAVINGS BANKS

The Trustee Savings Banks (Current Account Deposits) (Limits) (Amendment) Order 1969

Laid before Parliament in draft

Made - - -		11*th July* 1969
Coming into Operation		14*th July* 1969

The Treasury, in exercise of the powers conferred upon them by section 12 of the Trustee Savings Banks Act 1954(**a**), as having effect by virtue of section 9 of the Trustee Savings Banks Act 1964(**b**) and paragraph 2 of schedule 2 to that Act, and of all other powers enabling them in that behalf, hereby make the following Order:—

1. This Order may be cited as the Trustee Savings Banks (Current Account Deposits) (Limits) (Amendment) Order 1969, and shall come into operation on 14th July 1969.

2. The Interpretation Act 1889(**c**) shall apply for the interpretation of this Order as it applies for the interpretation of an Act of Parliament.

3. The Trustee Savings Banks (Current Account Deposits) (Limits) Order 1965(**d**) shall be amended by substituting in article 1 thereof, for the figures "£5,000", the figures "£10,000".

Joseph Harper,
B. K. O'Malley,
Two of the Lords Commissioners
of Her Majesty's Treasury.

11th July 1969.

(**a**) 1954 c. 63.
(**c**) 1889 c. 63.
(**b**) 1964 c. 4.
(**d**) S.I. 1965/574 (1965 I, p. 1797).

EXPLANATORY NOTE

(*This Note is not part of the Order.*)

The Trustee Savings Banks (Current Account Deposits) (Limits) Order 1965 imposed a limit of £5,000 on the amount which any person may have at any time in current account deposits in a trustee savings bank in his own name or jointly with another person. This Order increases the limit to £10,000.

STATUTORY INSTRUMENTS

1969 No. 944

AGRICULTURE

The Agricultural Lime Scheme (Extension of Period) Order 1969

Laid before Parliament in draft

Made - - - -   11*th July* 1969

The Minister of Agriculture, Fisheries and Food, the Secretary of State for Scotland (being the Secretary of State concerned with agriculture in Scotland) and the Secretary of State for the Home Department (being the Secretary of State concerned with agriculture in Northern Ireland) in exercise of the powers vested in them by section 2 of the Agriculture (Miscellaneous Provisions) Act 1954**(a)** and of all other powers enabling them in that behalf, with the approval of the Treasury, hereby make the following Order.

Citation and Interpretation

1.—(1) This Order may be cited as the Agricultural Lime Scheme (Extension of Period) Order 1969.

(2) The Interpretation Act 1889**(b)** shall apply to the interpretation of this Order as it applies to the interpretation of an Act of Parliament.

Extension of Period for Contributions

2.   The period during which any cost must have been incurred in order that contributions may be payable in respect of it under section 1 of the Agriculture Act 1937**(c)**, as amended by section 97 of the Agriculture Act 1947**(d)**, is hereby extended until the end of July 1974.

In Witness whereof the official seal of the Minister of Agriculture, Fisheries and Food is hereunto affixed on 3rd July 1969.

(L.S.)   *Cledwyn Hughes,*

Minister of Agriculture, Fisheries and Food.

Given under the seal of the Secretary of State for Scotland on 4th July 1969.

(L.S.)   *William Ross,*

Secretary of State for Scotland.

Given under the hand of the Secretary of State for the Home Department on 7th July 1969.

James Callaghan,

Secretary of State for the Home Department.

Approved on 11th July 1969.

Joseph Harper,

B. K. O'Malley,

Two of the Lords Commissioners of Her Majesty's Treasury.

(a) 1954 c. 39.   (b) 1889 c. 63.   (c) 1937 c. 70.   (d) 1947 c. 48.

EXPLANATORY NOTE

(This Note is not part of the Order.)

Contributions towards the cost of acquiring and transporting lime for use on agricultural land and spreading it on such land are payable in accordance with a scheme made under the Agriculture Act 1937, as amended by the Agriculture Act 1947. The prescribed period during which such contributions may be made is due to expire on the 31st July 1969.

This Order extends by five years, ending on the 31st July 1974, the period during which contributions may be made.

STATUTORY INSTRUMENTS

1969 No. 953

PRICES AND INCOMES

The Awards and Settlements (Temporary Continuation of Standstill) (No. 2) Order 1969

Made - - -	*14th July* 1969
Laid before Parliament	*17th July* 1969
Coming into Operation	*18th July* 1969

Whereas by virtue of a reference to the National Board for Prices and Incomes under section 2(1) of the Prices and Incomes Act 1966(**a**) (the text whereof was published on 18th March 1969 in both the London and the Edinburgh Gazettes) the implementation of the settlement described in Article 2 hereof relating to the pay of workers in the exhibition industry was forbidden by section 15(2) of that Act ;

And whereas before the said implementation ceased to be so forbidden a report of the Board on the said reference was published on 18th June 1969(**b**) with a recommendation adverse to the implementation of the said settlement ;

And whereas by virtue of the said recommendation and subsections (1) and (2)(*a*) of section 1 of the Prices and Incomes Act 1967(**c**) the said section 15(2) continued to apply to the implementation of the said settlement as it applied up to the date of publication of the said report :

Now, therefore, the Secretary of State, having given notice under section 1(2)(*a*) of the said Act of 1967 within a period of ten days after the date of the said publication, of a proposal to make this Order, and having taken into consideration representations duly made in pursuance of the said notice, in exercise of the powers conferred on her by section 1(2)(*b*) of the said Act of 1967, as amended by section 3(2) of the Prices and Incomes Act 1968(**d**), and of all other powers enabling her in that behalf, hereby makes the following Order :—

1.—(1) This Order, which may be cited as the Awards and Settlements (Temporary Continuation of Standstill) (No. 2) Order 1969, shall come into operation on 18th July 1969.

(2) The Interpretation Act 1889(**e**) shall apply for the interpretation of this Order as it applies for the interpretation of an Act of Parliament.

(**a**) 1966 c. 33.   (**b**) Report No. 117 entitled "Pay and conditions of workers in the Exhibition Contracting Industry" (Cmnd. 4088).

(**c**) 1967 c. 53.   (**d**) 1968 c. 42.   (**e**) 1889 c. 63.

2. The Secretary of State hereby directs that section 15(2) of the Prices and Incomes Act 1966 shall continue to apply to forbid the implementation up to and including 17th February 1970 of the undermentioned settlement, that is to say :—

the settlement reached on 7th February 1969 by the National Joint Council for the Exhibition Industry providing, amongst other things, for—

(*a*) increases in the hourly rates of wages of craftsmen and labourers of fourpence and threepence respectively ; and

(*b*) a productivity bonus of ten shillings per day (including week-end working) for all operatives covered by the said National Joint Council employed in shops and exhibition halls.

14th July 1969.

Barbara Castle,

First Secretary of State and
Secretary of State for Employment and Productivity.

EXPLANATORY NOTE

(*This Note is not part of the Order.*)

This Order, which has effect from 18th July 1969, provides for the further continuation until 17th February 1970 of the standstill on the implementation of a settlement relating to the pay of certain workers employed in the Exhibition Contracting Industry.

STATUTORY INSTRUMENTS

1969 No. 954

ROAD TRAFFIC

The Goods Vehicles (Production of Test Certificates) Regulations 1969

Made - - -	*14th July* 1969
Laid before Parliament	*22nd July* 1969
Coming into Operation	*1st August* 1969

The Minister of Transport, in exercise of his powers under section 14(9) of the Road Safety Act 1967(a), as amended by section 148 of the Transport Act 1968(b) and by section 18(2) of the Vehicle and Driving Licences Act 1969(c), and of all other enabling powers, after consultation with representative organisations in accordance with the provisions of section 260(2) of the Road Traffic Act 1960(d) as applied by section 29(6) of the said Act of 1967, hereby makes the following Regulations :—

1. These Regulations shall come into operation on the 1st August 1969, and may be cited as the Goods Vehicles (Production of Test Certificates) Regulations 1969.

2.—(1) In these Regulations the following expressions have the meanings hereby respectively assigned to them :—

"the 1967 Act" means the Road Safety Act 1967 ;

"the Plating and Testing regulations" means the Goods Vehicles (Plating and Testing) Regulations 1968(e), as amended (f).

(2) The Interpretation Act 1889(g) shall apply for the interpretation of these Regulations as it applies for the interpretation of an Act of Parliament.

3. Where application is made on or after 1st October 1969 and before 1st April 1970 for a licence under the Vehicles (Excise) Act 1962(h) for any motor vehicle, being a goods vehicle to which section 14(2) of the 1967 Act applies and of a class specified in paragraph 1, 2 or 3 in Part I of, or in paragraph 1 or 2 in Part II of, Schedule 4 to the Plating and Testing regulations, the licence shall not be granted unless—

(*a*) there is produced an effective goods vehicle test certificate in force for the vehicle ; or

---

(a) 1967 c.30.   (b) 1968 c.73.
(c) 1969 c.27.   (d) 8 & 9 Eliz. 2. c.16.
(e) S.I. 1968/601 (1968 I, p.1372).
(f) The relevant amending instrument is S.I. 1968/1854 (1968 III, p. 4880).
(g) 52 & 53 Vict. c.63.   (h) 10 & 11 Eliz. 2. c.13.

(b) such a declaration as is specified in the Schedule to these Regulations is made ; or

(c) there is produced in respect of the vehicle a certificate of temporary exemption issued by virtue of Regulation 57 of the Plating and Testing regulations which exempts the vehicle from the provisions of section 14(2) of the 1967 Act for a period which includes the date on which the licence is to come into force.

4. Without prejudice to the provisions of the last preceding Regulation, where application is made on or after 1st April 1970 for a licence under the Vehicles (Excise) Act 1962 for any motor vehicle, being a goods vehicle to which section 14(2) of the 1967 Act applies and of a class specified in Part I or II of Schedule 4 to the Plating and Testing regulations, the licence shall not be granted unless—

(a) there is produced an effective goods vehicle test certificate in force for the vehicle ; or

(b) such a declaration as is specified in the Schedule to these Regulations is made ; or

(c) there is produced in respect of the vehicle a certificate of temporary exemption issued by virtue of Regulation 57 of the Plating and Testing regulations which exempts that vehicle from the provisions of section 14(2) of the 1967 Act for a period which includes the date on which the licence is to come into force.

Given under the Official Seal of the Minister of Transport the 14th July 1969.

(L.S.)

Richard Marsh,
Minister of Transport,

SCHEDULE

FORM OF DECLARATION

I DECLARE that the vehicle, of which the registration mark/chassis or serial number/identification mark is...................................and for which I have made application for a licence for the period commencing................................and ending................................, is not intended to be used during the period for which the licence is to be in force except—

(a) for a purpose prescribed in Regulation 53(4) of the Goods Vehicles (Plating and Testing) Regulations 1968, or

(b) in an area prescribed in Regulation 55 of the Goods Vehicles (Plating and Testing) Regulations 1968, being an area to which that Regulation applies.

Usual signature ....

Full Name ....
(block letters)

Address ....

....

....

In the case of a
partnership,
limited company
or other legal
entity state
capacity in which   Capacity ....
declaration is made
and name of   Name ....
that partnership,
company or   Date ....
entity

EXPLANATORY NOTE

(This Note is not part of the Regulations.)

These Regulations provide that where application is made for a licence under the Vehicles (Excise) Act 1962 for a motor vehicle, being a goods vehicle required under section 14(2) of the Road Safety Act 1967 to have a goods vehicle test certificate and of a class specified in Schedule 4 to the Goods Vehicles (Plating and Testing) Regulations 1968, the applicant must, before the licence will be granted, produce either a goods vehicle test certificate relating to the vehicle which shall be in force on the date on which the licence is to come into force or a certificate of temporary exemption exempting the vehicle from the provisions of section 14(2) of the above Act of 1967 for a period which includes the date on which the licence is to come into force, or also make the declaration prescribed by the Regulations as to proposed limited use of the vehicle. The Regulations have effect in two stages:—

(a) on and after 1st October 1969, the foregoing requirements preliminary to the grant of a licence will apply to the goods vehicles concerned in the case of those not based in Scotland, if they were first registered before 1st January 1961, or in the case of those so based, if they were first registered before 1st January 1958 (Reg. 3);

(b) on and after 1st April 1970, those requirements will apply to all the goods vehicles concerned, being motor vehicles either registered before 1st January 1968 or, if manufactured before that date, not registered before 1st January 1969 (Reg. 4).

1969 No. 955 (S. 76)

LEGAL AID AND ADVICE, SCOTLAND

The Legal Aid (Extension of Proceedings) (Scotland) Regulations 1969

Made - - - -	*9th June* 1969
Laid before Parliament	*16th June* 1969
Coming into Operation	*1st August* 1969

In exercise of the powers conferred on me by sections 1 and 15 of the Legal Aid (Scotland) Act 1967(**a**), and of all other powers enabling me in that behalf, I hereby make the following regulations:—

1.—(1) These regulations may be cited as the Legal Aid (Extension of Proceedings) (Scotland) Regulations 1969 and shall come into operation on 1st August 1969.

(2) The Interpretation Act 1889(**b**) shall apply for the interpretation of these regulations as it applies for the interpretation of an Act of Parliament.

2. Notwithstanding anything in paragraph 1 of Part II of Schedule 1 to the Legal Aid (Scotland) Act 1967, the making of a counterclaim for defamation or verbal injury in proceedings for which legal aid may be given shall not of itself affect any right of the defender to the counterclaim to legal aid in the proceedings and legal aid may be granted to enable him to defend such counterclaim.

William Ross,
One of Her Majesty's
Principal Secretaries of State.

St. Andrew's House,
 Edinburgh.
9th June 1969.

EXPLANATORY NOTE

(This Note is not part of the Regulations.)

These Regulations vary the proceedings in connection with which legal aid may be given to make legal aid available in certain proceedings which are partly in respect of defamation or verbal injury.

(**a**) 1967 c. 43. (**b**) 1889 c. 63.

STATUTORY INSTRUMENTS

1969 No. 962

MERCHANDISE MARKS

The Motor Vehicles (Designation of Approval Marks) (No. 2) Regulations 1969

Made - - - -	*14th July* 1969
Laid before Parliament	*24th July* 1969
Coming into Operation	*28th July* 1969

The Minister of Transport (hereinafter referred to as "the Minister"), in exercise of his powers under section 47(1) of the Road Traffic Act 1962(**a**), as amended by paragraph 4 of Schedule 1 to the Trade Descriptions Act 1968(**b**), and as applied by section 146 of the Transport Act 1968(**c**), and of all other enabling powers and, by virtue of section 52(2) of the Road Traffic Act 1962, after consultation with representative organisations in accordance with the provisions of section 260(2) of the Road Traffic Act 1960(**d**), hereby makes the following Regulations:—

1.—(1) These Regulations shall come into operation on the 28th July 1969 and may be cited as the Motor Vehicles (Designation of Approval Marks) (No. 2) Regulations 1969.

(2) In these Regulations the expression "the International Agreement of 1958" means the Agreement concerning the adoption of uniform conditions of approval and reciprocal recognition of approval for motor vehicle equipment and parts concluded at Geneva on 20th March 1958(**e**), and as amended(**f**), to which the United Kingdom is a party(**g**).

(3) The Interpretation Act 1889(**h**) shall apply for the interpretation of these Regulations as it applies for the interpretation of an Act of Parliament.

2.—(1) The Minister hereby designates as an approval mark a marking which is in the same form as and of a size not less than the marking shown in the diagram in Part I of Schedule 1 to these Regulations subject, however, to the provisions of Part II of that Schedule, the said marking being one for which the International Agreement of 1958 by virtue of the Regulation specified in Part III of that Schedule and annexed to that Agreement makes such provision as is mentioned in section 146(1)(*a*)(ii) and (*b*) of the Transport Act 1968 in relation to a motor vehicle fitted with certain parts consisting of radio interference suppression equipment on the vehicle.

(a) 10 & 11 Eliz. 2. c. 59.   (b) 1968 c. 29.
(c) 1968 c. 73.   (d) 8 & 9 Eliz. 2. c. 16.
(e) Cmnd. 2535.   (f) Cmnd. 3562.
(g) By instrument of accession dated 14th January 1963 deposited with the Secretary-General of the United Nations on 15th January 1963.
(h) 52 & 53 Vict. c. 63.

(2) The Minister hereby designates as an approval mark a marking which is in the same form as and of a size not less than the marking shown in the diagram in Part I of Schedule 2 to these Regulations subject, however, to the provisions of Part II of that Schedule, the said marking being one for which the International Agreement of 1958 by virtue of the Regulation specified in Part III of that Schedule and annexed to that Agreement makes such provision as is mentioned in section 146(1)(a)(ii) and (b) of the Transport Act 1968 in relation to a motor vehicle fitted with certain latches and hinges on the side doors of the vehicle.

(3) The Minister hereby designates as an approval mark a marking which is in the same form as and of a size not less than the marking shown in the diagram in Part I of Schedule 3 to these Regulations subject, however, to the provisions of Part II of that Schedule, the said marking being one for which the International Agreement of 1958 by virtue of the Regulation specified in Part III of that Schedule and annexed to that Agreement makes such provision as is mentioned in section 146(1)(a)(ii) and (b) of the Transport Act 1968 in relation to a motor vehicle fitted with certain parts consisting of the steering mechanism of the vehicle.

Given under the Official Seal of the Minister of Transport the 14th July 1969.

(L.S.)

Richard Marsh,
Minister of Transport

SCHEDULE 1

PART I

DIAGRAM SHOWING MARKING

1OR-2439

PART II

1. The number shown inside the circle in the marking in the above diagram will be varied, where appropriate, to be the number assigned to each Contracting State party to the International Agreement of 1958 and applying the Regulation specified in Part III of this Schedule.

2. The number which is shown outside the circle in the said marking will be varied, where appropriate, to be the number allotted by a competent authority to distinguish the manufacturer of the type of motor vehicle concerned being a motor vehicle fitted with certain parts consisting of radio interference suppression equipment on the vehicle.

PART III

Regulation No. 10
UNIFORM PROVISIONS CONCERNING THE APPROVAL OF VEHICLES WITH REGARD TO RADIO INTERFERENCE SUPPRESSION.

SCHEDULE 2

PART I

DIAGRAM SHOWING MARKING

11 R-2439

PART II

1. The number shown inside the circle in the marking in the above diagram will be varied, where appropriate, to be the number assigned to each Contracting State party to the International Agreement of 1958 and applying the Regulation specified in Part III of this Schedule.

2. The number which is shown outside the circle in the said marking will be varied, where appropriate, to be the number allotted by a competent authority to distinguish the manufacturer of the type of motor vehicle concerned being a motor vehicle fitted with certain latches and hinges on the side doors of the vehicle.

PART III

REGULATION No. 11

UNIFORM PROVISIONS CONCERNING THE APPROVAL OF VEHICLES WITH REGARD TO THE STRENGTH OF DOOR LATCHES AND HINGES.

SCHEDULE 3

PART I

DIAGRAM SHOWING MARKING

12R-2439

PART. II

1. The number shown inside the circle in the marking in the above diagram will be varied, where appropriate, to be the number assigned to each Contracting State party to the International Agreement of 1958 and applying the Regulation specified in Part III of this Schedule.

2. The number which is shown outside the circle in the said marking will be varied, where appropriate, to be the number allotted by a competent authority to distinguish the manufacturer of the type of motor vehicle concerned being a motor vehicle fitted with certain parts consisting of the steering mechanism of the vehicle.

PART III

Regulation No. 12

UNIFORM PROVISIONS CONCERNING THE APPROVAL OF VEHICLES WITH REGARD TO THE PROTECTION OF THE DRIVER AGAINST THE STEERING MECHANISM IN THE EVENT OF IMPACT.

EXPLANATORY NOTE

(This Note is not part of the Regulations.)

Section 47(1) of the Road Traffic Act 1962, as applied by section 146 of the Transport Act 1968, enacts that where any international agreement to which the United Kingdom is a party provides—

(*a*) for markings to be applied to a motor vehicle to indicate that the vehicle is fitted with motor vehicle parts within the meaning of the said section 47 of any description and either—

    (i) that the parts conform with a type approved by any country; or

    (ii) that the vehicle is such that as so fitted it conforms with a type so approved; and

(*b*) for motor vehicles bearing those markings to be recognised as complying with the requirements imposed by the law of another country,

the Minister of Transport may by regulations designate the markings as approval marks.

Section 47 of the Road Traffic Act 1962, as amended by Schedule 1 to the Trade Descriptions Act 1968, also provides, *inter alia*, that any markings so designated shall be deemed for the purposes of the latter Act to be a trade description and that it shall be an offence under that Act to apply an approval mark without proper authority.

The Regulations designate for the purposes of the said section 47, as so applied and amended, as approval marks, markings complying with the provisions of Schedule 1 or Schedule 2 or Schedule 3 to these Regulations and in respect of which the International Agreement of 1958 (referred to in the Regulations) and the Regulations specified in Part III of each of the Schedules to these Regulations and annexed to that Agreement makes such provision as is mentioned in (*a*)(ii) and (*b*) above as respects motor vehicles fitted with motor vehicle parts. The motor vehicle parts concerned (in the case of a marking complying with the provisions of Schedule 1 to these Regulations) consist of radio interference suppression equipment and (in the case of a marking complying with Schedule 2 to these Regulations) are the latches and hinges on the side doors of the vehicle and (in the case of a marking complying with Schedule 3 to these Regulations) consist of the steering mechanism.

STATUTORY INSTRUMENTS

1969 No. 963

MINES AND QUARRIES

The Mines (Notification of Dangerous Occurrences) (Amendment) Order 1969

Made - - - -	14*th July* 1969
Laid before Parliament	23*rd July* 1969
Coming into Operation	1*st August* 1969

Whereas the Minister of Power is of opinion that the special class of occurrences at mines which is hereinafter specified is of so dangerous a nature as to render it expedient that notice should be given under section 116 of the Mines and Quarries Act 1954(a) as modified by the Mines and Quarries (Tips) Act 1969(b) in every case thereof:

Now, therefore, the Minister in pursuance of the powers conferred upon him by sections 117(1) and 173 of the Mines and Quarries Act 1954 and section 1 of and Schedule 1 to the Mines and Quarries (Tips) Act 1969 and of all other powers him enabling hereby orders as follows:—

1.—(1) This Order may be cited as the Mines (Notification of Dangerous Occurrences) (Amendment) Order 1969 and shall come into operation on 1st August 1969.

(2) The Interpretation Act 1889(c) applies for the interpretation of this Order as it applies for the interpretation of an Act of Parliament, and as if this Order and the Order hereby revoked were Acts of Parliament.

2.—(1) The Mines (Notification of Dangerous Occurrences) Order 1959(d) shall have effect subject to the modifications specified in this article.

(2) For sub-paragraph (*t*) of article 3 inserted by the Mines (Notification of Dangerous Occurrences) (Amendment) Order 1967(e) there shall be inserted the following sub-paragraph:—

" (*t*) any movement of material or any fire or any other event indicates that a tip to which Part I of the Mines and Quarries (Tips) Act 1969 applies is, or is likely to become, insecure."

and the Mines (Notification of Dangerous Occurrences) (Amendment) Order 1967 is accordingly hereby revoked.

(3) In article 4(1) after the words " in paragraph (*e*) " there shall be inserted the words " or (*t*) ".

Dated 14th July 1969.

Roy Mason,
Minister of Power.

(a) 1954 c. 70.   (b) 1969 c. 10.   (c) 1889 c. 63.   (d) S.I. 1959/2117 (1959 I, p. 1786.)
(e) S.I. 1967/1522 (1967 III, p. 4244.)

EXPLANATORY NOTE

(This Note is not part of the Order.)

This Order supersedes the Mines (Notification of Dangerous Occurrences) (Amendment) Order 1967 on the coming into operation of Part I of the Mines and Quarries (Tips) Act 1969.

SBN 11 840039 8